Why can't we remember anything from those first few years of life? (p. 202)

What affects gender bias in the workplace, and how is this changing? (pp. 109, 110)

How can sex, sleep, exercise, and stimulating environments help the brain repair itself? (pp. 48, 57, 76)

Can self-control really boost academic and career success, and also health and well-being? How can we strengthen our self-control? (pp. 91, 170, 295)

How do our experiences affect the way our genes express themselves? (pp. 71–72, 73, 85–86, 246–247, 354, 378, 398, 405)

Why does it feel so painful to be excluded, ignored, or shunned? (pp. 267–268)

How can we get a better night's sleep? (p. 60)

What causes those frustrating tip-of-the-tongue memory problems? (p. 210)

Why is there controversy over attention-deficit/hyperactivity disorder? (pp. 376–377)

Are memories of childhood sexual abuse often repressed? If so, can they be recovered? (p. 214)

(See inside the back cover for more of this text's application questions.)

PSYCHOLOGY
in Everyday Life

fourth edition

DAVID G. MYERS

Hope College
Holland, Michigan

C. NATHAN DEWALL

University of Kentucky
Lexington, Kentucky

worth publishers
Macmillan Learning

New York

caracterdesign/Vetta/Getty Images

Vice President, Social Sciences: Charles Linsmeier
Executive Editor: Carlise Stembridge
Development Editors: Christine Brune, Nancy Fleming,
    Trish Morgan, Danielle Slevens
Assistant Editor: Katie Pachnos
Executive Marketing Manager: Katherine Nurre
Marketing Assistant: Morgan Ratner
Executive Media Editor: Noel Hohnstine
Media Editor: Laura Burden
Media Editorial Assistant: Nik Toner
Supplements Editor: Betty Probert
Director, Content Management Enhancement: Tracey Kuehn
Managing Editor, Sciences and Social Sciences: Lisa Kinne
Project Editor: Won McIntosh
Director of Digital Production: Keri deManigold
Senior Media Producer: Chris Efstratiou
Media Producer: Eve Conte
Senior Production Supervisor: Sarah Segal
Senior Photo Editor: Robin Fadool
Photo Research Assistant: Candice Cheesman
Director of Design, Content Management: Diana Blume
Interior and Cover Design: Blake Logan
Cover Illustration: Evelyn Pence
Interior Illustrations: Shawn Barber, Keith Kasnot, Matthew McAdams,
    Evelyn Pence, Don Stewart
Art Manager: Matthew McAdams
Composition: Lumina Datamatics
Printing and Binding: LSC Communications

Cover Photo: caracterdesign/Vetta/Getty Images
Chapter Opener Photo Credits for Contents: FilippoBacci/Getty Images; Cultura/Getty
Images; DigitalVision/Getty Images; Blend Images/Getty Images; Adam Hester/Blend
Images/Getty Images; E+/Getty Images; Caiaimage/Sam Edwards/OJO+/Getty Images;
Blend Images/Getty Images; © Hero Images/Getty Images; Tetra Images/Getty Images;
Taxi/Getty Images; Rex Features/AP Images; Delphine Le Berre/Moment Select/Getty
Images; Ryan McVay/Stone/Getty Images

Library of Congress Control Number: 2016945699

ISBN-13: 978-1-319-01373-8
ISBN-10: 1-319-01373-2

Worth Publishers
One New York Plaza
Suite 4500
New York, NY 10004-1562
MacmillanLearning.com

[DM] In memory of Janet Gallaher Myers, 1939–2016, with gratitude for her love and joy.

[ND] For Nichole DeWall, my loving sister who taught me how to read, how to laugh, and how to believe in myself.

DAVID MYERS received his B.A. in chemistry from Whitworth University, and his psychology Ph.D. from the University of Iowa. He has spent his career at Hope College in Michigan, where he has taught dozens of introductory psychology sections. Hope College students have invited him to be their commencement speaker and voted him "outstanding professor."

His research and writings have been recognized by the Gordon Allport Intergroup Relations Prize, by a 2010 Honored Scientist award from the Federation of Associations in Behavioral & Brain Sciences, by a 2010 Award for Service on Behalf of Personality and Social Psychology, by a 2013 Presidential Citation from APA Division 2, by his 2015 election as an American Association for the Advancement of Science Fellow, and by three honorary doctorates.

With support from National Science Foundation grants, Myers' scientific articles have appeared in three dozen scientific periodicals, including *Science, American Scientist, Psychological Science,* and the *American Psychologist.* In addition to his scholarly writing and his textbooks for introductory and social psychology, he also digests psychological science for the general public. His writings have appeared in four dozen magazines, from *Today's Education* to *Scientific American.* He also has authored five general audience books, including *The Pursuit of Happiness* and *Intuition: Its Powers and Perils.*

David Myers has chaired his city's Human Relations Commission, helped found a thriving assistance center for families in poverty, and spoken to hundreds of college, community, and professional groups worldwide.

Drawing on his experience, he also has written articles and a book *(A Quiet World)* about hearing loss, and he is advocating a transformation in American assistive listening technology (see HearingLoop.org). For his leadership, he received an American Academy of Audiology Presidential Award in 2011, and the Hearing Loss Association of America Walter T. Ridder Award in 2012.

David and Carol Myers have raised two sons and a daughter, and have one granddaughter.

David, in South Africa with daughter Laura, a "sociobehavioural scientist" at the University of Cape Town's Desmond Tutu HIV Foundation.

NATHAN DEWALL is professor of psychology and director of the Social Psychology Lab at the University of Kentucky. He received his bachelor's degree from St. Olaf College, a master's degree in social science from the University of Chicago, and a master's degree and Ph.D. in social psychology from Florida State University. DeWall received the College of Arts and Sciences Outstanding Teaching Award, which recognizes excellence in undergraduate and graduate teaching. The Association for Psychological Science identified DeWall as a "Rising Star" for "making significant contributions to the field of psychological science."

DeWall conducts research on close relationships, self-control, and aggression. With funding from the National Institutes of Health and the National Science Foundation, he has published over 180 scientific articles and chapters. DeWall's research awards include the SAGE Young Scholars Award from the Foundation for Personality and Social Psychology, the Young Investigator Award from the International Society for Research on Aggression, and the Early Career Award from the International Society for Self and Identity. His research has been covered by numerous media outlets, including *Good Morning America,* the *Wall Street Journal, Newsweek, Atlantic Monthly,* the *New York Times,* the *Los Angeles Times,* the *Harvard Business Review, USA Today,* and National Public Radio. He has lectured nationally and internationally, including in Hong Kong, China, the Netherlands, England, Greece, Hungary, Sweden, and Australia.

Nathan is happily married to Alice DeWall and is the proud father of Beverly "Bevy" DeWall. He enjoys playing with his two golden retrievers, Finnegan and Atticus. In his spare time, he writes novels, watches sports, tends his chickens and goats, and runs and runs and runs. He has braved all climates—from freezing to ferocious heat—to complete over 1000 miles' worth of ultramarathons, including the Vol State 500K in 2016.

Brief Contents

Contents

CHAPTER 4

Sex, Gender, and Sexuality 107

CHAPTER 5

Sensation and Perception 133

Preface

PSYCHOLOGY IS FASCINATING, and so relevant to our everyday lives. Psychology's insights enable us to be better students, more tuned-in friends and partners, more effective co-workers, and wiser parents. With this new edition, we hope to captivate students with what psychologists are learning about our human nature, to help them think more like psychological scientists, and, as the title implies, to help them relate psychology to their own lives—their thoughts, feelings, and behaviors.

For those of you familiar with other Myers/DeWall introductory psychology texts, you may be surprised at how different this text is. We have created this very brief, uniquely student-friendly book with supportive input from hundreds of instructors and students (by way of surveys, focus groups, content and design reviews, and class testing). Compacting our introduction of psychology's key topics keeps both the length and the price manageable. And we write with the goal of making psychology accessible to all students, regardless of their personal or academic backgrounds. It has been gratifying to hear from instructors who have been delighted to find that this affordable, accessible text offers a complete, college-level survey of the field that they can offer proudly to their students.

What's New in the Fourth Edition?

In addition to thorough updating of every chapter, with new infographic "Thinking Critically About" features, this fourth edition offers exciting new activities in the teaching package.

Hundreds of New Research Citations

Our ongoing scrutiny of dozens of scientific periodicals and science news sources, enhanced by commissioned reviews and countless e-mails from instructors and students, enables integrating our field's most important, thought-provoking, and student-relevant new discoveries. Part of the pleasure that sustains this work is learning something new every day! See MacmillanLearning.com/PEL4eContent for a chapter-by-chapter list of significant **Content Changes.**

"Thinking Critically About" Infographic features

We worked with an artist to create infographic critical thinking features. (In many cases, these new infographics replace a more static boxed essay in the previous edition.) Several dozen instructors reviewed this feature, often sharing it with their students, and they were unanimously supportive. Students seem to enjoy engaging this visual tool for thinking critically about key psychological concepts (parenting styles, gender bias, group polarization, introversion, lifestyle changes, and more). A picture can indeed be worth a thousand words! (See **FIGURE 1** for an example.)

"Assess Your Strengths" Activities for LaunchPad

With the significantly revised **Assess Your Strengths** activities, students apply what they are learning from the text to their own lives and experiences by considering key "strengths." For each of these activities, we [DM and ND] start by offering a personalized video introduction, explaining how that strength ties in to the content of the chapter. Next, we ask students to assess themselves on the strength (critical thinking, quality of sleep, self-control, relationship-building, healthy belonging, hope, and more) using scales developed by researchers across psychological science. After showing students their results, we offer tips for nurturing that strength in students' own lives. Finally, students take a quiz to help solidify their learning.

These activities reside in **Launch-Pad**, an online resource designed to help achieve better course results. Launch-Pad for *Psychology in Everyday Life,* Fourth Edition, also includes **LearningCurve** formative assessment and the "Immersive Learning: How Would You Know?" activities described next. For details, see p. xxii and LaunchPadWorks.com. For this new edition, you will see that we've offered callouts from the text pages to especially pertinent, helpful resources elsewhere in LaunchPad. (See **FIGURE 2** for a sample.)

"Immersive Learning: How Would You Know?" Research Activities

We [ND and DM] created these online activities to engage students in the scientific process, showing them how psychological research begins with a question, and how key decision points can alter the meaning and value of a psychological study. In a fun, interactive environment, students learn about important aspects of research design and interpretation, and develop scientific literacy and critical thinking skills in the process. I [ND] have enjoyed taking the lead on this project and sharing my research experience and enthusiasm with students. Topics include: "How

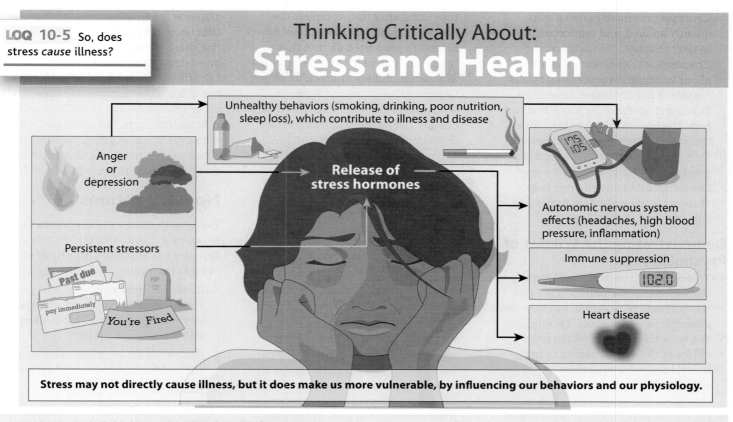

LOQ 10-5 So, does stress *cause* illness?

Thinking Critically About:
Stress and Health

Unhealthy behaviors (smoking, drinking, poor nutrition, sleep loss), which contribute to illness and disease

Anger or depression

Persistent stressors

Past due
pay immediately
You're Fired
RIP

Release of stress hormones

Autonomic nervous system effects (headaches, high blood pressure, inflammation)

Immune suppression
102.0

Heart disease

Stress may not directly cause illness, but it does make us more vulnerable, by influencing our behaviors and our physiology.

FIGURE 1 Sample "Thinking Critically About" infographic from Chapter 10

LaunchPad To review the classic conformity studies and experience a simulated experiment, visit LaunchPad's *PsychSim 6: Everybody's Doing It!*

FIGURE 2 Sample LaunchPad callout from Chapter 1

Would You Know If a Cup of Coffee Can Warm Up Relationships?"; "How Would You Know If People Can Learn to Reduce Anxiety?"; and "How Would You Know If Schizophrenia Is Inherited?"

What Continues in the Fourth Edition?

Eight Guiding Principles

Despite all the exciting changes, this new edition retains its predecessors' voice, as well as much of the content and or-ganization. It also retains the goals—the guiding principles—that have animated all of the Myers texts:

Facilitating the Learning Experience

1. **To teach critical thinking** By presenting research as intellectual detective work, we illustrate an inquiring, analytical mind-set. Whether students are studying development, cognition, or social behavior, they will become involved in, and see the rewards of, critical reasoning. Moreover, they will discover how an empirical approach can help them evaluate competing ideas and claims for highly publicized phenomena—ranging from ESP and alternative therapies to group differences in intelligence and repressed and recovered memories. Our new "Thinking Critically About" infographic features help engage students in this learning.

2. **To integrate principles and applications** Throughout—by means of anecdotes, case histories, and the posing of hypothetical situations—we relate the findings of basic research to their applications and implications. Where psychology can illuminate pressing human issues—be they racism and sexism, health and happiness, or violence and war—we have not hesitated to shine its light. Our newly revised "Assess Your Strengths" activities invite students to apply important concepts to their own lives, and to learn ways to develop key personal strengths.

3. **To reinforce learning at every step** Everyday examples and rhetorical questions encourage students to process the material actively.

Concepts presented earlier are frequently applied, and reinforced, in later chapters. For instance, in Chapter 1, students learn that much of our information processing occurs outside of our conscious awareness. Ensuing chapters drive home this concept. Numbered Learning Objective Questions, Retrieve + Remember self-tests throughout each chapter, a marginal glossary, and Chapter Review key terms lists and self-tests help students learn and retain important concepts and terminology.

Demonstrating the Science of Psychology

4. **To exemplify the process of inquiry** We strive to show students not just the outcome of research, but how the research process works. Throughout, the book tries to excite the reader's curiosity. It invites readers to imagine themselves as participants in classic experiments. Several chapters introduce research stories as mysteries that progressively unravel as one clue after another falls into place. Our new "Immersive Learning: How Would You Know?" activities in LaunchPad encourage students to think about research questions and how they may be studied effectively.

5. **To be as up-to-date as possible** Few things dampen students' interest as quickly as the sense that they are reading stale news. While retaining psychology's classic studies and concepts, we also present the discipline's most important recent developments. In this edition, 619 references are dated 2013–2016. Likewise, new photos and new everyday examples are drawn from today's world.

6. **To put facts in the service of concepts** Our intention is not to fill students' intellectual file drawers with facts, but to reveal psychology's major concepts—to teach students how to think, and to offer psychological ideas worth thinking about. In each chapter, we place emphasis on those concepts we hope students will carry with them long after they complete the course. Always, we try to follow Albert Einstein's purported dictum that "everything should be made as simple as possible, but not simpler." Learning Objective Questions and Retrieve + Remember questions throughout each chapter help students focus on the most important concepts.

Promoting Big Ideas and Broadened Horizons

7. **To enhance comprehension by providing continuity** Many chapters have a significant issue or theme that links subtopics, forming a thread that ties the chapter together. The Learning chapter conveys the idea that bold thinkers can serve as intellectual pioneers. The Thinking, Language, and Intelligence chapter raises the issue of human rationality and irrationality. The Psychological Disorders chapter conveys empathy for, and understanding of, troubled lives. Other threads, such as cognitive neuroscience, dual processing, and cultural and gender diversity, weave throughout the whole book, and students hear a consistent voice.

8. **To convey respect for human unity and diversity** Throughout the book, readers will see evidence of our human kinship in our shared biological heritage—our common mechanisms of seeing and learning, hungering and feeling, loving and hating. They will also better understand the dimensions of our diversity—our individual diversity in development and aptitudes, temperament and personality, and disorder and health; and our cultural diversity in attitudes and expressive styles, child raising and care for the elderly, and life priorities.

The Writing

As with the third edition, we've written this book to be optimally accessible. The vocabulary is sensitive to students' widely varying reading levels and backgrounds. (A Spanish language *Glosario* at the back of the book offers additional assistance for ESL Spanish speakers.) And this book is briefer than many texts on the market, making it easier to fit into one-term courses. *Psychology in Everyday Life* offers a complete survey of the field, but it is a more manageable survey, with an emphasis on the most humanly significant concepts. We continually asked ourselves while working, "Would an educated person need to know this? Would this help students live better lives?"

No Assumptions

Even more than in other Myers/DeWall texts, we have written *Psychology in Everyday Life* with the diversity of student readers in mind.

- *Gender:* Extensive coverage of gender roles and gender identity and the increasing diversity of choices men and women can make.

- *Culture:* No assumptions about readers' cultural backgrounds or experiences.

- *Economics:* No references to backyards, summer camp, vacations.

- *Education:* No assumptions about past or current learning environments; writing is accessible to all.

- *Physical Abilities:* No assumptions about full vision, hearing, movement.

- *Life Experiences:* Examples are included from urban, suburban, and rural/outdoor settings.

- *Family Status:* Examples and ideas are made relevant for all students, whether they have children or are still living at home, are married or cohabiting or single; no assumptions about sexual orientation.

Four Big Ideas

In the general psychology course, it can be a struggle to weave psychology's disparate parts into a cohesive whole for students, and for students to make sense of all the pieces. In *Psychology in Everyday Life,* we have introduced four of psychology's big ideas as one possible way to make connections among all the concepts. These ideas are presented in Chapter 1 and gently integrated throughout the text.

1. Critical Thinking Is Smart Thinking

We love to write in a way that gets students thinking and keeps them active as they read. Students will see how the science of psychology can help them evaluate competing ideas and highly publicized claims—ranging from intuition, subliminal persuasion, and ESP to alternative therapies, attention-deficit/hyperactivity disorder, and repressed and recovered memories.

In *Psychology in Everyday Life*, students have many opportunities to learn or practice critical thinking skills. (See **TABLE 1** for a complete list of this text's coverage of critical thinking topics.)

- *Chapter 1 takes a unique, critical thinking approach to introducing students to psychology's research methods.* Understanding the weak points of our everyday intuition and common sense helps students see the need for psychological science. Critical thinking is introduced as a key term in this chapter (page 8).

- *"Thinking Critically About . . ." infographic features* are found in each chapter. This feature models for students a critical approach to some key issues in psychology. For example, see "Thinking Critically About: The Stigma of Introversion" (Chapter 12) or "Thinking Critically About: The Internet as Social Amplifier" (Chapter 11).

- *Detective-style stories* throughout the text get students thinking critically about psychology's key research questions. In Chapter 8, for example, we present as a puzzle the history of discoveries about where and how language happens in the brain. We guide students through the puzzle, showing them how researchers put all the pieces together.

- *"Try this" and "think about it"* style discussions and side notes keep students active in their study of each

---

TABLE 1 Critical Thinking

Critical thinking coverage can be found on the following pages:

A scientific model for studying psychology, pp. 174–175
Are intelligence tests biased?, pp. 251–252
Are personality tests able to predict behavior?, p. 362
Attachment style, development of, pp. 83–86
Attention-deficit/hyperactivity disorder (ADHD), p. 377
Can memories of childhood sexual abuse be repressed and then recovered?, p. 214
Causation and the violence-viewing effect, pp. 189–190
Classifying psychological disorders, pp. 379–380
Confirmation bias, p. 223
Continuity vs. stage theories of development, pp. 68–69
Correlation and causation, pp. 16–17, 87, 92, 101
Critical thinking defined, p. 8
Critiquing the evolutionary perspective on sexuality, pp. 126–127
Discovery of hypothalamus reward centers, p. 42
Do lie detectors lie?, p. 276
Do other species have language?, pp. 236–237
Do other species share our cognitive abilities?, pp. 230–231
Do video games teach, or release, violence?, p. 334

Does meditation enhance health?, pp. 300–301
Effectiveness of alternative psychotherapies, p. 428
Emotion and the brain, pp. 37, 39–42
Emotional intelligence, p. 240
Evolutionary science and human origins, pp. 128–129
Extrasensory perception, pp. 162–163
Fear of flying vs. probabilities, p. 225
Freud's contributions, pp. 355–357
Gender bias in the workplace, p. 110
Genetic and environmental influences on schizophrenia, pp. 403–404
Group differences in intelligence, pp. 248–252
Hindsight bias, pp. 11–12
How do nature and nurture shape prenatal development?, pp. 70–72
How do twin and adoption studies help us understand the effects of nature and nurture?, pp. 74–75
How does the brain process language?, pp. 234–235
How much is gender socially constructed vs. biologically influenced?, pp. 111–115
How valid is the Rorschach inkblot test?, p. 355

Human curiosity, pp. 2, 3
Humanistic perspective, evaluating, p. 359
Hypnosis: dissociation or social influence?, pp. 157–158
Importance of checking fears against facts, p. 225
Interaction of nature and nurture in overall development, p. 68
Is dissociative identity disorder a real disorder?, pp. 407–408
Is psychotherapy effective?, pp. 426–427
Is repression a myth?, p. 356
Limits of case studies, naturalistic observation, and surveys, p. 16
Limits of intuition, pp. 10–12
Nature, nurture, and perceptual ability, pp. 151–152
Overconfidence, pp. 12, 226
Parenting styles, p. 87
Posttraumatic stress disorder (PTSD), pp. 382–383
Powers and limits of parental involvement on development, pp. 93–94
Powers and perils of intuition, pp. 227–228
Problem-solving strategies, pp. 222–223
Psychic phenomena, pp. 3, 162–163
Psychology: a discipline for critical thought, pp. 11, 14, 16

Religious involvement and longevity, pp. 301–302
Scientific attitude, p. 3
Scientific method, pp. 12–14
Sexual desire and ovulation, p. 116
Similarities and differences in social power between men and women, pp. 109, 110
Stress and cancer, p. 290
Stress and health, p. 292
Subliminal sensation and persuasion, p. 136
Technology and "big data" observations, p. 15
The divided brain, pp. 48–50
Therapeutic lifestyle change, p. 431
The stigma of introversion, p. 361
The Internet as social amplifier, p. 326
Using more than 10 percent of our brain, p. 46
Using psychology to debunk popular beliefs, p. 8
Values and psychology, pp. 21–23
What does selective attention teach us about consciousness?, pp. 51–53
What factors influence sexual orientation?, pp. 121–124
What is the connection between the brain and the mind?, p. 38
Wording effects, pp. 15–16

chapter. We often encourage students to imagine themselves as participants in experiments. In Chapter 11, for example, students take the perspective of participants in a Solomon Asch conformity experiment and, later, in one of Stanley Milgram's obedience experiments. We've also asked students to join the fun by taking part in activities they can try along the way. Here are two examples: In Chapter 5, they try out a quick sensory adaptation activity. In Chapter 9, they test the effects of maintaining different facial expressions.

- **Critical examinations of pop psychology** spark interest and provide important lessons in thinking critically about everyday topics. For example, Chapter 5 includes a close examination of ESP, and Chapter 7 addresses the controversial topic of repression of painful memories.

2. Behavior Is a Biopsychosocial Event

Students will learn that we can best understand human behavior if we view it from three levels—the biological, psychological, and social-cultural. This concept is introduced in Chapter 1 and revisited throughout the text. Readers will see evidence of our human kinship. Yet they will also better understand the dimensions of our diversity—our *individual* diversity, our *gender* diversity, and our *cultural* diversity. **TABLE 2**

TABLE 2 Culture and Multicultural Experience

Coverage of *culture and multicultural experience* can be found on the following pages:

Academic achievement, pp. 249–251, 296
Achievement motivation, p. B-4
Adolescence, onset and end of, pp. 94–95
Aggression, pp. 332–333
Animal learning, p. 231
Animal research, views on, p. 22
Beauty ideals, p. 337
Biopsychosocial approach, pp. 7, 68, 111–115, 366, 378
Body image, p. 406
Child raising, pp. 86–88
Cognitive development of children, p. 82
Collectivism, p. 319
Crime and stress hormone levels, p. 408
Cultural values
  child raising and, pp. 86–88
  morality and, p. 90
  psychotherapy and, p. 429
Culture
  defined, p. 9
  emotional expression and, pp. 278–280
  intelligence test bias and, p. 251
  the self and, pp. 369–371
Deindividuation, p. 324
Depression
  and suicide, p. 400
  risk of, p. 397
Developmental similarities across cultures, p. 68
Discrimination, pp. 327–328
Dissociative identity disorder, p. 407
Division of labor, p. 114
Divorce rate, p. 99

Dysfunctional behavior diagnoses, pp. 376–378
Eating disorders, p. 378
Enemy perceptions, p. 342
Expressions of grief, p. 101
Family environment, p. 92
Family self, sense of, pp. 86–88
Father's presence
  pregnancy and, p. 120
  violence and, p. 333
Flow, pp. B-1–B-2
Foot-in-the-door phenomenon, p. 316
Framing, and organ donation, p. 227
Fundamental attribution error, p. 314
Gender roles, pp. 110, 113–114
Gender
  aggression and, pp. 108–109
  communication and, p. 109
  sex drive and, p. 116
General adaptation syndrome, p. 287
Groupthink, pp. 325–326
Happiness, pp. 303, 305, 306–307
HIV/AIDS, pp. 118, 290
Homosexuality, attitudes toward, p. 121
Identity formation, pp. 91–92
Individualism, pp. 314, 319, 324
  ingroup bias, p. 329
  moral development and, p. 90
Intelligence, p. 238
  group differences in, pp. 248–252
  test scores, p. 249
Intelligence testing, pp. 240–242
Interracial dating, p. 327
Job satisfaction, p. B-5
Just-world phenomenon, p. 329

Language development, p. 234
Leadership, p. B-7
Life cycle, p. 68
Marriage, pp. 338–339
Mating preferences, p. 126
Mental disorders and stress, p. 378
Mere exposure effect, p. 335
Migration, p. 267
Motivation, p. 260
Naturalistic observation, pp. 14–15
Need to belong, pp. 266–267
Obedience, p. 321
Obesity, p. 264
  and sleep loss, p. 265
Optimism, p. 296
Ostracism, p. 267
Parent-teen relations, pp. 92–93
Partner selection, p. 337
Peace, promoting, pp. 342–343
Personal control, p. 294
Personality traits, p. 360
Phobias, p. 382
Physical attractiveness, p. 337
Poverty, explanations of, p. 315
Power differences between men and women, pp. 109, 110
Prejudice, pp. 327–330
  automatic, pp. 327–328
  contact, cooperation, and, pp. 342–343
  forming categories, p. 330
  group polarization and, p. 325
  racial, pp. 316, 327–328
  subtle versus overt, pp. 327–328
  unconscious, Supreme Court's recognition of, p. 328
Prosocial behavior, pp. 188–189
Psychoactive drugs, pp. 393–394

Psychological disorders, pp. 376–378
  treatment of, p. 429
Race-influenced perceptions, pp. 327–328
Racial similarities, pp. 249–251
Religious involvement and longevity, p. 301
Resilience, p. 438
Risk assessment, p. 224
Scapegoat theory, p. 329
Schizophrenia, pp. 403–405
Self-esteem, pp. 307, 367
Self-serving bias, p. 368
Separation anxiety, p. 84
Serial position effect, p. 207
Sexual risk-taking among teens, pp. 119–120
Social clock variation, p. 100
Social influence, pp. 319, 321–322
Social loafing, p. 324
Social networking, p. 268
Social support, p. 302
Social trust, p. 86
Social-cultural psychology, p. 6
Stereotype threat, pp. 251–252
Stereotypes, pp. 327, 329
Substance use disorders, pp. 386–394
  rates of, p. 386
Susto, p. 378
Taijin-kyofusho, p. 378
Taste preference, p. 263
Terrorism, pp. 224, 225
Trauma, pp. 356, 426
Universal expressions, p. 8
Video game playing
  compulsive, p. 386
  effects of, p. 334
Weight, p. 264
Well-being, p. 307

provides a list of integrated coverage of the cross-cultural perspective on psychology. **TABLE 3** lists the coverage of the psychology of women and men. Significant gender and cross-cultural examples and research are presented within the narrative. In addition, an abundance of photos showcases the diversity of cultures within North America and across the globe. These photos and their informative captions bring the pages to life, broadening students' perspectives in applying psychological science to their own world and to others' worlds across the globe.

TABLE 3 Psychology of Women and Men

Coverage of the *psychology of women and men* can be found on the following pages:

Age and decreased fertility, p. 96
Aggression, pp. 108–109, 331
  testosterone and, p. 331
Alcohol use and sexual assault, p. 387
Alcohol use disorder, p. 387
Alcohol, women's greater physical vulnerability, p. 387
Attraction, pp. 335–339
Beauty ideals, pp. 336–337
Bipolar disorder, p. 395
Body image, p. 406
Brain scans, and sex-reassignment surgery, p. 115
Depression, pp. 396–400
  among girls, p. 92
  higher vulnerability of women, pp. 396–399
  seasonal pattern, p. 394
Eating disorders, p. 108
Emotion, p. 277
  ability to detect, p. 277
  expressiveness, p. 277
  identification of as masculine or feminine, p. 277
Empathy, p. 277
Father's presence
  pregnancy rates and, p. 120
  lower sexual activity and, p. 120
Freud's views on gender identity development, p. 352
Gender, pp. 8–10
  anxiety and, p. 396
  biological influences on, pp. 111–113
  changes in society's thinking about, pp. 114, 128
  social-cultural influences on, pp. 113–115
  workplace bias and, p. 110
Gender differences, pp. 8–10, 108–111
  rumination and, p. 399
  evolutionary perspectives on, pp. 124–127
  intelligence and, pp. 248–249
  sexuality and, p. 125
Gender discrimination, p. 328
Gender identity, development of, pp. 114–115
  in transgender individuals, p. 115
Gender roles, p. 114
Gender schema theory, p. 114
Gender similarities, pp. 108–111
Gender typing, p. 114
Generalized anxiety disorder, p. 381
HIV/AIDS, women's vulnerability to, p. 118
Hormones and sexual behavior, pp. 116–117

Human sexuality, pp. 116–120
Leadership styles, p. 110
Learned helplessness, pp. 398–399
Love
  companionate, pp. 338–339
  passionate, p. 338
Marriage, pp. 98–99
Motor development, infant massage and, p. 77
Mating preferences, pp. 125–126
Maturation, pp. 88–89, 94
Menarche, p. 88
Menopause, p. 96
Pain, women's greater sensitivity to, p. 156
Physical attractiveness, pp. 336–337
Posttraumatic stress disorder, p. 383
Puberty, pp. 88–89
  early onset of, p. 88
Relationship equity, p. 339
Responses to stress, p. 288
Schizophrenia, p. 402
Sex, pp. 8, 116–120
Sex and gender, p. 108
Sex chromosomes, p. 111
Sex drive, gender differences, pp. 117–118, 125
Sex hormones, pp. 111, 116
Sex-reassignment, pp. 107, 113, 115
Sexual activity and aging, p. 97
Sexual activity, teen girls' regret, p. 119
Sexual arousal, gender and gay-straight differences, p. 123
Sexual intercourse among teens, pp. 119–120
Sexual orientation, pp. 121–124
Sexual response cycle, p. 116
Sexual response, alcohol-related expectation and, p. 387
Sexual scripts, p. 333
Sexuality, natural selection and, pp. 125–126
Sexualization of girls, p. 120
Sexually explicit media, p. 333
Sexually transmitted infections, p. 118
Similarities and differences between men and women, pp. 108–111
Social clock, p. 100
Social connectedness, pp. 109–111
Social power, p. 109
Spirituality and longevity, p. 301
Substance use disorder and the brain, p. 387
Teen pregnancy, pp. 119–120
Violent crime, p. 108
Vulnerability to psychological disorders, p. 108
Women in psychology, pp. 2, 4

3. We Operate With a Two-Track Mind (Dual Processing)

Today's psychological science explores our *dual-processing* capacity. Our perception, thinking, memory, and attitudes all operate on two levels: the level of fully aware, conscious processing, and the behind-the-scenes level of unconscious processing. Students may be surprised to learn how much information we process outside of our awareness. Discussions of sleep (Chapter 2), perception (Chapter 5), cognition (Chapter 8), emotion (Chapter 9), and attitudes and prejudice (Chapter 11) provide some particularly compelling examples of what goes on in our mind's downstairs.

4. Psychology Explores Human Strengths as Well as Challenges

Students will learn about the many troublesome behaviors and emotions psychologists study, as well as the ways psychologists work with those who need help. Yet students will also learn about the *beneficial* emotions and traits that psychologists study, and the ways psychologists (some as part of the new *positive psychology* movement—see **TABLE 4**) attempt to nurture those traits in others. After studying with this text, students may find themselves living improved day-to-day lives. See, for example, tips for better sleep in Chapter 2, parenting suggestions throughout Chapter 3, information to help with romantic relationships in Chapters 3, 4, 11 and elsewhere, and tips for greater happiness in Chapter 10. Students may also find themselves doing better in their courses. See, for example, following this preface, "Time Management: Or, How to

TABLE 4 Examples of Positive Psychology	
Coverage of *positive psychology* topics can be found in the following chapters:	
Topic	**Chapter**
Altruism/compassion	3, 8, 11, 12, 14
Coping	10
Courage	11
Creativity	6, 8, 11, 12
Emotional intelligence	9, 11
Empathy	3, 6, 10, 11, 14
Flow	10, App B
Gratitude	9, 10
Happiness/life satisfaction	3, 9, 10, 11
Humility	11
Humor	10
Justice	3, 11
Leadership	11, 12, App B
Love	3, 4, 9, 10, 11, 12, 13, 14
Morality	3
Optimism	10, 12
Personal control	10
Resilience	3, 10, 11, 14
Self-discipline	3, 8, 9, 12, App B
Self-awareness	10
Self-efficacy	10, 12
Self-esteem	3, 4, 9, 11, 12
Spirituality	3, 4, 10
Toughness (grit)	8, App B
Wisdom	3, 8, 12

Be a Great Student and Still Have a Life"; "Use Psychology to Become a Stronger Person—and a Better Student" at the end of Chapter 1; "Improving Memory" in Chapter 7; and the helpful study tools throughout the text based on the documented testing effect. Students may learn to nurture their own strengths by completing the newly revised "Assess Your Strengths" activities in Launch-Pad.

Everyday Life Applications

Throughout this text, as its title suggests, we relate the findings of psychology's research to the real world. This edition includes:

- chapter-ending "In Your Everyday Life" questions, helping students make the concepts more meaningful (and memorable).

- "Assess Your Strengths" personal self-assessments in LaunchPad, allowing students to actively apply key principles to their own experiences.

- fun notes and quotes in small boxes throughout the text, applying psychology's findings to sports, literature, world religions, music, and more.

- an emphasis throughout the text on critical thinking in everyday life, including the "Statistical Reasoning in Everyday Life" appendix, helping students to become more informed consumers and everyday thinkers.

- added emphasis on *clinical* applications. *Psychology in Everyday Life* offers a great sensitivity to clinical issues throughout the text. For example, Chapter 13, Psychological Disorders, includes lengthy coverage of substance-related disorders, with guidelines for determining substance use disorder. See **TABLE 5** for a listing of coverage of clinical psychology concepts and issues throughout the text.

See inside the front and back covers (or at the beginning of the e-Book) for a listing of students' top-rated applications to everyday life from this text.

Scattered throughout this book, students will find interesting and informative review notes and quotes from researchers and others that will encourage them to be active learners and to apply their new knowledge to everyday life.

Study System Follows Best Practices From Learning and Memory Research

This text's learning system harnesses the *testing effect*, which documents the benefits of actively retrieving information through self-testing (**FIGURE 3**). Thus, each chapter offers 12 to 15 **Retrieve + Remember** questions interspersed throughout (**FIGURE 4**). Creating these *desirable difficulties* for students along the way optimizes the testing effect, as does *immediate feedback* (via answers that are available after attempting to answer each question).

In addition, each main section of text begins with a numbered question that establishes a **learning objective** and directs student reading. The Chapter Review section repeats these questions as a further self-testing opportunity

FIGURE 3 How to learn and remember
For a 5-minute animated guide to more effective studying, visit tinyurl.com/HowToRemember.

Retrieve + Remember

- What does a good theory do?

ANSWER: 1. It organizes observed facts. 2. It implies hypotheses that offer testable predictions and, sometimes, practical applications. 3. It often stimulates further research.

- Why is replication important?

ANSWER: When others are able to repeat (replicate) studies and produce similar results, psychologists can have more confidence in the original findings.

FIGURE 4 Sample of Retrieve + Remember feature

TABLE 5 Clinical Psychology

Coverage of *clinical psychology* can be found on the following pages:

Abused children, risk of psychological disorder among, p. 174
Alcohol use and aggression, p. 332
Alzheimer's disease, pp. 33, 195, 264
Anxiety disorders, pp. 380–382
Autism spectrum disorder, pp. 80–81, 108, 223, 238
Aversive conditioning, pp. 421–422
Behavior modification, p. 422
Behavior therapies, pp. 419–422
Big Five, use in understanding personality disorders, p. 362
Bipolar disorder, pp. 395–396
Brain damage and memory loss, p. 208
Brain scans, p. 38
Brain stimulation therapies, pp. 434–436
Childhood trauma, effect on mental health, p. 86
Client-analyst relationship in psychoanalysis, pp. 416–417
Client-therapist relationship, p. 429
Clinical psychologists, pp. 5–6
Cognitive therapies, pp. 422–424
eating disorders and, pp. 423–424
Culture and values in psychotherapy, p. 429

Depression:
adolescence and, p. 92
heart disease and, pp. 291–292
homosexuality and, p. 121
mood-memory connection and, p. 207
outlook and, p. 399
self-esteem and, pp. 17, 92
social exclusion and, p. 93
unexpected loss and, p. 101
Dissociative and personality disorders, pp. 406–409
Dissociative identity disorder, therapist's role, pp. 407–408
Drug therapies, pp. 18–19, 432–434
DSM-5, p. 379
Eating disorders, pp. 405–406
Emotional intelligence, p. 240
Evidence-based clinical decision making, p. 428
Exercise, therapeutic effects of, pp. 298–299, 431
Exposure therapies, pp. 420–421
Generalized anxiety disorder, p. 381
Grief therapy, p. 101
Group and family therapies, p. 425
Historical treatment of mental illness, p. 416
Hospitals, clinical psychologists and, p. 416
Humanistic therapies, pp. 418–419

Hypnosis and pain relief, pp. 157–158
Intelligence scales and stroke rehabilitation, p. 242
Lifestyle change, therapeutic effects of, p. 431
Loss of a child, psychiatric hospitalization and, p. 101
Major depressive disorder, pp. 394–395
Medical model of mental disorders, p. 378
Neurotransmitter imbalances and related disorders, pp. 33–34
Nurturing strengths, pp. 358–359
Obsessive-compulsive disorder, p. 382
Operant conditioning, p. 422
Ostracism, pp. 267–268
Panic disorder, pp. 381–382
Person-centered therapy, p. 419
Personality inventories, pp. 361–362
Personality testing, pp. 361–362
Phobias, p. 382
Physical and psychological treatment of pain, pp. 155–158
Posttraumatic stress disorder, pp. 382–383
Psychiatric labels and bias, pp. 379–380
Psychoactive drugs, types of, pp. 385–386

Psychoanalysis, pp. 416–418
Psychodynamic theory, pp. 350–353
Psychodynamic therapy, pp. 417–418
Psychological disorders, pp. 375–380
are those with disorders dangerous?, pp. 409–410
classification of, pp. 379–380
gender differences in, p. 108
preventing, and building resilience, pp. 436–438
Psychotherapy, pp. 416–417
effectiveness of, pp. 426–427
Rorschach inkblot test, p. 355
Savant syndrome, pp. 238–239
Schizophrenia, pp. 401–405
parent-blaming and, p. 93
risk of, pp. 403–405
Self-actualization, p. 357
Self-injury, pp. 400–401
Sex-reassignment surgery, pp. 113, 115
Sleep disorders, pp. 58–60
Spanked children, risk for aggression among, p. 181
Substance use disorders and addictive behaviors, pp. 385–394
Suicide, pp. 400–401
Testosterone replacement therapy, p. 116
Tolerance, withdrawal, and addiction, p. 386

(with answers a click away in the e-Book, or in the printed Appendix D, Complete Chapter Reviews). The Chapter Review section also offers a page-referenced list of **Terms and Concepts to Remember** (set up as a self-test in the e-Book), and **Chapter Test** questions in multiple formats to promote optimal retention.

Each chapter closes with **In Your Everyday Life** questions, designed to help students make the concepts more personally meaningful, and therefore more memorable. These questions are also well designed to function as group discussion topics. The text offers hundreds of interesting **applications** to help students see just how applicable psychology's concepts are to everyday life.

These features enhance the Survey-Question-Read-Retrieve-Review (SQ3R) format. Chapter outlines allow students to *survey* what's to come. Learning objective *questions* encourage students to *read* actively. Periodic Retrieve + Remember sections and the Chapter Review (with repeated Learning Objective Questions, Key Terms and Concepts list, and a complete Chapter Test) encourage students to test themselves by *retrieving* what they know and *reviewing* what they don't. (See Figure 4 for a Retrieve + Remember sample.)

Our LearningCurve formative quizzing in LaunchPad is built on these principles as well, allowing students to develop a personalized learning plan.

A Design Students Love

In response to unanimous support from students across previous editions, the new fourth edition retains the easy-to-read three-column design with a clean look that makes navigation easy. Our three-column format is rich with visual support. It responds to students' expectations, based on what they have told us about their reading, both online and in print. The narrow column width eliminates the strain of reading across a wide page. Illustrations appear near the pertinent text narrative, which helps students see them in the appropriate context. Key terms are defined near where they are introduced, and always in a corner of the page.

key terms Look for complete definitions of each important term in a page corner near the term's introduction in the narrative.

In written reviews, students have compared our three-column design with a traditional one-column design (without knowing which was ours). They have unanimously preferred the three-column design. It was, they said, "less intimidating" and "less overwhelming," and it "motivated" them to read on.

Multimedia for *Psychology in Everyday Life,* Fourth Edition

Psychology in Everyday Life, Fourth Edition, boasts impressive multimedia options. For more information about any of these choices, visit our online catalog at MacmillanLearning.com/PEL4eContent.

LaunchPad

LaunchPad (LaunchPadWorks.com) was carefully designed to solve key challenges in the course (see **FIGURE 5**). LaunchPad gives students everything they need to prepare for class and exams, while giving instructors everything *they* need to quickly set up a course, shape the content to their syllabus, craft presentations and lectures, assign and assess homework, and guide the progress of individual students and the class as a whole.

- **An interactive e-Book** integrates the text and all student media, including the *"Assess Your Strengths"* activities, *"Immersive Learning: How Would You Know?"* activities, and *PsychSim 6* tutorials.

- **LearningCurve adaptive quizzing** gives individualized question sets and feedback based on each student's correct and incorrect responses. All the questions are tied back to the e-Book to encourage students to read the book in preparation for class time and exams.

- **PsychSim 6** has arrived! Tom Ludwig's (Hope College) fabulous new tutorials further strengthen LaunchPad's abundance of helpful student activity resources.

- The new **Video Assignment Tool** makes it easy to assign and assess video-based activities and projects, and provides a convenient way for students to submit video coursework.

- **LaunchPad Gradebook** gives a clear window on performance for the whole class, for individual students, and for individual assignments.

- A **streamlined interface** helps students manage their schedule of assignments, while *social commenting tools* let them connect with classmates, and learn from one another.

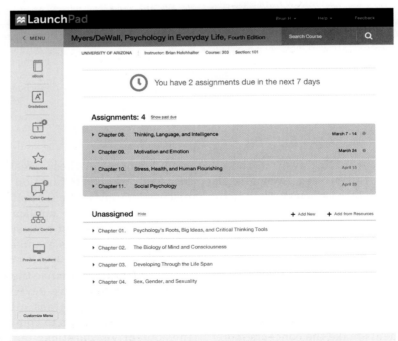

FIGURE 5 Sample from LaunchPad

24/7 help is a click away, accessible from a link in the upper right-hand corner.

- We [DM and ND] curated **optional pre-built chapter units,** which can be used as is or customized. Or choose not to use them and build your course from scratch.

- **Book-specific instructor resources** include PowerPoint sets, textbook graphics, lecture and activity suggestions, test banks, and more.

- LaunchPad offers **easy LMS integration** into your school's learning management system.

Faculty Support and Student Resources

- **Instructor's Resources** available in LaunchPad

- **Lecture Guides** available in LaunchPad

- **Macmillan Community** (Community.Macmillan.com) Created *by* instructors *for* instructors, this is an ideal forum for interacting with fellow educators—including Macmillan authors—in your discipline. Join ongoing conversations about everything from course prep and presentations to assignments and assessments to teaching with media, keeping pace with—and influencing—new directions in your field. Includes exclusive access to classroom resources, blogs, webinars, professional development opportunities, and more.

- Enhanced course management solutions (including course cartridges)

- e-Book in various available formats

Video and Presentation

- The **Video Collection** is now the single resource for all videos for introductory psychology from Worth Publishers. Available on flash drive and in LaunchPad, this includes more than 130 clips.

- **Interactive Presentation Slides for Introductory Psychology** is an extraordinary series of PowerPoint® lectures. This is a dynamic, yet easy-to-use way to engage students during classroom presentations of core psychology topics. This collection provides opportunities for discussion and interaction, and includes an unprecedented number of embedded video clips and animations.

Assessment

- **LearningCurve** quizzing in LaunchPad

- Diploma Test Banks, downloadable from LaunchPad and our online catalog

- Chapter Quizzes in LaunchPad

- Clicker Question Presentation Slides now in PowerPoint®

Print

- *Study Guide,* by Richard O. Straub

- *Pursuing Human Strengths: A Positive Psychology Guide,* Second Edition, by Martin Bolt and Dana S. Dunn

- *Critical Thinking Companion,* Third Edition, by Jane S. Halonen and Cynthia Gray

- FABBS Foundation's *Psychology and the Real World: Essays Illustrating Fundamental Contributions to Society,* Second Edition, edited by Morton Ann Gernsbacher and James R. Pomerantz

- *The Horse That Won't Go Away: Clever Hans, Facilitated Communication, and the Need for Clear Thinking,* by Scott O. Lilienfeld, Susan A. Nolan, and Thomas Heinzen

- *The Psychology Major's Companion: Everything You Need to Know to Get Where You Want to Go,* by Dana S. Dunn and Jane S. Halonen

- *The Worth Expert Guide to Scientific Literacy: Thinking Like a Psychological Scientist,* by Kenneth D. Keith and Bernard C. Beins

- *Collaboration in Psychological Science: Behind the Scenes,* by Richard Zweigenhaft and Eugene Borgida

APA Assessment Tools

In 2011, the American Psychological Association (APA) approved the new **Principles for Quality Undergraduate Education in Psychology.** These broad-based principles and their associated recommendations were designed to "produce psychologically literate citizens who apply the principles of psychological science at work and at home." (See apa.org/education/undergrad/principles.aspx.)

APA's more specific **2013 Learning Goals and Outcomes,** from their *Guidelines for the Undergraduate Psychology Major,* Version 2.0, were designed to gauge progress in students graduating with psychology majors. (See apa.org/ed/precollege/about/psymajor-guidelines.pdf.) Many psychology departments use these goals and outcomes to help establish their own benchmarks for departmental assessment purposes.

Some instructors are eager to know whether a given text for the introductory course helps students get a good start at achieving these APA benchmarks. **TABLE 6** outlines the way *Psychology in Everyday Life,* Fourth Edition, could help you to address the 2013 APA Learning Goals and Outcomes in your department. In addition, the Test Bank questions for *Psychology in Everyday Life,* Fourth Edition, are all keyed to these APA Learning Goals and Outcomes.

An APA working group in 2013 drafted guidelines for **Strengthening the Common Core of the Introductory Psychology**

TABLE 6 *Psychology in Everyday Life,* Fourth Edition, Corresponds to 2013 APA Learning Goals

Relevant Feature from *Psychology in Everyday Life,* Fourth Edition	APA Learning Goals				
	Knowledge Base in Psychology	Scientific Inquiry and Critical Thinking	Ethical and Social Responsibility in a Diverse World	Communication	Professional Development
Text content	•	•	•	•	•
Four Big Ideas in Psychology as integrating themes	•	•	•		•
"Thinking Critically About" features	•	•	•		•
Learning Objective Questions previewing main sections	•	•		•	
Retrieve + Remember sections throughout	•	•	•	•	•
In Your Everyday Life questions at end of each chapter	•	•	•		•
"Try this"-style activities integrated throughout	•	•		•	•
Chapter Tests	•	•		•	
Statistical Reasoning in Everyday Life appendix		•		•	•
Psychology at Work appendix	•	•	•	•	•
Subfields of Psychology appendix, with Careers in Psychology online appendix	•		•		•
LaunchPad with LearningCurve formative quizzing	•	•	•	•	•
"Assess Your Strengths" feature in LaunchPad	•	•	•	•	•
"Immersive Learning: How Would You Know?" activities in LaunchPad	•	•	•	•	•

Course (tinyurl.com/14dsdx5). Their goals were to "strike a nuanced balance providing flexibility yet guidance." The group noted that "a mature science should be able to agree upon and communicate its unifying core while embracing diversity."

MCAT Now Includes Psychology

Since 2015, the Medical College Admission Test (MCAT) has devoted 25 percent of its questions to the "Psychological, Social, and Biological Foundations of Behavior," with most of those questions coming from the psychological science taught in introductory psychology courses. From 1977 to 2014, the MCAT focused on biology, chemistry, and physics. Hereafter, reported the *Preview Guide for MCAT 2015,* the exam will also recognize "the importance of socio-cultural and behavioral determinants of health and health outcomes." The exam's new psychology section includes the breadth of topics in this text. For example, see **TABLE 7,** which outlines the precise correlation between this text's coverage of Emotion and of Stress, and the corresponding portion of the MCAT exam. To improve their MCAT preparation, I [ND] have taught premedical students an intensive course covering the topics that appear in this text. For a complete pairing of the new MCAT psychology topics with this book's contents, see MacmillanLearning.com/PEL4eContent. In addition, the Test Bank questions for *Psychology in Everyday Life,* Fourth Edition, are keyed to the new MCAT.

TABLE 7 Sample MCAT Correlation with *Psychology in Everyday Life*, Fourth Edition

MCAT 2015	*Psychology in Everyday Life*, Fourth Edition, Correlations	
Content Category 6C: Responding to the world		Page Number
Emotion	Emotion: Arousal, Behavior, and Cognition; Embodied Emotion; Expressed and Experienced Emotion	270–283
Three components of emotion (i.e., cognitive, physiological, behavioral)	Emotion: Arousal, Behavior, and Cognition	270–273
Universal emotions (e.g., fear, anger, happiness, surprise, joy, disgust, and sadness)	The Basic Emotions	273–274
	Culture and Emotion—including the universal emotions	278–279
Adaptive role of emotion	Emotion as the body's adaptive response	270
	Emotions and the Autonomic Nervous System	274
Theories of emotion		
James-Lange theory	*James-Lange Theory: Arousal Comes Before Emotion*	271
Cannon-Bard theory	*Cannon-Bard Theory: Arousal and Emotion Happen at the Same Time*	271
Schachter-Singer theory	*Schachter and Singer Two-Factor Theory: Arousal + Label = Emotion*	271–272
The role of biological processes in perceiving emotion	Emotions and the Autonomic Nervous System	274
Brain regions involved in the generation and experience of emotions	The Physiology of Emotions	274
	Zajonc, LeDoux, and Lazarus: Emotion and the Two-Track Brain	272–273
The role of the limbic system in emotion	*Emotions and the Autonomic Nervous System*	274
	Physiological differences among specific emotions	274–275
Emotion and the autonomic nervous system	Emotions and the Autonomic Nervous System	274
Physiological markers of emotion (signatures of emotion)	The Physiology of Emotions	274–276
Stress	Stress, Health, and Human Flourishing	284–311
The nature of stress	Stress: Some Basic Concepts	286–288
Appraisal	*Stress appraisal*	286
Different types of stressors (i.e., cataclysmic events, personal)	*Stressors—Things That Push Our Buttons*	286–287
Effects of stress on psychological functions	*Stress Reactions—From Alarm to Exhaustion*	287–288
Stress outcomes/response to stressors	Stress Reactions—From Alarm to Exhaustion	287–288
Physiological	Stress Reactions—From Alarm to Exhaustion	287–288
	Stress Effects and Health	288–292
Emotional	*Stress and Heart Disease—The Effects of Personality Type, The Effects of Pessimism and Depression*	290–292
	Coping With Stress	293–298
	Posttraumatic Stress Disorder	382–385
Behavioral	Stress Reactions—From Alarm to Exhaustion	287–288
	Coping With Stress	293–298
Managing stress (e.g., exercise, relaxation techniques, spirituality)	Managing Stress Effects—aerobic exercise, relaxation and meditation, faith communities	298–302

In Appreciation

Aided by input from thousands of instructors and students over the years, this has become a better, more effective, more accurate book than two authors alone (these authors at least) could write. Our indebtedness continues to the innumerable researchers who have been so willing to share their time and talent to help us accurately report their research, and to the hundreds of instructors who have taken the time to offer feedback.

Our gratitude extends to the colleagues who contributed criticism, corrections, and creative ideas related to the content, pedagogy, and format of this new edition and its teaching package. For their expertise and encouragement, and the gift of their time to the teaching of psychology, we thank the reviewers and consultants listed here.

Matthew Alcala
Santa Ana College

Burton Beck
Pensacola State College

LaQuisha Beckum
De Anza College

Gina Bell
Santa Barbara City College

Bucky Bhadha
Pasadena City College

Gerald Braasch
McHenry County College

T. L. Brink
Cosumnes River College

Eric Bruns
Campbellsville University

Carrie Canales
West Los Angeles College

Michael Cassens
Irvine Valley College

Wilson Chu
Cerritos College

Jeffrey Cooley
University of Wisconsin–Oshkosh

Amy Cunningham
San Diego Mesa College

Robert DuBois
Waukesha County Technical College

Michael Fantetti
Western New England University

Jessica Fede
Johnson and Wales University

Perry Fuchs
University of Texas at Arlington

Marcus Galle
University of Texas Rio Grande Valley

Caroline Gee
Saddleback College

Emily Germain
Southern Wesleyan University

Pavithra Giridharan
Middlesex Community College

Allyson Graf
Elmira College

Philippe Gross
Kapi'olani Community College

Christopher Hayashi
Southwestern College

Ann Hennessey
Los Angeles Pierce College

Julia Hoigaard
Fullerton College

Lindsay Holland
Chattanooga State Community College

Michael Huff
College of the Canyons

Lynn Ingram
University of North Carolina, Wilmington

Linda Johnson
Butte College

Andrew Kim
Citrus College

Kristie Knows His Gun
George Fox University

Misty Kolchakian
Mt. San Antonio College

Linda Krajewski
Norco College

Marika Lamoreaux
Georgia State University

Kelly Landman
Delaware County Community College

Karen Markowitz
Grossmont College

Jan Mendoza
Golden West College

Peter Metzner
Vance-Granville Community College

Josh Muller
College of the Sequoias

Hayley Nelson
Delaware County Community College

David Oberleitner
University of Bridgeport

Susan O'Donnell
George Fox University

Ifat Pelad
College of the Canyons

Lien Pham
Orange Coast College

Debra Phoenix Maher
Orange Coast College

Jack Powell
University of Hartford

Joseph Reish
Tidewater Community College

Ja Ne't Rommero
Mission College

Edie Sample
Metropolitan Community College-Elkorn Valley Campus

Meridith Selden
Yuba College

Aya Shigeto
Nova Southeastern University

Michael Skibo
Westchester Community College

Bradley Stern
Cosumnes River College

Leland Swenson
California Polytechnic State University, San Luis Obispo

Shawn Ward
Le Moyne College

Jane Whitaker
University of the Cumberlands

Judith Wightman
Kirkwood Community College

Ellen Wilson
University of Wisconsin–Oshkosh

We appreciate the guidance offered by the following teaching psychologists, who reviewed and offered helpful feedback on the development of our "Assess Your Strengths" LaunchPad activities, or on our new "Immersive Learning: How Would You Know?" feature in LaunchPad. (See LaunchPadWorks.com.)

"Assess Your Strengths" Activity Reviewers

Malinde Althaus, *Inver Hills Community College*

TaMetryce Collins, *Hillsborough Community College, Brandon*

Lisa Fosbender, *Gulf Coast State College*

Kelly Henry, *Missouri Western State University*

Brooke Hindman, *Greenville Technical College*

Natalie Kemp, *University of Mount Olive*

David Payne, *Wallace Community College*

Tanya Renner, *Kapi'olani Community College*

Lillian Russell, *Alabama State University, Montgomery*

Amy Williamson, *Moraine Valley Community College*

"Immersive Learning: How Would You Know?" Activity Reviewers

Pamela Ansburg, *Metropolitan State University of Denver*

Makenzie Bayles, *Jacksonville State University*

Lisamarie Bensman, *University of Hawai'i at Manoa*

Jeffrey Blum, *Los Angeles City College*

Pamela Costa, *Tacoma Community College*

Jennifer Dale, *Community College of Aurora*

Michael Devoley, *Lone Star College, Montgomery*

Rock Doddridge, *Asheville-Buncombe Technical Community College*

Kristen Doran, *Delaware County Community College*

Nathaniel Douda, *Colorado State University*

Celeste Favela, *El Paso Community College*

Nicholas Fernandez, *El Paso Community College*

Nathalie Franco, *Broward College*

Sara Garvey, *Colorado State University*

Nichelle Gause, *Clayton State University*

Michael Green, *Lone Star College, Montgomery*

Christine Grela, *McHenry County College*

Rodney Joseph Grisham, *Indian River State College*

Toni Henderson, *Langara College*

Jessica Irons, *James Madison University*

Darren Iwamoto, *Chaminade University of Honolulu*

Jerwen Jou, *University of Texas, Pan American*

Rosalyn King, *Northern Virginia Community College, Loudoun Campus*

Claudia Lampman, *University of Alaska, Anchorage*

Mary Livingston, *Louisiana Tech University*

Christine Lofgren, *University of California, Irvine*

Thomas Ludwig, *Hope College*

Theresa Luhrs, *DePaul University*

Megan McIlreavy, *Coastal Carolina University*

Elizabeth Mosser, *Harford Community College*

Robin Musselman, *Lehigh Carbon Community College*

Kelly O'Dell, *Community College of Aurora*

William Keith Pannell, *El Paso Community College*

Eirini Papafratzeskakou, *Mercer County Community College*

Jennifer Poole, *Langara College*

James Rodgers, *Hawkeye Community College*

Regina Roof-Ray, *Harford Community College*

Lisa Routh, *Pikes Peak Community College*

Conni Rush, *Pittsburg State University*

Randi Smith, *Metropolitan State University of Denver*

Laura Talcott, *Indiana University, South Bend*

Cynthia Turk, *Washburn University*

Parita Vithlani, *Harford Community College*

David Williams, *Spartanburg Community College*

We offer thanks to the three dozen instructors who thoughtfully responded to our new edition planning survey, from the following schools:

Allan Hancock College

Antelope Valley College

Bakersfield College

Barstow Community College

Bristol Community College

California State University, Chico

California State University, Long Beach

Cerritos College

Chaffey College

Chandler Gilbert Community College

Dallas County Community College

John Carroll University

Johnson & Wales University

Lincoln University

Middlesex Community College

North Lake College

Northampton Community College

Northern Essex College

Northern Kentucky University

Paradise Valley Community College

Pensacola State College

Rowan University

Sierra College

Suffolk County Community College

Tennessee State University

University of Wisconsin-Milwaukee

Upper Iowa University

Utica College

Valdosta State University

Yuba College

And we appreciate the input from the students who helped us select the best of the application questions from the text, to appear inside the front and back covers of this new edition. Those students represent the following schools:

College of St. Benedict

Cornell University

Creighton University

Fordham University

George Washington University

Hofstra University

Hope College

James Madison University

State University of New York at Geneseo

University of Kentucky

University of New Hampshire

At Worth Publishers a host of people played key roles in creating this fourth edition.

Noel Hohnstine and Laura Burden coordinated production of the huge media component for this edition, including the fun Assess Your Strengths activities. Betty Probert effectively edited and produced print and media supplements and, in the process, also helped fine-tune the whole book. Katie Pachnos provided invaluable support in commissioning and organizing the multitude of reviews, e-mailing information to professors, and handling numerous other daily tasks related to the book's development and production. Lee McKevitt did a splendid job of laying out each page. Robin Fadool and Candice Cheesman worked together to locate the myriad photos. Art Manager Matthew McAdams coordinated our working with artist Evelyn Pence to create the wonderful new "Thinking Critically About" infographics.

Tracey Kuehn, Director of Content Management Enhancement, displayed tireless tenacity, commitment, and impressive organization in leading Worth's gifted artistic production team and coordinating editorial input throughout the production process. Project Editor Won McIntosh and Senior Production Supervisor Sarah Segal masterfully kept the book to its tight schedule, and Director of Design Diana Blume and Senior Design Manager Blake Logan skillfully created the beautiful new design program.

As you can see, although this book has two authors it is a *team* effort. A special salute is due to two of our book development editors, who have invested so much in creating *Psychology in Everyday Life*. My [DM] longtime editor Christine Brune saw the need for a very short, accessible, student-friendly introductory psychology text, and she energized and guided the rest of us in bringing her vision to reality. Development editor Nancy Fleming is one of those rare editors who is gifted at "thinking big" about a chapter—and with a kindred spirit to our own—while also applying her sensitive, graceful, line-by-line touches. Her painstaking, deft editing was a key part of achieving the hoped-for brevity and accessibility. Development Editors Trish Morgan and Danielle Slevens also amazed us with their meticulous focus, impressive knowledge, and helpful editing. And Deborah Heimann did an excellent job with the copyediting.

To achieve our goal of supporting the teaching of psychology, this teaching package not only must be authored, reviewed, edited, and produced, but also made available to teachers of psychology, with effective guidance and professional and friendly servicing close at hand. For their exceptional success in doing all this, our author team is grateful to Macmillan Learning's professional sales and marketing team. We are especially grateful to Executive Marketing Manager Kate Nurre, Senior Marketing Manager Lindsay Johnson, and Learning Solutions Specialist Nicki Trombley both for their tireless efforts to inform and guide our teaching colleagues about our efforts to assist their teaching, and for the joy of working with them.

At Hope College, the supporting team members for this edition included Kathryn Brownson, who researched countless bits of information and edited and proofed hundreds of pages. Kathryn is a knowledgeable and sensitive adviser on many matters, and Sara Neevel is our high-tech manuscript developer, par excellence. At the University of Kentucky, Lorie Hailey has showcased a variety of indispensable qualities, including a sharp eye and a strong work ethic.

Again, I [DM] gratefully acknowledge the editing assistance and mentoring of my writing coach, poet Jack Ridl, whose influence resides in the voice you will be hearing in the pages that follow. He, more than anyone, cultivated my delight in dancing with the language, and taught me to approach writing as a craft that shades into art. Likewise, I [ND] am grateful to my intellectual hero and mentor, Roy Baumeister, who taught me how to hone my writing and embrace the writing life.

After hearing countless dozens of people say that this book's resource package has taken their teaching to a new level, we reflect on how fortunate we are to be a part of a team in which everyone has produced on-time work marked by the highest professional standards. For their remarkable talents, their long-term dedication, and their friendship, we thank John Brink, Thomas Ludwig, Richard Straub, Sue Frantz, and Jim Cuellar.

And we have enjoyed our ongoing work with each other! It has been a joy for me [DM] to welcome Nathan into this project. Nathan's fresh insights and contributions are enriching this book as we work together on each chapter. With support from our wonderful editors, this is a team project. In addition to our work together on the textbook, Nathan and I contribute to the monthly Teaching Current Directions in Psychological Science column in the APS *Observer* (tinyurl.com/MyersDeWall). I [DM] also blog at TalkPsych.com, where I share exciting new findings, everyday applications, and observations on all things psychology.

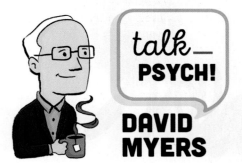

talk_ PSYCH!

DAVID MYERS

Finally, our gratitude extends to the many students and instructors who have written to offer suggestions, or just an encouraging word. It is for them, and those about to begin their study of psychology, that we have done our best to introduce the field we love.

*   *   *

The day this book went to press was the day we started gathering information and ideas for the next edition. Your input will influence how this book continues to evolve. So, please, do share your thoughts.

Hope College
Holland, Michigan 49422-9000 USA
DavidMyers.org
myers@hope.edu
@DavidGMyers

University of Kentucky
Lexington, Kentucky 40506-0044 USA
NathanDeWall.com
nathan.dewall@uky.edu
@cndewall

Time Management

OR, HOW TO BE A GREAT STUDENT AND STILL HAVE A LIFE

Richard O. Straub, University of Michigan, Dearborn

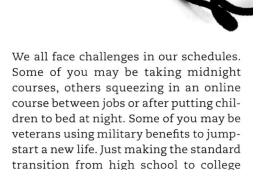

How Are You Using Your Time Now?

Design a Better Schedule
Plan the Term
Plan Your Week
More Tips for Effective Scheduling

Make Every Minute of Your Study Time Count
Take Useful Class Notes
Create a Study Space That Helps You Learn
Set Specific, Realistic Daily Goals
Use SQ3R to Help You Master This Text
Don't Forget About Rewards!

Do You Need to Revise Your New Schedule?
Are You Doing Well in Some Courses But Not in Others?
Have You Received a Poor Grade on a Test?
Are You Trying to Study Regularly for the First Time and Feeling Overwhelmed?

We all face challenges in our schedules. Some of you may be taking midnight courses, others squeezing in an online course between jobs or after putting children to bed at night. Some of you may be veterans using military benefits to jump-start a new life. Just making the standard transition from high school to college can be challenging enough.

How can you balance all of your life's demands and be successful? Time management. Manage the time you have so that you can find the time you need.

In this section, I will outline a simple, four-step process for improving the way you make use of your time.

1. Keep a time-use diary to understand how you are using your time. You may be surprised at how much time you're wasting.

2. Design a new schedule for using your time more effectively.

3. Make the most of your study time so that your new schedule will work for you.

4. If necessary, refine your new schedule, based on what you've learned.

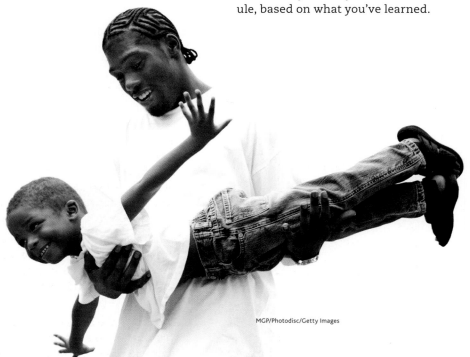

MGP/Photodisc/Getty Images

How Are You Using Your Time Now?

Although everyone gets 24 hours in the day and seven days in the week, we fill those hours and days with different obligations and interests. If you are like most people, you probably use your time wisely in some ways, and not so wisely in others. Answering the questions in **TABLE 1** can help you find trouble spots—and hopefully more time for the things that matter most to you.

The next thing you need to know is how you *actually* spend your time. To find out, record your activities in a *time-use diary* for one week. Be realistic. Take notes on how much time you spend attending class, studying, working, commuting, meeting personal and family needs, fixing and eating meals, socializing (don't forget texting and social networking), exercising, and anything else that occupies your time, including life's small practical tasks, which can take up plenty of your 24/7. As you record your activities, take notes on how you are feeling at various times of the day. When does your energy slump, and when do you feel most energetic?

Design a Better Schedule

Take a good look at your time-use diary. Where do you think you may be wasting time? Do you spend a lot of time commuting, for example? If so, could you use that time more productively? If you take public transportation, commuting is a great time to read and test yourself for review.

Did you remember to include time for meals, personal care, work schedules, family commitments, and other fixed activities?

How much time do you sleep? In the battle to meet all of life's daily commitments and interests, we tend to treat sleep as optional. Do your best to manage your life so that you can get enough sleep to feel rested. You will feel better and be healthier, and you will also do better academically and in relationships with your family and friends. (You will read more about this in Chapter 2.)

Are you dedicating enough time for focused study? Take a last look at your notes to see if any other patterns pop out. Now it's time to create a new and more efficient schedule.

Plan the Term

Before you draw up your new schedule, think ahead. Use your phone's calendar feature, or buy a portable calendar that covers the entire school term, with a writing space for each day. Using the course outlines provided by your instructors, enter the dates of all exams, term-paper deadlines, and other important assignments. Also be sure to enter your own long-range personal plans (work and family commitments, etc.). Keep your calendar up-to-date, refer to it often, and change it as needed. Through this process, you will develop a regular schedule that will help you achieve success.

Plan Your Week

To pass those exams, meet those deadlines, and keep up with your life outside of class, you will need to convert your long-term goals into a daily schedule. Be realistic—you will be living with this routine for the entire school term. Here are some more things to add to your calendar.

1. Enter your class times, work hours, and any other fixed obligations. Be thorough. Allow plenty of time for such things as commuting, meals, and laundry.

2. Set up a study schedule for each course. Remember what you learned about yourself in the study habits survey (Table 1) and your time-use diary.

3. After you have budgeted time for studying, fill in slots for other obligations, exercise, fun, and relaxation.

TABLE 1 Study Habits Survey

Answer the following questions, writing *Yes* or *No* for each line.

1. Do you usually set up a schedule to budget your time for studying, work, recreation, and other activities?

2. Do you often put off studying until time pressures force you to cram?

3. Do other students seem to study less than you do, but get better grades?

4. Do you usually spend hours at a time studying one subject, rather than dividing that time among several subjects?

5. Do you often have trouble remembering what you have just read in a textbook?

6. Before reading a chapter in a textbook, do you skim through it and read the section headings?

7. Do you try to predict test questions from your class notes and reading?

8. Do you usually try to summarize in your own words what you have just finished reading?

9. Do you find it difficult to concentrate for very long when you study?

10. Do you often feel that you studied the wrong material for a test?

Thousands of students have participated in similar surveys. Students who are fully realizing their academic potential usually respond as follows: (1) yes, (2) no, (3) no, (4) no, (5) no, (6) yes, (7) yes, (8) yes, (9) no, (10) no. Do your responses fit that pattern? If not, you could benefit from improving your time management and study habits.

© Hero Images/Corbis

More Tips for Effective Scheduling

There are a few other things you will want to keep in mind when you set up your schedule.

Spaced study is more effective than massed study. If you need 3 hours to study one subject, for example, it's best to divide that into shorter periods spaced over several days.

Alternate subjects, but avoid interference. Alternating the subjects you study in any given session will keep you fresh and will, surprisingly, increase your ability to remember what you're learning in each different area. Studying similar topics back-to-back, however, such as two different foreign languages, could lead to interference in your learning. (You will hear more about this in Chapter 7.)

Determine the amount of study time you need to do well in each course. The time you need depends on the difficulty of your courses and the effectiveness of your study methods. Ideally, you would spend at least 1 to 2 hours studying for each hour spent in class. Increase your study time slowly by setting weekly goals that will gradually bring you up to the desired level.

Create a schedule that makes sense. Tailor your schedule to meet the demands of each course. For the course that emphasizes lecture notes, plan a daily review of your notes soon after each class. If

you are evaluated for class participation (for example, in a language course), allow time for a review just before the class meets. Schedule study time for your most difficult (or least motivating) courses during hours when you are the most alert and distractions are fewest.

Schedule open study time. Life can be unpredictable. Emergencies and new obligations can throw off your schedule. Or you may simply need some extra time for a project or for review in one of your courses. Try to allow for some flexibility in your schedule each week.

Following these guidelines will help you find a schedule that works for you!

Make Every Minute of Your Study Time Count

How do you study from a textbook? Many students simply read and reread in a passive manner. As a result, they remember the wrong things—the catchy stories but not the main points that show up later in test questions. To make things worse, many students take poor notes during class. Here are some tips that will help you get the most from your class and your text.

Take Useful Class Notes

Good notes will boost your understanding and retention. Are yours thorough? Do they form a sensible outline of each lecture? If not, you may need to make some changes.

Keep Each Course's Notes Separate and Organized

Keeping all your notes for a course in one location will allow you to flip back and forth easily to find answers to questions.

Three options are (1) separate notebooks for each course, (2) clearly marked sections in a shared ring binder, or (3) carefully organized folders if you opt to take notes electronically. For the print options, removable pages will allow you to add new information and weed out past mistakes. Choosing notebook pages with lots of space, or using mark-up options in electronic files, will allow you to add comments when you review and revise your notes after class.

Use an Outline Format

Use numbers for major points, letters for supporting arguments, and so on. (See **FIGURE 1** for a sample.) In some courses, taking notes will be easy, but some instructors may be less organized, and you will have to work harder to form your outline.

Clean Up Your Notes After Class

Try to reorganize your notes soon after class. Expand or clarify your comments and clean up any hard-to-read scribbles while the material is fresh in your mind. Write important questions in the margin, or by using an electronic markup feature, next to notes that answer them. (For example: "What are the sleep stages?") This will help you when you review your notes before a test.

Create a Study Space That Helps You Learn

It's easier to study effectively if your work area is well designed.

Organize Your Space

Work at a desk or table, not on your bed or a comfy chair that will tempt you to nap.

Minimize Distractions

Turn the TV off, turn off your phone, and close Facebook and other distracting windows on your computer. If you must listen to music to mask outside noise, play soft instrumentals, not vocal selections that will draw your mind to the lyrics.

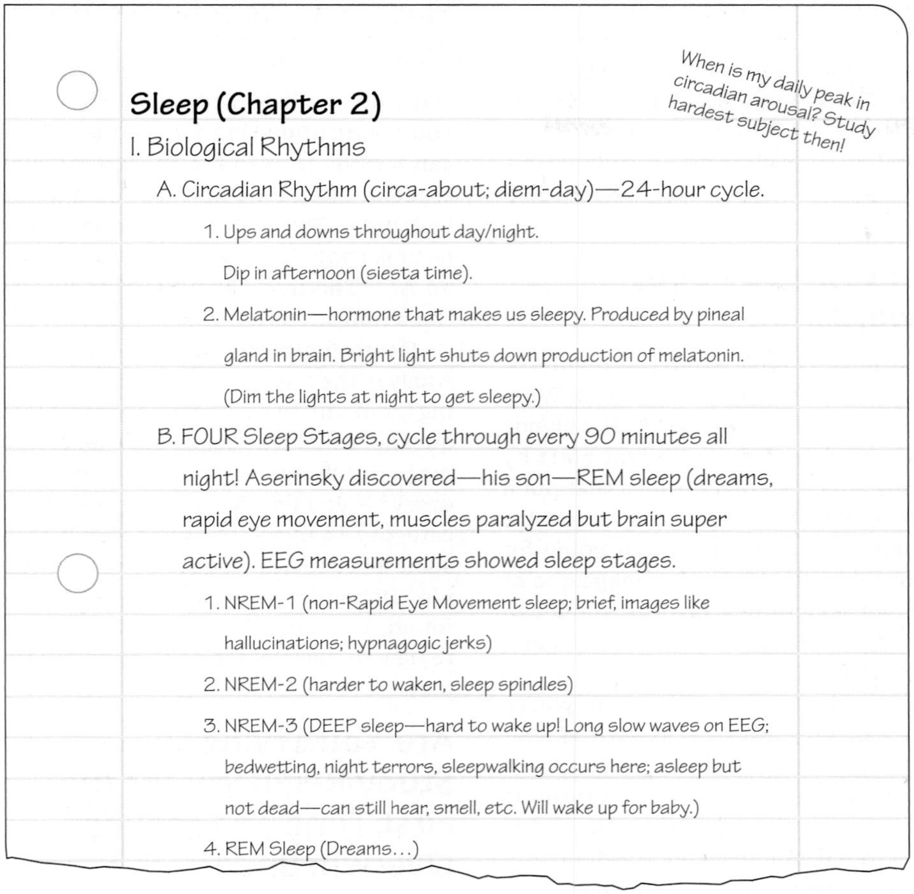

Sleep (Chapter 2)

I. Biological Rhythms

A. Circadian Rhythm (circa-about; diem-day)—24-hour cycle.

1. Ups and downs throughout day/night.
Dip in afternoon (siesta time).

2. Melatonin—hormone that makes us sleepy. Produced by pineal gland in brain. Bright light shuts down production of melatonin. (Dim the lights at night to get sleepy.)

B. FOUR Sleep Stages, cycle through every 90 minutes all night! Aserinsky discovered—his son—REM sleep (dreams, rapid eye movement, muscles paralyzed but brain super active). EEG measurements showed sleep stages.

1. NREM-1 (non-Rapid Eye Movement sleep; brief, images like hallucinations; hypnagogic jerks)

2. NREM-2 (harder to waken, sleep spindles)

3. NREM-3 (DEEP sleep—hard to wake up! Long slow waves on EEG; bedwetting, night terrors, sleepwalking occurs here; asleep but not dead—can still hear, smell, etc. Will wake up for baby.)

4. REM Sleep (Dreams...)

When is my daily peak in circadian arousal? Study hardest subject then!

FIGURE 1 Sample class notes in outline form Here is a sample from a student's notes taken in outline form from a lecture on sleep.

Ask Others to Honor Your Quiet Time

Tell roommates, family, and friends about your new schedule. Try to find a study place where you are least likely to be disturbed.

Set Specific, Realistic Daily Goals

The simple note "7–8 P.M.: Study Psychology" is too broad to be useful. Instead, break your studying into manageable tasks. For example, you will want to subdivide large reading assignments. If you aren't used to studying for long periods, start with relatively short periods of concentrated study, with breaks in between. In this text, for example, you might decide to read one major section before each break. Limit your breaks to 5 or 10 minutes to stretch or move around a bit.

Your attention span is a good indicator of whether you are pacing yourself successfully. At this early stage, it's important to remember that you're in training. If your attention begins to wander, get up immediately and take a short break. It is better to study effectively for 15 minutes and then take a break than to fritter away 45 minutes out of your study hour. As your endurance develops, you can increase the length of study periods.

Use SQ3R to Help You Master This Text

David Myers and Nathan DeWall organized this text by using a system called SQ3R (Survey, Question, Read, Retrieve, Review). Using SQ3R can help you to understand what you read, and to retain that information longer.

Applying SQ3R may feel at first as though it's taking more time and effort to "read" a chapter, but with practice, these steps will become automatic.

You will hear more about SQ3R in Chapter 1.

Survey

Before you read a chapter, survey its key parts. Scan the chapter outline. Note that main sections have numbered Learning Objective Questions to help you focus. Pay attention to headings, which indicate important subtopics, and to words set in bold type.

Surveying gives you the big picture of a chapter's content and organization. Understanding the chapter's logical sections will help you break your work into manageable pieces in your study sessions.

Question

As you survey, don't limit yourself to the numbered Learning Objective Questions that appear throughout the chapter. Jotting down additional questions of your own will cause you to look at the material in a new way. (You might, for example, scan this section's headings and ask "What does 'SQ3R' mean?") Information becomes easier to remember when you make it personally meaningful. Trying to answer your questions while reading will keep you in an active learning mode.

Read

As you read, keep your questions in mind and actively search for the answers. If you come to material that seems to answer an important question that you haven't jotted down, stop and write down that new question.

Be sure to read everything. Don't skip photo or art captions, graphs, tables, or quotes. An idea that seems vague when you read about it may become clear when you see it in a graph or table. Keep in mind that instructors sometimes base their test questions on figures and tables.

And take advantage of the new "Thinking Critically About" infographic features that will help you learn about key concepts.

Retrieve

When you have found the answer to one of your questions, close your eyes and mentally recite the question and its answer. Then write the answer next to the question in your own words. Trying to explain something in your own words will help you figure out where there are gaps in your understanding. These kinds of opportunities to practice *retrieving* develop the skills you will need when you are taking exams. If you study without ever putting your book and notes aside, you may develop false confidence about what you know. With the material available, you may be able to recognize the correct answer to your questions. But will you be able to recall it later, when you take an exam without having your mental props in sight?

Test your understanding as often as you can. Testing yourself is part of successful learning, because the act of testing forces your brain to work at remembering, thus establishing the memory more permanently (so you can find it later for the exam!). Use the self-testing opportunities throughout each chapter, including the periodic Retrieve + Remember items. Also take advantage of the self-testing that is available through LaunchPad (LaunchPadWorks.com).

Review

After working your way through the chapter, read over your questions and your written answers. Take an extra few minutes to create a brief written summary covering all of your questions and answers. At the end of the chapter, you should take advantage of three important opportunities for self-testing and review—a list of the chapter's Learning Objective Questions for you to try answering before checking Appendix D in the printed text, or the answers that are a click away in the e-Book; a list of the chapter's key terms

for you to try to define before checking the referenced page in the printed text, or completing the key terms self-test in the e-Book; and a final Chapter Test that covers all of the key chapter concepts (with answers in Appendix E in the printed text or a click away in the e-Book).

Don't Forget About Rewards!

If you have trouble studying regularly, giving yourself a reward may help. What kind of reward works best? That depends on what you enjoy. You might start by making a list of 5 or 10 things that put a smile on your face. Spending time with a loved one, taking a walk or going for a bike ride, relaxing with a magazine or novel, or watching a favorite show can provide immediate rewards for achieving short-term study goals.

To motivate yourself when you're having trouble sticking to your schedule, allow yourself an immediate reward for completing a specific task. If running makes you smile, change your shoes, grab a friend, and head out the door! You deserve a reward for a job well done.

Do You Need to Revise Your New Schedule?

What if you've lived with your schedule for a few weeks, but you aren't making progress toward your academic and personal goals? What if your studying hasn't paid off in better grades? Don't despair and abandon your program, but do take a little time to figure out what's gone wrong.

Are You Doing Well in Some Courses But Not in Others?

Perhaps you need to shift your priorities a bit. You may need to allow more study time for chemistry, for example, and less time for some other course.

Have You Received a Poor Grade on a Test?

Did your grade fail to reflect the effort you spent preparing for the test? This can happen to even the hardest-working student, often on a first test with a new instructor. This common experience can be upsetting. "What do I have to do to get an A?" "The test was unfair!" "I studied the wrong material!"

Try to figure out what went wrong. Analyze the questions you missed, dividing them into two categories: class-based questions and text-based questions. How many questions did you miss in each category? If you find far more errors in one category than in the other, you'll have some clues to help you revise your schedule. Depending on the pattern you've found, you can add extra study time to review of class notes or to studying the text.

Are You Trying to Study Regularly for the First Time and Feeling Overwhelmed?

Perhaps you've set your initial goals too high. Remember, the point of time management is to identify a regular schedule that will help you achieve success. Like any skill, time management takes practice. Accept your limitations and revise your schedule to work slowly up to where you know you need to be—perhaps adding 15 minutes of study time per day.

* * *

I hope that these suggestions help make you more successful academically, and that they enhance the quality of your life in general. Having the necessary skills makes any job a lot easier and more pleasant. Let me repeat my warning not to attempt to make too drastic a change in your lifestyle immediately. Good habits require time and self-discipline to develop. Once established, they can last a lifetime.

REVIEW

Time Management: Or, How to Be a Great Student and Still Have a Life

1. How Are You Using Your Time Now?

   - Identify your areas of weakness.
   - Keep a time-use diary.
   - Record the time you actually spend on activities.
   - Record your energy levels to find your most productive times.

2. Design a Better Schedule

   - Decide on your goals for the term and for each week.
   - Enter class times, work times, social times (for family and friends), and time needed for other obligations and for practical activities.
   - Tailor study times to avoid interference and to meet each course's needs.

3. Make Every Minute of Your Study Time Count

   - Take careful class notes (in outline form) that will help you recall and rehearse material covered in lectures.
   - Try to eliminate distractions to your study time, and ask friends and family to help you focus on your work.
   - Set specific, realistic daily goals to help you focus on each day's tasks.
   - Use the SQ3R system (survey, question, read, retrieve, review) to master material covered in your text.
   - When you achieve your daily goals, reward yourself with something that you value.

4. Do You Need to Revise Your New Schedule?

   - Allocate extra study time for courses that are more difficult, and a little less time for courses that are easy for you.
   - Study your test results to help determine a more effective balance in your schedule.
   - Make sure your schedule is not too ambitious. Gradually establish a schedule that will be effective for the long term.

SURVEY THE CHAPTER

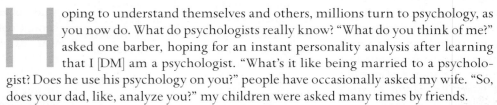

Psychology's Roots, Big Ideas, and Critical Thinking Tools

Hoping to understand themselves and others, millions turn to psychology, as you now do. What do psychologists really know? "What do you think of me?" asked one barber, hoping for an instant personality analysis after learning that I [DM] am a psychologist. "What's it like being married to a psychologist? Does he use his psychology on you?" people have occasionally asked my wife. "So, does your dad, like, analyze you?" my children were asked many times by friends.

Perhaps you've seen psychologists portrayed on television, in movies, or on popular websites. They seem to spend their time analyzing personality, examining crime scenes, testifying in court, and offering advice about parenting, love, happiness, and overcoming personal problems. Do psychologists do all these things? Yes, and much more. Consider some of the questions psychologists study that you may also wonder about:

- Have you ever found yourself reacting to something as one of your biological parents would—perhaps in a way you vowed you *never* would—and then wondered how much of your personality you inherited? *How much are we shaped by our genes, and how much by our home and community environments?*

- Have you ever worried about how to act among people of a different culture, race, gender, or sexual orientation? *In what ways are we alike as members of the human family? How do we differ?*

- Have you ever awakened from a nightmare and, with a wave of relief, wondered why you had such a crazy dream? *How often, and why, do we dream?*

- Have you ever played peekaboo with a 6-month-old and wondered why the baby finds your "disappearing act" so delightful? *What do babies actually perceive and think?*

- Have you ever wondered what leads to success in life? *Are some people just born smarter? Can we make it on intelligence alone? What about creativity and emotional intelligence? How about self-control?*

- Have you ever become depressed or anxious and wondered whether you'll ever feel "normal"? *What triggers our bad moods—and our good ones? What's the line between a normal mood swing and a psychological disorder?*

As you will see, psychological science has produced some fascinating and sometimes surprising answers to these questions. Psychology's roots are broad, reaching back into philosophy and biology, and its branches now spread out across the world.

FilippoBacci/Getty Images

1

Psychology's Roots

Once upon a time, on a planet in our neighborhood of the universe, there came to be people. These creatures became intensely interested in themselves and one another. They wondered, "Who are we? Why do we think and feel and act as we do? And how are we to understand—and to manage—those around us?"

To be human is to be curious about ourselves and the world around us. The ancient Greek naturalist and philosopher Aristotle (384–322 B.C.E.) wondered about learning and memory, motivation and emotion, perception and personality. We may chuckle at some of his guesses, like his suggestion that a meal makes us sleepy by causing gas and heat to collect around the source of our personality, the heart. But credit Aristotle with asking the right questions.

Psychology asks similar questions. But today's psychologists search for answers differently, by scientifically studying how we act, think, and feel. (See Thinking Critically About: The Scientific Attitude.)

Psychological Science's Birth and Development

LOQ 1-2 How has psychology's focus changed over time?[1]

Psychology as we know it was born on a December day in 1879, in a small, third-floor room at a German university. There, Wilhelm Wundt and his assistants created a machine to measure how long it took people to press a telegraph key after hearing a ball hit a platform (Hunt, 1993).[2]

(Most hit the key in about one-tenth of a second.) Wundt's attempt to measure "atoms of the mind"—the fastest and simplest mental processes—was psychology's first experiment. And that modest third-floor room took its place in history as the first psychological laboratory.

Psychology's earliest pioneers— "Magellans of the mind," Morton Hunt (1993) called them—came from many disciplines and countries. Wundt was both a philosopher and a physiologist. Charles Darwin, who proposed evolutionary psychology, was an English naturalist. Ivan Pavlov, who taught us much about learning, was a Russian physiologist. Sigmund Freud, a famous personality theorist and therapist, was an Austrian physician. Jean Piaget, who explored children's developing minds, was a Swiss biologist. William James, who shared his love of psychology in his 1890 textbook, was an American philosopher.

Few of psychology's early pioneers were women. In the late 1800s, psychology, like most fields, was a man's world. William James helped break that mold when he accepted Mary Whiton Calkins into his graduate seminar. Although Calkins went on to outscore all the male students on the Ph.D. exams, Harvard University denied her the degree she had earned. In its place, she was told, she could have a degree from Radcliffe College, Harvard's undergraduate "sister" school for women. Calkins resisted the unequal treatment and turned down the offer. But she continued her research on memory, which her colleagues honored in 1905 by electing her the first female president of the American Psychological Association (APA). Animal behavior researcher Margaret Floy Washburn became the first woman to officially receive a psychology Ph.D. and the second, in 1921, to become an APA president.

The rest of the story of psychology— the story this book tells—develops at many levels, in the hands of many people, with interests ranging from therapy to the study of nerve cell activity. As you might expect, agreeing on a definition of psychology has not been easy.

> **behaviorism** the view that psychology (1) should be an objective science that (2) studies behavior without reference to mental processes. Most psychologists today agree with (1) but not with (2).
>
> **humanistic psychology** historically important perspective that emphasized human growth potential.

For the early pioneers, *psychology* was defined as "the science of mental life." And so it continued until the 1920s, when the first of two larger-than-life American psychologists dismissed this idea. John B. Watson, and later B. F. Skinner, insisted that *psychology* must be "the scientific study of observable *behavior*." What you cannot observe and measure, they said, you cannot scientifically study. You cannot observe a sensation, a feeling, or a thought, but you *can* observe and record people's *behavior* as they are *conditioned*—as they respond to and learn in different situations. Many agreed, and **behaviorism**[3] became one of psychology's two major forces well into the 1960s.

The other major force was *Freudian psychology*, which emphasized our unconscious thought processes and our emotional responses to childhood experiences. Some students wonder: Is psychology mainly about Freud's teachings on unconscious sexual conflicts and the mind's defenses against its own wishes and impulses? *No.* Psychology is much more, though Freudian psychology did have an impact. (In chapters to come, we'll look more closely at Freud and others mentioned here.)

As the behaviorists had rejected the early 1900s definition of *psychology*, other groups in the 1960s rejected the behaviorists' definition. The **humanistic psychologists**, led by Carl Rogers and Abraham Maslow, found both behaviorism and Freudian psychology too limiting. Rather than focusing on conditioned responses or childhood

---

1. Throughout this book you will find numbered questions that preview main sections and suggest your learning goal, or objective. Keep the question in mind as you read the section to make sure that you are following the main point of the discussion. These Learning Objective Questions are repeated at the end of each chapter as a self-test, and answered in Appendix D, Complete Chapter Reviews, at the end of this book.

2. This book's information sources are cited in parentheses, with name and date. Every citation can be found in the end-of-book References, with complete documentation.

3. Throughout the text, important concepts are boldfaced. As you study, you can find these terms defined in a boxed section nearby, and in the Glossary and Glosario at the end of the book.

Thinking Critically About:
The Scientific Attitude
Three basic attitudes helped make modern science possible.

1 CURIOSITY:

Research begins with a passion to explore and understand, without misleading or being misled. No matter how crazy an idea sounds, the scientist asks,

Does it work?
When put to the test, can its predictions be confirmed?

Can some people read minds?

Are stress levels related to health and well-being? ○

○ *No one has yet been able to demonstrate extrasensory mind-reading.*

○ *Many studies have found that higher stress relates to poorer health.*

2 SKEPTICISM:

Ask
"What do you mean?"
and
"How do you know?"

Skeptical testing can reveal which claim best matches the facts. Sifting reality from fantasy requires a healthy skepticism—an attitude that is not cynical (doubting everything), but also not gullible (believing everything).

Do our facial expressions and body postures affect how we actually feel? ○

Do parental behaviors determine children's sexual orientation— or not? ○

○ *Our facial expressions and body postures can affect how we feel.*

○ *As you will see in Chapter 4, there is not a relationship between parental behaviors and a child's sexual orientation.*

3 HUMILITY:

Researchers can make mistakes, and so must be willing to be surprised and follow new ideas. What matters is not our opinions, but the truths revealed in response to our questioning. If people or other animals don't behave as our ideas predict, then so much the worse for our ideas.

The rat is always right.

WILHELM WUNDT (1832–1920) Wundt established the first psychology laboratory at the University of Leipzig, Germany.

WILLIAM JAMES (1842–1910) AND MARY WHITON CALKINS (1863–1930) James was a legendary teacher-writer of psychology. Among his students was Mary Whiton Calkins, who became famous for her memory research and for being the first woman president of the American Psychological Association.

MARGARET FLOY WASHBURN (1871–1939) After Harvard refused to grant Calkins the degree she had earned, Washburn became the first woman to receive a psychology Ph.D. She focused on animal behavior research in *The Animal Mind*.

memories, Rogers and Maslow stressed people's growth potential. They drew attention to our needs for love and acceptance and to the ways that an environment can help or hinder personal growth.

Another group searching for a new path in the 1960s pioneered a *cognitive revolution*, which led the field back to its early interest in mental processes. **Cognitive psychology** today continues its scientific exploration of how we perceive, process, and remember informa-

tion, and of how thinking and emotion interact in anxiety, depression, and other disorders. The marriage of cognitive psychology (the science of the mind) and neuroscience (the science of the brain) gave birth to **cognitive neuroscience.** This specialty, with researchers in many disciplines, studies the brain activity underlying mental activity.

Today's psychology builds upon the work of many earlier scientists and schools of thought. To include psychology's concern with observable behavior

and with inner thoughts and feelings, we now define **psychology** as the *science of behavior and mental processes.*

Let's unpack this definition. *Behavior* is anything a human or nonhuman animal *does*—any action we can observe and record. Yelling, smiling, blinking, sweating, talking, and questionnaire marking are all observable behaviors. *Mental processes* are the internal states— such as thoughts, beliefs, and feelings—that we *infer* from behavior. When you observe someone yelling, you may

JOHN B. WATSON (1878–1958) AND ROSALIE RAYNER (1898–1935) Working with Rayner, Watson championed psychology as the scientific study of behavior. He and Rayner showed that fear could be learned, in experiments on a baby who became famous as "Little Albert." (More about Watson's controversial study in Chapter 6.)

B. F. SKINNER (1904–1990) This leading behaviorist rejected the idea of studying inner thoughts and feelings. He believed psychology should study how consequences shape behavior.

SIGMUND FREUD (1856–1939) The controversial ideas of this famous personality theorist and therapist influenced twentieth-century psychology and culture.

infer the person's mental state (angry or excited).

The key word in psychology's definition is *science*. Psychology, as we will stress again and again, is less a set of findings than a way of asking and answering questions. Our aim, then, is not merely to report results but also to show you how psychologists play their game, weighing opinions and ideas. And we hope you, too, will learn how to play the game—to think smarter when explaining events and making choices in your own life.

Retrieve + Remember[4]

- Describe the three parts of the scientific attitude.

  ANSWER: The scientific attitude combines (1) curiosity about the world around us, (2) skepticism about unproven claims and ideas, and (3) humility about our own understanding. These three traits guide psychologists as they consider ideas and test them with scientific methods. Ideas that don't hold up will then be discarded.

- What event defined the start of scientific psychology?

  ANSWER: Scientific psychology began in Germany in 1879, when Wilhelm Wundt opened the first psychology laboratory.

- How did the cognitive revolution affect the field of psychology?

  ANSWER: It led the field back to its early interest in mental processes and made them acceptable topics for scientific study.

LaunchPad is a research-based online learning tool that will help you excel in this course. Visit LaunchPad to take advantage of self-tests, interactive simulations, IMMERSIVE LEARNING "How Would You Know?" activities, and Assess Your Strengths personal self-assessments. For an introduction to LaunchPad, including how to get in and use its helpful resources, go to LaunchPadWorks.com. In LaunchPad, you will find resources collected by chapter. Additional resources may be found by clicking on the "Resources" star in the left column.

4. Study Tip: Memory research reveals a testing effect. We retain information much better if we actively retrieve it by self-testing and rehearsing. To boost your learning and memory, take advantage of the Retrieve + Remember self-tests you will find throughout this text.

LaunchPad For an excellent tour of psychology's roots, view the 9.5-minute *Video: The History of Psychology.*

Contemporary Psychology

LOQ 1-3 What are psychology's current perspectives, and what are some of its subfields?

Psychologists' wide-ranging interests make it hard to picture a psychologist at work. You might start by imagining a neuroscientist probing an animal's brain, an intelligence researcher studying how quickly infants become bored with a familiar scene, or a therapist listening closely to a client's anxieties. Psychologists examine behavior and mental processes from many viewpoints, which are described in **TABLE 1.1**. These perspectives range from the biological to the social-cultural, and their settings range from the laboratory to the clinic. But all share a common goal: *describing and explaining behavior and the mind underlying it.*

Psychology also relates to many other fields. You'll find psychologists teaching not only in psychology departments but also in medical schools, law schools, business schools, and theological seminaries. You'll see them working in hospitals, factories, and corporate offices. In this course, you will hear about

- *biological psychologists* exploring the links between brain and mind.
- *developmental psychologists* studying our changing abilities from womb to tomb.
- *cognitive psychologists* experimenting with how we perceive, think, and solve problems.
- *personality psychologists* investigating our persistent traits.
- *social psychologists* exploring how we view and affect one another.

- *counseling psychologists* helping people cope with personal and career challenges by recognizing their strengths and resources.
- *health psychologists* investigating the psychological, biological, and behavioral factors that promote or impair our health.
- *clinical psychologists* assessing and treating people with mental, emotional, and behavior disorders. (By contrast, *psychiatrists* are medical doctors who also prescribe drugs when treating psychological disorders.)
- *industrial-organizational psychologists* studying and advising on workplace-related behaviors and system and product designs.
- *community psychologists* working to create social and physical environments that are healthy for all.

Psychology is both a science and a profession. Some psychologists conduct *basic research,* to build the field's knowledge base. Others conduct *applied research,* tackling practical problems. Many do both.

Psychology also influences modern culture. Knowledge transforms us. After learning about psychology's findings, people less often judge psychological disorders as moral failures. They less often regard women as men's inferiors. They less often view children as ignorant, willful beasts in need of taming.

cognitive psychology the study of mental processes, such as occur when we perceive, learn, remember, think, communicate, and solve problems.

cognitive neuroscience the interdisciplinary study of the brain activity linked with mental activity (including perception, thinking, memory, and language).

psychology the science of behavior and mental processes.

TABLE 1.1 Psychology's Current Perspectives

Perspective	Focus	Sample Questions	Examples of Subfields Using This Perspective
Neuroscience	How the body and brain enable emotions, memories, and sensory experiences	How do pain messages travel from the hand to the brain? How is blood chemistry linked with moods and motives?	Biological; cognitive; clinical
Evolutionary	How the natural selection of traits passed down from one generation to the next has promoted the survival of genes	How has our evolutionary past influenced our modern-day mating preferences? Why do humans learn some fears so much more easily than others?	Biological; developmental; social
Behavior genetics	How our genes and our environment influence our individual differences	To what extent are psychological traits such as intelligence, personality, sexual orientation, and optimism products of our genes? Of our environment?	Personality; developmental; legal/forensic
Psychodynamic	How behavior springs from unconscious drives and conflicts	How can someone's personality traits and disorders be explained in terms of their childhood relationships?	Clinical; counseling; personality
Behavioral	How we learn observable responses	How do we learn to fear particular objects or situations? What is the most effective way to alter our behavior, say, to lose weight or stop smoking?	Clinical; counseling; industrial-organizational
Cognitive	How we encode, process, store, and retrieve information	How do we use information in remembering? Reasoning? Solving problems?	Cognitive neuroscience; clinical; counseling; industrial-organizational
Social-cultural	How behavior and thinking vary across situations and cultures	How are we alike as members of one human family? How do we differ as products of our environment?	Developmental; social; clinical; counseling

And as thinking changes, so do actions. "In each case," noted Hunt (1990, p. 206), "knowledge has modified attitudes, and, through them, behavior." Once aware of psychology's well-researched ideas—about how body and mind connect, how we construct our perceptions, how we learn and remember, how people across the world are alike and differ—your own mind may never be quite the same.

The New Yorker Collection, 1986, J.B. Handelsman from cartoonbank.com

"I'm a social scientist, Michael. That means I can't explain electricity or anything like that, but if you ever want to know about people I'm your man."

Paul Sakuma, File/AP Photo

Brad Barket/AP Photo

LIFE AFTER STUDYING PSYCHOLOGY The study of psychology and its critical thinking strategies have helped prepare people for varied occupations. Facebook CEO Mark Zuckerberg majored in psychology and computer science while at Harvard. Comedian Jon Stewart was a psychology major at William and Mary. What path might psychology open for you?

LaunchPad Want to learn more? See Appendix C, Subfields of Psychology, at the end of this book, and go to LaunchPad's regularly updated *Careers in Psychology* resource to learn about the many interesting options available to those with bachelor's, master's, and doctoral degrees in psychology.

PSYCHOLOGY IN COURT Forensic psychologists apply psychology's principles and methods in the criminal justice system. They may consult on witnesses, or testify about a defendant's state of mind and future risk.

1. *Critical thinking* The scientific attitude prepares us to think smarter—to examine assumptions, consider the source, uncover hidden values, weigh evidence, and test conclusions. Science-aided thinking is smart thinking.

2. *The biopsychosocial approach* We can view human behavior from three levels—the biological, psychological, and social-cultural. We share a biologically rooted human nature. Yet cultural and psychological influences fine-tune our assumptions, values, and behaviors.

3. *The two-track mind* Today's psychological science explores our *dual-processing* capacity. Our perception, thinking, memory, and attitudes all operate on two levels: a conscious, aware track, and an unconscious, automatic, unaware track. It has been a surprise to learn how much information processing happens without our awareness.

4. *Exploring human strengths* Psychology today focuses not only on understanding and offering relief from troublesome behaviors and emotions, but also on understanding and developing the emotions and traits that help us to thrive.

Let's consider these four ideas, one by one.

Retrieve + Remember

- The _____ perspective in psychology focuses on how behavior and thought differ from situation to situation and from culture to culture.

  ANSWER: social-cultural

- The _____ perspective emphasizes how we learn observable responses.

  ANSWER: behavioral

Four Big Ideas in Psychology

LOQ 1-4 What four big ideas run throughout this book?

Woven throughout this book are four of psychology's big ideas.

PSYCHOLOGY: A SCIENCE AND A PROFESSION Psychologists experiment with, observe, test, and treat behavior. Here we see psychologists testing a child, measuring emotion-related physiology, and doing face-to-face therapy.

Big Idea 1: Critical Thinking Is Smart Thinking

Whether reading an online article or swapping ideas with others, **critical thinkers** ask questions. *How do they know that? Who benefits from this? Is the conclusion based on a personal story and gut feelings, or on evidence? How do we know one event caused the other? How else could we explain things?*

From a Twitter feed:
"The problem with quotes on the Internet is that you never know if they're true."
Abraham Lincoln

In psychology, critical thinking has led to some surprising findings. Believe it or not . . .

- massive losses of brain tissue early in life may have few long-term effects (see Chapter 2).
- within days, newborns can recognize their mother's odor (Chapter 3).
- after brain damage, some people can learn new skills, yet at the mind's conscious level be unaware that they have these skills (Chapter 7).
- most of us—male and female, old and young, wealthy and not wealthy, with and without disabilities—report roughly the same levels of personal happiness (Chapter 10).
- an electric shock delivered to the brain (electroconvulsive therapy) may relieve severe depression when all else has failed (Chapter 14).

This same critical thinking has also debunked some popular beliefs. When we let the evidence speak for itself, we learn that . . .

- sleepwalkers are *not* acting out their dreams (Chapter 2).
- our past experiences are *not* recorded word for word in our brain. Neither brain stimulation nor hypnosis will let us "hit the replay button" and relive long-buried memories (Chapter 7).

- most of us do *not* suffer from low self-esteem, and high self-esteem is not all good (Chapter 12).
- opposites do not generally attract (Chapter 11).

In later chapters, you'll see many more examples in which psychology's critical thinking has challenged old beliefs and led us onto new paths.

Big Idea 2: Behavior Is a Biopsychosocial Event

Each of us is part of a larger social system—a family, a group, a society. But each of us is also made up of smaller systems, such as our nervous system and body organs, which are composed of still smaller systems—cells, molecules, and atoms.

If we study this complexity with simple tools, we may end up with partial answers. Consider the many ways of explaining horrific school shootings. Is it because the shooters have brain disorders or genetic tendencies that cause them to be violent? Because they have observed brutality and mayhem in the media or played violent video games? Because they live in a gun-toting society? Each of these is a partial truth, but none is a full answer. For the best possible view, we need to use many *levels of analysis*. The **biopsychosocial approach** integrates three levels: biological, psychological, and social-cultural. Each level's viewpoint gives us a valuable insight into a behavior or mental process. Each asks different questions and has limits, but together they offer the most complete picture.

Suppose we wanted to study gender differences in a group of people. *Gender* is not the same as *sex*. *Gender* refers to the traits and behaviors we *expect* from a boy or girl, or a man or woman in a specific culture. *Sex* refers to the biological characteristics people inherit, thanks to their genes. To study gender similarities and differences, we would want to know about biological influences. But we would also want to understand how the group's **culture**—the shared ideas and behaviors that one generation passes on to the next—views gender. Critical thinking has taught psychologists to be careful about making statements about people in general if the evidence comes from studies done in only one time and place. Participants in many studies have come from the "WEIRD" cultures—Western, Educated, Industrial, Rich, and

Roy Tuft/National Geographic/Getty Images

Antonia Brune

A SMILE IS A SMILE THE WORLD AROUND Throughout this book, you will see examples not only of our cultural and gender diversity, but also of the similarities that define our shared human nature. People in different cultures vary in when and how often they smile, but a naturally happy smile means the same thing anywhere in the world.

CULTURE AND KISSING Kissing crosses cultures. Yet how we do it varies. Imagine yourself kissing someone on the lips. Do you tilt your head right or left? People in Western cultures read from left to right. About two-thirds of Western couples also kiss right, as in William and Kate's famous kiss and in Auguste Rodin's sculpture, *The Kiss*. People reading Hebrew and Arabic read from right to left, and in one study 77 percent of those readers kissed tilting left (Shaki, 2013).

Democratic (Henrich et al., 2010). We are also increasingly aware that the categories we use to divide people—including "gender" and "sex"—are socially constructed. As we will see in Chapter 4, many individuals' *gender identity* differs from their biological sex.

Even with this much information about people's gender and culture, our view would be incomplete. We would also need some understanding of how the *individuals* in a group differ from one another because of their personal abilities and learning.

Studying all these influences in various people around the world, researchers have found some gender differences—in what we dream, in how we express and detect emotion, and in our risk for alcohol use disorder, eating disorders, and depression. Psychologically as well as biologically, we differ. But research shows we are also alike. Whether female or male, we learn to walk at about the same age. We experience the same sensations of light and sound. We remember vivid emotional events and forget everyday details. We feel the same pangs of hunger, desire, and fear. We exhibit similar overall intelligence and well-being.

Psychologists have used the biopsychosocial approach to study many of the field's big questions. One of the biggest and most persistent is the **nature–nurture issue:** How do we judge the contributions of *nature* (biology) and *nurture* (experience)? Today's psychologists explore this age-old question by asking, for example:

- How are intelligence and personality differences influenced by heredity and by environment?
- Is our *sexual orientation* written in our genes or learned through our experiences?

A NATURE-MADE NATURE–NURTURE EXPERIMENT Identical twins (left) have the same genes. This makes them ideal participants in studies designed to shed light on hereditary and environmental influences on personality, intelligence, and other traits. Fraternal twins (right) have different genes but often share the same environment. Twin studies provide a wealth of findings—described in later chapters—showing the importance of both nature and nurture.

critical thinking thinking that does not blindly accept arguments and conclusions. Rather, it examines assumptions, uncovers hidden values, weighs evidence, and assesses conclusions.

biopsychosocial approach an approach that integrates different but complementary views from biological, psychological, and social-cultural viewpoints.

culture the enduring behaviors, ideas, attitudes, values, and traditions shared by a group of people and handed down from one generation to the next.

nature–nurture issue the age-old controversy over the relative influence of genes and experience in the development of psychological traits and behaviors. Today's psychological science sees traits and behaviors arising from the interaction of nature and nurture.

- Can life experiences affect the expression of our genes?
- Should we treat depression as a disorder of the brain or a disorder of thought—or both?

In most cases, *nurture works on what nature provides.* Our species has been graced with a great biological gift: an enormous ability to learn and adapt. Moreover (and you will read this over and over in the pages that follow), every psychological event—every thought, every emotion—is also a biological event. Thus, depression can be both a brain disorder *and* a thought disorder. (You'll learn more about this in Chapter 13.)

Big Idea 3: We Operate With a Two-Track Mind (Dual Processing)

Mountains of new research reveal that our brain works on two tracks. Our conscious mind *feels* like our body's chief executive, and in fact we do process much information on our brain's conscious track, with full awareness. But at the same time, a surprisingly large unconscious, automatic track is processing information outside of our awareness. Thinking, memory, perception, language, and attitudes all operate on these two tracks. Today's researchers call it **dual processing.** We know more than we know we know.

Vision is a great example of our dual processing. As science often reveals, truth can be stranger than fiction.

During a stay at Scotland's University of St. Andrews, I [DM] came to know research psychologists Melvyn Goodale and David Milner (2004, 2006). A local woman, whom they studied and call D. F., was overcome by carbon monoxide one day. The resulting brain damage left her unable to consciously perceive objects. Yet she *acted* as if she *could* see them. Slip a postcard into a mail slot? She could do so without error. Report the width of a block in front of her? No, but she could grasp it with just the right finger-thumb distance. How could a

woman who is perceptually blind grasp and guide objects accurately? A scan of D. F.'s brain revealed the answer.

The eye sends information to different brain areas, and each of these areas has a different task. A scan of D. F.'s brain revealed normal activity in an area concerned with reaching for and grasping objects, but not in another area concerned with consciously recognizing objects. A few other patients have a reverse pattern of damage. As you might expect, their symptoms are the reverse of D. F.'s. They can see and recognize objects, but they have difficulty pointing toward or grasping them.

We think of our vision as one system: We look. We see. We respond to what we see. Actually, vision is a two-track system. Our *visual perception track* enables us to think about the world—to recognize things and to plan future actions. Our *visual action track* guides our moment-to-moment actions.

This big idea—that much of our everyday thinking, feeling, sensing, and acting operates outside our awareness—may be a strange new idea for you. It was for me [DM]. I long believed that my own intentions and deliberate choices ruled my life. In many ways they do. But as you will see in later chapters, there is much, much more to being human.

Big Idea 4: Psychology Explores Human Strengths as Well as Challenges

Psychology's first hundred years focused on understanding and treating troubles, such as abuse and anxiety, depression and disease, prejudice and poverty. Much of today's psychology continues the exploration of such challenges. Without slighting the need to repair damage and cure disease, Martin Seligman and others (2002, 2005, 2011) have called for more research on *human flourishing.* These psychologists call their approach **positive psychology.** They believe that happiness is a by-product of a pleasant, engaged, and meaningful life. Thus, positive psychology focuses on building

a "good life" that engages our skills, and a "meaningful life" that points beyond ourselves. Positive psychology uses scientific methods to explore

- *positive emotions,* such as satisfaction with the past, happiness with the present, and optimism about the future.
- *positive character traits,* such as creativity, courage, compassion, integrity, self-control, leadership, wisdom, and spirituality. Current research examines the roots and fruits of such qualities, sometimes by studying the lives of individuals who offer striking examples.
- *positive institutions,* such as healthy families, supportive neighborhoods, effective schools, and socially responsible media.

Will psychology have a more positive mission in this century? Can it help us all to flourish? An increasing number of scientists worldwide believe it can.

Why Do Psychology?

Many people feel guided by their *intuition*—by what they feel in their gut. "Buried deep within each and every one of us, there is an instinctive, heartfelt awareness that provides—if we allow it to—the most reliable guide," offered Britain's Prince Charles (2000).

The Limits of Intuition and Common Sense

LOQ 1-5 How does our everyday thinking sometimes lead us to the wrong conclusion?

Prince Charles has much company, judging from the long list of pop-culture discussions of "intuitive managing," "intuitive trading," and "intuitive healing." Intuition is indeed important. Research shows that our thinking, memory, and attitudes operate on two levels—conscious and unconscious. More than we realize, much of our mental life happens automatically, off screen. Like jumbo jets, we fly mostly on autopilot.

But intuition can lead us astray. Our gut feelings may tell us that lie detectors work and that eyewitnesses recall events accurately. But as you will see in chapters to come, hundreds of findings challenge these beliefs.

Hunches are a good starting point, even for smart thinkers. But thinking critically means checking assumptions, weighing evidence, inviting criticism, and testing conclusions. Does the death penalty prevent murders? Whether your gut tells you *Yes* or *No*, you need more evidence. You might ask, *Do states with a death penalty have lower homicide rates? After states pass death-penalty laws, do their homicide rates drop? Do homicide rates rise in states that abandon the death penalty?* If we ignore the answers to such questions (which the evidence suggests are *No, No,* and *No*), our intuition may steer us down the wrong path.

With its standards for gathering and sifting evidence, psychological science helps us avoid errors and think smarter. Before moving on to our study of how psychologists use psychology's methods in their research, let's look more closely at three common flaws in intuitive thinking—*hindsight bias, overconfidence,* and *perceiving patterns in random events.*

Kevin C. Cox/Getty Images

"THE WORST PLAY CALL IN SUPER BOWL HISTORY"? Seattle Seahawks coach Pete Carroll was widely ridiculed after calling an ill-fated pass play with his team inches from victory at the end of the 2015 Super Bowl. With 25 seconds and three downs remaining, but with only one timeout, Carroll correctly reasoned that there was time for only two running plays. Thus the attempted (and intercepted) pass was a free third play (and with lower odds of an interception than a fumble). Alas, the improbable happened and, in hindsight, Carroll was lampooned. In life as in sports, successful decisions later seem "gutsy" and failed ones seem "stupid."

Did We Know It All Along? Hindsight Bias

Some people think psychology merely proves what we already know and then dresses it in jargon: "You get paid for using fancy methods to tell me what my grandmother knew?" But consider how

easy it is to draw the bull's-eye after the arrow strikes. After the football game, we credit the coach if a "gutsy play" wins the game and fault the coach for the same "stupid play" if it doesn't. After a war or an election, its outcome usually seems obvious. Although history may therefore seem like a series of predictable events, the actual future is seldom foreseen. No one's diary recorded, "Today the Hundred Years War began."

This **hindsight bias** (also called the *I-knew-it-all-along phenomenon*) is easy to demonstrate by giving half the members of a group a true psychological finding, and giving the other half the opposite result. Tell the first group, for example: "Psychologists have found that separation weakens romantic attraction. As the saying goes, 'Out of sight, out of mind.'" Ask them to imagine why this might be true. Most people can, and nearly all will then view this true finding as unsurprising—just common sense. Tell the second group the opposite: "Psychologists have found that separation strengthens romantic attraction. As the saying goes, 'Absence makes the heart grow fonder.'" People given this *false* statement can also easily imagine it, and most will also see it as unsurprising. When opposite findings both seem like common sense, we have a problem!

More than 800 scholarly papers have shown hindsight bias in people young and old from across the world (Roese & Vohs, 2012). Hindsight errors in what we recall and how we explain it show why we need psychological research. Just asking people how and why they felt or acted

UPI/U.S. Coast Guard/Landov

HINDSIGHT BIAS When drilling the Deepwater Horizon oil well in 2010, BP employees took some shortcuts and ignored some warning signs, without intending to harm any people, the environment, or their company's reputation. *After* the resulting Gulf oil spill, with the benefit of hindsight, the foolishness of those judgments became obvious.

dual processing the principle that our mind processes information at the same time on separate conscious and unconscious tracks.

positive psychology the scientific study of human functioning, with the goals of discovering and promoting strengths and virtues that help individuals and communities to thrive.

hindsight bias the tendency to believe, after learning an outcome, that we could have predicted it. (Also known as the *I-knew-it-all-along phenomenon.*)

as they did can be misleading. Why? Not because common sense is usually wrong, but because common sense describes, after the fact, what *has* happened better than it predicts what *will* happen.

Nevertheless, although sometimes mistaken, Grandma's intuition is often right. As the late baseball great Yogi Berra (1925–2015) once said, "You can observe a lot by watching." (We have Berra to thank for other gems, such as "Nobody ever comes here—it's too crowded," and "If the people don't want to come out to the ball-park, nobody's gonna stop 'em.") We're all behavior watchers, and sometimes we get it right. Many people believe that love breeds happiness, and it does. (We have what Chapter 9 calls a deep "need to belong.")

Overconfidence

We humans also tend to be *overconfident*—we think we know more than we do. Consider these three word puzzles (called anagrams), which people like you were asked to unscramble in one study (Goranson, 1978).

> WREAT → WATER
> ETRYN → ENTRY
> GRABE → BARGE

About how many seconds do you think it would have taken you to unscramble each anagram? Knowing the answer makes us overconfident. Surely the solution would take only 10 seconds or so? In reality, the average problem solver spends 3 minutes, as you also might, given a similar puzzle without the solution: OCHSA. (When you're ready, check your answer against the footnote below.[5])

> Fun anagram solutions from Wordsmith (www.wordsmith.org):
>
> Snooze alarms = Alas! No more z's
>
> Dormitory = dirty room
>
> Slot machines = cash lost in 'em

Are we any better at predicting our social behavior? At the beginning of the school year, one study had students predict their own behavior (Vallone et al., 1990).

Would they drop a course, vote in an upcoming election, call their parents regularly (and so forth)? On average, the students felt 84 percent sure of their self-predictions. But later quizzes about their actual behavior showed their predictions were correct only 71 percent of the time. Even when they were 100 percent sure of themselves, their self-predictions were wrong 15 percent of the time.

Perceiving Order in Random Events

We have a built-in eagerness to make sense of our world. People see a face on the Moon, hear Satanic messages in music, or perceive the Virgin Mary's image on a grilled cheese sandwich. Even in random, unrelated data we often find patterns, because *random sequences often don't look random* (Falk et al., 2009; Nickerson, 2002, 2005). Flip a coin 50 times and you may be surprised at the streaks of heads or tails. In actual random sequences, patterns and streaks (such as repeating numbers) occur more often than people expect (Oskarsson et al., 2009). That also makes it hard for people to generate random-like sequences. When embezzlers try to simulate random digits, their nonrandom patterns can alert fraud experts (Poundstone, 2014).

Some happenings, such as winning the lottery twice, seem so amazing that we struggle to believe they are due to chance. But as statisticians have noted, "with a large enough sample, any outrageous thing is likely to happen" (Diaconis & Mosteller, 1989). An event that happens to but 1 in 1 billion people every day occurs about 7 times a day, more than 2500 times a year.

> **LaunchPad** IMMERSIVE LEARNING
> Consider how scientific inquiry can help you think smarter about hot streaks in sports with LaunchPad's *How Would You Know If There Is a Hot Hand in Basketball?*

The point to remember: We trust our intuition more than we should. Our intuitive thinking is flawed by three powerful tendencies—hindsight bias,

BIZARRE SEQUENCE OF COMPUTER-GENERATED RANDOM NUMBERS

© 1990 by Sidney Harris/American Scientist magazine.

Bizarre looking, perhaps. But actually no more unlikely than any other number sequence.

overconfidence, and perceiving patterns in random events. But scientific thinking can help us sift reality from illusion.

Retrieve + Remember

- Why, after friends start dating, do we often feel that we *knew* they were meant to be together?

ANSWER: We often suffer from hindsight bias—after we've learned a situation's outcome, that outcome seems familiar and therefore obvious.

How Do Psychologists Ask and Answer Questions?

Psychologists try to avoid the pitfalls of intuitive thinking by using the *scientific method*. They observe events, form theories, and then refine their theories in the light of new observations.

The Scientific Method

LOQ 1-6 How do theories advance psychological science?

Chatting with friends and family, we often use *theory* to mean "mere hunch." In science, a **theory** *explains* behaviors or events by offering ideas that *organize* what we have observed. By organizing

---

5. The solution to the OCHSA anagram is CHAOS.

isolated facts, a theory simplifies. There are too many facts about behavior to remember them all. By linking facts to underlying principles, a theory offers a useful summary. It connects many small dots so that a clear picture emerges.

A theory about the effects of sleep on memory, for example, helps us organize countless sleep-related observations into a short list of principles. Imagine that we observe over and over that people with good sleep habits tend to answer questions correctly in class, and they do well at test time. We might therefore theorize that sleep improves memory. So far so good: Our principle neatly summarizes a list of observations about the effects of a good night's sleep.

Yet no matter how reasonable a theory may sound—and it does seem reasonable to suggest that sleep could improve memory—we must put it to the test. A good theory produces testable *predictions*, called **hypotheses**. Such predictions specify what results (what behaviors or events) would support the theory and what results would cast doubt on the theory. To test our theory about the effects of sleep on memory, our hypothesis might be that when sleep deprived, people will remember less from the day before. To test that hypothesis, we might assess how well people remember course materials they studied before a good night's sleep, or before a shortened night's sleep (**FIGURE 1.1**). The results will either support our theory or lead us to revise or reject it.

Our theories can bias our observations. The urge to see what we expect to see is always present, both inside and outside the laboratory. Having theorized that better memory springs from more sleep, we may see what we expect: We may perceive sleepy people's comments as less insightful.

As a check on their biases, psychologists use **operational definitions** when they report their studies. "Sleep deprived," for example, may be defined as "2 or more hours less" than the person's natural sleep. These exact descriptions will allow anyone to **replicate** (repeat) the research. Other people can then re-create the study with different participants and in different situations. If they get similar results, we can be more confident that the findings are reliable.

Replication is an essential part of good science. When 270 psychologists recently worked together to redo 100 psychological studies, the results made news: Only 36 percent of the results were replicated (Open Science Collaboration, 2015). (None of the non-reproducible findings appears in this text.) But then another team of scientists found most of the failed replications flawed and "the reproducibility of psychological science" to be "quite high" (Gilbert et al., 2016). Other fields, including medicine, also have seeming issues with nonreplicated findings (Collins & Tabak, 2014). Especially when based on a small sample, a single failure to replicate can itself need replication (Maxwell et al., 2015). In all scientific fields, replication either confirms findings, or enables us to correct or refine our knowledge.

> "Failure to replicate is not a bug; it is a feature. It is what leads us along the path—the wonderfully twisty path—of scientific discovery."
>
> Lisa Feldman Barrett, "Psychology Is Not in Crisis," 2015

Let's summarize. A good theory:

- effectively *organizes* a range of self-reports and observations.

- leads to clear *predictions* that anyone can use to check the theory or to create practical applications of it.

- often stimulates replications and more research that supports the theory (as happened with sleep and memory studies, as you'll see in Chapter 2), or leads to a revised theory that better *organizes* and predicts what we observe.

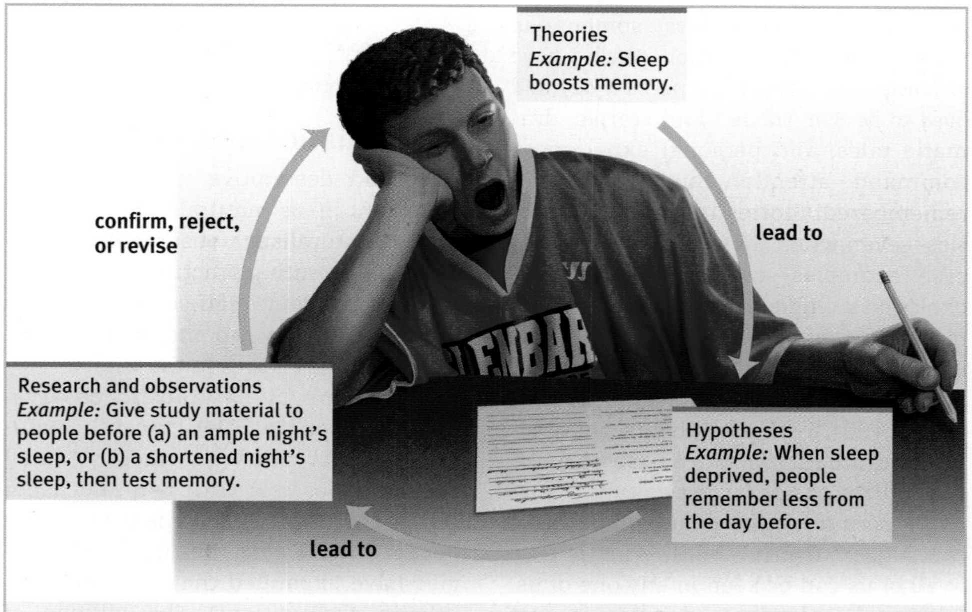

confirm, reject, or revise

Theories
Example: Sleep boosts memory.

lead to

Hypotheses
Example: When sleep deprived, people remember less from the day before.

lead to

Research and observations
Example: Give study material to people before (a) an ample night's sleep, or (b) a shortened night's sleep, then test memory.

FIGURE 1.1 The scientific method A self-correcting process for asking questions and observing nature's answers.

theory an explanation using principles that organize observations and predict behaviors or events.

hypothesis a testable prediction, often implied by a theory.

operational definition a carefully worded statement of the exact procedures (operations) used in a research study. For example, *human intelligence* may be operationally defined as what an intelligence test measures.

replication repeating the essence of a research study, usually with different participants in different situations, to see whether the basic finding can be reproduced.

We can test our hypotheses and refine our theories in several ways.

- *Descriptive* methods describe behaviors, often by using (as we will see) case studies, naturalistic observations, or surveys.
- *Correlational* methods associate different factors. (You'll see the word *factor* often in descriptions of research. It refers to anything that contributes to a result.)
- *Experimental* methods manipulate, or vary, factors to discover their effects.

To think critically about popular psychology claims, we need to understand the strengths and weaknesses of these methods. (For more information about some of the statistical methods that psychological scientists use in their work, see Appendix A, Statistical Reasoning in Everyday Life.)

Retrieve + Remember

- What does a good theory do?

ANSWER: 1. It *organizes* observed facts. 2. It implies hypotheses that offer testable predictions and, sometimes, practical applications. 3. It often stimulates further research.

- Why is replication important?

ANSWER: When others are able to repeat (replicate) studies and produce similar results, psychologists can have more confidence in the original findings.

Description

LOQ 1-7 How do psychologists use case studies, naturalistic observations, and surveys to observe and describe behavior, and why is random sampling important?

In daily life, we all observe and describe other people, trying to understand why they think, feel, and act as they do. Professional psychologists do much the same, though more objectively and systematically, using

- *case studies* (in-depth analyses of individuals or groups).
- *naturalistic observations* (watching and recording individual

or group behavior in a natural setting).

- *surveys* and interviews (self-reports in which people answer questions about their behavior or attitudes).

The Case Study

A **case study** examines one individual or group in depth, in the hope of revealing things true of us all. Some examples: Medical case studies of people who lost specific abilities after damage to certain brain regions gave us much of our early knowledge about the brain. Jean Piaget, the pioneer researcher on children's thinking, carefully watched and questioned just a few children. Studies of only a few chimpanzees jarred our beliefs about what other species can understand and communicate.

Intensive case studies are sometimes very revealing. They often suggest directions for further study, and they show us what *can* happen. But individual cases may also mislead us. The individual being studied may be *atypical* (not like those in the larger population). Viewing such cases as general truths can lead to false conclusions. Indeed, anytime a researcher mentions a finding (*Smokers die younger: 95 percent of men over 85 are nonsmokers*), someone is sure to offer an exception (*Well, I have an uncle who smoked two packs a day and lived to be 89*). These vivid stories, dramatic tales, and personal experiences command attention and are easily remembered. Stories move us, but stories—even when they are psychological case examples—can mislead. A psychologist's single case of someone who reportedly changed from gay to straight is *not* evidence that sexual orientation is a choice. As psychologist Gordon Allport (1954, p. 9) said, "Given a thimbleful of [dramatic] facts we rush to make generalizations as large as a tub."

The point to remember: Individual cases can suggest fruitful ideas. What is true of all of us can be seen in any one of us. But just because something is true of one of us (the atypical uncle), we should not assume it is true of all of us (most

FREUD AND LITTLE HANS Sigmund Freud's case study of 5-year-old Hans' extreme fear of horses led Freud to his theory of childhood sexuality. Freud believed Hans' intense fear of being bitten by a horse had its roots in the boy's unconscious desire for his mother and his fear of being castrated by his rival father. As Chapter 12 will explain, today's psychological science does not support Freud's theory of childhood sexuality. It does, however, agree that much of the human mind operates outside our conscious awareness.

long-term smokers *do* suffer ill health and early deaths). To uncover general truths, we must look to methods beyond the case study.

Retrieve + Remember

- We cannot assume that case studies always reveal general principles that apply to all of us. Why not?

ANSWER: Case studies focus on one individual or group, so we can't know for sure whether the principles observed would apply to a larger population.

Naturalistic Observation

A second descriptive method records behavior in a natural environment. These **naturalistic observations** may describe parenting practices in different cultures, students' self-seating patterns in American lunchrooms, or chimpanzee family structures in the wild.

The scope of naturalistic observations is expanding. Until recently, naturalistic observation was mostly "small science"—possible with pen and paper rather than fancy equipment and a big budget (Provine, 2012). But new technologies have expanded the scope of naturalistic observations. The billions of people entering personal information on sites such as Facebook, Twitter, and

Google have created a huge new opportunity for "big data" observations. To track the ups and downs of human moods, one study counted positive and negative words in 504 million Twitter messages from 84 countries (Golder & Macy, 2011). When were people happiest? As **FIGURE 1.2** shows, spirits seemed to rise on weekends, shortly after waking, and in the evenings. (Are late Saturday evenings often a happy time for you, too?) Another study found that the proportion of negative emotion words (especially anger-related words) in 148 million tweets from 1347 U.S. counties predicted the counties' heart disease rates (Eichstaedt et al., 2015). How well did it predict heart disease rates? Better than other traditional predictors, such as smoking and obesity.

Smart-phone apps and body-worn sensors are also offering new ways to collect data. Using such tools, researchers can track willing volunteers' locations, activities, and opinions—without interfering with the person's activity. In one study, 79 introductory psychology students donned electronically activated recording devices (EARs) (Mehl et al., 2010). For up to four days, the EARs

captured 30-second snippets of the students' waking hours, turning on every 12.5 minutes. By the end of the study, researchers had eavesdropped on more than 23,000 half-minute life slices. Was happiness related to having simple talks or deeply involved conversations? The happiest participants avoided small talk and embraced meaningful conversations. Happy people would rather talk than tweet. Does that surprise you?

Like the case study method, naturalistic observation does not *explain* behavior. It *describes* it. Nevertheless, descriptions can be revealing: The starting point of any science is description.

Retrieve + Remember

- What are the advantages and disadvantages of naturalistic observation, such as the EARs study?

ANSWER: In the EARs study, researchers were able to carefully observe and record naturally occurring behaviors outside the artificial environment of a laboratory. However, they were not able to explain the behaviors because they could not control all the factors that may have influenced them.

The Survey

A **survey** looks at many cases in less depth, asking people to report their own behavior or opinions. Questions about everything from sexual practices to political opinions are put to the public. In recent surveys,

- Saturdays and Sundays have been the week's happiest days (confirming what the Twitter researchers found using naturalistic observation) (Stone et al., 2012).

- 1 in 5 people across 22 countries reported believing that alien beings have come to Earth and now walk among us disguised as humans (Ipsos, 2010).

- 68 percent of all humans—some 4.6 billion people—say that religion is important in their daily lives (from Gallup World Poll data analyzed by Diener et al., 2011).

But asking questions is tricky, and the answers often depend on the way you word your questions and on who answers them.

WORDING EFFECTS Even subtle changes in the wording of questions can have major effects. Should violence be allowed to appear in children's television programs? People are much more likely to approve "not allowing" such things than "forbidding" or "censoring" them. In one national survey, only 27 percent of Americans approved of "government censorship" of media sex and violence, though 66 percent approved of "more restrictions on what is shown on television" (Lacayo, 1995).

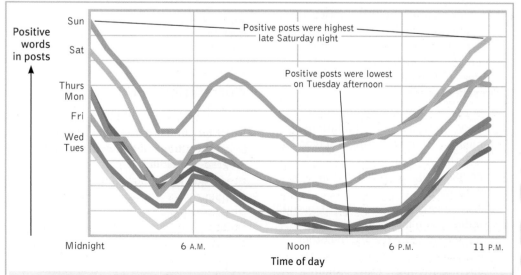

FIGURE 1.2 Twitter message moods by time and by day This graph illustrates how, without knowing anyone's identity, research can use "big data" to study human behavior on a huge scale. Many options are possible, such as an association between mood and weather, or the spread of ideas through social networks. (Data from Golder & Macy, 2011.)

case study a descriptive technique in which one individual or group is studied in depth in the hope of revealing universal principles.

naturalistic observation a descriptive technique of observing and recording behavior in naturally occurring situations without trying to change or control the situation.

survey a descriptive technique for obtaining the self-reported attitudes or behaviors of a group, usually by questioning a representative, *random sample* of that group.

People are much more approving of "aid to the needy" than of "welfare," and of "revenue enhancers" than of "taxes." Wording is a delicate matter, and some words can trigger positive or negative reactions. Critical thinkers will reflect on how a question's phrasing might affect the opinions people express.

RANDOM SAMPLING For an accurate picture of a group's experiences and attitudes, there's only one game in town. In a *representative sample*, a smaller group can accurately reflect the larger **population** you want to study and describe.

So how do you obtain a representative sample? Say you want to survey the total student population at your school to get their reaction to an upcoming tuition increase. To be sure your sample represents the whole student population, you will want to choose a **random sample,** in which every person in the entire population has an equal chance of being picked. You would not want to ask for volunteers, because those extra-nice students who step forward to help would not necessarily be a random sample of all the students. But you could assign each student a number, and then use a random number generator to select a sample.

> With very large samples, estimates become quite reliable. E is estimated to represent 12.7 percent of the letters in written English. E, in fact, is 12.3 percent of the 925,141 letters in Melville's *Moby-Dick*, 12.4 percent of the 586,747 letters in Dickens' *A Tale of Two Cities,* and 12.1 percent of the 3,901,021 letters in 12 of Mark Twain's works (Chance News, 1997).

Time and money will affect the size of your sample, but you would try to involve as many people as possible. Why? Because large representative samples are better than small ones. (But a smaller representative sample of 100 is better than a larger unrepresentative sample of 500.)

Political pollsters sample voters in national election surveys just this way. Using only 1500 randomly sampled people, drawn from all areas of a country, they can provide a remarkably accurate snapshot of the nation's opinions. Without random sampling, large

samples—including call-in phone samples and TV or website polls—often give misleading results.

The point to remember: Before accepting survey findings, think critically. Consider the wording of the questions and the sample. The best basis for generalizing is from a random sample of a population.

Retrieve + Remember

- What is an unrepresentative sample, and how do researchers avoid it?

ANSWER: An unrepresentative sample is a group that does not represent the population being studied. *Random sampling* helps researchers form a representative sample, because each member of the population has an equal chance of being included.

Correlation

LOQ 1-8 What are positive and negative correlations, and how can they lead to prediction but not cause-effect explanation?

Describing behavior is a first step toward predicting it. Naturalistic observations and surveys often show us that one trait or behavior relates to another. In such cases, we say the two **correlate.** A statistical measure (the *correlation coefficient*) helps us figure how closely two things vary together, and thus how well either one *predicts* the other. Knowing how much aptitude tests *correlate* with school success tells us how well the scores *predict* school success.

- A *positive correlation* (above 0 to +1.00) indicates a *direct* relationship, meaning that two things increase together or decrease together. Across people, height correlates positively with weight.

- A *negative correlation* (below 0 to –1.00) indicates an *inverse* relationship: As one thing increases, the other decreases. The number of hours spent watching TV and playing video games each week correlates negatively with grades. Negative correlations can go as low as –1.00. This means that, like children on

opposite ends of a teeter-totter, one set of scores goes down precisely as the other goes up.

- A coefficient near zero is a weak correlation, indicating little or no relationship.

The point to remember: A correlation coefficient helps us see the world more clearly by revealing the extent to which two things relate.

Retrieve + Remember

- Indicate whether each of the following statements describes a positive correlation or a negative correlation.

1. The more husbands viewed Internet pornography, the worse their marital relationships (Muusses et al., 2015).
2. The less sexual content teens saw on TV, the less likely they were to have sex (Collins et al., 2004).
3. The longer children were breast-fed, the greater their later academic achievement (Horwood & Fergusson, 1998).
4. The more income rose among a sample of poor families, the fewer symptoms of mental illness their children experienced (Costello et al., 2003).

ANSWERS: 1. negative, 2. positive, 3. positive, 4. negative

LaunchPad For an animated tutorial on correlations, visit LaunchPad's *Concept Practice: Positive and Negative Correlations.*

Correlation and Causation

Consider some recent headlines:

- "Study finds that increased parental support for college results in lower grades" (Jaschik, 2013)

- "People with mental illness more likely to be smokers, study finds" (Belluck, 2013)

- "Teenagers who don't get enough sleep at higher risk for mental health problems" (Rodriguez, 2015)

What shall we make of these correlations? Do they indicate that students would achieve more if their parents supported them less? That stopping smoking would improve mental health? That more sleep would produce better mental health?

No, because such correlations do not come with built-in cause-effect arrows. In two recent studies, sexual hook-ups correlated with college women's experiencing depression; delaying sexual intimacy correlated with positive outcomes such as greater relationship satisfaction and stability (Fielder et al., 2013; Willoughby et al., 2014). Do these findings mean that sexual restraint causes better outcomes? It might. But in this case, as in many others, causation might work the other way around (more depressed people are more likely to hook up). Alternatively, some third factor, such as lower impulsivity, might underlie both sexual restraint and psychological well-being.

But correlations do help us predict. Here's an example: Self-esteem correlates negatively with (and therefore predicts) depression. (The lower people's self-esteem, the more they are at risk for depression.) But does that mean low self-esteem *causes* depression? If you think the answer is *Yes,* you are not alone. We all find it hard to resist thinking that associations prove causation. But no matter how strong the relationship, they do not!

How else might we explain the negative correlation between self-esteem and depression? As **FIGURE 1.3** suggests, we'd get the same correlation between low self-esteem and depression if depression caused people to be down on themselves. And we'd also get that correlation if something else—a third factor such as heredity or some awful event—caused *both* low self-esteem and depression.

This point is so important—so basic to thinking smarter with psychology—

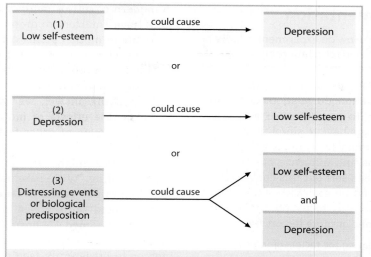

FIGURE 1.3 Three possible cause-effect relationships People low in self-esteem are more likely to report depression than are those high in self-esteem. One possible explanation of this negative correlation is that a bad self-image causes depressed feelings. But, as this diagram shows, other cause-effect relationships are possible.

that it merits one more example, this one from a survey of over 12,000 adolescents. The more those teens felt loved by their parents, the less likely they were to behave in unhealthy ways—having early sex, smoking, abusing alcohol and drugs, behaving violently (Resnick et al., 1997). "Adults have a powerful effect on their children's behavior right through the high school years," gushed an Associated Press (AP) news report on the study. But *correlations don't prove causation.* Thus, the AP could as well have said, "Children's behavior has a powerful effect on their parents' feelings toward them."

The point to remember (turn up the volume here): *Correlation indicates the* possibility *of a cause-effect relationship, but it does not prove causation.* Knowing that two events are associated does not tell us anything about which causes the other. Remember this principle and you will be wiser as you read and hear news of scientific studies.

"When scientists communicate with each other, they . . . are cautious about oversimplifying results and speaking beyond the data. But when science is . . . fed to the public, the nuance and uncertainty is often lost."

Clay Routledge, "What Scientists Know and Need to Share with the Public," 2015

© Nancy Brown/Getty Images

Retrieve + Remember

• Length of marriage correlates with hair loss in men. Does this mean that marriage causes men to lose their hair (or that balding men make better husbands)?

ANSWER: In this case, as in many others, a third factor can explain the correlation: Golden anniversaries and baldness both accompany aging.

population all those in a group being studied, from which samples may be drawn. (*Note:* Except for national studies, this does *not* refer to a country's whole population.)

random sample a sample that fairly represents a population because each member has an equal chance of inclusion.

correlation a measure of the extent to which two events vary together, and thus of how well either one predicts the other. The *correlation coefficient* is the mathematical expression of the relationship, ranging from −1.00 to +1.00, with 0 indicating no relationship.

Experimentation

LOQ 1-9 How do experiments clarify or reveal cause-effect relationships?

Descriptions, even with big data, don't prove causation. Correlations don't prove causation. To isolate cause and effect, psychologists have to simplify the world. In our everyday lives, many things affect our actions and influence our thoughts. Psychologists sort out this complexity by using **experiments.** With experiments, researchers can focus on the possible effects of one or more factors by

- *manipulating the factors of interest.*
- *holding constant ("controlling") other factors.*

Let's consider a few experiments to see how this works.

Random Assignment: Minimizing Differences

Researchers have compared infants who are breast-fed with those who are bottle-fed with formula. Some studies, but not others, show that children's intelligence test scores are a tad higher if they were breast-fed (von Stumm & Plomin, 2015; Walfisch et al., 2014). The longer they were breast-fed, the higher their later scores (Jedrychowski et al., 2012; Victora et al., 2015). So we can say that mother's milk may *correlate* modestly but positively with later intelligence. But what does this mean? Do smarter mothers (who

Lane Oatey/Getty Images

in modern countries more often breast-feed) have smarter children? Or do the nutrients in mother's milk contribute to brain development? Even big data from a million or a billion mothers and their offspring wouldn't tell us.

To find the answer, we would have to isolate the effects of mother's milk from the effects of other factors, such as mother's age, education, and intelligence. How might we do that? By experimenting. With parental permission, one British research team directly experimented with breast milk. They **randomly assigned** 424 hospitalized premature infants either to formula feedings or to breast-milk feedings (Lucas et al., 1992). By doing this, they created two otherwise similar groups:

- an **experimental group,** in which babies received the treatment (breast milk).
- a contrasting **control group** without the treatment.

Random assignment (whether by means of a random-number generator or by the flip of a coin) minimizes any preexisting differences between the two groups. If one-third of the volunteers for an experiment can wiggle their ears, then about one-third of the people in each group will be ear wigglers. So, too, with age, intelligence, attitudes, and other characteristics, which will be similar in the experimental and control groups. When groups are formed by random assignment, and they differ at the experiment's end, we can assume the treatment had an effect.

Is breast best? The British experiment found that, at least for premature infants, breast milk is indeed best for developing intelligence. On intelligence tests taken at age 8, those nourished with breast milk scored significantly higher than those who had been formula-fed.

The point to remember: Unlike correlational studies, which uncover *naturally occurring* relationships, an experiment *manipulates* (varies) a factor to determine its effect.

The Double-Blind Procedure: Eliminating Bias

In the breast-milk experiment, babies didn't have expectations that could affect the experiment's outcome. Adults do have expectations.

Consider: Three days into a cold, many of us start taking vitamin C tablets. If we find our cold symptoms lessening, we may credit the pills. But after a few days, most colds are naturally on their way out. Was the vitamin C cure truly effective? To find out, we could experiment.

And that is precisely what investigators do to judge whether new drug treatments and new methods of psychotherapy are effective (Chapter 14). They use random assignment to form the groups. An experimental group receives the treatment, such as a medication. A control group receives a **placebo** (an inactive substance—perhaps a look-alike pill with no drug in it). Often, the people who take part in these studies are *blind* (uninformed) about which treatment, if any, they are receiving.

Many studies use a **double-blind procedure**—neither those taking part in the study nor those collecting the data know which group is receiving the treatment. In such studies, researchers can check a treatment's actual effects apart from the participants' belief in its healing powers and the staff's enthusiasm for its potential. Just *thinking* you are getting a treatment can boost your spirits, relax your body, and relieve your symptoms. This **placebo effect** is well documented in reducing pain, depression, and anxiety (Kirsch, 2010). Athletes have run faster when given a fake performance-enhancing drug (McClung & Collins, 2007). Decaf-coffee drinkers have reported increased vigor and alertness—when they thought their brew had caffeine in it (Dawkins et al., 2011). People have felt better after receiving a phony mood-enhancing drug (Michael et al., 2012). And the more expensive the placebo, the more "real" it seems—a fake pill that cost $2.50 worked better than one costing 10 cents (Waber et al., 2008). So what do you think happens when people have

"If I don't think it's going to work, will it still work?"

repeatedly received a placebo and have repeatedly reported decreased pain? Even when they learn they are taking a placebo, they continue to report reduced pain (Schafer et al., 2015). To know how effective a therapy really is, researchers must control for a possible placebo effect.

Retrieve + Remember

- What measures do researchers use to prevent the *placebo effect* from confusing their results?

ANSWER: Research designed to prevent the *placebo effect* randomly assigns participants to an *experimental group* (which receives the real treatment) or a *control group* (which receives a placebo). A double-blind procedure prevents people's beliefs and hopes from affecting the results, because neither the participants nor those collecting the data know who receives the placebo. A comparison of the results will show whether the real treatment produces better results than *belief* in that treatment.

Independent and Dependent Variables

Here is an even more potent example: The drug Viagra was approved for use after 21 clinical trials. One trial was an experiment in which researchers randomly assigned 329 men with erectile disorder to either an experimental group (Viagra takers) or a control group (placebo takers). The pills looked identical, and the procedure was double-blind—neither the men taking the pills nor the people giving them knew who received the placebo.

The result: Viagra worked. At peak doses, 69 percent of Viagra-assisted attempts at intercourse were successful, compared with 22 percent for men receiving the placebo (Goldstein et al., 1998).

This simple experiment manipulated just one factor—the drug (Viagra versus no Viagra). We call the manipulated factor an **independent variable:** We can vary it *independently* of other factors, such as the men's age, weight, and personality. These other factors, which could influence a study's results, are called **confounding variables.** Thanks to random assignment, the confounding variables should be roughly equal in both groups.

Note the distinction between random sampling (discussed earlier in relation to surveys) and random assignment (depicted in Figure 1.4). Through random sampling, we may represent a population effectively, because each member of that population has an equal chance of being selected (sampled) for participation in our research. Random assignment ensures accurate representation among the research groups, because each participant has an equal chance of being placed in (assigned to) any of the groups. This helps control outside influences so that we can determine cause and effect.

Experiments examine the effect of one or more independent variables on some behavior or mental process that can be measured. We call this kind of affected behavior the **dependent variable** because it can vary *depending* on what takes place during the experiment. Experimenters give both variables precise *operational definitions.* They specify exactly how the

- independent variable (in this study, the precise drug dosage and timing) was manipulated.

- dependent variable (in this study, the men's responses to questions about their sexual performance) was measured.

Operational definitions answer the "What do you mean?" question with a level of precision that enables others to replicate (repeat) the study.

Let's see how this works with the British breast-milk experiment (**FIGURE 1.4**). A *variable* is anything that can vary (infant nutrition, intelligence). Experiments aim to *manipulate* an *independent* variable (type of milk), *measure* a *dependent* variable (later intelligence test score), and control *confounding* variables. An experiment has at least two different groups: an *experimental group* (infants who received breast milk) and a *comparison* or *control group* (infants who did not receive breast milk). *Random assignment*

experiment a method in which researchers vary one or more factors (independent variables) to observe the effect on some behavior or mental process (the dependent variable). By random assignment of participants, researchers aim to control other factors.

random assignment assigning participants to experimental and control groups by chance, thus minimizing any preexisting differences between the groups.

experimental group in an experiment, the group exposed to the treatment, that is, to one version of the independent variable.

control group in an experiment, the group *not* exposed to the treatment; the control group serves as a comparison with the experimental group for judging the effect of the treatment.

placebo [pluh-SEE-bo; Latin for "I shall please"] an inactive substance or condition that is sometimes given to those in a control group in place of the treatment given to the experimental group.

double-blind procedure in an experiment, a procedure in which both the participants and the research staff are ignorant (blind) about who has received the treatment or a placebo.

placebo effect results caused by expectations alone.

independent variable in an experiment, the factor that is manipulated; the variable whose effect is being studied.

confounding variable a factor other than the factor being studied that might influence a study's results.

dependent variable in an experiment, the factor that is measured; the variable that may change when the independent variable is manipulated.

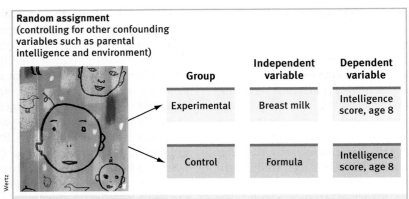

FIGURE 1.4 Experimentation To study cause and effect, psychologists control for confounding variables by randomly assigning some participants to an experimental group, others to a control group. Measuring the dependent variable (intelligence score in later childhood) will determine the effect of the independent variable (type of milk).

works to *control* all other (confounding) variables by equating the groups before any manipulation begins. In this way, an experiment tests the effect of at least one independent variable (what we manipulate) on at least one dependent variable (the outcome we measure).

In another experiment, psychologists tested whether landlords' perceptions of an applicant's ethnicity would influence the availability of rental housing. The researchers sent identically worded e-mails to 1115 Los Angeles–area landlords (Carpusor & Loges, 2006). They varied the sender's name to imply different ethnic groups: "Patrick McDougall," "Said Al-Rahman," and "Tyrell Jackson." Then they tracked the percentage of landlords' positive replies. How many e-mails triggered invitations to view the apartment? For McDougall, 89 percent; for Al-Rahman, 66 percent; and for Jackson, 56 percent.

"[We must guard] against not just racial slurs, but . . . against the subtle impulse to call Johnny back for a job interview, but not Jamal."

Barack Obama, *Eulogy for Clementa Pinckney,*
June 26, 2015

How Would You Know Which Research Design to Use?

Throughout this book, you will read about amazing psychological science discoveries. **TABLE 1.2** compares the features of psychology's main research methods. In later chapters, you will read about other research designs, including twin studies (Chapter 3) and cross-sectional and longitudinal research (Appendix A). But how do we know fact from fiction? How do psychological scientists choose research methods and design their studies in ways that pro-

vide meaningful results? Understanding how research is done—how testable questions are developed and studied—is key to appreciating all of psychology.

In psychological research, no questions are off limits, except untestable ones. Does free will exist? Are people born evil? Is there an afterlife? Psychologists can't test those questions, but they *can* test whether free will beliefs, aggressive personalities, and a belief in life after death influence how people think, feel, and act (Dechesne et al., 2003; Shariff et al., 2014; Webster et al., 2014).

Having chosen their question, psychologists then select the most appropriate research design—experimental, correlational, case study, naturalistic observation, twin study, longitudinal, or cross-sectional—and determine how to set it up most effectively. They consider how much money and time are available, ethical issues, and other limitations. For example, it wouldn't be ethical for a researcher studying child development to use the experimental method and randomly assign children to loving versus punishing homes.

To help you build your understanding, your critical thinking, and your scientific literacy skills, we created IMMERSIVE LEARNING research activities in LaunchPad. In these *"How Would You Know?"* activities, you get to play the role of the researcher, making choices about the best ways to test interesting questions. Some examples: How Would You Know If Having Children Relates to Being Happier?, How Would You Know If a Cup of Coffee Can Warm Up Relationships?, and How Would You Know If People Can Learn to Reduce Anxiety?

TABLE 1.2	Comparing Research Methods			
Research Method	**Basic Purpose**	**How Conducted**	**What Is Manipulated**	**Weaknesses**
Descriptive	To observe and record behavior	Do case studies, naturalistic observations, or surveys	Nothing	No control of variables; single cases may be misleading.
Correlational	To detect naturally occurring relationships; to assess how well one variable predicts another	Collect data on two or more variables; no manipulation	Nothing	Does not specify cause and effect.
Experimental	To explore cause and effect	Manipulate one or more factors; use random assignment	The independent variable(s)	Sometimes not possible for practical or ethical reasons.

Next, psychological scientists decide how to measure the behavior or mental process being studied. For example, researchers could measure aggressive behavior by measuring participants' willingness to blast a stranger with intense noise.

Researchers want to have confidence in their findings, so they carefully consider confounding variables—factors other than those being studied that may affect their interpretation of results.

Psychological research is a fun and creative adventure. Researchers *design* each study, *measure* target behaviors, *interpret* results, and learn more about the fascinating world of behavior and mental processes along the way.

LaunchPad To review and test your understanding of experimental methods and concepts, visit LaunchPad's *Concept Practice: The Language of Experiments,* and the interactive *PsychSim 6: Understanding Psychological Research.* For a 9.5-minute video synopsis of psychology's scientific research strategies, visit LaunchPad's *Video: Research Methods.*

Predicting Everyday Behavior

LOQ 1-10 How can simplified laboratory experiments help us understand general principles of behavior?

When you see or hear about psychology research, do you ever wonder whether people's behavior in a research laboratory will predict their behavior in real life? Does detecting the blink of a faint red light in a dark room say anything useful about flying a plane at night? Or, suppose an experiment shows that a man aroused by viewing a violent, sexually explicit film will then be more willing to push buttons that he thinks will electrically shock a woman. Does that really say anything about whether violent pornography makes men more likely to abuse women?

Before you answer, consider this. The experimenter *intends* to simplify reality—to create a mini-environment that imitates and controls important features of everyday life. Just as a wind tunnel lets airplane designers re-create airflow forces under controlled conditions, a laboratory experiment lets psychologists re-create psychological forces under controlled conditions.

An experiment's purpose is not to re-create the exact behaviors of everyday life, but to test *theoretical principles* (Mook, 1983). In aggression studies, deciding whether to push a button that delivers a shock may not be the same as slapping someone in the face, but the principle is the same. *It is the resulting principles—not the specific findings—that help explain everyday behaviors.* Many investigations have shown that principles derived in the laboratory do typically generalize to the everyday world (Anderson et al., 1999).

The point to remember: Psychological science focuses less on specific behaviors than on revealing general principles that help explain many behaviors.

Psychology's Research Ethics

LOQ 1-11 Why do psychologists study animals, and what ethical guidelines safeguard human and animal research participants? How do personal values influence psychology's research and applications?

We have reflected on how a scientific approach can restrain hidden biases. We have seen how case studies, naturalistic observations, and surveys help us describe behavior. We have noted that correlational studies assess the association between two factors, showing how well one predicts the other. We have examined the logic underlying experiments, which use controls and random assignment to isolate the effects of independent variables on dependent variables.

Hopefully, you are now prepared to understand what lies ahead and to think critically about psychological matters. But before we plunge in, let's address some common questions about psychology's ethics and values.

Retrieve + Remember

- In the rental housing experiment discussed in this section, what was the independent variable? The dependent variable?

ANSWER: The independent variable, which the researchers manipulated, was the implied ethnicity of the applicants' names. The dependent variable, which researchers measured, was the rate of positive responses from the landlords.

- Match the term on the left with the description on the right.

1. double-blind procedure
2. random sampling
3. random assignment

a. helps researchers generalize from a small set of survey responses to a larger population

b. helps minimize preexisting differences between experimental and control groups

c. controls for the placebo effect; neither researchers nor participants know who receives the real treatment

ANSWERS: 1. c, 2. a, 3. b

- Why, when testing a new drug to control blood pressure, would we learn more about its effectiveness from giving it to half the participants in a group of 1000 than to all 1000 participants?

ANSWER: We learn more about the drug's effectiveness when we can compare the results of those who took the drug (the experimental group) with the results of those who did not (the control group). If we gave the drug to all 1000 participants, we would have no way of knowing whether the drug is serving as a placebo or is actually medically effective.

Studying and Protecting Animals

Many psychologists study nonhuman animals because they find them fascinating. They want to understand how different species learn, think, and behave. Psychologists also study animals to learn about people. We humans are not *like* animals; we *are* animals, sharing a common biology. Animal experiments have therefore led to treatments for human diseases—insulin for diabetes, vaccines to prevent polio and rabies, transplants to replace defective organs.

Humans are more complex. But the same processes by which we learn are present in rats, monkeys, and even sea slugs. The simplicity of the sea slug's nervous system is precisely what makes it so revealing of the neural mechanisms of learning.

> "Rats are very similar to humans except that they are not stupid enough to purchase lottery tickets."
> Dave Barry, July 2, 2002

Sharing such similarities, should we respect rather than experiment on our animal relatives? The animal protection movement protests the use of animals in psychological, biological, and medical research. Out of this heated debate, two issues emerge.

The basic question: Is it right to place the well-being of humans above that of other animals? In experiments on stress and cancer, is it right that mice get tumors in the hope that people might not? Should some monkeys be exposed to an HIV-like virus in the search for an AIDS vaccine? Humans raise and slaughter 56 billion animals a year (Worldwatch Institute, 2013). Is this use and consumption of other animals as natural as the behavior of carnivorous hawks, cats, and whales?

If we decide to give human life top priority, a second question emerges: What safeguards should protect the well-being of animals in research? One survey asked animal researchers if they supported government regulations protecting research animals. Ninety-eight percent supported such protection for primates, dogs, and cats. And 74 percent also backed regulations providing for the humane care of rats and mice (Plous & Herzog, 2000). Many professional associations and funding agencies already have such guidelines. British Psychological Society (BPS) guidelines call for housing animals under reasonably natural living conditions, with companions for social animals (Lea, 2000). American Psychological Association (APA) guidelines state that researchers must ensure the "comfort, health, and humane treatment" of animals and minimize "infection, illness, and pain" (APA, 2002). Most universities screen research proposals, often through an animal care ethics committee, and laboratories are regulated and inspected.

Animals have themselves benefited from animal research. After measuring stress hormone levels in samples of millions of dogs brought each year to animal shelters, research psychologists devised handling and stroking methods to reduce stress and ease the dogs' move to adoptive homes (Tuber et al., 1999). Other studies have helped improve care and management in animals' natural habitats. By revealing our behavioral kinship with animals and the remarkable intelligence of chimpanzees, gorillas, and other animals, experiments have led to increased empathy and protection for other species. At its best, a psychology concerned for humans and sensitive to animals serves the welfare of both.

Studying and Protecting Humans

What about human participants? Does the image of white-coated scientists seeming to deliver electric shocks trouble you? Actually, most psychological studies are free of such stress. Blinking lights, flashing words, and pleasant

ANIMAL RESEARCH BENEFITING ANIMALS Psychologists have helped enrich zoo animal environments (Weir, 2013). Thanks partly to research on the benefits of novelty, control, and stimulation, these gorillas have enjoyed an improved quality of life in New York's Bronx Zoo.

social interactions are more common. Moreover, psychology's experiments are mild compared with the stress and humiliation often inflicted in the media "experiments" of reality TV shows. In one episode of *The Bachelor*, a man dumped his new fiancée on camera, at the producers' request, for the woman who earlier had finished second (Collins, 2009).

Occasionally, though, researchers do temporarily stress or deceive people. This happens only when they believe it is unavoidable. Some experiments won't work if participants know everything beforehand. (Wanting to be helpful, they might try to confirm the researcher's predictions.)

The APA and Britain's BPS ethics codes urge researchers to

- obtain the participants' **informed consent** to participate.

- protect participants from out-of-the-ordinary harm and discomfort.

- keep information about individual participants confidential.

- fully **debrief** participants (explain the research afterward).

As noted earlier in relation to nonhuman animals, most universities have ethics committees that screen research proposals and safeguard participants' well-being.

Values in Psychology

Values affect what we study, how we study it, and how we interpret results. Consider our choice of research topics. Should we study worker productivity or worker morale? Sex discrimination or gender differences? Conformity or independence? Values can also color "the facts"—our observations and interpretations. Sometimes we see what we want or expect to see (**FIGURE 1.5**).

Even the words we use to describe traits and tendencies can reflect our values. Labels describe and labels evaluate. One person's *rigidity* is another's *consistency*. One person's "undocumented worker" is another's "illegal alien." One person's *faith* is another's *fanaticism*. One country's *enhanced interrogation techniques* become *torture* when practiced by an enemy. Our words—*firm* or *stubborn, careful* or *picky, discreet* or *secretive*—reveal our attitudes.

Applied psychology also contains hidden values. If you defer to "professional" guidance—on raising children, achieving self-fulfillment, coping with sexual feelings, getting ahead at work—you are accepting value-laden advice. A science of behavior and mental processes can help us reach our goals, but it cannot decide what those goals should be.

Others have a different worry about psychology: that it is becoming dangerously powerful. Might psychology, they ask, be used to manipulate people?

Office of Public Affairs at Columbia University, publication permission granted by Columbia University Archives, Columbia Library

PSYCHOLOGY SPEAKS In making its historic 1954 school desegregation decision, the U.S. Supreme Court cited the expert testimony and research of psychologists Kenneth Clark and Mamie Phipps Clark (1947). The Clarks reported that, when given a choice between Black and White dolls, most African-American children chose the White doll. This choice seemed to indicate that the children had absorbed and accepted anti-Black prejudice.

Knowledge, like all power, can be used for good or evil. Nuclear power has been used to light up cities—and to demolish them. Persuasive power has been used to educate people—and to deceive them. Although psychology does indeed have the power to deceive, its purpose is to enlighten. Every day, psychologists explore ways to enhance learning, creativity, and compassion. Psychology speaks to many of our world's great problems—war, climate change, prejudice, family crises, crime—all of which involve attitudes and behaviors. Psychology also speaks to our deepest longings—for nourishment, for love, for happiness. And, as you have seen, one of the new developments in this field—positive psychology—has as its goal exploring and promoting human strengths. Many of life's questions are beyond psychology, but even a first psychology course can shine a bright light on some very important ones.

Retrieve + Remember

- How are animal subjects and human research participants protected?

ANSWER: Animal protection laws, laboratory regulation and inspection, and local and university ethics committees (which screen research proposals) attempt to safeguard animal welfare. International psychological organizations urge researchers to obtain *informed consent* from human participants, and to protect them from greater-than-usual harm and discomfort, treat their personal information confidentially, and *debrief* them fully at the end of the experiment.

informed consent giving people enough information about a study to enable them to decide whether they wish to participate.

debriefing after an experiment ends, explaining to participants the study's purpose and any deceptions researchers used.

Mike Kemp/Getty Images

FIGURE 1.5 What do you see? Our expectations influence what we perceive. Did you see a duck or a rabbit? Show some friends this image with the rabbit photo covered up and see if they are more likely to perceive a duck instead. (Shepard, 1990.)

Use Psychology to Become a Stronger Person—and a Better Student

LOQ 1-12 How can psychological principles help you learn, remember, and thrive?

In chapters to come, we will offer evidence-based suggestions that you can use to live a happy, effective, flourishing life. As we will see, people who live happy, thriving lives

- *manage their time to get a full night's sleep.* Unlike sleep-deprived people, who live with fatigue and gloomy moods, well-rested people live with greater energy, alertness, and productivity.
- *make space for exercise.* Aerobic activity not only increases health and energy, it also is an effective remedy for mild to moderate depression and anxiety.
- *set long-term goals, with daily aims.* Flourishing people take time each day to work toward their goals—and, after doing so for a month, often find that their daily practice becomes a habit.
- *have a "growth mind-set."* Rather than seeing their abilities as fixed, they view their mental abilities as like a muscle—something that grows stronger with effortful use.
- *prioritize relationships.* We humans are social animals. We flourish when connected in close relationships. We are both happier and healthier when supported by (and supporting) caring friends.

Psychology's research also shows how we can learn and retain information. Most students assume that the way to cement new learning is to reread. Do you? If so, you may be surprised to hear that repeated self-testing and rehearsal of previously studied material helps even more. Memory researchers call this the **testing effect** (Roediger & Karpicke, 2006). (This is also known as the *retrieval practice effect*

or as *test-enhanced learning*.) In one study, students learned 40 Swahili words. Later, those who had been tested repeatedly recalled the words' meaning much better than did others who had spent the same time restudying the 40 words (Karpicke & Roediger, 2008). In college classrooms and elsewhere, frequent quizzing and self-testing have boosted retention (Pennebaker et al., 2013; Rowland, 2014).

We have designed this book to help you benefit from the testing effect and other memory research findings. As you will see in Chapter 7, to master information you must *actively process it.* Your mind is not like your stomach, something to be filled passively. Your mind is more like a muscle that grows stronger with exercise. People learn and remember best when they put material into their own words, rehearse it, and then retrieve and review it again.

The **SQ3R** study method converts these principles into practice (McDaniel et al., 2009; Robinson, 1970). SQ3R is an acronym—an abbreviation formed from the first letter of each of its five steps: Survey, Question, Read, Retrieve,[6] Review.

To study a chapter, first *survey,* taking a bird's-eye view. Use the colorful two-page chapter opening to visually survey the upcoming content. Scan the headings, and notice how the chapter is organized.

Before you read each main section, try to answer its numbered Learning Objective *Question* (for this section: "How can psychological principles help you learn, remember, and thrive?"). By testing your understanding *before* you read the section, you will discover what you don't yet know.

Then *read,* actively searching for the answer to the question. At each sitting, read only as much of the chapter (usually a single main section) as you can absorb without tiring. Read actively and think critically. Ask your own questions. Take notes. Relate the ideas to your personal experiences and to your own life. Does the idea support or challenge your assumptions? How convincing is the evidence?

Having read a section, *retrieve* its main ideas—"Active retrieval promotes meaningful learning" (Karpicke, 2012). So test yourself—even better, test yourself repeatedly. To get you started, we offer periodic Retrieve + Remember questions throughout each chapter (see, for example, the questions at the end of this section). After trying to answer these questions, check the answers (printed upside-down beneath the questions), and reread the material as needed. Researchers have found that "trying and failing to retrieve the answer is actually helpful to learning" (Roediger & Finn, 2010). Testing yourself after you read will help you learn and retain the information more effectively.

Finally, *review:* Read over any notes you have taken, again with an eye on the chapter's organization, and quickly review the whole chapter. Write or say what a concept is before rereading the material to check your understanding.

Survey, question, read, retrieve, review. We have organized this book's chapters to help you use the SQ3R study system. Each chapter begins with a *survey* of the content to come. Headings and Learning Objective *Questions* suggest issues and concepts you should consider as you move through the section. The length of the sections is controlled so you can easily *read* them. The Retrieve + Remember questions will challenge you to *retrieve* what you have learned, and thus better remember it. You can find complete chapter *reviews* in Appendix D. Additional self-test questions in a variety of formats appear together at the end of each chapter. You'll also find there a list of In Your Everyday Life questions that will help make the chapter's concepts more meaningful, and therefore more memorable.

Four additional study tips may further boost your learning:

Distribute your study time. One of psychology's oldest findings is that *if you want to retain information, spaced practice is better than massed practice.* So space your practice time over several study periods—perhaps one hour a day, six days a week—rather than cramming it into one week-long or

---

6. Also sometimes called "Recite."

all-night study blitz. You'll remember material better if you read just one main section (not the whole chapter) in a single sitting. Then turn to something else.

Spacing your study sessions requires discipline and knowing how to manage your time. Richard O. Straub explains time management in a helpful preface at the beginning of this text.

Learn to think critically. Whether you are reading or listening to class discussions, think smart. Try to spot people's assumptions and values. Can you detect a bias underlying an argument? Weigh the evidence. Is it a personal story that might not represent the whole group? Or is it scientific evidence based on sound experiments? Assess conclusions. Are other explanations possible?

Process class information actively. Listen for a lecture's main ideas and sub-ideas. *Write them down.* Ask questions during and after class. In class, as in your own study, process the information actively and you will understand and retain it better. How can you make

the information your own? Take notes in your own words. Make connections between what you read and what you already know. Tell someone else about it. (As any teacher will confirm, to teach is to remember.)

Overlearn. Psychology tells us that we tend to be overconfident—we overestimate how much we know. You may understand a chapter as you read it, but that feeling of familiarity can trick you. Overlearning helps you retain new information. By using the Retrieve + Remember opportunities, you can carve out extra study time for testing your knowledge.

Memory experts offer the bottom line for how to improve your retention and your grades (Bjork & Bjork, 2011, p. 63):

> Spend less time on the input side and more time on the output side, such as summarizing what you have read from memory or getting together with friends and asking each other questions. Any activities that involve testing yourself—that is, activities that require you to retrieve or generate

information, rather than just representing information to yourself—will make your learning both more durable and flexible.

Retrieve + Remember

- The _____ _____ describes the improved memory that results from repeated retrieval (as in self-testing) rather than from simple rereading of new information.

  ANSWER: testing effect

- What does SQ3R mean?

  ANSWER: SQ3R is an acronym—an abbreviation formed by the first letters in five words: Survey, Question, Read, Retrieve, and Review.

testing effect enhanced memory after retrieving, rather than simply rereading, information. Also sometimes called the *retrieval practice effect* or *test-enhanced learning*.

SQ3R a study method incorporating five steps: *S*urvey, *Q*uestion, *R*ead, *R*etrieve, *R*eview.

CHAPTER REVIEW

Psychology's Roots, Big Ideas, and Critical Thinking Tools

Test yourself by taking a moment to answer each of these Learning Objective Questions (repeated here from within the chapter). Then turn to Appendix D, Complete Chapter Reviews, to check your answers. Research suggests that trying to answer these questions on your own will improve your long-term memory of the concepts (McDaniel et al., 2009).

Psychology's Roots

1-1: What are the three key elements of the scientific attitude, and how do they support scientific inquiry?

1-2: How has psychology's focus changed over time?

1-3: What are psychology's current perspectives, and what are some of its subfields?

Four Big Ideas in Psychology

1-4: What four big ideas run throughout this book?

Why Do Psychology?

1-5: How does our everyday thinking sometimes lead us to the wrong conclusion?

How Do Psychologists Ask and Answer Questions?

1-6: How do theories advance psychological science?

1-7: How do psychologists use case studies, naturalistic observations, and surveys to observe and describe behavior, and why is random sampling important?

1-8: What are positive and negative correlations, and how can they lead to prediction but not cause-effect explanation?

1-9: How do experiments clarify or reveal cause-effect relationships?

1-10: How can simplified laboratory experiments help us understand general principles of behavior?

Psychology's Research Ethics

1-11: Why do psychologists study animals, and what ethical guidelines safeguard human and animal research participants? How do personal values influence psychology's research and applications?

Use Psychology to Become a Stronger Person—and a Better Student

1-12: How can psychological principles help you learn, remember, and thrive?

TERMS AND CONCEPTS TO REMEMBER

Test yourself on these terms by trying to write down the definition in your own words before flipping back to the referenced page to check your answer.

behaviorism, p. 2

humanistic psychology, p. 2

cognitive psychology, p. 5

cognitive neuroscience, p. 5

psychology, p. 5

critical thinking, p. 9

biopsychosocial approach, p. 9

culture, p. 9

nature–nurture issue, p. 9

dual processing, p. 11

positive psychology, p. 11

hindsight bias, p. 11

theory, p. 13

hypothesis, p. 13

operational definition, p. 13

replication, p. 13

case study, p. 15

naturalistic observation, p. 15

survey, p. 15

population, p. 17

random sample, p. 17

correlation, p. 17

experiment, p. 19

random assignment, p. 19

experimental group, p. 19

control group, p. 19

placebo [pluh-SEE-bo], p. 19

double-blind procedure, p. 19

placebo effect, p. 19

independent variable, p. 19

confounding variable, p. 19

dependent variable, p. 19

informed consent, p. 23

debriefing, p. 23

testing effect, p. 25

SQ3R, p. 25

CHAPTER TEST

Test yourself repeatedly throughout your studies. This will not only help you figure out what you know and don't know; the testing itself will help you learn and remember the information more effectively thanks to the *testing effect.*

1. In 1879, in psychology's first experiment, _____ and his students measured the time lag between hearing a ball hit a platform and pressing a key.

2. In the early twentieth century, _____ redefined psychology as "the science of observable behavior."

   a. John B. Watson

   b. Abraham Maslow

   c. William James

   d. Sigmund Freud

3. A psychologist treating emotionally troubled adolescents at a local mental health agency is most likely to be a(n)

   a. research psychologist.

   b. psychiatrist.

   c. industrial-organizational psychologist.

   d. clinical psychologist.

4. A mental health professional with a medical degree who can prescribe medication is a _____.

5. A psychologist doing research from the _____ perspective might be interested in how our blood chemistry affects our moods and motives.

   a. psychodynamic   c. neuroscience

   b. behavioral   d. social-cultural

6. How can critical thinking help you evaluate claims in the media, even if you're not a scientific expert on the issue?

7. Nature is to nurture as

   a. personality is to intelligence.

   b. biology is to experience.

   c. intelligence is to biology.

   d. psychological traits are to behaviors.

8. "Nurture works on what nature provides." Describe what this means, using your own words.

9. _____ _____ is the principle that our mind processes information on two tracks at the same time—one with our full awareness and the other outside of our awareness.

10. Martin Seligman and other researchers who explore various aspects of human flourishing refer to their field of study as _____ _____.

11. _____ _____ refers to our tendency to perceive events as predictable and obvious after the fact.

12. As scientists, psychologists

    a. keep their methods private so others will not repeat their research.

    b. assume the truth of articles published in leading scientific journals.

    c. reject evidence that competes with traditional findings.

    d. put competing ideas to the test and collect evidence.

13. Theory-based predictions are called _____.

14. Which of the following is NOT one of the *descriptive* methods psychologists use to study behavior?

    a. A case study   c. Correlational research

    b. Naturalistic observation d. A phone survey

15. You wish to survey a group of people who will reflect the views of the country's entire adult population. To do this, you will need to question a _____ sample of the population, in which each person has an equal chance of being chosen.

16. A study finds that the more childbirth training classes women attend, the less pain medication they require during childbirth. This finding can be stated as a _____ (positive/negative) correlation.

17. Knowing that two events correlate provides

    a. a basis for prediction.

    b. an explanation of why the events are related.

    c. proof that as one increases, the other also increases.

    d. an indication that an underlying third factor is at work.

18. Here are some recently reported correlations, with interpretations drawn by journalists. Knowing just these correlations, can you come up with other possible explanations for each of these?

    a. Alcohol use is associated with violence. (One interpretation: Drinking causes, or triggers, aggressive behavior.)

    b. Educated people live longer, on average, than less-educated people. (One interpretation: Education lengthens life and improves health.)

    c. Teens engaged in team sports are less likely to use drugs, smoke, have sex, carry weapons, and eat junk food than are teens who do not engage in team sports. (One interpretation: Team sports encourage healthy living.)

    d. Adolescents who frequently see smoking in movies are more likely to smoke. (One interpretation: Movie stars' behavior influences teens.)

19. To explain behaviors and clarify cause and effect, psychologists use _____.

20. To test the effect of a new drug on depression, researchers randomly assign people to control and experimental groups. People in the control group take a pill that contains no medication. This pill is a _____.

21. In a double-blind procedure,

    a. only the participants know whether they are in the control group or the experimental group.

    b. experimental and control group members will be carefully matched for age, sex, income, and education level.

    c. neither the participants nor the researchers know who is in the experimental group or control group.

    d. someone separate from the researcher will ask people to volunteer for the experimental group or the control group.

22. A researcher wants to know whether noise level affects workers' blood pressure. In one group, she varies the level of noise in the environment and records participants' blood pressure. In this experiment, the level of noise is the _____ _____.

23. The laboratory environment is designed to

    a. exactly re-create the events of everyday life.

    b. re-create psychological forces under controlled conditions.

    c. provide a safe place.

    d. reduce the use of animals and humans in psychological research.

24. In defending their experimental research with animals, psychologists have noted that

    a. animals' biology and behavior can tell us much about our own.

    b. animals are fascinating creatures and worthy of study.

    c. animal experiments sometimes help animals as well as humans.

    d. all of these statements are correct.

Find answers to these questions in Appendix E, in the back of the book.

IN YOUR EVERYDAY LIFE

Answering these questions will help you make these concepts more personally meaningful, and therefore more memorable.

1. How would you have defined *psychology* before taking this class?

2. Imagine that someone claims she can interpret your dreams or can speak to the dead. How could critical thinking help you check her claims?

3. Which of the four big ideas is most interesting to you? What was it that attracted your attention to that idea?

4. What about psychology has surprised you the most so far?

5. If you could conduct a study on any psychological question, which would you choose? How would you do it?

6. What other questions or concerns do you have about psychology?

Use 📖 LearningCurve to create your personalized study plan, which will direct you to the resources that will help you most in 📖 LaunchPad.

SURVEY THE CHAPTER

The Biology of Mind and Consciousness

How long would it take you to learn and remember 25,000 streets and their connections? London taxi driver trainees take two to four years to master this maze before they are allowed to drive one of the city's famous black cabs. Only half of these trainees will pass the difficult final test. But big rewards await those who do: increased status, better income, and an enlarged hippocampus. As the drivers' street memory grows, so does their brain's spatial memory center. Bus drivers, who navigate a smaller set of roads, gain no similar neural rewards (Maguire et al., 2000, 2006).

Our brain is constantly changing. Over millions of years, our brain evolved in ways that helped our ancestors survive and reproduce. Our individual brains also continue to adapt. Through repeated practice, musicians, ballerinas, and jugglers experience unique brain changes that improve their performance (Draganski et al., 2004; Hänggi et al., 2010; Herholz & Zatorre, 2012). They are not alone. The brain you're born with is not the brain you will die with.

So, everything psychological is also biological. Our thoughts, feelings, and actions influence blood pressure, hormone release, and health. And yet our biology guides all that we do. You love, laugh, and cry with your body. Without your body—your brain, your heart, your genes—you truly would be nobody. To think, feel, or act without a body would be like running without legs. Our psychology and biology interact.

We may talk separately of biological influences and psychological influences, but they are two sides of the same coin. In combination with social-cultural influences, they form the *biopsychosocial approach,* one of this text's Four Big Ideas. In later chapters, we'll look at how those influences interact in our development (Chapter 3), our sensory perceptions (Chapter 5), our learning and memory (Chapters 7 and 8), and our well-being (Chapters 10 and 13). In this chapter, we explore these interactions in our two-track mind.

The Brain: A Work in Progress

LOQ LearningObjectiveQuestion

2-1 How do biology and experience interact?

Your brain is sculpted not only by your genes but also by your experiences. Under the surface of your awareness, your brain is constantly changing, building new pathways as it adjusts to new experiences. This neural change is called **plasticity,** and it continues throughout your life (Gutchess, 2014). Plasticity is part of what makes the human brain unique (Gómez-Robles et al., 2015). More than for any other species, our brain is designed to change. By having a flexible brain, we can adapt to new social, cultural, and other environmental factors. Our brain is a work in progress.

Consider the case of Daniel Kish. He is an enthusiastic mountain biker and a skilled cook. Daniel is also completely blind. To "see" his surroundings, he learned to use echolocation—clicking his tongue and listening to the sound's reverberation. "I don't use my eyes [to see]," Daniel says. "I use my brain" (Kish, 2015). And so he does. Blind echolocation experts, such as Kish, use the brain's visual centers to navigate their surroundings (Thaler et al., 2011, 2014).

How does our brain create our mind? Such questions fascinate **biological psychologists,** who study the links between biological (genetic, neural, hormonal) processes and psychological processes. In **cognitive neuroscience,** people from many fields join forces to study the connections between brain activity and mental processes. One of the great mysteries these scientists are trying to solve is *consciousness*—what it is and how it works. (More on this to come.)

Around the world, researchers are unlocking the mysteries of how our brain uses electrical and chemical processes to take in, organize, interpret, store, and use information. One giant study, the

THE MIND'S EYE Daniel Kish, who is completely blind, enjoys going for walks in the woods. To stay safe, he uses echolocation—the same navigation method used by bats and dolphins. By clicking his tongue and listening to the sound's reverberation, Kish engages his brain's visual centers. Although Kish is blind, his brain helps him "see."

$40 million Human Connectome Project, is mapping long-distance brain fiber connections in search of "what makes us uniquely human and what makes every person different from all others" (2013; Gorman 2014). To be learning about the brain now is like studying geography while the early explorers were mapping the world.

Our own exploration of the brain starts small and builds—from nerve cells to brain functions to brain states, including sleeping and dreaming.

"You're certainly a lot less fun since the operation."

Neural Communication

LOQ 2-2 What are the parts of a neuron, and what is an *action potential*?

The human body is complexity built from simplicity. Our amazing internal communication system is formed by basic building blocks: **neurons,** or nerve cells. Throughout life, new neurons are born and unused ones wither away (Shors, 2014).

A Neuron's Structure

Neurons differ, but each consists of a *cell body* and its branching fibers (**FIGURE 2.1**). The neuron's often-bushy **dendrite** fibers receive messages and conduct them toward the cell body. From there, the cell's single **axon** fiber sends out messages to other neurons or to muscles or glands (**FIGURE 2.2**). Dendrites listen. Axons speak.

The messages neurons carry are electrical signals, or nerve impulses, called **action potentials.** These impulses travel down axons at different speeds. Supporting our billions of nerve cells are nine times as many spidery **glial cells** ("glue cells"). Neurons are like queen bees—on their own, they cannot feed or sheathe themselves. Glial cells are worker bees. They provide nutrients and *myelin*—the layer of fatty tissue that insulates some neurons. They also guide neural connections and clean up after neurons send messages to one another. Glia play a role in information

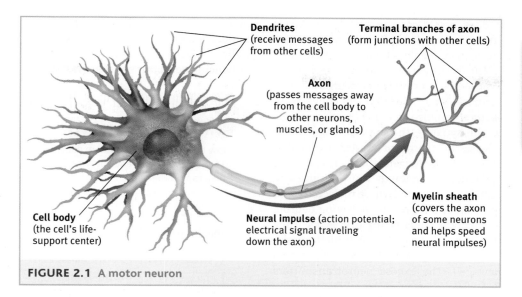

Dendrites (receive messages from other cells)

Terminal branches of axon (form junctions with other cells)

Axon (passes messages away from the cell body to other neurons, muscles, or glands)

Cell body (the cell's life-support center)

Neural impulse (action potential; electrical signal traveling down the axon)

Myelin sheath (covers the axon of some neurons and helps speed neural impulses)

FIGURE 2.1 A motor neuron

processing—learning, thinking, and memory (Fields, 2011; Martín et al., 2015).

Some action potentials trudge along at a sluggish 2 miles per hour, and others race along at 200 or more miles per hour. Can you guess which reacts faster, a human brain or a high-speed computer? The computer wins every time. Even our brain's top speed is 3 million times slower than electricity zipping through a wire. Thus, unlike the nearly instant reactions of a computer, your "quick" reaction to a sudden event, such as a child darting in front of your car, may take a quarter-second or more. Your brain is vastly more complex than a computer, but slower at executing simple responses. And your reflexes would be slower yet if you were an elephant. The round-trip time for a message that begins with a yank on an elephant's tail and then travels to its brain and back to the tail is 100 times longer than in the body of a tiny shrew (More et al., 2010).

Neurons interweave so tightly that even with a microscope, you would have trouble seeing where one ends and another begins. But end they do, at meeting places called **synapses.** At these points, two neurons are separated by a tiny *synaptic gap* less than a millionth of an inch wide. "Like elegant ladies air-kissing so as not to muss their makeup, dendrites and axons don't quite touch," noted poet Diane Ackerman (2004). How, then, does a neuron send information across the tiny gap? The answer is one of the important scientific discoveries of our age.

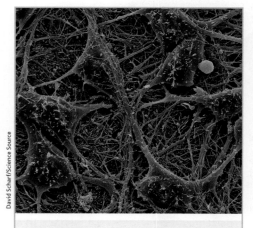

David Scharf/Science Source

FIGURE 2.2 **Neurons communicating** When we learn about neurons, we often see them one at a time to learn their parts. But our billions of neurons exist in a vast and densely interconnected web. One neuron's terminal branches send messages to neighboring dendrites. Read on to learn more about this complex and fascinating electrochemical communication process.

"All information processing in the brain involves neurons 'talking to' each other at synapses."

Neuroscientist Solomon H. Snyder, 1984

Retrieve + Remember

- When a neuron fires an action potential, the information travels through the axon, the dendrites, and the cell body, but not in that order. Place these three structures in the correct order.

ANSWER: dendrites, cell body, axon

How Neurons Communicate

LOQ 2-3 How do neurons communicate?

Each neuron is itself a miniature decision-making device, reacting to signals it receives from hundreds, even thousands, of other neurons. Most of these signals are *excitatory,* somewhat like pushing a neuron's gas pedal. Others are *inhibitory,* more like pushing its brake.

plasticity the brain's ability to change, especially during childhood, by reorganizing after damage or by building new pathways based on experience.

biological psychology the scientific study of the links between biological and psychological processes.

cognitive neuroscience the interdisciplinary study of the brain activity linked with cognition (including perception, thinking, memory, and language).

neuron a nerve cell; the basic building block of the nervous system.

dendrites neuron extensions that receive messages and conduct them toward the cell body.

axon the neuron extension that sends messages to other neurons or to muscles and glands.

action potential a nerve impulse; a brief electrical charge that travels down an axon.

glial cells (glia) cells in the nervous system that support, nourish, and protect neurons; they also play a role in learning, thinking, and memory.

synapse [SIN-aps] the junction between the axon tip of a sending neuron and the dendrite or cell body of a receiving neuron. The tiny gap at this junction is called the *synaptic gap* or *synaptic cleft.*

If the excitatory signals exceed the inhibitory signals by a minimum intensity, or **threshold,** the combined signals trigger an action potential. (Think of it this way: If the excitatory party animals outvote the inhibitory party poopers, the party's on.) The neuron fires, sending an impulse down its axon, carrying information to another cell. Neurons then need a tiny break before they can fire again. This resting pause, called a **refractory period,** lasts fractions of a second.

A neuron's firing doesn't vary in intensity. The neuron's reaction is an **all-or-none response.** Like guns, neurons either fire or they don't. How, then, do we distinguish a big hug from a gentle touch? A strong stimulus (the hug) can trigger *more* neurons to fire, and to fire more often. But it does not affect the action potential's strength or speed. Squeezing a trigger harder won't make a bullet bigger or faster.

When the action potential reaches the axon's end, your body performs an amazing trick. Your neural system converts an *electrical* impulse into a *chemical* message. At the synapse, the impulse triggers the release of **neurotransmitter** molecules, chemical messengers that can cross the synaptic gap (**FIGURE 2.3**). Within one 10,000th of a second, these molecules bind to receptor sites on the receiving neuron, as neatly as keys fitting into locks. They then act as excitatory or inhibitory signals, and the process begins again in this new cell. The excess neurotransmitters finally drift away, are broken down by enzymes, or are reabsorbed by the sending neuron—a process called **reuptake.** Some antidepressant medications work by partially blocking the reuptake of mood-enhancing neurotransmitters (**FIGURE 2.4**).

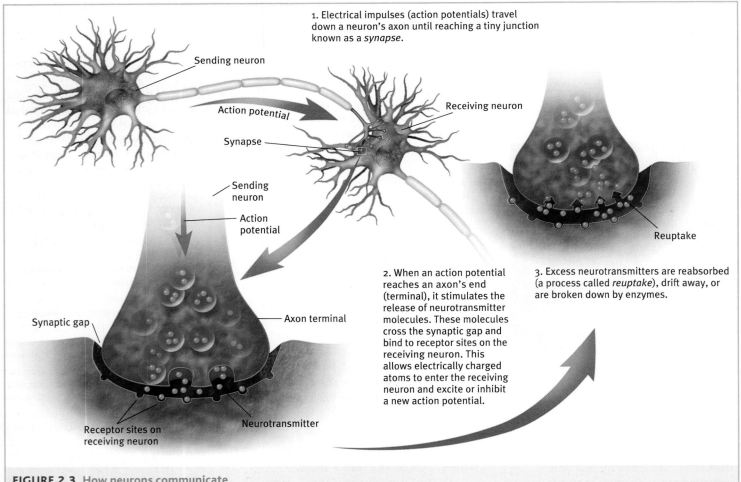

1. Electrical impulses (action potentials) travel down a neuron's axon until reaching a tiny junction known as a *synapse.*

Sending neuron

Action potential

Receiving neuron

Synapse

Sending neuron

Action potential

Axon terminal

Synaptic gap

Receptor sites on receiving neuron

Neurotransmitter

Reuptake

2. When an action potential reaches an axon's end (terminal), it stimulates the release of neurotransmitter molecules. These molecules cross the synaptic gap and bind to receptor sites on the receiving neuron. This allows electrically charged atoms to enter the receiving neuron and excite or inhibit a new action potential.

3. Excess neurotransmitters are reabsorbed (a process called *reuptake*), drift away, or are broken down by enzymes.

FIGURE 2.3 How neurons communicate

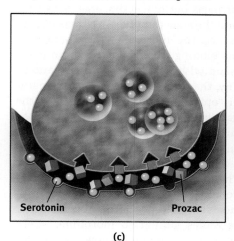

Message is sent across synaptic gap.

Message is received; excess serotonin molecules are reabsorbed by sending neuron.

Prozac partially blocks normal reuptake of the neurotransmitter serotonin; excess serotonin in synapse enhances its mood-lifting effect.

Sending neuron
Action potential
Synaptic gap
Receiving neuron
Serotonin molecule
Receptor
Reuptake
Serotonin
Prozac

(a)   (b)   (c)

FIGURE 2.4 **Biology of antidepressants** Selective serotonin reuptake inhibitors (SSRIs) are popularly prescribed antidepressants. They relieve depression by partially blocking the reuptake of the neurotransmitter serotonin. Shown here is the action of the SSRI Prozac.

How Neurotransmitters Influence Us

LOQ 2-4 How do neurotransmitters affect our mood and behavior?

Dozens of different neurotransmitters have their own pathways in the brain. As they travel along these paths, they carry specific but different messages that influence our motions and emotions. *Dopamine* levels, for example, influence our movement, learning, attention, and feelings of pleasure and reward. *Serotonin* levels can make us more or less moody, hungry, sleepy, or aroused. **TABLE 2.1** outlines the effects of these and other neurotransmitters.

"When it comes to the brain, if you want to see the action, follow the neurotransmitters."
Neuroscientist Floyd Bloom, 1993

In Chapter 1, we promised to show you how psychologists play their game. Here's an example. An exciting neurotransmitter discovery emerged when researchers attached a radioactive tracer to morphine, an **opiate** drug that elevates mood and eases pain (Pert & Snyder, 1973). (Radioactive tracers send out

Need to know

TABLE 2.1 Some Neurotransmitters and Their Functions

Neurotransmitter	Function	Examples of Malfunctions
Acetylcholine (ACh)	Enables muscle action, learning, and memory	With Alzheimer's disease, ACh-producing neurons deteriorate.
Dopamine	Influences movement, learning, attention, and emotion	Oversupply linked to schizophrenia. Undersupply linked to tremors and decreased mobility in Parkinson's disease.
Serotonin	Affects mood, hunger, sleep, and arousal	Undersupply linked to depression. Some drugs that raise serotonin levels are used to treat depression.
Norepinephrine	Helps control alertness and arousal	Undersupply can depress mood.
GABA (gamma-aminobutyric acid)	A major inhibitory neurotransmitter	Undersupply linked to seizures, tremors, and insomnia.
Glutamate	A major excitatory neurotransmitter; involved in memory	Oversupply can overstimulate brain, producing migraines or seizures (which is why some people avoid MSG, monosodium glutamate, in food).
Endorphins	Neurotransmitters that influence the perception of pain or pleasure	Oversupply with opiate drugs can suppress the body's natural endorphin supply.

threshold the level of stimulation required to trigger a neural impulse.

refractory period in neural processing, a brief resting pause that occurs after a neuron has fired; subsequent action potentials cannot occur until the axon returns to its resting state.

all-or-none response a neuron's reaction of either firing (with a full-strength response) or not firing.

neurotransmitters neuron-produced chemicals that cross the synaptic gap to carry messages to other neurons or to muscles and glands.

reuptake a neurotransmitter's reabsorption by the sending neuron.

opiate a chemical, such as opium, morphine, or heroin, that depresses neural activity, temporarily lessening pain and anxiety.

harmless but detectable energy as they pass through the body.) As researchers tracked the morphine, they noticed it was binding to receptors in brain areas linked with mood and pain sensations. Why, they wondered, would these natural "opiate receptors" exist? Might the brain have these chemical locks because our body produces a natural key—some built-in painkiller—to open them?

Further work revealed the answer. When we are in pain or exercising vigorously, the brain does, indeed, produce several types of neurotransmitter molecules similar to morphine. These natural opiates, now known as **endorphins** (short for *endogenous* [produced within] *morphine*), help explain why we can be unaware of pain after an extreme injury. They also explain the painkilling effects of acupuncture, and the good feeling known as "runner's high" (Boecker et al., 2008).

If our natural endorphins lessen pain and boost mood, why not amplify this effect by flooding the brain with artificial opiates, such as heroin and morphine? Because the brain does a chemical balancing act. When flooded with artificial opiates, it may shut down its own "feel-good" chemistry. If the artificial opiates are then withdrawn, the brain will be deprived of any form of relief. Nature charges a price for suppressing the body's own neurotransmitter production.

Throughout this book, you'll hear more about the many roles neurotransmitters play in our daily lives. But let's first continue our journey into the brain.

Retrieve + Remember

- The endorphins, serotonin, and dopamine are all chemical messengers called

  _____ .

  ANSWER: neurotransmitters

LaunchPad For an illustrated review of neural communication, visit LaunchPad's *PsychSim 6: Neural Messages*.

The Nervous System

LOQ 2-5 What are the two major divisions of the nervous system, and what are their basic functions?

To live is to take in information from the world and the body's tissues, to make decisions, and to send back information and orders to the body's tissues. All this happens thanks to your body's **nervous system** (**FIGURE 2.5**). Your brain and spinal cord form the **central nervous system (CNS)**, your body's decision maker. Your **peripheral nervous system (PNS)** gathers information from other body parts and transmits CNS decisions to the rest of your body.

Nerves are electrical cables formed from bundles of axons. They link your central nervous system with your body's sensory receptors, muscles, and glands. Your optic nerve, for example, bundles a million axons into a single cable carrying messages from each eye to your brain (Mason & Kandel, 1991). Information travels in your nervous system through three types of neurons.

- **Sensory neurons** carry messages from your body's tissues and sensory receptors inward to your spinal cord and brain for processing.
- **Motor neurons** carry instructions from your central nervous system outward to your body's muscles and glands.
- **Interneurons** within your brain and spinal cord communicate with one another and process information between the sensory input and motor output.

Your complexity resides mostly in your interneuron systems. Your nervous system has a few million sensory neurons, a few million motor neurons, and billions and billions of interneurons.

The Peripheral Nervous System

The peripheral nervous system has two parts—somatic and autonomic. Your **somatic nervous system** monitors sensory input and triggers motor output,

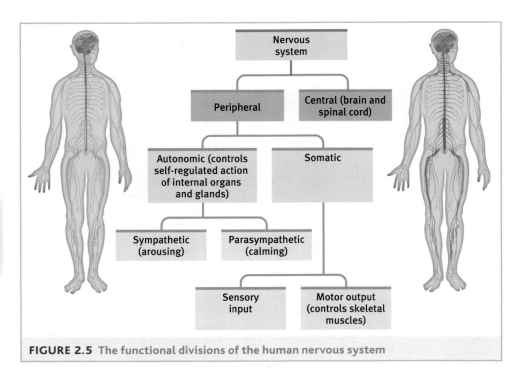

FIGURE 2.5 The functional divisions of the human nervous system

controlling your skeletal muscles (which is why it is also called the *skeletal nervous system*). As you reach the end of this page, your somatic nervous system will report the information to your brain and then carry back instructions that will trigger your hand to reveal the next page. Your **autonomic nervous system (ANS)** controls your glands and the muscles of your internal organs, including those of your heart and digestive system. Like an automatic pilot, this system may be consciously overridden, but usually it operates on its own (autonomously).

Within your autonomic nervous system, two subdivisions help you cope with challenges (**FIGURE 2.6**). If something alarms or challenges you (perhaps giving a speech), your **sympathetic nervous system** will arouse you, making you more alert, energetic, and ready for action. It will increase your heartbeat, blood pressure, and blood-sugar level. It will also slow your digestion and cool you with perspiration. When the stress dies down (the speech is over), your **parasympathetic nervous system** will calm you, conserving your energy as it decreases your heartbeat, lowers your blood sugar, and so on. In everyday situations, the sympathetic and parasympathetic divisions work together to steady our internal state.

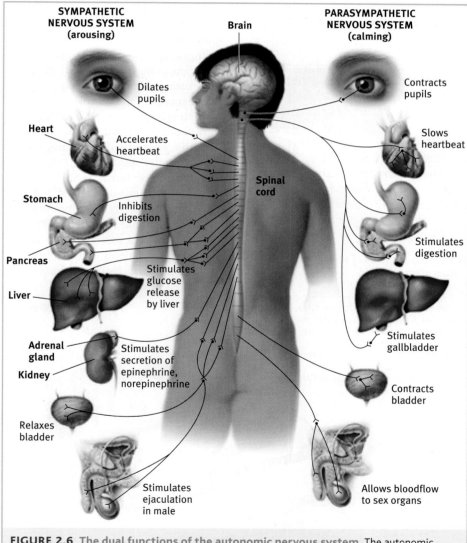

SYMPATHETIC NERVOUS SYSTEM (arousing)

Brain

PARASYMPATHETIC NERVOUS SYSTEM (calming)

Dilates pupils

Contracts pupils

Heart

Accelerates heartbeat

Slows heartbeat

Spinal cord

Stomach

Inhibits digestion

Stimulates digestion

Pancreas

Stimulates glucose release by liver

Liver

Adrenal gland

Stimulates secretion of epinephrine, norepinephrine

Kidney

Stimulates gallbladder

Contracts bladder

Relaxes bladder

Stimulates ejaculation in male

Allows bloodflow to sex organs

FIGURE 2.6 The dual functions of the autonomic nervous system The autonomic nervous system controls the more autonomous (or self-regulating) internal functions. Its sympathetic division arouses and expends energy. Its parasympathetic division calms and conserves energy, allowing routine maintenance activity. For example, sympathetic stimulation accelerates heartbeat, whereas parasympathetic stimulation slows it.

endorphins [en-DOR-fins] "morphine within"—natural, opiate-like neurotransmitters linked to pain control and to pleasure.

nervous system the body's speedy, electrochemical communication network, consisting of all the nerve cells of the central and peripheral nervous systems.

central nervous system (CNS) the brain and spinal cord.

peripheral nervous system (PNS) the sensory and motor neurons connecting the central nervous system to the rest of the body.

nerves bundled axons that form neural cables connecting the central nervous system with muscles, glands, and sense organs.

sensory neuron neuron that carries incoming information from the body's tissues and sensory receptors to the brain and spinal cord.

motor neuron neuron that carries outgoing information from the brain and spinal cord to the muscles and glands.

interneuron neurons within the brain and spinal cord; communicate internally and process information between sensory inputs and motor outputs.

somatic nervous system peripheral nervous system division that controls the body's skeletal muscles. Also called the *skeletal nervous system*.

autonomic [aw-tuh-NAHM-ik] nervous system (ANS) peripheral nervous system division that controls the glands and the muscles of the internal organs (such as the heart). Its *sympathetic* subdivision arouses; its *parasympathetic* subdivision calms.

sympathetic nervous system autonomic nervous system subdivision that arouses the body, mobilizing its energy.

parasympathetic nervous system autonomic nervous system subdivision that calms the body, conserving its energy.

I [DM] recently experienced my ANS in action. Before sending me into an MRI (magnetic resonance imaging) machine for a shoulder scan, the technician asked if I had ever had claustrophobia (panic feelings when confined). "No, I'm fine," I assured her, with perhaps a hint of macho swagger. Moments later, my sympathetic nervous system had a different idea. I found myself on my back, stuck deep inside a coffin-sized box and unable to move. Claustrophobia overtook me. My heart began pounding and I felt a desperate urge to escape. Just as I was about to cry out for release, I felt my calming parasympathetic nervous system kick in. My heart rate slowed and my body relaxed, though my arousal surged again before the 20-minute confinement ended. "You did well!" the technician said, unaware of my ANS roller-coaster ride.

Retrieve + Remember

- Match the type of neuron to its description.

Type
1. Motor neurons
2. Sensory neurons
3. Interneurons

Description
a. carry incoming messages from sensory receptors to the CNS.
b. communicate within the CNS and between incoming and outgoing messages.
c. carry outgoing messages from the CNS to muscles and glands.

ANSWERS: 1. c, 2. a, 3. b

- What bodily changes does your ANS (autonomic nervous system) direct before and after you give an important speech?

ANSWER: Responding to this challenge, your ANS' *sympathetic* division will arouse you. It increases your heartbeat, raises your blood pressure and blood sugar, slows your digestion, and cools you with perspiration. After you give the speech, your ANS' *parasympathetic* division will reverse these effects.

The Central Nervous System

From neurons "talking" to other neurons arises the complexity of the central nervous system's brain and spinal cord.

It is the *brain* that enables our humanity—our thinking, feeling, and acting. Tens of billions of neurons, each communicating with thousands of other neurons, yield an ever-changing wiring diagram. By one estimate, based on small tissue samples, our brain has some 86 billion neurons (Azevedo et al., 2009; Herculano-Houzel, 2012).

The brain's neurons cluster into work groups called *neural networks,* much as people cluster into cities rather than spreading themselves evenly across the nation (Kosslyn & Koenig, 1992). Neurons network with close neighbors by means of short, fast connections. Learning—to

"The body is made up of millions and millions of crumbs."

© Tom Swick/Cartoonstock.com

play a guitar, speak a foreign language, solve a math problem—occurs as experience strengthens those connections. Neurons that fire together wire together.

The other part of the central nervous system, the *spinal cord,* is a two-way highway connecting the peripheral nervous system and the brain. Some nerve fibers carry incoming information from your senses to your brain, while others carry outgoing motor-control information to your body parts. The neural pathways governing our **reflexes,** our automatic responses to stimuli, illustrate the spinal cord's work. A simple spinal reflex pathway is composed of a single sensory neuron and a single motor neuron. These often communicate through an interneuron. The knee-jerk response, for example, involves one such simple pathway. A headless warm body could do it (**FIGURE 2.7**).

When people suffer damage to the top of their spinal cord, their brain is truly out of touch with their body. They lose all sensation and voluntary movement in body regions that connect to the spinal cord below its injury. Given a doctor's knee-reflex test, their foot would respond with a jerk, but they would not feel the doctor's tap.

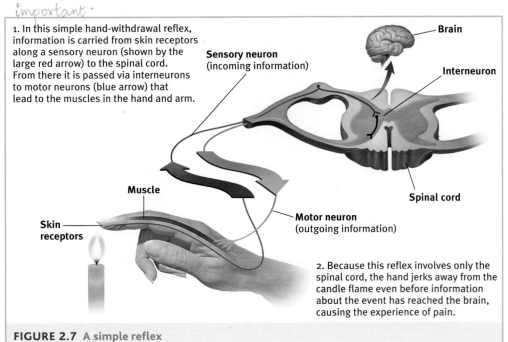

1. In this simple hand-withdrawal reflex, information is carried from skin receptors along a sensory neuron (shown by the large red arrow) to the spinal cord. From there it is passed via interneurons to motor neurons (blue arrow) that lead to the muscles in the hand and arm.

Brain

Sensory neuron (incoming information)

Interneuron

Spinal cord

Motor neuron (outgoing information)

Muscle

Skin receptors

2. Because this reflex involves only the spinal cord, the hand jerks away from the candle flame even before information about the event has reached the brain, causing the experience of pain.

FIGURE 2.7 A simple reflex

Men paralyzed below the waist may be capable of an erection (a simple reflex) if their genitals are stimulated (Goldstein, 2000). Women who are similarly paralyzed may respond with vaginal lubrication. But, depending on where and how completely their spinal cord is severed, people may have no genital responses to erotic images and no genital feeling (Kennedy & Over, 1990; Sipski et al., 1999). To produce physical pain or pleasure, sensory information must reach the brain.

The Endocrine System

LOQ 2-6 How does the endocrine system transmit information and interact with the nervous system?

So far, we have focused on the body's speedy electrochemical information system. But your body has a second communication system, the **endocrine system** (**FIGURE 2.8**). Glands in this system secrete **hormones,** another form of chemical messenger. Hormones travel through our bloodstream and influence many aspects of our life—growth, reproduction, metabolism, and mood.

Some hormones are chemically identical to neurotransmitters. The endocrine system and nervous system are therefore close relatives. Both produce molecules that act on receptors elsewhere. Like many relatives, they also differ. The speedier nervous system zips messages from eyes to brain to hand in a fraction of a second. Endocrine messages trudge along in the bloodstream, taking several seconds or more to travel from the gland to the target tissue. The nervous system transmits information to specific receptor sites with text-message speed. The endocrine system is more like delivering an old-fashioned letter.

But slow and steady sometimes wins the race. The effects of endocrine messages tend to outlast those of neural messages. Have you ever felt angry long after the cause of your angry feelings was resolved (say, your friend apologized for her rudeness)? You may have experienced an "endocrine hangover" from lingering emotion-related hormones. Angry feelings can hang on, even when we've chosen to move past them. When this happens, we need a little time to simmer down. Consider what happens behind the scenes when you hear burglar-like noises outside your window. Your ANS may order your **adrenal glands** to release *epinephrine* and *norepinephrine* (also called *adrenaline* and *noradrenaline*). In response, your heart rate, blood pressure, and blood sugar will rise, giving you a surge of energy known as the *fight-or-flight response*. When the "burglar" turns out to be a playful friend, the hormones—and your alert, aroused feelings—will linger a while.

The endocrine glands' control center is the **pituitary gland.** This pea-sized structure, located in the brain's core, is controlled by a nearby brain area, the *hypothalamus* (more on that shortly). The pituitary releases a number of hormones. One is a growth hormone that stimulates physical development. Another is *oxytocin,* which enables contractions during birthing, milk flow in nursing, and orgasm. Oxytocin also promotes social interactions. When couples bond, or when we experience feelings of group togetherness or social trust, oxytocin's pleasant presence is paving the way (De Dreu et al., 2010; Zak, 2012).

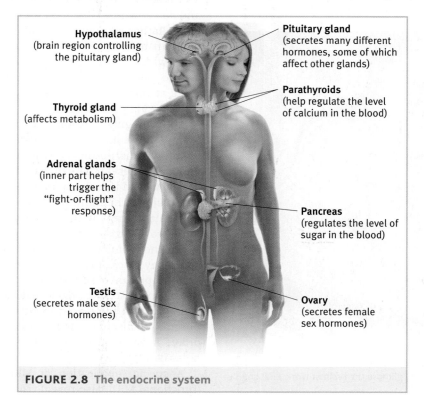

Hypothalamus (brain region controlling the pituitary gland)

Thyroid gland (affects metabolism)

Adrenal glands (inner part helps trigger the "fight-or-flight" response)

Testis (secretes male sex hormones)

Pituitary gland (secretes many different hormones, some of which affect other glands)

Parathyroids (help regulate the level of calcium in the blood)

Pancreas (regulates the level of sugar in the blood)

Ovary (secretes female sex hormones)

FIGURE 2.8 The endocrine system

reflex a simple, automatic response to a sensory stimulus, such as the knee-jerk response.

endocrine [EN-duh-krin] system the body's "slow" chemical communication system; a set of glands that secrete hormones into the bloodstream.

hormones chemical messengers that are manufactured by the endocrine glands, travel through the bloodstream, and affect other tissues.

adrenal [ah-DREEN-el] glands a pair of endocrine glands that sit just above the kidneys and secrete hormones (epinephrine and norepinephrine) that help arouse the body in times of stress.

pituitary gland the most influential endocrine gland. Under the influence of the hypothalamus, the pituitary regulates growth and controls other endocrine glands.

Pituitary secretions also direct other endocrine glands to release their hormones. The pituitary, then, is a master gland (whose own master is the hypothalamus). For example, under the brain's influence, the pituitary triggers your sex glands to release sex hormones. These in turn influence your brain and behavior.

This feedback system (brain → pituitary → other glands → hormones → body and brain) reveals the interplay between the nervous and endocrine systems. The nervous system directs endocrine secretions, which then affect the nervous system. In charge of this whole electrochemical orchestra is that master conductor we call the brain.

Retrieve + Remember

- Why is the pituitary gland called the "master gland"?

ANSWER: Responding to signals from the hypothalamus, the pituitary releases hormones that trigger other endocrine glands to secrete hormones, which in turn influence our brain and our behavior.

- How are the nervous and endocrine systems alike, and how do they differ?

ANSWER: Both of these communication systems produce chemical molecules that act on the body's receptors to influence our behavior and emotions. The endocrine system, which secretes hormones into the bloodstream, delivers its messages much more slowly than the speedy nervous system, and the effects of the endocrine system's messages tend to linger much longer than those of the nervous system.

The Brain

When you think *about* your brain, you're thinking *with* your brain—sending billions of neurotransmitter molecules across trillions of synapses. Indeed, say neuroscientists, "the mind is what the brain does" (Minsky, 1986).

Tools of Discovery— Having Our Head Examined

LOQ 2-7 What are some techniques for studying the brain?

For most of human history, we had no device high-powered yet gentle enough to reveal a living brain's activity. In the

past, brain injuries provided clues to brain-mind connections. For example, physicians had noted that damage to one side of the brain often caused paralysis on the body's opposite side, and they correctly guessed that the body's right side is wired to the brain's left side, and vice versa. Other early observers linked vision problems with damage to the back of the brain, and speech problems with damage to the left-front brain. Gradually, a map of the brain began to emerge.

Now a new generation of mapmakers is at work charting formerly unknown territory, stimulating various brain parts and watching the results. Some use microelectrodes to snoop on the messages of individual neurons. Some attach larger electrodes to the scalp to eavesdrop with an **EEG (electroencephalograph)** on the chatter of billions of neurons. Others use scans that peer into the thinking, feeling brain and give us a Superman-like ability to see what's happening.

The **PET (positron emission tomography) scan** tracks a temporarily radio-

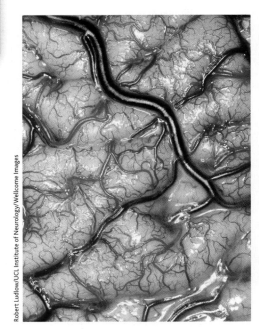

A LIVING HUMAN BRAIN EXPOSED Today's neuroscience tools enable us to "look under the hood" and glimpse the brain at work, enabling the mind.

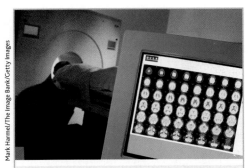

FIGURE 2.9 The PET scan To obtain a PET scan, researchers inject volunteers with a low and harmless dose of a short-lived radioactive sugar. Detectors around the person's head pick up the release of gamma rays from the sugar, which has concentrated in active brain areas. A computer then processes and translates these signals into a map of the brain at work.

active form of the sugar glucose. Your brain accounts for only about 2 percent of your body weight. But this control center—the heart of your smarts—uses 20 percent of your body's energy. Because active neurons gobble glucose, a PET scan can track the radioactivity and detect where this "food for thought" goes. Rather like weather radar showing rain activity, PET-scan "hot spots" show which brain areas are most active as the person solves math problems, looks at images of faces, or daydreams (**FIGURE 2.9**).

MRI (magnetic resonance imaging) scans capture images of brain structures by briefly disrupting activity in brain molecules. Researchers first position the person's head in a strong magnetic field, which aligns the spinning atoms of brain molecules. Then, with a brief pulse of radio waves, they disrupt the spinning. When the atoms return to their normal spin, they give off signals that provide a detailed picture of soft tissues, including the brain. MRI scans have revealed, for example, that some people with schizophrenia, a disabling psychological disorder, have enlarged fluid-filled brain areas (**FIGURE 2.10**).

A special application of MRI, **fMRI (functional MRI)**, also reveals the brain's

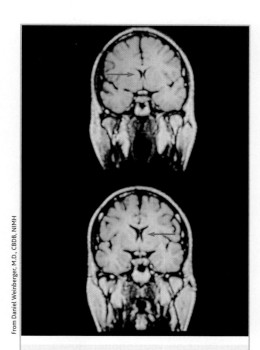

FIGURE 2.10 MRI scan of a healthy individual (top) and a person with schizophrenia (bottom) Note the enlarged ventricle, the fluid-filled brain region at the tip of the arrow in the image on the bottom.

From Daniel Weinberger, M.D., CBDB, NIMH

functions. Where the brain is especially active, blood goes. By comparing MRI scans taken less than a second apart, researchers can watch parts of the brain activate as a person thinks or acts in certain ways. As the person looks at a photo, for example, the fMRI shows blood rushing to the back of the brain, which processes visual information (see Figure 2.19). This technology enables a very crude sort of mind reading. Neuroscientists scanned 129 people's brains as they did eight different mental tasks (such as reading, gambling, and rhyming). Later, viewing another person's brain images, they were able, with 80 percent accuracy, to identify which of these mental tasks the person was doing (Poldrack et al., 2009).

What the telescope did for astronomy, these brain-snooping tools are doing for psychology. By revealing how the living, working brain divides its labor, these tools have taught us more about the brain in the past 30 years than we had learned in the prior 30,000 years.

Retrieve + Remember

- Match the scanning technique with the correct description.

Technique
1. fMRI scan   3. MRI scan
2. PET scan

Description
a. tracks radioactive glucose to reveal brain *activity*.
b. tracks successive images of brain tissue to show brain *function*.
c. uses magnetic fields and radio waves to show brain *anatomy*.

ANSWERS: 1.b, 2.a, 3.c

Older Brain Structures

Brain structures determine our abilities. In sharks and other primitive vertebrates (animals with backbones), a not-so-complex brain mainly handles basic survival functions: breathing, resting, and feeding. In lower mammals, such as rodents, a more complex brain enables emotion and greater memory. In advanced mammals, such as humans, a brain that processes more information also enables the ability to plan ahead.

The brain's increasing complexity arises from new systems built on top of the old, much as new layers cover old ones in Earth's landscape. Digging down, one discovers the fossil remnants of the past—brainstem components performing for us much as they did for our distant ancestors. Let's start with the brain's base and work up.

The Brainstem

LOQ 2-8 What structures make up the brainstem, and what are the functions of the brainstem, thalamus, reticular formation, and cerebellum?

The **brainstem** is the brain's oldest and innermost region. Its base is the **medulla,** the slight swelling in the

EEG (electroencephalograph) a device that uses electrodes placed on the scalp to record waves of electrical activity sweeping across the brain's surface. (The record of those brain waves is an *electroencephalogram*.)

PET (positron emission tomography) scan a view of brain activity showing where a radioactive form of glucose goes while the brain performs a given task.

MRI (magnetic resonance imaging) a technique that uses magnetic fields and radio waves to produce computer-generated images of soft tissue. MRI scans show brain anatomy.

fMRI (functional MRI) a technique for revealing bloodflow and, therefore, brain activity by comparing successive MRI scans. fMRI scans show brain function.

brainstem the oldest part and central core of the brain, beginning where the spinal cord swells as it enters the skull; responsible for automatic survival functions.

medulla [muh-DUL-uh] the base of the brainstem; controls heartbeat and breathing.

Stefan Klein/imagebroker/Alamy

spinal cord just after it enters the skull (**FIGURE 2.11**). Here lie the controls for your heartbeat and breathing. Just above the medulla sits the *pons,* which helps coordinate movements and control sleep. As some severely brain-damaged patients illustrate, we need no higher brain or conscious mind to orchestrate our heart's pumping and our lungs' breathing. The brainstem handles those tasks. If a cat's brainstem is severed from the rest of the brain above it, the animal will still live and breathe. It will even run, climb, and groom (Klemm, 1990). But cut off from the brain's higher regions, it won't *purposefully* run or climb to get food.

The brainstem is a crossover point. Here, you'll find a peculiar sort of cross-wiring, with most nerves to and from each side of the brain connecting to the body's opposite side. Thus, the right brain controls the left side of the body, and vice versa (**FIGURE 2.12**). This cross-wiring is one of the brain's many surprises.

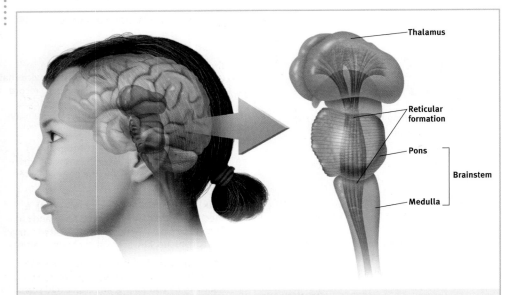

FIGURE 2.11 The brainstem and thalamus The brainstem, including the pons and medulla, is an extension of your spinal cord. The thalamus is attached to its top. The reticular formation passes through both structures.

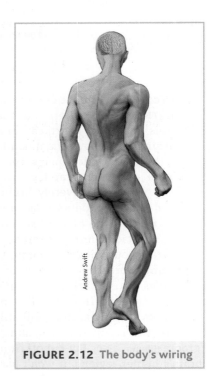

FIGURE 2.12 The body's wiring

‑

Retrieve + Remember

• The _____ is a crossover point where nerves from the left side of the brain are mostly linked to the right side of the body, and vice versa.

ANSWER: brainstem

The Thalamus

Sitting at the top of the brainstem is the **thalamus,** which acts as the brain's sensory control center. This joined pair of egg-shaped structures receives information from all your senses except smell. It then forwards those messages to their final destination in other brain regions that deal with seeing, hearing, tasting, and touching. Your thalamus also receives some higher brain regions' replies, which it forwards to your medulla and cerebellum for processing. For sensory information, your thalamus is something like Chicago's O'Hare International Airport, a hub through which traffic flows in and out on its way to various locations.

The Reticular Formation

Inside the brainstem, between your ears, lies your **reticular ("netlike") formation.** This neuron network extends upward from your spinal cord, through your brainstem, and into your thalamus (see Figure 2.11). As sensory messages travel from your spinal cord to your thalamus, this long structure acts as a filter, relaying important information to other brain areas.

The reticular formation also controls arousal, as researchers discovered in 1949. Electrically stimulating the reticular formation of a sleeping cat almost instantly produced an awake, alert animal (Moruzzi & Magoun, 1949). When a cat's reticular formation was cut off from higher brain regions, without damaging nearby sensory pathways, the effect was equally dramatic. The cat lapsed into a coma and never woke up.

The Cerebellum

At the rear of the brainstem is the **cerebellum,** meaning "little brain," which is what its two wrinkled halves resemble (**FIGURE 2.13**). This baseball-sized structure plays an important role in a lot that happens just outside your awareness. Quickly answer these questions. How long have you been reading this text? Does music sound better on your TV or on your phone? How's your mood today?

If you answered those questions easily, thank your cerebellum. It helps you judge time, discriminate textures and sounds, and control your emotions (Bower & Parsons, 2003). Your cerebellum also coordinates voluntary movement. When a soccer player masterfully controls the ball, give the cerebellum some credit. If you injured your cerebellum or drugged it with alcohol, you would have trouble walking, keeping your balance, or shaking hands. The cerebellum also helps process and store memories for things you cannot consciously recall, such as how to ride a bicycle. (Stay tuned for more about this in Chapter 7.)

* * *

Note: These older brain functions all occur without any conscious effort. Once again, we see one of our Big Ideas at work: *Our two-track brain processes most information outside of our awareness.* We are aware of the *results* of our brain's labor (say, our current visual experience) but not of *how* we construct the visual image. Likewise, whether we are asleep or awake, our brainstem manages its life-sustaining functions, freeing our newer brain regions to think, talk, dream, or savor a memory.

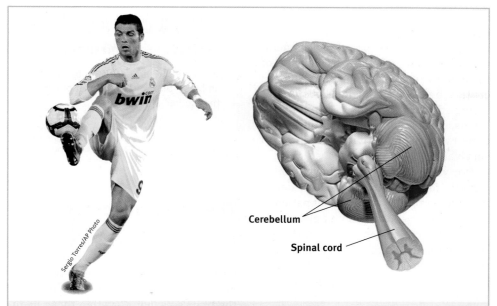

FIGURE 2.13 **The brain's organ of agility** Hanging at the back of the brain, the cerebellum coordinates our voluntary movements, as when soccer star Cristiano Ronaldo controls the ball.

Retrieve + Remember

- In what brain region would damage be most likely to (1) disrupt your ability to skip rope? (2) disrupt your ability to hear? (3) perhaps leave you in a coma? (4) cut off the very breath and heartbeat of life?

ANSWERS: 1. cerebellum, 2. thalamus, 3. reticular formation, 4. medulla

The Limbic System

LOQ 2-9 What are the structures and functions of the limbic system?

We've traveled through the brain's oldest parts, but we've not yet reached its newest and highest regions, the *cerebral hemispheres* (the two halves of the brain). Before we do, we must pass the **limbic system,** which lies between the oldest and newest brain areas (*limbus* means "border"). The limbic system contains the *amygdala,* the *hypothalamus,* and the *hippocampus* (**FIGURE 2.14**).

THE AMYGDALA The **amygdala**—two lima-bean-sized neural clusters—enable aggression and fear. In 1939, researchers

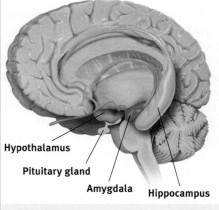

FIGURE 2.14 **The limbic system** This neural system sits between your brain's older parts and its cerebral hemispheres. The limbic system's hypothalamus controls the nearby pituitary gland.

surgically removed a rhesus monkey's amygdala, turning the normally ill-tempered animal into the most mellow of creatures (Klüver & Bucy, 1939).

What, then, might happen if we electrically stimulated the amygdala of a normally mellow domestic animal, such as a cat? Do so in one spot and the cat prepares to attack, hissing with its back arched, its pupils wide, its hair on end. Move the electrode only slightly within

the amygdala, cage the cat with a small mouse, and now it cowers in terror.

Many experiments have confirmed the amygdala's role in processing emotions and perceiving rage and fear. Monkeys and humans with amygdala damage become less fearful of strangers (Harrison et al., 2015). After her amygdala was destroyed by a rare genetic disease, one woman no longer experienced fear. Facing a snake, speaking in public, even being threatened with a gun—she's not afraid (Feinstein et al., 2013).

But a critical thinker should be careful here. The brain is not neatly organized into structures that reflect specific behaviors and feelings. When we feel afraid or act aggressively, many areas of our brain become active, not just the amygdala. If you destroy a car's battery, you won't be able to start the engine. Yet the battery is merely one link in the whole working system.

Retrieve + Remember

- Electrical stimulation of a cat's amygdala provokes angry reactions, suggesting the amygdala's role in aggression. Which ANS division is activated by such stimulation?

ANSWER: the sympathetic nervous system

thalamus [THAL-uh-muss] the brain's sensory control center, located on top of the brainstem; directs sensory messages to the cortex and transmits replies to the cerebellum and medulla.

reticular formation nerve network running through the brainstem and into the thalamus; plays an important role in controlling arousal.

cerebellum [sehr-uh-BELL-um] the "little brain" at the rear of the brainstem; functions include processing sensory input, coordinating movement output and balance, and enabling nonverbal learning and memory.

limbic system neural system (including the *amygdala, hypothalamus,* and *hippocampus*) located below the cerebral hemispheres; associated with emotions and drives.

amygdala [uh-MIG-duh-la] two lima-bean-sized neural clusters in the limbic system; linked to emotion.

THE HYPOTHALAMUS Just below (*hypo*) your thalamus is your **hypothalamus,** an important link in the command chain that helps your body maintain a steady internal state. Some neural clusters in the hypothalamus influence hunger. Others regulate thirst, body temperature, and sexual behavior.

To monitor your body state, the hypothalamus tunes in to your blood chemistry and any incoming orders from other brain parts. For example, picking up signals from your brain's information-processing center, the *cerebral cortex,* that you are thinking about sex, your hypothalamus will secrete hormones. These hormones will in turn trigger the nearby "master" gland of the endocrine system, your pituitary (see Figure 2.14), to influence your sex glands to release *their* hormones. These hormones will intensify the thoughts of sex in your cerebral cortex. (Once again, we see the interplay between the nervous and endocrine systems. The brain influences the endocrine system, which in turn influences the brain.)

A remarkable discovery about the hypothalamus illustrates how progress in science often occurs—when curious, smart-thinking investigators keep an open mind. Two young psychologists, James Olds and Peter Milner (1954), were trying to implant an electrode in a rat's reticular formation when they made a magnificent mistake. They placed the electrode incorrectly (Olds, 1975). Curiously, the rat, as though seeking more stimulation, kept returning to the location where it had been stimulated by this misplaced electrode. When Olds and Milner discovered that they had actually placed the device in a region of the hypothalamus, they realized they had stumbled upon a brain center that provides pleasurable rewards. In later studies, rats allowed to control their own stimulation in this and other *reward centers* in the brain did so at a feverish pace—pressing a pedal up to 1000 times an hour, until they dropped from exhaustion.

Animal researchers have discovered similar reward centers in or near the hypothalamus in goldfish, dolphins, monkeys, and other species. One general reward system triggers the release of the neurotransmitter dopamine. Specific centers help us enjoy the pleasures of eating, drinking, and sex. Animals, it seems, come equipped with built-in systems that reward activities essential to survival.

Do we humans also have limbic centers for pleasure? Some evidence indicates we do. To calm violent patients, one neurosurgeon implanted electrodes in such limbic system areas. Although those patients reported mild pleasure, they—unlike Olds and Milner's rats—were not driven to a frenzy (Deutsch, 1972; Hooper & Teresi, 1986). And some studies reveal that stimulating the human brain's reward circuits may trigger more *desire* than pure enjoyment (Kringelbach & Berridge, 2012).

THE HIPPOCAMPUS The **hippocampus**—a seahorse-shaped brain structure—processes conscious, *explicit* memories of facts and events. Surgery or injury that removes the hippocampus also removes the ability to form or retrieve these conscious memories. Children who survive a hippocampal brain tumor will later struggle to remember new information (Jayakar et al., 2015). Birds with a damaged hippocampus will be unable to recall where they buried seeds (Kamil & Cheng, 2001; Sherry & Vaccarino, 1989). National Football League players who experience a concussion may later have a shrunken hippocampus and poor memory (Strain et al., 2015).

Later in this chapter, we'll see how the hippocampus helps store the day's experiences while we sleep. In Chapter 7, we'll explore how the hippocampus interacts with our frontal lobes to create our conscious memory.

* * *

FIGURE 2.15 locates the brain areas we've discussed—as well as the cerebral cortex, our next topic and the final stop on our journey through the brain.

The Cerebral Cortex

Older brain networks sustain basic life functions and enable memory, emotions, and basic drives. High above these older structures are the *cerebrum*—two large hemispheres that contribute 85 percent of the brain's weight. Covering those hemispheres, like bark on a tree, is the **cerebral cortex,** a thin surface layer of interconnected neurons. In our brain's evolutionary history, the cerebral cortex is a relative newcomer. Its newer neural networks form specialized work teams that enable your thinking, sensing, and speaking. The cerebral cortex is your brain's thinking crown, your body's ultimate control and information-processing center.

Structure of the Cortex

LOQ 2-10 What are the four lobes of the cerebral cortex, and where are they located?

If you opened a human skull, exposing the brain, you would see a wrinkled organ, shaped somewhat like an oversized walnut. Without these wrinkles, a flattened cerebral cortex would require triple the area—roughly that of a large pizza. The brain's left and right hemispheres are filled mainly with axons connecting the cortex to the brain's other regions. The cerebral cortex—that thin surface layer—contains some 20 to 23 billion nerve cells and 300 trillion synaptic connections (de Courten-Myers, 2005). Being human takes a lot of nerve.

Each hemisphere's cortex is subdivided into four *lobes,* separated by deep folds (**FIGURE 2.16**). You can roughly trace the four lobes, starting with both hands on your forehead. The **frontal lobes** lie

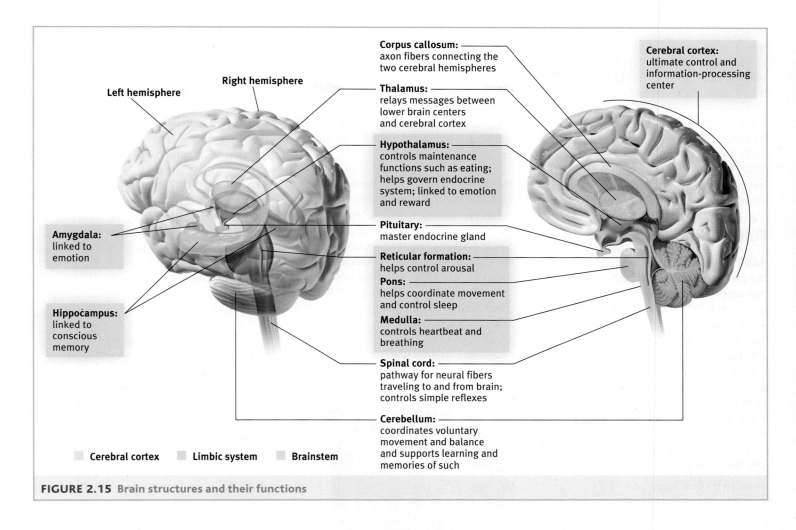

Corpus callosum: axon fibers connecting the two cerebral hemispheres

Thalamus: relays messages between lower brain centers and cerebral cortex

Hypothalamus: controls maintenance functions such as eating; helps govern endocrine system; linked to emotion and reward

Cerebral cortex: ultimate control and information-processing center

Left hemisphere

Right hemisphere

Amygdala: linked to emotion

Pituitary: master endocrine gland

Reticular formation: helps control arousal

Pons: helps coordinate movement and control sleep

Medulla: controls heartbeat and breathing

Hippocampus: linked to conscious memory

Spinal cord: pathway for neural fibers traveling to and from brain; controls simple reflexes

Cerebellum: coordinates voluntary movement and balance and supports learning and memories of such

■ Cerebral cortex   ■ Limbic system   ■ Brainstem

FIGURE 2.15 Brain structures and their functions

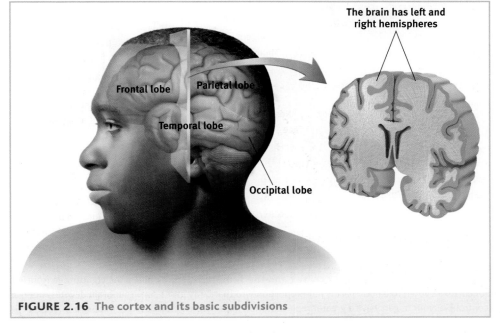

The brain has left and right hemispheres

Frontal lobe   Parietal lobe

Temporal lobe

Occipital lobe

FIGURE 2.16 The cortex and its basic subdivisions

hypothalamus [hi-po-THAL-uh-muss] a neural structure lying below *(hypo)* the thalamus; directs several maintenance activities (eating, drinking, body temperature), helps govern the endocrine system via the pituitary gland, and is linked to emotion and reward.

hippocampus a neural center located in the limbic system; helps process for storage explicit (conscious) memories of facts and events.

cerebral [seh-REE-bruhl] cortex a thin layer of interconnected neurons covering the cerebral hemispheres; the body's ultimate control and information-processing center.

frontal lobes the portion of the cerebral cortex lying just behind the forehead; involved in speaking and muscle movements and in making plans and judgments.

directly behind your forehead. As you move your hands over the top of your head, toward the rear, you're sliding over your **parietal lobes**. Continuing to move down, toward the back of your head, you'll slide over your **occipital lobes**. Now move each hand forward, to the sides of your head, and just above each ear you'll find your **temporal lobes**. Each hemisphere has these four lobes. Each lobe carries out many functions. And many functions require the cooperation of several lobes.

Functions of the Cortex

LOQ 2-11 What are the functions of the motor cortex, somatosensory cortex, and association areas?

More than a century ago, surgeons found damaged areas of the cerebral cortex during autopsies of people who had been partially paralyzed or speechless. This rather crude evidence was interesting, but it did not prove that *specific* parts of the cortex control complex functions like movement or speech. A laptop with a broken power cord might go dead, but we would be fooling ourselves if we thought we had "localized" the Internet in the cord.

MOTOR FUNCTIONS Early scientists had better luck showing simple brain-behavior links. In 1870, for example, German physicians Gustav Fritsch and Eduard Hitzig made an important discovery. By electrically stimulating parts of an animal's cortex, they could make other parts of its body move. The movement happened only when they stimulated an arch-shaped region at the back of the frontal lobe, running roughly ear-to-ear across the top of the brain. Moreover, if they stimulated this region in the left hemisphere, the right leg would move. And if they stimulated part of the right hemisphere, the opposite leg—on the left—reacted. Fritsch and Hitzig had discovered what is now called the **motor cortex.**

Lucky for brain surgeons and their patients, the brain has no sensory receptors. Knowing this, in the 1930s, Otfrid Foerster and Wilder Penfield were able to map the motor cortex in hundreds of wide-awake patients by stimulating different cortical areas and observing the body's responses. They discovered that body areas requiring precise control, such as the fingers and mouth, occupied the greatest amount of cortical space (**FIGURE 2.17**).

As is so often the case in science, new answers have triggered new questions. Might electrodes implanted in

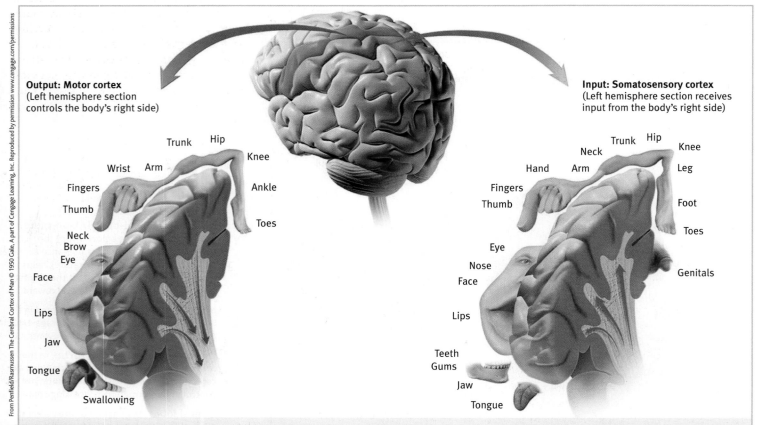

FIGURE 2.17 **Left hemisphere tissue devoted to each body part in the motor cortex and the somatosensory cortex** As you can see from this classic though inexact representation, the amount of cortex devoted to a body part is not proportional to that body part's size. Your brain devotes more tissue to sensitive areas and to areas requiring precise control. So, your fingers have a greater representation in the cortex than does your upper arm.

the motor cortex identify what neurons control specific activities? If so, could people learn to mentally control these implanted devices, perhaps to direct a robotic limb? Clinical trials are now under way with people who have severe paralysis or have lost a limb (Andersen et al., 2010; Nurmikko et al., 2010). Some who received implants have indeed learned to control robotic limbs (Collinger et al., 2013; Hochberg et al., 2012).

Retrieve + Remember

- Try moving your right hand in a circular motion, as if polishing a car. Then start your right foot doing the same motion as your hand. Now reverse the right foot's motion, but not the hand's. Finally, try moving the *left* foot opposite to the right hand.

  1. Why is reversing the right foot's motion so hard?
  2. Why is it easier to move the left foot opposite to the right hand?

ANSWERS: 1. The right limbs' activities interfere with each other because both are controlled by the same (left) side of your brain. 2. Opposite sides of your brain control your left and right limbs, so the reversed motion causes less interference.

SENSORY FUNCTIONS The motor cortex sends messages out to the body. What parts of the cortex receive incoming messages from our senses of touch and movement? Penfield supplied the answer. An area now called the **somatosensory cortex** receives this sensory input. It runs parallel to the motor cortex and just behind it, at the front of the parietal lobes (see Figure 2.17). Stimulate a point on the top of this band of tissue, and a person may report being touched on the shoulder. Stimulate some point on the side, and the person may feel something on the face.

The more sensitive a body region, the larger the somatosensory area devoted to it. Why do we kiss with our lips rather than rub elbows? Our supersensitive lips project to a larger brain area than do our arms (see Figure 2.17). Similarly, rats have a large brain area devoted to their whisker sensations, and owls to their hearing sensations.

Your somatosensory cortex is a very powerful tool for processing information from your skin senses—such as touch and temperature—and from movements of your body parts. But this parietal lobe area isn't the only part of your cortex that receives input from your senses. After surgeons removed a large tumor from his right *occipital lobe,* in the back of his brain, a friend of mine [DM's] became blind to the left half of his field of vision. Why? Because in an intact brain, visual information travels from the eyes to the *visual cortex,* in the occipital lobes (**FIGURE 2.18**). From your occipital lobes, visual information travels to other areas that specialize in tasks such as identifying words, detecting emotions, and recognizing faces (**FIGURE 2.19**).

If you have normal vision, you might see flashes of light or dashes of color if stimulated in your occipital lobes. (In a sense, we *do* have eyes in the back of our head!)

Any sound you now hear is processed by your *auditory cortex* in your

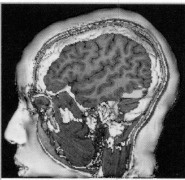

Neurolmage, Vol. 4, V.P. Clark, K. Keill, J. Ma, Maisog, S. Courtney, L. G. Ungerleider, and J. V. Haxby, Functional Magnetic Resonance Imaging of Human Visual Cortex during Face Matching: A Comparison with Positron Emission Tomography, August 1996, with permission from Elsevier.

FIGURE 2.19 The brain in action As this person looks at a photo, the fMRI (functional MRI) scan shows increased activity (color represents increased bloodflow) in the visual cortex in the occipital lobes. When the person stops looking, the region instantly calms down.

temporal lobes (just above your ears; see Figure 2.18). Most of this auditory information travels a roundabout route from one ear to the auditory receiving area above your opposite ear. If stimulated in your auditory cortex, you alone might hear a sound. People with schizophrenia sometimes have auditory **hallucinations** (false sensory experiences).

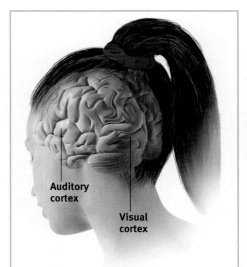

FIGURE 2.18 The visual cortex and auditory cortex The visual cortex in the occipital lobes at the rear of your brain receives input from your eyes. The auditory cortex, in your temporal lobes—above your ears—receives information from your ears.

parietal [puh-RYE-uh-tuhl] lobes the portion of the cerebral cortex lying at the top of the head and toward the rear; receives sensory input for touch and body position.

occipital [ahk-SIP-uh-tuhl] lobes the portion of the cerebral cortex lying at the back of the head; includes areas that receive information from the visual fields.

temporal lobes the portion of the cerebral cortex lying roughly above the ears; includes areas that receive information from the ears.

motor cortex the cerebral cortex area at the rear of the frontal lobes; controls voluntary movements.

somatosensory cortex the cerebral cortex area at the front of the parietal lobes; registers and processes body touch and movement sensations.

hallucination a false sensory experience, such as hearing something in the absence of an external auditory stimulus.

MRI scans taken during these hallucinations show active auditory areas in the temporal lobes (Lennox et al., 1999).

ASSOCIATION AREAS So far, we have pointed out small areas of the cortex that receive messages from our senses, and other small areas that send messages to our muscles. Together, these areas occupy about one-fourth of the human brain's thin, wrinkled cover. What, then, goes on in the remaining vast regions of the cortex? In these **association areas,** neurons are busy with higher mental functions—many of the tasks that make us human. Electrically probing an association area won't trigger any observable response. So, unlike the somatosensory and motor areas, association area functions can't be neatly mapped. Does this mean we don't use them? See Thinking Critically About: Using More Than 10 Percent of Our Brain.

Association areas are found in all four lobes. In the forward part of the frontal lobes, the *prefrontal cortex* enables judgment, planning, and processing of new memories. People with damaged frontal lobes may have intact memories, high intelligence test scores, and great cake-baking skills. Yet they would not be able to plan ahead to *begin* baking a cake for a loved one's birthday (Huey et al., 2006).

Frontal lobe damage can alter personality, as it did in the famous case study of railroad worker Phineas Gage. One afternoon in 1848, Gage, then 25 years old, was using an iron rod to pack gunpowder into a rock. A spark ignited the gunpowder, shooting the rod up through his left cheek and out the top of his skull, causing massive damage to his frontal lobes (**FIGURE 2.20a**). To everyone's amazement, he was immediately able to sit up and speak. After the wound healed, he returned to work. But friendly, soft-spoken Gage was now irritable, profane, and dishonest. The accident had destroyed frontal lobe areas that enable control over emotions (Van Horn et al., 2012). This person, said his friends, was "no longer Gage." His mental abilities and memories were unharmed, but his personality was not. (Gage later lost his railroad job, but, over time, he adapted to his injury and found work as a stagecoach driver [Macmillan & Lena, 2010].)

Without the frontal lobe brakes on his impulses, Gage became less inhibited. When his frontal lobes ruptured, his moral compass seemed to disconnect from his behavior. Studies of others with damaged frontal lobes reveal

Thinking Critically About:
Using More Than 10 Percent of Our Brain

LOQ 2-12 Do we really use only 10 percent of our brain?

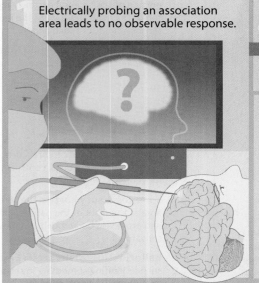

1 Electrically probing an association area leads to no observable response.

2 This vast association area "silence" has led to the false claim that we really use only 10 percent of our brain— *"one of the hardiest weeds in the garden of psychology."* [1]

3 Is there really a 90 percent chance that a bullet to your brain would land in an unused area?

← **No.**

4 Brain-damaged animals and humans bear witness: Association areas interpret, integrate, and act on sensory information and link it with stored memories. More intelligent animals have larger association areas.

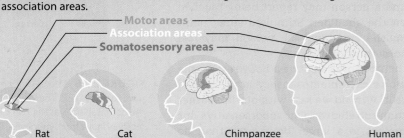

Motor areas
Association areas
Somatosensory areas

Rat　　Cat　　Chimpanzee　　Human

1. McBurney, 1996, p. 44

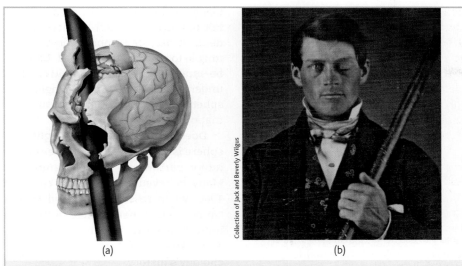

(a)   (b)

Collection of Jack and Beverly Wilgus

FIGURE 2.20 A blast from the past (a) Phineas Gage's skull was kept as a medical record. Using measurements and modern neuroimaging techniques, researchers have reconstructed the probable path of the rod through Gage's brain (Van Horn et al., 2012). (b) This photo shows Gage after his accident. (The image has been reversed to show the features correctly. Early photos, including this one, were actually mirror images.)

similar losses—their moral judgments seem untouched by normal emotions. Would you agree with the idea of pushing someone in front of a runaway train to save five others? Most people would not, but those with damage to the prefrontal cortex often do (Koenigs et al., 2007). The frontal lobes help steer us away from violent actions (Molenberghs et al., 2015; Yang & Raine, 2009). In 1972, Cecil Clayton lost 20 percent of his left frontal lobe in a sawmill accident. His intelligence test score dropped to an elementary school level. He became increasingly impulsive. In 1996, he shot and killed a deputy sheriff. In 2015, when he was 74, the State of Missouri executed him (Williams, 2015).

Damage to association areas in other lobes would result in different losses. If a stroke or head injury destroyed part of your parietal lobes, you might lose mathematical and spatial reasoning (Ibos & Freedman, 2014). If the damaged area was on the underside of the right temporal lobe, which lets you recognize faces, you would still be able to describe facial features and to recognize someone's sex and approximate age. Yet you would be strangely unable to identify the person as, say, Taylor Swift or even your grandmother.

Nevertheless, brain scans show that complex mental functions don't reside in any one spot in your brain. Performing simple tasks may activate tiny patches of your brain, far less than 10 percent. During a complex task, a scan would

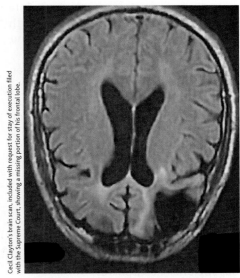

Cecil Clayton's brain scan, included with request for stay of execution filed with the Supreme Court, showing a missing portion of his frontal lobe.

MISSING FRONTAL LOBE BRAKES With part of his left frontal lobe (in this downward-facing brain scan) lost to injury, Cecil Clayton became more impulsive and killed a deputy sheriff. Nineteen years later, his state executed him for this crime.

show many islands of brain activity working together—some running automatically in the background, and others under conscious control (Chein & Schneider, 2012). Memory, language, and attention are the products of interaction among distinct brain areas (Knight, 2007). Ditto for religious experience—there is no simple "God spot." More than 40 brain regions become active in different religious states, such as prayer and meditation (Fingelkurts & Fingelkurts, 2009).

Retrieve + Remember

- Why are association areas important?

ANSWER: Association areas are involved in higher mental functions—interpreting, integrating, and acting on information processed in other areas.

The Power of Plasticity: Responding to Damage

LOQ 2-13 How does the brain modify itself after some kinds of damage?

Earlier, we learned about the brain's *plasticity*—how our brain adapts to new situations. What happens when we experience mishaps, big and little? Let's explore the brain's ability to modify itself after damage.

Brain-damage effects were discussed in several places in this chapter. Most can be traced to two hard facts. (1) Severed brain and spinal cord neurons, unlike cut skin, usually do not repair themselves. If a spinal cord is severed, the person will probably be paralyzed permanently. (2) Some brain functions seem forever linked to specific areas. A newborn with damage to facial recognition areas on both temporal lobes was never able to recognize faces (Farah et al., 2000).

association areas cerebral cortex areas involved primarily in higher mental functions, such as learning, remembering, thinking, and speaking.

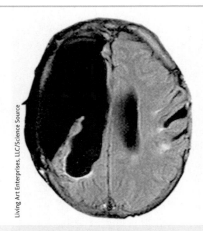

FIGURE 2.21 Brain plasticity This 6-year-old had surgery to end her life-threatening seizures. Although most of an entire hemisphere was removed (see MRI of hemispherectomy above), her remaining hemisphere compensated by putting other areas to work. One Johns Hopkins medical team reflected on the child hemispherectomies they had performed. Although use of the opposite arm was compromised, the team reported being "awed" by how well the children had retained their memory, personality, and humor (Vining et al., 1997). The younger the child, the greater the chance that the remaining hemisphere can take over the functions of the one that was surgically removed (Choi, 2008; Danelli et al., 2013).

But there is good news: The brain often attempts self-repair by *reorganizing* existing tissue. Some brain tissue—especially in a young child's brain—can reorganize even after serious damage (Kolb, 1989) (**FIGURE 2.21**). If a slow-growing left-hemisphere tumor disrupts language, the right hemisphere may take over the task (Thiel et al., 2006). If a finger is lost, the somatosensory cortex that received its input will begin to pick up signals from the neighboring fingers, which then become more sensitive (Oelschläger et al., 2014). Blindness or deafness makes unused brain areas available for other uses (Amedi et al., 2005). This plasticity helps explain why deaf people who learned sign language before another language may have better-than-average peripheral and motion detection (Bosworth & Dobkins, 1999; Shiell et al., 2014). An area of the temporal lobe is normally dedicated to hearing. But without stimulation from sounds, it is free to process other signals, such as those from the visual system.

Although self-repair by reorganizing is more common, the brain some-

times tries to mend itself through **neurogenesis**—producing new neurons. Researchers have found baby neurons deep in the brains of adult mice, birds, monkeys, and humans (Jessberger et al., 2008). These neurons may then migrate elsewhere and form connections with neighboring neurons (Aimone et al., 2010; Egeland et al., 2015; Gould, 2007).

Might new drugs spur the production of new nerve cells? Right now, companies are working on such possibilities, so stay tuned. In the meantime, we can all benefit from natural aids to neurogenesis, such as exercise, sex, and sleep (Iso et al., 2007; Leuner et al., 2010; Pereira et al., 2007; Stranahan et al., 2006).

Our Divided Brain

LOQ 2-14 What is a split brain, and what does it reveal about the functions of our two brain hemispheres?

Our brain's look-alike left and right hemispheres serve different functions. This *lateralization* is clear after some types of brain damage. Language processing, for

example, seems to reside mostly in your left hemisphere. A left-hemisphere accident, stroke, or tumor could leave you unable to read, write, or speak. You might be unable to reason, do arithmetic, or understand others. Similar right hemisphere damage seldom has such dramatic effects.

Does this mean that the right hemisphere is just along for the ride—a silent junior partner or "minor" hemisphere? Many believed this was the case until 1960, when researchers found that the "minor" right hemisphere was not so limited after all. The unfolding of this discovery is a fascinating chapter in psychology's history.

Splitting the Brain: One Skull, Two Minds

In 1961, two neurosurgeons believed that the uncontrollable seizures of some patients with severe epilepsy was caused by abnormal brain activity bouncing back and forth between the two cerebral hemispheres. If so, they wondered, could they end this biological tennis game by cutting through the **corpus callosum**, the wide band of axon fibers connecting the two hemispheres and carrying messages between them (**FIGURE 2.22**)? The neurosurgeons knew that psychologists Roger Sperry, Ronald Myers, and Michael Gazzaniga had divided cats' and monkeys' brains in this manner, with no serious ill effects.

So the surgeons operated. The result? The seizures all but disappeared. The patients with these **split brains** were surprisingly normal, their personality and intellect hardly affected. Waking from surgery, one even joked that he had a "splitting headache" (Gazzaniga, 1967). By sharing their experiences, these patients have greatly expanded our understanding of interactions between the intact brain's two hemispheres.

To appreciate these studies, we need to focus for a minute on the peculiar nature of our visual wiring, illustrated in **FIGURE 2.23**. Note that each eye receives sensory information from the entire

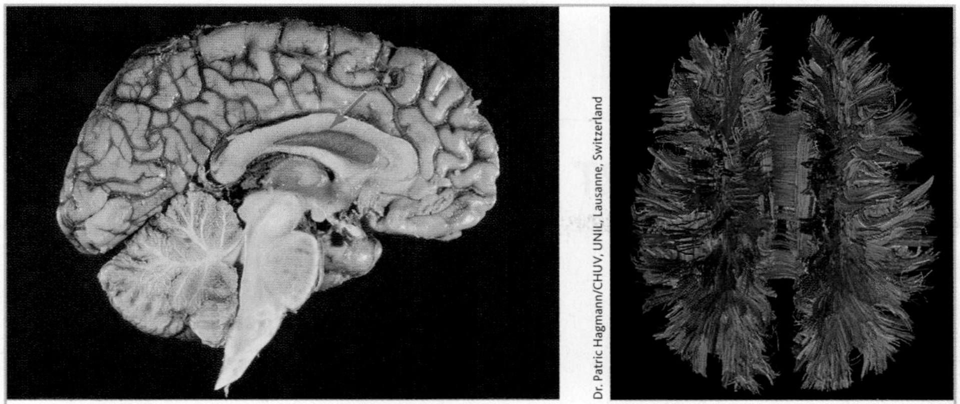

Martin M. Rotker/Science Source

Dr. Patric Hagmann/CHUV, UNIL, Lausanne, Switzerland

FIGURE 2.22 **The corpus callosum** This large band of neural fibers connects the two brain hemispheres. To photograph the half brain above left, a surgeon separated the hemispheres by cutting through the corpus callosum (see blue arrow) and lower brain regions. The high-resolution diffusion spectrum image above right, showing a top-facing brain from above, reveals brain neural networks within the two hemispheres, and the corpus callosum neural bridge between them.

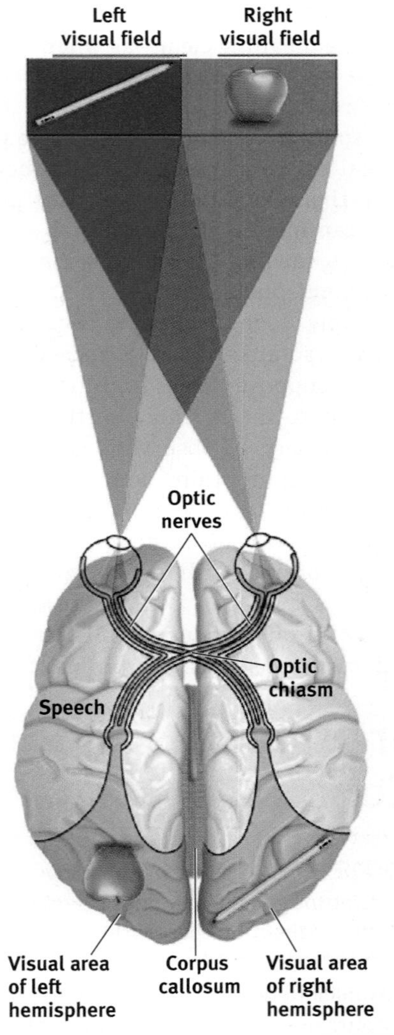

FIGURE 2.23 **The information highway from eye to brain**

visual field. But information from the left half of your field of vision goes to your right hemisphere, and information from the right half of your visual field goes to your left hemisphere. In an intact brain, data received by either hemisphere are quickly transmitted to the other side, across the corpus callosum.

In a person with a severed corpus callosum, this information sharing does not take place. Because the surgery had cut the communication lines between the patient's two hemispheres, Sperry and Gazzaniga were able to quiz each hemisphere separately. They could send information to the patient's left hemisphere by having the person stare at a dot and by then flashing a stimulus (a word or photo) to the right of the dot. To send a message to the right hemisphere, they would flash the item to the left of the dot. (If they tried to do this with you, the hemisphere receiving the information would instantly pass the news to the other side of your intact brain.)

In an early experiment, Gazzaniga (1967, 2016) flashed the word *HEART* across the screen in such a way that *HE* appeared to the left of the dot, and *ART* appeared to the right (**FIGURE 2.24b**). Asked to *say* what they had seen, the patients reported the letters sent to the left hemisphere, which usually controls speech—*"ART."* Asked to point *with their left hand* to what they had seen, they were startled when that hand (controlled by the right hemisphere) pointed to *"HE"* (Figure 2.24c). One skull was housing two minds.

A few people who have had split-brain surgery have for a time been bothered by the unruly independence of their left hand. It seems the left hand truly didn't know what the right hand was doing. One hand might unbutton a shirt while the other buttoned it, or put grocery store items back on the shelf after the other hand put them in the cart. It was as if each hemisphere was thinking, "I've half a mind to wear my green (blue) shirt today." Indeed, said Sperry (1964), split-brain surgery leaves people "with two separate minds." (Reading these reports, can you imagine a patient playing a solitary game of "rock, paper, scissors"—left hand versus right?)

What happens when the "two minds" disagree? If a split-brain patient follows an order ("Walk") sent to the right hemisphere, the left hemisphere won't know why the legs start walking. But if asked, the left hemisphere doesn't say "I don't know." Instead, it instantly invents—and apparently believes—an explanation ("I'm going into the house to get a Coke"). Thus, Gazzaniga (1988), who has called split-brain patients "the most fascinating people on Earth," concluded that the conscious left hemisphere resembles an interpreter that instantly constructs theories to explain our behavior. There goes our brain, running on autopilot as usual. It feels and acts and later explains itself (Kahneman, 2011).

neurogenesis the formation of new neurons.

corpus callosum [KOR-pus kah-LOW-sum] a large band of neural fibers connecting the two brain hemispheres and carrying messages between them.

split brain a condition in which the brain's two hemispheres have been isolated by surgery that cut the fibers (mainly those of the corpus callosum) connecting them.

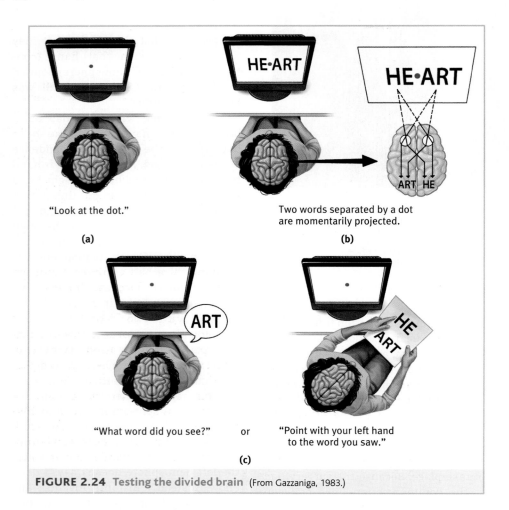

"Look at the dot."

(a)

Two words separated by a dot are momentarily projected.

(b)

"What word did you see?"   or   "Point with your left hand to the word you saw."

(c)

FIGURE 2.24 Testing the divided brain (From Gazzaniga, 1983.)

Retrieve + Remember

- (1) If we flash a red light to the right hemisphere of a person with a split brain, and flash a green light to the left hemisphere, will each observe its own color? (2) Will the person be aware that the colors differ? (3) What will the person verbally report seeing?

ANSWERS: 1. yes, 2. no, 3. green

Right-Left Differences in Intact Brains

So, what about the 99.99+ percent of us with undivided brains? Does each of *our* hemispheres also perform distinct functions? The short answer is *Yes*. If you were performing a *perceptual* task, a brain scan would show increased activity (brain waves, bloodflow, and glucose consump-

tion) in your *right* hemisphere. If you were speaking or doing math calculations, the scan would show increased activity in your *left* hemisphere.

A dramatic demonstration of lateralization happens before some types of brain surgery. To locate the patient's language centers, the surgeon injects a sedative into the neck artery feeding blood to the left hemisphere, which usually controls speech. Before the injection, the patient is lying down, arms in the air, chatting with the doctor. Can you predict what probably happens when the drug puts the left hemisphere to sleep? Within seconds, the patient's right arm falls limp. If the left hemisphere is controlling language, the patient will be speechless until the drug wears off.

To the brain, language is language, whether spoken or signed. Just as hearing

people usually use the left hemisphere to process spoken language, deaf people usually use the left hemisphere to process sign language (Corina et al., 1992; Hickok et al., 2001). Thus, a left-hemisphere stroke disrupts a deaf person's signing, much as it disrupts a hearing person's speaking (Corina, 1998). The same brain area is involved in both. (For more on how the brain enables language, see Chapter 8.)

Let's not forget that our left and right brain hemispheres work together. The left hemisphere is good at making quick, exact interpretations of language. But the right hemisphere excels in *making inferences* (reasoned conclusions) (Beeman & Chiarello, 1998; Bowden & Beeman, 1998; Mason & Just, 2004). It also *helps fine-tune our speech* to make meaning clear—as when we say "Let's eat, Grandpa," instead of "Let's eat Grandpa!" (Heller, 1990). And it *helps orchestrate our self-awareness*. People with partial paralysis sometimes stubbornly deny their condition. They may claim they can move a paralyzed limb—if the damage causing the paralysis is in the right hemisphere (Berti et al., 2005).

Simply looking at the two hemispheres, so alike to the naked eye, who would suppose they each contribute uniquely to the harmony of the whole? Yet a variety of observations—of people with split brains and those with intact brains, and even of other species' brains—leaves little doubt. We have unified brains with specialized parts (Hopkins & Cantalupo, 2008; MacNeilage et al., 2009). And one product of all that brain activity is consciousness, our next topic.

Brain States and Consciousness

LOQ 2-15 What do we mean by *consciousness,* and how does selective attention direct our perceptions?

Consciousness is our awareness of ourselves and our environment (Paller & Suzuki, 2014). Consciousness enables us to exert voluntary control and to communicate our mental states to others. When we learn a complex concept or behavior, it is consciousness that focuses our attention. It lets us assemble information from many sources as we reflect on the past, adapt to the present, and plan for the future.

Can consciousness persist in a permanently motionless body? Possibly, depending on the underlying condition. A hospitalized 23-year-old woman showed no outward signs of conscious awareness (Owen, 2014; Owen et al., 2006). But when researchers asked her to *imagine* playing tennis, fMRI scans revealed activity in a brain area that normally controls arm and leg movements. Even in a motionless body, the researchers concluded, the brain—and the mind— may still be active (**FIGURE 2.25**).

> "I am a brain, Watson. The rest of me is a mere appendix."
>
> Sherlock Holmes, in Arthur Conan Doyle's "The Adventure of the Mazarin Stone," 1921

Consciousness is not located in any one small brain area. Conscious awareness is a product of coordinated, brain-wide activity (Chennu et al., 2014; Gaillard et al., 2009; Schurger et al., 2010). In a brain scan, your awareness of a loved one's presence would appear as a pattern of strong signals bouncing back and forth among many brain areas (Blanke, 2012; Boly et al., 2011; Olivé et al., 2015). Our brain is a whole system, and our mental experiences arise from coordinated brain activity.

When we consciously focus on a new or complex task, our brain uses **sequential processing,** giving full attention to one thing at a time. But sequential processing is only one track in the two-track mind. Even while your conscious awareness is intensely focused elsewhere, your mind's other track is taking care of routine business (breathing and heart function, body balance, and hundreds of other tasks) by means of **parallel processing.** Some "80 to 90 percent of what we do is unconscious," says Nobel Laureate and memory expert Eric Kandel (2008).

INSADCO Photography/Alamy

ALTERED STATES OF CONSCIOUSNESS In addition to normal, waking awareness, consciousness comes to us in altered states. These include meditating, daydreaming, sleeping, and drug-induced hallucinating.

In addition to normal waking awareness, consciousness comes to us in altered states, aspects of which are discussed in other chapters—hypnosis in Chapter 5, for example, and consciousness-altering drugs in Chapter 13. Here we take a close look at the role

of attention, and two altered states we all experience—sleep and dreams.

Selective Attention

Your conscious awareness focuses, like a flashlight beam, on a *very* small part of all that you experience. Psychologists call this **selective attention.** Until reading this sentence, you were unaware that your nose is jutting into your line of vision. Now, suddenly, the spotlight shifts, and your nose stubbornly intrudes on the words before you.

> **consciousness** our awareness of ourselves and our environment.
>
> **sequential processing** the processing of one aspect of a problem at a time; used when we focus attention on new or complex tasks.
>
> **parallel processing** the processing of many aspects of a problem simultaneously; the brain's natural mode of information processing for many functions.
>
> **selective attention** focusing conscious awareness on a particular stimulus.

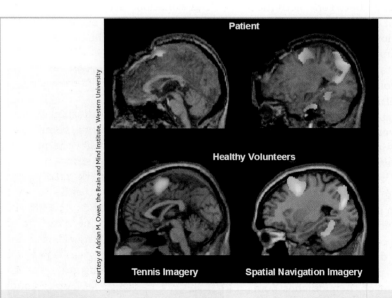

Courtesy of Adrian M. Owen, the Brain and Mind Institute, Western University

FIGURE 2.25 Evidence of awareness? When asked to imagine playing tennis or navigating her home, a noncommunicative patient's brain (top) exhibited activity similar to a healthy person's brain (bottom). Researchers wonder if such fMRI scans might enable a "conversation" with some unresponsive patients, by instructing them, for example, to answer *yes* to a question by imagining playing tennis (top and bottom left), and *no* by imagining walking around their home (top and bottom right).

While focusing on these words, you've also been blocking other parts of your environment from awareness, though your normal side vision would let you see them easily. You can change that. As you stare at the X below, notice what surrounds these sentences (the edges of the page, the desktop, the floor).

X

Chat on your phone, text, or tweak your playlist while driving, and your selective attention will shift back and forth between the road and its electronic competition. Indeed, it shifts more than we realize. One study left people in a room for 28 minutes, free to surf the Internet and to control and watch a TV. How many times did their attention shift between the two? Participants guessed it was about 15 times. Not even close! The actual number (verified by eye-tracking equipment) was 120 (Brasel & Gips, 2011).

> "Has a generation of texters, surfers, and twitterers evolved the enviable ability to process multiple streams of novel information in parallel? Most cognitive psychologists doubt it."
> Steven Pinker, "Not at All," 2010

Rapid toggling between activities is today's great enemy of sustained, focused attention. When we switch attentional gears, especially when we shift complex tasks like noticing and avoiding cars around us, we pay a toll—a slight and sometimes fatal delay in coping (Rubenstein et al., 2001).

When a driver attends to a conversation, activity in brain areas vital to driving decreases an average of 37 percent (Just et al., 2008). Chatting or texting—something 1 in 4 drivers admits doing—has been present in about 28 percent of traffic accidents (NSC, 2010; Pew, 2011). One video cam study of teen drivers found that driver distraction from passengers or phones occurred just before 58 percent of their crashes (AAA, 2015). Phone use is the bigger distraction. Talking with passengers raises the risk of an accident 1.6 above normal. Using a cell phone (even a hands-free set) carries a risk 4 times higher than normal—

"I wasn't texting. I was building this ship in a bottle."

equal to the risk of drunk driving (McEvoy et al., 2005, 2007).

Talking is distracting, but texting wins the danger game. In an 18-month video cam study that tracked the driving habits of long-haul truckers, their risk of a collision was 23 times greater when they were texting (Olson et al., 2009). Mindful of such findings, most U.S. states now ban texting while driving.

LaunchPad | Visit LaunchPad to watch the thought-provoking *Video—Automatic Skills: Disrupting a Pilot's Performance.*

Our conscious attention is so powerfully selective that we become "blind" to all but a tiny sliver of the immense ocean of visual stimuli constantly before us. In one famous study, people watched a one-minute video of basketball players, three in black shirts and three in white shirts, tossing a ball (Becklen & Cervone, 1983; Neisser, 1979). Researchers told the viewers to press a key each time they saw a black-shirted player pass the ball. Most viewers were so intent on their task that they failed to notice a young woman carrying an umbrella stroll across the screen midway through the clip (**FIGURE 2.26**). During a replay, they were amazed to see her! With their attention focused elsewhere, the viewers suffered from **inattentional blindness.** In another study, two smart-aleck researchers had a gorilla-suited assistant thump his chest and move through the swirl of players. Did he steal the show? *No*—half the pass-counting viewers failed to see him, too (Simons & Chabris, 1999).

The invisible gorilla struck again in a study of 24 radiologists who were asked to search for signs of cancer in lung scans. All but 4 of them missed the little image of a gorilla embedded in the scan (Drew et al., 2013). They did, however, spot the much tinier groups of cancer cells, which were the focus of their attention.

Given that most of us miss people strolling by in gorilla suits while our attention is focused elsewhere, imagine the fun that others can have by distracting us. Misdirect our attention and we will miss the hand slipping into the pocket. "Every time you perform a magic trick, you're engaging in experimental psychology," says magician Teller, a master of mind-messing methods (2009). Clever thieves know this, too. One psychologist was surprised by a woman exposing herself. Only later did he realize her crime partner had picked his pocket (Gallace, 2012).

Magicians also exploit our **change blindness** (a form of inattentional blindness). With a dramatic flourish, they direct our selective attention away from other changes being made. So, too, in laboratory experiments, where viewers failed to notice that, after a brief visual interruption, a big Coke bottle had disappeared, a railing had risen, clothing had changed color—and construction

DRIVEN TO DISTRACTION In driving-simulation experiments, people whose attention is diverted by texting and cell-phone conversation make more driving errors.

FIGURE 2.26 Selective inattention Viewers who were attending to basketball tosses among the black-shirted players usually failed to notice the umbrella-toting woman sauntering across the screen (Neisser, 1979).

workers had changed places (**FIGURE 2.27**) (Chabris & Simons, 2010; Resnick et al., 1997). Out of sight, out of mind.

LaunchPad For more on change blindness, watch the 3-minute *Video: Visual Attention.*

The point to remember: Our conscious mind is in one place at a time. But outside our conscious awareness, the other track of our two-track mind remains active—even during sleep, as we see next.

Retrieve + Remember

- Explain three attentional principles that magicians may use to fool us.

ANSWER: *Our selective attention* allows us to focus on only a limited portion of our surroundings. *Inattentional blindness* explains why we don't perceive some things when we are distracted. And *change blindness* happens when we fail to notice a relatively unimportant change in our environment. All these principles help magicians fool us, as they direct our attention elsewhere to perform their tricks.

Sleep and Dreams

Each night, we lose consciousness and slip into sleep. We may feel "dead to the world," but we are not. Our perceptual window remains open a crack, and our two-track mind continues to process information outside our conscious awareness. We move around on the bed but manage not to fall out. And if someone speaks our name, our unconscious body will perk up. Although the roar of my [ND's] neighborhood garbage truck leaves me undisturbed, my baby's cry will shatter my sleep. Our auditory cortex responds to sound stimuli during sleep (Kutas, 1990).

Sleep's mysteries puzzled scientists for centuries. Now, in laboratories around the world, some of these mysteries are being solved as people sleep, attached to recording devices, while others observe. By recording brain waves and muscle movements, and by watching and sometimes waking sleepers, researchers are glimpsing things that a thousand years of common sense never told us.

FIGURE 2.27 Change blindness While a man (in red) provides directions to a construction worker, two experimenters rudely pass between them carrying a door. During this interruption, the original worker switches places with another person wearing different-colored clothing. Most people, focused on their direction giving, do not notice the switch (Simons & Levin, 1998).

Biological Rhythms and Sleep

LOQ 2-16 What is the *circadian rhythm,* and what are the stages of our nightly sleep cycle?

Like the ocean, life has its rhythmic tides. Let's look more closely at two of these biological rhythms—our 24-hour biological clock and our 90-minute sleep cycle.

CIRCADIAN RHYTHM Try pulling an all-nighter, or working an occasional night shift. You'll feel groggiest in the middle of the night but may gain new energy when your normal wake-up time arrives. This happens thanks to your body's internal biological clock, its **circadian rhythm** (from the Latin *circa,* "about," and *diem,* "day"). Your wake-up call is a sign that your internal clock is doing its job—keeping you roughly in tune with the 24-hour cycle of day and night. As morning approaches, body temperature rises. Then it peaks during the day, dips for a time in early afternoon (when many people take naps), and begins to drop again in the evening. Thinking is sharpest and memory most accurate when we are at our daily peak in circadian arousal.

Age and experience can alter our circadian rhythm. Most 20-year-olds are evening-energized "owls," with performance improving across the day (May & Hasher, 1998). After age 20, our clocks begin to shift. Most older adults are morning-loving "larks," with performance declining as the day wears on (Roenneberg et al., 2004). Women, if they have children, but

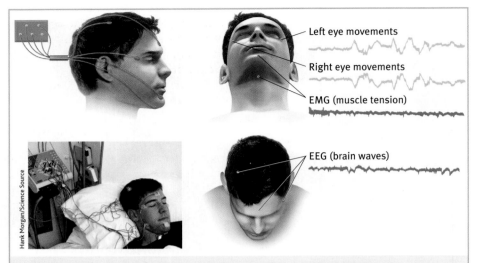

FIGURE 2.28 Measuring sleep activity Sleep researchers measure brain-wave activity, eye movements, and muscle tension with electrodes that pick up weak electrical signals from the brain, eyes, and facial muscles. (From Dement, 1978.)

Left eye movements

Right eye movements

EMG (muscle tension)

EEG (brain waves)

Hank Morgan/Science Source

also as they go through menopause, morph into larks slightly earlier than men (Leonhard & Randler, 2009; Randler & Bausback, 2010). Most retirement homes are quiet by mid-evening, when the night has hardly begun for many young adults.

SLEEP STAGES Sooner or later, sleep overtakes us all, and consciousness fades as different parts of our brain's cortex stop communicating (Massimini et al., 2005). Yet the sleeping brain is active and has its own biological rhythm. About every 90 minutes, we cycle through distinct sleep stages. This basic fact came to light after 8-year-old Armond Aserinsky went to bed one night in 1952. His father, Eugene, needed to test an electroencephalograph he had repaired that day (Aserinsky, 1988; Seligman & Yellen, 1987). Placing electrodes near Armond's eyes to record the rolling eye movements then believed to occur during sleep, Aserinsky watched the machine go wild, tracing deep zigzags on the graph paper. Could the machine still be broken? As the night proceeded and the activity recurred, Aserinsky realized that the periods of fast, jerky eye movements were accompanied by energetic brain activity. Awakened during one

Peter Chadwick/Science Source

Eric Isselée/Shutterstock

such episode, Armond reported having a dream. Aserinsky had discovered what we now know as **REM sleep** (rapid *eye movement* sleep).

Similar procedures used with thousands of volunteers showed the cycles were a normal part of sleep (Kleitman, 1960). To appreciate these studies, imagine yourself as a participant. As the hour grows late, you feel sleepy and get ready for bed. A researcher comes in and tapes electrodes to your scalp (to detect your brain waves), on your chin (to detect muscle tension), and just outside the corners of your eyes (to detect eye movements) (**FIGURE 2.28**). Other devices will record your heart rate, breathing rate, and genital arousal.

When you are in bed with your eyes closed, the researcher in the next room sees on the EEG the relatively slow **alpha waves** of your awake but relaxed state (**FIGURE 2.29**). As you adapt to all this equipment, you grow tired. Then, in a moment you won't remember, your breathing slows and you slip into **sleep.** The EEG now shows the irregular brain waves of the non-REM sleep stage called *NREM-1* sleep (Silber et al., 2008).

During this brief NREM-1 sleep you may experience fantastic images resembling hallucinations. You may have a

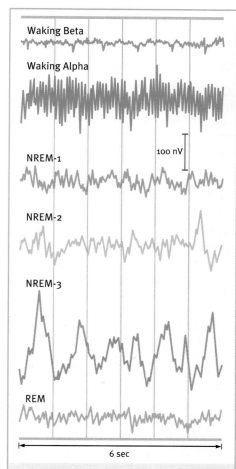

FIGURE 2.29 Brain waves and sleep stages The beta waves of an alert, waking state and the regular alpha waves of an awake, relaxed state differ from the slower, larger delta waves of deep NREM-3 sleep. Although the rapid REM sleep waves resemble the near-waking NREM-1 sleep waves, the body is more internally aroused during REM sleep than during NREM sleep.

sensation of falling (at which moment your body may suddenly jerk) or of floating weightlessly. These are *hypnagogic* sensations (from the Greek root words meaning "leading to sleep"). Your brain may later treat them as real memories. People who claim they were abducted by aliens—often shortly after getting into bed—commonly recall being floated off from (or pinned down on) their beds (Clancy, 2005).

You then relax more deeply and begin about 20 minutes of *NREM-2* sleep. The EEG will show bursts of rapid, rhythmic brain-wave activity. Although you could still be awakened without too much difficulty, you are now clearly asleep.

Then you enter the deep sleep of NREM-3. During this slow-wave sleep, which lasts for about 30 minutes, your brain emits large, slow **delta waves.** You would be hard to awaken. (It is at the end of this stage that children may wet the bed.)

LaunchPad To better understand EEG readings and their relationship to consciousness, sleep, and dreams, experience the tutorial and simulation at LaunchPad's *PsychSim 6: EEG and Sleep Stages.*

REM SLEEP About an hour after you first dive into sleep, a strange thing happens. You reverse course. From NREM-3, you head back through NREM-2 (where you'll ultimately spend about half your night). You then enter the most puzzling sleep phase—REM sleep (**FIGURE 2.30**).

circadian [ser-KAY-dee-an] rhythm our internal biological clock; regular bodily rhythms (for example, of temperature and wakefulness) that occur on a 24-hour cycle.

REM sleep rapid eye movement sleep; a recurring sleep stage during which vivid dreams commonly occur. Also known as *paradoxical sleep,* because the muscles are relaxed (except for minor twitches) but other body systems are active.

alpha waves relatively slow brain waves of a relaxed, awake state.

sleep a periodic, natural loss of consciousness—as distinct from unconsciousness resulting from a coma, general anesthesia, or hibernation. (Adapted from Dement, 1999.)

delta waves large, slow brain waves associated with deep sleep.

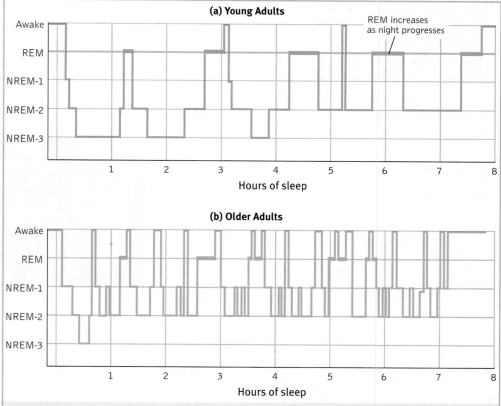

FIGURE 2.30 The stages in a typical night's sleep People pass through a multistage sleep cycle several times each night. As the night goes on, the periods of deep sleep diminish and REM sleep increases. As people age, sleep becomes more fragile, with awakenings more common (Kamel & Gammack, 2006; Neubauer, 1999).

And the show begins. For about 10 minutes, your brain waves become rapid and saw-toothed, more like those of the nearly awake NREM-1 sleep. But unlike NREM-1, during REM sleep your heart rate rises and your breathing becomes rapid and irregular. Every half-minute or so, your eyes dart around in a brief burst of activity behind your closed lids. These eye movements announce the beginning of a dream—often emotional, usually story-like, and richly hallucinatory.

Except during very scary dreams, your genitals become aroused during REM sleep. You have an erection or increased vaginal lubrication and clitoral engorgement, regardless of whether the dream's content is sexual (Karacan et al., 1966). Men's common "morning erection" stems from the night's last REM period, often just before waking. (Many men who have occasional erectile problems get sleep-related erections, suggesting the problem is not between their legs.)

During REM sleep, your brain's motor cortex is active but your brainstem blocks its messages. This leaves your muscles relaxed, so much so that, except for an occasional finger, toe, or facial twitch, you are essentially paralyzed. Moreover, you cannot easily be awakened. REM sleep is thus sometimes called *paradoxical* sleep. The body is internally aroused, with waking-like brain activity, but externally calm—except for those darting eyes

"Boy are my eyes tired! I had REM sleep all night long."

Horses, which spend 92 percent of each day standing and can sleep standing, must lie down for muscle-paralyzing REM sleep (Morrison, 2003).

As the night goes on, the 90-minute sleep cycle repeats itself over and over—with one difference. Deep NREM-3 sleep grows shorter and disappears, and REM and NREM-2 sleep periods get longer (see Figure 2.30). By morning, we have spent 20 to 25 percent of an average night's sleep—some 100 minutes—in REM sleep. In sleep lab studies, 37 percent of participants have reported rarely or never having dreams "that you can remember the next morning" (Moore, 2004). Yet even they, more than 80 percent of the time, could recall a dream if awakened during REM sleep. Each year, we spend about 600 hours experiencing some 1500 dreams. Over a typical lifetime, this adds up to more than 100,000 dreams—all swallowed by the night but not acted out, thanks to REM's protective paralysis.

Why Do We Sleep?

LOQ 2-17 How do our sleep patterns differ? What five theories describe our need to sleep?

True or false? "Everyone needs 8 hours of sleep." *False.* The first clue to how much sleep a person needs is their age. Newborns often sleep two-thirds of their day, most adults no more than one-third. But there is more to our sleep differences than age.

Some adults thrive on fewer than 6 hours a night. Others regularly rack up 9 hours or more. Some of us are awake between nightly sleep periods, breaking the night into a "first sleep" and a "second sleep" (Randall, 2012). And for those who can nap, a 15-minute midday snooze can be as effective as an additional hour at night (Horne, 2011). Heredity influences sleep patterns, and researchers are tracking the sleep-regulating genes in humans and other animals (Donlea et al., 2009; Hor & Tafti, 2009; Mackenzie et al., 2015).

Retrieve + Remember

- Why would communal sleeping provide added protection for these soldiers?

  ANSWER: Each soldier cycles through the sleep stages independently. So, it is very likely that at any given time, at least one will be in an easily awakened stage in the event of a threat.

- What are the four sleep stages, and in what order do we normally travel through those stages?

  ANSWER: REM, NREM-1, NREM-2, NREM-3; normally we move through NREM-1, then NREM-2, then NREM-3, then back up through NREM-2 before we experience REM sleep.

- Can you match the cognitive experience with the sleep stage?

  1. NREM-1   a. story-like dreams
  2. NREM-3   b. fleeting images
  3. REM   c. minimal awareness

ANSWERS: 1. b, 2. c, 3. a

"Maybe 'Bring Your Pillow To Work Day' wasn't such a good idea."

But let's not forget another of this book's Big Ideas: *Biological, psychological, and social-cultural influences interact.* We can see this interaction in sleep patterns. Thanks to modern lighting, shift work, and social media diversions, many who would have gone to bed at 9:00 P.M. a century ago are now up until 11:00 P.M. or later. Those extra hours awake are often subtracted from sleep time. In Britain, Canada, Germany, Japan, and the United States, adults average 6½ to 7 hours of sleep a night on workdays, and 7 to 8 hours on other days (National Sleep Foundation, 2013).

In a 2013 Gallup poll, 40 percent of Americans reported getting 6 hours or less sleep at night (Jones, 2013).

Whether for work or play, bright light can disrupt our biological clock, tricking the brain into thinking night is morning. The process begins in our eyes' retinas, which contain light-sensitive proteins. Bright light sets off an internal alarm by activating these proteins, which then signal a brain structure called the **suprachiasmatic nucleus** (**FIGURE 2.31**). This brain structure in turn decreases production of the sleep-inducing hormone *melatonin* (Chang et al., 2015; Gandhi et al., 2015). This process can put sports teams at a disadvantage. One study of more than 24,000 Major League Baseball games found that teams who had crossed three time zones before playing a series had nearly a 60 percent chance of losing their first game (Winter et al., 2009).

SLEEP THEORIES So our sleep patterns differ from person to person and from culture to culture. But why do we *need* to sleep? Psychologists offer five possible reasons.

1. *Sleep protects.* When darkness shut down the day's hunting, gathering, and social activities, our distant ancestors were better off asleep in a cave, out of harm's way. Those who didn't wander around dark cliffs were more likely to leave descendants. This fits a broader principle: Sleep patterns tend to suit a species' place in nature. Animals with the greatest need to graze and the least

> **suprachiasmatic nucleus (SCN)** a pair of cell clusters in the hypothalamus that controls circadian rhythm. In response to light, the SCN adjusts melatonin production, thus modifying our feelings of sleepiness.

ability to hide tend to sleep less (see **FIGURE 2.32**). Animals also sleep less, with no ill effects, during times of mating and migration (Siegel, 2012).

2. *Sleep helps us recover.* Sleep helps restore the immune system and repair brain tissue. Bats and many other small animals burn a lot of calories, producing *free radicals*, molecules that are toxic to neurons. Sleep sweeps away this toxic waste (Xie et al., 2013). Sleeping gives resting neurons time to repair, rewire, and reorganize themselves (Gilestro et al., 2009; Tononi & Cirelli, 2013). Think of it this way: When consciousness leaves your house, workers come in for a makeover, saying "Good night. Sleep tidy."

3. *Sleep helps us restore and rebuild fading memories of the day's experiences.* Sleep strengthens neural connections and replays recent learning (Yang et al., 2014). During sleep, the brain shifts memories from temporary storage in the hippocampus to permanent storage in areas of the cortex (Diekelmann & Born, 2010; Racsmány et al., 2010). Children and adults trained to perform tasks recall them better after a night's sleep, or even after

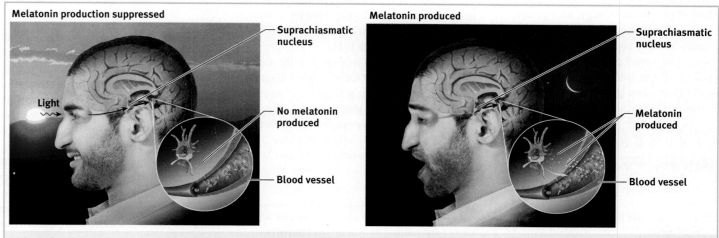

FIGURE 2.31 The biological clock Light striking the eye's retina signals the suprachiasmatic nucleus (SCN) to suppress production of the sleep hormone melatonin. At night, the SCN quiets down, allowing release of melatonin into the bloodstream.

20 hours
Kruglov_Orda/Shutterstock

16 hours
Courtesy of Andrew D. Myers

12 hours
Utekhina Anna/Shutterstock

10 hours
Steffen Foerster
Photography/Shutterstock

8 hours
Rubberball/Vetta/Getty
Images

4 hours
Eric Isselée/Shutterstock

2 hours
pandapaw/Shutterstock

FIGURE 2.32 Animal sleep time Would you rather be a brown bat and sleep 20 hours a day or a giraffe and sleep 2 hours a day? (Data from NIH, 2010.)

a short nap, than after several hours awake (Friedrich et al., 2015; Kurdziel et al., 2013; Stickgold & Ellenbogen, 2008). Sleep, it seems, strengthens memories in a way that being awake does not.

4. **Sleep feeds creative thinking.** A full night's sleep boosts our thinking and learning. After working on a task, then sleeping on it, people solve problems more insightfully than do those who stay awake (Barrett, 2011; Sio et al., 2013). They also are better at spotting connections among novel pieces of information (Ellenbogen et al., 2007). To think smart and see connections, it often pays to sleep on it.

> "Sleep faster, we need the pillows."
> Yiddish proverb

5. **Sleep supports growth**. During deep sleep, the pituitary gland releases a hormone we need for muscle development. A regular full night's sleep can *"dramatically improve your athletic ability"* (Maas & Robbins, 2010). Well-rested athletes have faster reaction times, more energy, and greater endurance. Teams that build 8 to 10 hours of daily sleep into their training show improved performance.

Given all the benefits of sleep, it's no wonder that sleep loss—our next topic of discussion—hits us so hard.

Retrieve + Remember

- What five theories explain our need for sleep?

ANSWER: (1) Sleep has survival value. (2) Sleep helps restore the immune system and repair brain tissue. (3) During sleep we strengthen memories. (4) Sleep fuels creativity. (5) Sleep plays a role in the growth process.

Sleep Deprivation and Sleep Disorders

LOQ 2-18 How does sleep loss affect us, and what are the major sleep disorders?

Sleep commands roughly one-third of our lives—some 25 years, on average. With enough sleep, we awaken refreshed and in a better mood. We work more efficiently and accurately. But when our body yearns for sleep and does not get it, we feel terrible. Trying to stay awake, we will eventually lose. In the tiredness battle, sleep always wins.

THE EFFECTS OF SLEEP LOSS Today, more than ever, our sleep patterns leave us not only sleepy but drained of energy and feelings of well-being. This tiredness tendency has grown so steadily that some researchers have labeled current times as the "Great Sleep Recession" (Keyes et al., 2015). After a series of 5-hour nights, we run up a sleep debt that won't be wiped out by one long snooze. "The brain keeps an accurate count of sleep debt for at least two weeks," reported sleep researcher William Dement (1999, p. 64).

College students are especially sleep deprived. In one national survey, 69 percent reported "feeling tired" or "having little energy" on at least several days in the two previous weeks (AP, 2009). Small wonder so many fall asleep in class. The going needn't get boring for students to start snoring.

LaunchPad To see whether you are one of the many sleep-deprived students, visit LaunchPad's *Assess Your Strengths self-assessment quiz, Sleep Deprivation*.

Sleep loss also affects our mood. Tired often equals crabby—less sleep predicts more conflicts in students' friendships and romantic relationships (Gordon & Chen, 2014; Tavernier & Willoughby, 2014). Sleep loss can also predict depression, as one study of 15,500 young people, ages 12 to 18, showed. Risk of depression was 71 percent higher for teens who slept 5 or fewer hours a night, compared with those who slept 8 hours or more (Gangwisch et al., 2010). The link does not reflect an effect of depression on sleep. In long-term studies, sleep loss predicts depression, not vice versa (Gregory et al., 2009). REM sleep's processing of emotional experiences helps protect against depression (Walker & van der Helm, 2009). After a good night's sleep, we often do feel better the next day.

Chronic sleep loss can suppress the immune system, lowering our resistance to illness. With fewer immune cells, we are less able to battle viral infections and cancer (Möller-Levet et al., 2013; Motivala & Irwin, 2007). One experiment exposed volunteers to a cold virus. Those who had been averaging less than 7 hours of sleep a night were three times more likely to develop the cold than were those sleeping 8 or more hours a night (Cohen et al., 2009). Sleep's protective effect may help explain why people who sleep 7 to 8 hours a night tend to outlive their sleep-deprived agemates (Dew et al., 2003; Parthasarathy et al., 2015).

When sleepy frontal lobes confront visual attention tasks, reactions slow and errors increase (Caldwell, 2012; Lim & Dinges, 2010). For drivers in an unexpected situation, slow responses can spell disaster. Drowsy driving has contributed to an estimated one of six deadly American traffic accidents (AAA, 2010). One 2-year study examined the driving accident rates of more than 20,000 Virginia 16- to 18-year-olds in two major cities. In one city, the high schools started 75 to 80 minutes later than in the other. The late starters had about 25 percent fewer crashes (Vorona et al., 2011).

Deliberate manipulation of driver fatigue on the road would be illegal and unethical. But twice each year, most North Americans participate in a revealing sleep-manipulation experiment: We "spring forward" to daylight savings time and "fall back" to standard time. A search of millions of Canadian and U.S. records showed that accidents increased immediately after the spring-forward change, which shortens sleep (Coren, 1996) (**FIGURE 2.33**). The same spring-forward effect appeared in another study, which showed that tired people are more likely to "cyberloaf"—to fritter away time online. On the Monday after daylight savings time begins, entertainment-related Google searches have been 3.1 percent higher than on the preceding Monday, and 6.4 percent higher than on the following Monday (Wagner et al., 2012).

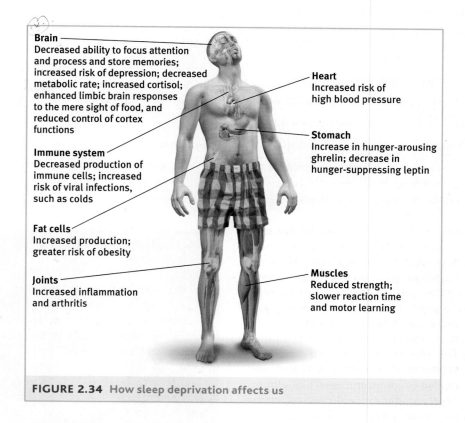

FIGURE 2.34 How sleep deprivation affects us

So sleep loss can destroy our mood, lower our resistance to infection, and decrease driver safety. It can also make us gain weight. Children and adults who sleep less than normal are heavier than average. And in recent decades, people have been sleeping less and weighing more (Shiromani et al., 2012). Here's how it happens. Sleep deprivation

- increases *ghrelin,* a hunger-arousing hormone, and decreases its hunger-suppressing partner, *leptin* (Shilsky et al., 2012).
- decreases metabolic rate, a gauge of energy use (Buxton et al., 2012).
- increases production of *cortisol,* a stress hormone that triggers fat production.
- enhances limbic brain responses to the mere sight of food (Benedict et al., 2012; Greer et al., 2013; St-Onge et al., 2012).

These effects may help explain the weight gain common among sleep-deprived college students.

FIGURE 2.34 summarizes the effects of sleep deprivation. But there is good news! Psychologists have discovered a treatment that strengthens memory, increases concentration, boosts mood, moderates hunger, reduces obesity, fortifies the disease-fighting immune

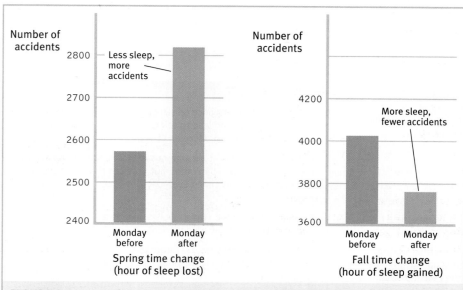

FIGURE 2.33 **Less sleep = more accidents** On the Monday after the spring time change, when people lose one hour of sleep, accidents increased, as compared with the Monday before. In the fall, traffic accidents normally increase because of greater snow, ice, and darkness, but they diminished after the time change. (Data from Coren, 1996.)

TABLE 2.2 Some Natural Sleep Aids

- Exercise regularly but not in the late evening. (Late afternoon is best.)
- Avoid caffeine after early afternoon, and avoid food and drink near bedtime. The exception would be a glass of milk, which provides raw materials for the manufacture of serotonin, a neurotransmitter that fosters sleep.
- Relax before bedtime, using dimmer light.
- Sleep on a regular schedule (rise at the same time even after a restless night) and avoid long naps.
- Hide time displays so you aren't tempted to check repeatedly.
- Reassure yourself that temporary sleep loss causes no great harm.
- Focus your mind on nonarousing, engaging thoughts, such as song lyrics, TV programs, or vacation travel (Gellis et al., 2013).
- If all else fails, settle for less sleep, either going to bed later or getting up earlier.

system, and lessens the risk of fatal accidents. Even better news: The treatment feels good, it can be self-administered, the supplies are limitless, and it's free! If you are a typical college-age student, often going to bed near 2:00 A.M. and dragged out of bed 6 hours later by the dreaded alarm, the treatment is simple: Add 15 minutes to your sleep each night until you feel more like a rested and energized student and less like a zombie. For some additional tips on getting better quality sleep, see **TABLE 2.2**.

> Some students sleep like the fellow who stayed up all night to see where the Sun went. (Then it dawned on him.)

MAJOR SLEEP DISORDERS Do you have trouble sleeping when anxious or excited? Most of us do. (*Warning:* A smart phone tucked under your pillow as an alarm clock

DID BRAHMS NEED HIS OWN LULLABIES? Cranky, overweight, and nap-prone, classical composer Johannes Brahms exhibited common symptoms of sleep apnea (Margolis, 2000).

increases the likelihood that you'll have a bad night's sleep.) An occasional loss of sleep is nothing to worry about. But for those who have a major sleep disorder—**insomnia, narcolepsy, sleep apnea,** *sleepwalking, sleeptalking,* or *night terrors*—trying to sleep can be a nightmare. (See **TABLE 2.3** for a summary of these disorders.)

Dreams

LOQ 2-19 What do we dream about, and what are five explanations of *why* we dream?

Now playing at an inner theater near you: the premiere showing of a sleeping person's dream. This never-before-seen mental movie features engaging characters wrapped in a plot that is original and unlikely, yet seemingly real.

REM **dreams** are vivid, emotional, and often bizarre (Loftus & Ketcham, 1994). Waking from one, we may wonder how our brain can so creatively, colorfully, and completely construct this inner world. Caught for a moment between our dreaming and waking consciousness, we may even be unsure which world is real. A 4-year-old may awaken and scream for his parents, terrified of the bear in the house.

> "I love to sleep. Do you? Isn't it great? It really is the best of both worlds. You get to be alive and unconscious."
>
> Comedian Rita Rudner, 1993

TABLE 2.3 Sleep Disorders

Disorder	Rate	Description	Effects
Insomnia	1 in 10 adults; 1 in 4 older adults	Ongoing difficulty falling or staying asleep.	Chronic tiredness. Reliance on sleeping pills and alcohol, which reduce REM sleep and lead to tolerance—a state in which increasing doses are needed to produce an effect.
Narcolepsy	1 in 2000 adults	Sudden attacks of overwhelming sleepiness.	Risk of falling asleep at a dangerous moment. Narcolepsy attacks usually last less than 5 minutes, but they can happen at the worst and most emotional times. Everyday activities, such as driving, require extra caution.
Sleep apnea	1 in 20 adults	Stopping breathing repeatedly while sleeping.	Fatigue and depression (as a result of slow-wave sleep deprivation), and obesity (especially among men).
Sleepwalking/sleeptalking	1–15 in 100 in the general population	Doing normal waking activities (sitting up, walking, speaking) during NREM-3 sleep.	Few serious concerns. People return to their beds on their own or with the help of a family member, rarely remembering their trip the next morning.
Night terrors	1 in 100 adults; 1 in 30 children	Appearing terrified, talking nonsense, sitting up, or walking around during NREM-3 sleep; different from nightmares.	Doubling of a child's heart and breathing rates during the attack. Luckily, children remember little or nothing of the fearful event the next day. As people age, night terrors become more and more rare.

Each of us spends about six years of our life in dreams—adventures that remain locked behind our moving eyelids and usually vanish with the new day. The discovery of the link between REM sleep and dreaming gave us a key to that lock. Now, instead of relying on a dreamer's hazy recall hours or days after waking, researchers can catch dreams as they happen. They can awaken people during or within 3 minutes after a REM sleep period and hear a vivid account.

WHAT WE DREAM Few REM dreams are sweet. For both women and men, 8 in 10 are bad dreams (Domhoff, 2007). Common themes are failing in an attempt to do something; being attacked, pursued, or rejected; or experiencing misfortune (Hall et al., 1982). Dreams with sexual imagery occur less often than you might think. In one study, only 1 in 10 dreams among young men and 1 in 30 among young women had sexual overtones (Domhoff, 1996). More commonly, our dreams feature people and places from the day's nonsexual experiences (De Koninck, 2000).

A popular sleep myth: If you dream you are falling and hit the ground (or if you dream of dying), you die. Unfortunately, those who could confirm these ideas are not around to do so. Many people, however, have had such dreams and are alive to report them.

Our two-track mind continues to monitor our environment while we sleep. Sensory stimuli—a particular odor or a phone's ringing—may be instantly woven into the dream story. In a classic experiment, researchers lightly sprayed cold water on dreamers' faces (Dement & Wolpert, 1958). Compared with sleepers who did not get the cold-water treatment, these people were more likely to dream about a waterfall, a leaky roof, or even about being sprayed by someone.

WHY WE DREAM Dream theorists have proposed several explanations of why we dream, including these five:

1. *To satisfy our own wishes.* In 1900, Sigmund Freud offered what he thought was "the most valuable of all the discoveries it has been my good fortune to make." He proposed that dreams act as a safety valve, discharging feelings that the dreamer could not express in public. He called the dream's remembered story line its **manifest content**. For Freud, this apparent content was a censored, symbolic version of the dream's underlying meaning—the **latent content,** or unconscious drives and wishes that would be threatening if expressed directly. Although most dreams have no openly sexual imagery, Freud believed most adult dreams could be "traced back by analysis to erotic wishes." Thus, a gun appearing in a dream could be a penis in disguise.

Freud's critics say it is time to wake up from Freud's dream theory, which they regard as a scientific nightmare. Scientific studies offer "no reason to believe any of Freud's specific claims about dreams and their purposes," said dream researcher William Domhoff (2003). Maybe a dream about a gun is really just a dream about a gun. Legend has it that even Freud, who loved to smoke cigars, agreed that "sometimes, a cigar is just a cigar." Other critics have noted that dreams could be interpreted in many different ways. Freud's wish-fulfillment theory of dreams has in large part given way to other theories.

2. *To file away memories.* The *information-processing* perspective proposes that dreams may help sift, sort, and secure the day's events in our memory. Some studies support this view. When tested the day after learning a task, those who had slept undisturbed did better than those who had been deprived of both slow-wave and REM sleep (Stickgold, 2012).

Brain scans confirm the link between REM sleep and memory. Brain regions that were active as rats learned to navigate a maze (or as people learned to identify the difference between objects) were active again later during REM sleep (Louie & Wilson, 2001; Maquet, 2001). So precise were these activity patterns that scientists could tell where in the maze the rat would be if awake.

Students, take note. Sleep researcher Robert Stickgold (2000) believes many students suffer from a kind of sleep bulimia, sleep deprived on weekdays and binge sleeping on the weekend. He warned, "If you don't get good sleep and enough sleep after you learn new stuff, you won't integrate it effectively into your memories." That helps explain why high school students with top grades slept about 25 minutes longer each night than their lower-achieving classmates (Wolfson & Carskadon, 1998). Sacrificing sleep time to study actually worsens academic performance by making it harder the next day to understand class material or do well on a test (Gillen-O'Neel et al., 2013).

3. *To develop and preserve neural pathways.* Dreams—the brain activity linked to REM sleep—may give the sleeping brain a workout that helps it develop. As we'll see in Chapter 3, stimulating experiences preserve and expand the brain's neural pathways. Infants, whose neural networks are fast developing, spend much of their abundant sleep time in REM sleep.

4. *To make sense of neural static.* Other theories propose that dreams are born when random neural activity spreads upward from the brainstem (Antrobus, 1991; Hobson, 2003, 2004, 2009). Our ever-alert brain attempts to make sense of the activity, pasting the random bits of information into a meaningful image.

insomnia recurring problems in falling or staying asleep.

narcolepsy a sleep disorder in which a person has uncontrollable sleep attacks, sometimes lapsing directly into REM sleep.

sleep apnea a sleep disorder in which a sleeping person repeatedly stops breathing until blood oxygen is so low the person awakens just long enough to draw a breath.

dream a sequence of images, emotions, and thoughts passing through a sleeping person's mind.

manifest content according to Freud, the remembered story line of a dream.

latent content according to Freud, the underlying meaning of a dream.

Brain scans taken while people were dreaming have revealed increased activity in the emotion-related limbic system and in areas that process visual images (Schwarz, 2012). Damage either of these areas and dreaming itself may be impaired (Domhoff, 2003).

5. *To reflect cognitive development.* Some dream researchers dispute these theories. Instead, they see dreams as a reflection of brain maturation and cognitive development (Domhoff, 2010, 2011; Foulkes, 1999). For example, before age 9, children's dreams seem more like a slide show and less like an active story in which the child is an actor. Dreams at all ages tend to feature the kind of thinking and talking we demonstrate when awake. They seem to draw on our current knowledge and concepts we understand.

Despite their differences, today's dream researchers agree on one thing: We need REM sleep. Deprived of it in sleep labs or in real life, people return more and more quickly to the REM stage when finally allowed to sleep undisturbed. They literally sleep like babies—with increased REM sleep, known as **REM rebound.** Withdrawing REM-suppressing sleeping pills also increases REM sleep, often with nightmares.

Retrieve + Remember

• What five theories explain why we dream?

ANSWER: (1) Freud's wish fulfillment (dreams as a psychic safety valve), (2) information processing (dreams sort the day's events and form memories), (3) physiological function (dreams pave neural pathways), (4) making sense of neural static (REM sleep triggers random neural activity that the mind weaves into stories), (5) cognitive development (dreams reflect the dreamer's developmental stage)

* * *

We have glimpsed the truth of this chapter's overriding principle: *Biological and psychological explanations of behavior are partners, not competitors.* We are privileged to live in a time of breathtaking discovery about the interplay of our biology and our behavior and mental processes. Yet what is unknown still dwarfs what is known. We can describe the brain. We can learn the functions of its parts. We can study how the parts communicate. We can observe sleeping and waking brains. But how do we get mind out of meat? How does the electrochemical whir in a hunk of tissue the size of a head of lettuce give rise to a feeling of joy, a creative idea, or a crazy dream?

The mind seeking to understand the brain—that is indeed among the ultimate scientific challenges. And so it will always be. To paraphrase scientist John Barrow, a brain simple enough to be understood is too simple to produce a mind able to understand it.

> **REM rebound** the tendency for REM sleep to increase following REM sleep deprivation.

CHAPTER REVIEW

The Biology of Mind and Consciousness

Test yourself by taking a moment to answer each of these Learning Objective Questions (repeated here from within the chapter). Then turn to Appendix D, Complete Chapter Reviews, to check your answers. Research suggests that trying to answer these questions on your own will improve your long-term memory of the concepts (McDaniel et al., 2009).

The Brain: A Work in Progress

2-1: How do biology and experience interact?

Neural Communication

2-2: What are the parts of a neuron, and what is an *action potential?*

2-3: How do neurons communicate?

2-4: How do neurotransmitters affect our mood and behavior?

The Nervous System

2-5: What are the two major divisions of the nervous system, and what are their basic functions?

The Endocrine System

2-6: How does the endocrine system transmit information and interact with the nervous system?

The Brain

2-7: What are some techniques for studying the brain?

2-8: What structures make up the brainstem, and what are the functions of the brainstem, thalamus, reticular formation, and cerebellum?

2-9: What are the structures and functions of the limbic system?

2-10: What are the four lobes of the cerebral cortex, and where are they located?

2-11: What are the functions of the motor cortex, somatosensory cortex, and association areas?

2-12: Do we really use only 10 percent of our brain?

2-13: How does the brain modify itself after some kinds of damage?

2-14: What is a split brain, and what does it reveal about the functions of our two brain hemispheres?

Brain States and Consciousness

2-15: What do we mean by *consciousness,* and how does selective attention direct our perceptions?

2-16: What is the *circadian rhythm,* and what are the stages of our nightly sleep cycle?

2-17: How do our sleep patterns differ? What five theories describe our need to sleep?

2-18: How does sleep loss affect us, and what are the major sleep disorders?

2-19: What do we dream about, and what are five explanations of *why* we dream?

TERMS AND CONCEPTS TO REMEMBER

Test yourself on these terms by trying to write down the definition in your own words before flipping back to the referenced page to check your answer.

plasticity, p. 31
biological psychology, p. 31
cognitive neuroscience, p. 31
neuron, p. 31
dendrites, p. 31
axon, p. 31
action potential, p. 31
glial cells (glia), p. 31
synapse [SIN-aps], p. 31
threshold, p. 33
refractory period, p. 33
all-or-none response, p. 33
neurotransmitters, p. 33
reuptake, p. 33
opiate, p. 33
endorphins [en-DOR-fins], p. 35
nervous system, p. 35
central nervous system (CNS), p. 35
peripheral nervous system (PNS), p. 35
nerves, p. 35

sensory neuron, p. 35
motor neuron, p. 35
interneuron, p. 35
somatic nervous system, p. 35
autonomic [aw-tuh-NAHM-ik] nervous system (ANS), p. 35
sympathetic nervous system, p. 35
parasympathetic nervous system, p. 35
reflex, p. 37
endocrine [EN-duh-krin] system, p. 37
hormones, p. 37
adrenal [ah-DREEN-el] glands, p. 37
pituitary gland, p. 37
EEG (electroencephalograph), p. 39
PET (positron emission tomography) scan, p. 39
MRI (magnetic resonance imaging), p. 39

fMRI (functional MRI), p. 39
brainstem, p. 39
medulla [muh-DUL-uh], p. 39
thalamus [THAL-uh-muss], p. 41
reticular formation, p. 41
cerebellum [sehr-uh-BELL-um], p. 41
limbic system, p. 41
amygdala [uh-MIG-duh-la], p. 41
hypothalamus [hi-po-THAL-uh-muss], p. 43
hippocampus, p. 43
cerebral [seh-REE-bruhl] cortex, p. 43
frontal lobes, p. 43
parietal [puh-RYE-uh-tuhl] lobes, p. 45
occipital [ahk-SIP-uh-tuhl] lobes, p. 45
temporal lobes, p. 45
motor cortex, p. 45
somatosensory cortex, p. 45
hallucination, p. 45
association areas, p. 47
neurogenesis, p. 49

corpus callosum [KOR-pus kah-LOW-sum], p. 49
split brain, p. 49
consciousness, p. 51
sequential processing, p. 51
parallel processing, p. 51
selective attention, p. 51
inattentional blindness, p. 53
change blindness, p. 53
circadian [ser-KAY-dee-an] rhythm, p. 55
REM sleep, p. 55
alpha waves, p. 55
sleep, p. 55
delta waves, p. 55
suprachiasmatic nucleus (SCN), p. 57
insomnia, p. 61
narcolepsy, p. 61
sleep apnea, p. 61
dream, p. 61
manifest content, p. 61
latent content, p. 61
REM rebound, p. 62

CHAPTER TEST

Test yourself repeatedly throughout your studies. This will not only help you figure out what you know and don't know; the testing itself will help you learn and remember the information more effectively thanks to the *testing effect*.

1. The neuron fiber that passes messages through its branches to other neurons or to muscles and glands is the _____.

2. The tiny space between the axon of one neuron and the dendrite or cell body of another is called the
   a. axon terminal.   c. synaptic gap.
   b. branching fiber.   d. threshold.

3. Regarding a neuron's response to stimulation, the intensity of the stimulus determines
   a. whether or not an impulse is generated.
   b. how fast an impulse is transmitted.
   c. how intense an impulse will be.
   d. whether reuptake will occur.

4. In a sending neuron, when an action potential reaches an axon terminal, the impulse triggers the release of chemical messengers called _____.

5. Endorphins are released in the brain in response to
   a. morphine or heroin.
   b. pain or vigorous exercise.
   c. the all-or-none response.
   d. all of the above.

6. The autonomic nervous system
   a. is also referred to as the *skeletal nervous system*.
   b. controls the glands and the muscles of our internal organs.
   c. is a voluntary system under our conscious control.
   d. monitors sensory input and triggers motor output.

7. The sympathetic nervous system arouses us for action and the parasympathetic nervous system calms us down. Together, the two systems make up the _____ nervous system.

8. The neurons of the spinal cord are part of the _____ nervous system.

9. The most influential endocrine gland, known as the "master gland," is the
   a. pituitary.
   b. hypothalamus.
   c. thyroid.
   d. pancreas.

10. The _____ _____ secrete(s) epinephrine and norepinephrine, helping to arouse the body during times of stress.

11. The part of the brainstem that controls heartbeat and breathing is the
    a. cerebellum.
    b. medulla.
    c. cortex.
    d. thalamus.

12. The thalamus functions as a
    a. memory bank.
    b. balance center.
    c. breathing regulator.
    d. sensory control center.

13. The lower brain structure that governs arousal is the
    a. spinal cord.
    b. cerebellum.
    c. reticular formation.
    d. medulla.

14. The part of the brain that coordinates voluntary movement and enables nonverbal learning and memory is the _____.

15. Two parts of the limbic system are the amygdala and the
    a. cerebral hemispheres.
    b. hippocampus.
    c. thalamus.
    d. pituitary.

16. A cat's ferocious response to electrical brain stimulation would lead you to suppose the electrode had touched the _____.

17. The neural structure that most directly regulates eating, drinking, and body temperature is the
    a. endocrine system.
    b. hypothalamus.
    c. hippocampus.
    d. amygdala.

18. The initial reward center discovered by Olds and Milner was located in the _____.

19. If a neurosurgeon stimulated your right motor cortex, you would most likely
    a. see light.
    b. hear a sound.
    c. feel a touch on the right arm.
    d. move your left leg.

20. How do different neural networks communicate with one another to let you respond when a friend greets you at a party?

21. Which of the following body regions has the greatest representation in the somatosensory cortex?
    a. Upper arm
    b. Toes
    c. Lips
    d. All regions are equally represented.

22. The "uncommitted" areas that make up about three-fourths of the cerebral cortex are called _____ _____.

23. Judging and planning are enabled by the _____ lobes.

24. Plasticity is especially evident in the brains of
    a. split-brain patients.
    b. young adults.
    c. young children.
    d. right-handed people.

25. An experimenter flashes the word HERON across the visual field of a man whose corpus callosum has been severed. HER is transmitted to his right hemisphere and ON to his left hemisphere. When asked to indicate what he saw, the man says he saw _____, but his left hand points to _____.

26. Studies of people with split brains and brain scans of those with undivided brains indicate that the left hemisphere excels in
    a. processing language.
    b. visual perceptions.
    c. making inferences.
    d. neurogenesis.

27. Damage to the brain's right hemisphere is most likely to reduce a person's ability to
    a. recite the alphabet rapidly.
    b. make inferences.
    c. understand verbal instructions.
    d. solve arithmetic problems.

28. Failure to see visible objects because our attention is occupied elsewhere is called _____ _____.

29. Inattentional blindness is a product of our _____ attention.

30. Our body temperature tends to rise and fall in sync with a biological clock, which is referred to as our _____ _____.

31. During the NREM-1 sleep stage, a person is most likely to experience

    a. deep sleep.

    b. hallucinations.

    c. night terrors or nightmares.

    d. rapid eye movements.

32. The brain emits large, slow delta waves during _____ sleep.

33. As the night progresses, what happens to the REM stage of sleep?

34. Which of the following is NOT one of the reasons that have been proposed to explain why we need sleep?

    a. Sleep has survival value.

    b. Sleep helps us recuperate.

    c. Sleep rests the eyes.

    d. Sleep plays a role in the growth process.

35. What is the difference between narcolepsy and sleep apnea?

36. In interpreting dreams, Freud was most interested in their

    a. information-processing function.

    b. physiological function.

    c. manifest content, or story line.

    d. latent content, or hidden meaning.

37. Which dream theory best explains why we often dream of daily things we've seen or done?

38. _____ _____ is the tendency for REM sleep to increase following REM sleep deprivation.

Find answers to these questions in Appendix E, in the back of the book.

IN YOUR EVERYDAY LIFE

Answering these questions will help you make these concepts more personally meaningful, and therefore more memorable.

1. Can you think of a time when endorphins may have saved you or a friend from feeling intense pain? What happened?

2. Think back to a time when you felt your autonomic nervous system kick in. What was your body preparing you for?

3. Do you remember feeling the lingering effects of hormones after a really stressful event? How did it feel? How long did it last?

4. In what ways has learning about the physical brain influenced your thoughts about human nature?

5. If most information in the brain is processed outside of our awareness, how can we ever really know ourselves?

6. What important experiences have influenced your brain development? How do you imagine that your genes and your environment have interacted to make you different from other people?

7. Why do you think our brain evolved into so many interconnected structures with varying functions?

8. Can you think of a time when you focused your attention so completely on one thing that you did not notice something else? What happened?

9. Do you ever text, watch TV, or talk on the phone while studying? What impact do you think this multitasking has on your learning?

10. What have you learned about sleep that you could apply to yourself?

11. Which explanation for why we dream makes the most sense to you? How well does it explain your own dreams?

Use ⌂ LearningCurve to create your personalized study plan, which will direct you to the resources that will help you most in ⌂ LaunchPad.

SURVEY THE CHAPTER

Developing Through the Life Span

3

Life is a journey, from womb to tomb. So it is for me [DM], and so it will be for you. My story, and yours, began when a man and a woman together contributed 20,000+ genes to an egg that became a unique person. Those genes contained the codes for the building blocks that, with astonishing precision, formed our bodies and predisposed our traits. My grandmother gave to my mother a rare hearing-loss pattern, which she, in turn, passed on to me (the least of her gifts). My father was a good-natured extravert, and sometimes I forget to stop talking. As a child, my talking was slowed by painful stuttering, for which Seattle Public Schools provided speech therapy.

Along with my parents' nature, I also received their nurture. Like you, I was born into a particular culture, with its own way of viewing the world. My values have been shaped by a family culture filled with talking and laughter, by a religious culture that speaks of love and justice, and by an academic culture that encourages critical thinking (asking, *What do you mean? How do you know?*).

We are formed by our genes, and by our contexts, so our stories will differ. But in many ways we are each like nearly everyone else on Earth. Being human, you and I have a need to belong. My mental video library, which began after age 4, is filled with scenes of social attachment. Over time, my attachments to parents loosened as peer friendships grew. After lacking confidence to date in high school, I fell in love with a college classmate and married at age 20. Natural selection disposes us to survive and pass on our genes. Sure enough, two years later a child entered our lives, and I experienced a new form of love that surprised me with its intensity.

But life is marked by change. That child now lives 2000 miles away, and one of his two siblings calls South Africa her home. The tight rubber bands linking parent and child have loosened, as yours likely have as well.

Change also marks most vocational lives. I spent my teen years working in the family insurance agency, then became a premed chemistry major and a hospital aide. After discarding my half-completed medical school applications, I found my calling as a psychology professor and author. I predict that in 10 years you, too, will be doing things not in your current plan.

Stability also marks our development. When I look in the mirror I do not see the person I once was, but I feel like the person I have always been. I am the same person who, as a late teen, played basketball and discovered love. A half-century later, I still play basketball. And I still love—with less passion but more security—the life partner with whom I have shared life's griefs and joys.

We experience a continuous self, but that self morphs through stages—typically growing up, raising children, enjoying a career, and, eventually, life's final stage, which will demand my presence. As I make my way through this cycle of life to death, I am mindful that life's journey is a continuing process of development. That process is seeded by nature and shaped by nurture, animated by love and focused by work, begun with wide-eyed curiosity and completed, for those blessed to live to a good old age, with peace and never-ending hope.

Across the life span, we grow from newborn to toddler to teen to mature adult. At each stage of life there are physical, cognitive, and social milestones. Let's begin by exploring three key themes in developmental psychology.

Developmental Psychology's Major Issues

LOQ **L**earning**O**bjective**Q**uestion

3-1 What are the three major issues studied by developmental psychologists?

Why do researchers find human development interesting? Like most of the rest of us, they want to understand more about how we've become our current selves, and how we may change in the years ahead. **Developmental psychology** examines our physical, cognitive, and social development across the life span, with a focus on three major issues:

1. *Nature and nurture:* How does our genetic inheritance (our *nature*) interact with our experiences (our *nurture*) to influence our development?

2. *Continuity and stages:* What parts of development are gradual and continuous, like riding an escalator? What parts change abruptly in separate stages, like climbing rungs on a ladder?

3. *Stability and change:* Which of our traits persist through life? How do we change as we age?

Nature and Nurture

The unique gene combination created when our mother's egg absorbed our father's sperm helped form us as individuals. Genes predispose both our shared humanity and our individual differences.

But it also is true that our experiences form us. Our families and peer relationships teach us how to think and act. Even differences initiated by our nature may be amplified by our nurture. We are not formed by either nature or nurture, but by the interaction between them. Biological, psychological, and social-cultural forces interact.

Mindful of how others differ from us, however, we often fail to notice the similarities stemming from our shared biology. Regardless of our culture, we humans share the same life cycle. We speak to our infants in similar ways and respond similarly to their coos and cries (Bornstein et al., 1992a,b). All over the world, the children of warm and supportive parents feel better about themselves and are less hostile than are the children of punishing and rejecting parents (Farruggia et al., 2004; Rohner, 1986; Scott et al., 1991). Although ethnic groups have differed in some ways, including average school achievement, the differences are "no more than skin deep" (Rowe et al., 1994). To the extent that family structure, peer influences, and parental education predict behavior in one of these ethnic groups, they do so for the others as well. Compared with the person-to-person differences within groups, the differences between groups are small. We share a human nature.

Continuity and Stages

Do adults differ from infants as a giant redwood differs from its seedling—differences mostly created by constant, gradual growth? Or do we change in some ways as a caterpillar differs from a butterfly—in distinct stages?

Researchers who focus on experience and learning typically view development as a slow, ongoing process. Those who emphasize the influence of our biology tend to see development as a process of maturation, as we pass through a series of stages or steps, guided by instructions programmed into our genes. Progress through the various stages may be quick or slow, but we all pass through the stages in the same order.

Are there clear-cut stages of psychological development, as there are physical stages such as walking before running? The stage theories we will consider—of Jean Piaget on cognitive development, Lawrence Kohlberg on moral development, and Erik Erikson on psychosocial development—propose developmental phases (summarized in **FIGURE 3.1**). But we will also see that some research casts doubt on the idea that life passes through neatly defined age-linked stages.

Although many modern developmental psychologists do not identify as stage theorists, the stage concept remains useful. The human brain does experience growth spurts during childhood and puberty that correspond roughly to Piaget's stages (Thatcher et al., 1987). And stage theories help us focus our attention on the forces and interests that affect us at different points in the life span. This close attention can help us understand how people of one age think and act differently when they arrive at a later age.

TOO MUCH COFFEE MAN BY SHANNON WHEELER

Stages of the life cycle

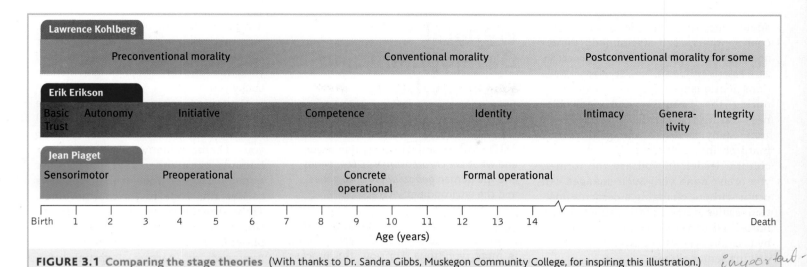

Lawrence Kohlberg		
Preconventional morality	Conventional morality	Postconventional morality for some

Erik Erikson							
Basic Trust	Autonomy	Initiative	Competence	Identity	Intimacy	Genera-tivity	Integrity

Jean Piaget			
Sensorimotor	Preoperational	Concrete operational	Formal operational

Birth 1 2 3 4 5 6 7 8 9 10 11 12 13 14 Death

Age (years)

FIGURE 3.1 Comparing the stage theories (With thanks to Dr. Sandra Gibbs, Muskegon Community College, for inspiring this illustration.) *important*

Stability and Change

As we follow lives through time, do we find more evidence for stability or change? If reunited with a long-lost grade-school friend, do we instantly realize that "it's the same old Andy"? Or do people we once befriended later seem like total strangers? (At least one man I [DM] know would choose the second option. He failed to recognize a former classmate at his 40-year college reunion. That upset classmate was his long-ago first wife!)

Developmental psychologists' research shows that we experience both stability and change. People predict that they will not change much in the future (Quoidbach et al., 2013). In some ways, they are correct. Some of our characteristics, such as *temperament* (emotional excitability), are very stable. When a research team studied 1000 people from age 3 to 32, they were struck by the consistency of temperament and emotionality across time (Slutske et al., 2012). Out-of-control 3-year-olds were the most likely, at age 32, to be out-of-control gamblers. Other research showed that the widest smilers in childhood and college photos were, years later, the adults most likely to enjoy enduring marriages (Hertenstein et al., 2009). And conscientious 12-year-olds tend to be, 40 years later, more occupationally successful (Spengler et al., 2015).

SMILES PREDICT MARITAL STABILITY In one study of 306 college graduates, 1 in 4 with yearbook expressions like the one on the left later divorced. Only 1 in 20 with smiles like the one on the right divorced (Hertenstein et al., 2009).

We cannot, however, predict all of our eventual traits based on our early years (Kagan, 1998; Kagan et al., 1978). Some traits, such as social attitudes, are much less stable than temperament, especially during the impressionable late adolescent years (Krosnick & Alwin, 1989; Rekker et al., 2015). And older children and adolescents can learn new ways of coping. It is true that delinquent children later have higher rates of work problems, substance abuse, and crime, but many confused and troubled children blossom into mature, successful adults (Moffitt et al., 2002; Roberts et al., 2001; Thomas & Chess, 1986). Happily for them, life is a process of becoming.

In some ways, we *all* change with age. Most shy, fearful toddlers begin opening up by age 4. In the years after

As adults grow older, there is continuity of self.

> **developmental psychology** a branch of psychology that studies physical, cognitive, and social change throughout the life span.

adolescence, most people become more conscientious, self-disciplined, agreeable, and self-confident (Lucas & Donnellan, 2011; Roberts et al., 2003, 2006; Shaw et al., 2010). Conscientiousness increases especially during the twenties, and agreeableness during the thirties (Srivastava et al., 2003). Many a 20-year-old goof-off has matured into a 40-year-old business or cultural leader. (If you are the former, you aren't done yet.) Such changes can occur without changing a person's position *relative to others* of the same age. The hard-driving young adult may mellow by later life, yet still be a relatively hard-driving senior citizen.

Life requires *both* stability and change. Stability increasingly marks our personality as we age (Briley & Tucker-Drob, 2014). ("As at 7, so at 70," says a Jewish proverb.) And stability gives us our identity. It lets us depend on others and be concerned about the healthy development of the children in our lives. Our trust in our ability to change gives us hope for a brighter future and lets us adapt and grow with experience.

Retrieve + Remember

- Developmental researchers who consider how biological, psychological, and social-cultural forces interact are focusing on _____ and _____.

  ANSWERS: nature; nurture

- Developmental researchers who emphasize learning and experience are supporting _____; those who emphasize biological maturation are supporting _____.

  ANSWERS: continuity; stages

- What findings in psychology support (1) the stage theory of development and (2) the idea of stability in personality across the life span?

  ANSWER: (1) Stage theory is supported by the work of Piaget (cognitive development), Kohlberg (moral development), and Erikson (psychosocial development). (2) Some traits, such as temperament, do exhibit remarkable stability across many years. But we do change in other ways, such as in our social attitudes.

Prenatal Development and the Newborn

Conception

LOQ 3-2 How does conception occur, and what are *chromosomes, DNA, genes,* and the human *genome*? How do genes and the environment interact?

Nothing is more natural than a species reproducing itself, yet nothing is more wondrous. For you, the process began when your mother's ovary released a mature egg—a cell roughly the size of the period at the end of this sentence. The 250 million or more sperm deposited by your father then began their race upstream. Like space voyagers approaching a huge planet, the sperm approached a cell 85,000 times their own size. Only a small number reached the egg. Those that did released enzymes that ate away the egg's protective coating (**FIGURE 3.2**a). As soon as one sperm broke through that coating (Figure 3.2b), the egg's surface blocked out the others. Before half a day passed, the egg nucleus and the sperm nucleus fused. The two became one. Consider it your most fortunate of moments. Among 250 million sperm, the one needed to make you, in combination with that one particular egg, won the race, and so also for each of your ancestors through all human history. Lucky you.

Contained within the new single cell is a master code. This code will interact with your experience, creating you—a being in many ways like all other humans, but in other ways like no other human. Each of your trillions of cells carries this code in its **chromosomes.** These threadlike structures contain the **DNA** we hear so much about. **Genes** are pieces of DNA, and they can be active *(expressed)* or inactive. External influences can "turn on" genes much as a cup of hot water lets a teabag express its flavor. When turned on, your genes will provide the code for creating protein molecules, your body's building blocks. **FIGURE 3.3** summarizes the elements that make up your **heredity.**

Genetically speaking, every other human is close to being your identical twin. It is our shared genetic profile—our human **genome**—that makes us humans, rather than chimpanzees, bananas, or tulips. "Your DNA and mine are 99.9 percent the same," noted former Human Genome Project director Francis Collins (2007). "At the DNA level, we are clearly all part of one big worldwide family."

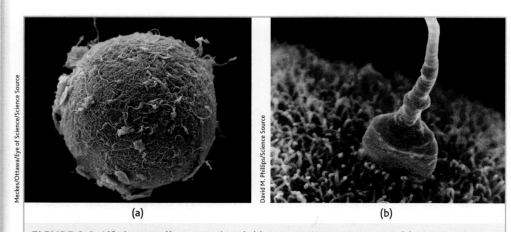

FIGURE 3.2 Life is sexually transmitted (a) Sperm cells surround an egg. (b) As one sperm penetrates the egg's jellylike outer coating, a series of events begins that will cause sperm and egg to fuse into a single cell. If all goes well, that cell will subdivide again and again to emerge 9 months later as a 100-trillion-cell human being.

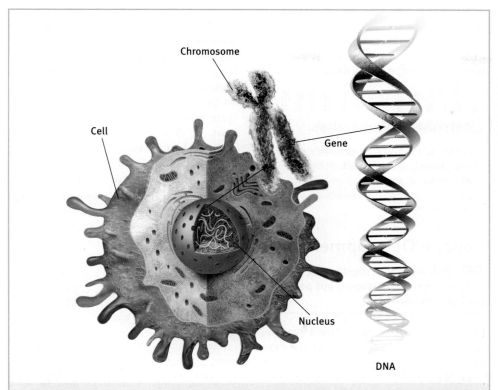

THE NURTURE OF NATURE Parents everywhere wonder: Will my baby grow up to be peaceful or aggressive? Homely or attractive? Successful or struggling at every step? What comes built in, and what is nurtured—and how? Research reveals that nature and nurture together shape our development—every step of the way.

FIGURE 3.3 The genes: Their location and composition Contained in the nucleus of each cell in your body are chromosomes. Each chromosome contains a coiled chain of the molecule DNA. Genes are DNA segments that, when expressed (turned on), direct the production of proteins and influence our individual biological development.

"We share half our genes with the banana."
Evolutionary biologist Robert May, president of Britain's Royal Society, 2001

The slight person-to-person variations found at particular gene sites in the DNA give clues to our uniqueness. They help explain why one person has a disease that another does not, why one person is tall and another short, why one is anxious and another calm. Most

of our traits are influenced by many genes. How tall you are, for example, reflects the height of your face, the length of your leg bones, and so forth. Each of those is influenced by different genes. Traits such as intelligence, happiness, and aggressiveness are similarly influenced by a whole orchestra of genes (Holden, 2008).

Our human differences are also shaped by our **environment**—by every external influence, from maternal nutrition while in the womb, to social support while nearing the tomb. Your height, for example, may be influenced by your diet.

How do heredity and environment **interact?** Let's imagine two babies with two different sets of genes. Malia is a beautiful child and is also sociable and easygoing. Kalie is plain, shy, and cries constantly. Malia's pretty, smiling face attracts more affectionate and stimulating care. This in turn helps her develop

into an even warmer and more outgoing person. Kalie's fussiness often leaves her caregivers tired and stressed. As the two children grow older, Malia, the more naturally outgoing child, often seeks activities and friends that increase her social confidence. Shy Kalie has few friends and becomes even more withdrawn. *Our genetically influenced traits affect how others respond.* And vice versa, *our environments trigger gene activity.* Nature and nurture interact.

"Thanks for almost everything, Dad."

chromosomes threadlike structures made of DNA molecules that contain the genes.

DNA (deoxyribonucleic acid) a molecule containing the genetic information that makes up the chromosomes.

genes the biochemical units of heredity that make up the chromosomes; segments of DNA.

heredity the genetic transfer of characteristics from parents to offspring.

genome the complete instructions for making an organism, consisting of all the genetic material in that organism's chromosomes.

environment every external influence, from prenatal nutrition to social support in later life.

interaction the interplay that occurs when the effect of one factor (such as environment) depends on another factor (such as heredity).

The field of **epigenetics** explores the nature–nurture meeting place. *Epigenetics* means "in addition to" or "above and beyond" genetics. This field studies how the environment can cause genes to become either active (expressed) or inactive (not expressed). Genes can influence development, but the environment can switch genes on or off.

The molecules that trigger or block genetic expression are called *epigenetic marks*. When one of these molecules attaches to part of a DNA segment, it instructs the cell to ignore any gene present in that DNA stretch (**FIGURE 3.4**).

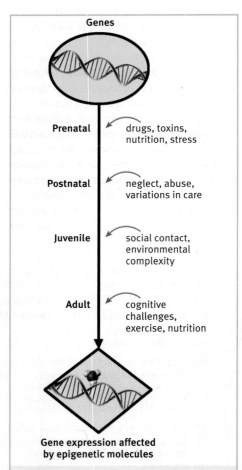

Genes

Prenatal — drugs, toxins, nutrition, stress

Postnatal — neglect, abuse, variations in care

Juvenile — social contact, environmental complexity

Adult — cognitive challenges, exercise, nutrition

Gene expression affected by epigenetic molecules

FIGURE 3.4 How environment influences gene expression Beginning in the womb, life experiences lay down *epigenetic marks*, which are often organic molecules. These molecules can block the expression of any gene in the DNA segment they affect. (Research from Champagne, 2010.)

Diet, drugs, stress, and other experiences can affect these epigenetic molecules. Thus, from conception onward, heredity and experience dance together.

Retrieve + Remember

- Put the following cell structures in order from largest to smallest: DNA, chromosome, gene.

ANSWER: chromosome, DNA, gene

Prenatal Development

LOQ 3-3 How does life develop before birth, and how do *teratogens* put prenatal development at risk?

How many fertilized eggs, called **zygotes**, survive beyond the first 2 weeks? Fewer than half (Grobstein, 1979; Hall, 2004). For the survivors, one cell becomes two, then four—each just like the first—until this cell division has produced some 100 identical cells within the first week. Then the cells begin to specialize. ("I'll become a brain, you become intestines!")

About 10 days after conception, the zygote attaches to the wall of the mother's uterus. So begins about 37 weeks of the closest human relationship. The tiny clump of cells forms two parts.

The inner cells become the **embryo** (**FIGURE 3.5**). Many of the outer cells become the *placenta*, the life-link transferring nutrition and oxygen between embryo and mother. Over the next 6 weeks, the embryo's organs begin to form and function. The heart begins to beat. By 9 weeks after conception, an embryo looks unmistakably human. It is now a **fetus** (Latin for "offspring" or "young one"). During the sixth month, organs will develop enough to give the fetus a good chance to survive and thrive if born prematurely.

Prenatal development

Zygote: Conception to 2 weeks
Embryo: 2 weeks through 8 weeks
Fetus: 9 weeks to birth

Remember: *Heredity and environment interact.* This is true even in the prenatal period. The placenta not only transfers nutrients and oxygen from mother to fetus, it also screens out many harmful substances. But some slip by. **Teratogens**, agents such as viruses and drugs, can damage an embryo or fetus. This is one reason pregnant women are advised not to drink alcoholic beverages or smoke cigarettes. A pregnant woman never drinks or smokes alone. When alcohol enters her bloodstream and that

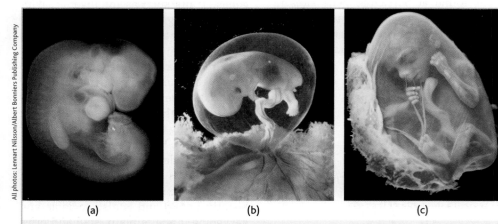

All photos: Lennart Nilsson/Albert Bonniers Publishing Company

(a)   (b)   (c)

FIGURE 3.5 Prenatal development (a) The embryo grows and develops rapidly. At 40 days, the spine is visible and the arms and legs are beginning to grow. (b) By the start of the ninth week, when the fetal period begins, facial features, hands, and feet have formed. (c) As the fetus enters the sixteenth week, its 3 ounces could fit in the palm of your hand.

of her fetus, it reduces activity in both their central nervous systems.

Even light drinking or occasional binge drinking can affect the fetal brain (Braun, 1996; Ikonomidou et al., 2000; Marjonen et al., 2015; Sayal et al., 2009). Persistent heavy drinking puts the fetus at risk for birth defects and for future behavior and intelligence problems. For 1 in about 700 children, the effects are visible as **fetal alcohol syndrome (FAS),** the most serious of all fetal alcohol spectrum disorders, marked by lifelong physical and mental abnormalities (May et al., 2014). The fetal damage may occur because alcohol has an epigenetic effect. It leaves chemical marks on DNA that switch genes to abnormal on or off states (Liu et al., 2009). Smoking during pregnancy also leaves epigenetic scars that weaken infants' ability to handle stress (Stroud et al., 2014). Some stress in early life prepares us to cope with later adversity. But substantial prenatal stress puts a child at increased risk for later health problems.

PREPARED TO FEED AND EAT Animals, including humans, are predisposed to respond to their offsprings' cries for nourishment.

basis of reflexes.) New parents are often in awe of the finely tuned set of reflexes by which their baby gets food. When something touches their cheek, babies turn toward that touch, open their mouth, and actively *root* for a nipple. Finding one, they quickly close on it and begin *sucking*. (Failing to find satisfaction, the hungry baby may cry—a behavior parents find highly unpleasant, and very rewarding to relieve.) Other reflexes that helped our ancestors survive include the *startle* reflex (when arms and legs spring out, quickly followed by fist clenching and loud crying) and the surprisingly strong *grasping* reflex, both of which may have helped infants stay close to their mothers.

Even as newborns, we search out sights and sounds linked with other humans. We turn our heads in the direction of human voices. We prefer to look at objects 8 to 12 inches away. Wonder of wonders, that just happens to be about the distance between a mother's eyes and those of her nursing infant (Maurer & Maurer, 1988). We gaze longer at a drawing of a face-like image (**FIGURE 3.6**).

We seem especially tuned in to that human who is our mother. Can newborns distinguish their own mother's smell in a sea of others? Indeed they can. Within days after birth, our brain has picked up and stored the smell of our mother's body (MacFarlane, 1978). What's more, that smell preference lasts. One experiment was able to show this, thanks to some French nursing mothers who had used a chamomile-scented balm to prevent nipple soreness

(Delaunay-El Allam et al., 2010). Twenty-one months later, their toddlers preferred playing with chamomile-scented toys! Other toddlers who had not sniffed the scent while breast feeding did not show this preference. (Hmm. Will adults, who as babies associated chamomile scent with their mother's breast, become devoted chamomile tea drinkers?)

So, very young infants are competent. They smell and hear well. They see what they need to see. They are already using their sensory equipment to learn. Guided by biology and experience, those sensory and perceptual abilities will continue to develop steadily over the next months.

Retrieve + Remember

- The first two weeks of prenatal development is the period of the _____. The period of the _____ lasts from 9 weeks after conception until birth. The time between those two prenatal periods is considered the period of the _____.

ANSWERS: zygote; fetus; embryo

LaunchPad For an interactive review of prenatal development, see LaunchPad's *PsychSim 6: Conception to Birth.* LaunchPad also offers the 8-minute *Video: Prenatal Development.*

The Competent Newborn

LOQ 3-4 What are some of the newborn's abilities and traits?

Having survived prenatal hazards, we arrive as newborns with automatic **reflex** responses ideally suited for our survival. (Recall Chapter 2's discussion of the neural

epigenetics the study of environmental influences on gene expression that occur without a DNA change.

zygote the fertilized egg; it enters a 2-week period of rapid cell division and develops into an embryo.

embryo the developing human organism from about 2 weeks after fertilization through the second month.

fetus the developing human organism from 9 weeks after conception to birth.

teratogen [tuh-RAT-uh-jen] an agent, such as a chemical or virus, that can reach the embryo or fetus during prenatal development and cause harm.

fetal alcohol syndrome (FAS) physical and mental abnormalities in children caused by a pregnant woman's heavy drinking. In severe cases, signs include a small, out-of-proportion head and abnormal facial features.

reflex a simple, automatic response to a sensory stimulus.

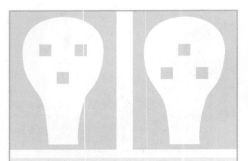

FIGURE 3.6 Newborns' preference for faces When shown these two images with the same three elements, newborns spent nearly twice as many seconds looking at the face-like image on the left (Johnson & Morton, 1991). Newborns—average age 53 minutes in one study—seem to have an inborn preference for looking toward faces (Mondloch et al., 1999).

Yet, as most parents will tell you after having their second child, babies differ. One clear difference is in **temperament**—whether intense and fidgety, or easygoing and quiet. From the first weeks of life, some babies are irritable, intense, and unpredictable. Others are cheerful and relaxed, with predictable feeding and sleeping schedules (Chess & Thomas, 1987). Temperament is genetically influenced (Picardi et al., 2011; Raby et al., 2012). This effect appears in physical differences: Anxious, inhibited infants have high and variable heart rates. They become very aroused when facing new or strange situations (Kagan & Snidman, 2004; Roque et al., 2012).

Our biologically rooted temperament also helps form our enduring personality (McCrae et al., 2000, 2007; Rothbart, 2007). This effect can be seen in identical twins, who have more similar personalities—including temperament—than do fraternal twins.

Twin and Adoption Studies

LOQ 3-5 How do twin and adoption studies help us understand the effects of nature and nurture?

For about 1 in 270 sets of parents, pregnancy news brings a bonus. Detection of two heartbeats reveals that the zygote,

during its early days of development, has split into two (**FIGURE 3.7**). If all goes well, some 32 weeks later two genetically identical babies will emerge from their underwater world.

Identical (*monozygotic*) **twins** are nature's own human clones. They develop from a single fertilized egg, and they share the same genes. They also share the same uterus, and usually the same birth date and cultural history. **Fraternal** (*dizygotic*) **twins** develop from two separate fertilized eggs. As womb-mates, they share the same prenatal environment but not the same genes. Genetically, they are no more similar than nontwin brothers and sisters.

How might researchers use twins to study the influences of nature and nurture? To do so, they would need to

- vary the home environment while controlling heredity.
- vary heredity while controlling the home environment.

Happily for our purposes, nature has done this work for us.

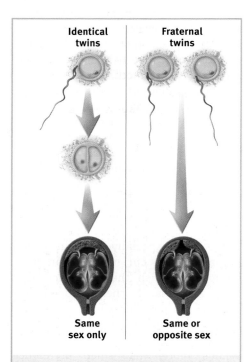

FIGURE 3.7 Same fertilized egg, same genes; different eggs, different genes Identical twins develop from a single fertilized egg, fraternal twins from two different eggs.

LaunchPad See LaunchPad's *Video: Twin Studies* for a helpful tutorial animation.

Identical Versus Fraternal Twins

Identical twins have identical genes. Do these shared genes mean that identical twins also *behave* more similarly than fraternal twins (Bouchard, 2004)? Studies of over 14.5 million twin pairs worldwide provide a consistent answer. Identical twins are more similar than fraternal twins in their abilities, personal traits, and interests (Polderman et al., 2015).

Next question: Could shared experiences rather than shared genes explain these similarities? Again, twin studies give some answers.

Separated Twins

On a chilly February morning in 1979, some time after divorcing his first wife, Linda, Jim Lewis awoke next to his second wife, Betty. Determined to make this marriage work, Jim left love notes to Betty around the house. As he lay there he thought about his son, James Alan, and his faithful dog, Toy.

Jim loved his basement woodworking shop where he built furniture, including a white bench circling a tree. Jim also liked to drive his Chevy, watch stock-car racing, and drink Miller Lite beer. Except for an occasional migraine, Jim was healthy. His blood pressure was a little high, perhaps related to his chain-smoking. He had gained weight but had shed some of the extra pounds. After a vasectomy, he was done having children.

What was extraordinary about Jim Lewis, however, was that at that moment (we are not making this up) there was another man named Jim for whom all these things were also true.[1] This other Jim—Jim Springer—just happened, 38 years earlier, to have been Jim Lewis' womb-mate. Thirty-seven days after

---

1. Actually, this description of the two Jims errs in one respect: Jim Lewis named his son James Alan. Jim Springer named his James Allan.

Image labels in Figure 3.7: Identical twins / Fraternal twins / Same sex only / Same or opposite sex

their birth, these genetically identical twins were separated and adopted by two blue-collar families. They grew up with no contact until the day Jim Lewis received a call from his genetic clone (who, having been told he had a twin, set out to find him).

One month later, the brothers became the first of 137 separated twin pairs tested by psychologist Thomas Bouchard and his colleagues (Miller, 2012b). Given tests measuring their personality, intelligence, heart rate, and brain waves, the Jim twins were virtually as alike as the same person tested twice. Their voice patterns were so similar that, hearing a playback of an earlier interview, Jim Springer guessed "That's me." Wrong—it was Jim Lewis.

This and other research on separated identical twins supports the idea that genes matter.

Twin similarities do not impress Bouchard's critics, however. If you spent hours with a complete stranger

Beth Eberth, St. Bonaventure University, St. Bonaventure, N.Y.

TRUE BROTHERS The identical friars Julian and Adrian Reister—two "quiet, gentle souls"—both died of heart failure, at age 92, on the same day in 2011.

comparing your individual behaviors and life histories, wouldn't you also discover many coincidental similarities? Moreover, critics note, identical twins share an appearance and the responses it evokes, so they have probably had similar experiences. Bouchard replies that the life choices made by separated fraternal twins are not as dramatically similar as those made by separated identical twins.

Biological Versus Adoptive Relatives

The separated-twin studies control heredity while varying environment. Nature's second type of real-life experiment—adoption—controls environment while varying heredity. Adoption creates two groups: genetic relatives (biological parents and siblings) and environmental relatives (adoptive parents and siblings). For any given trait we study, we can therefore ask three questions:

- How much do adopted children resemble their biological parents, who contributed their genes?

- How much do they resemble their adoptive parents, who contribute a home environment?

- While sharing a home environment, do adopted siblings also come to share traits?

By providing children with loving, nurturing homes, adoption matters. Yet researchers asking these questions about *personality* agree on one stunning finding, based on studies of hundreds of adoptive families. *Nontwin siblings who grow up together, whether biologically related or not, do not much resemble one another in personality* (McGue & Bouchard, 1998; Plomin et al., 1988; Rowe, 1990). In traits such as outgoingness and agreeableness, people who have been adopted are more similar to their biological parents than to their caregiving adoptive parents.

As we discuss throughout this book, twin and adoption study results shed light on how nature and nurture interact to influence intelligence, disordered behavior, and many other traits.

Infancy and Childhood

As a flower develops in accord with its genetic instructions, so do we humans. **Maturation**—the orderly sequence of biological growth—dictates much of our shared path. We stand before we walk. We use nouns before adjectives. Severe deprivation or abuse can slow development, yet genetic growth patterns are inborn. Maturation (nature) sets the basic course of development; experience (nurture) adjusts it. Genes and scenes interact.

Physical Development

LOQ 3-6 During infancy and childhood, how do the brain and motor skills develop?

Brain Development

In your mother's womb, your developing brain formed nerve cells at the explosive rate of nearly one-quarter million

temperament a person's characteristic emotional reactivity and intensity.

identical (monozygotic) twins twins who develop from a single fertilized egg that splits in two, creating two genetically identical siblings.

fraternal (dizygotic) twins twins who develop from separate fertilized eggs. They are genetically no closer than nontwin brothers and sisters, but they share a prenatal environment.

maturation biological growth processes leading to orderly changes in behavior, mostly independent of experience.

per minute. Your brain and your mental abilities developed together. On the day you were born, you had most of the brain cells you would ever have. However, the wiring among these cells—your nervous system—was immature. After birth, these neural networks had a wild growth spurt, branching and linking in patterns that would eventually enable you to walk, talk, and remember. This rapid development helps explain why infant brain size increases rapidly in the early days after birth (Holland et al., 2014).

From ages 3 to 6, the most rapid brain growth was in your frontal lobes, the seat of reasoning and planning. During those years, your ability to control your attention and behavior developed rapidly (Garon et al., 2008; Thompson-Schill et al., 2009). Last to develop were your association areas—those linked with thinking, memory, and language. As they developed, your mental abilities surged (Chugani & Phelps, 1986; Thatcher et al., 1987). The neural pathways supporting language and agility continued their rapid growth into puberty. Then, a use-it-or-lose-it *pruning process* began to shut down unused links and strengthen others (Paus et al., 1999; Thompson et al., 2000).

> "It is a rare privilege to watch the birth, growth, and first feeble struggles of a living human mind."
>
> Annie Sullivan, in Helen Keller's *The Story of My Life*, 1903

Your genes laid down the basic design of your brain, rather like the lines of a

THE BABY EXPERIMENT Researchers deploy every technology they can to understand infant brains, and what happens when development goes awry.

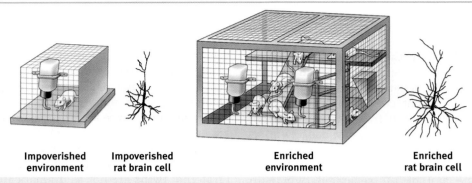

Impoverished environment   Impoverished rat brain cell   Enriched environment   Enriched rat brain cell

FIGURE 3.8 **Experience affects brain development** In this experiment, some rats lived alone in an environment without playthings. Others lived together in an environment enriched with playthings that changed daily. In 14 of 16 repetitions of the experiment, rats in the enriched setting developed more cerebral cortex (relative to the rest of the brain's tissue) than was found in those raised in the impoverished environment (Renner & Rosenzweig, 1987; Rosenzweig, 1984).

coloring book. Experience fills in the details (Kenrick et al., 2009). So how do early experiences shape the brain? Some fascinating experiments separated young rats into two groups (Renner & Rosenzweig, 1987; Rosenzweig, 1984). Rats in one group lived alone, with little to interest or distract them. The other rats shared a cage, complete with objects and activities that might exist in a natural "rat world" (**FIGURE 3.8**). Compared with the "loner" rats, those that lived in an enriched environment developed a heavier and thicker brain cortex.

The environment's effect was so great that if you viewed brief video clips, you could tell from the rats' activity and curiosity whether they had lived in solitary confinement or in the enriched setting (Renner & Renner, 1993). After 60 days in the enriched environment, some rats' brain weight increased 7 to 10 percent. The number of synapses, forming the networks between the cells (see Figure 3.8), mushroomed by about 20 percent (Kolb & Whishaw, 1998). The enriched environment literally increased brain power.

Touching or massaging infant rats and premature human babies has similar benefits (Field, 2010; Sarro et al., 2014). In hospital intensive care units, medical staff now massage premature infants to help them develop faster neurologically, gain weight more rapidly, and go home sooner. Preemies who have had skin-to-skin contact with their mothers sleep better, experience less stress, and show better cognitive development 10 years later (Feldman et al., 2014).

Nature and nurture interact to sculpt our synapses. Brain maturation provides us with a wealth of neural connections. Experience—sights and smells, touches and tastes, music and movement—activates and strengthens some neural pathways while others weaken from disuse. Similar to paths through a forest, less-traveled neural pathways gradually disappear and popular ones are broadened (Gopnik et al., 2015).

During early childhood—while excess connections are still available—youngsters can most easily master another language. We seem to have a **critical period** for some skills. Lacking any exposure to spoken, written, or signed language before adolescence, a person will never master any language (see Chapter 8). Likewise, lacking visual experience during the early years, a person whose vision is restored by cataract removal will never achieve normal perceptions (Gregory, 1978; Wiesel, 1982) (more on this in Chapter 5). Without that early visual stimulation, the brain cells normally assigned to vision will die during the pruning process or be used for other purposes. For normal brain development, early stimulation is critical. The maturing brain's rule: Use it or lose it.

The brain's development does not, however, end with childhood. Throughout life, whether we are learning to text friends or write textbooks, we perform with increasing skill as our learning changes our brain tissue (Ambrose, 2010).

Motor Development

Babies gain control over their movements as their nervous system and muscles mature. Motor skills emerge, and with occasional exceptions, their sequence is universal. Babies roll over before they sit unsupported. They usually crawl before they walk. The recommended infant *back-to-sleep position* (putting babies to sleep on their backs to reduce the risk of a smothering crib death) has been associated with somewhat later crawling but not with later walking (Davis et al., 1998; Lipsitt, 2003).

There are, however, individual differences in timing. Consider walking. In the United States, 90 percent of all babies walk by age 15 months. But 25 percent walk by 11 months, and 50 percent within a week after their first birthday (Frankenburg et al., 1992). In some regions of Africa, the Caribbean, and India, caregivers often massage and exercise babies. This can speed up the process of learning to walk (Karasik et al., 2010).

Genes guide motor development. Identical twins typically begin walking on nearly the same day (Wilson, 1979). The rapid development of the cerebellum (at the back of the brain; see Chapter 2) helps create our eagerness to walk at about age 1. Maturation is likewise important for mastering other physical skills, including bowel and bladder control. Before a child's muscles and nerves mature, no amount of pleading or punishment will produce successful toilet training.

PHYSICAL DEVELOPMENT Sit, crawl, walk, run—the sequence of these motor development milestones is the same the world around, though babies reach them at varying ages.

> ### Retrieve + Remember
>
> - The biological growth process, called _____, explains why most children begin walking by about 12 to 15 months.
>
>   ANSWER: maturation

Brain Maturation and Infant Memory

Can you recall your third birthday party? Most people cannot. Psychologists call this blank space in our conscious memory *infantile amnesia*. Although we *consciously* recall little from before age 4, our brain was processing and storing information during that time. How do we know that? To see how developmental psychologists study thinking and learning in very young children, consider a surprise discovery.

In 1965, Carolyn Rovee-Collier was finishing her doctoral work in psychology. She was a new mom, whose colicky 2-month-old, Benjamin, could be calmed by moving a mobile hung above his crib. Weary of hitting the mobile, she strung a cloth ribbon connecting the mobile to Benjamin's foot. Soon, he was kicking his foot to move the mobile.

Thinking about her unintended home experiment, Rovee-Collier realized that, contrary to popular opinion in the 1960s, babies can learn. To know for sure that little Benjamin wasn't just a whiz kid, Rovee-Collier repeated the experiment with other infants (Rovee-Collier, 1989, 1999). Sure enough, they, too, soon kicked more when hitched to a mobile, both on the day of the experiment and the day after. They had learned the link between a moving leg and a moving mobile. If, however, she hitched them to a different mobile the next day, the infants showed no learning. Their actions indicated that they remembered the original mobile and recognized the difference. Moreover, when tethered to the familiar mobile a month later, they remembered the association and again began kicking.

Traces of forgotten childhood languages may also persist. One study

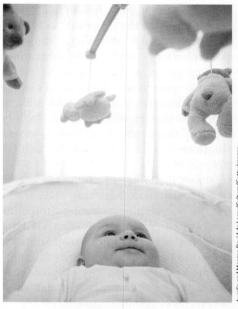

INFANT AT WORK Babies only 3 months old can learn that kicking moves a mobile, and they can retain that learning for a month (Rovee-Collier, 1989, 1997).

tested English-speaking British adults who had spoken Hindi (an Indian language) or Zulu (an African language) in their childhood. Although they had no conscious memory of those languages, they could, up to age 40, relearn subtle Hindi or Zulu sound contrasts that other English speakers could *not* learn (Bowers et al., 2009). What the conscious mind does not know and cannot express in words, the nervous system and our two-track mind somehow remembers.

Cognitive Development

LOQ 3-7 From the perspectives of Piaget, Vygotsky, and today's researchers, how does a child's mind develop?

Somewhere on your journey from egghood to childhood, you became conscious. When was that? Psychologist Jean Piaget [pee-ah-ZHAY] spent a half-century searching for answers to

critical period a period early in life when exposure to certain stimuli or experiences is needed for proper development.

such questions. He studied children's **cognition**—all the mental activities associated with thinking, knowing, remembering, and communicating. Thanks partly to his pioneering work, we now understand that a child's mind is not a miniature model of an adult's. Children reason *differently*, in "wildly illogical ways about problems whose solutions are self-evident to adults" (Brainerd, 1996).

Piaget's interest in children's cognitive development began in 1920, when he was developing questions for children's intelligence tests in Paris. Looking over the test results, Piaget noticed something interesting. At certain ages, children made strikingly similar mistakes. Where others saw childish mistakes, Piaget saw intelligence at work.

Piaget's studies led him to believe that a child's mind develops through a series of stages. This upward march begins with the newborn's simple reflexes, and it ends with the adult's abstract reasoning power. Moving through these stages, Piaget believed, is like climbing a ladder. A child can't easily move to a higher rung without first having a firm footing on the one below.

JEAN PIAGET (1896–1980) "If we examine the intellectual development of the individual or of the whole of humanity, we shall find that the human spirit goes through a certain number of stages, each different from the other" (1930).

FIGURE 3.9 A changing marriage schema Twenty-five years ago, most people had a schema of marriage as a union between a man and a woman. In 2001, the Netherlands was the first country to change its marriage laws to accommodate same-sex marriage. By 2015, over twenty other countries, including the United States, had also legalized same-sex marriage.

Tools for thinking and reasoning differ in each stage. Thus, you can tell an 8-year-old that "getting an idea is like having a light turn on in your head," and the child will understand. A 2-year-old won't get the analogy. But an adult mind likewise can reason in ways that an 8-year-old won't understand.

Piaget believed that the force driving us up this intellectual ladder is our struggle to make sense of our experiences. His core idea was that "children are active thinkers, constantly trying to construct more advanced understandings of the world" (Siegler & Ellis, 1996). Part of this active thinking is building **schemas,** which are concepts or mental molds into which we pour our experiences.

To explain how we use and adjust our schemas, Piaget proposed two more concepts. First, we **assimilate** new experiences—we interpret them in terms of our current understandings (schemas). Having a simple schema for dog, for example, a toddler may call all four-legged animals dogs. But as we interact with the world, we also adjust, or **accommodate,** our schemas to incorporate information provided by new experiences. Thus, the child soon learns that the original dog schema is too broad and accommodates by refining the category.

By adulthood we have built countless schemas, ranging from what a dog is to what love is (**FIGURE 3.9**).

Piaget's Theory and Current Thinking

Piaget believed that children construct their understanding of the world as they interact with it. Their minds go through spurts of change, he believed, followed by greater stability as they move from one level to the next. In his view, cognitive development consisted of four major stages—*sensorimotor, preoperational, concrete operational,* and *formal operational.*

SENSORIMOTOR STAGE The **sensorimotor stage** begins at birth and lasts to nearly age 2. In this stage, babies take in the world through their senses and actions—through looking, hearing, touching, mouthing, and grasping. As their hands and limbs begin to move, they learn to make things happen.

Very young babies seem to live in the present. Out of sight is out of mind. In one test, Piaget showed an infant an appealing toy and then flopped his hat over it. Before the age of 6 months, the infant acted as if the toy no longer existed. Young infants lack **object permanence**—the awareness that objects continue to exist when out of

FIGURE 3.10 Object permanence Infants younger than 6 months seldom understand that things continue to exist when they are out of sight. But for this older infant, out of sight is definitely not out of mind.

sight (**FIGURE 3.10**). By about 8 months, infants begin to show that they do remember things they can no longer see. If you hide a toy, an 8-month-old will briefly look for it. Within another month or two, the infant will look for it even after several seconds have passed.

So does object permanence in fact blossom suddenly at 8 months, much as tulips blossom in spring? Today's researchers think not. They believe object permanence unfolds gradually, and they view development as more continuous than Piaget did.

They also think that young children are more competent than Piaget and his followers believed. Young children think like little scientists, testing ideas and learning from patterns (Gopnik et al., 2015). For example, infants seem to have an inborn grasp of simple physical laws—they have "baby physics." Like adults staring in disbelief at a magic trick (the "*Whoa!*" look), infants look longer at an unexpected, impossible, or unfamiliar scene—a car seeming to pass through a solid object. They also stare longer at a ball stopping in midair, or at an object that seems to magically disappear (Baillargeon, 1995, 2008; Shuwairi & Johnson, 2013; Stahl & Feigenson, 2015). Even as babies, we had a lot on our minds.

PREOPERATIONAL STAGE Piaget believed that until about age 6 or 7, children are in a **preoperational stage**—able to represent things with words and images, but too young to perform *mental operations* (such as imagining an action and mentally reversing it).

Conservation Consider a 5-year-old who tells you there is too much milk in a tall, narrow glass. "Too much" may become just right if you pour that milk into a short, wide glass. Focusing only on the height dimension, the child cannot perform the operation of mentally pouring the milk back into the tall glass. Before about age 6, said Piaget, young children lack the concept of **conservation**—the idea that the amount remains the same even if it changes shape (**FIGURE 3.11**).

Pretend Play A child who can think in symbols can begin to enjoy *pretend play*. Although Piaget did not view the change from one stage to another as an abrupt shift, symbolic thinking occurs at an earlier age than he supposed. One researcher showed children a model of a room and hid a miniature stuffed dog behind its miniature couch (DeLoache & Brown, 1987). The 2½-year-olds easily remembered where to find the miniature toy in the model, but that knowledge didn't transfer to the real world. They could not use the model to locate an actual stuffed dog behind a couch in a real room. Three-year-olds—only 6 months older—usually went right to the actual stuffed animal in the real room, showing they *could* think of the model as a symbol for the room.

LaunchPad For quick video examples of children being tested for conservation, visit LaunchPad's *Concept Practice: Piaget and Conservation*.

cognition all the mental activities associated with thinking, knowing, remembering, and communicating.

schema a concept or framework that organizes and interprets information.

assimilation interpreting our new experiences in terms of our existing schemas.

accommodation adapting our current understandings (schemas) to incorporate new information.

sensorimotor stage in Piaget's theory, the stage (from birth to nearly 2 years of age) during which infants know the world mostly in terms of their sensory impressions and motor activities.

object permanence the awareness that things continue to exist even when not perceived.

preoperational stage in Piaget's theory, the stage (from about 2 to 6 or 7 years of age) in which a child learns to use language but cannot yet perform the mental operations of concrete logic.

conservation the principle (which Piaget believed to be a part of concrete operational reasoning) that properties such as mass, volume, and number remain the same despite changes in shapes.

FIGURE 3.11 Piaget's test of conservation This visually focused preoperational child does not yet understand the principle of conservation. When the milk is poured into a tall, narrow glass, it suddenly seems like "more" than when it was in the shorter, wider glass. In another year or so, she will understand that the amount stays the same even though it looks different.

Egocentrism Piaget also taught us that preschool children are **egocentric:** They have difficulty imagining things from another's point of view. Asked to "show Mommy your picture," 2-year-old Gabriella holds the picture up facing her own eyes. Told to hide, 3-year-old Gray puts his hands over his eyes, assuming that if he can't see you, you can't see him. When a TV-watching preschooler blocks your view of the screen, the child probably assumes that you see what she sees. At this age, children simply are not yet able to take another's viewpoint. Even we adults may overestimate the extent to which others share our views. Have you ever mistakenly assumed that something would be clear to a friend because it was clear to you? Or sent an e-mail mistakenly thinking that the receiver would "hear" your "just kidding" intent (Epley et al., 2004; Kruger et al., 2005)? As children, we were even more prone to such egocentricism.

Theory of Mind When Little Red Riding Hood realized her "grandmother" was really a wolf, she swiftly revised her ideas about the creature's intentions and raced away. Preschoolers develop this ability to read others' mental states when they begin forming a **theory of mind.**

When children can imagine another person's viewpoint, all sorts of new skills emerge. They can tease, because they now understand what makes a playmate angry. They may be able to convince a sibling to share. Knowing what might make a parent buy a toy, they may try to persuade. Children who have an advanced ability to understand others' minds tend to be more popular (Slaughter et al., 2015).

Between about ages 3 and 4½, children worldwide use their new theory-of-mind skills to realize that others may hold false beliefs (Callaghan et al., 2005; Rubio-Fernandez & Geurts, 2013; Sabbagh et al., 2006). One research team asked preschoolers what was inside a Band-Aid box (Jenkins & Astington, 1996). Expecting Band-Aids, the children were surprised to see that the box contained pencils. Then came the theory-of-mind question. Asked what a child who had never seen the box would think was inside, 3-year-olds typically answered "pencils." By age 4 to 5, children knew better. They anticipated their friends' false belief that the box would hold Band-Aids.

Children with **autism spectrum disorder (ASD)** have an *impaired theory of mind* (Rajendran & Mitchell, 2007; Senju et al., 2009). They have difficulty reading and remembering other people's thoughts and feelings. Most children learn that another child's pouting mouth signals sadness, and that twinkling eyes mean happiness or mischief. A child with ASD fails to understand these signals (Boucher et al., 2012; Frith & Frith, 2001).

AUTISM SPECTRUM DISORDER This speech-language pathologist is helping a boy with ASD learn to form sounds and words. ASD is marked by limited communication ability and difficulty understanding others' states of mind.

ASD has differing levels of severity. "High-functioning" individuals generally have normal intelligence, and they often have an exceptional skill or talent in a specific area. But they lack social and communication skills, and they tend to become distracted by minor and unimportant stimuli (Remington et al., 2009). Those at the spectrum's lower end struggle to use language.

Biological factors, including genetic influences and abnormal brain development, contribute to ASD (Blanken et al., 2015; Colvert et al., 2015; Makin, 2015a). Childhood measles, mumps, and rubella (MMR) vaccinations do not (Demicheli et al., 2012). Based on a fraudulent 1998 study—"the most damaging medical hoax of the last 100 years" (Flaherty, 2011)—some parents were misled into thinking that the childhood MMR vaccine increased risk of ASD. The unfortunate result was a drop in vaccination rates and an increase in cases of measles and mumps. Some

EGOCENTRISM IN ACTION "Look, Granddaddy, a match!" So said my [DM's] granddaughter, Allie, at age 4, when showing me two memory game cards with matching pictures—that faced her.

"AUTISM" CASE NUMBER 1 In 1943, Donald Gray Triplett, an "odd" child with unusual gifts and social weaknesses, was the first person to receive the diagnosis of "autism." (After a 2013 change in the diagnosis manual, his condition is now called autism spectrum disorder.) In 2010, at age 77, Triplett was still living in his family home and Mississippi town, where he often played golf (Donvan & Zucker, 2010).

unvaccinated children suffered long-term harm or even death.

ASD afflicts about four boys for every girl (Lai et al., 2015). Children exposed to high levels of the male sex hormone *testosterone* in the womb may develop more masculine and ASD-related traits (Auyeung et al., 2009). Psychologist Simon Baron-Cohen argues that ASD represents an "extreme male brain" (2008, 2009). Although there is some overlap between the sexes, he believes that boys are better "systemizers." They tend to understand things according to rules or laws, as in mathematical and mechanical systems. Girls, he thinks, are naturally predisposed to be "empathizers." They tend to be better at reading facial expressions and gestures (van Honk et al., 2011). But this typical sex difference disappears among those with ASD (Baron-Cohen et al., 2015).

Why is reading faces so difficult for those with ASD? The underlying cause seems to be poor communication among brain regions that normally work together to let us take another's viewpoint. This effect appears to result from ASD-related genes interacting with the environment (State & Šestan, 2012).

CONCRETE OPERATIONAL STAGE By about age 7, said Piaget, children enter the **concrete operational stage.** Given concrete (physical) materials, they begin to grasp conservation. Understanding that change

in form does not mean change in quantity, they can mentally pour milk back and forth between glasses of different shapes. They also enjoy jokes that allow them to use this new understanding:

> Mr. Jones went into a restaurant and ordered a whole pizza for his dinner. When the waiter asked if he wanted it cut into 6 or 8 pieces, Mr. Jones said, "Oh, you'd better make it 6, I could never eat 8 pieces!" (McGhee, 1976)

Piaget believed that during the concrete operational stage, children become able to understand simple math and conservation. When my [DM's] daughter, Laura, was 6, I was astonished at her inability to reverse simple arithmetic. Asked, "What is 8 plus 4?" she required 5 seconds to compute "12," and another 5 seconds to then compute 12 minus 4. By age 8, she could answer a reversed question instantly.

FORMAL OPERATIONAL STAGE By age 12, said Piaget, our reasoning expands to include abstract thinking. We are no longer limited to purely concrete reasoning, based on actual experience. As children approach adolescence, many become capable of abstract *if . . . then* thinking: *If* this happens, *then* that will happen. Piaget called this new systematic reasoning ability **formal operational** thinking. (Stay tuned for more about adolescents' thinking abilities later in this chapter.) **TABLE 3.1** summarizes the four stages in Piaget's theory.

egocentrism in Piaget's theory, the preoperational child's difficulty taking another's point of view.

theory of mind people's ideas about their own and others' mental states—about their feelings, perceptions, and thoughts, and the behaviors these might predict.

autism spectrum disorder (ASD) a disorder that appears in childhood and is marked by significant deficiencies in communication and social interaction, and by rigidly fixated interests and repetitive behaviors.

concrete operational stage in Piaget's theory, the stage of cognitive development (from about 7 to 11 years of age) during which children gain the mental operations that enable them to think logically about concrete events.

formal operational stage in Piaget's theory, the stage of cognitive development (normally beginning about age 12) during which people begin to think logically about abstract concepts.

PRETEND PLAY

TABLE 3.1	Piaget's Stages of Cognitive Development	
Typical Age Range	**Stage and Description**	**Key Accomplishments**
Birth to nearly 2 years	*Sensorimotor* Experiencing the world through senses and actions (looking, hearing, touching, mouthing, and grasping)	• Object permanence • Stranger anxiety
About 2 to 6 or 7 years	*Preoperational* Representing things with words and images; using intuitive rather than logical reasoning	• Pretend play • Egocentrism
About 7 to 11 years	*Concrete operational* Thinking logically about concrete events; grasping concrete analogies and performing arithmetical operations	• Conservation • Mathematical transformations
About 12 through adulthood	*Formal operational* Reasoning abstractly	• Abstract logic • Potential for mature moral reasoning

An Alternative Viewpoint: Vygotsky and the Social Child

As Piaget was forming his theory of cognitive development, Russian psychologist Lev Vygotsky was also studying how children think and learn. He noted that by age 7, children are more able to think and solve problems with words. They do this, he said, by no longer thinking aloud. Instead they internalize their culture's language and rely on inner speech (Fernyhough, 2008). Parents who say *"No, no, Bevy!"* when pulling her hand away from a cake are giving their child a self-control tool. When Bevy later needs to resist temptation, she may likewise think *"No, no, Bevy!"* Talking to themselves, whether out loud or inside their heads, helps children to control their behavior and emotions and to master new skills. (Adults who motivate themselves using self-talk—"You can do it!"—also experience better performance [Kross et al., 2014].)

Piaget emphasized how the child's mind grows through interaction with the physical environment. Vygotsky emphasized how the child's mind grows through interaction with the *social* environment. If Piaget's child was a young scientist, Vygotsky's was a young apprentice. By guiding children and giving them new words, parents and others provide a temporary *scaffold* from which children can step to higher levels of thinking (Renninger & Granott, 2005). Language is an important ingredient of social guidance, and it provides the building blocks for thinking, noted Vygotsky. (For more on children's development of language, see Chapter 8.)

Reflecting on Piaget's Theory

What remains of Piaget's ideas about the child's mind? Plenty. *Time* magazine singled him out as one of the twentieth century's 20 most influential scientists and thinkers. And a survey of British psychologists rated him as the last century's greatest psychologist (*The Psychologist*, 2003). Piaget identified significant cognitive milestones and stimulated worldwide interest in how the mind develops. His emphasis was less on the ages at which children typically reach specific milestones than on their sequence. Studies around the globe, from Algeria to North America, have confirmed that human cognition unfolds basically in the sequence Piaget described (Lourenco & Machado, 1996; Segall et al., 1990).

However, today's researchers see development as more continuous than did Piaget. By detecting the beginnings of each type of thinking at earlier ages, they have revealed conceptual abilities Piaget missed. Moreover, they see formal logic as a smaller part of cognition than he did. Piaget would not be surprised that today, as part of our own cognitive development, we are adapting his ideas to accommodate new findings.

Piaget's insights can nevertheless help teachers and parents understand young children. Remember this: Young children cannot think with adult logic and cannot take another's viewpoint. What seems simple and obvious to us—getting off a teeter-totter will cause a friend on the other end to crash—may never occur to a 3-year-old. Also remember that children are not empty containers waiting to be filled with knowledge. By building on what children already know, we can engage them in concrete demonstrations and stimulate them to think for themselves. Finally, accept children's cognitive immaturity as adaptive. It is nature's strategy for keeping children close to protective adults and providing time for learning and socialization (Bjorklund & Green, 1992).

LEV VYGOTSKY (1896–1934) Vygotsky, pictured here with his daughter, was a Russian developmental psychologist. He studied how a child's mind feeds on the language of social interaction.

James V. Wertsch/Washington University

Retrieve + Remember

- Object permanence, pretend play, conservation, and abstract logic are developmental milestones for which of Piaget's stages, respectively?

  ANSWER: Object permanence for the sensorimotor stage, pretend play for the preoperational stage, conservation for the concrete operational stage, and abstract logic for the formal operational stage.

- Match each developmental ability (1–6) to the correct cognitive developmental stage (a–d).

  a. Sensorimotor
  b. Preoperational
  c. Concrete operational
  d. Formal operational

  1. Thinking about abstract concepts, such as "freedom."
  2. Enjoying imaginary play (such as dress-up).
  3. Understanding that physical properties stay the same even when objects change form.
  4. Having the ability to reverse math operations.
  5. Understanding that something is not gone for good when it disappears from sight, as when Mom "disappears" behind the shower curtain.
  6. Having difficulty taking another's point of view (as when blocking someone's view of the TV).

  ANSWERS: 1. d, 2. b, 3. c, 4. c, 5. a, 6. b

LaunchPad For a 7-minute synopsis of Piaget's concepts, see LaunchPad's *Video: Cognitive Development.*

Social Development

From birth, babies all over the world are normally very social creatures, developing an intense bond with their caregivers. Infants come to prefer familiar faces and voices, then to coo and gurgle when given their mother's or father's attention. Have you ever wondered why tiny infants can happily be handed off to admiring visitors, but after a certain age pull back? By about 8 months, soon after object permanence emerges and children become mobile, a curious thing happens: They develop **stranger anxiety.** When handed to a stranger they may cry and reach for a parent: "No! Don't leave me!" At about this age, children have schemas for familiar faces—mental images of how caregivers should look. When the new face does not fit one of these remembered images, they become distressed (Kagan, 1984). Once again, we see an important principle: *The brain, mind, and social-emotional behavior develop together.*

Origins of Attachment

LOQ 3-8 How do the bonds of attachment form between caregivers and infants?

One-year-olds typically cling tightly to a parent when they are frightened or expect separation. Reunited after being apart, they often shower the parent with smiles and hugs. This striking parent-infant **attachment** bond is a powerful survival impulse that keeps infants close to their caregivers.

Infants normally become attached to people—typically their parents—who are comfortable and familiar. For many years, psychologists reasoned that infants grew attached to those who satisfied their need for nourishment. It made sense. But an accidental finding overturned this idea.

STRANGER ANXIETY A newly emerging ability to evaluate people as unfamiliar and possibly threatening helps protect babies 8 months and older.

During the 1950s, University of Wisconsin psychologists Harry Harlow and Margaret Harlow bred monkeys for their learning studies. Shortly after birth, they separated the infants from their mothers and placed each infant in an individual cage with a cheesecloth baby blanket (Harlow et al., 1971). Then came a surprise: When their soft blankets were taken to be washed, the infant monkeys became distressed.

Imagine yourself as one of the Harlows, trying to figure out why the monkey infants were so intensely attached to their blankets. Psychologists believed that infants became attached to those who nourish them. Might comfort instead be the key? How could you test that idea? The Harlows decided to pit the drawing power of a food source against the contact comfort of the blanket by creating two artificial mothers. One was a bare wire cylinder with a wooden head and an attached feeding bottle. The other was a cylinder wrapped with terry cloth.

For the monkeys, it was no contest. They overwhelmingly preferred the comfy cloth mother (**FIGURE 3.12**). Like anxious infants clinging to their live mothers, the monkey babies would cling to their cloth mothers when

anxious. When exploring their environment, they used her as a *secure base.* They acted as though they were attached to her by an invisible elastic band that stretched only so far before pulling them back. Researchers soon learned that other qualities—rocking, warmth, and feeding—made the cloth mother even more appealing.

Human infants, too, become attached to parents who are soft and warm and who rock, pat, and feed. Much parent-infant emotional communication occurs via touch (Hertenstein et al., 2006), which can be either soothing (snuggles) or arousing (tickles). The human parent also provides a safe haven for a distressed child and a secure base from which to explore.

FIGURE 3.12 The Harlows' mothers The Harlows' infant monkeys much preferred contact with a comfortable cloth mother, even while feeding from a nourishing wire mother.

stranger anxiety the fear of strangers that infants commonly display, beginning by about 8 months of age.

attachment an emotional tie with another person; shown in young children by their seeking closeness to their caregiver and showing distress on separation.

Attachment Differences

LOQ 3-9 Why do secure and insecure attachments matter, and how does an infant's ability to develop basic trust affect later relationships?

Children's attachments differ. To study these differences, Mary Ainsworth (1979) designed the *strange situation* experiment. She observed mother-infant pairs at home during their first six months. Later she observed the 1-year-old infants in a strange situation (usually a laboratory playroom) with and without their mothers. Such research shows that about 60 percent of infants and young children display *secure attachment* (Moulin et al., 2014). In their mother's presence, they play comfortably, happily exploring their new environment. When she leaves, they become upset. When she returns, they seek contact with her.

Other infants show *insecure attachment,* marked by either anxiety or avoidance of trusting relationships. These infants are less likely to explore their surroundings. Anxiously attached infants may cling to their mother. When she leaves, they might cry loudly and remain upset. Avoidantly attached infants seem not to notice or care about her departure and return (Ainsworth, 1973, 1989; Kagan, 1995; van IJzendoorn & Kroonenberg, 1988).

Ainsworth and others found that sensitive, responsive mothers—those who noticed what their babies were doing and responded appropriately—had infants who were securely attached (De Wolff & van IJzendoorn, 1997). Insensitive, unresponsive mothers—mothers who attended to their babies when they felt like doing so but ignored them at other times—often had infants who were insecurely attached. The Harlows' monkey studies, with unresponsive artificial mothers, produced even more striking effects. When put in strange situations without their artificial mothers, the deprived infants were terrified (**FIGURE 3.13**).

Today's climate of greater respect for animal welfare would prevent primate studies like the Harlows'. Many

FIGURE 3.13 Social deprivation and fear In the Harlows' experiments, monkeys raised with artificial mothers were terror-stricken when placed in strange situations without those mothers.

now remember Harry Harlow as the researcher who tortured helpless monkeys. But others support the Harlows' work. "Harry Harlow, whose name has [come to mean] cruel monkey experiments, actually helped put an end to cruel child-rearing practices," said primatologist Frans de Waal (2011). Harry Harlow defended their methods: "Remember, for every mistreated monkey there exist a million mistreated children." He expressed the hope that his research would sensitize people to child abuse and neglect.

So caring parents matter. But is attachment style the *result* of parenting? Or are other factors also at work?

TEMPERAMENT AND ATTACHMENT

How does *temperament*—a person's characteristic emotional reactivity and intensity—affect attachment style? As we saw earlier in this chapter, temperament is genetically influenced.

Some babies tend to be difficult—irritable, intense, and unpredictable. Others are easy—cheerful, relaxed, and feeding and sleeping on predictable schedules (Chess & Thomas, 1987). Parenting studies that neglect such inborn differences, critics say, might as well be "comparing foxhounds reared in kennels with poodles reared in apartments" (Harris, 1998). To separate the effects of nature and nurture on attachment, we would need to vary parenting while controlling temperament. (Pause and think: If you were the researcher, how might you do this?)

One researcher's solution was to randomly assign 100 temperamentally difficult infants to two groups. Half of the 6- to 9-month-olds were in the experimental group, in which mothers received personal training in sensitive responding. The other half were in a control group, in which mothers did not receive this training (van den Boom, 1990, 1995). At 12 months of age, 68 percent of the infants in the first group were rated securely attached, as were only 28 percent of the control group infants. Other studies support the idea that such programs can increase parental sensitivity and, to some extent, infant attachment security (Bakermans-Kranenburg et al., 2003; Van Zeijl et al., 2006). Nature and nurture interact.

Children's anxiety over separation from parents peaks at around 13 months, then gradually declines (Kagan, 1976). This happens whether they live with one parent or two, are cared for at home or in day care, live in North America, Guatemala, or the Kalahari Desert. As the power of early attachment relaxes,

PARENTING IS FOR DADS, TOO Emperor penguin dads may lose half their body weight over the two months they spend keeping a precious egg warm during the harsh Antarctic winter. After mom returns from the sea, both parents take turns caring for and feeding the chick.

we humans begin to move out into a wider range of situations. We communicate with strangers more freely. And we stay attached emotionally to loved ones despite distance.

At all ages, we are social creatures. But as we mature, our secure base and safe haven shift—from parents to peers and partners (Cassidy & Shaver, 1999). We gain strength when someone offers, by words and actions, a safe haven: "I will be here. I am interested in you. Come what may, I will actively support you" (Crowell & Waters, 1994).

LaunchPad | Consider how researchers have studied temperament and personality with LaunchPad's *IMMERSIVE LEARNING: How Would You Know If Personality Runs in the Genes?*

ATTACHMENT STYLES AND LATER RELATIONSHIPS Developmental psychologist Erik Erikson (1902–1994), working with his wife, Joan Erikson (1902–1997), believed that securely attached children approach life with a sense of **basic trust**—a sense that the world is predictable and reliable. This lifelong attitude of trust rather than fear, they said, flows from children's interactions with sensitive, loving caregivers.

Do our early attachments form the foundation for adult relationships, including our comfort with *intimacy?* Many researchers now believe they do (Birnbaum et al., 2006; Fraley et al., 2013). People who report that they had secure relationships with their parents tend to enjoy secure friendships (Gorrese & Ruggieri, 2012). Children with secure, responsive mothers tend to have good grades and strong friendships (Raby et al., 2014).

Feeling insecurely attached to others during childhood may take either of two main forms (Fraley et al., 2011). One is anxiety, in which people constantly crave acceptance but are overly alert to signs of possible rejection. The other is avoidance, in which people experience discomfort getting close to others and tend to keep their distance. An anxious attachment style can annoy relationship partners. An avoidant style decreases commitment and increases conflict (DeWall et al., 2011; Li & Chan, 2012).

Deprivation of Attachment

If secure attachment fosters social trust, what happens when circumstances prevent a child from forming any attachments? In all of psychology, there is no sadder research literature. Some of these babies were raised in institutions without a regular caregiver's stimulation and attention. Others were locked away at home under conditions of abuse or extreme neglect. Most were withdrawn, frightened, even speechless. Those abandoned in Romanian orphanages during the 1980s looked "frighteningly like Harlow's monkeys" (Carlson, 1995). The longer they were institutionalized, the more they bore lasting emotional scars (Chisholm, 1998; Nelson et al., 2009).

The Harlows' monkeys bore similar scars if raised in total isolation, without even an artificial mother. As adults, when placed with other monkeys their age, they either cowered in fright or lashed out in aggression. When they reached sexual maturity, most were incapable of mating. Females who did have babies were often neglectful, abusive, even murderous toward them.

In humans, too, the unloved sometimes become the unloving. Some 30 percent of those who have been abused do later abuse their own children. This is four times the U.S. national rate of child abuse (Dumont et al., 2007; Widom, 1989a,b). Abuse victims have a doubled risk of later depression (Nanni et al., 2012). They are especially at risk for depression if they carry a gene variation that spurs stress-hormone production (Bradley et al., 2008). As we will see again and again, behavior and emotion arise from a particular environment interacting with particular genes.

Recall that, depending on our experience, genes may or may not be expressed (active). Epigenetics studies show that experience puts molecular marks on genes that influence their expression. Severe child abuse, for example, can affect the expression of genes (Romens et al., 2015). Extreme childhood trauma can also leave footprints on the brain.

> **basic trust** according to Erik Erikson, a sense that the world is predictable and trustworthy; said to be formed during infancy by appropriate experiences with responsive caregivers.

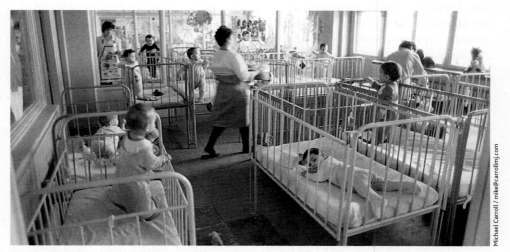

THE DEPRIVATION OF ATTACHMENT In this 1980s Romanian orphanage, the 250 children between ages 1 and 5 outnumbered caregivers 15 to 1. When such children were tested years later they had lower intelligence scores and double the 20 percent rate of anxiety symptoms found in children assigned to quality foster care settings (Bick et al., 2015; Kumsta et al., 2015; Nelson et al., 2009, 2014).

Normally placid golden hamsters that are repeatedly threatened and attacked while young grow up to be cowards when caged with same-sized hamsters, or bullies when caged with weaker ones (Ferris, 1996). Young children who are terrorized through bullying, physical abuse, or wartime atrocities (being beaten, witnessing torture, and living in constant fear) often suffer other lasting wounds. Many have reported nightmares, depression, and an adolescence troubled by substance abuse, binge eating, or aggression (Kendall-Tackett, 2004; Lereya et al., 2015; Polusny & Follette, 1995; Trickett & McBride-Chang, 1995). So too with childhood sexual abuse. Especially if severe and prolonged, it places children at increased risk for health problems, psychological disorders, substance abuse, and criminality (Freyd et al., 2005; Tyler, 2002).

Still, many children successfully survive abuse. It's true that most abusive parents—and many condemned murderers—were indeed abused. It's also true that most children growing up in harsh conditions don't become violent criminals or abusive parents. Indeed, hardship short of trauma often boosts mental toughness (Seery, 2011). And though growing up poor puts children at risk for some social problems, growing up rich puts them at risk for other troubles. Wealthy children are at greater risk for substance abuse, eating disorders, anxiety, and depression (Lund & Dearing, 2012; Luthar et al., 2013). When you face adversity, consider the silver lining. Your coping may strengthen your *resilience*—your tendency to bounce back and go on to lead a better life.

Parenting Styles

LOQ 3-10 What are the four main parenting styles?

Child-raising practices vary. Some parents are strict, some are lax. Some show little affection, some liberally hug and kiss. How do parenting differences affect children?

The most heavily researched aspect of parenting has been how, and to what extent, parents seek to control their children. Parenting styles can be described as a combination of two traits: how *responsive* and how *demanding* parents are (Kakinami et al., 2015). Investigators have identified four parenting styles (Baumrind, 1966, 1967; Steinberg, 2001):

1. *Authoritarian* parents are *coercive*. They set the rules and expect obedience: "Don't interrupt." "Keep your room clean." "Don't stay out late or you'll be grounded." "Why? Because I said so."

2. *Permissive* parents are *unrestraining*. They make few demands and use little punishment. They may be unwilling to set limits.

3. *Negligent* parents are *uninvolved*. They are neither demanding nor responsive. They are careless, inattentive, and do not seek a close relationship with their children.

4. *Authoritative* parents are *confrontive*. They are both demanding and responsive. They exert control by setting rules, but especially with older children, they encourage open discussion and allow exceptions.

For more on parenting styles and their associated outcomes, see Thinking Critically About: Parenting Styles.

Remember, too, that parenting doesn't happen in a vacuum. One of the forces that influences parenting styles is culture.

CULTURE AND CHILD RAISING Culture, as we noted in Chapter 1, is the set of enduring behaviors, ideas, attitudes, values, and traditions shared by a group of people and handed down from one generation to the next (Brislin, 1988). In Chapter 4, we'll explore the effects of culture on gender. In later chapters, we'll consider the influence of culture on social interactions and psychological disorders. For now, let's look at the way that child-raising practices reflect cultural values.

Cultural values vary from place to place and, even in the same place, from one time to another. Do you prefer children who are independent, or children who comply with what others think?

The Westernized culture of the United States today favors independence. "You are responsible for yourself," Western families and schools tell their children. "Follow your conscience. Be true to yourself. Discover your gifts." In recent years, some Western parents have gone further, telling their children, "You are more special than other children" (Brummelman et al., 2015). Western cultural values used to place greater priority on obedience, respect, and sensitivity to others (Alwin, 1990; Remley, 1988). "Be true to your traditions," parents then taught their children. "Be loyal to your heritage and country. Show respect toward your parents and other superiors." Cultures can change.

Children across place and time have thrived under various child-raising systems. Upper-class British parents traditionally handed off routine caregiving to nannies, then sent their 10-year-olds away to boarding school. Many Americans now give children their own bedrooms and entrust them to day care.

Many Asian and African cultures place less value on independence and more on a strong sense of *family self*. They feel that what shames the child shames the family, and what brings

CULTURES VARY Parents everywhere care about their children, but raise and protect them differently depending on the surrounding culture. Parents raising children in New York City keep them close. In smaller, close-knit communities, such as Scotland's Orkney Islands' town of Stromness, social trust has enabled parents to park their toddlers outside shops.

LOQ 3-11 What outcomes are associated with each parenting style?

Thinking Critically About:
Parenting Styles—
Too Hard, Too Soft, Too Uncaring, and Just Right?

Researchers have identified **four parenting styles**,[1] which have been associated with varying outcomes.

1 Authoritarian parents

Children with less social skill and self-esteem, and a brain that overreacts when they make mistakes [2]

2 Permissive parents

Children who are more aggressive and immature [3]

HOWEVER, Correlation ≠ Causation!
What other factors might explain this parenting-competence link? For example, might children with positive characteristics be more likely to bring out positive parenting methods?

3 Negligent parents

Children with poor academic and social outcomes [4]

4 Authoritative parents

Children with the highest self-esteem, self-reliance, self-regulation, and social competence [5]

1. Kakinami et al., 2015. 2. Meyer et al., 2015. 3. Luyckx et al., 2011. 4. Pinquart, 2015; Steinberg et al., 1994. 5. Baumrind, 1996, 2013; Buri et al.,1988; Coopersmith, 1967; Sulik et al., 2015.

honor to the family brings honor to the self. These cultures also value emotional closeness, and infants and toddlers may sleep with their mothers and spend their days close to a family member (Morelli et al., 1992; Whiting & Edwards, 1988). Sending children away would have been shocking to a traditional African Gusii family. Their babies nursed freely but spent most of the day on their mother's or siblings' back, with lots of body contact but little face-to-face and language interaction. If the mother became pregnant again, the toddler was weaned and handed over to another family member. Westerners may wonder about the negative effects of the lack of verbal interaction, but then the Gusii may in turn have wondered about Western mothers pushing their babies around in strollers and putting them in playpens and car seats (Small, 1997). Such diversity in child raising cautions us against presuming that our culture's way is the only way to raise children successfully.

Retrieve + Remember

- The four parenting styles may be described as "too hard, too soft, too uncaring, and just right." Which parenting style goes with which of these descriptions, and why?

ANSWER: The authoritarian style would be described as too hard, the permissive style too soft, the negligent style too uncaring, and the authoritative style just right. Parents using the authoritative style tend to have children with high self-esteem, self-reliance, self-regulation, and social competence.

Adolescence

During **adolescence** we morph from child to adult. Adolescence starts with a physical event—bodily changes that mark the beginning of sexual maturity. It ends with a social event—

At a five-year high school reunion, former best friends may be surprised at their differences; a decade or more later, they may have trouble sustaining a conversation.

independent adult status, which means that in cultures where teens are self-supporting, adolescence hardly exists.

Physical Development

LOQ 3-12 How is adolescence defined, and what major physical changes occur during adolescence?

Adolescence begins with **puberty**, the time when we mature sexually. Puberty follows a surge of hormones, which may intensify moods and which trigger a series of bodily changes, outlined in Chapter 4.

Early versus late maturing. Just as in the earlier life stages, we all go through the same *sequence* of changes in puberty. All girls, for example, develop breast buds and pubic hair before *menarche*, their first menstrual period. The *timing* of such changes is less predictable. Some girls start their growth spurt at 9, some boys as late as age 16. How do girls and boys experience early versus late maturation?

For boys, early maturation has mixed effects. Boys who are stronger and more athletic during their early teen years tend to be more popular, self-assured, and independent, though also more

at risk for alcohol use, delinquency, and premature sexual activity (Conley & Rudolph, 2009; Copeland et al., 2010; Lynne et al., 2007). For girls, early maturation can be a challenge (Mendle et al., 2007). If a young girl's body and hormone-fed feelings are too far beyond her emotional maturity and her friends' physical development and experiences, she may search out older teens or may suffer teasing or sexual harassment (Ge & Natsuaki, 2009).

The teenage brain. An adolescent's brain is also a work in progress. This is the time when unused neurons and their connections are pruned (Blakemore, 2008). What we don't use, we lose.

As teens mature, their frontal lobes also continue to develop. But frontal lobe maturation lags behind the development of the emotional limbic system. When puberty's hormonal surge combines with limbic system development and unfinished frontal lobes, it's no wonder teens feel stressed. Impulsiveness, risky behaviors, and emotional storms—slamming doors and turning up the music—happen (Casey et al., 2008; Casey & Caudle, 2013; Fuhrmann et al., 2015). Not yet fully equipped for making long-term plans and curbing impulses, young teens may give in to the lure of smoking. Teens typically know the risks of smoking, fast driving, and unprotected sex. They just, reasoning from their gut, weigh the benefits of risky behaviors more heavily (Reyna & Farley, 2006; Steinberg, 2010). Teens find rewards more exciting than adults do. So they seek thrills without a fully developed brake pedal controlling their impulses (Chick, 2015) (**FIGURE 3.14**).

"Young man, go to your room and stay there until your cerebral cortex matures."

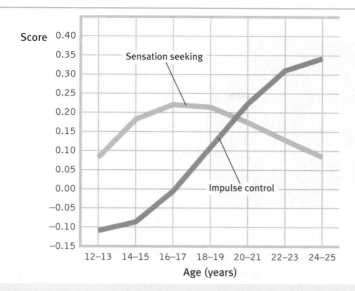

FIGURE 3.14 **Impulse control lags reward seeking** Surveys of more than 7000 American 12- to 24-year-olds reveal that thrill seeking peaks in the mid-teens. Impulse control develops more slowly as frontal lobes mature. (National Longitudinal Study of Youth and Children and Young Adults survey data presented by Steinberg, 2013.)

So, when Junior drives recklessly and academically self-destructs, should his parents reassure themselves that "he can't help it; his frontal cortex isn't yet fully grown"? They can at least take hope: The brain with which Junior begins his teens differs from the brain with which he will end his teens. Unless he slows his brain development with heavy drinking, his frontal lobes will continue maturing until about age 25 (Beckman, 2004). Better communication between the frontal lobes and other brain regions will bring improved judgment, impulse control, and the ability to plan for the long term.

In 2004, the American Psychological Association (APA) joined seven other medical and mental health associations in filing U.S. Supreme Court briefs arguing against the death penalty for 16- and 17-year-olds. They presented evidence for the teen brain's immaturity "in areas that bear upon adolescent decision making." Brain scans of young teens reveal that frontal lobe immaturity is most evident among juvenile offenders and drug users (Shannon et al., 2011; Whelan et al., 2012). Teens are "less guilty by reason of adolescence," suggested psychologist Laurence Steinberg and law professor Elizabeth Scott (2003; Steinberg et al., 2009).

In 2005, by a 5-to-4 margin, the Court agreed, declaring juvenile death penalties unconstitutional.

"I helped a so-called friend commit armed robbery and murder. . . . I was just 17 years old. . . . Been in prison for over 20 years . . . longer than I was ever free. . . . I am among the 300 plus "Juvenile Lifers" . . . in Michigan prisons. I learned and matured a lot since my time incarcerated. I experience great remorse and regret over the tragedy that I ashamedly participated in. But I salvage this experience by learning and growing from it."

M. H., Michigan prison inmate, personal correspondence, 2015

Cognitive Development

LOQ 3-13 How did Piaget, Kohlberg, and later researchers describe cognitive and moral development during adolescence?

During the early teen years, reasoning is often self-focused. Adolescents may think their private experiences are unique, something parents just couldn't understand: "But, Mom, *you* don't really know how it feels to be in love" (Elkind, 1978). Capable of thinking about their own thinking and about other people's thinking, they also begin imagining what other people are thinking about *them*. (They might worry less if they understood their peers' similar self-focus.) Gradually, though, most begin to reason more abstractly.

Developing Reasoning Power

When adolescents achieve the intellectual peak Jean Piaget called *formal operations*, they apply their new abstract thinking tools to the world around them. They may debate human nature, good and evil, truth and justice. Having left behind the concrete images of early

DEMONSTRATING THEIR REASONING ABILITY Although on opposite sides of the immigration policy debate, these teens are all demonstrating their ability to think logically about abstract topics. According to Piaget, they are in the final cognitive stage, formal operations.

childhood, they may search for spirituality and a deeper meaning of life (Boyatzis, 2012; Elkind, 1970). They can now reason logically. They can spot hypocrisy and detect inconsistencies in others' reasoning (Peterson et al., 1986). (Can you remember having a heated debate with your parents? Did you perhaps even vow silently never to lose sight of your own ideals?)

Developing Morality

Two crucial tasks of childhood and adolescence are determining right from wrong and developing character—the psychological muscles for controlling impulses. To be a moral person is to *think* morally and *act* accordingly. Jean Piaget and Lawrence Kohlberg proposed that moral reasoning guides moral actions. A more recent view builds on psychology's game-changing new recognition that much of our functioning occurs not on the "high road" of deliberate, conscious thinking but on the "low road" of unconscious, automatic thinking. Our morality provides another demonstration of our two-track mind.

MORAL REASONING Piaget (1932) believed that children's moral judgments build on their cognitive development. Agreeing with Piaget, Lawrence Kohlberg (1981, 1984) sought to describe the development of *moral reasoning,* the thinking that occurs as we consider right and wrong. Kohlberg posed moral dilemmas—for example, should a person steal medicine to save a loved one's life? He then asked children, adolescents, and adults whether the action was right or wrong. He believed their answers would give evidence of stages of moral thinking. His findings led him to propose three basic levels of moral thinking: preconventional, conventional, and postconventional (**TABLE 3.2**). Kohlberg claimed these levels form a moral ladder. As with all stage theories, the sequence never changes. We begin on the bottom rung and rise to varying heights, where we may place others' comfort above our own (Crockett et al., 2014). Kohlberg's critics have noted that his postconventional level is culturally limited. It appears mostly among people

MORAL REASONING Some Staten Island, New York, residents faced a moral dilemma in 2012 when Superstorm Sandy caused disastrous flooding. Should they risk their lives to try to rescue family, friends, and neighbors in dangerously flooded areas? Their reasoning likely reflected different levels of moral thinking, even if they behaved similarly.

who prize *individualism*—giving priority to one's own goals (Eckensberger, 1994; Miller & Bersoff, 1995). This theory, add its critics, is biased against *collectivist* (group-centered) societies, such as China and India, which place more value on group goals.

MORAL INTUITION According to psychologist Jonathan Haidt [HITE] (2002, 2006, 2010) much of our morality is rooted in *moral intuitions*—"quick gut feelings." In this view, the mind makes moral judgments quickly and automatically. We *feel* elevation—a tingly, warm, glowing feeling in the chest—when seeing people display exceptional generosity, compassion, or courage. Such feelings in turn trigger moral reasoning, says Haidt.

This viewpoint on morality finds support in a study of moral decisions. Imagine seeing a runaway trolley headed for five people. All will certainly be killed unless you throw a switch that diverts the trolley onto another track, where it will kill one person. Should you throw the switch? Most say *Yes*. Kill one, save five.

Now imagine the same dilemma, with one change. This time, your opportunity to save the five requires you to push a large stranger onto the tracks, where he will die as his body stops the trolley. Kill one, save five? The logic is the same, but most say *No*. Seeking to understand why, researchers used brain imaging to spy on people's neural responses as they considered such problems (Greene et al., 2001). Despite the identical logic, only the body-pushing type of moral choice activated their brain's emotion areas. The point: Emotions feed moral intuitions.

While the new research shows that moral intuitions can beat moral reasoning, other research reaffirms the importance of moral reasoning (Johnson, 2014). The religious and moral reasoning of the Amish, for example, shapes their practices of forgiveness, communal life, and modesty (Narvaez, 2010). Joshua Greene (2010) likens our moral cognition to our phone's camera. Usually, we rely on the automatic point-and-shoot mode. But sometimes we use reason to manually override the camera's automatic impulse.

MORAL ACTION Today's character-education programs focus both on moral reasoning and on *doing* the right thing. In service-learning programs, where teens have tutored, cleaned up their neighborhoods, and assisted older adults, everyone has benefited. The teens' sense of competence and their desire to serve have increased, and their school absenteeism and drop-out rates have decreased (Andersen, 1998; Piliavin, 2003). Moral action feeds moral attitudes.

TABLE 3.2	Kohlberg's Levels of Moral Thinking	
Level (approximate age)	**Focus**	**Example**
Preconventional morality (before age 9)	Self-interest; obey rules to avoid punishment or gain concrete rewards.	"If you save your dying wife, you'll be a hero."
Conventional morality (early adolescence)	Uphold laws and rules to gain social approval or maintain social order.	"If you steal the drug for her, everyone will think you're a criminal."
Postconventional morality (adolescence and beyond)	Actions reflect belief in basic rights and self-defined ethical principles.	"People have a right to live."

"This might not be ethical. Is that a problem for anybody?"

These programs also teach the self-discipline needed to restrain one's own impulses—to delay small pleasures now to earn bigger rewards later. Those who have learned to *delay gratification* have become more socially responsible, academically successful, and productive (Daly et al., 2015; Funder & Block, 1989; Sawyer et al., 2015). What inspired researchers to study delay of gratification? It began with Walter Mischel's observations of his three preschool daughters' "remarkable progression" in self-control. To explore this further, Mischel conducted one of psychology's most famous experiments (Mischel, 2014; Mischel et al., 1988, 1989). He gave 4-year-old preschoolers a choice between one marshmallow now, or two marshmallows when he returned a few minutes later. The children who had the willpower to delay gratification went on to have higher college completion rates and incomes, and less often suffered addiction problems.

Retrieve + Remember

- According to Kohlberg, _____ morality focuses on self-interest, _____ morality focuses on self-defined ethical principles, and _____ morality focuses on upholding laws and social rules.

ANSWERS: preconventional; postconventional; conventional

- How has Kohlberg's theory of moral reasoning been criticized?

ANSWER: Kohlberg's work reflected an individualist worldview, so his theory is less culturally universal than he supposed.

Social Development

LOQ 3-14 What are the social tasks and challenges of adolescence?

Erik Erikson (1963) believed that we must resolve a specific crisis at each stage of life. Thus, each stage has its own *psychosocial* task. Young children wrestle with issues of *trust*, then *autonomy* (independence), then *initiative*. School-age children strive for *competence*—feeling able and productive. The adolescent's task

COMPETENCE VS. INFERIORITY

is to blend past, present, and future possibilities into a clearer sense of self. Adolescents wonder, "Who am I as an individual? What do I want to do with my life? What values should I live by? What do I believe in?" Such questions, said Erikson, are part of the adolescent's *search for identity* (TABLE 3.3).

Forming an Identity

To refine their sense of identity, adolescents in Western cultures usually try out different "selves" in different situations. They may act out one self at home, another with friends, and still another at school or online. Sometimes these separate worlds overlap. Do you remem-

INTIMACY VS. ISOLATION

TABLE 3.3 Erikson's Stages of Psychosocial Development

Stage (approximate age)	Issue	Description of Task
Infancy (to 1 year)	Trust vs. mistrust	If needs are dependably met, infants develop a sense of basic trust.
Toddlerhood (1 to 3 years)	Autonomy vs. shame and doubt	Toddlers learn to exercise their will and do things for themselves, or they doubt their abilities.
Preschool (3 to 6 years)	Initiative vs. guilt	Preschoolers learn to initiate tasks and carry out plans, or they feel guilty about their efforts to be independent.
Elementary school (6 years to puberty)	Competence vs. inferiority	Children learn the pleasure of applying themselves to tasks, or they feel inferior.
Adolescence (teen years into 20s)	Identity vs. role confusion	Teenagers work at refining a sense of self by testing roles and then integrating them to form a single identity, or they become confused about who they are.
Young adulthood (20s to early 40s)	Intimacy vs. isolation	Young adults struggle to form close relationships and to gain the capacity for intimate love, or they feel socially isolated.
Middle adulthood (40s to 60s)	Generativity vs. stagnation	In middle age, people discover a sense of contributing to the world, usually through family and work, or they may feel a lack of purpose.
Late adulthood (late 60s and up)	Integrity vs. despair	Reflecting on their lives, older adults may feel a sense of satisfaction or failure.

ber having your friend world and family world bump into each other, and wondering, "Which self should I be? Which is the real me?" Most of us make peace with our various selves. In time, we blend them into a stable and comfortable sense of who we are—an **identity.**

For both adolescents and adults, our group identities are often formed by how we differ from those around us. When living in Britain, I [DM] become conscious of my Americanness. When spending time in Hong Kong, I [ND] become conscious of my minority White race. When surrounded by women, we are both mindful of our male gender identity. For international students, for those of a minority ethnic group, for gay and transgender people, or for people with a disability, a **social identity** often forms around their distinctiveness.

But not always. Erikson noticed that some adolescents bypass this period. Some forge their identity early, simply by taking on their parents' values and expectations. Others may adopt the identity of a particular peer group—jocks, preps, geeks, band kids, debaters.

Cultural values may influence teens' search for an identity. Traditional, more collectivist cultures teach adolescents who they are, rather than encouraging them to decide on their own. In individualist Western cultures, young people may continue to try out possible roles well into their late teen years, when many people begin attending college or working full time. During the early to mid-teen years, self-esteem typically falls and, for girls, depression scores often increase. Then, during the late teens and twenties, self-image bounces back (Chung et al., 2014; Orth et al., 2015; Wagner et al., 2013). Agreeableness and emotional stability also increase during late adolescence and early adulthood (Klimstra et al., 2009; Lucas & Donnellan, 2011).

Erikson believed that adolescent identity formation (which continues into adulthood) is followed in young adulthood by a developing capacity for **intimacy,** the ability to form emotionally close relationships. With a clear and comfortable sense of who you are, said Erikson, you are ready for close relationships. Such relationships are, for most of us, a source of great pleasure.

LaunchPad For an interactive self-assessment of your own identity, see LaunchPad's *PsychSim 6: Who Am I?*

Parent and Peer Relationships

LOQ 3-15 How do parents and peers influence adolescents?

As adolescents in Western cultures seek to form their own identities, they begin to pull away from their parents (Shanahan et al., 2007). The preschooler who can't be close enough to her mother, who loves to touch and cling to her, becomes the 14-year-old who wouldn't be caught dead holding hands with Mom. The transition occurs gradually, but this period is typically a time when parental influence wanes and peer influence grows. As ancient Greek philosopher Aristotle long ago recognized, we humans are "the social animal." At all ages, but especially during childhood and the teen years, we seek to fit in with our groups and are influenced by them (Harris, 1998, 2002).

When researchers used a beeper to sample the daily experiences of American teens, they found them unhappiest when alone and happiest when with friends (Csikszentmihalyi & Hunter, 2003). Teens who start smoking typically have smoker friends who offer cigarettes (J. S. Rose et al., 1999; R. J. Rose et al., 2003). A *selection effect* partly influences this; those who smoke (or don't) may select as friends those who also smoke (or don't). Put two teens together and their brains become supersensitive to reward (Albert et al., 2013). This increased activation helps explain why teens take more driving risks when with friends than they do alone (Chein et al., 2011).

By adolescence, parent-child arguments occur more often, usually over ordinary things—household chores, bedtime, homework (Tesser et al., 1989). For a minority of families, these arguments lead to real splits and great stress

"I'm fourteen, Mom, I don't do hugs."

(Steinberg & Morris, 2001). But most disagreements are at the level of harmless bickering. With sons, the issues often are behavior problems, such as acting out or hygiene. For daughters, the conflict commonly involves relationships, such as dating and friendships (Schlomer et al., 2011). Nevertheless, most adolescents—6000 of them in 10 countries, from Australia to Bangladesh to Turkey—have said they like their parents (Offer et al., 1988). They often report, "We usually get along but . . ." (Galambos, 1992; Steinberg, 1987).

Positive parent-teen relations and positive peer relations often go hand in hand. High school girls who had the most affectionate relationships with their mothers tended also to enjoy the most intimate friendships with girlfriends (Gold & Yanof, 1985). And teens who felt close to their parents have tended to be healthy and happy and to do well in school (Resnick et al., 1997). But pause now to think critically. Look what happens if you state this association another way: Teens in trouble are more likely to have tense relationships with parents and other adults. Remember: *Correlations don't prove cause and effect.*

As we saw earlier, heredity does much of the heavy lifting in forming individual temperament and personality differences. Parents and peers influence teens' behaviors and attitudes.

When with peers, teens discount the future and focus more on immediate rewards (O'Brien et al., 2011). Most teens are herd animals. They talk, dress, and act more like their peers than their parents. What their friends are, they often become, and what "everybody's doing," they often do. Part of what everybody's doing is networking—a lot. U.S. teens typically send 30 text messages daily and average 145 Facebook friends (Pew, 2015). They tweet, post videos to Snapchat, and share pictures on Instagram. Online communication prompts intimate self-disclosure, both for better (support groups) and for worse (online predators and extremist groups) (Subrahmanyam & Greenfield, 2008; Valkenburg & Peter, 2009). A Facebook study of all English-language users revealed that it took parent users and their children 371 days on average to "friend" each other (Burke et al., 2013).

Both online and in real life, for those who feel bullied and excluded by their peers, the pain is acute. Most excluded teens "suffer in silence.... A small number act out in violent ways against their classmates" (Aronson, 2001). The pain of exclusion also persists. In one large study, those who were bullied as children showed poorer physical health and greater psychological distress 40 years later (Takizawa et al., 2014)! Peer approval matters.

Teens see their parents as having more influence in other areas—for example, in shaping their religious faith and in thinking about college and career choices (*Emerging Trends,* 1997). A Gallup Youth Survey revealed that most share their parents' political views (Lyons, 2005).

Nine times out of ten, it's all about peer pressure.

HOW MUCH CREDIT OR BLAME DO PARENTS DESERVE? Parents usually feel enormous satisfaction in their children's successes, and feel guilt or shame over their failures. They beam over the child who wins an award. They wonder where they went wrong with the child who is repeatedly called into the principal's office. Freudian psychiatry and psychology have been among the sources of such ideas, by blaming problems from asthma to schizophrenia on "bad mothering." Society has reinforced parent blaming. Believing that parents shape their offspring as a potter molds clay, people readily praise parents for their children's virtues and blame them for their children's vices.

But do parents really damage these future adults by being (take your pick from the toxic-parenting lists) overbearing—or uninvolved? Pushy—or weak? Overprotective—or distant? Are children really so easily wounded? If so, should we then blame our parents for our failings, and ourselves for our children's failings? Or does all the talk of wounding fragile children through normal parental mistakes trivialize the brutality of real abuse?

Parents do matter. The power of parenting is clearest at the extremes: the abused who become abusive, the neglected who become neglectful, the loved but firmly handled children who become self-confident and socially competent. The power of the family environment also appears in the remarkable academic and vocational successes of children of people who fled from Vietnam and Cambodia—successes attributed to close-knit, supportive, even demanding families (Caplan et al., 1992).

Yet in personality measures, shared environmental influences from the womb onward typically account for less than 10 percent of children's personality differences. In the words of Robert Plomin and Denise Daniels (1987; Plomin, 2011), "Two children in the same family are [apart from their shared genes] as different from one another as are pairs of children selected randomly from the population."

identity our sense of self; according to Erikson, the adolescent's task is to solidify a sense of self by testing and blending various roles.

social identity the "we" aspect of our self-concept; the part of our answer to "Who am I?" that comes from our group memberships.

intimacy in Erikson's theory, the ability to form close, loving relationships; a primary developmental task in early adulthood.

"So I blame you for everything—whose fault is that?"

To developmental psychologist Sandra Scarr (1993), this meant that "parents should be given less credit for kids who turn out great and blamed less for kids who don't." Knowing that children are not easily sculpted by parental nurture, perhaps parents can relax a bit more and love their children for who they are.

The genetic leash may limit the family environment's influence on personality, but does it mean that adoptive parenting is a fruitless venture? *No.* As a new adoptive parent, I [ND] especially find it heartening to know that parents do influence their children's attitudes, values, manners, politics, and faith (Reifman & Cleveland, 2007). A pair of adopted children or identical twins *will,* if raised together, have more similar religious beliefs, especially during adolescence (Kelley & De Graaf, 1997; Koenig et al., 2005; Rohan & Zanna, 1996).

Child neglect, abuse, and parental divorce are rare in adoptive homes, in part because adoptive parents are carefully screened. Despite a slightly greater risk of psychological disorder, most adopted children thrive, especially when adopted as infants (Benson et al., 1994; Wierzbicki, 1993).

ADOPTION MATTERS As country music singer Faith Hill and Apple co-founder Steve Jobs have known, children benefit from one of the biggest gifts of love: adoption.

Seven in eight report feeling strongly attached to one or both adoptive parents. As children of self-giving parents, they themselves grow up to be more self-giving than average (Sharma et al., 1998). Many score higher than their biological parents and raised-apart biological siblings on intelligence tests, and most grow into happier and more stable adults (Kendler et al., 2015; van IJzendoorn et al., 2005). Regardless of personality differences between parents and their adoptees, children benefit from adoption. Parenting matters!

The investment in raising a child buys many years of joy and love, but also of worry and irritation. Yet for most people who become parents, a child is one's biological and social legacy—one's personal investment in the human future. To paraphrase psychiatrist Carl Jung, we reach backward into our parents and forward into our children, and through their children into a future we will never see, but about which we must therefore care.

Retrieve + Remember

- What is the *selection effect,* and how might it affect a teen's decision to join sports teams at school?

ANSWER: Adolescents tend to select similar others and to sort themselves into like-minded groups. For an athletic teen, this could lead to finding other athletic teens and joining school teams together.

Emerging Adulthood

LOQ 3-16 What is emerging adulthood?

In the Western world, adolescence now roughly equals the teen years. At earlier times, and in other parts of the world today, this slice of life has been much smaller (Baumeister & Tice, 1986). Shortly after sexual maturity, teens would assume adult responsibilities and status. The event might be celebrated with an elaborate initiation—a public rite of passage. The new adult would then work, marry, and have children.

Where schooling became compulsory, independence was put on hold until after graduation. And as educational goals rose, so did the age of independence. Adolescents are now taking more time to finish college, leave the nest, and establish careers. In 1960, three-quarters of all U.S. women and two-thirds of all U.S. men had, by age 30, finished school, left home, become financially independent, married, and had a child. Today, fewer than half of 30-year-old women and one-third of 30-year-old men have met these five milestones (Henig, 2010).

Delayed independence has overlapped with an earlier onset of puberty, widening the once-brief gap between child and adult (**FIGURE 3.15**). In well-off communities, the time from 18 to the mid-twenties is an increasingly not-yet-settled phase of life, now often called **emerging adulthood** (Arnett, 2006, 2007).

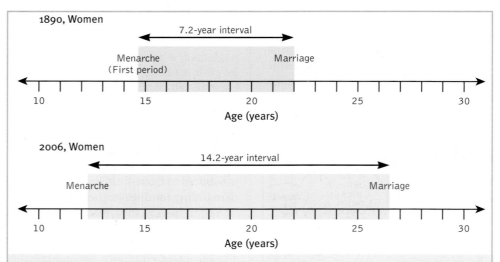

FIGURE 3.15 The transition to adulthood is being stretched from both ends In the 1890s, the average interval between a woman's first menstrual period and marriage, which typically marked a transition to adulthood, was about 7 years. Over a century later in industrialized countries, that gap had widened to about 14 years (Finer & Philbin, 2014; Guttmacher Institute, 1994). Although many adults are unmarried, later marriage combines with prolonged education and earlier menarche to help stretch out the transition to adulthood.

"When I was your age, I was an adult."

No longer adolescents, these emerging adults, having not yet assumed adult responsibilities and independence, feel "in between." Those in college or the job market after high school may be setting their own goals and managing their own time more than ever before. Yet they may still be living in their parents' home, unable to afford their own place and perhaps still emotionally dependent as well. Recognizing today's more gradually emerging adulthood, the U.S. government now allows children up to age 26 to remain on their parents' health insurance (Cohen, 2010).

such statements about the adult years is much more difficult. If we know that James is a 1-year-old and Jamal is a 10-year-old, we can say a great deal about each child. Not so with adults who differ by a decade. A 20-year-old may be a parent who supports a child or a child who gets an allowance. A new mother may be 25 or 45. A boss may be 30 or 60.

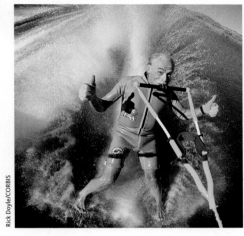

Rick Doyle/CORBIS

ADULT ABILITIES VARY WIDELY In 2012, George Blair maintained his place in the record books as the world's oldest barefoot water skier. He is shown here in 2002 when he first set the record, at age 87. (He died in 2013 at age 98.)

early *adulthood* (roughly twenties and thirties), *middle adulthood* (to age 65), and *late adulthood* (the years after 65). Remember, though, that within each of these stages, people vary widely in physical, psychological, and social development.

Physical Development

LOQ 3-17 How do our bodies and sensory abilities change from early to late adulthood?

Early Adulthood

Our physical abilities—our muscular strength, reaction time, sensory keenness, and cardiac output—all crest by our mid-twenties. Like the declining daylight at the end of summer, the pace of our physical decline is a slow creep. Athletes are often the first to notice. Baseball players peak at about age 27—with 60 percent of Most Valuable Player awardees since 1985 coming ±2 years of that (Silver, 2012). But few of the rest of us notice. Unless our daily lives require us to be in top physical condition, we hardly perceive the early signs of decline.

Middle Adulthood

During early and middle adulthood, physical vigor has less to do with age than with a person's health and exercise habits. Sedentary 25-year-olds may find themselves huffing and puffing up two flights of stairs. When they make it to the top and glance out the window, they may see their physically fit 50-year-old neighbor jog by on a daily 4-mile run.

Physical decline is gradual, but as most athletes know, the pace of that decline gradually picks up. As a lifelong basketball player, I [DM] find myself increasingly not racing for that loose ball. The good news is that even diminished vigor is enough for normal activities.

Retrieve + Remember

• Match the psychosocial development stage below (1–8) with the issue that Erikson believed we wrestle with at that stage (a–h).

1. Infancy
2. Toddlerhood
3. Preschool
4. Elementary school
5. Adolescence
6. Young adulthood
7. Middle adulthood
8. Late adulthood

a. Generativity vs. stagnation
b. Integrity vs. despair
c. Initiative vs. guilt
d. Intimacy vs. isolation
e. Identity vs. role confusion
f. Competence vs. inferiority
g. Trust vs. mistrust
h. Autonomy vs. shame and doubt

ANSWERS: 1. g, 2. h, 3. c, 4. f, 5. e, 6. d, 7. a, 8. b

Adulthood

The unfolding of our lives continues across the life span. Earlier in this chapter, we considered what we all share in life's early years. Making

Nevertheless, our life courses are in some ways similar. Physically, cognitively, and especially socially, we differ at age 60 from our 25-year-old selves. In the discussion that follows, we recognize these differences and use three terms:

emerging adulthood a period from about age 18 to the mid-twenties, when many in Western cultures are no longer adolescents but have not yet achieved full independence as adults.

Aging also brings a gradual decline in fertility. For a 35- to 39-year-old woman, the chances of getting pregnant after a single act of intercourse are only half those of a woman 19 to 26 (Dunson et al., 2002). Women experience **menopause,** the end of the menstrual cycle, usually within a few years of age 50. There is no male menopause—no end of fertility or sharp drop in sex hormones. Men experience a more gradual decline in sperm count, testosterone level, and speed of erection and ejaculation.

Late Adulthood

Is old age "more to be feared than death" (Juvenal, *Satires*)? Or is life "most delightful when it is on the downward slope" (Seneca, *Epistulae ad Lucilium*)? What is it like to grow old?

Although physical decline begins in early adulthood, we are not usually acutely aware of it until later in life. Vision changes. We have trouble seeing fine details, and our eyes take longer to adapt to changes in light levels. As the eye's pupil shrinks and its lens grows cloudy, less light reaches the *retina*—the light-sensitive inner portion of the eye.

In fact, a 65-year-old retina receives only about one-third as much light as its 20-year-old counterpart (Kline & Schieber, 1985). Thus, to see as well as a 20-year-old when reading or driving, a 65-year-old needs three times as much light.

Aging also levies a tax on the brain. The small, gradual net loss of brain cells begins in early adulthood. By age 80, the brain has lost about 5 percent of its former weight. Some of the brain regions that shrink during aging are the areas important for memory (Schacter, 1996; Ritchie et al., 2015). No wonder adults feel older after taking a memory test. "[It's like] aging 5 years in 5 minutes," joked one research team (Hughes et al., 2013). The frontal lobes, which help restrain impulsivity, also shrink, which helps explain older people's occasional blunt questions ("Have you put on weight?") or inappropriate comments (von Hippel, 2007, 2015). Happily for us, there is still some *plasticity* in the aging brain. It partly compensates for what it loses by recruiting and reorganizing neural networks (Park & McDonough, 2013).

"I am still learning."

Michelangelo, 1560, at age 85

Up to the teen years, we process information with greater and greater speed (Fry & Hale, 1996; Kail, 1991). But compared with teens and young adults, older people take a bit more time to react, to solve perceptual puzzles, even to remember names (Bashore et al., 1997; Verhaeghen & Salthouse, 1997). This neural processing lag is greatest on complex tasks (Cerella, 1985; Poon, 1987). At video games, most 70-year-olds are no match for a 20-year-old.

But there is some good news. A study of identical twin pairs—in which only one of the two exercised—shows that exercise slows aging (Rottensteiner et al., 2015). Physical exercise enhances muscles, bones, and energy and helps to prevent obesity and heart disease. It also stimulates brain cell development and neural connections (Erickson et al., 2010; Pereira et al., 2007). That may help explain why sedentary older adults randomly assigned to aerobic exercise programs exhibit enhanced memory, sharpened judgment, and reduced risk of severe cognitive decline (DeFina et al., 2013; Liang et al., 2010; Nagamatsu et al., 2013; Vidoni et al., 2015). Exercise also promotes *neurogenesis* (the birth of new nerve cells) in the hippocampus, a brain region important for memory.

Exercise also helps maintain the *telomeres,* which protect the ends of chromosomes (Erickson, 2009; Leslie, 2011; Loprinzi et al., 2015). With age, telomeres wear down, much as the tip of a shoelace frays. Smoking, obesity, or stress can speed up this wear. Children who suffer frequent abuse or bullying exhibit shortened telomeres as biological scars (Shalev et al., 2013). As telomeres shorten, aging cells may die without being replaced with perfect genetic copies (Epel, 2009).

The message is clear: We are more likely to rust from disuse than to wear out from overuse. Fit bodies support fit minds.

Muscle strength, reaction time, and stamina also diminish noticeably in late adulthood. The fine-tuned senses of smell, hearing, and distance perception that we took for granted in our twenties

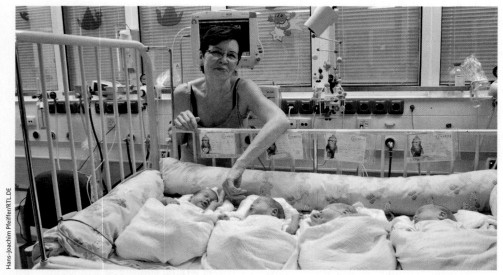

Hans-Joachim Pfeiffer/RTL.DE

NOT YOUR AVERAGE MOM Annegret Raunigk shocked the world when, at age 65 (and with the help of modern science), she gave birth to quadruplets, who joined 13 siblings. Some people celebrated. Others scorned her decision to have children at such an advanced age. Raunigk has defended her decision, noting, "I was fit to have them and I am fit to care for them" (Hall, 2016).

and thirties will become distant memories. In later life, the stairs get steeper, the print gets smaller, and other people seem to mumble more.

For those growing older, there is both bad and good news about health. The bad news: The body's disease-fighting immune system weakens, putting older adults at higher risk for life-threatening ailments, such as cancer and pneumonia. The good news: Thanks partly to a lifetime's collection of antibodies, those over 65 suffer fewer short-term ailments, such as common flu and cold viruses. One study found they were half as likely as 20-year-olds and one-fifth as likely as preschoolers to suffer upper respiratory flu each year (National Center for Health Statistics, 1990). No wonder older workers have lower absenteeism rates (Rhodes, 1983).

For both men and women, sexual activity also remains satisfying after middle age. When does sexual desire diminish? In one sexuality survey, age 75 was the point when most women and nearly half the men reported little sexual desire (DeLamater, 2012; DeLamater & Sill, 2005). In another study, 75 percent of those surveyed nevertheless reported being sexually active into their eighties (Schick et al., 2010).

> "The things that stop you having sex with age are exactly the same as those that stop you riding a bicycle (bad health, thinking it looks silly, no bicycle)."
>
> Alex Comfort, *The Joy of Sex*, 2002

Cognitive Development

Aging and Memory

LOQ 3-18 How does memory change with age?

As we age, we remember some things well. Looking back in later life, adults asked to recall the one or two most important events over the last half-century tend to name events from their teens or twenties (Conway et al., 2005; Rubin et al., 1998). Whatever people experienced

around this time of life—the Vietnam War, the 9/11 terrorist attacks, the election of the first Black U.S. president—gets remembered (Pillemer, 1998; Schuman & Scott, 1989). Our teens and twenties are also the time when we experience many of our big "firsts"—our first date, first job, first day at college, first meeting our romantic partner's parents.

Early adulthood is indeed a peak time for some types of learning and remembering. Consider one experiment in which 1205 people were invited to learn some names (Crook & West, 1990). They watched video clips in which 14 strangers said their names, using a common format: "Hi, I'm Larry." Then those strangers reappeared and gave additional details. For example, they said "I'm from Philadelphia," which gave viewers more visual and voice cues for remembering the person's name. After a second and third replay of the introductions, everyone remembered more names, but younger adults consistently remembered more names than older adults. How well older people remember depends in part on the task. When asked to *recognize* words they had

menopause the end of menstruation. In everyday use, it can also mean the biological transition a woman experiences from before until after the end of menstruation.

earlier tried to memorize, people showed only a slight decline in memory. When asked to *recall* that information without clues, however, the decline was greater (**FIGURE 3.16**).

No matter how quick or slow we are, remembering seems also to depend on the type of information we are trying to retrieve. If the information is meaningless—nonsense syllables or unimportant events—then the older we are, the more errors we make. If the information is *meaningful,* older people's rich web of existing knowledge will help them to hold it. But they may take longer than younger adults to *produce* the words and things they know. Older adults also more often experience tip-of-the-tongue forgetting (Ossher et al., 2012). Quick-thinking game show winners are usually young or middle-aged adults (Burke & Shafto, 2004).

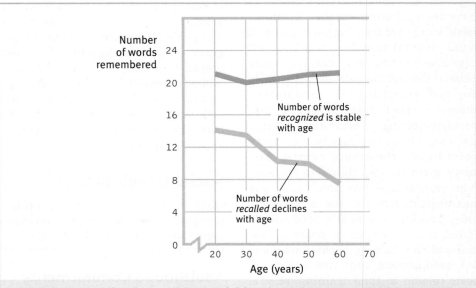

FIGURE 3.16 Recall and recognition in adulthood In this experiment, the ability to *recall* new information declined during early and middle adulthood, but the ability to *recognize* new information did not. (Data from Schonfield & Robertson, 1966.)

Chapter 8 explores another dimension of cognitive development: intelligence. As we will see, **cross-sectional studies** (comparing people of different ages) and **longitudinal studies** (restudying the same people over time) have identified mental abilities that do and do not change as people age. Age is less a predictor of memory and intelligence than is the nearness of death. Knowing whether someone is 8 months or 8 years from a natural death, regardless of age, gives a clue to that person's mental ability. In the last three or four years of life and especially as death approaches, negative feelings and the rate of cognitive decline typically increase (Vogel et al., 2013; Wilson et al., 2007). Researchers call this near-death drop *terminal decline* (Backman & MacDonald, 2006). As death approaches, our goals also shift. We're driven less to learn and more to connect socially (Carstensen, 2011).

📱 **LaunchPad**   See LaunchPad's *Video: Longitudinal and Cross-Sectional Studies* for a helpful tutorial animation.

Sustaining Mental Abilities

Psychologists who study the aging mind have been debating whether "brain-fitness" computer training programs can build "mental muscles" and hold off cognitive decline. Our brain remains plastic throughout life (Gutchess, 2014). So, can exercising our brain—with memory, visual tracking speed, and problem-solving exercises—prevent us from losing our minds? "At every point in life, the brain's natural plasticity gives us the ability to improve how our brains function," said one neuroscientist-entrepreneur (Merzenich, 2007). One study of nearly 3000 people found that 10 cognitive training sessions, with follow-up booster sessions, led to improved cognitive scores on tests related to their training (Boron et al., 2007; Willis et al., 2006).

Based on such findings, some computer game makers have been marketing

The New Yorker Collection Kaamran Hafeez from cartoonbank.com

"I've been working out for six months, but all my gains have been in cognitive function."

daily brain-exercise programs for older people. But other researchers, after reviewing all the available studies, advise caution (Melby-Lervåg & Hulme, 2013; Redick et al., 2013; Salthouse, 2010; Shipstead et al., 2012a,b). A British study of 11,430 people who either completed one of two sets of brain-training activities over six weeks, or instead completed a control task, confirms the limited benefits. Although the training improved the practiced skills, it did not boost overall cognitive fitness (Makin, 2015b; Owens et al., 2010). In 2016, the maker of one prominent brain-training program, Lumosity, was fined $2 million for deceiving customers about the program's supposed benefits. "Lumosity preyed on consumers' fears about age-related cognitive decline," said the Federal Trade Commission's Jessica Rich (Federal Trade Commission, 2016). "But Lumosity simply did not have the science to back up its ads."

Social Development

LOQ 3-19 What are adulthood's two primary commitments, and how do chance events and the social clock influence us?

Adulthood's Commitments

Two basic aspects of our lives dominate adulthood. Erik Erikson called them *intimacy* (forming close relationships) and

generativity (being productive and supporting future generations). Sigmund Freud (1935/1960) put it most simply: The healthy adult, he said, is one who can *love* and *work*.

LOVE We typically flirt, fall in love, and commit—one person at a time. "Pair-bonding is a trademark of the human animal," observed anthropologist Helen Fisher (1993). From an evolutionary perspective, this pairing makes sense. Parents who cooperated to nurture their children to maturity were more likely to have their gene-carrying children survive and reproduce.

Romantic attraction is often influenced by chance encounters (Bandura, 1982). Psychologist Albert Bandura (2005) recalled the true story of a book editor who came to one of Bandura's lectures on the "Psychology of Chance Encounters and Life Paths"—and ended up marrying the woman who happened to sit next to him.

Bonds of love are most satisfying and enduring when two adults share similar interests and values and offer mutual emotional and material support.

Andersen Ross/ Blend Images/Alamy

LOVE Intimacy, attachment, commitment—love by whatever name—is central to healthy and happy adulthood.

One of the ties that binds couples is *self-disclosure*—revealing intimate aspects of oneself to others (see Chapter 11). There also appears to be "vow power." Straight and gay romantic relationships sealed with commitment more often endure (Balsam et al., 2008; Rosenfeld, 2014).

The chances that a marriage will last also increase when couples marry after age 20 and are well educated. Compared with their counterparts of 30 years ago, people in Western countries *are* better educated and marrying later (Wolfinger, 2015). These trends may help explain why the American divorce rate, which surged from 1960 to 1980, has since leveled off and even slightly declined in some areas (Schoen & Canudas-Romo, 2006). Despite the drop in divorce, our standards have risen. Both men and women now expect more than an enduring bond when they marry. Most hope for a mate who is a wage earner, caregiver, intimate friend, and warm and responsive lover (Finkel et al., 2015a).

Historically, couples have met at school, on the job, or through family and friends. Thanks to the Internet, many couples now meet online. As one recent national survey revealed, nearly a quarter of heterosexual couples and some two-thirds of same-sex couples found one another online (**FIGURE 3.17**).

Might test-driving life together in a "trial marriage" reduce divorce risk? In one Gallup survey of American twenty-somethings, 62 percent thought it would (Whitehead & Popenoe, 2001). In reality, in Europe, Canada, and the United States, those living together before marriage have had *higher* rates of divorce and marital troubles than those who have not lived together (Jose et al., 2010; Manning & Cohen, 2012; Stanley et al., 2010). The risk appears greatest for those who live together before becoming engaged (Goodwin et al., 2010; Rhoades et al., 2009). These couples tend to be initially less committed to the ideal of enduring marriage, and they become even less marriage-supporting while living together.

Nonetheless, the institution of marriage endures. Ninety-five percent of Americans have either married or want to (Newport & Wilke, 2013). And marriage is a predictor of happiness, sexual satisfaction, income, and mental health (Scott et al., 2010). Neighborhoods with high marriage rates typically have low rates of crime, delinquency, and emotional disorders among children. Since 1972, surveys of more than 50,000 Americans have revealed that 40 percent of married adults report being "very happy," compared with 23 percent of unmarried adults. Lesbian couples, too, report greater well-being than those who are single (Peplau & Fingerhut, 2007; Wayment & Peplau, 1995).

Often, love bears children. For most people, this most enduring of life changes is a happy event—one that adds meaning, joy, and occasional stress (S. K. Nelson et al., 2013; Witters, 2014). "I feel an overwhelming love for my children unlike anything I feel for anyone else," said 93 percent of American mothers in a national survey (Erickson & Aird, 2005). Many fathers feel the same. A few weeks after the birth of my first child, I [DM] was suddenly struck by a realization: "So *this* is how my parents felt about me!"

Children eventually leave home. This departure is a significant and sometimes difficult event. But for most people, an empty nest is a happy place (Adelmann et al., 1989; Gorchoff et al., 2008). Many parents experience a "postlaunch honeymoon," especially if they maintain close relationships with their children (White & Edwards, 1990). As Daniel Gilbert (2006) concluded, "The only known symptom of 'empty nest syndrome' is increased smiling."

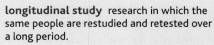 To explore the connection between parenting and happiness, visit LaunchPad's IMMERSIVE LEARNING: *How Would You Know If Having Children Relates to Being Happier?*

WORK Having work that fits your interests provides a sense of competence and accomplishment. For many adults, the answer to "Who are you?" depends a great deal on the answer to "What do you do?"

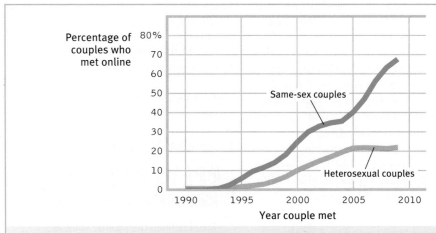

FIGURE 3.17 **The changing way Americans meet their partners** A national survey of 2452 straight couples and 462 gay and lesbian couples reveals the increasing role of the Internet. (Data from Rosenfeld, 2013; Rosenfeld & Thomas, 2012.)

cross-sectional study research in which people of different ages are compared with one another.

longitudinal study research in which the same people are restudied and retested over a long period.

JOB SATISFACTION AND LIFE SATISFACTION Work can provide us with a sense of identity and competence and opportunities for accomplishment. Perhaps this is why challenging and interesting occupations enhance people's happiness.

Choosing a career path is difficult, especially during bad economic times. (See Appendix B: Psychology at Work for more on building work satisfaction.)

For both men and women, there exists a **social clock**—a culture's definition of "the right time" to leave home, get a job, marry, have children, and retire. It's the expectation people have in mind when saying "I married early" or "I started college late." Today the clock still ticks, but people feel freer about keeping their own time.

Well-Being Across the Life Span

LOQ 3-20 What factors affect our well-being in later life?

To live is to grow older. This moment marks the oldest you have ever been and the youngest you will henceforth be. That means we all can look back with satisfaction or regret, and forward with hope or dread. When asked what they would have done differently if they could relive their lives, people most often answer, "taken my education more seriously and worked harder at it" (Kinnier & Metha, 1989; Roese & Summerville, 2005). Other regrets—"I should have told my father I loved him," "I regret that I never went to Europe"—have also focused less on mistakes made than on the things one *failed* to do (Gilovich & Medvec, 1995).

How will you look back on your life 10 years from now? Are you making choices that someday you will recollect with satisfaction?

From the teens to midlife, people's sense of identity, confidence, and self-esteem typically grows stronger (Huang, 2010; Robins & Trzesniewski, 2005). The popular image of the midlife crisis—an early-forties man who leaves his family for a younger romantic partner and a hot sports car—is more myth than reality (Hunter & Sundel, 1989; Mroczek & Kolarz, 1998). In later life, challenges arise. Income often shrinks. Work is often taken away. The body declines. Recall fades. Energy wanes. Family members and friends die or move away. The great enemy, death, looms ever closer.

Prior to the very end, however, the over-65 years are not notably unhappy: Self-esteem, for example, remains stable (Wagner et al., 2013). The Gallup Organization asked 658,038 people worldwide to rate their lives on a ladder from 0 ("the worst possible life") to 10 ("the best possible life"). Age—from 15 to over 90 years—gave no clue to life satisfaction (Morrison et al., 2014).

"At 20 we worry about what others think of us. At 40 we don't care what others think of us. At 60 we discover they haven't been thinking about us at all."

Anonymous

If anything, positive feelings, supported by better emotional control, tend to grow after midlife, and negative feelings decline (Stone et al., 2010; Urry & Gross, 2010). Compared with younger Chinese and American adults, older adults are *more* attentive to positive news (Isaacowitz, 2012; Wang et al., 2015b). Like people of all ages, older adults are happiest when not alone (**FIGURE 3.18**). Older adults experience fewer problems in their relationships—less attachment anxiety, stress, and anger (Chopik et al., 2013; Fingerman & Charles, 2010; Stone et al., 2010). With age, we become more stable and more accepting (Carstensen et al., 2011; Shallcross et al., 2013).

Throughout the life span, the bad feelings tied to negative events fade faster than the good feelings linked with positive events (Walker et al., 2003). This leaves most older people with the comforting feeling that life, on balance, has been mostly good. As the years go by, feelings mellow (Brose et al., 2015). Highs become less high, lows less low.

Retrieve + Remember

- Freud defined the healthy adult as one who is able to _____ and to _____.

ANSWERS: love; work

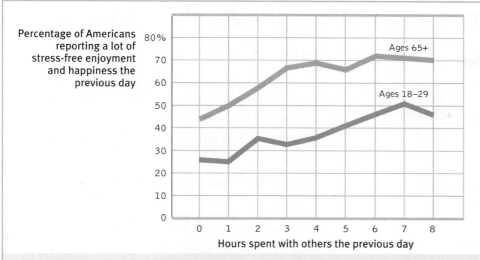

FIGURE 3.18 Humans are social creatures Both younger and older adults report greater happiness when spending time with others. (Note, this correlation could also reflect happier people being more social.) (Gallup survey data reported by Crabtree, 2011.)

Death and Dying

LOQ 3-21 How do people vary in their responses to a loved one's death?

Warning: If you begin reading the next paragraph, you will die.

But of course, if you hadn't read this, you would still die in due time. Death is our unavoidable end. Most of us will also have to cope with the death of a close relative or friend. Normally, the most difficult separation is from the death of one's spouse or partner—a loss suffered by four times more women than men. When, as usually happens, death comes at an expected late-life time—the "right time" on the social clock—the grieving usually passes.

Grief is especially severe when a loved one's death comes suddenly and before its expected time. The sudden illness or accident that claims a 45-year-old life partner or a child may trigger a year or more of memory-filled mourning. Eventually, this may give way to a mild depression (Lehman et al., 1987).

For some, the loss is unbearable. One study tracked more than 17,000 people who had suffered the death of a child under 18. In the five years following that death, 3 percent of them were hospitalized for the first time in a psychiatric unit. This rate is 67 percent higher than the rate recorded for parents who had not lost a child (Li et al., 2005).

> "Love—why, I'll tell you what love is: It's you at 75 and her at 71, each of you listening for the other's step in the next room, each afraid that a sudden silence, a sudden cry, could mean a lifetime's talk is over."
>
> Brian Moore, *The Luck of Ginger Coffey*, 1960

Why do grief reactions vary so widely? Some cultures encourage public weeping and wailing. Others expect mourners to hide their emotions. In all cultures, some individuals grieve more intensely and openly. Some popular beliefs, however, are not confirmed by scientific studies:

- Those who immediately express the strongest grief do not purge their grief faster (Bonanno & Kaltman, 1999; Wortman & Silver, 1989). However, grieving parents who try to protect their partner by "staying strong" and not discussing their child's death may actually prolong the grieving (Stroebe et al., 2013).

- Grief therapy and self-help groups offer support, but there is similar healing power in the passing of time, the support of friends, and the act of giving support and help to others (Baddeley & Singer, 2009; Brown et al., 2008; Neimeyer & Currier, 2009). After a spouse's death, those who talk often with others or who receive grief counseling adjust about as well as those who grieve more privately (Bonanno, 2009; Stroebe et al., 2005).

- Terminally ill and grief-stricken people do not go through identical stages, such as denial before anger (Friedman & James, 2008; Nolen-Hoeksema & Larson, 1999). Given similar losses, some people grieve hard and long, others grieve less (Ott et al., 2007).

Facing death with dignity and openness helps people complete the life cycle with a sense of life's meaningfulness and unity—the sense that their existence has been good and that life and death are parts of an ongoing cycle. Although death may be unwelcome, life itself can be affirmed even at death. This is especially so for people who review their lives not with despair but with what Erik Erikson called a sense of *integrity*—a feeling that one's life has been meaningful and worthwhile.

Retrieve + Remember

- What are some of the most significant challenges and rewards of growing old?

ANSWER: Challenges: decline of muscular strength, reaction times, stamina, sensory keenness, cardiac output, and immune system functioning; Risk of cognitive decline increases. Rewards: positive feelings tend to grow; negative emotions are less intense; and anger, stress, worry, and social-relationship problems decrease.

social clock the culturally preferred timing of social events such as marriage, parenthood, and retirement.

CHAPTER REVIEW

Developing Through the Life Span

Test yourself by taking a moment to answer each of these Learning Objective Questions (repeated here from within the chapter). Then turn to Appendix D, Complete Chapter Reviews, to check your answers. Research suggests that trying to answer these questions on your own will improve your long-term memory of the concepts (McDaniel et al., 2009).

Developmental Psychology's Major Issues

3-1: What are the three major issues studied by developmental psychologists?

Prenatal Development and the Newborn

3-2: How does conception occur, and what are *chromosomes, DNA, genes,* and the human *genome*? How do genes and the environment interact?

3-3: How does life develop before birth, and how do *teratogens* put prenatal development at risk?

3-4: What are some of the newborn's abilities and traits?

3-5: How do twin and adoption studies help us understand the effects of nature and nurture?

Infancy and Childhood

3-6: During infancy and childhood, how do the brain and motor skills develop?

3-7: From the perspectives of Piaget, Vygotsky, and today's researchers, how does a child's mind develop?

3-8: How do the bonds of attachment form between caregivers and infants?

3-9: Why do secure and insecure attachments matter, and how does an infant's ability to develop basic trust affect later relationships?

3-10: What are the four main parenting styles?

3-11: What outcomes are associated with each parenting style?

Adolescence

3-12: How is adolescence defined, and what major physical changes occur during adolescence?

3-13: How did Piaget, Kohlberg, and later researchers describe cognitive and moral development during adolescence?

3-14: What are the social tasks and challenges of adolescence?

3-15: How do parents and peers influence adolescents?

3-16: What is emerging adulthood?

Adulthood

3-17: How do our bodies and sensory abilities change from early to late adulthood?

3-18: How does memory change with age?

3-19: What are adulthood's two primary commitments, and how do chance events and the social clock influence us?

3-20: What factors affect our well-being in later life?

3-21: How do people vary in their responses to a loved one's death?

TERMS AND CONCEPTS TO REMEMBER

Test yourself on these terms by trying to write down the definition in your own words before flipping back to the referenced page to check your answer.

developmental psychology, p. 69

chromosomes, p. 71

DNA (deoxyribonucleic acid), p. 71

genes, p. 71

heredity, p. 71

genome, p. 71

environment, p. 71

interaction, p. 71

epigenetics, p. 73

zygote, p. 73

embryo, p. 73

fetus, p. 73

teratogen [tuh-RAT-uh-jen], p. 73

fetal alcohol syndrome (FAS), p. 73

reflex, p. 73

temperament, p. 75

identical (monozygotic) twins, p. 75

fraternal (dizygotic) twins, p. 75

maturation, p. 75

critical period, p. 77

cognition, p. 79

schema, p. 79

assimilation, p. 79

accommodation, p. 79

sensorimotor stage, p. 79

object permanence, p. 79

preoperational stage, p. 79

conservation, p. 79

egocentrism, p. 81

theory of mind, p. 81

autism spectrum disorder (ASD), p. 81

concrete operational stage, p. 81

formal operational stage, p. 81

stranger anxiety, p. 83

attachment, p. 83

basic trust, p. 85

adolescence, p. 89

puberty, p. 89

identity, p. 93

social identity, p. 93

intimacy, p. 93

emerging adulthood, p. 95

menopause, p. 97

cross-sectional study, p. 99

longitudinal study, p. 99

social clock, p. 101

CHAPTER TEST

Test yourself repeatedly throughout your studies. This will not only help you figure out what you know and don't know; the testing itself will help you learn and remember the information more effectively thanks to the *testing effect*.

1. The three major issues that interest developmental psychologists are nature/nurture, stability/change, and _____/_____.

2. Although development is lifelong, there is stability of personality over time. For example,

   a. most personality traits emerge in infancy and persist throughout life.

   b. temperament tends to remain stable throughout life.

   c. few people change significantly after adolescence.

   d. people tend to undergo greater personality changes as they age.

3. The threadlike structures made largely of DNA molecules are called _____.

4. A small segment of DNA is referred to as a _____.

5. When the mother's egg and the father's sperm unite, each contributes

   a. one chromosome pair.

   b. 23 chromosomes.

   c. 23 chromosome pairs.

   d. 25,000 chromosomes.

6. Body organs first begin to form and function during the period of the _____; within 6 months, during the period of the _____, the organs are sufficiently functional to allow a good chance to survive and thrive.

   a. zygote; embryo

   b. zygote; fetus

   c. embryo; fetus

   d. placenta; fetus

7. Chemicals that the placenta isn't able to screen out that may harm an embryo or fetus are called _____.

8. Stroke a newborn's cheek and the infant will root for a nipple. This illustrates

   a. a reflex.

   b. nurture.

   c. a preference.

   d. continuity.

9. Fraternal twins result when

   a. a single egg is fertilized by a single sperm and then splits.

   b. a single egg is fertilized by two sperm and then splits.

   c. two eggs are fertilized by two sperm.

   d. two eggs are fertilized by a single sperm.

10. _____ twins share the same DNA.

11. Adoption studies seek to understand genetic influences on personality. They do this mainly by

    a. comparing adopted children with nonadopted children.

    b. evaluating whether adopted children's personalities more closely resemble those of their adoptive parents or their biological parents.

    c. studying the effect of prior neglect on adopted children.

    d. studying the effect of children's age at adoption.

12. _____ studies explore how experiences put molecular marks on genes that trigger or block their expression.

13. Between ages 3 and 6, the human brain experiences the greatest growth in the _____ lobes, which we use for rational planning and which aid memory.

14. Which of the following is true of motor-skill development?

    a. It is determined solely by genetic factors.

    b. The sequence, but not the timing, is universal.

    c. The timing, but not the sequence, is universal.

    d. It is determined solely by environmental factors.

15. Why can't we consciously recall how we learned to walk when we were infants?

16. Use Piaget's first three stages of cognitive development to explain why young children are not just miniature adults in the way they think.

17. Although Piaget's stage theory continues to inform our understanding of children's thinking, many researchers believe that

    a. Piaget's "stages" begin earlier and development is more continuous than he realized.

    b. children do not progress as rapidly as Piaget predicted.

    c. few children progress to the concrete operational stage.

    d. there is no way of testing much of Piaget's theoretical work.

18. An 8-month-old infant who reacts to a new babysitter by crying and clinging to his father's shoulder is showing _____ _____.

19. In a series of experiments, the Harlows found that monkeys raised with artificial mothers tended, when afraid, to cling to their cloth mother, rather than to a wire mother holding the feeding bottle. Why was this finding important?

20. From the very first weeks of life, infants differ in their characteristic emotional reactions, with some infants being intense and anxious, while others are easygoing and relaxed. These differences are usually explained as differences in _____.

21. Adolescence is marked by the onset of

    a. an identity crisis.

    b. puberty.

    c. separation anxiety.

    d. parent-child conflict.

22. According to Piaget, a person who can think logically about abstractions is in the _____ stage.

23. In Erikson's stages, the primary task during adolescence is

    a. attaining formal operations.

    b. forging an identity.

    c. developing a sense of intimacy with another person.

    d. living independent of parents.

24. Some developmental psychologists refer to the period that occurs in some Western cultures from age 18 to the mid-twenties and beyond (up to the time of full adult independence) as _____ _____.

25. By age 65, a person would be most likely to experience a cognitive decline in the ability to

    a. recall and list all the important terms and concepts in a chapter.

    b. select the correct definition in a multiple-choice question.

    c. recall their own birth date.

    d. practice a well-learned skill, such as knitting.

26. How do cross-sectional and longitudinal studies differ?

27. Freud defined the healthy adult as one who is able to love and work. Erikson agreed, observing that the adult struggles to attain intimacy and _____.

28. Contrary to what many people assume,

    a. older people are much less happy than adolescents are.

    b. we become less happy as we move from our teen years into midlife.

    c. positive feelings tend to grow after midlife.

    d. those whose children have recently left home—the empty nesters—have the lowest level of happiness of all groups.

Find answers to these questions in Appendix E, in the back of the book.

IN YOUR EVERYDAY LIFE

Answering these questions will help you make these concepts more personally meaningful, and therefore more memorable.

1. What impresses you the most about infants' abilities, and why?

2. What do you think about the idea that, genetically speaking, we are all nearly identical twins?

3. What kinds of mistakes do you think parents of the past made? What mistakes do you think today's parents might be making?

4. What skills did you practice the most as a child? Which have you continued to use? How do you think this affected your brain development?

5. Imagine your friend says, "Personality (or intelligence) is in the genes." How would you respond?

6. What are the most positive or most negative things you remember about your own adolescence? Who do you credit or blame more—your parents or your peers?

7. Think about a difficult decision you had to make as a teenager. What did you do? Would you do things differently now?

8. What do you think makes a person an adult? Do you feel like an adult? Why or why not?

9. Imagining the future, how do you think you might change? How might you stay the same?

Use 🏊 LearningCurve to create your personalized study plan, which will direct you to the resources that will help you most in 🏊 LaunchPad.

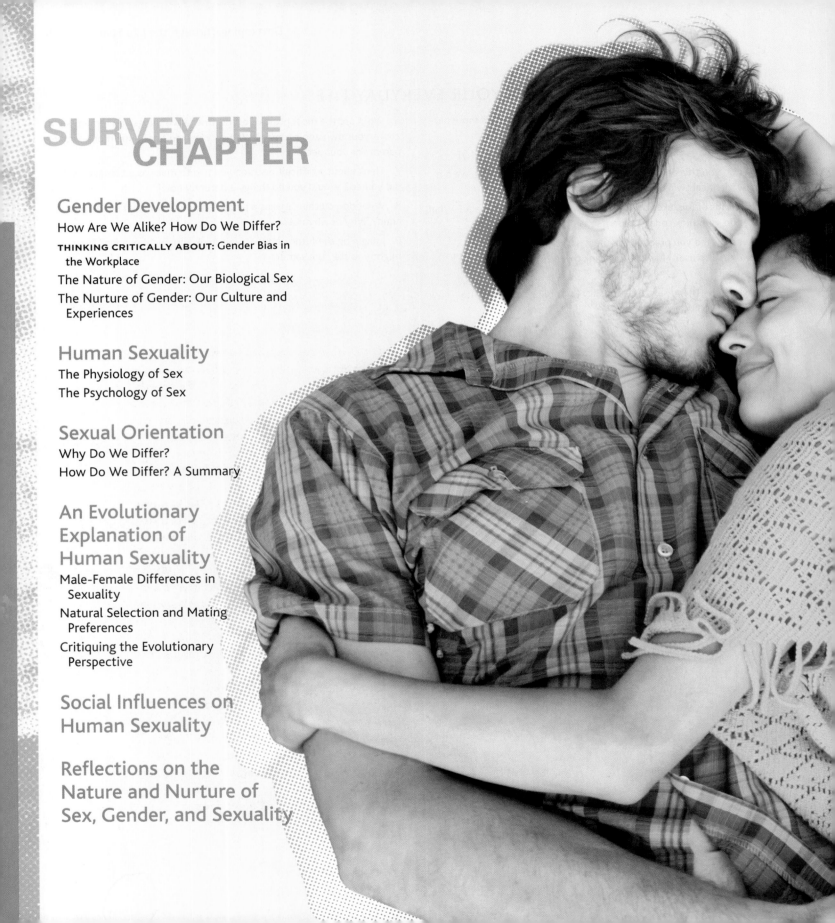

SURVEY THE CHAPTER

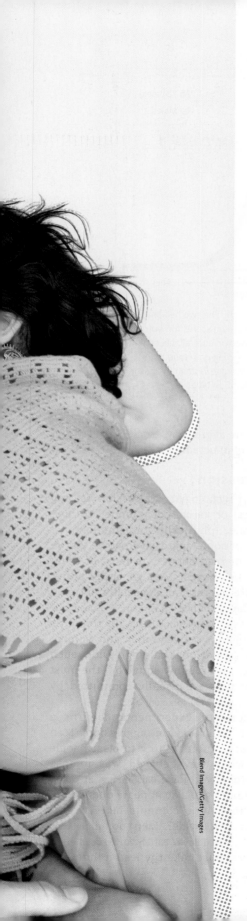

Blend Images/Getty Images

Sex, Gender, and Sexuality

We humans can't resist the urge to organize our world into distinct categories. We divide people, who may reflect an ethnic mix, into "Black," "White," "Asian," or "Hispanic." We eagerly identify people as either male or female. Before or at your birth, everyone wanted to know: "Is it a boy or a girl?" The answer described your *sex*, your biological status, defined by your genes and your anatomy.

For most people, those biological traits also help define their *gender*—their culture's expectations about what it means to be male or female. But there are exceptions. Occasionally a person's *gender identity*—their sense of being male or female—differs from their assigned sex. Writer Mark Morris (2015) reports that this is the case for his famous father, Jan Morris: "My father . . . is transgender. He always knew that he was, underneath, a girl, and my mother knew this when they married in 1949." In 1973, his father had gender reassignment surgery and ever since has been "she" to family and friends. After the gender reassignment, British law (which forbade same-sex marriage) required his father and mother—who "continued to live together in a remarkably strong marital bond"—to divorce. Years later, when same-sex marriages finally became legal, they remarried.

More recently, the public has followed the journey of Caitlyn Jenner, the Olympic decathlon champion whose transition from Bruce Jenner made headlines. Cases like those of Morris and Jenner make us wonder: How do nature and nurture interact to form our unique gender identities? In this chapter, we'll see what researchers tell us about how alike we are as males and females, and how and why we differ. We'll gain insight from psychological science about the psychology and biology of sexual attraction and sexual intimacy. And, as part of the journey, we'll see how evolutionary psychologists explain our sexuality.

Let's start at the beginning. What is gender, and how does it develop?

Gender Development

4-1 How does the meaning of *gender* differ from the meaning of *sex*?

Simply said, your body defines your **sex**. Your mind defines your **gender**. But your mind's understanding of gender arises from the interplay between your biology and your experiences (Eagly & Wood, 2013). Before we consider that interplay in more detail, let's take a closer look at some ways that males and females are both similar and different.

How Are We Alike? How Do We Differ?

LOQ **4-2** What are some ways in which males and females tend to be alike and to differ?

Whether male or female, each of us receives 23 chromosomes from our mother and 23 from our father. Of those 46 chromosomes, 45 are *unisex*—the same for males and females. Our similar biology helped our evolutionary ancestors face similar adaptive challenges. Both men and women needed to survive, reproduce, and avoid predators, and so today we are in most ways alike. Do you identify yourself as male, female, or some combination of the two? No matter your answer, you gave no clues to your vocabulary, happiness, or ability to see, hear, learn, and remember. Whether male or female, we are, on average, similarly creative and intelligent. We feel the same emotions and longings (Hyde, 2014). Our "opposite" sex is, in reality, our very similar sex.

But in some areas, males and females do differ, and differences command attention. Some much-talked-about gender differences (like the difference in self-esteem shown in **FIGURE 4.1**) are actually quite modest (Zell et al., 2015). Others are more striking. The average

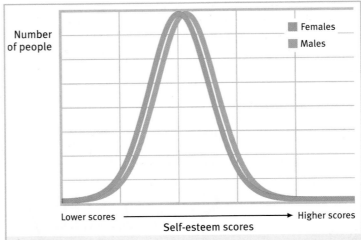

FIGURE 4.1 Different? Yes, but not by much The two bell-shaped curves in this graph show the distribution of self-esteem scores for women (red) and men (blue). These are average scores based on all available samples (Hyde, 2005). As you can see, the variation *among* women or *among* men is much greater than the difference *between* the average woman (highest point on red line) and the average man (highest point on blue line).

girl enters puberty about a year earlier than the average boy, and a woman's life span is 5 years longer. She expresses emotions more freely, smiling and crying more. And in Facebook updates, she more often mentions "love" and being "sooo excited!!!" (Fischer & LaFrance, 2015; Schwartz et al., 2013). She can detect fainter odors, receives offers of help more often, and can become sexually re-aroused sooner after orgasm. She also has twice the risk of developing depression and anxiety and 10 times the risk of developing an eating disorder. Yet the average man is 4 times more likely to die by suicide or to develop alcohol use disorder. His "more likely" list also includes autism spectrum disorder (ASD), color-deficient vision, and attention-deficit/hyperactivity disorder (ADHD). And as an adult, he is more at risk for antisocial personality disorder. Male or female, each has its own share of risks.

Gender similarities and differences appear throughout this book. For now, let's take a closer look at three gender differences. Although individuals vary greatly, the *average* male and female differ in aggression, social power, and social connectedness.

Aggression

To a psychologist, **aggression** is any physical or verbal act intended to hurt someone (physically or emotionally). Think of some aggressive people you've heard or read about. Are most of them men? Likely yes. Men generally admit to more aggression, especially extreme physical violence (Bushman & Huesmann, 2010; Wölfer & Hewstone, 2015). In romantic relationships between men and women, minor acts of physical aggression, such as slaps, are roughly equal, but the most violent acts are usually committed by men (Archer, 2000; Johnson, 2008).

Laboratory experiments confirm a gender difference in aggression. Men have been more willing to blast people with what they believed was intense and prolonged noise (Bushman et al., 2007). The gender gap also appears outside the laboratory. Who commits more violent crimes worldwide? Men do (Antonaccio et al., 2011; Caddick & Porter, 2012; Frisell et al., 2012). Men also take the lead in hunting, fighting, warring, and supporting war (Liddle et al., 2012; Wood & Eagly, 2002, 2007).

Here's another question: Think of examples of people harming others by passing along hurtful gossip, or by shutting someone out of a social group or situation. Were most of those people men? Perhaps not. Those behaviors are acts of **relational aggression,** and women are slightly more likely than men to commit them (Archer, 2004, 2007, 2009).

Social Power

Imagine walking into a job interview. You sit down and peer across the table at your two interviewers. The unsmiling person on the left oozes self-confidence and independence and maintains steady eye contact. The person on the right gives you a warm, welcoming smile but makes less eye contact and seems to expect the other interviewer to take the lead.

Which interviewer is male?

If you said the person on the left, you're not alone. Around the world, from Nigeria to New Zealand, people have perceived gender differences in power (Williams & Best, 1990). Indeed, in most societies men *do* place more importance on power and achievement and *are* socially dominant (Gino et al., 2015; Schwartz & Rubel-Lifschitz, 2009).

> "Because it's 2015."
>
> Canadian Prime Minister Justin Trudeau, when asked why he chose a gender-balanced cabinet

For more on this topic, see Thinking Critically About: Gender Bias in the Workplace.

Social Connectedness

Whether male or female, we humans cherish social connections. We all have a *need to belong* (more on this in Chapter 9). But males and females satisfy this need in different ways (Baumeister, 2010). Males tend to be *independent*. Even as children, males typically form large play groups. Boys' games brim with activity and competition, with little intimate discussion

(Rose & Rudolph, 2006). As adults, males enjoy side-by-side activities, and their conversations often focus on problem solving (Tannen, 1990; Wright, 1989).

Scans of more than 1400 brains show no big differences between the sexes. "Human brains cannot be categorized into two distinct classes: male brain/female brain" (Joel et al., 2015). Brain scans do, however, suggest a subtle difference: A woman's brain, more than a man's, is wired in a way that enables social relationships (Ingalhalikar et al., 2013). This may help explain why females tend to be more *interdependent*. As children, they compete less and imitate social relationships more (Maccoby, 1990; Roberts, 1991). They usually play in small groups, often with one friend. As teens, girls spend less time alone and more time with friends (Wong & Csikszentmihalyi, 1991). Compared with their male counterparts, teen girls average twice as many daily texts and, in late adolescence, spend more time on social networking sites (Lenhart, 2012; Pryor et al., 2007, 2011). Girls' and women's friendships are more intimate, with more conversation that explores relationships (Maccoby, 2002).

More than a half-million people's responses to questions about their interests indicated that "men prefer working with things and women prefer working with people" (Su et al., 2009). Men's search for solutions and actions may contribute to their interest in working with computers. American college men are seven times more likely than women to declare an interest in computer science (Pryor et al., 2011). And consider another big-data analysis, of more than 700 million words collected from Facebook messages: Men used more work-related words, and women used more family-related words (Schwartz et al., 2013). In the workplace, women are less often driven by money and status, and they more often opt for reduced work hours (Pinker, 2008). For many, family obligations loom large. In recent years, fathers have been doing more child care, but mothers still

DEADLY RELATIONAL AGGRESSION Sladjana Vidovic was a high school student who committed suicide after suffering constant relational aggression by bullies.

do nearly twice as much (CEA, 2014; Parker & Wang, 2013; Pew, 2015).

Take a minute now to think about the last time you felt worried or hurt and wanted to talk with someone who would understand. Was that person male or female? At such times, most people turn to women, who are said to *tend and befriend* (Tamres et al., 2002; Taylor, 2002). They support others, and they, more than men, turn to others for support. Both men and women have reported that their friendships with women are more intimate, enjoyable, and nurturing (Kuttler et al., 1999; Rubin, 1985; Sapadin, 1988).

Gender differences in both social connectedness and power are greatest in

---

sex in psychology, the biologically influenced characteristics by which people define *male* and *female*.

gender in psychology, the socially influenced characteristics by which people define *men* and *women*.

aggression any act intended to harm someone physically or emotionally.

relational aggression an act of aggression (physical or verbal) intended to harm a person's relationship or social standing.

Thinking Critically About:
Gender Bias
in the Workplace

LOQ 4-3 What factors contribute to gender bias in the workplace?

Differences in PERCEPTION

Among politicians who seem power-hungry, women are less successful than men.[1]

She's so aggressive!

He's so take-charge!

Most political leaders are men:

Men held 78% of seats in the world's governing parliaments in 2015.[2]

men

Political leaders

women

People around the world tend to see men as more powerful.[3]

When groups form, whether as juries or companies, leadership tends to go to males.[4]

Differences in COMPENSATION

Women in traditionally male occupations have received less than their male colleagues.[5]

Medicine U.S. salary disparity between male and female physicians:[6]

$150,053 women

$211,526 men

Academia Female research grant applicants have received lower "quality of researcher" ratings and have been less likely to be funded.[7] (But as we will see, gender attitudes and roles are changing.)

Differences in CHILD-CARE RESPONSIBILITY

Mothers still do nearly **twice** as much child care as **fathers**.[8]

What else contributes to WORKPLACE GENDER BIAS?

Social norms

In most societies, men place more importance on power and achievement, and are socially dominant.[9]

Leadership styles

Men are more directive, telling people what to do and how to do it.

Women are more democratic, welcoming others' input in decision making.[10]

Interaction styles

Men are more likely to offer opinions.[11]

Women are more likely to express support.[11]

Everyday behavior

Men are more likely to talk assertively, interrupt, initiate touches, and stare.[12]

Women smile and apologize more than men.[12]

Yet GENDER ROLES VARY WIDELY across place and time.

Women are increasingly represented in leadership (now 50% of Canada's cabinet ministers) and in the workforce. In 1963, the Harvard Business School admitted its first women students. Among its Class of 2016, 41% were women.[13] In 1960, women were 6% of U.S. medical students. Today they are about half.[14]

1. Okimoto & Brescoll, 2010.   2. IPU, 2015.   3. Williams & Best, 1990.   4. Colarelli et al., 2006.   5. Willett et al., 2015.   6. Census Bureau, 2014. 7. van der Lee et al., 2015.
8. Parker & Wang, 2013; Pew, 2015; CEA, 2014.   9. Schwartz & Rubel-Lifschitz, 2009; Gino et al., 2015.   10. Eagly & Carli, 2007; van Engen & Willemsen, 2004.
11. Aries, 1987; Wood, 1987.   12. Leaper & Ayres, 2007; Major et al., 1990; Schumann & Ross, 2010. 13. Peck, 2015. 14. AAMC, 2014.

EVERY MAN FOR HIMSELF, OR TEND AND BEFRIEND? Sex differences in the way we interact with others begin to appear at a very young age.

late adolescence and early adulthood—the prime years for dating and mating. By their teen years, girls become less assertive and more flirtatious, and boys appear more dominant and less expressive (Chaplin, 2015). In adulthood, after the birth of a first child, attitudes and behavior differences often peak. Mothers especially may become more traditional (Ferriman et al., 2009; Katz-Wise et al., 2010).

By age 50, most parenting-related gender differences subside. Men become less domineering and more empathic. Women—especially those with paid employment—become more assertive and self-confident (Kasen et al., 2006; Maccoby, 1998).

So, although women and men are more alike than different, there are some behavior differences between the average woman and man. Are such differences dictated by our biology? Shaped by our cultures and other experiences? Do we vary in the extent to which we are male or female? Read on.

Retrieve + Remember

• _____ (Men/Women) are more likely to commit relational aggression, and _____ (men/women) are more likely to commit physical aggression.

ANSWERS: Women; men

The Nature of Gender: Our Biological Sex

LOQ 4-4 How do sex hormones influence prenatal and adolescent development, and what is an *intersex* condition?

In many physical ways, men and women are similar. We sweat to cool down, guzzle an energy drink or coffee to get going in the morning, search for darkness and quiet to sleep. When looking for a mate, we also prize many of the same traits—someone who is "kind," "honest," and "intelligent." But, say evolutionary psychologists, in mating-related domains, guys act like guys whether they're chimpanzees or elephants, rural peasants or corporate presidents (Geary, 2010).

Biology does not *dictate* gender, but it can influence it in two ways:

• *Genetically*—males and females have differing *sex chromosomes*.

• *Physiologically*—males and females have differing concentrations of *sex hormones*, which trigger other anatomical differences.

These influences began to form you long before you were born.

Prenatal Sexual Development

Six weeks after you were conceived, you and someone of the other sex looked much the same. Then, as your genes kicked in, your biological sex became more apparent. Whether you are male or female, your mother's contribution to your twenty-third chromosome pair—the two sex chromosomes—was an **X chromosome.** It was your father's contribution that determined your sex. From him, you received the 1 chromosome out of 46 that is not unisex—either another X chromosome, making you female, or a **Y chromosome,** making you male.

About seven weeks after conception, a single gene on the Y chromosome throws a master switch. "Turned on," this switch triggers the testes to develop and to produce **testosterone,** the main androgen (male hormone) that promotes male sex organ development. (Females also have testosterone, but less of it.) Later, during the fourth and fifth prenatal months, sex hormones bathe the fetal brain and tilt its wiring toward female or male patterns (Hines, 2004; Udry, 2000).

Adolescent Sexual Development

During adolescence, boys and girls enter **puberty** and mature sexually. A surge of hormones triggers a two-year period of rapid physical development, beginning at about age 11 in girls and age 12 in boys, and visible male-female differences

---

X chromosome the sex chromosome found in both men and women. Females typically have two X chromosomes; males typically have one. An X chromosome from each parent produces a female child.

Y chromosome the sex chromosome typically found only in males. When paired with an X chromosome from the mother, it produces a male child.

testosterone the most important male sex hormone. Both males and females have it, but the additional testosterone in males stimulates the growth of the male sex organs during the fetal period and the development of the male sex characteristics during puberty.

puberty the period of sexual maturation, when a person becomes capable of reproducing.

emerge. Hints of this upcoming puberty, such as enlarging testes, appear earlier (Herman-Giddens et al., 2012). A year or two before physical changes are visible, boys and girls often feel the first stirrings of sexual attraction (McClintock & Herdt, 1996).

Girls' slightly earlier entry into puberty can at first propel them to greater height than boys of the same age (**FIGURE 4.2**). But boys catch up when they begin puberty, and by age 14 they are usually taller than girls. During these growth spurts, the **primary sex characteristics**—the reproductive organs and external genitalia—develop dramatically. So do the nonreproductive **secondary sex characteristics.** Girls develop breasts and larger hips. Boys' facial hair begins growing and their voices deepen. Pubic and underarm hair emerge in both girls and boys (**FIGURE 4.3**).

> Pubertal boys may not at first like their sparse beard. (But then it grows on them.)

For boys, puberty's landmark is the first ejaculation, which often occurs during sleep (as a "wet dream"). This event, called **spermarche,** usually happens by about age 14.

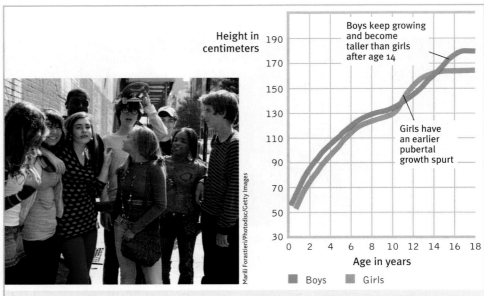

FIGURE 4.2 **Height differences** Throughout childhood, boys and girls are similar in height. At puberty, girls surge ahead briefly, but then boys, on average, overtake them at about age 14. (Data from Tanner, 1978.) Recent studies suggest that sexual development and growth spurts are now beginning somewhat earlier than was the case a half-century ago (Herman-Giddens et al., 2001).

In girls, the landmark is the first menstrual period, **menarche,** usually within a year of age 12½ (Anderson et al., 2003). Genes play a major role in predicting when girls will have their first period (Perry et al., 2014). But environment matters, too. Early menarche is more likely following stresses related to father absence, sexual abuse, insecure attachments, or a history of a mother's smoking during pregnancy (DelPriore & Hill, 2013; Rickard et al., 2014; Shrestha et al., 2011). In various countries, girls are developing breasts earlier (sometimes before age 10)

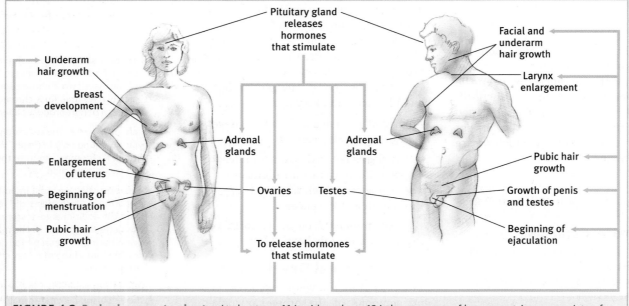

FIGURE 4.3 **Body changes at puberty** At about age 11 in girls and age 12 in boys, a surge of hormones triggers a variety of visible physical changes.

and reaching puberty earlier than in the past. Suspected triggers include increased body fat, diets filled with hormone-mimicking chemicals, and, possibly, greater stress due to family disruption (Biro et al., 2010, 2012; Herman-Giddens et al., 2012).

Girls prepared for menarche usually view it as a positive life transition (Chang et al., 2009). Most women recall the onset of their first menstrual period with mixed emotions—pride, excitement, embarrassment, and apprehension (Greif & Ulman, 1982; Woods et al., 1983). Men report mostly positive emotional reactions to spermarche (Fuller & Downs, 1990).

LaunchPad | For a 7-minute discussion of sexual development, visit LaunchPad's *Video: Gender Development.*

Sexual Development Variations

Nature may blur the biological line between males and females. Sometimes a fetus is exposed to unusual levels of sex hormones or is especially sensitive to those hormones. These **intersex** individuals may be born with unusual combinations of male and female chromosomes, hormones, and anatomy. A genetic male, for example, may be born with normal male hormones and testes but no penis or a very small one. Such individuals may struggle to identify their gender identity.

In the past, medical professionals often recommended *sex-reassignment surgery* to create a clear sex identity for such children. One study reviewed 14 cases of genetic boys who had undergone early sex-reassignment surgery and been raised as girls. Of those cases, 6 later declared themselves male, 5 were living as females, and 3 reported an unclear gender identity (Reiner & Gearhart, 2004). Today, experts generally recommend postponing surgery until a child's naturally developing physical appearance and gender identity become clear.

These conditions raise the question: What makes a *biological* male or female? In 2015, this question made the sports pages when Indian sprinter Dutee Chand was found to have natural testosterone levels higher than most females. The International Association of Athletics Federations suspended Chand, forcing her to miss several events. The Court of Arbitration for Sport finally ruled in favor of Chand, allowing her to continue to compete as a woman.

In one famous case, a little boy lost his penis during a botched circumcision. His parents followed a psychiatrist's advice to raise him as a girl rather than as a dam-

Rafiq Maqbool/AP Images

DEBATING THE BIOLOGICAL MALE-FEMALE DISTINCTION The higher-than-normal testosterone levels of female sprinter Dutee Chand prompted the sporting world to temporarily deny her participation in several competitions.

aged boy. So, with male chromosomes and hormones and female upbringing, did nature or nurture form this child's gender identity? Although raised as a girl, "Brenda" Reimer was not like most other girls. "She" didn't like dolls. She tore her dresses with rough-and-tumble play. At puberty she wanted no part of kissing boys. Finally, Brenda's parents explained what had happened, whereupon "Brenda" immediately rejected the assigned female identity. He cut his hair and chose a male name, David. He eventually married a woman and became a stepfather. And, sadly, he later committed suicide (Colapinto, 2000). *The bottom line:* "Sex matters," concluded the National Academy of Sciences (2001). Sex-related genes and physiology "result in behavioral and cognitive differences between males and females." Yet environmental factors matter, too, as we will see next. Nature and nurture work together.

The Nurture of Gender: Our Culture and Experiences

LOQ 4-5 How do gender roles and gender identity differ?

For many people, biological sex and gender exist together in harmony. Biology draws the outline, and culture paints the

---

primary sex characteristics the body structures (ovaries, testes, and external genitalia) that make sexual reproduction possible.

secondary sex characteristics nonreproductive sexual traits, such as female breasts and hips, male voice quality, and body hair.

spermarche [sper-MAR-key] first ejaculation.

menarche [meh-NAR-key] first menstrual period.

intersex a condition present at birth; possessing biological sexual characteristics of both sexes.

details. The physical traits that define a newborn as male or female are the same worldwide. But the gender traits that define how men (or boys) and women (or girls) should act, interact, and feel about themselves differ from one time and place to another.

Gender Roles

Cultures shape our behaviors by defining how we ought to behave in a particular social position, or **role**. We can see this shaping power in **gender roles**—the social expectations that guide our behavior as men or as women. Gender roles shift over time and they differ from place to place.

In just a thin slice of history, gender roles have undergone an extreme makeover, worldwide. At the beginning of the twentieth century, only one country in the world—New Zealand—granted women the right to vote (Briscoe, 1997). Effective 2015, all countries granted that right. A century ago, American women could not vote in national elections, serve in the military, or divorce a husband without cause. And if a woman worked for pay, she would more likely have been a midwife or a servant than a surgeon or a college professor. Now, more U.S. women than men graduate from college, and nearly half the workforce is female (DOL, 2015). This trend will likely continue. For example, in the STEM fields (science, technology, engineering, and mathematics), men currently hold most faculty positions (Ceci et al., 2014; Sheltzer & Smith, 2014). But when researchers invited U.S. professors to recommend candidates for STEM positions, most said they preferred hiring the highly qualified women over the equally qualified men (Williams & Ceci, 2015). The modern economy has produced jobs that rely not on brute strength but on social intelligence, open communication, and the ability to sit still and focus (Rosin, 2010). What changes might the next hundred years bring?

Take a minute to check your own gender expectations. Would you agree that "When jobs are scarce, men should

"Sex brought us together, but gender drove us apart."

have more rights to a job"? In the United States, Britain, and Spain, a little over 12 percent of adults agree. In Nigeria, Pakistan, and India, about 80 percent of adults agree (Pew, 2010). This question taps people's views on the idea that men and women should be treated equally. We're all human, but my, how our views differ. Northern European countries offer the greatest gender equity, Middle Eastern and North African countries the least (UN, 2015).

"You cannot put women and men on an equal footing. It is against nature. They were created differently."

Recep Tayyip Erdoğan, President of Turkey, 2014

THE GENDERED TSUNAMI In Sri Lanka, Indonesia, and India, the gendered division of labor helps explain the excess of female deaths from the 2004 tsunami. In some villages, 80 percent of those killed were women, who were mostly at home while the men were more likely to be at sea fishing or doing out-of-the-home chores (Oxfam, 2005).

How Do We Learn Gender?

A *gender role* describes how others expect us to think, feel, and act. Our **gender identity** is our personal sense of being male, female, or, occasionally, some combination of the two. How do we develop that personal viewpoint?

Social learning theory assumes that we acquire our gender identity in childhood, by observing and imitating others' gender-linked behaviors and by being rewarded or punished for acting in certain ways. ("Tatiana, you're such a good mommy to your dolls"; "Big boys don't cry, Armand.") But some critics think there's more to gender identity than imitating parents and being rewarded for certain responses. They ask us to consider how much **gender typing**—taking on a traditional male or female role—varies from child to child (Tobin et al., 2010).

Parents do help to transmit their culture's views on gender. In one analysis of 43 studies, parents with traditional gender views were more likely to have gender-typed children who shared their culture's expectations about how males and females should act (Tenenbaum & Leaper, 2002). But no matter how much parents encourage or discourage traditional gender behavior, children may drift toward what feels right to them. Some organize themselves into "boy worlds" and "girl worlds," each guided by their understanding of the rules. Other children seem to prefer **androgyny:** A blend of male and female roles feels right to them. Androgyny has benefits. As adults, androgynous people are more adaptable. They are more flexible in their actions and in their career choices (Bem, 1993). They tend to bounce back more easily from bad events. They accept themselves and are depressed less often (Lam & McBride-Chang, 2007; Mosher & Danoff-Burg, 2008; Ward, 2000).

How we *feel* matters, but so does how we *think*. Early in life, we all form *schemas,* or concepts that help us make sense of our world. Our *gender schemas* organize our experiences of male-female characteristics and help us think about our gender identity, about who we are (Bem, 1987, 1993; Martin et al., 2002).

As young children, we were "gender detectives" (Martin & Ruble, 2004). Before our first birthday, we knew the difference between a male and female voice or face (Martin et al., 2002). After we turned 2, language forced us to label the world in terms of gender. English classifies people as *he* and *she*. Other languages classify objects as masculine ("*le train*") or feminine ("*la table*").

Once children grasp that two sorts of people exist—and that they are of one of these two sorts—they search for clues about gender. In every culture, people communicate their gender in many ways. Their *gender expression* drops hints not only in their language but also in their clothes, toys, books, media, and games. Having picked up such clues, 3-year-olds may divide the human world in half. They will then like their own kind better and seek them out for play. "Girls," they may decide, are the ones who watch *My Little Pony* and have long hair. "Boys" watch *Transformers* battles and don't wear dresses. Armed with their newly collected "proof," they then adjust their behaviors to fit their concept of gender. These stereotypes are most rigid at about age 5 or 6. If the new neighbor is a boy, a 6-year-old girl may assume that she cannot share his interests. In a young child's life, gender looms large.

For a **transgender** person, gender identity differs from the behaviors or traits considered typical for that person's biological sex (APA, 2010; Bockting, 2014). From childhood onward, a person may feel like

THE SOCIAL LEARNING OF GENDER Children observe and imitate parental models.

Courtesy of David Myers

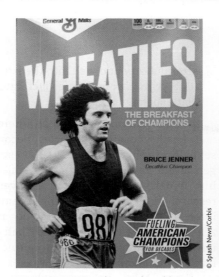

"Call me Caitlyn"
BRUCE BISSINGER *Photo by* ANNIE LEIBOVITZ

© Splash News/Corbis

Polaris Images/Newscom

TRANSGENDER Olympic decathlon champion and reality TV star Bruce Jenner became the world's most famous transgender person and an Internet sensation after transitioning to Caitlyn Jenner.

a male in a female body, or a female in a male body (Olson et al., 2015). In most countries, it's not easy being transgender. In a national survey of lesbian, gay, bisexual, and transgender Americans, 71 percent saw "some" or "a lot" of social acceptance for gay men, and 85 percent said the same for lesbians. But only 18 percent saw similar acceptance for transgender people (Sandstrom, 2015).

Transgender people may attempt to align their outward appearance with their internal gender identity by dressing as a person of the other biological sex typically would. Some transgender people are also *transsexual*: They prefer to live as members of the other birth sex. Brain scans reveal that those (about 75 percent men) who seek medical sex-reassignment have some neural tracts that differ from those of nontransgender men and women (Kranz et al., 2014; Van Kesteren et al., 1997). Note that *gender identity* is distinct from *sexual orientation* (the direction of one's sexual attraction). Transgender people may be sexually attracted to people of the other birth sex (*heterosexual*), the same birth sex (*homosexual*), both sexes (*bisexual*), or to no one at all (*asexual*). Your sexual orientation, as some say, is who you fantasize going to bed *with*; your gender identity is who you go to bed *as*.

> "The more I was treated as a woman, the more woman I became."
>
> Writer Jan Morris, male-to-female transsexual, 1974

Retrieve + Remember

- What are gender roles, and what do their variations tell us about our human capacity for learning and adaptation?

ANSWER: *Gender roles* are social rules or norms for accepted and expected male and female behaviors. Gender roles vary widely in different cultures and over time, which is proof that we are able to learn and adapt to the social demands of different environments.

LaunchPad For a 6.5-minute exploration of one pioneering transgender person's journey, see LaunchPad's *Video: Renée Richards—A Long Journey*.

role a set of expectations (norms) about a social position, defining how those in the position ought to behave.

gender role a set of expected behaviors, attitudes, and traits for males or for females.

gender identity our sense of being male, female, or some combination of the two.

social learning theory the theory that we learn social behavior by observing and imitating and by being rewarded or punished.

gender typing the acquisition of a traditional masculine or feminine role.

androgyny displaying both traditional masculine and feminine psychological characteristics.

transgender an umbrella term describing people whose gender identity or expression differs from that associated with their birth sex.

Human Sexuality

As you've probably noticed, we can hardly talk about gender without talking about our sexuality. For all but the tiny fraction of us considered **asexual**, dating and mating become a high priority from puberty on. Our sexual feelings and behaviors reflect both physiological and psychological influences.

In a British survey of 18,876 people, 1 percent were seemingly asexual, having "never felt sexually attracted to anyone at all" (Bogaert, 2004, 2006b, 2012, 2015). People identifying as asexual are, however, nearly as likely as others to report masturbating, noting that it feels good, reduces anxiety, or "cleans out the plumbing."

The Physiology of Sex

Unlike hunger, sex is not an actual *need*. (Without it, we may feel like dying, but we will not.) Yet sex is a part of life. Had this not been so for all your ancestors, you would not be reading this book. Sexual motivation is nature's clever way of making people procreate, thus enabling our species' survival. As the pleasure we take in eating is nature's method of ensuring we nourish our bodies, so the desires and pleasures of sex are nature's way of driving us to preserve and spread our genes. Life is sexually transmitted.

Hormones and Sexual Behavior

LOQ 4-6 How do hormones influence human sexual motivation?

Among the forces driving sexual behavior are the *sex hormones*. As we noted earlier, the main male sex hormone is *testosterone*. The main female sex hormones are the **estrogens**, such as *estradiol*. Sex hormones influence us at many points in the life span:

- During the prenatal period, they direct our development as males or females.
- During puberty, a sex hormone surge ushers us into adolescence.

- After puberty and well into the late adult years, sex hormones facilitate sexual behavior.

In most mammals, sexual interest and fertility overlap. Females become sexually receptive when their estrogen levels peak at ovulation. By injecting female animals with estrogens, researchers can increase their sexual interest. Hormone injections do not affect male animals' sexual behavior as easily because male hormone levels are more constant (Piekarski et al., 2009). Nevertheless, male hamsters that have had their testosterone-making testes surgically removed gradually lose much of their interest in receptive females. They gradually regain it if injected with testosterone.

Hormones do influence human sexuality, but more loosely. Researchers are exploring and debating whether women's mating preferences change across the menstrual cycle (Gildersleeve et al., 2014; Wood et al., 2014). At ovulation, women's estrogens surge, as does their testosterone, though not as much. (Recall that women have testosterone, though less than men have.) Some evidence suggests that, among women with mates, sexual desire rises slightly at this time—a change men can sometimes detect in women's behaviors and voices (Haselton & Gildersleeve, 2011).

More than other mammalian females, women are responsive to their testosterone levels (van Anders, 2012). If a woman's natural testosterone level drops, as happens with removal of the ovaries or adrenal glands, her sexual interest may plummet (Davison & Davis, 2011; Lindau et al., 2007). But testosterone-replacement therapy can often restore sexual desire, arousal, and activity (Braunstein et al., 2005; Buster et al., 2005; Petersen & Hyde, 2011).

Testosterone-replacement therapy also increases sexual functioning in men with abnormally low testosterone levels (Khera et al., 2011). But normal ups and downs in testosterone levels (from man to man and hour to hour) have little effect on sexual drive (Byrne, 1982). In fact, male hormones sometimes vary in *response* to sexual

stimulation (Escasa et al., 2011). One Australian study tested whether the presence of an attractive woman would affect heterosexual male skateboarders' performance. The result? Their testosterone surged, as did their riskier moves and crash landings (Ronay & von Hippel, 2010). Thus, sexual arousal can be a *cause* as well as a result of increased testosterone.

Large hormonal surges or declines do affect men's and women's desire. These shifts take place at two predictable points in the life span, and sometimes at an unpredictable third point:

1. *During puberty, the surge in sex hormones triggers development of sex characteristics and sexual interest.* If this hormonal surge is prevented, sex characteristics and sexual desire do not develop normally (Peschel & Peschel, 1987). This happened in Europe during the 1600s and 1700s, when boy sopranos were castrated to preserve their high voices for Italian opera.

2. *In later life, estrogen and testosterone levels fall.* Women experience menopause, males a more gradual change (Chapter 3). Sex remains a part of life, but as sex hormone levels decline, sexual fantasies and intercourse decline as well (Leitenberg & Henning, 1995).

3. *For some, surgery or drugs may cause hormonal shifts.* After surgical castration, men's sex drive typically falls as testosterone levels decline sharply (Hucker & Bain, 1990). When male sex offenders took a drug that reduced their testosterone level to that of a boy before puberty, they also lost much of their sexual urge (Bilefsky, 2009; Money et al., 1983).

To recap, we might compare human sex hormones, especially testosterone, to the fuel in a car. Without fuel, a car will not run. But if the fuel level is at least adequate, adding more won't change how the car runs. This isn't a perfect comparison, because hormones and sexual motivation influence each other. But it does suggest that biology alone cannot fully explain human sexual behavior.

Hormones are the essential fuel for our sex drive. But psychological stimuli turn on the engine, keep it running, and shift it into high gear. Let's now see just where that drive usually takes us.

Retrieve + Remember

- The primary male sex hormone is _____. The primary female sex hormones are the _____.

ANSWERS: testosterone; estrogens

The Sexual Response Cycle

LOQ 4-7 What is the human *sexual response cycle,* and how can sexual dysfunctions interfere with this cycle?

As we noted in Chapter 1, science often begins by carefully observing behavior. Sexual behavior is no exception. In the 1960s, two researchers—gynecologist-obstetrician William Masters and his colleague, Virginia Johnson (1966)—made headlines with their observations of sexual behavior. They recorded the physiological responses of 382 female and 312 male volunteers who came to their lab to masturbate or have intercourse. With the help of this atypical sample of people able and willing to display arousal and orgasm while scientists observed, the researchers identified a four-stage **sexual response cycle:**

1. *Excitement:* The genital areas fill with blood, causing a woman's clitoris and a man's penis to swell. A woman's vagina expands and secretes lubricant. Her breasts and nipples may enlarge.

2. *Plateau:* Excitement peaks as breathing, pulse, and blood pressure rates continue to rise. A man's penis becomes fully engorged—to an average 5.6 inches, among 1661 men who measured themselves for condom fitting (Herbenick et al., 2014). Some fluid—frequently containing enough live sperm to enable conception—may appear at its tip. A woman's vaginal secretion continues to increase, and her clitoris retracts. Orgasm feels imminent.

3. *Orgasm:* Muscles contract all over the body. Breathing, pulse, and blood pressure rates continue to climb. Men and women don't differ much in the delight they receive from sexual release. PET scans have shown that the same brain regions were active in men and women during orgasm (Holstege et al., 2003a,b).

4. *Resolution:* The body gradually returns to its unaroused state as genital blood vessels release their accumulated blood. This happens relatively quickly if orgasm has occurred, relatively slowly otherwise. (It's like the nasal tickle that goes away rapidly if you have sneezed, slowly otherwise.) Men then enter a **refractory period,** a resting period that lasts from a few minutes to a day or more. During this time, they cannot achieve another orgasm. Women have a much shorter refractory period, enabling them to have more orgasms if restimulated during or soon after resolution.

> As you learned in Chapter 2's discussion of neural processing, the "refractory period" is also a brief resting pause that occurs after a neuron has fired.

> A nonsmoking 50-year-old male has about a 1-in-a-million chance of a heart attack during any hour. This increases to merely 2-in-a-million in the two hours during and following sex (with no increase for those who exercise regularly). Compared with risks associated with heavy exertion or anger (see Chapter 10), this risk seems not worth losing sleep (or sex) over (Jackson, 2009; Muller et al., 1996).

Sexual Dysfunctions

Masters and Johnson had two goals: to describe the human sexual response cycle, and to understand and treat problems that prevent people from completing that cycle. **Sexual dysfunctions** consistently impair sexual arousal or functioning. Some involve sexual motivation—the person lacks sexual energy and/or does not become aroused. For men, one common problem (and the subject of many TV commercials) is **erectile disorder,** an inability to have or maintain an erection. Another is *premature ejaculation,* reaching a sexual climax before the man or his partner wishes. For some women, pain during intercourse may prevent them from completing the sexual response cycle. Others may experience **female orgasmic disorder,** distress over rarely or never having an orgasm. In surveys of some 35,000 American women, about 4 in 10 reported a sexual problem, such as female orgasmic disorder or low desire. Only about 1 in 8 said that the problem caused them personal distress (Lutfey et al., 2009; Shifren et al., 2008). Most women who have reported sexual distress have connected it with their emotional relationship with their sexual partner (Bancroft et al., 2003).

Psychological and medical therapies can help people with sexual dysfunctions (Frühauf et al., 2013). Behaviorally oriented therapy, for example, can help men learn ways to control their urge to ejaculate, or help women learn to bring themselves to orgasm. Starting with the introduction of Viagra in 1998, erectile

asexual having no sexual attraction to others.

estrogens sex hormones, such as estradiol, that contribute to female sex characteristics and are secreted in greater amounts by females than by males. Estrogen levels peak during ovulation. In nonhuman mammals this promotes sexual receptivity.

sexual response cycle the four stages of sexual responding described by Masters and Johnson—excitement, plateau, orgasm, and resolution.

refractory period in human sexuality, a resting pause that occurs after orgasm, during which a man cannot achieve another orgasm.

sexual dysfunction a problem that consistently impairs sexual arousal or functioning.

erectile disorder inability to develop or maintain an erection due to insufficient bloodflow to the penis.

female orgasmic disorder distress due to infrequently or never experiencing orgasm.

disorder has been routinely treated by taking a pill. Some modestly effective drug treatments for *female sexual interest/ arousal disorder* are also available.

Sexually Transmitted Infections

LOQ 4-8 How can sexually transmitted infections be prevented?

Every day, more than 1 million people worldwide acquire a *sexually transmitted infection (STI; also called STD, for sexually transmitted disease)* (WHO, 2013). "Compared with older adults," reports the Centers for Disease Control (2016b), "sexually active adolescents aged 15–19 years and young adults aged 20–24 years are at higher risk." Teenage girls, for example, are at heightened risk because their anatomy is not fully mature and their level of protective antibodies is lower (Dehne & Riedner, 2005; Guttmacher Institute, 1994).

To understand the mathematics of infection, imagine this scenario. Over the course of a year, Pat has sex with 9 people. By that time, each of Pat's partners has had sex with 9 other people, who in turn have had sex with 9 others. How many partners—including "phantom" sex partners (past partners of partners) will Pat have? The actual number—511—is more than five times the estimate given by the average student (Brannon & Brock, 1993).

Condoms are very effective in blocking the spread of some STIs. The effects were clear when Thailand promoted condom use by commercial sex workers. Over a 4-year period, condom use soared from 14 to 94 percent. During that time, the number of bacterial STIs reported each year plummeted 93 percent—from 410,406 to 27,362 (WHO, 2000).

Condoms offer only limited protection against certain skin-to-skin STIs, such as herpes. But their ability to reduce other risks has saved lives (NIH, 2001). When used by people with an infected partner, condoms have been 80 percent effective in preventing transmission of HIV (*human immunodeficiency virus*—the virus that causes

AIDS—*acquired immune deficiency syndrome*) (Weller & Davis-Beaty, 2002; WHO, 2003). AIDS can be transmitted by other means, such as needle sharing during drug use, but its sexual transmission is most common. Many people think oral sex is "safe sex," but it carries a significant risk. It is linked to STIs, such as the *human papillomavirus (HPV)*, and risks rise with the number of sexual partners (Ballini et al., 2012; Gillison et al., 2012). Most HPV infections can now be prevented if people are vaccinated before they become sexually active.

Half of all humans with HIV (and one-fourth of Americans with HIV) are women. Women's proportion of the worldwide AIDS population has grown, for several reasons. The virus is passed from man to woman much more often than from woman to man. A man's semen can carry more of the virus than can a woman's vaginal and cervical secretions. The HIV-infected semen can also linger in a woman's vagina and cervix, increasing her exposure time (Allen & Setlow, 1991; WHO, 2015).

Just over half of Americans with AIDS are between ages 30 and 49 (CDC, 2013). Given AIDS' long incubation period, this means that many were infected in their teens and twenties. In 2012, the death of 1.6 million people with AIDS worldwide left behind countless grief-stricken partners and millions of orphaned children (UNAIDS, 2013). In sub-Saharan Africa, home to two-thirds of those with HIV, medical treatment to extend life and care for the dying is sapping social resources.

Retrieve + Remember

- Someone who is distressed by impaired sexual arousal may be diagnosed with a _____ _____.

ANSWER: sexual dysfunction

- From a biological perspective, HIV is passed more readily from women to men than from men to women. True or false?

ANSWER: False. HIV is transmitted more easily and more often from men to women.

The Psychology of Sex

LOQ 4-9 How do external and imagined stimuli contribute to sexual arousal?

Biological factors powerfully influence our sexual motivation and behavior. But despite our shared biology, human sexual motivation and behavior vary widely—over time, across place, and among individuals. So social and psychological factors exert a great influence as well (**FIGURE 4.4**).

What motivates people to have sex? The 281 (by one count) expressed reasons have ranged widely—from "to get closer to God" to "to get my boyfriend to shut up" (Buss, 2008; Meston & Buss, 2007). One thing is certain: Our most important sex organ may be the one resting above our shoulders. Our sophisticated brain enables sexual arousal both from what is real and from what is imagined.

External Stimuli

Men and women become aroused when they see, hear, or read erotic material (Heiman, 1975; Stockton & Murnen, 1992). In men more than in women, *feelings* of sexual arousal closely mirror their (more obvious) physical genital responses (Chivers et al., 2010).

People may find sexual arousal either pleasing or disturbing. (Those who wish to control their arousal often limit their exposure to arousing material, just as those wishing to avoid overeating limit their exposure to tempting food cues.) With repeated exposure to any stimulus, including an erotic stimulus, our response lessens—we *habituate*. During the 1920s, when Western women's rising hemlines first reached the knee, many male hearts fluttered when viewing a woman's leg. Today, many men wouldn't notice.

Can exposure to sexually explicit material have lingering negative effects? Researchers have found that it can, in two areas especially.

- *Believing rape is acceptable:* In some studies, people have viewed scenes in which women were forced to have sex and appeared to enjoy it. Those viewers were more accepting of the

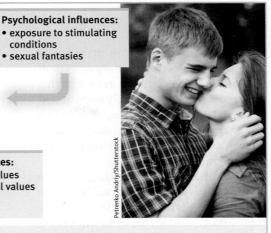

Biological influences:
• sexual maturity
• sex hormones, especially testosterone

Psychological influences:
• exposure to stimulating conditions
• sexual fantasies

Sexual motivation

Social-cultural influences:
• family and societal values
• religious and personal values
• cultural expectations
• media

Petrenko Andriy/Shutterstock

FIGURE 4.4 Levels of analysis for sexual motivation Our sexual motivation is influenced by biological factors, but psychological and social-cultural factors play an even bigger role.

false idea that many women want to be overpowered. Male viewers also expressed more willingness to hurt women and to commit rape after viewing these scenes (Allen et al., 1995, 2000; Foubert et al., 2011; Malamuth & Check, 1981; Zillmann, 1989).

• *Reducing satisfaction with a partner's appearance or with a relationship:* After viewing images or X-rated films of sexually attractive women and men, people have judged an average person, their own partner, or their spouse as less attractive. And they have found their own relationship less satisfying (Kenrick & Gutierres, 1980; Kenrick et al., 1989; Lambert et al., 2012; Weaver et al., 1984). Perhaps reading or watching erotica's unlikely scenarios may create expectations few men and women can fulfill.

GUESS
FLY TO FLORIDA $159
I'M TRYING TO STAY SEXUALLY SATISFIED WITH MY WIFE BUT IT'S TOUGH.
SINGER
MAGAZINES
SPORTS ILLUSTRATED
VOGUE
BEDS
GEORGE
A LURE
© Andy Singer

Imagined Stimuli

Sexual arousal and desire can also be products of our imagination. People left with no genital sensation after a spinal cord injury can still feel sexual desire, and many engage in sexual intercourse (Donohue & Gebhard, 1995; Sipski et al., 1999; Willmuth, 1987).

Both men and women (about 95 percent of each) report having sexual fantasies, which for a few women can produce orgasms (Komisaruk & Whipple, 2011). Men, regardless of sexual orientation, tend to have more frequent, more physical, and less romantic fantasies (Schmitt et al., 2012). They also prefer less personal and faster-paced sexual content in books and videos (Leitenberg & Henning, 1995).

Does fantasizing about sex indicate a sexual problem or dissatisfaction? *No.* If anything, sexually active people have *more* sexual fantasies.

Sexual Risk Taking and Teen Pregnancy

LOQ 4-10 What factors influence teenagers' sexual behaviors and use of contraceptives?

Thanks to decreased sexual activity and increased protection, teen pregnancy rates are declining (CDC, 2016b). Yet compared with European teens, American teens have a higher pregnancy rate (Sedgh et al., 2015). What environmental factors contribute to sexual risk taking among teens?

MINIMAL COMMUNICATION ABOUT BIRTH CONTROL Many teens are uncomfortable discussing birth control with parents, partners, and peers. But teens who talk freely and openly with their parents and with their partner in an exclusive relationship are more likely to use contraceptives (Aspy et al., 2007; Milan & Kilmann, 1987).

"Condoms should be used on every conceivable occasion."

Anonymous

IMPULSIVE SEXUAL BEHAVIOR Among sexually active 12- to 17-year-old American girls, 72 percent said they regretted having had sex (Reuters, 2000). When sexually aroused, people perform poorly on measures of impulse control (Macapagal et al., 2011). If passion overwhelms intentions (either to delay using contraceptives or to delay having sex), unplanned sexual activity may result in pregnancy (Ariely & Loewenstein, 2006; Gerrard & Luus, 1995; MacDonald & Hynie, 2008).

ALCOHOL USE Among late teens and young adults, most sexual hook-ups (casual encounters outside of a relationship) occur after alcohol use, often without knowing consent (Fielder et al., 2013; Garcia et al., 2013; Johnson & Chen, 2015). Those who use alcohol prior to sex are also less likely to use condoms (Kotchick et al., 2001). Alcohol disarms normal restraints by depressing the brain centers that control judgment, inhibition, and self-awareness.

MASS MEDIA INFLUENCES The more sexual content adolescents and young adults view or read, the more likely they are to perceive their peers as sexually active, to develop sexually permissive

---

AIDS (acquired immune deficiency syndrome) a life-threatening, sexually transmitted infection caused by the *human immunodeficiency virus* (HIV). AIDS depletes the immune system, leaving the person vulnerable to infections.

attitudes, and to experience early intercourse (Escobar-Chaves et al., 2005; Kim & Ward, 2012; Parkes et al., 2013). These perceptions of peer norms (what "everybody else" is doing) influence teens' sexual behavior (Lyons et al., 2015; van de Bongardt et al., 2015). And they come in part from the popular media, which help write the **social scripts** that shape our views of how to act in certain situations. So what sexual scripts do today's media write on our minds? Sexual content appears in approximately 85 percent of movies, 82 percent of TV programs, 59 percent of music videos, and 37 percent of music

Apic/Moviepix/Getty Images

KEEPING ABREAST OF HYPERSEXUALITY
An analysis of the 60 top-selling video games found 489 characters, 86 percent of whom were males (like most of the game players). The female characters were much more likely than the male characters to be "hypersexualized"— partially nude or revealingly clothed, with large breasts and tiny waists (Downs & Smith, 2010). Such depictions can lead to unrealistic expectations about sexuality and contribute to the early sexualization of girls. The American Psychological Association suggests countering this by teaching girls to "value themselves for who they are rather than how they look" (APA, 2007).

lyrics (Ward et al., 2014). Twenty percent of middle school students, and 44 percent of 18- to 24-year-olds, report having received a "sext"—a sexually explicit text (Lenhart & Duggan, 2014; Rice et al., 2014). Online dating sites, such as Tinder, enable young people to seek out quick hook-ups with little emotional investment.

Media influences can either increase or decrease sexual risk taking. One long-term study asked more than a thousand 12- to 14-year-olds what movies they had seen. Then, after those teens reached age 18, researchers again asked them about their sexual experiences (O'Hara et al., 2012). (The study controlled for other factors that predict early sexual activity, such as personal and family characteristics.) The result? The more the adolescents had viewed movies with high sexual content, the greater was their sexual risk taking. They started earlier, had more partners, and used condoms inconsistently. Another study analyzed the effect of MTV's series *16 and Pregnant,* which portrayed the consequences of unprotected sex and the challenges of having a child. By analyzing viewership and pregnancy rates over time in specific areas, researchers concluded that the program led to a 6 percent reduction in the national teen pregnancy rate (Kearney & Levine, 2014).

What are the characteristics of teens who delay having sex?

- *High intelligence* Teens with high rather than average intelligence test scores more often delayed sex, partly because they considered possible negative consequences and were more focused on future achievements than on here-and-now pleasures (Harden & Mendle, 2011).
- *Religious engagement* Actively religious teens, especially young women, often reserve sexual activity for adulthood (Hull et al., 2011; Štulhofer et al., 2011). The most common reason U.S. teens give for not having sex is that it conflicts with their "religion or morals" (Guttmacher Institute, 2012).

- *Father presence* Studies that followed hundreds of New Zealand and U.S. girls from age 5 to 18 found that having Dad around reduces the risk of teen pregnancy. A father's presence was linked to lower sexual activity before age 16 and to lower teen pregnancy rates (Ellis et al., 2003).
- *Participation in service learning programs* Teens who volunteered as tutors or teachers' aides, or participated in community projects, have had lower pregnancy rates than other teens randomly assigned to control groups (Kirby, 2002; O'Donnell et al., 2002). Does service learning promote a sense of personal competence, control, and responsibility? Does it encourage more future-oriented thinking? Or does it simply reduce opportunities for unprotected sex? Researchers don't have those answers yet.

* * *

In the rest of this chapter, we will consider two special topics: *sexual orientation* (the direction of our sexual interests), and evolutionary psychology's explanation of our sexuality.

Retrieve + Remember

- What factors influence our sexual motivation and behavior?

ANSWER: Influences include biological factors such as sexual maturity and sex hormones, psychological factors such as environmental stimuli and fantasies, and social-cultural factors such as values and expectations.

- Which THREE of the following five factors contribute to unplanned teen pregnancies?

  a. Alcohol use
  b. Higher intelligence level
  c. Father absence
  d. Mass media models
  e. Participating in service learning programs

ANSWERS: a, c, d

Sexual Orientation

LOQ 4-11 What has research taught us about sexual orientation?

As noted earlier in this chapter, we express the *direction* of our sexual interest in our **sexual orientation**—our enduring sexual attraction toward others. Sexual orientation varies from exclusive interest in our own sex to complete interest in the other sex, with most people in one of those two distinct categories (Norris et al., 2015). Those of us attracted to people of

- our own sex have a *homosexual* (gay or lesbian) orientation.
- the other sex have a *heterosexual* (straight) orientation.
- both sexes have a *bisexual* orientation.

Cultures vary in their attitudes toward same-sex attractions. "Should society accept homosexuality?" *Yes,* say 88 percent of Spaniards, 80 percent of Canadians, 60 percent of Americans, and 1 percent of Nigerians (Pew, 2013). Women everywhere are more accepting than men. Yet whether a culture condemns or accepts same-sex unions, heterosexuality prevails and bisexuality and homosexuality exist. In most African countries, same-sex relationships are illegal. Yet the ratio of people who are lesbian, gay, or bisexual "is no different from other countries in the rest of the world," reports the Academy of Science of South Africa (2015). A large number of Americans—13 percent of women and 5 percent of men—say they have had some same-sex sexual contact during their lives (Chandra et al., 2011). Still more have had an occasional same-sex fantasy. Far fewer (3.4 percent) identify themselves as lesbian, gay, bisexual, or transgender (Gates & Newport, 2012; Ward et al., 2014).

How many people in Europe and the United States are exclusively homosexual? About 10 percent, as the popular press has often assumed? Nearly 20 percent, as Americans, on average, estimated in a 2013 survey (Jones et al., 2014)? Actually, the figure is about 3 or 4 percent of men and 2 percent of women (Chandra et al., 2011; Herbenick et al., 2010; Savin-Williams et al., 2012). Bisexuality is rarer, at less than 1 percent (Ward et al., 2014). In one survey of 7076 Dutch adults, only 12 people said they were actively bisexual (Sandfort et al., 2001).

> In tribal cultures in which homosexual behavior is expected of all boys before marriage, heterosexuality nevertheless persists (Hammack, 2005; Money, 1987). As this illustrates, homosexual *behavior* does not always indicate a homosexual *orientation.*

What does it feel like to have same-sex attractions in a majority straight culture? If you are heterosexual, imagine that you have found "the one"—a perfect partner of the other sex. How would you feel if you weren't sure who you could trust with knowing you had these feelings? How would you react if you overheard people telling crude jokes about straight people, or if most movies, TV shows, and advertisements showed only same-sex relationships? How would you like hearing that many people wouldn't vote for a political candidate who favors other-sex marriage? And how would you feel if children's organizations and adoption agencies thought you might not be safe or trustworthy because you're attracted to people of the other sex?

Facing such reactions, some gays and lesbians may at first try to ignore or deny their feelings, hoping their desires will go away. But they don't go away. Especially during adolescence or when rejected by their parents, people may struggle against their same-sex attractions. Without social support, these teens' self-esteem may fall, and feelings of anxiety and depression may increase (Becker et al., 2014; Kwon, 2013). Some may consider suicide (Plöderl et al., 2013; Ryan et al., 2009; Wang et al., 2012). Later, people may even try to change their nonheterosexual orientation through psychotherapy, willpower, or prayer. But the feelings typically persist, as do those of heterosexual people—who are

DRIVEN TO SUICIDE In 2010, Rutgers University student Tyler Clementi jumped off this bridge after his roommate secretly recorded and broadcast his intimate encounter with another man on the Internet. Reports then surfaced of other gay teens who had reacted in a similarly tragic fashion after being taunted. Since 2010, Americans—especially those under 30—have been increasingly supportive of those with same-sex orientations.

similarly unable to change (Haldeman, 1994, 2002; Myers & Scanzoni, 2005).

Today's psychologists therefore view sexual orientation as neither willfully chosen nor willfully changed. "Efforts to change sexual orientation are unlikely to be successful and involve some risk of harm," declared a 2009 American Psychological Association report. In 1973, the American Psychiatric Association dropped homosexuality from its list of "mental illnesses." In 1993, The World Health Organization did the same, as did Japan's and China's psychiatric associations in 1995 and 2001.

social script culturally modeled guide for how to act in various situations.

sexual orientation an enduring sexual attraction toward members of one's own sex (homosexual orientation), the other sex (heterosexual orientation), or both sexes (bisexual orientation).

Sexual orientation in some ways is like handedness. Most people are one way, some the other. A very few are truly ambidextrous. Regardless, the way we are endures, especially in men (Chivers, 2005; Diamond, 2008; Dickson et al., 2013). Women's sexual orientation tends to be less strongly felt and more variable (Baumeister, 2000). This may help explain why more women than men report having had at least one same-sex sexual contact, even though males' homosexuality rate exceeds the female rate (Chandra et al., 2011).

Why Do We Differ?

So, if we do not choose our sexual orientation and (especially for males) cannot change it, where do these preferences come from? See if you can predict the answers (Yes or No) to these questions:

1. Is homosexuality linked with problems in a child's relationships with parents, such as with an overpowering mother and a weak father, or a possessive mother and a hostile father?

2. Does homosexuality involve a fear or hatred of people of the other sex, leading individuals to direct their desires toward members of their own sex?

3. Is sexual orientation linked with levels of sex hormones currently in the blood?

4. As children, were most homosexuals molested, seduced, or otherwise sexually victimized by an adult homosexual?

Hundreds of studies have indicated that the answers to these questions have been No, No, No, and No (Storms, 1983). In a search for possible environmental influences on sexual orientation, Kinsey Institute investigators interviewed nearly 1000 homosexual and 500 heterosexual people. They assessed almost every imaginable psychological cause of homosexuality—parental relationships, childhood sexual experiences, peer relationships, and dating experiences (Bell et al., 1981; Hammersmith, 1982). Their findings: Homosexual people were no more likely than heterosexual people to have been smothered by maternal love or neglected

PERSONAL VALUES AFFECT SEXUAL ORIENTATION LESS THAN THEY AFFECT OTHER FORMS OF SEXUAL BEHAVIOR Compared with people who rarely attend religious services, for example, those who attend regularly are one-third as likely to have lived together before marriage. They also report having had many fewer sex partners. But (if male) they are just as likely to be homosexual (Smith, 1998).

by their father. And consider this: If "distant fathers" were more likely to produce homosexual sons, then shouldn't boys growing up in father-absent homes more often be gay? (They are not.) And shouldn't the rising number of such homes have led to a noticeable increase in the gay population? (It has not.) Most children raised by gay or lesbian parents grow up to be heterosexual and well-adjusted adults (Gartrell & Bos, 2010).

Note that the scientific question is not "What causes homosexuality?" (or "What causes heterosexuality?") but "What causes differing sexual orientations?" In pursuit of answers, psychological science compares the backgrounds and physiology of people whose sexual orientations differ.

What have we learned from a half-century's theory and research? If there are environmental factors that influence sexual orientation after we're born, we haven't yet found them. The lack of evidence for environmental influences on homosexuality has led researchers to explore several lines of biological evidence:

- Same-sex attraction in other species
- Gay-straight brain differences
- Genetic influences
- Prenatal influences

SAME-SEX ATTRACTION IN OTHER SPECIES In Boston's Public Gardens, caretakers solved the mystery of why a much-loved swan couple's eggs never hatched. Both swans were female. In New York City's Central Park Zoo, penguins Silo and Roy spent several years as devoted same-sex partners. Same-sex sexual behaviors have also been observed in several hundred other species, including grizzlies, gorillas, monkeys, flamingos, and owls (Bagemihl, 1999). Among rams, for example, some 7 to 10 percent (to sheep-breeding ranchers, the "duds") display same-sex attraction by shunning ewes and seeking to mount other males (Perkins & Fitzgerald, 1997). Homosexual behavior seems a natural part of the animal world.

GAY-STRAIGHT BRAIN DIFFERENCES Might the structure and function of heterosexual and homosexual brains differ? With this question in mind, researcher Simon LeVay (1991) studied sections of the hypothalamus taken from deceased heterosexual and homosexual people. (The hypothalamus is a brain structure linked to sexual behavior.) As a gay scientist, LeVay wanted to do "something connected with my gay identity." To avoid biasing the results, he did a blind study: He didn't know which donors were gay or straight. After nine months of peering through his microscope at a cell cluster that varied in size among donors, he consulted the donor records. The cell cluster

JULIET AND JULIET Boston's beloved swan couple, "Romeo and Juliet," were discovered actually to be, as are many other animal partners, a same-sex pair.

was reliably larger in heterosexual men than in women and homosexual men. "I was almost in a state of shock," LeVay said (1994). "I took a walk by myself on the cliffs over the ocean. I sat for half an hour just thinking what this might mean."

It should not surprise us that brains differ with sexual orientation. Remember, *everything psychological is also biological*. But when did the brain difference begin? At conception? During childhood or adolescence? Did experience produce the difference? Or was it genes or prenatal hormones (or genes activating prenatal hormones)?

LeVay does not view this cell cluster as an "on-off button" for sexual orientation. Rather, he believes it is an important part of a brain pathway that is active during sexual behavior. He agrees that sexual behavior patterns could influence the brain's anatomy. Neural pathways in our brain do grow stronger with use. In fish, birds, rats, and humans, brain structures vary with experience— including sexual experience (Breedlove, 1997). But LeVay believes it more likely that brain anatomy influences sexual orientation. His hunch seems confirmed by the discovery of a similar difference between the male sheep that do and do not display same-sex attraction (Larkin et al., 2002; Roselli et al., 2002, 2004). Moreover, such differences seem to develop soon after birth, perhaps even before birth (Rahman & Wilson, 2003).

> "Gay men simply don't have the brain cells to be attracted to women."
>
> Simon LeVay, *The Sexual Brain*, 1993

Since LeVay's brain *structure* discovery, other researchers have reported additional differences in the way that gay and straight brains *function*. One is in an area of the hypothalamus that governs sexual arousal (Savic et al., 2005). When straight women were given a whiff of a scent derived from men's sweat (which contains traces of male hormones), this area became active. Gay men's brains responded similarly to the men's scent. Straight men's brains did not. For them, only a female scent triggered the arousal response. In a similar study, lesbians' responses differed from those of straight women (Kranz & Ishai, 2006; Martins et al., 2005). Researcher Qazi Rahman (2015) sums it up: Compared to heterosexuals, "gay men appear, on average, more 'female typical' in brain pattern responses and lesbian women are somewhat more 'male typical.'"

GENETIC INFLUENCES Three lines of evidence suggest a genetic influence on sexual orientation.

- *Homosexuality seems to run in families:* Homosexuality appears more often in some families than in others (Mustanski & Bailey, 2003). Several studies have found that (1) homosexual men tend to have more homosexual relatives on their mother's than on their father's side, and (2) their heterosexual maternal relatives tend to produce more offspring than do the maternal relatives of heterosexual men (Camperio-Ciani et al., 2004, 2009; Camperio-Ciani & Pellizzari, 2012; VanderLaan & Vasey, 2011; VanderLaan et al., 2012).

- *Gene and chromosome studies:* In genetic studies of fruit flies, altering a single gene has changed the flies' sexual orientation and behavior (Dickson, 2005). During courtship, females pursued females and males pursued males (Demir & Dickson, 2005). In humans, it's likely that multiple genes, possibly interacting with other influences, shape human sexual orientation. In search of factors, researchers studied the genes of 409 pairs of gay brothers. They found links between sexual orientation and two chromosome areas. One of those chromosomes is transmitted through the mother's line (Sanders et al., 2015).

- *Twin studies:* Identical twins (who have identical genes) are somewhat more likely than fraternal twins (whose genes are not identical) to share a homosexual orientation (Alanko et al., 2010; Lángström et al., 2010). However, sexual orientation differs in many identical twin pairs (especially female twins). This means that other factors besides genes must play a role.

PRENATAL INFLUENCES Twins share not only genes, but also a prenatal environment. Recall that in the womb, sex hormones direct our development as male or female. A critical period for human brain development occurs in the second trimester (Ellis & Ames, 1987; Garcia-Falgueras & Swaab, 2010; Meyer-Bahlburg, 1995). A fetus (either male or female) exposed to typical female hormone levels during this period may be attracted to males in later life. When pregnant sheep were injected with testosterone during a similar critical period, their female offspring later showed homosexual behavior (Money, 1987).

> "Modern scientific research indicates that sexual orientation is . . . partly determined by genetics, but more specifically by hormonal activity in the womb."
>
> Glenn Wilson and Qazi Rahman, *Born Gay: The Psychobiology of Sex Orientation*, 2005

A second important prenatal influence is the curious *older-brother effect*. Men with older brothers are somewhat more likely to be gay—about one-third more likely for each additional older brother (Blanchard, 2004, 2008a,b, 2014; Bogaert, 2003). If the odds of homosexuality are roughly 2 percent among first sons, they would rise to nearly 3 percent among second sons, 4 percent for third sons, and so on for each additional older brother (**FIGURE 4.5**).

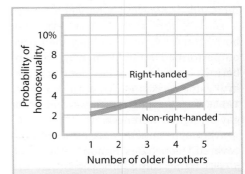

FIGURE 4.5 The older-brother effect These approximate curves depict a man's likelihood of homosexuality as a function of the number of biological (not adopted) older brothers he has (Blanchard 2008a; Bogaert, 2006a). This correlation has been found in several studies, but only among right-handed men (as about 9 in 10 men are).

The older-brother effect seems to be biological. It does not occur among adopted brothers (Bogaert, 2006a). One possible explanation is that male fetuses may produce a substance that triggers a defensive response in the mother's immune system. After each pregnancy with a male fetus, antibodies in her system may grow stronger and may prevent the fetal brain from developing in a typical male pattern. Curiously, the older-brother effect is found only among right-handed men.

How Do We Differ?
A Summary

Taken together, the brain, genetic, and prenatal findings offer strong support for a biological explanation of sexual orientation (LeVay, 2011; Rahman & Koerting, 2008). Additional support comes from other gay-straight differences. Gays and lesbians appear to fall midway between straight females and males on several traits (LeVay, 2011; Rahman & Koerting, 2008). From birth on, gay males tend to be shorter and lighter than straight males. Women in same-sex marriages were mostly heavier than average at birth (Bogaert, 2010; Frisch & Zdravkovic, 2010). Gay-straight spatial abilities also differ. On mental rotation tasks such as the one in **FIGURE 4.6,** straight men tend to outscore straight women. The scores of gay men and lesbians fall in between (Rahman & Koerting, 2008; Rahman et al., 2004). But both straight women and gay men have outperformed straight men at remembering objects' spatial locations in memory game tasks (Hassan & Rahman, 2007). **TABLE 4.1** summarizes these and other gay-straight differences.

Although "much remains to be discovered," concludes Simon LeVay (2011, p. xvii), "the same processes that are involved in the biological development of our bodies and brains as male or female are also involved in the development of sexual orientation."

"There is no sound scientific evidence that sexual orientation can be changed."
UK Royal College of Psychiatrists, 2009

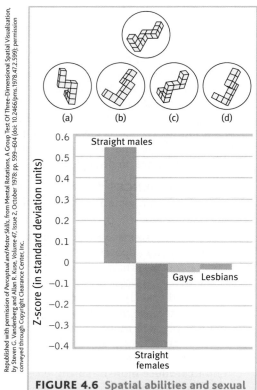

Republished with permission of *Perceptual and Motor Skills,* from *Mental Rotations, A Group Test Of Three-Dimensional Spatial Visualization,* by Steven G. Vandenberg and Allan R. Kuse, Volume 47, Issue 2, October 1978: pp. 599–604 (doi: 10.2466/pms.1978.47.2.599); permission conveyed through Copyright Clearance Center, Inc.

FIGURE 4.6 **Spatial abilities and sexual orientation** Which of the four figures can be rotated to match the target figure at the top? Straight males tend to find this an easier task than do straight females, with gays and lesbians falling in between. (From Rahman et al., 2004, with 60 people tested in each group.)

Answer: Figures a and d.

Retrieve + Remember
• Which THREE of the following five factors have researchers found to have an effect on sexual orientation?
   a. An overpowering mother
   b. Size of a certain cell cluster in the hypothalamus
   c. Prenatal hormone exposure
   d. A weak or distant father
   e. For right-handed men, having multiple older biological brothers

ANSWERS: b, c, e

LaunchPad For an 8-minute overview of the biology of sexual orientation, see LaunchPad's *Video: Homosexuality and the Nature–Nurture Debate.*

An Evolutionary Explanation of Human Sexuality

LOQ 4-12 How might an evolutionary psychologist explain male-female differences in sexuality and mating preferences?

Having faced many similar challenges throughout history, males and females have adapted in similar ways.

TABLE 4.1	Biological Correlates of Sexual Orientation

Gay-straight trait differences
Sexual orientation is part of a package of traits. Studies—some in need of replication—indicate that homosexuals and heterosexuals differ in the following biological and behavioral traits:

• spatial abilities	• gender nonconformity
• fingerprint ridge counts	• age of onset of puberty in males
• auditory system development	• sleep length
• handedness	• physical aggression
• occupational preferences	• walking style
• relative finger lengths	

On average (the evidence is strongest for males), results for gays and lesbians fall between those of straight men and straight women. Three biological influences—brain, genetic, and prenatal—may contribute to these differences.

Brain differences
• One hypothalamic cell cluster is smaller in women and gay men than in straight men.
• Gay men's hypothalamus reacts as do straight women's to the smell of sex-related hormones.

Genetic influences
• Shared sexual orientation is higher among identical twins than among fraternal twins.
• Sexual attraction in fruit flies can be genetically manipulated.
• Male homosexuality often appears to be transmitted from the mother's side of the family.

Prenatal influences
• Altered prenatal hormone exposure may lead to homosexuality in humans and other animals.
• Men with several older biological brothers are more likely to be gay, possibly due to a maternal immune-system reaction.

We eat the same foods, avoid the same predators, and perceive, learn, and remember in much the same way. It is only in areas where we have faced differing adaptive challenges—most obviously in behaviors related to reproduction—that we differ, say **evolutionary psychologists.**

Male-Female Differences in Sexuality

And differ we do. Consider sex drives. Both men and women are sexually motivated, some women more so than many men. Yet, on average, who thinks more about sex? Masturbates more often? Initiates more sex? Views more pornography? The answers worldwide—*men, men, men,* and *men* (Baumeister et al., 2001; Lippa, 2009; Petersen & Hyde, 2010). To see if you can predict such gender differences, take the quiz in **TABLE 4.2.**

Many gender similarities and differences transcend sexual orientation. Compared with lesbians, gay men (like straight men) report more responsiveness to visual sexual stimuli and more concern with their partner's physical attractiveness (Bailey et al., 1994; Doyle, 2005; Schmitt, 2007). Gay male couples also report having sex more often than do lesbian couples (Peplau & Fingerhut, 2007). And (also

"Not tonight, I have a concussion."

like straight men) gay men report more interest in uncommitted sex. Although men are roughly two-thirds of the gay population, they are only 36 percent of same-sex legal partners in marriages, civil unions, or domestic partnerships (Badgett & Mallory, 2014).

> "It's not that gay men are oversexed; they are simply men whose male desires bounce off other male desires rather than off female desires."
>
> Steven Pinker, *How the Mind Works,* 1997

Natural Selection and Mating Preferences

Natural selection is nature selecting traits and appetites that contribute to survival and reproduction. Thanks to random genetic mutations, our ancestors were born with varied traits, some

of which helped them to survive and reproduce. Eventually, these characteristics became widespread. Evolutionary psychologists use this natural selection principle to explain how men and women differ more in the bedroom than in the boardroom. Our natural yearnings, they say, are our genes' way of reproducing themselves. "Humans are living fossils—collections of mechanisms produced by prior selection pressures" (Buss, 1995).

Why do women tend to be choosier than men when selecting sexual partners? Women have more at stake. To send their genes into the future, a woman must—at a minimum—conceive and protect a fetus growing inside her body for up to nine months. And unlike men, women are limited in how many children they can have between puberty and menopause. No surprise, then, that heterosexual women prefer stick-around dads over likely cads. Partners who stick around can offer their joint offspring support and protection. Heterosexual women are attracted to tall men with slim waists and broad

> **evolutionary psychology** the study of how our behavior and mind have changed in adaptive ways over time due to natural selection.
>
> **natural selection** the principle that, among the range of inherited trait variations, the ones most likely to be passed on to succeeding generations are those that increase the organism's chances of surviving and reproducing in its environment.

TABLE 4.2	Predict the Responses		

Researchers asked samples of U.S. adults whether they agreed or disagreed with the following statements. For each item give your best guess about the percentage who agreed with the statement.

Statement	Percentage of males who agreed	Percentage of females who agreed
1. If two people really like each other, it's all right for them to have sex even if they've known each other for a very short time.	_____	_____
2. I can imagine myself being comfortable and enjoying "casual" sex with different partners.	_____	_____
3. Affection was the reason I first had intercourse.	_____	_____
4. I think about sex every day, or several times a day.	_____	_____
5. Pornography is "morally acceptable."	_____	_____

Answers: (1) males, 58 percent; females, 34 percent; (2) males, 48 percent; females, 12 percent; (3) males, 25 percent; females, 48 percent; (4) males, 54 percent; females, 19 percent; (5) males, 43 percent; females, 25 percent

Sources: (1) Pryor et al., 2005; (2) Bailey et al., 2000; (3 and 4) Research from Laumann et al., 1994; (5) Dugan, 2015

shoulders—all signs of reproductive success (Mautz et al., 2013). And they prefer men who seem mature, dominant, bold, and wealthy (Asendorpf et al., 2011; Conroy-Beam et al., 2015; Gangestad & Simpson, 2000). One study of hundreds of Welsh pedestrians asked people to rate a driver pictured at the wheel of a humble Ford Fiesta or a swanky Bentley. Men said a female driver was equally attractive in both cars. Women, however, found a male driver more attractive if he was in the luxury car (Dunn & Searle, 2010). If you put a man in a mating mind-set, how will he try to show he is a "catch"? He'll buy showy items, express aggressive intentions, and take risks (Baker & Maner, 2009; Griskevicius et al., 2009; Shan et al., 2012; Sundie et al., 2011).

📱 **LaunchPad** To listen to experts discuss evolutionary psychology and sex differences, visit LaunchPad's *Video: Evolutionary Psychology and Sex Differences.*

The data are in, say evolutionists: Men pair widely; women pair wisely. And what traits do straight men find desirable?

For heterosexual men, some desired traits, such as a woman's smooth skin and youthful shape, cross place and time (Buss, 1994). Mating with such women might increase a man's chances of sending his genes into the future. And sure enough, men feel most attracted to women whose waist is roughly a third narrower than their hips—a sign of future fertility (Perilloux et al., 2010). Even blind men show this preference for women with a low waist-to-hip ratio (Karremans et al., 2010).

There is a principle at work here, say evolutionary psychologists: Nature selects behaviors that increase genetic success. As mobile gene machines, we are designed to prefer whatever worked for our ancestors in their environments. They were predisposed to act in ways that would produce children, grandchildren, and beyond. Had they not been, we wouldn't be here. And as carriers of their genetic legacy, we are similarly predisposed.

THE MATING GAME Evolutionary psychologists are not surprised that older men, and not just Johnny Depp (pictured with Amber Heard, who is 23 years younger), often prefer younger women whose features suggest fertility.

Why might "gay genes" persist? Same-sex couples cannot naturally reproduce. Evolutionary psychologists suggest a possible answer: the *fertile females* theory. The theory goes like this. As we noted earlier, women relatives of homosexual men have tended to have larger-than-normal families. Perhaps, then, the genes that dispose women to be strongly attracted (or attractive) to men—and to have more children—also dispose some men to be attracted to men (LeVay, 2011). Thus, there may actually be biological wisdom to genes that dispose some men to love other men.

Critiquing the Evolutionary Perspective

LOQ 4-13 What are the key criticisms of evolutionary explanations of human sexuality, and how do evolutionary psychologists respond?

Most psychologists agree that natural selection prepares us for survival and reproduction. But critics say there is a weakness in the reasoning evolutionary psychologists use to explain our mating preferences. Let's consider how an evolutionary psychologist might explain the findings in a startling study (Clark & Hatfield, 1989), and how a critic might object.

In this experiment, someone posing as a stranger approached people of the other sex and remarked, "I have been noticing you around campus. I find you to be very attractive." The "stranger" then asked a question, which was sometimes "Would you go to bed with me tonight?"

What percentage of men and women do you think agreed to this offer? An evolutionary explanation of genetic differences in sexuality would predict that women would be choosier than men in selecting their sexual partners. If so, the women in this experiment should be less willing to hop into bed with a complete stranger. Indeed, not a single woman agreed—but 70 percent of the men did. A repeat of this study in France produced a similar result (Guéguen, 2011). The research seemed to support an evolutionary explanation.

Or did it? Critics note that evolutionary psychologists start with an effect—in this case, that men are more likely to accept casual sex offers—and work backward to explain what happened. What if research showed the opposite effect? If men refused an offer for casual sex, might we not reason that men who partner with one woman for life make better fathers, whose children more often survive?

Other critics ask why we should try to explain today's behavior based on decisions our ancestors made thousands of

years ago. Don't cultural expectations also bend the genders? Behavior differences between men and women are smaller in cultures with greater gender equality (Eagly, 2009; Eagly & Wood, 1999). Such critics believe that *social learning theory* offers a better, more immediate explanation for these results. We all learn *social scripts* by watching and imitating others in our cultures. Women may learn that sexual encounters with strangers are dangerous, and that casual sex may not offer much sexual pleasure (Conley, 2011). This explanation of the study's effects proposes that women react to sexual encounters in ways that their modern culture teaches them. And men's reactions may reflect the social scripts taught them: "Real men" take advantage of every opportunity to have sex.

LaunchPad To experience a demonstration and explanation of evolutionary psychology and mating preferences, visit LaunchPad's *PsychSim 6: Dating and Mating*.

A third criticism focuses on the social consequences of accepting an evolutionary explanation. Are heterosexual men truly hard-wired to have sex with any woman who approaches them? If so, does this mean that men have no moral responsibility to remain faithful to their partners? Does this explanation excuse men's sexual aggression—"boys will be boys"—because of our evolutionary history?

Evolutionary psychologists agree that much of who we are is *not* hard-wired. Our destiny is not written in our genes. "Evolution forcefully rejects a genetic determinism," insisted one research team (Confer et al., 2010). Evolutionary psychologists also remind us that men and women, having faced similar adaptive problems, are far more alike than different. Natural selection has prepared us to be flexible. We humans have a great capacity for learning and social progress. We adjust and respond to varied environments. We adapt and survive, whether we live in the Arctic or the desert.

Evolutionary psychologists also agree with their critics that some traits and behaviors, such as suicide, are hard to explain in terms of natural selection (Barash, 2012; Confer et al., 2010). But they ask us to remember evolutionary psychology's scientific goal: to explain behaviors and mental traits by offering testable predictions using principles of natural selection. We may, for example, predict that people are more likely to perform favors for those who share their genes or can later return those favors. Is this true? (The answer is *Yes*.) And evolutionary psychologists remind us that the study of how we *came to be* need not dictate how we *ought to be*. Understanding our tendencies can help us overcome them.

Retrieve + Remember

- How do evolutionary psychologists explain gender differences in sexuality?

ANSWER: Evolutionary psychologists theorize that females have inherited their ancestors' tendencies to be more cautious sexually because of the challenges associated with incubating and nurturing offspring. Males have inherited a tendency to be more casual about sex, because their act of fathering requires a smaller investment.

- What are the three main criticisms of the evolutionary explanation of human sexuality?

ANSWER: (1) It starts with an effect and works backward to propose an explanation. (2) This explanation may overlook the effects of cultural expectations and socialization. (3) Men could use such explanations to rationalize their negative behavior toward women.

Social Influences on Human Sexuality

LOQ 4-14 What role do social factors play in our sexuality?

Scientific research on human sexuality does not aim to define the personal meaning of sex in our own lives. We could know every available fact about sex—that the initial spasms of male and female orgasm come at 0.8-second

intervals, that systolic blood pressure rises some 60 points and respiration rate reaches 40 breaths per minute, that female nipples expand 10 millimeters at the peak of sexual arousal—but fail to understand the human significance of sexual intimacy.

Intimacy expresses our social nature. One study of 2035 married people found that couples who reported being in a deeply committed relationship before having sex also reported greater relationship satisfaction and stability—and better sex than those who had sex very early in their relationship (Busby et al., 2010; Galinsky & Sonenstein, 2013). For both men and women, but especially for women, sex is more satisfying (more orgasms, less regret) for those in a committed relationship, rather than a sexual hook-up (Armstrong et al., 2012; Garcia et al., 2012, 2013). Partners who share regular meals are more likely than one-time dinner companions to understand what seasoning touches suit each other's food tastes. So, too, with the touches of loyal partners who share a bed.

Sex is a socially significant act. Men and women can achieve orgasm alone. Yet most people find greater satisfaction after intercourse and orgasm with their loved one (Brody & Tillmann, 2006). Sex at its human best is life uniting and love renewing.

Reflections on the Nature and Nurture of Sex, Gender, and Sexuality

LOQ 4-15 How do nature, nurture, and our own choices influence gender roles and sexuality?

Our ancestral history helped form us as a species. Where there is variation, natural selection, and heredity, there will be evolution. Our genes form us. This is a great truth about human nature.

But our culture and experiences also shape us. If their genes and hormones predispose males to be more physically aggressive than females, culture can amplify this gender difference with norms that reward macho men and gentle women. If men are encouraged toward roles that demand physical power, and women toward more nurturing roles, each may act accordingly. By exhibiting the actions expected of those who fulfill such roles, men and women shape their own traits. Presidents in time become more presidential, servants more servile. Gender roles similarly shape us.

In many modern cultures, gender roles are merging. Brute strength is becoming less and less important for power and status (think Mark Zuckerberg and Hillary Clinton). From 1965 to 2013, women soared from 9 percent to 47 percent of U.S. medical students (AAMC, 2014). In 1965, U.S. married women devoted eight times as many hours to housework as did their husbands. By 2011, this gap had shrunk to less than twice as many (Parker & Wang, 2013). Such swift changes signal that biology does not fix gender roles.

If nature and nurture jointly form us, are we "nothing but" the product of nature and nurture? Are we rigidly determined?

We *are* the product of nature and nurture, but we're also an open system. Genes are all-pervasive but not all-powerful. People may reject their evolutionary role as transmitters of genes and choose not to reproduce. Culture, too, is all-pervasive but not all-powerful. People may defy peer pressures and do the opposite of the expected.

We can't excuse our failings by blaming them solely on bad genes or bad influences. In reality, we are both creatures and creators of our worlds. So many things about us—including our gender identity and mating behaviors—are the products of our genes and environments. Yet the future-shaping stream of causation runs through our

San Diego Museum of Man, photograph by Rose Tyson

CULTURE MATTERS As this exhibit at San Diego's Museum of Man illustrates, children learn their culture. A baby's foot can step into any culture.

present choices. Our decisions today design our environments tomorrow. The human environment is not like the weather—something that just happens. We are its architects. Our hopes, goals, and expectations influence our future. And that is what enables cultures to vary and to change. Mind matters.

* * *

We know from our correspondence that some readers feel troubled by the naturalism and evolutionism of contemporary science. They worry that a science of behavior (and evolutionary science in particular) will destroy our sense of the beauty, mystery, and spiritual significance of the human creature. For those concerned, we offer some reassuring thoughts.

When Isaac Newton explained the rainbow in terms of light of differing wavelengths, British poet John Keats feared that Newton had destroyed the rainbow's mysterious beauty. Yet, nothing about the science of optics need diminish our appreciation for the drama of a rainbow arching across a rain-darkened sky.

When Galileo assembled evidence that the Earth revolved around the Sun, not vice versa, he did not offer absolute proof for his theory. Rather, he offered an explanation that pulled together a variety of observations, such as the changing shadows cast by the Moon's mountains. His explanation eventually won the day because it described and explained things in a way that made sense, that hung together. Darwin's theory of evolution likewise offers an organizing principle that makes sense of many observations.

Many people of faith find the scientific idea of human origins fits with their own spirituality. In 2014, Pope Francis welcomed a science-religion dialogue, saying, "Evolution in nature is not inconsistent with the notion of creation, because evolution requires the creation of beings that evolve."

Meanwhile, many people of science are awestruck at the emerging understanding of the universe and the human creature. It boggles the mind—the entire universe popping out of a point some 14 billion years ago, and instantly inflating to cosmological size. Had the energy of this Big Bang been the tiniest bit less, the universe would have collapsed back on itself. Had it been the tiniest bit more, the result would have been a soup too thin to support life. Had gravity been a teeny bit stronger or weaker, or had the weight of a carbon proton been a wee bit different, our universe just wouldn't have worked.

What caused this almost-too-good-to-be-true, finely tuned universe? Why is there something rather than nothing? How did it come to be, in the words of Harvard-Smithsonian astrophysicist Owen Gingerich (1999), "so extraordinarily right, that it seemed the universe had been expressly designed to produce intelligent, sentient beings"? Is there a benevolent superintelligence behind it all? On such matters, a humble, awed, scientific silence is appropriate, suggested philosopher Ludwig Wittgenstein: "Whereof one cannot speak, thereof one must be silent."

Rather than fearing science, we can welcome its enlarging our understanding and awakening our sense of awe. In a short 4 billion years, life on Earth has come from nothing to structures as complex as a 6-billion-unit strand of DNA and the incomprehensible intricacy of the human brain. Nature seems cunningly and ingeniously devised to produce extraordinary, self-replicating, information-processing systems—us (Davies, 2007). Although we appear to have been created from dust, over eons of time, the end result is a priceless creature, one rich with potential beyond our imagining.

CHAPTER REVIEW

Sex, Gender, and Sexuality

Test yourself by taking a moment to answer each of these Learning Objective Questions (repeated here from within the chapter). Then turn to Appendix D, Complete Chapter Reviews, to check your answers. Research suggests that trying to answer these questions on your own will improve your long-term memory of the concepts (McDaniel et al., 2009).

Gender Development

4-1: How does the meaning of *gender* differ from the meaning of *sex?*

4-2: What are some ways in which males and females tend to be alike and to differ?

4-3: What factors contribute to gender bias in the workplace?

4-4: How do sex hormones influence prenatal and adolescent development, and what is an *intersex* condition?

4-5: How do gender roles and gender identity differ?

Human Sexuality

4-6: How do hormones influence human sexual motivation?

4-7: What is the human *sexual response cycle,* and how can sexual dysfunctions interfere with this cycle?

4-8: How can sexually transmitted infections be prevented?

4-9: How do external and imagined stimuli contribute to sexual arousal?

4-10: What factors influence teenagers' sexual behaviors and use of contraceptives?

Sexual Orientation

4-11: What has research taught us about sexual orientation?

An Evolutionary Explanation of Human Sexuality

4-12: How might an evolutionary psychologist explain male-female differences in sexuality and mating preferences?

4-13: What are the key criticisms of evolutionary explanations of human sexuality, and how do evolutionary psychologists respond?

Social Influences on Human Sexuality

4-14: What role do social factors play in our sexuality?

Reflections on the Nature and Nurture of Sex, Gender, and Sexuality

4-15: How do nature, nurture, and our own choices influence gender roles and sexuality?

TERMS AND CONCEPTS TO REMEMBER

Test yourself on these terms by trying to write down the definition in your own words before flipping back to the referenced page to check your answers.

CHAPTER TEST

Test yourself repeatedly throughout your studies. This will not only help you figure out what you know and don't know; the testing itself will help you learn and remember the information more effectively thanks to the *testing effect*.

1. Psychologists define _____ as the biologically influenced characteristics by which people define males and females. The socially influenced characteristics by which people define men and women is _____.

2. Females and males are very similar to each other. But one way they differ is that

   a. females are more physically aggressive than males.

   b. males are more democratic than females in their leadership roles.

   c. as children, females tend to play in small groups, while males tend to play in large groups.

   d. females are more likely to commit suicide.

3. A fertilized egg will develop into a boy if it receives a/n _____ chromosome from its father.

4. Primary sex characteristics relate to _____; secondary sex characteristics refer to _____.

   a. spermarche; menarche

   b. breasts and facial hair; ovaries and testes

   c. emotional maturity; hormone surges

   d. reproductive organs; nonreproductive traits

5. On average, girls begin puberty at about the age of _____, boys at about the age of _____.

6. A person born with sexual anatomy that differs from typical male or female anatomy may be considered _____.

7. *Gender role* refers to our

   a. personal sense of being male or female.

   b. culture's expectations about the "right" way for males and females to behave.

   c. assigned birth sex—our chromosomes and anatomy.

   d. unisex characteristics.

8. Our sense of being male, female, or some combination of the two is known as our _____ _____.

9. A striking effect of hormonal changes on human sexual behavior is the

   a. end of sexual desire in men over 60.

   b. sharp rise in sexual interest at puberty.

   c. decrease in women's sexual desire at the time of ovulation.

   d. increase in testosterone levels in castrated males.

10. In describing the sexual response cycle, Masters and Johnson noted that

    a. a plateau phase follows orgasm.

    b. men experience a refractory period during which they cannot experience orgasm.

    c. the feeling that accompanies orgasm is stronger in men than in women.

    d. testosterone is released equally in women and men.

11. Using condoms during sex _____ (does/doesn't) reduce the risk of getting HIV and _____ (does/doesn't) fully protect against skin-to-skin STIs.

12. An example of an external stimulus that might influence sexual behavior is

    a. the level of testosterone in the bloodstream.

    b. the onset of puberty.

    c. a sexually explicit film.

    d. an erotic fantasy or dream.

13. Evolutionary psychologists are most likely to focus on

    a. how we differ from one another.

    b. the social consequences of learned behaviors.

    c. the natural selection of traits that helped our ancestors survive and reproduce.

    d. cultural expectations about the "right" ways for men and women to behave.

Find answers to these questions in Appendix E, in the back of the book.

IN YOUR EVERYDAY LIFE

Answering these questions will help you make these concepts more personally meaningful, and therefore more memorable.

1. How gender-typed are you? What has influenced your feelings of masculinity, femininity, or some combination of the two?

2. What strategy might be effective for reducing teen pregnancy?

3. Surveys show that about 40 percent of Americans believe society should not accept same-sex marriages. Yet, acceptance of nonheterosexual orientation is increasing, especially among young people. Why do you think so many Americans disapprove of same-sex relationships? And why do you think support for same-sex relationships has increased?

4. Has reading about the causes of sexual orientation influenced your views? If so, in what ways?

5. What do you think about the evolutionary perspective on sexual behavior? To what extent do you think genetics affect our sexual behavior?

Use 📖 LearningCurve to create your personalized study plan, which will direct you to the resources that will help you most in 📖 LaunchPad.

SURVEY THE CHAPTER

Adam Hester/Blend Images/Getty Images

Sensation and Perception

5

"I have perfect vision," explains the writer and teacher Heather Sellers. Her vision may be perfect, but her perception is not. In her book, *You Don't Look Like Anyone I Know,* she tells of awkward moments resulting from her lifelong *prosopagnosia*—face blindness (Sellers, 2010).

> In college, on a date at the Spaghetti Station, I returned from the bathroom and plunked myself down in the wrong booth, facing the wrong man. I remained unaware he was not my date even as my date (a stranger to me) accosted Wrong Booth Guy, and then stormed out. . . . I do not recognize myself in photos or videos. I can't recognize my stepsons in the soccer pick-up line; I failed to determine which husband was mine at a party, in the mall, at the market.

People sometimes see Sellers as snobby or cold. "Why did you walk past me?" a neighbor might later ask. Hoping to avoid offending others, Sellers sometimes fakes recognition. She smiles at people she passes, in case she knows them. Or she may pretend to know the person with whom she is talking. But there is an upside to these perception failures. When she runs into someone who previously irritated her, she typically feels no ill will. She doesn't recognize the person.

Unlike Sellers, most of us have a functioning area on the underside of our brain's right hemisphere that helps us recognize a familiar human face as soon as we detect it—in only one-seventh of a second (Jacques & Rossion, 2006). This ability is an example of a broader principle. *Nature's sensory gifts enable each animal to obtain essential information.* Some other examples:

- Human ears are most sensitive to sound frequencies that include human voices, especially a baby's cry.
- Frogs, which feed on flying insects, have cells in their eyes that fire only in response to small, dark, moving objects. A frog could starve to death knee-deep in motionless flies. But let one zoom by and the frog's "bug detector" cells snap awake. (As Kermit the Frog said, "Time's fun when you're having flies.")
- Male silkworm moths' odor receptors can detect one-billionth of an ounce of chemical sex attractant per second—released by a female one mile away (Sagan, 1977). That is why there continue to be silkworms.

In this chapter, we'll look more closely at what psychologists have learned about how we sense and perceive the world around us. We begin with some basic principles that apply to all our senses.

Basic Concepts of Sensation and Perception

5-1 What are *sensation* and *perception*? What do we mean by *bottom-up processing* and *top-down processing*?

Sellers' curious mix of "perfect vision" and face blindness illustrates the distinction between *sensation* and *perception*. When she looks at a friend, her **sensation** is normal. Her senses detect the same information yours would, and they transmit that information to her brain. And her **perception**—the processes by which her brain organizes and interprets the sensory input—is *almost* normal. Thus, she may recognize people from their hair, walk, voice, or peculiar build, just not from their face. Her experience is much like the struggle any human would have trying to recognize a specific penguin.

Under normal circumstances, your sensory and perceptual processes work together to help you decipher the world around you.

- **Bottom-up processing** starts at the very basic level of sensory receptors (more on those later) and works up to higher levels of processing.
- **Top-down processing** creates meaning from the sensory input by drawing on your experience and expectations.

As your brain absorbs the information in **FIGURE 5.1**, bottom-up processing enables your sensory systems to detect the lines, angles, and colors that form the flower and leaves. Using top-down processing, you interpret what your senses detect.

But how do you do it? How do you create meaning from the blizzard of sensory stimuli bombarding your body 24 hours a day? Meanwhile, in a silent, cushioned, inner world, your brain floats in utter darkness. By itself, it sees nothing.

FIGURE 5.1 What's going on here? Our sensory and perceptual processes work together to help us sort out complex images, including the hidden couple in Sandro Del-Prete's drawing, *The Flowering of Love*.

It hears nothing. It feels nothing. *So, how does the world out there get in?*

To phrase the question scientifically: How do we construct our representations of the external world? How do a campfire's flicker, crackle, and smoky scent activate pathways in our brain? And how, from this living neurochemistry, do we create our conscious experience of the fire's motion and temperature, its aroma and beauty? In search of answers, let's look at some processes that cut across all our sensory systems.

From Outer Energy to Inner Brain Activity

LOQ 5-2 What three steps are basic to all our sensory systems?

Every second of every day, your sensory systems perform an amazing feat: They convert one form of energy into another. Vision processes light energy. Hearing processes sound waves. All your senses

- *receive* sensory stimulation, often with the help of specialized receptor cells.

- *transform* that stimulation into neural impulses.
- *deliver* the neural information to your brain.

The process of converting one form of energy into another form that your brain can use is **transduction.** Later in this chapter, we'll focus on individual sensory systems. How do we see? Hear? Feel pain? Taste? Smell? Keep our balance? In each case, we'll consider these three steps—receiving, transforming, and delivering the information to the brain.

First, though, let's explore some strengths and weaknesses in our ability to detect and interpret stimuli in the vast sea of energy around us.

Retrieve + Remember

- What is the rough distinction between sensation and perception?

ANSWER: *Sensation* is the bottom-up process by which your sensory receptors and nervous system receive and represent stimuli. *Perception* is the top-down process by which your brain creates meaning by organizing and interpreting what your senses detect.

Thresholds

LOQ 5-3 How do absolute thresholds and difference thresholds differ?

At this moment, we are being struck by X-rays and radio waves, ultraviolet and infrared light, and sound waves of very high and very low frequencies. To all of these we are blind and deaf. Other animals with differing needs detect a world beyond our human experience. Migrating birds stay on course aided by an internal magnetic compass. Bats and dolphins locate prey using sonar, bouncing sounds off objects. Bees navigate on cloudy days by detecting aspects of sunlight we cannot see.

Our senses open the shades just a crack, giving us only a tiny glimpse of the energy around us. But for our needs, this is enough.

Absolute Thresholds

To some kinds of stimuli we are amazingly sensitive. Standing atop a mountain on a dark, clear night, most of us could see a candle flame atop another mountain 30 miles away. We could feel the wing of a bee falling on our cheek. We could smell a single drop of perfume in a three-room apartment (Galanter, 1962).

Our awareness of these faint stimuli illustrates our **absolute thresholds**—the minimum stimulation needed to detect a particular light, sound, pressure, taste, or odor 50 percent of the time. To test your absolute threshold for sounds, a hearing specialist would send tones, at varying levels, into each of your ears and record whether you could hear each tone. The test results would show the point where, for any sound frequency, half the time you could detect the sound and half the time you could not. That 50-50 point would define your absolute threshold.

Stimuli you cannot detect 50 percent of the time are **subliminal**—below your absolute threshold (**FIGURE 5.2**).

Eric Isselée/Shutterstock

To consider their effects, see Thinking Critically About: Subliminal Sensation and Subliminal Persuasion.

LaunchPad See LaunchPad's *Video: Experiments* for a helpful tutorial animation about the experimental research method.

Difference Thresholds

To function effectively, we need absolute thresholds low enough to allow us to detect important sights, sounds, textures, tastes, and smells. Many of life's important decisions also depend on our ability to detect small differences among stimuli. A musician must detect tiny differences when tuning an instrument. Parents must detect the sound of their own child's voice amid other children's voices. Even after I [DM] had lived two years in Scotland, all lambs' *baas* sounded alike to my ears. But not to their mother's, as I observed. After shearing, each ewe would streak directly to the *baa* of her lamb amid the chorus of other distressed lambs.

The LORD is my shepherd;
I shall not want.
He maketh me to lie down
in green pastures:
he leadeth me
beside the still waters.
He restoreth my soul:
he leadeth me
in the paths of righteousness
for his name's sake.
Yea, though I walk through the valley
of the shadow of death,
I will fear no evil;
for thou art with me;
thy rod and thy staff
they comfort me.
Thou preparest a table before me
in the presence of mine enemies:
thou anointest my head with oil,
my cup runneth over.
Surely goodness and mercy
shall follow me
all the days of my life:
and I will dwell
in the house of the LORD
for ever.

THE DIFFERENCE THRESHOLD In this classic poem, the Twenty-third Psalm, each line of typeface increases slightly in size. How many lines did you read before experiencing a *just noticeable difference*?

The **difference threshold** (or the *just noticeable difference [jnd]*) is the minimum difference a person can detect between two stimuli half the time. That detectable difference increases with the size of

sensation the process by which our sensory receptors and nervous system receive and represent stimulus energies from our environment.

perception the process by which our brain organizes and interprets sensory information, transforming it into meaningful objects and events.

bottom-up processing analysis that begins with the sensory receptors and works up to the brain's integration of sensory information.

top-down processing information processing guided by higher-level mental processes, as when we construct perceptions drawing on our experience and expectations.

transduction changing one form of energy into another. In sensation, the transforming of stimulus energies, such as sights, sounds, and smells, into neural impulses our brain can interpret.

absolute threshold the minimum stimulus energy needed to detect a particular stimulus 50 percent of the time.

subliminal below a person's absolute threshold for conscious awareness.

difference threshold the minimum difference between two stimuli required for detection 50 percent of the time. We experience the difference threshold as a *just noticeable difference* (or *jnd*).

Dan Dunkley/Science Source

FIGURE 5.2 Absolute threshold Can I detect this sound? An *absolute threshold* is the intensity at which a person can detect a stimulus half the time. Hearing tests locate these thresholds for various frequencies. Stimuli below your absolute threshold are subliminal.

LOQ 5-4 How are we affected by subliminal stimuli?

Thinking Critically About:
Subliminal Sensation and Subliminal Persuasion

We can be affected by *subliminal* sensations —stimuli so weak that we don't consciously notice them.

Researchers use **priming** to activate unconscious associations.

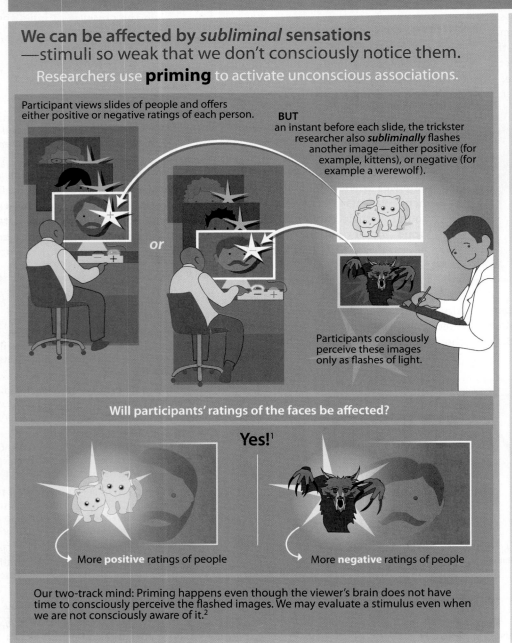

Participant views slides of people and offers either positive or negative ratings of each person.

BUT an instant before each slide, the trickster researcher also **subliminally** flashes another image—either positive (for example, kittens), or negative (for example a werewolf).

Participants consciously perceive these images only as flashes of light.

or

Will participants' ratings of the faces be affected?

Yes![1]

More **positive** ratings of people

More **negative** ratings of people

Our two-track mind: Priming happens even though the viewer's brain does not have time to consciously perceive the flashed images. We may evaluate a stimulus even when we are not consciously aware of it.[2]

So, we can be *primed*, but can we be *persuaded* by subliminal stimuli, for example to lose weight, stop smoking, or improve our memories?

Quiz 100%

Audio and video messages subliminally (without recipients' conscious awareness) announce:

"I am thin,"
"Cigarette smoke tastes bad,"
and
"I do well on tests. I have total recall of information."

Results from 16 experiments[3] showed no powerful, enduring influence on behavior. Not one of the recordings helped more than a placebo, which works only because we believe it will.

1. Krosnick et al., 1992.   2. Ferguson & Zayas, 2009.   3. Greenwald, 1992; Greenwald et al., 1991.

the stimulus. If we listen to our music at 40 decibels, we might detect an added 5 decibels. But if we increase the volume to 110 decibels, we probably won't then detect an additional 5-decibel change.

In the late 1800s, Ernst Weber noted something so simple and so useful that we still refer to it as **Weber's law**. It states that for an average person to perceive a difference, two stimuli must differ by a constant minimum *percentage* (not a constant amount). The exact percentage varies, depending on the stimulus. Two lights, for example, must differ in intensity by 8 percent. Two objects must differ in weight by 2 percent. And two tones must differ in frequency by only 0.3 percent (Teghtsoonian, 1971).

Retrieve + Remember

- Using sound as your example, show how these concepts differ: absolute threshold, subliminal stimulation, and difference threshold.

ANSWER: *Absolute threshold* is the minimum stimulation needed to detect a particular sound (such as an approaching bike on the sidewalk behind you) 50 percent of the time. *Subliminal stimulation* happens when, without your awareness, your sensory system processes a sound that is below your absolute threshold. A *difference threshold* is the minimum difference needed to distinguish between two stimuli (such as between the sound of a bike and the sound of a runner coming up behind you).

Sensory Adaptation

LOQ 5-5 What is the function of sensory adaptation?

Sitting down on the bus, you are overwhelmed by your seatmate's heavy perfume. You wonder how she can stand it, but within minutes you no longer notice. **Sensory adaptation** has come to your rescue. When constantly exposed to an unchanging stimulus, we become less aware of it because our nerve cells fire less frequently. (To experience sensory adaptation, roll up your sleeve. You will feel it—but only for a few moments.)

> "We need above all to know about changes; no one wants or needs to be reminded 16 hours a day that his shoes are on."
>
> Neuroscientist David Hubel (1979)

Why, then, if we stare at an object without flinching, does it not vanish from sight? Because, unnoticed by us, our eyes are always moving. This continual flitting from one spot to another ensures that stimulation on the eyes' receptors is always changing.

What if we actually could stop our eyes from moving? Would sights seem to vanish, as odors do? To find out, psychologists have designed clever instruments that maintain a constant image on the eye's inner surface. Imagine that we have fitted a volunteer, Mary, with such an instrument—a miniature projector mounted on a contact lens (**FIGURE 5.3a**). When Mary's eye moves, the image from the projector moves as well. So everywhere that Mary looks, the scene is sure to go.

If we project images through this instrument, what will Mary see? At first, she will see the complete image. But within a few seconds, as her sensory system begins to tire, things will get weird. Bit by bit, the image will vanish, only to reappear and then disappear—often in fragments (Figure 5.3b).

Although sensory adaptation reduces our sensitivity, it offers an important benefit. It frees us to focus on informative changes in our environment without being distracted by background chatter. The attention-grabbing power of changing stimulation helps explain why television's cuts, edits, zooms, pans, and sudden noises are so hard to ignore. One TV researcher marveled at television's ability to distract, even during interesting conversations: "I cannot for the life of me stop from periodically glancing over to the screen" (Tannenbaum, 2002).

Sensory adaptation influences our perceptions of emotions, too. By creating a 50-50 morphed blend of an angry and a scared face, researchers showed that our visual system adapts to an unchanging facial expression by becoming less responsive to that expression (Butler et al., 2008) (**FIGURE 5.4**).

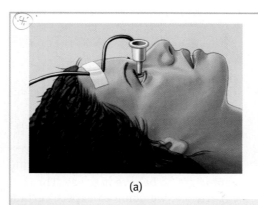

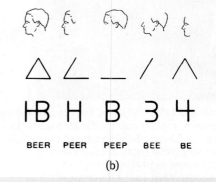

BEER · PEER · PEEP · BEE · BE

(a)　(b)

FIGURE 5.3 Sensory adaptation: Now you see it, now you don't (a) A projector mounted on a contact lens makes the projected image move with the eye. (b) At first, the person sees the whole image. Then, as the eye grows accustomed to the unchanging stimulus, the image begins to break into fragments that fade and reappear. (From "Stabilized images on the retina," by R. M. Pritchard. Copyright © 1961 Scientific American, Inc. All Rights Reserved.)

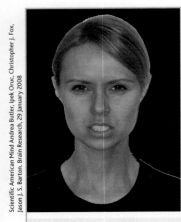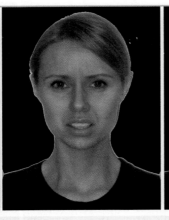

Scientific American Mind Andrea Butler, Ipek Oruc, Christopher J. Fox, Jason J. S. Barton. Brain Research, 29 January 2008

FIGURE 5.4 **Emotion adaptation** Gaze at the angry face on the left for 20 to 30 seconds, then look at the center face (looks scared, yes?). Then gaze at the scared face on the right for 20 to 30 seconds, and again, return to the center face (now looks angry, yes?). (From Butler et al., 2008.)

Keystone/Hulton Archive/Getty Images

FIGURE 5.5 **Believing is seeing** What do you perceive? Is this Nessie, the Loch Ness monster, or a log?

The effect is created by our brain, not by our retinas. How do we know this? Because the illusion also works when we view either side image with one eye, and the center image with the other eye.

The point to remember: Our sensory receptors are alert to novelty; bore them with repetition and they free our attention for more important things. We will see this principle again and again: *We perceive the world not exactly as it is, but as it is useful for us to perceive it.*

Retrieve + Remember

- Why is it that after wearing shoes for a while, you cease to notice them (until questions like this draw your attention back to them)?

ANSWER: The shoes provide constant stimulation. Thanks to *sensory adaptation*, we tend to focus primarily on changing stimuli.

YOUR BRAIN'S DRESS CODE How could one dress capture the world's attention? In 2015, a woman took a picture of a dress she planned to wear to a wedding. What began as a social networking post became a global sensation, leading millions to wonder: What color is the dress? Although the dress is actually blue and black, a survey of 1400 people showed that 43 percent saw the dress as white and gold, blue and brown, or blue and gold (Lafer-Sousa et al., 2015). People's differing color perceptions correlate with differing brain activity (Schlaffke et al., 2015).

Perceptual Set

LOQ 5-6 How do our expectations, contexts, motivations, and emotions influence our perceptions?

To see is to believe. As we less fully appreciate, to believe is to see. Through experience, we come to expect certain results. Those expectations may give us a **perceptual set,** a set of mental tendencies and assumptions that affects, top-down, what we hear, taste, feel, and see. In 1972, a British newspaper

published "the most amazing pictures ever taken"—of a lake "monster" in Scotland's Loch Ness. If this information creates in you the same expectations it did in most of the paper's readers, you, too, will see a monster in a similar photo in **FIGURE 5.5**. But when a skeptical researcher approached the photos with different expectations, he saw a curved tree limb—as had others the day the photo was shot (Campbell, 1986). What a difference a new perceptual set makes.

When shown the phrase

Mary had a

a little lamb

many people perceive what they expect and miss the repeated word. Did you?

The New Yorker Collection, 2002, Leo Cullum from cartoonbank.com

IT'S AMAZING HOW PEOPLE SLOW DOWN WHEN YOU POINT A HAIR DRYER AT THEM.

To believe is also to hear. Consider the kindly airline pilot who, on a takeoff run, looked over at his unhappy co-pilot and said, "Cheer up." Expecting to hear the usual "Gear up," the co-pilot promptly raised the wheels—before they left the ground (Reason & Mycielska, 1982).

Our expectations can also influence our taste perceptions. In one experiment, preschool children, by a 6-to-1 margin, thought french fries tasted better when served in a McDonald's bag rather than a plain white bag (Robinson et al., 2007). Another experiment invited bar patrons to sample free beer (Lee et al., 2006). When researchers added a few drops of vinegar to a brand-name beer and called it "MIT brew," the tasters preferred it—unless they had been told they were drinking vinegar-laced beer. In that case, they expected, and usually experienced, a worse taste. In both cases, people's past experiences (tastes they had enjoyed, and positive associations with prestigious institutions such as MIT) led them to form concepts, or *schemas,* that they then used to interpret new stimuli.

Context, Motivation, and Emotion

Perceptual set influences how we interpret stimuli. But our immediate context, and the motivation and emotion we bring to a situation, also affect our interpretations.

CONTEXT EFFECTS Social psychologist Lee Ross invited us to recall our own perceptions in different contexts: "Ever notice that when you're driving you hate pedestrians, the way they saunter through the crosswalk, almost daring you to hit them, but when you're walking you hate drivers?" (Jaffe, 2004).

Some other examples of the power of context:

- When holding a gun, people become more likely to perceive another person as also gun-toting—a perception that has led to the shooting of some unarmed people

FIGURE 5.6 Culture and context effects What is above the woman's head? In one classic study, most rural East Africans questioned said the woman was balancing a metal box or can on her head (a typical way to carry water at that time). They also perceived the family as sitting under a tree. Westerners, used to running water and boxlike houses with corners, were more likely to perceive the family as being indoors, with the woman sitting under a window (Gregory & Gombrich, 1973).

who were actually holding their phone or wallet (Witt & Brockmole, 2012).

- Imagine hearing a noise interrupted by the words "eel is on the wagon." Likely you would actually perceive the first word as *wheel*. Given "eel is on the orange," you would more likely hear *peel*. In each case, the context creates an expectation that, top-down, influences our perception (Grossberg, 1995). Depending on our perceptual set, "rhapsody" may become "rap city," "sects" may become "sex," and "meteorologist" may be heard as the muscular "meaty urologist."

- Cultural context helps form our perceptions, so it's not surprising that people from different cultures view things differently, as in **FIGURE 5.6.**

- How is the woman in **FIGURE 5.7** feeling?

MOTIVATION Motives give us energy as we work toward a goal. Like context, they can bias our interpretations of neutral stimuli. Consider these findings.

FIGURE 5.7 What emotion is this? (See Figure 5.8.)

- Desirable objects, such as a water bottle viewed by a thirsty person, seem closer than they really are (Balcetis & Dunning, 2010).

perceptual set a mental predisposition to perceive one thing and not another.

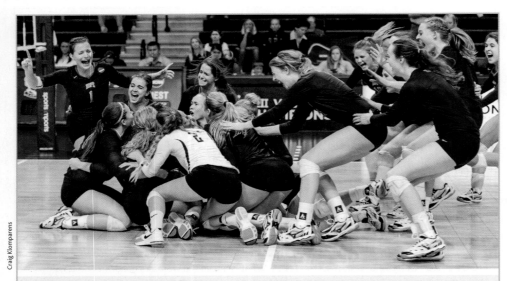

FIGURE 5.8 Context makes clearer The Hope College volleyball team celebrates its national championship winning moment.

Craig Klomparens

- A softball appears bigger when players are hitting well (Witt & Proffitt, 2005).

EMOTION Other clever experiments have demonstrated that emotions can shove our perceptions in one direction or another.

- Hearing sad music can tilt the mind toward hearing a spoken word as *mourning* rather than *morning,* as *die* rather than *dye,* as *pain* rather than *pane* (Halberstadt et al., 1995).

- A hill seems less steep to people who feel others understand them (Oishi et al., 2013).

- A harmful action, such as robbery, seems more serious to those who have just listened to irritating (and anger-cuing) music (Seidel & Prinz, 2013).

The moral of all these examples? *Much of what we perceive comes not just from what's "out there," but also from what's behind our eyes and between our ears.* Through top-down processing, our experiences, assumptions, and expectations—and even our context, motivation, and emotions—can shape and color our views of reality.

Retrieve + Remember

- Does *perceptual set* involve bottom-up or top-down processing? Why?

ANSWER: It involves top-down processing, because it draws on our experiences, assumptions, and expectations when interpreting stimuli.

* * *

The processes we've discussed so far are features shared by all our sensory systems. Let's turn now to the ways those systems are unique. We'll start with our most prized and complex sense, vision.

Vision: Sensory and Perceptual Processing

Your eyes receive light energy and transform it into neural messages that your brain then processes into what you consciously see. How does such a taken-for-granted yet remarkable thing happen?

Light Energy and Eye Structures

LOQ 5-7 What are the characteristics of the energy we see as visible light? What structures in the eye help focus that energy?

The Stimulus Input: Light Energy

When you look at a bright red tulip, what strikes your eyes are not bits of the color red but pulses of energy that your visual system *perceives* as red. What we see as visible light is but a thin slice of the wide spectrum of electromagnetic energy shown in **FIGURE 5.9**. On one end of this spectrum are the short gamma waves, no longer than the diameter of an atom. On the other end are the mile-long waves of radio transmission. In between is the narrow band visible to us. Other portions are visible to other animals. Bees, for instance, cannot see what we perceive as red but they can see ultraviolet light.

Light travels in waves, and the shape of those waves influences what we see. Light's **wavelength** is the distance from one wave peak to the next (**FIGURE 5.10a**). Wavelength determines **hue**—the color we experience, such as a tulip's red petals. A light wave's **amplitude,** or height, determines its **intensity**—the amount of energy the wave contains. Intensity influences brightness (Figure 5.10b).

Understanding the characteristics of the physical energy we see as light is one part of understanding vision. But to appreciate *how* we transform that energy into color and meaning, we need to know more about vision's window—the eye.

The Eye

What color are your eyes? Asked this question, most people describe their *iris,* the doughnut-shaped ring of muscle that controls the size of your *pupil.* Your iris is so distinctive that an iris-scanning

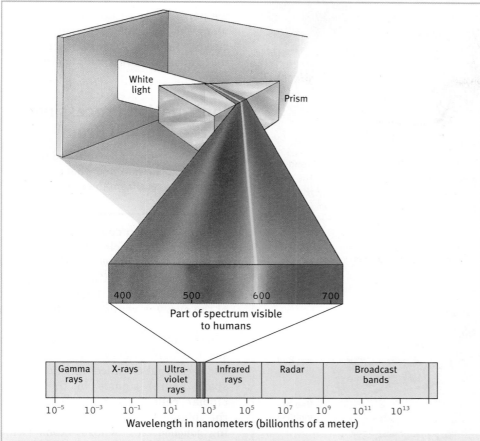

FIGURE 5.9 The wavelengths we see What we see as light is only a tiny slice of a wide spectrum of electromagnetic energy. The wavelengths visible to the human eye (shown enlarged) extend from the shorter waves of blue-violet light to the longer waves of red light.

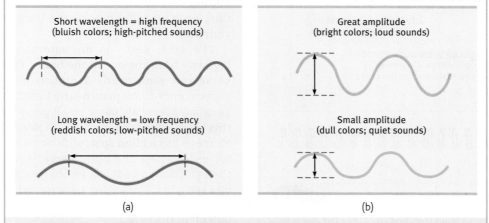

FIGURE 5.10 The physical properties of waves (a) Waves vary in *wavelength* (the distance between successive peaks). *Frequency,* the number of complete wavelengths that can pass a point in a given time, depends on the length of the wave. The shorter the wavelength, the higher the frequency. Wavelength determines the *perceived color* of light (and also the *pitch* of sound). (b) Waves also vary in *amplitude,* the height from peak to trough (top to bottom). Wave amplitude determines the perceived *brightness* of colors (and also the *intensity* of sounds).

machine can confirm your identity. Your sensitive iris can also reveal some of your thoughts and emotions. When you feel disgust or are about to answer *No,* your iris constricts, making your pupil smaller (de Gee et al., 2014; Goldinger & Papesh, 2012). When you're feeling amorous, your iris dilates, enlarging your pupil and signaling your interest. But the iris' main job is controlling the amount of light entering your eye.

After passing through your pupil, light hits the lens in your eye. The lens then focuses the light rays into an image on your eyeball's inner surface, the **retina.** For centuries, scientists knew that an image of a candle passing through a small opening will cast an upside-down, mirror image on a dark wall behind. They wondered how, if the eye's structure casts this sort of image on the retina (as in **FIGURE 5.11**), can we see the world right side up?

Eventually the answer became clear: The retina doesn't "see" a whole image. Rather, its millions of receptor cells behave like the prankster engineering students who make news by taking a car apart and rebuilding it in a friend's third-floor bedroom. The retina's millions of cells convert the particles of light energy into neural impulses and forward those to the brain. The brain reassembles them into what

wavelength the distance from the peak of one light wave or sound wave to the peak of the next.

hue the dimension of color that is determined by the wavelength of light; what we know as the color names *blue, green,* and so forth.

intensity the amount of energy in a light wave or sound wave, which influences what we perceive as brightness or loudness. Intensity is determined by the wave's amplitude (height).

retina the light-sensitive inner surface of the eye; contains the receptor rods and cones plus layers of neurons that begin the processing of visual information.

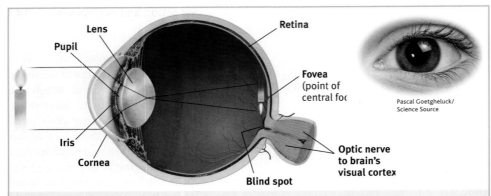

FIGURE 5.11 The eye Light rays reflected from a candle pass through the cornea, pupil, and lens. The curve and thickness of the lens change to bring nearby or distant objects into focus on the retina. Rays from the top of the candle strike the bottom of the retina. Those from the left side of the candle strike the right side of the retina. The candle's image appears on the retina upside down and reversed.

Pascal Goetgheluck/Science Source

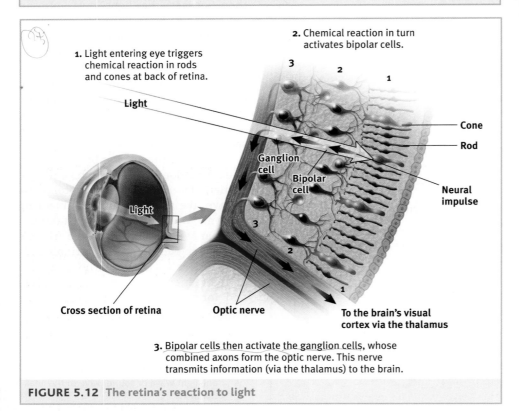

1. Light entering eye triggers chemical reaction in rods and cones at back of retina.

2. Chemical reaction in turn activates bipolar cells.

3. Bipolar cells then activate the ganglion cells, whose combined axons form the optic nerve. This nerve transmits information (via the thalamus) to the brain.

FIGURE 5.12 The retina's reaction to light

Retrieve + Remember

FIGURE 5.13 The blind spot To demonstrate your blind spot, first close your left eye, look at the spot above, and move your face away to a distance at which one of the cars disappears (which one do you predict it will be?). Repeat with your right eye closed—and note that now the other car disappears. Can you explain why?

ANSWER: Your blind spot is on the nose side of each retina, which means that objects to your right may fall onto the right eye's blind spot. Objects to your left may fall on the left eye's blind spot. The blind spot does not normally impair your vision, because your eyes are moving and because one eye catches what the other misses.

we perceive as an upright object. And along the way, visual information processing moves through increasingly more abstract levels, all at astonishing speed.

Information Processing in the Eye and Brain

LOQ 5-8 How do the rods and cones process information, and what path does information take from the eye to the brain?

Imagine that you could follow a single light-energy particle after it entered your eye. First, you would thread your way through your retina's sparse outer layer of cells. Then, reaching the back of the eye, you would meet the retina's buried receptor cells, the **rods** and **cones** (**FIGURE 5.12**). There, you would see the light energy trigger chemical changes. That chemical reaction would spark neural signals in the nearby bipolar cells. You could then watch the bipolar cells activate neighboring *ganglion cells,* whose axons twine together like strands of a rope to form the **optic nerve.** After a momentary stopover at the thalamus, rather like changing planes in Chicago, the information will fly on to the final destination, your visual cortex, at the back of your brain.

The optic nerve is an information highway from the eye to the brain. This nerve can send nearly 1 million messages at once through its nearly 1 million ganglion fibers. We pay a small price for this high-speed connection, however. Your eye has a **blind spot,** with no receptor cells, where the optic nerve leaves the eye (**FIGURE 5.13**). Close one eye. Do you see a black hole? *No,* because, without seeking your approval, your brain will fill in the hole.

The retina's two types of receptor cells, rods and cones, differ in where they're found and in what they do (**TABLE 5.1**). Cones cluster in and around the *fovea,* the retina's area of central focus. Many cones have their own hotline to the brain. One cone transmits a precise message to a single bipolar cell, which relays it to the visual cortex. Thanks to cones, you can see fine details and perceive color—but not at night. In dim light, cones don't function well.

Rods, which are located around the outer regions (the periphery) of your retina, remain sensitive in dim light. If cones are soloists, rods perform as a chorus. They enable black-and-white vision. Rods have no hotlines to the brain. Several rods pool their faint energy output and funnel it onto a single bipolar cell, which sends the combined message to your brain.

Stop for a minute and experience the rod-cone difference. Pick a word in

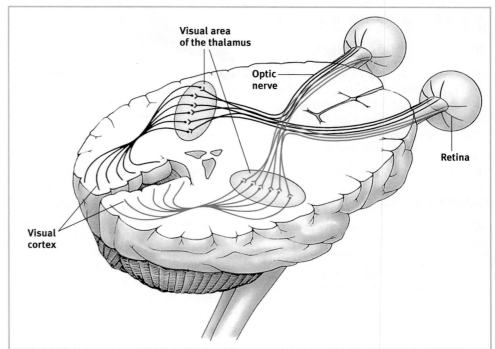

FIGURE 5.14 **Pathway from the eyes to the visual cortex** The retina's ganglion axons form the optic nerve. In the thalamus, the optic nerve axons pass messages to other neurons that run to the visual cortex.

Omikron/Science Source

TABLE 5.1 Receptors in the Human Eye: Rod-Shaped Rods and Cone-Shaped Cones

	Cones	Rods
Number	6 million	120 million
Location in retina	Center	Periphery
Sensitivity in dim light	Low	High
Color sensitivity	High	Low
Detail sensitivity	High	Low

this sentence and stare directly at it, focusing its image on the cones in the center of your eye. Notice that words a few inches off to the side appear blurred? They lack detail because their image is striking your retina's outer regions, where most rods are found. Thus, when driving or biking, rods help you detect a car in your peripheral vision well before you perceive its details.

So, cones and rods each provide a special sensitivity: Cones are sensitive to detail and color. Rods are sensitive to faint light and peripheral motion. But these receptor cells do more than simply pass along electrical impulses. They begin processing sensory information by coding and analyzing it. (In a frog's eye, for example, the "bug detector" cells that fire when they respond to moving fly-like objects are found in the retina's third neural layer.) After this

round of processing, information travels up your optic nerve, headed toward a specific location in your visual cortex in the back of your brain. In an important stop on that journey, the optic nerve links up with neurons in the thalamus (**FIGURE 5.14**).

rods retinal receptors that detect black, white, and gray, and are sensitive to movement; necessary for peripheral and twilight vision, when cones don't respond.

cones retinal receptors that are concentrated near the center of the retina; in daylight or well-lit conditions, cones detect fine detail and give rise to color sensations.

optic nerve the nerve that carries neural impulses from the eye to the brain.

blind spot the point at which the optic nerve leaves the eye; this part of the retina is "blind" because it has no receptor cells.

Retrieve + Remember

- Some night-loving animals, such as toads, mice, rats, and bats, have impressive night vision thanks to having many more_____ (rods/cones) than _____ (rods/cones) in their retinas. These creatures probably have very poor _____ (color/black-and-white) vision.

  ANSWERS: rods; cones; color

- Cats are able to open their _____ much wider than we can, which allows more light into their eyes so they can see better at night.

  ANSWER: pupils

Color Processing

LOQ 5-9 How do we perceive color in the world around us?

We talk as though objects possess color: "A tomato is red." Recall the old question, "If a tree falls in the forest and no one hears it, does it make a sound?" We can ask the same of color: If no one sees the tomato, is it red?

The answer is *No*. First, the tomato is everything *but* red, because it *rejects* (reflects) the long wavelengths of red. Second, the tomato's color is our mental construction. As the famous physicist Sir Isaac Newton (1704) observed more than three centuries ago, "The [light] rays are not colored." Color, like all aspects of vision, lives not in the object but in the theater of our brain. Even while dreaming, we may perceive things in color.

One of vision's most basic and intriguing mysteries is how we see the world in color. How, from the light energy striking your retina, does your brain construct your experience of color—and of so many colors?

Modern detective work on the mystery of color vision began in the nineteenth century, when Hermann von Helmholtz built on the insights of an English physicist, Thomas Young. The clue that led to their breakthrough was the knowledge that any color can be created by combining the light waves of three primary colors—red, green, and blue. Young and von Helmholtz reasoned that the eye must therefore have three types of receptors, one for each color.

Years later, researchers confirmed the **Young-Helmholtz trichromatic (three-color) theory.** By measuring the response of various cones to different color stimuli, they found that the retina does indeed have three types of color receptors. Each type is especially sensitive to the wavelengths of one of three colors, and those colors are, in fact, red, green, and blue. When light stimulates combinations of these cones, we see other colors. For example, the retina has no separate receptors especially sensitive to yellow. But when red and green wavelengths stimulate both red-sensitive and green-sensitive cones, we see yellow.

By one estimate, we can see differences among more than 1 million color variations (Neitz et al., 2001). At least most of us can. About 1 person in 50 is "colorblind." That person is usually male, because the defect is genetically sex linked. Most people with color-deficient vision are not actually blind to all colors. They simply have trouble perceiving the difference between red and green. They don't have three-color vision. Instead, perhaps unknown to them (because their lifelong vision *seems* normal), their retinas' red- or green-sensitive cones, or sometimes both, don't function properly (**FIGURE 5.15**).

But why do people blind to red and green often still see yellow? And why does yellow appear to be a pure color, not a mixture of red and green, the way purple is of red and blue? As Ewald Hering soon noted, trichromatic theory leaves some parts of the color vision mystery unsolved.

FIGURE 5.15 Color-deficient vision People with red-green deficiency had trouble perceiving the teams in a 2015 Buffalo Bills versus New York Jets football game. "For the 8 percent of American men like me that are red-green colorblind, this game is a nightmare to watch," tweeted one fan. "Everyone looks like they're on the same team," said another.

Hering, a physiologist, found a clue in *afterimages*. Stare at a green square for a while and then look at a white sheet of paper, and you will see red, green's opponent color. Stare at a yellow square and its opponent color, blue, will appear on the white paper. (To experience this, try the flag demonstration in **FIGURE 5.16**.) Hering proposed that color vision must involve two additional processes: one responsible for red-versus-green perception, and the other for blue-versus-yellow.

A century later, researchers confirmed Hering's proposal, now called the **opponent-process theory.** They found that color vision depends on three pairs of opponent retinal processes—*red-green*, *yellow-blue*, and *white-black*. As impulses travel to the visual cortex, some neurons in both the retina and the thalamus are "turned on" by red but "turned off" by green. Others are turned on by green but off by red (DeValois & DeValois, 1975). Like red and green marbles sent down a narrow tube, "red" and "green" messages cannot both travel at once. Red and green are thus opponents, so we see either red or green, not a mixture of reddish green. But red and blue travel in separate channels, so we are able to see a reddish-blue, or purple.

How does opponent-process theory help us understand afterimages, such

FIGURE 5.16 Afterimage effect Stare at the center of the flag for a minute and then shift your eyes to the dot in the white space beside it. What do you see? (After tiring your neural response to black, green, and yellow, you should see their opponent colors.) Stare at a white wall and note how the size of the flag grows with the projection distance.

Young-Helmholtz trichromatic (three-color) theory the theory that the retina contains three different types of color receptors—one most sensitive to red, one to green, one to blue. When stimulated in combination, these receptors can produce the perception of any color.

opponent-process theory the theory that opposing retinal processes (red-green, yellow-blue, white-black) enable color vision. For example, some cells are "turned on" by green and "turned off" by red; others are turned on by red and off by green.

feature detectors nerve cells in the brain that respond to specific features of a stimulus, such as shape, angles, or movement.

as in the flag demonstration? Here's the answer (for the green changing to red):

- First, you stared at green bars, which tired the green part of the green-red pairing in your eyes.
- Then you stared at a white area. White contains all colors, including red.
- Because you had tired your green response, only the red part of the green-red pairing fired normally.

The present solution to the mystery of color vision is therefore roughly this: *Color processing occurs in two stages.*

1. The retina's red, green, and blue cones respond in varying degrees to different color stimuli, as the Young-Helmholtz trichromatic theory suggested.

Retrieve + Remember

- What are two key theories of color vision? Do they contradict each other, or do they make sense together? Explain.

ANSWER: The *Young-Helmholtz trichromatic theory* shows that the retina contains color receptors for red, green, and blue. The *opponent-process theory* shows that we have opponent-process cells in the retina and thalamus for red-green, yellow-blue, and white-black. These theories make sense together. They outline two stages of color vision: (1) The retina's receptors for red, green, and blue respond to different color stimuli. (2) The receptors' signals are then processed by the opponent-process cells on their way to the visual cortex in the brain.

2. The cones' responses are then processed by opponent-process cells, as Hering's opponent-process theory proposed.

LaunchPad For an interactive review and demonstration of these color vision principles, visit LaunchPad's *PsychSim 6: Colorful World*.

Feature Detection

LOQ 5-10 What are *feature detectors,* and what do they do?

Scientists once compared the brain to a movie screen, on which the eye projected images. But along came David Hubel and Torsten Wiesel (1979), who showed that at an early stage, our visual processing system takes images apart and later reassembles them. Hubel and Wiesel received a Nobel Prize for their work on **feature detectors,** nerve cells in the brain that respond to a scene's specific features—to particular edges, lines, angles, and movements. These specialized nerve cells in the visual cortex pass this specific information to other cortical areas, where teams of cells (*supercell clusters*) respond to more complex patterns, such as recognizing faces. The resulting brain activity varies depending on what's viewed. Thus, with the help of brain scans, "we can tell if a person is looking at a shoe, a chair, or a face," noted one researcher (Haxby, 2001).

One temporal lobe area by your right ear enables you to perceive faces and, thanks to a specialized neural network, to recognize them from many viewpoints (Connor, 2010). If this region is damaged, people still may recognize other forms and objects, but, like Heather Sellers, they cannot recognize familiar faces. How do we know this? In part because in laboratory experiments, researchers have used magnetic pulses to disrupt that brain area, producing a temporary loss of face recognition. The interaction between feature detectors and supercells provides instant analyses of objects in the world around us.

WELL-DEVELOPED SUPERCELLS In this 2011 World Cup match, USA's Abby Wambach instantly processed visual information about the positions and movements of Brazil's defenders and goalkeeper and somehow managed to get the ball around them all and into the net.

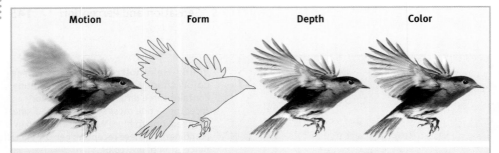

FIGURE 5.17 Parallel processing Studies of patients with brain damage suggest that the brain delegates the work of processing motion, form, depth, and color to different areas. After taking a scene apart, the brain integrates these parts into a whole perceived image.

Parallel Processing

LOQ 5-11 How does the brain use parallel processing to construct visual perceptions?

One of the most amazing aspects of visual information processing is the brain's ability to divide a scene into its parts. Using **parallel processing,** your brain assigns different teams of nerve cells the separate tasks of simultaneously processing a scene's movement, form, depth, and color (**FIGURE 5.17**). You then construct your perceptions by integrating the work of these different visual teams (Livingstone & Hubel, 1988).

Destroy or disable the neural workstation for a visual subtask, and something peculiar results, as happened to "Mrs. M." (Hoffman, 1998). After a stroke damaged areas near the rear of both sides of her brain, she could not perceive movement. People in a room seemed "suddenly here or there but I [had] not seen them moving." Pouring tea into a cup was a challenge because the fluid appeared frozen—she could not perceive it rising in the cup. Brain damage often reveals the importance of the parallel processing that operates, beyond our awareness, in our normal everyday life.

* * *

Think about the wonders of visual processing. As you read this page, the letters reflect light rays onto your retina, which then sends formless nerve impulses to several areas of your brain, which integrate the information and decode its meaning. The amazing result: we have transferred information across time and space, from our minds to your mind (**FIGURE 5.18**). That all of this happens instantly, effortlessly, and continuously is awe-inspiring.

> "I am fearfully and wonderfully made."
> King David, Psalm 139:14

Perceptual Organization

LOQ 5-12 What was the main message of Gestalt psychology, and how do figure-ground and grouping principles help us perceive forms?

It's one thing to understand how we see colors and shapes. But how do we organize and interpret those sights (or sounds or tastes or smells) so that they become *meaningful* perceptions—a rose in bloom, a familiar face, a sunset?

Early in the twentieth century, a group of German psychologists noticed that people who are given a cluster of sensations tend to organize them into a **gestalt,** a German word meaning a "form" or a "whole." As we look straight ahead, we cannot separate the perceived scene into our left and right fields of view. Our conscious perception is, at every moment, one whole, seamless scene. Consider **FIGURE 5.19.** The individual elements of this figure, called a

Retrieve + Remember

- What is the rapid sequence of events that occurs when you see and recognize the crouching animal in Figure 5.18?

ANSWER: Light waves reflect off the image and travel into your eyes. Receptor cells in your retina convert the light waves' energy into millions of neural impulses sent to your brain. Your brain's detector cells and work teams process the different parts of this visual input—including color, depth, movement, and form—on separate but parallel paths. Your brain pools the results and produces a meaningful image, which it compares to previously stored images. You recognize the image—a crouching tiger.

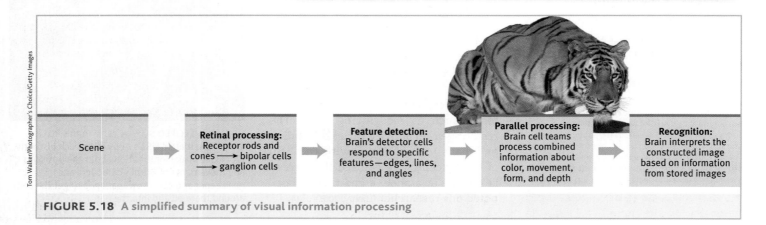

| Scene | → | **Retinal processing:** Receptor rods and cones → bipolar cells → ganglion cells | → | **Feature detection:** Brain's detector cells respond to specific features—edges, lines, and angles | → | **Parallel processing:** Brain cell teams process combined information about color, movement, form, and depth | → | **Recognition:** Brain interprets the constructed image based on information from stored images |

Tom Walker/Photographer's Choice/Getty Images

FIGURE 5.18 A simplified summary of visual information processing

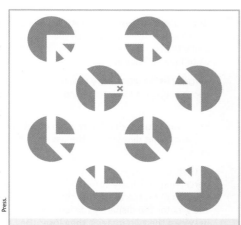

FIGURE 5.19 A Necker cube What do you see: circles with white lines, or a cube? If you stare at the cube, you may notice that it reverses location, moving the tiny X in the center from the front edge to the back. At times, the cube may seem to float forward, with circles behind it. At other times, the circles may become holes through which the cube appears, as though it were floating behind them. There is far more to perception than meets the eye.

Necker cube, are really nothing but eight blue circles, with three white lines meeting near the center. When we view all these elements together, however, we see a cube that sometimes reverses direction. The Necker cube nicely illustrates a famous saying of Gestalt psychologists: *In perception, the whole may exceed the sum of its parts.*

Over the years, the Gestalt psychologists demonstrated many principles we use to organize our sensations into perceptions. Underlying all of them is a basic truth: *Our brain does more than register information about the world.* Perception is not just opening a shutter and letting a picture print itself on the brain. We filter incoming information and we construct perceptions. Mind matters.

How Do We Perceive Form?

Imagine designing a video-computer system that, like your eye-brain system, could recognize faces at a glance. What abilities would it need? To start with, the video-computer system would need to perceive **figure-ground**—to separate faces from their backgrounds. In our eye-brain system, this is our first perceptual task—perceiving any object (the *figure*) as distinct from its surroundings (the *ground*). As you read, the words are the figure; the white space is the ground. This perception applies to our hearing, too. As you hear voices at a party, the one you attend to becomes the figure; all others are part of the ground. Sometimes, the same stimulus can trigger more than one perception, as in **FIGURE 5.20,** where the figure-ground relationship continually reverses. First we see the vase, then the faces, but we always perceive a figure standing out from a ground.

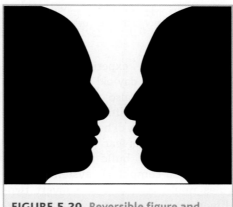

FIGURE 5.20 Reversible figure and ground A classic example: a vase or two faces?

While telling figure from ground, we (and our video-computer system) must also organize the figure into a *meaningful* form. Some basic features of a scene—such as color, movement, and light-dark contrast—we process instantly and automatically (Treisman, 1987). Our mind brings order and form to other stimuli by following certain rules for **grouping,** also identified by the Gestalt psychologists. These rules, which we apply even as infants and even in our touch perceptions, illustrate how the perceived whole differs from the sum of its parts (Gallace & Spence, 2011; Quinn et al., 2002; Rock & Palmer, 1990). Three examples:

Proximity We group nearby figures together. We see not six separate lines, but three sets of two lines:

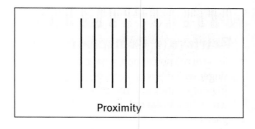

Proximity

Continuity We perceive smooth, continuous patterns rather than discontinuous ones. This pattern could be a series of alternating semicircles, but we perceive it as two continuous lines—one wavy, one straight:

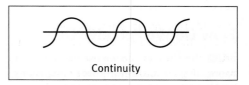

Continuity

Closure We fill in gaps to create a complete, whole object. Thus, we assume that the circles on the left are complete but partially blocked by the (illusory) triangle. Add nothing more than little lines to close off the circles, and your brain stops constructing a triangle:

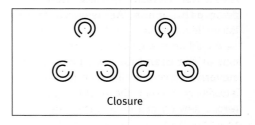

Closure

parallel processing processing many aspects of a problem or scene at the same time; the brain's natural mode of information processing for many functions, including vision.

gestalt an organized whole. Gestalt psychologists emphasized our tendency to integrate pieces of information into meaningful wholes.

figure-ground the organization of the visual field into objects (the *figures*) that stand out from their surroundings (the *ground*).

grouping the perceptual tendency to organize stimuli into meaningful groups.

How Do We Perceive Depth?

LOQ 5-13 How do we use binocular and monocular cues to see in three dimensions, and how do we perceive motion?

Our brain performs many amazing tricks, but one of its best is **depth perception.** From the two-dimensional images falling on our retinas, our brain creates three-dimensional perceptions that let us estimate the distance of an oncoming car or the height of a faraway house. How do we acquire this ability? Are we born with it? Do we learn it?

As Eleanor Gibson picnicked on the rim of the Grand Canyon, her scientific curiosity kicked in. She wondered, *Would a toddler peering over the rim perceive the dangerous drop-off and draw back?* To answer that question and others, Gibson and Richard Walk (1960) designed a series of experiments using a **visual cliff**—a model of a cliff with a "drop-off" area that was covered by sturdy glass. They placed 6- to 14-month-olds on the edge of the "cliff" and had their mothers coax the infants to crawl out onto the glass (**FIGURE 5.21**). Most infants refused to do so, indicating that they could perceive depth.

Had they *learned* to perceive depth? Crawling, no matter when it begins, seems to increase an infant's fear of heights (Adolph et al., 2014; Campos et al., 1992). But depth perception is also partly innate. Mobile newborn animals—even those

FIGURE 5.21 Visual cliff Eleanor Gibson and Richard Walk devised this miniature cliff with a glass-covered drop-off to determine whether crawling infants and newborn animals can perceive depth. Even when coaxed, infants refuse to climb onto the glass over the cliff.

with no visual experience (including young kittens, a day-old goat, and newly hatched chicks)—also refuse to venture across the visual cliff. Thus, biology prepares us to be wary of heights, and experience amplifies that fear.

If we were to build this ability into our video-computer system, what rules might enable it to convert two-dimensional images into a single three-dimensional perception? A good place to start would be the depth cues our brain receives from information supplied by one or both of our eyes.

BINOCULAR CUES People who see with two eyes perceive depth thanks partly to **binocular cues.** Here's an example. With both eyes open, hold two pens or pencils in front of you and touch their tips together. Now do so with one eye closed. A more difficult task, yes?

We use binocular cues to judge the distance of nearby objects. One such cue is **retinal disparity.** Because your eyes are about 2½ inches apart, your retinas receive slightly different images of the world. By comparing these two images, your brain can judge how close an object is to you. The greater the disparity (the difference) between the two retinal images, the closer the object. Try

it. Hold your two index fingers, with the tips about half an inch apart, directly in front of your nose, and your retinas will receive quite different views. If you close one eye and then the other, you can see the difference. (You can also create a finger sausage, as in **FIGURE 5.22.**) At a greater distance—say, when you hold your fingers at arm's length—the disparity is smaller.

We could easily include retinal disparity in our video-computer system. Moviemakers do so by filming a scene with two cameras placed a few inches apart. Viewers then watch the film through glasses that allow the left eye to see only the image from the left camera, and the right eye to see only the image from the right camera. The resulting effect, as 3-D movie fans know, mimics or exaggerates normal retinal disparity, giving the perception of depth.

MONOCULAR CUES How do we judge whether a person is 10 or 100 yards away? Retinal disparity won't help us here, because there won't be much difference between the images cast on our right and left retinas. At such distances, we depend on **monocular cues** (depth cues available to each eye separately). See **FIGURE 5.23** for some examples.

---

depth perception the ability to see objects in three dimensions, although the images that strike the retina are two-dimensional; allows us to judge distance.

visual cliff a laboratory device for testing depth perception in infants and young animals.

binocular cue a depth cue, such as retinal disparity, that depends on the use of two eyes.

retinal disparity a binocular cue for perceiving depth. By comparing images from the two eyes, the brain computes distance—the greater the disparity (difference) between the two images, the closer the object.

monocular cue a depth cue, such as interposition or linear perspective, available to either eye alone.

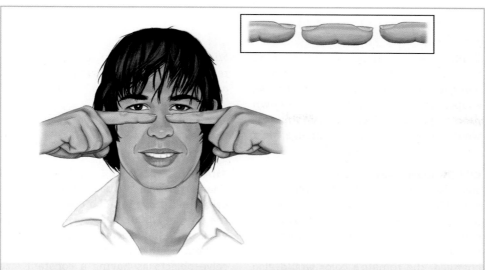

FIGURE 5.22 **The floating finger sausage** Hold your two index fingers about 5 inches in front of your eyes, with their tips half an inch apart. Now look beyond them and note the weird result. Move your fingers out farther and the retinal disparity—and the finger sausage—will shrink.

"I can't go on living with such lousy *depth perception!*"

RELATIVE HEIGHT We perceive objects higher in our field of vision as farther away. Because we assume the lower part of a figure-ground illustration is closer, we perceive it as figure (Vecera et al., 2002). Turn the illustration upside down and the black will become ground, like a night sky.

Direction of passenger's motion ⟶

RELATIVE MOTION As we move, objects that are actually stable may appear to move. If while riding on a bus you fix your gaze on some point—say, a house—the objects beyond the fixation point will appear to move with you. Objects in front of the point will appear to move backward. The farther an object is from the fixation point, the faster it will seem to move.

RELATIVE SIZE If we assume two objects are similar in size, most people perceive the one that casts the smaller retinal image as farther away.

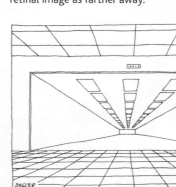

LINEAR PERSPECTIVE Parallel lines appear to meet in the distance. The sharper the angle of convergence, the greater the perceived distance.

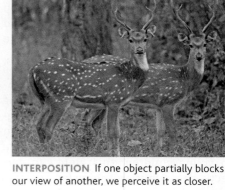

INTERPOSITION If one object partially blocks our view of another, we perceive it as closer.

LIGHT AND SHADOW Shading produces a sense of depth consistent with our assumption that light comes from above. If you turn this illustration upside down, the hollow will become a hill.

FIGURE 5.23 Monocular depth cues

LaunchPad For animated demonstrations and explanations of these cues, visit LaunchPad's *Concept Practice: Depth Cues.*

Retrieve + Remember

- How do we normally perceive depth?

ANSWER: We are normally able to perceive depth thanks to (1) binocular cues (which are based on our retinal disparity), and (2) monocular cues (which include relative height, relative size, interposition, linear perspective, light and shadow, and relative motion).

How Do We Perceive Motion?

Imagine that you could perceive the world as having color, form, and depth but that you could not see motion. You would be unable to bike or drive, and writing, eating, and walking would be a challenge.

Normally your brain computes motion based partly on its assumption that shrinking objects are moving away (not getting smaller) and enlarging objects are approaching. But you are imperfect at motion perception. In young children, this ability to correctly perceive approaching (and enlarging) vehicles is not yet fully developed, which puts them at risk for pedestrian accidents (Wann et al., 2011).

It's not just children who have occasional difficulties with motion perception. Our adult brain is sometimes tricked into believing what it is not seeing. When large and small objects move at the same speed, the large objects appear to move more slowly. Thus, trains seem to move slower than cars, and jumbo jets seem to land more slowly than smaller jets.

Perceptual Constancy

LOQ 5-14 How do perceptual constancies help us construct meaningful perceptions?

So far, we have noted that our video-computer system must perceive objects as we do—as having a distinct form, location, and perhaps motion. Its next task is to recognize objects without being deceived by changes in their color, shape, or size. We call this top-down process **perceptual constancy.** This feat would be an enormous challenge for a video-computer system.

COLOR CONSTANCY Our experience of color depends on an object's *context*. This would be clear if you viewed an isolated tomato through a paper tube over the course of the day. As the light—and thus the tomato's reflected wavelengths—changed, the tomato's color would also seem to change. But if you discarded the paper tube and viewed the tomato as one item in a salad bowl, its color would remain roughly constant as the lighting shifted. This perception of consistent color is known as **color constancy.**

We see color thanks to our brain's ability to decode the meaning of the light reflected by an object *relative to the objects surrounding it.* **FIGURE 5.24** dramatically illustrates the ability of a blue object to appear very different in three different contexts. Yet we have no trouble seeing these disks as blue. Paint manufacturers have learned this lesson. Knowing that your perception of a paint color will be determined by other colors in your home, many now offer trial samples you can test in that context. The take-home lesson: *Comparisons govern our perceptions.*

"From there to here, from here to there, funny things are everywhere."

Dr. Seuss, *One Fish, Two Fish, Red Fish, Blue Fish,* 1960

SHAPE AND SIZE CONSTANCIES Thanks to *shape constancy,* we usually perceive the form of familiar objects, such as the door in **FIGURE 5.25,** as constant even while our retinas receive changing images of them. Thanks to *size constancy,* we perceive objects as having a constant size even while our distance from them varies. We assume a car is large enough to carry people, even when we see its tiny image from two blocks away. This assumption also shows the close connection between perceived distance and perceived size. Perceiving an object's distance gives us cues to its size. Likewise, knowing its general size—that the object is a car—provides us with cues to its distance.

Even in size-distance judgments, however, we consider an object's context. This interplay between perceived size and perceived distance helps explain several well-known illusions, including the *Moon illusion.* The Moon looks up to 50 percent larger when near the horizon than when high in the sky.

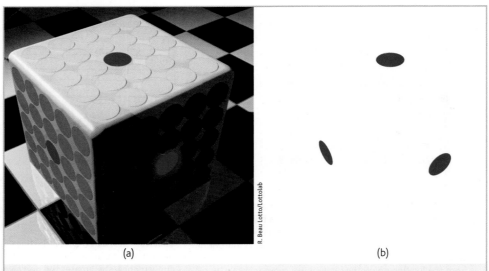

R. Beau Lotto/Lottolab

(a)   (b)

FIGURE 5.24 Color depends on context (a) Believe it or not, these three blue disks are identical in color. (b) Remove the surrounding context and see what results.

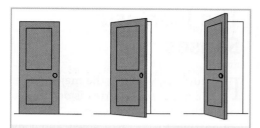

FIGURE 5.25 Shape constancy An opening door looks more and more like a trapezoid. Yet we still perceive it as a rectangle.

Can you imagine why? One reason is that monocular cues to an object's distance make the horizon Moon appear farther away. If it's farther away, our brain assumes, it must be larger than the Moon high in the night sky (Kaufman & Kaufman, 2000). Take away the distance cues—by looking at the horizon Moon through a paper tube—and the object will immediately shrink.

Mistaken judgments like these reveal the workings of our normally effective perceptual processes. The perceived relationship between distance and size is usually valid. But under special circumstances it can lead us astray.

Form perception, depth perception, and perceptual constancies illuminate how we organize our visual experiences. Perceptual organization applies to our other senses, too. Listening to an unfamiliar language, we have trouble hearing where one word stops and the next one begins. Listening to our own language, we automatically hear distinct words. We even organize a string of letters—THEDOGATEMEAT—into words that make an understandable phrase, more likely "The dog ate meat" than "The do gate me at" (McBurney & Collings, 1984). Perception, however, is more than organizing stimuli. Perception also requires what would be another big challenge to our video-computer system: interpretation—finding meaning in what we perceive.

LaunchPad To experience more visual illusions, and to understand what they reveal about how you perceive the world, visit LaunchPad's *PsychSim 6: Visual Illusions.*

Perceptual Interpretation

The debate over whether our perceptual abilities spring from our nature or our nurture has a long history. To what extent do we *learn* to perceive? German philosopher Immanuel Kant (1724–1804) maintained that knowledge comes from our inborn ways of organizing sensory experiences. Psychology's findings support this idea. We do come equipped to process sensory information. But British philosopher John Locke (1632–1704) argued that through our experiences we also learn to perceive the world. Psychology also supports this idea. We do learn to link an object's distance with its size. So, just how important is experience? How much does it shape our perceptual interpretations?

Experience and Visual Perception

LOQ 5-15 What does research on restored vision, sensory restriction, and perceptual adaptation reveal about the effects of experience on perception?

RESTORED VISION AND SENSORY RESTRICTION Writing to John Locke, a friend wondered what would happen if "a man born blind, and now adult, [was] taught by his touch to distinguish between a cube and a sphere." Could he, if made to see, visually distinguish the two? Locke's answer was *No*, because the man would never have learned to see the difference.

This question has since been put to the test with a few dozen adults who, though blind from birth, later gained sight (Gregory, 1978; Huber et al., 2015; von Senden, 1932). Most were born with cataracts—clouded lenses that allowed them to see only light and shadows, rather as a sighted person might see a foggy image through a Ping-Pong ball sliced in half. After cataract surgery, the patients could tell the difference between figure and ground, and they could sense colors. This suggests that we are born with these aspects of perception. But much as Locke supposed, they often could not visually recognize objects that were familiar by touch.

LEARNING TO SEE At age 3, Mike May lost his vision in an explosion. Decades later, after a new cornea restored vision to his right eye, he got his first look at his wife and children. Alas, although signals were now reaching his visual cortex, it lacked the experience to interpret them. May could not recognize expressions, or faces, apart from features such as hair. Yet he can see an object in motion and has learned to navigate his world and to marvel at such things as dust floating in sunlight (Abrams, 2002; Gorlick, 2010).

Seeking to gain more control than is provided by clinical cases, researchers have outfitted infant kittens and monkeys with goggles through which they could see only diffuse, unpatterned light (Wiesel, 1982). After infancy, when the goggles were removed, the animals' reactions were much like those of humans born with cataracts. They could distinguish color and brightness but not form. Their eyes were healthy. Their retinas still sent signals to their visual cortex. But without early stimulation, the brain's cortical cells had not developed normal connections. Thus, the animals remained functionally blind to shape.

perceptual constancy perceiving objects as unchanging (having consistent color, brightness, shape, and size) even as illumination and retinal images change.

color constancy perceiving familiar objects as having consistent color, even if changing illumination alters the wavelengths reflected by the object.

Surgery on blind children in India reveals that children blind from birth can benefit from cataract surgery. Although their vision may never be as sharp as normal, the younger they are, the more they will benefit (Sinha, 2013). There is a *critical period* for normal sensory and perceptual development—a limited time when exposure to certain stimuli or experiences is required.

In humans and other animals, similar sensory restrictions later in life do no permanent harm. When researchers cover an adult animal's eye for several months, its vision will be unaffected after the eye patch is removed. When surgeons remove cataracts that developed during late adulthood, most people are thrilled at the return to normal vision.

PERCEPTUAL ADAPTATION Given a new pair of glasses, we may feel a little strange, even dizzy. Within a day or two, we adjust. Our **perceptual adaptation** to changed visual input makes the world seem normal again. But imagine wearing a far more dramatic pair of new glasses—one that shifts the apparent location of objects 40 degrees to the left. When you toss a ball to a friend, it sails off to the left. Walking forward to shake hands with someone, you veer to the left.

Courtesy of Hubert Dolezal

PERCEPTUAL ADAPTATION "Oops, missed," thought researcher Hubert Dolezal as he attempted a handshake while viewing the world through inverting goggles. Yet, believe it or not, kittens, monkeys, and humans can adapt to an upside-down world.

Could you adapt to this distorted world? Not if you were a baby chicken. When fitted with such lenses, baby chicks continue to peck where food grains *seem* to be (Hess, 1956; Rossi, 1968). But we humans adapt to distorting lenses quickly. Within a few minutes, your throws would again be accurate, your stride on target. Remove the lenses and you would experience an aftereffect. At first your throws would err in the opposite direction, sailing off to the right. But again, within minutes you would adjust.

Indeed, given an even more radical pair of glasses—one that literally turns the world upside down—you could still adapt. Psychologist George Stratton (1896) experienced this when he invented, and for eight days wore, a device that flipped left to right and up to down, making him the first person to experience a right-side-up retinal image while standing upright. The ground was up; the sky was down.

At first, when Stratton wanted to walk, he found himself searching for his feet, which were now "up." Eating was nearly impossible. He became nauseated and depressed. But he persisted, and by the eighth day he could comfortably reach for an object and walk without bumping into things. When Stratton finally removed the headgear, he readapted quickly. So did research participants who also wore such optical gear—while riding a motorcycle, skiing the Alps, or flying an airplane (Dolezal, 1982; Kohler, 1962). By actively moving about in their topsy-turvy world, they adapted to their new context and learned to coordinate their movements. Later, they readapted to normal life.

So do we learn to perceive the world? In part we do, as we constantly adjust to changed sensory input. Research on critical periods teaches us that early nurture sculpts what nature has provided. In less dramatic ways, nurture continues to do this throughout our lives. Experience guides, sustains, and maintains the pathways in our brain that enable our perceptions.

The Nonvisual Senses

For humans, vision is the major sense. More of our brain cortex is devoted to vision than to any other sense. Yet without hearing, touch, taste, smell, and body position and movement, our experience of the world would be vastly diminished.

Hearing

Like our other senses, our hearing, or **audition,** helps us adapt and survive. Hearing provides information and enables relationships. It lets us communicate invisibly, shooting unseen air waves across space and receiving the same from others. Hearing loss is therefore an invisible disability. To not catch someone's name, to not grasp what someone is asking, and to miss the hilarious joke is to be deprived of what others know, and sometimes to feel excluded. (As a person with hearing loss, I [DM] know the feeling.)

Most of us, however, can hear a wide range of sounds, and the ones we hear best are those in the range of the human voice. With normal hearing, we are remarkably sensitive to faint sounds, such as a child's whimper. (If our ears were only slightly more sensitive, we would hear a constant hiss from the movement of air molecules.) We also are acutely sensitive to sound differences. Among thousands of possible voices, we easily distinguish an unseen friend's. Moreover, hearing is fast. Your reaction to a sudden sound is at least 10 times faster than your response when you suddenly see something "from the corner of your eye, turn your head toward it, recognize it, and respond to it" (Horowitz, 2012). A fraction of a second after such events stimulate your ear's receptors, millions of neurons are working together to extract the essential features, compare them with past experience, and identify the sound (Freeman, 1991). For hearing as for seeing, we wonder: How do we do it?

Sound Waves: From the Environment Into the Brain

LOQ 5-16 What are the characteristics of the air pressure waves that we hear as sound?

Hit a piano key and you unleash the energy of sound waves. Moving molecules of air, each bumping into the next, create waves of compressed and expanded air, like ripples on a pond circling out from a tossed stone. Our ears detect these brief air pressure changes.

Like light waves, sound waves vary in shape. The height, or *amplitude*, of sound waves determines their perceived *loudness*. Their length, or **frequency**, determines the **pitch** (the high or low tone) we experience. Long waves have low frequency—and low pitch. Short waves have high frequency—and high pitch. Sound waves produced by a referee's whistle are much shorter and faster than those produced by a truck horn.

We measure sounds in *decibels*, with zero decibels representing the lowest level detectable by human ears. Normal

THE SOUNDS OF MUSIC A violin's short, fast waves create a high pitch. The longer, slower waves of a cello or bass create a lower pitch. Differences in the waves' height, or amplitude, also create differing degrees of loudness. (To review the physical properties of light and sound waves, see Figure 5.10.)

conversation registers at about 60 decibels. A whisper falls at about 20 decibels, and a jet plane passing 500 feet overhead registers at about 110 decibels. Prolonged exposure to any sounds above 85 decibels can produce hearing loss. Tell that to football fans of the NFL's Kansas City Chiefs who, in 2014, broke the Guinness World Record for the noisiest stadium at 142 decibels (Liberman, 2015). Hear today, gone tomorrow.

Retrieve + Remember

- The amplitude of a sound wave determines our perception of _____ (loudness/pitch).

ANSWER: loudness

- The longer the sound waves, the _____ (lower/higher) their frequency and the _____ (lower/higher) their pitch.

ANSWERS: lower; lower

Decoding Sound Waves

LOQ 5-17 How does the ear transform sound energy into neural messages?

How does vibrating air morph into nerve impulses that your brain can decode as sounds?

The process begins when sound waves entering your *outer ear* trigger a mechanical chain reaction. Your outer ear channels the waves into your *auditory canal*, where they bump against your *eardrum*, causing this tight membrane to vibrate (**FIGURE 5.26a**).

In your **middle ear**, three tiny bones (the *hammer, anvil,* and *stirrup*) pick up the vibrations and transmit them to the **cochlea**, a snail-shaped tube in your **inner ear.**

The incoming vibrations then cause the cochlea's membrane-covered opening (the *oval window*) to vibrate, sending ripples through the fluid inside the cochlea (Figure 5.26b). The ripples bend the *hair cells* lining the *basilar membrane* on the cochlea's surface, much as wind bends wheat stalks in a field.

The hair cell movements in turn trigger impulses in nerve cells, whose axons combine to form the *auditory nerve*. The auditory nerve carries the impulses to your thalamus and then on to your *auditory cortex* in your brain's temporal lobe.

From vibrating air, to tiny moving bones, to fluid waves, to electrical impulses to the brain: You hear!

Perhaps the most magical part of the hearing process is the hair cells—"quivering bundles that let us hear" thanks to their "extreme sensitivity and extreme speed" (Goldberg, 2007). A cochlea has 16,000 of these cells, which sounds like a lot until we compare that with an eye's 130 million or so receptors. But consider a hair cell's responsiveness. Deflect the tiny bundles of *cilia* on its tip by only the width of an atom, and the alert hair cell will trigger a neural response (Corey et al., 2004).

Damage to the cochlea's hair cell receptors or their associated nerves can cause **sensorineural hearing loss** (or nerve deafness). Occasionally, disease

---

perceptual adaptation the ability to adjust to changed sensory input, including an artificially displaced or even inverted visual field.

audition the sense or act of hearing.

frequency the number of complete wavelengths that pass a point in a given time (for example, per second).

pitch a tone's experienced highness or lowness; depends on frequency.

middle ear the chamber between the eardrum and cochlea containing three tiny bones (hammer, anvil, and stirrup) that concentrate the vibrations of the eardrum on the cochlea's oval window.

cochlea [KOHK-lee-uh] a coiled, bony, fluid-filled tube in the inner ear; sound waves traveling through the cochlear fluid trigger nerve impulses.

inner ear the innermost part of the ear, containing the cochlea, semicircular canals, and vestibular sacs.

sensorineural hearing loss hearing loss caused by damage to the cochlea's receptor cells or to the auditory nerves; the most common form of hearing loss, also called *nerve deafness*.

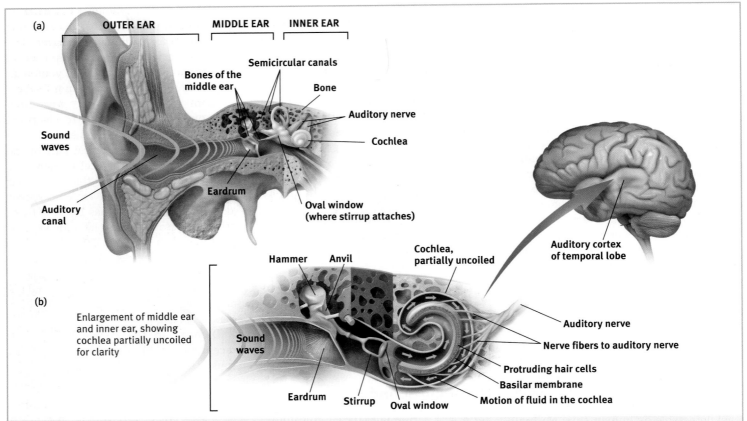

FIGURE 5.26 Hear here: How we transform sound waves into nerve impulses that our brain interprets (a) The outer ear funnels sound waves to the eardrum. The bones of the middle ear (hammer, anvil, and stirrup) amplify and relay the eardrum's vibrations through the oval window into the fluid-filled cochlea. (b) As shown in this detail of the middle and inner ear, the resulting pressure changes in the cochlear fluid cause the basilar membrane to ripple, bending the hair cells on its surface. Hair cell movements trigger impulses at the base of the nerve cells, whose fibers join together to form the auditory nerve. That nerve sends neural messages to the thalamus and on to the auditory cortex.

damages hair cell receptors, but more often the culprits are biological changes linked with heredity and aging, or prolonged exposure to ear-splitting noise or music. Sensorineural hearing loss is more common than **conduction hearing loss,** which is caused by damage to the mechanical system that conducts sound waves to the cochlea.

Hair cells have been compared to carpet fibers. Walk around on them and they will spring back. But leave a heavy piece of furniture on them and they may never rebound. As a general rule, any noise we cannot talk over (loud machinery, fans screaming at a sports event, music blasting at maximum volume) may be harmful, especially if we are exposed to it often or for a long time (Roesser, 1998). And if our ears ring after

such experiences, we have been bad to our unhappy hair cells. As pain alerts us to possible bodily harm, ringing in the ears alerts us to possible hearing damage. It is hearing's version of bleeding.

Worldwide, 1.23 billion people are challenged by hearing loss (Global Burden of Disease, 2015). Since the early 1990s, teen hearing loss has risen by a third and now affects 1 in 5 teens (Shargorodsky et al., 2010). Teen boys more than teen girls or adults blast themselves with loud volumes for long periods (Zogby, 2006). (Does it surprise you that men's hearing tends to be less acute than women's?) People who spend many hours behind a power mower, above a jackhammer, or in a loud club should wear earplugs, or they risk needing a hearing aid later. "Condoms or, safer yet, abstinence," say

sex educators. "Earplugs or walk away," say hearing educators.

Nerve deafness cannot be reversed. For now, the only way to restore hearing is a sort of bionic ear—a **cochlear implant.** Some 50,000 people, including some 30,000 children, receive these electronic devices each year (Hochmair, 2013). The implants translate sounds into electrical signals that, wired into the cochlea's nerves, transmit sound information to the brain. When given to deaf kittens and human infants, cochlear implants have seemed to trigger an "awakening" of brain areas normally used in hearing (Klinke et al., 1999; Sireteanu, 1999). They can help children become skilled in oral communication (especially if they receive them as preschoolers or ideally before age 1) (Dettman et al., 2007; Schorr et al., 2005).

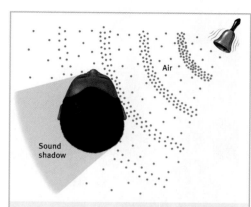

FIGURE 5.27 Why two ears are better than one Sound waves strike one ear sooner and more intensely than the other. From this information, our brain can compute the sound's location. As you might therefore expect, people who lose all hearing in one ear often have difficulty locating sounds.

How Do We Locate Sounds?

Why don't we have one big ear—perhaps above our one nose? "All the better to hear you with," as the wolf said to Little Red Riding Hood. Our two ears are about 6 inches apart, and they pick up two slightly different messages. Say a car to your right honks (**FIGURE 5.27**). Your right ear will receive a more *intense* sound. It will also receive the sound slightly *sooner* than your left ear. Because sound travels 750 miles per hour, the intensity difference and the time lag will be very small—just 0.000027 second! Lucky for us, our supersensitive sound system can detect such tiny differences (Brown & Deffenbacher, 1979; Middlebrooks & Green, 1991).

LaunchPad For an interactive review of how we perceive sound, visit LaunchPad's *PsychSim 6: The Auditory System.* For an animated explanation, visit LaunchPad's *Concept Practice: The Auditory Pathway.*

Touch

LOQ 5-18 What are the four basic touch sensations, and how do we sense touch?

If you had to lose one sense, which would you give up? If you could have only one, which would you keep?

Although not the first sense to come to mind, touch might be a good choice for keeping. Right from the start, touch enables our development. Infant monkeys allowed to see, hear, and smell—but not touch—their mother become desperately unhappy (Suomi et al., 1976). Those separated by a screen with holes that allow touching are much less miserable. Premature babies gain weight faster and go home sooner if they are stimulated by hand massage (Field et al., 2006). As adults, we still yearn to touch—to kiss, to stroke, to snuggle.

Humorist Dave Barry was perhaps right to joke that your skin "keeps people from seeing the inside of your body, which is repulsive, and it prevents your organs from falling onto the ground." But skin does much more. Our "sense of touch" is actually a mix of four basic and distinct skin senses: *pressure, warmth, cold,* and *pain.* Other skin sensations are variations of these four. For example, stroking side-by-side pressure spots creates a tickle. Repeated gentle stroking of a pain spot creates an itching sensation. Touching side-by-side cold and pressure spots triggers a sense of wetness (which you can experience by touching dry, cold metal).

Touch sensations involve more than feelings on our skin, however. A soft touch on the leg evokes a different cortical

THE PRECIOUS SENSE OF TOUCH As William James wrote in his *Principles of Psychology* (1890), "Touch is both the alpha and omega of affection."

response when a straight man believes he was caressed by an attractive woman rather than by another man (Gazzola et al., 2012). Such responses show how quickly our thinking brain influences our sensory responses. This thought-feeling interaction also appears in the ways we experience and respond to pain.

Pain—What Is It and How Can We Control It?

LOQ 5-19 What biological, psychological, and social-cultural influences affect our experience of pain? How do placebos, distraction, and hypnosis help control pain?

Be thankful for occasional pain. Pain is your body's way of telling you something has gone wrong. Drawing your attention to a burn, a break, or a sprain, pain orders you to change your behavior—"Stay off that ankle!" The rare people born without the ability to feel pain may experience severe injury or even death before early adulthood. Without the discomfort that makes us shift positions, their joints can fail from excess strain. Without the warnings of pain, infections can run wild and injuries multiply (Neese, 1991).

Many more people live with chronic pain, which is rather like an alarm that won't shut off. Persistent backaches, arthritis, headaches, and cancer-related pain prompt two questions: What is pain? And how might we control it?

Our feeling of pain reflects both *bottom-up* sensations and *top-down* cognition. Pain is a biopsychosocial event (Hadjistavropoulos et al., 2011). As such, pain experiences vary widely, from group to group and from person to person.

conduction hearing loss a less common form of hearing loss, caused by damage to the mechanical system that conducts sound waves to the cochlea.

cochlear implant a device for converting sounds into electrical signals and stimulating the auditory nerve through electrodes threaded into the cochlea.

"PAIN IS A GIFT." So said a doctor studying Ashlyn Blocker. Ashlyn has a rare genetic mutation that prevents her from feeling pain. As a child, she ran around for two days on a broken ankle. She has put her hands on a hot machine and burned the flesh off. And she has reached into boiling water to retrieve a dropped spoon. "Everyone in my class asks me about it, and I say, 'I can feel pressure, but I can't feel pain.' *Pain!* I cannot feel it!" (Heckert, 2012).

BIOLOGICAL INFLUENCES Pain is a physical event produced by your senses. But pain differs from some of your other sensations. No one type of stimulus triggers pain, the way light triggers vision. And no specialized receptors process pain signals, the way the rods and cones in your eyes react to light rays. Instead, you have sensory receptors *(nociceptors),* mostly in your skin, which detect hurtful temperatures, pressure, or chemicals.

Your experience of pain also depends in part on the genes you inherited and on your physical characteristics. Women are more sensitive to pain than are men—and their senses of hearing and smell also tend to be more sensitive (Ruau et al., 2012; Wickelgren, 2009).

But pain is not merely a physical event in which injured nerves send impulses to a specific brain area—like pulling on a rope to ring a bell. With pain, as with sights and sounds, the brain sometimes gets its signals crossed. And when it does, the brain can actually create pain, as it does in *phantom limb sensations* following a limb amputation. Without sensory input, the brain may misinterpret other neural activity. As a dreamer may see with eyes closed, so 7 in 10 such people feel pain or movement in limbs that no longer exist (Melzack, 1992, 2005).

Phantoms may haunt other senses, too. People with hearing loss often experience the sound of silence: *tinnitus,* a phantom sound of ringing in the ears. Those who lose vision to glaucoma, cataracts, diabetes, or macular degeneration may experience phantom sights—nonthreatening hallucinations (Ramachandran & Blakeslee, 1998). And damage to nerves in the systems for tasting and smelling can give rise to phantom tastes or smells, such as ice water that seems sickeningly sweet or fresh air that reeks of rotten food (Goode, 1999). The point to remember: *We see, hear, taste, smell, and feel pain with our brain.*

PSYCHOLOGICAL INFLUENCES One powerful influence on our perception of pain is the attention we focus on it. Athletes, focused on winning, may perceive pain differently and play through it. After a tackle in the first half of a competitive game, Swedish professional soccer player Mohammed Ali Khan said he "had a bit of pain" but thought it was "just a bruise." He played on. In the second half he was surprised to learn from an attending doctor that his leg was broken. The pain in sprain is mainly in the brain.

We also seem to edit our *memories* of pain. The pain we experience may not be the pain we remember. In experiments, and after medical procedures, people overlook how long a pain lasted. Their memory snapshots instead record two points: the peak moment of pain, and how much pain they felt at the *end*. In one experiment, people put one hand in painfully cold water for 60 seconds, and then the other hand in the same painfully cold water for 60 seconds, followed by a slightly less painful 30 seconds

DISTRACTED FROM THE PAIN Halfway through his lap of the 2012 Olympics 1600-meter relay, Manteo Mitchell (top) broke one of his leg bones—and kept running.

more (Kahneman et al., 1993). Which experience would you expect they recalled as most painful?

Curiously, when asked which trial they would prefer to repeat, most preferred the longer trial, with more net pain—but less pain at the end. Physicians have used this principle with patients undergoing colon exams—lengthening the discomfort by a minute, but lessening its intensity at the end (Kahneman, 1999). Patients experiencing this taper-down treatment later recalled the exam as less painful than did those whose pain ended abruptly. (As a painful root canal is coming to an end, if the oral surgeon asks if you'd like to go home, or to have a few more minutes of milder discomfort, there's a case to be made for prolonging your hurt.) Endings matter.

SOCIAL-CULTURAL INFLUENCES Pain is a product of our attention, our expectations, and our culture (Gatchel et al., 2007; Reimann et al., 2010). Not surprisingly, then, our perception of pain varies with our social situation and our cultural traditions. We tend to feel more pain when others seem to be experiencing pain

(Symbaluk et al., 1997). When people felt empathy for another's pain, their own brain activity partly mirrored the activity of the actual brain in pain (Singer et al., 2004).

CONTROLLING PAIN If pain is where body meets mind—if pain is both a physical and a psychological event—then it should be treatable both physically and psychologically. Depending on the symptoms, pain control therapies may include drugs, surgery, acupuncture, electrical stimulation, massage, exercise, hypnosis, relaxation training, and thought distraction.

We have some built-in pain controls, too. Our brain releases a natural painkiller—*endorphins*—in response to severe pain or even vigorous exercise. The release of these neurotransmitters has a soothing effect so that the pain we experience may be greatly reduced. People who carry a gene that boosts the normal supply of endorphins are less bothered by pain, and their brain is less responsive to it (Zubieta et al., 2003). Others, who carry a gene that disrupts the neural pain circuit, may be unable to experience pain (Cox et al., 2006). Such discoveries point the

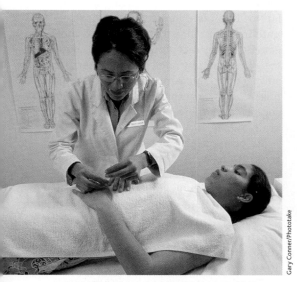

ACUPUNCTURE: A JAB WELL DONE This acupuncturist is attempting to help this woman gain relief from back pain by using needles on points of the patient's hand.

Gary Conner/Phototake

way toward future pain medications that mimic these genetic effects.

> "Pain is increased by attending to it."
>
> Charles Darwin, *The Expression of the Emotions in Man and Animals*, 1872

Even *placebos* can help, by dampening the central nervous system's attention and responses to painful experiences—mimicking painkilling drugs (Eippert et al., 2009; Wager & Atlas, 2013). After being injected in the jaw with a stinging saltwater solution, men in one experiment received a placebo. They had been told it would relieve pain, and it did—they immediately felt better. "Nothing" worked. Their belief in the fake painkiller triggered their brain to respond by dispensing endorphins, indicated by activity in an area that releases the natural painkillers (Scott et al., 2007; Zubieta et al., 2005).

When endorphins combine with distraction, amazing things can happen. Have you ever had a health care professional suggest that you focus on a pleasant image ("Think of a warm, comfortable environment") or perform some task ("Count backward by 3s")? These are effective ways to activate brain pathways that decrease pain and increase tolerance (Edwards et al., 2009). For burn victims receiving painful wound care, an even more effective distraction is escaping into a computer-generated 3-D world. Functional MRI (fMRI) scans reveal that playing in virtual reality reduces the brain's pain-related activity (Hoffman, 2004).

Better yet, research suggests, maximize pain relief by combining a placebo with distraction (Buhle et al., 2012), and amplify their effects with **hypnosis.** Imagine you are about to be hypnotized. The hypnotist invites you to sit back, fix your gaze on a spot high on the wall, and relax. You hear a quiet, low voice suggest, "Your eyes are growing tired . . . Your eyelids are becoming heavy . . . now heavier and heavier . . . They are beginning to close . . . You are becoming more deeply relaxed . . . Your breathing is now deep and regular . . . Your muscles are becoming more and more relaxed. Your whole

body is beginning to feel like lead." After a few minutes of this hypnotic induction, you may experience hypnosis.

Hypnotists have no magical mind-control power; they merely focus people on certain images or behaviors. To some extent, we are all open to suggestion. But highly hypnotizable people—such as the 20 percent who can carry out a suggestion not to react to an open bottle of smelly ammonia—are especially suggestible and imaginative (Barnier & McConkey, 2004; Silva & Kirsch, 1992).

Can hypnosis relieve pain? *Yes.* Hypnosis inhibits pain-related brain activity. In surgical experiments, hypnotized patients have required less medication, recovered sooner, and left the hospital earlier than unhypnotized control patients (Askay & Patterson, 2007; Hammond, 2008; Spiegel, 2007). Nearly 10 percent of us can become so deeply hypnotized that even major surgery can be performed without anesthesia. Half of us can gain at least some relief from hypnosis. The surgical use of hypnosis has flourished in Europe, where one Belgian medical team has performed more than 5000 surgeries with a combination of hypnosis, local anesthesia, and a mild sedative (Song, 2006). Hypnosis has also lessened some forms of chronic pain (Adachi et al., 2014).

But how does hypnosis work? Psychologists have proposed two explanations.

- *Social influence theory* contends that hypnosis is a form of social influence—a by-product of normal social and mental processes (Lynn et al., 1990, 2015; Spanos & Coe, 1992). In this view, hypnotized people, like actors caught up in a role, begin to feel and behave in ways appropriate for "good hypnotic subjects." They may allow the hypnotist to direct their attention and fantasies away from pain.

hypnosis a social interaction in which one person (the hypnotist) suggests to another person (the subject) that certain perceptions, feelings, thoughts, or behaviors will spontaneously occur.

• *Dissociation theory* proposes that hypnosis is a special dual-processing state of *dissociation*—a split between normal sensations and conscious awareness. Dissociation theory seeks to explain why, when no one is watching, hypnotized people may carry out **posthypnotic suggestions** (which are made during hypnosis but carried out after the person is no longer hypnotized) (Perugini et al., 1998). It also offers an explanation for why people hypnotized for pain relief may show brain activity in areas that receive sensory information, but not in areas that normally process pain-related information (Rainville et al., 1997). *Selective attention* may also be at work (Chapter 2). Brain scans show that hypnosis increases activity in the brain's attention systems

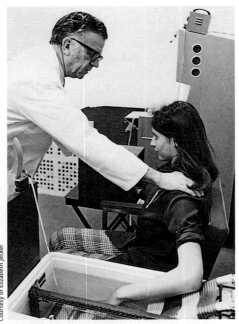

Courtesy of Elizabeth Jecker

DISSOCIATION OR SOCIAL INFLUENCE? This hypnotized woman being tested by famous researcher Ernest Hilgard showed no pain when her arm was placed in an ice bath. But asked to press a key if some part of her felt the pain, she did so. To Hilgard (1986, 1992), this was evidence of dissociation, or divided consciousness. The social influence perspective, however, maintains that people responding this way are caught up in playing the role of "good subject."

(Oakley & Halligan, 2013). Thus, hypnosis doesn't block the sensory input itself, but it may block our attention to those stimuli. This helps explain why injured soldiers, caught up in battle, may feel little or no pain until they reach safety.

So, is hypnosis to be explained as normal social influence or a special dissociative state? As the debate continues, stay tuned for further research.

Retrieve + Remember

- Which of the following options has NOT been proven to reduce pain?
  a. Distraction
  b. Hypnosis
  c. Phantom limb sensations
  d. Endorphins

ANSWER: c

Taste

LOQ 5-20 In what ways are our senses of taste and smell similar, and how do they differ?

Like touch, our sense of taste involves several basic sensations. Taste's sensations were once thought to be *sweet, sour, salty,* and *bitter,* with all others stemming from a mixture of these four (McBurney & Gent, 1979). Then, as researchers searched for specialized fibers for those four taste sensations, they discovered a fifth sensation—the savory, meaty taste of *umami.* You may have experienced umami as the flavor enhancer monosodium glutamate (MSG), often used in Chinese or Thai food.

Tastes give us pleasure, but they also help us survive. Pleasant tastes attracted our ancestors to foods rich in energy or protein (see **TABLE 5.2**). Unpleasant tastes warned them away from new foods that might be toxic. The taste preferences of today's 2- to 6-year-olds reflect this inherited biological wisdom. At this age, children are typically fussy

TABLE 5.2	The Survival Functions of Basic Tastes
Taste	**Indicates**
Sweet	Energy source
Salty	Sodium essential to physiological processes
Sour	Potentially toxic acid
Bitter	Potential poisons
Umami	Proteins to grow and repair tissue

eaters and often turn away from new meat dishes or bitter-tasting vegetables, such as spinach and brussels sprouts (Cooke et al., 2003). But learning—another tool in our early ancestors' survival kit—comes to the aid of frustrated parents across the globe. When given repeated small tastes of disliked new foods, children usually learn to accept them (Wardle et al., 2003). We come to like what we eat. German babies who were bottle-fed vanilla-flavored milk became adults with a striking preference for vanilla flavoring (Haller et al., 1999).

Taste is a chemical sense. Look into a mirror and you'll see little bumps on the top and sides of your tongue. Each bump contains 200 or more taste buds. Each taste bud contains a pore that catches food chemicals. In each taste bud pore, 50 to 100 taste receptor cells project antenna-like hairs that sense food molecules. Some receptors respond mostly to sweet-tasting molecules, others to salty-, sour-, umami-, or bitter-tasting ones. Each receptor transmits its message to a matching partner cell in your brain (Barretto et al., 2015).

It doesn't take much to trigger receptor responses. If a stream of water is pumped across your tongue, the addition of a concentrated salty or sweet taste for only one-tenth of a second will get your attention (Kelling & Halpern, 1983). When a friend asks for "just a taste" of your soft drink, you can squeeze off the straw after a mere instant.

Taste receptors reproduce themselves every week or two, so if hot food burns your tongue, it hardly matters. However, as you grow older, it may matter more, because the number of taste buds in your mouth will decrease, as will your taste sensitivity (Cowart, 1981). (No wonder adults enjoy strong-tasting foods that children resist.) Smoking and alcohol can speed up the loss of taste buds.

There's more to taste than meets the tongue. Our expectations also influence what we taste. When told a sausage roll was "vegetarian," people in one experiment judged it inferior to its identical partner labeled "meat" (Allen et al., 2008). In another experiment, hearing that a wine cost $90 rather than its real $10 price made it taste better and triggered more activity in a brain area that responds to pleasant experiences (Plassman et al., 2008).

Smell

Inhale, exhale. Between birth's first inhale and death's last exhale, about 500 million breaths of life-sustaining air will bathe your nostrils in a stream of scent-laden molecules. The resulting experience of smell (olfaction) is strikingly intimate. With every breath, we inhale something of whatever or whoever it is we smell.

Smell, like taste, is a chemical sense. We smell something when molecules of a substance carried in the air reach a tiny cluster of receptor cells at the top of each nasal cavity. These 20 million olfactory receptors, waving like sea anemones on a reef, respond selectively—to the aroma of a cake baking, to a wisp of smoke, to a friend's fragrance. Bypassing the brain's sensory control center, the thalamus, they instantly alert the brain.

LaunchPad For an animated explanation of how we smell, visit LaunchPad's *Concept Practice: Sense of Smell.*

Odor molecules come in many shapes and sizes—so many, in fact, that it takes hundreds of different receptors, designed by a large family of genes, to recognize these molecules (Miller, 2004). We do not have one distinct receptor for each detectable odor. Instead, receptors on the surface of nasal cavity neurons work in different combinations to send

messages to the brain, activating different patterns in the olfactory cortex (Buck & Axel, 1991). As the English alphabet's 26 letters can combine to form many words, so olfactory receptors can produce different patterns to identify an estimated 1 trillion different odors (Bushdid et al., 2014). These combinations of olfactory receptors, activating different neuron patterns, allow us to detect the difference between fresh-brewed and hours-old coffee (Zou & Buck, 2006).

Aided by smell, a mother fur seal returning to a beach crowded with pups will find her own. Human mothers and nursing infants also quickly learn to recognize each other's scents (McCarthy, 1986). A smell's appeal—or lack of it—depends in part on learned associations (Herz, 2001). In the United States, people associate the smell of wintergreen with candy and gum, and they tend to like it. In Great Britain, wintergreen is often associated with medicine, and people find it less appealing.

Our sense of smell is less impressive than our senses of seeing and hearing. Looking out across a garden, we see its forms and colors in wonderful detail and hear a variety of birds singing. Yet we smell few of the garden's scents without sticking our nose directly into the blossoms. We also have trouble recalling odors by name. But we have a remarkable capacity to recognize long-forgotten smells and their associated personal tales (Engen, 1987; Schab, 1991). The smell of the sea, the scent of a perfume, or the

THE NOSE KNOWS Humans have some 20 million olfactory receptors. A bloodhound has 220 million (Herz, 2007).

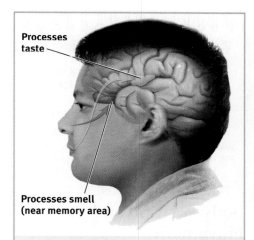
FIGURE 5.28 Taste, smell, and memory Information from the taste buds (yellow arrow) travels to an area between the frontal and temporal lobes of the brain. It registers in an area not far from where the brain receives information from our sense of smell, which interacts with taste. The brain's circuitry for smell (red area) also connects with areas involved in memory storage, which helps explain why a smell can trigger a memory.

smell can trigger memory.

aroma of a favorite relative's kitchen can bring to mind a happy time.

Our brain's circuitry helps explain an odor's power to evoke feelings, memories, and behaviors (**FIGURE 5.28**). A hotline runs between the brain area that receives information from the nose and other brain centers associated with emotions and memories. In experiments, people have become more suspicious when exposed to a fishy smell during a trust game (Lee & Schwarz, 2012). When exposed to a sweet taste, others became sweeter on their romantic partners and more helpful to others (Meier et al., 2012; Ren et al., 2015). And when riding on a train car with the citrus scent of a cleaning product, people left less trash behind (de Lange et al., 2012).

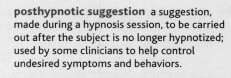
posthypnotic suggestion a suggestion, made during a hypnosis session, to be carried out after the subject is no longer hypnotized; used by some clinicians to help control undesired symptoms and behaviors.

Body Position and Movement

LOQ 5-21 How do we sense our body's position and movement?

Using only the five familiar senses we have so far considered, you could not put food in your mouth, stand up, or reach out and touch someone. Nor could you perform the "simple" act of taking one step forward. That act requires feedback from, and instructions to, some 200 muscles, and it engages brain power that exceeds the mental activity involved in reasoning. Like all your other voluntary movements, taking a step is possible because of your sense of **kinesthesia**, which keeps you aware of your body parts' position and movement. You came equipped with millions of position and motion sensors in muscles, tendons, and joints all over your body. These sensors provide constant feedback to your brain. Twist your wrist one degree, and your brain receives an immediate update.

You can momentarily imagine being blind or deaf. Close your eyes, plug your ears, and experience the dark stillness. But what would it be like to live without the benefits of kinesthesia? Ian Waterman of Hampshire, England, knows. In 1972, at age 19, Waterman contracted a rare viral infection that destroyed the nerves that enabled his sense of light touch and of body position and movement. People with this condition report feeling disconnected from their body, as though it is dead, not real, not theirs (Sacks, 1985). With long practice, Waterman has learned to walk and eat—by visually focusing on his

limbs and directing them accordingly. But if the lights go out, he crumples to the floor (Azar, 1998).

Vision interacts with kinesthesia for you, too. Stand with your right heel in front of your left toes. Easy. Now close your eyes and try again. Did you wobble?

A companion **vestibular sense** works hand in hand with kinesthesia to monitor your head's (and thus your body's) position and movement. Two structures in your inner ear join forces to help you maintain your balance. The first, your *semicircular canals*, look like a three-dimensional pretzel (Figure 5.26a). The second structure is the pair of *vestibular sacs* connecting those canals with the cochlea. These sacs contain fluid that moves when your head rotates or tilts. This movement stimulates hair-like receptors, which send messages to your cerebellum at the back of your brain, enabling you to sense your body position and maintain your balance.

If you twirl around and then come to an abrupt halt, it takes a few seconds for the fluid in your semicircular canals and for your kinesthetic receptors to return to their neutral state. The aftereffect fools your dizzy brain with the sensation that you're still spinning. This illustrates a principle underlying perceptual illusions: Mechanisms that normally give us an accurate experience of the world can, under special conditions, fool us.

BODIES IN SPACE These high school competitive cheer team members can thank their inner ears for the information that enables their brains to monitor their bodies' position so expertly.

Understanding how we get fooled provides clues to how our perceptual system works.

Sensory Interaction

LOQ 5-22 How does sensory interaction influence our perceptions, and what is *embodied cognition?*

We have seen that vision and kinesthesia interact. Actually, all our senses eavesdrop on one another (Rosenblum, 2013). This is **sensory interaction** at work. One sense can influence another.

Consider how smell sticks its nose into the business of taste. Hold your nose, close your eyes, and have someone feed you various foods. You may be unable to tell a slice of apple from a chunk of raw potato. A piece of steak may taste like cardboard. Without their smells, a cup of cold coffee and a glass of red wine may seem the same. To savor a taste, we normally breathe the aroma through our nose—which is why eating is not much fun when you have a bad cold. Smell can also enhance our taste: A strawberry odor intensifies our perception of a drink's sweetness. Even touch can influence taste. Depending on its texture, a potato chip "tastes" fresh or stale (Smith, 2011). Smell + texture + taste = flavor.

Hearing and vision may similarly interact. We can see a tiny flicker of light more easily if it is paired with a short burst of sound (Kayser, 2007). The reverse is also true: We can hear soft sounds more easily if they are paired with a visual cue (**FIGURE 5.29**). If I [DM], a person with hearing loss, watch a video with on-screen captions, I have no trouble hearing the words I see. But if I then decide

FIGURE 5.29 Face-to-face Seeing the speaker forming the words, which Apple's FaceTime video-chat feature allows, makes those words easier to understand for hard-of-hearing listeners (Knight, 2004).

I don't need the captions, and turn them off, I will quickly realize I do need them. The eyes guide the ears.

So our senses interact. But what happens if they disagree? What if our eyes *see* a speaker form one sound but our ears *hear* another sound? Surprise: Our brain may perceive a third sound that blends both inputs. Seeing mouth movements for *ga* while hearing *ba,* we may perceive *da.* This is known as the *McGurk effect,* after one of its discoverers (McGurk & MacDonald, 1976). For all of us, lip reading is part of hearing.

We have seen that our perceptions have two main ingredients: Our bottom-up sensations and our top-down cognitions (such as expectations, attitudes, thoughts, and memories). But let's return to our starting point in this chapter. In everyday life, sensation and perception are two points on a continuum. We think from within a body. It's not surprising, then, that the brain circuits processing our bodily sensations may sometimes interact with brain circuits responsible for cognition. The result is **embodied cognition.** Here are some examples from a few playful experiments.

- *Physical warmth may promote social warmth.* After holding a warm drink rather than a cold one, people were more likely to rate someone more warmly, feel closer to them, and behave more generously (IJzerman & Semin, 2009; Williams & Bargh, 2008).

- *Social exclusion can literally feel cold.* After being given the cold shoulder by others, people judged the room

to be colder than did those who had been treated warmly (Zhong & Leonardelli, 2008).

- *Judgments of others may also mimic body sensations.* Sitting at a wobbly desk and chair makes others' relationships seem less stable (Kille et al., 2013).

🖥 **LaunchPad** Are you wondering how researchers test these kinds of questions? Try LaunchPad's *IMMERSIVE LEARNING: How Would You Know If a Cup of Coffee Can Warm Up Relationships?*

As we attempt to decipher our world, our brain blends inputs from multiple channels. For many people, an odor—perhaps of mint or chocolate—can evoke a sensation of taste. But in a few rare individuals, the brain circuits for two or more senses become joined in a condition called *synesthesia,* where one sort of sensation (such as hearing sound) produces another (such as seeing color). Thus, hearing music may activate color-sensitive cortex regions and trigger a sensation of color (Brang et al., 2008; Hubbard et al., 2005). Seeing the number 3 may evoke a taste sensation (Ward, 2003).

kinesthesia [kin-ehs-THEE-zhuh] the system for sensing the position and movement of individual body parts.

vestibular sense the sense of body movement and position, including the sense of balance.

sensory interaction the principle that one sense may influence another, as when the smell of food influences its taste.

embodied cognition the influence of bodily sensations, gestures, and other states on cognitive preferences and judgments.

* * *

For a summary of our sensory systems, see **TABLE 5.3.**

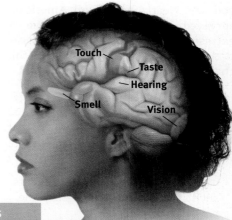

TABLE 5.3 Summarizing the Senses

Sensory System	Source	Receptors	Key Brain Areas
Vision	Light waves striking the eye	Rods and cones in the retina	Occipital lobes
Hearing	Sound waves striking the outer ear	Cochlear hair cells in the inner ear	Temporal lobes
Touch	Pressure, warmth, cold, harmful chemicals	Receptors *(nociceptors),* mostly in the skin, which detect pressure, warmth, cold, and pain	Somatosensory cortex
Taste	Chemical molecules in the mouth	Basic tongue receptors for sweet, sour, salty, bitter, and umami	Frontal temporal lobe border
Smell	Chemical molecules breathed in through the nose	Millions of receptors at top of nasal cavities	Olfactory bulb
Body position— kinesthesia	Any change in position of a body part, interacting with vision	Kinesthetic sensors in joints, tendons, and muscles	Cerebellum
Body movement— vestibular sense	Movement of fluids in the inner ear caused by head/ body movement	Hair-like receptors in the ears' semicircular canals and vestibular sacs	Cerebellum

ESP—Perception Without Sensation?

LOQ 5-23 What are the claims of ESP, and what have most research psychologists concluded after putting these claims to the test?

The river of perception is fed by streams of sensation, cognition, and emotion. If perception is the product of these three sources, what can we say about **extrasensory perception (ESP)**, which claims that perception can occur apart from sensory input?

The answer depends in part on who you ask. Nearly half of all Americans surveyed believe we are capable of extrasensory perception (AP, 2007; Moore, 2005). The most testable and, for this chapter, most relevant ESP claims are

- *telepathy*: mind-to-mind communication.
- *clairvoyance*: perceiving remote events, such as a house on fire in another state.
- *precognition*: perceiving future events, such as an unexpected death in the next month.

Closely linked is *psychokinesis,* or "mind over matter," such as using mind power alone to raise a table or affect the roll of a die. (The claim is illustrated by the wry request, "Will all those who believe in psychokinesis please raise my hand?")

Most research psychologists and scientists—including 96 percent of the scientists in one U.S. National Academy of Sciences survey—have been skeptical of ESP claims (McConnell, 1991). No greedy—or charitable—psychic has been able to choose the winning lottery jackpot ticket, or make billions on the stock market. In 30 years, unusual predictions have almost never come true, and psychics have virtually never anticipated any of the year's headline events (Emery, 2004, 2006). Why, despite a $50 million reward, could no psychics help

locate Osama bin Laden after the 9/11 terrorist attacks? (And where were they on 9/10 when we needed them?)

What about the hundreds of visions offered by psychics working with the police? These have been no more accurate than guesses made by others (Nickell, 1994, 2005; Radford, 2010; Reiser, 1982). Their sheer volume does, however, increase the odds of an occasional correct guess, which psychics can then report to the media.

Are everyday people's "visions" any more accurate? Do our dreams predict the future, or do they only seem to do so when we recall or reconstruct them in light of what has already happened? After aviator Charles Lindbergh's baby son was kidnapped and murdered in 1932, but before the body was discovered, two psychologists invited people to report their dreams about the child (Murray & Wheeler, 1937). How many replied? 1300. How many accurately saw the child dead? 65. How many also correctly anticipated the body's location—buried among trees? Only 4. Although this number was surely no better than chance, to those 4 dreamers, the accuracy of their apparent prior knowledge must have seemed uncanny.

Given the billions of events in the world each day, and given enough days,

Will you marry me, live happily for 3 years, become bored, pretend to be taking a pottery class but actually be having an affair, then agree to go to marriage counseling to stay together for the sake of our hyperactive son, Derrick?

WHEN PSYCHICS PROPOSE

BIZARRO © 2014 Dan Piraro, Dist. By King Features

some stunning coincidences are sure to occur. By one careful estimate, chance alone would predict that more than a thousand times a day, someone on Earth will think of another person and then, within the next five minutes, learn of that person's death (Charpak & Broch, 2004). Thus, when explaining an astonishing event, we should "give chance a chance" (Lilienfeld, 2009). With enough time and enough people, the improbable becomes inevitable.

> "A person who talks a lot is sometimes right."
> Spanish proverb

When faced with claims of mind reading or out-of-body travel or communication with the dead, how can we separate bizarre ideas from those that sound strange but are true? At the heart of science is a simple answer: *Test them to see if they work.* If they do, so much the better for the ideas. If they don't, so much the better for our skepticism.

How might we test ESP claims in a controlled, reproducible experiment? An experiment differs from a staged demonstration. In the laboratory, the experimenter controls what the "psychic" sees and hears. On stage, the "psychic" controls what the audience sees and hears.

Daryl Bem, a respected social psychologist, once joked that "a psychic is an actor playing the role of a psychic" (1984). Yet this one-time skeptic has reignited hopes for scientific evidence of ESP with nine experiments that seemed to show people anticipating future events (Bem, 2011). In one, for example, people guessed when an erotic scene would appear on a screen in one of two randomly selected positions. Participants guessed right 53.1 percent of the time, beating 50 percent by a small but statistically significant margin.

Bem's research survived critical reviews by a top-tier journal. But other critics found the methods "badly flawed" (Alcock, 2011) or the statistical analyses "biased" (Wagenmakers et al., 2011). Still others predicted the results could not be

Courtesy of Claire Cole

TESTING PSYCHIC POWERS IN THE BRITISH POPULATION Psychologists created a "mind machine" to see if people could influence or predict a coin toss (Wiseman & Greening, 2002). Using a touch-sensitive screen, visitors to British festivals were given four attempts to call heads or tails, playing against a computer that kept score. By the time the experiment ended, nearly 28,000 people had predicted 110,959 tosses—with 49.8 percent correct.

who can demonstrate a single, reproducible ESP event. (To silence those who say pigs can't talk would take but one talking pig.) So far, no such person has emerged.

Retrieve + Remember

- If an ESP event occurred under controlled conditions, what would be the next best step to confirm that ESP really exists?

ANSWER: The ESP event would need to be reproduced in other scientific studies.

* * *

Most of us will never know what it is like to see colorful music, to be incapable of feeling pain, or to be unable to recognize the faces of friends and family. But within our ordinary sensation and perception lies much that is truly extraordinary. More than a century of research has revealed many secrets of sensation and perception. For future generations of researchers, though, there remain profound and genuine mysteries to solve.

repeated by "independent and skeptical researchers" (Helfand, 2011).

Anticipating such skepticism, Bem has made his research materials available to anyone who wishes to replicate his studies. Multiple attempts have met with minimal success, and the debate continues (Bem et al., 2014; Galak et al., 2012; Ritchie et al., 2012; Wagenmakers, 2014). Regardless, science is doing its work. It has been open to a finding that challenges its assumptions. And then, through follow-up research, it has assessed the validity of the findings. And that is how science sifts crazy-sounding ideas, leaving most on the historical waste heap while occasionally surprising us.

One skeptic, magician James Randi, has had a long-standing offer of $1 million to be given "to anyone who proves a genuine psychic power under proper observing conditions" (Randi, 1999; Thompson, 2010). French, Australian, and Indian groups have made similar offers of up to 200,000 euros (CFI, 2003). Large as these sums are, the scientific seal of approval would be worth far more. To silence those who say there is no ESP, one need only produce a single person

extrasensory perception (ESP) the controversial claim that perception can occur apart from sensory input; includes telepathy, clairvoyance, and precognition.

CHAPTER REVIEW

Sensation and Perception

Test yourself by taking a moment to answer each of these Learning Objective Questions (repeated here from within the chapter). Then turn to Appendix D, Complete Chapter Reviews, to check your answers. Research suggests that trying to answer these questions on your own will improve your long-term memory of the concepts (McDaniel et al., 2009).

Basic Concepts of Sensation and Perception

5-1: What are *sensation* and *perception?* What do we mean by *bottom-up processing* and *top-down processing?*

5-2: What three steps are basic to all our sensory systems?

5-3: How do absolute thresholds and difference thresholds differ?

5-4: How are we affected by subliminal stimuli?

5-5: What is the function of sensory adaptation?

5-6: How do our expectations, contexts, motivations, and emotions influence our perceptions?

Vision: Sensory and Perceptual Processing

5-7: What are the characteristics of the energy we see as visible light? What structures in the eye help focus that energy?

5-8: How do the rods and cones process information, and what path does information take from the eye to the brain?

5-9: How do we perceive color in the world around us?

5-10: What are *feature detectors,* and what do they do?

5-11: How does the brain use parallel processing to construct visual perceptions?

5-12: What was the main message of Gestalt psychology, and how do figure-ground and grouping principles help us perceive forms?

5-13: How do we use binocular and monocular cues to see in three dimensions, and how do we perceive motion?

5-14: How do perceptual constancies help us construct meaningful perceptions?

5-15: What does research on restored vision, sensory restriction, and perceptual adaptation reveal about the effects of experience on perception?

The Nonvisual Senses

5-16: What are the characteristics of the air pressure waves that we hear as sound?

5-17: How does the ear transform sound energy into neural messages?

5-18: What are the four basic touch sensations, and how do we sense touch?

5-19: What biological, psychological, and social-cultural influences affect our experience of pain? How do placebos, distraction, and hypnosis help control pain?

5-20: In what ways are our senses of taste and smell similar, and how do they differ?

5-21: How do we sense our body's position and movement?

Sensory Interaction

5-22: How does sensory interaction influence our perceptions, and what is *embodied cognition?*

ESP—Perception Without Sensation?

5-23: What are the claims of ESP, and what have most research psychologists concluded after putting these claims to the test?

TERMS AND CONCEPTS TO REMEMBER

Test yourself on these terms by trying to write down the definition in your own words before flipping back to the referenced page to check your answer.

sensation, p. 135
perception, p. 135
bottom-up processing, p. 135
top-down processing, p. 135
transduction, p. 135
absolute threshold, p. 135
subliminal, p. 135
difference threshold, p. 135
priming, p. 137
Weber's law, p. 137
sensory adaptation, p. 137
perceptual set, p. 139
wavelength, p. 141
hue, p. 141

intensity, p. 141
retina, p. 141
rods, p. 143
cones, p. 143
optic nerve, p. 143
blind spot, p. 143
Young-Helmholtz trichromatic (three-color) theory, p. 145
opponent-process theory, p. 145
feature detectors, p. 145
parallel processing, p. 147
gestalt, p. 147
figure-ground, p. 147
grouping, p. 147
depth perception, p. 148

visual cliff, p. 148
binocular cue, p. 148
retinal disparity, p. 148
monocular cue, p. 148
perceptual constancy, p. 151
color constancy, p. 151
perceptual adaptation, p. 153
audition, p. 153
frequency, p. 153
pitch, p. 153
middle ear, p. 153
cochlea [KOHK-lee-uh], p. 153
inner ear, p. 153

sensorineural hearing loss, p. 153
conduction hearing loss, p. 155
cochlear implant, p. 155
hypnosis, p. 157
posthypnotic suggestion, p. 159
kinesthesia [kin-ehs-THEE-see-a], p. 161
vestibular sense, p. 161
sensory interaction, p. 161
embodied cognition, p. 161
extrasensory perception (ESP), p. 163

CHAPTER TEST

Test yourself repeatedly throughout your studies. This will not only help you figure out what you know and don't know; the testing itself will help you learn and remember the information more effectively thanks to the *testing effect*.

1. Sensation is to _____ as perception is to _____.

   a. absolute threshold; difference threshold
   b. bottom-up processing; top-down processing
   c. interpretation; detection
   d. grouping; priming

2. The process by which we organize and interpret sensory information is called _____.

3. Subliminal stimuli are

   a. too weak to be processed by the brain.
   b. consciously perceived more than 50 percent of the time.
   c. always strong enough to affect our behavior at least 75 percent of the time.
   d. below our absolute threshold for conscious awareness.

4. Another term for *difference threshold* is the _____ _____ _____.

5. Weber's law states that for a difference to be perceived, two stimuli must differ by

   a. a fixed or constant energy amount.
   b. a constant minimum percentage.
   c. a constantly changing amount.
   d. more than 7 percent.

6. Sensory adaptation helps us focus on

   a. visual stimuli.
   b. auditory stimuli.
   c. constant features of the environment.
   d. important changes in the environment.

7. Our perceptual set influences what we perceive. This mental tendency reflects our

   a. experiences, assumptions, and expectations.
   b. sensory adaptation.
   c. priming ability.
   d. difference thresholds.

8. The characteristic of light that determines the color we experience, such as blue or green, is _____.

9. The amplitude of a light wave determines our perception of _____.
   a. brightness.
   b. color.
   c. meaning.
   d. distance.

10. The blind spot in your retina is located where
    a. there are rods but no cones.
    b. there are cones but no rods.
    c. the optic nerve leaves the eye.
    d. the bipolar cells meet the ganglion cells.

11. Cones are the eye's receptor cells that are especially sensitive to _____ light and are responsible for our _____ vision.
    a. bright; black-and-white
    b. dim; color
    c. bright; color
    d. dim; black-and-white

12. Two theories together account for color vision. The Young-Helmholtz trichromatic theory shows that the eye contains _____, and Hering's theory accounts for the nervous system's having _____.
    a. opposing retinal processes; three pairs of color receptors
    b. opponent-process cells; three types of color receptors
    c. three pairs of color receptors; opposing retinal processes
    d. three types of color receptors; opponent-process cells

13. What mental processes allow you to perceive a lemon as yellow?

14. The cells in the visual cortex that respond to certain lines, edges, and angles are called _____ _____.

15. The brain's ability to process many aspects of an object or a problem simultaneously is called _____ _____.

16. Our tendencies to fill in the gaps and to perceive a pattern as continuous are two different examples of the organizing principle called
    a. interposition.
    b. depth perception.
    c. shape constancy.
    d. grouping.

17. In listening to a concert, you attend to the star performer and perceive the other musicians as accompaniment. This illustrates the organizing principle of
    a. figure-ground.
    b. shape constancy.
    c. grouping.
    d. depth perception.

18. The visual cliff experiments suggest that
    a. infants have not yet developed depth perception.
    b. crawling human infants and very young animals perceive depth.
    c. we have no way of knowing whether infants can perceive depth.
    d. unlike other species, humans are able to perceive depth in infancy.

19. Depth perception underlies our ability to
    a. group similar items in a gestalt.
    b. perceive objects as having a constant shape or form.
    c. judge distances.
    d. fill in the gaps in a figure.

20. Two examples of _____ depth cues are interposition and linear perspective.

21. Perceiving a tomato as consistently red, despite lighting shifts, is an example of
    a. shape constancy.
    b. perceptual constancy.
    c. a binocular cue.
    d. continuity.

22. After surgery to restore vision, patients who had been blind from birth had difficulty
    a. recognizing objects by touch.
    b. recognizing objects by sight.
    c. distinguishing figure from ground.
    d. distinguishing between bright and dim light.

23. In experiments, people have worn glasses that turned their visual fields upside down. After a period of adjustment, they learned to function quite well. This ability is called _____ _____.

24. The snail-shaped tube in the inner ear, where sound waves are converted into neural activity, is called the _____.

25. What are the basic steps in transforming sound waves into perceived sound?

26. The sensory receptors that are found mostly in the skin and that detect hurtful temperatures, pressure, or chemicals are called _____.

27. We have specialized nerve receptors for detecting which five tastes? How did this ability aid our ancestors?

28. _____ is your sense of body position and movement. Your _____ _____ specifically monitors your head's movement, with sensors in the inner ear.

29. Why do you feel a little dizzy immediately after a roller-coaster ride?

30. A food's aroma can greatly enhance its taste. This is an example of

   a. sensory adaptation.

   b. synesthesia.

   c. kinesthesia.

   d. sensory interaction.

31. Which of the following ESP events is supported by solid, replicable scientific evidence?

   a. Telepathy

   b. Clairvoyance

   c. Precognition

   d. None of these answers

Find answers to these questions in Appendix E, in the back of the book.

IN YOUR EVERYDAY LIFE

Answering these questions will help you make these concepts more personally meaningful, and therefore more memorable.

1. What types of sensory adaptation have you experienced in the last 24 hours?

2. Can you recall a time when your expectations influenced how you perceived a person (or group of people)? What happened?

3. People often compare the human eye to a camera. Do you think this is an accurate comparison? Why or why not?

4. What would your life be like without perceptual constancy?

5. How would you respond if, after you were injured, a friend said, "The pain is just in your head"?

Use [icon] LearningCurve to create your personalized study plan, which will direct you to the resources that will help you most in [icon] LaunchPad.

SURVEY THE CHAPTER

Learning

6

In the early 1940s, University of Minnesota graduate students Marian Breland and Keller Breland witnessed the power of a new learning technology. Their mentor, B. F. Skinner, would become famous for *shaping* rat and pigeon behaviors, by delivering well-timed rewards as the animals inched closer and closer to a desired behavior. Impressed with Skinner's results, the Brelands began shaping the behavior of cats, chickens, parakeets, turkeys, pigs, ducks, and hamsters (Bailey & Gillaspy, 2005). The rest is history. The company they formed spent the next half-century training more than 15,000 animals from 140 species for movies, traveling shows, amusement parks, corporations, and the government.

While writing about animal trainers, Amy Sutherland wondered if shaping had uses closer to home (2006a,b). If baboons could be trained to skateboard and elephants to paint, might "the same techniques . . . work on that stubborn but lovable species, the American husband"? Step by step, she "began thanking Scott if he threw one dirty shirt into the hamper. If he threw in two, I'd kiss him [and] as he basked in my appreciation, the piles became smaller." After two years of "thinking of my husband as an exotic animal species," she reported, "my marriage is far smoother, my husband much easier to love."

Like husbands and other animals, much of what we do we learn from experience. Indeed, nature's most important gift may be our *adaptability*—our capacity to learn new behaviors that help us cope with our changing world. We can learn how to build grass huts or snow shelters, submarines or space stations, and thereby adapt to almost any environment.

Learning breeds hope. What is learnable we may be able to teach—a fact that encourages animal trainers, and also parents, educators, and coaches. What has been learned we may be able to change by new learning—an assumption underlying stress management and counseling programs. No matter how unhappy, unsuccessful, or unloving we are, we can learn and change.

No topic is closer to the heart of psychology than *learning,* the process of acquiring, through experience, new and relatively enduring information or behaviors. (Learning acquires information, and memory—our next chapter topic—retains it.) In earlier chapters we considered the learning of sleep patterns, of gender roles, of visual perceptions. In later chapters we will see how learning shapes our thoughts, our emotions, our personality, and our attitudes.

How Do We Learn?

LOQ Learning**O**bjective**Q**uestion

6-1 How do we define *learning,* and what are some basic forms of learning?

By **learning,** we humans are able to adapt to our environments. We learn to expect and prepare for significant events such as food or pain *(classical conditioning).* We learn to repeat acts that bring good results and to avoid acts that bring bad results *(operant conditioning).* We learn new behaviors by observing events and by watching other people, and through language, we learn things we have neither experienced nor observed *(cognitive learning).* But *how* do we learn?

One way we learn is by *association.* Our minds naturally connect events that occur in sequence. Suppose you see and smell freshly baked bread, eat some, and find it satisfying. The next time you see and smell fresh bread, you will expect that eating it will again be satisfying. So, too, with sounds. If you associate a sound with a frightening consequence, hearing the sound alone may trigger your fear. As one 4-year-old said after watching a TV character get mugged, "If I had heard that music, I wouldn't have gone around the corner!" (Wells, 1981).

Learned associations also feed our habitual behaviors (Wood et al., 2014b). Habits can form when we repeat behaviors in a given context—sleeping in the same comfy position in bed, biting our nails in class, eating buttery popcorn in the movie theater. As behavior becomes linked with the context, our next experience of that context will evoke our habitual response. Especially when our willpower is depleted, as when we're mentally fatigued, we tend to fall back on our habits—good or bad (Graybiel & Smith, 2014; Neal et al., 2013). To increase our self-control, to connect our resolutions with positive outcomes, the key is forming "beneficial habits" (Galla & Duckworth, 2015). How long does it take to form a beneficial habit? To find out, researchers asked 96 university students to choose some healthy behavior,

such as running before dinner or eating fruit with lunch, and to perform it daily for 84 days. The students also recorded whether the behavior felt automatic (something they did without thinking and would find hard not to do). When did the behaviors turn into habits? After about 66 days, on average (Lally et al., 2010). Is there something you'd like to make a routine or essential part of your life? Just do it every day for two months, or a bit longer for exercise, and you likely will find yourself with a new habit. This happened for both of us—with a midday workout [DM] or late afternoon run [ND] having long ago become an automatic daily routine.

Other animals also learn by association. To protect itself, the sea slug *Aplysia* withdraws its gill when squirted with water. If the squirts continue, as happens naturally in choppy water, the withdrawal response weakens. But if the sea slug repeatedly receives an electric shock just after being squirted, its protective response to the squirt instead grows stronger. The animal has learned that the squirt signals an upcoming shock.

Complex animals can learn to link outcomes with their own responses. An aquarium seal will repeat behaviors, such as slapping and barking, that prompt people to toss it a herring.

By linking two events that occur close together, the sea slug and the seal are exhibiting **associative learning.** The sea slug associated the squirt with an upcoming shock. The seal associated its slapping and barking with a herring treat. Each animal has learned something important to its survival: anticipating the immediate future.

This process of learning associations is *conditioning.* It takes two main forms:

- In *classical conditioning,* we learn to associate two stimuli and thus to anticipate events. (A **stimulus** is any event or situation that evokes a response.) We learn that a flash of lightning will be followed by a crack of thunder, so when lightning flashes nearby, we start to brace ourselves (**FIGURE 6.1**). We associate stimuli that we do not control, and we automatically respond. This is called **respondent behavior.**

- In *operant conditioning,* we learn to associate an action (our behavior) and its consequence. Thus, we (and other animals) learn to repeat acts followed by good results (**FIGURE 6.2**) and to avoid acts followed by bad results. These associations produce **operant behaviors.**

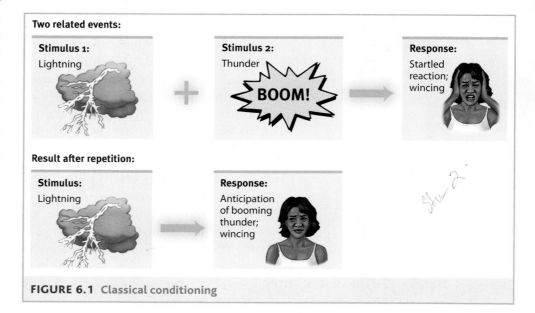

Two related events:

Stimulus 1: Lightning **+** **Stimulus 2:** Thunder BOOM! → **Response:** Startled reaction; wincing

Result after repetition:

Stimulus: Lightning → **Response:** Anticipation of booming thunder; wincing

FIGURE 6.1 Classical conditioning

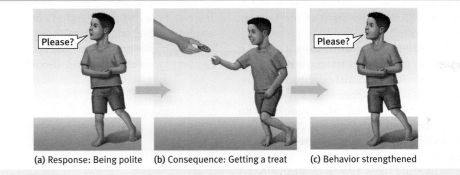

(a) Response: Being polite   (b) Consequence: Getting a treat   (c) Behavior strengthened

FIGURE 6.2 Operant conditioning

Conditioning is not the only form of learning. Through **cognitive learning** we acquire mental information that guides our behavior. *Observational learning,* one form of cognitive learning, lets us learn from others' experiences. Chimpanzees, for example, sometimes learn behaviors merely by watching others. If one animal sees another solve a puzzle and gain a food reward, the observer may perform the trick more quickly. So, too, in humans: We look and we learn.

Retrieve + Remember

- Why are habits, such as having something sweet with that cup of coffee, so hard to break?

ANSWER: Habits form when we repeat behaviors in a given context and, as a result, learn associations—often without our awareness. For example, we may have eaten a sweet pastry with a cup of coffee often enough to associate the flavor of the coffee with the treat, so that the cup of coffee alone just doesn't seem right anymore!

Classical Conditioning

For many people, the name Ivan Pavlov (1849–1936) rings a bell. His early twentieth-century experiments—now psychology's most famous research—are classics. The process he explored we justly call **classical conditioning.**

Pavlov's Experiments

LOQ 6-2 What is *classical conditioning,* and how does it demonstrate associative learning?

For his studies of digestion, Pavlov (who held a medical degree) earned Russia's first Nobel Prize. But his novel experiments on learning, which consumed the last three decades of his life, earned Pavlov his place in history.

Pavlov's new direction came when his creative mind focused on what seemed to others an unimportant detail. Without fail, putting food in a dog's mouth caused the animal to drool—to *salivate.* Moreover, the dog began salivating not only to the taste of the food but also to the mere sight of the food or the

IVAN PAVLOV "Experimental investigation . . . should lay a solid foundation for a future true science of psychology" (1927).

food dish. The dog even drooled at the sight of the person delivering the food or the sound of that person's approaching footsteps. At first, Pavlov considered these "psychic secretions" an annoyance. Then he realized they pointed to a simple but important form of learning.

Pavlov and his assistants tried to imagine what the dog was thinking and feeling as it drooled in anticipation of the food. This only led them into useless debates. So, to make their studies more objective, they experimented. To rule out other possible influences, they isolated the dog in a small room, placed it in a harness, and attached a device to measure its saliva. Then, from the next room, they presented food. First, they slid in a food bowl. Later, they blew meat powder into the dog's mouth at a precise moment. Finally, they paired various **neutral stimuli (NS)**—events the dog could see or hear but didn't associate with food—with food in the dog's mouth. If a sight or sound regularly signaled the arrival of food, would the dog learn the link? If so, would it begin salivating in anticipation of the food?

learning the process of acquiring, through experience, new and relatively enduring information or behaviors.

associative learning learning that certain events occur together. The events may be two stimuli (as in classical conditioning) or a response and its consequences (as in operant conditioning).

stimulus any event or situation that evokes a response.

respondent behavior behavior that occurs as an automatic response to some stimulus.

operant behavior behavior that operates on the environment, producing consequences.

cognitive learning the acquisition of mental information, whether by observing events, by watching others, or through language.

classical conditioning a type of learning in which we learn to link two or more stimuli and anticipate events.

neutral stimulus (NS) in classical conditioning, a stimulus that evokes no response before conditioning.

PEANUTS

Peanuts reprinted with permission of United Features Syndicate

The answers proved to be *Yes* and *Yes*. Just before placing food in the dog's mouth to produce salivation, Pavlov sounded a tone. After several pairings of tone and food, the dog got the message. Anticipating the meat powder, it began salivating to the tone alone. In later experiments, a buzzer, a light, a touch on the leg, even the sight of a circle set off the drooling.

A dog doesn't *learn* to salivate in response to food in its mouth. Rather, food in the mouth automatically, *unconditionally*, triggers this response. Thus, Pavlov called the drooling an **unconditioned response (UR)**. And he called the food an **unconditioned stimulus (US)**.

Salivating in response to a tone, however, is learned. Because it is *conditional* upon the dog's linking the tone with the food (**FIGURE 6.3**), we call this response the **conditioned response (CR)**. The stimulus that used to be neutral (in this case, a previously meaningless tone that now triggers drooling) is the **conditioned stimulus (CS)**. Remembering the difference between these two kinds of stimuli and responses is easy: Conditioned = learned; *unconditioned* = *unlearned*.

If Pavlov's demonstration of associative learning was so simple, what did he do for the next three decades? What discoveries did his research factory publish in his 532 papers on salivary conditioning (Windholz, 1997)? He and his associates explored five major conditioning processes: *acquisition, extinction, spontaneous recovery, generalization,* and *discrimination.*

Remember:
NS = Neutral Stimulus
US = Unconditioned Stimulus
UR = Unconditioned Response
CS = Conditioned Stimulus
CR = Conditioned Response

Retrieve + Remember

- An experimenter sounds a tone just before delivering an air puff that causes your eye to blink. After several repetitions, you blink to the tone alone. What is the NS? The US? The UR? The CS? The CR?

ANSWERS: NS = tone before conditioning; US = air puff; UR = blink to air puff; CS = tone after conditioning; CR = blink to tone

BEFORE CONDITIONING

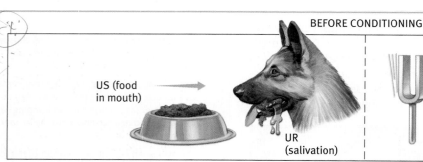

US (food in mouth) → UR (salivation)

An unconditioned stimulus (US) produces an unconditioned response (UR).

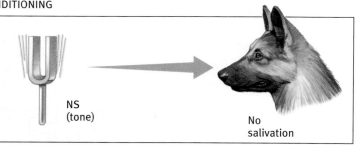

NS (tone) → No salivation

A neutral stimulus (NS) produces no salivation response.

DURING CONDITIONING

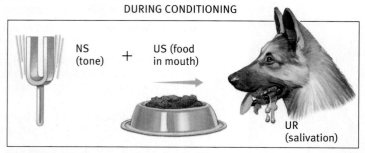

NS (tone) + US (food in mouth) → UR (salivation)

The US is repeatedly presented just after the NS. The US continues to produce a UR.

AFTER CONDITIONING

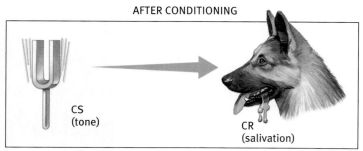

CS (tone) → CR (salivation)

The previously neutral stimulus alone now produces a conditioned response (CR), thereby becoming a conditioned stimulus (CS).

FIGURE 6.3 Pavlov's classic experiment Pavlov presented a neutral stimulus (a tone) just before an unconditioned stimulus (food in mouth). The neutral stimulus then became a conditioned stimulus, producing a conditioned response.

Acquisition

LOQ 6-3 What parts do acquisition, extinction, spontaneous recovery, generalization, and discrimination play in classical conditioning?

Acquisition is the first stage in classical conditioning. This is the point when Pavlov's dogs learned the link between the NS (the tone, the light, the touch) and the US (the food). To understand this stage, Pavlov and his associates wondered: How much time should pass between presenting the neutral stimulus and the food? In most cases, not much—half a second usually works well.

What do you suppose would happen if the food (US) appeared before the tone (NS) rather than after? Would conditioning occur? Not likely. With only a few exceptions, conditioning doesn't happen when the NS follows the US. *Remember, classical conditioning is biologically adaptive because it helps humans and other animals prepare for good or bad events.* To Pavlov's dogs, the originally neutral tone became a CS after signaling an important biological event—the arrival of food (US). To deer in the forest, the snapping of a twig (CS) may signal a predator's approach (US).

More recent research on male Japanese quail shows how a CS can signal another important biological event (Domjan, 1992, 1994, 2005). Just before presenting a sexually approachable female quail, the researchers turned on a red light. Over time, as the red light continued to announce the female's arrival, the light caused the male quail to become excited. They developed a preference for their cage's red-light district. When a female appeared, they mated with her more quickly and released more semen and sperm (Matthews et al., 2007). This capacity for classical conditioning gives the quail a reproductive edge.

Eric Isselée/Shutterstock

Can objects, sights, and smells associated with sexual pleasure become conditioned stimuli for human sexual arousal, too? Indeed they can (Byrne, 1982; Hoffman, 2012). Onion breath does not usually produce sexual arousal (**FIGURE 6.4**). But when repeatedly paired with a passionate kiss, it can become a CS and do just that. The larger lesson: *Conditioning helps an animal survive and reproduce—by responding to cues that help it gain food,* avoid dangers, locate mates, and produce offspring (Hollis, 1997). Learning makes for yearning.

Extinction and Spontaneous Recovery

What would happen, Pavlov wondered, if after conditioning, the CS occurred repeatedly without the US? If the tone sounded again and again, but no food appeared, would the tone still trigger drooling? The answer was mixed.

unconditioned response (UR) in classical conditioning, an unlearned, naturally occurring response (such as salivation) to an unconditioned stimulus (US) (such as food in the mouth).

unconditioned stimulus (US) in classical conditioning, a stimulus that unconditionally—naturally and automatically—triggers a response (UR).

conditioned response (CR) in classical conditioning, a learned response to a previously neutral (but now conditioned) stimulus (CS).

conditioned stimulus (CS) in classical conditioning, an originally irrelevant stimulus that, after association with an unconditioned stimulus (US), comes to trigger a conditioned response (CR).

acquisition in classical conditioning, the initial stage, when we link a neutral stimulus and an unconditioned stimulus so that the neutral stimulus begins triggering the conditioned response. (In operant conditioning, the strengthening of a reinforced response.)

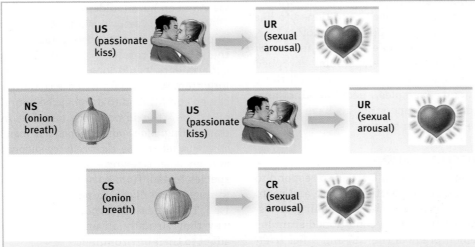

FIGURE 6.4 An unexpected CS Psychologist Michael Tirrell (1990) recalled: "My first girlfriend loved onions, so I came to associate onion breath with kissing. Before long, onion breath sent tingles up and down my spine. Oh what a feeling!"

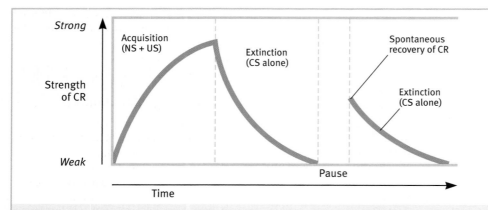

FIGURE 6.5 **Acquisition, extinction, and spontaneous recovery** The rising curve (simplified here) shows the CR rapidly growing stronger as the NS becomes a CS due to repeated pairing with the US *(acquisition)*. The CR then weakens rapidly as the CS is presented alone *(extinction)*. After a pause, the (weakened) CR reappears *(spontaneous recovery)* .

The dogs salivated less and less, a reaction known as **extinction**—a drop-off in responses when a CS (tone) no longer signals an upcoming US (food). But the dogs began drooling to the tone again if Pavlov scheduled several tone-free hours. This **spontaneous recovery**—the reappearance of a (weakened) CR after a pause—suggested to Pavlov that extinction was *suppressing* the CR rather than eliminating it (**FIGURE 6.5**).

Retrieve + Remember

- The first step of classical conditioning, when an NS becomes a CS, is called _____. When a US no longer follows the CS, and the CR becomes weakened, this is called _____.

ANSWERS: acquisition; extinction

Generalization

Pavlov and his students noticed that a dog conditioned to the sound of one tone also responded somewhat to the sound of a new and different tone. Likewise, a dog conditioned to salivate when rubbed would also drool a bit when scratched or when touched on a different body part (Windholz, 1989). This tendency to respond similarly to stimuli that resemble the CS is called **generalization**.

Generalization can be adaptive, as when toddlers who learn to fear moving cars also become afraid of moving trucks and motorcycles. And generalized fears can linger. One Argentine writer who had been tortured recalled flinching with fear years later at the sight of black shoes—his first glimpse of his torturers as they approached his cell. This generalized fear response was found in laboratory studies comparing abused and nonabused children (Pollak et al., 1998). When an angry face appeared on a computer screen, abused children's brain-wave responses were dramatically stronger and longer lasting. And when a face that we've been conditioned to like (or dislike) is morphed into another face, we also have some tendency to like (or dislike) the vaguely similar morphed face (Gawronski & Quinn, 2013). In all these human examples, people's emotional reactions to one stimulus have generalized to similar stimuli.

Discrimination

Pavlov's dogs also learned to respond to the sound of a particular tone and *not* to other tones. This learned ability to *distinguish* between a conditioned stimulus (which predicts the US) and other irrelevant stimuli is called **discrimination**. Being able to recognize differences is adaptive. Slightly different stimuli can

be followed by vastly different results. Facing a guard dog, your heart may race; facing a guide dog, it probably will not.

Retrieve + Remember

- What conditioning principle is affecting the snail's affections?

"I don't care if she's a tape dispenser. I love her."

ANSWER: generalization

Pavlov's Legacy

LOQ 6-4 Why is Pavlov's work important, and how is it being applied?

What remains today of Pavlov's ideas? A great deal. Most psychologists now agree that classical conditioning is a basic form of learning. Judged with today's knowledge of the biological and cognitive influences on conditioning, Pavlov's ideas were incomplete. But if we see further than Pavlov did, it is because we stand on his shoulders.

Why does Pavlov's work remain so important? If he had merely taught us that old dogs can learn new tricks, his experiments would long ago have been forgotten. Why should we care that dogs can be conditioned to drool at the sound of a tone? The importance lies first in this finding: *Many other responses to many other stimuli can be classically conditioned in many other creatures*—in fact, in every species tested, from earthworms to fish to dogs to monkeys to people (Schwartz, 1984). Thus, classical conditioning is one way that virtually all animals learn to adapt to their environment.

Second, *Pavlov showed us how a process such as learning can be studied objectively*. He was proud that his methods were not based on guesswork about a dog's mind. The salivary response is a behavior we can measure in cubic centimeters of saliva. Pavlov's success therefore suggested a scientific model for how the young field of psychology might proceed. That model was to isolate the basic building blocks of complex behaviors and study them with objective laboratory procedures.

Retrieve + Remember

- If the aroma of cake baking makes your mouth water, what is the US? The CS? The CR?

ANSWERS: The cake is the US. The associated aroma is the CS. Salivation to the aroma is the CR.

LaunchPad To review Pavlov's classic work and to play the role of experimenter in classical conditioning research, visit LaunchPad's *PsychSim 6: Classical Conditioning.* See also a 3-minute recreation of Pavlov's lab in the *Video: Pavlov's Discovery of Classical Conditioning.*

Classical Conditioning in Everyday Life

Other chapters in this text—on motivation and emotion, stress and health, psychological disorders, and therapy—show how Pavlov's principles can influence human health and well-being. Two examples:

- Drugs given as cancer treatments can trigger nausea and vomiting. Patients may then develop classically conditioned nausea (and sometimes anxiety) to the sights, sounds, and smells associated with the clinic (Hall, 1997). Merely entering the clinic's waiting room or seeing the nurses can provoke these feelings (Burish & Carey, 1986).

- Former drug users often feel a craving when they are again in the drug-using context. They associate particular people or places with previous highs. Thus, drug counselors advise their clients to steer clear of people and settings that may trigger these cravings (Siegel, 2005).

Does Pavlov's work help us understand our own emotions? John B. Watson thought so. He believed that human emotions and behaviors, though biologically influenced, are mainly a bundle of conditioned responses (1913). Working with an 11-month-old, Watson and his graduate student Rosalie Rayner (1920; Harris, 1979) showed how specific fears might be conditioned. Like most infants, "Little Albert" feared loud noises but not white rats. Watson and Rayner presented a white rat and, as Little Albert reached to touch it, struck a hammer against a steel bar just behind the infant's head. After seven repeats of seeing the rat and hearing the frightening noise, Albert burst into tears at the mere sight of the rat. Five days later, he had generalized this startled fear reaction to the sight of a rabbit, a dog, and a sealskin coat, but not to dissimilar objects.

For years, people wondered what became of Little Albert. Detective work by Russell Powell and his colleagues (2014) found that the child of one of the campus hospital's wet nurses matched Little Albert's description. The child, William Albert Barger, went by Albert B.—precisely the name used by Watson and Rayner. This Albert died in 2007. He was an easygoing person, though, perhaps coincidentally, he had an aversion to dogs. Albert died without ever knowing of his role in psychology's history.

People also wondered what became of Watson. After losing his Johns Hopkins professorship over an affair with Rayner (whom he later married), he joined an advertising agency as the company's resident psychologist. There, he used his knowledge of associative learning in many successful advertising campaigns. One of them, for Maxwell House, helped make the "coffee break" an American custom (Hunt, 1993).

The treatment of Little Albert would be unethical by today's standards. Also, some psychologists had difficulty repeating Watson and Rayner's findings with other children. Nevertheless, Little Albert's learned fears led many psychologists to wonder whether each of us might be a walking storehouse of conditioned emotions. If so, might extinction procedures or new conditioning help us change our unwanted responses to emotion-arousing stimuli?

LaunchPad See LaunchPad's *Video: Research Ethics* for a helpful tutorial animation.

Comedian-writer Mark Malkoff extinguished his fear of flying by doing just that. With support from an airline, he faced his fear. Living on an airplane for 30 days and taking 135 flights, he spent 14 hours a day in the air. After a week and a half, Malkoff's fear had faded, and he began playing games with fellow passengers (NPR, 2009). (His favorite: He'd put one end of a toilet paper roll in the toilet, unroll the rest down the aisle, and flush—sucking down the whole roll in 3 seconds.) In Chapters 13 and 14, we will see more examples of how psychologists use behavioral techniques such as *counterconditioning* to treat emotional disorders and promote personal growth.

extinction in classical conditioning, the weakening of a conditioned response when an unconditioned stimulus does not follow a conditioned stimulus. (In operant conditioning, the weakening of a response when it is no longer reinforced.)

spontaneous recovery the reappearance, after a pause, of an extinguished conditioned response.

generalization in classical conditioning, the tendency, after conditioning, to respond similarly to stimuli that resemble the conditioned stimulus. (In operant conditioning, *generalization* occurs when our responses to similar stimuli are also reinforced.)

discrimination in classical conditioning, the learned ability to distinguish between a conditioned stimulus and other irrelevant stimuli. (In operant conditioning, the ability to distinguish responses that are reinforced from those that are not.)

Retrieve + Remember

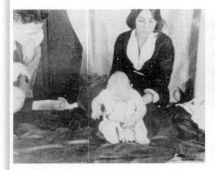

Archives of the History of American Psychology, The Center for the History of Psychology, The University of Akron

- In Watson and Rayner's experiments, "Little Albert" learned to fear a white rat after repeatedly experiencing a loud noise as the rat was presented. In these experiments, what was the US? The UR? The NS? The CS? The CR?

ANSWERS: The US was the loud noise; the UR was the fear response to the noise; the NS was the rat before it was paired with the noise; the CS was the rat after the pairing; the CR was fear of the rat.

Retrieve + Remember

- With classical conditioning, we learn associations between events we _____ (do/do not) control. With operant conditioning, we learn associations between our behavior and _____ (resulting/random) events.

ANSWERS: do not; resulting

Operant Conditioning

LOQ 6-5 What is *operant conditioning,* and how is operant behavior reinforced and shaped?

It's one thing to classically condition a dog to drool at the sound of a tone, or a child to fear a white rat. To teach an elephant to walk on its hind legs or a child to say *please,* we must turn to another type of learning—*operant conditioning.*

Classical conditioning and operant conditioning are both forms of associative learning. But their differences are straightforward:

- In *classical conditioning,* an animal (dog, child, sea slug) forms associations between two events it does not control. Classical conditioning involves *respondent behavior*—automatic responses to a stimulus (such as salivating in response to meat powder and later in response to a tone).

- In **operant conditioning,** animals associate their own actions with consequences. Actions followed by

a rewarding event increase; those followed by a punishing event decrease. Behavior that *operates* on the environment to *produce* rewarding or punishing events is called *operant behavior.*

We can therefore distinguish our classical from our operant conditioning by asking two questions. *Are we learning associations between events we do not control* (classical conditioning)? *Or are we learning associations between our behavior and resulting events* (operant conditioning)?

Skinner's Experiments

B. F. Skinner (1904–1990) was a college English major who had set his sights on becoming a writer. Then, seeking a new direction, he became a graduate student in psychology, and, eventually, modern *behaviorism's* most influential and controversial figure.

Skinner's work built on a principle that psychologist Edward L. Thorndike (1874–1949) called the **law of effect:** Rewarded behavior tends to be repeated (**FIGURE 6.6**). From this starting point, Skinner went on to develop experiments that would reveal principles of *behavior control.* By shaping pigeons' natural walking and pecking behaviors, for example, Skinner was able to teach them such unpigeon-like behaviors as walking in a figure 8, playing Ping-Pong, and keeping a missile on course by pecking at a screen target. With operant conditioning, pigeons can

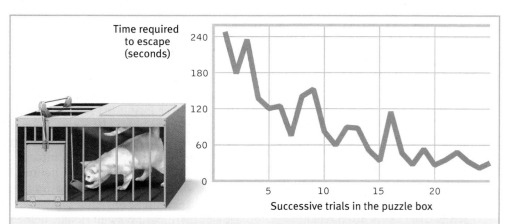

FIGURE 6.6 Cat in a puzzle box Thorndike used a fish reward to entice cats to find their way out of a puzzle box through a series of maneuvers. The cats' performance tended to improve with successive trials, illustrating Thorndike's *law of effect.* (Data from Thorndike, 1898.)

BIRD BRAINS SPOT TUMORS After being rewarded with food when correctly spotting breast tumors, pigeons became as skilled as humans at discriminating cancerous from healthy tissue.

display "remarkable ability" at identifying malignant tumors in breast cancer images (Levenson et al., 2015).

For his studies, Skinner designed an **operant chamber,** popularly known as a *Skinner box* (**FIGURE 6.7**). The box has a bar or button that an animal presses or pecks to release a food or water reward. It also has a device that records these responses. This design creates a stage on which rats and other animals act out Skinner's concept of **reinforcement:** any event that strengthens (increases the frequency of) a preceding response. What is reinforcing depends on the animal and the conditions. For people, it may be praise, attention, or a paycheck.

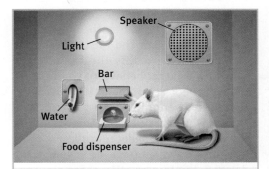

FIGURE 6.7 A Skinner box Inside the box, the rat presses a bar for a food reward. Outside, measuring devices (not shown here) record the animal's accumulated responses.

For hungry and thirsty rats, food and water work well. Skinner's experiments have done far more than teach us how to pull habits out of a rat. They have explored the precise conditions that foster efficient and enduring learning.

Shaping Behavior

Imagine that you wanted to condition a hungry rat to press a bar. Like Skinner, you could tease out this action with **shaping,** gradually guiding the rat's actions toward the desired behavior. First, you would watch how the animal naturally behaves, so that you could build on its existing behaviors. You might give the rat a bit of food each time it approaches the bar. Once the rat is approaching regularly, you would give the treat only when it moves close to the bar, then closer still. Finally, you would require it to touch the bar to get food. By rewarding *successive approximations,* you reinforce responses that are ever-closer to the final desired behavior. By giving rewards only for desired behaviors and ignoring all other responses, researchers and animal trainers gradually shape complex behaviors.

Shaping can also help us understand what nonverbal organisms perceive. Can a dog see red and green? Can a baby hear the difference between lower- and higher-pitched tones? If we can shape them to respond to one stimulus and not to another, then we know they can perceive the difference. Such experiments have even shown that some nonhuman animals can form concepts. When experimenters reinforced pigeons for pecking after seeing a human face, but not after seeing other images, the pigeons learned to recognize human faces (Herrnstein & Loveland, 1964). After being trained to discriminate among classes of events or objects—flowers, people, cars, chairs—pigeons were usually able to identify the category in which a new pictured object belonged (Bhatt et al., 1988; Wasserman, 1993).

Skinner noted that we continually reinforce and shape others' everyday behaviors, though we may not mean to do so. Isaac's whining annoys his dad, but look how his dad typically responds:

Isaac: *Could you take me to the mall?*

Dad: *(Continues reading paper.)*

Isaac: *Dad, I need to go to the mall.*

Dad: *(distracted) Uh, yeah, just a minute.*

Isaac: *DAAAD! The mall!!*

Dad: *Show me some manners! Okay, where are my keys . . .*

Isaac's whining is reinforced, because he gets something desirable—a trip to the mall. Dad's response is reinforced, because it ends something *aversive* (unpleasant)—Isaac's whining.

Or consider a teacher who sticks gold stars on a wall chart beside the names of children scoring 100 percent on spelling tests. As everyone can then see, some children always score 100 percent. The others, who take the same test and may have worked harder than the academic all-stars, get no stars. Using operant conditioning principles, what advice could you offer the teacher to help all students do their best work?[1]

---

1. You might advise the teacher to shape students by reinforcing them all for gradual improvements, as their spelling gets closer and closer to the goal.

operant conditioning a type of learning in which a behavior becomes more probable if followed by a reinforcer or is diminished if followed by a punisher.

law of effect Thorndike's principle that behaviors followed by favorable consequences become more likely, and that behaviors followed by unfavorable consequences become less likely. *looking for a desired outcome*

operant chamber in operant conditioning research, a chamber (also known as a *Skinner box*) containing a bar or key that an animal can manipulate to obtain a food or water reinforcer; attached devices record the animal's rate of bar pressing or key pecking.

reinforcement in operant conditioning, any event that *strengthens* the behavior it follows.

shaping an operant conditioning procedure in which reinforcers guide actions closer and closer toward a desired behavior.

Levenson RM, Krupinski EA, Navarro VM, Wasserman EA (2015). Pigeons (Columba livia) as Trainable Observers of Pathology and Radiology Breast Cancer Images. PLoS ONE 10(11): e0141357.

Types of Reinforcers

LOQ 6-6 How do positive and negative reinforcement differ, and what are the basic types of reinforcers?

Up to now, we've mainly been discussing **positive reinforcement,** which strengthens a response by *presenting* a typically *pleasurable* stimulus immediately afterward. But, as the whining Isaac story shows us, there are two basic kinds of reinforcement (**TABLE 6.1**). **Negative reinforcement** strengthens a response by *reducing or removing* something *undesirable or unpleasant.* Isaac's whining was *positively* reinforced, because Isaac got something desirable—a trip to the mall. His dad's response to the whining (doing what Isaac wanted) was *negatively* reinforced, because it got rid of something undesirable—Isaac's annoying whining. Similarly, taking aspirin may relieve your headache, and hitting *snooze* will silence your irritating alarm. These welcome results provide negative reinforcement and increase the odds that you will repeat these behaviors. For those with drug addiction, the negative reinforcement of ending withdrawal pangs can be a compelling reason to resume using (Baker et al., 2004).

Note that *negative reinforcement is not punishment.* (Some friendly advice: Repeat the italicized words in your mind.) Rather, negative reinforcement—psychology's most misunderstood concept—*removes* a punishing event. Think of negative reinforcement as something that provides relief—from that child's whining, a bad headache, or an annoying alarm. *The point to remember:* Whether it works by getting rid of something we *don't* enjoy or by giving us something we *do* enjoy, *reinforcement is any consequence that strengthens behavior.*

Retrieve + Remember

• How is operant conditioning at work in this cartoon?

THIS IS GREAT!

I'LL HAVE TO WAKE UP CRYING IN THE MIDDLE OF THE NIGHT MORE OFTEN

ANSWER: The baby negatively reinforces her parents' behavior when she stops crying once they grant her wish. Her parents positively reinforce her cries by letting her sleep with them.

Will Burgess/Reuters/Landov

REINFORCERS VARY WITH CIRCUMSTANCES What is reinforcing (a heat lamp) to one animal (a cold meerkat) may not be to another (a penguin). What is reinforcing in one situation (a cold snap at the Taronga Zoo in Sydney) may not be in another (a sweltering summer day).

PRIMARY AND CONDITIONED REINFORCERS Getting food when hungry or having a painful headache go away is innately (naturally) satisfying. These **primary reinforcers** are unlearned. **Conditioned reinforcers,** also called *secondary reinforcers,* get their power through learned associations with primary reinforcers. If a rat in a Skinner box learns that a light reliably signals a food delivery, the rat will work to turn on the light. The light has become a secondary reinforcer linked with food. Our lives are filled with conditioned reinforcers—money, good grades, a pleasant tone of voice—each of which has been linked with a more basic reward—food, shelter, safety, social support.

IMMEDIATE AND DELAYED REINFORCERS In shaping experiments, rats are conditioned with immediate rewards. You want the rat to press the bar. So, when it sniffs the bar (a step toward the target behavior), you immediately give it a food pellet. If a distraction delays your giving the rat its prize, the rat won't learn to link the bar sniffing with the food pellet reward.

Unlike rats, humans *do* respond to delayed reinforcers. We associate the paycheck at the end of the week, the good grade at the end of the semester, the trophy at the end of the season with our earlier actions. Indeed, learning to

TABLE 6.1	Ways to Increase Behavior	
Operant Conditioning Term	**Description**	**Examples**
Positive reinforcement	Add a desirable stimulus	Pet a dog that comes when you call it; pay the person who paints your house.
Negative reinforcement	Remove an aversive stimulus	Take painkillers to end pain; fasten seat belt to end loud beeping.

"Oh, not bad. The light comes on, I press the bar, they write me a check. How about you?"

control our impulses in order to achieve more valued rewards is a big step toward maturity (Logue, 1998a,b). Chapter 3 described a famous finding in which some children did curb their impulses and delay gratification, choosing two marshmallows later over one now. Those same children achieved greater educational and career success later in life (Mischel, 2014).

Sometimes, however, small but immediate pleasures (the enjoyment of watching late-night TV, for example) are more attractive than big but delayed rewards (feeling rested for a big exam tomorrow). For many teens, the immediate gratification of impulsive, unprotected sex wins over the delayed gratification of safe sex or saved sex (Loewenstein & Furstenberg, 1991). And for too many of us, the immediate rewards of today's gas-guzzling vehicles, air travel, and air conditioning win over the bigger future consequences of climate change, rising seas, and extreme weather.

Reinforcement Schedules

LOQ 6-7 How do continuous and partial reinforcement schedules affect behavior?

In most of our examples, the desired response has been reinforced every time it occurs. But **reinforcement schedules** vary. With **continuous reinforcement,** learning occurs rapidly, which makes it the best choice for mastering a behavior. But there's a catch: Extinction also occurs rapidly. When reinforcement stops—when we stop delivering

food after the rat presses the bar—the behavior soon stops (extinguishes). If a normally dependable candy machine fails to deliver a chocolate bar twice in a row, we stop putting money into it (although a week later we may exhibit spontaneous recovery by trying again).

Real life rarely provides continuous reinforcement. Salespeople don't make a sale with every pitch. But they persist because their efforts are occasionally rewarded. And that's the good news about **partial (intermittent) reinforcement** schedules, in which responses are sometimes reinforced, sometimes not. Learning is slower than with continuous reinforcement, but *resistance to extinction* is greater. Imagine a pigeon that has learned to peck a key to obtain food. If you gradually phase out the food delivery until it occurs only rarely, in no predictable pattern, the pigeon may peck 150,000 times without a reward (Skinner, 1953). Slot machines reward gamblers in much the same way—occasionally and unpredictably. And like pigeons, slot players keep trying, again and again. With intermittent reinforcement, hope springs eternal.

Lesson for parents: Partial reinforcement also works with children. What happens when we occasionally give in to children's tantrums for the sake of peace and quiet? We have intermittently reinforced the tantrums. This is the best way to make a behavior persist.

Skinner (1961) and his collaborators compared four schedules of partial reinforcement. Some are rigidly fixed, some unpredictably variable (**TABLE 6.2**).

Fixed-ratio schedules reinforce behavior after a set number of responses. Coffee shops may reward us with a free drink after every 10 purchased. In the laboratory, rats may be reinforced on a fixed ratio of, say, one food pellet for every 30 responses. Once conditioned, the rats will pause only briefly to munch

on the pellet before returning to a high rate of responding.

Variable-ratio schedules provide reinforcers after an unpredictable number of responses. This unpredictable reinforcement is what slot-machine players and fly fishers experience. And it's what makes gambling and fly fishing so hard to extinguish even when they don't produce the desired results. Because reinforcers increase as the number of responses increases, variable-ratio schedules produce high rates of responding.

positive reinforcement increases behaviors by presenting positive stimuli, such as food. A positive reinforcer is anything that, when *presented* after a response, strengthens the response.

negative reinforcement increases behaviors by stopping or reducing negative stimuli, such as shock. A negative reinforcer is anything that, when *removed* after a response, strengthens the response. (*Note:* Negative reinforcement is *not* punishment.)

primary reinforcer an event that is innately reinforcing, often by satisfying a biological need.

conditioned reinforcer (also known as *secondary reinforcer*) an event that gains its reinforcing power through its link with a primary reinforcer.

reinforcement schedule a pattern that defines how often a desired response will be reinforced.

continuous reinforcement reinforcing a desired response every time it occurs.

partial (intermittent) reinforcement reinforcing a response only part of the time; results in slower acquisition but much greater resistance to extinction than does continuous reinforcement.

fixed-ratio schedule in operant conditioning, a reinforcement schedule that reinforces a response only after a specified number of responses.

variable-ratio schedule in operant conditioning, a reinforcement schedule that reinforces a response after an unpredictable number of responses.

TABLE 6.2   Schedules of Partial Reinforcement

	Fixed	Variable
Ratio	*Every so many:* reinforcement after every *n*th behavior, such as buy 10 coffees, get 1 free, or pay workers per product unit produced	*After an unpredictable number:* reinforcement after a random number of behaviors, as when playing slot machines or fly fishing
Interval	*Every so often:* reinforcement for behavior after a fixed time, such as Tuesday discount prices	*Unpredictably often:* reinforcement for behavior after a random amount of time, as when checking our phone for a message

Fixed-interval schedules reinforce the first response after a fixed time period. Pigeons on a fixed-interval schedule peck more rapidly as the time for reinforcement draws near. People waiting for an important letter check more often as delivery time approaches. A hungry cook peeks into the oven frequently to see if cookies are brown. This produces a choppy stop-start pattern rather than a steady rate of response.

Variable-interval schedules reinforce the first response after unpredictable time intervals. At unpredictable times, a food pellet rewarded Skinner's pigeons for persistence in pecking a key. Like the longed-for message that finally rewards persistence in rechecking our phone, variable-interval schedules tend to produce slow, steady responding. This makes sense, because there is no knowing when the waiting will be over.

In general, response rates are higher when reinforcement is linked to the number of responses (a ratio schedule) rather than to time (an interval schedule). But responding is more consistent when reinforcement is unpredictable (a variable schedule) than when it is predictable (a fixed schedule).

Animal behaviors differ, yet Skinner (1956) contended that the reinforcement principles of operant conditioning are universal. It matters little, he said, what response, what reinforcer, or what species you use. The effect of a given reinforcement schedule is pretty much the same: "Pigeon, rat, monkey, which is which? It doesn't matter. . . . Behavior shows astonishingly similar properties."

Retrieve + Remember

- People who send spam are reinforced by which schedule? Home bakers checking the oven to see if the cookies are done are on which schedule? Coffee shops that offer a free drink after every 10 drinks purchased are using which reinforcement schedule?

ANSWERS: Spammers are reinforced on a variable-ratio schedule (after a varying number of messages). Cookie checkers are reinforced on a fixed-interval schedule. Coffee drink programs use a fixed-ratio schedule.

Punishment

LOQ 6-8 How does punishment differ from negative reinforcement, and how does punishment affect behavior?

Reinforcement increases a behavior; **punishment** does the opposite. A *punisher* is any consequence that *decreases* the frequency of the behavior it follows (**TABLE 6.3**). Swift and sure punishers can powerfully restrain unwanted behaviors. The rat that is shocked after touching a forbidden object and the child who is burned by touching a hot stove will learn not to repeat those behaviors.

Criminal behavior, much of it impulsive, is also influenced more by swift and sure punishers than by the threat of severe sentences (Darley & Alter, 2013). Thus, when Arizona introduced an exceptionally harsh sentence for first-time drunk drivers, the drunk-driving rate changed very little. But when Kansas City police patrols started patrolling a high crime area to increase the swiftness and sureness of punishment, that city's crime rate dropped dramatically.

What do punishment studies tell us about parenting practices? Should we physically punish children to change their behavior? Many psychologists and supporters of nonviolent parenting say No, pointing out four major drawbacks of physical punishment (Gershoff, 2002; Marshall, 2002).

1. *Punished behavior is suppressed, not forgotten. This temporary state may (negatively) reinforce parents' punishing behavior.* The child swears, the parent swats, the parent hears no more swearing and feels the punishment successfully stopped the behavior. No wonder spanking is a hit with so many parents—with 70 percent of American adults agreeing that sometimes children need a "good, hard spanking" (Child Trends, 2013).

2. *Punishment teaches discrimination among situations.* In operant conditioning, discrimination occurs when we learn that some responses, but not others, will be reinforced. Did the punishment effectively end the child's swearing? Or did the child simply learn that while it's not okay to swear around the house, it's okay elsewhere?

TABLE 6.3   Ways to Decrease Behavior

Type of Punisher	Description	Examples
Positive punishment	Administer an aversive stimulus	Spray water on a barking dog; give a traffic ticket for speeding.
Negative punishment	Withdraw a rewarding stimulus	Take away a misbehaving teen's driving privileges; revoke a library card for nonpayment of fines.

3. *Punishment can teach fear.* In operant conditioning, *generalization* occurs when our responses to similar stimuli are also reinforced. A punished child may associate fear not only with the undesirable behavior but also with the person who delivered the punishment or the place it occurred. Thus, children may learn to fear a punishing teacher and try to avoid school, or may become more anxious (Gershoff et al., 2010). For such reasons, most European countries and most U.S. states now ban hitting children in schools and child-care institutions (EndCorporalPunishment.org). As of 2015, 47 countries outlaw hitting by parents, giving children the same legal protection given to adults.

4. *Physical punishment may increase aggression by modeling violence as a way to cope with problems.* Studies find that spanked children are at increased risk for aggression (MacKenzie et al., 2013). We know, for example, that many aggressive delinquents and abusive parents come from abusive families (Straus et al., 1997).

Some researchers question this logic. Physically punished children may be more aggressive, they say, for the same reason that people who have undergone psychotherapy are more likely to suffer depression—because they had preexisting problems that triggered the treatments (Ferguson, 2013; Larzelere, 2000; Larzelere et al., 2004). Which is the chicken and which is the egg? Correlations don't hand us an answer.

LaunchPad See LaunchPad's *Video: Correlational Studies* for a helpful tutorial animation.

The debate continues. Some researchers note that frequent spankings predict future aggression—even when studies control for preexisting bad behavior (Taylor et al., 2010a). Other researchers believe that lighter spank-

CHILDREN SEE, CHILDREN DO? Children who often experience physical punishment tend to display more aggression.

David Strickler/The Image Works

ings pose less of a problem (Baumrind et al., 2002; Larzelere & Kuhn, 2005). That is especially so if physical punishment is used only as a backup for milder disciplinary tactics, and if it is combined with a generous dose of reasoning and reinforcing.

Parents of delinquent youths may not know how to achieve desirable behaviors without screaming, hitting, or threatening their children with punishment (Patterson et al., 1982). Training programs can help them translate dire threats ("Apologize right now or I'm taking that cell phone away!") into positive incentives ("You're welcome to have your phone back when you apologize"). Stop and think about it. Aren't many threats of punishment just as forceful, and perhaps more effective, when rephrased positively? Thus, "If you don't get your homework done, I'm not giving you money for a movie!" could be phrased more positively as . . . .

In classrooms, too, teachers can give feedback by saying "No, but try this . . ." and "Yes, that's it!" Such responses reduce unwanted behavior while reinforcing more desirable alternatives. Remember: *Punishment tells you what not to do; reinforcement tells you what to do.*

What punishment often teaches, said Skinner, is how to avoid it. The bottom line: *Most psychologists now favor an emphasis on reinforcement.* Notice people doing something right and affirm them for it.

fixed-interval schedule in operant conditioning, a reinforcement schedule that reinforces a response only after a specified time has elapsed.

variable-interval schedule in operant conditioning, a reinforcement schedule that reinforces a response at unpredictable time intervals.

punishment an event that decreases the behavior it follows.

Retrieve + Remember

- Fill in the blanks below with one of the following terms: negative reinforcement (NR), positive punishment (PP), and negative punishment (NP). The first answer, positive reinforcement (PR), is provided for you.

Type of Stimulus	Give It	Take It Away
Desired (for example, a teen's use of the car):	1. PR	2.
Undesired/aversive (for example, an insult):	3.	4.

ANSWERS: 1. PR (positive reinforcement); 2. NP (negative punishment); 3. PP (positive punishment); 4. NR (negative reinforcement)

Skinner's Legacy

LOQ 6-9 Why were Skinner's ideas controversial, and how might his operant conditioning principles be applied at school, at work, in parenting, and for self-improvement?

B. F. Skinner stirred a hornet's nest with his outspoken beliefs. He repeatedly insisted that external influences (not internal thoughts and feelings) shape behavior. And he urged people to use operant conditioning principles to influence others' behavior at school, work, and home. Knowing that behavior is shaped by its results, he argued that we should use rewards to evoke more desirable behavior.

Skinner's critics objected, saying that by neglecting people's personal freedom and trying to control their actions, he treated them as less than human. Skinner's reply: External consequences already control people's behavior. So why not steer those consequences toward human betterment? Wouldn't reinforcers be more humane than the punishments used in homes, schools, and prisons? And if it is humbling to think that our history has shaped us,

---

⚙ LaunchPad | To review and experience simulations of operant conditioning, visit LaunchPad's *PsychSim 6: Operant Conditioning* and also *PsychSim 6: Shaping.*

B. F. SKINNER "I am sometimes asked, 'Do you think of yourself as you think of the organisms you study?' The answer is yes. So far as I know, my behavior at any given moment has been nothing more than the product of my genetic endowment, my personal history, and the current setting" (1983).

---

doesn't this very idea also give us hope that we can shape our future?

Applications of Operant Conditioning

In later chapters we will see how psychologists apply operant conditioning principles to help people reduce high blood pressure or gain social skills. Reinforcement techniques are also at work in schools, workplaces, and homes, and these principles can support our self-improvement as well (Flora, 2004).

AT SCHOOL More than 50 years ago, Skinner and others worked toward a day when "machines and textbooks" would shape learning in small steps, by immediately reinforcing correct responses. Such machines and texts, they said, would revolutionize education and free teachers to focus on each student's special needs. "Good instruction demands two things," said Skinner (1989). "Students must be told immediately whether what they do is right or wrong and, when right, they must be directed to the step to be taken next."

Skinner might be pleased to know that many of his ideals for education are now possible. Teachers used to find it difficult to pace material to each student's rate of learning, and to provide prompt feedback. Online adaptive quizzing, such as the LearningCurve system available with this text, does both. Students move through quizzes at their own pace, according to their own level of understanding. And they get immediate feedback on their efforts, including personalized study plans.

AT WORK Skinner's ideas also show up in the workplace. Knowing that reinforcers influence productivity, many organizations have invited employees to share the risks and rewards of company ownership. Others have focused on reinforcing a job well done. Rewards are most likely to increase productivity if the desired performance is both well defined and achievable. How might managers successfully motivate their employees? *Reward specific, achievable behaviors, not vaguely defined "merit."*

Operant conditioning also reminds us that reinforcement should be *immediate*. IBM legend Thomas Watson understood. When he observed an achievement, he wrote the employee a check on the spot (Peters & Waterman, 1982). But rewards don't have to be material, or lavish. An effective manager may simply walk the floor and sincerely praise people for good work, or write notes of appreciation for a completed project. As Skinner said, "How much richer would the whole world be if the reinforcers in daily life were more effectively contingent on productive work?"

IN PARENTING As we have seen, parents can learn from operant conditioning practices. Parent-training researchers remind us that by saying "Get ready for bed" and then caving in to protests or defiance, parents reinforce such whining and arguing. Exasperated, they may then yell or make threatening gestures. When the child, now frightened, obeys, that in turn reinforces the parents' angry behavior. Over time, a destructive parent-child relationship develops.

To disrupt this cycle, parents should remember the basic rule of shaping: *Notice people doing something right and affirm them for it.* Give children attention and other reinforcers when they are behaving *well* (Wierson & Forehand, 1994). Target a specific behavior, reward it, and watch it increase. When children misbehave or are defiant, do not yell at or hit them. Simply explain what they did wrong and give them a time-out.

TO CHANGE YOUR OWN BEHAVIOR Want to stop smoking? Eat less? Study or exercise more? To reinforce your own desired behaviors and extinguish the undesired ones, psychologists suggest applying operant conditioning in five steps.

1. *State a realistic goal in measurable terms and announce it.* You might, for example, aim to boost your study time by an hour a day. Share that goal with friends to increase your commitment and chances of success.

2. *Decide how, when, and where you will work toward your goal.* Take time to plan. Those who list specific steps

"I wrote another five hundred words. Can I have another cookie?"

showing how they will reach their goals more often achieve them (Gollwitzer & Oettingen, 2012).

3. *Monitor how often you engage in your desired behavior.* You might log your current study time, noting under what conditions you do and don't study. (When I [DM] began writing textbooks, I logged how I spent my time each day and was amazed to discover how much time I was wasting. I [ND] experienced a similar rude awakening when I started tracking my daily writing hours.)

4. *Reinforce the desired behavior.* To increase your study time, give yourself a reward (a snack or some activity you enjoy) only after you finish your extra hour of study. Agree with your friends that you will join them for weekend activities only if you have met your realistic weekly studying goal.

5. *Reduce the rewards gradually.* As your new behaviors become habits, give yourself a mental pat on the back instead of a cookie.

Retrieve + Remember

- Ethan constantly misbehaves at preschool even though his teacher scolds him repeatedly. Why does Ethan's misbehavior continue, and what can his teacher do to stop it?

ANSWER: If Ethan is seeking attention, the teacher's scolding may be reinforcing rather than punishing. To change Ethan's behavior, his teacher could offer reinforcement (such as praise) each time he behaves well. The teacher might encourage Ethan toward increasingly appropriate behavior through shaping, or by rephrasing rules as rewards instead of punishments ("You can have a snack if you play nicely with the other children," rather than "You will not get a snack if you misbehave!" [punishment]).

LaunchPad Conditioning principles may also be applied in clinical settings. Explore some of these applications in LaunchPad's *IMMERSIVE LEARNING: How Would You Know If People Can Learn to Reduce Anxiety?*

Contrasting Classical and Operant Conditioning

LOQ 6-10 How does classical conditioning differ from operant conditioning?

Both classical and operant conditioning are forms of *associative learning* (**TABLE 6.4**). In both, we *acquire* behaviors that may later become *extinct* and then *spontaneously reappear*. We often *generalize* our responses but learn to *discriminate* among different stimuli.

Classical and operant conditioning also differ: Through classical conditioning, we associate different events that we don't control, and we respond automatically (*respondent behaviors*). Through operant conditioning, we link our behaviors—which act on our environment to produce rewarding or punishing events (*operant behaviors*)—with their consequences.

As we shall see next, our *biology* and our *thought processes* influence both classical and operant conditioning.

Retrieve + Remember

- Salivating in response to a tone paired with food is a(n) _____ behavior; pressing a bar to obtain food is a(n) _____ behavior.

ANSWERS: respondent; operant

Biology, Cognition, and Learning

From drooling dogs, running rats, and pecking pigeons, we have learned much about the basic processes of learning. But conditioning principles don't tell us the whole story. Once again we see one of psychology's big ideas at work. Our learning is the product of the interaction of biological, psychological, and social-cultural influences.

Biological Limits on Conditioning

LOQ 6-11 What limits does biology place on conditioning?

Evolutionary theorist Charles Darwin proposed that *natural selection* favors traits that aid survival. In the middle of the twentieth century, researchers

---

TABLE 6.4	Comparison of Classical and Operant Conditioning	
	Classical Conditioning	**Operant Conditioning**
Basic idea	Learning associations between events we don't control	Learning associations between our own behavior and its consequences
Response	Involuntary, automatic	Voluntary, operates on environment
Acquisition	Associating events; NS is paired with US and becomes CS	Associating response with a consequence (reinforcer or punisher)
Extinction	CR decreases when CS is repeatedly presented alone	Responding decreases when reinforcement stops
Spontaneous recovery	The reappearance, after a rest period, of an extinguished CR	The reappearance, after a rest period, of an extinguished response
Generalization	Responding to stimuli similar to the CS	Responding to similar stimuli to achieve or prevent a consequence
Discrimination	Learning to distinguish between a CS and other stimuli that do not signal a US	Learning that some responses, but not others, will be reinforced

further showed that there are **biological constraints** (limits) on learning. Each species comes predisposed (biologically prepared) to learn those things crucial to its survival.

Limits on Classical Conditioning

A discovery by John Garcia and Robert Koelling in the 1960s helped end a popular and widely held belief in psychology: that environments rule our behavior. Part of this idea was that almost any stimulus (whether a taste, sight, or sound) could serve equally well as a conditioned stimulus. Garcia and Koelling's work put that idea to the test and proved it wrong. They noticed that rats would avoid a taste—but not sights or sounds—associated with becoming sick, even hours later (1966). This response, which psychologists call *taste aversion*, makes adaptive sense. For rats, the easiest way to identify tainted food is to taste it. Taste aversion makes it tough to wipe out an invasion of "bait-shy" rats by poisoning. After being sickened by the bait, they are biologically prepared to avoid that taste ever after.

JOHN GARCIA As the laboring son of California farmworkers, Garcia attended school only in the off-season during his early childhood years. After entering junior college in his late twenties, and earning his Ph.D. in his late forties, he received the American Psychological Association's Distinguished Scientific Contribution Award "for his highly original, pioneering research in conditioning and learning." He was also elected to the National Academy of Sciences.

Humans, too, seem biologically prepared to learn some things rather than others. If you become violently ill four hours after eating a tainted hamburger, you will probably develop an aversion to the taste of hamburger. But you usually won't avoid the sight of the associated restaurant, its plates, the people you were with, or the music you heard there.

Though Garcia and Koelling's taste-aversion research began with the discomfort of some laboratory animals, it later enhanced the welfare of many others. In one taste-aversion study, coyotes and wolves were tempted into eating sheep carcasses laced with a sickening poison. Ever after, they avoided sheep meat (Gustavson et al., 1974, 1976). Two wolves penned with a live sheep seemed actually to fear it. These studies not only saved the sheep from their predators, but also saved the sheep-shunning coyotes and wolves from angry ranchers and farmers. In later experiments, conditioned taste aversion has successfully prevented baboons from raiding African gardens, raccoons from attacking chickens, and ravens and crows from feeding on crane eggs. In all these cases, research helped preserve both the prey and their predators (Dingfelder, 2010; Garcia & Gustavson, 1997).

Such research supports Darwin's principle that natural selection favors traits that aid survival. Our ancestors who readily learned taste aversions were unlikely to eat the same toxic food again and were more likely to survive and leave descendants. Nausea, like anxiety, pain, and other bad feelings, serves a good purpose. Like a car's low-oil warning light, each alerts the body to a threat (Davidson & Riley, 2015; Neese, 1991).

This tendency to learn behaviors favored by natural selection may help explain why we humans seem naturally disposed to learn associations between the color red and sexuality. Female primates display red when nearing ovulation. In human females, enhanced blood flow during sexual excitation may produce a red blush. Does the frequent pairing of red and sex—with

ANIMAL TASTE AVERSION As an alternative to killing wolves and coyotes that prey on sheep, some ranchers have sickened the animals with lamb laced with a drug to help them develop a taste aversion.

Valentine's hearts, red-light districts, and red lipstick—naturally enhance heterosexual men's attraction to women? Experiments (**FIGURE 6.8**) indicate that it does (Elliot et al., 2013; Pazda & Elliot, 2012).

Retrieve + Remember

- How did Garcia and Koelling's taste-aversion studies help disprove the belief that almost any stimulus (tastes, sights, sounds) could serve equally well as a conditioned stimulus?

ANSWER: Garcia and Koelling demonstrated that rats may learn an aversion to tastes, on which their survival depends, but not to sights or sounds.

Limits on Operant Conditioning

As with classical conditioning, nature sets limits on each species' capacity for operant conditioning. Science fiction writer Robert Heinlein (1907–1988) said it well: "Never try to teach a pig to sing; it wastes your time and annoys the pig."

We most easily learn and retain behaviors that reflect our biological predispositions. Thus, using food as a reinforcer, you could easily condition a hamster to dig or to rear up, because these are among the animal's natural food-searching behaviors. But you won't be so successful if you use food

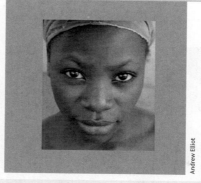

FIGURE 6.8 Romantic red In a series of experiments that controlled for other factors (such as the brightness of the image), heterosexual men found women more attractive and sexually desirable when framed in red (Elliot & Niesta, 2008). Women have also been observed to wear red during their fertile days, and to perceive other women in red as more sexually receptive (Eisenbruch et al., 2015; Pazda et al., 2014). The phenomenon has been found not only in North America and Europe, but also in the West African nation of Burkina Faso (Elliot et al., 2013).

JOHN B. WATSON Watson (1924) admitted to "going beyond my facts" when offering his famous boast: "Give me a dozen healthy infants, well-formed, and my own specified world to bring them up in and I'll guarantee to take any one at random and train him to become any type of specialist I might select—doctor, lawyer, artist, merchant-chief, and, yes, even beggar-man and thief, regardless of his talents, penchants, tendencies, abilities, vocations, and race of his ancestors."

to try to shape face washing and other hamster behaviors that normally have no link to food or hunger (Shettleworth, 1973). Similarly, you could easily teach pigeons to flap their wings to avoid being shocked, and to peck to obtain food. That's because fleeing with their wings and eating with their beaks are natural pigeon behaviors. However, pigeons have a hard time learning to peck to avoid a shock, or to flap their wings to obtain food (Foree & LoLordo, 1973). The principle: *Our biology predisposes us to learn associations that are naturally adaptive.*

NATURAL ATHLETES Animals can most easily learn and retain behaviors that draw on their biological predispositions, such as horses' inborn ability to move around obstacles with speed and agility.

Cognitive Influences on Conditioning

LOQ 6-12 How do cognitive processes affect classical and operant conditioning?

Cognition and Classical Conditioning

John B. Watson, the "Little Albert" researcher, was one of many psychologists who built on Ivan Pavlov's work. Pavlov and Watson shared many beliefs. They avoided "mentalistic" concepts (such as consciousness) that referred to inner thoughts, feelings, and motives (Watson, 1913). They also maintained that the basic laws of learning are the same for all animals—whether dogs or humans. Thus, the science of psychology should study how organisms respond to stimuli in their environments, said Watson. "Its theoretical goal is the prediction and control of behavior." This view—that psychology should be an objective science based on observable behavior—was called **behaviorism.** Behaviorism influenced North American psychology during the first half of the twentieth century.

Later research has shown that Pavlov's and Watson's views of learning underestimated two important sets of influences. The first, as we have seen, is the way that biological predispositions limit our learning. The second is the effect of our *cognitive processes*—our thoughts, perceptions, and expectations—on learning.

The early behaviorists believed that rats' and dogs' learned behaviors were mindless mechanisms, so there was no need to consider cognition. But experiments have shown that animals can learn the *predictability* of an event (Rescorla & Wagner, 1972). If a shock always is preceded by a tone, and then may also be preceded by a light that accompanies the tone, a rat will react with fear to the tone but not to the light. Although the light is always followed by the shock, it adds no new information; the tone is a better predictor. It's as if the animal learns an *expectancy*, an awareness of how likely it is that the US will occur.

Cognition matters in humans, too. For example, people being treated for alcohol use disorder may be given alcohol spiked with a nauseating drug. However, their *awareness* that the drug, not the

biological constraints evolved biological tendencies that predispose animals' behavior and learning. Thus, certain behaviors are more easily learned than others.

behaviorism the view that psychology (1) should be an objective science that (2) studies behavior without reference to mental processes. Most research psychologists today agree with (1) but not with (2).

alcohol, causes the nausea tends to weaken the association between drinking alcohol and feeling sick, making the treatment less effective. In classical conditioning, it is—especially with humans—not simply the CS-US pairing, but also the thought that counts.

Cognition and Operant Conditioning

B. F. Skinner acknowledged the biological underpinnings of behavior and the existence of private thought processes. Nevertheless, many psychologists criticized him for discounting cognition's importance.

A mere eight days before dying of leukemia in 1990, Skinner stood before those of us attending the American Psychological Association convention. In this final address, he again rejected the growing belief that presumed cognitive processes have a necessary place in the science of psychology and even in our understanding of conditioning. For Skinner, thoughts and emotions were behaviors that follow the same laws as other behaviors.

Nevertheless, the evidence of cognitive processes cannot be ignored. For example, rats exploring a maze, given no obvious rewards, seem to develop a **cognitive map,** a mental representation of the maze. In one study, when an experimenter placed food in the maze's goal box, these roaming rats ran the maze as quickly as (and even faster than) other rats that had always been rewarded with food for reaching the goal. Like people sightseeing in a new town, the exploring rats seemingly experienced **latent learning** during their earlier tours. Their latent learning became evident only when they had some reason to demonstrate it.

The cognitive perspective shows the limits of rewards. Promising people a

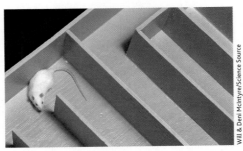

LATENT LEARNING Animals, like people, can learn from experience, with or without reinforcement. In a classic experiment, rats in one group repeatedly explored a maze, always with a food reward at the end. Rats in another group explored the maze with no food reward. But once given a food reward at the end, rats in the second group thereafter ran the maze as quickly as (and even faster than) the always-rewarded rats (Tolman & Honzik, 1930).

reward for a task they already enjoy can backfire. Excessive rewards can destroy **intrinsic motivation**—the desire to do something well, for its own sake. In experiments, rewarding children with toys or candy for reading shortens the time they spend reading (Marinak & Gambrell, 2008). It is as if they think, "If I have to be bribed into doing this, it must not be worth doing for its own sake."

To sense the difference between intrinsic motivation and **extrinsic motivation** (behaving in certain ways to gain external rewards or to avoid threatened punishment), think about your experience in this course. Are you feeling pressured to finish this reading before a deadline? Worried about your grade? Eager for the credits that will count toward graduation? If *Yes*, then you are extrinsically motivated (as, to some extent, almost all students must be). Are you also finding the material interesting? Does learning it make you feel more competent? If there were no grade at stake, might you be curious enough to want to learn the material for its own sake? If *Yes*, intrinsic

motivation also fuels your efforts. People who focus on their work's meaning and significance not only do better work, but ultimately earn more extrinsic rewards (Wrzesniewski et al., 2014).

Nevertheless, extrinsic rewards that signal a job well done—rather than to bribe or to control someone—can be effective (Boggiano et al., 1985). "Most improved player" awards, for example, can boost feelings of competence and increase enjoyment of a sport. Rightly administered, rewards can improve performance and spark creativity (Eisenberger & Rhoades, 2001; Henderlong & Lepper, 2002). And extrinsic rewards—such as the admissions, scholarships, and jobs that often follow hard work and academic achievement—are here to stay.

To sum up, **TABLE 6.5** compares the biological and cognitive influences on classical and operant conditioning.

Retrieve + Remember

- Latent learning is an example of what important idea?

ANSWER: The success of operant conditioning is affected not just by environmental cues, but also by cognitive factors.

Learning by Observation

LOQ 6-13 How does observational learning differ from associative learning? How may observational learning be enabled by mirror neurons?

Cognition supports **observational learning**, in which higher animals learn without direct experience, by watching and imitating others. A child who sees his sister burn her fingers on a hot stove

TABLE 6.5	Biological and Cognitive Influences on Conditioning	
	Classical Conditioning	**Operant Conditioning**
Biological influences	Biological tendencies limit the types of stimuli and responses that can easily be associated. Involuntary, automatic.	Animals most easily learn behaviors similar to their natural behaviors; associations that are not naturally adaptive are not easily learned.
Cognitive influences	Thoughts, perceptions, and expectations can weaken the association between the CS and the US.	Animals may develop an expectation that a response will be reinforced or punished; latent learning may occur without reinforcement.

learns, without getting burned himself, that hot stoves can burn us. We learn our native languages and all kinds of other specific behaviors by observing and imitating others, a process called **modeling.**

Picture this scene from an experiment by Albert Bandura, the pioneering researcher of observational learning (Bandura et al., 1961). A preschool child works on a drawing. In another part of the room, an adult builds with Tinkertoys. As the child watches, the adult gets up and for nearly 10 minutes pounds, kicks, and throws around the room a large, inflated Bobo doll, yelling, "Sock him in the nose. . . . Hit him down. . . . Kick him."

The child is then taken to another room filled with appealing toys. Soon the experimenter returns and tells the child she has decided to save these good toys "for the other children." She takes the now-frustrated child to a third room containing a few toys, including a Bobo doll. Left alone, what does the child do?

Compared with other children in the study, those who viewed the model's actions were much more likely to lash out at the doll. Apparently, observing the aggressive outburst lowered their inhibitions. But *something more* was also at work, for the children often imitated the very acts they had observed and

ALBERT BANDURA "The Bobo doll follows me wherever I go. The photographs are published in every introductory psychology text and virtually every undergraduate takes introductory psychology. I recently checked into a Washington hotel. The clerk at the desk asked, 'Aren't you the psychologist who did the Bobo doll experiment?' I answered, 'I am afraid that will be my legacy.' He replied, 'That deserves an upgrade. I will put you in a suite in the quiet part of the hotel'" (2005). A recent analysis of citations, awards, and textbook coverage identified Bandura as the world's most eminent psychologist (Diener et al., 2014).

used the very words they had heard (**FIGURE 6.9**).

LaunchPad For 3 minutes of classic footage, see LaunchPad's *Video: Bandura's Bobo Doll Experiment.*

That "something more," Bandura suggested, was this: By watching models, we *vicariously* (in our imagination) experience what they are experiencing.

cognitive map a mental image of the layout of one's environment.

latent learning learning that is not apparent until there is an incentive to demonstrate it.

intrinsic motivation a desire to perform a behavior well for its own sake.

extrinsic motivation a desire to perform a behavior to gain a reward or avoid punishment.

observational learning learning by observing others.

modeling the process of observing and imitating a specific behavior.

Through *vicarious reinforcement* or *vicarious punishment*, we learn to anticipate a behavior's consequences in situations like those we are observing. We are especially likely to experience models' outcomes vicariously if we identify with them—if we perceive them as

- similar to ourselves.
- successful.
- admirable.

Functional MRI (fMRI) scans show that when people observe someone winning a reward, their own brain reward systems become active, much as if they themselves had won the reward (Mobbs et al., 2009). Even our learned fears may extinguish as we

Courtesy of Albert Bandura, Stanford University

FIGURE 6.9 The famous Bobo doll experiment Notice how the children's actions directly imitate the adult's.

observe another safely navigating the feared situation (Golkar et al., 2013).

Mirrors and Imitation in the Brain

In one of those quirky events that appear in the growth of science, researchers made an amazing discovery.

On a 1991 hot summer day in Parma, Italy, a lab monkey awaited its researchers' return from lunch. The researchers had implanted a monitoring device in the monkey's brain, in a frontal lobe region important for planning and acting out movements. The device would alert the researchers to activity in that region. When the monkey moved a peanut into its mouth, for example, the device would buzz. That day, the monkey stared as one of the researchers entered the lab carrying an ice cream cone in his hand. As the researcher raised the cone to lick it, the monkey's monitor buzzed—as if the motionless monkey had itself made some movement (Blakeslee, 2006; Iacoboni, 2009). The same buzzing had been heard earlier, when the monkey watched humans or other monkeys move peanuts to their mouths.

This quirky event, the researchers believed, marked an amazing discovery: a previously unknown type of neuron (Rizzolatti et al., 2002, 2006). In their view, these **mirror neurons** provided a neural basis for everyday imitation and observational learning. When a monkey grasps, holds, or tears something, these neurons fire. They likewise fire when the monkey observes another doing so. When one monkey sees, these neurons mirror what another monkey does. (Other researchers continue to debate the existence and importance of mirror neurons and related brain networks [Gallese et al., 2011; Hickok, 2014].)

It's not just monkey business. Imitation occurs in various animal species, but it is most striking in humans. Our catchphrases, fashions, ceremonies, foods, traditions, morals, and fads all spread by one person copying another. Children and even infants are natural imitators (Marshall & Meltzoff, 2014). Shortly after birth, babies may imitate adults

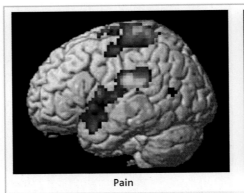
Pain

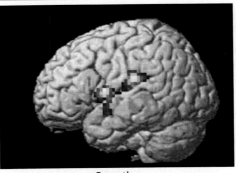
Empathy

FIGURE 6.10 Experienced and imagined pain in the brain Brain activity related to actual pain (left) is mirrored in the brain of an observing loved one (right). Empathy in the brain shows up in areas that process emotions, but not in the areas that register physical pain.

who stick out their tongue. By 8 to 16 months, infants imitate various novel gestures (Jones, 2007). By age 12 months, they begin looking where an adult is looking (Meltzoff et al., 2009). And by 14 months, children imitate acts modeled on TV (Meltzoff & Moore, 1997). Even as 2½-year-olds, when many of their mental abilities are near those of adult chimpanzees, young humans surpass chimps at social tasks such as imitating another's solution to a problem (Herrmann et al., 2007). Children see, children do.

Because of the brain's responses, emotions are contagious. As we observe others' postures, faces, voices, and writing styles, we unconsciously mimic them. And by doing that, we grasp others' states of mind and we feel what they are feeling (Bernieri et al., 1994; Ireland & Pennebaker, 2010).

Seeing a loved one's pain, our faces mirror the loved one's emotion. And so do our brains. In the fMRI scan in **FIGURE 6.10,** the pain imagined by an empathic romantic partner triggered some of the same brain activity experienced by the loved one in actual pain (Singer et al., 2004). Even fiction reading may trigger such activity, as we indirectly experience the feelings and actions described (Mar & Oatley, 2008; Speer et al., 2009). In one experiment, university students read a fictional fellow student's description of overcoming obstacles to vote. A week later, those who read the first-person account were more likely to vote in a presidential primary election (Kaufman & Libby, 2012). In other experiments, reading about Harry Potter and his acceptance of people such as the "Mudbloods" reduced

prejudice against immigrants, refugees, and gay people (Vezzali et al., 2015).

So real are these mental instant replays that we may remember an action we have observed as an action we have actually performed (Lindner et al., 2010). The bottom line: *Brain activity underlies our intensely social nature.*

Applications of Observational Learning

LOQ 6-14 What is the impact of prosocial modeling and of antisocial modeling?

So the big news from Bandura's studies and the mirror-neuron research is that we look, we mentally imitate, and we learn. Models—in our family, our neighborhood, or the media we consume—may have effects, good and bad.

Prosocial Effects

The good news is that **prosocial** (positive, helpful) **behavior** models can have prosocial effects. One research team found that across seven countries, viewing prosocial TV, movies, and video games boosted later helping behavior (Prot et al., 2014). Real people who model nonviolent, helpful behavior can also prompt similar behavior in others. India's Mahatma Gandhi and America's Martin Luther King, Jr., both drew on the power of modeling, making nonviolent action a powerful force for social change in both countries (Matsumoto et al., 2015). Parents are also powerful models. European Christians who risked their lives to

A MODEL CAREGIVER This girl is learning orphan-nursing skills, as well as compassion, by observing her mentor in this Humane Society program. As the sixteenth-century proverb states, "Example is better than precept."

rescue Jews from the Nazis usually had a close relationship with at least one parent who modeled a strong moral or humanitarian concern. This was also true for U.S. civil rights activists in the 1960s (London, 1970; Oliner & Oliner, 1988).

Models are most effective when their actions and words are consistent. To encourage children to read, read to them and surround them with books and people who read. To increase the odds that your children will practice your religion, worship and attend religious activities with them. Sometimes, however, models say one thing and do another. Many parents seem to operate according to the principle "Do as I *say*, not as I *do*." Experiments suggest that children learn to do both (Rice & Grusec, 1975; Rushton, 1975). Exposed to a hypocrite, they tend to imitate the hypocrisy—by doing what the model did and saying what the model said.

Antisocial Effects

The bad news is that observational learning may also have *antisocial effects*. This helps us understand why abusive parents might have aggressive children, and why many men who beat their wives had wife-battering fathers (Stith et al., 2000). Critics note that such aggressiveness could be genetic. But with monkeys, we know it can be environmental. In study after study, young monkeys separated from their mothers and subjected to high levels of aggression grew up to be aggressive themselves (Chamove, 1980). The lessons we

learn as children are not easily unlearned as adults, and they are sometimes visited on future generations.

TV shows, movies, and online videos are sources of observational learning. While watching TV and videos, children may "learn" that bullying is an effective way to control others, that free and easy sex brings pleasure without later misery or disease, or that men should be tough and women gentle. And they have ample time to learn such lessons. During their first 18 years, most children in developed countries spend more time watching TV shows than they spend in school. In the United States, the average teen watches TV shows more than 4 hours a day; the average adult, 3 hours (Robinson & Martin, 2009; Strasburger et al., 2010).

Viewers are learning about life from a rather peculiar storyteller, one with a taste for violence. During one closely studied year, nearly 6 in 10 U.S. network and cable programs featured violence. Of those violent acts, 74 percent went unpunished, and the victims' pain was usually not shown. Nearly half the events were portrayed as "justified," and nearly half the attackers were attractive (Donnerstein, 1998). These conditions define the recipe for the violence-viewing effect,

described in many studies (Donnerstein, 1998, 2011).

In 2012, a well-armed man targeted young children and their teachers in a horrifying mass shooting at Connecticut's Sandy Hook Elementary School. Was the American media correct in wondering whether the killer was influenced by the violent video games found stockpiled in his home? (See Thinking Critically About: The Effects of Viewing Media Violence.)

Screen time's greatest effect may stem from what it displaces. Children and adults who spend several hours a day in front of a screen spend that many fewer hours in other pursuits—talking, studying, playing, reading, or socializing in real time with friends. What would you have done with your extra time if you had spent even half as many hours in front of a screen, and how might you therefore be different?

> **mirror neuron** a neuron that fires when we perform certain actions and when we observe others performing those actions; a neural basis for imitation and observational learning.
>
> **prosocial behavior** positive, constructive, helpful behavior. The opposite of antisocial behavior.

Retrieve + Remember

- Jason's parents and older friends all smoke, but they advise him not to. Juan's parents and friends don't smoke, but they say nothing to deter him from doing so. Will Jason or Juan be more likely to start smoking?

  ANSWER: Jason may be more likely to smoke, because observational learning studies suggest that children tend to do as others do and say what they say.

- Match the learning examples (items 1–5) to the following concepts (a–e):

  a. Classical conditioning
  b. Operant conditioning
  c. Latent learning
  d. Observational learning
  e. Biological predispositions

  1. Knowing the way from your bed to the bathroom in the dark
  2. Speaking the language your parents speak
  3. Salivating when you smell brownies in the oven
  4. Disliking the taste of chili after becoming violently sick a few hours after eating chili
  5. Your dog racing to greet you on your arrival home

  ANSWERS: 1. c (You've probably learned your way by *latent learning*.) 2. d (*Observational learning* may have contributed to your imitating the language modeled by your parents.) 3. a (Through *classical conditioning* you have associated the smell with the anticipated tasty result.) 4. e (You are *biologically predisposed* to develop a conditioned taste aversion to foods associated with illness.) 5. b (Through *operant conditioning* your dog may have come to associate approaching excitedly with attention, petting, and a treat.)

Thinking Critically About:
The Effects of Viewing Media Violence

LOQ 6-15 What is the violence-viewing effect?

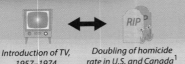 *Introduction of TV, 1957–1974* ⟷ *Doubling of homicide rate in U.S. and Canada[1]*

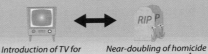 *Introduction of TV for White South Africans in 1975* ⟷ *Near-doubling of homicide rate in South Africa[1]*

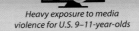 *Heavy exposure to media violence for U.S. 9–11-year-olds* ⟷ *Increased fighting, and more violent behavior later as teens[2]*

BUT, CORRELATION ≠ CAUSATION!

Experimental studies have also found that media violence viewing can **cause** aggression:
Viewing violence (compared to entertaining nonviolence) ➡ participants react more cruelly when provoked. (Effect is strongest if the violent person is attractive, the violence seems justified and realistic, the act goes unpunished, and the viewer does not see pain or harm caused.)

What prompts the *violence-viewing effect*?

1 IMITATION:

Watching violent cartoons ➡ Sevenfold increase in violent play[3]

Limited exposure to violent programs ➡ Reduced aggressive behavior[4]

2 DESENSITIZATION:

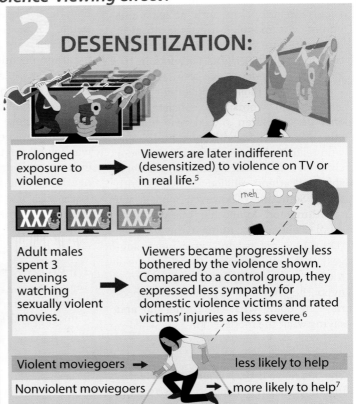

Prolonged exposure to violence ➡ Viewers are later indifferent (desensitized) to violence on TV or in real life.[5]

XXX XXX XXX ----- meh.

Adult males spent 3 evenings watching sexually violent movies. ➡ Viewers became progressively less bothered by the violence shown. Compared to a control group, they expressed less sympathy for domestic violence victims and rated victims' injuries as less severe.[6]

Violent moviegoers ➡ less likely to help
Nonviolent moviegoers ➡ more likely to help[7]

- **APA Task Force on Violent Media (2015)** found that the "research demonstrates a consistent relation between violent video game use and increases in aggressive behavior, aggressive cognitions and aggressive affect, and decreases in prosocial behavior, empathy and sensitivity to aggression."

- **American Academy of Pediatrics (2009)** has advised pediatricians that "media violence can contribute to aggressive behavior, desensitization to violence, nightmares, and fear of being harmed."

1. Centerwall, 1989. 2. Boxer at al., 2009; Gentile et al., 2011; Gentile & Bushman, 2012. 3. Boyatzis et al., 1995. 4. Christakis et al., 2013. 5. Fanti et al., 2009; Rule & Ferguson, 1986. 6. Mullin & Linz, 1995. 7. Bushman & Anderson, 2009.

CHAPTER REVIEW

Learning

Test yourself by taking a moment to answer each of these Learning Objective Questions (repeated here from within the chapter). Then turn to Appendix D, Complete Chapter Reviews, to check your answers. Research suggests that trying to answer these questions on your own will improve your long-term memory of the concepts (McDaniel et al., 2009).

How Do We Learn?

6-1: How do we define *learning*, and what are some basic forms of learning?

Classical Conditioning

6-2: What is *classical conditioning*, and how does it demonstrate associative learning?

6-3: What parts do acquisition, extinction, spontaneous recovery, generalization, and discrimination play in classical conditioning?

6-4: Why is Pavlov's work important, and how is it being applied?

Operant Conditioning

6-5: What is *operant conditioning,* and how is operant behavior reinforced and shaped?

6-6: How do positive and negative reinforcement differ, and what are the basic types of reinforcers?

6-7: How do continuous and partial reinforcement schedules affect behavior?

6-8: How does punishment differ from negative reinforcement, and how does punishment affect behavior?

6-9: Why were Skinner's ideas controversial, and how might his operant conditioning principles be applied at school, at work, in parenting, and for self-improvement?

6-10: How does classical conditioning differ from operant conditioning?

Biology, Cognition, and Learning

6-11: What limits does biology place on conditioning?

6-12: How do cognitive processes affect classical and operant conditioning?

Learning by Observation

6-13: How does observational learning differ from associative learning? How may observational learning be enabled by mirror neurons?

6-14: What is the impact of prosocial modeling and of antisocial modeling?

6-15: What is the violence-viewing effect?

TERMS AND CONCEPTS TO REMEMBER

Test yourself on these terms by trying to write down the definition in your own words before flipping back to the referenced page to check your answer.

learning, p. 171
associative learning, p. 171
stimulus, p. 171
respondent behavior, p. 171
operant behavior, p. 171
cognitive learning, p. 171
classical conditioning, p. 171
neutral stimulus (NS), p. 171
unconditioned response (UR), p. 173
unconditioned stimulus (US), p. 173
conditioned response (CR), p. 173

conditioned stimulus (CS), p. 173
acquisition, p. 173
extinction, p. 175
spontaneous recovery, p. 175
generalization, p. 175
discrimination, p. 175
operant conditioning, p. 177
law of effect, p. 177
operant chamber, p. 177
reinforcement, p. 177
shaping, p. 177
positive reinforcement, p. 179

negative reinforcement, p. 179
primary reinforcer, p. 179
conditioned reinforcer, p. 179
reinforcement schedule, p. 179
continuous reinforcement, p. 179
partial (intermittent) reinforcement, p. 179
fixed-ratio schedule, p. 179
variable-ratio schedule, p. 179
fixed-interval schedule, p. 181
variable-interval schedule, p. 181

punishment, p. 181
biological constraints, p. 185
behaviorism, p. 185
cognitive map, p. 187
latent learning, p. 187
intrinsic motivation, p. 187
extrinsic motivation, p. 187
observational learning, p. 187
modeling, p. 187
mirror neuron, p. 189
prosocial behavior, p. 189

CHAPTER TEST

Test yourself repeatedly throughout your studies. This will not only help you figure out what you know and don't know; the testing itself will help you learn and remember the information more effectively thanks to the *testing effect*.

1. Learning is defined as "the process of acquiring, through experience, new and relatively enduring _____ or _____."

2. Two forms of associative learning are classical conditioning, in which we associate _____, and operant conditioning, in which we associate _____.

   a. two or more responses; a response and consequence

   b. two or more stimuli; two or more responses

   c. two or more stimuli; a response and consequence

   d. two or more responses; two or more stimuli

3. In Pavlov's experiments, the tone started as a neutral stimulus, and then became a(n) _____ stimulus.

4. Dogs have been taught to salivate to a circle but not to a square. This process is an example of _____.

5. After Watson and Rayner classically conditioned Little Albert to fear a white rat, the child later showed fear in response to a rabbit, a dog, and a sealskin coat. This illustrates

   a. extinction.

   b. generalization.

   c. spontaneous recovery.

   d. discrimination between two stimuli.

6. "Sex sells!" is a common saying in advertising. Using classical conditioning terms, explain how sexual images in advertisements can condition your response to a product.

7. Thorndike's law of effect was the basis for _____ 's work on operant conditioning and behavior control.

8. One way to change behavior is to reward natural behaviors in small steps, as they get closer and closer to a desired behavior. This process is called _____.

9. Your dog is barking so loudly that it's making your ears ring. You clap your hands, the dog stops barking, your ears stop ringing, and you think to yourself, "I'll have to do that when he barks again." The end of the barking was for you a

   a. positive reinforcer.

   b. negative reinforcer.

   c. positive punishment.

   d. negative punishment.

10. How could your psychology instructor use negative reinforcement to encourage you to pay attention during class?

11. Reinforcing a desired response only some of the times it occurs is called _____ reinforcement.

12. A restaurant is running a special deal. After you buy four meals at full price, your fifth meal will be free. This is an example of a _____ schedule of reinforcement.

    a. fixed-ratio

    b. variable-ratio

    c. fixed-interval

    d. variable-interval

13. The partial reinforcement schedule that reinforces a response after unpredictable time periods is a _____ - _____ schedule.

14. An old saying notes that "a burnt child dreads the fire." In operant conditioning, the burning would be an example of a

    a. primary reinforcer.

    b. negative reinforcer.

    c. punisher.

    d. positive reinforcer.

15. Which research showed that conditioning can occur even when the unconditioned stimulus (US) does not immediately follow the neutral stimulus (NS)?

    a. The Little Albert experiment

    b. Pavlov's experiments with dogs

    c. Watson's behaviorism studies

    d. Garcia and Koelling's taste-aversion studies

16. Taste-aversion research has shown that some animals develop aversions to certain tastes but not to sights or sounds. This finding supports

    a. Pavlov's demonstration of generalization.

    b. Darwin's principle that natural selection favors traits that aid survival.

    c. Watson's belief that psychologists should study observable behavior, not mentalistic concepts.

    d. the early behaviorists' view that any organism can be conditioned to any stimulus.

17. Evidence that cognitive processes play an important role in learning comes in part from studies in which rats running a maze develop a _____ _____ of the maze.

18. Rats that explored a maze without any reward were later able to run the maze as well as other rats that had received food rewards for running the maze. The rats that had learned without reinforcement demonstrated _____.

19. Children learn many social behaviors by imitating parents and other models. This type of learning is called _____.

20. According to Bandura, we learn by watching models because we experience _____ reinforcement or _____ punishment.

21. Parents are most effective in getting their children to imitate them if

    a. their words and actions are consistent.

    b. they have outgoing personalities.

    c. one parent works and the other stays home to care for the children.

    d. they carefully explain why a behavior is acceptable in adults but not in children.

22. Some scientists believe that the brain has _____ neurons that enable observation and imitation.

23. Most experts agree that repeated viewing of TV violence

    a. makes all viewers significantly more aggressive.

    b. has little effect on viewers.

    c. is a risk factor for viewers' increased aggression.

    d. makes viewers angry and frustrated.

    Find answers to these questions in Appendix E, in the back of the book.

IN YOUR EVERYDAY LIFE

Answering these questions will help you make these concepts more personally meaningful, and therefore more memorable.

1. How have your emotions or behaviors been classically conditioned?

2. Can you recall a time when a teacher, coach, family member, or employer helped you learn something by shaping your behavior in little steps until you achieved your goal?

3. Think of a bad habit of yours or of a friend. How could you or your friend use operant conditioning to break it?

4. Is your behavior in this class influenced more by intrinsic motivation or extrinsic motivation?

5. Who has been a significant role model for you? What did you learn from observing this person? Are you a role model for someone else?

Use ≋ LearningCurve to create your personalized study plan, which will direct you to the resources that will help you most in ≋ LaunchPad.

SURVEY THE CHAPTER

Memory

Memory is learning we save over time. Imagine being unable to form new conscious memories. This was life for Henry Molaison, or H. M. (as psychologists knew him until his 2008 death). In 1953, surgeons removed much of H. M.'s hippocampus in order to stop severe seizures. He remained intelligent and did daily crossword puzzles. Yet from that point on he lived an unusual inner life. "I've known H. M. since 1962," reported one neuroscientist, "and he still doesn't know who I am" (Corkin, 2005, 2013). For about 20 seconds during a conversation he could keep something in mind. When distracted, he would lose what was just said or what had just occurred. Thus, he never could name the current president of the United States (Ogden, 2012).

My [DM's] own father suffered a similar problem after a small stroke at age 92. His upbeat personality was unchanged. He enjoyed poring over family photo albums and telling stories about his pre-stroke life. But he could not tell me what day of the week it was, or what he'd had for dinner. Told repeatedly of his brother-in-law's recent death, he was surprised and saddened each time he heard the news.

Some disorders slowly strip away memory. Alzheimer's disease affects millions of people, usually later in life. What begins as difficulty remembering new information progresses into an inability to do everyday tasks. Family members and close friends become strangers. Complex speech becomes simple sentences. The brain's memory centers, once strong, become weak and wither away (Desikan et al., 2009). Over a period typically lasting several years, people become unknowing and unknowable. Such is the tragedy of lost memory.

At the other extreme are people who would be gold medal winners in a memory Olympics. Russian journalist Solomon Shereshevskii, or S, had merely to listen while other reporters scribbled notes (Luria, 1968). The average person could parrot back a string of 7 or so numbers. If numbers were read about 3 seconds apart in an otherwise silent room, S could repeat up to 70. Moreover, he could recall them (and words, too) backward as easily as forward. His accuracy was perfect, even when recalling a list 15 years later. "Yes, yes," he might recall. "This was a series you gave me once when we were in your apartment. . . . You were sitting at the table and I in the rocking chair. . . . You were wearing a gray suit. . . ."

Amazing? Yes, but consider your own impressive memory. You remember countless faces, places, and happenings; tastes, smells, and textures; voices, sounds, and songs. In one study, students listened to snippets—a mere four-tenths of a second—from popular songs. How often did they recognize the artist and song? More than 25 percent of the time (Krumhansl, 2010). We often recognize songs as quickly as we recognize a familiar voice. So, too, with faces and places. In another experiment, people were exposed to 2800 images for only 3 seconds each. Later, viewing these and other images in a second round, they spotted the repeats with 82 percent accuracy (Konkle et al., 2010). Some super-recognizers display an extraordinary ability to recognize faces. Eighteen months after viewing a video of an armed robbery, one such police officer spotted and arrested the robber walking on a busy street (Davis et al., 2013).

How do we accomplish such memory feats? How can we remember things we have not thought about for years, yet forget the name of someone we met a minute ago? How are our memories stored in our brain? Why, when we ask you later in this chapter, will you be likely to have trouble recalling this sentence: *"The angry rioter threw the rock at the window"?* In this chapter, we'll consider these fascinating questions and more, including some tips on how we can improve our own memories.

Studying Memory

LOQ **L**earning**O**bjective**Q**uestion

7-1 What is *memory,* and how do information-processing models help us study memory?

Be thankful for **memory**—your storehouse of accumulated learning. Your memory enables you to recognize family, speak your language, find your way home, and locate food and water. Your memory allows you to enjoy an experience and then mentally replay it and enjoy it again. Without memory, you could not savor past achievements, nor feel guilt or anger over painful past events. You would instead live in an endless present, each moment fresh. Each person would be a stranger, every language foreign, every task—dressing, cooking, biking—a new challenge. You would even be a stranger to yourself, lacking that ongoing sense of self that extends from your distant past to your momentary present.

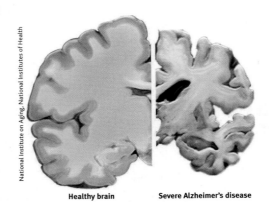

National Institute on Aging, National Institutes of Health

Healthy brain   **Severe Alzheimer's disease**

EXTREME FORGETTING Alzheimer's disease severely damages the brain, and in the process strips away memory.

Earlier, in the Sensation and Perception chapter, we considered one of psychology's big questions: How does the world out there enter your brain? In this chapter we consider a related question: How does your brain pluck information out of the world around you and store it for a lifetime of use? Said simply, how does your brain construct your memories?

To help clients imagine future buildings, architects create miniature models. Similarly, psychologists create models of memory to help us think about how our brain forms and retrieves memories. An *information-processing model* compares human memory to a computer's operation. It assumes that, to remember something, we must

- get information into our brain, a process called **encoding.**
- retain that information, a process called **storage.**
- later get the information back out, a process called **retrieval.**

Let's take a closer look.

An Information-Processing Model

LOQ **7-2** What is the three-stage information-processing model, and how has later research updated this model?

Richard Atkinson and Richard Shiffrin (1968) proposed that we form memories in three stages.

1. We first record to-be-remembered information as a fleeting **sensory memory.**

2. From there, we process information into **short-term memory,** where we encode it through *rehearsal.*

3. Finally, information moves into **long-term memory** for later retrieval.

Other psychologists later updated this model with important newer concepts, including *working memory* and *automatic processing* (**FIGURE 7.1**).

Working Memory

So much active processing takes place in the middle stage that psychologists now prefer the term **working memory.** In Atkinson and Shiffrin's original model, the second stage appeared to be a temporary shelf for holding recent thoughts and experiences. We now know that this working-memory stage is where your brain actively processes important information, making sense of new input and linking it with long-term memories. It also works in the opposite direction, processing already stored information. When you process verbal

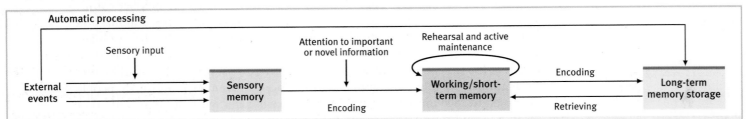

FIGURE 7.1 A modified three-stage processing model of memory Atkinson and Shiffrin's classic three-step model helps us to think about how memories are processed, but today's researchers recognize other ways long-term memories form. For example, some information slips into long-term memory via a "back door," without our consciously attending to it *(automatic processing).* And so much active processing occurs in the short-term memory stage that many now prefer to call that stage *working memory.*

information, your *active* working memory connects new information to what you already know or imagine (Cowan, 2010; Kail & Hall, 2001). If you hear someone say "eye-scream," you may encode it as "ice cream" or "I scream," depending on both the context (snack shop or horror film) and your experience.

For most of you, what you are reading enters your working memory through vision. You may also silently repeat the information using auditory rehearsal. Integrating these memory inputs with your existing long-term memory requires focused attention.

Without focused attention, information often fades. If you think you can look something up later, you attend to it less and forget it more quickly. In one experiment, people read and typed new information they would later need, such as "An ostrich's eye is bigger than its brain." If they knew the information would be available online, they invested less energy in remembering it, and they remembered it less well (Sparrow et al., 2011; Wegner & Ward, 2013). Online, out of mind.

Retrieve + Remember

- How does the *working memory* concept update the classic Atkinson-Shiffrin three-stage information-processing model?

ANSWER: The newer idea of a *working memory* emphasizes the active processing that we now know takes place in Atkinson-Shiffrin's short-term memory stage. While the Atkinson-Shiffrin model viewed short-term memory as a temporary holding space, working memory plays a key role in processing new information and connecting it to previously stored information.

- What are two basic functions of working memory?

ANSWER: (1) Active processing of incoming visual and auditory information, and (2) focusing our spotlight of attention.

LaunchPad For a 14-minute explanation and demonstration of our memory systems, visit LaunchPad's *Video: Models of Memory.*

Building Memories: Encoding

Our Two-Track Memory System

LOQ 7-3 How do implicit and explicit memories differ?

As we have seen throughout this text, our mind operates on two tracks. This theme appears again in the way we process memories:

- On one track, information skips the Atkinson-Shiffrin stages and barges directly into storage, without our awareness. These **implicit memories** (also called *nondeclarative memories*) form without our conscious effort. Implicit memories, formed through **automatic processing,** bypass the conscious encoding track.

- On the second track, we process our **explicit memories** of the facts and experiences we can consciously know and declare. (Explicit memories are also called *declarative memories.*) We encode explicit memories through conscious, **effortful processing.** The Atkinson-Shiffrin model helps us understand how this memory track operates.

Our two-track mind, then, helps us encode, retain, and recall information through both automatic and effortful tracks. Let's begin by seeing how automatic processing assists the formation of implicit memories.

Automatic Processing and Implicit Memories

LOQ 7-4 What information do we process automatically?

Your implicit memories include automatic skills (such as how to ride a bike) and classically conditioned *associations.* If attacked by a dog in childhood, years later you may, without recalling the conditioned association, automatically tense up as a dog approaches.

Without conscious effort, you also automatically process information about

- *space.* While studying, you often encode the place on a page where certain material appears. Later, when you want to retrieve the information, you may visualize its location on the page.

---

memory the persistence of learning over time through the encoding, storage, and retrieval of information.

encoding the process of getting information into the memory system.

storage the process of retaining encoded information over time.

retrieval the process of getting information out of memory storage.

sensory memory the immediate, very brief recording of sensory information in the memory system.

short-term memory activated memory that holds a few items briefly (such as the seven digits of a phone number while calling) before the information is stored or forgotten.

long-term memory the relatively permanent and limitless storehouse of the memory system. Includes knowledge, skills, and experiences.

working memory a newer understanding of short-term memory that adds conscious, active processing of incoming auditory and visual-spatial information, and of information retrieved from long-term memory.

implicit memory retention of learned skills, or classically conditioned associations, without conscious awareness. (Also called *nondeclarative memory.*)

automatic processing unconscious encoding of everyday information, such as space, time, and frequency, and of well-learned information, such as word meanings.

explicit memory retention of facts and personal events you can consciously retrieve. (Also called *declarative memory.*)

effortful processing encoding that requires attention and conscious effort.

time. While you are going about your day, your brain is working behind the scenes, jotting down the sequence of your day's events. Later, if you realize you've left your coat somewhere, you can call up that sequence and retrace your steps.

frequency. Your behind-the-scenes mind also keeps track of how often things have happened, thus enabling you to realize, "This is the third time I've run into her today!"

Your two-track mind processes information efficiently. As one track automatically tucks away routine details, the other track focuses on conscious, effortful processing. This division of labor illustrates the **parallel processing** we've also seen in Chapter 2 and Chapter 5. Mental feats such as thinking, vision, and memory may seem to be single abilities, but they are not. Rather, your brain assigns different subtasks to separate areas for simultaneous processing.

Effortful Processing and Explicit Memories

Automatic processing happens effortlessly. When you see words in your native language, you can't help but register their meaning. *Learning* to read was not automatic. You at first worked hard to pick out letters and connect them to certain sounds. But with experience and practice, your reading became automatic. Imagine now learning to read sentences in reverse:

.citamotua emoceb nac gnissecorp luftroffE

At first, this requires effort, but with practice it becomes more automatic. We develop many skills in this way: driving, texting, and speaking a new language. With practice, these tasks become automatic.

Sensory Memory

LOQ 7-5 How does sensory memory work?

Sensory memory (recall Figure 7.1) is the first stage in forming explicit memo-

FIGURE 7.2 Total recall—briefly When George Sperling (1960) flashed a group of letters similar to this for one-twentieth of a second, people could recall only about half the letters. But when signaled to recall a particular row immediately after the letters had disappeared, they could do so with near-perfect accuracy.

ries. A memory-to-be enters by way of the senses, feeding very brief images of scenes, or echoes of sounds, into our working memory. But sensory memory, like a lightning flash, is fleeting. How fleeting? In one experiment, people viewed three rows of three letters each for only one-twentieth of a second (**FIGURE 7.2**). Then the nine letters disappeared. How many letters could people recall? Only about half of them.

Was it because they had too little time to see them? *No*—the researcher demonstrated that people actually had seen, and could recall, all the letters, but only briefly (Sperling, 1960). He sounded a tone immediately *after* flashing the nine letters. A high tone directed people to report the top row of letters; a medium tone, the middle row; a low tone, the bottom row. With these cues, they rarely missed a letter, showing that all nine were briefly available for recall.

This fleeting sensory memory of the flashed letters was an *iconic memory.* For a few tenths of a second, our eyes retain a picture-image memory of a scene. Then our visual field clears quickly, and new images replace old ones. We also have a fleeting sensory memory of sounds. It's called *echoic memory,* because the sound echoes in our mind for 3 or 4 seconds.

Short-Term Memory Capacity

LOQ 7-6 What is our short-term memory capacity?

Recall that short-term memory refers to what we can briefly retain. The related idea of working memory also includes our active processing, as our brain makes sense of incoming information and links it with stored memories. What are the limits of what we can hold in this middle short-term stage?

Memory researcher George Miller (1956) proposed that we can store about seven bits of information (give or take two) in this middle stage. Miller's Magical Number Seven is psychology's contribution to the list of magical sevens—the seven wonders of the world, the seven seas, the seven deadly sins, the seven primary colors, the seven musical scale notes, the seven days of the week—seven magical sevens. After Miller's 2012 death, his daughter recalled his best moment of golf: "He made the one and only hole-in-one of his life at the age of 77, on the seventh green . . . with a seven iron. He loved that" (quoted by Vitello, 2012).

Other researchers have confirmed that we can, if nothing distracts us, recall about seven digits, or about six letters or five words (Baddeley et al., 1975). How quickly do our short-term memories disappear? To find out how quickly, researchers asked people to remember groups of three consonants, such as CHJ (Peterson & Peterson, 1959). To prevent rehearsal, they distracted them (asking them, for example, to start at 100 and count backward by threes). Without active processing, people's short-term memories of the consonants disappeared. After 3 seconds, they recalled the letters only about half the time. After 12 seconds, they seldom recalled them at all (**FIGURE 7.3**).

Working-memory capacity varies, depending on age and other factors.

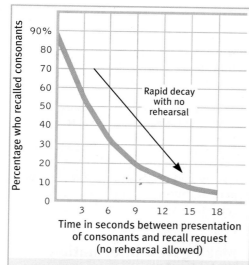

FIGURE 7.3 Short-term memory decay Unless rehearsed, verbal information may be quickly forgotten. (Data from Peterson & Peterson, 1959; see also Brown, 1958.)

Compared with children and older adults, young adults have more working-memory capacity. Having a large working-memory capacity—the ability to juggle multiple items while processing information—tends to help them retain more information after sleep and to solve problems more creatively (De Dreu et al., 2012; Fenn & Hambrick, 2012; Wiley & Jarosz, 2012). Even so, whatever our age, our work is better and more efficient when we focus on one task at a time, without distractions. *The bottom line:* It's probably a bad idea to try to watch TV, text your friends, and write a psychology paper all at the same time (Willingham, 2010)!

LaunchPad For a review of memory stages and a test of your own short-term memory capacity, visit LaunchPad's *PsychSim 6: Short-Term Memory.*

Effortful Processing Strategies

LOQ 7-7 What are some effortful processing strategies that can help us remember new information?

Let's recap. To form an explicit memory (a lasting memory of a fact or an experience) it helps to *focus our attention* and *make a conscious effort* to remember. But our working-memory desktop has limited space, and images, sounds, and other distractions compete for our attention.

We can boost our ability to form new explicit memories by using specific effortful processing strategies, such as *chunking* and *mnemonics.*

- *Chunking:* When we **chunk** information, we organize items into familiar, manageable units. Glance for a few seconds at row 1 of **FIGURE 7.4**, then look away and try to draw those forms. Impossible, yes? But you can easily reproduce row 2, which is just as complex. And row 4 is probably much easier to remember than row 3, although both contain the same letters. As you can see, chunking information helps us to recall it more easily.

1.   M Ɔ ∧ S Я W ⊥

2.   W G V S R M T

3.   VRESLI UEGBN GSORNW CDOUL LWLE NTOD WTO
4.   SILVER BEGUN WRONGS CLOUD WELL DONT TWO

5.   SILVER BEGUN WRONGS CLOUD DONT TWO
     HALF MAKE WELL HAS A
     EVERY IS RIGHT A DONE LINING

6.   WELL BEGUN IS HALF DONE
     EVERY CLOUD HAS A SILVER LINING
     TWO WRONGS DONT MAKE A RIGHT

FIGURE 7.4 Chunking effects Organizing information into meaningful units, such as letters, words, and phrases, helps us recall it more easily (Hintzman, 1978).

parallel processing the processing of many aspects of a problem at the same time; the brain's natural mode of information processing for many functions.

chunking organizing items into familiar, manageable units; often occurs automatically.

mnemonics [nih-MON-iks] memory aids, especially techniques that use vivid imagery and organizational devices.

Chunking usually occurs so naturally that we take it for granted. Try remembering 43 individual numbers and letters. It would be impossible, unless chunked into, say, seven meaningful chunks—such as "Try remembering 43 individual numbers and letters!" ☺

- *Mnemonics:* In ancient Greece, scholars and public speakers needed memory aids to help them encode long passages and speeches. They developed **mnemonics,** which often rely on vivid imagery. We are particularly good at remembering mental pictures. Concrete words that create these mental images are easier to remember than other words that describe abstract ideas. (When we quiz you later, which three of these words—*bicycle, void, cigarette, inherent, fire, process*—will you most likely recall?) Do you still recall the rock-throwing rioter sentence mentioned at the beginning of this chapter? If so, it is probably not only because of the meaning you encoded but also because the sentence painted a mental image.

Memory whizzes understand the power of such systems. Star performers in the World Memory Championships do not usually have exceptional intelligence. Rather, they are superior at using mnemonic strategies (Maguire et al., 2003). Frustrated by his ordinary memory, science writer Joshua Foer wanted to see how much he could improve it. After a year of intense practice, he won the U.S. Memory Championship by memorizing a pack of 52 playing cards in under two minutes. How did Foer do it? He added vivid new details to memories of a familiar place—his childhood home. Each card, presented in any order, could then match up with the clear picture in his head. As the test subject of his own wild memory experiment, he learned that "you don't have to be memorizing packs of playing cards to benefit from a little bit of insight into how your mind works" (Foer, 2011a,b).

* * *

Effortful processing requires closer attention and effort, and chunking and mnemonics help us form meaningful and accessible memories. But memory researchers have also discovered other important influences on how we capture information and hold it in memory.

Retrieve + Remember

- What is the difference between *automatic* and *effortful* processing, and what are some examples of each?

ANSWER: *Automatic* processing occurs unconsciously (automatically) for such things as the sequence and frequency of a day's events, and reading and understanding words in our own language(s). *Effortful* processing requires us to focus attention and make an effort, as when we work hard to learn new material in class, or new lines for a play.

- At which of Atkinson-Shiffrin's three memory stages would iconic and echoic memory occur?

ANSWER: sensory memory

Spaced Study and Self-Assessment

LOQ 7-8 Why is cramming ineffective, and what is the *testing effect?* Why is it important to make new information meaningful?

We retain information better when our encoding is spread over time. Psychologists call this the **spacing effect,** and more than 300 experiments have confirmed that *distributed practice* produces better long-term recall (Cepeda et al., 2006). *Massed practice* (cramming) can produce speedy short-term learning

and feelings of confidence. But to paraphrase pioneering memory researcher Hermann Ebbinghaus (1850–1909), those who learn quickly also forget quickly. You'll retain material better if, rather than cramming, you space your study, with reviewing time later. How much later? If you need to remember something 10 days from now, practice it again tomorrow. If you need to remember something 6 months from now, practice it again a month from now (Cepeda et al., 2008). The spacing effect is one of psychology's most reliable findings, and it extends to motor skills and online game performance (Stafford & Dewar, 2014). Memory researcher Henry Roediger (2013) sums it up: "Hundreds of studies have shown that distributed practice leads to more durable learning." Distributing your learning over several months, rather than over a shorter term, can help you retain information for a lifetime.

One effective way to distribute practice is *repeated self-testing,* often called the **testing effect** (Roediger & Karpicke, 2006). Testing does more than assess learning; it improves it (Brown et al., 2014). In this text, for example, the Retrieve + Remember questions and Chapter Tests offer self-testing opportunities. Better to practice retrieval (as any exam will demand) than to merely reread material (which may lull you into a false sense of mastery). Happily, "retrieval practice (or testing) is [a] powerful and general strategy for learning" (Roediger, 2013). No

MAKING THINGS MEMORABLE
For suggestions on how to apply the *testing effect* to your own learning, watch this 5-minute animation: tinyurl.com/HowToRemember.

wonder daily online quizzing improves introductory psychology students' course performance (Pennebaker et al., 2013).

Here is another sentence we will ask you about later: The fish attacked the swimmer.

The point to remember: Spaced study and self-assessment beat cramming and rereading. Practice may not make perfect, but smart practice—occasional rehearsal with self-testing—makes for lasting memories.

Making New Information Meaningful

Spaced practice helps, but if new information is not meaningful or related to your experience, you will have trouble processing it. Imagine being asked to remember this passage (Bransford & Johnson, 1972):

> The procedure is actually quite simple. First you arrange things into different groups. Of course, one pile may be sufficient depending on how much there is to do. . . . After the procedure is completed one arranges the materials into different groups again. Then they can be put into their appropriate places. Eventually they will be used once more and the whole cycle will then have to be repeated. However, that is part of life.

When some students heard the paragraph you just read, without a meaningful context, they remembered little of it. Others were told the paragraph described doing laundry (something meaningful to them). They remembered much more of it—as you probably could now after rereading it.

Can you repeat the sentence about the angry rioter (from this chapter's opening section)?

Was the sentence "The angry rioter threw the rock *through* the window" or "The angry rioter threw the rock *at* the window"? If the first looks more correct, you—like the participants in the original study—may have recalled the meaning you encoded, not the words that were written (Brewer, 1977). In making such mistakes, our minds are like theater directors who, given a raw script, imagine a finished stage production (Bower & Morrow, 1990).

We can avoid some encoding errors by translating what we see and hear into personally meaningful terms. From his experiments on himself, Hermann Ebbinghaus estimated that, compared with learning nonsense material, learning meaningful material required one-tenth the effort. As another memory researcher noted, "The time you spend thinking about material you are reading and relating it to previously stored material is about the most useful thing you can do in learning any new subject matter" (Wickelgren, 1977, p. 346).

The point to remember: You can profit from taking time to find personal meaning in what you are studying.

Retrieve + Remember

- Which strategies are better for long-term retention: cramming and rereading material, or spreading out learning over time and repeatedly testing yourself?

ANSWER: Although cramming and rereading may lead to short-term gains in knowledge, distributed practice and repeated self-testing will result in the greatest long-term retention.

Memory Storage

LOQ 7-9 What is the capacity of long-term memory? Are our long-term memories processed and stored in specific locations?

In Arthur Conan Doyle's *A Study in Scarlet,* Sherlock Holmes offers a popular theory of memory capacity:

> I consider that a man's brain originally is like a little empty attic, and you have to stock it with such furniture as you choose. . . . It is a mistake to think that that little room has elastic walls and can distend to any extent. Depend upon it, there comes a time when for every addition of knowledge you forget something that you knew before.

Contrary to Holmes' "memory model," our capacity for storing long-term memories has no real limit. Many endure for a lifetime. Our brains are not like attics, which, once filled, can store more items only if we discard old ones.

Retaining Information in the Brain

I [DM] marveled at my aging mother-in-law, a retired pianist and organist. At age 88, her blind eyes could no longer read music. But let her sit at a keyboard and she would flawlessly play any of hundreds of hymns, including ones she had not thought of for 20 years. Where did her brain store those thousands of note patterns?

For a time, some surgeons and memory researchers marveled at what appeared to be vivid memories triggered by stimulating the brain during surgery. Did this prove that our whole past, not just well-practiced music, is "in there," just waiting to be relived? Further research disproved this idea. The vivid flashbacks were actually new creations of a stressed brain, not real memories (Loftus & Loftus, 1980). We do not store information in single, specific spots, as libraries store their books. As with perception, language, emotion, and much more, memory requires brain networks. Many parts of our brain interact as we encode, store, and retrieve information.

Explicit Memory System: The Hippocampus and Frontal Lobes

LOQ 7-10 What roles do the hippocampus and frontal lobes play in memory processing?

Separate brain regions process our explicit and implicit memories. We know this from scans of the brain in action, and from autopsies of people who suffered different types of memory loss.

Explicit, conscious memories are either **semantic** (facts and general knowledge) or **episodic** (experienced events). New explicit memories of these

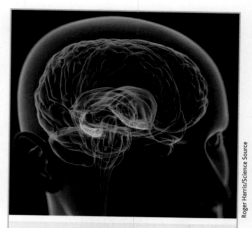

FIGURE 7.5 The hippocampus Explicit memories for facts and episodes are processed in the hippocampus (orange structure) and fed to other brain regions for storage.

Roger Harris/Science Source

facts and episodes are laid down via the **hippocampus,** a limbic system neural center that is our brain's equivalent of a "save" button (**FIGURE 7.5**). Brain scans reveal activity in the hippocampus and nearby brain networks as people form explicit memories of names, images, and events (Squire & Wixted, 2011; Wang et al., 2014). Your hippocampus acts as a loading dock where your brain registers and temporarily stores aspects of an event—its smell, feel, sound, and location.

spacing effect the tendency for distributed study or practice to yield better long-term retention than is achieved through massed study or practice.

testing effect enhanced memory after retrieving, rather than simply rereading, information. Also sometimes referred to as the *retrieval practice effect* or *test-enhanced learning.*

semantic memory explicit memory of facts and general knowledge; one of our two conscious memory systems (the other is *episodic memory*).

episodic memory explicit memory of personally experienced events; one of our two conscious memory systems (the other is *semantic memory*).

hippocampus a neural center located in the limbic system; helps process explicit memories for storage.

HIPPOCAMPUS HERO Among animals, one contender for champion memorist would be a mere birdbrain—the Clark's Nutcracker—which during winter and spring can locate up to 6000 caches of pine seed it had previously buried (Shettleworth, 1993).

Then, like older files shifted to a store-room, memories migrate for storage elsewhere. This storage process is called **memory consolidation.**

Your brain's right and left frontal lobes store different information. Recalling a password and holding it in working memory, for example, would activate your left frontal lobe. Calling up a visual image of last night's party would more likely activate your right frontal lobe.

A good night's sleep supports memory consolidation, both in humans and in rats. In experiments, rats have learned the location of a tasty new food. If their hippocampus is removed 3 hours after they locate the food, no long-term memory will form (Tse et al., 2007). If their hippocampus is removed 48 hours later, after doing its work, they still remember that location. During sleep, the hippocampus and brain cortex display rhythmic patterns of activity, as if they were talking to each other (Ji & Wilson, 2007; Mehta, 2007). Researchers suspect that the brain is replaying the day's experiences as it transfers them to the cortex for long-term storage.

Implicit Memory System: The Cerebellum and Basal Ganglia

LOQ 7-11 What roles do the cerebellum and basal ganglia play in memory processing?

You could lose your hippocampus and still—thanks to automatic processing—lay down *implicit* memories of newly conditioned associations and skills. Memory loss following brain damage left one patient unable to recognize her physician as, each day, he shook her hand and introduced himself. One day, after reaching for his hand, she yanked hers back, for the physician had pricked her with a tack in his palm. When he next introduced himself, she refused to shake his hand but couldn't explain why. Having been *classically conditioned,* she just wouldn't do it (LeDoux, 1996). Implicitly, she felt what she could not explain.

Your *cerebellum,* a brain region extending out from the rear of your brainstem, plays an important role in forming and storing memories created by classical conditioning. People with a damaged cerebellum cannot develop some conditioned reflexes. They can't, for example, link a tone with an oncoming puff of air, so they don't blink just before the puff, as anyone else would learn to do (Daum & Schugens, 1996; Green & Woodruff-Pak, 2000). Implicit memory formation needs the cerebellum.

Your memories of physical skills—walking, cooking, dressing—are also implicit memories. Your *basal ganglia,* deep brain structures involved in motor movement, help form your memories for these skills (Mishkin, 1982; Mishkin et al., 1997). If you have learned how to ride a bike, thank your basal ganglia.

Although not part of our conscious adult memory system, the reactions and skills we learned during infancy reach far into our future. Can you remember learning to talk and walk as a baby? If you cannot, you are not alone. As adults, our *conscious* memory of our first four years is largely blank, an experience called *infantile amnesia.* To form and store

explicit memories, we need a command of language and a well-developed hippocampus. Before age 4, we don't have those learning tools.

Retrieve + Remember

• Which parts of the brain are important for *implicit* memory processing, and which parts play a key role in *explicit* memory processing?

ANSWER: The cerebellum and basal ganglia are important for *implicit* memory processing. The hippocampus and frontal lobes are key to *explicit* memory formation.

• Your friend has experienced brain damage in an accident. He can remember how to tie his shoes but has a hard time remembering anything you tell him during a conversation. How can implicit vs. explicit information processing explain what's going on here?

ANSWER: Our *explicit* conscious memories of facts and episodes differ from our *implicit* memories of skills (such as tying shoelaces) and classically conditioned responses. The parts of the brain involved in explicit memory processing may have sustained damage in the accident, while the parts involved in implicit memory processing appear to have escaped harm.

The Amygdala, Emotions, and Memory

LOQ 7-12 How do emotions affect our memory processing?

Arousal can sear certain events into the brain (Birnbaum et al., 2004; McGaugh, 2015; Strange & Dolan, 2004). Excitement or stress (perhaps at a time you performed in front of a crowd) triggers your glands to produce stress hormones. By making more glucose energy available to fuel brain activity, stress hormones signal the brain that something important is happening. Stress hormones also focus memory. They provoke the *amygdala* (two limbic system, emotion-processing clusters) to boost activity in the brain's memory-forming areas (Buchanan, 2007; Kensinger, 2007) (**FIGURE 7.6**).

The resulting emotions often persist without our conscious awareness of

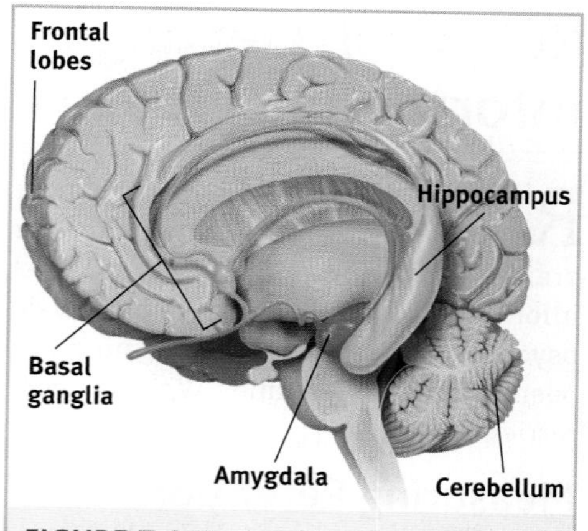

FIGURE 7.6 Review key memory structures in the brain
Frontal lobes and *hippocampus:* explicit memory formation
Cerebellum and *basal ganglia:* implicit memory formation
Amygdala: emotion-related memory formation

what caused them, as one clever experiment demonstrated. The participants were patients with hippocampal damage, which left them unable to form new explicit memories. Researchers first showed them a sad film, and later a happy film. Although these viewers could not consciously recall the films, the sad or happy emotion lingered (Feinstein et al., 2010).

After a horrific experience—a school shooting, a house fire, a rape—vivid memories of the event may intrude again and again. The result is "stronger, more reliable memories" (McGaugh, 1994, 2003). The persistence of such memories is adaptive. They alert us to future dangers. By giving us a mental tunnel vision of the remembered event, they reduce our attention to minor details and focus our attention on the central event (Mather & Sutherland, 2012). Whatever captures our attention gets recalled well, at the expense of the surrounding context.

Why are some memories so much stronger than others? Emotion-triggered hormonal changes help explain why we long remember exciting or shocking events, such as our first kiss or our whereabouts when learning of a loved one's death. Psychologists call them **flashbulb memories.** It's as if the brain commands, "Capture this!" In a 2006 Pew survey, 95 percent of American adults said they could recall exactly where they were or what they were doing when they first heard the news of the 9/11 terrorist attacks. With time, some errors crept in (compared with earlier reports taken right after 9/11). Mostly, however, people's memories of 9/11 remained consistent over the next two to three years (Conway et al., 2009; Hirst et al., 2009; Kvavilashvili et al., 2009).

Which is more important—your experiences or your memories of them?

Dramatic experiences remain clear in our memory in part because we rehearse them. We think about them and describe them to others. Memories of our best experiences, which we enjoy recalling and recounting, also endure (Storm & Jobe, 2012; Talarico & Moore, 2012). One study invited 1563 Boston Red Sox and New York Yankees fans to recall the baseball championship games between their two teams in 2003 (Yankees won) and 2004 (Red Sox won). Fans recalled much better the game their team won (Breslin & Safer, 2011).

Synaptic Changes

LOQ 7-13 How do changes at the synapse level affect our memory processing?

As you read this chapter and learn about memory processes, your brain is changing. Activity in some brain pathways is increasing. Neural network connections are forming and strengthening. Changes are taking place at your *synapses*—the sites where nerve cells communicate with one another by means of chemical messengers (neurotransmitters). Experience alters the brain's neural networks (see Chapter 3).

Eric Kandel and James Schwartz (1982) were able to catch a new memory leaving tracks in neurons of the California sea slug. This simple animal's nerve cells

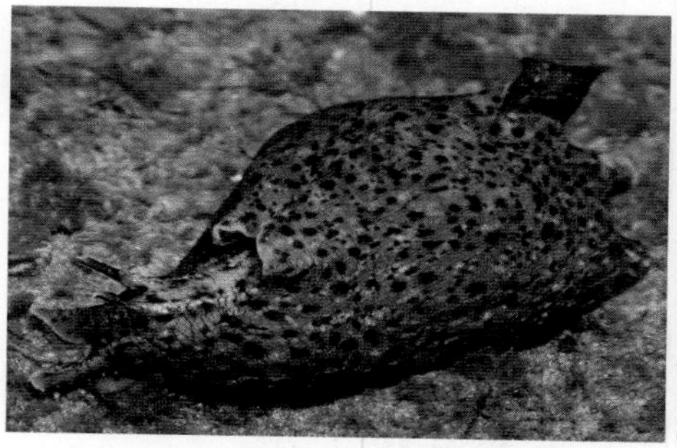

© Donna Ikenberry/Art Directors & TRIP Alamy

MEMORY SLUG The much-studied California sea slug, *Aplysia,* has increased our understanding of the neural basis of learning and memory.

are unusually large, and researchers have been able to observe how they change during learning. Using electric shocks, they have classically conditioned sea slugs to withdraw their gills when squirted with water, much as we might jump at the sound of a firecracker. By observing the slugs' neural connections before and after this conditioning, Kandel and Schwartz pinpointed changes. As a slug learns, it releases more of the neurotransmitter *serotonin* into certain neurons. These cells' synapses then become more efficient at transmitting signals. Experience and learning can increase—even double—the number of synapses, even in slugs (Kandel, 2012). No wonder the brain area that processes spatial memory grows larger as London taxi driver trainees learn to navigate the city's complicated maze of streets (Woolett & Maguire, 2011).

As synapses become more efficient, so do neural networks. Sending neurons now release their neurotransmitters more easily. Receiving neurons may grow additional receptor sites. This increased neural efficiency, called **long-term potentiation (LTP),** enables learning and memory (Lynch, 2002; Whitlock et al., 2006).

memory consolidation the neural storage of a long-term memory.

flashbulb memory a clear memory of an emotionally significant moment or event.

long-term potentiation (LTP) an increase in a cell's firing potential. Believed to be a neural basis for learning and memory.

Several lines of evidence confirm that LTP is a physical basis for memory:

- Rats given a drug that enhanced synaptic efficiency (LTP) learned to run a maze with half the usual number of mistakes (Service, 1994).

- Drugs that block LTP interfere with learning (Lynch & Staubli, 1991).

- Mice that could not produce an enzyme needed for LTP could not learn their way out of a maze (Silva et al., 1992).

After LTP has occurred, an electric current passing through the brain won't erase old memories. Before LTP, the same current can wipe out very recent memories. This often happens when severely depressed people receive electroconvulsive therapy (Chapter 14). Sports concussions can also wipe out recent memories. Football players and boxers knocked unconscious typically have no memory of events just before the blow to the head (Yarnell & Lynch, 1970). Their working memory had no time to process the information into long-term memory before the shutdown.

Recently, I [DM] did a little test of memory consolidation. While on an operating table for a basketball-related tendon repair, I was given a face mask and soon could smell the anesthesia gas. "So how much longer will I be with you?" I asked the anesthesiologist. My last moment of memory was her answer: "About 10 seconds." My brain spent that 10 seconds consolidating a memory for her words, but could not tuck any further memory away before I was out cold.

FIGURE 7.7 summarizes the brain's two-track memory processing and storage system for implicit (automatic) and explicit (effortful) memories. *The bottom line:* Learn something and you change your brain a little.

Retrieve + Remember

- Which brain area responds to stress hormones by helping to create stronger memories?

  ANSWER: the amygdala

- Increased efficiency at the synapses is evidence of the neural basis of learning and memory. This is called _____-_____ _____.

  ANSWER: long-term potentiation

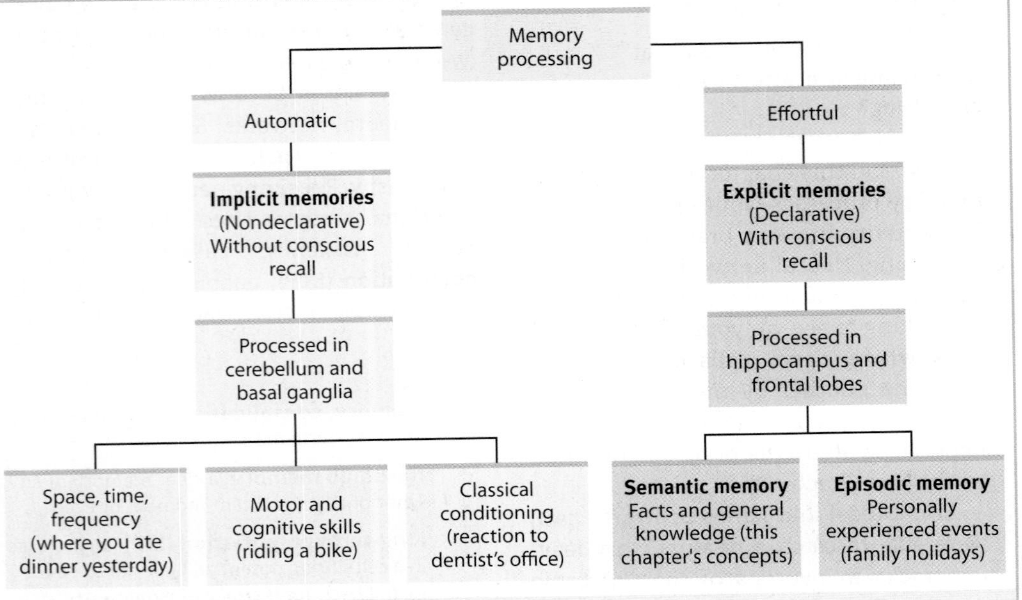

Retrieval: Getting Information Out

Remembering an event requires more than getting information into our brain and storing it there. To use that information, we must retrieve it. How do psychologists test whether learning has been retained over time? What triggers retrieval?

Measuring Retention

LOQ 7-14 How do psychologists assess memory with recall, recognition, and relearning?

Memory is learning that persists over time. Three types of evidence indicate whether something has been learned and retained:

- **Recall**—*retrieving* information out of storage and into your conscious awareness. Example: a fill-in-the-blank question.

- **Recognition**—*identifying* items you previously learned. Example: a multiple-choice question.

- **Relearning**—*learning something more quickly* when you learn it a second or later time. Example: Reviewing the first weeks of course work to prepare for your final exam, you will relearn the material more easily than you did originally.

Long after you cannot recall most of your high school classmates, you may still be able to recognize their yearbook pictures and spot their names in a list of names. One research team found that people who had graduated 25 years earlier could not *recall* many of their old classmates, but they could *recognize* 90 percent of their pictures and names (Bahrick et al., 1975).

Our recognition memory is quick and vast. "Is your friend wearing a new or old outfit?" Old. "Is this 5-second movie clip from a film you've ever seen?" Yes. "Have you ever seen this face before?" No. Before our mouth can form an answer to any of millions of such questions, our mind knows, and knows that it knows.

FIGURE 7.7 Our two memory systems

National News/ZUMAPRESS.com/Newscom

recall memory demonstrated by retrieving information learned earlier, as on a fill-in-the-blank test.

recognition memory demonstrated by identifying items previously learned, as on a multiple-choice test.

relearning memory demonstrated by time saved when learning material a second time.

REMEMBERING THINGS PAST Even if Taylor Swift and Leonardo DiCaprio had not become famous, their high school classmates would most likely still recognize them in these photos.

And it's not just humans who have shown remarkable memory for faces (**FIGURE 7.8**).

Our response speed when recalling or recognizing information indicates memory strength, as does our speed at *relearning*. Memory explorer Ebbinghaus showed this long ago by studying his own learning and memory.

Put yourself in Ebbinghaus' shoes. How could you produce new items to learn? Ebbinghaus' answer was to form a list of all possible nonsense syllables by sandwiching a vowel between two consonants. Then, for a particular experiment, he would randomly select a sample of the syllables, practice them, and test himself. To get a feel for his experiments, rapidly read aloud the following list, repeating it eight times (from Baddeley, 1982). Then, without looking, try to recall the items:

JIH, BAZ, FUB, YOX, SUJ, XIR, DAX, LEQ, VUM, PID, KEL, WAV, TUV, ZOF, GEK, HIW.

The day after learning such a list, Ebbinghaus recalled only a few of the syllables. But were they entirely forgotten? *No.* The more often he practiced the list aloud on Day 1, the fewer times he would have to practice it to *relearn* it on Day 2 (**FIGURE 7.9**).

The point to remember: Tests of recognition and of time spent relearning demonstrate that *we remember more than we can recall.*

FIGURE 7.9 Ebbinghaus' retention curve The more times he practiced a list of nonsense syllables on Day 1, the less time he required to *relearn* it on Day 2. Speed of relearning is one way to measure whether something was learned and retained. (Data from Baddeley, 1982.)

As rehearsal increases, relearning time decreases

FIGURE 7.8 Other animals also display face smarts After food rewards are repeatedly associated with some sheep faces, but not with others, sheep remember those faces for two years (Kendrick & Feng, 2011).

Retrieve + Remember

- Multiple-choice questions test our
  a. recall.
  b. recognition.
  c. learning
  d. sensory memory.

ANSWER: b

- Fill-in-the-blank questions test our _____.

ANSWER: recall

- If you want to be sure to remember what you're learning for an upcoming test, would it be better to use *recall* or *recognition* to check your memory? Why?

ANSWER: It would be better to test your memory with *recall* (such as with short-answer or fill-in-the-blank self-test questions) rather than *recognition* (such as with multiple-choice questions). Recalling information is harder than recognizing it. So if you can recall it, that means your retention of the material is better than if you could only recognize it. Your chances of test success are therefore greater.

Retrieval Cues

LOQ 7-15 How do external events, internal moods, and order of appearance affect memory retrieval?

Imagine a spider suspended in the middle of her web, held up by the many strands extending outward from her in all directions to different points. You could begin at any one of these anchor points and follow the attached strand to the spider.

Retrieving a memory is similar. Memories are held in storage by a web of associations, each piece of information connected to many others. Suppose you encode into your memory the name of the person sitting next to you in class. With that name, you will also encode other bits of information, such as your surroundings, mood, seating position, and so on. These bits serve as **retrieval cues,** anchor points for pathways you can follow to access your classmate's name when you need to recall it later. The more retrieval cues you've encoded, the better your chances of finding a path to the memory suspended in this web of information.

The best retrieval cues come from associations you form at the time you encode a memory—smells, tastes, and sights that can call up your memory of the associated person or event. When trying to recall something, you may mentally place yourself in the original context. For most of us, that includes visual information. After losing his sight, British scholar John Hull (1990, p. 174) described his difficulty recalling such details:

> I knew I had been somewhere, and had done particular things with certain people, but where? I could not put the conversations . . . into a context. There was no background, no features against which to identify the place. Normally, the memories of people you have spoken to during the day are stored in frames which include the background.

LaunchPad For an 8-minute summary of how we access what's stored in our brain, visit LaunchPad's *Video: Memory Retrieval.*

Priming

Often associations are activated without your awareness. Seeing or hearing the word *rabbit* can activate associations with *hare,* even though you may not recall having seen or heard *rabbit* (**FIGURE 7.10**). Although this process, called **priming,** happens without your conscious awareness, it can influence your attitudes and your behavior.

Want to impress your friends with your new knowledge? Ask them three rapid-fire questions:

1. What color is snow?
2. What color are clouds?
3. What do cows drink?

If they answer *milk* to the third question, you have demonstrated priming.

Context-Dependent Memory

Have you noticed? Putting yourself back in the context where you experienced something can prime your memory retrieval. Remembering, in many ways, is an action that depends on our environment (Palmer, 1989). Childhood memories may surface when you visit your childhood home. In one study, scuba

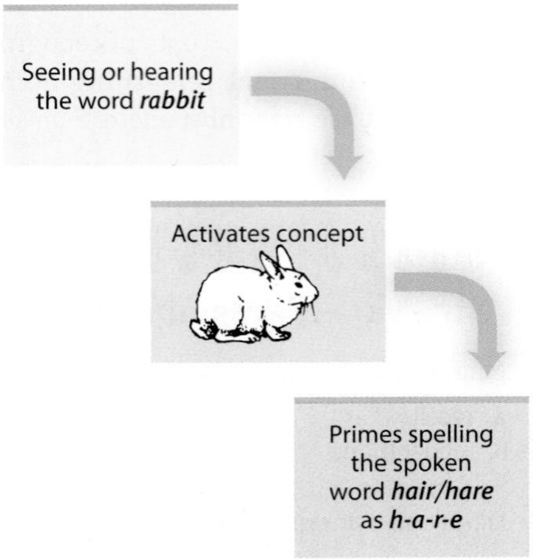

FIGURE 7.10 Priming—awakening associations After seeing or hearing *rabbit,* we are later more likely to spell the spoken word "hair/hare" as *h-a-r-e* (Bower, 1986). Associations unconsciously activate related associations. This process is called priming.

divers listened to a list of words in two different settings, either 10 feet underwater or sitting on the beach (Godden & Baddeley, 1975). Later, the divers recalled more words when they were tested in the same place.

By contrast, experiencing something outside the usual setting can be confusing. Have you ever run into a former teacher in an unusual place, such as at the store? Maybe you recognized the person but struggled to figure out who it was and how you were acquainted. Our memories are *context-dependent* and are affected by the cues we have associated with that context.

State-Dependent Memory

State-dependent memory is closely related to context-dependent memory. What we learn in one state—be it drunk or sober—may be more easily recalled when we are again in that state. What people learn when drunk they don't recall well in *any* state (alcohol disrupts memory storage). But they recall it slightly better when again drunk. Someone who hides money when drunk may forget the location until drunk again.

Moods also influence what we remember (Gaddy & Ingram, 2014). Being happy primes sweet memories. Being angry or depressed primes sour ones. Say you have a terrible evening. Your date canceled, you lost your phone, and now a new red sweatshirt somehow made its way into your white laundry batch. Your bad mood may trigger other unhappy memories. If a friend or family member walks in at this point, your mind may fill with bad memories of that person.

This tendency to recall events that fit our mood is called **mood-congruent memory.** If put in a great mood— whether under hypnosis or just by the day's events (a World Cup soccer victory for German participants in one study)— people recall the world through rose-colored glasses (DeSteno et al., 2000; Forgas et al., 1984; Schwarz et al., 1987). They recall their behaviors as competent and effective. They view other people as kind and giving. And they're sure happy events happen more often than unhappy ones.

Knowing this mood-memory connection, we should not be surprised that in some studies, *currently* depressed people have recalled their parents as rejecting and punishing. *Formerly* depressed people have described their parents in more positive ways—much as do those who have never been depressed (Lewinsohn & Rosenbaum, 1987; Lewis, 1992). Similarly, adolescents' ratings of parental warmth in one week have offered few clues to how they would rate their parents six weeks later (Bornstein et al., 1991). When teens were down, their parents seemed cruel. As moods brightened, those devil parents became angels.

Mood effects on retrieval help explain why our moods persist. When happy, we recall happy events and see the world as a happy place, which prolongs our good mood. When depressed, we recall sad events, which darkens our view of current events. For those predisposed to depression, this process can help maintain a vicious, dark cycle. Moods magnify.

Serial Position Effect

Another memory-retrieval quirk, the **serial position effect,** explains why you may have large holes in your memory of a list of recent events. Imagine it's your first day in a new job, and your manager is introducing co-workers. As you meet each person, you silently repeat everyone's name, starting from the beginning. As the last person smiles and turns away, you hope you'll be able to greet your new co-workers by name the next day.

Don't count on it. Because you have spent more time rehearsing the earlier names than the later ones, those are the names you'll probably recall more easily the next day. In experiments, when people viewed a list of items (words, names, dates, even experienced odors) and immediately tried to recall them in any order, they fell prey to the serial position effect (Reed, 2000). They briefly recalled the last items especially quickly and well (a *recency effect*), perhaps because those last items were still in working memory. But

"I can't remember what we're arguing about, either. Let's keep yelling, and maybe it will come back to us."

after a delay, when their attention was elsewhere, their recall was best for the first items (a *primacy effect;* see **FIGURE 7.11**).

Retrieve + Remember

- What is priming?

ANSWER: *Priming* is the activation (often without our awareness) of associations.

- When we are tested immediately after viewing a list of words, we tend to recall the first and last items best. This is known as the _____ _____ effect.

ANSWER: serial position

---

retrieval cue any stimulus (event, feeling, place, and so on) linked to a specific memory.

priming the activation, often unconsciously, of particular associations in memory.

mood-congruent memory the tendency to recall experiences that are consistent with your current good or bad mood.

serial position effect our tendency to recall best the last and first items in a list.

Forgetting

LOQ 7-16 Why do we forget?

If a memory-enhancing pill ever becomes available, it had better not be too effective. To discard the clutter of useless information—outfits worn last month, your old phone number, restaurant orders already cooked and served—is surely a blessing (Nørby, 2015). Remember meeting the Russian memory whiz S earlier in this chapter? His junk heap of memories dominated his conscious mind. He had difficulty thinking abstractly—generalizing, organizing, evaluating. So does Jill Price, whose incredibly accurate memory of her

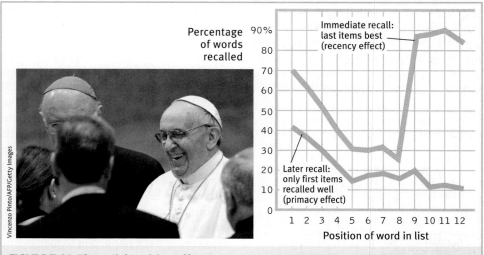

FIGURE 7.11 The serial position effect Immediately after Pope Francis made his way through this receiving line of special guests, he would probably have recalled the names of the last few people best *(recency effect)*. But later he may have been able to recall the first few people best *(primacy effect)*.

THE WOMAN WHO CAN'T FORGET Jill Price, with writer Bart Davis, told her story in a 2008 published memoir. Price remembers every day of her life since age 14 with detailed clarity, including both the joys and the hurts. Researchers have identified enlarged brain areas in people with super memory (Ally et al., 2013; LePort et al., 2012).

life's events has been studied and verified. She reports that her super-memory interferes with her life, with one memory cuing another (McGaugh & LePort, 2014; Parker et al., 2006): "It's like a running movie that never stops."

More often, however, our quirky memories fail us when we least expect it. My [DM's] own memory can easily call up such episodes as that wonderful first kiss with the woman I love, or trivial facts like the air mileage from London to Detroit. Then it abandons me when I discover that I have failed to encode, store, or retrieve a student's name or the spot where I left my sunglasses.

As we process information, we sift, change, or lose most of it (**FIGURE 7.12**).

"Oh, is that today?"

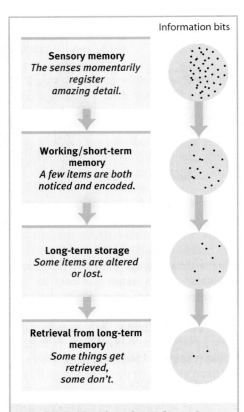

Information bits

Sensory memory
The senses momentarily register amazing detail.

Working/short-term memory
A few items are both noticed and encoded.

Long-term storage
Some items are altered or lost.

Retrieval from long-term memory
Some things get retrieved, some don't.

FIGURE 7.12 When do we forget? Forgetting can occur at any memory stage. When we process information, we filter, alter, or lose much of it.

Forgetting and the Two-Track Mind

For some, memory loss is severe and permanent, as it was for Henry Molaison (H. M.), whom you met earlier in this chapter. Molaison could recall his past, but he could not form new conscious memories. Neurologist Oliver Sacks (1933–2015) described another patient, Jimmie, who was stuck in 1945, the year of his brain injury. When Jimmie gave his age as 19, Sacks set a mirror before him: "Look in the mirror and tell me what you see. Is that a 19-year-old looking out from the mirror?" (Sacks, 1985, pp. 26–27)

Jimmie turned pale, gripped the chair, cursed, then became frantic: "What's going on? What's happened to me? Is this a nightmare? Am I crazy? Is this a joke?" When his attention was directed to some children playing baseball, his panic ended, the dreadful mirror forgotten.

"Waiter, I'd like to order, unless I've eaten, in which case bring me the check."

Sacks showed Jimmie a photo from *National Geographic*. "What is this?" he asked.

"It's the Moon," Jimmie replied.

"No, it's not," Sacks answered. "It's a picture of the Earth taken from the Moon."

"Doc, you're kidding! Someone would've had to get a camera up there!"

"Naturally."

"Hell! You're joking—how the hell would you do that?" Jimmie's wonder was that of a bright young man from the 1940s, amazed by his travel back to the future.

Careful testing of these unique people reveals something even stranger. Although they cannot recall new facts or anything they have done recently, they can learn new skills and can be classically conditioned. Shown hard-to-find figures in pictures (in the *Where's Waldo?* series), they can quickly spot them again later. They can find their way to the bathroom, though without being able to tell you where it is. They can master mirror-image writing, jigsaw puzzles, and even complicated job skills (Schacter, 1992, 1996; Xu & Corkin, 2001). However, *they do all these things with no awareness of having learned them.* They suffer **amnesia.**

Molaison and Jimmie lost their ability to form new explicit memories, but their automatic processing ability remained intact. They could learn *how* to do something, but they had no conscious recall of learning their new skill. Such sad cases confirm that we have two distinct memory systems, controlled by different parts of the brain.

For most of us, forgetting is a less drastic process. Let's consider some of the reasons we forget.

LaunchPad For a 6-minute example of another dramatic case—of an accomplished musician who has lost the ability to form new memories—visit LaunchPad's *Video—Clive Wearing: Living Without Memory.*

Encoding Failure

Much of what we sense we never notice, and what we fail to encode, we will never remember (**FIGURE 7.13**). Age can affect encoding ability. When young adults encode new information, areas of their brain jump into action. In older adults, these areas are slower to respond. Learning and retaining a new neighbor's name or mastering a new smart phone becomes more of a challenge. This encoding lag helps explain age-related memory decline (Grady et al., 1995).

But no matter how young we are, we pay conscious attention to only a limited portion of the vast number of sights and sounds bombarding us. Consider: You have surely seen the Apple logo thousands of times. Can you draw it? In one study, only 1 of 85 UCLA students (including 52 Apple users) could do so accurately (Blake et al., 2015). Without encoding effort, many might-have-been memories never form.

Storage Decay

Even after encoding something well, we may later forget it. That master of nonsense-syllable learning, Hermann Ebbinghaus, also studied how long memories last. After learning his lists of nonsense syllables, such as YOX and JIH, he measured how much he remembered at various times, from 20 minutes to 30 days

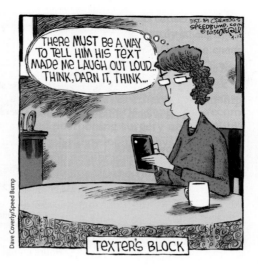

Dave Coverly/Speed Bump

THERE MUST BE A WAY TO TELL HIM HIS TEXT MADE ME LAUGH OUT LOUD... THINK, DARN IT, THINK...

TEXTER'S BLOCK

later. The result was his famous forgetting curve: *The course of forgetting is rapid at first, then levels off with time* (Wixted & Ebbesen, 1991).

People studying Spanish as a foreign language showed this forgetting curve for Spanish vocabulary (Bahrick, 1984). Compared with others who had just completed a high school or college Spanish course, people 3 years out of school had forgotten much of what they had learned. However, what they remembered then, they still remembered 25 and more years later. Their forgetting had leveled off (**FIGURE 7.14**).

One explanation for these forgetting curves is a gradual fading of the physical **memory trace,** which is a physical change in the brain as a memory forms.

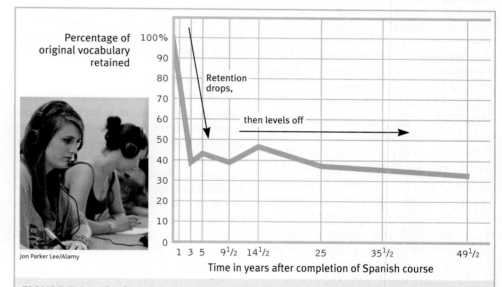

Jon Parker Lee/Alamy

FIGURE 7.14 The forgetting curve for Spanish learned in school Compared with people just completing a Spanish course, those 3 years out of the course remembered much less (on a vocabulary recognition test). Compared with the 3-year group, however, those who studied Spanish even longer ago did not forget much more. (Data from Bahrick, 1984.)

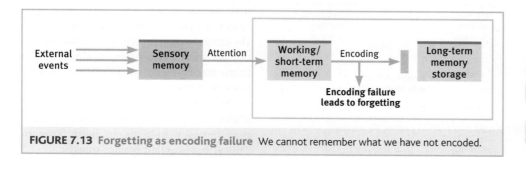

FIGURE 7.13 Forgetting as encoding failure We cannot remember what we have not encoded.

amnesia literally "without memory"—a loss of memory, often due to brain trauma, injury, or disease.

memory trace lasting physical change in the brain as a memory forms.

Researchers are getting closer to solving the mystery of the physical storage and decay of memories. But memories fade for many reasons, including other learning that disrupts our retrieval.

Retrieval Failure

We can compare forgotten events to books you can't find in your local library. Some aren't available because they were never acquired (not encoded). Others have been discarded (stored memories decay).

But there is a third possibility. The book—or memory—may be out of reach because we don't have enough information to access it. For example, what causes frustrating "tip-of-the-tongue" forgetting? (Deaf people fluent in sign language may experience a parallel "tip-of-the-fingers" feeling [Thompson et al., 2005].) These are retrieval problems (**FIGURE 7.15**). Given retrieval cues ("*It begins with an M*"), you may easily retrieve the memory. Older adults more frequently have these frustrating tip-of-the-tongue experiences (Abrams, 2008; Salthouse & Mandell, 2013).

Here's a question to test your memory. Do you recall the second sentence we asked you to remember—about the swimmer? If not, does the word *shark* serve as a retrieval cue? Experiments show that *shark* (the image you probably visualized) more readily retrieves the image you stored than does the sentence's actual word, *fish* (Anderson et al., 1976). (The sentence was "*The fish attacked the swimmer.*")

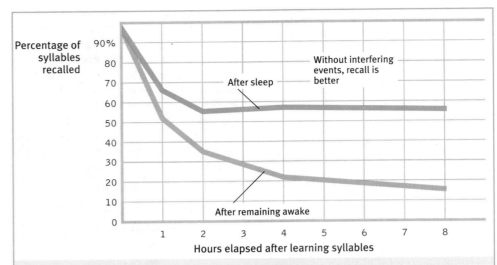

FIGURE 7.16 Retroactive interference People forgot more when they stayed awake and experienced other new material. (Data from Jenkins & Dallenbach, 1924.)

Retrieval problems occasionally stem from interference and even from motivated forgetting.

Interference

As you collect more and more information, your mental attic never fills, but it gets cluttered. Sometimes the clutter interferes, as new and old learning bump into each other and compete for your attention. **Proactive** (forward-acting) **interference** occurs when an older memory makes it more difficult to remember new information. If you buy a new combination lock, your well-rehearsed old combination may interfere with your retrieval of the new one.

Retroactive (backward-acting) **interference** occurs when new learning disrupts your memory of older information.

If someone sings new words to the tune of an old song, you may have trouble remembering the original. It is rather like a second stone being tossed in a pond, disrupting the waves rippling out from the first.

New learning in the hour before we fall asleep suffers less retroactive interference because the chances of disruption are few (Diekelmann & Born, 2010; Nesca & Koulack, 1994). Researchers first discovered this in a now-classic experiment (Jenkins & Dallenbach, 1924). Day after day, two people each learned some nonsense syllables. When they tried to recall them after a night's sleep, they could retrieve more than half the items (**FIGURE 7.16**). But when they learned the material and then stayed awake and involved with other activities, they forgot more, and sooner.

The hour before sleep is a good time to commit information to memory (Scullin & McDaniel, 2010), but not the *seconds* just before sleep (Wyatt & Bootzin, 1994). And if you're considering learning *while* sleeping, forget it. We have little memory for information played aloud in the room during sleep, although our ears do register it (Wood et al., 1992).

Old and new information do not always compete, of course. Knowing Latin may actually help us to learn French. This effect is called *positive transfer*.

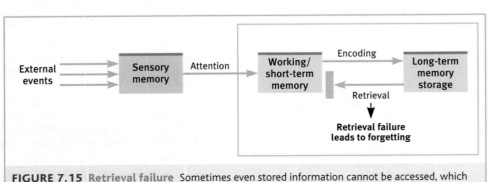

FIGURE 7.15 Retrieval failure Sometimes even stored information cannot be accessed, which leads to forgetting.

LaunchPad | To experience a demonstration and explanation of interference effects on memory, visit LaunchPad's *PsychSim 6: Forgetting*.

Motivated Forgetting

To remember our past is often to revise it. Years ago, the huge cookie jar in my [DM's] kitchen was jammed with freshly baked cookies. Still more were cooling across racks on the counter. A day later, not a crumb was left. Who had taken them? During that time, my wife, three children, and I were the only people in the house. So while memories were still fresh, I conducted a little memory test. Andy admitted wolfing down as many as 20. Peter thought he had eaten 15. Laura guessed she had stuffed her then-6-year-old body with 15 cookies. My wife, Carol, recalled eating 6. I remembered consuming 15 and taking 18 more to the office. We sheepishly accepted responsibility for 89 cookies. Still we had not come close; there had been 160.

Why were our estimates so far off? Was our cookie confusion an *encoding* problem? (Did we just not notice what we had eaten?) Was it a *storage* problem? (Might our memories of cookies, like Ebbinghaus' memory of nonsense syllables, have melted away almost as fast as the cookies themselves?) Or was the information still intact but not *retrievable* because it would be embarrassing to remember?

Sigmund Freud might have argued that our memory systems self-censored this information. He proposed that we **repress** painful or unacceptable memories to protect our self-concept and to minimize anxiety. But the repressed memory lingers, he believed, and can be retrieved by some later cue or during therapy. Repression was central to Freud's psychoanalytic theory (more on that in Chapter 12) and was a popular idea in mid-twentieth century psychology and beyond. An American study revealed that 81 percent of university students, and 60 to 90 percent of therapists (depending on their perspective), believe "traumatic memories

are often repressed" (Patihis et al., 2014a,b). However, increasing numbers of memory researchers think repression rarely, if ever, occurs. People succeed in forgetting unwanted neutral information (yesterday's parking place), but they struggle to forget emotional events (Payne & Corrigan, 2007). Thus, we may have intrusive memories of the very same traumas we would most like to forget.

Retrieve + Remember

- What are three ways we forget, and how does each of these happen?

  ANSWER: (1) *Encoding failure:* Unattended information never entered our memory system. (2) *Storage decay:* Information fades from our memory. (3) *Retrieval failure:* We cannot access stored information accurately, sometimes due to interference or motivated forgetting.

- You will experience less _____ (proactive/retroactive) interference if you learn new material in the hour before sleep than you will if you learn it before turning to another subject.

  ANSWER: retroactive

- Freud believed that we _____ unacceptable memories to minimize anxiety.

  ANSWER: repress

Memory Construction Errors

LOQ 7-17 How do misinformation, imagination, and source amnesia influence our memory construction? How do we decide whether a memory is real or false?

Memory is not exact. Like scientists who infer a dinosaur's appearance from its remains, we infer our past from stored tidbits of information plus what we later imagined, expected, saw, and heard. We don't just retrieve memories; we reweave them (Gilbert, 2006). Our memories are like Wikipedia pages, capable of continuous revision. When we "replay" a memory, we often replace the original with a slightly modified

This is one of those beautiful summer days when I'm flooded with memories of things that never happened to me.

SIPRESS

David Sipress

version (Hardt et al., 2010). (Memory researchers call this **reconsolidation.**) So, in a sense, said Joseph LeDoux (2009), "your memory is only as good as your last memory. The fewer times you use it, the more [unchanged] it is." This means that, to some degree, all memory is false (Bernstein & Loftus, 2009).

Despite knowing all this, I [DM] recently rewrote my own past. It happened at an international conference, where memory researcher Elizabeth Loftus (2012) was demonstrating how memory works. Loftus showed us a handful of individual faces that we were later to identify, as if in a police lineup. Then she showed us some pairs of faces, one face we had seen earlier and one we had not, and asked us to identify the one we had seen. But one pair she had slipped in included *two* new faces, one of which was rather *like* a face we had seen earlier. Most of us understandably

proactive interference the forward-acting disruptive effect of older learning on the recall of *new* information.

retroactive interference the backward-acting disruptive effect of newer learning on the recall of *old* information.

repression in psychoanalytic theory, the basic defense mechanism that banishes from consciousness the thoughts, feelings, and memories that arouse anxiety.

reconsolidation a process in which previously stored memories, when retrieved, are potentially altered before being stored again.

but wrongly identified this face as one we had previously seen. To climax the demonstration, when she showed us the originally seen face and the previously chosen wrong face, most of us picked the wrong face! As a result of our memory reconsolidation, we—an audience of psychologists who should have known better—had replaced the original memory with a false memory.

Clinical researchers have experimented with memory reconsolidation. People recalled a traumatic or negative experience and then had the reconsolidation of that memory disrupted, with a drug or brief, painless electroconvulsive shock (Kroes et al., 2014; Lonergan, 2013). Someday it might become possible to erase your memory of a specific traumatic experience—by reactivating that memory and then disrupting its storage. Would you wish for this? If brutally assaulted, would you welcome having your memory of the attack and its associated fears deleted?

Misinformation and Imagination Effects

In more than 200 experiments involving more than 20,000 people, Loftus has shown how eyewitnesses reconstruct their memories when questioned after a crime or an accident. In one important study, two groups of people watched a film clip of a traffic accident and then answered questions about what they had seen (Loftus & Palmer, 1974).

Those asked, "About how fast were the cars going when they *smashed* into each other?" gave higher speed estimates than those asked, "About how fast were the cars going when they *hit* each other?" A week later, when asked whether they recalled seeing any broken glass, people who had heard *smashed* in the leading (suggestive) version of the question were more than twice as likely to report seeing glass fragments (**FIGURE 7.17**). In fact, the film showed no broken glass.

> "Memory is insubstantial. Things keep replacing it. Your batch of snapshots will both fix and ruin your memory. . . . You can't remember anything from your trip except the wretched collection of snapshots."
>
> Annie Dillard, "To Fashion a Text," 1988

In many follow-up experiments around the world, others have witnessed an event. Then they have received or not received misleading information about it. And then they have taken a memory test. The repeated result is a **misinformation effect.** Exposed to misleading information, we tend to misremember (Loftus et al., 1992). Coke cans become peanut cans. Breakfast cereal becomes eggs. A clean-shaven man morphs into a man with a mustache.

Just hearing a vivid retelling of an event may implant false memories. One experiment falsely suggested to some Dutch university students that, as children, they had become ill after eating spoiled egg salad (Geraerts et al., 2008). After

absorbing that suggestion, they were less likely to eat egg salad sandwiches, both immediately and four months later.

Even repeatedly *imagining* fake actions and events can create false memories. Canadian university students were asked to recall two events from their past. One event actually happened; the other was a false event that involved committing a crime, such as assaulting someone with a weapon. Initially, none of the lawful students remembered breaking the law. But after repeated interviewing, 70 percent of students reported a detailed false memory of having committed the crime (Shaw & Porter, 2015).

Should we be surprised that digitally altered photos have produced the same result? In experiments, researchers have altered photos from a family album to show some family members taking a hot-air balloon ride. After viewing these photos (rather than photos showing just the balloon), children "remembered" the faked experience. And days later, they reported even richer details of their false memories (Strange et al., 2008; Wade et al., 2002).

In British and Canadian university surveys, nearly one-fourth of students have reported personal memories that they later realized were not accurate (Mazzoni et al., 2010). I [DM] empathize. For decades, my cherished earliest memory was of my parents getting off the bus and walking to our house, bringing my baby brother home from the hospital. When, in middle age, I shared that memory with my father, he assured me they did *not* bring their newborn home on the Seattle Transit System. The human mind, it seems, comes with built-in Photoshopping software.

Source Amnesia

What is the weakest part of a memory? Its source. Have you ever recognized someone but had no idea where you had met the person? Or dreamed about an event and later wondered whether it really happened? Or misrecalled *how* you learned about something

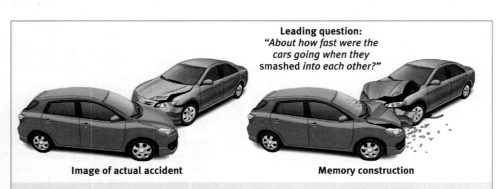

FIGURE 7.17 Memory construction In this experiment, people viewed a film clip of a car accident (left). Those who later were asked a leading question recalled a more serious accident than they had witnessed (Loftus & Palmer, 1974).

Leading question:
"About how fast were the cars going when they smashed into each other?"

Image of actual accident   Memory construction

(Henkel et al., 2000)? If so, you experienced **source amnesia**—you retained the memory of the event but not of its context. Source amnesia, along with the misinformation effect, is at the heart of many false memories. Authors and songwriters sometimes suffer from it. They think an idea came from their own creative imagination, when in fact they are unintentionally plagiarizing something they earlier read or heard.

Psychologist Donald Thompson became part of his own research on memory distortion when police brought him in for questioning about a rape. Although he was a near-perfect match to the victim's memory of the rapist, Thompson had an airtight alibi. Just before the rape occurred, he was being interviewed on live TV and could not possibly have made it to the crime scene. Then it came to light that the victim had been watching the interview—ironically about face recognition—and had experienced source amnesia. She had confused her memories of Thompson with those of the rapist (Schacter, 1996).

Source amnesia also helps explain **déjà vu** (French for "already seen"). Two-thirds of us have experienced this fleeting, eerie sense that "I've been in this exact situation before." The key to déjà vu seems to be that we are familiar with a stimulus or one like it but can't recall where we ran into it before (Cleary, 2008). Normally, we experience a feeling of *familiarity* (thanks to temporal lobe processing) before we consciously remember details (thanks to hippocampus and frontal lobe processing). Sometimes, though, we may have a feeling of familiarity without conscious recall. As our amazing brain tries to make sense of this source amnesia, we get an eerie feeling that we're reliving some earlier part of our life.

> "Do you ever get that strange feeling of vujà dé? Not déjà vu; vujà dé. It's the distinct sense that, somehow, something just happened that has never happened before. Nothing seems familiar. And then suddenly the feeling is gone. Vujà dé."
>
> Comedian George Carlin (1937–2008), *Funny Times*, December 2001

Retrieve + Remember

- What—given the commonness of source amnesia—might life be like if we remembered all our daily experiences and all our dreams?

ANSWER: Real experiences would be confused with those we dreamed. When seeing someone we know, we might therefore be unsure whether we were reacting to something they previously did or to something we dreamed they did.

Recognizing False Memories

We often are confident of our inaccurate memories. Because the misinformation effect and source amnesia happen outside our awareness, it is hard to separate false memories from real ones (Schooler et al., 1986). Perhaps you can recall describing a childhood experience to a friend and filling in memory gaps with reasonable guesses. We all do it. After more retellings, those guessed details—now absorbed into your memory—may feel as real as if you had actually observed them (Roediger et al., 1993). False memories, like fake diamonds, seem so real. False memories can be persistent. Imagine that we were to read aloud a list of words such as *candy, sugar, honey,* and *taste.* Later, we ask you to recognize those words in a larger list. If you are at all like the people in a famous experiment (Roediger & McDermott, 1995), you would err three out of four times—by falsely remembering a new but similar word, such as *sweet.* We more easily remember the *gist*—the general idea—than the words themselves.

Memory construction errors can help us understand why some people have been sent to prison for crimes they never committed. Of 337 people who were later proven not guilty by DNA testing, 71 percent had been convicted because of faulty eyewitness identification (Innocence Project, 2015; Smalarz & Wells, 2015). "Hypnotically refreshed" memories of crimes often contain similar errors.

If a hypnotist asks leading questions ("*Did you hear loud noises?*"), witnesses may weave that false information into their memory of the event. Memory construction errors also seem to be at work in many "recovered" memories of childhood abuse. See Thinking Critically About: Can Memories of Childhood Sexual Abuse Be Repressed and Then Recovered?

LaunchPad To participate in a simulated experiment on false memory formation, and to review related research, visit LaunchPad's *PsychSim 6: Can You Trust Your Memory?* For a 5-minute demonstration and explanation of a false memory experiment, visit LaunchPad's *Video: Creating False Memories—A Laboratory Study.*

Children's Eyewitness Recall

LOQ 7-19 How reliable are young children's eyewitness descriptions?

If memories can be sincere, yet sincerely wrong, how can jurors decide cases in which children's memories of sexual abuse are the only evidence?

Stephen Ceci (1993) thinks "it would be truly awful to ever lose sight of the enormity of child abuse." Yet Ceci and Maggie Bruck's (1993, 1995) studies have made them aware of how easily children's memories can be molded. For example, they asked 3-year-olds to show on anatomically correct dolls where a pediatrician had touched them. Of the children who had not received genital examinations, 55 percent pointed to either genital or anal areas.

---

misinformation effect when a memory has been corrupted by misleading information.

source amnesia faulty memory for how, when, or where information was learned or imagined.

déjà vu that eerie sense that "I've experienced this before." Cues from the current situation may unconsciously trigger retrieval of an earlier experience.

Thinking Critically About:
Can Memories of Childhood Sexual Abuse Be Repressed and Then Recovered?

LOQ 7-18 Why have reports of repressed and recovered memories been so hotly debated?

Two Possible Tragedies:

1. People doubt childhood sexual abuse survivors who tell their secret.

2. Innocent people are falsely accused, as therapists prompt "recovered" memories of childhood sexual abuse:

*"Victims of sexual abuse often have your symptoms. So maybe you were abused and **repressed** the memory. Let's see if I can help you recover the memory, by digging back and visualizing your trauma."*

 Well-intentioned therapist

Misinformation effect and **source amnesia:** Client may form image of threatening person.

With *rehearsal* (repeated therapy sessions), the image grows more vivid.

Client is stunned, angry, and ready to confront or sue the remembered abuser.

Accused person is equally stunned and vigorously denies the accusation.

Professional organizations (including the American Medical, American Psychological, and American Psychiatric Associations) are working to find sensible common ground to resolve psychology's "memory war": [1]

• **Childhood sexual abuse happens** and can leave its victims at risk for problems ranging from sexual dysfunction to depression.[2] But there is no "survivor syndrome"—no group of symptoms that lets us spot victims of sexual abuse.[3]

• **Injustice happens.** Innocent people have been falsely convicted. And guilty people have avoided punishment by casting doubt on their truth-telling accusers.

• **Forgetting happens.** Children abused when very young may not have understood the meaning of their experience or remember it. Forgetting long-ago good and bad events is an ordinary part of everyday life.

• **Recovered memories are common.** Cued by a remark or an experience, we may recover pleasant or unpleasant memories of long-forgotten events. But does the unconscious mind *forcibly repress* painful experiences, and can these experiences be *recovered* by therapist-aided techniques?[4] Memories that surface naturally are more likely to be true.[5]

• **Memories of events before age 4 are unreliable.** As noted earlier, *infantile amnesia* results from not yet developed brain pathways. Most psychologists therefore doubt "recovered" memories of abuse during infancy.[6] The older a child was when suffering sexual abuse, and the more severe the abuse, the more likely it is to be remembered.[7]

• **Memories "recovered" under hypnosis are especially unreliable.**

• **Memories, whether real or false, can be emotionally upsetting.** What was born of mere suggestion can become, like an actual event, a stinging memory that drives bodily stress.[8]

Psychologists question whether *repression* ever occurs. (See Chapter 12 for more on this concept—the cornerstone of Freud's theory and of so much popular psychology.)

Traumatic experiences (witnessing a loved one's murder, being terrorized by a hijacker or rapist, losing everything in a natural disaster) → **TYPICALLY LEAD TO** → **vivid, persistent, haunting memories**[9]

---

1. Patihis et al., 2014a. 2. Freyd et al., 2007. 3. Kendall-Tackett et al., 1993. 4. McNally & Geraerts, 2009. 5. Geraerts et al., 2007. 6. Gore-Felton et al., 2000; Knapp & VandeCreek, 2000. 7. Goodman et al., 2003. 8. McNally, 2003, 2007. 9. Porter & Peace, 2007.

In other experiments, the researchers studied the effect of suggestive interviewing techniques (Bruck & Ceci, 1999, 2004). In one study, children chose a card from a deck of possible happenings, and an adult then read the card to them. For example, "Think real hard, and tell me if this ever happened to you. Can you remember going to the hospital with a mousetrap on your finger?" In weekly interviews, the same adult repeatedly asked children to think about several real and fictitious events. After 10 weeks of this, a new adult asked the same questions. The stunning result: 58 percent of preschoolers produced false (often vivid) stories about one or more events they had never experienced (Ceci et al., 1994). Here's one:

> My brother Colin was trying to get Blowtorch [an action figure] from me, and I wouldn't let him take it from me, so he pushed me into the wood pile where the mousetrap was. And then my finger got caught in it. And then we went to the hospital, and my mommy, daddy, and Colin drove me there, to the hospital in our van, because it was far away. And the doctor put a bandage on this finger.

Given such detailed stories, professional psychologists who specialize in interviewing children could not reliably separate the real memories from the false ones. Nor could the children themselves. The child quoted above, reminded that his parents had told him several times that the mousetrap event never happened—that he had imagined it—protested. "But it really did happen. I remember it!"

We shouldn't forget that children can be accurate eyewitnesses. When a neutral person has asked nonleading

questions soon after the event, using words the children could understand, children often accurately recalled what happened and who did it (Goodman & Quas, 2008; Pipe et al., 2004).

Retrieve + Remember

- Imagine being a jury member in a trial for a parent accused of sexual abuse based on a recovered memory. What insights from memory research should you offer the jury?

ANSWER: It will be important to remember the key points agreed upon by most researchers and professional associations: Sexual abuse, injustice, forgetting, and memory construction all happen; recovered memories are common; memories from our first four years are unreliable; memories claimed to be recovered through hypnosis or drug influence are especially unreliable; and memories, whether real or false, can be emotionally upsetting.

LaunchPad Consider how researchers have studied these issues with Launch-Pad's *IMMERSIVE LEARNING: How Would You Know If People's Memories Are Accurate?*

Improving Memory

LOQ 7-20 How can you use memory research findings to do better in this course and in others?

Biology's findings benefit medicine. Botany's findings benefit agriculture. Can psychology's research on memory benefit your performance in class and on tests? You bet! Here, for easy reference, is a summary of research-based suggestions that can help you remember information when you need it. The SQ3R—Survey, Question, Read, Retrieve, Review—study technique introduced in Chapter 1 includes several of these strategies:

Rehearse repeatedly. To master material, remember the *spacing effect* and use *distributed*

THINKING AND MEMORY What's the best way to retain new information? Think actively as you read. That includes rehearsing and relating ideas and making the material personally meaningful.

(spaced) practice. To learn a concept, give yourself many separate study sessions. Take advantage of life's little intervals—riding a bus, walking across campus, waiting for class to start. New memories are weak; exercise them and they will strengthen. To memorize specific facts or figures, research has shown that you should "rehearse the name or number you are trying to memorize, wait a few seconds, rehearse again, wait a little longer, rehearse again, then wait longer still and rehearse yet again. The waits should be as long as possible without losing the information" (Landauer, 2001). Rehearsal will help you retain material. As the *testing effect* has shown, it pays to study actively. Take lecture notes by hand. That way you will summarize the material in your own words, which will lead to better retention than typing the lecture word for word on your laptop. "The pen is mightier than the keyboard," note researchers Pam Mueller and Daniel Oppenheimer (2014).

In the discussion of mnemonics, we gave you six words and told you we would quiz you about them later. How many of those words can you now recall? Of these, how many are concrete, vivid-image words? How many describe abstract ideas? (You can check your list against the one below.)

Bicycle, void, cigarette, inherent, fire, process

Make the material meaningful. You can build a network of retrieval cues by taking notes in your own words, and then increase these cues by forming as many associations as possible. Apply the concepts to your own life. Form images. Understand and organize information. Relate the material to what you already know or have experienced. As William James (1890) suggested, "Knit each new thing on to some acquisition already there." Mindlessly repeating someone else's words without taking the time to really understand what they mean won't supply many retrieval cues. On an exam, you may find yourself stuck when a question uses terms different from the ones you memorized.

Activate retrieval cues. Remember the importance of *context-dependent* and state-dependent memory. Mentally re-create the situation in which your original learning occurred. Imagine returning to the same location and being in the same mood. Jog your memory by allowing one thought to cue the next.

Use mnemonic devices. Make up a story that uses *vivid images* of the items. *Chunk* information for easier retrieval.

Minimize proactive and retroactive interference. Study before sleeping. Do not schedule back-to-back study times for topics that are likely to interfere with each other, such as Spanish and French.

Sleep more. During sleep, the brain reorganizes and *consolidates* information for long-term memory. Sleep deprivation disrupts this process (Frenda et al., 2014). Even 10 minutes of waking rest enhances memory of what we have read (Dewar et al., 2012). So, after a period of hard study, you might just sit or lie down for a few minutes before tackling the next subject.

Test your own knowledge, both to rehearse it and to find out what you don't yet know. The *testing* effect is real, and it is powerful. Don't become overconfident because you can *recognize* information.

Test your *recall* using the Retrieve + Remember items found throughout each chapter, and the numbered Learning Objective Questions and Chapter Test questions at the end of each chapter. Outline sections using a blank page. Define the terms and concepts listed at each chapter's end before turning back to their definitions. Take practice tests; the online resources that accompany many texts, including LaunchPad for this text, are a good source for such tests.

Retrieve + Remember

- Which memory strategies can help you study smarter and retain more information?

ANSWER: Spend more time rehearsing or actively thinking about the material to boost long-term recall. Schedule spaced (not crammed) study times. Make the material personally meaningful, with well-organized and vivid associations. Refresh your memory by returning to contexts and moods that activate retrieval cues. Use mnemonic devices. Minimize interference. Plan for a complete night's sleep. Test yourself repeatedly—retrieval practice is a proven retention strategy.

CHAPTER REVIEW

Memory

Test yourself by taking a moment to answer each of these Learning Objective Questions (repeated here from within the chapter). Then turn to Appendix D, Complete Chapter Reviews, to check your answers. Research suggests that trying to answer these questions on your own will improve your long-term memory of the concepts (McDaniel et al., 2009).

Studying Memory

7-1: What is *memory,* and how do information-processing models help us study memory?

7-2: What is the three-stage information-processing model, and how has later research updated this model?

Building Memories: Encoding

7-3: How do implicit and explicit memories differ?

7-4: What information do we process automatically?

7-5: How does sensory memory work?

7-6: What is our short-term memory capacity?

7-7: What are some effortful processing strategies that can help us remember new information?

7-8: Why is cramming ineffective, and what is the *testing effect?* Why is it important to make new information meaningful?

Memory Storage

7-9: What is the capacity of long-term memory? Are our long-term memories processed and stored in specific locations?

7-10: What roles do the hippocampus and frontal lobes play in memory processing?

7-11: What roles do the cerebellum and basal ganglia play in memory processing?

7-12: How do emotions affect our memory processing?

7-13: How do changes at the synapse level affect our memory processing?

Retrieval: Getting Information Out

7-14: How do psychologists assess memory with recall, recognition, and relearning?

7-15: How do external events, internal moods, and order of appearance affect memory retrieval?

Forgetting

7-16: Why do we forget?

Memory Construction Errors

7-17: How do misinformation, imagination, and source amnesia influence our memory construction? How do we decide whether a memory is real or false?

7-18: Why have reports of repressed and recovered memories been so hotly debated?

7-19: How reliable are young children's eyewitness descriptions?

Improving Memory

7-20: How can you use memory research findings to do better in this course and in others?

TERMS AND CONCEPTS TO REMEMBER

Test yourself on these terms by trying to write down the definition in your own words before flipping back to the referenced page to check your answer.

CHAPTER TEST

Test yourself repeatedly throughout your studies. This will not only help you figure out what you know and don't know; the testing itself will help you learn and remember the information more effectively thanks to the *testing effect*.

1. The psychological terms for taking in information, retaining it, and later getting it back out are _____, _____, and _____.

2. The concept of working memory
   a. clarifies the idea of short-term memory by focusing on the active processing that occurs in this stage.
   b. splits short-term memory into two substages—sensory memory and working memory.
   c. splits short-term memory into two areas—working (retrievable) memory and inaccessible memory.
   d. clarifies the idea of short-term memory by focusing on space, time, and frequency.

3. Sensory memory may be visual (_____ memory) or auditory (_____ memory).

4. Our short-term memory for new information is limited to about _____ items.

5. Memory aids that use visual imagery or other organizational devices are called _____.

6. The hippocampus seems to function as a
   a. temporary processing site for explicit memories.
   b. temporary processing site for implicit memories.
   c. permanent storage area for emotion-based memories.
   d. permanent storage area for iconic and echoic memories.

7. Hippocampus damage typically leaves people unable to learn new facts or recall recent events. However, they may be able to learn new skills, such as riding a bicycle, which is an _____ (explicit/implicit) memory.

8. Long-term potentiation (LTP) refers to
   a. emotion-triggered hormonal changes.
   b. the role of the hippocampus in processing explicit memories.
   c. an increase in a cell's firing potential.
   d. aging people's potential for learning.

9. A psychologist who asks you to write down as many objects as you can remember having seen a few minutes earlier is testing your _____.

10. Specific odors, visual images, emotions, or other associations that help us access a memory are examples of _____ _____.

11. When you feel sad, why might it help to look at pictures that reawaken some of your best memories?

12. When tested immediately after viewing a list of words, people tend to recall the first and last items more readily than those in the middle. When retested after a delay, they are most likely to recall
    a. the first items on the list.
    b. the first and last items on the list.
    c. a few items at random.
    d. the last items on the list.

13. When forgetting is due to encoding failure, information has not been transferred from
    a. the environment into sensory memory.
    b. sensory memory into long-term memory.
    c. long-term memory into short-term memory.
    d. short-term memory into long-term memory.

14. Ebbinghaus' "forgetting curve" shows that after an initial decline, memory for novel information tends to
    a. increase slightly.
    b. decrease noticeably.
    c. decrease greatly.
    d. level out.

15. The hour before sleep is a good time to memorize information, because going to sleep after learning new material minimizes _____ interference.

16. Freud proposed that painful or unacceptable memories are blocked from consciousness through a mechanism called _____.

17. One reason false memories form is our tendency to fill in memory gaps with our reasonable guesses and assumptions, sometimes based on misleading information. This tendency is an example of
    a. proactive interference.
    b. the misinformation effect.
    c. retroactive interference.
    d. the forgetting curve.

18. Eliza's family loves to tell the story of how she "stole the show" as a 2-year-old, dancing at her aunt's wedding reception. Even though she was so young, Eliza says she can recall the event clearly. How is this possible?

19. We may recognize a face at a social gathering but be unable to remember how we know that person. This is an example of _____ _____.

20. When a situation triggers the feeling that "I've been here before," you are experiencing _____ _____.

21. Children can be accurate eyewitnesses if
    a. interviewers give the children hints about what really happened.
    b. a neutral person asks nonleading questions soon after the event.
    c. the children have a chance to talk with involved adults before the interview.
    d. interviewers use precise technical and medical terms.

22. Psychologists involved in the study of memories of abuse tend to *disagree* with each other about which of the following statements?
    a. Memories of events that happened before age 4 are not reliable.
    b. We tend to repress extremely upsetting memories.
    c. Memories can be emotionally upsetting.
    d. Sexual abuse happens.

Find answers to these questions in Appendix E, in the back of the book.

IN YOUR EVERYDAY LIFE

Answering these questions will help you make these concepts more personally meaningful, and therefore more memorable.

1. What has your memory system encoded, stored, and retrieved today?

2. How do you make psychology terms more personally meaningful so you remember them better? Could you do this more often?

3. Can you recall a time when stress helped you remember something? Has stress ever made it more difficult to remember something?

4. In what ways do you notice your moods coloring your memories, perceptions, or expectations?

5. Most people wish for a better memory. Is that true of you? Do you ever wish you were better at forgetting certain memories?

6. If you were on a jury in a trial involving recovered memories of abuse, do you think you could be impartial? Would it matter whether the defendant was a parent accused of sexual abuse, or a therapist being sued for creating a false memory?

7. Think of a memory you frequently recall. How might you have changed it without conscious awareness?

8. Which of the study and memory strategies suggested at the end of this chapter do you plan to try first?

Use 📖 LearningCurve to create your personalized study plan, which will direct you to the resources that will help you most in 📖 LaunchPad.

SURVEY THE CHAPTER

8

Thinking, Language, and Intelligence

Throughout history, we humans have celebrated our wisdom and be-moaned our foolishness. In this book we likewise marvel at both our abilities and our errors. As our brain develops, our mind blossoms. We move from the amazing abilities of the newborn, to the logic of adolescence, to the wisdom of older age. Our sensory systems gather count-less sensations, convert them into nerve impulses, and send them to multiple brain sites, forming meaningful perceptions. Meanwhile, our two-track mind is processing, interpreting, and storing vast amounts of information, with and without our awareness. Not bad for the cabbage-sized three pounds of wet tis-sue jammed inside our skull.

Yet we are also sometimes simple-minded or error-prone. Our species is kin to the other animals, influenced by the same principles that produce learning in rats, pigeons, and even slugs. Sometimes our thinking fails us. We not-so-wise humans are easily fooled by perceptual illusions, fake psychic claims, and false memories.

In this chapter, we find more examples of these two images—the ratio-nal and irrational human. We will consider thinking, and how we use—and sometimes ignore or misuse—information about the world around us. We will look at our gift for language and why and how it develops. And we will reflect on intelligence. How deserving are we of the meaning of our species' name, *Homo sapiens*—wise human?

Thinking

Concepts

LOQ LearningObjectiveQuestion

8-1 What is cognition, and what are the functions of concepts?

Psychologists who study **cognition** focus on the mental activities associated with thinking, knowing, remembering, and communicating information. One of these activities is forming **concepts**—mental groupings of similar objects, events, ideas, or people. The concept *chair* includes many items— a baby's high chair, a reclining chair, a dentist's chair.

Concepts simplify our thinking. Imagine life without them. We could not ask a child to "throw the ball" because there would be no concept of *throw* or *ball*. We could not say "They were angry." We would have to describe expressions and words. Concepts such as *ball* and *anger* give us much information with little mental effort.

We often form our concepts by developing a **prototype**—a mental image or best example of a category (Rosch, 1978). People more quickly agree that "a robin is a bird" than that "a penguin is a bird." For most of us, the robin is the "birdier" bird; it more closely resembles our *bird* prototype. When something closely matches our prototype of a concept, we readily recognize it as an example of the concept.

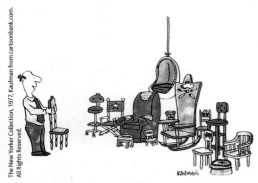

"Attention, everyone! I'd like to introduce the newest member of our family."

Sometimes, though, our experiences don't match up neatly with our prototypes. When this happens, our category boundaries may blur. Is a 17-year-old female a girl or a woman? Is a whale a fish or a mammal? Is a tomato a fruit? Because a tomato fails to match our *fruit* prototype, we are slower to recognize it as a fruit.

Similarly, when symptoms don't fit one of our disease prototypes, we are slow to perceive an illness (Bishop, 1991). People whose heart attack symptoms (shortness of breath, exhaustion, a dull weight in the chest) don't match their *heart attack* prototype (sharp chest pain) may not seek help. Concepts speed and guide our thinking. But they don't always make us wise.

Solving Problems

LOQ 8-2 What cognitive strategies help us solve problems, and what tendencies work against us?

One tribute to our rationality is our impressive problem-solving skill. What's the best route around this traffic jam? How should we handle a friend's criticism? How can we get in the house without our keys?

Some problems we solve through *trial and error*. Thomas Edison tried thousands of light bulb filaments before stumbling upon one that worked. For other problems, we use **algorithms,** step-by-step procedures that guarantee a solution. But following the steps in an algorithm takes time and effort—sometimes a lot of time and effort. To find a word using the 10 letters in *SPLOYOCHYG*, for example, you could construct a list, with each letter in each of the 10 positions. But your list of 907,200 different combinations would be very long! In such cases, we often resort to **heuristics,** simpler thinking strategies. Thus, you might reduce the number of options in the *SPLOYOCHYG* example by grouping letters that often appear together (*CH* and *GY*) and avoiding rare combinations (such as *YY*). By using heuristics and

then applying trial and error, you may hit on the answer. Have you guessed it?[1]

Sometimes we puzzle over a problem, with no feeling of getting closer to the answer. Then, suddenly the pieces fall together in a flash of **insight**—an abrupt, true-seeming, and often satisfying solution (Topolinski & Reber, 2010). Ten-year-old Johnny Appleton had one of these Aha! moments and solved a problem that had stumped many adults. How could they rescue a young robin that had fallen into a narrow, 30-inch-deep hole in a cement-block wall? Johnny's solution: Slowly pour in sand, giving the bird enough time to keep its feet on top of the constantly rising mound (Ruchlis, 1990).

Bursts of brain activity accompany sudden flashes of insight (Kounios & Beeman, 2009; Sandkühler & Bhattacharya, 2008). In one study, researchers asked people to think of a word that forms a compound word or phrase with each of three words in a set (such as *pine, crab,* and *sauce*). When people knew the answer, they were to press a button, which would sound a bell. (Need a hint? The word is a fruit.[2]) About half the solutions arrived by a sudden Aha! insight. Before the Aha! moment, the problem solvers' frontal lobes (which are involved in focusing attention) were active. Then, at the instant of discovery, there was a burst of activity in their right temporal lobe, just above the ear (**FIGURE 8.1**).

Insight gives us a happy sense of satisfaction. The joy of a joke is similarly a sudden "I get it!" reaction to a double meaning or a surprise ending: "You don't need a parachute to skydive. You only need a parachute to skydive twice." Comedian Groucho Marx was a master at this: "I once shot an elephant in my pajamas. How he got into my pajamas I'll never know."

Insightful as we are, other cognitive tendencies may lead us astray.

---

1 Answer to SPLOYOCHYG problem: PSYCHOLOGY

2 The word is *apple*: pineapple, crabapple, applesauce.

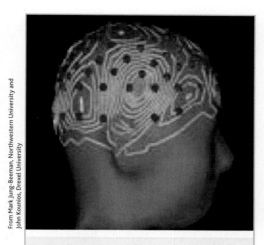

FIGURE 8.1 **The Aha! moment** A burst of right temporal lobe EEG activity (yellow area) accompanied insight solutions to word problems (Jung-Beeman et al., 2004). The red dots show placement of the EEG electrodes. The light gray lines show patterns of brain activity during insight.

Confirmation bias is our tendency to seek evidence *for* our ideas more eagerly than we seek evidence *against* them (Klayman & Ha, 1987; Skov & Sherman, 1986). Peter Wason (1960) demonstrated confirmation bias in a now-classic study. He gave students a set of three numbers (2-4-6) and told them the sequence was based on a rule. Their task was to guess the rule. (It was simple: Each number must be larger than the one before it.) Before giving their answers, students formed their own three-number sets, and Wason told them whether their sets worked with his rule. When they felt certain they had the rule, they could announce it. The result? Most students formed a wrong idea ("Maybe it's counting by twos") and then searched only for evidence confirming the wrong rule (by testing 6-8-10, 100-102-104, and so forth). They were seldom right but never in doubt.

In real life, this tendency can have grave results. Having formed a belief—that vaccines cause (or do not cause) autism spectrum disorder, that people can (or cannot) change their sexual orientation, that gun control does (or does not) save lives—we prefer information

that supports our belief. And once we get hung up on an incorrect view of a problem, it's hard to approach it from a different angle. This obstacle to problem solving is called **fixation,** an inability to come to a fresh perspective. Can you solve the matchstick problem in **FIGURE 8.2?** (See the solution in **FIGURE 8.3.**)

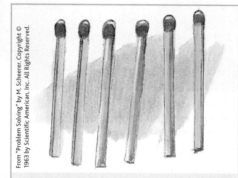

FIGURE 8.2 **The matchstick problem** How would you arrange six matches to form four equilateral triangles?

Making Good (and Bad) Decisions and Judgments

LOQ 8-3 What is intuition, and how can the availability heuristic influence our decisions and judgments?

Each day we make hundreds of judgments and decisions. *(Should I take a jacket? Can I trust this person? Should I shoot the basketball or pass to the player who's hot?)* As we judge the odds and make our decisions, we seldom take the time and effort to reason systematically. We just follow our **intuition,** our fast, automatic, unreasoned feelings and thoughts. After interviewing leaders in government, business, and education, one social psychologist concluded that they often made decisions without considered thought and reflection. How did they usually reach their decisions? "If you ask, they are likely to tell you . . . they do it mostly *by the seat of their pants*" (Janis, 1986).

Quick-Thinking Heuristics

When we need to make snap judgments, the mental shortcuts we call *heuristics* enable quick thinking without conscious awareness. As cognitive psychologists Amos Tversky and Daniel Kahneman (1974) showed, these automatic, intuitive strategies, although generally helpful, can sometimes lead even the smartest people into quick but dumb decisions.[3]

---

[3] Tversky and Kahneman's joint work on decision making received a 2002 Nobel Prize; sadly, only Kahneman was alive to receive the honor.

cognition all the mental activities associated with thinking, knowing, remembering, and communicating.

concept a mental grouping of similar objects, events, ideas, or people.

prototype a mental image or best example of a category. Matching new items to a prototype provides a quick and easy method for sorting items into categories (as when you compare a feathered creature to a prototypical bird, such as a robin).

algorithm a methodical, logical rule or procedure that guarantees you will solve a particular problem. Contrasts with the usually speedier—but also more error-prone—use of *heuristics*.

heuristic a simple thinking strategy that often allows you to make judgments and solve problems efficiently; usually speedier but also more error-prone than *algorithms*.

insight a sudden realization of the solution to a problem; contrasts with strategy-based solutions.

confirmation bias a tendency to search for information that supports your preconceptions and to ignore or distort evidence that contradicts them.

fixation in thinking, the inability to see a problem from a new perspective; an obstacle to problem solving.

intuition an effortless, immediate, automatic feeling or thought, as contrasted with explicit, conscious reasoning.

"In creating these problems, we didn't set out to fool people. All our problems fooled us, too." (Amos Tversky, 1985)

Carsten Rehder/POOL/EPA/Newscom

"Intuitive thinking [is] fine most of the time. . . . But sometimes that habit of mind gets us in trouble." (Daniel Kahneman, 2005)

From "Problem Solving" by M Scheerer. Copyright © 1963 by Scientific American, Inc. All Rights Reserved.

FIGURE 8.3 Solution to the matchstick problem Were you, by chance, fixated on two-dimensional solutions? Solving problems often requires taking a new angle on the situation.

Consider the **availability heuristic,** which operates when we estimate how common an event is, based on its mental availability. Anything that makes information "pop" into mind—its vividness, recentness, or distinctiveness—can make it seem commonplace. Casinos know this. They entice us to gamble by broadcasting wins with noisy bells and flashing lights. The big losses are soundlessly invisible.

The availability heuristic can distort our judgments of other people. If people from a particular ethnic or religious group commit a terrorist act, as happened on September 11, 2001, our readily available memory of the dramatic event may shape our impression of the whole group. Even during that horrific year, terrorist acts claimed comparatively few lives. Despite the much greater risk of death from other causes (**FIGURE 8.4**), the vivid image of 9/11 terror came more easily to mind. Emotion-laden images of terror fed our fears (Sunstein, 2007). Thus, if terrorists were to kill 1000 people in the United States this year, Americans would be mighty afraid. And yet they would have reason to be 30 times more afraid of homicidal, suicidal, and accidental death by guns, which take more than 30,000 lives annually. *The bottom line:* We often fear the wrong things (see Thinking Critically About: The Fear Factor).

Over 40 nations have sought to harness the positive power of vivid, memorable images by putting eye-catching warnings and graphic photos on cigarette packages (Riordan, 2013). This campaign has worked (Huang et al., 2013). Why?

FIGURE 8.4 Risk of death from various causes in the United States, 2001 (Data assembled from various government sources by Marshall et al., 2007.)

Risk of death

- Auto accident: 1 in 6029
- Suicide: 1 in 9310
- Terrorist attack: 1 in 97,927
- Homicide: 1 in 25,123
- Accidental choking: 1 in 94,371
- Pedestrian accident: 1 in 46,960

Cause of death

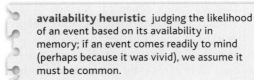

availability heuristic judging the likelihood of an event based on its availability in memory; if an event comes readily to mind (perhaps because it was vivid), we assume it must be common.

Thinking Critically About:
The Fear Factor

9/11 terrorist attacks ⟶ Many people fear flying more than driving.

HOWEVER:

2010 ⟶ 2012

Americans are vastly more likely to die in a vehicle accident than on a scheduled flight.[1]

65,249 people died in U.S. car or light truck accidents; **zero** died on scheduled airline flights.

In the three months after 9/11, **FEAR OF FLYING** led more Americans to travel by car, and some to die:[2]

Number of U.S. traffic deaths

Oct.-Dec. 2001: 353 excess deaths

Number of traffic deaths, 2001

Average number of traffic deaths, 1996-2000

3600
3400
3200
3000
2800
2600
2400
2200

Jan Feb Mar Apr May Jun Jul Aug Sep Oct Nov Dec

In the year following 9/11, these researchers estimated, 1500 Americans had "lost their lives on the road by trying to avoid the risk of flying."

WHY DO WE FEAR THE WRONG THINGS?

1. We fear what our ancestral history has prepared us to fear: Snakes, lizards, and spiders combined now kill a tiny fraction of the number killed by modern-day threats, such as cars and cigarettes. Ancestral risks also prepare us to fear confinement and heights, and therefore flying.

2. We fear what we cannot control: Driving we control; flying we do not.

3. We fear what is immediate. Dangers of flying are mostly in the moments of takeoff and landing. Dangers of driving are spread across many moments, each trivially dangerous.

4. Thanks to the *availability heuristic*, we fear what is most readily available in memory: Vivid images of horrific airline crashes feed our judgments of risk.

Shark attacks kill ~1 American per year.
"Vivid image!"

Heart disease kills 800,000 Americans per year.
"Harder to visualize"

People may fear sharks more than cigarettes or the effects of an unhealthy diet.[3]

We remember and fear **disasters** (hurricanes, earthquakes) that kill people dramatically, in bunches.

We fear too little the **less dramatic and ongoing threats** that claim lives one by one:

• In an average day, guns kill 92 Americans — in homicides, suicides, and accidents.[4] Yet renewed calls for U.S. gun control tend to follow the well-publicized, mass shootings.

• Worldwide, 500,000 children die each year from diarrhea, with tragically little notice.

"If it's in the news, don't worry about it. The very definition of news is 'something that hardly ever happens.'"[5]

1. National Safety Council, 2015. 2. Gigerenzer, 2004, 2006; Gaissmaier & Gigerenzer, 2012. 3. Daley, 2011. 4. Xu et al., 2016. 5. Schneier, 2007.

DRAMATIC DEATHS IN BUNCHES BREED CONCERN AND FEAR With scenes from the 2015 terrorist attacks in Paris, San Bernardino (California), and elsewhere flooding people's minds, 27 percent of Americans identified terrorism as their biggest worry—up from 8 percent just before the Paris attacks (Reuters, 2015). The hijacking of our rationality by fears of terrorist guns (when other risks, such as driving or influenza, kill so many more) highlights an important piece of scientific news: *We often fear the wrong things.*

Because we reason emotionally—we overfeel and underthink. In one experiment, donations to a starving 7-year-old were greater when her image appeared alone, without statistics describing the millions of needy African children like her (Small et al., 2007). Dramatic outcomes make us gasp; probabilities we hardly grasp.

Retrieve + Remember

- Why can news be described as "something that hardly ever happens"? How does knowing this help us assess our fears?

ANSWER: If a tragic event such as a plane crash makes the news, it grabs our attention more than the much more common bad events, such as traffic accidents. Knowing this, we can worry less about unlikely events and think more about improving the safety of our everyday activities. (For example, we can wear a seat belt when in a vehicle and use the crosswalk when walking.)

Overconfidence: Was There Ever Any Doubt?

LOQ 8-5 How are our decisions and judgments affected by overconfidence, belief perseverance, and framing?

Sometimes our decisions and judgments go awry because we are more confident than correct. When answering factual questions such as "Is absinthe a liqueur or a precious stone?" only 60 percent of people in one study answered correctly. (It's a licorice-flavored liqueur.) Yet those answering felt, on average, 75 percent confident (Fischhoff et al., 1977). This tendency to overestimate our accuracy is **overconfidence.**

Classrooms are full of overconfident students who expect to finish

PREDICT YOUR OWN BEHAVIOR When will you finish reading this chapter?

assignments and write papers ahead of schedule (Buehler et al., 1994, 2002). In fact, such projects generally take about twice the number of days predicted. We also are overconfident about our future free time (Zauberman & Lynch, 2005). Surely we'll have more free time next month than we do today. So we happily accept invitations, only to discover we're just as busy when the day rolls around. And believing we'll surely have more money next year, we take out loans or buy on credit. Despite our past overconfident predictions, we remain overly confident of our next one.

Overconfidence affects us at the group level, too. History is full of leaders who, when waging war, were more confident than correct. In politics, overconfidence feeds extreme political views. Sometimes the less we know, the more definite we sound.

Nevertheless, overconfidence can have adaptive value. Believing that their decisions are right and they have time to spare, self-confident people tend to live happily. They make tough decisions more easily, and they seem competent (Anderson et al., 2012).

Our Beliefs Live On— Sometimes Despite Evidence

Our overconfidence is startling. Equally startling is **belief perseverance**—our tendency to cling to our beliefs even when the evidence proves us wrong. Consider a classic study of people with opposing views of the death penalty (Lord et al., 1979). Both sides were asked to read the same material—two new research reports. One report showed that the death penalty lowers the crime rate; the other that it has no effect. Each side was impressed by the study supporting its own beliefs, and each was quick to criticize the other study. Thus, showing the two groups the *same* mixed evidence actually *increased* their disagreement about the value of capital punishment.

So how can smart thinkers avoid belief perseverance? A simple remedy is to *consider the opposite.* In a repeat of the death penalty study, researchers asked some participants to be "as *objective* and *unbiased* as possible" (Lord et al., 1984). This plea did nothing to reduce people's biases. They also asked another group to consider "whether you would have made the same high or low evaluations had exactly the same study produced results on the *other* side of the issue." In this group, people's views did change. After imagining the *opposite* findings, they judged the evidence in a much less biased way.

The more we come to appreciate why our beliefs might be true, the more tightly we cling to them. Once we have explained to ourselves why candidate X or Y will be a better commander-in-chief, we tend to ignore evidence that challenges our belief. Prejudice persists. Once beliefs take root, it takes stronger evidence to change them than it did to create them. Beliefs often persevere.

Framing: Let's Put It This Way . . .

Framing—the way we present an issue—can be a powerful tool of persuasion. Governments know this. Both Britain and the United States have been exploring ways to gently nudge people in healthy directions (Fox & Tannenbaum, 2015). Consider how the framing of options can affect perceptions (Benartzi & Thaler, 2013; Thaler & Sunstein, 2008):

- *Choosing to live or die.* Imagine two surgeons explaining the risk of an upcoming surgery. One explains that during this type of surgery, 10 percent of patients die. The other explains that 90 percent survive. The information is the same. The effect is not. In real-life surveys, patients and physicians overwhelmingly say the risk seems greater when they hear that 10 percent *die* (Marteau, 1989; McNeil et al., 1988; Rothman & Salovey, 1997).

- *Choosing to be an organ donor.* In many European countries, as well as in the United States, people renewing their driver's license can decide whether to

be organ donors. In some countries, the assumed answer is *Yes*, unless you opt out. Nearly 100 percent of the people in these opt-out countries agree to be donors. In countries where the assumed answer is *No*, fewer than half have agreed to be donors (Hajhosseini et al., 2013; Johnson & Goldstein, 2003).

- *Making students happier.* One economist's students were upset by a "hard" exam, on which the class average was 72 out of 100. So on the next exam, he made the highest possible score 137 points. Although the class average score of 96 was only 70 percent correct, "the students were delighted." (The number 96 felt so much better than 72.) So he continued the reframed exam results thereafter (Thaler, 2015).

The point to remember: Framing can influence our decisions.

The Perils and Powers of Intuition

LOQ 8-6 How do smart thinkers use intuition?

We have seen how our unreasoned thinking can plague our efforts to solve problems, assess risks, and make wise decisions. Moreover, these perils of intuition persist even when people are offered extra pay for thinking smart or when asked to justify their answers. And they persist even among those with high intelligence, including expert physicians, clinicians, and U.S. federal intelligence agents (Reyna et al., 2013; Shafir & LeBoeuf, 2002; Stanovich & West, 2008).

But psychological science is also revealing intuition's powers:

- *Intuition is analysis "frozen into habit"* (Simon, 2001). It is implicit (unconscious) knowledge—what we've learned and recorded in our brains but can't fully explain (Chassy & Gobet, 2011; Gore & Sadler-Smith, 2011). We see this ability to size up a situation and react in an eyeblink in chess

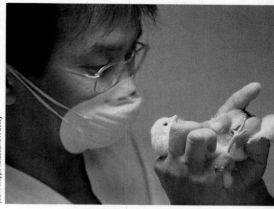

HMM . . . MALE OR FEMALE? When acquired expertise becomes an automatic habit, as it is for experienced chicken sexers, it feels like intuition. At a glance, they just know, yet cannot easily tell you how they know.

masters playing speed chess, when they intuitively know the right move (Burns, 2004). We see it in the smart and quick judgments of seasoned nurses, firefighters, art critics, and car mechanics. We see it in skilled athletes who react without thinking. Indeed, conscious thinking may disrupt well-practiced movements, leading skilled athletes to choke under pressure, as when shooting free throws (Beilock, 2010). And we would see this instant intuition in you, too, for anything in which you have developed a deep and special knowledge, based on experience.

- *Intuition is usually adaptive.* Our fast and frugal heuristics let us intuitively assume that fuzzy-looking objects are far away—which they usually are, except on foggy mornings. Our learned associations surface as gut

overconfidence the tendency to be more confident than correct—to overestimate the accuracy of our beliefs and judgments.

belief perseverance clinging to beliefs even after evidence has proven them wrong.

framing the way an issue is posed; framing can significantly affect decisions and judgments.

feelings, right or wrong: Seeing a stranger who looks like someone who has harmed or threatened us in the past, we may automatically react with distrust. Newlyweds' implicit attitudes to their new spouses likewise predict their future marital happiness (McNulty et al., 2013).

- *Intuition is huge.* Unconscious automatic influences are constantly affecting our judgments (Custers & Aarts, 2010). Imagine participating in this decision-making experiment (Strick et al., 2010). You've been assigned to one of three groups that will receive complex information about four apartment options. Members of the first group will state their choice immediately after reading the information. Those in the second group will analyze the information before choosing one of the options. Your group, the third, will consider the information but then be distracted for a time before giving your decision. Which group will make the smartest decision?

Did you guess the second group would make the best choice? Most people do, believing that the more complex the choice, the smarter it is to make decisions rationally rather than intuitively (Inbar et al., 2010). Actually, the third group made the best choice in this real-life experiment. When making complex decisions, we benefit by letting a problem "incubate" while we attend to other things (Dijksterhuis & Strick, 2016). Facing a difficult decision involving a lot of facts, we're wise to gather all the information we can, and then say, "Give me some time *not* to think about this." By taking time even to sleep on it, we let our unconscious mental machinery work, and then await the intuitive result of this automatic processing. Thanks to our ever-active brain, nonconscious thinking (reasoning, problem solving, decision making, planning) is surprisingly wise (Creswell et al., 2013; Hassin, 2013; Lin & Murray, 2015).

Critics remind us, however, that with most complex tasks, deliberate, conscious thought helps (Lassiter et al., 2009; Newell, 2015; Nieuwenstein et al., 2015; Payne et al., 2008). With many sorts of problems, smart thinkers may initially fall prey to an intuitive option but then reason their way to a better answer. Consider a random coin flip. If someone flipped a coin six times, which of the following sequences of heads (H) and tails (T) would seem most likely: HHHTTT or HTTHTH or HHHHHH?

Daniel Kahneman and Amos Tversky (1972) reported that most people believe HTTHTH would be the most likely random sequence. (Ask someone to predict six coin tosses and they will likely tell you a sequence like this.) Actually, each of these exact sequences is equally likely (or, you might say, equally unlikely).

The bottom line: Our two-track mind makes sweet harmony as smart, critical thinking listens to the creative whispers of our vast unseen mind and then evaluates evidence, tests conclusions, and plans for the future.

Thinking Creatively

LOQ 8-7 What is creativity, and what fosters it?

Creativity is the ability to produce ideas that are both novel and valuable (Hennessey & Amabile, 2010). Consider Princeton mathematician Andrew Wiles' incredible, creative moment. Pierre de Fermat (1601–1665), a mischief-loving genius, dared scholars to match his solutions to various number theory problems. Three centuries later, one of those problems continued to baffle the greatest mathematical minds, even after a $2 million prize (in today's money) had been offered for cracking the puzzle.

Wiles had searched for the answer for more than 30 years and reached the brink of a solution. One morning in 1994, out of the blue, an "incredible revelation"

Peter Muhly/AFP/Getty Images

INDUSTRIOUS CREATIVITY Researcher Sally Reis (2001) found that notably creative women were typically "intelligent, hard working, imaginative, and strong willed" as girls. In her acceptance speech for the 2013 Nobel Prize for Literature, author Alice Munro, shown here, spoke about creativity as hard work. "Stories are so important in the world.... [The part that's hardest is] when you go over the story and realize how bad it is.... [T]hat is when you really have to get to work on it. And for me, it always seemed the right thing to do."

struck him. "It was so . . . beautiful . . . so simple and so elegant. I couldn't understand how I'd missed it. . . . It was the most important moment of my working life" (Singh, 1997, p. 25).

Creativity like Wiles' requires a certain level of *aptitude* (ability to learn). But creativity is more than school smarts, and it requires a different kind of thinking. Aptitude tests (such as the SAT) typically require **convergent thinking**—an ability to provide a single correct answer. Creativity tests *(How many uses can you think of for a brick?)* require **divergent thinking**—the ability to consider many different options and to think in novel ways.

Robert Sternberg and his colleagues (1988, 2003; Sternberg & Lubart, 1991, 1992) believe creativity has five ingredients.

1. *Expertise*—a solid knowledge base—furnishes the ideas, images, and phrases we use as mental building blocks. The more blocks we have, the more novel ways we can combine them. Wiles' well-developed base of mathematical knowledge gave him access to many combinations of ideas and methods.

2. *Imaginative thinking skills* give us the ability to see things in novel ways, to recognize patterns, and to make connections. Wiles' imaginative solution combined two partial solutions.

3. A *venturesome personality* seeks new experiences, tolerates gray areas, takes risks, and stays focused despite obstacles. Wiles said he worked in near-isolation from the mathematics community, partly to stay focused and avoid distraction. This kind of focus and dedication is an enduring trait.

4. *Intrinsic motivation* (as explained in Chapter 6) arises internally rather than from external rewards or pressures (extrinsic motivation) (Amabile & Hennessey, 1992). Creative people seem driven by the pleasure and challenge of the work itself, not by meeting deadlines, impressing people, or making money. As Wiles said, "I was so obsessed by this problem that . . .

I was thinking about it all the time—[from] when I woke up in the morning to when I went to sleep at night" (Singh & Riber, 1997).

5. A *creative environment* sparks, supports, and refines creative ideas. Colleagues are an important part of creative environments. In one study of 2026 leading scientists and inventors, the best known of them had challenging and supportive relationships with colleagues (Simonton, 1992). Many creative environments also minimize stress and foster focused awareness (Byron & Khazanchi, 2011). While on a retreat in a monastery, Jonas Salk solved a problem that led to the polio vaccine. Later, when he designed the Salk Institute, he provided quiet spaces where scientists could think and work without interruption (Sternberg, 2006).

Would you like some research-based tips to boost your own creative process? Try these:

- *Develop your expertise.* What do you care about most? What do you enjoy doing? Follow your passion by broadening your knowledge base and becoming an expert at your special interest. The more you know, the more building blocks you'll have to combine in new and creative ways.

- *Allow time for ideas to hatch.* Think hard on a problem, but then set it aside and come back to it later. During periods of inattention ("sleeping on a problem"), automatic processing can help associations to form (Zhong et al., 2008).

- *Set aside time for your mind to roam freely.* Creativity springs from "defocused attention" (Simonton, 2012a, b). So detach from attention-grabbing television, social networking, and video gaming. Jog, go for a long walk, or meditate. Serenity seeds spontaneity.

- *Experience other cultures and ways of thinking.* Viewing life from a different perspective sets the creative juices flowing. Students who spend time in another country and embrace their host culture are more adept at working out creative solutions to problems (Lee et al., 2012; Tadmor et al., 2012). Even getting out of your neighborhood and exposing yourself to multicultural experiences fosters flexible thinking. Although immigrants face many challenges, developing a sense of being different from others can inspire creativity (Kim et al., 2013; Ritter et al., 2012).

* * *

TABLE 8.1 summarizes the cognitive processes and strategies discussed in this section.

"For the love of God, is there a doctor in the house?"

WELL, I TOLD YOU TO ADD YEAST TO YOUR SHAMPOO.

IMAGINATIVE THINKING Cartoonists often display creativity as they see things in new ways or make unusual connections.

creativity the ability to produce new and valuable ideas.

convergent thinking narrowing the available solutions to determine the single best solution to a problem.

divergent thinking expanding the number of possible solutions to a problem; creative thinking that branches out in different directions.

TABLE 8.1   Comparing Cognitive Processes and Strategies

Process or Strategy	Description	Powers	Perils
Algorithm	Methodical rule or procedure	Guarantees solution	Requires time and effort
Heuristic	Simple thinking shortcut, such as the availability heuristic (which estimates likelihood based on how easily events come to mind)	Lets us act quickly and efficiently	Puts us at risk for errors
Insight	Sudden Aha! reaction	Provides instant realization of solution	May not happen
Confirmation bias	Tendency to search for support for our own views and ignore contradictory evidence	Lets us quickly recognize supporting evidence	Hinders recognition of contradictory evidence
Fixation	Inability to view problems from a new angle	Focuses thinking	Hinders creative problem solving
Intuition	Fast, automatic feelings and thoughts	Is based on our experience; huge and adaptive	Can lead us to overfeel and underthink
Overconfidence	Overestimating the accuracy of our beliefs and judgments	Allows us to be happy and to make decisions easily	Puts us at risk for errors
Belief perseverance	Ignoring evidence that proves our beliefs are wrong	Supports our enduring beliefs	Closes our mind to new ideas
Framing	Wording a question or statement so that it evokes a desired response	Can influence others' decisions	Can produce a misleading result
Creativity	Ability to produce novel and valuable ideas	Produces new products	May distract from structured, routine work

Retrieve + Remember

- Match the process or strategy listed below (1–10) with its description (a–j).

1. Algorithm
2. Intuition
3. Insight
4. Heuristic
5. Fixation
6. Confirmation bias
7. Overconfidence
8. Creativity
9. Framing
10. Belief perseverance

a. Inability to view problems from a new angle; focuses thinking but hinders creative problem solving.

b. Step-by-step rule or procedure that guarantees the solution but requires time and effort.

c. Your fast, automatic, effortless feelings and thoughts based on your experience; adaptive but can lead you to overfeel and underthink.

d. Simple thinking shortcut that lets you act quickly and efficiently but puts you at risk for errors.

e. Sudden Aha! reaction that instantly reveals the solution.

f. Tendency to search for support for your own views and to ignore evidence that opposes them.

g. Holding on to your beliefs even after they are proven wrong; closing your mind to new ideas.

h. Overestimating the accuracy of your beliefs and judgments; allows you to be happier and to make decisions easily, but puts you at risk for errors.

i. Wording a question or statement so that it produces a desired response; can mislead people and influence their decisions.

j. The ability to produce novel and valuable ideas.

ANSWERS: 1. b, 2. c, 3. e, 4. d, 5. a, 6. f, 7. h, 8. j, 9. i, 10. g

Do Other Species Share Our Cognitive Skills?

LOQ 8-8 What do we know about thinking in other species?

Other species are smarter than many humans realize. Neuroscientists have agreed that "nonhuman animals, including all mammals and birds" possess the neural networks "that generate consciousness" (Low, 2012). Consider, then, what animal brains can do.

USING CONCEPTS AND NUMBERS Black bears have learned to sort pictures into animal and nonanimal categories, or concepts (Vonk et al., 2012). The great apes—a group that includes chimpanzees and gorillas—also form concepts, such as *cat* and *dog*. After monkeys have learned these concepts, certain frontal lobe neurons in their brains fire in response to new "cat-like" images, others to new "dog-like" images (Freedman et al., 2001). Even pigeons—mere birdbrains—can sort objects (pictures of cars, cats, chairs, flowers) into categories. Shown a picture of a never-before-seen chair, pigeons will reliably peck a key that represents *chairs* (Wasserman, 1995).

Until his death in 2007, Alex, an African Grey parrot, displayed jaw-dropping numerical skills. He categorized and named objects (Pepperberg, 2009, 20012, 2013). He could comprehend numbers up to 8. He could speak the number of objects. He could add two small clusters of objects and announce the sum. He could indicate which of two numbers was greater. And he gave correct answers when shown various groups of objects. Asked, for example, "What color four?" (meaning "What's the color of the objects of which there are four?"), he could speak the answer.

DISPLAYING INSIGHT We are not the only creatures to display insight. Psychologist Wolfgang Köhler (1925) placed a piece of fruit and a long stick outside the cage of a chimpanzee named Sultan, beyond his reach. Inside the cage, he placed a short stick, which Sultan grabbed, using it to try to reach the fruit. After several failed attempts, the chimpanzee dropped the stick and seemed to survey the situation. Then suddenly (as if thinking "Aha!"), Sultan jumped up and seized the short stick again. This time, he used it to pull in the longer stick, which he then used to reach the fruit.

Birds, too, have displayed insight. One experiment brought to life one of Aesop's fables (ancient Greek stories), in which a thirsty crow is unable to reach the water in a partly filled pitcher. See the crow's solution (exactly as in the fable) in **FIGURE 8.5**.

USING TOOLS AND TRANSMITTING CULTURE Like humans, other animals invent behaviors and transmit cultural patterns to their observing peers and offspring (Boesch-Achermann & Boesch, 1993). Forest-dwelling chimpanzees select different tools for different purposes—a heavy stick for making holes, a light, flexible stick for fishing for termites, a pointed stick for roasting marshmallows. (Just kidding: They don't roast marshmallows, but they have surprised us with their sophisticated tool use [Sanz

FIGURE 8.5 Tool-using animals (a) Crows studied by (yes) Christopher Bird and Nathan Emery (2009) quickly learned to raise the water level in a tube and nab a floating worm by dropping stones into the water. (b) One male chimpanzee in Sweden's Furuvik Zoo was observed every morning collecting stones into a neat little pile, which later in the day he used as ammunition to pelt visitors (Osvath & Karvonen, 2012).

et al., 2004].) Researchers have found at least 39 local customs related to chimpanzee tool use, grooming, and courtship (Whiten & Boesch, 2001). One group may slurp termites directly from a stick, another group may pluck them off individually. One group may break nuts with a stone, while their neighbors use a piece of wood. These group differences, along with differing communication and hunting styles, are the chimpanzee version of cultural diversity.

Chimpanzees have shown altruism, cooperation, and group aggression. Like humans, they will kill their neighbor to gain land, and they grieve over dead relatives (C. A. Anderson et al., 2010; D. Biro et al., 2010; Mitani et al., 2010). Elephants have demonstrated self-awareness by recognizing themselves in a mirror. They have also displayed their abilities to learn, remember, discriminate smells, empathize, cooperate, teach, and spontaneously use tools (Byrne et al., 2009).

So there is no question that other species display many remarkable cognitive skills. Are they also capable of what we humans call language, the topic we consider next?

Language

Imagine an alien species that could pass thoughts from one head to another merely by setting air molecules in motion between them. Actually, we are those creatures! When we speak, we send air-pressure waves banging against other people's eardrums as we transfer thoughts from our brain into theirs. We sometimes sit for hours "listening to other people make noise as they exhale, because those hisses and squeaks contain *information*" (Pinker, 1998). And depending on how you vibrate the air after opening your own mouth, you may get a scowl or a kiss.

Language is our spoken, written, or signed words, and the ways we meaningfully combine them. When I [DM] created this paragraph, my fingers on a keyboard triggered electronic signals

> **language** our spoken, written, or signed words, and the ways we combine them to communicate meaning.

that morphed into the squiggles in front of you. As you read these squiggles, they trigger nerve impulses that travel to areas of your brain that decode the meaning. Thanks to our shared language, information has just moved from my mind to yours. With language, we humans can transmit civilization's knowledge from one generation to the next. Many animals know only what they see. Thanks to language, we know much that we've never seen and that our ancestors never knew.

Language also connects us. If you were able to keep only one cognitive ability, what would it be? Without sight or hearing, you could still have friends, family, and a job. But without language, could you have these things? "Language is so fundamental to our experience, so deeply a part of being human, that it's hard to imagine life without it" (Boroditsky, 2009).

Language Development

LOQ 8-9 What are the milestones in language development, and when is the critical period for learning language?

Make a quick guess: How many words did you learn in your native language between your first birthday and your high school graduation? Although you use only 150 words for about half of what you say, you probably learned about 60,000 words (Bloom, 2000; McMurray, 2007). That averages (after age 2) nearly 3500 words each year, or nearly 10 each day! How you did it—how those 3500 words could so far outnumber the roughly 200 words your schoolteachers consciously taught you each year—is one of the great human wonders.

Could you even now state the rules of *syntax* (the correct way to string words together to form sentences) for the language(s) you speak fluently? Most of us cannot. Yet before you were able to add 2 + 2, you were creating your own original sentences and applying these rules. As a preschooler, your ability to understand and speak your language(s)

was so great it would put to shame college students struggling to learn a new language.

We humans have an astonishing knack for language. Without blinking, we sample tens of thousands of words in our memory, effortlessly combine them with near-perfect syntax, and spew them out, three words a second (Vigliocco & Hartsuiker, 2002). We rarely form sentences in our minds before we speak them. We organize them on the fly as we speak. And while doing all this, we also fine-tune our language to our social and cultural setting. *(How far apart should we stand? Is it OK to interrupt?)* Given how many ways we can mess up, it's amazing that we master this social dance. When and how does it happen?

When Do We Learn Language?

RECEPTIVE LANGUAGE Children's language development moves from simplicity to complexity. Infants start without language (*in fantis* means "not speaking"). Yet by 4 months of age, babies can recognize differences in speech sounds (Stager & Werker, 1997). They can also read lips, preferring to look at a face that matches a sound. They can recognize that *ah* comes from wide open lips and *ee* from a mouth with corners pulled back (Kuhl & Meltzoff, 1982). This marks the beginning of the development of babies' *receptive language,* their ability to understand what is said to and about them. At 7 months and beyond, babies grow in their power to break language they hear into individual words—which adults find difficult when listening to an unfamiliar language.

PRODUCTIVE LANGUAGE Babies' *productive language,* their ability to produce words, matures after their receptive language. Before nurture molds their speech, nature allows a wide range of possible sounds in the **babbling stage,** around 4 months of age. In this stage,

Jaimie Duplass/Shutterstock

they seem to sample all the sounds they can make, such as *ah-goo.* Babbling is not an imitation of adult speech. We know this because babbling includes sounds from languages not spoken in the household. From this early babbling, a listener could not identify an infant as being, say, French, Korean, or Ethiopian. Do deaf infants babble in sign language? They do, especially if they have deaf parents whose signing they observe (Petitto & Marentette, 1991).

By about 10 months old, infants' babbling has changed so that a trained ear can identify the household language (de Boysson-Bardies et al., 1989). Without exposure to other languages, babies lose their ability to discriminate and produce sounds and tones found outside their native language (Meltzoff et al., 2009; Pallier et al., 2001). Thus, by adulthood those who speak only English cannot discriminate certain sounds in Japanese speech. Nor can Japanese adults with no training in English hear the difference between the English *r* and *l.* For a Japanese-speaking adult, *la-la-ra-ra* may sound like the same syllable repeated.

Around their first birthday, most children enter the **one-word stage.** They know that sounds carry meanings. They now begin to use sounds—usually only one barely recognizable syllable, such as *ma* or *da*—to communicate meaning. But family members learn to understand, and gradually the infant's language sounds more like the family's language. Across the world, baby's first words are often nouns that label objects or people (Tardif et al., 2008). At this one-word stage, a single word (*"Doggy!"*) may equal a sentence (*"Look at the dog out there!"*).

At about 18 months, children's word learning explodes, jumping from about a word each week to a word each day. By their second birthday, most have entered the **two-word stage** (**TABLE 8.2**).

TABLE 8.2   Summary of Language Development

Month (approximate)	Stage
4	Babbles many speech sounds ("ah-goo")
10	Babbling; resembles household language ("ma-ma")
12	One-word stage ("Kitty!")
24	Two-word stage ("Get ball.")
24+	Rapid development into complete sentences

Sidney Harris/Science Cartoons Plus

"Got idea. Talk better. Combine words. Make sentences."

They start uttering two-word sentences in **telegraphic speech.** Like today's texts or yesterday's telegrams that charged by the word (TERMS ACCEPTED. SEND MONEY), a 2-year-old's speech contains mostly nouns and verbs (*"Want juice"*). Also like telegrams, their speech follows rules of syntax, arranging words in a sensible order. English-speaking children typically place adjectives before nouns—*white house* rather than *house white.* Spanish reverses this order, as in *casa blanca.*

Moving out of the two-word stage, children quickly begin speaking in longer phrases (Fromkin & Rodman, 1983). By early elementary school, children understand complex sentences. They can enjoy a joke with a double meaning: "You never starve in the desert because of all the sand-which-is there."

CRITICAL PERIODS What might happen if a child gets a late start on learning a particular language? This is not uncommon for children who have surgery to enable hearing, or who are adopted by a family in another country. For these late bloomers, language development follows the same sequence, though the pace is often faster (Ertmer et al., 2007; Snedeker et al., 2007). But there is a limit on how long language learning can be delayed.

Childhood seems to represent a *critical* (or "sensitive") *period* for mastering certain aspects of language before the language-learning window closes (Hernandez & Li, 2007; Lenneberg, 1967). That window closes gradually. Deaf children who gain hearing with cochlear implants by age 2 develop better oral speech than do those who receive implants after age 4 (Greers, 2004). For both deaf and hearing children, later-than-usual exposure to language—at age 2 or 3—unleashes their brain's idle language capacity, producing a rush of language. But there is no similar rush of learning if children are not exposed to either a spoken or a signed language until age 7. Such deprived children lose their ability to master *any* language.

The impact of early experience is evident in language learning in children who have been deaf from birth. More than 90 percent of such children have parents who are not deaf and who do not use sign language. These children typically are not exposed to signed language during their early years. Those who learn to sign as teens or adults can master basic words and learn to order them. But they are not as fluent as native signers in using and understanding subtle differences in **grammar** (Newport, 1990).

After the language window closes, even learning a second language becomes more difficult. Have you learned a second language as an adult? If so, you almost certainly speak it with the accent of your first, and perhaps with imperfect grammar. This difficulty appeared in one study of Korean and Chinese immigrants (Johnson & Newport, 1991). Their task was to read 276 English sentences, such as *"Yesterday the hunter shoots a deer,"* and to decide whether each sentence was grammatically correct or incorrect. All had lived in the United States for approximately 10 years. Some had arrived as very young children, others as adults. As **FIGURE 8.6** reveals, those who had learned their second language early learned it best. The older we are when moving to a new country, the harder it is to learn the new language and culture (Cheung et al., 2011; Hakuta et al., 2003). Cognitive psychologist Stephen Kosslyn (2008) summed it up nicely. "Children can learn multiple languages without an accent and with good grammar, if they are exposed to the language before puberty. But after puberty, it's very difficult to learn a second language so well. Similarly, when I first went to Japan, I was told not even to bother trying to bow, that there were something like a dozen different bows and I was always going to 'bow with an accent.'"

babbling stage beginning at about 4 months, the stage of speech development in which an infant spontaneously utters various sounds, many at first unrelated to the household language.

one-word stage the stage in speech development, from about age 1 to 2, during which a child speaks mostly in single words.

two-word stage beginning about age 2, the stage in speech development during which a child speaks mostly in two-word sentences.

telegraphic speech early speech stage in which a child speaks in compressed sentences, like a telegram—"want milk" or "Daddy go store"—using mostly nouns and verbs.

grammar in a specific language, a system of rules that enables us to communicate with and understand others.

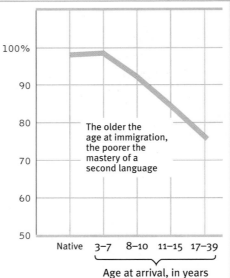

Percentage correct on grammar test

The older the age at immigration, the poorer the mastery of a second language

Age at arrival, in years

A.E. Araiza/Arizona Daily Star/AP Photo

FIGURE 8.6 Our ability to learn a new language diminishes with age Young children have a readiness to learn language. Ten years after coming to the United States, Asian immigrants took an English grammar test. Those who arrived before age 8 understood American English grammar as well as native speakers did. Those who arrived later did not. (Data from Johnson & Newport, 1991.)

Susan Meiselas/Magnum Photos

CREATING A LANGUAGE Brought together as if on a desert island (actually a school), Nicaragua's young deaf children over time drew upon sign gestures from home to create their own Nicaraguan Sign Language, complete with words and intricate grammar. Our biological predisposition for language does not create language in a vacuum. But activated by a social context, nature and nurture work creatively together (Osborne, 1999; Sandler et al., 2005; Senghas & Coppola, 2001).

Retrieve + Remember

- What is the difference between *receptive* and *productive* language, and when do children normally hit these milestones in language development?

ANSWER: Infants normally start developing *receptive language skills* (ability to understand what is said to and about them) around 4 months of age. Then, starting with babbling at 4 months and beyond, infants normally start building *productive language skills* (ability to produce sounds and eventually words).

- Why is it so difficult to learn a new language in adulthood?

ANSWER: Our brain's *critical period* for language learning is in childhood, when we can absorb language structure almost effortlessly. As we move past that stage in our brain's development, our ability to learn a new language drops dramatically.

Retrieve + Remember

- What was Noam Chomsky's explanation of language development?

ANSWER: Chomsky maintained that all languages share a universal grammar, and humans are biologically predisposed to learn whatever language they experience.

How Do We Learn Language?

The world's 6000+ languages are structurally very diverse (Evans & Levinson, 2009). Linguist Noam Chomsky has argued that all languages nevertheless share some basic elements, which he calls a *universal grammar*. All human languages have nouns, verbs, and adjectives as basic building blocks. Moreover, said Chomsky, we humans are born with a built-in readiness—a predisposition—to learn grammar rules. This helps explain why preschoolers pick up language so readily and use grammar so well. It happens so

naturally—as naturally as birds learn to fly—that training hardly helps.

No matter what our language is, we start speaking mostly in nouns (*kitty, da-da*) rather than verbs and adjectives (Bornstein et al., 2004). We are not, however, born with a built-in *specific* language. Most babies born in Mexico learn to speak Spanish, not Chinese. And whatever language we experience as children, whether spoken or signed, we readily learn its specific grammar and vocabulary (Bavelier et al., 2003). Once again, we see biology and experience working together.

The Brain and Language

LOQ 8-10 What brain areas are involved in language processing and speech?

We think of speaking and reading, or writing and reading, or singing and speaking as merely different examples of the same general ability—language. But consider this curious finding: Damage to any one of several areas of the brain's cortex can impair language. Even more curious, some people with brain damage can speak fluently but cannot read (despite good vision). Others can understand what they read but cannot speak. Still others can write but not read, read

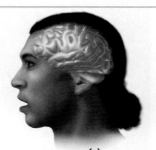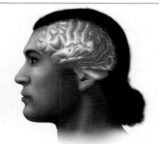

(a)
Speaking words
(Broca's area and
the motor cortex)

(b)
Hearing words
(auditory cortex and
Wernicke's area)

FIGURE 8.7 Brain activity when speaking and hearing words

but not write, read numbers but not letters, or sing but not speak. To sort out this puzzle required a lot of smart thinking by many different scientists, all seeking to answer the same question: How does the brain process language?

In 1865, French physician Paul Broca discovered that after damage to a specific area of the left frontal lobe (later called **Broca's area**) a person would struggle to *speak* words, yet could often sing familiar songs with ease. A decade later, German investigator Carl Wernicke discovered that after damage to a specific area of the left temporal lobe **(Wernicke's area),** people were unable to *understand* others' words and could speak only meaningless words.

Today's neuroscience has confirmed brain activity in Broca's and Wernicke's areas during language processing **(FIGURE 8.7)**. But we now know that the brain processes language in other areas as well. Although you experience language as a single, unified stream, functional MRI (fMRI) scans would show that your brain is busily multitasking and networking. Different brain areas are activated by nouns and verbs (or objects and actions); by different vowels; by stories of visual versus motor experiences; by who spoke and what was said; and by many other stimuli (Perrachione et al., 2011; Shapiro et al., 2006; Speer et al., 2009). Moreover, if you're lucky enough to be fluent in two languages, your hardworking brain assigns those two functions to

two different sets of neural networks. One processes your native language, and the other handles your second language (Perani & Abutalebi, 2005).

The big point to remember: In processing language, as in other forms of information processing, the brain operates by dividing its mental functions—speaking, perceiving, thinking, remembering—into smaller tasks. Your conscious experience of reading this page *seems* to be one task, but many different neural networks are pooling their work to compute each word's form, sound, and meaning (Posner & Carr, 1992).

LaunchPad To review research on left- and right-hemisphere language processing—and to test your own processing speed—see LaunchPad's *PsychSim 6: Dueling Hemispheres.* Consider how researchers have learned about the benefits of speaking more than one language with LaunchPad's *IMMERSIVE LEARNING: How Would You Know If There Is a Bilingual Advantage?*

Retrieve + Remember

• _____ _____ is the part of the brain that, if damaged, might impair your ability to speak words. If you damage _____ _____, you might impair your ability to understand language.

ANSWERS: Broca's area; Wernicke's area

Thinking Without Language

LOQ 8-11 How can thinking in images be useful?

To turn on the cold water in your bathroom, in which direction do you turn the handle? To answer, you probably thought not in words but in images—perhaps a mental picture of your hand turning the faucet.

Indeed, we often think in images. Mental practice relies on thinking in images. One year after placing second in a worldwide piano competition, pianist Liu Chi Kung was imprisoned during China's cultural revolution. Soon after his release, after seven years without touching a piano, Liu was back on tour. The critics judged his playing to be better than ever, and his fans wondered how he had continued to develop without practice. "I did practice," said Liu, "every day. I rehearsed every piece I had ever played, note by note, in my mind" (Garfield, 1986).

One experiment on the benefits of mental rehearsal observed the University of Tennessee women's basketball team (Savoy & Beitel, 1996). Over 35 games, researchers tracked the team's skill at shooting free throws following standard physical practice or mental practice. After physical practice, the team scored about 52 percent of their shots. After mental practice, that score rose to 65 percent. During mental practice, players had repeatedly imagined making free throws under various conditions, including being "trash-talked" by the opposition. In a dramatic conclusion, Tennessee won that season's national

Broca's area controls language expression; an area of the frontal lobe, usually in the left hemisphere, that directs the muscle movements involved in speech.

Wernicke's area controls language reception; a brain area involved in language comprehension and expression; usually in the left temporal lobe.

championship game in overtime, thanks in part to their free-throw shooting.

Once you have learned a skill, even *watching* that skill happen triggers brain activity in the same areas that are active when you actually use the skill. As ballet dancers watch ballet videos, fMRI scans show their brain dancing along (Calvo-Merino et al., 2004). Just *imagining* a physical experience, such as pain, can have similar results. Imagined pain activates the same neural networks that are active during *actual* pain (Grèzes & Decety, 2001).

Can mental rehearsal also help you reach your academic goals? Definitely! One study demonstrated this with two groups of introductory psychology students facing a midterm exam one week later (Taylor et al., 1998). (Students not engaged in any mental rehearsal formed a control group.) The first group spent five minutes each day imagining themselves scanning the posted grade list, seeing their *A,* beaming with joy, and feeling proud. This daily *outcome simulation* had little effect, adding only 2 points to their average exam score. The second group spent five minutes each day imagining themselves effectively studying—reading the chapters, going over notes, eliminating distractions, declining an offer to go out. This daily *process simulation* paid off. In real life, this group began studying sooner, spent more time at it, and beat the other group's average score by 8 points.

The point to remember: To benefit from your fantasy time, it's better to imagine *how* to reach your goal than to focus on your desired destination.

Retrieve + Remember

- What is mental practice, and how can it help you to prepare for an upcoming event?

ANSWER: Mental practice uses visual imagery to mentally rehearse future behaviors, activating some of the same brain areas used during the actual behaviors. Imagining the details of the process is more effective than visualizing only your end goal.

LaunchPad To experience your own thinking as (a) manipulating words and (b) manipulating images, see LaunchPad's *PsychSim 6: My Head Is Spinning!*

Do Other Species Have Language?

LOQ 8-12 What do we know about other species' capacity for language?

Humans have long and proudly claimed that language sets us above all other animals. "When we study human language, we are approaching what some might call the 'human essence,' the qualities of mind that are, so far as we know, unique [to humans]" (Chomsky, 1972). Is it true that humans, alone, have language?

Animals display great powers of understanding and communicating. Vervet monkeys sound different alarm cries for different predators: a barking call for a leopard, a cough for an eagle, and a chuttering for a snake. Hearing the leopard alarm, other vervets climb the nearest tree. Hearing the eagle alarm, they rush into the bushes. Hearing the snake chutter, they stand up and scan the ground (Byrne, 1991). To indicate complex alarms, monkeys may combine 6 different calls. Specific types of threats (eagle, leopard, falling tree, neighboring group) may trigger a 25-call sequence (Balter, 2010). But are such communications language?

Psychologists Allen Gardner and Beatrix Gardner (1969) were among the earliest to address this question in scientific experiments using sign language. In the late 1960s, they aroused enormous scientific and public interest with their work with Washoe, a young chimpanzee. After four years, Washoe could use 132 signs. By her life's end in 2007, she was using 250 signs (Metzler, 2011; Sanz et al., 1998). One *New York Times* reporter, having learned sign language from his deaf parents, visited Washoe and exclaimed, "Suddenly I realized I was conversing with a member of another species in my native tongue."

COMPREHENDING CANINE Border collie Rico had a vocabulary of 200 human words. If asked to retrieve a toy with a name he had never heard, Rico would pick out a new toy from a group of familiar items (Kaminski et al., 2004). Hearing that name for the second time four weeks later, Rico more often than not would retrieve the same toy. Another border collie, Chaser, has set an animal record by learning 1022 object names (Pilley & Reid, 2011). Like a 3-year-old child, she can also categorize them by function and shape. She can "fetch a ball" or "fetch a doll."

During the 1970s, more and more reports came in. Some chimpanzees were stringing signs together to form sentences. Washoe, for example, signed "You me go out, please." Some word combinations seemed very creative—saying *water bird* for "swan" or *apple which-is orange* for "orange" (Patterson, 1978; Rumbaugh, 1977).

But by the late 1970s, other psychologists were growing skeptical. Were the chimps language champs or were the researchers chumps? Consider the skeptics' points:

- Ape vocabularies and sentences are simple, rather like those of a 2-year-old child. And apes gain their limited vocabularies only with great difficulty (Wynne, 2004, 2008). Speaking or signing children can easily soak up dozens of new words each week, and 60,000 by adulthood.

- Chimpanzees can make signs or push buttons in sequence to get a reward. But pigeons, too, can peck a sequence of keys to get grain (Straub et al., 1979). The apes' signing might be nothing

IS THIS LANGUAGE? Chimpanzees' ability to express themselves in American Sign Language raises questions about the very nature of language. Here, the trainer is asking, "What is this?" The sign in response is "Baby." Does the response constitute language?

Paul Fusco/Magnum Photos

more than aping their trainers' signs and learning that certain arm movements produce rewards (Terrace, 1979).

- Studies of perceptual set (see Chapter 5) show that when information is unclear, we tend to see what we want or expect to see. Interpreting chimpanzee signs as language may be little more than the trainers' wishful thinking (Terrace, 1979). When Washoe signed *water bird,* she may have been separately naming *water* and *bird.*

- "Give orange me give eat orange me eat orange . . ." is a far cry from the mastery of syntax in a 3-year-old's sentences (Anderson, 2004; Pinker, 1995). To the child, "You tickle" and "Tickle you" communicate different ideas. A chimpanzee, lacking human syntax, might use the same sequence of signs for both phrases.

Controversy can stimulate progress, as it did in this case. Studies of animal communication and the possibility of nonhuman language continued. An early and surprising finding was that Washoe's adopted son, Loulis, had picked up 68 signs, simply by observing Washoe and three other language-trained chimps signing together (Fouts, 1992, 1997). Even more stunning was a report that Kanzi, a bonobo with a reported 384-word vocabulary, could

understand syntax in spoken English (Savage-Rumbaugh et al., 1993, 2009). Kanzi has responded appropriately when asked, "Can you show me the light?" and "Can you bring me the [flash] light?" and "Can you turn the light on?" Given stuffed animals and asked—for the first time— to "make the dog bite the snake," he put the snake to the dog's mouth.

How should we interpret such studies? Are humans the only language-using species? If by *language* we mean verbal or signed expression of complex grammar, most psychologists would now agree that humans alone possess language. If we mean, more simply, an ability to communicate through a meaningful sequence of symbols, then apes are indeed capable of language.

One thing is certain. Studies of animal language and thinking have moved psychologists toward a greater appreciation of other species' remarkable abilities (Friend, 2004; Rumbaugh & Washburn, 2003; Wilson et al., 2014). In the past, many psychologists doubted that other species could plan, form concepts, count, use tools, or show compassion (Thorpe, 1974). Today, thanks to animal researchers, we know better. Other animals exhibit insight, show family loyalty, communicate with one another, care for one another, and transmit cultural patterns across generations. Working out what this means for the moral rights of other animals is an unfinished task.

* * *

Thinking about other species' abilities brings us back to a question raised earlier

in this chapter: How smart are we? Do we deserve the label *Homo sapiens*—wise human? Let's pause to issue a report card. On decision making and risk assessment, our smart but error-prone species might rate a B–. On problem solving, where humans are inventive yet subject to confirmation bias and fixation, we would probably receive better marks, perhaps a B+. On creativity and cognitive skills, our divergent thinking and quick (though sometimes faulty) heuristics would earn us an A–. And when it comes to language and the processing that occurs outside of consciousness, the awestruck experts would surely award the human species an A+.

Retrieve + Remember

- If your dog barks at a stranger at the door, does this qualify as language? What if the dog yips in a telltale way to let you know she needs to go out?

ANSWER: These are definitely communications. But if language consists of words and the grammatical rules we use to combine them to communicate meaning, few scientists would label a dog's barking and yipping as language.

LaunchPad   For more case studies of intelligent communication and problem solving among orangutans, elephants, and killer whales, see LaunchPad's 6-minute *Video: How Intelligent Are Animals?* See also *Video: Case Studies* for a helpful tutorial animation on this type of research method.

Intelligence

School boards, courts, and scientists debate the use and fairness of tests that assess people's mental abilities and assign them a score. One of psychology's most heated questions has been whether each of us has some general mental capacity that can be measured and expressed as a number.

In this section, we consider some findings from more than a century of

"Although humans make sounds with their mouths and occasionally look at each other, there is no solid evidence that they actually communicate with each other."

ScienceCartoonsPlus.com

research, as psychologists have searched for answers to these questions and more:

- What is intelligence? Is it one general ability, or many different abilities?
- How can we best assess intelligence?
- How do nature (heredity) and nurture (environment) together weave the fabric of intelligence?
- What intelligence test score similarities and differences exist among groups, and what accounts for those differences?

What Is Intelligence?

LOQ 8-13 How do psychologists define *intelligence,* and what are the arguments for general intelligence *(g)?*

Intelligence is not a quality like height or weight, which has the same meaning in all generations, worldwide. People assign the term *intelligence* to the qualities that enable success in their own time and place (Sternberg & Kaufman, 1998). In Cameroon's equatorial forest, intelligence may be understanding the medicinal qualities of local plants. In a North American high school, it may be mastering difficult concepts in tough courses. In both places, **intelligence** is the ability to learn from experience, solve problems, and use knowledge to adapt to new situations.

You probably know some people with talents in science or history, and others gifted in athletics, art, music, or dance. You may also know a terrific artist who is stumped by the simplest math problem, or a brilliant math student with little talent for writing term papers. Are all these people intelligent? Could you rate their intelligence on a single scale? Or would you need several different scales? Simply put: Is intelligence a single overall ability or several specific abilities?

Spearman's General Intelligence *(g)*

Charles Spearman (1863–1945) believed we have one **general intelligence** (often shortened to *g*) that is at the heart of our smarts, from sailing the sea to sailing through school. People often have special, outstanding abilities, he noted, but those who score high in one area (such as verbal ability) typically score above average in other areas (such as spatial or reasoning ability). Spearman's belief stemmed in part from his work with *factor analysis,* a statistical tool that searches for clusters of related items.

In Spearman's view, mental abilities are much like physical abilities. The ability to run fast is distinct from the eye-hand coordination required to throw a ball on target. Yet there remains some tendency for good things to come packaged together. Running speed and throwing accuracy, for example, often correlate, thanks to general athletic ability. Similarly, intelligence involves distinct abilities, which correlate enough to define a small general intelligence factor (the common skill set we call the *g* factor). Or to say this in the language of contemporary neuroscience, we have many distinct neural networks that enable our many varied abilities. Our brain coordinates all that activity, and the result is *g* (Hampshire et al., 2012).

Theories of Multiple Intelligences

LOQ 8-14 How do Gardner's and Sternberg's theories of multiple intelligences differ, and what criticisms have they faced?

Other psychologists, particularly since the mid-1980s, have proposed that the definition of *intelligence* should be broadened, beyond the idea of academic smarts.

GARDNER'S MULTIPLE INTELLIGENCES

Howard Gardner (1983, 2006, 2011; Davis et al., 2011) views intelligence as multiple abilities that come in different packages. Brain damage, he notes, may destroy one ability but leave others intact. He sees other evidence of multiple intelligences in people with **savant syndrome.** Despite their island of brilliance, these people often score low on intelligence tests and may have limited or no language ability

ISLANDS OF GENIUS: SAVANT SYNDROME
After a brief helicopter ride over Singapore followed by five days of drawing, British savant artist Stephen Wiltshire accurately reproduced a view of the city from memory.

(Treffert & Wallace, 2002). Some can render incredible works of art or music. Others can compute numbers with amazing speed and accuracy, or identify almost instantly the day of the week that matches any given date in history (Miller, 1999).

About four in five people with savant syndrome are males. Many also have *autism spectrum disorder (ASD),* a developmental disorder. The late memory whiz Kim Peek (who did not have ASD) inspired the movie *Rain Man.* In 8 to 10 seconds, Peek could read and remember a page. During his lifetime, he memorized 9000 books, including Shakespeare's plays and the Bible. He absorbed details of maps and could provide GPS-like travel directions within

---

intelligence the ability to learn from experience, solve problems, and use knowledge to adapt to new situations.

general intelligence (g) a general intelligence factor that, according to Spearman and others, underlies specific mental abilities and is therefore measured by every task on an intelligence test.

savant syndrome a condition in which a person otherwise limited in mental ability has an exceptional specific skill, such as in computation or drawing.

FIGURE 8.8 **Gardner's eight intelligences** Gardner has also proposed existential intelligence (the ability to ponder deep questions about life) as a ninth possible intelligence.

any major U.S. city. Yet he could not button his clothes, and he had little capacity for abstract concepts. Asked by his father at a restaurant to lower his voice, he slid down in his chair to lower his voice box. Asked for Lincoln's Gettysburg Address, he responded, "227 North West Front Street. But he only stayed there one night—he gave the speech the next day" (Treffert & Christensen, 2005).

Gardner has identified a total of eight *relatively independent intelligences,* including the verbal and mathematical aptitudes assessed by standardized tests (**FIGURE 8.8**). (He has also proposed a ninth possibility—existential intelligence—the ability to think in depth about deep questions in life.) Thus, the computer programmer, the poet, the street-smart adolescent, and the basketball team's play-making

point guard exhibit different kinds of intelligence (Gardner, 1998). To Gardner, a general intelligence score is like the overall rating of a city—it tells you something but doesn't give you much specific information about the city's schools, streets, or nightlife.

> "You have to be careful, if you're good at something, to make sure you don't think you're good at other things that you aren't necessarily so good at. . . . Because I've been very successful at [software development] people come in and expect that I have wisdom about topics that I don't."
> Bill Gates, 1998

STERNBERG'S THREE INTELLIGENCES

Robert Sternberg (1985, 2011) agrees with Gardner that there is more to real-world success than traditional intelligence and that we have multiple intelligences.

But Sternberg's *triarchic theory* proposes three, not eight or nine, intelligences:

- *Analytical intelligence* (school smarts: traditional academic problem solving)
- *Creative intelligence* (trailblazing smarts: the ability to adapt to new situations and generate novel ideas)
- *Practical intelligence* (street smarts: skill at handling everyday tasks that may be poorly defined, with multiple solutions)

Gardner and Sternberg differ in some areas, but they agree on two important points: Multiple abilities can contribute to life success, and varieties of giftedness bring spice to life and challenges for education. Trained to appreciate such variety, many teachers have applied multiple intelligence theories in their classrooms.

"You're wise, but you lack tree smarts."

CRITICISMS OF MULTIPLE INTELLIGENCE THEORIES Wouldn't it be wonderful if the world were so just that a weakness in one area would be balanced by genius in another? Alas, say critics, the world is not just (Ferguson, 2009; Scarr, 1989). Research using factor analysis has confirmed that there is a general intelligence factor: *g* matters (Johnson et al., 2008). It predicts performance on various complex tasks and in various jobs (Arneson et al., 2011; Gottfredson, 2002a,b, 2003a,b). Youths' intelligence test scores predict their income decades later (Zagorsky, 2007).

But we do well to remember that the recipe for success is not simple. As in so many realms of life, success has two ingredients: *can do* (ability) and *will do* (motivation) (Lubinski, 2009a). High intelligence may get you into a profession (via the schools and training programs that open doors). *Grit*—your motivation and drive—will make you successful once you're there.

Highly successful people tend to be conscientious, well connected, and doggedly energetic. These qualities often translate into dedicated hard work. Researchers report a *10-year rule*: Expert performers—in chess, dancing, sports, computer programming, music, and medicine—have all spent about a decade in intense, daily practice (Ericsson & Pool, 2016; Simon & Chase, 1973). Becoming a professional musician, for example, requires primarily native ability (Macnamara et al., 2014). But it also requires years of practice— totalling about 11,000 hours on average, and *at least* 3000 hours (Campitelli & Gobet, 2011). (For more on how

self-disciplined grit feeds success, see Appendix B.) The recipe for success is a gift of nature plus a whole lot of nurture.

Retrieve + Remember

- How does the existence of savant syndrome support Gardner's theory of multiple intelligences?

ANSWER: People with savant syndrome have limited mental ability overall but possess one or more exceptional skills. According to Howard Gardner, this suggests that our abilities come in separate packages rather than being fully expressed by one general intelligence that covers all our talents.

Emotional Intelligence

LOQ 8-15 What four abilities make up emotional intelligence?

Some psychologists have further explored our nonacademic *social intelligence*—the know-how involved in understanding social situations and managing ourselves successfully (Cantor & Kihlstrom, 1987). Psychologist Edward Thorndike first proposed the concept in 1920, noting that "the best mechanic in a factory may fail as a foreman for lack of social intelligence" (Goleman, 2006, p. 83).

A critical part of social intelligence, **emotional intelligence**, includes four abilities (Mayer et al., 2002, 2011, 2012):

- *Perceiving* emotions (recognizing them in faces, music, and stories)
- *Understanding* emotions (predicting them and how they may change and blend)
- *Managing* emotions (knowing how to express them in varied situations)
- *Using* emotions to enable adaptive or creative thinking

Emotionally intelligent people are both socially aware and self-aware. They avoid being hijacked by overwhelming depression, anxiety, or anger. They can read others' emotions and know what to say to soothe a grieving friend, encourage a workmate, and manage a conflict.

Those who score high on managing emotions enjoy higher-quality interac-

tions with friends, and they perform modestly better on the job (Lopes et al., 2004; O'Boyle et al., 2011). On and off the job, they can delay gratification in favor of long-range rewards. They are also emotionally happy and physically healthy (Sánchez-Álvarez et al., 2015; Schutte et al., 2007). Thus, emotionally intelligent people tend to succeed in career, marriage, and parenting situations where academically smarter, but emotionally less intelligent people may fail (Ciarrochi et al., 2006).

* * *

TABLE 8.3 summarizes these theories of intelligence.

Assessing Intelligence

LOQ 8-16 What is an intelligence test, and how do achievement and aptitude tests differ?

An **intelligence test** assesses a person's mental aptitudes and compares them with those of others, using numerical scores. We can test people's mental abilities in two ways, depending on what we want to know.

- **Achievement tests** are designed to measure what people have learned. Your final exam will measure what you learned in this class.
- **Aptitude tests** are designed to assess what people will be able to learn; they are meant to predict future behavior.

So, how do psychologists design these tests, and why should we believe in the results?

What Do Intelligence Tests Test?

LOQ 8-17 When and why were intelligence tests created, and how do today's tests differ from early intelligence tests?

Barely more than a century ago, psychologists began designing tests to assess people's mental abilities. Modern intelligence testing traces its birth to early twentieth-century France.

TABLE 8.3   Comparing Theories of Intelligence

Theory	Summary	Strengths	Other Considerations
Spearman's general intelligence (g)	A basic intelligence predicts our abilities in many different academic areas.	Different abilities, such as verbal and spatial, do have some tendency to correlate.	Human abilities are too varied to be presented as a single general intelligence factor.
Gardner's multiple intelligences	Our abilities are best classified into eight or nine independent intelligences, which include a broad range of skills beyond traditional school smarts.	Intelligence is more than just verbal and mathematical skills. Other equally important abilities help us adapt.	Should all abilities be considered *intelligences?* Shouldn't some be called less vital *talents?*
Sternberg's triarchic theory	Our intelligence is best classified into three areas that predict real-world success: analytical, creative, and practical.	These three areas cover the different aptitudes we call intelligence.	These three areas may be less independent than Sternberg thought and may actually share an underlying g factor.
Emotional intelligence	Social intelligence contributes to life success. Emotional intelligence is a key aspect, consisting of perceiving, understanding, managing, and using emotions.	The four components that predict social success.	Does this stretch the concept of intelligence too far?

ALFRED BINET: PREDICTING SCHOOL ACHIEVEMENT With a new French law that required all children to attend school, officials knew that some children, including many newcomers to Paris, would need special classes. But how could the schools make fair judgments about children's learning potential? Teachers might assess children who had little prior education as slow learners. Or they might sort children into classes on the basis of their social backgrounds. To avoid such bias, France's minister of public education gave psychologist Alfred Binet the task of designing fair tests.

In 1905, Binet and his student, Théodore Simon, first presented their work (Nicolas & Levine, 2012). They began by assuming that all children follow the same course of intellectual development but that some develop more rapidly. A "dull" child should therefore score much like a typical younger child, and a "bright" child like a typical older child. Binet and Simon now had a clear goal. They would measure each child's **mental age,** the level of performance typically associated with a certain *chronological age* (age in years). Average 8-year-olds, for example, have a mental age of 8. An 8-year-old with a below-average mental age (perhaps performing at the level of a typical 6-year-old) would struggle with schoolwork considered normal for 8-year-olds.

ALFRED BINET (1857–1911) Adaptations of Binet's pioneering intelligence test were sometimes used to discriminate against immigrant and minority groups. But his intent was simply to match children with appropriate schooling.

Binet and Simon tested a variety of reasoning and problem-solving questions on Binet's two daughters, and then on "bright" and "backward" Parisian schoolchildren. The items they developed predicted how well French children would handle their schoolwork.

Binet hoped his test would be used to improve children's education. But he also feared it would be used to label children and limit their opportunities (Gould, 1981).

LEWIS TERMAN: MEASURING INNATE INTELLIGENCE Binet's fears were realized soon after his death in 1911, when others adapted his tests for use as a numerical measure of inherited intelligence. Lewis Terman (1877–1956), a Stanford University professor, tried the Paris-developed questions and age norms with California schoolchildren but found they worked poorly. So he adapted some items, added others, and established new standards for various ages. He also extended the upper end of the test's range from teenagers to "superior adults." He gave his revision the name it still has today—the **Stanford-Binet.**

emotional intelligence the ability to perceive, understand, manage, and use emotions.

intelligence test a method for assessing an individual's mental aptitudes and comparing them with those of others, using numerical scores.

achievement test a test designed to assess what a person has learned.

aptitude test a test designed to predict a person's future performance; *aptitude* is the capacity to learn.

mental age a measure of intelligence test performance devised by Binet; the level of performance typically associated with children of a certain chronological age. Thus, a child who does as well as an average 8-year-old is said to have a mental age of 8.

Stanford-Binet the widely used American revision (by Terman at Stanford University) of Binet's original intelligence test.

Terman assumed that intelligence tests revealed a fixed mental capacity present from birth. He also assumed that some ethnic groups were naturally more intelligent than others. And he supported the controversial *eugenics* movement, which promoted selective breeding and sterilization as a means of protecting and improving human genetic quality.

German psychologist William Stern's contribution to intelligence testing was the famous term **intelligence quotient,** or **IQ.** The IQ was simply a person's mental age divided by chronological age and multiplied by 100 to get rid of the decimal point. Thus, an average child, whose mental age (8) and chronological age (8) are the same, has an IQ of 100. But an 8-year-old who answers questions at the level of a typical 10-year-old has an IQ of 125:

$$IQ = \frac{\text{mental age of 10}}{\text{chronological age of 8}} \times 100 = 125$$

The original IQ formula worked fairly well for children but not for adults. (Should a 40-year-old who does as well on the test as an average 20-year-old be assigned an IQ of only 50?) Most current intelligence tests, including the Stanford-Binet, no longer compute an IQ (though the term IQ still lingers in everyday vocabulary as short for "intelligence test score"). Instead, they assign a score that represents a test-taker's performance *relative to the average performance* (which is arbitrarily set at 100) of others the same age. Most people—about 68 percent of those taking an intelligence test—fall between 85 and 115. (We'll return to these figures shortly, in the discussion of the *normal curve.*)

DAVID WECHSLER: TESTING SEPARATE STRENGTHS Psychologist David Wechsler created what is now the most widely used individual intelligence test, the **Wechsler Adult Intelligence Scale (WAIS).** There is a version for school-age children (the *Wechsler Intelligence Scale for Children* [WISC]), and another for preschool children (Evers et al., 2012).

The WAIS (2008 edition) consists of 15 subtests, broken into verbal and performance areas. Here is a sample:

- *Similarities*—Considering the commonality of two objects or concepts, such as "In what way are wool and cotton alike?"
- *Vocabulary*—Naming pictured objects, or defining words ("What is a guitar?")
- *Block design*—Visual abstract processing, such as "Using the four blocks, make one just like this."
- *Letter-number sequencing*—On hearing a series of numbers and letters, repeat the numbers in ascending order, and then the letters in alphabetical order: "R-2-C-1-M-3."

The WAIS yields both an overall intelligence score and separate scores for verbal comprehension, perceptual organization, working memory, and processing speed. Striking differences among these scores can provide clues to strengths or weaknesses. For example,

MATCHING PATTERNS Block design puzzles test visual abstract processing ability. Wechsler's individually administered intelligence test comes in forms suited for adults and children.

a person who scores low on verbal comprehension but has high scores on other subtests may have a reading or language disability. Other comparisons can help health care workers design a therapy plan for a stroke patient. In such ways, these tests help realize Binet's aim: to identify opportunities for improvement and strengths that teachers and others can build upon.

Retrieve + Remember

- An employer with a pool of applicants for a single position wants to know each applicant's potential. To determine that, she should use an _____ (achievement/aptitude) test. That same employer wishing to test the effectiveness of a new, on-the-job training program would be wise to use an _____ (achievement/aptitude) test.

  ANSWERS: aptitude; achievement

- What did Binet hope to achieve by establishing a child's *mental age*?

  ANSWER: Binet hoped that knowing the child's *mental age* (the age that typically corresponds to a certain level of performance) would help identify appropriate school placement.

- What is the IQ of a 4-year-old with a mental age of 5?

  ANSWER: 125 (5 ÷ 4 × 100 = 125)

Three Tests of a "Good" Test

LOQ 8-18 What is a normal curve, and what does it mean to say that a test has been standardized and is reliable and valid?

To be widely accepted, a psychological test must be *standardized, reliable,* and *valid.* The Stanford-Binet and Wechsler tests meet these requirements.

WAS THE TEST STANDARDIZED? The number of questions you answer correctly on an intelligence test would reveal almost nothing. To know how well you performed, you would need some basis for comparison. That's why test-makers give new tests to a representative sample of people. The scores from this pretested group become the basis for future comparisons. If you then take the test following the same procedures, your score will be meaningful when compared with others. This process is called **standardization.**

One way to compare scores is to graph them. No matter what trait we measure—height, weight, or mental aptitude—people's scores tend to form a bell-shaped pattern called the *bell curve,* or **normal curve.** The curve's highest point is the average score. Moving out from the average, toward either extreme, we find fewer and fewer people.

On an intelligence test, the average score has a value of 100 (**FIGURE 8.9**). For the Stanford-Binet and the Wechsler tests, your score would indicate whether your performance fell above or below that average. A score of 130, for example, would indicate that only 2.5 percent of all test-takers had scores higher than yours. About 95 percent of all people score within 30 points above or 30 points below 100.

IS THE TEST RELIABLE? Knowing how your score compares with those in the standardization group still won't tell you much unless the test has **reliability.** A reliable test gives consistent scores, no matter who takes the test or when they take it. To check a test's reliability, researchers test many people many times. They may retest people using the same test, or they may split the test in half and see whether odd-question scores and even-question scores agree. If the two sets of scores generally agree—if they *correlate*—the test is reliable. The higher the correlation, the more reliable the test.

The tests we have considered—the Stanford-Binet, the WAIS, and the WISC—all are very reliable after early childhood. When retested, people's scores generally match their first score closely—even over a lifetime (Deary et al., 2004, 2009).

IS THE TEST VALID? A **valid** test measures or predicts what it promises. A test can be reliable but not valid. Imagine buying a tape measure with faulty markings. If you use it to measure people's heights, your results will be very reliable. No matter how many times you measure, people's heights will be the same. But your faulty height results will not be valid.

Valid tests have **content validity** when they measure what they are supposed to measure. The road test for a driver's license has content validity because it samples the tasks a driver routinely faces. A course exam has content validity if it tests what you learned in the course.

But we also expect intelligence tests to have **predictive validity**. Intelligence tests should predict future performance, and to some extent, they do.

LaunchPad See LaunchPad's *Video: Correlational Studies* for a helpful tutorial animation.

High and Low Scorers—How Do They Differ?

LOQ 8-19 What are the traits of people who score at the low and high extremes on intelligence tests?

One way to glimpse the validity and significance of any test is to compare people who score at the two extremes of the

intelligence quotient (IQ) defined originally as the ratio of mental age *(ma)* to chronological age *(ca)* multiplied by 100 (thus, IQ = *ma* ÷ *ca* × 100). On contemporary intelligence tests, the average performance for a given age is assigned a score of 100.

Wechsler Adult Intelligence Scale (WAIS) the WAIS and its companion versions for children are the most widely used intelligence tests; contains verbal and performance (nonverbal) subtests.

standardization defining uniform testing procedures and meaningful scores by comparison with the performance of a pretested group.

normal curve the bell-shaped curve that describes the distribution of many physical and psychological attributes. Most scores fall near the average, and fewer and fewer scores lie near the extremes.

reliability the extent to which a test yields consistent results, as assessed by the consistency of scores on two halves of the test, on alternative forms of the test, or on retesting.

validity the extent to which a test measures or predicts what it is supposed to. (See also *content validity* and *predictive validity*.)

content validity the extent to which a test samples the behavior that is of interest.

predictive validity the success with which a test predicts the behavior it is designed to predict.

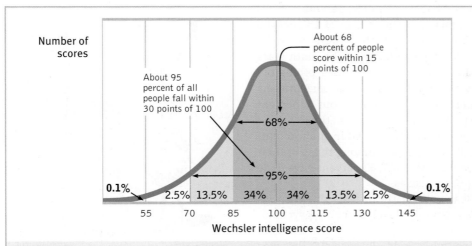

FIGURE 8.9 The normal curve Scores on aptitude tests tend to form a normal, or bell-shaped, curve around an average score. For the Wechsler scale, for example, the average score is 100.

normal curve. As Figure 8.9 shows, about 5 percent of intelligence test-takers score at the extremes—2.5 percent higher than 130, and 2.5 percent lower than 70. If a test is valid, the two extreme groups should differ noticeably. On intelligence tests, they do.

THE LOW EXTREME A low intelligence test score alone does not mean that a person has the developmental condition now known as an **intellectual disability** (formerly called *mental retardation*). Intellectual disability is a condition that is apparent before age 18. It sometimes has a known physical cause. **Down syndrome,** for example, is a disorder of varying intellectual and physical severity caused by an extra copy of chromosome 21. People diagnosed with a mild intellectual disability—those just below the 70 score—may be able to live independently.

The American Association on Intellectual and Developmental Disabilities guidelines list two requirements for assigning a diagnosis of intellectual disability:

- The person's intelligence test score indicates performance below 98 percent of test-takers (Schalock et al., 2010).

MAINSTREAMING IN CHILE Most Chilean children with Down syndrome attend separate schools for students with special needs. However, this boy attends the Altamira School, where children with differing abilities share the classroom.

Claudia Daut/Reuters

- The person has difficulty adapting to the normal demands of independent living, as expressed in three areas, or skills: *conceptual* (such as language, reading, and concepts of money, time, and number); *social* (such as interpersonal skills, being socially responsible, following basic rules and laws, avoiding being victimized); and *practical* (such as health and personal care, occupational skill, and travel).

THE HIGH EXTREME Children whose intelligence test scores indicate extraordinary academic gifts mostly thrive. In one famous project begun in 1921, Lewis Terman studied more than 1500 California schoolchildren with IQ scores over 135. These high-scoring children (later called the "Termites") were healthy, well-adjusted, and unusually successful academically (Friedman & Martin, 2012; Koenen et al., 2009; Lubinski, 2009a). Their success continued over the next seven decades. Most attained high levels of education, and many were doctors, lawyers, professors, scientists, and writers (Austin et al., 2002; Holahan & Sears, 1995).

Other studies have focused on young people who aced the SAT. One group of 1650 math whizzes had at age 13 scored in the top quarter of 1 percent of their age group. By their fifties, those individuals had claimed 681 patents (Lubinski et al., 2014). Another group of 13-year-old verbal aptitude high scorers were by age 38 twice as likely as the math stars to have become humanities professors or written a novel (Kell et al., 2013). Among Americans in general, about 1 percent earn doctorates. But for the 12- and 13-year-olds who scored in the top hundredth of 1 percent among those of their age taking the SAT, 63 percent have done so (Lubinski, 2009b).

Jean Piaget, the twentieth century's most famous developmental psychologist, might have felt right at home with these whiz kids. By age 15, he was already publishing scientific articles on mollusks (Hunt, 1993).

Retrieve + Remember

- What are the three requirements that a psychological test must meet in order to be widely accepted? Explain.

ANSWER: A psychological test must be *standardized* (pretested on a representative sample of people), *reliable* (yielding consistent results), and *valid* (measuring and predicting what it is supposed to).

The Nature and Nurture of Intelligence

Intelligence runs in families. But why? Are our intellectual abilities mostly inherited? Or are they molded by our environment?

Heredity and Intelligence

LOQ 8-20 What does it mean when we say that a trait is heritable? What do twin and adoption studies tell us about the nature and nurture of intelligence?

Heritability is the portion of the *variation among individuals* that we can assign to genes. Estimates of the heritability of intelligence range from 50 to 80 percent (Calvin et al., 2012; Johnson et al., 2009; Neisser et al., 1996). Does this mean that we can assume that 50 percent of *your* intelligence is due to your genes, and the rest

"I told my parents that if grades were so important they should have paid for a smarter egg donor."

The New Yorker Collection, 1999, Donald Reilly from cartoonbank.com

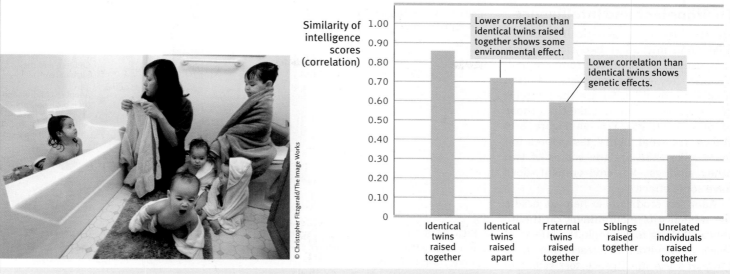

FIGURE 8.10 Intelligence: Nature and nurture The most genetically similar people have the most similar intelligence scores. Remember: 1.00 indicates a perfect correlation; zero indicates no correlation at all. (Data from McGue et al., 1993.)

to your environment? *No.* Heritability is a tricky concept. *The important point to remember:* Heritability never applies to an *individual*, only to *why people in a group differ from one another.*

The heritability of intelligence varies from study to study. To see why, consider humorist Mark Twain's fantasy of raising boys in barrels until age 12, feeding them through a hole. Let's take his joke a step further and say we'll give all those boys an intelligence test at age 12. Since their *environments* were all equal, any differences in their test scores could only be due to their heredity. In this "study," heritability would be 100 percent. But what if a mad scientist cloned 100 boys and raised them in drastically different environments (some in barrels and others in mansions)? In this case, their *heredity* would be equal, so any test-score differences could only be due to their environment. The environmental effect would be 100 percent, and heritability would be zero.

In real life, psychologists can't clone people to study the effects of heredity and environment. But as we noted in Chapter 3, nature has done that work for us. Identical twins share the same genes. Do they also share the same mental abilities?

As you can see from **FIGURE 8.10,** which summarizes many studies, the answer is *Yes.* Even when identical twins are adopted by two different families, their intelligence test scores are nearly the same. When they grow up together, their scores are nearly as similar as those of one person taking the same test twice (Haworth et al., 2009; Lykken, 1999; Plomin et al., 2016). Identical twins are also very similar in specific talents, such as music, math, and sports (Vinkhuyzen et al., 2009).

Although genes matter, there is no known "genius" gene. When 200 researchers pooled their data on 126,559 people, all the gene variations analyzed accounted for only about 2 percent of the differences in educational achievement (Rietveld et al., 2013). The search for smart genes continues, but this much is

clear: Many, many genes contribute to intelligence (Bouchard, 2014). Intelligence is thus like height (Johnson, 2010). Working together, 54 specific gene variations account for only 5 percent of our individual height differences.

intellectual disability a condition of limited mental ability, indicated by an intelligence test score of 70 or below and difficulty adapting to the demands of life. (Formerly referred to as *mental retardation.*)

Down syndrome a condition of mild to severe intellectual disability and associated physical disorders caused by an extra copy of chromosome 21.

heritability the portion of variation among people in a group that we can attribute to genes. The heritability of a trait may vary, depending on the population and the environment.

Retrieve + Remember

- A check on your understanding of heritability: If environments become more equal, the heritability of intelligence would

  a. increase.   b. decrease.   c. be unchanged.

ANSWER: a. (Heritability—variation explained by genetic influences—will increase as environmental variation decreases.)

Environment and Intelligence

Fraternal twins are genetically no more alike than any other two siblings. But they usually share an environment and, because they are the same age, are often treated more alike. So are their intelligence test scores more alike than those of other siblings? *Yes*—as Figure 8.10 shows, fraternal twins' test scores are more alike than are the scores of two other siblings. So environment does have some effect.

Adoption studies also help us assess the influence of environment on intelligence. Seeking to untangle the effects of genes and environment, researchers have compared the intelligence test scores of adopted children with those of their

- *biological parents* (who provided their genes).
- *adoptive parents* (who provided their home environment).
- *adoptive siblings* (who shared that home environment).

Several studies suggest that a shared environment exerts a modest influence on intelligence test scores.

- The intelligence scores of "virtual twins"—same-age children adopted as infants and raised together as siblings—correlate at a level higher than chance: +0.28 (Segal et al., 2012).
- Adoption from poverty into middle-class homes enhances children's intelligence test scores (Nisbett et al., 2012). One large Swedish study looked at this effect among children adopted into wealthier families with more educated parents. The adopted children's scores were higher, by an average of 4.4 points, than those of their not-adopted biological siblings (Kendler et al., 2015).
- Adoption of mistreated or neglected children also enhances their intelligence scores (van IJzendoorn & Juffer, 2005, 2006).

So during childhood, adoptive siblings' test scores correlate modestly.

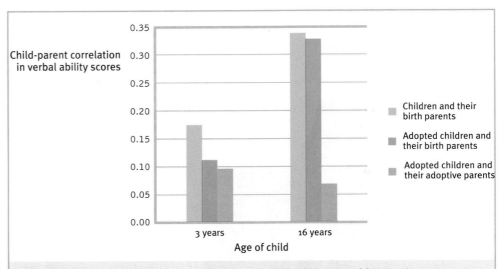

FIGURE 8.11 In verbal ability, whom do adopted children resemble? As the years went by in their adoptive families, children's verbal ability scores became more like their *biological* parents' scores. (Data from Plomin & DeFries, 1998.)

What do you think happens as the years go by and adopted children settle in with their adoptive families? Would you expect the shared-home-environment effect to grow stronger, and the shared-gene effect to shrink?

If you said *Yes*, we have a surprise for you. Mental similarities between adopted children and their adoptive families *lessen* with age. By adulthood they drop to roughly zero (McGue et al., 1993). Genetic influences—not environmental ones—become more apparent as we accumulate life experience. Identical twins' similarities, for example, continue or increase into their eighties (Deary et al., 2009). Similarly, in verbal ability, adopted children become more like their biological parents as the years go by (**FIGURE 8.11**). Who would have guessed?

LaunchPad   See LaunchPad's *Video: Twin Studies* for a helpful tutorial animation.

Gene-Environment Interactions

LOQ 8-21 How can environmental influences affect cognitive development?

We have seen that biology and experience intertwine. (Recall from Chapter 3 that *epigenetics* is the field that studies this nature–nurture meeting place.)

Suppose that, thanks to your genes, you are just slightly taller and quicker than others (Flynn, 2003, 2007). If you try out for a basketball team, you will more likely be picked. Once on the team, you will probably play more often than others (getting more practice and experience) and you will receive more coaching. The same would be true for your separated identical twin—who might, not just for genetic reasons, also become a basketball star. With mental abilities, as with physical abilities, *our genes shape the experiences that shape us*. If you have a natural aptitude for academics, you will more likely stay in school, read books, and ask questions—all of which will increase your brain power. In these gene-environment interactions, small genetic advantages can trigger social experiences that multiply your original skills.

Sometimes, however, environmental conditions work in reverse, depressing cognitive development. Severe deprivation leaves footprints on the brain, as J. McVicker Hunt (1982) observed in one Iranian orphanage. The typical child Hunt observed there could not sit up unassisted at age 2 or walk at age 4. The little care the infants received was not in response to their crying, cooing, or other behaviors, so the children developed little sense of personal control over their environment. They were instead becoming passive "glum lumps." Extreme deprivation was crushing native intelligence—a finding confirmed by other studies of children raised in poorly run orphanages in Romania and elsewhere (C. A. Nelson et al., 2009, 2013; van IJzendoorn et al., 2008).

Mindful of the effect of early experiences and early intervention, Hunt began a training program for the Iranian caregivers, teaching them to play language-fostering games with 11 infants. They learned to imitate the babies' babbling. They engaged them in vocal follow-the-leader. And, finally, they taught the infants sounds from the Persian language. The results were dramatic. By 22 months of age, the infants could name more than 50 objects and body parts. They so charmed visitors that most were adopted—an impressive new success rate for the orphanage.

If extreme conditions—malnutrition, sensory deprivation, and social isolation—can slow normal brain development, could the reverse also be true? Could normal brain development be amplified by providing an "enriched" environment? Most experts are doubtful (Bruer, 1999; DeLoache et al., 2010; Reichert et al., 2010). There is no recipe for fast-forwarding a normal infant into a genius. All babies should have normal exposure to

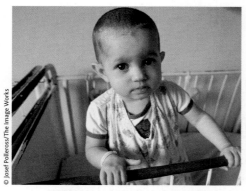

DEVASTATING NEGLECT Some Romanian orphans, such as this child in the Leaganul Pentru Copii orphanage in 1990, had minimal interaction with caregivers and suffered delayed development.

sights, sounds, and speech. Beyond that, developmental psychologist Sandra Scarr's (1984) verdict is still widely shared: "Parents who are very concerned about providing special educational lessons for their babies are wasting their time."

Later in childhood, however, some forms of enrichment can pay intelligence-score dividends (Protzko et al., 2013). Motivation can even affect test scores. When promised money for doing well, adolescents have scored higher on intelligence tests (Duckworth et al., 2011).

So, environmental influences can foster or diminish cognitive skills. But what is the general trend? On our journey from womb to tomb, does our intelligence change or remain stable?

Intelligence Across the Life Span

Stability or Change?

LOQ 8-22 How stable are intelligence test scores over the life span, and how do psychologists study this question?

Intelligence endures. By age 4, children's intelligence test scores begin to predict their adolescent and adult scores. By late adolescence, intelligence and other aptitude scores display remarkable stability. How do we know this?

- **Cross-sectional studies** compare people of different ages with one another.
- **Longitudinal studies** restudy and retest the same people over a long period of time.

Scottish researcher Ian Deary and his colleagues (2004, 2009b, 2013) set a record for a long-term study, and their story is one of psychology's great tales. On June 1, 1932, Scotland did what no other nation has done before or since. To identify working-class children who would benefit from further education, the government gave every child born in Scotland in 1921 an intelligence test—87,498 eleven-year-olds in all.

On June 1, 1997, sixty-five years later to the day, Patricia Whalley, the wife of Deary's co-worker, Lawrence Whalley, discovered the test results on dusty storeroom shelves at the Scottish Council for Research in Education, not far from Deary's Edinburgh University office. "This will change our lives," Deary replied when Whalley told him the news. And so it has, with dozens of studies of the stability and the predictive capacity of these early test results. For example, 542 survivors from the 1932 test group were retested at age 80 (Deary et al., 2004). After nearly 70 years of varied life experiences, the correlation between the test-takers' two sets of scores was striking (**FIGURE 8.12**). Ditto when 106 survivors were retested at age 90 (Deary et al., 2013).

Higher-scoring children and adults also tend to live healthier and longer lives. Why might this be the case? Deary (2008) offered four possible explanations:

- Intelligence gives people better access to more education, better jobs, and a healthier environment.
- Intelligence encourages healthy living: less smoking, better diet, more exercise.
- Prenatal events or early childhood illnesses could influence both intelligence and health.
- A "well-wired body," as evidenced by fast reaction speeds, may foster both intelligence and longer life.

So, intelligence scores are strikingly *stable*. And high intelligence is a predictor of health and long life. Yet, with age, our knowledge and our mental agility change, as we see next.

---

cross-sectional study research in which people of different ages are compared with one another.

longitudinal study research in which the same people are restudied and retested over a long period.

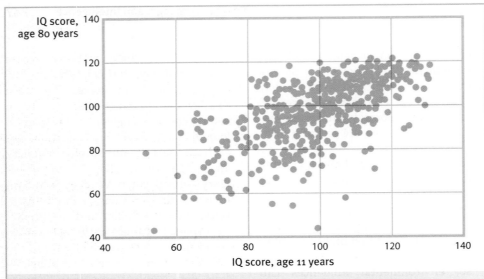

FIGURE 8.12 Intelligence endures When Ian Deary and his colleagues retested 80-year-old Scots, using an intelligence test they had taken as 11-year-olds, their scores across seven decades correlated +0.66, as shown here. (Data from Deary et al., 2004.) When 106 survivors were again retested at age 90, the correlation with their age 11 scores was +0.54 (Deary et al., 2013).

LaunchPad See LaunchPad's *Video: Longitudinal and Cross-Sectional Studies* for a helpful tutorial animation. And explore how researchers have studied aging and intelligence with LaunchPad's *How Would You Know If Intelligence Changes With Age?*

Crystallized and Fluid Intelligence

LOQ 8-23 What are crystallized and fluid intelligence, and how does aging affect them?

What happens to our intellectual powers as we age? The answer to that question depends on the task and the type of ability it represents.

- **Crystallized intelligence**—our accumulated knowledge, as reflected in vocabulary and word-power tests—*increases* as we age, up to old age.

- **Fluid intelligence**—our ability to reason speedily and abstractly, as when solving unfamiliar logic problems—*decreases* beginning in the twenties and thirties. It declines slowly until about age 75 or so, and then more rapidly, especially after age 85 (Cattell, 1963; Horn, 1982; Salthouse, 2009, 2013).

With age we lose and we win. We lose recall memory and processing speed, but we gain vocabulary and knowledge (**FIGURE 8.13**). In older adulthood, our social

reasoning skills increase. We are better able to see many different viewpoints, to appreciate the limits of knowledge, and to offer helpful wisdom in times of conflict (Grossmann et al., 2010). Our decisions also become less distorted by negative emotions such as anxiety, depression, or anger (Blanchard-Fields, 2007; Carstensen & Mikels, 2005).

These life-span differences in mental abilities help explain why older adults are less likely to embrace new technologies (Charness & Boot, 2009; Pew, 2015). They also help explain some curious findings about creativity. Mathematicians and scientists produce much of their most creative work during their late twenties or early thirties, when fluid intelligence is at its peak (Jones et al., 2014). Prose authors, historians, and philosophers, who depend more on crystallized intelligence, tend to produce their best work in their forties, fifties, and beyond (Simonton, 1988, 1990).

Group Differences in Intelligence Test Scores

If there were no group differences in aptitude scores, psychologists would have no debate over hereditary and environmental influences. But there are group differences. What are they? And what do they mean?

Gender Similarities and Differences

LOQ 8-24 How and why do the genders differ in mental ability scores?

As in everyday life, in science it is differences, not similarities, that excite interest. Compared with the many ways men and women are physically alike, our intelligence differences are minor. In the 1932 testing of all Scottish 11-year-olds, for example, girls' average intelligence score was 100.6 and boys' was 100.5 (Deary et al., 2003, 2009). So far as *g* is concerned, boys and girls, and men and women, are the same species.

Yet, most people find differences more newsworthy. Girls outpace boys in spelling, verbal fluency, and locating objects (Voyer & Voyer, 2014). They are better emotion detectors and are more sensitive to touch, taste, and color (Halpern et al., 2007). In math computation and overall math performance, girls and boys hardly differ (Else-Quest et al., 2010; Hyde & Mertz, 2009; Lindberg et al., 2010). But in tests of spatial ability and complex math problems, boys outperform girls.

Males' mental ability scores also vary more than females'. Worldwide, boys outnumber girls at both the low extreme and the high extreme (Brunner et al., 2013).

Retrieve + Remember

- Researcher A is well funded to learn about how intelligence changes over the life span. Researcher B wants to study the intelligence of people who are now at various life stages. Which researcher should use the cross-sectional method and which should use the longitudinal method?

ANSWER: Researcher A should develop a *longitudinal study* to examine how intelligence changes in the same people over the life span. Researcher B should develop a *cross-sectional study* to examine the intelligence of people now at various life stages.

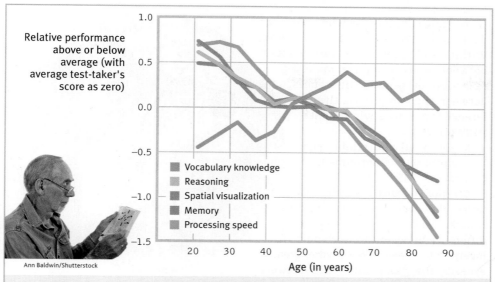

Relative performance above or below average (with average test-taker's score as zero)

Ann Baldwin/Shutterstock

- Vocabulary knowledge
- Reasoning
- Spatial visualization
- Memory
- Processing speed

Age (in years)

FIGURE 8.13 With age, we lose and we win. Studies reveal that word power grows with age, while fluid intelligence declines. (Data from Salthouse, 2010.)

crystallized intelligence your accumulated knowledge and verbal skills; tends to increase with age.

fluid intelligence your ability to reason speedily and abstractly; tends to decrease with age, especially during late adulthood.

of our ancestral mothers may have benefited more from a keen memory for the location of edible plants. That legacy lives today in women's superior memory for objects and their location.

But social expectations and opportunities also matter. In Russia, Asia, and the Middle East—where science and engineering are not considered masculine subjects—15-year-old girls slightly outperformed boys on an international science exam. In North America and Britain, boys scored higher (Fairfield, 2012). More gender-equal cultures, such as Sweden and Iceland, exhibit little of the gender math gap found in gender-unequal cultures, such as Turkey and Korea (Guiso et al., 2008). As we have seen in so many areas of life, experience matters.

Boys, for example, are more often found in special education classes, but also among those scoring very high on the SAT math test.

The most reliable male edge appears in spatial ability tests like the one shown in **FIGURE 8.14** (Maeda & Yoon, 2013; Wei et al., 2012). To solve the problem, you must quickly rotate three-dimensional objects in your mind. Today, such skills help when fitting suitcases into a car trunk, playing chess, or doing certain types of geometry problems. Evolutionary psychologists believe these same skills would have had survival value for our ancestral fathers, helping them track prey and make their way home (Geary, 1995, 1996; Halpern et al., 2007). The survival

Racial and Ethnic Similarities and Differences

LOQ 8-25 How and why do racial and ethnic groups differ in mental ability scores?

Fueling the group-differences debate are two other disturbing but agreed-upon facts:

- Racial and ethnic groups differ in their average intelligence test scores.
- High-scoring people (and groups) are more likely to achieve high levels of education and income.

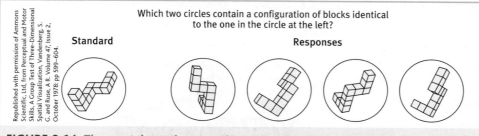

Republished with permission of Ammons Scientific, Ltd, from Perceptual and Motor Skills, A Group Test of Three-Dimensional Spatial Visualization, Vandenberg, S. G. and Ruse, A. R. Volume 47, Issue 2, October 1978: pp 599–604.

Which two circles contain a configuration of blocks identical to the one in the circle at the left?

Standard

Responses

FIGURE 8.14 The mental rotation test This is a test of spatial abilities. (From Vandenberg & Kuse, 1978.) See answer below.

ANSWER: The first and fourth responses.

© Larry Williams/Corbis

There are many group differences in average intelligence test scores. New Zealanders of European descent outscore native Maori New Zealanders. Israeli Jews outscore Israeli Arabs. Most Japanese outscore most Burakumin, a stigmatized Japanese minority. And White Americans have outscored Black Americans. This Black-White difference has been somewhat smaller in recent years, especially among children (Dickens & Flynn, 2006; Nisbett, 2009).

One more agreed-upon fact is that *group* differences provide little basis for judging individuals. Worldwide, women outlive men by four years, but knowing that you are male or female won't tell us much about how long you will live.

We have seen that heredity contributes to *individual* differences in intelligence. But group differences in a heritable trait may be entirely environmental, as in our earlier boys-in-barrels versus boys-in-mansions example. Consider one of nature's experiments: Allow some children to grow up hearing their culture's dominant language, while others, born deaf, do not. Then give both groups an intelligence test rooted in the dominant language. The result? No surprise. Those with expertise in the dominant language will score higher than those who were born deaf (Braden, 1994; Steele, 1990; Zeidner, 1990). Within each group, the differences between individuals are mainly a reflection of genetic differences. Between the two groups, the difference is mainly environmental (**FIGURE 8.15**).

Might racial and ethnic gaps be similarly environmental? Consider:

Genetics research reveals that under the skin, we humans are remarkably alike. The average genetic difference between two Icelandic villagers or between two Kenyans greatly exceeds the group difference between Icelanders and Kenyans (Cavalli-Sforza et al., 1994; Rosenberg et al., 2002). Moreover, looks can deceive. Light-skinned Europeans and dark-skinned Africans are genetically closer than are dark-skinned Africans and dark-skinned Aboriginal Australians.

Race is not a neatly defined biological category. Many social scientists think *race* is no longer a meaningful term. They view race primarily as a social category without well-defined physical boundaries. Each racial group, they point out, blends seamlessly into its geographical neighbors (Helms et al., 2005; Smedley & Smedley,

NATURE'S OWN MORPHING Nature draws no sharp boundaries between races, which blend gradually one into the next around the Earth. But the human urge to classify causes people to socially define themselves in racial categories, which may become catchall labels for physical features, social identity, and nationality.

2005). Moreover, with increasingly mixed ancestries, fewer and fewer people fit neatly into any one category, and more and more identify themselves as multiracial (Pauker et al., 2009).

Within the same population, there are generation-to-generation differences in test

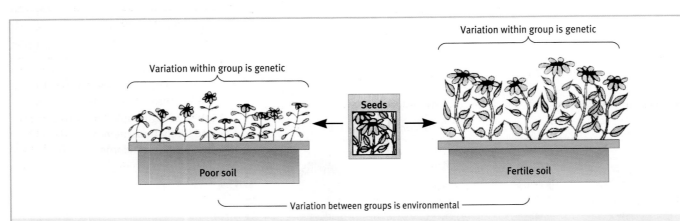

FIGURE 8.15 Group differences and environmental impact Even if the variation between members within a group reflects genetic differences, the average difference between groups may be wholly due to environment. Imagine that seeds from the same mixture are sown in different soils. Although height differences *within* each window box of flowers will be genetic, the height difference *between* the two groups will be environmental. (Inspired by Lewontin, 1976.)

scores. Test scores of today's better-fed, better-educated, and more test-prepared population exceed the scores of the 1930s population (Flynn, 2012; Pietschnig & Voracek, 2015; Trahan et al., 2014). The two generations differ by a greater margin than the intelligence test score of the average White today exceeds that of the average Black. The average intelligence test performance of today's sub-Saharan Africans is the same as that of British adults in 1948. No one credits generation-to-generation differences to genetics.

Given the same information, Blacks and Whites show similar information-processing skills. Research findings indicate that cultural differences in access to information may account for racial differences in intelligence test performance (Fagan & Holland, 2007).

Schools and culture matter. Countries whose economies create a large wealth gap between rich and poor also tend to have a large rich-versus-poor intelligence test score gap (Nisbett, 2009). Moreover, educational policies—such as kindergarten attendance, school discipline, and instructional time per year—predict national differences in intelligence and knowledge tests (Rindermann & Ceci, 2009). Math achievement, aptitude test differences, and especially grades may reflect conscientiousness more than competence (Poropat, 2014). Asian students, who have outperformed North American students on such tests, have also spent 30 percent more time in school and much more time in and out of school studying math (Geary et al., 1996; Larson & Verma, 1999; Stevenson, 1992).

In different eras, different ethnic groups have experienced golden ages—periods of remarkable achievement. Twenty-five hundred years ago, it was the Greeks and the Egyptians, then the Romans. In the eighth and ninth centuries, genius seemed to reside in the Arab world. Five hundred years ago, the Aztecs and North Europeans took the lead. Today, we marvel at Asian technological genius and Jewish cultural success. Cultures rise and fall over centuries. Genes do not.

That fact makes it difficult to believe in the natural genetic superiority of any racial or ethnic group.

Retrieve + Remember

- If our society were to change dramatically, so that it offered perfect environmental equality, would the heritability of intelligence test scores then be 100 percent, or zero?

ANSWER: Perfect environmental equality would create 100 percent heritability, because genes alone would account for any human differences.

Are Intelligence Test Questions Biased?

LOQ 8-26 Are intelligence tests biased and discriminatory? How does stereotype threat affect test-takers' performance?

Knowing there are group differences in intelligence test scores leads us to wonder whether those differences are built into the tests. Are intelligence tests biased? The answer depends on how we define *bias*.

One way a test can be biased is if scores are influenced by a person's cultural experience. This in fact happened to Eastern European immigrants in the early 1900s. Lacking the experience to answer questions about their new culture, many were classified as "feeble-minded."

The *scientific* meaning of *bias* hinges on a test's validity. A valid intelligence test should predict future behavior for all groups of test-takers, not just for some. For example, if the SAT accurately predicted the college achievement of women but not that of men, then the test would be biased. Almost all psychologists agree that in this scientific sense, the major U.S. aptitude tests are *not* biased (Berry & Zhao, 2015; Neisser et al., 1996; Wigdor & Garner, 1982). Their predictive validity is roughly the same for women and men, for various races,

and for rich and poor. If an intelligence test score of 95 predicts slightly below-average grades, that rough prediction usually applies equally to all groups of test-takers.

As you've seen in so many contexts in this text, expectations and attitudes influence perceptions and behaviors. For intelligence test-makers, they can introduce bias. And for intelligence test-takers, expectations and attitudes can become self-fulfilling prophecies.

STEREOTYPE THREAT If you worry that your group or "type" often doesn't do well on a certain kind of test, your self-doubts and self-monitoring may hijack your working memory and hurt your performance (Schmader, 2010). This self-confirming concern that you will be judged based on a negative viewpoint is called **stereotype threat,** and it may impair your attention and learning (Inzlicht & Kang, 2010; Rydell et al., 2010).

In one study, equally capable men and women took a difficult math test. The women did not do as well as the men—except when they had been led to expect that women usually do as well as men on the test (Spencer et al., 1997). Without this helpful hint, these women apparently expected they would not do well. This feeling then led them to live *down* to their own expectations. Stereotype threat appeared again when Black students were reminded of their race just before taking verbal aptitude tests and performed worse (Steele et al., 2002). Negative stereotypes may undermine people's academic potential (Nguyen & Ryan, 2008; Walton & Spencer, 2009).

Stereotype threat helps explain why Blacks have scored higher when tested by Blacks than when tested by Whites (Danso & Esses, 2001; Inzlicht & Ben-Zeev, 2000).

 stereotype threat a self-confirming concern that you will be judged based on a negative stereotype.

It gives us insight into why women have scored higher on math tests with no male test-takers present, and why women's online chess performance drops sharply when they think they are playing a male opponent (Maass et al., 2008).

Could remedial "minority support" programs function as a stereotype that can erode performance? Some researchers believe they can, by giving students the message that they probably won't succeed. College programs that challenge minority students to believe in their potential, to increase their sense of belonging, or to focus on the idea that intelligence is not fixed have had good results. Students' grades were markedly higher, and their dropout rates lower (Walton & Cohen, 2011; Wilson, 2006).

Believing that intelligence is changeable, rather than biologically fixed, can foster a *growth mind-set*—a focus on learning and growing (Dweck, 2012a,b, 2015a,b, 2016). In programs fostering a growth mind-set, young teens learn that the brain is like a muscle that grows stronger with use as neuron connections grow: "Learning how to do a new kind of problem grows your math brain!" Receiving praise for effort rather than ability helps them understand the link between hard work and success (Gunderson et al, 2013). They also become more resilient when others frustrate them (Paunesku et al., 2015; Yeager et al., 2013, 2014). Indeed, superior achievements in fields from sports to science to music arise from the combination of ability, opportunity, and disciplined effort (Ericsson et al., 2007).

More than 300 studies of college and university students confirm the point. Ability + opportunity + motivation = success. High school students' math achievements and college students' grades reflect their aptitude but also

their self-discipline, their belief in the power of effort, and a curious "hungry mind" (Credé & Kuncel, 2008; Murayama et al., 2013; Richardson et al., 2012; von Stumm et al., 2011). Indian-Americans won all nine national spelling bee contests between 2008 and 2016. This achievement was likely influenced by a cultural belief that strong effort will meet with success (Rattan et al., 2012). To reach your potential, the formula is simple: Believe in your ability to learn and apply yourself with sustained effort.

Retrieve + Remember

- What is the difference between a test that is biased culturally and a test that is biased in terms of its validity?

ANSWER: A test may be *culturally biased* if higher scores are achieved by those with certain cultural experiences. That same test may not be biased in terms of *validity* if it predicts what it is supposed to predict. For example, the SAT may be culturally biased in favor of those with experience in the U.S. school system, but it does still accurately predict U.S. college success.

- What psychological principle helps explain why women tend to perform more poorly when they believe their online chess opponent is male?

ANSWER: stereotype threat

* * *

Perhaps, then, these should be our goals for tests of mental abilities:

- *Realize the benefits Alfred Binet foresaw*—to enable schools to recognize who might profit most from early intervention.

- *Remain alert to Binet's fear*—that intelligence test scores may be misinterpreted as literal measures of a person's enduring worth and potential.

U.S. SPELLING CHAMPS Vanya Shivashankar, 13, and Gokul Venkatachalam, 14, celebrate their co-winning the 2015 Scripps National Spelling Bee. Vanya correctly spelled "scherenschnitte" and Gokul "nunatak."

- *Remember that the competence that general intelligence tests sample is important.* Without such tests, those who decide on jobs and admissions would rely more on other considerations, such as personal opinion. But these tests reflect only one aspect of personal competence. Our practical intelligence and emotional intelligence matter, too, as do other forms of creativity, talent, and character.

The point to remember: There are many ways of being successful: Our differences are variations of human adaptability. Life's great achievements result not only from abilities (and fair opportunity) but also from motivation. Competence + Diligence = Accomplishment.

What time is it now? When you were reading about overconfidence, did you underestimate or overestimate how quickly you would finish the chapter?

Thinking, Language, and Intelligence

Test yourself by taking a moment to answer each of these Learning Objective Questions (repeated here from within the chapter). Then turn to Appendix D, Complete Chapter Reviews, to check your answers. Research suggests that trying to answer these questions on your own will improve your long-term memory of the concepts (McDaniel et al., 2009).

Thinking

8-1: What is cognition, and what are the functions of concepts?

8-2: What cognitive strategies help us solve problems, and what tendencies work against us?

8-3: What is intuition, and how can the availability heuristic influence our decisions and judgments?

8-4: What factors exaggerate our fear of unlikely events?

8-5: How are our decisions and judgments affected by overconfidence, belief perseverance, and framing?

8-6: How do smart thinkers use intuition?

8-7: What is creativity, and what fosters it?

8-8: What do we know about thinking in other species?

Language

8-9: What are the milestones in language development, and when is the critical period for learning language?

8-10: What brain areas are involved in language processing and speech?

8-11: How can thinking in images be useful?

8-12: What do we know about other species' capacity for language?

Intelligence

8-13: How do psychologists define *intelligence,* and what are the arguments for general intelligence *(g)?*

8-14: How do Gardner's and Sternberg's theories of multiple intelligences differ, and what criticisms have they faced?

8-15: What four abilities make up emotional intelligence?

8-16: What is an intelligence test, and how do achievement and aptitude tests differ?

8-17: When and why were intelligence tests created, and how do today's tests differ from early intelligence tests?

8-18: What is a normal curve, and what does it mean to say that a test has been standardized and is reliable and valid?

8-19: What are the traits of people who score at the low and high extremes on intelligence tests?

8-20: What does it mean when we say that a trait is heritable? What do twin and adoption studies tell us about the nature and nurture of intelligence?

8-21: How can environmental influences affect cognitive development?

8-22: How stable are intelligence test scores over the life span, and how do psychologists study this question?

8-23: What are crystallized and fluid intelligence, and how does aging affect them?

8-24: How and why do the genders differ in mental ability scores?

8-25: How and why do racial and ethnic groups differ in mental ability scores?

8-26: Are intelligence tests biased and discriminatory? How does stereotype threat affect test-takers' performance?

TERMS AND CONCEPTS TO REMEMBER

Test yourself on these terms by trying to write down the definition in your own words before flipping back to the referenced page to check your answer.

cognition, p. 223

concept, p. 223

prototype, p. 223

algorithm, p. 223

heuristic, p. 223

insight, p. 223

confirmation bias, p. 223

fixation, p. 223

intuition, p. 223

availability heuristic, p. 224

overconfidence, p. 227

belief perseverance, p. 227

framing, p. 227

creativity, p. 229

convergent thinking, p. 229

divergent thinking, p. 229

language, p. 231

babbling stage, p. 233

one-word stage, p. 233

two-word stage, p. 233

telegraphic speech, p. 233

grammar, p. 233

Broca's area, p. 235

Wernicke's area, p. 235

intelligence, p. 238

general intelligence *(g)*, p. 238

savant syndrome, p. 238

intelligence test, p. 241

emotional intelligence, p. 241

achievement test, p. 241

aptitude test, p. 241

mental age, p. 241

Stanford-Binet, p. 241

intelligence quotient (IQ), p. 243

Wechsler Adult Intelligence Scale (WAIS), p. 243

standardization, p. 243

normal curve, p. 243

reliability, p. 243

validity, p. 243

content validity, p. 243

predictive validity, p. 243

intellectual disability, p. 245

Down syndrome, p. 245

heritability, p. 245

cross-sectional study, p. 247

longitudinal study, p. 247

crystallized intelligence, p. 249

fluid intelligence, p. 249

stereotype threat, p. 251

CHAPTER TEST

Test yourself repeatedly throughout your studies. This will not only help you figure out what you know and don't know; the testing itself will help you learn and remember the information more effectively thanks to the testing effect.

1. A mental grouping of similar things is called a _____.

2. The most systematic procedure for solving a problem is a(n) _____.

3. Oscar describes his political beliefs as "strongly liberal," but he has decided to explore opposing viewpoints. How might he be affected by confirmation bias and belief perseverance in this effort?

4. A major obstacle to problem solving is fixation, which is a(n)

   a. tendency to base our judgments on vivid memories.

   b. tendency to wait for insight to occur.

   c. inability to view a problem from a new perspective.

   d. rule of thumb for judging the likelihood of an event in terms of our mental image of it.

5. Terrorist attacks in Paris and San Bernardino made Americans, in the words of one senator, "really scared and worried"—and more fearful of being victimized by terrorism than of other greater threats. Such exaggerated fears after dramatic events illustrate the _____ heuristic.

6. When consumers respond more positively to ground beef described as "75 percent lean" than to the same product labeled "25 percent fat," they have been influenced by _____.

7. Which of the following is NOT a characteristic of a creative person?

   a. Expertise

   b. Extrinsic motivation

   c. A venturesome personality

   d. Imaginative thinking skills

8. Children reach the one-word stage of speech development at about

   a. 4 months.

   b. 6 months.

   c. 1 year.

   d. 2 years.

9. When young children speak in short phrases using mostly verbs and nouns, this is referred to as _____ _____.

10. According to Chomsky, all languages share a(n) _____ _____.

11. Most researchers agree that apes can

    a. communicate through symbols.

    b. reproduce most human speech sounds.

    c. master language in adulthood.

    d. surpass a human 3-year-old in language skills.

12. Charles Spearman suggested we have one _____ _____ underlying success across a variety of intellectual abilities.

13. The existence of savant syndrome seems to support

    a. Sternberg's distinction among three types of intelligence.

    b. criticism of multiple intelligence theories.

    c. Gardner's theory of multiple intelligences.

    d. Thorndike's view of social intelligence.

14. Sternberg's three types of intelligence are _____, _____, and _____.

15. Emotionally intelligent people tend to

    a. seek immediate gratification.

    b. understand their own emotions but not those of others.

    c. understand others' emotions but not their own.

    d. succeed in their careers.

16. The IQ of a 6-year-old with a measured mental age of 9 would be

    a. 67.

    b. 133.

    c. 86.

    d. 150.

17. The Wechsler Adult Intelligence Scale (WAIS) is best able to tell us

    a. what part of an individual's intelligence is determined by genetic inheritance.

    b. whether the test-taker will succeed in a job.

    c. how the test-taker compares with other adults in vocabulary and arithmetic reasoning.

    d. whether the test-taker has specific skills for music and the performing arts.

18. The Stanford-Binet, the Wechsler Adult Intelligence Scale, and the Wechsler Intelligence Scale for Children yield consistent results, for example on retesting. In other words, these tests have high _____.

19. The strongest support for heredity's influence on intelligence is the finding that
    a. identical twins, but not other siblings, have nearly identical intelligence test scores.
    b. the correlation between intelligence test scores of fraternal twins is not higher than that for other siblings.
    c. mental similarities between adopted siblings increase with age.
    d. children in impoverished families have similar intelligence scores.

20. To say that the heritability of intelligence is about 50 percent means that 50 percent of
    a. an individual's intelligence is due to genetic factors.
    b. the similarities between two groups of people are attributable to genes.
    c. the variation in intelligence within a group of people is attributable to genetic factors.
    d. intelligence is due half to the mother's genes and half to the father's genes.

21. The environmental influence that has the clearest, most profound effect on intellectual development is
    a. exposing normal infants to enrichment programs before age 1.
    b. growing up in an economically disadvantaged home or neighborhood.
    c. being raised in conditions of extreme deprivation.
    d. being an identical twin.

22. Use the concepts of crystallized and fluid intelligence to explain why writers tend to produce their most creative work later in life, while scientists often hit their peak much earlier.

23. Which of the following is NOT a possible explanation for the fact that more intelligent people tend to live longer, healthier lives?
    a. Intelligence makes it easier to access more education, better jobs, and a healthier environment.
    b. Intelligence encourages a more health-promoting lifestyle.
    c. Intelligent people have slower reaction times, making it less likely that they will put themselves at risk.
    d. Prenatal events or early childhood illnesses could influence both intelligence and health.

24. In prosperous country X everyone eats all they want. In country Y the rich are well fed, but the poor have very little to eat. In which country will the heritability of body weight be greater?

25. _____ _____ can lead to poor performance on tests by undermining test-takers' belief that they can do well on the test.

Find answers to these questions in Appendix E, in the back of the book.

IN YOUR EVERYDAY LIFE

Answering these questions will help you make these concepts more personally meaningful, and therefore more memorable.

1. What are the things you fear? Are some of those fears out of proportion to statistical risk? Are there other areas of your life where you need to take more precautions?

2. Can you recall a time when contradictory information challenged one of your views? Was it hard for you to consider the opposite view? Did you change your mind?

3. How could you use mental practice to improve your performance in some area of your life?

4. Can you think of a time when you believed an animal was communicating with you? How might you put that to a test?

5. The concept of multiple intelligences suggests that different people have different gifts. What are yours?

6. How have environmental influences shaped your ability to reach your academic potential?

Use ⟨⟩ LearningCurve to create your personalized study plan, which will direct you to the resources that will help you most in ⟨⟩ LaunchPad.

SURVEY THE CHAPTER

Motivation and Emotion

9

ow well I [DM] remember asking my first discussion question in a new introductory psychology class. Several hands rose, along with one left foot. The foot belonged to Chris Klein, who was the unlikeliest person to have made it to that class. At birth, Chris suffered oxygen deprivation that required 40 minutes of CPR. "One doctor wanted to let him go," recalls his mother.

The result was severe cerebral palsy. With damage to the brain area that controls muscle movement, Chris is unable to control his constantly moving hands. He cannot feed, dress, or care for himself. And he cannot speak. But what Chris can control are his keen mind and his left foot. With that blessed foot, he controls the joystick on his motorized wheelchair. Using his left big toe, he can type sentences, which his communication system can store, send, or speak. And Chris has *motivation*—lots of motivation.

When Chris was a high school student in suburban Chicago, three teachers doubted he would be able to leave home for college. Yet he persisted, and, with much support, came to my college called Hope. Five years later, as his left foot drove him across the stage to receive his diploma, his admiring classmates gave him a spontaneous standing ovation.

Today, Chris is an inspirational speaker for schools, churches, and community events, giving "a voice to those that have none, and a helping hand to those with disabilities." He is writing a book, *Lessons from the Big Toe*. And he has found love and married.

Few of us face Chris Klein's challenges. But we all seek to direct our energy in ways that will produce satisfaction and success. We are moved by our feelings along the way, and we inspire them in others. We are pushed by biological motives, such as hunger, and by social ones, such as the need to belong. Chris Klein's strong will to live, learn, and love highlights the close ties between our own *motivations* and *emotions,* which energize, direct, and enrich our lives.

Motivational Concepts

LOQ Learning**O**bjective**Q**uestion

9-1 What is *motivation*, and what are three key perspectives that help us understand motivated behaviors?

Our **motivations** arise from the interplay between nature (the bodily "push") and nurture (the "pulls" from our personal experiences, thoughts, and culture). Our motives drive our behavior. That is usually, but not always, for the better. Addictions, for example, may drive people to satisfy harmful cravings instead of those for food, safety, and social support.

Let's consider three perspectives that psychologists have used to understand motivated behaviors.

A MOTIVATED MAN: CHRIS KLEIN To see and hear Chris presenting his story, visit tinyurl.com/ChrisPsychStudent.

Drives and Incentives

Drive-reduction theory makes three assumptions:

- We have **physiological needs,** such as the need for food or water.
- If a need is not met, it creates a *drive,* an aroused, motivated state, such as hunger or thirst.
- That drive pushes us to reduce the need by, say, eating or drinking.

| Need (food, water) | ➡ | Drive (hunger, thirst) | ➡ | Drive-reducing behaviors (eating, drinking) |

FIGURE 9.1 Drive-reduction theory Drive-reduction motivation arises from homeostasis—our body's natural tendency to maintain a steady internal state. Thus, if we are water deprived, our thirst drives us to drink and to restore the body's normal state.

The goal of this three-step process (**FIGURE 9.1**), from need to drive-reducing behavior, is **homeostasis,** our body's natural tendency to maintain a steady internal state. (*Homeostasis* means "staying the same.") For example, our body regulates its temperature in a way similar to a room's thermostat. Both systems monitor temperature and feed information to a control device. If the room's temperature cools, the control device switches on the furnace. Likewise, if our body's temperature cools, our blood vessels narrow to conserve warmth, and we search for warmer clothes or a warmer environment.

We also are pulled by **incentives**—environmental stimuli that attract or repel us, depending on our individual learning histories. If you a r e hungry, the aroma of good food will motivate you. Whether that aroma comes from fresh-baked bread or fresh-toasted ants will depend on your culture and experience.

When there is both a need and an incentive, we feel strongly driven. You've skipped lunch and you can smell bread baking in your friend's kitchen. You will feel a strong drive to satisfy your hunger, and the baking bread will be a powerful incentive that will motivate your actions.

For each motive, we can therefore ask, "How are we pushed by our inborn bodily needs and pulled by incentives in the environment?"

Arousal Theory

We are much more than homeostatic systems, however. When we are aroused, we are physically energized, or tense. Some motivated behaviors actually *increase* rather than decrease arousal. Well-fed animals with no clear, need-based drive will leave a safe shelter to explore and gain information. Curiosity drives monkeys to monkey around trying to figure out how to unlock a latch that opens nothing, or how to open a window that allows them to see outside their room (Butler, 1954). Curiosity drives newly mobile infants to check out every corner of the house. It drives the scientists whose work this text discusses. And it strongly drives some individuals, such as mountain adventurer George Mallory. Asked why he wanted to climb Mount Everest, *The New York Times* reported that Mallory answered, "Because it is there." Those who, like Mallory, enjoy high arousal are most likely to enjoy intense music, novel foods, and risky behaviors (Roberti et al., 2004; Zuckerman, 1979, 2009).

We humans hunger for information (Biederman & Vessel, 2006). When we find that all our biological needs have been met, we feel bored and seek stimulation to increase our arousal. When left alone in a room for 6 to 15 minutes, many university students even give themselves electric shocks rather than do nothing (Wilson et al., 2014). Yet *too* much stimulation brings stress and sends us looking for ways to decrease arousal. Arousal theory describes this search for the right arousal level, a search that energizes and directs our behavior.

Two early twentieth-century psychologists studied the relationship of arousal to performance. They identified the **Yerkes-Dodson law:** *Moderate arousal leads to optimal performance* (Yerkes & Dodson, 1908). When taking an exam, for example, it pays to be moderately aroused—alert but not trembling

Katie Green/MLIVE.COM/Landov

DRIVEN BY CURIOSITY Young monkeys and children are fascinated by the unfamiliar. Their drive to explore maintains an optimum level of arousal and is one of several motives that do not fill any immediate physiological need.

with nervousness. (If already anxious, remember that a caffeine drink may make you even more jumpy.) Between bored low arousal and anxious hyper-arousal lies a well-lived life. Optimal arousal levels depend on the task, with more difficult tasks requiring lower arousal for best performance (Hembree, 1988) (**FIGURE 9.2**).

A Hierarchy of Needs

Some needs are more important than others. At this moment, with your needs for air and food hopefully satisfied, other motives are directing your behavior. But if you were deprived of nourishment, your hunger would take over your thoughts. Just ask the semi-starved people of the fictional Panem, whose districts, represented by a boy and girl selected by lottery, must compete in mortal *Hunger Games*. Food matters. Yet in Panem, as in our world, we do not live by bread alone. People also have needs for safety, connection, and self-worth.

Abraham Maslow (1970) viewed human motives as a pyramid—a **hierarchy of needs** (**FIGURE 9.3**). At the pyramid's base are physiological needs, such as those for food. If those are unmet, life is a hunger game. Only after these needs are met, said Maslow (1971), do we try to meet our need for safety, and then to satisfy our needs to give and receive love and to enjoy self-esteem. At the peak of the pyramid are the highest human needs. At the *self-actualization* level, people seek to realize their own potential. At the very top is *self-transcendence*, which Maslow proposed near the end of his life. At this level, some people strive for meaning, purpose, and identity in a way that is *transpersonal*—beyond (*trans*) the self (Koltko-Rivera, 2006).

FIGURE 9.2 Optimal arousal varies with difficulty of the task being performed

Retrieve + Remember

- Performance peaks at lower levels of arousal for difficult tasks, and at higher levels for easy or well-learned tasks. (1) How might this phenomenon affect runners? (2) How might this phenomenon affect anxious test-takers facing a difficult exam? (3) How might the performance of anxious students be affected by relaxation training?

ANSWERS: (1) Well-practiced runners tend to excel when aroused by competition. (2) High anxiety about a difficult exam may disrupt test-takers' performance. (3) Teaching anxious students how to relax before an exam can enable them to perform better.

motivation a need or desire that energizes and directs behavior.

drive-reduction theory the idea that a physiological need creates an aroused state (a drive) that motivates us to satisfy the need.

physiological need a basic bodily requirement.

homeostasis a tendency to maintain a balanced or constant internal state; the regulation of any aspect of body chemistry, such as blood glucose, around a particular level.

incentive a positive or negative environmental stimulus that motivates behavior.

Yerkes-Dodson law the principle that performance increases with arousal only up to a point, beyond which performance decreases.

hierarchy of needs Maslow's pyramid of human needs; at the base are physiological needs. These basic needs must be satisfied before higher-level safety needs, and then psychological needs, become active.

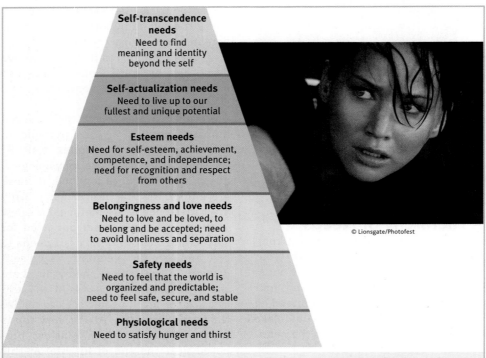

- **Self-transcendence needs**
  Need to find meaning and identity beyond the self

- **Self-actualization needs**
  Need to live up to our fullest and unique potential

- **Esteem needs**
  Need for self-esteem, achievement, competence, and independence; need for recognition and respect from others

- **Belongingness and love needs**
  Need to love and be loved, to belong and be accepted; need to avoid loneliness and separation

- **Safety needs**
  Need to feel that the world is organized and predictable; need to feel safe, secure, and stable

- **Physiological needs**
  Need to satisfy hunger and thirst

© Lionsgate/Photofest

FIGURE 9.3 Maslow's hierarchy of needs Reduced to semistarvation by their rulers, inhabitants of Suzanne Collins' fictional nation of Panem hunger for food and survival. *Hunger Games* heroine Katniss Everdeen expresses higher-level needs for actualization and transcendence, and in the process inspires the nation.

There are exceptions to Maslow's hierarchy. For example, people have starved themselves to make a political statement. Nevertheless, some needs are indeed more basic than others. In poorer nations, money—and the food and shelter it buys—more strongly commands attention and predicts feelings of well-being. In wealthy nations, where most are able to meet their basic needs, social connections (such as home-life satisfaction) better predict well-being (Oishi et al., 1999).

Let's take a closer look now at two specific motives: the basic-level motive, *hunger,* and the higher-level *need to belong.* As you read about these motives, watch for ways that incentives (the psychological "pull") interact with bodily needs (the biological "push") (**TABLE 9.1**).

TABLE 9.1 Classic Motivation Theories

Theory	Its Big Idea
Drive-reduction theory	Physiological needs (such as hunger and thirst) create an aroused state that drives us to reduce the need (for example, by eating or drinking).
Arousal theory	Our need to maintain an optimal level of arousal motivates behaviors that meet no physiological need (such as our yearning for stimulation and our hunger for information).
Maslow's hierarchy of needs	We prioritize survival-based needs and then social needs more than the needs for esteem and meaning.

LaunchPad To test your understanding of the hierarchy of needs, visit Launch-Pad's *Concept Practice: Building Maslow's Hierarchy.*

Retrieve + Remember

- After hours of driving alone in an unfamiliar city, you finally see a diner. Although it looks deserted and a little creepy, you stop because you are *really* hungry and thirsty. How would Maslow's hierarchy of needs explain your behavior?

ANSWER: According to Maslow, our drives to meet the physiological needs of hunger and thirst take priority over safety needs, prompting us to take risks at times.

Hunger

As dieters know, physiological needs are powerful. Their strength was vividly demonstrated when Ancel Keys and his research team (1950) did a now-classic study with wartime conscientious objectors. First, they fed 200 adult male volunteers normally for three months. Then, for six months, they cut this food level in half for 36 of them. The effects soon became visible. Without thinking about it, these men began conserving energy. They appeared sluggish and dull. Eventually, their body weights stabilized at about 25 percent below their starting weights.

As Maslow might have guessed, the men became obsessed with food. They talked about it. They daydreamed about it. They collected recipes, read cookbooks, and feasted their eyes on tasty but forbidden food. Focused on their unmet basic need, they lost interest in sex and social activities. One man reported, "If we see a show, the most interesting [parts are] scenes where people are eating. I couldn't laugh at the funniest picture in the world, and love scenes are completely dull." As journalist Dorothy Dix (1861–1951) observed, "Nobody wants to kiss when they are hungry."

"Never hunt when you're hungry."

Motives can capture our consciousness. When we're hungry, thirsty, fatigued, or sexually aroused, little else seems to matter. When we're not, food, water, sleep, or sex just don't seem like such big things in life, now or ever. (You may recall from Chapter 7 a parallel effect of our current good or bad mood on our memories.) Shop for food on an empty stomach and you are more likely to see those jelly-filled doughnuts as just what you've always loved and will be wanting tomorrow. *Motives matter mightily.*

The Physiology of Hunger

LOQ 9-2 What physiological factors cause us to feel hungry?

Deprived of a normal food supply, Keys' volunteers were clearly hungry. What triggers hunger? Is it the pangs of an empty stomach? So it seemed to

A. L. Washburn. Working with Walter Cannon, Washburn agreed to swallow a balloon that was attached to a recording device (Cannon & Washburn, 1912) (**FIGURE 9.4**). When inflated to fill his stomach, the balloon tracked his stomach contractions. Washburn supplied information about his *feelings* of hunger by pressing a key each time he felt a hunger pang. The discovery: When Washburn felt hungry, he was indeed having stomach contractions.

Can hunger exist without stomach pangs? To answer that question, researchers removed some rats' stomachs and created a direct path to their small intestines (Tsang, 1938). Did the rats continue to eat? Indeed they did. Some hunger similarly persists in humans whose stomachs have been removed as a treatment for ulcers or cancer. So the pangs of an empty stomach cannot be the *only* source of hunger. What else might trigger hunger?

Body Chemistry and the Brain

Somehow, somewhere, your body is keeping tabs on the energy it takes in and the energy it uses. This balancing act enables you to maintain a stable body weight. A major source of energy in your body is the **glucose** circulating in your bloodstream. If your blood glucose level drops, you won't consciously feel the lower blood sugar. But your brain, which automatically monitors your blood chemistry and your body's internal state, will trigger your feeling of hunger.

How does the brain sound the alarm? The work is done by several neural areas, some housed deep in the brain within the *hypothalamus* (**FIGURE 9.5**). This neural traffic intersection includes areas that influence eating. In one neural area (called the *arcuate nucleus*), a center pumps out appetite-stimulating hormones, and another center pumps out appetite-suppressing hormones. When researchers stimulate this appetite-enhancing center, well-fed animals

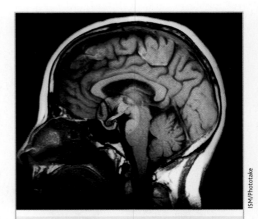

FIGURE 9.5 The hypothalamus The hypothalamus (colored orange) performs various body maintenance functions. One of these functions is control of hunger.

glucose the form of sugar that circulates in the blood and provides the major source of energy for body tissues. When its level is low, we feel hunger.

Washburn swallows balloon, which measures stomach contractions.

Washburn presses key each time he feels hungry.

Stomach contractions

Hunger pangs

0 1 2 3 4 5 6 7 8 9 10
Time in minutes

FIGURE 9.4 Monitoring stomach contractions (From Cannon, 1929.)

will begin to eat. If they destroy the area, even starving animals lose interest in food. The opposite occurs when the appetite-suppressing area is stimulated: The animal will stop eating. Destroy this area and animals can't stop eating and will become obese (Duggan & Booth, 1986; Hoebel & Teitelbaum, 1966) (**FIGURE 9.6**).

Blood vessels connect the hypothalamus to the rest of the body, so it can respond to our current blood chemistry and other incoming information. One of its tasks is monitoring levels of appetite hormones, such as *ghrelin*, a hunger-arousing hormone secreted by an empty stomach. When people have surgery for severe obesity, surgeons seal off or remove part of the stomach. The remaining stomach then produces much less ghrelin, and the person's appetite lessens (Ammori, 2013; Lemonick, 2002). Other appetite hormones include *insulin, leptin, orexin,* and *PYY.* **FIGURE 9.7** describes how they influence your feelings of hunger.

The interaction of appetite hormones and brain activity suggests that the body has a "weight thermostat." When

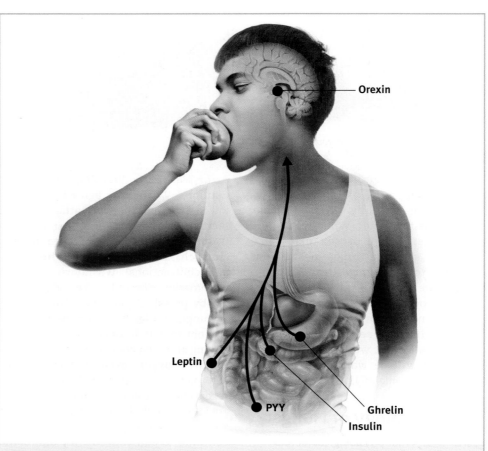

FIGURE 9.7 The appetite hormones

- *Ghrelin:* Hormone secreted by empty stomach; sends "I'm hungry" signals to the brain.
- *Insulin:* Hormone secreted by pancreas; controls blood glucose.
- *Leptin:* Protein hormone secreted by fat cells; when abundant, causes brain to increase metabolism and decrease hunger.
- *Orexin:* Hunger-triggering hormone secreted by hypothalamus.
- *PYY:* Digestive tract hormone; sends "I'm *not* hungry" signals to the brain.

Voisin/Phanie/Science Source

FIGURE 9.6 Evidence for the brain's control of eating The fat mouse on the left has nonfunctioning receptors in the appetite-suppressing part of the hypothalamus.

semistarved rats fall below their normal weight, this system signals their bodies to restore the lost weight. It's like fat cells cry out, "Feed me!" and start grabbing glucose from the bloodstream (Ludwig & Friedman, 2014). Hunger increases and energy output decreases. If body weight rises—as happens when rats are force-fed—hunger decreases and energy output increases. In this way, rats (and humans) tend to hover around a stable weight, or **set point,** influenced in part by heredity (Keesey & Corbett, 1983).

We humans (and other species, too) vary in our **basal metabolic rate,** a measure of how much energy we use to maintain basic body functions when our body is at rest. But we share a common response to decreased food intake: Our basal metabolic rate drops. So it did for the participants in Keys' experiment. After 24 weeks of semistarvation, they stabilized at three-quarters of their normal weight, although they were taking in only *half* their previous calories. How did their bodies achieve this dieter's nightmare? They reduced the amount of energy they were using—partly by being less active, but partly because their basal metabolic rate dropped by 29 percent.

Some researchers have suggested that the idea of a biologically *fixed* set point is too rigid to explain why slow, steady changes in body weight can alter a person's set point (Assanand et al., 1998), or why, when we have unlimited access to various tasty foods, we tend to overeat and gain weight (Raynor & Epstein, 2001). Thus, some researchers prefer the looser term *settling point* to indicate the level at which a person's weight settles in response to caloric intake and energy use. As we will see next, environment matters as well as biology.

🎮 **LaunchPad** For an interactive and visual tutorial on the brain and eating, visit LaunchPad's *PsychSim 6: Hunger and the Fat Rat.*

Retrieve + Remember

- Hunger occurs in response to _____ (low/high) blood glucose and _____ (low/high) levels of ghrelin.

ANSWERS: low; high

The Psychology of Hunger

LOQ 9-3 How do cultural and situational factors affect our taste preferences and eating habits?

Our internal hunger games are pushed by our body chemistry and brain activity. Yet there is more to hunger than meets the stomach. This was strikingly apparent when trickster researchers tested two patients who had no memory for events occurring more than a minute ago (Rozin et al., 1998). If offered a second lunch 20 minutes after eating a normal lunch, both patients readily ate it . . . and usually a third meal offered 20 minutes after they finished the second. This suggests that one part of our decision to eat is our memory of the time of our last meal. As time passes, we think about eating again, and that thought triggers feelings of hunger. Psychological influences on eating behavior affect all of us at some point.

"Never get a tattoo when you're drunk and hungry."

Taste Preferences: Biology and Culture

Both body cues and environment influence our feelings of hunger and what we hunger for—our taste preferences. When feeling tense or depressed, do you crave starchy, carbohydrate-laden foods? High-carb foods, such as pasta, chips, and sweets, help boost levels of the neurotransmitter serotonin, which has calming effects. When stressed, both rats and many humans find it extra rewarding to scarf Oreos (Artiga et al., 2007; Sproesser et al., 2014).

Our preferences for sweet and salty tastes are genetic and universal. Other taste preferences are learned. People given highly salted foods, for example, develop a liking for excess salt (Beauchamp, 1987). People who become violently ill after eating a particular food often develop a dislike of it. (The frequency of children's illnesses provides many chances for them to learn to avoid certain foods.)

Our culture teaches us what foods are acceptable. Many Japanese people enjoy *nattó*, a fermented soybean dish that "smells like the marriage of ammonia and a tire fire," reports smell expert Rachel Herz (2012). Asians, she adds, are often repulsed by what many Westerners love—"the rotted bodily fluid of an ungulate" (a.k.a. cheese, some varieties of which have the same bacteria and odor as stinky feet).

We also may learn to prefer some tastes because they are adaptive. In hot climates, where food spoils more quickly, recipes often include spices that slow the growth of bacteria (**FIGURE 9.8**).

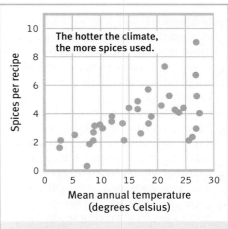

FIGURE 9.8 **Hot cultures like hot spices** (Sherman & Flaxman, 2001)

India averages nearly 10 spices per meat recipe, Finland 2 spices. Pregnancy-related food dislikes—and the nausea associated with them—are another example of adaptive taste preferences. These dislikes peak about the tenth week, when the developing embryo is most vulnerable to toxins.

Rats tend to avoid unfamiliar foods (Sclafani, 1995). So do we, especially those that are animal-based. This surely was adaptive for our ancestors by protecting them from potentially toxic substances.

Tempting Situations

Would it surprise you to know that situations also control your eating? Some examples:

- *Friends and food* Do you eat more when eating with others? Most of us do (Herman et al., 2003; Hetherington et al., 2006). The presence of others tends to amplify our natural behavior tendencies. (This is *social facilitation* and you'll hear more about it in Chapter 11.)

set point the point at which your "weight thermostat" may be set. When your body falls below this weight, increased hunger and a lowered metabolic rate may combine to restore lost weight.

basal metabolic rate the body's resting rate of energy output.

• *Serving size is significant* Researchers studied the effects of portion size by offering people varieties of free snacks (Geier et al., 2006). In an apartment lobby, they laid out full or half pretzels, big or little Tootsie Rolls, or a small or large serving scoop by a bowl of M&M's. Their consistent result: Offered a supersized portion, people put away more calories. Offered pasta, people eat more when given a bigger plate (Van Ittersum & Wansink, 2012). Offered ice cream, people take and eat more when given a big bowl and big scoop. They pour and drink more from short, wide glasses than from tall, narrow glasses. Portion size matters.

• *Selections stimulate* Food variety promotes eating. Offered a dessert buffet, people eat more than they do when choosing a portion from one favorite dessert. And they take more of easier-to-reach foods on buffet lines (Marteau et al., 2012). For our early ancestors, eating more when foods were abundant and varied was adaptive. Consuming a wide range of vitamins and minerals and storing fat offered protection later, during winter cold or famine. When bad times hit, they could eat less, hoarding their small food supply until winter or famine ended (Polivy et al., 2008; Remick et al., 2009).

• *Nudging nutrition* One research team quadrupled carrots taken by offering schoolchildren carrots before they picked up other foods in a lunch line (Redden et al., 2015). A planned new school lunch tray will put fruits and veggies up front, and spread the main dish out in a shallow compartment to make it look bigger (Wansink, 2014). Such "nudges" support U.S. President Barack Obama's 2015 executive order to use "behavioral science insights to better serve the American people."

LaunchPad Consider how researchers test some of these ideas with Launch-Pad's *IMMERSIVE LEARNING: How Would You Know If Using Larger Dinner Plates Makes People Gain Weight?*

Retrieve + Remember

• After an 8-hour hike without food, your long-awaited favorite dish is placed in front of you, and your mouth waters in anticipation. Why?

ANSWER: You have learned to respond to the sight and aroma that signal the food about to enter your mouth. Both *physiological cues* (low blood sugar) and *psychological cues* (anticipation of the tasty meal) heighten your experienced hunger.

Obesity and Weight Control

LOQ 9-4 What factors predispose some people to become and remain obese?

Obesity has physical health risks, but it can also be socially toxic, by affecting both how you feel about yourself and how others treat you. In fat-disapproving cultures, obese 6- to 9-year olds are 60 percent more likely to suffer bullying (Lumeng et al., 2010). Adult obesity is linked with lower psychological well-being, increased depression, and discrimination in employment (de Wit et al., 2010; Luppino et al., 2010; Riffkin, 2014). Yet few overweight people win the battle of the bulge. Why? And why do some people gain weight while others eat the same amount and seldom add a pound?

The Survival Value—and Health Risks—of Fat

The answers lie partly in our history. Fat is stored energy. It is a fuel reserve that can carry us through times when food is scarce. (Think of that spare tire around the middle as an energy storehouse—biology's counterpart to a hiker's waist-borne snack pack.) In impoverished Europe in earlier centuries, and in parts of the world today, plumpness has signaled wealth and social status (Furnham & Baguma, 1994; Swami, 2015; Swami et al., 2011).

Our hungry distant ancestors were well served by a simple rule: *When you find energy-rich fat or sugar, eat it!* That rule is no longer adaptive in a world where unhealthy processed foods are abundantly available. Pretty much everywhere this book is being read, people have a growing problem. Worldwide, obesity has more than doubled since 1980, with 1.9 billion adults now overweight. Some 600 million are *obese*, which is defined as a *body mass index (BMI)* of 30 or more (Swinburn et al., 2011; WHO, 2015). (See tinyurl.com/GiveMyBMI to calculate your BMI.) In the United States, 36 percent of adults are obese (Flegal et al., 2012).

Significant obesity can shorten your life, reduce your quality of life, and increase your health care costs (Kitahara et al., 2014). It increases the risk of diabetes, high blood pressure, heart disease, gallstones, arthritis, and certain types of cancer. Women's obesity has been linked to a higher risk of late-life cognitive decline, including Alzheimer's disease and brain tissue loss (Bruce-Keller et al., 2009; Whitmer et al., 2008). In one experiment, memory performance improved 12 weeks after severely obese people had weight-loss surgery and lost significant weight. Those *not* having the surgery showed some further cognitive decline (Gunstad et al., 2011).

So why don't obese people just drop that excess baggage? Because their bodies fight back.

A SLUGGISH METABOLISM Once we become fat, we require less food to maintain our weight than we did to gain it. Compared with muscle tissue, fat has a lower metabolic rate—it takes less

"Remember when we used to have to fatten the kids up first?"

food energy to maintain. When an overweight person's body drops below its previous set (or settling) point, the person's hunger increases and metabolism decreases. The body adapts to what it perceives as starvation by burning fewer calories. Blame your brain for weight regain (Cornier, 2011).

Lean people and overweight people differ in their rates of resting metabolism. Lean people seem naturally disposed to move about, and in doing so, they burn more calories. Overweight people tend to sit still longer and conserve their energy (Levine et al., 2005). This helps explain why two people of the same height and age can maintain the same weight, even if one of them eats much more than the other does. (Who said life is fair?)

A GENETIC HANDICAP It's true: Our genes influence the size of our jeans. Consider:

- Adopted children share meals with their adoptive siblings and parents. Yet their body weights more closely resemble those of their biological family (Grilo & Pogue-Geile, 1991).

- Identical twins have closely similar weights, even when raised apart (Plomin et al., 1997; Stunkard et al., 1990). Fraternal twins' weights are much less similar. Such findings suggest that genes explain two-thirds of the person-to-person differences in body mass (Maes et al., 1997).

As with other behavior traits, there is no one "weight gene." Rather, many genes (including nearly 100 genes identified in a recent study) each contribute small effects (Locke et al., 2015).

LaunchPad See LaunchPad's *Video: Twin Studies* for a helpful tutorial animation.

SLEEP, FRIENDS, FOOD, ACTIVITY— THEY ALL MATTER! Genes tell an important part of the obesity story. But environmental factors are mighty important, too.

Studies in Europe, Japan, and the United States show that children and adults who suffer from *sleep loss* are more at risk for obesity (Keith et al., 2006; Nedeltcheva et al., 2010; Taheri, 2004; Taheri et al., 2004). Deprived of sleep, our bodies produce less leptin (which reports body fat to the brain) and more ghrelin (the appetite-stimulating stomach hormone).

Social influence is another factor. One 32-year study of 12,067 people found them most likely to become obese when a friend became obese (Christakis & Fowler, 2007). The odds of becoming obese almost tripled when the obese friend was a close one. Moreover, the correlation among friends' weights was not simply a matter of seeking out similar people as friends.

Friends matter, but evidence that environment influences weight comes from eating disorders research (see Chapter 13), and especially from our fattening world (**FIGURE 9.9**). What explains this growing problem? Changing food consumption and activity levels are at work. Our lifestyles may now approach those of animal feedlots, where farmers fatten animals by giving them lots of food and little exercise. We are eating more and moving less. In the United States, jobs requiring moderate physical activity declined from about 50 percent in 1960 to 20 percent in 2011 (Church et al., 2011).

Stadiums, theaters, and subway cars—but not airplanes—are widening seats to accommodate the new "bottom" line (Hampson, 2000; Kim & Tong, 2010). Washington State Ferries abandoned a 50-year-old standard: "Eighteen-inch butts are a thing of the past" (Shepherd, 1999). New York City, facing a large problem with Big Apple bottoms, has mostly replaced 17.5-inch bucket-style subway seats with bucketless seats (Hampson, 2000). In the end, today's people need more room.

* * *

The obesity research findings reinforce a familiar lesson from Chapter 8's study of intelligence. There can be high levels of *heritability* (genetic influence on individual differences) without heredity being the only explanation of group differences. Genes mostly determine why one person today is heavier than another. Environment mostly determines why people today are heavier than their counterparts 50 years ago.

Our eating behavior once again demonstrates one of this book's big ideas: Biological, psychological, and social-cultural factors interact. We have seen many biological and psychological forces working against those who want to shed excess pounds. Indeed, short of drastic weight-loss surgery, what most people lose on weight-loss programs in the short term they regain in the long run (Mann et al., 2015). For tips on shedding unwanted weight, see **TABLE 9.2**.

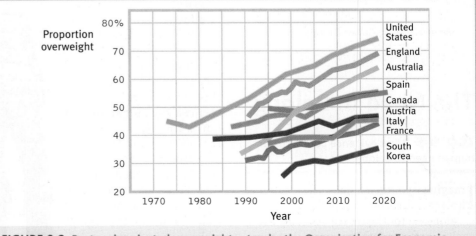

FIGURE 9.9 Past and projected overweight rates, by the Organisation for Economic Co-operation and Development

TABLE 9.2 Waist Management

People struggling with obesity should seek medical evaluation and guidance. For others who wish to lose weight, researchers have offered these tips:

- **Begin only if you feel motivated and self-disciplined.** Permanent weight loss usually requires a lifelong change in eating habits combined with increased exercise.

- **Exercise and get enough sleep.** Especially when supported by 7 to 8 hours of sleep a night, exercise empties fat cells, builds muscle, speeds up metabolism, helps lower your settling point, and reduces stress and stress-induced craving for carbohydrate-rich comfort foods (Bennett, 1995; Kolata, 1987; Thompson et al., 1982).

- **Minimize exposure to tempting food cues.** Food shop on a full stomach. Keep tempting foods out of the house, and tuck away special-occasion foods.

- **Limit variety and eat healthy foods.** Given more variety, people consume more. So eat simple meals with vegetables, fruits, and whole grains. Healthy fats, such as those found in olive oil and fish, help regulate appetite (Taubes, 2001, 2002). Water- and vitamin-rich veggies can fill the stomach with few calories. Better crispy greens than Krispy Kremes.

- **Reduce portion sizes.** Serve food with smaller bowls, plates, and utensils.

- **Don't starve all day and eat one big meal at night.** This common eating pattern slows metabolism. Moreover, those who eat a balanced breakfast are, by late morning, more alert and less fatigued (Spring et al., 1992).

- **Beware of the binge.** Drinking alcohol or feeling anxious or depressed can unleash the urge to eat (Herman & Polivy, 1980). And men especially should note that eating slowly can lead to eating less (Martin et al., 2007).

- **Before eating with others, decide how much you want to eat.** Eating with friends can distract us from monitoring our own eating (Ward & Mann, 2000).

- **Remember, most people occasionally lapse.** A lapse need not become a full collapse.

- **Connect to a support group.** Join with others, either face-to-face or online, to share goals and progress updates (Freedman, 2011).

AMERICAN IDLE: COUCH POTATOES BEWARE— TV WATCHING CORRELATES WITH OBESITY Over time, lifestyles have become less active. As TV watching (and other screen time) has increased, so has the percentage of overweight people in Britain, Canada, and the United States (Pagani et al., 2010). As televisions have become flatter, people have become fatter.

Retrieve + Remember

- Why can two people of the same height, age, and activity level maintain the same weight, even if one of them eats much less than the other does?

ANSWER: Individuals have very different set points and genetically influenced metabolism levels, causing them to burn calories differently.

The Need to Belong

LOQ 9-5 What evidence points to our human need to belong?

Imagine yourself like the fictional Robinson Crusoe, dropped on an island . . . alone . . . for the rest of your life. Food, shelter, and comfort are yours—but there is not a single fellow human around, no way to connect with loved ones, no story but your own. Do you savor the stress-free serenity?

Surely not. We are what the ancient Greek philosopher Aristotle called the *social animal*. Cut off from friends or family—alone in prison or in a new school or in a foreign land—most people feel keenly their lost connections with important others. Although some people are more social than others, this deep *need to belong* seems a key human motivation (Baumeister & Leary, 1995). Facebook founder Mark Zuckerberg (2012) understands this need, noting that Facebook "was built to accomplish a social mission—to make the world more open and connected." And connect we do.

Photodisc/Getty Images

The Benefits of Belonging

Social bonds boosted our ancestors' chances of survival. These bonds motivated caregivers to keep children close, protecting them from threats (Esposito et al., 2013). As adults, those who formed attachments were more likely to reproduce and co-nurture their offspring to maturity. To be "wretched" literally means, in its Middle English origin (*wrecched*), to be without kin nearby.

Survival also was supported by cooperation. In solo combat, our ancestors were not the toughest predators. But as hunters, they learned that eight hands were better than two. As food gatherers, they gained protection from their enemies by traveling in groups. Those who felt a need to belong survived and reproduced most successfully, and their genes now rule.

People in every society on Earth belong to groups (and,

as Chapter 11 explains, prefer and favor "us" over "them"). With the need to belong satisfied by close, supportive relationships, we feel included, accepted, and loved, and our self-esteem rides high. Indeed, *self-esteem* is a measure of how valued and accepted we feel (Leary, 2012). When our need for relatedness is satisfied in balance with two other basic psychological needs—*autonomy* (a sense of personal control) and *competence*—the result is a deep sense of well-being (Deci & Ryan, 2002, 2009; Milyavskaya et al., 2009). To feel free, capable, and connected is to enjoy a good life.

Is it surprising, then, that so much of our social behavior aims to increase our feelings of belonging? To win friendship and avoid rejection, we generally conform to group standards. We monitor our behavior, hoping to make a good impression. We spend billions on clothes, cosmetics, and diet and fitness aids—all motivated by our search for love and acceptance.

Thrown together in groups at school, at work, on a hiking trip, we behave like magnets, moving closer, forming bonds. Parting, we feel distress. We promise to call, to write, to come back for reunions.

THE NEED TO CONNECT Six days a week, thousands of women from the Philippines work as domestic helpers in Hong Kong households. On Sundays, they throng to the central business district to picnic, dance, sing, talk, and laugh. "Humanity could stage no greater display of happiness," reported one observer (*Economist*, 2001).

By drawing a sharp circle around "us," the need to belong feeds both deep attachments and menacing threats. Out of our need to define a "we" come loving families, faithful friendships, and team spirit, but also teen gangs, ethnic rivalries, and fanatic nationalism.

Even when bad relationships break, people suffer. In one 16-nation survey, and in repeated U.S. surveys, separated and divorced people have been half as likely as married people to say they were "very happy" (Inglehart, 1990; NORC, 2007). Divorce also predicts earlier mortality. In an analysis of 755,000 divorces in 11 different countries, divorce was associated with dying earlier (Sbarra et al., 2011). After such separations, loneliness and anger—and sometimes even a strange desire to be near the former partner— linger (Spielmann et al., 2015). For those in abusive relationships, the fear of being alone sometimes seems worse than the certainty of emotional or physical pain.

Children who move through a series of foster homes also know the fear of being alone. After repeated breaks in budding attachments, children may have difficulty forming deep attachments (Oishi & Schimmack, 2010). The evidence is clearest at the extremes—children who grow up in institutions without a sense of belonging to anyone, or who are locked away at home and severely neglected. As we saw in Chapter 3, most become pathetic creatures, withdrawn, frightened, even speechless.

No matter how secure our early years were, we all experience anxiety, loneliness, jealousy, or guilt when something threatens or dissolves our social ties. Many of life's best moments occur when close relationships begin: making a new friend, falling in love, having a baby. And many of life's worst moments happen when close relationships end (Jaremka et al., 2011). At such times, we may feel life is empty, pointless, and we may overeat to fill that emptiness (Yang et al., 2016). For those moving alone to new places, the stress and loneliness can be depressing. After years of placing individual refugee and immigrant

families in isolated communities, U.S. agencies today encourage *chain migration* (Pipher, 2002). The second Syrian refugee family settling in a town generally has an easier adjustment than the first.

The Pain of Being Shut Out

Sometimes our need to belong is denied. Can you recall a time when you felt excluded or ignored or shunned? Perhaps you were unfriended or ignored online. Or perhaps others gave you the silent treatment, avoided you, looked away, mocked you, or shut you out in some other way.

This is **ostracism**—social exclusion (Williams, 2007, 2009). Worldwide, humans use many forms of ostracism—exile, imprisonment, solitary confinement— to punish, and therefore control, social behavior. For children, even a brief time-out in isolation can be punishing. Among prisoners, half of all suicides occur among those experiencing the extreme exclusion of solitary confinement (Goode, 2012).

ENDURING THE PAIN OF OSTRACISM White cadets at the United States Military Academy at West Point ostracized Henry Flipper for years, hoping he would drop out. He somehow resisted their cruelty and in 1877 became the first African-American West Point graduate.

ostracism deliberate social exclusion of individuals or groups.

Being shunned threatens our need to belong (Vanhalst et al., 2015; Wirth et al., 2010). Lea, a lifelong victim of the silent treatment by her mother and grandmother, described the effect. "It's the meanest thing you can do to someone, especially if you know they can't fight back. I never should have been born." Like Lea, people often respond to ostracism with efforts to restore their acceptance, depressed moods, and then withdrawal. Prisoner William Blake (2013) has spent more than a quarter-century in solitary confinement. "I cannot fathom how dying any death could be harder and more terrible than living through all that I have been forced to endure," he observed. To many, social exclusion is a sentence worse than death.

> "Do we really think it makes sense to lock so many people alone in tiny cells for 23 hours a day, sometimes for months or even years at a time? . . . And if those individuals are ultimately released, how are they ever going to adapt?"
>
> U.S. President Barack Obama, July 14, 2015, expressing bipartisan concerns about the solitary confinement of some 75,000 American prisoners

Rejected and powerless, people may seek new friends. Or they may turn nasty, as did college students made to feel rejected in one series of experiments (Gaertner et al., 2008; Twenge et al., 2001, 2007). Some students were told that a personality test they had taken showed that they were "the type likely to end up alone later in life." Others heard that people they had met didn't want them in a group that was forming. Still others heard good news. These lucky people would have "rewarding relationships throughout life," or "everyone chose you as someone they'd like to work with." How did students react after being told they weren't wanted or would end up alone? They were much more likely to engage in self-defeating behaviors and to underperform on aptitude tests. When later interacting with those who had excluded them, they also were more likely to act in mean or aggressive ways (blasting people with noise, for example). "If intelligent, well-adjusted, successful . . . students can turn aggressive in response to a small laboratory

experience of social exclusion," noted the research team, "it is disturbing to imagine the aggressive tendencies that might arise from . . . chronic exclusion from desired groups in actual social life." (At the end of the experiments, the study was fully explained and the *debriefed* participants left feeling reassured.)

Ostracism is a real pain. Brain scans show increased activity in areas that also activate in response to physical pain (Lieberman & Eisenberger, 2015; Rotge et al., 2015). That helps explain another surprising finding. The pain reliever acetaminophen (as in Tylenol), taken to relieve physical pain, also lessens social pain (DeWall et al., 2010). Psychologically, we seem to experience social pain with the same emotional unpleasantness that marks physical pain. And across cultures, we use the same words (for example, *hurt, crushed*) for social pain and physical pain (MacDonald & Leary, 2005).

The opposite of ostracism—feelings of love—activate brain areas associated with rewards and satisfaction. Loved ones activate a brain region that dampens feelings of physical pain (Eisenberger et al., 2011). In one experiment, university students felt markedly less pain when looking at their beloved's picture, rather than at someone else's photo (Younger et al., 2010).

The bottom line: Social isolation and rejection foster depressed moods or emotional numbness, and they can trigger aggression (Bernstein & Claypool, 2012; Gerber & Wheeler, 2009). They can put us at risk for mental decline and ill health (Cacioppo & Hawkley, 2009). But love is a natural painkiller. When feelings of acceptance and connection build, so do self-esteem, positive feelings, and the desire to help rather than hurt others (Buckley & Leary, 2001).

Connecting and Social Networking

LOQ 9-6 How does social networking influence us?

As social creatures, we live for connection. Researcher George Vaillant (2013) was asked what he had learned from studying 238 Harvard University men from the 1930s to the end of their lives. He replied, "Happiness is love." A South African Zulu saying captures the idea: *Umuntu ngumuntu ngabantu*—"a person is a person through other persons."

Mobile Networks and Social Media

Look around and see humans connecting: talking, tweeting, texting, posting, chatting, social gaming, e-mailing. The changes in how we connect have been fast and vast.

- At the end of 2015, the world had 7.4 billion people and more than 7 billion mobile cell-phone subscriptions (ITU, 2016). But phone talking now accounts for less than half of U.S. mobile network traffic (Wortham, 2010). Speedy texting is not really writing, said one observer (McWhorter, 2012), but rather a new form of conversation—"fingered speech."

- The typical U.S. teen with a cell phone sends 30 texts a day (Lenhart, 2015). For many, it's as though friends are always present. Half of 18- to 29-year-olds with a smart phone check it multiple times per hour, and "can't imagine . . . life without [it]" (Newport, 2015; Saad, 2015).

- How many of us are using social networking sites? Among 2014's

---

Retrieve + Remember

- How have students reacted in studies where they were made to feel rejected and unwanted? What helps explain these results?

ANSWER: They engaged in more self-defeating behaviors, underperformed on aptitude tests, and displayed less empathy and more aggression. These students' basic *need to belong* seems to have been disrupted.

entering American college students, 94 percent were (Eagan et al., 2014). With so many of your friends on a social network, its lure becomes hard to resist. Such is our need to belong. Check in or miss out.

The Net Result: Social Effects of Social Networking

By connecting like-minded people, the Internet serves as a social amplifier. In times of social crisis or personal stress, it provides information and supportive connections. For better or for worse, it enables people to compare their lives with others (Verduyn et al., 2015). The Internet also functions as a matchmaker. (I [ND] can attest to this. I met my wife online.) As electronic communication has become a basic part of life, researchers have explored how it has affected our relationships.

HAVE SOCIAL NETWORKING SITES MADE US MORE, OR LESS, SOCIALLY ISOLATED? Lonely people have tended to spend greater-than-average time online (Bonetti et al., 2010; Stepanikova et al., 2010). But the Internet also offers opportunities for new social networks. (I [DM] am now connected to other hearing-technology advocates worldwide.) Social networking is also mostly strengthening our connections with the variety of people we already know (DiSalvo, 2010; Ugander et al., 2012; Valkenburg & Peter, 2009). If your social networking helps you connect with friends, stay in touch with extended fam-

ily, or find support when facing challenges, then you are not alone (Rainie et al., 2011). So social networks connect us. But they can also, as you've surely noticed, become gigantic time- and attention-sucking distractions. The net result may be an imbalance between face-to-face and online social connection.

Image Source/SuperStock

DOES ELECTRONIC COMMUNICATION STIMULATE HEALTHY SELF-DISCLOSURE? *Self-disclosure* is sharing ourselves—our joys, worries, and weaknesses—with others. As we will see in Chapter 10, confiding in others can be a healthy way of coping with day-to-day challenges. When communicating electronically rather than face-to-face, we often are less focused on others' reactions. We are less self-conscious and thus less inhibited. Sometimes this is taken to an extreme, as when teens send photos of themselves they later regret, bullies hound a victim, or hate groups post messages promoting bigotry or crimes. More often, however, the increased self-disclosure serves to deepen friendships (Valkenburg & Peter, 2009).

DOES SOCIAL NETWORKING PROMOTE NARCISSISM? Narcissism is self-esteem gone wild. Narcissistic people are self-important, self-focused, and self-promoting. Personality tests may assess narcissism with items such as "I like to be the center of attention." People with high narcissism test scores are especially active on social networking sites. They collect more superficial "friends." They post more staged, glamorous selfies. They retaliate more to negative comments. And, not surprisingly, they *seem* more narcissistic to strangers viewing their pages (Buffardi & Campbell, 2008; Weiser, 2015).

For narcissists, social networking sites are more than a gathering place; they are a feeding trough. In one study, college students were *randomly assigned*

either to edit and explain their online profiles for 15 minutes, or to use that time to study and explain a Google Maps routing (Freeman & Twenge, 2010). After completing their tasks, all were tested. Who then scored higher on a narcissism measure? Those who had spent the time focused on themselves.

📱 **LaunchPad** See LaunchPad's *Video: Random Assignment* for a helpful tutorial animation.

Maintaining Balance and Focus

It will come as no surprise that excessive online socializing and gaming have been associated with lower grades (Chen & Fu, 2008; Kaiser Family Foundation, 2010). In one U.S. survey, 47 percent of the heaviest users of the Internet and other media were receiving mostly C grades or lower, as were just 23 percent of the lightest users (Kaiser Family Foundation, 2010).

In today's world, each of us is challenged to maintain a healthy balance between our real-world and online time. Experts offer some practical suggestions:

- *Monitor your time.* Keep a log of how you use your time. Then ask yourself, "Does my time use reflect my priorities? Am I spending more or less time online than I intended? Is my time online interfering with school or work performance? Have family or friends commented on this?"

- *Monitor your feelings.* Ask yourself, "Am I emotionally distracted by my online interests? When I disconnect and move to another activity, how do I feel?"

- *"Hide" from your more distracting online friends when necessary.* And in your own postings, practice the golden rule. Before you post, ask yourself, "Is this something I'd care about reading if someone else posted it?"

"The women on these dating sites don't seem to believe I'm a prince."

narcissism excessive self-love and self-absorption.

"It keeps me from looking at my phone every two seconds."

- *When studying, get in the habit of checking your phone only once per hour.* Selective attention—the flashlight of your mind—can be in only one place at a time. When we try to do two things at once, we don't do either one of them very well (Willingham, 2010). If you want to study or work productively, resist the temptation to always be available. Disable sound alerts, vibration, and pop-ups, which can hijack your attention just when you've managed to get focused. (To avoid distraction, I [DM] am proofing and editing this chapter in a coffee shop without Wi-Fi.)

- *Try a social networking fast* (give it up for an hour, a day, or a week) *or a time-controlled social media diet* (check in only after homework is done, or only during a lunch break). Take notes on what you're losing and gaining on your new "diet."

- *Refocus by taking a nature walk.* People learn better after a peaceful walk in a park, which—unlike a walk on a busy street—refreshes our capacity for focused attention (Berman et al., 2008).

As psychologist Steven Pinker (2010a) said, "The solution is not to bemoan technology but to develop strategies of self-control, as we do with every other temptation in life."

Retrieve + Remember

- Social networking tends to _____ (strengthen/weaken) your relationships with people you already know, and _____ (increase/decrease) your self-disclosure.

ANSWERS: strengthen; increase

Emotion: Arousal, Behavior, and Cognition

LOQ 9-7 What are the three parts of an emotion, and what theories help us to understand our emotions?

Motivated behavior is often connected to powerful emotions. My [DM's] own need to belong was unforgettably disrupted one day when I went to a huge store and brought along Peter, my toddler first-born child. As I set Peter down on his feet for a moment to do some paperwork, a passerby warned, "You'd better be careful or you'll lose that boy!" Not more than a few breaths later, I turned and found no Peter beside me.

With mild anxiety, I peered around one end of the customer service counter. No Peter in sight. With slightly more anxiety, I peered around the other end. No Peter there, either. Now, with my heart pounding, I circled the neighboring counters. Still no Peter anywhere. As anxiety turned to panic, I began racing up and down the store aisles. He was nowhere to be found. Seeing my alarm, the store manager used the public-address system to ask customers to assist in looking for a missing

Courtesy of David Myers

child. Soon after, I passed the customer who had warned me. "I told you that you were going to lose him!" he now scorned. With visions of kidnapping (strangers routinely admired that beautiful child), I braced for the possibility that my neglect had caused me to lose what I loved above all else, and—dread of all dreads—that I might have to return home and face my wife without our only child. Never before or since have I felt such panic.

But then, as I passed the counter yet again, there he was, having been found and returned by some obliging customer! In an instant, the arousal of terror spilled into ecstasy. Clutching my son, with tears suddenly flowing, I found myself unable to speak my thanks and stumbled out of the store awash in grateful joy.

Where do such emotions come from? Why do we have them? What are they made of? Emotions don't exist just to give us interesting experiences. They are our body's adaptive response, supporting our survival. When we face challenges, emotions focus our attention and energize our action (Cyders & Smith, 2008). Our heart races. Our pace quickens. All our senses go on high alert. Receiving unexpected good news, we may find our eyes tearing up. We raise our hands in triumph. We feel joy and a newfound confidence.

As my panicked search for Peter illustrates, **emotions** are a mix of

- *bodily arousal* (heart pounding),
- *expressive behaviors* (quickened pace), and
- *conscious experience,* including thoughts (*"Is this a kidnapping?"*) and feelings (fear, panic, joy).

Psychologists' task is fitting these three pieces together. To do that, we need answers to two big questions:

1. A chicken-and-egg debate: Does your bodily arousal come *before* or *after* your emotional feelings? (Did I first notice my racing heart and faster step, and then feel terror about losing Peter? Or did my sense of fear come first, stirring my heart and legs to respond?)

2. How do *thinking* (cognition) and *feeling* interact? Does cognition always come before emotion? (Did I think about a kidnapping threat before I reacted emotionally?)

Historical theories of emotion, as well as current research, have tried to answer these questions.

Historical Emotion Theories

The psychological study of emotion began with the first question: How do bodily responses relate to emotions? Two historical theories provided different answers.

James-Lange Theory: Arousal Comes Before Emotion

Common sense tells most of us that we cry because we are sad, lash out because we are angry, tremble because we are afraid. First comes conscious awareness, then the feeling. But to psychologist William James, an early explorer of human feelings, this commonsense view of emotion had things backward. Rather, "We feel sorry because we cry, angry because we strike, afraid because we tremble" (1890, p. 1066). James' idea was also proposed by Danish physiologist Carl Lange, and so is called the **James-Lange theory.** James and Lange would have guessed that I noticed my racing heart and then, shaking with fright, felt the whoosh of emotion—that my feeling of fear *followed* my body's response.

Cannon-Bard Theory: Arousal and Emotion Happen at the Same Time

Physiologist Walter Cannon (1871–1945) disagreed with James and Lange. Does a racing heart signal fear, anger, or love? The body's responses—heart rate, perspiration, and body temperature—are too similar to *cause* the different emotions, said Cannon. He and another physiologist, Philip Bard, concluded that our bodily responses and experienced

JOY EXPRESSED IS JOY FELT According to the James-Lange theory, we don't just smile because we share our teammates' joy. We also share the joy because we are smiling with them.

Matt Sullivan/Reuters/Landov

emotions occur simultaneously. So, according to the **Cannon-Bard theory,** my heart began pounding *as* I experienced fear. The emotion-triggering stimulus traveled to my sympathetic nervous system, causing my body's arousal. *At the same time,* it traveled to my brain's cortex, causing my awareness of my emotion. My pounding heart did not cause my feeling of fear, nor did my feeling of fear cause my pounding heart. Bodily responses and experienced emotions are separate.

But are they really independent from each other? The Cannon-Bard theory has been challenged by studies of people with severed spinal cords, including a survey of 25 injured World War II soldiers (Hohmann, 1966). Those with *lower-spine injuries,* who had lost sensation only in their legs, reported little change in their emotions' intensity. Those with *high spinal cord injury,* who could feel nothing below the neck, did report changes. Some reactions were

much less intense than before the injuries. Anger, one man with a high spinal cord injury confessed, "just doesn't have the heat to it that it used to. It's a mental kind of anger." Other emotions, those expressed mostly in body areas above the neck, were felt *more* intensely. These men reported increases in weeping, lumps in the throat, and getting choked up when saying good-bye, worshipping, or watching a touching movie. Such evidence has led some researchers to view feelings as "mostly shadows" of our bodily responses and behaviors (Damasio, 2003).

But our emotions also involve cognition (Averill, 1993; Barrett, 2006). Here we arrive at psychology's second big emotion question: How do thinking and feeling interact? Whether we fear the man behind us on the dark street depends entirely on whether we interpret his actions as threatening or friendly.

Schachter-Singer Two-Factor Theory: Arousal + Label = Emotion

Stanley Schachter and Jerome Singer (1962) demonstrated that how we assess, or *appraise,* our experiences matters greatly. Our physical reactions and our thoughts (perceptions, memories, and interpretations) together create emotion. In their **two-factor theory,** emotions

emotion a response of the whole organism, involving (1) bodily arousal, (2) expressive behaviors, and (3) conscious experience.

James-Lange theory the theory that our experience of emotion is our awareness of our physiological responses to an emotion-arousing stimulus.

Cannon-Bard theory the theory that an emotion-arousing stimulus simultaneously triggers (1) physiological responses and (2) the subjective experience of emotion.

two-factor theory Schachter and Singer's theory that to experience emotion we must (1) be physically aroused and (2) cognitively label the arousal.

therefore have two ingredients: *physical arousal* and *cognitive appraisal*. An emotional experience, they argued, requires a conscious interpretation of arousal.

Sometimes our arousal spills over from one event to the next, influencing our response. Imagine arriving home after a fast run and finding a message that you got a longed-for job. With arousal lingering from the run, will you feel more excited than you would be if you heard this news after staying awake all night studying?

To explore this *spillover effect*, Schachter and Singer injected college men with *epinephrine*, a hormone that triggers feelings of arousal. Picture yourself as a participant. After receiving the injection, you go to a waiting room. You find yourself with another person (actually someone working with the experimenters) who is acting either joyful or irritated. As you observe this accomplice, you begin to feel your heart race, your body flush, and your breathing become more rapid. If you had been told to expect these effects from the injection, what would you feel? The actual volunteers felt little emotion—because they assumed their arousal was caused by the drug. But if you had been told the injection would produce no effects, what would you feel? Perhaps you would react as another group of participants did. They "caught" the apparent emotion of the other person in the waiting room. They became happy if the accomplice was acting joyful, and testy if the accomplice was acting irritated.

We can experience a stirred-up state as one emotion or another, depending on how we interpret and label it. Dozens of experiments have demonstrated this effect (Reisenzein, 1983; Sinclair et al., 1994; Zillmann, 1986). As one happiness researcher noted, "Feelings that one interprets as fear in the presence of a sheer drop may be interpreted as lust in the presence of a sheer blouse" (Gilbert, 2006).

The point to remember: Arousal fuels emotion; cognition channels it.

THE SPILLOVER EFFECT Arousal from a soccer match can fuel anger, which can descend into rioting or other violent confrontations.

📺 **LaunchPad**   For a 4-minute demonstration of the relationship between arousal and cognition, see LaunchPad's *Video: Emotion = Arousal Plus Interpretation*.

Zajonc, LeDoux, and Lazarus: Emotion and the Two-Track Brain

Is the heart always subject to the mind? Must we *always* interpret our arousal before we can experience an emotion?

No, said Robert Zajonc (1923–2008) [ZI-yence]. He argued that we actually have many emotional reactions apart from, or even before, our interpretation of a situation (Zajonc, 1980, 1984). Can you recall liking something or someone immediately, without knowing why? These reactions often reflect the automatic processing that takes place in our two-track mind.

Our emotional responses are the final step in a process that can follow two different pathways in our brain, both via the thalamus. Some emotions, especially our more complex feelings, like hatred and love, travel a "high road" to the brain's cortex (**FIGURE 9.10**). There, we analyze and label information before we order a response via the amygdala (an emotion-control center).

But sometimes our emotions (especially simple likes, dislikes, and fears) take what Joseph LeDoux (2002, 2015) has called the "low road." This neural shortcut bypasses the cortex (Figure 9.10b). Following the low road, a fear-provoking stimulus travels from the eye or the ear directly to the amygdala. This shortcut

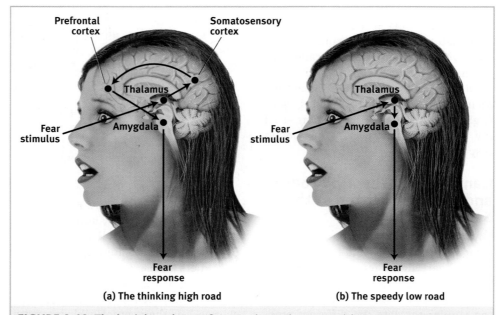

(a) The thinking high road

(b) The speedy low road

FIGURE 9.10 The brain's pathways for emotions The two-track brain processes sensory input on two different pathways. (a) Some input travels to the cortex (via the thalamus) for analysis and is then sent to the amygdala. (b) Other input travels directly to the amygdala (via the thalamus) for an instant emotional reaction.

enables our greased-lightning emotional response ("Life in danger!") before our brain interprets the exact source of danger. Like speedy reflexes (that also operate apart from the brain's thinking cortex), the amygdala's reactions are so fast that we may not be aware of what's happened (Dimberg et al., 2000).

The amygdala's structure makes it easier for our feelings to hijack our thinking than for our thinking to rule our feelings (LeDoux & Armony, 1999). It sends more neural projections up to the cortex than it receives back. In the forest, we can jump when we hear rustling in nearby bushes and leave it to our cortex (via the high road) to decide later whether the sound was made by a snake or by the wind. Such experiences support Zajonc's belief that *some* of our emotional reactions involve no deliberate thinking.

Emotion researcher Richard Lazarus (1991, 1998) agreed that our brain processes vast amounts of information without our conscious awareness, and that some emotional responses do not require *conscious* thinking. Much of our emotional life operates via the automatic, speedy low road. But, he asked, how would we *know* what we are reacting to if we did not in some way appraise the situation? The appraisal may be effortless and we may not be conscious of it, but it is still a mental function. To know whether a stimulus is good or bad, the brain must have some idea of what it is (Storbeck et al., 2006). Thus, said Lazarus, emotions arise when we *appraise* an event as harmless or dangerous, whether we truly *know* it is or not. We appraise the sound of the rustling bushes as the presence of a threat. Later, we learn that it was "just the wind."

Let's sum up (see also **TABLE 9.3**). As Zajonc and LeDoux have demonstrated, some emotional responses—especially simple likes, dislikes, and fears—involve no conscious thinking. When I [ND] see a big spider trapped behind glass, I experience fear, even though I know the spider can't hurt me. Such responses are difficult to alter by changing our thinking. Within a fraction of a second, we may automatically perceive one person as more likable or trustworthy than another (Willis & Todorov, 2006). This instant appeal can even influence our political decisions if we vote (as many people do) for the candidate we *like* over the candidate expressing positions closer to our own (Westen, 2007).

But other emotions—including moods such as depression, and complex feelings such as hatred and love—are greatly affected by our interpretations, memories, and expectations. For these emotions, we have more conscious control. As you will see in Chapter 11, learning to *think* more positively about ourselves and the world around us can help us *feel* better.

Embodied Emotion

Whether you are falling in love or grieving a loved one's death, you need little convincing that emotions involve the body. Feeling without a body is like breathing without lungs. Some physical responses are easy to notice; others happen without your awareness. Indeed, many take place at the level of your brain's neurons.

The Basic Emotions

LOQ 9-8 What are some basic emotions?

Carroll Izard (1977) isolated 10 basic emotions: joy, interest-excitement, surprise, sadness, anger, disgust, contempt, fear, shame, and guilt. Most are present in

TABLE 9.3	Summary of Emotion Theories	
Theory	**Explanation of Emotions**	**Example**
James-Lange	Our awareness of our specific bodily responses to emotion-arousing stimuli	We observe our heart racing after a threat and then feel afraid.
Cannon-Bard	Bodily responses + simultaneous subjective experience	Our heart races at the same time that we feel afraid.
Schachter-Singer	Two factors: general arousal + a conscious cognitive label	We may label our arousal as fear or excitement, depending on context.
Zajonc; LeDoux	Instant, before cognitive appraisal	We automatically feel startled by a sound in the forest before labeling it as a threat.
Lazarus	Appraisal ("Is it dangerous or not?")—sometimes without our awareness—defines emotion	The sound is "just the wind."

infancy (**FIGURE 9.11**). Other research-ers believe that pride and love are also basic emotions (Shaver et al., 1996; Tracey & Robins, 2004). But Izard has argued that they are combinations of the basic 10, with love, for example, being a mixture of joy and interest-excitement. Another issue: Do our different emotions have distinct arousal footprints? (In other words, does our body know the difference between fear and anger?) Before answering that question, let's review what happens in your autonomic nervous system when your body becomes aroused.

Emotions and the Autonomic Nervous System

LOQ 9-9 What is the link between emotional arousal and the autonomic nervous system?

As we saw in Chapter 2, in a crisis, the *sympathetic division* of your *autonomic nervous system (ANS)* mobilizes your body for action (**FIGURE 9.12**). It triggers your adrenal glands to release stress hormones. To provide energy, your liver pours extra sugar into your bloodstream. To help burn the sugar, your breathing rate increases to supply needed oxygen. Your heart rate and blood pressure increase. Your digestion slows, allowing blood to move away from your internal organs and toward your muscles. With blood sugar driven into the large muscles, running becomes easier. Your pupils open wider, letting in more light. To cool your stirred-up body, you perspire. If you were wounded, your blood would clot more quickly.

After your next crisis, think of this: Without any conscious effort, your body's response to danger is wonderfully coordinated and adaptive—preparing you for *fight or flight*. When the crisis passes, the *parasympathetic division* of your ANS gradually calms your body, as stress hormones slowly leave your bloodstream.

The Physiology of Emotions

LOQ 9-10 How do our body states relate to specific emotions?

Imagine conducting an experiment, measuring the body's responses to different emotions. In each of four rooms, you have someone watching a movie. In the first, the person is viewing a horror show. In the second, the viewer watches an anger-provoking film. In the third, someone is watching a sexually arousing film. In the fourth, the person is viewing an utterly boring movie. From the control center, you are tracking each person's physical responses, measuring perspiration, breathing, and heart rate. Do you think you could tell who is frightened? Who is angry? Who is sexually aroused? Who is bored?

With training, you could probably pick out the bored viewer. But spotting the bodily differences among fear, anger, and sexual arousal would be much more difficult (Barrett, 2006). Different emotions can share common biological signatures.

> "No one ever told me that grief felt so much like fear. I am not afraid, but the sensation is like being afraid. The same fluttering in the stomach, the same restlessness, the yawning. I keep on swallowing."
>
> C. S. Lewis, *A Grief Observed*, 1961

Despite similar bodily responses, sexual arousal, fear, and anger *feel* different to us, and they often *look* different to others. We may appear "paralyzed with fear" or "ready to explode."

With the help of sophisticated laboratory tools, researchers have pinpointed some subtle indicators of different emotions (Lench et al., 2011). The finger temperatures and hormone secretions that accompany fear do sometimes differ from those that accompany rage (Ax, 1953; Levenson, 1992). Fear and joy stimulate different facial muscles. During fear, your brow muscles tense. During joy, muscles in your cheeks and under your eyes pull into a smile (Witvliet & Vrana, 1995).

SCARY THRILLS Intense, happy excitement and panicky fear involve similar physiological arousal. That allows us to flip rapidly between the two emotions.

Brain scans and EEGs reveal that some emotions also differ in their brain circuits (Panksepp, 2007). When you experience negative emotions such as disgust, your right frontal cortex is more active than your left frontal cortex. People who are prone to depression, or who have generally negative personalities, also show more activity in their right frontal lobe (Harmon-Jones et al., 2002). One not-unhappy wife reported that her husband, who had lost part of his right frontal lobe in brain surgery, became less irritable and more affectionate (Goleman, 1995). My [DM's] father, after a right-hemisphere stroke at age 92, lived the last two years of his life with happy gratitude and nary a complaint or negative emotion.

When you experience positive moods—when you are enthusiastic, energized, and happy—your left frontal lobe will be more active. Increased left frontal lobe activity is found in people with positive personalities—jolly infants and alert, energetic, and persistently goal-directed adults (Davidson & Begley, 2012; Urry et al., 2004). When you're happy and you know it, your brain will surely show it.

(a) Joy (mouth forming smile, cheeks lifted, twinkle in eye)

(b) Anger (brows drawn together and downward, eyes fixed, mouth squarish)

(c) Interest (brows raised or knitted, mouth softly rounded, lips may be pursed)

(d) Disgust (nose wrinkled, upper lip raised, tongue pushed outward)

(e) Surprise (brows raised, eyes widened, mouth rounded in oval shape)

(f) Sadness (brows' inner corners raised, mouth corners drawn down)

(g) Fear (brows level, drawn in and up, eyelids lifted, mouth corners retracted)

FIGURE 9.11 Some naturally occurring infant emotions To identify the emotions generally present in infancy, Carroll Izard analyzed the facial expressions of infants.

Autonomic Nervous System Controls Physiological Arousal

Sympathetic division (arousing)		Parasympathetic division (calming)
Pupils dilate	EYES	Pupils get smaller
Decreases	SALIVATION	Increases
Perspires	SKIN	Dries
Increases	RESPIRATION	Decreases
Speeds up	HEART	Slows
Slows	DIGESTION	Speeds up
Increased stress hormones	ADRENAL GLANDS	Decreased stress hormones
Reduced	IMMUNE SYSTEM FUNCTIONING	Enhanced

FIGURE 9.12 Emotional arousal In a crisis, the Autonomic Nervous System's sympathetic division arouses us. When the crisis passes, the parasympathetic division calms us.

Thinking Critically About:
Lie Detection

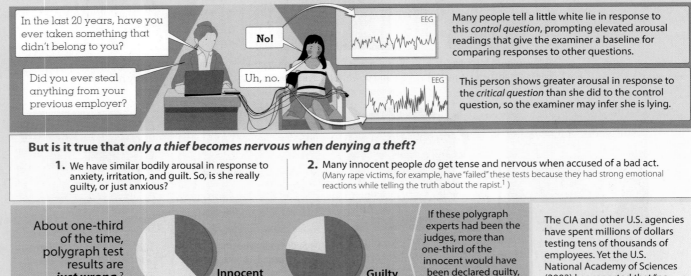

***Polygraphs* measure emotion-linked changes in breathing, heart rate, and perspiration. Can we use these results to detect lies?**

In the last 20 years, have you ever taken something that didn't belong to you?

Did you ever steal anything from your previous employer?

No!

Uh, no.

EEG

Many people tell a little white lie in response to this *control question*, prompting elevated arousal readings that give the examiner a baseline for comparing responses to other questions.

EEG

This person shows greater arousal in response to the *critical question* than she did to the control question, so the examiner may infer she is lying.

But is it true that *only a thief becomes nervous when denying a theft*?

1. We have similar bodily arousal in response to anxiety, irritation, and guilt. So, is she really guilty, or just anxious?

2. Many innocent people *do* get tense and nervous when accused of a bad act. (Many rape victims, for example, have "failed" these tests because they had strong emotional reactions while telling the truth about the rapist.[1])

About one-third of the time, polygraph test results are ***just wrong***.[2]

Innocent people

Guilty people

○ Judged innocent by polygraph ● Judged guilty by polygraph

If these polygraph experts had been the judges, more than one-third of the innocent would have been declared guilty, and one-fourth of the guilty would have gone free.

The CIA and other U.S. agencies have spent millions of dollars testing tens of thousands of employees. Yet the U.S. National Academy of Sciences (2002) has reported that "no spy has ever been caught [by] using the polygraph."

The ***guilty knowledge test* is more effective**. Innocent people are seldom wrongly judged to be lying.

Questions focus on specific crime-scene details known only to the police and the guilty person. [3] (If a camera and computer had been stolen, for example, only a guilty person should react strongly to the brand names of the stolen items.)

1. Lykken, 1991.   2. Kleinmuntz & Szucko, 1984.   3. Ben-Shakhar & Elaad, 2003.

To sum up, we can't easily see differences in emotions from tracking heart rate, breathing, and perspiration. But facial expressions and brain activity can vary from one emotion to another. So do we, like Pinocchio, give off telltale signs when we lie? Can a *lie detector*—a **polygraph**—reveal lies? For more on that question, see Thinking Critically About: Lie Detection.

Expressed and Experienced Emotion

There is a simple method of detecting people's emotions: Read their body language, listen to their voice tones, and study their faces. People's expressive behavior reveals their emotion. Does this nonverbal language vary with culture, or is it the same everywhere? And do our expressions influence what we feel?

Detecting Emotion in Others

LOQ 9-12 How do we communicate nonverbally? How do women and men differ in these abilities?

All of us communicate without words. Westerners "read" a firm handshake as evidence of an outgoing, expressive personality (Chaplin et al., 2000). A glance can communicate intimacy, while darting eyes may signal anxiety (Kleinke, 1986; Perkins et al., 2012). When two people are passionately in love, they typically spend time—quite a bit of time—gazing into each other's eyes (Bolmont et al., 2014; Rubin, 1970). Would such gazes stir these feelings between strangers? To find out, researchers asked male-female (and presumed heterosexual) pairs of strangers to gaze intently for 2 minutes either at each other's hands or into each other's eyes. After separating, the eye gazers reported feeling a tingle of attraction and affection (Kellerman et al., 1989).

Most of us read nonverbal cues fairly well. Shown 10 seconds of video from the end of a speed-dating interaction, people can often detect whether one person is attracted to the other (Place et al., 2009). We are adept at detecting a subtle smile (Maher et al., 2014). We are especially good at detecting nonverbal threats. A single angry face will "pop out" of a crowd (Fox et al., 2000; Hansen & Hansen, 1988; Öhman et al., 2001).

A SILENT LANGUAGE OF EMOTION Hindu classic dance uses the face and body to effectively convey 10 different emotions (Hejmadi et al., 2000).

Despite our brain's emotion-detecting skill, we find it difficult to detect deceiving expressions (Porter & ten Brinke, 2008). The behavioral differences between liars and truth tellers are too slight for most of us to detect (Hartwig & Bond, 2011). When researchers summarized 206 studies of sorting truth from lies, people were just 54 percent accurate—barely better than a coin toss (Bond & DePaulo, 2006). Are experts more skilled at spotting lies? No. With the possible exception of police professionals in high-stakes situations, even they don't beat chance by much (Bond & DePaulo, 2008; O'Sullivan et al., 2009).

Some of us are, however, more skilled than others at reading emotions. In one study, hundreds of people were asked to name the emotion displayed in brief film clips. The clips showed portions of a person's emotionally expressive face or body, sometimes accompanied by a garbled voice (Rosenthal et al., 1979). For example, one 2-second scene revealed only the face of an upset woman. After watching the scene, viewers would state whether the woman was criticizing someone for being late or was talking about her divorce. Given such "thin slices," women have generally been the better emotion detectors (Hall, 1984, 1987). The female advantage emerges early in development. Female infants, children, and adolescents have outperformed males in many studies (McClure, 2000).

Women's skill at decoding emotions may help explain why women tend to respond with and express greater emotion (Fischer & LaFrance, 2015; Vigil, 2009). In studies of 23,000 people from 26 cultures, women more than men have reported themselves open to feelings (Costa et al., 2001). Children show the same gender difference: Girls express stronger emotions than boys do (Chaplin & Aldao, 2013). That helps explain the extremely strong perception (nearly all 18- to 29-year-old Americans in one survey) that emotionality is "more true of women" (Newport, 2001).

One exception: Quickly—imagine an angry face. What gender is the person? If you're like 3 in 4 Arizona State University students in the original study, you imagined a male (Becker et al., 2007). And when a gender-neutral face was made to look angry, most people perceived it as male. If the face was smiling, they were more likely to perceive it as female (**FIGURE 9.13**). Anger strikes most people as a more masculine emotion.

Are there gender differences in empathy? If you have *empathy,* you identify with others and imagine what it must be like to walk in their shoes. You rejoice with those who rejoice and weep with those who weep. In surveys, women are far more likely than men to describe themselves as empathic. But measures of body responses, such as one's heart rate while seeing another's distress, reveal a much smaller gender gap (Eisenberg & Lennon, 1983; Rueckert et al., 2010).

Nevertheless, females are somewhat more likely to *express* empathy—to display more emotion when observing someone else's emotions. As **FIGURE 9.14** shows, this gender difference was clear when men and women watched film clips that were sad (children with a dying parent), happy (slapstick comedy), or frightening (a man nearly falling off the ledge of a tall building) (Kring & Gordon, 1998; Vigil, 2009). Women also more deeply experience emotional events, such as viewing pictures of mutilations. (Brain scans show more activity in areas sensitive to emotion.) Women also tend to remember the scenes better three weeks later (Canli et al., 2002).

Retrieve + Remember

• _____ (Women/Men) report experiencing emotions more deeply, and they tend to be more adept at reading nonverbal behavior.

ANSWER: Women

polygraph a machine, commonly used in attempts to detect lies, that measures some bodily responses (such as changes in perspiration, heart rate, and breathing) accompanying emotion.

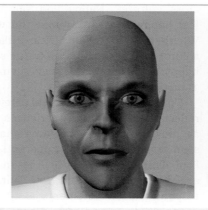
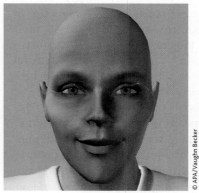

FIGURE 9.13 Male or female? Researchers manipulated a gender-neutral face. People were more likely to see it as a male when it wore an angry expression, and as a female when it wore a smile (Becker et al., 2007).

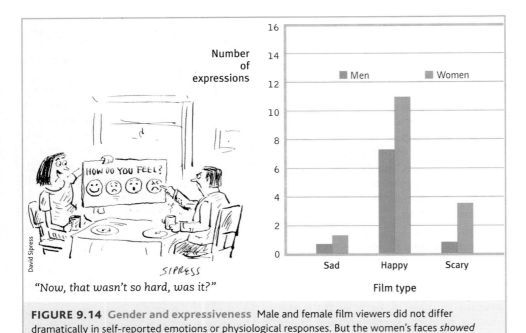

FIGURE 9.14 **Gender and expressiveness** Male and female film viewers did not differ dramatically in self-reported emotions or physiological responses. But the women's faces *showed* much more emotion. (Data from Kring & Gordon, 1998.)

Culture and Emotion

LOQ 9-13 How are nonverbal expressions of emotion understood within and across cultures?

The meaning of *gestures* varies from culture to culture. U.S. President Richard Nixon learned this while traveling in Brazil. He made the North American "A-OK" sign before a welcoming crowd, not knowing it was a crude insult in that country. In 1968, North Korea publicized photos of supposedly happy officers from a captured U.S. Navy spy ship. In the photo, three men had raised their middle fingers, telling their captors—who didn't recognize the cultural gesture—it was a "Hawaiian good luck sign" (Fleming & Scott, 1991).

Do *facial expressions* also have different meanings in different cultures? To find out, researchers showed photographs of some facial expressions to people in different parts of the world and asked them to guess the emotion (Ekman, 1994; Ekman & Friesen, 1975; Ekman et al., 1987; Izard, 1977, 1994). You can try this matching task yourself by pairing the six emotions with the six faces in **FIGURE 9.15**.

Regardless of your cultural background, you probably did pretty well. A smile's a smile the world around. Ditto for sadness, and to a lesser extent the other basic expressions (Jack et al., 2012). (There is no culture where people frown when they are happy.) We do slightly better when judging emotional displays from our own culture (Elfenbein & Ambady, 2002, 2003a,b). Nevertheless, the outward signs of emotion are generally the same across cultures.

Musical expressions of emotions also cross cultures. Happy and sad music feel happy and sad around the world. Whether you live in an African village or a European city, fast-paced music seems happy, and slow-paced music seems sad (Fritz et al., 2009).

Do these shared emotional categories reflect shared *cultural* experiences, such as movies and TV programs that are seen around the world? Apparently not. Paul Ekman and Wallace Friesen (1971) asked isolated people in New Guinea to respond to such statements as, "Pretend your child has died." When North American college students viewed the recorded responses, they easily read the New Guineans' facial reactions.

So we can say that facial muscles speak a fairly universal language. This discovery would not have surprised Charles Darwin (1809–1882). In *The Expression of the Emotions in Man and Animals* (1872), Darwin argued that in prehistoric times, before our ancestors communicated in words, they communicated threats, greetings, and submission with facial expressions. Such expressions helped them survive and became part of our shared heritage (Hess & Thibault, 2009). A sneer, for example, retains elements of an animal's baring its teeth in a snarl. Emotional expressions may enhance our survival in other ways, too. Surprise raises our eyebrows and widens our eyes, helping us take in more information. Disgust wrinkles our nose, closing out foul odors.

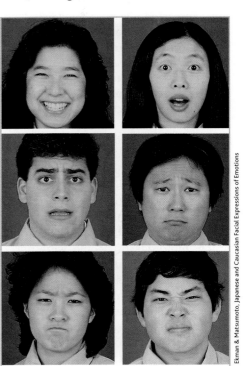

FIGURE 9.15 **Culture-specific or culturally universal expressions?** As people of differing cultures, do our faces speak differing languages? Which face expresses disgust? Anger? Fear? Happiness? Sadness? Surprise? (From Matsumoto & Ekman, 1989.) See inverted answers below.

From left to right, top to bottom: happiness, surprise, fear, sadness, anger, disgust.

UNIVERSAL EMOTIONS No matter where on Earth you live, you have no trouble knowing which photo depicts English soccer player Michael Owen and his fans feeling crushing disappointment (after he missed a goal) and triumphant celebration (after he scored one).

Smiles are social as well as emotional events. Olympic gold medalists typically don't smile when they are awaiting their award ceremony. But they wear broad grins when interacting with officials and facing the crowd and cameras (Fernández-Dols & Ruiz-Belda, 1995). Even natively blind athletes, who have never observed smiles, display social smiles in such situations (Matsumoto & Willingham, 2006, 2009).

"For news of the heart, ask the face."
Guinean proverb

Although we humans share a universal facial language, it has been adaptive for us to interpret faces in particular contexts (**FIGURE 9.16**). People judge an angry face set in a frightening situation as afraid, and a fearful face set in a painful situation as pained (Carroll & Russell, 1996). Movie directors harness this tendency by creating scenes and soundtracks that amplify our perceptions of particular emotions.

Smiles are also cultural events. In the United States, people of European descent tend to display excitement; in China, people are more likely to emphasize calmness (Tsai et al., 2006). These cultural differences shape facial expressiveness (Tsai et al., 2016). Compared with their counterparts in China, European-American leaders express excited smiles over six times more frequently in their official photos (**FIGURE 9.17**). If we're happy and we know it, our culture will teach us how to show it.

FIGURE 9.16 We read faces in context Whether we perceive the man in the top row as disgusted or angry depends on which body his face appears on (Aviezer et al., 2008). In the second row, tears on a face make its expression seem sadder (Provine et al., 2009).

📖 **LaunchPad** For a 4-minute demonstration of our universal facial language, see LaunchPad's *Video: Emotions and Facial Expression.*

Retrieve + Remember

• Are people more likely to differ culturally in their interpretations of facial expressions, or of gestures?

ANSWER: gestures

Peter Probst/Alamy

Vincent Yu/AP Photo

FIGURE 9.17 Culture and smiling U.S. Vice President Joe Biden and Chinese President Xi Jinping illustrate a cultural difference in facial expressiveness.

The Effects of Facial Expressions

LOQ 9-14 How do facial expressions influence our feelings?

As famed psychologist William James (1890) struggled with feelings of depression and grief, he came to believe that we can control our emotions by going "through the outward movements" of any emotion we want to experience. "To feel cheerful," he advised, "sit up cheerfully, look around cheerfully, and act as if cheerfulness were already there."

Was James right? Can our outward expressions and movements trigger our inner feelings and emotions? You can test his idea: Fake a big grin. Now scowl. Can you feel the "smile therapy" difference? Participants in dozens of experiments have felt a difference. For example, researchers tricked students into making a frowning expression by asking them to "contract these muscles" and "pull your brows together" (Laird, 1974, 1984; Laird et al., 1989). (The students thought they were helping the researchers attach facial electrodes.) The result? The students reported feeling a little angry.

So, too, for other basic emotions. For example, people reported feeling more fear than anger, disgust, or sadness when made to construct a fearful expression (Duclos et al., 1989). (They were told, "Raise your eyebrows. And open your eyes wide. Move your whole head back, so that your chin is tucked in a little bit, and let your mouth relax and hang open a little.") This **facial feedback effect** has been found many times, in many places, for many basic emotions (**FIGURE 9.18**). Just activating one of the smiling muscles by holding a pen in the teeth (rather than gently in the mouth, which produces a neutral expression) makes stressful situations less upsetting (Kraft & Pressman, 2012). When happy we smile, and when smiling we become happier.

So, your face is more than a billboard that displays your feelings; it also feeds your feelings. No wonder some depressed patients reportedly feel better after between-the-eyebrows Botox injections that freeze their frown muscles (Wollmer et al., 2012). Botox paralysis of the frowning muscles also slows people's reading of sadness- or anger-related sentences, and it slows activity

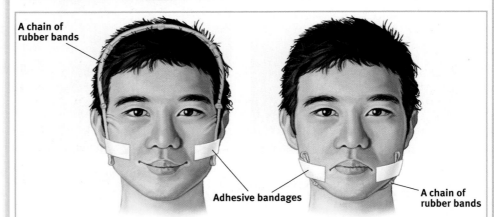

Retrieve + Remember

A chain of rubber bands

Adhesive bandages

A chain of rubber bands

FIGURE 9.18 How to make people smile without telling them to smile Do as Kazuo Mori and Hideko Mori (2009) did with students in Japan: Attach rubber bands to the sides of the face with adhesive bandages, and then run them either over the head or under the chin. (1) Based on the facial feedback effect, how might students in this experiment report feeling when the rubber bands raise their cheeks as though in a smile? (2) How might they report feeling when the rubber bands pull their cheeks downward?

ANSWERS: (1) Most report feeling more happy than sad when their cheeks are raised upward. (2) Most report feeling more sad than happy when their cheeks are pulled downward.

in emotion-related brain circuits (Havas et al., 2010; Hennenlotter et al., 2008).

Other studies have noted a similar *behavior feedback effect* (Carney et al., 2015; Flack, 2006). Try it. Walk for a few minutes with short, shuffling steps, keeping your eyes downcast. Now walk around taking long strides, with your arms swinging and your eyes looking straight ahead. Can you feel your mood shift? Going through the motions awakens the emotions.

You can use your understanding of feedback effects to become more empathic—to feel what others feel. See what happens if you let your own face mimic another person's expression.

Acting as another acts helps us feel what another feels (Vaughn & Lanzetta, 1981). Indeed, natural mimicry of others' emotions helps explain why emotions are contagious (Dimberg et al., 2000; Neumann & Strack, 2000). Positive, upbeat Facebook posts create a ripple effect, leading Facebook friends to also express more positive emotions (Kramer, 2012).

* * *

We have seen how our motivated behaviors, triggered by the forces of nature and nurture, often go hand in hand with emotional responses. Our psychological emotions likewise come equipped with physical reactions. Nervous about

an upcoming date, we feel stomach butterflies. Anxious over public speaking, we head for the bathroom. Smoldering over a family conflict, we get a splitting headache. Negative emotions and the prolonged high arousal that may accompany them can tax the body and harm our health. You'll hear more about this in Chapter 10. In that chapter, we'll also take a closer look at the emotion of happiness.

 facial feedback effect the tendency of facial muscle states to trigger corresponding feelings such as fear, anger, or happiness.

CHAPTER REVIEW

Motivation and Emotion

Test yourself by taking a moment to answer each of these Learning Objective Questions (repeated here from within the chapter). Then turn to Appendix D, Complete Chapter Reviews, to check your answers. Research suggests that trying to answer these questions on your own will improve your long-term memory of the concepts (McDaniel et al., 2009).

Motivational Concepts

9-1: What is *motivation*, and what are three key perspectives that help us understand motivated behaviors?

Hunger

9-2: What physiological factors cause us to feel hungry?

9-3: How do cultural and situational factors affect our taste preferences and eating habits?

9-4: What factors predispose some people to become and remain obese?

The Need to Belong

9-5: What evidence points to our human need to belong?

9-6: How does social networking influence us?

Emotion: Arousal, Behavior, and Cognition

9-7: What are the three parts of an emotion, and what theories help us to understand our emotions?

Embodied Emotion

9-8: What are some basic emotions?

9-9: What is the link between emotional arousal and the autonomic nervous system?

9-10: How do our body states relate to specific emotions?

9-11: How effective are polygraphs in using body states to detect lies?

Expressed and Experienced Emotion

9-12: How do we communicate nonverbally? How do women and men differ in these abilities?

9-13: How are nonverbal expressions of emotion understood within and across cultures?

9-14: How do facial expressions influence our feelings?

TERMS AND CONCEPTS TO REMEMBER

Test yourself on these terms by trying to write down the definition in your own words before flipping back to the referenced page to check your answer.

motivation, p. 259
drive-reduction theory, p. 259
physiological need, p. 259

homeostasis, p. 259
incentive, p. 259
Yerkes-Dodson law, p. 259

hierarchy of needs, p. 259
glucose, p. 261
set point, p. 263
basal metabolic rate, p. 263
ostracism, p. 267
narcissism, p. 269

emotion, p. 271
James-Lange theory, p. 271
Cannon-Bard theory, p. 271
two-factor theory, p. 271
polygraph, p. 277
facial feedback effect, p. 281

CHAPTER TEST

Test yourself repeatedly throughout your studies. This will not only help you figure out what you know and don't know; the testing itself will help you learn and remember the information more effectively thanks to the *testing effect*.

1. An example of a physiological need is _____. An example of a psychological drive is _____.

   a. hunger; a "push" to find food

   b. a "push" to find food; hunger

   c. curiosity; a "push" to reduce arousal

   d. a "push" to reduce arousal; curiosity

2. Jan walks into a friend's kitchen, smells bread baking, and begins to feel very hungry. The smell of baking bread is a(n) _____ (incentive/drive).

3. _____ theory attempts to explain behaviors that do NOT reduce physiological needs.

4. With a challenging task, such as taking a difficult exam, performance is likely to peak when arousal is

   a. very high.

   b. moderate.

   c. very low.

   d. absent.

5. According to Maslow's hierarchy of needs, our most basic needs are physiological, including the need for food and water; just above these are _____ needs.

   a. safety

   b. self-esteem

   c. belongingness

   d. self-transcendence

6. Journalist Dorothy Dix once remarked, "Nobody wants to kiss when they are hungry." Which motivation theory best supports her statement?

7. According to the concept of set point, our body maintains itself at a particular weight level. This "weight thermostat" is an example of _____.

8. Which of the following is a genetically predisposed response to food?

   a. An aversion to eating cats and dogs

   b. An interest in novel foods

   c. A preference for sweet and salty foods

   d. An aversion to carbohydrates

9. The blood sugar _____ provides the body with energy. When it is _____ (low/high), we feel hungry.

10. The rate at which your body expends energy while at rest is referred to as the _____ _____ rate.

11. Obese people find it very difficult to lose weight permanently. This is due to several factors, including the fact that

    a. it takes more energy to maintain weight than it did to gain it.

    b. the set point of obese people is lower than average.

    c. with dieting, metabolism increases.

    d. there is a genetic influence on body weight.

12. Sanjay recently adopted the typical college diet high in processed fat and sugar. He knows he may gain weight, but he figures it's no big deal because he can lose the extra pounds in the future. How would you evaluate Sanjay's plan?

13. Which of the following is NOT part of the evidence presented to support the view that humans are strongly motivated by a need to belong?

    a. Students who rated themselves as "very happy" also tended to have satisfying close relationships.

    b. Social exclusion—such as exile or solitary confinement—is considered a severe form of punishment.

    c. As adults, adopted children tend to resemble their biological parents.

    d. Children who are extremely neglected become withdrawn, frightened, and speechless.

14. What are some ways to manage our social networking time successfully?

15. The _____-_____ theory of emotion maintains that a physiological response happens BEFORE we know what we are feeling.

16. Assume that after spending an hour on a treadmill, you receive a letter saying that your scholarship request has been approved. The two-factor theory of emotion would predict that your physical arousal will

    a. weaken your happiness.

    b. intensify your happiness.

    c. transform your happiness into relief.

    d. have no particular effect on your happiness.

17. Zajonc and LeDoux maintain that some emotional reactions occur before we have had the chance to consciously label or interpret them. Lazarus noted the importance of how we appraise events. These psychologists differ in the emphasis they place on _____ in emotional responses.

    a. physical arousal

    b. the hormone epinephrine

    c. cognitive processing

    d. learning

18. What does a polygraph measure and why are its results questionable?

19. When people are induced to assume fearful expressions, they often report feeling a little fear. This result is known as the _____ _____ effect.

20. Aiden has a bad cold and finds himself shuffling to class with his head down. How might his posture, as well as his cold, affect his emotional well-being?

Find answers to these questions in Appendix E, in the back of the book.

IN YOUR EVERYDAY LIFE

Answering these questions will help you make these concepts more personally meaningful, and therefore more memorable.

1. How often do you satisfy what Maslow called "self-actualization" needs? What about "self-transcendence" needs?

2. Does boredom ever motivate you to do things just to figure out something new? When was the last time that happened, and what did you find?

3. Do you usually eat only when your body sends hunger signals? How much does the sight or smell of delicious food tempt you even when you're full?

4. Have you or a loved one ever tried unsuccessfully to lose weight? What happened? What weight-loss strategies might have been more successful?

5. Do your connections on social media increase your sense of belonging? At busy times, what strategies do you use to maintain balance and focus?

6. Can you remember a time when you began to feel upset or uneasy and only later labeled those feelings? What was that like?

7. Can you think of a recent time when you noticed your body's reactions to a stressful experience? How did you interpret the situation? What emotion did you feel?

8. Imagine one situation in which you would like to change the way you feel. How could you do so by altering your facial expressions or the way you carry yourself?

Use **LearningCurve** to create your personalized study plan, which will direct you to the resources that will help you most in **LaunchPad**.

SURVEY THE CHAPTER

10

Stress, Health, and Human Flourishing

For many students, the transition to college (or back to college) has not been easy. College is a happy time, but it presents challenges. Debt piles up. Deadlines loom. New relationships form, and sometimes fail. Family demands continue. Big exams or class presentations make you tense. Stuck in traffic, late to class or work, your mood may turn sour. It's enough to give you a headache or disrupt your sleep. No wonder 85 percent of college students have reported occasional or frequent stress during the past three months (AP, 2009).

Stress often strikes without warning. Imagine being 21-year-old Ben Carpenter on the world's wildest and fastest wheelchair ride. As he crossed an intersection on a sunny summer afternoon in 2007, the light changed. A large truck, whose driver didn't see him, started moving into the intersection. As they bumped, Ben's wheelchair turned to face forward, and its handles got stuck in the truck's grille. Off they went, the driver unable to hear Ben's cries for help.

As they sped down the highway about an hour from my [DM's] home, passing motorists caught the bizarre sight of a truck pushing a wheelchair at 50 miles per hour and started calling 911. (The first caller: "You are not going to believe this. There is a semitruck pushing a guy in a wheelchair on Red Arrow highway!") Lucky for Ben, one passerby was an undercover police officer. Pulling a quick U-turn, he followed the truck to its destination a couple of miles from where the wild ride had started, and informed the disbelieving driver that he had a passenger hooked in his grille. "It was very scary," said Ben.

In this chapter we explore stress—what it is, how it affects us, and how we can reduce it. Then we'll take a close look at happiness—an important measure of whether we are flourishing. Let's begin with some basic terms.

Stress: Some Basic Concepts

LOQ LearningObjectiveQuestion

10-1 How does our appraisal of an event affect our stress reaction, and what are the three main types of stressors?

Stress is a slippery concept. In everyday life, we may use the word to describe threats or challenges ("Ben was under a lot of stress") or to describe our responses to those events ("Ben experienced acute stress"). Psychologists use more precise terms. The challenge or event (Ben's dangerous truck ride) is a *stressor*. Ben's physical and emotional responses are a *stress reaction*. And the process by which he interprets the threat is *stress*.

Thus, **stress** is the process of appraising an event as threatening or challenging, and responding to it (Lazarus, 1998). If you have prepared for an important math test, you may welcome it as a challenge. You will be aroused and focused, and you will probably do well (**FIGURE 10.1**). Championship athletes, successful entertainers, motivated students, and great teachers and leaders all thrive and excel when aroused by a challenge (Blascovich & Mendes, 2010; Wang et al., 2015).

Stressors that we appraise as threats, not challenges, can instead lead to strong negative reactions. If prevented from preparing for your math test, you will appraise the disruption as a threat, and your response will be distress.

Extreme or prolonged stress can harm us. Demanding jobs that mentally exhaust workers also damage their physical health (Huang et al., 2010). Pregnant women with overactive stress systems tend to have shorter pregnancies, which pose health risks for their infants (Entringer et al., 2011).

So there is an interplay between our head and our health. Before we explore that interplay, let's take a closer look at types of stressors and stress reactions.

Stressors—Things That Push Our Buttons

Stressors fall into three main types: catastrophes, significant life changes, and daily hassles. All can be toxic—they can increase our risk of disease and death.

Catastrophes

Catastrophes are unpredictable large-scale events, such as earthquakes, floods, wildfires, and storms. Even though we often give aid and comfort to one another after such events, the damage to emotional

and physical health is significant. In surveys taken in the three weeks after the 9/11 terrorist attacks, for example, 58 percent of Americans said they were experiencing greater than average arousal and anxiety (Silver et al., 2002). And those who watched a lot of 9/11 television footage had worse health outcomes two to three years later (Silver et al., 2013).

Significant Life Changes

During catastrophes, misery often has company. But during significant life changes, we may experience stress alone. Even happy life changes, such as graduating from college or marrying the love of your life, can be stressful. So can other personal events—leaving home, having a loved one die, getting divorced, or taking on student debt. These life changes often happen during young adulthood. The stress of those years was clear in a recent survey that asked, "Are you trying to take on too many things at once?" Who reported the highest stress levels? Women and younger adults (APA, 2009). About half of people in their twenties, but only one-fifth of those over 65, reported experiencing stress during "a lot of the day yesterday" (Newport & Pelham, 2009).

How does stress related to life changes affect our health? Long-term studies indicate that people recently widowed, fired, or divorced are more disease-prone (Dohrenwend et al., 1982; Sbarra et al., 2015; Strully, 2009). In one study of 96,000 widowed people, their risk of death doubled in the week following their partner's death (Kaprio et al., 1987). Experiencing a cluster of crises (perhaps losing a job and an important relationship while falling behind in schoolwork) puts one even more at risk.

Daily Hassles

Events don't have to remake our lives to cause stress. Stress also comes from *daily hassles*—dead cell phones, lost keys, irritating housemates, and too many things to do (Lazarus, 1990; Pascoe & Richman, 2009; Ruffin, 1993). Some people simply shrug off

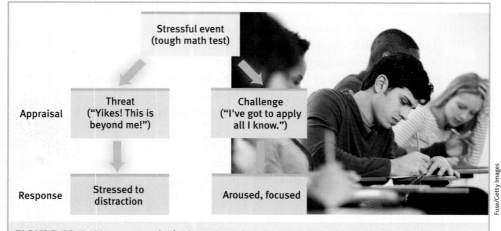

FIGURE 10.1 Stress appraisal The events of our lives flow through a psychological filter. How we appraise an event influences how much stress we experience and how effectively we respond.

such hassles. Others find them hard to ignore. This is especially the case for the many Americans who wake up each day facing budgets that won't stretch to the next payday, housing problems, solo parenting, poor health, and discrimination. Such stressors can take a toll on physical and mental well-being (DeLongis et al., 1982, 1988; Piazza et al., 2013; Sin et al., 2015).

> "It's not the large things that send a man to the madhouse . . . no, it's the continuing series of small tragedies . . . not the death of his love but the shoelace that snaps with no time left."
>
> American author Charles Bukowski (1920–1994)

Stress Reactions—From Alarm to Exhaustion

LOQ 10-2 How does the body respond to stress?

Our response to stress is part of a unified mind-body system. Walter Cannon (1929) first realized this in the 1920s. He found that extreme cold, lack of oxygen, and emotion-arousing events all trigger an outpouring of stress hormones from the adrenal glands. When your brain sounds an alarm, your *sympathetic nervous system* (Chapter 2) responds. It increases your heart rate and respiration, diverts blood from your digestive organs to your skeletal muscles, dulls your feeling of pain, and releases sugar and fat from your body's stores. All this prepares your body for the wonderfully adaptive **fight-or-flight response** (see Figure 9.12 in Chapter 9). By fighting or fleeing, we increase our chances of survival.

Hans Selye (1936, 1976) extended Cannon's findings. His studies of animals' reactions to various stressors, such as electric shock and surgery, helped make stress a major concept in both psychology and medicine. Selye discovered that the body's adaptive response to stress was so general that it was like a single burglar alarm that sounds, no matter what intrudes. He named this response the **general adaptation syndrome (GAS),** and he saw it as a three-stage process (**FIGURE 10.2**). Here's how those stages, or phases, might look if you suffered a physical or emotional trauma:

- In Phase 1, you have an *alarm reaction,* as your sympathetic nervous system suddenly activates. Your heart rate soars. Blood races to your skeletal muscles. You feel the faintness of shock.

- During Phase 2, *resistance,* your temperature, blood pressure, and respiration remain high. With your resources mobilized, you are ready to resist the trauma—to fight back. Your adrenal glands pump stress hormones into your bloodstream. You are fully engaged, summoning all your resources to meet the challenge.

---

stress the process by which we perceive and respond to certain events, called *stressors,* that we appraise as threatening or challenging.

fight-or-flight response an emergency response, including activity of the sympathetic nervous system, that mobilizes energy and activity for attacking or escaping a threat.

general adaptation syndrome (GAS) Selye's concept of the body's adaptive response to stress in three stages—alarm, resistance, exhaustion.

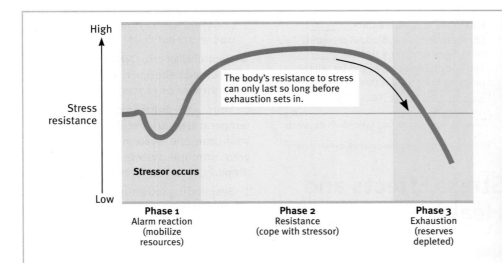

High

Stress resistance

The body's resistance to stress can only last so long before exhaustion sets in.

Stressor occurs

Low

Phase 1
Alarm reaction
(mobilize resources)

Phase 2
Resistance
(cope with stressor)

Phase 3
Exhaustion
(reserves depleted)

Luis Hidalgo/AP Photo

Chile's Presidency/AP Photo

FIGURE 10.2 Selye's general adaptation syndrome When a gold and copper mine in Chile collapsed in 2010, family and friends rushed to the scene, fearing the worst. Many of those holding vigil outside the mine were nearly exhausted with the stress of waiting and worrying. Then—good news! After 18 days, they learned that all 33 of the miners inside were alive and well.

• In Phase 3, constant stress causes *exhaustion*. As time passes, with no relief from stress, your reserves begin to run out. Your body copes well with temporary stress, but prolonged stress can damage it. You become more vulnerable to illness or even, in extreme cases, collapse and death. In one study, former prisoners of war, who experienced constant stress and suffering, died sooner than their fellow soldiers not taken captive (Solomon et al., 2014). Rats show similar patterns. The most fearful and easily stressed rats die about 15 percent sooner than their more confident counterparts (Cavigelli & McClintock, 2003).

We respond to stress in other ways, too. One response is common after a loved one's death: Withdraw. Pull back. Conserve energy. Faced with an extreme disaster, such as a car sinking in a body of water, some people become paralyzed by fear. They stay strapped in their seatbelt instead of swimming to safety. Another option for dealing with stress is to seek out those who need support (Lim & DeSteno, 2016). Perhaps you have participated in this **tend-and-befriend response** by contributing help after a natural disaster.

TENDING TO TRAUMA Arizona's 2013 wildfires claimed the lives of 19 elite firefighters. Juliann Ashcroft's (left) husband, Andrew, was among those lost. Women suffering such tragedies often show a tend-and-befriend coping response by joining together and nurturing each other.

Krista Kennell/AFP/Getty Images

The tend-and-befriend response is found especially among women (Taylor, 2006; Taylor et al., 2000). Facing stress, men more often than women tend to socially withdraw, turn to alcohol, or become emotionally insensitive (Bodenmann et al., 2015). Women more often respond to stress by nurturing and banding together, which may be due to *oxytocin*. This stress-moderating hormone is associated with pair-bonding in animals and is released by cuddling, massage, and breast feeding in humans (Taylor, 2006). Women in distressed relationships also have higher levels of oxytocin, however, which may help them seek out and receive support from others (Taylor et al., 2010b).

It often pays to spend our physical and mental resources in fighting or fleeing an external threat. But we do so at a cost. When our stress is momentary, the cost is small. When stress persists, we may pay a much higher price, with lowered resistance to infections and other threats to mental and physical health.

Retrieve + Remember

• Stress response system: When alerted to a negative, uncontrollable event, our _____ nervous system arouses us. Heart rate and respiration _____ (increase/decrease). Blood is diverted from digestion to the skeletal _____. The body releases sugar and fat. All this prepares the body for the _____-_____-_____ response.

ANSWERS: sympathetic; increase; muscles; fight-or-flight

Stress Effects and Health

LOQ 10-3 How does stress influence our immune system?

How do you try to stay healthy? Avoid sneezers? Get extra rest? Wash your hands? You should add stress management to that list. Why? Because, as we

have seen throughout this text, everything psychological is also biological. Stress is no exception. Stress contributes to high blood pressure and headaches. Stress also leaves us less able to fight off disease. To manage stress, we need to understand these connections.

The field of **psychoneuroimmunology** studies our mind-body interactions (Kiecolt-Glaser, 2009). That mouthful of a word makes sense when said slowly. Your emotions (*psycho*) affect your brain (*neuro*), which controls the endocrine hormones that influence your disease-fighting *immune* system. And this field is the study of (*ology*) those interactions. Let's start by focusing on the immune system.

Your immune system resembles a complex security system. When it functions properly, it keeps you healthy by capturing and destroying bacteria, viruses, and other invaders. Four types of cells carry out these search-and-destroy missions (**FIGURE 10.3**):

• *B lymphocytes* release antibodies that fight bacterial infections.

• *T lymphocytes* attack cancer cells, viruses, and foreign substances—even "good" ones, such as transplanted organs.

• *Macrophage* ("big eater") *cells* identify, trap, and destroy harmful invaders and worn-out cells.

• *Natural killer cells* (NK cells) attack diseased cells (such as those infected by viruses or cancer).

Your age, nutrition, genetics, body temperature, and stress all influence your immune system's activity. When your immune system doesn't function properly, it can err in two directions:

1. Responding too strongly, it may attack the body's own tissues, causing some forms of arthritis or an allergic reaction. Women have stronger immune systems than men do, making them less likely to get infections. But this very strength also puts women at higher risk for self-attacking diseases, such as lupus and multiple sclerosis (Nussinovitch & Schoenfeld, 2012; Schwartzman-Morris & Putterman, 2012).

R.legosyn/Shutterstock

Intruders!

Is it a bacterial infection?

Response: Send in *B lymphocytes*, such as this one shown in front of a macrophage.

CNRI/Science Source

Is it a cancer cell, virus, or other "foreign substance"?

Response: Send in *T lymphocytes*, such as this one.

NIBSC/Science Source

Is it some other harmful intruder, or perhaps a worn-out cell needing to be cleaned up?

Are there diseased cells (such as those infected by viruses or cancer) that need to be cleared out?

Response: Send in *macrophages*, such as the large one shown here, which is about to trap and destroy a tiny bacterium (lower right).

Lennart Nilsson/Boehringer Ingelheim International GmbH

Response: Send in *natural killer cells* (NK cells) such as the two shown here attacking a cell infected by cancer.

Eye of Science/Science Source

FIGURE 10.3   A simplified view of immune responses

2. Underreacting, the immune system may allow a bacterial infection to flare, a dormant herpes virus to erupt, or cancer cells to multiply. Surgeons may deliberately suppress a patient's immune system to protect transplanted organs (which the body treats as foreign invaders).

A flood of stress hormones can also suppress the immune system. In laboratories, immune suppression appears when animals are stressed by physical restraints, unavoidable electric shocks, noise, crowding, cold water, social defeat, or separation from their mothers (Maier et al., 1994). In one such study, monkeys

were housed with new roommates—three or four new monkeys—each month for six months (Cohen et al., 1992). If you know the stress of adjusting to even one new roommate, you can imagine how trying it would be to repeat this experience monthly. By the experiment's end, the socially stressed monkeys' immune systems were weaker than those of other monkeys left in stable groups.

Human immune systems react similarly. Three examples:

- *Surgical wounds heal more slowly in stressed people.* In one experiment, two groups of dental students received punch wounds (small holes punched in the skin). Punch-wound healing was 40 percent slower in the group wounded three days before a major exam than in the group wounded during summer vacation (Kiecolt-Glaser et al., 1998).

- *Stressed people develop colds more readily.* Researchers dropped a cold virus in the noses of people with high and low life-stress scores (**FIGURE 10.4**). Among those living stress-filled lives, 47 percent developed colds. Among those living relatively free of stress, only 27 percent did (Cohen et al., 2003, 2006; Cohen & Pressman, 2006).

- *Vaccines are less effective with stress.* Nurses gave older adults a flu vaccine and then measured how well their bodies fought off bacteria and viruses. The vaccine was most effective among those who experienced low stress (Segerstrom et al., 2012).

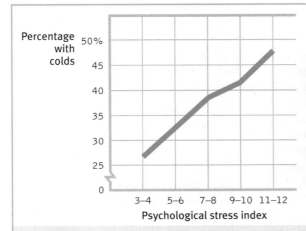

Laurent/Yakou/Science Source

FIGURE 10.4   Stress and colds   People with the highest life stress scores were also most vulnerable when exposed to an experimentally delivered cold virus (Cohen et al., 1991).

tend-and-befriend response   under stress, people (especially women) often provide support to others *(tend)* and bond with and seek support from others *(befriend)*.

psychoneuroimmunology   the study of how psychological, neural, and endocrine processes combine to affect our immune system and health.

The stress effect on immunity makes sense. It takes energy to track down invaders, produce swelling, and maintain fevers (Maier et al., 1994). Stress hormones drain this energy away from the disease-fighting lymphocytes. When you are ill, your body demands less activity and more sleep, in part to cut back on the energy your muscles usually use. Stress does the opposite. During an aroused fight-or-flight reaction, your stress responses draw energy away from your disease-fighting immune system and send it to your muscles and brain (see Figure 9.12 in Chapter 9). This competing energy need leaves you more open to illness.

© D. Hurst/Alamy

The bottom line: Stress does not make us sick. But it does reduce our immune system's ability to function, and that leaves us less able to fight infection.

Let's look now at how stress might affect AIDS, cancer, and heart disease.

Retrieve + Remember

- _____ focuses on mind-body interactions, including the effects of psychological, neural, and endocrine functioning on the immune system and overall health.

ANSWER: Psychoneuroimmunology

- What general effect does stress have on our health?

ANSWER: Stress tends to reduce our immune system's ability to function properly. So, those who regularly experience higher stress also have a higher risk of physical illness.

Stress and AIDS

We know that stress suppresses immune system functioning. What does this mean for people suffering from AIDS (acquired immune deficiency syndrome)? People with AIDS already have a damaged immune system. The name of the virus that triggers AIDS tells us that. "HIV" stands for *human immunodeficiency virus*.

Stress can't give people AIDS. But could stress and negative emotions speed the transition from HIV infection to AIDS in someone already infected? Might stress predict a faster decline in those with AIDS? An analysis of 33,252 participants from around the world suggests the answer to both questions is *Yes* (Chida & Vedhara, 2009). The greater the stress that HIV-infected people experience, the faster their disease progresses.

Could reducing stress help control AIDS? The answer again appears to be *Yes*. Although drug treatments are more effective, educational programs, grief support groups, talk therapy, relaxation training, and exercise programs that reduce distress have all had good results for HIV-positive people (Baum & Posluszny, 1999; McCain et al., 2008; Schneiderman, 1999).

Stress and Cancer

Stress does not create cancer cells. But in a healthy, functioning immune system, lymphocytes, macrophages, and NK cells search out and destroy cancer cells and cancer-damaged cells. If stress weakens the immune system, might this weaken a person's ability to fight off cancer? To find out, researchers implanted tumor cells in rodents. Next, they exposed some of the rodents to uncontrollable stress (for example, inescapable shocks). Compared with their unstressed counterparts, the stressed rodents developed cancer more often, experienced tumor growth sooner, and grew larger tumors (Sklar & Anisman, 1981).

Does this stress-cancer link apply to humans? The results are generally the same (Lutgendorf & Andersen, 2015). Some studies have found that people are at increased risk for cancer within a year after experiencing depression, helplessness, or grief. In one large study, the risk of colon cancer was 5.5 times greater among people with a history of workplace stress than among those who did not report such problems. The difference was not due to group differences in age, smoking, drinking, or physical characteristics (Courtney et al., 1993). There are exceptions, though. Other studies have found no link between stress and a risk of cancer in humans (Edelman & Kidman, 1997; Fox, 1998; Petticrew et al., 1999, 2002). Concentration camp survivors and former prisoners of war, for example, do not have elevated cancer rates. So this research story is still being written.

There is a danger in overstating the link between attitudes and cancer. Can you imagine how a woman dying of breast cancer might react to a report on the effects of stress on the speed of decline in cancer patients? She could wrongly blame herself for her illness. ("If only I had been more expressive, relaxed, and hopeful.") Her loved ones could become haunted by the notion that they caused her illness. ("If only I had been less stressful for my mom.")

> "I didn't give myself cancer."
> Mayor Barbara Boggs Sigmund (1939–1990), Princeton, New Jersey

It's important enough to repeat: *Stress does not create cancer cells.* At worst, stress may affect their growth by weakening the body's natural defenses against multiplying cancer cells (Lutgendorf et al., 2008; Nausheen et al., 2010; Sood et al., 2010). Although a relaxed, hopeful state may enhance these defenses, we should be aware of the thin line that divides science from wishful thinking. The powerful biological processes at work in advanced cancer or AIDS are not likely to be completely derailed by avoiding stress or maintaining a relaxed but determined spirit (Anderson, 2002; Kessler et al., 1991).

LaunchPad For a 7-minute demonstration of the links between stress, cancer, and the immune system, visit LaunchPad's *Video: Fighting Cancer—Mobilizing the Immune System.*

Stress and Heart Disease

LOQ 10-4 How does stress increase coronary heart disease risk?

Depart from reality for a moment. In this new world, you wake up each day, eat your breakfast, and check the news.

Among the headlines, you see that four 747 jumbo jet airplanes crashed again yesterday, killing another 1642 passengers. You finish your breakfast, grab your bag, and head out the door. It's just an average day.

Replace airplane crashes with **coronary heart disease,** the United States' leading cause of death, and you have re-entered reality. About 610,000 Americans die annually from heart disease (CDC, 2016a). Heart disease occurs when the blood vessels that nourish the heart muscle gradually close. High blood pressure and a family history of the disease increase the risk. So do smoking, obesity, an unhealthy diet, physical inactivity, and a high cholesterol level.

Stress and personality also play a big role in heart disease. The more psychological trauma people experience, the more their bodies generate *inflammation*, which is associated with heart and other health problems, as well as depression (Haapakoski et al., 2015; O'Donovan et al., 2012). Plucking a hair and measuring its level of *cortisol* (a stress hormone) can help indicate whether a child has experienced prolonged stress or predict whether an adult will have a future heart attack (Karlén et al., 2015; Pereg et al., 2011; Vliegenthart et al., 2016).

The Effects of Personality Type

In a classic study, Meyer Friedman, Ray Rosenman, and their colleagues measured the blood cholesterol level and clotting speed of 40 U.S. male tax accountants during unstressful and stressful times of year (Friedman & Ulmer, 1984). From January through March, the accountants showed normal results. But as the accountants began scrambling to finish their clients' tax returns before the April 15 filing deadline, their cholesterol and clotting measures rose to dangerous levels. In May and June, with the deadline passed, their health measures returned to normal. Stress predicted heart attack risk for the accountants, with rates going up during their most stressful times. Blood pressure also rises as students approach stressful exams (Conley & Lehman, 2012).

So, are some of us at high risk of stress-related coronary disease? To answer this question, the researchers who studied the tax accountants launched a classic nine-year *longitudinal study* of more than 3000 healthy men, aged 35 to 59. The researchers interviewed each man for 15 minutes, noting his work and eating habits, manner of talking, and other behavioral patterns. Some of the men were competitive, hard-driving, impatient, time-conscious, super-motivated, verbally aggressive, and easily angered. These men were labeled **Type A.** The roughly equal number who were more easygoing they called **Type B.** Which group do you suppose turned out to be the most coronary-prone?

Nine years later, 257 men in the study had suffered heart attacks, and 69 percent of them were Type A. Moreover, not one of the "pure" Type Bs—the most mellow and laid-back of their group—had suffered a heart attack.

As often happens in science, this exciting discovery provoked enormous public interest. But after that initial honeymoon period, researchers wanted to know more. Was the finding reliable? If so, what exactly is so toxic about the Type A profile: Time-consciousness? Competitiveness? Anger? Further research revealed the answer. Type A's toxic core is negative emotions—especially anger (Smith, 2006; Williams, 1993). Type A individuals are more often "combat ready." When these people are threatened or challenged by a stressor, they react aggressively. As their often active sympathetic nervous system redistributes blood-flow to the muscles, it pulls blood away from internal organs. One of these internal organs, the liver, which normally removes cholesterol and fat from the blood, can't do its job. Excess cholesterol and fat continue to circulate in the blood and are deposited around the heart. Further stress—sometimes conflicts brought on by their own traits—may trigger altered heart rhythms. In people with weakened hearts, this altered pattern can cause sudden death (Kamarck & Jennings, 1991). Our heart and mind interact.

> *"The fire you kindle for your enemy often burns you more than him."*
>
> **Chinese proverb**

Hundreds of other studies of young and middle-aged men and women have confirmed that people who react with anger over little things are the most coronary-prone (Chida & Hamer, 2008; Chida & Steptoe, 2009). As researchers have noted, rage "seems to lash back and strike us in the heart muscle" (Spielberger & London, 1982).

In recent years, another personality type has interested stress and heart disease researchers. Type A individuals direct their negative emotion toward dominating others. People with another personality type—*Type D*—suppress their negative emotion to avoid social disapproval. The negative emotion these Type D individuals experience during social interactions is mainly *distress* (Denollet, 2005; Denollet et al., 1996). In one analysis of 12 studies, having a Type D personality significantly increased risk for mortality and nonfatal heart attack (Grande et al., 2012).

---

coronary heart disease the clogging of the vessels that nourish the heart muscle; the leading cause of death in the United States and many other countries.

Type A Friedman and Rosenman's term for competitive, hard-driving, impatient, verbally aggressive, and anger-prone people.

Type B Friedman and Rosenman's term for easygoing, relaxed people.

© PhotoSpin Inc/ Alamy

The Effects of Pessimism and Depression

Pessimism, the tendency to judge a glass as half empty instead of half full, increases the risk for heart attack. One U.S. longitudinal study of 1306 men (ages 40 to 90) measured pessimism levels. Those who reported higher levels of pessimism were twice as likely to experience a fatal or nonfatal heart attack ten years later (Kubzansky et al., 2001) **(FIGURE 10.5)**.

Depression, too, can be lethal, as the evidence from many studies has shown (Wulsin et al., 1999). Three examples:

- Nearly 4000 English adults (ages 52 to 79) provided mood reports from a single day. Compared with those in a good mood on that day, those in a blue mood were twice as likely to be dead five years later (Steptoe & Wardle, 2011).

- In a U.S. survey of 164,102 adults, those who had experienced a heart attack were twice as likely to report also having been depressed at some point in their lives (Witters & Wood, 2015).

- People with high scores for depression in the years following a heart attack were four times more likely than their low-scoring counterparts to develop further heart problems (Frasure-Smith & Lesperance, 2005).

It is still unclear why depression poses such a serious risk for heart disease, but this much seems clear: Depression is disheartening.

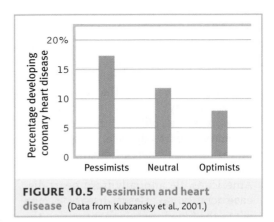

FIGURE 10.5 **Pessimism and heart disease** (Data from Kubzansky et al., 2001.)

* * *

In many ways stress can affect our health. (See Thinking Critically About: Stress and Health.) Our stress-related susceptibility to disease is a price we pay for the benefits of stress. Stress enriches our lives. It arouses and motivates us. An unstressed life would not be challenging or productive.

LaunchPad To consider how researchers have studied these issues, visit LaunchPad's *IMMERSIVE LEARNING: How Would You Know If Stress Increases Risk of Disease?*

LOQ 10-5 So, does stress *cause* illness?

Thinking Critically About:
Stress and Health

Anger or depression

Persistent stressors

Past due

pay immediately

You're Fired

Unhealthy behaviors (smoking, drinking, poor nutrition, sleep loss), which contribute to illness and disease

Release of stress hormones

Autonomic nervous system effects (headaches, high blood pressure, inflammation)

Immune suppression

Heart disease

Stress may not directly cause illness, but it does make us more vulnerable, by influencing our behaviors and our physiology.

Coping With Stress

LOQ 10-6 What are two basic ways that people cope with stress?

Stressors are unavoidable. That's the reality we live with. One way we can develop our strengths and protect our health is to learn better ways to **cope** with our stress.

We need to find new ways to feel, think, and act when we are dealing with stressors. We address some stressors directly, with **problem-focused coping.** For example, if our impatience leads to a family fight, we may go directly to that family member to work things out. We tend to use problem-focused strategies when we feel a sense of control over a situation and think we can change the circumstances, or at least change ourselves to deal with the circumstances more capably.

We turn to **emotion-focused coping** when we cannot—or *believe* we cannot—change a situation. If, despite our best efforts, we cannot get along with a family member, we may relieve stress by confiding in friends and reaching out for support and comfort.

Emotion-focused strategies can benefit our long-term health, as when we attempt to gain emotional distance from a damaging relationship or keep busy with hobbies to avoid thinking about an old addiction. Emotion-focused strategies can also be maladaptive, however, as when students worried about not keeping up with the reading in class go out to party or play video games to get it off their mind. Sometimes a problem-focused strategy (catching up with the reading) will reduce stress more effectively and promote long-term health and satisfaction.

Our success in coping depends on several factors. Let's look at four of them: personal control, an optimistic outlook, social support, and finding meaning in life's ups and downs.

Retrieve + Remember

- To cope with stress, we tend to use ________-focused (emotion/problem) strategies when we feel in control of our world. When we believe we cannot change a situation, we may try to relieve stress with ________-focused (emotion/problem) strategies.

ANSWERS: problem; emotion

coping reducing stress using emotional, cognitive, or behavioral methods.

problem-focused coping attempting to reduce stress directly—by changing the stressor or the way we interact with that stressor.

emotion-focused coping attempting to reduce stress by avoiding or ignoring a stressor and attending to emotional needs related to our stress reaction.

personal control our sense of controlling our environment rather than feeling helpless.

learned helplessness the hopelessness and passive resignation an animal or person learns when unable to avoid repeated aversive events.

Personal Control, Health, and Well-Being

LOQ 10-7 How does our sense of control influence stress and health?

Personal control refers to how much we perceive having control over our environment. Psychologists study the effect of personal control (or any personality factor) in two ways:

1. They *correlate* people's feelings of control with their behaviors and achievements.
2. They *experiment,* by raising or lowering people's sense of control and noting the effects.

At times, we all feel helpless, hopeless, and depressed after experiencing a series of bad events beyond our control. For some animals and people, a series of uncontrollable events creates a state of **learned helplessness,** with feelings of passive resignation (**FIGURE 10.6**). In one series of experiments, dogs were strapped in a harness and given repeated shocks, with no opportunity to avoid them (Seligman & Maier, 1967). When later placed in another situation where they *could* escape the punishment by simply leaping a hurdle, the dogs cowered as if without hope. Other dogs that had been able to escape the first shocks reacted differently. They had learned they were in control, and in the new situation they easily escaped the shocks (Seligman & Maier, 1967). In other experiments, people have shown similar patterns of learned helplessness (Abramson et al., 1978, 1989; Seligman, 1975).

Learned helplessness is a dramatic form of loss of control. But we've all felt a loss of control at times. Our health can suffer as our level of stress hormones (such as *cortisol*) rise, our blood pressure increases, and our immune responses weaken (Rodin, 1986; Sapolsky, 2005). One study found these effects among nurses, who reported their workload and their level of personal control on the job. The greater their workload, the higher their cortisol level and blood pressure—but *only* among nurses who reported little control over their environment (Fox et al., 1993). Stress effects have also been observed among captive animals. Those in captivity are more prone to disease than their wild counterparts,

Uncontrollable bad events → Perceived lack of control → Generalized helpless behavior

FIGURE 10.6 Learned helplessness When animals and people experience no control over repeated bad events, they often learn helplessness.

which have more control over their lives (Roberts, 1988). Similar effects are found when humans are crowded together in high-density neighborhoods, prisons, and even college dorms (Fleming et al., 1987; Fuller et al., 1993; Ostfeld et al., 1987). Feelings of control drop, and stress hormone levels and blood pressure rise.

Proposals to improve health and morale by increasing control have included (Humphrey et al., 2007; Ruback et al., 1986; Warburton et al., 2006):

- Allowing prisoners to move chairs and control room lights and the TV.
- Having workers participate in decision making. Simply allowing people to personalize their workspace has been linked with higher (55 percent) engagement with their work (Krueger & Killham, 2006).
- Offering nursing home patients choices about their environment. In one famous study, 93 percent of nursing home patients who were encouraged to exert more control became more alert, active, and happy (Rodin, 1986).

"Perceived control is basic to human functioning," concluded researcher Ellen Langer (1983, p. 291). "For the young and old alike," she suggested, environments

HAPPY TO HAVE CONTROL   This family is finally experiencing the joy of having their own new home, after working on the building—alongside Habitat for Humanity volunteers—for several months.

should enhance people's sense of control over their world. No wonder mobile devices and online streaming, which enhance our control of the content and timing of our entertainment, are so popular.

Google has incorporated these principles effectively. Each week, Google employees can spend 20 percent of their working time on projects they find personally interesting. This Innovation Time Off program has increased employees' personal control over their work environment. It has also paid off: Gmail was developed this way.

The power of personal control also appears at the national level. People thrive when they live in conditions of personal freedom and empowerment. For example, citizens of stable democracies report higher levels of happiness (Inglehart et al., 2008).

So, some freedom and control are better than none. But does ever-increasing choice breed ever-happier lives? Some researchers have suggested that today's Western cultures offer an "excess of freedom"—too many choices. The result can be decreased life satisfaction, increased depression, or even behavior paralysis (Schwartz, 2000, 2004). In one study, people offered a choice of one of 30 brands of jam or chocolate were less satisfied with their decision than were others who had chosen from only 6 options (Iyengar & Lepper, 2000). This *tyranny of choice* brings information overload and a greater likelihood that we will feel regret over some of the things we left behind. (Do you, too, ever waste time agonizing over too many choices?)

Who Controls Your Life?

Do you believe that your life is out of control? That the world is run by a few powerful people? That getting a good job depends mainly on being in the right place at the right time? Or do you more strongly believe that you control your own fate? That each of us can influence our government's decisions? That being a success is a matter of hard work?

Hundreds of studies have compared people who differ in their perceptions of control:

- Those who have an **external locus of control** believe that chance or outside forces control their fate.
- Those who have an **internal locus of control** believe they control their own destiny.

EXTREME SELF-CONTROL   Our ability to exert self-control increases with practice, and some of us have practiced more than others! Magician David Blaine (top) endured standing in a block of ice (in which a small space had been carved out for him) for nearly 62 hours for a stunt in New York's Times Square. A number of performing artists make their living as very convincing human statues, as does this actress (bottom) performing on The Royal Mile in Edinburgh, Scotland.

Does it matter which view we hold? In study after study comparing people with these two viewpoints, the "internals" have achieved more in school and work, acted more independently, enjoyed better health, and felt less depressed (Lefcourt, 1982; Ng et al., 2006). In one long-term study of more than 7500 people, those who had expressed a more internal locus of control at age 10 exhibited less obesity, lower blood pressure, and less distress at age 30 (Gale et al., 2008).

Another way to say that we believe we are in control of our own life is to say we have *free will*, or that we can control our own willpower. Studies show that people who believe in their freedom learn better, enjoy making decisions, perform better at work, and behave more helpfully (Clark et al., 2014; Feldman et al., 2014a; Stillman et al., 2010).

So we differ in our perceptions of whether we have control over our world. Compared with their parents' generation, more young Americans now express an external locus of control (Twenge et al., 2004). This shift may help explain an associated increase in rates of depression and other psychological disorders (Twenge et al., 2010).

Coping With Stress by Boosting Self-Control

Google trusted its belief in the power of personal control, and the company and its employees reaped the benefits. Could we reap similar benefits by actively managing our own behavior? One place to start might be increasing our **self-control**—the ability to control impulses and delay immediate gratification. Strengthening our self-control may not pay off with a Gmail invention, but self-control has been linked to health and well-being (Moffitt et al., 2011; Tangney et al., 2004). People with more self-control earn higher income, get better grades, and enjoy good health (Kuhnle et al., 2012; Moffitt et al., 2011). In one study that followed eighth-graders over a school year, better self-control was more than twice as important as intelligence score in

predicting academic success (Duckworth & Seligman, 2005).

Self-control constantly changes—from day to day, hour to hour, and even minute to minute. We can compare self-control to a muscle: It weakens after use, recovers after rest, and grows stronger with exercise (Baumeister & Tierney, 2012; Hagger et al., 2010; Vohs & Baumeister, 2011).

When you use your self-control, you have less of it available to use when you need it later (Grillon et al., 2015; Vohs et al., 2012). In one experiment, hungry people who had resisted eating tempting chocolate chip cookies abandoned a frustrating task sooner than people who had not resisted the cookies (Baumeister et al., 1998b). When people feel provoked, those who have used up their self-control energy have acted more aggressively toward strangers and intimate partners (DeWall et al., 2007). In one experiment, frustrated participants with low self-control energy stuck more pins into a doll that represented their romantic partner. Participants whose self-control energy was left intact used fewer pins (Finkel et al., 2012a).

Exercising self-control uses up the brain energy needed for mental focus (Wagner et al., 2013). Might sugar provide a solution to self-control fatigue? Sugar not only tastes good, it also improves mental control (Chambers et al., 2009). In several studies, giving sugar (in naturally rather than artificially sweetened lemonade) had a sweet effect: It reduced people's aggression and impulsive decision making (Pfundmair et al., 2015; Wang & Dvorak, 2010). Even dogs experiencing self-control energy loss seemed to bounce back after this sweet treatment (Miller et al., 2010). But researchers do not encourage candy bar diets to improve self-control. Just rinsing your mouth with a sugary liquid can activate the brain's self-control centers (Hagger & Chatzisarantis, 2013; Sanders et al., 2012). You will get the boost in self-control without the bulge in your waistline.

Weakened mental energy after exercising self-control is a short-term effect. The long-term effect of exercising self-

control is *strengthened* self-control, much as a hard physical workout leaves you temporarily tired out but stronger in the long term. Strengthened self-control improves people's performance on laboratory tasks as well as their self-management of eating, drinking, smoking, and household chores (Oaten & Cheng, 2006a,b).

The point to remember: Develop self-discipline in one area of your life, and your strengthened self-control may spill over into other areas as well, making for a healthier, happier, and more successful life (Tuk et al., 2015).

Is the Glass Half Full or Half Empty?

LOQ 10-8 How do optimists and pessimists differ, and why does our outlook on life matter?

Another part of coping with stress is our outlook—how we perceive the world. **Optimists** agree with statements such as, "In uncertain times, I usually expect the best" (Scheier & Carver, 1992). Optimists expect to have control, to cope well with stressful events, and to enjoy good health (Aspinwall & Tedeschi, 2010; Boehm & Kubzansky, 2012; Hernandez et al., 2015). **Pessimists**, as noted earlier, don't share these expectations. They expect things to go badly (Aspinwall & Tedeschi, 2010; Carver et al., 2010; Rasmussen et al., 2009). And when

---

external locus of control the perception that chance or outside forces beyond our personal control determine our fate.

internal locus of control the perception that we control our own fate.

self-control the ability to control impulses and delay short-term gratification for greater long-term rewards.

optimism the anticipation of positive outcomes. Optimists are people who expect the best and expect their efforts to lead to good things.

pessimism the anticipation of negative outcomes. Pessimists are people who expect the worst and doubt that their goals will be achieved.

bad things happen, pessimists believe they knew it all along. They lacked the necessary skills ("I can't do this"). The situation prevented them from doing well ("There is nothing I can do about it"). They expected the worst and their expectations were fulfilled.

Optimism, like a feeling of personal control, pays off. Optimists respond to stress with smaller increases in blood pressure, and they recover more quickly from heart bypass surgery. And during the stressful first few weeks of classes, U.S. law school students who were optimistic ("It's unlikely that I will fail") enjoyed better moods and stronger immune systems (Segerstrom et al., 1998). When American dating couples wrestle with conflicts, optimists and their partners see each other as engaging constructively. They tend to feel more supported and satisfied with the resolution and with their relationship (Srivastava et al., 2006). Optimism also predicts well-being and success elsewhere, including China and Japan (Qin & Piao, 2011).

Is an optimistic outlook related to living a longer life? Possibly. One research team followed 941 Dutch people, aged 65 to 85, for nearly a decade (Giltay et al., 2004, 2007). They split the sample into four groups according to their optimism scores. Only 30 percent of those with the highest optimism died during the study,

Positive expectations often motivate eventual success.

"We just haven't been flapping them hard enough."

© PhotosIndia.com LLC/Alamy

compared with 57 percent of those with the lowest optimism.

The optimism–long-life correlation also appeared in a famous study of 180 American Catholic nuns. At about 22 years of age, each of these women had written a brief autobiography. In the decades that followed, they lived similar lifestyles. Those who had expressed happiness, love, and other positive feelings in their autobiographies lived an average of seven years longer than did the more negative nuns (Danner et al., 2001). By age 80, only 24 percent of the most positive-spirited had died, compared with 54 percent of those expressing few positive emotions.

Optimism runs in families, so some people truly are born with a sunny, hopeful outlook. If one identical twin is optimistic, the other often will be as well (Bates, 2015; Mosing et al., 2009). One genetic marker of optimism is a gene that enhances the social-bonding hormone oxytocin (Saphire-Bernstein et al., 2011).

Positive thinking pays dividends, but so does a dash of realism (Schneider, 2001). Realistic anxiety over possible *future* failures—worrying about being able to pay a bill on time, or fearing you will do badly on an exam—can cause you to try extra hard to avoid failure (Goodhart, 1986; Norem, 2001; Showers, 1992). Students concerned about failing an upcoming

exam may study more, and therefore outperform equally able but more confident peers. This may help explain the impressive academic achievements of some Asian-American students. Compared with European-Americans, these students express somewhat greater pessimism (Chang, 2001). Success requires enough optimism to provide hope and enough pessimism to keep you on your toes.

Excessive optimism can blind us to real risks (Weinstein, 1980, 1982, 1996). Most college students display an *unrealistic optimism*. They view themselves as less likely than their average classmate to develop drinking problems, drop out of school, or have a heart attack. Many credit-card users choose cards with low fees and high interest, causing them to pay more because they are unrealistically optimistic that they will always pay off the monthly balance (Yang et al., 2006). Blinded by optimism, people young

Mark Andersen/Rubberball/Getty Images

LAUGHTER AMONG FRIENDS IS GOOD MEDICINE Laughter arouses us, massages muscles, and then leaves us feeling relaxed (Robinson, 1983). Humor (though not hostile sarcasm) may defuse stress, ease pain, and strengthen immune activity (Ayan, 2009; Berk et al., 2001; Dunbar et al., 2011; Kimata, 2001). People who laugh a lot have also tended to have lower rates of heart disease (Clark et al., 2001).

and old echo the statement famed basketball player Magic Johnson made (1992) after contracting HIV: "I didn't think it could happen to me."

> "God grant us the serenity to accept the things we cannot change, courage to change the things we can, and wisdom to know the difference."
>
> Alcoholics Anonymous Serenity Prayer (attributed to Reinhold Niebuhr)

Social Support

LOQ 10-9 How do social support and finding meaning in life influence health?

Which of these factors has the strongest association with poor health: smoking 15 cigarettes daily, being obese, being inactive, or lacking strong social connections? This is a trick question, because each factor has a roughly similar impact (Cacioppo & Patrick, 2008). That's right! *Social support*—feeling liked and encouraged by intimate friends and family—promotes both happiness and health. It helps you cope with stress. Not having this support can affect your health as much as smoking nearly a pack per day.

Seven massive international investigations that followed thousands of people over several years reached similar conclusions. Although *individualist* (individual-focused) and *collectivist* (group-focused) cultures vary in how much value they place on social support, it is universally related to greater happiness (Brannan et al., 2013; Chu et al., 2010; Gable et al., 2012). People supported by close relationships are also less likely to die early (Shor et al., 2013). These relationships may be with friends, family, fellow students or workers, members of our faith community, or some other support group. Even pets can help us cope with stress.

Happy marriages bathe us in social support. One seven-decade-long study found that at age 50, healthy aging is better predicted by a good marriage than by a low cholesterol level (Vaillant, 2002). On the flip side, divorce is a predictor of poor health. In one analysis of 32 studies involving more than 6.5 million people,

PETS ARE FRIENDS, TOO Pets can provide social support. Having a pet may increase the odds of survival after a heart attack, relieve depression among people with AIDS, and lower blood pressure and other coronary risk factors (Allen, 2003; McConnell et al., 2011; Wells, 2009). To lower blood pressure, pets are no substitute for effective drugs and exercise. But for people who enjoy animals, and especially for those who live alone, pets are a healthy pleasure (Allen, 2003).

Photos.com/Getty Images

divorced people were 23 percent more likely to die early (Sbarra et al., 2011). But it's less marital status than marital *quality* that predicts health—to about the same extent as a healthy diet and physical activity do (Robles, 2015; Robles et al., 2014).

Social support helps us fight illness in at least two ways. First, it calms our cardiovascular system, which lowers blood pressure and stress hormone levels (Baron et al., 2016; Uchino et al., 1996, 1999). To see if social support might calm people's response to threats, one research team subjected happily married women, while lying in an fMRI machine, to the threat of electric shock to an ankle (Coan et al., 2006). During the experiment, some women held their husband's hand. Others held a stranger's hand or no hand at all. While awaiting the occasional shocks, the women's brains reacted differently. Those who held their husband's hand had less activity in threat-responsive areas. This soothing benefit was greatest for women reporting the highest-quality marriages. A follow-up experiment suggested that simply viewing a supportive romantic partner's picture was enough to reduce painful discomfort (Master et al., 2009). One study of women with ovarian cancer suggests that social support may slow the progression of cancer. Researchers found that women with the highest levels of social support had the lowest levels of a stress hormone linked to cancer progression.

Social support helps us cope with stress in a second way. It helps us fight illness by fostering stronger *immune functioning*. We have seen that stress puts us at risk for disease by stealing disease-fighting energy from our immune system. Social support seems to reboot our immune system. In one series of studies, research participants with strong support systems showed greater resistance to cold viruses (Cohen, 2004; Cohen et al., 1997). After inhaling nose drops loaded with a cold virus, two groups of healthy volunteers were isolated and observed for five days. (The volunteers each received $800 to endure this experience.) The researchers then took a cold hard look at the results. After controlling for age, race, sex, smoking, and other health habits, they found that people

with close social ties in their everyday lives were least likely to catch a cold. If they did catch one, they produced less mucus. People whose daily life included frequent hugs likewise experienced fewer cold symptoms and less symptom severity (Cohen et al., 2015). The effect of social ties is nothing to sneeze at!

When we are trying to cope with stressors, social ties can tug us toward or away from our goal. Are you trying to exercise more, drink less, quit smoking, or eat better? If so, think about whether your social network can help or hinder you. That social net covers not only the people you know but friends of your friends, and friends of their friends. That's three degrees of separation between you and the most remote people. This means that people you have never met can influence your thoughts, feelings, and actions without your awareness (Christakis & Fowler, 2009; Kim et al., 2015).

Finding Meaning

Catastrophes and significant life changes can leave us confused and distressed as we try to make sense of what happened. At such times, an important part of coping with stress is finding meaning in life—some redeeming purpose in our suffering (Guo et al., 2013; Taylor, 1983). Unemployment is very threatening, but it may free up time to spend with children. The loss of a loved one may force us to expand our social network. A heart attack may trigger a shift toward healthy, active living. Some have argued that the search for meaning is fundamental. We constantly seek to maintain meaning when our expectations are not met (Heine el al., 2006). As psychiatrist Viktor Frankl (1962), who survived a Nazi concentration camp, observed, "Life is never made unbearable by circumstances, but only by lack of meaning and purpose."

Close relationships offer an opportunity for "open heart therapy"—a chance to confide painful feelings and sort things out (Frattaroli, 2006). Talking about things that push our buttons may arouse us in the short term. But in the long term, it calms us by reducing our physical stress responses (Lieberman et al., 2007; Mendolia & Kleck, 1993; Niles et al., 2015). After we gain distance from a stressful event, talking or writing about the experience helps us make sense of it and find meaning in it (Esterling et al., 1999). In one study, 33 Holocaust survivors spent two hours recalling their experiences, many in intimate detail never before disclosed (Pennebaker et al., 1989). In the weeks following, most watched a video of their recollections and showed it to family and friends. Those who were most self-disclosing had the most improved health 14 months later. Confiding is good for the body and the soul. Another study surveyed surviving spouses of people who had committed suicide or died in car accidents. Those who bore their grief alone had more health problems than those who could share it with others (Pennebaker & O'Heeron, 1984).

Managing Stress Effects

Having a sense of control, nurturing an optimistic outlook, building our social support, and finding meaning can help us *experience* less stress and thus improve our health. What do we do when we cannot avoid stress? At such times, we need to *manage* our stress. Aerobic exercise, relaxation, meditation, and active spiritual engagement may help us gather inner strength and lessen stress effects.

Aerobic Exercise

LOQ 10-10 How well does aerobic exercise help us manage stress and improve well-being?

It's hard to find a medicine that works for most people most of the time. But **aerobic exercise**—sustained activity that increases heart and lung fitness—

THE MOOD BOOST When energy or spirits are sagging, few things reboot the day better than exercising, as I [DM] can confirm from my noontime basketball, and as I [ND] can confirm from my running.

is one of these rare near-perfect "medicines." Estimates vary, but moderate exercise adds to your quantity of life— two additional years, on average—as well as to your quality of life, with more energy, better mood, and stronger relationships (Flueckiger et al., 2016; Hogan et al., 2015; Seligman, 1994; Wang et al., 2011).

Throughout this book, we have revisited one of psychology's basic themes: Heredity and environment interact. Physical activity can weaken the influence of genetic risk factors for obesity. In one analysis of 45 studies, that risk fell by 27 percent (Kilpeläinen et al., 2012). Exercise also helps fight heart disease. It strengthens your heart, increases bloodflow, keeps blood vessels open, lowers overall blood pressure, and reduces the hormone and blood pressure reaction to stress (Ford, 2002; Manson, 2002). Compared with inactive adults, people who exercise suffer half as many heart attacks (Powell et al., 1987; Visich & Fletcher, 2009). Exercise makes the muscles hungry for the fats that, if not used by the muscles, contribute to clogged arteries (Barinaga, 1997).

Many studies suggest that aerobic exercise reduces stress, depression, and anxiety. People who exercise at least

30 minutes, three times a week manage stressful situations better, have more self-confidence and energy, and feel less depressed and anxious than their inactive peers (Rebar et al., 2015; Smits et al., 2011). In one study of over 650,000 American adults, walking 150 minutes per week predicted living seven more years (Moore et al., 2012). Going from active exerciser to couch potato can increase risk for depression—by 51 percent in two years for the women in one study (Wang et al., 2011). But we could state these observations another way: Stressed and depressed people exercise less. It's that old correlation problem again—cause and effect are not clear.

To sort out cause and effect, researchers experiment. They randomly assign people either to an aerobic exercise group or to a control group. Next, they measure whether aerobic exercise (compared with a control activity that doesn't involve exercise) produces a change in stress, depression, anxiety, or some other health-related outcome. In one such experiment (McCann & Holmes, 1984), researchers randomly assigned mildly depressed female college students to one of three groups:

- Group 1 completed an aerobic exercise program.
- Group 2 completed a relaxation program.
- Group 3 functioned as a pure control group and did not complete any special activity.

As **FIGURE 10.7** shows, 10 weeks later the women in the aerobic exercise program reported the greatest decrease in depression. Many of them had, quite literally, run away from their troubles.

Another experiment randomly assigned depressed people to an exercise group, an antidepressant group, or a placebo pill group. Again, exercise diminished depression levels. And it did so as effectively as antidepressants, with longer-lasting effects (Hoffman et al., 2011). Aerobic exercise counteracts depression in two ways. First, it increases arousal. Second, it does naturally what some prescription drugs do chemically: It increases the brain's serotonin activity.

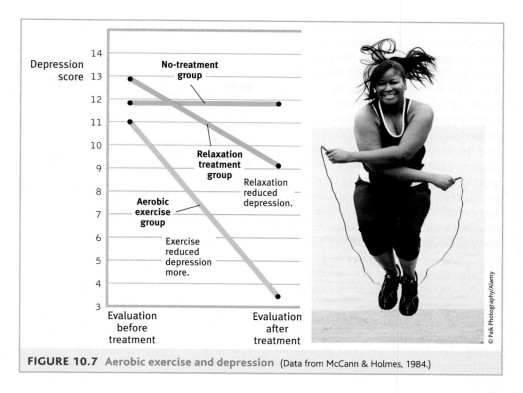

FIGURE 10.7 Aerobic exercise and depression (Data from McCann & Holmes, 1984.)

More than 150 other studies have confirmed that exercise reduces depression and anxiety. What is more, toned muscles filter out depression-causing toxins (Agudelo et al., 2014). Aerobic exercise has therefore taken a place, along with antidepressant drugs and psychotherapy, on the list of effective treatments for depression and anxiety (Arent et al., 2000; Berger & Motl, 2000; Dunn et al., 2005).

LaunchPad See LaunchPad's *Video: Random Assignment* for a helpful tutorial animation about this important part of effective research design.

Relaxation and Meditation

LOQ 10-11 In what ways might relaxation and meditation influence stress and health?

Sit with your back straight, getting as comfortable as you can. Breathe a deep, single breath of air through your nose. Now exhale that air through your mouth as slowly as you can. As you exhale, repeat a focus word, phrase, or prayer—something from your own belief system. Do this five times. Do you feel more relaxed?

Why Relaxation Is Good

Like aerobic exercise, relaxation can improve our well-being. Did you notice in Figure 10.7 that women in the relaxation treatment group also experienced reduced depression? More than 60 studies have found that relaxation procedures can also provide relief from headaches, high blood pressure, anxiety, and insomnia (Nestoriuc et al., 2008; Stetter & Kupper, 2002).

Researchers have even used relaxation to help Type A heart attack survivors reduce their risk of future attacks (Friedman & Ulmer, 1984). They randomly assigned hundreds of these middle-aged men to one of two groups. The first group received standard advice from cardiologists about medications, diet,

aerobic exercise sustained activity that increases heart and lung fitness; may also reduce depression and anxiety.

and exercise habits. The second group received similar advice, but they also were taught ways of modifying their lifestyle. They learned to slow down and relax by walking, talking, and eating more slowly. They learned to smile at others and laugh at themselves. They learned to admit their mistakes, to take time to enjoy life, and to renew their religious faith. The training paid off spectacularly (**FIGURE 10.8**). During the next three years, the lifestyle modification group had half as many repeat heart attacks as did the first group. A British study supported this finding. Lifestyle modification cut the risk of heart attack in half over 13 years for heart-attack-prone people (Eysenck & Grossarth-Maticek, 1991).

Time may heal all wounds, but relaxation can help speed that process. In one study, surgery patients were randomly assigned to two groups. Both groups received standard treatment, but the second group also experienced a 45-minute relaxation exercise and received relaxation recordings to use before and after surgery. A week after surgery, patients in the second group reported lower stress and showed better wound healing (Broadbent el al., 2012).

Learning to Reflect and Accept

Meditation is a modern practice with a long history in a variety of world religions. Meditation was originally used to reduce suffering and improve awareness, insight, and compassion. Numerous studies have confirmed the psychological benefits of meditation (Goyal et al., 2014; Rosenberg et al., 2015; Sedlmeier et al., 2012), including **mindfulness meditation**, which has today found a new home in stress management programs. If you were taught this practice, you would relax and silently attend to your inner state, without judging it (Kabat-Zinn, 2001). You would sit down, close your eyes, and mentally scan your body from head to toe. Zooming in on certain body parts and responses, you would remain aware and accepting. You would also pay attention to your breathing, attending to each breath as if it were a material object.

Practicing mindfulness may improve many health measures. In one study of 1140 people, some received mindfulness-based therapy for several weeks. Others did not. Levels of anxiety and depression were lower among those who received the therapy (Hofmann et al., 2010). In another study, mindfulness training

Djomas/Shutterstock

improved immune system functioning and coping in a group of women newly diagnosed with early-stage breast cancer (Witek-Janusek et al., 2008). Mindfulness practices have also been linked with reductions in sleep problems, cigarette use, binge eating, and alcohol and other substance abuse (Bowen et al., 2006; Brewer et al., 2011; Cincotta et al., 2011; de Dios et al., 2012; Kristeller et al., 2006).

So, what's going on in the brain as we practice mindfulness? Correlational and experimental studies offer three explanations for how mindfulness helps us make positive changes:

- *It strengthens connections among regions in our brain.* The affected regions are those associated with focusing our attention, processing what we see and hear, and being reflective and aware (Berkovich-Ohana et al., 2014; Ives-Deliperi et al., 2011; Kilpatrick et al., 2011).

- *It activates brain regions associated with more reflective awareness* (Davidson et al., 2003; Way et al., 2010). When labeling emotions, mindful people show less activation in the amygdala, a brain region associated with fear, and more activation in the prefrontal cortex, which aids emotion regulation (Creswell et al., 2007).

- *It calms brain activation in emotional situations.* This lower activation was clear in one study in which participants watched two movies— one sad, one neutral. Those in the control group, who were not trained in mindfulness, showed strong

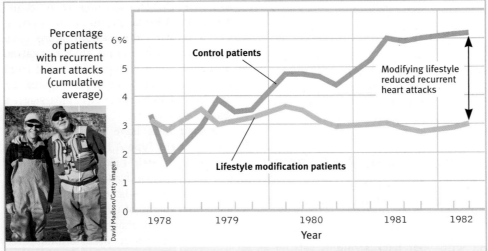

FIGURE 10.8 Recurrent heart attacks and lifestyle modification The San Francisco Recurrent Coronary Prevention Project offered counseling from a cardiologist to survivors of heart attacks. Those who were also guided in modifying their Type A lifestyle suffered fewer repeat heart attacks. (Data from Friedman & Ulmer, 1984.)

differences in brain activation when watching the two movies. Those who had received mindfulness training showed little change in brain response to the two movies (Farb et al., 2010). Emotionally unpleasant images also trigger weaker electrical brain responses in mindful people than in their less mindful counterparts (Brown et al., 2013). A mindful brain is strong, reflective, and calm.

Exercise and meditation are not the only routes to healthy relaxation. Massage helps relax both premature infants (Chapter 3) and those suffering pain (Chapter 5), and it also helps reduce depression (Hou et al., 2010).

Faith Communities and Health

LOQ 10-12 Does religious involvement relate to health?

A wealth of studies has revealed another curious correlation, called the *faith factor* (Koenig et al., 2012). Religiously active people tend to live longer than those who are not religiously active. In one 16-year study, researchers tracked 3900 Israelis living in one of two groups of communities (Kark et al., 1996). The first group contained 11 religiously orthodox collective settlements. The second group contained 11 matched, nonreligious collective settlements. The researchers found that "belonging to a religious collective was associated with

© MaRoDee Photography/Alamy   Fuse/Jupiterimages   Sura Nualpradid/Shutterstock   casejustin/Shutterstock

© Georgios Kollidas/Alamy   Georgios Kollidas/Shutterstock   ppart/Shutterstock

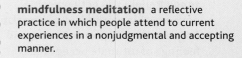

FIGURE 10.9 **Predictors of longer life: Not smoking, frequent exercise, and regular religious attendance** One 28-year study followed more than 5200 adults (Oman et al., 2002; Strawbridge, 1999; Strawbridge et al., 1997). After adjusting for age and education, the researchers found that not smoking, regular exercise, and religious attendance all predicted a lowered risk of death in any given year. Women attending weekly religious services, for example, were only 54 percent as likely to die in a typical study year as were nonattenders.

a strong protective effect" not explained by age or economic differences. In every age group, religious community members were about half as likely to have died as were those in the nonreligious community.

How should we interpret such findings? Remember that correlation does not mean causation. What other factors might explain these protective effects? Here's one possibility: Women are more religiously active than men, and women outlive men. Does religious involvement reflect this gender-longevity link?

No. Although the spirituality-longevity correlation is stronger among women, it also appears among men (McCullough et al., 2000; McCullough & Laurenceau, 2005). In study after study—some lasting 28 years, and some studying more than 20,000 people—the faith factor holds (Chida et al., 2009; Hummer et al., 1999; Schnall et al., 2010). And it holds after researchers control for age, sex, race, ethnicity, education, and region. In one study, this effect translated into a life expectancy of 83 years for those who regularly attended religious services, and only 75 years for nonattenders (**FIGURE 10.9**).

Does this mean that nonattenders who start attending services and change nothing else will live longer? Again, the answer is *No*. But we can say that religious involvement *predicts* health and longevity, just as nonsmoking and exercise do.

mindfulness meditation a reflective practice in which people attend to current experiences in a nonjudgmental and accepting manner.

Religiously active people have demonstrated healthier immune functioning, fewer hospital admissions, and, for people with AIDS, fewer stress hormones and longer survival (Ironson et al., 2002; Koenig & Larson, 1998; Lutgendorf et al., 2004).

Can you imagine why religiously active people might be healthier and live longer than others? Here are three factors that help explain the correlation:

- *Healthy lifestyles* Religiously active people have healthier lifestyles. For example, they smoke and drink less (Islam & Johnson, 2003; Koenig & Vaillant, 2009; Koopmans et al., 1999). In one Gallup survey of 550,000 Americans, 15 percent of the very religious were smokers, compared with 28 percent of nonreligious people (Newport et al., 2010). But healthy lifestyles are not the complete answer. In studies that have controlled for unhealthy behaviors, such as inactivity and smoking, about 75 percent of the life-span difference remained (Musick et al., 1999).

- *Social support* Those who belong to a faith community have access to a support network. When misfortune strikes, religiously active people can turn to each other. Moreover, religions encourage marriage, another predictor of health and longevity. In the Israeli religious settlements, for example, divorce has been almost nonexistent. But even after controlling for social support, gender, unhealthy behaviors, and preexisting health problems, much of the original religious engagement correlation remains (Chida et al., 2009; George et al., 2000; Kim-Yeary et al., 2012; Powell et al., 2003).

- *Positive emotions* Researchers speculate that a third set of influences helps protect religiously active people from stress and enhance their well-being (**FIGURE 10.10**). Religiously active people have a stable worldview, a sense of hope for the long-term future, and feelings of ultimate acceptance.

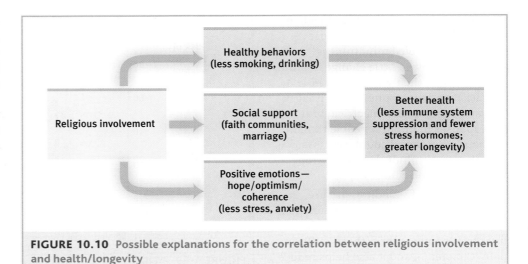

FIGURE 10.10 Possible explanations for the correlation between religious involvement and health/longevity

They may also benefit from the relaxed meditation of prayer or other religious observances. Taken together, these positive emotions, expectations, and practices may have a protective effect on well-being.

* * *

Let's summarize what we've learned so far: Sustained emotional reactions to stressful events can be damaging. However, some qualities and influences can help us cope with life's challenges by making us emotionally and physically stronger. These include a sense of control, an optimistic outlook, relaxation, healthy habits, social support, a sense of meaning, and spirituality (**FIGURE 10.11**).

In the remainder of this chapter, we'll take a closer look at our pursuit of happiness and how it relates to our human flourishing.

Retrieve + Remember

- What are some of the tactics that help people manage the stress they cannot avoid?

ANSWER: aerobic exercise, relaxation procedures, mindfulness meditation, and religious engagement

Happiness

LOQ 10-13 What are the causes and consequences of happiness?

In *The How of Happiness*, psychologist Sonja Lyubomirsky (2008) tells the true story of Randy. By any measure, Randy lived a hard life. His dad and best friend both died by suicide. Growing up, his mother's boyfriend treated him poorly. Randy's first wife was unfaithful, and they divorced. Despite these setbacks, Randy is a happy person whose endless optimism can light up a room. He remarried and enjoys being a stepfather to three boys. His work life is rewarding. Randy says he survived his life stressors by seeing the "silver lining in the cloud."

Overcoming serious challenges, as Randy did, people may feel a stronger sense of self-esteem and a deeper sense of purpose. Tough challenges, especially early in life, can foster personal growth and emotional **resilience** (Landauer & Whiting, 1979).

Are you a person who makes everyone around you smile and laugh? Have you, like Randy, bounced back from serious challenges and become stronger because of it? Our state of happiness or unhappiness colors our thoughts and our

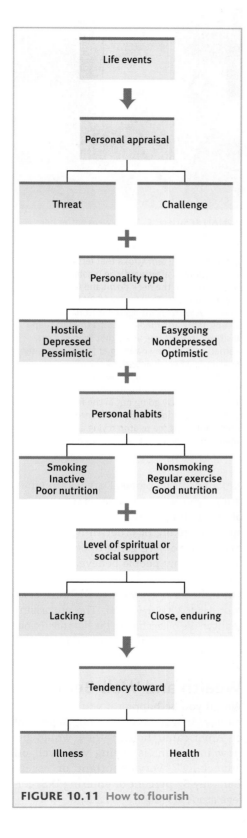

FIGURE 10.11 How to flourish

actions. Happy people perceive the world as a safer place. Their eyes are drawn toward emotionally positive information (Raila et al., 2015). They are more decisive and cooperate more easily. They live healthier and more energized and satisfied lives (Boehm et al., 2015; De Neve et al., 2013; Mauss et al., 2011; Stellar et al., 2015). We all get gloomy sometimes. When that happens, life as a whole may seem depressing and meaningless. Let your mood brighten, and your thinking broadens and becomes more playful and creative (Baas et al., 2008; Forgas, 2008; Fredrickson, 2013). Your relationships, your self-image, and your hopes for the future seem more promising.

This helps explain why college students' happiness helps predict their life course. In one study, which surveyed thousands of U.S. college students in 1976 and restudied them at age 37, happy students had gone on to earn significantly more money than their less-happy-than-average peers (Diener et al., 2002). In another, the happiest 20-year-olds were not only more likely to marry, but also less likely to divorce (Stutzer & Frey, 2006).

Moreover—and this is one of psychology's most consistent findings—when we feel happy we become more helpful. Psychologists call it the **feel-good, do-good phenomenon** (Salovey, 1990). Happiness doesn't just feel good, it does good. In study after study, a mood-boosting experience (finding money, succeeding on a challenging task, recalling a happy event) has made people more likely to give money, pick up someone's dropped papers, volunteer time, and do other good deeds.

The reverse is also true: Doing good promotes feeling good. One survey of more than 200,000 people in 136 countries found that, pretty much everywhere, people report feeling happier after spending money on others rather than themselves (Aknin et al., 2013; Dunn et al., 2014). Why does doing good feel so good? It strengthens our social relationships (Aknin et al., 2015; Yamaguchi et al., 2015).

Some happiness coaches and instructors harness this force by asking their clients to perform a daily "random act of kindness" and to record how it made them feel.

William James was writing about the importance of happiness ("the secret motive for all [we] do") as early as 1902. With the rise of *positive psychology* in the twenty-first century (Chapter 1), the study of happiness has become a main area of research. It is a key part of one of our big ideas in this text: Psychology explores human strengths as well as challenges. Part of happiness research is the study of **subjective well-being**—our feelings of happiness (sometimes defined as a high ratio of positive to negative feelings) or sense of satisfaction with life. This information, combined with objective measures of well-being, such as a person's physical and economic condition, helps us make more informed quality-of-life judgments.

The Short Life of Emotional Ups and Downs

Are some days of the week happier than others? In what may be psychology's biggest-ever data sample, one social psychologist (Kramer, 2010—at my [DM's] request and in cooperation with Facebook) did a naturalistic observation of emotion words in "billions" of status updates. After eliminating exceptional days, such as holidays, he tracked the frequency of positive and negative emotion words by day of the week. The days

resilience the personal strength that helps most people cope with stress and recover from adversity and even trauma.

feel-good, do-good phenomenon our tendency to be helpful when already in a good mood.

subjective well-being self-perceived happiness or satisfaction with life. Used along with measures of objective well-being (for example, physical and economic indicators) to judge our quality of life.

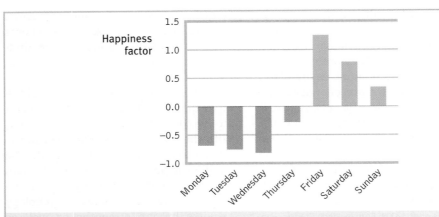

FIGURE 10.12 Using web science to track happy days Adam Kramer (2010) tracked positive and negative emotion words in many "billions" (the exact number is proprietary information) of status updates of U.S. Facebook users between September 7, 2007, and November 17, 2010.

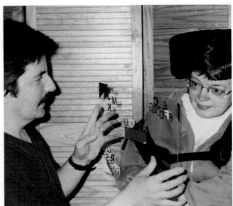

HUMAN RESILIENCE Seven weeks after her 1994 wedding, Anna Putt of South Midlands, England, shown here with her husband, Des, suffered a brainstem stroke that left her "locked in." For months afterward, she recalled, "I was paralyzed from the neck down and was unable to communicate. These were VERY frightening times. But with encouragement from family, friends, faith, and medical staff, I tried to keep positive." In the three years that followed, she learned to "talk" (by nodding at letters), to steer an electric wheelchair with her head, and to use a computer (by nodding while wearing spectacles that guide a cursor). Despite her paralysis, she has reported, "I enjoy going out in the fresh air. My motto is 'Don't look back, move forward.' God would not want me to stop trying and I have no intention of doing so. Life is what you make of it!"

with the most positive moods? Friday and Saturday (**FIGURE 10.12**). Similar analyses of questionnaire responses and 59 million Twitter messages found Friday to Sunday the week's happiest days (Golder & Macy, 2011; Helliwell & Wang, 2015, Young & Lim, 2014). For you, too?

LaunchPad See LaunchPad's *Video: Naturalistic Observation* for a helpful tutorial animation about this type of research design.

Over the long run, our emotional ups and downs tend to balance out. This is true even over the course of the day. Positive emotion rises over the early to middle part of most days and then drops off (Kahneman et al., 2004; Watson, 2000). So, too, with day-to-day moods. A stressful event—an argument, a sick child, a car problem—triggers a bad mood. No surprise there. But by the next day, the gloom nearly always lifts (Affleck et al., 1994; Bolger et al., 1989; Stone & Neale, 1984). If anything, people tend to bounce back from a bad day to a *better*-than-usual good mood the following day. Even when negative events drag us down for longer periods, our bad mood usually ends. We may feel that our heart has broken during a romantic breakup, but eventually the wound heals.

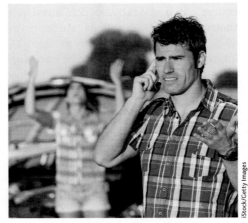

TAKE HEART! TOMORROW WILL BE A NEW DAY Car trouble can happen at the worst possible times. But this man's bad mood will almost certainly clear by tomorrow, when he may even experience a better-than-normal good mood.

Grief over the loss of a loved one or anxiety after a severe trauma can linger. But usually, even tragedy is not permanently depressing. People who have become blind or paralyzed may not completely recover their previous well-being, but those with an agreeable personality have usually recovered near-normal levels of day-to-day happiness (Boyce & Wood, 2011). So have those forced to go on kidney dialysis or to have permanent colostomies (Gerhart et al., 1994; Riis et al., 2005; Smith et al., 2009a). Even if you become paralyzed,

explained psychologist Daniel Kahneman (2005), "you will gradually start thinking of other things, and the more time you spend thinking of other things, the less miserable you are going to be." Contrary to what many people believe, even most patients "locked in" a motionless body do not indicate they want to die (Nizzi et al., 2012; Smith & Delargy, 2005). The surprising reality: *We overestimate the duration of our emotions and underestimate our resilience—our ability to bounce back.*

Wealth and Well-Being

Would you be happier if you made more money? In a 2006 Gallup poll, 73 percent of Americans thought they would be. How important is "Being very well off financially"? "Very important" or "essential," say 82 percent of entering U.S. college students (Eagen et al., 2016).

Money does buy happiness, up to a point. Having enough money to buy your way out of hunger and to enable a sense of control over your life predicts greater happiness (Fischer & Boer, 2011). Money's power to buy happiness also depends on your current income. A $1000 annual wage increase would do a lot more for the average person in a very poor country than for the average person in a very rich one. But once one has enough money for comfort and security, piling up more and more matters less and less.

Consider: During the last four decades, the average U.S. citizen's buying power almost tripled—enabling larger homes and twice as many cars per person, not to mention iPads and smart phones. Did it also buy more happiness? As **FIGURE 10.13** shows, Americans have become no happier. In 1957, some 35 percent said

they were "very happy," as did slightly fewer—33 percent—in 2014. Ditto China, where living standards have risen but happiness has not (Davey & Rato, 2012; Easterlin et al., 2012). These findings lob a bombshell at modern materialism: *Economic growth in wealthy countries has provided no apparent boost to morale or social well-being.*

"But on the positive side, money can't buy happiness—so who cares?"

"Researchers say I'm not happier for being richer, but do you know how much researchers make?"

Why Can't Money Buy More Happiness?

Why is it that, for those who are not poor, more and more money does not buy more and more happiness? More

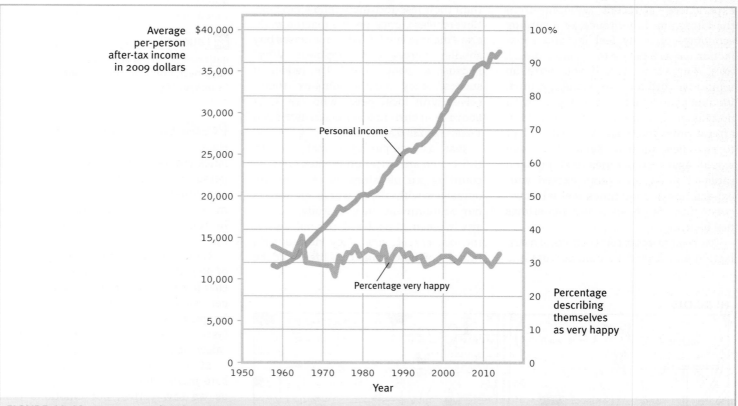

FIGURE 10.13 Does money buy happiness? It surely helps us to avoid certain types of pain. Yet, though average buying power has almost tripled since the 1950s, Americans' reported happiness has remained almost unchanged. (Happiness data from National Opinion Research Center surveys; income data from *Historical Statistics of the United States and Economic Indicators*.)

generally, why do our emotions seem to be attached to elastic bands that pull us back from highs or lows? Psychology has proposed two answers. Each suggests that happiness is relative.

My Happiness Is Relative to My Own Experience

We tend to judge new events by comparing them with our past experiences. Psychologists call this the **adaptation-level phenomenon.** Our past experiences act as *neutral* levels—sounds that seem neither loud nor soft, temperatures that seem neither hot nor cold, events that seem neither pleasant nor unpleasant. We then notice and react to variations up or down from these levels.

So, could we ever create a permanent social paradise? Probably not (Campbell, 1975; Di Tella et al., 2010). People who have experienced a recent windfall—from the lottery, an inheritance, or a surging economy—typically feel joy and satisfaction (Diener & Oishi, 2000; Gardner & Oswald, 2007). You would, too, if you woke up tomorrow with all your wishes granted. Wouldn't you love to live in a world with no bills, no ills, and perfect grades? But after a time, you would gradually adapt to this new normal. Before long, you would again sometimes feel joy and satisfaction (when events exceed your expectations), sometimes feel let down (when they fall below), and sometimes feel neutral.

The point to remember: Feelings of satisfaction and dissatisfaction, success and

failure are judgments we make about ourselves, based partly on our prior experience (Rutledge et al., 2014).

My Happiness Is Relative to Your Success

We are always comparing ourselves with others. And whether we feel good or bad depends on our perception of just how successful those others are (Lyubomirsky, 2001). We are slow-witted or clumsy only when others are smarter or more graceful. When we sense that we are worse off than others with whom we compare ourselves, we experience **relative deprivation.**

When expectations soar above achievements, we feel disappointed. Thus, the middle- and upper-income people in a given country, who can compare themselves with the relatively poor, tend to have greater life satisfaction than their less-fortunate fellow citizens. Nevertheless, once people reach a moderate income level, further increases buy smaller increases in happiness. Why? Because as people climb the ladder of success, they mostly compare themselves with local peers who are at or above their current level (Gruder, 1977; Suls & Tesch, 1978; Zell & Alicke, 2010).

Just as comparing ourselves with those who are better off creates envy, so counting our blessings as we compare ourselves with those worse off boosts our contentment. In one study, university women considered others' suffering (Dermer et al., 1979). They viewed vivid images of how grim city life could be

"Money won't make you happy, Waldron. So instead of a raise, I'm giving you a Prozac."

in 1900. They imagined and then wrote about various personal tragedies, such as being burned and disfigured. Later, the women expressed greater satisfaction with their own lives. Similarly, when mildly depressed people have read about someone who was even more depressed, they felt somewhat better (Gibbons, 1986). "I cried because I had no shoes," states a Persian saying, "until I met a man who had no feet."

LaunchPad For a 6.5-minute examination of historical and modern views of happiness, visit LaunchPad's *Video: The Search for Happiness.*

Predictors of Happiness

Happy people share many characteristics (**TABLE 10.1**). But what makes one person so filled with joy, day after day, and others so gloomy? Here, as in so many other areas, the answer is found in the interplay between nature and nurture.

Genes matter. Studies of hundreds of identical and fraternal twins indicate that heredity accounts for about 50 percent of the difference among people's happiness ratings (Gigantesco et al., 2011; Lykken & Tellegen, 1996). Identical twins raised apart are often similarly happy.

But our personal history and our culture matter, too. On the personal level, as we saw earlier, our emotions tend to balance around a level defined by our experiences. On the cultural level, groups vary in the traits they value. Self-

HI & LOIS

TABLE 10.1 Happiness Is . . .	
Researchers Have Found That Happy People Tend to	**However, Happiness Seems Not Much Related to Other Factors, Such as**
Have high self-esteem (in individualist countries).	Age.
Be optimistic, outgoing, and agreeable.	Gender (women are more often depressed, but also more often joyful).
Have close, positive, and lasting relationships.	Physical attractiveness.
Have work and leisure that engage their skills.	
Have an active religious faith (especially in more religious cultures).	
Sleep well and exercise.	

Sources: DeNeve & Cooper, 1998; Diener et al., 2003, 2011; Headey et al., 2010; Lucas et al., 2004; Myers, 1993, 2000; Myers & Diener, 1995, 1996; Steel et al., 2008. Veenhoven (2014) offers a database of 13,000+ correlates of happiness at WorldDatabaseofHappiness.eur.nl.

"I could cry when I think of the years I wasted accumulating money, only to learn that my cheerful disposition is genetic."

esteem matters more to Westerners, who value individualism. Social acceptance and harmony matter more in cultures that stress family and community, such as in Japan (Diener et al., 2003; Fulmer et al., 2010; Uchida & Kitayama, 2009).

Depending on our genes, our outlook, and our recent experiences, our happiness seems to vary around our "happiness set point." Some of us seem to be ever upbeat; others, more negative. Even so, our satisfaction with life can change (Lucas & Donnellan, 2007). As researchers studying human strengths will tell you, happiness rises and falls, and we can control some of the factors that make us more or less happy (Sin & Lyubomirsky, 2009).

If we can enhance our happiness on an *individual* level, could we use happiness research to refocus our *national* priorities? Many psychologists believe we could. Many political leaders agree: 43 nations have begun measuring their citizens' well-being (Diener et al., 2015). Happy societies are not only prosperous but are also places where people trust one another, feel free, and enjoy close relationships (Helliwell et al., 2013; Oishi & Schimmack, 2010; Sachs, 2012). Thus, when debating such issues as economic inequality, tax rates, divorce laws, and health care, people's psychological well-being should be a prime consideration. Such measures may help guide nations toward policies that decrease stress, foster human flourishing, and promote "the pursuit of happiness."

Scientifically Proven Ways to Have a Happier Life[1]

Your happiness, like your cholesterol level, is genetically influenced. Yet as cholesterol is also influenced by diet and exercise, so happiness is to some extent under your personal control (Nes, 2010; Sin & Lyubomirsky, 2009). Here are 10 research-based suggestions for building your personal strengths to increase your satisfaction with life.

1. ***Take control of your time.*** Happy people feel in control of their lives. To master your use of time, set goals and divide them into daily aims.

This may be frustrating at first, because we all tend to overestimate how much we will accomplish in any given day. The good news is that we generally underestimate how much we can accomplish in a year, given just a little progress every day.

2. ***Act happy.*** As you saw in Chapter 9, people who have been manipulated into a smiling expression felt better. So put on a happy face. Talk as if you feel positive self-esteem, are optimistic, and are outgoing. We can often act our way into a happier state of mind.

3. ***Seek work and leisure that engage your skills.*** Happy people often are in a zone called *flow*—absorbed in tasks that challenge but don't overwhelm them. Passive forms of leisure (watching TV) often provide less flow experience than exercising, socializing, or expressing your musical interests. And frequent small positive experiences make for more lasting happiness than big but rare positive events.

---

1. Digested from David G. Myers, *The Pursuit of Happiness* (Harper).

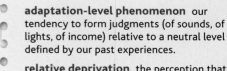

adaptation-level phenomenon our tendency to form judgments (of sounds, of lights, of income) relative to a neutral level defined by our past experiences.

relative deprivation the perception that we are worse off relative to those with whom we compare ourselves.

RubberBall Selects/Alamy

4. *Buy shared experiences rather than things.* Compared with money spent on stuff, money buys more happiness when spent on experiences that you look forward to, enjoy, remember, and talk about (Carter & Gilovich, 2010; Kumar & Gilovich, 2013). This is especially so for socially shared experiences (Caprariello & Reis, 2013). The shared experience of a family vacation may cost a lot, but, as pundit Art Buchwald said, "The best things in life aren't things."

5. *Join the "movement" movement.* Aerobic exercise can relieve mild depression and anxiety as it promotes health and energy. Sound minds reside in sound bodies.

6. *Give your body the sleep it wants.* Happy people live active lives yet save time for renewing sleep. Many people—high school and college students, especially—suffer from sleep debt. The result is fatigue, diminished alertness, and gloomy moods. If you sleep now, you'll smile later.

7. *Give priority to close relationships.* Confiding is good for soul and body. Those who care deeply about you can help you weather difficult times. Compared with unhappy people, happy people engage in less small talk and more meaningful conversations (Mehl et al., 2010). You can nurture your closest relationships by not taking your loved ones for granted. This means being as kind to them as you are to others, affirming them, playing together, and sharing together.

8. *Focus beyond self.* Reach out to those in need. Happiness increases helpfulness (those who feel good do good). But doing good also makes us feel good.

9. *Count your blessings and record your gratitude.* Keeping a gratitude journal heightens well-being (Davis et al., 2016). Each day, savor the good moments and positive events and record why they occurred. Express your gratitude to others.

10. *Nurture your spiritual self.* For many people, faith provides a support community, a reason to focus beyond self, and a sense of purpose and hope. That helps explain why people active in faith communities report greater-than-average happiness and often cope well with crises.

Retrieve + Remember

- Which of the following factors does NOT predict self-reported happiness?
  a. Age
  b. Personality traits
  c. Sleep and exercise
  d. Active religious faith

ANSWER: a. Age does NOT effectively predict happiness levels. Better predictors are personality traits, sleep and exercise, and religious faith.

CHAPTER REVIEW

Stress, Health, and Human Flourishing

Test yourself by taking a moment to answer each of these Learning Objective Questions (repeated here from within the chapter). Then turn to Appendix D, Complete Chapter Reviews, to check your answers. Research suggests that trying to answer these questions on your own will improve your long-term memory of the concepts (McDaniel et al., 2009).

Stress: Some Basic Concepts

10-1: How does our appraisal of an event affect our stress reaction, and what are the three main types of stressors?

10-2: How does the body respond to stress?

Stress Effects and Health

10-3: How does stress influence our immune system?

10-4: How does stress increase coronary heart disease risk?

10-5: So, does stress *cause* illness?

Coping With Stress

10-6: What are two basic ways that people cope with stress?

10-7: How does our sense of control influence stress and health?

10-8: How do optimists and pessimists differ, and why does our outlook on life matter?

10-9: How do social support and finding meaning in life influence health?

Managing Stress Effects

10-10: How well does aerobic exercise help us manage stress and improve well-being?

10-11: In what ways might relaxation and meditation influence stress and health?

10-12: Does religious involvement relate to health?

Happiness

10-13: What are the causes and consequences of happiness?

TERMS AND CONCEPTS TO REMEMBER

Test yourself on these terms by trying to write down the definition in your own words before flipping back to the referenced page to check your answer.

stress, p. 287

fight-or-flight response, p. 287

general adaptation syndrome (GAS), p. 287

tend-and-befriend response, p. 289

psychoneuroimmunology, p. 289

coronary heart disease, p. 291

Type A, p. 291

Type B, p. 291

coping, p. 293

problem-focused coping, p. 293

emotion-focused coping, p. 293

personal control, p. 293

learned helplessness, p. 293

external locus of control, p. 295

internal locus of control, p. 295

self-control, p. 295

optimism, p. 295

pessimism, p. 295

aerobic exercise, p. 299

mindfulness meditation, p. 301

resilience, p. 303

feel-good, do-good phenomenon, p. 303

subjective well-being, p. 303

adaptation-level phenomenon, p. 307

relative deprivation, p. 307

CHAPTER TEST

Test yourself repeatedly throughout your studies. This will not only help you figure out what you know and don't know; the testing itself will help you learn and remember the information more effectively thanks to the *testing effect*.

1. Selye's general adaptation syndrome (GAS) consists of an alarm reaction followed by _____, then _____.

2. When faced with stress, women are more likely than men to exhibit the _____-and-_____ response.

3. The number of short-term illnesses and stress-related psychological disorders was higher than usual in the months following an earthquake. Such findings suggest that
   a. daily hassles have adverse health consequences.
   b. experiencing a very stressful event increases a person's vulnerability to illness.
   c. the amount of stress a person feels is directly related to the number of stressors experienced.
   d. daily hassles don't influence our physical or psychological health, but catastrophes can be toxic.

4. Which of the following is NOT one of the three main types of stressors?
   a. Catastrophes
   b. Significant life changes
   c. Daily hassles
   d. Loss of personal control

5. Stress can suppress the immune system by prompting a decrease in the release of _____, the immune cells that ordinarily attack bacteria, viruses, cancer cells, and other foreign substances.

6. Research has shown that people are at increased risk for cancer a year or so after experiencing depression, helplessness, or bereavement. In describing this link, researchers are quick to point out that
   a. accumulated stress causes cancer.
   b. anger is the negative emotion most closely linked to cancer.
   c. stress does not create cancer cells, but it weakens the body's natural defenses against them.
   d. feeling optimistic about chances of survival increases the likelihood of a cancer patient's recovery.

7. A Chinese proverb warns, "The fire you kindle for your enemy often burns you more than him." How is this true of Type A individuals?

8. The components of the Type A personality that have been linked most closely to coronary heart disease are anger and other _____ feelings.

9. When faced with a situation over which you feel you have little control, it is most effective to use _____ (emotion/problem)-focused coping.

10. Research has shown that a dog will respond with learned helplessness if it has received repeated shocks and has had
    a. the opportunity to escape.
    b. no control over the shocks.
    c. pain or discomfort.
    d. no food or water prior to the shocks.

11. When elderly patients take an active part in managing their own care and surroundings, their morale and health tend to improve. Such findings indicate that people do better when they experience an _____ (internal/external) locus of control.

12. People who have close relationships are less likely to die prematurely than those who do not, supporting the idea that
    a. social ties can be a source of stress.
    b. gender influences longevity.
    c. Type A behavior is responsible for many premature deaths.
    d. social support has a beneficial effect on health.

13. Because it triggers the release of mood-boosting neurotransmitters such as serotonin, _____ exercise raises energy levels and helps alleviate depression and anxiety.

14. Research on the faith factor has found that
    a. pessimists tend to be healthier than optimists.
    b. our expectations influence our feelings of stress.
    c. religiously active people tend to outlive those who are not religiously active.
    d. religious engagement promotes social isolation and repression.

15. One of the most consistent findings of psychological research is that happy people are also
    a. more likely to express anger.
    b. generally luckier than others.
    c. concentrated in the wealthier nations.
    d. more likely to help others.

16. After moving to a new apartment, you find the street noise irritatingly loud, but after a while, it no longer bothers you. This reaction illustrates the

    a. relative deprivation principle.

    b. adaptation-level phenomenon.

    c. feel-good, do-good phenomenon.

    d. importance of mindfulness meditation.

17. A philosopher observed that we cannot escape envy, because there will always be someone more successful, more accomplished, or richer with whom to compare ourselves. In psychology, this observation is embodied in the _____ _____ principle.

Find answers to these questions in Appendix E, in the back of the book.

IN YOUR EVERYDAY LIFE

Answering these questions will help you make these concepts more personally meaningful, and therefore more memorable.

1. In what ways have you experienced the stress adaptation phases of alarm, resistance, and exhaustion in your life as a student?

2. Do you think you are Type A, Type B, or somewhere in between? In what ways has this been helpful to you, and in what ways has this been a challenge?

3. Can you remember a time when you felt better after discussing a problem with a loved one, or even after playing with your pet? How did it help you to cope?

4. What strategies have you used to cope with stress in your own life? How well are they working? What other strategies could you try?

5. How much control do you feel you have over your life? What changes could you make to increase your sense of control?

6. Were you surprised by any of the findings related to happiness? What things might you change in your life to increase your own happiness?

Use 🔁 **LearningCurve** to create your personalized study plan, which will direct you to the resources that will help you most in 🔁 **LaunchPad**.

SURVEY THE CHAPTER

Taxi/Getty Images

Social Psychology

On a winter day in 1569, Dirk Willems faced a moment of decision. He had just escaped from prison, where he was facing torture and death for belonging to a persecuted religious minority. Willems fled across an ice-covered pond in Asperen, Holland, with his stronger and heavier jailer close behind. Then, suddenly, the jailer fell through the ice. Unable to climb out, he pleaded for Willems' help to escape the icy waters.

Rather than racing to freedom, Willems acted with ultimate selflessness: He turned back and rescued his pursuer. The jailer, following orders, took Willems back to prison where, a few weeks later, Willems was burned alive. For his martyrdom, present-day Asperen has named a street in honor of its folk hero (Toews, 2004).

What drives people to feel and act so heartlessly toward those, like Willems, who differ from them? What motivates the selflessness of so many who have died trying to save others?

What leads us to like or even love another? Do birds of a feather flock together—or do opposites attract? Does absence make the heart grow fonder—or does out of sight more often mean out of mind? Do good looks attract us—or does a good personality matter more?

As such questions demonstrate, we are social animals. We may assume the worst or the best in others. We may approach them with closed fists or open arms. But as the novelist Herman Melville remarked, "We cannot live for ourselves alone. Our lives are connected by a thousand invisible threads." In this chapter, we explore some of these connections and see how social psychologists study them.

What Is Social Psychology's Focus?

LOQ   **L**earning **O**bjective **Q**uestion

11-1 What are three main focuses of social psychology?

Social psychologists use *scientific methods* to study how we *think about, influence,* and *relate to* one another. When the unexpected occurs, we want to understand why people act as they do. Personality psychologists (Chapter 12) study the personal traits and processes that explain why *different people* may act differently *in a given situation.* (Would you have acted as Willems did, helping the jailer out of the icy water?) Social psychologists study the social forces that explain why *the same person* may act differently in *different situations.* (Might Willems' jailer have released him if the circumstances had been different?)

Social Thinking

When we try to explain people's actions, our search for answers often leaves us with two choices. We can attribute behavior to a person's stable, enduring traits. Or we can attribute behavior to the situation (Heider, 1958). Our explanations, or *attributions,* affect our feelings and actions.

AN ETCHING OF DIRK WILLEMS BY DUTCH ARTIST JAN LUYKEN (from *Martyrs Mirror,* 1685)

Mennonite Library and Archives/Bethel College

The Fundamental Attribution Error

LOQ **11-2** How does the fundamental attribution error describe how we tend to explain others' behavior compared with our own?

In class, we notice that Juliette seldom talks. Over coffee, Jack talks nonstop. That must be the sort of people they are, we decide. Juliette must be shy and Jack outgoing. Are they? Perhaps. People do have enduring personality traits. But often our explanations are wrong. We fall prey to the **fundamental attribution error:** We give too much weight to the influence of personality and too little to the influence of situations. In class, Jack may be as quiet as Juliette. Catch Juliette at a party and you may hardly recognize your quiet classmate.

📖 **LaunchPad** | For a quick interactive tutorial, visit LaunchPad's *Concept Practice: Making Attributions.*

Researchers demonstrated this tendency in an experiment with college students (Napolitan & Goethals, 1979). They had students talk, one at a time, with a young woman who acted either cold and critical or warm and friendly. Before the talks, researchers told half the students that the woman's behavior would be normal and natural. They told the other half the truth—that they had instructed her to *act* friendly (or unfriendly).

Did hearing the truth affect students' impressions of the woman? Not at all! If the woman acted friendly, both groups decided she really was a warm person. If she acted unfriendly, both decided she really was a cold person. In other words, they attributed her behavior to her personal traits, *even when they were told that her behavior was part of the experimental situation.*

The fundamental attribution error appears more often in some cultures than in others. Individualist Westerners more often attribute behavior to people's personal traits. People in East Asian cultures are more sensitive to the power of situations (Masuda & Kitayama, 2004; Riemer et al., 2014). This difference appeared in experiments in which people were asked to view scenes, such as a big fish swimming. Americans focused more on the individual fish; Japanese people focused on the whole scene (Chua et al., 2005; Nisbett, 2003).

To see how easily we make the fundamental attribution error, answer this question: Is your psychology instructor shy or outgoing?

If you're tempted to answer "outgoing," remember that you know your instructor from one situation—the classroom, where teaching demands talking. Your instructor (who observes his or her own behavior not only in the classroom, but also with family, friends, and colleagues) might say, "Me, outgoing? It all depends on the situation. In class or with good friends, yes, I'm outgoing. But at professional meetings I'm really rather shy." Outside the classroom, professors seem less professorial, students less studious.

When we explain *our own* behavior, we are sensitive to how behavior changes with the situation (Idson & Mischel, 2001). We also are sensitive to the power of the situation when we explain the behavior of people we have seen in many different contexts. So, when are we most likely to commit the fundamental attribution error? The odds are highest when a stranger acts badly. Having never seen this person in other situations, we assume he must be a bad person. But outside the stadium, that red-faced man screaming at the referee may be a great neighbor and a good father.

Could we broaden our thinking by taking another person's view? To test this idea, researchers have reversed the perspectives of *actor* and *observer*. They filmed two people interacting, with a camera behind each person. Then they showed each person a replay of their interaction—filmed from the other person's perspective. Sure enough, this reversed participants' attributions of the behaviors. Seeing the world from the actor's perspective, the observers better appreciated the situation. Taking the observer's point of view, the actors became more aware of their own personal style (Lassiter & Irvine, 1986; Storms, 1973). Becoming aware of our style of attribution can also help us rid ourselves of negative thinking. When people with depression realize they explain their actions through a negative lens, they can begin to love and accept themselves (Rubenstein et al., 2016).

Reflecting on our past selves of 5 or 10 years ago also switches our perspective. Our present self adopts the observer's perspective and attributes our past behavior mostly to our traits (Pronin & Ross, 2006). In another 5 or 10 years, your current self may seem like another person.

The way we explain others' actions, attributing them to the person or the situation, can have important real-life effects (Fincham & Bradbury, 1993; Fletcher et al., 1990). A person must decide whether another's warm greeting reflects friendliness or romantic interest. A jury must decide whether a shooting was an act of self-defense or a brutal attack. A voter must judge whether a candidate's

promises are sincere or soon to be forgotten. A partner must decide whether a loved one's acid-tongued remark reflects a bad day or a serious rejection.

Finally, consider the social effects of attribution. How should we explain poverty or unemployment? In Britain, India, Australia, and the United States, political conservatives have tended to attribute responsibility to the personal traits of the poor and unemployed (Furnham, 1982; Pandey et al., 1982; Wagstaff, 1982; Zucker & Weiner, 1993). "People generally get what they deserve. Anybody who tries hard can still get ahead." In experiments, after reflecting on the power of choice—either by recalling their own choices or taking note of another's choices—people are less bothered by inequality. They are more likely to think people get what they deserve (Savani & Rattan, 2012). Those not asked to consider the power of choice are more likely to blame past and present situations. So are political liberals.

The point to remember: Our attributions—to someone's personal traits or to the situation—have real consequences.

PERSONAL VERSUS SITUATIONAL ATTRIBUTIONS Should the 2015 slaughter of nine African-Americans attending a church Bible study in Charleston be attributed to the shooter's personal traits? ("There is one person to blame here. A person filled with hate," said South Carolina governor Nikki Haley.) To America's gun culture? ("At some point, we as a country will have to reckon with the fact that this type of mass violence does not happen in other advanced countries . . . with this kind of frequency," said President Obama.) Or to both?

© Richard Ellis/Alamy

Attitudes and Actions

LOQ **11-3** What is an attitude, and how do attitudes and actions affect each other?

Attitudes are feelings, often based on our beliefs, that can influence how we respond to particular objects, people, and events. If we *believe* someone is mean, we may *feel* dislike for the person and *act* unfriendly. That helps explain a noteworthy finding. If people in a country intensely dislike the leaders of another country, their country is more likely to produce terrorist acts against that country (Krueger & Malecková, 2009). Hateful attitudes breed violent behavior.

Attitudes Affect Actions

Knowing that public attitudes affect public policies, people on both sides of any debate aim to *persuade*. Persuasion efforts generally take two forms:

- **Peripheral route persuasion** uses unimportant cues to trigger speedy, emotion-based judgments. Beautiful and famous people can affect people's attitudes about everything from perfume to climate change.

- **Central route persuasion** offers evidence and arguments in hopes of motivating careful thinking. This form works well for people who are naturally analytical or involved in an issue.

social psychology the scientific study of how we think about, influence, and relate to one another.

fundamental attribution error the tendency, when analyzing others' behavior, to overestimate the influence of personal traits and underestimate the effects of the situation.

attitude feelings, often based on our beliefs, that predispose us to respond in a particular way to objects, people, and events.

peripheral route persuasion occurs when people are influenced by unimportant cues, such as a speaker's attractiveness.

central route persuasion occurs when interested people focus on the arguments and respond with favorable thoughts.

Attitudes affect our behavior, but other factors, including the situation, also influence behavior. For example, in roll-call votes requiring politicians to state their support or opposition publicly, situational pressures can control behavior. Politicians may vote as their supporters demand, despite privately disagreeing with those demands (Nagourney, 2002).

When are attitudes most likely to affect behavior? Under these conditions (Glasman & Albarracin, 2006):

- External influences are minimal.
- The attitude is stable.
- The attitude is specific to the behavior.
- The attitude is easily recalled.

One experiment used vivid, easily recalled information to persuade people that sustained tanning put them at risk for future skin cancer. One month later, 72 percent of the participants, and only 16 percent of those in a waitlist control group, had lighter skin (McClendon & Prentice-Dunn, 2001). Changed attitudes can change behavior.

Actions Affect Attitudes

People also come to believe in what they have stood up for. Many streams of evidence confirm that *attitudes follow behavior* (**FIGURE 11.1**).

FOOT-IN-THE-DOOR PHENOMENON

How would you react if someone got you to act against your beliefs? Would you change your beliefs? Many people do. During the Korean war, many U.S. prisoners were held in Chinese communist camps. Without using brutality, the Chinese captors gained prisoners' cooperation in various activities. Some merely did simple tasks to gain privileges. Others made radio appeals and false confessions. Still others informed on other prisoners and revealed U.S. military information. When the war ended, 21 prisoners chose to stay with the communists. More returned home "brainwashed"—convinced that communism was good for Asia.

FIGURE 11.1 Attitudes follow behavior Cooperative actions, such as those performed by people on sports teams (including Germany, shown here celebrating their World Cup 2014 victory), feed mutual liking. Such attitudes, in turn, promote positive behavior.

Jeff J. Mitchell/Getty Images

How did the Chinese captors achieve these amazing results? A key ingredient was their effective use of the **foot-in-the-door phenomenon.** They knew that people who agree to a small request will find it easier to agree later to a larger one. The Chinese began with harmless requests, such as copying a trivial statement. Gradually, they made bigger demands (Schein, 1956). The next statement to be copied might contain a list of the flaws of capitalism. Then, to gain privileges, the prisoners took part in group discussions, wrote self-criticisms, or made public confessions. After taking this series of small steps, some of the Americans changed their beliefs to be more in line with their public acts. The point is simple. To get people to agree to something big, start small and build (Cialdini, 1993). A trivial act makes the next act easier. Telling a small lie paves the way to telling a bigger lie. Give in to a temptation and the next temptation becomes harder to resist.

In dozens of experiments, researchers have coaxed people into acting against their attitudes or violating their moral standards, with the same result. Doing becomes believing. After giving in to a request to harm an innocent victim—by making nasty comments or delivering presumed electric shocks—people begin to look down on their victim. After speaking or writing in support of a position they have doubts about, they begin to believe their own words.

Fortunately, the principle that attitudes follow behavior works as well for good deeds as for bad. After U.S. schools were desegregated and the 1964 Civil Rights Act was passed, White Americans expressed lower levels of racial prejudice. And as Americans in different regions came to *act* more alike—thanks to more uniform national standards against discrimination—they began to *think* more alike. Experiments confirm the observation: Moral action strengthens moral convictions.

ROLE-PLAYING AFFECTS ATTITUDES

How many new **roles** have you adopted recently? Becoming a college student is a new role. Perhaps you've started a new job, or a new relationship, or even become engaged or married. If so, you may have realized that people expected you to behave a little differently. At first, your behaviors may have felt phony, because you were acting a role. Soldiers may at first feel they are playing war games. Newlyweds may feel they are "playing house." Before long, however, what began as play-acting in the theater of life becomes you. (This fact is reflected in the Alcoholics Anonymous advice: "Fake it until you make it.")

Role-playing morphed into real life in one famous study in which male college students volunteered to spend time in a mock prison (Zimbardo, 1972). Stanford psychologist Philip Zimbardo randomly assigned some volunteers to be guards. He gave them uniforms, clubs, and whistles and instructed them to enforce certain rules. Others became prisoners, locked in barren cells and forced to wear humiliating outfits. For a day or two, the volunteers self-consciously played their roles. Then it became clear that the "play" had become real—too real. Most guards developed negative attitudes toward the prisoners. Some created cruel routines. One by one, the prisoners broke down, rebelled, or became passively resigned. After only six days, Zimbardo called off the study.

Although critics question the reliability of Zimbardo's results, there is evidence that role-playing can train people to become torturers in the real world (Griggs, 2014; Staub, 1989). Yet people differ. In Zimbardo's prison simulation, and in other atrocity-producing situations, some people gave in to the situation and others did not (Carnahan & McFarland, 2007; Haslam & Reicher, 2007, 2012; Mastroianni & Reed, 2006; Zimbardo, 2007). Persons and situations interact.

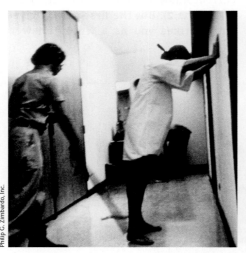 To view Philip Zimbardo's 14-minute illustration and explanation of his famous prison simulation, visit LaunchPad's *Video—The Stanford Prison Study: The Power of the Situation.*

COGNITIVE DISSONANCE: RELIEF FROM TENSION We have seen that actions can affect attitudes, sometimes turning prisoners of war into collaborators, doubters into believers, and guards into abusers. But why? One explanation is that when we become aware of a mismatch between our attitudes and actions, we experience mental discomfort, or *cognitive dissonance.* Indeed, the brain regions that become active when people experience cognitive conflict and negative arousal also become active when people experience cognitive dissonance (de Vries et al., 2015; Kitayama et al., 2013). To relieve this tension, according to Leon Festinger's **cognitive dissonance theory,** we often bring our attitudes into line with our actions.

Dozens of experiments have tested this attitudes-follow-behavior principle. Many have made people feel responsible for behavior that clashed with their attitudes. As a participant in one of these experiments, you might agree for a small sum of money to help a researcher by writing an essay that supports something you don't believe in (perhaps a tuition increase). Feeling responsible for your written statements (which don't reflect your attitudes), you would probably feel dissonance, especially if you thought an administrator would be reading your essay. How could you reduce the uncomfortable tension? One way would be to start believing your phony words. It's as if we tell ourselves, "If I chose to do it (or say it), I must believe in it." Thus, we may change our attitudes to help justify the act.

 To check your understanding of cognitive dissonance, visit LaunchPad's *Concept Practice: Cognitive Dissonance.*

The attitudes-follow-behavior principle can also help us become better people. We cannot control all our feelings, but we can influence them by altering our behavior. (Recall from Chapter 9 the emotional effects of facial expressions and of body postures.) If we are down in the dumps, we can do as cognitive therapists advise: We can talk in more positive, self-accepting ways with fewer self–put-downs. If we are unloving, we can become more loving. We can do thoughtful things, express affection, and give support.

The point to remember: Cruel acts shape the self. But so do acts of good will. Act as though you like someone, and you soon may. Changing our behavior can change how we think about others and how we feel about ourselves.

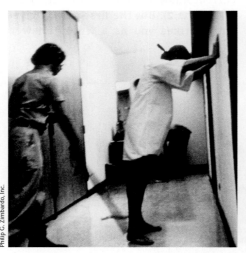

THE POWER OF THE SITUATION In his 1972 Stanford Prison simulation, Philip Zimbardo created a toxic situation (left). Those assigned to the guard role soon degraded the prisoners. In real life in 2004, some U.S. military guards tormented Iraqi prisoners at the U.S.-run Abu Ghraib prison (right). To Zimbardo (2004, 2007), it was a bad barrel rather than a few bad apples that led to the abuse: "When ordinary people are put in a novel, evil place, such as most prisons, Situations Win, People Lose."

foot-in-the-door phenomenon the tendency for people who have first agreed to a small request to comply later with a larger request.

role a set of expectations about a social position, defining how those in the position ought to behave.

cognitive dissonance theory the theory that we act to reduce the discomfort (dissonance) we feel when two of our thoughts (cognitions) clash. For example, when we become aware that our attitudes and our actions don't match, we may change our attitudes so that we feel more comfortable.

Retrieve + Remember

- Driving to school one snowy day, Marco narrowly misses a car that slides through a red light. "Slow down! What a terrible driver," he thinks to himself. Moments later, Marco himself slips through an intersection and yelps, "Wow! These roads are awful. The city plows need to get out here." What social psychology principle has Marco just demonstrated? Explain.

ANSWER: By attributing the other person's behavior to personal traits ("what a terrible driver") and his own to the situation ("these roads are awful!"), Marco has exhibited the fundamental attribution error.

- How do our attitudes and our actions affect each other?

ANSWER: Our attitudes often influence our actions, as we behave in ways consistent with our beliefs. However, our actions also influence our attitudes; we come to believe in what we have done.

- When people act in a way that is not in keeping with their attitudes, and then change their attitudes to match those actions, _____ _____ theory attempts to explain why.

ANSWER: cognitive dissonance

Social Influence

Social psychology's great lesson is the enormous power of social influence. We adjust our views to match the desires of those around us. We follow orders. We behave as others in our group behave. On campus, jeans are the dress code. On New York's Wall Street, dress suits are the norm. Let's examine the pull of these social strings. How strong are they? How do they operate? When do we break them?

Conformity and Obedience

LOQ 11-4 What do experiments on conformity and obedience reveal about the power of social influence?

Fish swim in schools. Birds fly in flocks. And humans, too, tend to go with their group—to think what it thinks and do what it does. Behavior is contagious.

If one of us laughs, coughs, yawns, scratches an itch, stares at the sky, or checks a cell phone, others in our group will often do the same (Holle et al., 2012). Even just reading about yawning increases people's yawning (Provine, 2012), as perhaps you've now noticed? Like the chameleon lizards that take on the color of their surroundings, we humans take on the emotional tones of those around us (Totterdell et al., 1998). We are natural mimics, unconsciously imitating others' expressions, postures, and voice tones.

Researchers demonstrated this *chameleon effect* in a clever experiment (Chartrand & Bargh, 1999). They had students work in a room beside another person, who was actually the experimenter's assistant. Sometimes the assistants rubbed their own face. Sometimes they shook their foot. Sure enough, the students tended to rub their face when with the face-rubbing person and shake their foot when with the foot-shaking person.

Automatic mimicry helps us to *empathize*, to feel what others feel. This helps explain why we feel happier around happy people than around depressed ones. The more we mimic, the greater our empathy, and the more people tend to like us (Chartrand & van Baaren, 2009; Lakin et al., 2008).

Group Pressure and Conformity

To study **conformity**—adjusting our behavior or thinking toward some group standard—Solomon Asch (1955) designed a simple test. As a participant in what you believe is a study of visual perception, you arrive in time to take a seat at a table with five other people. The experimenter asks the group to state, one by one, which of three comparison lines is identical to a standard line. You see clearly that the answer is Line 2, and you await your turn to say so. Your boredom begins to show when the next set of lines proves equally easy.

Now comes the third trial, and the correct answer seems just as clear-cut (**FIGURE 11.2**). But the first person gives what strikes you as a wrong answer:

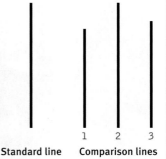

Standard line   Comparison lines

FIGURE 11.2 Asch's conformity experiments Which of the three comparison lines is equal to the standard line? What do you suppose most people would say after hearing five others say, "Line 3"? In this photo from one of Asch's experiments, the student in the center shows the severe discomfort that comes from disagreeing with the responses of other group members (in this case, accomplices of the experimenter).

"Line 3." When the second person and then the third and fourth give the same wrong answer, you sit up straight and squint. When the fifth person agrees with the first four, you feel your heart begin to pound. The experimenter then looks to you for your answer. Torn between the agreement voiced by the five others and the evidence of your own eyes, you feel tense and suddenly unsure of yourself. You wait a bit before answering, wondering whether you should suffer the pain of being the oddball. What answer do you give?

In Asch's experiments, college students experienced this conflict. Answering questions alone, they were wrong less than 1 percent of the time. But the odds were quite different when several others—people actually working for Asch—answered incorrectly. More than one-third of the time, these "intelligent and well-meaning" college students were then "willing to call white black" by going along with the group.

Experiments reveal that we are more likely to conform when we

- are made to feel incompetent or insecure.
- are in a group with at least three people.

Sanne Berg/iStock/360/Getty Images

TATTOOS: YESTERDAY'S NONCONFORMITY, TODAY'S CONFORMITY? As tattoos become perceived as fashion conformity, their popularity may wane.

- are in a group in which everyone else agrees. (If just one other person disagrees, we will almost surely disagree.)
- admire the group's status and attractiveness.
- have not already committed ourselves to any response.
- know that others in the group will observe our behavior.
- are from a culture that strongly encourages respect for social standards.

> "Have you ever noticed how one example—good or bad—can prompt others to follow? How one illegally parked car can give permission for others to do likewise? How one racial joke can fuel another?"
>
> Marian Wright Edelman,
> *The Measure of Our Success,* 1994

Why do we so often think what others think and do what they do? Why, when asked controversial questions, are students' answers more varied when using anonymous electronic clickers than when publicly raising hands (Stowell et al., 2010)? Why do we clap when others clap, eat as others eat, believe what others believe, even see what others see? Sometimes it's to avoid rejection or to gain social approval (Williams & Sommer, 1997). In such cases, we are responding to **normative social influence.** We are sensitive to social norms— understood rules for accepted and expected behavior—because the price we pay for being different can be severe. But sometimes we conform because we want to be accurate. We are responding to **informational social influence** when we accept others' opinions about reality. "Those who never retract their opinions love themselves more than they love truth," observed Joseph Joubert, an eighteenth-century French essayist.

Is conformity good or bad? The answer depends on whether people go along with what we believe. When people conform to our values, we applaud them for being "open-minded" and "sensitive" enough to be "responsive." When

they conform to others' values, we scorn their "blind, thoughtless" willingness to give in to others' wishes.

Our values, as we will see in Chapter 12, are influenced by our culture. Western Europeans and people in most English-speaking countries tend to prize *individualism.* People in many Asian, African, and Latin American countries place a higher value on *collectivism* (honoring group standards). It's perhaps not surprising, then, that in social influence experiments across 17 countries, conformity rates are lower in individualist cultures than in collectivist cultures (Bond & Smith, 1996). In the United States, for example, university students tend to see themselves as less conforming than others (Pronin et al., 2007). We are, in our own eyes, individuals amid a flock of sheep.

Retrieve + Remember

- Which of the following strengthens conformity to a group?
  a. Finding the group attractive
  b. Feeling secure
  c. Coming from an individualist culture
  d. Having already decided on a response

ANSWER: a

📔 **LaunchPad** To review the classic conformity studies and experience a simulated experiment, visit LaunchPad's *PsychSim 6: Everybody's Doing It!*

Obedience

Social psychologist Stanley Milgram (1963, 1974), a high school classmate of Phillip Zimbardo and later a student of Solomon

conformity adjusting our behavior or thinking to coincide with a group standard.

normative social influence influence resulting from a person's desire to gain approval or avoid disapproval.

informational social influence influence resulting from a person's willingness to accept others' opinions about reality.

Asch, knew that people often give in to social pressure. But how would they respond to outright commands? To find out, he undertook experiments that have become social psychology's most famous and most hotly debated.

Imagine yourself as one of the nearly 1000 people who took part in Milgram's 20 experiments. You have responded to an ad for participants in a Yale University psychology study of the effect of punishment on learning. Professor Milgram's assistant asks you and another person to draw slips from a hat to see who will be the "teacher" and who will be the "learner." You draw the "teacher" slip and are asked to sit down in front of a machine, which has a series of labeled switches. The "learner" is led to a nearby room and strapped into a chair. From the chair, wires run through the wall to your machine. You are given your task: Teach and then test the learner on a list of word pairs. If the learner gives a wrong answer, you are to flip a switch to deliver a brief electric shock. For the first wrong answer, you will flip the switch labeled "15 Volts—Slight Shock." With each additional error, you will move to the next higher voltage. The researcher demonstrates by flipping the first switch. Lights flash and an electric buzzing fills the air.

The experiment begins, and you deliver the shocks after the first and second wrong answers. If you continue, you hear the learner grunt when you flick the third, fourth, and fifth switches. After you flip the eighth switch ("120 Volts—Moderate Shock"), the learner cries out that the shocks are painful. After the tenth switch ("150 Volts—Strong Shock"), he begins shouting. "Get me out of here! I won't be in the experiment anymore! I refuse to go on!" You draw back, but the experimenter prods you. "Please continue—the experiment requires that you continue." You resist, but the experimenter insists, "It is absolutely essential that you continue," or "You have no other choice, you *must* go on."

If you obey, you hear the learner shriek in agony as you continue to raise the shock level after each new error. After the 330-volt level, the learner refuses to answer and falls silent. Still, the experimenter pushes you toward the final, 450-volt switch. Ask the question, he says, and if no correct answer is given, administer the next shock level.

Would you follow an experimenter's commands to shock someone? At what level would you refuse to obey? Before he started the experiments, Milgram asked people what they would do. Most people were sure they would stop playing such a sadistic-seeming role soon after the learner first indicated pain, certainly before he shrieked in agony. Forty psychiatrists agreed with that prediction when Milgram asked them. Were the predictions accurate? Not even close. When Milgram actually conducted the experiment with other men aged 20 to 50, he was amazed. More than 60 percent followed orders—right up to the last switch. When he ran a new study, with 40 new teachers and a learner who complained of a "slight heart condition," the results were the same. A full 65 percent of the new teachers obeyed every one of the experimenter's commands, right up to 450 volts (**FIGURE 11.3**).

How can we explain these findings? Could they be a product of the 1960s culture? Would people today be less likely to obey an order to hurt someone? *No.* When researchers replicated Milgram's basic experiment, 70 percent of the participants obeyed up to the 150-volt point (Burger, 2009). This is only a slight reduction from Milgram's 83 percent at that level. And in a French reality TV show replication, 81 percent of people, egged on by a cheering audience, obeyed and tortured a screaming victim (Beauvois et al., 2012).

Could Milgram's findings reflect some aspect of gender behavior found only in males? Again, the answer is *No.* In 10 later studies, women obeyed at rates similar to men (Blass, 1999).

Could the teachers have figured out the hoax—that no real shock was being delivered and the learner was in fact an assistant only pretending to feel pain? Did they realize the experiment was really testing their willingness to obey commands to inflict punishment? *No.* The teachers were typically genuinely distressed. They perspired, trembled, laughed nervously, and bit their lips.

In later experiments, Milgram discovered some conditions that did influence people's behavior. When he varied some details of the situation, the percentage of participants who fully obeyed ranged from 0 to 93 percent. Obedience was highest when

- the person giving the orders was close at hand and was perceived to be a legitimate authority figure.

- the authority figure was supported by a respected, well-known institution (Yale University).

- the victim was depersonalized or at a distance, even in another room. Similarly, many soldiers in combat either do not fire their rifles at an enemy they can see or do not aim them properly. Such refusals to kill are rare among those who kill from a distance. (Veterans who operated remotely piloted drones have suffered much less posttraumatic stress than have on-the-ground Afghanistan and Iraq war veterans [Miller, 2012a; Padgett, 1989].)

- there were no role models for defiance. (Teachers did not see any other participant disobey the experimenter.)

Stanley Milgram, from the film "Obedience." Rights held by Alexandra Milgram

STANLEY MILGRAM (1933–1984) This social psychologist's obedience experiments "belong to the self-understanding of literate people in our age" (Sabini, 1986).

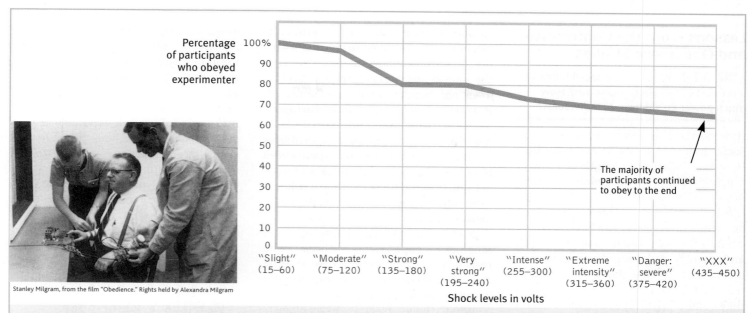

Percentage of participants who obeyed experimenter

Shock levels in volts

"Slight" (15–60) • "Moderate" (75–120) • "Strong" (135–180) • "Very strong" (195–240) • "Intense" (255–300) • "Extreme intensity" (315–360) • "Danger: severe" (375–420) • "XXX" (435–450)

The majority of participants continued to obey to the end

Stanley Milgram, from the film "Obedience." Rights held by Alexandra Milgram

FIGURE 11.3 Milgram's follow-up obedience experiment In a repeat of the earlier experiment, 65 percent of the adult male "teachers" fully obeyed the experimenter's commands to continue. They did so despite the "learner's" earlier mention of a heart condition, and despite hearing the learner's increasingly agonized protests as they administered what they believed were greater and greater voltages. (Data from Milgram, 1974.)

The power of legitimate, close-at-hand authorities is dramatically apparent in stories of those who followed orders to carry out the Nazis' Holocaust atrocities. Obedience alone does not explain the Holocaust; anti-Semitic ideology produced eager killers as well (Fenigstein, 2015; Mastroianni, 2015). But obedience was a factor. In the summer of 1942, nearly 500 middle-aged German reserve police officers were dispatched to German-occupied Jozefow, Poland. On July 13, the group's visibly upset commander informed his recruits, mostly family men, of their orders. They were to round up the village's Jews, who were said to be aiding the enemy. Able-bodied men would be sent to work camps, and all the rest were to be shot on the spot.

The commander gave the recruits a chance to refuse to participate in the executions. Only about a dozen immediately refused. Within 17 hours, the remaining 485 officers killed 1500 helpless women, children, and elderly, shooting them in the back of the head as they lay face down. Hearing the victims' pleas and seeing the gruesome results, some 20 percent of the officers did eventually disobey. They did so either by missing their victims or by hiding until the slaughter was over (Browning, 1992). In real life, as in Milgram's experiments, those who resisted did so early, and they were the minority.

Jeff Widener/AP Photo

STANDING UP FOR DEMOCRACY Some individuals—roughly one in three in Milgram's experiments—resist social pressure to act against their beliefs. This unarmed man in Beijing single-handedly challenged an advancing line of tanks in Tiananmen Square in 1989. This was one day after the Chinese government had suppressed a student uprising there.

"I was only following orders."

Adolf Eichmann, director of Nazi deportation of Jews to concentration camps

A different story played out in the French village of Le Chambon. There, villagers openly defied orders to cooperate with the "New Order." They sheltered French Jews and sometimes helped them escape across the Swiss border. The villagers' Protestant ancestors had themselves been persecuted. Their pastors had been teaching them to "resist whenever our adversaries will demand of us obedience contrary to the orders of the Gospel" (Rochat, 1993). Ordered by police to give a list of sheltered Jews, the head pastor modeled defiance. "I don't know of Jews, I only know of human beings." At great personal risk, the resisters made a commitment to defy. Throughout the war, they suffered from poverty and were punished for their disobedience. But they drew support from their beliefs, their role models, their interactions with one another, and their own early actions. They remained defiant to the war's end.

Lessons From the Conformity and Obedience Studies

LOQ 11-5 What do the social influence studies teach us about ourselves? How much power do we have as individuals?

How do the laboratory experiments on social influence relate to everyday life? How does judging the length of a line or flipping a shock switch relate to everyday social behavior? Psychology's experiments aim not to re-create the exact behaviors of everyday life but to explore what influences them. Solomon Asch and Stanley Milgram devised experiments that forced a choice: Do I remain true to my own standards, even when they conflict with expectations? That's a dilemma we all face.

In Milgram's experiments and their modern replications, participants were also torn. Should they respond to the pleas of the victim or the orders of the experimenter? Their moral sense warned them not to harm another. But that same sense also prompted them to obey the experimenter and to be a good research participant. With kindness and obedience on a collision course, obedience usually won.

These experiments demonstrated that strong social influences can make people conform to falsehoods or give in to cruelty. Milgram saw this as the most basic lesson of his work. "Ordinary people, simply doing their jobs, and without any particular hostility on their part, can become agents in a terrible destructive process" (1974, p. 6).

Using the foot-in-the-door technique, Milgram began with a little tickle of electricity and advanced step by step. In the minds of those throwing the switches, the small action became justified, making the next act tolerable.

In any society, great evils often grow out of people's acceptance of lesser evils. The Nazi leaders suspected that most German civil servants would resist shooting or gassing Jews directly. But they found them surprisingly willing to handle the paperwork of the Holocaust (Silver & Geller, 1978). Milgram found a similar reaction in his experiments. When he asked 40 men to give the learning test while someone else delivered the shocks, 93 percent agreed. Cruelty does not require devilish villains. All it takes is ordinary people corrupted by an evil situation. Ordinary students may follow orders to haze new members joining their group. Ordinary employees may follow orders to produce and market harmful products. Ordinary soldiers may follow orders to torture prisoners (Lankford, 2009).

In Jozefow and Le Chambon, as in Milgram's experiments, those who resisted usually did so early. After the first acts of obedience or resistance, attitudes began to follow and justify behavior.

What have social psychologists learned about the power of the individual? *Social control* (the power of the situation) and *personal control* (the power of the individual) interact. Much as water dissolves salt but not sand, so rotten situations turn some people into bad apples while others resist (Johnson, 2007).

People do resist. When feeling pressured, some react by doing the opposite of what is expected (Brehm & Brehm, 1981). Rosa Parks' refusal to sit at the back of the bus ignited the U.S. civil rights movement.

The power of one or two individuals to sway majorities is *minority influence* (Moscovici, 1985). In studies, one finding repeatedly stands out. When you are the minority, you are far more likely to sway the majority if you hold firmly to your position and don't waffle. This tactic won't make you popular, but it may make you influential, especially if your self-confidence stimulates others to consider why you react as you do. Even when a minority's influence is not yet visible, people may privately develop sympathy for the minority position and rethink their views (Wood et al., 1994). The powers of social influence are enormous, but so are the powers of the committed individual.

GANDHI As the life of Hindu nationalist and spiritual leader Mahatma Gandhi powerfully testifies, a consistent and persistent minority voice can sometimes sway the majority. Gandhi's nonviolent appeals and fasts helped win India's independence from Britain in 1947.

Retrieve + Remember

- In psychology's most famous obedience experiments, most participants obeyed an authority figure's demands to inflict presumed life-threatening shocks on an innocent person. Social psychologist _____ _____ conducted these experiments.

ANSWER: Stanley Milgram

- In the obedience experiments, people were most likely to follow orders in four situations. What were those situations?

ANSWER: The Milgram studies showed that people were most likely to follow orders when (a) the person giving the orders was nearby and was a legitimate authority figure, (b) the authority figure was supported by a respected institution, (c) the victim was not nearby, and (d) there were no models for defiance.

Group Influence

LOQ 11-6 How does the presence of others influence our actions, via social facilitation, social loafing, or deindividuation?

Imagine standing in a room, holding a fishing pole. Your task is to wind the reel as fast as you can. On some occasions you wind in the presence of another participant who is also winding as fast as possible. Will the other's presence affect your own performance?

In one of social psychology's first experiments, Norman Triplett (1898) found that adolescents would wind a fishing reel faster in the presence of someone doing the same thing. He and later social psychologists studied how the presence of others affects our behavior. Group influences operate both in simple groups—one person in the presence of another—and in more complex groups.

Social Facilitation

Triplett's finding—that our responses on an individual task are stronger in the presence of others—is called **social facilitation.** Later studies revealed that the presence of others sometimes helps and sometimes hurts performance (Guerin, 1986; Zajonc, 1965). Why? Because when others observe us, we become aroused, and this arousal amplifies our reactions. It strengthens our most likely response—the correct one on an easy task, an incorrect one on a difficult task. Thus, when others observe us, we perform well-learned tasks more quickly and accurately. But on new and difficult tasks, we perform less quickly and accurately.

SOCIAL FACILITATION Skilled athletes often find they are "on" before an audience. What they do well, they do even better when people are watching.

TABLE 11.1	Home Advantage in Team Sports	
Sport	Years	Home games won
Nippon League Baseball	1998–2009	53.6%
Major League Baseball	1903–2009	53.9%
National Hockey League	1917–2009	55.7%
International Rugby	1871–2009	56.9%
National Football League	1966–2009	57.3%
International Cricket	1877–2009	57.4%
National Basketball Association	1946–2009	60.5%
Women's National Basketball Association	2003–2009	61.7%
English Premier League Soccer	1993–2009	63.0%
NCAA Men's Basketball	1947–2009	68.8%
Major League Soccer	2002–2009	69.1%

Source: Data from Moskowitz & Wertheim, 2011.

This effect helps explain the home-team advantage. Studies of more than a quarter-million college and professional athletic events in various countries show that the home-team advantage is real (Allen & Jones, 2014; Jamieson, 2010). An enthusiastic audience seems to energize the home sports team. Home teams win about 6 in 10 games (**TABLE 11.1**). For most sports, home cooking is best.

The point to remember: What you do well, you are likely to do even better in front of an audience, especially a friendly audience. What you normally find difficult may seem all but impossible when you are being watched.

Social facilitation also helps explain a funny effect of crowding. Comedians and actors know that a "good house" is a full one. What they may not know is that crowding triggers arousal. Comedy routines that are mildly amusing to people in an uncrowded room seem funnier in a densely packed room (Aiello et al., 1983; Freedman & Perlick, 1979). In experiments, participants seated close to one another liked a friendly person even more and an unfriendly person even less (Schiffenbauer & Schiavo, 1976; Storms & Thomas, 1977). So, to increase the chances of lively interaction at your next event, choose a room or set up seating that will just barely hold all your guests.

Social Loafing

Does the presence of others have the same arousal effect when we perform a task as a group? In a team tug-of-war, do we exert more, less, or the same effort as in a one-on-one tug-of-war? If you said "less," you're right. In one experiment, students who believed three others were also pulling behind them exerted only 82 percent as much effort as when they knew they were pulling alone (Ingham et al., 1974). And consider what happened when blindfolded people seated in a group clapped or shouted as loudly as they could while hearing (through headphones) other people clapping or shouting (Latané, 1981). In one round of noise-making, the participants believed the researchers could identify their individual sounds. In another round, they believed their clapping and shouting was blended with other people's. When they thought they were part of a group effort, the participants produced about one-third less noise than when clapping "alone."

social facilitation improved performance on simple or well-learned tasks in the presence of others.

WORKING HARD, OR HARDLY WORKING? In group projects, social loafing often occurs, as individuals free ride on the efforts of others.

This lessened effort is called **social loafing** (Jackson & Williams, 1988; Latané, 1981). Experiments in the United States, India, Thailand, Japan, China, and Taiwan have found social loafing on various tasks. It was especially common among men in individualist cultures (Karau & Williams, 1993). What causes social loafing? Three things:

- People acting as part of a group feel less accountable, so they worry less about what others think of them.
- Group members may not believe their individual contributions make a difference (Harkins & Szymanski, 1989; Kerr & Bruun, 1983).
- Loafing is its own reward. When group members share equally in the benefits regardless of how much they contribute, some may slack off. (If you've worked on group assignments, you're probably already aware of this.) People who are not highly motivated, or who don't identify strongly with the group, may *free ride* on others' efforts.

Deindividuation

We've seen that the presence of others can arouse people, or it can make them feel less responsible. But sometimes the presence of others does both, triggering behavior that can range from a food fight to vandalism or rioting. This process of losing self-awareness and self-restraint is called **deindividuation.** It often occurs when group participation makes people feel *aroused* and *anonymous.* In one experiment, some female students dressed in Ku Klux Klan–style hoods that concealed their identity. Others in a control group did not wear the hoods. Those wearing hoods delivered twice as much electric shock to a victim (Zimbardo, 1970). (As in all such experiments, the "victim" did not actually receive the shocks.)

Deindividuation thrives, for better or for worse, in many different settings. The anonymity of online discussion boards and blog comment sections can unleash mocking or cruel words. Tribal warriors wearing face paints or masks have been more likely than those with exposed faces to kill, torture, or mutilate captured enemies (Watson, 1973). Online bullies, who would never say "You're the ugliest person I know" to someone's face, will hide behind their anonymity. When we shed self-awareness and self-restraint—whether in a mob, at a rock concert, at a ballgame, or at worship—we become more responsive to the group experience, bad or good. For a comparison of social facilitation, social loafing, and deindividuation, see **TABLE 11.2.**

Group Polarization

LOQ 11-7 How can group interaction enable group polarization?

Over time, differences between groups of college students tend to grow. If the first-year students at College X tend to be more politically conservative, and

TABLE 11.2 Behavior in the Presence of Others

Phenomenon	Social context	Psychological effect of others' presence	Behavioral effect
Social facilitation	Individual being observed	Increased arousal	Amplified dominant behavior, such as doing better what one does well (or doing worse what is difficult)
Social loafing	Group projects	Reduced feelings of responsibility when not individually accountable	Decreased effort
Deindividuation	Group setting that increases arousal and anonymity	Reduced self-awareness	Lowered self-restraint

DEINDIVIDUATION During England's 2011 riots and looting, rioters were disinhibited by social arousal and by the anonymity provided by darkness and their hoods and masks. Later, some of those arrested expressed bewilderment over their own behavior.

john t. fowler/Alamy

Lewis Whyld/PA Wire URN:11349922 Press Association via AP Image

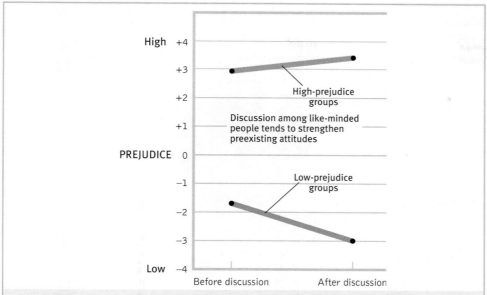

FIGURE 11.4 **Group polarization** If a group is like-minded, discussion strengthens its prevailing opinions. Talking over racial issues increased prejudice in a high-prejudice group of high school students and decreased it in a low-prejudice group. (Data from Myers & Bishop, 1970.)

those at College Y tend to be more politically liberal, those differences will probably be even greater by the time they graduate.

In each case, the beliefs and attitudes students bring to a group grow stronger as they discuss their views with others who share them. This process, called **group polarization,** can have positive results, as when low-prejudice students become even more accepting while discussing racial issues. It can also have negative results (**FIGURE 11.4**), as when high-prejudice students who discuss racial issues become more prejudiced (Myers & Bishop, 1970). While mixed-opinion groups moderate views, the echo chamber of like-minded groups polarizes.

Group polarization can feed extremism and even suicide terrorism. The terrorist mentality does not erupt suddenly on a whim (McCauley, 2002; McCauley & Segal, 1987; Merari, 2002). It usually begins slowly, among people who get together because of a grievance. As group members interact in isolation (sometimes with other "brothers" and "sisters" in camps), their views grow more and more extreme.

Increasingly, they divide the world into "us" against "them" (Moghaddam, 2005; Qirko, 2004).

The Internet provides an easily accessible medium for group polarization. I [DM] got my start in social psychology with experiments on group polarization. Never then did I imagine the potential dangers, or the creative possibilities, of polarization in *virtual* groups. (For more on this topic, see Thinking Critically About: The Internet as Social Amplifier.)

"I wonder if we might benefit from socializing more with those who don't harbor anti-government views."

Frank Cotham/The New Yorker Collection/Condé Nast

Groupthink

LOQ 11-9 How can group interaction enable groupthink?

So group interaction can influence our personal decisions. Can it also influence important national decisions? It can and it does. In one famous decision, it led to what is now known as the "Bay of Pigs fiasco." President John F. Kennedy and his advisers decided in 1961 to invade Cuba with 1400 CIA-trained Cuban exiles. When the invaders were easily captured and quickly linked to the U.S. government, the president wondered aloud, "How could we have been so stupid?"

Reading a historian's account of the ill-fated blunder, social psychologist Irving Janis (1982) found some clues in the invasion's decision-making process. The morale of the popular and recently elected president and his advisers was soaring. Their confidence was almost unlimited. To preserve the good feeling, group members with differing views kept quiet, especially after President Kennedy voiced his enthusiasm for the scheme. Since no one spoke strongly against the idea, everyone assumed the support was unanimous. **Groupthink** was at work: The desire for harmony had replaced realistic judgment.

Later studies showed that groupthink—fed by overconfidence, conformity, self-justification, and group

social loafing the tendency for people in a group to exert less effort when pooling their efforts toward attaining a common goal than when individually accountable.

deindividuation the loss of self-awareness and self-restraint occurring in group situations that foster arousal and anonymity.

group polarization strengthening of a group's preexisting attitudes through discussions within the group.

groupthink the mode of thinking that occurs when the desire for harmony in a decision-making group overrides a realistic appraisal of alternatives.

LOQ 11-8 What role does the Internet play in group polarization?

Thinking Critically About:
The Internet as Social Amplifier

The Internet connects like-minded people and strengthens their ideas.

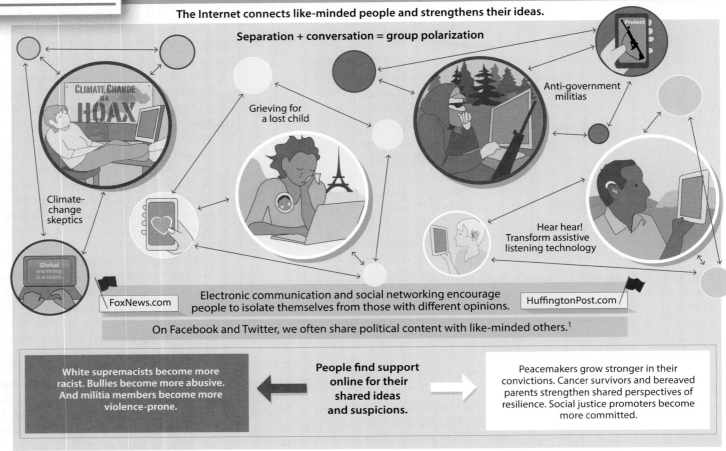

Separation + conversation = group polarization

Climate-change skeptics

Grieving for a lost child

Anti-government militias

Hear hear! Transform assistive listening technology

FoxNews.com — Electronic communication and social networking encourage people to isolate themselves from those with different opinions. — HuffingtonPost.com

On Facebook and Twitter, we often share political content with like-minded others.[1]

White supremacists become more racist. Bullies become more abusive. And militia members become more violence-prone.

People find support online for their shared ideas and suspicions.

Peacemakers grow stronger in their convictions. Cancer survivors and bereaved parents strengthen shared perspectives of resilience. Social justice promoters become more committed.

1. Bakshy et al., 2015; Barberá et. al., 2015.

---

polarization—contributed to other fiascos as well. Among them were the failure to anticipate the 1941 Japanese attack on Pearl Harbor; the escalation of the Vietnam war; the U.S. Watergate cover-up; the Chernobyl nuclear reactor accident (Reason, 1987); the U.S. space shuttle *Challenger* explosion (Esser & Lindoerfer, 1989); and the Iraq war, launched on the false idea that Iraq had weapons of mass destruction (U.S. Senate Select Committee on Intelligence, 2004).

How can we prevent groupthink? Leaders can welcome open debate, invite experts' critiques of developing plans, and assign people to identify possible problems.

The point to remember: Two heads are often better than one, especially when we encourage independent thinking and open debate.

Retrieve + Remember

- What is social facilitation, and under what circumstances is it most likely to occur?

  ANSWER: This improved performance in the presence of others is most likely to occur with a well-learned task, because the added arousal caused by an audience tends to strengthen the most likely response.

- People tend to exert less effort when working with a group than they would alone, which is called _____ _____.

  ANSWER: social loafing

- You are organizing a meeting of fiercely competitive political candidates and their supporters. To add to the fun, friends have suggested handing out masks of the candidates' faces for supporters to wear. What effect might these masks trigger?

  ANSWER: The anonymity provided by the masks, combined with the arousal of the competitive setting, might create *deindividuation* (lessened self-awareness and self-restraint).

- When like-minded groups discuss a topic, the existing opinions often grow stronger. This tendency is called _____ _____.

  ANSWER: group polarization

- When a group's desire for harmony overrides its realistic analysis of other options, _____ has occurred.

  ANSWER: groupthink

Social Relations

We have sampled how we *think about* and *influence* one another. Now we come to social psychology's third focus—how we *relate* to one another. What are the roots of prejudice? What causes us to harm or to help or to fall in love? How can we transform the closed fists of aggression into the open arms of compassion? We will ponder the bad and the good: from prejudice and aggression to attraction, altruism, and peacemaking.

Prejudice

LOQ 11-10 What are the three parts of prejudice, and how has prejudice changed over time?

Prejudice means "prejudgment." It is an unfair negative attitude toward some group. The target of the prejudice is often a different cultural, ethnic, or gender group.

Prejudice is a three-part mixture of

- *beliefs* (called **stereotypes**).
- *emotions* (for example, hostility, envy, or fear).
- *predispositions* to action (to discriminate).

> "Unhappily the world has yet to learn how to live with diversity."
>
> Pope John Paul II, Address to the United Nations, 1995

Some stereotypes may be at least partly accurate. If you presume that obese individuals usually have more health issues than healthy-weight individuals, you may be right. But to *believe* that obese people are gluttonous, and to *feel* dislike for an obese person is to be *prejudiced*; prejudice is a negative *attitude*. To ignore all the obese people on a dating site, or to reject an obese person as a potential job candidate, is to *discriminate*; **discrimination** is a negative *behavior*.

Our ideas influence what we notice and how we interpret events. In one classic 1970s study, most White participants who saw a White man shoving a Black

HOME-GROWN TERRORISM In the 14 years following the terror of September 11, 2001, many Americans feared attacks from foreign terrorists. Yet since that time, attacks by homegrown White supremacists and other non-Muslim extremists were nearly twice as likely (Shane, 2015)—as when a neo-Nazi slaughtered six people in a 2012 shooting at a Wisconsin Sikh temple.

man said they were "horsing around." When they saw a Black man shoving a White man, they interpreted the same act as "violent" (Duncan, 1976). The ideas we bring to a situation can color our perceptions.

How Prejudiced Are People?

Again and again throughout this book, we have seen that the human mind processes thoughts, memories, and attitudes on two different tracks. Sometimes that processing is *explicit*—on the radar screen of our awareness. More often, it is *implicit*—below the radar, out of sight. Prejudice involves both explicit and implicit negative attitudes toward people of a particular ethnic group, gender, sexual orientation, or viewpoint. Some examples:

EXPLICIT ETHNIC PREJUDICE To assess prejudice, we can observe what people say and what they do. Americans' expressed racial attitudes have changed dramatically in the last half-century. "It's all right for Blacks and Whites to date each other," agreed 48 percent of Americans in 1987 and 86 percent in 2012 (Pew, 2012). "Marriage between Blacks and Whites" was approved by 4 percent of Americans in 1958 and 87 percent in 2013 (Newport, 2013a).

Yet as *open* prejudice wanes, *subtle* prejudice lingers. Despite increased verbal support for interracial marriage, many people admit that in socially intimate settings (dating, dancing, marrying) they would feel uncomfortable with someone of another race. Subtle prejudice may also take the form of "micro-aggressions," such as race-related traffic stops or people's reluctance to choose a train seat next to someone of a different race (Wang et al., 2011b).

IMPLICIT ETHNIC PREJUDICE Prejudice can be not only subtle but also implicit, an automatic attitude that is more of an unthinking knee-jerk response than a decision. Consider these findings.

Implicit racial associations Even people who deny harboring racial prejudice may carry negative associations (Fisher & Borgida, 2012; Greenwald et al., 1998, 2015). For example, 9 in 10 White respondents took longer to identify pleasant words (such as *peace* and *paradise*) as "good" when the words were paired with Black-sounding names (such as *Latisha* and *Darnell*) rather than White-sounding names (such as *Katie* and *Ian*). Such tests are useful for studying automatic prejudice. But critics caution against using them to assess or label individuals as prejudiced (Oswald et al., 2015).

Race-influenced perceptions Our expectations influence our perceptions. Consider the 1998 shooting of an unarmed man, Amadou Diallo, in the doorway of his Bronx apartment building. The officers thought he had pulled a gun from his pocket. In fact, he had pulled out his wallet. Curious about this

---

prejudice an unfair and usually negative attitude toward a group and its members. Prejudice generally involves stereotyped beliefs, negative feelings, and a predisposition to discriminatory action.

stereotype a generalized (sometimes accurate but often overgeneralized) belief about a group of people.

discrimination unjustifiable negative behavior toward a group and its members.

tragic killing of an innocent man, several research teams created a similar situation (Correll et al., 2007, 2015; Greenwald et al., 2003; Plant & Peruche, 2005; Sadler et al., 2012a). They asked viewers to press buttons quickly to "shoot" or not shoot men who suddenly appeared on screen. Some of the on-screen men held a gun. Others held a harmless object, such as a flashlight or bottle. People (including both Blacks and Whites, and police officers) more often shot Black men holding the harmless object (**FIGURE 11.5**).

In a 2015 housing discrimination case, the U.S. Supreme Court recognized implicit bias research. They noted that "unconscious prejudices" can cause discrimination even when people do not consciously intend to discriminate. Are you sometimes aware that you have feelings you would rather not have about other people? If so, remember this: It is what we do with our feelings that matters. By monitoring our feelings and actions, and by replacing old habits with new ones based on new friendships, we can free ourselves of prejudice.

GENDER PREJUDICE Gender prejudice and discrimination persist, too. Despite gender equality in intelligence scores, people have tended to perceive their fathers as more intelligent than their mothers (Furnham & Wu, 2008). We pay more to those (usually men) who care for our streets than to those (usually women) who care for our children. Worldwide, women have been more likely to live in

HAVE RACE-INFLUENCED PERCEPTIONS ENABLED THE KILLINGS OF UNARMED BLACK MEN? Does automatic racial bias research help us understand the 2013 death of Trayvon Martin (shown here 7 months before he was killed)? As he walked alone to his father's fiancée's house in a gated Florida neighborhood, a suspicious resident started following him, leading to a confrontation and to Martin's being shot dead. Commentators wondered: Had Martin been an unarmed White teen, would he have been perceived and treated the same way?

poverty (Lipps, 1999). And among adults who cannot read, two-thirds are women (CIA, 2010).

Unwanted female infants are no longer left on a hillside to die of exposure, as was the practice in ancient Greece. Yet the normal male-to-female newborn ratio (105 to 100) hardly explains the world's estimated 163 million (say that number slowly) "missing women" (Hvistendahl, 2011). In many places, sons are valued more than daughters. There are 32 million more under-age-20 males than females in China, for example, so many bachelors will be unable to find mates (Zhu et al., 2009). A shortage of women also contributes to increased crime, violence, prostitution, and trafficking of women (Brooks, 2012).

SEXUAL ORIENTATION PREJUDICE In many places in the world, gays and lesbians cannot comfortably acknowledge who they are and whom they love (Katz-Wise & Hyde, 2012; United Nations, 2011). Dozens of countries have laws criminalizing same-sex relationships. Anti-gay prejudice, though rapidly declining in Western countries, persists. In national surveys, 39 percent of LGBT Americans reported having "been rejected by a friend or family member" because of their sexual orientation or gender identity. And 58 percent reported being "subject to slurs or jokes" (Pew, 2013). Worldwide, anti-gay attitudes are most common among men, older adults, and those less educated (Jäckle & Wenzelburger, 2015). When experimenters have sent thousands of resumés in response to employment ads, those whose past activities included "Treasurer, Progressive and Socialist Alliance" received more replies than those who had been "Treasurer, Gay and Lesbian Alliance" (Agerström et al., 2012; Bertrand & Mullainathan, 2003; Drydakis, 2009).

Social Roots of Prejudice

LOQ 11-11 What factors contribute to the social roots of prejudice, and how does scapegoating illustrate the emotional roots of prejudice?

Why does prejudice arise? Social inequalities and social divisions are partly responsible.

SOCIAL INEQUALITIES Some people have money, power, and prestige. Others do not. In this situation, the "haves" usually develop attitudes that justify things as they are. The **just-world phenomenon** assumes that good is rewarded and evil is punished. From this it is but a short

1. 2. 3.

FIGURE 11.5 Race primes perceptions In experiments by Keith Payne (2006), people viewed (1) a White or Black face, immediately followed by (2) a gun or hand tool, which was then followed by (3) a visual mask. Participants were more likely to misperceive a tool as a gun when it was preceded by a Black rather than White face.

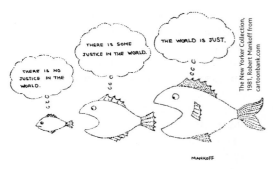

The New Yorker Collection, 1981, Robert Mankoff from cartoonbank.com

leap to assume that those who succeed must be good and those who suffer must be bad. Such reasoning enables the rich to see both their own wealth and the misfortune of the poor as justly deserved. When slavery existed in the United States, slaveholders developed attitudes that they used to "justify" slavery. They stereotyped the people they enslaved as naturally lazy, ignorant, and irresponsible. Stereotypes rationalize inequalities.

Victims of discrimination may react in ways that feed prejudice through the classic *blame-the-victim* dynamic (Allport, 1954). Do the circumstances of poverty breed a higher crime rate? If so, that higher crime rate can be used to justify discrimination against those who live in poverty.

US AND THEM: INGROUP AND OUTGROUP We have inherited our Stone Age ancestors' need to belong— to live and love in groups. We cheer for our groups, kill for them, die for them. Indeed, we define who we are partly in terms of our groups. Through our *social identities* we associate ourselves with certain groups and contrast ourselves with others (Dunham et al., 2013; Hogg, 2006; Turner, 2007). When Marc identifies himself as a man, an American, a political Independent, a Hudson Community College student, a Catholic, and a part-time letter carrier, he knows who he is, and so do we.

Evolution prepared us, when meeting strangers, to make instant judgments: friend or foe? Those from our group, those who look like us, and also those who *sound* like us—with accents like our own—we instantly tend to like, from childhood onward (Gluszek & Dovidio, 2010;

Kinzler et al., 2009). Mentally drawing a circle defines "us," the **ingroup**. But the social definition of who we are also states who we are not. People outside that circle are "them," the **outgroup**. An **ingroup bias**— a favoring of our own group—soon follows. Even forming us-them groups by tossing a coin creates this bias. In experiments, people have favored their own new group when dividing any rewards (Tajfel, 1982; Wilder, 1981). Discrimination often involves ingroup networking and mutual support—such as hiring a friend's child instead of a possibly more qualified candidate (Greenwald & Pettigrew, 2014). Less often, people discriminate because of outgroup hostility.

> "All good people agree,
> And all good people say
> All nice people, like Us, are We
> And everyone else is They."
> Rudyard Kipling, "We and They," 1926

Ingroup bias explains why active supporters of political parties may see what they expect to see (Cooper, 2010; Douthat, 2010). In the United States in the late 1980s, most Democrats believed inflation had risen under Republican president Ronald Reagan. (They were wrong: It had dropped.) In 2010, most Republicans believed that taxes had increased under Democratic president Barack Obama. (They were wrong: For most people, they had decreased.)

Emotional Roots of Prejudice

Prejudice springs not only from the divisions of society but also from the passions of the heart. **Scapegoat theory** proposes that when things go wrong, finding someone to blame can provide an outlet for anger. Following the 9/11 terrorist attacks, negative stereotypes blossomed. Some outraged people lashed out at innocent Arab-Americans. Others called for eliminating Saddam Hussein, the Iraqi leader whom Americans had been grudgingly tolerating but who had no role in the attacks. "Fear and anger create aggression, and aggression against citizens of different

ethnicity or race creates racism and, in turn, new forms of terrorism," noted Philip Zimbardo (2001).

Evidence for the scapegoat theory of prejudice comes from two sources:

- Prejudice levels tend to be high among economically frustrated people.
- In experiments, a temporary frustration increases prejudice. Students made to feel temporarily insecure have often restored their self-esteem by speaking badly of a rival school or another person (Cialdini & Richardson, 1980; Crocker et al., 1987). Those made to feel loved and supported have become more open to and accepting of others who differ (Mikulincer & Shaver, 2001).

Negative emotions nourish prejudice. When facing death, fearing threats, or experiencing frustration, we cling more tightly to our ingroup and our friends. The terror of death heightens patriotism. It also produces anger and aggression toward "them"—those who threaten our world (Pyszczynski et al., 2002, 2008).

Cognitive Roots of Prejudice

LOQ 11-12 What are the cognitive roots of prejudice?

Prejudice springs from a culture's divisions, the heart's passions, and also from the mind's natural workings. Stereotyped beliefs are a by-product of how we cognitively simplify the world.

---

just-world phenomenon the tendency to believe that the world is just and people therefore get what they deserve and deserve what they get.

ingroup "us"—people with whom we share a common identity.

outgroup "them"—those perceived as different or apart from our group.

ingroup bias the tendency to favor our own group.

scapegoat theory the theory that prejudice offers an outlet for anger by providing someone to blame.

FORMING CATEGORIES One way we simplify our world is to sort things into categories. A chemist sorts molecules into categories of "organic" and "inorganic." Therapists categorize psychological disorders. All of us categorize people by race, with mixed-race people often assigned to their minority identity. Despite his mixed-race background and being raised by a White mother and White grandparents, President Barack Obama has been perceived by White Americans as Black. Researchers believe this happens because, after learning the features of a familiar racial group, the observer's selective attention is drawn to the distinctive features of the less-familiar minority. In one study, New Zealanders viewed images of blended Chinese-Caucasian faces (Halberstadt et al., 2011). Some participants were of European descent; others were of Chinese descent. Those of European descent more readily classified ambiguous faces as Chinese (see **FIGURE 11.6**).

When we categorize people into groups, we often overestimate their similarities. "They"—the members of that other social or ethnic group—seem to look alike (Rhodes & Anastasi, 2012; Young et al., 2012). In personality and attitudes, too, they seem more alike than they really are, while "we" differ from one another (Bothwell et al., 1989). This greater recognition for own-race faces is called the **other-race effect** (also called the *cross-race effect* or *own-race bias*). It emerges during infancy, between 3 and 9 months of age (Anzures et al., 2013; Telzer et al., 2013).

Dave Coverly/Speed Bump

REMEMBERING VIVID CASES Cognitive psychologists tell us that we often judge the likelihood of events by recalling vivid cases that readily come to mind. In a classic experiment, researchers showed two groups of student volunteers lists containing information about 50 men (Rothbart et al., 1978). The first group's list included 10 men arrested for *nonviolent* crimes, such as forgery. The second group's list included 10 men arrested for *violent* crimes, such as assault. Later, both groups were asked how many men on their list had committed *any* sort of crime. The second group overestimated the number. Vivid—in this case violent—cases are readily available to our memory and feed our stereotypes (**FIGURE 11.7**).

BELIEVING THE WORLD IS JUST As noted earlier, people often justify their prejudices by blaming the victims. If the

world is just, they assume, people must get what they deserve. As one German civilian is said to have remarked when visiting the Bergen-Belsen concentration camp shortly after World War II, "What terrible criminals these prisoners must have been to receive such treatment."

People have a basic tendency to justify their culture's social systems (Jost et al., 2009; Kay et al., 2009). We're inclined to see the way things are as the way they ought to be. This natural conservatism makes it difficult to legislate major social changes, such as civil rights laws or Social Security or health care reform. But once such policies are in place, our "system justification" tends to preserve them.

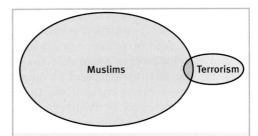

FIGURE 11.7 Vivid cases feed stereotypes The 9/11 Muslim terrorists created, in many minds, an exaggerated stereotype of Muslims as terrorism-prone. Actually, reported a U.S. National Research Council panel on terrorism, when offering this inexact illustration, most terrorists are not Muslim and "the vast majority of Islamic people have no connection with and do not sympathize with terrorism" (Smelser & Mitchell, 2002).

Dr. Jamin Halberstadt

| 100% Chinese | 80% Chinese 20% Caucasian | 60% Chinese 40% Caucasian | 40% Chinese 60% Caucasian | 20% Chinese 80% Caucasian | 100% Caucasian |

FIGURE 11.6 Categorizing mixed-race people When New Zealanders quickly classified 104 photos by race, those of European descent more often than those of Chinese descent classified the ambiguous middle two as Chinese (Halberstadt et al., 2011).

LaunchPad To review attribution research and experience a simulation of how stereotypes form, visit LaunchPad's *PsychSim 6: Not My Type*. And for a 6.5-minute synopsis of the cognitive and social psychology of prejudice, visit LaunchPad's *Video: Prejudice*.

Aggression

The most destructive force in our social relations is aggression. In psychology, **aggression** is any verbal or physical behavior intended to harm someone, whether it is passing along a vicious rumor or engaging in a physical attack.

Aggressive behavior emerges when biology interacts with experience. For a gun to fire, the trigger must be pulled. With some people, as with hair-trigger guns, it doesn't take much to trip an explosion. Let's look first at some biological factors that influence our thresholds for aggressive behavior. Then we'll turn to the psychological and social-cultural factors that pull the trigger.

The Biology of Aggression

LOQ 11-13 What biological factors predispose us to be aggressive?

Is aggression an unlearned instinct? The wide variation from culture to culture, era to era, and person to person argues against that idea. But biology does *influence* aggression at three levels—genetic, biochemical, and neural.

GENETIC INFLUENCES Genes influence aggression. We know this because animals have been bred for aggressiveness—sometimes for sport, sometimes for research. The effect of genes also

DO GUNS IN THE HOME SAVE OR TAKE MORE LIVES? In the last 40 years in the United States, well over 1 million people—more than all deaths in all wars in American history—have been killed by firearms in nonwar settings. Compared with people of the same sex, race, age, and neighborhood, those who keep a gun in the home (ironically, often for protection) have been twice as likely to be murdered and three times as likely to commit suicide (Anglemyer et al., 2014; Stroebe, 2013). States and countries with high gun ownership rates also tend to have high gun death rates (VPC, 2013).

appears in human *twin studies* (Kendler et al., 2015; Miles & Carey, 1997). If one identical twin admits to "having a violent temper," the other twin will often independently admit the same. Fraternal twins are much less likely to respond similarly. Researchers continue to search for genetic markers, or predictors, in those who commit the most violence (Ficks & Waldman, 2014). One is already well known and is carried by half the human race: the Y chromosome.

LaunchPad See LaunchPad's *Video: Twin Studies* for a helpful tutorial animation.

BIOCHEMICAL INFLUENCES Our genes engineer our individual nervous systems, which operate electrochemically. The hormone testosterone, for example, circulates in the bloodstream and influences the neural systems that control aggression. A raging bull becomes a gentle giant when castration reduces its testosterone level. And when injected with

testosterone, gentle, castrated mice once again become aggressive.

In humans, high testosterone is associated with irritability, assertiveness, impulsiveness, and low tolerance for frustration. These qualities make people somewhat more prone to aggressive responses when provoked or when competing for status (Dabbs et al., 2001; McAndrew, 2009; Montoya et al., 2012). Among both teenage boys and adult men, high testosterone levels have been linked with delinquency, hard drug use, and *aggressive-bullying* responses to frustration (Berman et al., 1993; Dabbs & Morris, 1990; Olweus et al., 1988). Drugs that sharply reduce testosterone levels subdue men's aggressive tendencies. As men age, their testosterone levels—and their aggressiveness—diminish. Hormonally charged, aggressive 17-year-olds mature into hormonally quieter and gentler 70-year-olds.

A LEAN, MEAN FIGHTING MACHINE—THE TESTOSTERONE-LADEN FEMALE HYENA The hyena's unusual embryology pumps testosterone into female fetuses. The result is revved-up young female hyenas who seem born to fight.

Another drug that sometimes circulates in the bloodstream—alcohol—also unleashes aggressive responses to frustration. Aggression-prone people are more likely to drink, and when intoxicated they are more likely to become violent (White et al., 1993). National crime data indicate that 73 percent of Russian homicides and 57 percent of U.S. homicides are alcohol-influenced (Landberg & Norström, 2011). Alcohol's effects are both biological and psychological. Just *thinking* you've been drinking alcohol can increase aggression (Bègue et al., 2009). But so, too, does unknowingly drinking an alcohol-laced beverage.

NEURAL INFLUENCES There is no one spot in the brain that controls aggression. Aggression is a complex behavior, and it occurs in particular contexts. But animal and human brains have neural systems that, given provocation, will either inhibit or facilitate aggression (Dambacher et al., 2015; Denson, 2011; Moyer, 1983). Consider:

- Researchers implanted a radio-controlled electrode in the brain of the domineering leader of a caged monkey colony. The electrode was in an area that, when stimulated, inhibits aggression. When researchers placed the control button for the electrode in the colony's

The New Yorker Collection, 1995, D. Reilly from cartoonbank.com

"It's a guy thing."

cage, one small monkey learned to push it every time the boss became threatening.

- A neurosurgeon implanted an electrode in the brain of a mild-mannered woman to diagnose a disorder. The electrode was in her amygdala, within her limbic system. Because the brain has no sensory receptors, she did not feel the stimulation. But at the flick of a switch, she snarled, "Take my blood pressure. Take it now," then stood up and began to strike the doctor.

- Studies of violent criminals have revealed diminished activity in the frontal lobes, which help control impulses. If the frontal lobes are damaged, inactive, disconnected, or not yet fully mature, aggression may be more likely (Amen et al., 1996; Davidson et al., 2000; Raine, 2013).

Psychological and Social-Cultural Influences on Aggression

LOQ 11-14 What psychological and social-cultural factors may trigger aggressive behavior?

Biological factors influence how easily aggression is triggered. But what psychological and social-cultural factors spark aggression?

AVERSIVE EVENTS Suffering sometimes builds character. In laboratory experiments, however, those made miserable have often made others miserable (Berkowitz, 1983, 1989). This reaction is called the **frustration-aggression principle.** Frustration creates anger, which can spark aggression. One Major League Baseball analysis of 27,667 hit-by-pitch incidents between 1960 and 2004 revealed this link (Timmerman, 2007). Pitchers were most likely to hit batters when

- they had been frustrated by the previous batter hitting a home run.

- the current batter hit a home run the last time at bat.

- a teammate of the pitcher had been hit by a pitch in the previous half-inning.

Other aversive stimuli—including hot temperatures, physical pain, personal insults, foul odors, cigarette smoke, and crowding—can also trigger anger. When people get overheated, they think, feel, and act more aggressively. In baseball games, the number of hit batters rises with the temperature (Reifman et al., 1991; see **FIGURE 11.8**). And in the wider world, many studies have found that throughout history, higher temperatures have predicted increased violent crime, spousal abuse, wars, and revolutions (Anderson et al., 1997; Hsiang et al., 2013). One projection, based on the available data, estimates that global warming of 4 degrees Fahrenheit (about 2 degrees Celsius) could induce tens of thousands of additional assaults and murders (Anderson et al., 2000; Anderson & Delisi, 2011). And that's before the added violence inducement from climate-change–related drought, poverty, food insecurity, and migration.

LaunchPad How have researchers studied these concepts? Learn more at LaunchPad's *Immersive Learning: How Would You Know If Hot Temperatures Cause Aggression?*

REINFORCEMENT AND MODELING Aggression may naturally follow aversive events, but learning can alter natural reactions. As Chapter 6 points out, we learn when our behavior is reinforced, and we learn by watching others. Children whose aggression successfully intimidates other children may become bullies. Animals that have successfully fought to get food or mates become increasingly ferocious. To foster a kinder, gentler world, we had best model and reward sensitivity and cooperation from an early age, perhaps by training parents to discipline without modeling violence.

Parent-training programs often advise parents to avoid modeling violence by not screaming and hitting

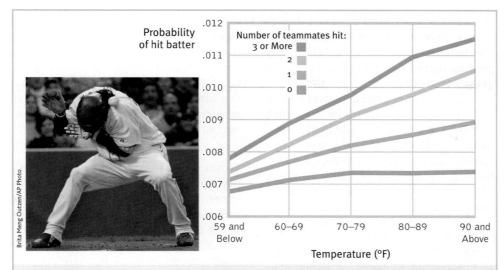

FIGURE 11.8 Temperature and retaliation Richard Larrick and his colleagues (2011) looked for occurrences of batters hit by pitchers during 4,566,468 pitcher-batter matchups across 57,293 Major League Baseball games since 1952. The probability of a hit batter increased if one or more of the pitcher's teammates had been hit, and also with temperature.

when frustrated by their children's bad behavior. Instead, parents should reinforce desirable behaviors and frame statements positively. ("When you finish loading the dishwasher, you can go play," rather than "If you don't load the dishwasher, there'll be no playing.")

"Why do we kill people who kill people to show that killing people is wrong?"
National Coalition to Abolish the Death Penalty, 1992

Different cultures model, reinforce, and evoke different tendencies toward violence. Some cultures encourage people to fight to defend their honor (Nowak et al., 2016). Crime rates have also been higher (and happiness lower) in times and places marked by a great income gap between rich and poor (Messias et al., 2011; Oishi et al., 2011; Wilkinson & Pickett, 2009). And high rates of violence and youth imprisonment have been found in cultures and families with minimal or no father care (Harper & McLanahan, 2004; Triandis, 1994).

MEDIA MODELS FOR VIOLENCE
Parents are not the only aggression models. In the United States and elsewhere, TV shows, films, video games, and the Internet offer supersized portions of violence. Repeatedly viewing on-screen

violence tends to make us less sensitive to cruelty (Montag et al., 2012). It also primes us to respond aggressively when provoked. And it teaches us **social scripts**—culturally provided mental files for how to act. When we find ourselves in new situations, uncertain how to behave, we rely on social scripts. After watching so many action films, adolescent boys may acquire a script that plays in their head when they face real-life conflicts. Challenged, they may "act like a man" by intimidating or eliminating the threat. More than 100 studies together confirm that people sometimes imitate what they've viewed. Watching risk-glorifying behaviors (dangerous driving, extreme sports, unprotected sex) increases viewers' real-life risk-taking (Fischer et al., 2011).

Music lyrics also write social scripts. In experiments, German university men who listened to woman-hating song lyrics administered the most hot chili sauce to a woman. Man-hating song lyrics had a similar effect on the aggressive behavior of women listeners (Fischer & Greitemeyer, 2006).

Sexual scripts in pornographic films can also be toxic. Repeatedly watching pornography makes sexual aggression

seem less serious (Harris, 1994). In one experiment, undergraduates viewed six brief, sexually explicit films each week for six weeks (Zillmann & Bryant, 1984). A control group viewed films with no sexual content during the same six-week period. Three weeks later, both groups read a newspaper report about a man convicted of raping a hitchhiker and were asked to suggest an appropriate prison term. Participants who viewed the sexually explicit films recommended sentences only half as long as those recommended by the control group.

While nonviolent sexual content affects aggression-related sexual attitudes, violent sexual content can increase men's readiness to actually behave aggressively toward women. A statement by 21 social scientists noted, "Pornography that portrays sexual aggression as pleasurable for the victim increases the acceptance of the use of coercion in sexual relations" (Surgeon General, 1986). Contrary to much popular opinion, viewing such scenes does not provide an outlet for bottled-up impulses. Rather, "in laboratory studies measuring short-term effects, exposure to violent pornography increases punitive behavior toward women."

To a lesser extent, nonviolent pornography can also influence aggression. One set of studies explored pornography's effects on aggression toward relationship partners. The result? Pornography consumption predicted both self-reported aggression and participants' willingness to deliver laboratory noise blasts to their partner (Lambert et al., 2011). Abstaining from customary pornography consumption decreased aggression. Abstaining from a favorite food did not.

frustration-aggression principle the principle that frustration—the blocking of an attempt to achieve some goal—creates anger, which can generate aggression.

social script a culturally modeled guide for how to act in various situations.

DO VIOLENT VIDEO GAMES TEACH SOCIAL SCRIPTS FOR VIOLENCE?

Experiments in North America, Western Europe, Singapore, and Japan indicate that playing positive games produces positive effects (Greitemeyer & Osswald, 2010, 2011; Prot et al., 2014). For example, playing *Lemmings*, where a goal is to help others, increases real-life helping. So, might a parallel effect occur after playing games that enact violence? Violent video games became an issue for public debate after teenagers in more than a dozen places seemed to mimic the carnage in the shooter games they had so often played (Anderson, 2004, 2013).

In 2002, three young men in Michigan spent part of a night drinking beer and playing *Grand Theft Auto III*. Using simulated cars, they ran down pedestrians, then beat them with fists, leaving a bloody body behind (Kolker, 2002). These young men then went out for a real drive. Spotting a 38-year-old man on a bicycle, they ran him down with their car, got out, stomped and punched him, and returned home to play the game some more. (The victim, a father of three, died six days later.)

Such violent mimicry causes some to wonder: What are the effects of actively role-playing aggression? Does it cause young people to become less sensitive to violence and more open to violent acts? Nearly 400 studies of 130,000 people offer an answer (Anderson et al., 2010a). Video games can prime aggressive thoughts, decrease empathy, and increase aggression. Adolescents and university students who spend the most hours playing violent video games have also tended to be the most physically aggressive (Anderson & Dill, 2000; Exelmans et al., 2015). (For example, they more often acknowledged having hit or attacked someone else.) And people randomly assigned to play a game involving bloody murders with groaning victims (rather than to play nonviolent *Myst*) became more hostile. On a follow-up task, they also were more likely to blast intense noise at a fellow student. Studies of young adolescents reveal that those who play a lot

of violent video games see the world as more hostile (Gentile, 2009; Hasan et al., 2013). Compared with nongaming kids, they get into more arguments and fights and get worse grades.

Ah, but is this merely because naturally hostile kids are drawn to such games? Apparently not. Comparisons of gamers and nongamers who scored low on hostility measures revealed a difference in the number of fights reported. Almost 4 in 10 violent-game players had been in fights. Only 4 in 100 of the nongaming kids reported fights (Anderson, 2004). Some researchers believe that, due partly to the more active participation and rewarded violence of game play, violent video games have even greater effects on aggressive behavior and cognition than do violent TV shows and movies (Anderson & Warburton, 2012).

Other researchers are unimpressed by such findings (Ferguson, 2014, 2015). They note that from 1996 to 2006, youth

Andrew Berwick via www.freak.no/Reuters/Landov

COINCIDENCE OR CAUSE? In 2011, Norwegian Anders Behring Breivik bombed government buildings in Oslo, and then went to a youth camp where he shot and killed 69 people, mostly teens. As a player of first-person shooter games, Breivik stirred debate when he commented that "I see MW2 *[Modern Warfare 2]* more as a part of my training-simulation than anything else." Did his violent game playing—and that of the 2012 mass murderer of Newtown, Connecticut's first-grade children—contribute to the violence, or was it a merely coincidental association? To explore such questions, psychologists experiment.

violence declined while video game sales increased. They argue that other factors—depression, family violence, peer influence—better predict aggression. The focused fun of game playing can also satisfy basic needs for a sense of competence, control, and social connection (Granic et al., 2014).

* * *

To sum up, research reveals biological, psychological, and social-cultural influences on aggressive behavior. Complex behaviors, including violence, have many causes, making any single explanation an oversimplification. Asking what causes violence is therefore like asking what causes cancer. Aspects of our biology, our psychology, and our social environment interact. Like so much else, aggression is a biopsychosocial phenomenon.

A happy concluding note: Historical trends suggest that the world is becoming less violent over time (Pinker, 2011). That people vary over time and place reminds us that environments differ. Yesterday's plundering Vikings have become today's peace-promoting Scandinavians. Like all behavior, aggression arises from the interaction of persons and situations.

Retrieve + Remember

- What psychological, biological, and social-cultural influences interact to produce aggressive behaviors?

ANSWER: Our biology (our genes, biochemistry, and neural systems—including testosterone and alcohol levels) influences our tendencies to be aggressive. Psychological factors (such as frustration, previous rewards for aggressive acts, and observation of others' aggression) can trigger any aggressive tendencies we may have. Social influences, such as exposure to violent media and cultural factors, can also affect our aggressive responses.

Attraction

Pause a moment and think about your relationships with two people—a close friend, and someone who has stirred in you feelings of romantic love. These special sorts of attachments help us cope with all other relationships. What is the psychological chemistry that binds us together? Social psychology suggests some answers.

The Psychology of Attraction

LOQ 11-15 Why do we befriend or fall in love with some people but not others?

We endlessly wonder how we can win others' affection and what makes our own affections flourish or fade. Does familiarity breed contempt or affection? Do birds of a feather flock together, or do opposites attract? Is it what's inside that counts, or does physical attractiveness matter greatly? To explore these questions, let's consider three ingredients of our liking for one another: proximity, physical attractiveness, and similarity.

PROXIMITY Before friendships become close, they must begin. Proximity—geographic nearness—is friendship's most powerful predictor. Being near another person gives us opportunities for aggression, but much more often it breeds liking. Study after study reveals that people are most inclined to like, and even to marry, those who are nearby. We are drawn to those who live in the same neighborhood, sit nearby in class, work in the same office, share the same parking lot, eat in the same dining hall. Look around. Mating starts with meeting.

Proximity breeds liking partly because of the **mere exposure effect.** Repeated exposure to novel stimuli increases our liking for them. By age three months, infants prefer photos of the race they most often see—usually their own race (Kelly et al., 2007). Mere exposure increases our liking not only for familiar faces, but also for nonsense syllables, musical selections, geometric figures, Chinese characters, and the letters of our own name (Moreland & Zajonc, 1982; Nuttin, 1987; Zajonc, 2001). People are even somewhat more likely to marry someone whose first or last name resembles their own (Jones et al., 2004).

So, within certain limits, familiarity feeds fondness (Bornstein, 1989, 1999; Finkel et al., 2015b). Researchers demonstrated this by having four equally attractive women silently attend a 200-student class for zero, 5, 10, or 15 class sessions (Moreland & Beach, 1992). At the end of the course, students viewed slides of each woman and rated her attractiveness. The most attractive? The ones they'd seen most often. These ratings would come as no surprise to the young Taiwanese man who wrote more than 700 letters to his girlfriend, urging her to marry him. She did marry—the mail carrier (Steinberg, 1993).

MODERN MATCHMAKING If you have not found a romantic partner in your immediate proximity, why not cast a wider net? Each year, an estimated 30 million people search for love on one of the 1500 online dating sites (Ellin, 2009). Online matchmaking seems to work mostly by expanding the pool of potential mates (Finkel et al., 2012a,b).

How effective are Internet matchmaking services? Compared with those formed in person, Internet-formed marriages are, on average, happier and less prone to separation or divorce (Cacioppo et al., 2013). Small wonder that one survey found a leading online matchmaker enabling more than 500 U.S. marriages a day (Harris Interactive, 2010). By one estimate, online dating now is responsible for about a fifth of U.S. marriages (Crosier et al., 2012).

Dating sites collect trait information, but that accounts for only a thin slice of what makes for successful long-term relationships. What matters more, say researchers, is what emerges only after two people get to know each other, such as how they communicate and resolve disagreements (Finkel et al., 2012a,b).

WHICH IS THE REAL SOFÍA VERGARA? The mere exposure effect applies even to ourselves. Because the human face is not perfectly symmetrical, the face we see in the mirror is not the same face our friends see. Most of us prefer the familiar mirror image, while our friends like the reverse (Mita et al., 1977). The person actress Sofía Vergara sees in the mirror each morning is shown at right, and that's the photo she would probably prefer. We might feel more comfortable with the reverse image (left), the one we see.

mere exposure effect the phenomenon that repeated exposure to novel stimuli increases liking of them.

Skeptics are calling for controlled studies. To establish that online matchmaking actually works, experiments need to split people into two groups. The *experimental group* gets matched using a dating site's matchmaking formula. The *control group* gets matched using randomly sorted information. If the dating site's formula works, those in the experimental group—who get a taste of its special matchmaking sauce—will enjoy the happiest relationships.

Speed dating pushes the search for romance into high gear. In a process pioneered by a matchmaking Jewish rabbi, people meet a succession of would-be partners, either in person or via webcam (Bower, 2009). After a 3- to 8-minute conversation, people move on to the next person. (In an in-person heterosexual meeting, one group—usually the women—remains seated while the other group circulates.) Those who want to meet again can arrange for future contacts.

Researchers have quickly realized that speed dating offers a unique opportunity for studying influences on our first impressions of potential romantic partners. Among recent findings are these:

- *People who fear rejection often provoke rejection.* After a 3-minute speed date, those who most feared rejection were least often selected for a follow-up date (McClure & Lydon, 2014).

"I'd like to meet the algorithm that thought we'd be a good match."

William Haefeli/The New Yorker Collection/Condé Nast

When Neanderthals fall in love.

By permission of Leigh Rubin and Creators Syndicate, Inc.

- *Given more options, people make more superficial choices.* They focus on more easily assessed characteristics, such as height and weight (Lenton & Francesconi, 2010, 2012). This was true even when researchers controlled for time spent with each partner.

- *Men wish for future contact with more of their speed dates; women tend to be choosier.* This gender difference disappears if the conventional roles are reversed, so that men stay seated while women circulate (Finkel & Eastwick, 2009).

PHYSICAL ATTRACTIVENESS So proximity offers contact. What most affects our first impressions? The person's sincerity? Intelligence? Personality? The answer is physical appearance. This finding is unnerving for those of us taught that "beauty is only skin deep" and "appearances can be deceiving."

In one early study, researchers randomly matched new students for a Welcome Week dance (Walster et al., 1966). Before the dance, the researchers gave each student a battery of personality and aptitude tests, and they rated each student's physical attractiveness. During the blind date, the couples danced and talked for more than two hours and then took a brief break to rate their dates. What determined whether they liked each other? Only one thing seemed to matter: appearance. Both the men and the women liked good-looking dates best. Women are more likely than men to say that another's looks don't affect them (Jonason et al., 2015; Lippa, 2007). But studies show that a man's looks do affect women's behavior (Eastwick et al., 2014a,b). In speed-dating experiments as in Tinder swipes, attractiveness influences first impressions for both sexes (Belot & Francesconi, 2006; Finkel & Eastwick, 2008).

Physical attractiveness also predicts how often people date and how popular they feel. We perceive attractive people as healthier, happier, more sensitive, more successful, and more socially skilled (Eagly et al., 1991; Feingold, 1992; Hatfield & Sprecher, 1986). Attractive, well-dressed people often make a favorable impression on potential employers, and they have tended to experience more success in their jobs (Cash & Janda, 1984; Langlois et al., 2000; Solomon, 1987). There is a premium for beauty in the workplace, and a penalty for plainness or obesity (Engemann & Owyang, 2005).

For those of us who find the importance of looks unfair and short-sighted, three other findings may be reassuring:

- First, people's attractiveness seems surprisingly unrelated to their self-esteem and happiness (Diener et al., 1995; Major et al., 1984). Unless we have just compared ourselves with superattractive people, few of us (thanks, perhaps, to the mere exposure effect) view ourselves as unattractive (Thornton & Moore, 1993).

- Second, strikingly attractive people are sometimes suspicious that praise for their work is simply a reaction to their looks. Less attractive people have been more likely to accept praise as sincere (Berscheid, 1981).

Percentage of Men and Women Who "Constantly Think About Their Looks"

	Men	Women
Canada	18%	20%
United States	17	27
Mexico	40	45
Venezuela	47	65

From Roper Starch survey, reported by McCool (1999).

- Third, for couples who were friends before lovers—who became romantically involved long after first meeting—looks were less important (Hunt et al., 2015). With slow-cooked love, looks mattered less and common interests mattered more.

Beauty is also in the eye of the culture. Hoping to look attractive, people across the globe have pierced and tattooed their bodies, lengthened their necks, bound their feet, and artificially lightened or darkened their skin and hair. Cultural ideals also change over time. In the United States, the soft, voluptuous Marilyn Monroe ideal of the 1950s has been replaced by today's lean yet busty ideal.

Do any aspects of heterosexual attractiveness cross place and time? *Yes.* As we noted in Chapter 4, men in many cultures, from Australia to Zambia, judge women as more attractive if they have a youthful, fertile appearance, suggested by a low waist-to-hip ratio (Karremans et al., 2010; Perilloux et al., 2010; Platek & Singh, 2010). Women feel attracted to healthy-looking men, but especially—and the more so when ovulating—to those who seem mature, dominant, masculine, and wealthy (Gallup & Frederick, 2010; Gangestad et al., 2010). But faces matter, too. When people rate opposite-sex faces and bodies separately, the face tends to be the better predictor of overall physical attractiveness (Currie & Little, 2009; Peters et al., 2007).

 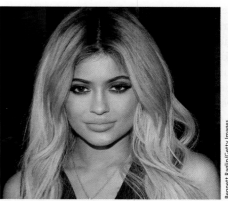

EXTREME MAKEOVER In affluent, beauty-conscious cultures, increasing numbers of people, such as reality TV star Kylie Jenner, have turned to cosmetic procedures to change their looks.

Our feelings also influence our attractiveness judgments. Imagine two people: One is honest, humorous, and polite. The other is rude, unfair, and abusive. Which one is more attractive? Most people perceive the person with the appealing traits as more attractive (Lewandowski et al., 2007). Or imagine being paired with an opposite-sex stranger who listened well to your self-disclosures (rather than seeming not tuned in to your thoughts and feelings). If you are heterosexual, might you feel a twinge of sexual attraction toward that person? Student volunteers did, in several experiments (Birnbaum & Reis, 2012). Our feelings influence our perceptions.

In a Rodgers and Hammerstein musical, Prince Charming asks Cinderella, "Do I love you because you're beautiful, or are you beautiful because I love you?" Chances are it's both. As we see our loved ones again and again, we notice their physical imperfections less, and their attractiveness grows more obvious (Beaman & Klentz, 1983; Gross & Crofton, 1977). Shakespeare said it in *A Midsummer Night's Dream*: "Love looks not with the eyes, but with the mind." Come to love someone and watch beauty grow.

SIMILARITY So you've met someone, and your appearance has made a decent first impression. What influences whether you will become friends? As you get to know each other, will the chemistry be better if you are opposites or if you are alike?

It makes a good story—extremely different types liking or loving each other: Frog and Toad in Arnold Lobel's books, Edward and Bella in the *Twilight* series. These stories delight us by expressing what we seldom experience. In real life, opposites retract (Montoya & Horton, 2013; Rosenbaum, 1986). Birds that flock together usually are of a feather. Compared with randomly paired people, friends and couples are far more likely to share attitudes, beliefs, and interests (and, for that matter, age, religion, race, education, intelligence, smoking behavior, and economic status). Journalist Walter Lippmann was right to suppose that love lasts "when the lovers love many things together, and not merely each other."

WHAT IS "ATTRACTIVE"? The answer varies by culture and over time. Yet some adult physical features, such as a healthy appearance and symmetrical face, seem attractive everywhere.

Proximity, attractiveness, and similarity are not the only forces that influence attraction. We also like those who like us. This is especially true when our self-image is low. When we believe someone likes us, we feel good and respond warmly. Our warm response in turn leads them to like us even more (Curtis & Miller, 1986). To be liked is powerfully rewarding.

Indeed, all the findings we have considered so far can be explained by a simple *reward theory of attraction*. We will like those whose behavior is rewarding to us, including those who are both able and willing to help us achieve our goals (Montoya & Horton, 2014). When people live or work in close proximity, it requires less time and effort to develop the friendship and enjoy its benefits. When people are attractive, they are aesthetically pleasing, and associating with them can be socially rewarding. When people share our views, they reward us by confirming our beliefs.

> ### Retrieve + Remember
> - People tend to marry someone who lives or works nearby. This is an example of proximity and the _____ _____ _____ in action.
>
>   ANSWER: mere exposure effect
> - How does being physically attractive influence others' perceptions?
>
>   ANSWER: Being physically attractive tends to elicit positive first impressions. People tend to assume that attractive people are healthier, happier, and more socially skilled than others are.

Romantic Love

LOQ 11-16 How does romantic love typically change as time passes?

Sometimes people move from first impressions, to friendship, to the more intense, complex, and mysterious state of romantic love. *Passionate love* mixes something new with something positive (Aron et al., 2000; Coulter & Malouff, 2013). We intensely desire to be with our partner

(Hatfield et al., 2015). When we see our partner, blood flows to a brain region linked to craving and obsession (Acevedo et al., 2012). But the intoxication of passionate love is often temporary. If love endures, *passionate love* will mellow into a lingering *companionate love* (Hatfield, 1988).

PASSIONATE LOVE A key ingredient of **passionate love** is arousal. The two-factor theory of emotion (Chapter 9) can help us understand this intense, positive state of feeling fully absorbed in another (Hatfield, 1988). That theory makes two assumptions:

- Emotions have two ingredients—physical arousal and cognitive appraisal.
- Arousal from any source can enhance an emotion, depending on how we interpret and label the arousal.

In one famous experiment, researchers studied people crossing two bridges above British Columbia's rocky Capilano River (Dutton & Aron, 1974, 1989). One, a swaying footbridge, was 230 feet above the rocks. The other was low and solid. The researchers had an attractive young woman stop men coming off each bridge and ask their help in filling out a short questionnaire. She then offered her phone number in case they wanted to hear more about her project. Which men accepted the number and later called the woman? Far more of those who had just crossed the high bridge—which left their hearts pounding. To experience a stirred-up state and to associate some of that feeling with a desirable person is to experience the pull of passion. Adrenaline makes the heart grow fonder. Sexual desire + a growing attachment = the passion of romantic love.

> "When two people are under the influence of the most violent, most insane, most delusive, and most transient of passions, they are required to swear that they will remain in that excited, abnormal, and exhausting condition continuously until death do them part."
>
> George Bernard Shaw, *Getting Married*, 1908

© Jason Love

Bill looked at Susan, Susan at Bill. Suddenly death didn't seem like an option. This was love at first sight.

COMPANIONATE LOVE Passionate romantic love seldom endures. The intense absorption in the other, the thrill of the romance, the giddy "floating on a cloud" feeling typically fade. Are the French correct in saying that "love makes the time pass and time makes love pass"? As love matures, it typically becomes a steadier **companionate love**—a deep, affectionate attachment (Hatfield, 1988). Like a passing storm, the flood of passion-feeding hormones (testosterone, dopamine, adrenaline) gives way. But another hormone, *oxytocin*, remains, supporting feelings of trust, calmness, and bonding with the mate. In the most satisfying of marriages, attraction and sexual desire endure, minus the obsession of early-stage romance (Acevedo & Aron, 2009).

There may be adaptive wisdom to this shift from passion to attachment (Reis & Aron, 2008). Passionate love often produces children, whose survival is aided by the parents' waning obsession with each other. Failure to appreciate passionate love's limited half-life can doom a relationship (Berscheid et al., 1984). Indeed, recognizing the short duration of passionate love, some societies judge such feelings to be a poor reason for marrying. Better, these cultures say, to choose (or have someone choose for you) a partner who shares your background and interests. Non-Western cultures, where people rate love less important for marriage, do have lower divorce rates (Levine et al., 1995). Do you think you could be happy in a marriage someone else arranged for you, by matching you with someone who shared your interests and traits? Many people in many cultures around the world live seemingly happy lives in such marriages.

One key to a satisfying and enduring relationship is **equity,** as both partners receive in proportion to what they give (Gray-Little & Burks, 1983; Van Yperen & Buunk, 1990). In one national survey, "sharing household chores" ranked third, after "faithfulness" and a "happy sexual relationship," on a list of nine things Americans associated with successful marriages. "I like hugs. I like kisses. But what I really love is help with the dishes," summarized the Pew Research Center (2007).

Equity's importance extends beyond marriage. Mutually sharing one's self and possessions, making decisions together, giving and getting emotional support, promoting and caring about each other's welfare—all these acts are at the core of every type of loving relationship (Sternberg & Grajek, 1984). It's true for lovers, for parent and child, and for close friends.

Another vital ingredient of loving relationships is **self-disclosure,** revealing

HI & LOIS

intimate details about ourselves—our likes and dislikes, our dreams and worries, our proud and shameful moments. As one person reveals a little, the other returns the gift. The first then reveals more, and on and on, as friends or lovers move to deeper intimacy (Baumeister & Bratslavsky, 1999).

One study marched pairs of students through 45 minutes of increasingly self-disclosing conversation—from "When did you last sing to yourself?" to "When did you last cry in front of another person? By yourself?" Others spent the time with small-talk questions, such as "What was your high school like?" (Aron et al., 1997). By the experiment's end, those experiencing the escalating intimacy felt remarkably close to their conversation partner, much closer than did the small-talkers.

In the mathematics of love, self-disclosing intimacy + mutually supportive equality = enduring companionate love.

Altruism

LOQ 11-17 What is altruism? When are we most—and least—likely to help?

Altruism is an unselfish concern for the welfare of others, such as Dirk Willems displayed when he rescued his jailer. Heroes are moral, courageous, and protective of those in need (Kinsella et al., 2015). Consider the heroic example of altruism that took place in a New York City subway station. Construction worker Wesley Autrey and his 6- and 4-year-old daughters were waiting for their train when they saw a nearby man collapse in a convulsion. The man then got up, stumbled to the platform's edge, and fell onto the tracks. With train headlights approaching, Autrey later recalled, "I had to make a split-second decision" (Buckley, 2007). His decision, as his girls looked on in horror, was to leap onto the track, push the man off the rails and

LOVE IS AN ANCIENT THING In 2007 near Rome, a 5000- to 6000-year-old "Romeo and Juliet" young couple was unearthed locked in embrace.

Retrieve + Remember

- How does the two-factor theory of emotion help explain *passionate love?*

ANSWER: Emotions consist of (1) physical arousal and (2) our interpretation of that arousal. Researchers have found that any source of arousal will be interpreted as passion in the presence of a desirable person.

- Two vital components for maintaining companionate love are _____ and _____-_____.

ANSWERS: equity; self-disclosure

passionate love an aroused state of intense positive absorption in another, usually present at the beginning of romantic love.

companionate love the deep affectionate attachment we feel for those with whom our lives are intertwined.

equity a condition in which people receive from a relationship in proportion to what they give to it.

self-disclosure revealing intimate aspects of ourselves to others.

altruism unselfish concern for the welfare of others.

into a foot-deep space between them, and lie on top of him. As the train screeched to a halt, five cars traveled just above his head, leaving grease on his knitted cap. When Autrey cried out, "I've got two daughters up there. Let them know their father is okay," the onlookers erupted into applause.

Such selfless goodness made New Yorkers proud to call that city home. Another New York story, four decades earlier, had a different ending. In 1964, a stalker repeatedly stabbed Kitty Genovese, then raped her as she lay dying outside her Queens, New York, apartment at 3:30 A.M. "Oh, my God, he stabbed me!" Genovese screamed into the early morning stillness. "Please help me!" Windows opened and lights went on as some neighbors heard her screams. Her attacker fled. Then he returned to stab and rape her again. Not until he had fled for good did anyone so much as call the police, at 3:50 A.M.

Bystander Intervention

In an emergency, some people intervene, as Wesley Autrey did, but others fail to offer help. Why do some people become heroes while others just stand and watch? Social psychologists John Darley and Bibb Latané (1968b) believed three conditions were necessary for bystanders to help (**FIGURE 11.9**). They must

- *notice* the incident.
- *interpret* the event as an emergency.
- *assume responsibility* for helping.

At each step, the presence of others can turn people away from the path that leads to helping. Darley and Latané (1968a) reached these conclusions after interpreting the results of a series of experiments. For example, they staged a fake emergency as students in separate laboratory rooms took turns speaking over an intercom. Only the person whose microphone was switched on could be heard. When his turn came, one student (who was actually working for the experimenters) pretended to

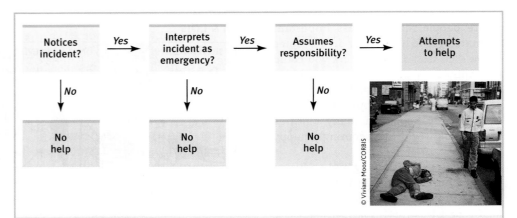

FIGURE 11.9 The decision-making process for bystander intervention Before helping, one must first notice an emergency, then correctly interpret it, and then feel responsible. (Information from Darley & Latané, 1968b.)

have an epileptic seizure, and he called for help.

How did the others react? As **FIGURE 11.10** shows, those who believed only they could hear the victim—and therefore thought they alone were responsible for helping him—usually went to his aid. Students who thought others could also hear the victim's cries were more likely to do nothing. When more people shared responsibility for helping—when no one person was clearly responsible—each listener was less likely to help.

LaunchPad For a review of research on emergency helping, visit LaunchPad's *Concept Practice: When Will People Help Others?*

Hundreds of additional experiments have confirmed this **bystander effect.** For example, researchers and their assistants took 1497 elevator rides in three cities and "accidentally" dropped coins or pencils in front of 4813 fellow passengers (Latané & Dabbs, 1975). When alone with the person in need, 40 percent helped; in the presence of five other bystanders, only 20 percent helped.

Observations of behavior in thousands of situations—relaying an emergency phone call, aiding a stranded motorist, donating blood, picking up

dropped books, contributing money, giving time, and more—show that the best odds of our helping someone occur when

- the person appears to need and deserve help.
- the person is in some way similar to us.
- the person is a woman.
- we have just observed someone else being helpful.
- we are not in a hurry.
- we are in a small town or rural area.
- we are feeling guilty.
- we are focused on others and not preoccupied.
- we are in a good mood.

This last result, that happy people are helpful people, is one of the most consistent findings in all of psychology. As poet Robert Browning (1868) observed, "Oh, make us happy and you make us good!" It doesn't matter how we are cheered. Whether by being made to feel successful and intelligent, by thinking happy thoughts, by finding money, or even by receiving a posthypnotic suggestion, we become more generous and more eager to help (Carlson et al., 1988).

So happiness breeds helpfulness. But it's also true that helpfulness breeds happiness. Helping those in need activates brain areas associated with

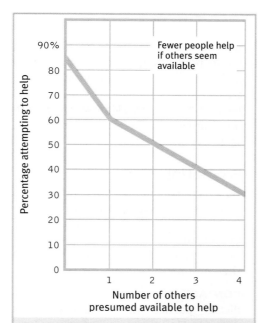

FIGURE 11.10 Responses to a simulated emergency When people thought they alone heard the calls for help from a person they believed to be having an epileptic seizure, they usually helped. But when they thought four others were also hearing the calls, fewer than one third responded. (Data from Darley & Latané, 1968a.)

reward (Harbaugh et al., 2007; Kawamichi et al., 2015). That helps explain a curious finding: People who give money away are happier than those who spend it almost entirely on themselves. In one experiment, researchers gave people an envelope with cash and instructions. Some were told to spend it on themselves, while others were told to spend it on others (Dunn et al., 2008; Dunn & Norton, 2013). Which group was happiest at the day's end? It was, indeed, those assigned to the spend-it-on-others condition.

Retrieve + Remember

- Why didn't anybody help Kitty Genovese? What social relations principle did this incident illustrate?

ANSWER: In the presence of others, an individual is less likely to notice a situation, correctly interpret it as an emergency, and then take responsibility for offering help. The Kitty Genovese case demonstrated this *bystander effect*, as each witness assumed many others were also aware of the event.

The Norms for Helping

LOQ 11-18 How do social norms explain helping behavior?

Why do we help? Sometimes we go to the aid of another because we have been socialized to do so, through norms that prescribe how we *ought* to behave (Everett et al., 2015). Through socialization, we learn the **reciprocity norm**: the expectation that we should return help, not harm, to those who have helped us. In our relations with others of similar status, the reciprocity norm compels us to give (in favors, gifts, or social invitations) about as much as we receive. People who are generously treated become more likely to be generous to a stranger—to "pay it forward" (Tsvetkova & Macy, 2014).

The reciprocity norm kicked in after Dave Tally, a Tempe, Arizona homeless man, found $3300 in a backpack an Arizona State University student had lost on his way to buy a used car (Lacey, 2010). Tally could have used the cash for food, shelter, and much-needed bike repairs. Instead, he turned the backpack in to the social service agency where he volunteered. To reciprocate Tally's help, the student thanked him with a monetary reward. Hearing about Tally's self-giving deeds, dozens of others also sent him money and job offers.

We also learn a **social-responsibility norm**: We should help those who depend on us. So we help young children and others who cannot give back as much as they receive. People who attend weekly religious services are often urged to practice the social-responsibility norm, and sometimes they do. Between 2006 and 2008, Gallup polls sampled more than 300,000 people across 140 countries, comparing the "highly religious" (who said religion was important to them and who had attended a religious service in the prior week) to the less religious. The highly religious, despite being poorer, were about 50 percent more likely to report having "donated money to a charity in the last month" and to have volunteered time to an organization (Pelham & Crabtree, 2008).

Positive social norms encourage generosity and enable group living. But conflicts often divide us.

Conflict and Peacemaking

LOQ 11-19 What social processes fuel conflict? How can we transform feelings of prejudice and conflict into behaviors that promote peace?

We live in surprising times. With astonishing speed, recent democratic movements have swept away totalitarian rule in Eastern European and Arab countries. Yet *every day*, the world continues to spend almost $5 billion for arms and armies—money that could have been used for housing, nutrition, education, and health care. Knowing that wars begin in human minds, psychologists have wondered: What in the human mind causes destructive conflict? How might the perceived threats of our differences be replaced by a spirit of cooperation?

To a social psychologist, a **conflict** is the perception that actions, goals, or ideas are incompatible. The elements of conflict are much the same, whether we are speaking of nations at war, cultural

bystander effect the tendency for any given bystander to be less likely to give aid if other bystanders are present.

reciprocity norm an expectation that people will help, not hurt, those who have helped them.

social-responsibility norm an expectation that people will help those dependent upon them.

conflict a perceived incompatibility of actions, goals, or ideas.

groups feuding within a society, or partners sparring in a relationship. In each situation, people become tangled in a destructive process that can produce results no one wants.

Enemy Perceptions

Psychologists have noticed a curious tendency: People in conflict form evil images of one another. These distorted images are so similar that we call them **mirror-image perceptions.** As we see "them"—untrustworthy, with evil intentions—so "they" see us.

Mirror-image perceptions can feed a vicious cycle of hostility. If Juan believes Maria is annoyed with him, he may snub her. In return, she may act annoyed, justifying his perceptions. As with individuals, so with countries. Perceptions can become **self-fulfilling prophecies**—beliefs that confirm themselves by influencing the other country to react in ways that seem to justify them.

Both individuals and nations tend to see their own actions as responses to provocation, not as the causes of what happens next. Perceiving themselves as returning tit for tat, they often hit back harder, as University College London volunteers did in one experiment (Shergill et al., 2003). After feeling pressure on their own finger, they were to use a mechanical device to press on another volunteer's finger. Although told to reciprocate with the same amount of pressure, they typically responded with about 40 percent more force than they had just experienced. Gentle touches soon escalated to hard presses. Volunteers felt confident that they were responding in kind, and their partners were the ones upping the pressure—much as when each child after a fight claims that "I just tapped him, but he hit me."

The point is not that truth must lie midway between two such views; one may be more accurate. The point is that enemy perceptions often form mirror

images. Moreover, as enemies change, so do perceptions. In American minds and media, the "bloodthirsty, cruel, treacherous" Japanese of World War II became "intelligent, hardworking, self-disciplined, resourceful allies" (Gallup, 1972).

Promoting Peace

How can we change perceptions and make peace? Can contact and cooperation transform the anger and fear fed by prejudice and conflict into peace-promoting attitudes? Research indicates that, in some cases, they can.

CONTACT Does it help to put two conflicting parties into close contact? It depends. Negative contact increases *dis*liking (Barlow et al., 2012). But positive contact—especially noncompetitive contact between parties with equal status, such as fellow store clerks—typically helps. Initially prejudiced co-workers of different races have, in such circumstances, usually come to accept one another. Across a quarter-million people studied in 38 nations, friendly contact with ethnic minorities, older people, and people with disabilities has usually led to less prejudice (Lemmer & Wagner, 2015; Pettigrew & Tropp, 2011). Some examples:

- With cross-racial contact, South African's interracial attitudes have moved "into closer alignment" (Dixon et al., 2007; Finchilescu & Tredoux, 2010).

- Heterosexuals' attitudes toward gay people are influenced not only by what they know but also by whom they know (Collier et al., 2012; Smith et al., 2009b). In surveys, the reason people most often give for becoming more supportive of same-sex marriage is "having friends, family, or acquaintances who are gay or lesbian" (Pew, 2013).

WHY DO GENOCIDES OCCUR? An estimated 800,000 people died during the Rwandan Genocide of 1994, when Hutu groups carried out mass killings of Tutsis. Social psychology research helps us understand some of the factors motivating genocides. We tend to categorize our world into us and them, and, when threatened, to feel greater animosity toward outside groups.

"You cannot shake hands with a clenched fist."
Indira Gandhi, 1971

FORMER UNITED NATIONS GENERAL SECRETARY, KOFI ANNAN: "Most of us have overlapping identities which unite us with very different groups. We *can* love what we are, without hating what—and who—we are *not*. We can thrive in our own tradition, even as we learn from others" (2001).

- Even indirect contact with an outgroup member (via reading a story or through a friend who has an outgroup friend) has reduced prejudice (Cameron & Rutland, 2006; Pettigrew et al., 2007).

However, contact is not always enough. In many schools, ethnic groups segregate themselves in lunch-rooms and on school grounds (Alexander & Tredoux, 2010; Clack et al., 2005; Schofield, 1986). People in each group often think they would welcome more contact with the other group, but they assume the other group does not share their interest (Richeson & Shelton, 2007). When these mirror-image untruths are corrected, friendships can form and prejudices melt.

COOPERATION To see if enemies could overcome their differences, researcher Muzafer Sherif (1966) manufactured a conflict. He separated 22 boys into two separate camp areas. Then he had the two groups compete for prizes in a series of activities. Before long, each group became intensely proud of itself and hostile to the other group's "sneaky," "smart-alecky stinkers." Food wars broke out. Cabins were ransacked. Fistfights had to be broken up by camp counselors. Brought together, the two groups avoided each other, except to taunt and threaten. Little did they know that within a few days, they would be friends.

Sherif accomplished this reconciliation by giving them **superordinate goals**—shared goals that could be achieved only through cooperation. When he arranged for the camp water supply to "fail," all 22 boys had to work together to restore the water. To rent a movie in those pre-Netflix days, they all had to pool their resources. To move a stalled truck, all the boys had to combine their strength, pulling and pushing together. Sherif used shared predicaments and goals to turn enemies into friends. What reduced conflict was not mere contact, but *cooperative* contact.

A shared predicament can have a powerfully unifying effect for other groups as well. Children and youth exposed to war, and minority group members facing rejection or discrimination, likewise develop strong ingroup identification (Bauer et al., 2014; Ramos et al., 2012).

At such times, cooperation can lead people to define a new, inclusive group that dissolves their former subgroups (Dovidio & Gaertner, 1999). If this were a social psychology experiment, you might seat members of two groups not on opposite sides, but alternately around a table. Give them a new, shared name. Have them work together. Then watch "us" and "them" become "we." After 9/11, one 18-year-old New Jersey man described this shift in his own social identity. "I just thought of myself as Black. But now I feel like I'm an American, more than ever" (Sengupta, 2001).

If superordinate goals and shared threats help bring rival groups together, might this principle bring people together in multicultural schools? Could interracial friendships replace competitive classroom situations with cooperative ones? Could cooperative learning maintain or even enhance student achievement? Experiments with teens from 11 countries confirm that, in each case, the answer is *Yes* (Roseth et al., 2008). In the classroom as in the sports arena, members of interracial groups who work together on projects typically come to feel friendly toward one another. Knowing this, thousands of teachers have made interracial cooperative learning part of their classroom experience.

The power of cooperative activity to make friends of former enemies has led psychologists to urge increased international exchange and cooperation. Some experiments have found that simply imagining the shared threat of climate change reduces international hostilities (Pyszczynski et al., 2012). From Brazilian tribes to European countries, formerly conflicting groups have managed to build interconnections, interdependence, and a shared social identity as they seek common goals (Fry, 2012). Let us then engage in mutually beneficial trade, working together to protect our common destiny on this fragile planet and becoming more aware that our hopes and fears are shared. By taking

---

mirror-image perceptions mutual views often held by conflicting people, as when each side sees itself as ethical and peaceful and views the other side as evil and aggressive.

self-fulfilling prophecy a belief that leads to its own fulfillment.

superordinate goals shared goals that override differences among people and require their cooperation.

such steps, we can change misperceptions that drive us apart and instead join together in a common cause based on common interests. As working toward shared goals reminds us, we are more alike than different.

Retrieve + Remember

- Why do sports fans tend to feel a sense of satisfaction when their archrival team loses? Why do such feelings, in other settings, make conflict resolution more challenging?

ANSWER: Sports fans may feel a part of an *ingroup* that sets itself apart from an *outgroup* (fans of the archrival team). *Ingroup bias* tends to develop, leading to prejudice and the view that the outgroup "deserves" misfortune. So, the archrival team's loss may seem justified. In conflicts, this kind of thinking is problematic, especially when each side in the conflict develops *mirror-image perceptions* of the other (distorted, negative images that are ironically similar).

- What are two ways to reconcile conflicts and promote peace?

ANSWER: Peacemakers should encourage equal-status contact and cooperation to achieve superordinate goals (shared goals that override differences).

CHAPTER REVIEW

Social Psychology

Test yourself by taking a moment to answer each of these Learning Objective Questions (repeated here from within the chapter). Then turn to Appendix D, Complete Chapter Reviews, to check your answers. Research suggests that trying to answer these questions on your own will improve your long-term memory of the concepts (McDaniel et al., 2009).

What Is Social Psychology's Focus?

11-1: What are three main focuses of social psychology?

Social Thinking

11-2: How does the fundamental attribution error describe how we tend to explain others' behavior compared with our own?

11-3: What is an attitude, and how do attitudes and actions affect each other?

Social Influence

11-4: What do experiments on conformity and obedience reveal about the power of social influence?

11-5: What do the social influence studies teach us about ourselves? How much power do we have as individuals?

11-6: How does the presence of others influence our actions, via social facilitation, social loafing, or deindividuation?

11-7: How can group interaction enable group polarization?

11-8: What role does the Internet play in group polarization?

11-9: How can group interaction enable groupthink?

Social Relations

11-10: What are the three parts of prejudice, and how has prejudice changed over time?

11-11: What factors contribute to the social roots of prejudice, and how does scapegoating illustrate the emotional roots of prejudice?

11-12: What are the cognitive roots of prejudice?

11-13: What biological factors predispose us to be aggressive?

11-14: What psychological and social-cultural factors may trigger aggressive behavior?

11-15: Why do we befriend or fall in love with some people but not others?

11-16: How does romantic love typically change as time passes?

11-17: What is altruism? When are we most—and least—likely to help?

11-18: How do social norms explain helping behavior?

11-19: What social processes fuel conflict? How can we transform feelings of prejudice and conflict into behaviors that promote peace?

TERMS AND CONCEPTS TO REMEMBER

Test yourself on these terms by trying to write down the definition in your own words before flipping back to the referenced page to check your answer.

social psychology, p. 315

fundamental attribution error, p. 315

attitude, p. 315

peripheral route persuasion, p. 315

central route persuasion, p. 315

foot-in-the-door phenomenon, p. 317

role, p. 317

cognitive dissonance theory, p. 317

conformity, p. 319

normative social influence, p. 319

informational social influence, p. 319

social facilitation, p. 323

social loafing, p. 325

deindividuation, p. 325

group polarization, p. 325

groupthink, p. 325

prejudice, p. 327

stereotype, p. 327

discrimination, p. 327

just-world phenomenon, p. 329

ingroup, p. 329

outgroup, p. 329

ingroup bias, p. 329

scapegoat theory, p. 329

other-race effect, p. 331

aggression, p. 331

frustration-aggression principle, p. 333

social script, p. 333

mere exposure effect, p. 335

passionate love, p. 339

companionate love, p. 339

equity, p. 339

self-disclosure, p. 339

altruism, p. 339

bystander effect, p. 341

reciprocity norm, p. 341

social-responsibility norm, p. 341

conflict, p. 341

mirror-image perceptions, p. 343

self-fulfilling prophecy, p. 343

superordinate goals, p. 343

CHAPTER TEST

Test yourself repeatedly throughout your studies. This will not only help you figure out what you know and don't know; the testing itself will help you learn and remember the information more effectively thanks to the testing effect.

1. If we encounter a person who appears to be high on drugs, and we make the fundamental attribution error, we will probably attribute the person's behavior to

   a. moral weakness or an addictive personality.

   b. peer pressure.

   c. the easy availability of drugs on city streets.

   d. society's acceptance of drug use.

2. We tend to agree to a larger request more readily if we have already agreed to a small request. This tendency is called the _____ - _____ - _____ - _____ phenomenon.

3. Jamal's therapist has suggested that Jamal should "act as if" he is confident, even though he feels insecure and shy. Which social psychological theory would best support this suggestion, and what might the therapist be hoping to achieve?

4. Researchers have found that a person is most likely to conform to a group if

   a. the group members have diverse opinions.

   b. the person feels competent and secure.

   c. the person admires the group's status.

   d. no one else will observe the person's behavior.

5. In Milgram's experiments, the rate of obedience was highest when

   a. the "learner" was at a distance from the "teacher."

   b. the "learner" was near the "teacher."

   c. other "teachers" refused to go along with the experimenter.

   d. the "teacher" disliked the "learner."

6. Dr. Huang, a popular music professor, delivers fascinating lectures on music history but gets nervous and makes mistakes when describing exam statistics in front of the class. Why does his performance vary by task?

7. In a group situation that fosters arousal and anonymity, a person sometimes loses self-consciousness and self-control. This phenomenon is called _____.

8. Sharing our opinions with like-minded others tends to strengthen our views, a phenomenon referred to as _____ _____.

9. Prejudice toward a group involves negative feelings, a tendency to discriminate, and overly generalized beliefs referred to as _____.

10. If several well-publicized murders are committed by members of a particular group, we may tend to react with fear and suspicion toward all members of that group. In other words, we

    a. blame the victim.

    b. overgeneralize from vivid, memorable cases.

    c. view the world as just.

    d. rationalize inequality.

11. The other-race effect occurs when we assume that other groups are _____ (more/less) homogeneous than our own group.

12. Evidence of a biochemical influence on aggression is the finding that

    a. aggressive behavior varies widely from culture to culture.

    b. animals can be bred for aggressiveness.

    c. stimulation of an area of the brain's limbic system produces aggressive behavior.

    d. a higher-than-average level of the hormone testosterone is associated with violent behavior in males.

13. When those who feel frustrated become angry and aggressive, this is referred to as the _____ - _____ _____.

14. Studies show that parents of delinquent young people tend to use beatings to enforce discipline. This suggests that aggression can be

    a. learned through direct rewards.

    b. triggered by exposure to violent media.

    c. learned through observation of aggressive models.

    d. caused by hormone changes at puberty.

15. Social scientists studying the effects of pornography have mostly agreed that violent pornography

    a. has little effect on most viewers.

    b. is the primary cause of reported and unreported rapes.

    c. leads viewers to be more accepting of coercion in sexual relations.

    d. has no effect, other than short-term arousal and entertainment.

16. The more familiar a stimulus becomes, the more we tend to like it. This exemplifies the _____ _____ effect.

17. A happy couple celebrating their 50th wedding anniversary is likely to experience deep _____ love, even though their _____ love has probably decreased over the years.

18. After vigorous exercise, you meet an attractive person, and you are suddenly seized by romantic feelings for that person. This response supports the two-factor theory of emotion, which assumes that emotions, such as passionate love, consist of physical arousal plus

    a. a reward.

    b. proximity.

    c. companionate love.

    d. our interpretation of that arousal.

19. Due to the bystander effect, a particular bystander is less likely to give aid if

    a. the victim is similar to the bystander in appearance.

    b. no one else is present.

    c. other people are present.

    d. the incident occurs in a deserted or rural area.

20. Our enemies often have many of the same negative impressions of us as we have of them. This exemplifies the concept of _____ - _____ perceptions.

21. One way of resolving conflicts and fostering cooperation is by giving rival groups shared goals that help them override their differences. These are called _____ goals.

Find answers to these questions in Appendix E, in the back of the book.

IN YOUR EVERYDAY LIFE

Answering these questions will help you make these concepts more personally meaningful, and therefore more memorable.

1. Do you have an attitude or tendency you would like to change? How could you use the attitudes-follow-behavior idea to change it?

2. What example of social influence have you experienced this week? How did you respond to the power of the situation?

3. What could you do to discourage social loafing in a group project assigned for a class?

4. What negative attitudes might professors and students have toward each other? What strategies might change those attitudes?

5. In what ways have you been affected by social scripts for aggression? How have TV shows or video games contributed such scripts?

6. To what extent have your closest relationships been affected by proximity, physical attractiveness, and similarity?

7. What could you do to motivate your friends to contribute their time or money to a cause that is important to you?

8. Think of a conflict between friends or family members. What strategies would you suggest to help them reconcile their relationships?

Use **LearningCurve** to create your personalized study plan, which will direct you to the resources that will help you most in **LaunchPad**.

SURVEY THE CHAPTER

Rex Features/AP Images

12

Personality

Lady Gaga dazzles millions with her unique musical arrangements, tantalizing outfits, and provocative performances. In shows around the world, Lady Gaga's most predictable feature is her unpredictability. She has worn a meat dress to an awards show, sported 16-inch heels to meet with U.S. President Barack Obama (who later described the interaction as "a little intimidating"), and wowed Super Bowl viewers with her performance of the national anthem.

Yet even Lady Gaga exhibits distinctive and enduring ways of thinking, feeling, and behaving. Her fans and critics can depend on her openness to new experiences and the energy she gets from the spotlight. And they can also rely on her painstaking dedication to her music and performances. She describes herself in high school as "very dedicated, very studious, and very disciplined." Now, in adulthood, she shows similar self-discipline: "I'm very detailed—every minute of the show has got to be perfect." This chapter focuses on the ways we all demonstrate unique and persisting patterns of thinking, feeling, and behaving—our *personality*.

Much of this book deals with personality. Earlier chapters considered biological influences on personality; personality development across the life span; how personality relates to learning, motivation, emotion, and health; and social influences on personality. The next chapter will study disorders of personality. This chapter focuses on personality itself—what it is and how researchers study it.

We begin with two historically important theories of personality that have become part of our cultural legacy: Sigmund Freud's *psychoanalytic theory* and the *humanistic approach*. These sweeping perspectives on human nature laid the foundation for later personality theorists and for what this chapter presents next: newer scientific explorations of personality. We'll look at the traits that define our uniqueness. We'll see how biology, psychology, and environment together influence personality. Finally, we'll note how our concept of self—that sense of "Who I am"—helps organize our thoughts, feelings, and behaviors.

What Is Personality?

12-1 What is *personality*, and what theories inform our understanding of personality?

Our **personality** is our characteristic pattern of thinking, feeling, and acting. Sigmund Freud's *psychoanalytic theory* proposed that childhood sexuality and unconscious motivations influence personality. (Freud's ideas inspired today's *psychodynamic theorists*.) The *humanistic theories* focused on our inner capacities for growth and self-fulfillment. Later theorists built upon these two broad perspectives. *Trait theories* examine characteristic patterns of behavior (traits). *Social-cognitive theories* explore the interaction between people's traits (including their thinking) and their social context. Let's begin with psychodynamic theories.

Psychodynamic Theories

Psychodynamic theories of personality view human behavior as a lively (dynamic) interaction between the conscious and unconscious mind, and they consider our related motives and conflicts. These theories came from Sigmund Freud's **psychoanalysis**—his theory of personality and the associated treatment techniques. Freud's work was the first to focus clinical attention on our unconscious mind.

Freud's Psychoanalytic Perspective: Exploring the Unconscious

LOQ **12-2** How did Sigmund Freud's treatment of psychological disorders lead to his view of the unconscious mind?

Freud was not psychology's most important figure, but he is definitely the most famous. Ask 100 people on the street to name a deceased psychologist, suggested Keith Stanovich (1996, p. 1), and "Freud would be the winner hands down." His influence lingers in books, movies, and psychological therapies. Who was Freud, what did he teach, and why do we still study his work?

Like all of us, Sigmund Freud was a product of his times. His Victorian era was a time of great discovery and scientific advancement, but it is also known today as a time of sexual repression and male dominance. Men's and women's roles were clearly defined, with male superiority assumed and only male sexuality generally acknowledged (discreetly).

After graduating from the University of Vienna medical school, Freud specialized in nervous disorders. Before long, he began hearing complaints that made no medical sense. One patient had lost all feeling in one hand. Yet there is no nerve pathway that, if damaged, would numb the entire hand and nothing else. Freud wondered: What could cause such disorders? His search for the answer led in a direction that would challenge our self-understanding.

Could these strange disorders have mental rather than physical causes? Freud decided they could. Many meetings with patients led to Freud's "discovery" of the **unconscious.** In Freud's view, this deep well keeps unacceptable thoughts, wishes, feelings, and memories hidden away so thoroughly that we are no longer aware of them. But despite our best efforts, bits and pieces of these ideas seep out. Thus, according to Freud, patients might have an odd loss of feeling in their hand because they have an unconscious fear of touching their genitals. Or their unexplained blindness might be caused by unconsciously not wanting to see something that makes them anxious.

Basic to Freud's theory was his belief that the mind is mostly hidden. Below the surface lies a large unconscious region where unacceptable passions and thoughts lurk. Freud believed we *repress* these unconscious feelings and ideas. We block them from awareness because admitting them would be too unsettling. Nevertheless, he said, these repressed feelings and ideas powerfully influence us.

For Freud, nothing was ever accidental. He saw the unconscious seeping not only into people's troubling symptoms but also, in disguised forms, into their work, their beliefs, and their daily habits. He also glimpsed the unconscious in slips of the tongue and pen, as when a financially stressed patient, not wanting any large pills, said, "Please do not give me any bills, because I cannot swallow them." Jokes, too, were expressions of repressed sexual and aggressive tendencies traveling in disguise. Dreams, he said, were the "royal road to the unconscious." He thought the dreams we remember are really censored versions of our unconscious wishes.

> "I know how hard it is for you to put food on your family."
>
> Former U.S. President George W. Bush, 2000

Hoping to unlock the door to the unconscious, Freud first tried hypnosis, but with poor results. He then turned to **free association,** telling patients to relax and say whatever came to mind, no matter how unimportant or silly. Freud believed that free association would trace a path from the troubled present into a patient's distant past. The chain of thought would lead back to the patient's

SIGMUND FREUD (1856–1939) "I was the only worker in a new field."

"Good morning, beheaded—uh, I mean beloved."

unconscious, the hiding place of painful past memories, often from childhood. His goal was to find these forbidden thoughts and release them.

Personality Structure

LOQ 12-3 What was Freud's view of personality?

In Freud's view, human personality arises from a conflict between impulse and restraint. People who evolved from "lower animals" are born with aggressive, pleasure-seeking urges, Freud famously said. He believed that as we are socialized, we internalize social restraints against these urges. Personality is the result of our efforts to resolve basic conflict—to express these impulses in ways that bring satisfaction without guilt or punishment.

To understand the mind's conflicts, Freud proposed three interacting systems: the *id*, *ego*, and *superego*. Psychologists have found it useful to view the mind's structure as an iceberg (**FIGURE 12.1**).

The **id** stores unconscious energy. It tries to satisfy our basic drives to survive, reproduce, and act aggressively. The id operates on the *pleasure principle:* It seeks immediate gratification. To understand the id's power, think of newborn infants crying out the moment they feel a need, wanting satisfaction now. Or think of people who abuse drugs, partying now rather than sacrificing today's

"Fifty is plenty."   *"Hundred and fifty."*

The ego struggles to reconcile the demands of superego and id, said Freud.

temporary pleasure for future success and happiness (Fernie et al., 2013; Friedel et al., 2014; Keough et al., 1999).

FIGURE 12.1 Freud's idea of the mind's structure Icebergs hide most of their bulk beneath the surface of the water. Psychologists often use this image to illustrate Freud's idea that the mind is mostly hidden beneath the conscious surface of our awareness. Note that the id is totally unconscious, but ego and superego operate both consciously and unconsciously. Unlike the parts of a frozen iceberg, however, the id, ego, and superego interact.

personality an individual's characteristic pattern of thinking, feeling, and acting.

psychodynamic theories view personality with a focus on the unconscious and the importance of childhood experiences.

psychoanalysis Freud's theory of personality that attributes thoughts and actions to unconscious motives and conflicts; the techniques used in treating psychological disorders by seeking to expose and interpret unconscious tensions.

unconscious according to Freud, a reservoir of mostly unacceptable thoughts, wishes, feelings, and memories. According to contemporary psychologists, information processing of which we are unaware.

free association in psychoanalysis, a method of exploring the unconscious in which the person relaxes and says whatever comes to mind, no matter how unimportant or embarrassing.

id a reservoir of unconscious psychic energy that, according to Freud, strives to satisfy basic sexual and aggressive drives. The id operates on the *pleasure principle*, demanding immediate gratification.

The mind's second part, the **ego**, operates on the *reality principle*. The ego is the conscious mind. It tries to satisfy the id's impulses in realistic ways that will bring long-term benefits rather than pain or destruction.

As the ego develops, the young child learns to cope with the real world. Around age 4 or 5, Freud theorized, a child's ego begins to recognize the demands of the **superego**, the voice of our moral compass, or *conscience*. The superego forces the ego to consider not only the real but also the ideal. It focuses on how one *ought* to behave in a perfect world. It judges actions and produces positive feelings of pride or negative feelings of guilt.

As you may have guessed, the superego's demands often oppose the id's. It is the ego's job to reconcile the two. As the personality's "executive," the ego juggles the impulsive demands of the id, the restraining demands of the superego, and the real-life demands of the external world.

Personality Development

LOQ 12-4 What developmental stages did Freud propose?

Freud believed that personality forms during life's first few years. He was convinced that children pass through a series of **psychosexual stages,** from oral to genital (**TABLE 12.1**). In each stage, the id's pleasure-seeking energies focus on an *erogenous zone,* a distinct pleasure-sensitive area of the body.

Freud believed that during the third stage, the *phallic stage,* boys develop unconscious sexual desires for their mother. They also feel jealousy and hatred for their father, who is a rival for their mother's attention. These feelings lead to guilt and a lurking fear that their father will punish them, perhaps by castration. Freud called this cluster of feelings the **Oedipus complex,** after the Greek legend of Oedipus, who unknowingly killed his father and married his mother. Some psychoanalysts in Freud's era believed that girls experience a parallel *Electra complex.*

TABLE 12.1	Freud's Psychosexual Stages
Stage	**Focus**
Oral (0–18 months)	Pleasure centers on the mouth—sucking, biting, chewing
Anal (18–36 months)	Pleasure focuses on bowel and bladder elimination; coping with demands for control
Phallic (3–6 years)	Pleasure zone is the genitals; coping with incestuous sexual feelings
Latency (6 to puberty)	A phase of dormant sexual feelings
Genital (puberty on)	Maturation of sexual interests

Children learn to cope with these feelings by repressing them, said Freud. They identify with the "rival" parent and try to become like him or her. It's as though something inside the child decides, "If you can't beat 'em, join 'em." This **identification** process strengthens children's superegos as they take on many of their parents' values. Freud believed that identification with the same-sex parent provides what psychologists now call our *gender identity*—our sense of being male, female, or some combination of the two.

Other conflicts could arise at other childhood stages. But whatever the stage, unresolved conflicts can cause trouble in adulthood. The result, Freud believed, would be **fixation,** locking the person's pleasure-seeking energies at the unresolved stage. A child who is either orally overindulged or orally deprived (perhaps

"Oh, for goodness' sake! Smoke!"

The New Yorker Collection, 1983, Charles Saxon from cartoonbank.com

by abrupt, early weaning) might become stalled at the oral stage, for example. As an adult, this orally fixated person might continue to seek oral gratification by smoking or excessive eating. In such ways, Freud suggested, the twig of personality is bent at an early age.

Defense Mechanisms

LOQ 12-5 How did Freud think people defended themselves against anxiety?

Anxiety, said Freud, is the price we pay for civilization. As members of social groups, we must control our sexual and aggressive impulses, not act them out. Sometimes the ego fears losing control of this inner war between the id and superego, which results in a dark cloud of generalized anxiety. We feel unsettled, but we don't know why.

Freud proposed that the ego distorts reality in an effort to protect itself from

"I heard that as soon as we become aware of our sexual impulses, whatever they are, we'll have to hide them."

ScienceCartoonsPlus.com

TABLE 12.2 Six Defense Mechanisms

Freud believed that *repression,* the basic mechanism that banishes anxiety-arousing impulses, enables other defense mechanisms, six of which are listed here.

Defense Mechanism	Unconscious Process Employed to Avoid Anxiety-Arousing Thoughts or Feelings	Example
Regression	Retreating to a more infantile psychosexual stage, where some psychic energy remains fixated.	A little boy reverts to the oral comfort of thumb sucking in the car on the way to his first day of school.
Reaction formation	Switching unacceptable impulses into their opposites.	Repressing angry feelings, a person displays exaggerated friendliness.
Projection	Disguising one's own threatening impulses by attributing them to others.	"The thief thinks everyone else is a thief" (an El Salvadoran saying).
Rationalization	Offering self-justifying explanations in place of the real, more threatening unconscious reasons for one's actions.	A habitual drinker says she drinks with her friends "just to be sociable."
Displacement	Shifting sexual or aggressive impulses toward a more acceptable or less threatening object or person.	A little girl kicks the family dog after her mother puts her in a time-out.
Denial	Refusing to believe or even perceive painful realities.	A partner denies evidence of his loved one's affair.

REGRESSION Children and young orangutans may regress if faced with a stressor, Freud believed, retreating to the comfort of earlier behaviors.

anxiety. **Defense mechanisms** help achieve this goal by disguising threatening impulses and preventing them from reaching consciousness. Note that, for Freud, *all defense mechanisms function indirectly and unconsciously.* Just as the body unconsciously defends itself against disease, so also does the ego unconsciously defend itself against anxiety. For example, **repression** banishes anxiety-arousing wishes and feelings from consciousness. According to Freud, *repression underlies all of the other defense mechanisms.* However, because repression is often incomplete, repressed urges may appear as symbols in dreams or as slips of the tongue in casual conversation. **TABLE 12.2** describes a sampling of six other well-known defense mechanisms.

Retrieve + Remember

- According to Freud's ideas about the three-part personality structure, the _____ operates on the *reality principle* and tries to balance demands in a way that produces long-term pleasure rather than pain; the _____ operates on the *pleasure principle* and seeks immediate gratification; and the _____ represents the voice of our internalized ideals (our *conscience*).

    ANSWERS: ego; id; superego

- In the psychoanalytic view, conflicts unresolved during one of the psychosexual stages may lead to _____ at that stage.

    ANSWER: fixation

- Freud believed that our defense mechanisms operate _____ (consciously/unconsciously) and defend us against _____.

    ANSWERS: unconsciously; anxiety

ego the largely conscious, "executive" part of personality that, according to Freud, balances the demands of the id, superego, and reality. The ego operates on the *reality principle,* satisfying the id's desires in ways that will realistically bring pleasure rather than pain.

superego the part of personality that, according to Freud, represents internalized ideals and provides standards for judgment (the conscience) and for future goals.

psychosexual stages the childhood stages of development (oral, anal, phallic, latency, genital) during which, according to Freud, the id's pleasure-seeking energies focus on distinct erogenous zones.

Oedipus [ED-uh-puss] complex according to Freud, a boy's sexual desires toward his mother and feelings of jealousy and hatred for the rival father.

identification the process by which, according to Freud, children incorporate their parents' values into their developing superegos.

fixation in personality theory, according to Freud, a lingering focus of pleasure-seeking energies at an earlier psychosexual stage, in which conflicts were unresolved.

defense mechanisms in psychoanalytic theory, the ego's protective methods of reducing anxiety by unconsciously distorting reality.

repression in psychoanalytic theory, the basic defense mechanism that banishes from consciousness the thoughts, feelings, and memories that arouse anxiety.

The Neo-Freudian and Later Psychodynamic Theorists

LOQ 12-6 Which of Freud's ideas did his followers accept or reject?

Freud's writings caused a lot of debate. Remember that Freud lived at a time when people seldom talked about sex, and certainly not unconscious sexual desires for one's parent. So it's no surprise that Freud was harshly criticized. In a letter to a trusted friend, Freud wrote, "In the Middle Ages, they would have burned me. Now they are content with burning my books" (Jones, 1957). Despite the controversy, Freud attracted followers. Several young, ambitious physicians formed an inner circle around the strong-minded Freud. These *neo-Freudians*, such as Alfred Adler, Karen Horney [HORN-eye], and Carl Jung [Yoong], adopted Freud's interviewing techniques and accepted his basic ideas:

- Personality has three parts: id, ego, and superego.
- The unconscious is key.
- Personality forms in childhood.
- We use defense mechanisms to ward off anxiety.

But the neo-Freudians differed from Freud in two important ways. First, they placed more emphasis on the role of the *conscious* mind. Second, they doubted that sex and aggression were all-consuming motivations. Instead, they tended to emphasize loftier motives and social interactions.

Jung believed that we have a **collective unconscious,** a common group of images, or *archetypes,* that developed from our species' universal experiences. Jung said that the collective unconscious explains why, for many people, spiritual concerns are deeply rooted and why people in different cultures share certain myths and images. Most of today's psychologists disagree with the idea of inherited experiences. But they do believe that our shared evolutionary history shaped some universal dispositions and that experience can leave *epigenetic* marks—affecting gene expression (Neel et al., 2016).

Some of Freud's ideas have been incorporated into the diverse perspectives that make up modern psychodynamic theory. Theorists and clinicians who study personality from a psychodynamic perspective assume, with Freud and with much support from today's psychological science, that much of our mental life is unconscious. They believe we often struggle with inner conflicts among our wishes, fears, and values, and respond defensively. And they agree that childhood shapes our personality and ways of becoming attached to others. But in other ways, they differ from Freud. "Most contemporary [psychodynamic] theorists and therapists are not wedded to the idea that sex is the basis of personality," noted psychologist Drew Westen (1996). They "do not talk about ids and egos, and do not go around classifying their patients as oral, anal, or phallic characters."

> "We don't see things as they are; we see things as we are."
>
> The Talmud

LaunchPad For a helpful, 9-minute overview, visit LaunchPad's *Video: Psychodynamic Theories of Personality.*

Assessing Unconscious Processes

LOQ 12-7 What are projective tests, how are they used, and how are they criticized?

Personality tests reflect the basic ideas of particular personality theories. So, what might be the assessment tool of choice for someone working in the Freudian tradition?

To find a way into the unconscious mind, you would need a sort of "psychological X-ray." The test would have to see through the top layer of social politeness, revealing hidden conflicts and impulses. **Projective tests** aim to provide this view by asking test-takers to describe an ambiguous image or tell a story about it. The image itself has no

ALFRED ADLER (1870–1937) Adler believed that childhood feelings of insecurity can drive behavior, triggering strivings for power and superiority. Adler coined the term *inferiority complex.*

KAREN HORNEY (1885–1952) Horney proposed that children's feelings of dependency give rise to feelings of helplessness and anxiety. These feelings trigger adult desires for love and security. Horney believed Freud's views of personality showed a masculine bias.

CARL JUNG (1875–1961) Jung shared Freud's view of the power of the unconscious. He also proposed a human *collective unconscious,* derived from our species' experiences in the distant past. Today's psychology rejects the idea that experiences can be inherited.

real meaning, but what the test-takers say about it offers a glimpse into their unconscious. (Recall that in Freudian theory, *projection* is a defense mechanism that disguises threatening impulses by "seeing" them in other people.) The **Thematic Apperception Test (TAT)** is one such test, in which people view images and then make up stories about them. For example, the TAT has been used to assess achievement motivation (Schultheiss et al., 2014). Shown a daydreaming boy, those who imagine he is fantasizing about an achievement are presumed to be projecting their own goals.

The most famous projective test, the **Rorschach inkblot test,** was introduced in 1921. Swiss psychiatrist Hermann Rorschach [ROAR-shock] based it on a game he and his friends played as children. They would drip ink on paper, fold it, and then say what they saw in the resulting blot (Sdorow, 2005). The assumption is that what you see in a series of 10 inkblots reflects your inner feelings and conflicts. Do you see predatory animals or weapons in **FIGURE 12.2**? Perhaps you have aggressive tendencies.

Is this a reasonable assumption? Let's see how well the Rorschach test measures up to the two primary criteria of a good test (Chapter 8):

- *Reliability* (consistency of results): Raters trained in different Rorschach scoring systems show little agreement (Sechrest et al., 1998).

- *Validity* (predicting what it's supposed to): The Rorschach test is not very

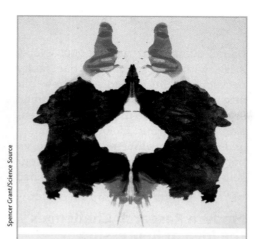

Spencer Grant/Science Source

FIGURE 12.2 The Rorschach test In this projective test, people tell what they see in a series of symmetrical inkblots. Some who use this test are confident that the interpretation of ambiguous images will reveal unconscious aspects of the test-taker's personality.

successful at predicting behavior or at discriminating between groups (for example, identifying who is suicidal and who is not). Inkblot results have diagnosed many normal adults as disordered (Wood, 2003; Wood et al., 2006).

The Rorschach test has neither much reliability nor great validity. But some clinicians value it as a source of suggestive leads, an icebreaker, or a revealing interview technique. Thus, the Rorschach test appears to have "the dubious distinction of being simultaneously the most cherished and most reviled of all psychological assessment instruments" (Hunsley & Bailey, 1999, p. 266).

Evaluating Freud's Psychoanalytic Perspective and Modern Views of the Unconscious

LOQ 12-8 How do today's psychologists view Freud's psychoanalysis?

"Many aspects of Freudian theory are indeed out of date, and they should be: Freud died in 1939, and he has been slow to undertake further revisions," observed one researcher (Westen, 1998). In Freud's time, there were no neurotransmitter or DNA studies. Decades of scientific breakthroughs in human

development, thinking, and emotion were yet to come. Criticizing Freud's theory by comparing it with current concepts is therefore, some say, like comparing Henry Ford's Model T with today's hybrid cars. (How tempting it always is to judge people in the past from our perspective in the present.)

But Freud's admirers and critics agree that recent research contradicts many of his specific ideas. Developmental psychologists now see our development as lifelong, not fixed in childhood. They doubt that infant brain networks are mature enough to process emotional trauma in the ways Freud assumed. Some think Freud overestimated parental influence and underestimated peer influence (and abuse). They also doubt that conscience and gender identity form as the child resolves the Oedipus complex at age 5 or 6. Our gender identity develops much earlier, and we become masculine or feminine even without a same-sex parent present. And they note that Freud's ideas about childhood sexuality arose from his female patients' stories of childhood sexual abuse. Some scholars suggest Freud doubted those stories, instead believing they reflected childhood sexual wishes and conflicts (Esterson, 2001; Powell & Boer, 1994).

Freud believed that dreams were the royal road to the unconscious, but they aren't. Modern dream researchers disagree with Freud's idea that dreams

© 1983 by Sidney Harris, American Scientist Magazine

"The forward thrust of the antlers shows a determined personality, yet the small sun indicates a lack of self-confidence. . . ."

collective unconscious Carl Jung's concept of a shared, inherited group of memories from our species' history.

projective test a personality test, such as the Rorschach, that provides an ambiguous image designed to trigger projection of the test-taker's unconscious thoughts or feelings.

Thematic Apperception Test (TAT) a projective test in which people express their inner feelings and interests through the stories they make up about ambiguous scenes.

Rorschach inkblot test the most widely used projective test; a set of 10 inkblots, designed by Hermann Rorschach; seeks to identify people's inner feelings by analyzing their interpretations of the blots.

disguise unfulfilled wishes lurking in our unconscious (Chapter 2). And slips of the tongue can be explained as competition between similar word choices in our memory network. Someone who says, "I don't want to do that—it's a lot of brothel" may simply be blending *bother* and *trouble* (Foss & Hakes, 1978).

Psychology's strength comes from its use of the same scientific method that biologists, chemists, and physicists use to test their theories. Psychologists must ask the same question about Freud's theory that they ask about other theories. Remember that a good theory organizes observations and predicts behaviors or events (Chapter 1). How does Freudian theory stand up to the scientific tests?

Freud's theory rests on few objective observations, and it has produced few hypotheses to verify or reject. For Freud, his own interpretations of patients' free associations, dreams, and slips of the tongue were evidence enough. Moreover, say the critics, Freud's theory offers after-the-fact explanations of behaviors and traits, but it fails to predict them. There is also no way to disprove this theory. If you feel angry when your mom dies, you illustrate his theory because "your unresolved childhood dependency needs are threatened." If you do not feel angry, you again illustrate his theory because "you are repressing your anger." That, say critics "is like betting on a horse after the race has been run" (Hall & Lindzey, 1978, p. 68).

Freud's supporters object. To criticize Freudian theory for not making testable predictions is, they say, like criticizing baseball for not being an aerobic exercise, something it was never intended to be. Freud never claimed that psychoanalysis was predictive science. He merely claimed that, looking back, psychoanalysts could find meaning in their clients' mental state (Rieff, 1979).

Freud's supporters also note that some of his ideas *are* enduring. It was Freud who drew our attention to the unconscious and the irrational, when such ideas were not popular. Today many researchers study our irrationality (Ariely, 2010; Thaler, 2015). Psychologist

Daniel Kahneman won a 2002 Nobel Prize with his studies of our faulty decision making. Freud also drew our attention to the importance of human sexuality. He made us aware of the tension between our biological impulses and our social well-being. He challenged our self-righteousness, pointed out our self-protective defenses, and reminded us of our potential for evil.

Modern Research Challenges the Idea of Repression

Psychoanalytic theory hinges on the assumption that our mind often *represses* offending wishes. Repression supposedly banishes emotions into the unconscious until they resurface, like long-lost books in a dusty attic. Today's memory researchers find that we do sometimes spare our egos by ignoring threatening information (Green et al., 2008). Yet they also find that repression, if it ever occurs, is a rare mental response to terrible trauma. "Repression folklore is . . . partly refuted, partly untested, and partly untestable," said Elizabeth Loftus (1995). Even those who have witnessed a parent's murder or survived Nazi death camps retain their unrepressed memories of the horror (Helmreich, 1992, 1994; Malmquist, 1986; Pennebaker, 1990). This led one prominent personality researcher to conclude, "Dozens of formal studies have yielded not a single convincing case of repression in the entire literature on trauma" (Kihlstrom, 2006).

Some researchers believe that extreme, prolonged stress, such as the stress some severely abused children experience, might disrupt memory by damaging the hippocampus (Schacter, 1996). But the far more common reality is that high stress and associated stress hormones *enhance* memory. Indeed, rape, torture, and other traumatic events haunt survivors, who experience unwanted flashbacks. They are seared onto the soul. "You see the babies," said Holocaust survivor Sally H. (1979). "You see the screaming mothers. You see hanging people. You sit and you see that face there. It's something you don't forget."

The Modern Unconscious Mind

LOQ 12-9 How has modern research developed our understanding of the unconscious?

Freud was right that we have limited access to all that goes on in our mind (Erdelyi, 1985, 1988, 2006; Kihlstrom, 1990). Our two-track mind has a vast out-of-sight realm. Some researchers even argue that "most of a person's everyday life is determined by unconscious thought processes" (Bargh & Chartrand, 1999). But the unconscious mind studied by cognitive researchers today is not the place Freud thought it was for storing our censored anxiety-producing thoughts and seething passions. Rather, it is a part of our two-track mind, where cooler information processing occurs without our awareness, such as

- the right-hemisphere brain activity that enables the split-brain patient's left hand to carry out an instruction the patient cannot verbalize (Chapter 2).

- the *parallel processing* of different aspects of vision and thinking, and the schemas that automatically control our perceptions and interpretations (Chapter 5).

- the *implicit memories* that operate without our conscious recall, even among those with amnesia (Chapter 7).

- the *emotions* we experience instantly, before conscious analysis (Chapter 9).

- the self-concept and *stereotypes* that automatically and unconsciously influence how we process information about ourselves and others (Chapter 11).

More than we realize, we fly on autopilot. Unconscious processing happens constantly. Like an enormous ocean, the unconscious mind is huge.

Research also supports two of Freud's defense mechanisms. For example, one study demonstrated *reaction formation* (trading unacceptable impulses for their opposite). Men who reported strong anti-gay attitudes experienced greater physiological arousal (measured erections) when watching videos of homosexual men having sex, even though they said the films did not make them sexually aroused (Adams et al., 1996). Likewise, some evidence suggests that people who unconsciously identify as homosexual—but who consciously identify as straight—report more negative attitudes toward gays and less support for pro-gay policies (Weinstein et al., 2012).

Freud's *projection* (attributing our own threatening impulses to others) has also been confirmed. People do tend to see their traits, attitudes, and goals in others (Baumeister et al., 1998b; Maner et al., 2005). Today's researchers call this the *false consensus effect*—the tendency to overestimate the extent to which others share our beliefs and behaviors. People who binge-drink or break speed limits tend to think many others do the same. However, defense mechanisms don't work exactly as Freud supposed. They seem motivated less by the sexual and aggressive impulses he imagined than by our need to protect our self-image.

Retrieve + Remember

- What are three big ideas that have survived from Freud's psychoanalytic theory? What are three ways in which Freud's theory has been criticized?

ANSWER: Freud is credited with first drawing attention to (1) the importance of childhood experiences, (2) the existence of the unconscious mind, and (3) our self-protective defense mechanisms. Freud's theory has been criticized as (1) not scientifically testable and offering after-the-fact explanations, (2) focusing too much on sexual conflicts in childhood, and (3) the idea of repression, which has not been supported by modern research.

- Which elements of traditional psychoanalysis have modern-day psychodynamic theorists and therapists retained, and which elements have they mostly left behind?

ANSWER: Today's psychodynamic theorists still tend to focus on childhood experiences and attachments, unresolved conflicts, and unconscious influences. However, they are not likely to focus on fixation at any psychosexual stage, or the idea that sexual issues are the basis of our personality.

Humanistic Theories

LOQ 12-10 How did humanistic psychologists view personality, and what was their goal in studying personality?

By the 1960s, some personality psychologists decided that their field needed fresh ideas and a new direction. They thought Freud's views were too negative. They were equally uncomfortable with the strict behaviorism of John Watson and B. F. Skinner (Chapter 6), judging it to be too mechanical. This movement helped produce *humanistic psychologists* such as Abraham Maslow (1908–1970) and Carl Rogers (1902–1987). They shifted the focus from disorders born out of dark conflicts to emphasizing ways *healthy* people strive for self-determination and self-realization. In contrast to behaviorism's objective laboratory experiments, they asked people to report their own experiences and feelings.

Abraham Maslow's Self-Actualizing Person

Abraham Maslow proposed that human motivations form a pyramid-shaped **hierarchy of needs** (Chapter 9). At the base are bodily needs. If those are met, we become concerned with the next-higher level of need, for personal safety. If we feel secure, we then seek to love, to be loved, and to love ourselves. With our love needs satisfied, we seek self-esteem (feelings of self-worth). Having achieved self-esteem, we strive for the top-level needs for **self-actualization** and **self-transcendence**. These motives, at the pyramid's peak, involve reaching our full potential.

Maslow (1970) formed his ideas by studying healthy, creative people rather than troubled clinical cases. His description of self-actualization grew out of his study of people, such as Abraham Lincoln, who had lived rich and productive lives. They were self-aware and self-accepting. They were open and

ABRAHAM MASLOW "Any theory of motivation that is worthy of attention must deal with the highest capacities of the healthy and strong person as well as with the defensive maneuvers of crippled spirits" (*Motivation and Personality*, 1970, p. 33).

spontaneous. They were loving and caring. They didn't worry too much about other people's opinions. Yet they were not self-centered. Curious about the world, they embraced uncertainties and stretched themselves to seek out new experiences (Kashdan, 2009). Once they focused their energies on a particular task, they often regarded that task as their life mission, or "calling" (Hall & Chandler, 2005). Most enjoyed a few deep relationships rather than many shallow ones. Many had been moved by spiritual or personal *peak experiences* that were beyond normal consciousness.

Maslow considered these to be mature adult qualities. These healthy people had outgrown their mixed feelings toward their parents. They had "acquired enough courage to be

hierarchy of needs Maslow's pyramid of human needs; at the base are physiological needs. These basic needs must be satisfied before higher-level safety needs, and then psychological needs, become active.

self-actualization according to Maslow, the psychological need that arises after basic physical and psychological needs are met and self-esteem is achieved; the motivation to fulfill our potential.

self-transcendence according to Maslow, the striving for identity, meaning, and purpose beyond the self.

unpopular, to be unashamed about being openly virtuous." Maslow's work with college students led him to believe that those likely to become self-actualizing adults were likable, caring young people who were "privately affectionate to those of their elders who deserve it," and "secretly uneasy about the cruelty, meanness, and mob spirit so often found in young people."

Carl Rogers' Person-Centered Perspective

Carl Rogers agreed that people have self-actualizing tendencies. Rogers' *person-centered perspective* held that people are basically good. Like plants, we are primed to reach our potential if we are given a growth-promoting environment. People nurture our growth, and we nurture theirs, he said, in three ways (Rogers, 1980).

- Being *genuine*. If we are genuine to another person, we are open with our own feelings. We drop our false fronts and are transparent and self-disclosing.

- Being *accepting*. If we are accepting, we offer the other person what Rogers called **unconditional positive regard.** This is an attitude of total acceptance. We value the person even knowing the person's failings. We all find it a huge relief to drop our pretenses, confess our worst feelings, and discover that we are still

"Just remember, son, it doesn't matter whether you win or lose—unless you want Daddy's love."

A father *not* offering unconditional positive regard.

accepted. In a good marriage, a close family, or an intimate friendship, we are free to be ourselves without fearing what others will think.

- Being *empathic*. If we are empathic, we share another's feelings and reflect that person's meanings back to them. "Rarely do we listen with real understanding, true empathy," said Rogers. "Yet listening, of this very special kind, is one of the most potent forces for change that I know."

Genuineness, acceptance, and empathy are, Rogers believed, the water, sun, and nutrients that enable people to grow like vigorous oak trees. For "as persons are accepted and prized, they tend to develop a more caring attitude toward themselves" (Rogers, 1980, p. 116). As persons are empathically heard, "it becomes possible for them to listen more accurately to the flow of inner experiencing."

Rogers called for genuineness, acceptance, and empathy in the relationship between therapist and client. But he also believed that these three qualities nurture growth between any two human beings—between leader and group member, teacher and student, manager and staff member, parent and child, friend and friend.

Writer Calvin Trillin (2006) recalls an example of parental genuineness and acceptance at a camp for children with severe disorders, where his wife, Alice, worked. L., a "magical child," had genetic diseases that meant she had to be tube-fed and could walk only with difficulty. Alice recalled,

> One day, when we were playing duck-duck-goose, I was sitting behind her and she asked me to hold her mail for her while she took her turn to be chased around the circle. It took her a while to make the circuit, and I had time to see that on top of the pile [of mail] was a note from her mom. Then I did something truly awful. . . . I simply had to know what this child's parents could have done to make her so spectacular, to make her the most optimistic, most enthusiastic, most hopeful human being I had ever encountered. I snuck a quick look at the note, and my eyes fell on this sentence: "If God had given us all of the children in the world

THE PICTURE OF EMPATHY Being open and sharing confidences is easier when the listener shows real understanding. Within such relationships we can relax and fully express our true selves.

to choose from, L., we would only have chosen you." Before L. got back to her place in the circle, I showed the note to Bud, who was sitting next to me. "Quick. Read this," I whispered. "It's the secret of life."

Maslow and Rogers would have smiled knowingly. For them, a central feature of personality is one's **self-concept**—all the thoughts and feelings we have in response to the question, "Who am I?" If our self-concept is positive, we tend to act and perceive the world positively. If it is negative—if in our own eyes we fall far short of our *ideal self*—we feel dissatisfied and unhappy. A worthwhile goal for therapists, parents, teachers, and friends is therefore to help others know, accept, and be true to themselves, said Rogers.

Assessing the Self

LOQ 12-11 How did humanistic psychologists assess a person's sense of self?

Humanistic psychologists sometimes assessed personality by asking people to fill out questionnaires that would evaluate their self-concept. One questionnaire, inspired by Carl Rogers, asked people to describe themselves both as they would *ideally* like to be and as they *actually* are. When the ideal and the actual self are nearly alike, said Rogers, the self-concept is positive. Assessing his clients' personal growth during therapy, he looked for closer and closer ratings of actual and ideal selves.

Some humanistic psychologists believed that any standardized assessment of personality, even a questionnaire, is depersonalizing. Rather than forcing the person to respond to narrow categories, these humanistic psychologists presumed that interviews and intimate conversation would provide a better understanding of each person's unique experiences. Some researchers believe our identity may be revealed using the *life story approach*—collecting a rich narrative detailing each person's unique life history (Adler et al., 2016; McAdams & Guo, 2015). A lifetime of stories can show more of a person's complete identity than can the responses to a few questions.

Evaluating Humanistic Theories

LOQ 12-12 How have humanistic theories influenced psychology? What criticisms have they faced?

Just as Freudian concepts have seeped into modern culture, humanistic psychology has had a far-reaching impact. Maslow's and Rogers' ideas have influenced counseling, education, child raising, and management. And they laid the groundwork for today's scientific *positive psychology* subfield (Chapter 1).

These theorists have also influenced—sometimes in unintended ways—much of today's popular psychology. Is a positive self-concept the key to happiness and success? Do acceptance and empathy nurture positive feelings about ourselves? Are people basically good and capable of improving? Many would answer *Yes, Yes,* and *Yes.* In 2006, U.S. high school students reported notably higher self-esteem and greater expectations of future career success than did students living in 1975 (Twenge & Campbell, 2008). When you hear talk about the importance of "loving your-

self," you can give some credit to the humanistic theories.

Many psychologists have criticized the humanistic perspective. First, said the critics, its concepts are vague and based on the theorists' personal opinions, rather than on scientific methods. Consider Maslow's description of self-actualizing people as open, spontaneous, loving, self-accepting, and productive. Is this a scientific description? Or is it merely a description of Maslow's own values and ideals, as viewed in his own personal heroes (Smith, 1978)? Imagine another theorist with a different set of heroes, such as the French military conqueror Napoleon and former U.S. Vice President Dick Cheney. This theorist might have described self-actualizing people as "desiring power," "willing to go to war," and "self-assured."

Other critics objected to the attitudes that humanistic psychology encourages. Rogers, for example, said, "The only question which matters is, 'Am I living in a way which is deeply satisfying to me, and which truly expresses me?'" (quoted by Wallach & Wallach, 1985). Imagine working on a group project with people who refuse to complete any task that is not deeply satisfying or does not truly express their identity. Such attitudes could lead to self-indulgence, selfishness, and a lack of moral restraint (Campbell & Specht, 1985; Wallach & Wallach, 1983).

Humanistic psychologists have replied that a secure, nondefensive self-acceptance is the important first step toward loving others. Indeed, people who recall feeling liked and accepted by a romantic partner—for who they are, not just for their achievements—report being happier in their relationships and acting more kindly toward their partner (Gordon & Chen, 2010).

A final criticism has been that humanistic psychology fails to appreciate our human capacity for evil (May, 1982). Faced with global climate change, overpopulation, terrorism, and the spread of nuclear weapons, we may be paralyzed by either of two ways of thinking. One is a naive optimism that denies the

threat ("People are basically good; everything will work out"). The other is a dark despair ("It's hopeless; why try?"). Action requires enough realism to fuel concern and enough optimism to provide hope. Humanistic psychology, said the critics, encourages the needed hope but not the equally necessary realism about threats.

Retrieve + Remember

- How did humanistic psychology provide a fresh perspective?

ANSWER: This movement sought to turn psychology's attention away from drives and conflicts and toward our growth potential. This focus on the way healthy people strive for self-determination and self-realization was in contrast to Freudian theory and strict behaviorism.

- What does it mean to be *empathic*? How about *self-actualized*? Which humanistic psychologists used these terms?

ANSWERS: To be empathic is to share and mirror another person's feelings. Carl Rogers believed that people nurture growth in others by being empathic. Abraham Maslow proposed that *self-actualization* is the motivation to fulfill one's potential, and one of the ultimate psychological needs (the other is self-transcendence).

Trait Theories

LOQ 12-13 How do psychologists use traits to describe personality?

Freudian and humanistic theories shared a common goal: Explain how our personality develops. They focused on the forces that act upon us. **Trait**

---

unconditional positive regard a caring, accepting, nonjudgmental attitude, which Rogers believed would help people develop self-awareness and self-acceptance.

self-concept all our thoughts and feelings about ourselves, in answer to the question, "Who am I?"

trait a characteristic pattern of behavior or a tendency to feel and act in a certain way, as assessed by self-report inventories and peer reports.

researchers, led by the work of Gordon Allport (1897–1967), have been less concerned with *explaining* traits than with *describing* them. They define personality as a *stable and enduring pattern of behavior*, such as Lady Gaga's openness to new experiences and self-discipline. These traits help describe her personality.

Exploring Traits

Imagine that you've been hired by an online dating service. Your job is to construct a questionnaire for a new app that will better help people describe themselves to those seeking dates and mates. With millions of people using such services each year, the need to understand and incorporate psychological science grows more important (Finkel et al., 2012a,b). What personality traits might give an accurate sense of the person filling out your questionnaire? You might begin by thinking of how we describe a pizza. We place a pizza along several trait dimensions. It's small, medium, or large; it has one or more toppings; it has a thin or thick crust. By likewise placing people on trait dimensions, we can begin to describe them.

"Russ is the sort of person who never wants to be alone with his thoughts."

Basic Factors

An even better way to identify our personality is to identify **factors**—clusters of behavior tendencies that occur together (McCabe & Fleeson, 2016). People who describe themselves as outgoing, for example, may also say that they like excitement and practical jokes and dislike quiet reading. This cluster of behaviors reflects a basic factor, or trait—in this case, *extraversion*. (For more about extraversion's opposite, see Thinking Critically About: The Stigma of Introversion.)

So how many traits will be just the right number for success with your dating questionnaire? If psychologists Hans Eysenck and Sybil Eysenck [EYE-zink] had been hired to do your job, they would have said two. They believed that we can reduce many normal human variations to two basic dimensions: Extraversion–introversion and emotional stability–instability (**FIGURE 12.3**). People in 35 countries, from China to Uganda to Russia, have taken the Eysenck Personality Questionnaire. The extraversion and emotionality factors emerged as basic personality dimensions (Eysenck, 1990, 1992).

Biology and Personality

As you may recall from the twin and adoption studies discussed in Chapter 3, our genes have much to say about the temperament and behavioral style that help define our personality. Children's shyness, for example, seems related to differences in their autonomic nervous systems. Infants with reactive autonomic nervous systems respond to stress with greater anxiety and inhibition (Kagan, 2010).

	UNSTABLE	
Moody		Touchy
Anxious		Restless
Rigid		Aggressive
Sober		Excitable
Pessimistic		Changeable
Reserved		Impulsive
Unsociable		Optimistic
Quiet		Active
INTROVERTED		**EXTRAVERTED**
Passive		Sociable
Careful		Outgoing
Thoughtful		Talkative
Peaceful		Responsive
Controlled		Easygoing
Reliable		Lively
Even-tempered		Carefree
Calm		Leadership
	STABLE	

FIGURE 12.3 Two personality dimensions Mapmakers can tell us a lot by using two axes (north–south and east–west). Two primary personality factors (extraversion–introversion and stability–instability) are similarly useful as axes for describing personality variation. Varying combinations define other, more specific traits (from Eysenck & Eysenck, 1963). Those who are naturally introverted, such as primatologist Jane Goodall, may be particularly gifted in field studies. Successful comedians, including Stephen Colbert, are often natural extraverts.

LOQ 12-14 What are some common misunderstandings about introversion?

Thinking Critically About:
The Stigma of Introversion

Western cultures prize extraversion:

Superheroes tend to be extraverted: Superman is bold and energetic. His introverted alter ego, Clark Kent, is mild-mannered and bumbling.

87% of Westerners want to be more extraverted. [1]

Being introverted seems to imply that we don't have the "right stuff." [2]

Take-charge Elastigirl saves the day in *The Incredibles*.

Attractive, successful people are presumed to be extraverts.

What is introversion?

Introversion is *not* shyness.
(Shy people remain quiet because they fear others will evaluate them negatively.)

Introverted people seek low levels of stimulation from their environment because they're ***sensitive***. For example, when given lemon juice, introverted people salivated more than extraverted people. [3]

Introversion may have benefits:

• Introverted leaders outperform extraverted leaders in some contexts, such as when their employees voice new ideas and challenge existing norms. [4]

• An analysis of 35 studies showed no correlation between extraversion and sales performance. [5]

• Many introverts prosper, including Abraham Lincoln, Mother Teresa, and Gandhi.

1. Hudson & Roberts, 2014. 2. Cain, 2012. 3. Corcoran, 1964. 4. Grant et al., 2011. 5. Barrick et al., 2001.

Brain activity appears to vary with personality as well. Brain-activity scans suggest that extraverts seek stimulation because their normal brain arousal is relatively low. Also, a frontal lobe area involved in restraining behavior is less active in extraverts than in introverts (Johnson et al., 1999).

Personality differences among dogs are as obvious to researchers as they are to dog owners. Such differences (in energy, affection, reactivity, and curious intelligence) are as evident, and as consistently judged, as personality differences among humans (Gosling et al., 2003; Jones & Gosling, 2005). Monkeys, bonobos, chimpanzees, orangutans, and even birds also have stable personalities (Weiss et al., 2006, 2015). Among the Great Tit (a European relative of the American

Erik Lam/Shutterstock

chickadee), bold birds more quickly inspect new objects and explore trees (Groothuis & Carere, 2005; Verbeek et al., 1994). Through selective breeding, researchers can produce bold or shy birds. Both have their place in natural history. In lean years, bold birds are more likely to find food; in abundant years, shy birds feed with less risk.

Assessing Traits

LOQ 12-15 What are personality inventories?

It helps to know that a potential date is an introvert or an extravert, or even that the person is emotionally stable or unstable. But wouldn't you like more information about the test-taker's personality before matching people as romantic partners? The **Minnesota Multiphasic Personality Inventory (MMPI)** might help.

Retrieve + Remember

• Which two primary dimensions did Hans Eysenck and Sybil Eysenck propose for describing personality variation?

ANSWER: introversion–extraversion and emotional stability–instability

factor a cluster of behavior tendencies that occur together.

Minnesota Multiphasic Personality Inventory (MMPI) the most widely researched and clinically used of all personality tests. Originally developed to identify emotional disorders (still considered its most appropriate use), this test is now used for many other screening purposes.

Personality inventories, including the famous MMPI, are long sets of questions covering a wide range of feelings and behaviors. Although the MMPI was originally developed to identify emotional disorders, it also assesses people's personality traits. Whereas most projective tests (such as the Rorschach) are scored subjectively, personality inventories are scored objectively. Objectivity does not, however, guarantee validity. People taking the MMPI for employment purposes can give the answers they know will create a good impression. But in so doing they may also score high on a *lie scale* that assesses faking (as when people respond *False* to a universally true statement, such as "I get angry sometimes"). The objectivity of the MMPI has contributed to its popularity and to its translation into more than 100 languages.

LaunchPad *IMMERSIVE LEARNING*
Might astrology hold the secret to our personality traits? To consider this question, visit LaunchPad's *How Would You Know If Astrologers Can Describe People's Personality?*

The Big Five Factors

LOQ 12-16 Which traits seem to provide the most useful information about personality variation?

Today's trait researchers rely on five factors (called the Big Five) to understand personality—conscientiousness, agreeableness, neuroticism, openness, and extraversion (**TABLE 12.3**) (Costa & McCrae, 2011; John & Srivastava, 1999). Work by Paul Costa, Robert McCrae, and others shows that where we fall on these five dimensions reveals much of what there is to say about our personality. Some clinical psychologists have begun to use the Big Five to understand personality disorder and dysfunction (Widiger et al., 2016).

As the dominant model in personality psychology, Big Five research has explored various questions:

- *How stable are these traits?* One research team analyzed 1.25 million participants ages 10 to 65. They learned that personality continues to develop and change through late childhood and adolescence. By adulthood, our traits have become fairly stable, though conscientiousness, agreeableness, openness, and extraversion continue to increase over the life span, and neuroticism (emotional instability) decreases (Soto et al., 2011).

- *Do we inherit these traits?* Roughly 40 percent of our individual differences on the Big Five can be credited to our genes (Vukasović & Bratko, 2015).

- *Do these traits reflect differing brain structure or function?* The size of different brain regions does correlate with several Big Five traits (DeYoung et al., 2010; Grodin & White, 2015). For example, those who score high on conscientiousness tend to have a larger frontal lobe area that aids in planning and controlling behavior. Brain connections also influence the Big Five traits (Adelstein et al., 2011). People high in openness have brains that are wired to experience intense imagination, curiosity, and fantasy.

- *Have levels of these traits changed over time?* Cultures change over time, which can influence shifts in personality. Within the United States and the Netherlands, extraversion and conscientiousness have increased over time (Mroczek & Spiro, 2003; Smits et al., 2011; Twenge, 2001).

- *How well do these traits apply to various cultures?* The Big Five dimensions describe personality in various cultures reasonably well (Schmitt et al., 2007; Vazsonyi et al., 2015; Yamagata et al., 2006). After studying people from 50 cultures, Robert McCrae and 79 co-researchers concluded that "features of personality traits are common to all human groups" (2005).

- *Do the Big Five traits predict our actual behavior? Yes.* For example, our traits appear in our language patterns. In blog posts, extraversion predicts use of personal pronouns (*we, our, us*). Agreeableness predicts positive-emotion words. Neuroticism predicts negative-emotion words (Yarkoni, 2010).

To find out how your personality measures up, try the brief self-assessment in **FIGURE 12.4**. If you work the Big Five traits into your dating questionnaire, your mission should be accomplished—if people act the same way at all times and in all situations, that is. Do they?

LaunchPad For an 8-minute demonstration of trait research, visit LaunchPad's *Video: Trait Theories of Personality.*

TABLE 12.3 The "Big Five" Personality Factors

Researchers use self-report inventories and peer reports to assess and score the Big Five personality factors.

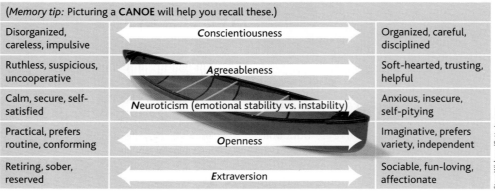

*(Memory tip: Picturing a **CANOE** will help you recall these.)*

Disorganized, careless, impulsive	**Conscientiousness**	Organized, careful, disciplined
Ruthless, suspicious, uncooperative	**Agreeableness**	Soft-hearted, trusting, helpful
Calm, secure, self-satisfied	**Neuroticism** (emotional stability vs. instability)	Anxious, insecure, self-pitying
Practical, prefers routine, conforming	**Openness**	Imaginative, prefers variety, independent
Retiring, sober, reserved	**Extraversion**	Sociable, fun-loving, affectionate

Source: Information from McCrae & Costa (1986, 2008).

Steve Wisbauer/Getty Images

How Do You Describe Yourself?

Describe yourself as you generally are now, not as you wish to be in the future. Describe yourself as you honestly see yourself, in relation to other people you know of the same sex and roughly the same age. Use the scale below to enter a number for each statement. Then, use the scoring guide at the bottom to see where you fall on the spectrum for each of the Big Five traits.

1	2	3	4	5
Very Inaccurate	Moderately Inaccurate	Neither Accurate Nor Inaccurate	Moderately Accurate	Very Accurate

1. ____Am the life of the party
2. ____Sympathize with others' feelings
3. ____Get stressed out easily
4. ____Am always prepared
5. ____Am full of ideas
6. ____Start conversations
7. ____Take time out for others
8. ____Follow a schedule
9. ____Worry about things
10. ____Have a vivid imagination

SCORING GUIDE SORTED BY BIG FIVE PERSONALITY TRAITS

Conscientiousness: statements 4, 8

Agreeableness: statements 2, 7

Neuroticism: statements 3, 9

Openness: statements 5, 10

Extraversion: statements 1, 6

How to score:
Separate your responses by each Big Five personality trait, as noted at left, and divide by two to obtain your score for each trait. So, for example, for the "Agreeableness" trait let's say you scored 3 for statement 2 ("Sympathize with others' feelings") and 4 for statement 7 ("Take time out for others"). That means on a scale from 1 to 5, your overall score for the "Agreeableness" trait is 3 + 4 = 7 ÷ 2 = 3.5.

FIGURE 12.4 The Big Five self-assessment Scale data from Goldberg, L. R. (1992). The development of markers for the Big-Five factor structure. *Psychological Assessment, 4,* 26–42.

Retrieve + Remember

- What are the Big Five personality factors, and why are they scientifically useful?

ANSWER: The Big Five personality factors are conscientiousness, agreeableness, neuroticism (emotional stability vs. instability), openness, and extraversion (CANOE). These factors may be objectively measured, they are relatively stable across the life span, and they apply to all cultures in which they have been studied.

Evaluating Trait Theories

LOQ 12-17 Does research support the consistency of personality traits over time and across situations?

To be useful indicators of personality, traits would have to persist over time and across situations. Friendly people, for example, would have to act friendly at different times and places. In some ways, our personality seems stable. Cheerful, friendly children tend to become cheerful, friendly adults. But it's also true that a fun-loving jokester can suddenly turn serious and respectful at a job interview. Major life events, such as becoming unemployed, can shift our personality from agreeable to slightly rude (Boyce et al., 2015). The personality traits we express change from one situation to another.

The Person-Situation Controversy

Many researchers have studied personality stability over the life span. A group of 152 long-term studies compared early trait scores with scores for the same traits seven years later. These comparisons were done for several different age groups, and for each group, the scores were positively correlated. But the correlations were strongest for comparisons done in adulthood. For young children, the correlation between early and later scores was +0.3. For college students, the correlation was +0.54. For 70-year-olds, the correlation was +0.73. (Remember that 0 indicates no relationship, and +1.0 would mean that one score perfectly predicts the other.)

As we grow older, our personality traits stabilize. Interests may change—the devoted collector of tropical fish may become the devoted gardener. Careers may change—the determined salesperson may become a determined social worker. Relationships may change—the hostile spouse may start over with a new partner. But most people recognize their traits as just who they are.

The consistency of specific *behaviors* from one situation to the next is another matter. People are not always predictable. What relationship would you expect to find between being conscientious on one occasion (say, showing up for class on time) and being conscientious on another occasion (say, avoiding unhealthy foods)? If you've noticed how outgoing you are in some situations and how reserved you are in others, perhaps you said, "Very little." That's what researchers have found—only a small correlation (Mischel, 1968, 2004; Sherman et al., 2015). This inconsistency makes personality traits weak predictors of behaviors. Personality traits predict a person's behavior *across many different situations.* They do not neatly predict a person's behavior *in any one specific situation* (Mischel, 1968, 1984; Mischel & Shoda, 1995).

If we remember such results, we will be more careful about labeling other people (Mischel, 1968, 2004). We will recognize how difficult it is to predict whether

personality inventory a questionnaire (often with *true-false* or *agree-disagree* items) on which people respond to items designed to gauge a wide range of feelings and behaviors; used to assess selected personality traits.

my hair over time

childhood

teens and twenties - experimentation

thirties and up   *mitra farmand*

It's not just personality that stabilizes with age.

someone is likely to violate parole, commit suicide, or be an effective employee. Years in advance, science can tell us the distance of the Earth from the Sun for any given date. A day in advance, meteorologists can often predict the weather. Yet psychologists have not yet solved the riddle of how you will feel and act tomorrow, or even a few hours from now.

Does this mean that psychological science has nothing meaningful to say about personality traits? *No!* Remember that traits do a good job at predicting people's *average* behavior (outgoingness, happiness, carelessness) over *many* situations (Epstein, 1983a,b).

Even when we try to restrain them, our traits may assert themselves. During my [DM] noontime pickup basketball games with friends, I keep vowing to cut back on my jabbering and joking. But without fail, the irrepressible chatterbox reoccupies my body moments later. I [ND] have a similar experience each time I try to stay quiet when riding in taxis, but somehow always end up chatting!

Our personality traits lurk in some unexpected places.

- *Music preferences:* Your playlist says a lot about your personality. Classical, jazz, blues, and folk music lovers tend to be open to experience and verbally intelligent. Extraverts tend to prefer upbeat and energetic music. Country, pop, and religious music lovers tend to be cheerful, outgoing, and conscientious (Langmeyer et al., 2012; Rentfrow & Gosling, 2003, 2006).

Written communications: Have you ever felt you could detect others' personality from their writing voice? You are right!! What a cool finding!!! ☺ From people's writing we can predict their levels of extraversion, neuroticism, and agreeableness (Gill et al., 2006; Park et al., 2015; Pennebaker, 2011). For example, those who score high in extraversion draw attention to themselves by using more first-person singular pronouns (*I* and *me*). Those high in neuroticism use more negative emotion words. And those high in agreeableness use fewer swear words.

- *Online and personal spaces:* Online profiles, blogs, websites, instant messaging accounts, and avatars are also a canvas for self-expression. People who seem most likeable on their Facebook page also seem most likeable in face-to-face meetings (Weisbuch et al., 2009). Your online self may indeed reflect the real you! Our living and working spaces also help us express our identity. They all offer clues to a person's extraversion, agreeableness, conscientiousness, and openness (Back et al., 2010; Fong & Mar, 2015; Gosling, 2008). Even mere photos, with their associated clothes, expressions, and postures, can give clues to personality (Naumann et al., 2009).

ROOM WITH A CUE Even at "zero acquaintance," people can catch a glimpse of others' personality from looking at their online and personal spaces. So, what's your read on this person's office?

In unfamiliar, formal situations—perhaps as a guest in the home of a person from another culture—our traits remain hidden as we carefully attend to social cues. In familiar, informal situations—just hanging out with friends—we feel more relaxed, and our traits emerge (Buss, 1989). In these informal situations, our expressive styles—our animation, manner of speaking, and gestures—are impressively consistent. Viewing "thin slices" of someone's behavior—such as seeing a photo for a mere fraction of a second or seeing three different 2-second video clips of a teacher in action—can tell us a lot about the person's basic personality traits (Ambady, 2010; Rule et al., 2009).

To sum up, we can say that the immediate situation powerfully influences our behavior, *especially when the situation makes clear demands* (Cooper & Withey, 2009). We can better predict drivers' behavior at traffic lights from knowing the color of the lights than from knowing the drivers' personalities. Averaging our behavior across many occasions does, however, reveal distinct personality traits. Traits exist, and they leave tracks in our lives. We differ. And our differences matter.

Retrieve + Remember

- How well do personality test scores predict our behavior? Explain.

ANSWER: Our scores on personality tests predict our *average* behavior across many situations much better than they predict our specific behavior in any given situation.

Social-Cognitive Theories

LOQ 12-18 How do social-cognitive theorists view personality development, and how do they explore behavior?

Reciprocal Influences

So, our personal traits interact with our environment to influence our behavior. Albert Bandura (1986, 2006, 2008) called this process **reciprocal determinism.**

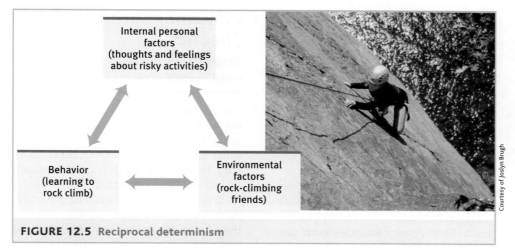

FIGURE 12.5 Reciprocal determinism

Courtesy of Joslyn Brugh

> **reciprocal determinism** the interacting influences of behavior, internal personal factors, and environment.
>
> **social-cognitive perspective** views behavior as influenced by the interaction between persons (and their thinking) and their social context.
>
> **self-efficacy** our sense of competence and effectiveness.

"Behavior, internal personal factors, and environmental influences," he said, "all operate as interlocking determinants of each other" (**FIGURE 12.5**).

The **social-cognitive perspective** on personality that Bandura proposed is especially focused on the many ways our individual traits and thoughts interact with our social world as we move from one situation to another. We bring a lot to any social situation we enter. We bring our past learning, often picked up through conditioning or by observing others. We bring our **self-efficacy**—our expectations about whether we will succeed in (and attempt) new challenges (Bandura, 1977). We also bring our ways of thinking about specific situations. But situations themselves place different demands on us. Most of us know the general social rules for acceptable behavior at a grandparent's funeral, for example. We also know that a different set of rules outlines what's acceptable at a friend's New Year's Eve party. In the end, our behavior in any situation is in part the result of our own characteristics and in part the result of the situation.

Roughly speaking, the short-term, outside influences on behavior are the focus of social psychology (Chapter 11), and the lasting, inner influences are the focus of personality psychology. In actuality, behavior always depends on the interaction of persons with situations.

We can see this interaction in people's relationships. For example, Rosa's romantic history (past behavior) influences her attitudes toward new relationships (internal factor), which affects how she now responds to Ryan (environmental factor). Social-cognitive theorists explore the *interaction* among the three sets of influence:

1. *Different people choose different environments.* What school do you attend? What do you read? What shows do you watch? What music do you listen to? With whom do you enjoy spending time? All these choices are part of an environment you are choosing, based partly on your personality (Ickes et al., 1997). We choose our environment, and it then shapes us.

2. *Our personalities shape how we interpret and react to events.* Anxious people tend to attend and react strongly to relationship threats (Campbell & Marshall, 2011). If we perceive the world as threatening, we will watch for threats and be prepared to defend ourselves.

3. *Our personalities help create situations to which we react.* How we view and treat people influences how they then treat us. If we expect that others will not like us, our desperate attempts to seek their approval might cause them to reject us. Depressed people often engage in

this excessive reassurance seeking, which may confirm their negative self-views (Coyne, 1976a,b).

In addition to the interaction of internal personal factors, the environment, and our behaviors, we also experience *gene-environment interaction* (Chapter 3). Our genetically influenced traits evoke certain responses from others, which may nudge us in one direction or another. In one classic study, those with the interacting factors of (1) having a specific gene associated with aggression, and (2) being raised in a difficult environment were most likely to demonstrate adult antisocial behavior (Caspi et al., 2002).

In such ways, we are both the products and the architects of our environments. Boiling water turns an egg hard and a noodle soft. Academic challenges turn one person into a success and another toward collapse (Harms et al., 2006). At every moment, our behavior is influenced by our biology, our social and cultural experiences, and our thought processes and traits (**FIGURE 12.6**).

Retrieve + Remember

- Albert Bandura proposed the _____-_____ perspective on personality, which emphasizes the interaction of people with their environment. To describe the interacting influences of behavior, thoughts, and environment, he used the term _____ _____.

ANSWERS: social-cognitive; reciprocal determinism

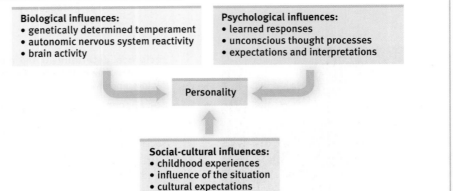

Biological influences:
• genetically determined temperament
• autonomic nervous system reactivity
• brain activity

Psychological influences:
• learned responses
• unconscious thought processes
• expectations and interpretations

Personality

Social-cultural influences:
• childhood experiences
• influence of the situation
• cultural expectations
• social support

FIGURE 12.6 The biopsychosocial approach to the study of personality

Assessing Behavior in Situations

To predict behavior, social-cognitive psychologists often observe behavior in realistic situations. Military and educational organizations and many Fortune 500 companies use such strategies (Bray & Byham, 1991, 1997; Eurich et al., 2009). AT&T has observed prospective managers doing simulated managerial work. Many colleges assess nursing students' potential by observing their clinical work, and evaluate potential faculty members' teaching abilities by observing them

teach. Most American cities with populations of 50,000 or more have used such strategies in evaluating police officers and firefighters (Lowry, 1997).

These assessment exercises have some limitations. They may not reveal less visible but important characteristics, such as inner achievement drive (Bowler & Woehr, 2006). These procedures do exploit a valid principle: The best way to predict future behavior is neither a personality test nor an interviewer's intuition; rather, *it is the person's past behavior patterns in similar situations* (Lyons et al., 2011; Mischel, 1981; Schmidt & Hunter, 1998).

Evaluating Social-Cognitive Theories

LOQ 12-19 What criticisms have social-cognitive theorists faced?

Social-cognitive theories of personality emphasize how situations affect, and are affected by, individuals. More than other personality theories (**TABLE 12.4**), they build from psychological research on learning and cognition.

Critics charge that social-cognitive theories focus so much on the situation that they fail to appreciate the person's inner traits. They note that in many instances our unconscious motives, our emotions, and our traits shine through. Personality traits have been shown to predict behavior at work, love, and play. Consider Percy Ray Pridgen and Charles Gill. Each faced the same situation: They had jointly won a $90 million lottery jackpot (Harriston, 1993). When Pridgen learned of the winning numbers, he began trembling uncontrollably, huddled with a friend behind a bathroom door while confirming the win, then sobbed. When Gill heard the news, he told his wife and then went to sleep.

Personality Theory	Key Proponents	Assumptions	View of Personality	Personality Assessment Methods
Psychoanalytic	Freud	Emotional disorders spring from unconscious dynamics, such as unresolved sexual and other childhood conflicts, and fixation at various developmental stages. Defense mechanisms fend off anxiety.	Personality consists of pleasure-seeking impulses (the id), a reality-oriented executive (the ego), and an internalized set of ideals (the superego).	Free association, projective tests, dream analysis
Psychodynamic	Adler, Horney, Jung	The unconscious and conscious minds interact. Childhood experiences and defense mechanisms are important.	The dynamic interplay of conscious and unconscious motives and conflicts shapes our personality.	Projective tests, therapy sessions
Humanistic	Rogers, Maslow	Rather than examining the struggles of sick people, it's better to focus on the ways healthy people strive for self-realization.	If our basic human needs are met, we will strive toward self-actualization. In a climate of unconditional positive regard, we can develop self-awareness and a more realistic and positive self-concept.	Questionnaires, therapy sessions
Trait	Allport, Eysenck, McCrae, Costa	We have certain stable and enduring characteristics, influenced by genetic predispositions.	Scientific study of traits has isolated important dimensions of personality, such as the Big Five traits (conscientiousness, agreeableness, neuroticism, openness, and extraversion).	Personality inventories
Social-Cognitive	Bandura	Our traits interact with the social context to produce our behaviors.	Conditioning and observational learning interact with cognition to create behavior patterns.	Our behavior in one situation is best predicted by considering our past behavior in similar situations.

TABLE 12.4 Comparing the Major Personality Theories

Exploring the Self

LOQ 12-20 Why has psychology generated so much research on the self? How important is self-esteem to our well-being?

We can think of our *self-image* as our internal view of our personality. Underlying this idea is the notion that the **self** is the center of personality—the organizer of our thoughts, feelings, and actions.

Consider the concept of *possible selves* (Cross & Markus, 1991; Markus & Nurius, 1986). Your possible selves include your visions of the self you dream of becoming—the rich self, the successful self, the loved and admired self. Your possible selves also include the self you fear becoming—the unemployed self, the academically failed self, the lonely and unpopular self. Possible selves motivate us to lay out specific goals that direct our energy effectively and efficiently (Landau et al., 2014). Middle school students whose families struggle financially are more likely to earn high grades if they have a clear vision of themselves succeeding in school (Duckworth et al., 2013).

> "The first step to better times is to imagine them."
> Chinese fortune cookie

Carried too far, our self-focus can lead us to fret that others are noticing and evaluating us. One of our favorite psychology experiments demonstrated this **spotlight effect** by having Cornell University students put on T-shirts featuring soft-rock star Barry Manilow, then enter a room with other students. Feeling self-conscious, the T-shirt

Gustavo Caballero/Getty Images

IF YOU CAN'T STAND THE HEAT . . . On the Food Network's *Chopped* show, contestants are pitted against one another in stressful situations. The entertaining episodes do illustrate a valid point: Seeing how potential chefs behave in such job-relevant situations helps predict their job performance.

wearers guessed that nearly half their peers would take note of the shirt as they walked in. In reality, only 23 percent did (Gilovich, 1996). *The point to remember:* We stand out less than we imagine, even with dorky clothes or bad hair, and even after a blunder like setting off a library alarm (Gilovich & Savitsky, 1999; Savitsky et al., 2001).

To turn down the brightness of the spotlight, we can use two strategies. The first is simply knowing about the spotlight effect. Public speakers perform better if they understand that their natural nervousness is not obvious (Savitsky & Gilovich, 2003). The second is to take the audience's perspective. When we imagine audience members empathizing with our situation, we tend to expect we will not be judged as harshly (Epley et al., 2002).

The Benefits of Self-Esteem

If we like our self-image, we probably have high **self-esteem**. This feeling of high self-worth will translate into more restful nights and less pressure to conform. We'll be

more persistent at difficult tasks. We'll be less shy, anxious, and lonely, and, in the future, we'll be more successful and just plain happier (Greenberg, 2008; Orth & Robins, 2014; Swann et al., 2007). Our self-esteem changes as we age. In one study of nearly 1 million people across 48 nations, self-esteem increased from adolescence to middle adulthood (Bleidorn et al., 2016).

Self-esteem is a household word. College students even report wanting high self-esteem more than food or sex (Bushman et al., 2011). But most research challenges the idea that high self-esteem is "the armor that protects kids" from life's problems (Baumeister, 2006, 2015; Dawes, 1994; Leary, 1999; Seligman, 1994, 2002). Problems and failures lower self-esteem. So, maybe self-esteem simply reflects reality. Maybe it's a side effect of meeting challenges and getting through difficulties. Maybe kids with high self-esteem do better in school because doing better in school raises their self-esteem. Maybe self-esteem is a gauge that reports the state of our relationships with others (Reitz et al., 2016). If so, isn't pushing the gauge artificially higher with empty compliments much like forcing a car's low-fuel gauge to display "full"?

If feeling good *follows* doing well, then giving praise in the absence of good performance may actually harm people. After receiving weekly self-esteem-boosting messages, struggling students earned *lower* than expected

Timothy Large/Shutterstock and © Trinity Mirror/Mirrorpix/Alamy grades (Forsyth et al., 2007). Other research showed that giving people random rewards hurt their productivity. Martin Seligman (2012) reported that "when good things occurred that weren't earned, like nickels coming out of slot machines, it did not increase people's well-being. It produced helplessness. People gave up and became passive."

There is, however, an important *effect* of low self-esteem. People who feel negatively about themselves also tend to behave negatively toward others (Amabile, 1983; Baumgardner et al., 1989; Pelham, 1993). Deflating a person's self-esteem produces similar effects. Researchers have temporarily lowered people's self-esteem—for example, by telling them they did poorly on a test or by insulting them. These participants were then more likely to insult others or to express racial prejudice (vanDellen et al., 2011; van Dijk et al., 2011; Ybarra, 1999). Self-image threat even increases unconscious racial bias (Allen & Sherman, 2011). But inflated self-esteem can also cause problems. When studying insult-triggered aggression, researchers found that "conceited, self-important individuals turn nasty toward those who puncture their bubbles of self-love" (Baumeister, 2001; Rasmussen, 2016). **Narcissistic** men and women forgive others less, take a game-playing approach to their romantic relationships, and engage in sexually forceful behavior (Blinkhorn et al., 2015; Bushman et al., 2003; Campbell et al., 2002; Exline et al., 2004).

Self-Serving Bias

LOQ 12-21 What evidence reveals self-serving bias, and how do defensive and secure self-esteem differ?

Imagine dashing to class, hoping not to miss the first few minutes. But you arrive five minutes late, huffing and puffing. As you sink into your seat, what thoughts go through your mind? Do you go through a negative door, thinking, "I hate myself" and "I'm worthless"? Or do you go through a positive door, saying to yourself, "At least I made it to class" and "I really tried to get here on time"?

Personality psychologists have found that most people choose the second door, which leads to positive self-thoughts. We have a good reputation with ourselves. We show a **self-serving bias**—a readiness to perceive ourselves favorably (Myers, 2010). Consider these two findings:

People accept more responsibility for good deeds than for bad, and for successes than for failures. When athletes succeed, they credit their own talent. When they fail, they blame poor weather, bad luck, lousy officials, or the other team's amazing performance. Most students who receive poor grades on a test blame the test or the instructor, not themselves. On insurance forms, drivers have explained accidents in such words as "As I reached an intersection, a hedge sprang up, obscuring my vision, and I did not see the other car" and "A pedestrian hit me and went under my car." The question "What have I done to deserve this?" is one we usually ask of our troubles, not our successes. Although a self-serving bias can lead us to avoid uncomfortable truths, it can also motivate us to approach difficult tasks with confidence instead of despair (Tomaka et al., 1992; von Hippel & Trivers, 2011).

> "If you are like most people, then like most people, you don't know you're like most people. Science has given us a lot of facts about the average person, and one of the most reliable of these facts is the average person doesn't see herself as average."
>
> Daniel Gilbert, *Stumbling on Happiness*, 2006

AND GOD CREATED SELF-WORTH

Most people see themselves as better than average. Compared with most other people, how nice are you? How easy to get along with? Where would you rank yourself, from the 1st to the 99th percentile? Most people put themselves well above the 50th percentile, the middle of the pack. This better-than-average effect appears for nearly any common, socially desirable behavior. Most business executives say they are more ethical than the average executive. At least 90 percent of business managers and college professors rate their performance as superior to that of their average peer. This tendency is less striking in Asia, where people tend to value modesty (Heine & Hamamura, 2007). Yet self-serving biases have been observed worldwide: among Dutch, Australian, and Chinese students; Japanese drivers; Indian Hindus; and French people of most walks of life. In every one of 53 countries surveyed, people expressed self-esteem above the midpoint of the most widely used scale (Schmitt & Allik, 2005). Brain scans reveal that the more people judge themselves as better than average, the less brain activation they show in regions that aid careful self-reflection (Beer & Hughes, 2010). It seems our brain's default setting is to think we are better than others.

Dear diary, Sorry to bother you again.

LOW SELF-ESTEEM

PEANUTS

Most people even see themselves as more immune than others to self-serving bias (Pronin, 2007). That's right, people believe they are above average at not believing they are above average. (Isn't psychology fun?) We also are quicker to believe flattering descriptions of ourselves than unflattering ones, and we are impressed with psychological tests that make us look good.

Self-serving bias often underlies conflicts, such as blaming a partner for relationship problems or an assistant for work problems. All of us tend to see our own group as superior (whether it's our school, our ethnic group, or our country). Ethnic pride fueled Nazi horrors and Rwandan genocide. No wonder religion and literature so often warn against the perils of self-love and pride.

If the self-serving bias is so common, why do so many people put themselves down? For four reasons:

1. Some negative thoughts—"How could I have been so stupid!"—*protect us from repeating mistakes*.

2. Self put-downs are sometimes meant to *prompt positive feedback*. Saying "No one likes me" may at least get you "But not everyone has met you!"

3. Put-downs can help *prepare us for possible failure*. The coach who talks about the superior strength of the upcoming opponent makes a loss understandable, a victory noteworthy.

4. We often put down *our old selves*, not our current selves (Wilson & Ross, 2001). Chumps yesterday, but champs today: "At 18, I was a jerk; today I'm more sensitive."

Despite our self-serving bias, all of us some of the time (and some of us much of the time) do feel inferior. As we saw in Chapter 10, this often happens when we compare ourselves with those who are a step or two higher on the ladder of status, looks, income, or ability. Olympians who win silver medals, barely missing gold, show greater sadness on the award podium compared with the bronze medal winners (Medvec et al., 1995). The more deeply and frequently we have such feelings, the more unhappy or even depressed we become. Positive self-esteem predicts happiness and *persistence after failure* (Baumeister et al., 2003). So maybe it helps that, for most people, thinking has a naturally positive bias.

Researchers have shown the value of separating self-esteem into two categories—*defensive* and *secure* (Kernis, 2003; Lambird & Mann, 2006; Ryan & Deci, 2004).

- *Defensive self-esteem is fragile.* Its goal is to sustain itself, which makes failures and criticism feel threatening. Defensive people may respond to such perceived threats with anger or aggression (Crocker & Park, 2004; Donnellan et al., 2005).

- *Secure self-esteem is sturdy.* It relies less on other people's evaluations. If we feel accepted for who we are, and not for our looks, wealth, or fame, we are free of pressures to succeed. We can focus beyond ourselves, losing ourselves in relationships and purposes larger than ourselves (Crocker & Park, 2004).

Secure self-esteem thus leads to greater quality of life. Such findings are in line with humanistic psychology's ideas about the benefits of a healthy self-image.

Retrieve + Remember

- What are the positive and negative effects of high self-esteem?

ANSWER: People who feel confident in their abilities are often happier, have greater motivation, and are less at risk for depression. Inflated self-esteem can lead to self-serving bias, greater aggression, and narcissism.

- The tendency to accept responsibility for success and blame circumstances or bad luck for failure is called _____-_____ _____.

ANSWER: self-serving bias

- _____ (Secure/Defensive) self-esteem is linked to more angry and aggressive behavior. _____ (Secure/Defensive) self-esteem is a healthier self-image that allows us to focus beyond ourselves and enjoy a higher quality of life.

ANSWERS: Defensive; Secure

Culture and the Self

LOQ 12-22 How do individualist and collectivist cultures differ in their values and goals?

The meaning of *self* varies from culture to culture. How much of your identity is defined by your social connections? Your answer may depend on your culture, and whether it gives greater priority to the *independent self* or to the *interdependent self*.

narcissism excessive self-love and self-absorption.

self-serving bias our readiness to perceive ourselves favorably.

If you are an **individualist,** you have an independent sense of "me," and an awareness of your unique personal convictions and values. Individualists give higher priority to personal goals. They define their identity mostly in terms of personal traits. They strive for personal control and individual achievement.

Although within cultures we vary, different cultures tend to emphasize either individualism or **collectivism** (Markus & Kitayama, 1991). Most Western countries, including the United States and Canada, lean toward individualism. Founded by settlers who wanted to differentiate themselves from others, Americans still cherish the "pioneer" spirit (Kitayama et al., 2010). Some 85 percent of Americans say it is possible "to pretty much be who you want to be" (Sampson, 2000). Being more self-contained, individualists also move in and out of social groups more easily. They change relationships, towns, and jobs with ease.

Over the past several decades, U.S. individualism has only increased. American high school and college students in 2012 reported greater interest in obtaining benefits for themselves and lower concern for others than ever before (Twenge et al., 2012). People in competitive, individualist cultures have more personal freedom (**TABLE 12.5**). They take more pride in personal achievements, are less geographically bound to their families, and enjoy more privacy. But the benefits of individualism may come at a cost: more loneliness, divorce, homicide, and stress-related disease (Popenoe, 1993; Triandis et al., 1988). People in individualist cultures also demand more romance and personal fulfillment in marriage, which puts relationships under more pressure (Dion & Dion, 1993). In one survey, "keeping romance alive" was rated as important to a good marriage by 78 percent of U.S. women but only 29 percent of Japanese women (*American Enterprise*, 1992).

If you are a collectivist, your identity may be closely tied to family, groups, and loyal friends. These connections define who you are. *Group identifications* provide a sense of belonging and a set of values in collectivist cultures. In return, collectivists have deeper, more stable attachments to their groups—their family, clan, or company. Elders receive great respect. In some collectivist cultures, disrespecting family elders violates the law. For example, the Law of the People's Republic of China on Protection of the Rights and Interests of the Elderly states that parents aged 60 or above can sue their sons and daughters if they fail to provide "for the elderly, taking care of them and comforting them, and cater[ing] to their special needs."

> Individualist motto: "The squeaky wheel gets the grease."
> Collectivist motto: "The quacking duck gets shot."

Collectivists are like athletes who take more pleasure in their team's victory than in their own performance.

COLLECTIVIST CULTURE Although the United States is largely individualist, many cultural subgroups remain collectivist. This is true for many Alaska Natives, who demonstrate respect for tribal elders, and whose identity springs largely from their group affiliations.

They find satisfaction in advancing their groups' interests, even when at the expense of personal needs. Preserving group spirit and avoiding social embarrassment are important goals. Collectivists therefore avoid direct confrontation, blunt honesty, and uncomfortable topics. They value humility, not self-importance (Bond et al., 2012). Instead of dominating conversations, collectivists hold back and display shyness when meeting strangers (Cheek & Melchior, 1990).

Collectivist cultures place less expectation or value than individualist cultures do on having a consistent, coherent self-concept. One's identity depends on others in this social context (Heine & Buchtel, 2009). Even if East Asians report inconsistency in their self-concept across different relationship partners, they generally still feel authentic

TABLE 12.5	Value Contrasts Between Individualism and Collectivism	
Concept	**Individualism**	**Collectivism**
Self	Independent (identity from individual traits)	Interdependent (identity from belonging to groups)
Life task	Discover and express your own uniqueness	Maintain connections, fit in, perform your role
What matters	Me—personal achievement and fulfillment; rights and liberties; self-esteem	Us—group goals and solidarity; social responsibilities and relationships; family duty
Coping method	Change reality	Adjust to reality
Morality	Defined by the individual (self-based)	Defined by social networks (duty-based)
Relationships	Many, often temporary or casual; confrontation is acceptable	Few, close and enduring; harmony is valued
Attributing behavior	Behavior reflects the individual's personality and attitudes	Behavior reflects social norms and roles

Sources: Information from Thomas Schoeneman (1994) and Harry Triandis (1994).

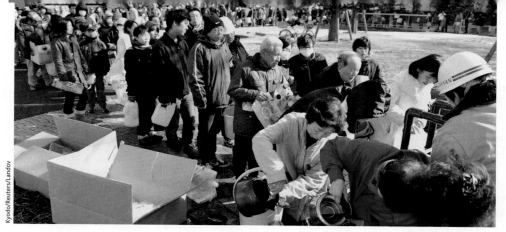

CONSIDERATE COLLECTIVISTS Japan's collectivist values, including duty to others and social harmony, were on display after the devastating 2011 earthquake and tsunami. Virtually no looting was reported, and residents remained calm and orderly, as shown here while waiting for drinking water.

Retrieve + Remember

• How do people in individualist and collectivist cultures differ?

ANSWER: Individualists give priority to personal goals over group goals and tend to define their identity in terms of their own personal attributes. Collectivists give priority to group goals over individual goals and tend to define their identity in terms of group identifications.

(English & Chen, 2011). In contrast, European-Americans are less likely to feel authentic if their self-concept changes across relationship partners.

* * *

From Freud's psychoanalysis and Maslow's and Rogers' humanistic perspective, to the trait and social-cognitive theories, to today's study of the self, our understanding of personality has come a long way! This is a good base from which to explore Chapter 13's questions: How and why do some people suffer from disordered thinking and emotions?

individualism giving priority to our own goals over group goals and defining our identity in terms of personal traits rather than group membership.

collectivism giving priority to the goals of our group (often our extended family or work group) and defining our identity accordingly.

CHAPTER REVIEW

Personality

Test yourself by taking a moment to answer each of these Learning Objective Questions (repeated here from within the chapter). Then turn to Appendix D, Complete Chapter Reviews, to check your answers. Research suggests that trying to answer these questions on your own will improve your long-term memory of the concepts (McDaniel et al., 2009).

What Is Personality?

12-1: What is *personality,* and what theories inform our understanding of personality?

Psychodynamic Theories

12-2: How did Sigmund Freud's treatment of psychological disorders lead to his view of the unconscious mind?

12-3: What was Freud's view of personality?

12-4: What developmental stages did Freud propose?

12-5: How did Freud think people defended themselves against anxiety?

12-6: Which of Freud's ideas did his followers accept or reject?

12-7: What are projective tests, how are they used, and how are they criticized?

12-8: How do today's psychologists view Freud's psychoanalysis?

12-9: How has modern research developed our understanding of the unconscious?

Humanistic Theories

12-10: How did humanistic psychologists view personality, and what was their goal in studying personality?

12-11: How did humanistic psychologists assess a person's sense of self?

12-12: How have humanistic theories influenced psychology? What criticisms have they faced?

Trait Theories

12-13: How do psychologists use traits to describe personality?

12-14: What are some common misunderstandings about introversion?

12-15: What are personality inventories?

12-16: Which traits seem to provide the most useful information about personality variation?

12-17: Does research support the consistency of personality traits over time and across situations?

Social-Cognitive Theories

12-18: How do social-cognitive theorists view personality development, and how do they explore behavior?

12-19: What criticisms have social-cognitive theorists faced?

Exploring the Self

12-20: Why has psychology generated so much research on the self? How important is self-esteem to our well-being?

12-21: What evidence reveals self-serving bias, and how do defensive and secure self-esteem differ?

12-22: How do individualist and collectivist cultures differ in their values and goals?

TERMS AND CONCEPTS TO REMEMBER

Test yourself on these terms by trying to write down the definition in your own words before flipping back to the referenced page to check your answer.

personality, p. 351
psychodynamic theories, p. 351
psychoanalysis, p. 351
unconscious, p. 351
free association, p. 351
id, p. 351
ego, p. 353
superego, p. 353
psychosexual stages, p. 353

Oedipus [ED-uh-puss] complex, p. 353
identification, p. 353
fixation, p. 353
defense mechanisms, p. 353
repression, p. 353
collective unconscious, p. 355
projective test, p. 355
Thematic Apperception Test (TAT), p. 355

Rorschach inkblot test, p. 355
hierarchy of needs, p. 357
self-actualization, p. 357
self-transcendence, p. 357
unconditional positive regard, p. 359
self-concept, p. 359
trait, p. 359
factor, p. 361
Minnesota Multiphasic Personality Inventory (MMPI), p. 361
personality inventory, p. 363

reciprocal determinism, p. 365
social-cognitive perspective, p. 365
self-efficacy, p. 365
self, p. 367
spotlight effect, p. 367
self-esteem, p. 367
narcissism, p. 369
self-serving bias, p. 369
individualism, p. 371
collectivism, p. 371

CHAPTER TEST

Test yourself repeatedly throughout your studies. This will not only help you figure out what you know and don't know; the testing itself will help you learn and remember the information more effectively thanks to the *testing effect*.

1. Freud believed that we may block painful or unacceptable thoughts, wishes, feelings, or memories from consciousness through an unconscious process called _____.

2. According to Freud's view of personality structure, the "executive" system, the _____, seeks to gratify the impulses of the _____ in more acceptable ways.
   a. id; ego
   b. ego; superego
   c. ego; id
   d. id; superego

3. Freud proposed that the development of the "voice of our moral compass" is related to the _____, which internalizes ideals and provides standards for judgments.

4. According to the psychoanalytic view of development, we all pass through a series of psychosexual stages, including the oral, anal, and phallic stages. Conflicts unresolved at any of these stages may lead to
   a. dormant sexual feelings.
   b. fixation at that stage.
   c. unconscious blocking of impulses.
   d. a distorted gender identity.

5. Freud believed that defense mechanisms are unconscious attempts to distort or disguise reality, all in an effort to reduce our _____.

6. _____ tests ask test-takers to respond to an ambiguous image, for example, by describing it or telling a story about it.

7. In general, neo-Freudians such as Adler and Horney accepted many of Freud's views but placed more emphasis than he did on
   a. development throughout the life span.
   b. the collective unconscious.
   c. the role of the id.
   d. social interactions.

8. Modern-day psychodynamic theorists and therapists agree with Freud about
   a. the existence of unconscious mental processes.
   b. the Oedipus complex.
   c. the predictive value of Freudian theory.
   d. the superego's role as the executive part of personality.

9. Which of the following is NOT part of the contemporary view of the unconscious?
   a. Repressed memories of anxiety-provoking events
   b. Stereotypes that influence our perceptions and interpretations
   c. Parallel processing that occurs without our conscious knowledge
   d. Instantly activated emotions and implicit memories of learned skills

10. Maslow's hierarchy of needs proposes that we must satisfy basic physiological and safety needs before we seek ultimate psychological needs, such as self-actualization. Maslow based his ideas on
    a. Freudian theory.
    b. his experiences with patients.
    c. a series of laboratory experiments.
    d. his study of healthy, creative people.

11. How might Freud and Rogers differ in their explanations of how the environment influences the development of a criminal?

12. The total acceptance Rogers advocated as part of a growth-promoting environment is called _____ _____ _____.

13. _____ theories of personality focus on describing characteristic behavior patterns, such as agreeableness or extraversion.

14. One famous personality inventory is the
 a. Extraversion–Introversion Scale.
 b. Person–Situation Inventory.
 c. MMPI.
 d. Rorschach.

15. Which of the following is NOT one of the Big Five personality factors?
 a. Conscientiousness **c.** Extraversion
 b. Anxiety **d.** Agreeableness

16. Our scores on personality tests best predict
 a. our behavior on a specific occasion.
 b. our average behavior across many situations.
 c. behavior involving a single trait, such as conscientiousness.
 d. behavior that depends on the situation or context.

17. The social-cognitive perspective proposes our personality is shaped by a process called reciprocal determinism, as personal factors, environmental factors, and behaviors interact. An example of an environmental factor is
 a. the presence of books in a home.
 b. a preference for outdoor play.
 c. the ability to read at a fourth-grade level.
 d. the fear of violent action on television.

18. Critics say that _____ - _____ personality theory is very sensitive to an individual's interactions with particular situations, but that it gives too little attention to the person's enduring traits.

19. Researchers have found that low self-esteem tends to be linked with life problems. How should this link be interpreted?
 a. Life problems cause low self-esteem.
 b. The answer isn't clear because the link is correlational and does not indicate cause and effect.
 c. Low self-esteem leads to life problems.
 d. Because of the self-serving bias, we must assume that external factors cause low self-esteem.

20. A fortune cookie advises, "Love yourself and happiness will follow." Is this good advice?

21. The tendency to overestimate others' attention to and evaluation of our appearance, performance, and mistakes is called the _____ _____.

22. Individualist cultures tend to value _____; collectivist cultures tend to value _____.
 a. interdependence; independence
 b. independence; interdependence
 c. solidarity; uniqueness
 d. duty; fulfillment

Find answers to these questions in Appendix E, in the back of the book.

IN YOUR EVERYDAY LIFE

Answering these questions will help you make these concepts more personally meaningful, and therefore more memorable.

1. How would you describe your personality? What are your typical patterns of thinking, feeling, and acting?

2. What did you think or know about Freud before you read this chapter? Have your thoughts changed now that you have learned more about him?

3. Think back to a conversation you had when you knew someone was just waiting for a turn to speak instead of listening to you. Now consider the last time someone heard you with empathy. How did those two experiences differ?

4. Has someone in your life accepted you unconditionally? Has this person helped you know yourself better or improve your self-image?

5. Where would you place yourself on the Big Five personality dimensions—conscientiousness, agreeableness, neuroticism, openness, and extraversion? Would your family and friends agree with you?

6. Look around your personal spaces, such as your bedroom, car, or your social media profiles. How do you think these spaces reflect your personality?

7. How have your experiences shaped your personality? How has your personality helped shape your environment?

8. What possible selves do you dream of—or fear—becoming? To what extent do these imagined selves motivate you now?

9. Do you consider yourself to be more of a collectivist or an individualist? How do you think this has influenced your behavior, emotions, and thoughts?

Use 📖 LearningCurve to create your personalized study plan, which will direct you to the resources that will help you most in 📖 LaunchPad.

SURVEY THE CHAPTER

Psychological Disorders

TABLE 13.1 Percentage of Americans Reporting Selected Psychological Disorders in the Past Year

Psychological Disorder	Percentage
Generalized anxiety disorder	3.1
Social anxiety disorder	6.8
Phobia of specific object or situation	8.7
Depressive disorders or bipolar disorder	9.5
Obsessive-compulsive disorder (OCD)	1.0
Schizophrenia	1.1
Posttraumatic stress disorder (PTSD)	3.5
Attention-deficit/hyperactivity disorder (ADHD)	4.1

Data from: National Institute of Mental Health, 2013.

Delphine Le Berre/Moment Select/Getty Images

I felt the need to clean my room at home in Indianapolis every Sunday and would spend four to five hours at it. I would take every book out of the bookcase, dust and put it back. At the time I loved doing it. Then I didn't want to do it anymore, but I couldn't stop. The clothes in my closet hung exactly two fingers apart. . . . I made a ritual of touching the wall in my bedroom before I went out because something bad would happen if I didn't do it the right way. I had a constant anxiety about it as a kid, and it made me think for the first time that I might be nuts.

Marc, diagnosed with obsessive-compulsive disorder (from Summers, 1996)

Whenever I get depressed it's because I've lost a sense of self. I can't find reasons to like myself. I think I'm ugly. I think no one likes me. . . . I become grumpy and short-tempered. Nobody wants to be around me. I'm left alone. Being alone confirms that I am ugly and not worth being with. I think I'm responsible for everything that goes wrong.

Greta, diagnosed with depression (from Thorne, 1993, p. 21)

Voices, like the roar of a crowd, came. I felt like Jesus; I was being crucified. It was dark. I just continued to huddle under the blanket, feeling weak, laid bare and defenseless in a cruel world I could no longer understand.

Stuart, diagnosed with schizophrenia (from Emmons et al., 1997)

Now and then, all of us feel, think, or act in ways that may resemble a psychological disturbance. We get anxious, depressed, withdrawn, or suspicious, just less intensely and more briefly. So it's no wonder that we sometimes see ourselves in the psychological disorders we study. "To study the abnormal is the best way of understanding the normal," said William James (1842–1910).

Personally or through friends or family, many of us will know the confusion and pain of unexplained physical symptoms, irrational fears, or a feeling that life is not worth living. Worldwide, some 450 million people suffer from mental or behavioral disorders (WHO, 2010). Among American college students, about 1 in 3 reports an apparent mental health problem (Eisenberg et al., 2011). This is slightly higher than the U.S. National Institute of Mental Health's estimate that 1 in 4 adult Americans has a "diagnosable mental disorder in a given year" (2013; **TABLE 13.1**). And, although rates and symptoms vary by culture, two of these disorders—major depressive disorder and schizophrenia—exist in every known society worldwide (Baumeister & Härter, 2007; Draguns, 1990a,b, 1997). This chapter examines these and other disorders. First, though, let's address some basic questions.

What Is a Psychological Disorder?

Most of us would agree that a family member who is depressed and stays mostly in bed for three months has a psychological disorder. But what should we say about a grieving father who can't resume his usual social activities three months after his child has died? Where do we draw the line between clinical depression and understandable grief? Between bizarre irrationality and zany creativity? Between abnormality and normality?

In their search for answers, theorists and clinicians ask:

- How should we *define* psychological disorders?
- How should we *understand* disorders? How do underlying biological factors contribute to disorder? How do troubling environments influence our well-being? And how do these effects of nature and nurture interact?
- How should we *classify* psychological disorders? How can we use labels to guide treatment without negatively judging people or excusing their behavior?

Defining Psychological Disorders

LOQ LearningObjectiveQuestion

13-1 How should we draw the line between normal behavior and psychological disorder?

A **psychological disorder** is a syndrome (a collection of symptoms) marked by a "clinically significant disturbance in an individual's cognitions, emotion regulation, or behavior" (American Psychiatric Association, 2013).

Such thoughts, emotions, or behaviors are *dysfunctional* or *maladaptive*—they interfere with normal day-to-day life. An

intense fear of spiders may be abnormal, but if it doesn't interfere with your life, it is not a disorder. Believing that your home must be thoroughly cleaned every weekend is not a disorder. But when cleaning rituals interfere with work and leisure, as Marc's did in this chapter's opening, they may be signs of a disorder. And occasional sad moods that persist and become disabling may likewise signal a psychological disorder.

Distress often accompanies dysfunctional thoughts, emotions, or behaviors. Marc, Greta, and Stuart were all distressed by their behaviors or emotions.

The diagnosis of specific disorders has varied from culture to culture and even over time in the same culture. The American Psychiatric Association classified homosexuality as a disorder until

Carol Beckwith

© Image Source/Corbis

CULTURE AND NORMALITY Young men of the West African Wodaabe tribe put on elaborate makeup and costumes to attract women. Young American men may buy flashy cars with loud stereos to do the same. Each culture may view the other's behavior as abnormal.

psychological disorder a syndrome marked by a clinically significant disturbance in a person's cognition, emotion regulation, or behavior.

attention-deficit/hyperactivity disorder (ADHD) a psychological disorder marked by extreme inattention and/or hyperactivity and impulsivity.

1973. By that point, most mental health workers no longer considered same-sex attraction as inherently dysfunctional or distressing, and it was removed from the list. On the other hand, high-energy children, who might have been viewed as normal youngsters running a bit wild in the 1970s, may today receive a diagnosis of **attention-deficit/hyperactivity disorder (ADHD)**. (See Thinking Critically About: ADHD—Normal High Energy or Disordered Behavior?) Times change, and research and clinical practices change, too.

Retrieve + Remember

- A lawyer is distressed by feeling the need to wash his hands 100 times a day. He has little time left to meet with clients, and his partners are wondering whether he is a risk to the firm. His behavior would probably be labeled disordered, because it is _____ —that is, it interferes with his day-to-day life.

ANSWER: dysfunctional or maladaptive

Understanding Psychological Disorders

LOQ 13-3 How do the medical model and the biopsychosocial approach influence our understanding of psychological disorders?

The way we view a problem influences how we try to solve it. In earlier times, people often thought that strange behaviors were evidence of strange forces at work. Had you lived during the Middle Ages, you might have said, "The devil

LOQ 13-2 Why is there controversy over attention-deficit/hyperactivity disorder?

Thinking Critically About: ADHD—
Normal High Energy
or
Disordered Behavior?

Diagnosis

Twice as often in BOYS as in girls

11%[1] **4- to 17-year-olds**

2.5%[2] **adults**

Symptoms

- extreme inattention
- hyperactivity
- impulsivity

SKEPTICS note:

Energetic child + boring school = ADHD overdiagnosis

- Children are not designed to sit for hours in chairs inside.
- Older students may seek out stimulant ADHD prescription drugs—"good-grade pills."[3]
- What are the long-term effects of drug treatment?
- Why the increased diagnoses?

SUPPORTERS note:

- More diagnoses reflect increased awareness.
- "ADHD is a real neurobiological disorder whose existence should no longer be debated."[4]
- ADHD is associated with abnormal brain activity patterns.[5]

Causes?

- Co-exists with learning disorder or with defiant and temper-prone behavior.
- Genetic[6]

Treatment:

- Stimulant drugs (Ritalin and Adderall) calm hyperactivity, increase ability to sit and focus.[7]
- Psychological therapies help with distress of ADHD.[8]

1. Schwarz & Cohen, 2013. 2. Simon et al., 2009. 3. Schwarz, 2012. 4. World Federation for Mental Health, 2005. 5. Barkley et al., 2002.
6. Nikolas & Burt, 2010; Poelmans et al., 2011; Volkow et al., 2009; Williams et al., 2010. 7. Barbaresi et al., 2007. 8. Fabiano et al., 2008.

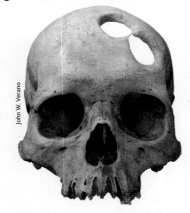

John W. Verano

YESTERDAY'S "THERAPY" Through the ages, psychologically disordered people have received brutal treatments. The hole drilled in the skull of this Stone Age patient may have been an attempt to release evil spirits and provide a cure. Did this patient survive the "cure"?

made him do it." To drive out demons, "mad" people were sometimes caged or given "therapies" such as beatings, genital mutilations, removal of teeth or lengths of intestine, or transfusions of animal blood (Farina, 1982).

Reformers such as Philippe Pinel (1745–1826) in France opposed such brutal treatments. Madness is not demon possession, he insisted, but a sickness of the mind caused by severe stress and inhumane conditions. Curing the sickness requires "moral treatment," including boosting patients' morale by unchaining them and talking with them. He and others worked to replace brutality with gentleness, isolation with activity, and filth with clean air and sunshine.

In some places, cruel treatments for mental illness—including chaining people to beds or locking them in spaces with wild animals—linger even today. In response, the World Health Organization has launched a plan to transform hospitals worldwide "into patient-friendly and humane places with minimum restraints" (WHO, 2014a).

The Medical Model

In the 1800s, a medical breakthrough prompted a new perspective on mental disorders. Researchers discovered that syphilis, a sexually transmitted infection, invades the brain and distorts the mind. This discovery triggered an excited search for physical causes of other mental disorders, and for treatments that would cure them. Hospitals replaced madhouses, and the **medical model** of mental disorders was born. This model is reflected in words we still use today. We speak of the mental *health* movement. A mental *illness* needs to be *diagnosed* on the basis of its *symptoms*. It needs to be *cured* through *therapy*, which may include *treatment* in a psychiatric *hospital*. Recent discoveries that abnormal brain structures and biochemistry contribute to some disorders have energized the medical perspective. A growing number of clinical psychologists now work in medical hospitals, where they collaborate with physicians to determine how the mind and body operate together.

The Biopsychosocial Approach

To call psychological disorders "sicknesses" tilts research heavily toward the influence of biology and away from the influence of our personal histories and social and cultural surroundings. But as we have seen throughout this text, our behaviors, our thoughts, and our feelings are formed by the interaction of our biology, our psychology, and our social-cultural environment. As individuals, we differ in the amount of stress we experience and in the ways we cope with stress. Cultures also differ in the sources of stress they produce and in the traditional ways of coping they provide. We are physically embodied and socially embedded.

The environment's influence can be seen in syndromes that are specific to certain cultures (Beardsley, 1994; Castillo, 1997). In Malaysia, for example, a sudden outburst of violent behavior is called *amok*, as in the English phrase "run amok." Traditionally, this aggression was believed to be the work of an evil spirit. Anxiety may also wear different faces in different cultures. In Latin American cultures, people may suffer from *susto*, a condition marked by severe anxiety, restlessness, and a fear of black magic. In Japanese culture, people may experience *taijin-kyofusho*—social anxiety about their appearance, combined with a readiness to blush and a fear of eye contact. The eating disorder *bulimia nervosa* occurs mostly in food-abundant Western cultures. Increasingly, however, such North American disorders, along with fast-food chains and processed foods, have spread across the globe (Watters, 2010).

Two other disorders—depression and schizophrenia—occur worldwide. From Asia to Africa and across the Americas, people with schizophrenia often act irrationally and speak in disorganized ways. Such disorders reflect genes and physiology, as well as psychological dynamics and cultural circumstances.

The biopsychosocial approach reminds us that mind and body work as one. Negative emotions contribute to physical illness, and abnormal physical processes contribute to negative emotions. As research on **epigenetics** shows, our DNA and our environment interact. In one environment, a gene will be *expressed*, but in another, it may lie dormant. For some, that will be the difference between developing a disorder or not developing it.

Retrieve + Remember

- Are psychological disorders universal or culture-specific? Explain with examples.

ANSWER: Some psychological disorders are culture-specific. For example, bulimia nervosa occurs mostly in food-rich Western cultures, and *taijin-kyofusho* appears largely in Japan. Other disorders, such as schizophrenia, are universal—they appear in all cultures.

- What is the biopsychosocial approach, and why is it important in our understanding of psychological disorders?

ANSWER: Biological, psychological, and social-cultural influences combine to produce psychological disorders. This approach helps us understand that our well-being is affected by the interaction of many forces: our genes, brain functioning, inner thoughts and feelings, and the influences of our social and cultural environment.

Classifying Disorders— and Labeling People

LOQ 13-4 How and why do clinicians classify psychological disorders, and why do some psychologists criticize the use of diagnostic labels?

In biology, classification creates order and helps us communicate. To say that an animal is a "mammal" tells us a great deal— that it is warm-blooded, has hair or fur, and produces milk to feed its young. In psychiatry and psychology, classification also tells us a great deal. To classify a person's disorder as "schizophrenia" implies that the person speaks in a disorganized way, has bizarre beliefs, shows either little emotion or inappropriate emotion, or is socially withdrawn. "Schizophrenia" is a quick way of describing a complex set of behaviors.

But diagnostic classification does more than give us a thumbnail sketch of a person's disordered behavior, thoughts, or feelings. In psychiatry and psychology, classification also attempts to *predict the disorder's future course* and to *suggest treatment*. And it *prompts research into causes*. To study a disorder we must first name and describe it.

The most common tool for describing disorders and estimating how often they occur is the American Psychiatric Association's 2013 *Diagnostic and Statistical Manual of Mental Disorders*, now

"I'm always like this, and my family was wondering if you could prescribe a mild depressant."

TABLE 13.2 Insomnia Disorder
• Feeling unsatisfied with amount or quality of sleep (trouble falling asleep, staying asleep, or returning to sleep)
• Sleep disruption causes distress or diminished everyday functioning
• Happens three or more nights each week
• Occurs during at least three consecutive months
• Happens even with sufficient sleep opportunities
• Independent from other sleep disorders (such as narcolepsy)
• Independent from substance use or abuse
• Independent from other mental disorders or medical conditions

Source: American Psychiatric Association, 2013.

in its fifth edition (**DSM-5**).[1] Physicians and mental health workers use the detailed listings in the DSM-5 to guide medical diagnoses and treatment. For example, a person may be diagnosed with and treated for *insomnia disorder* if he or she meets the criteria in **TABLE 13.2.**

In the new DSM-5, some diagnostic labels have changed. The conditions formerly called "autism" and "Asperger's syndrome" were combined under the label *autism spectrum disorder.* "Mental retardation" became *intellectual disability.* New categories, such as *hoarding disorder* and *binge-eating disorder,* were added.

In real-world tests (*field trials*) assessing the reliability of the new DSM-5 categories, some diagnoses have fared well and others have fared poorly (Freedman et al., 2013). Clinician agreement on adult *posttraumatic stress disorder* and childhood *autism spectrum disorder,* for example, was near 70 percent. (If one psychiatrist or psychologist diagnosed someone with one of these disorders, there was a 70 percent chance that another mental health worker would independently give the same diagnosis.) But for *antisocial personality disorder* and *generalized anxiety disorder,* agreement was closer to 20 percent.

Critics have long faulted the DSM manual for casting too wide a net and bringing "almost any kind of behavior within the compass of psychiatry" (Eysenck et al., 1983). Some now worry that the DSM-5's

even wider net will extend the pathologizing of everyday life—for example, by turning bereavement grief into a depressive disorder and childish fidgeting into ADHD (Frances, 2013, 2014). Others respond that relentless grief-related *depression* and enduring hyperactivity are genuine disorders (Kendler, 2011; Kupfer, 2012).

Other critics register a more basic complaint. At best, they say, these labels represent subjective, personal opinions. At worst, these labels represent personal opinions disguised as scientific judgments. Once we label a person, we view that person differently (Bathje & Pryor, 2011; Farina, 1982; Sadler et al., 2012b). Labels can change reality by putting us on alert for evidence that confirms our view. If we hear that a new co-worker is a difficult person, we may treat her suspiciously. She may in turn respond to us as a difficult person would. Teachers who were told certain students were "gifted" then

medical model the concept that diseases, in this case psychological disorders, have physical causes that can be *diagnosed, treated,* and, in most cases, *cured,* often through treatment in a *hospital.*

epigenetics the study of environmental influences on gene expression that occur without a DNA change.

DSM-5 the American Psychiatric Association's *Diagnostic and Statistical Manual of Mental Disorders,* Fifth Edition; a widely used system for classifying psychological disorders.

1. Many examples in this chapter were drawn from the case studies in a previous DSM edition.

acted in ways that brought out the creative behaviors they expected (Snyder, 1984). Labels can be self-fulfilling.

The biasing power of labels was clear in a now-classic study. David Rosenhan (1973) and seven others went to hospital admissions offices, complaining (falsely) of "hearing voices" saying *empty, hollow,* and *thud.* Apart from this complaint and giving false names and occupations, they answered questions truthfully. All eight of these healthy people were misdiagnosed with disorders.

Should we be surprised? Surely not. As one psychiatrist noted, if someone swallows blood, goes to an emergency room, and spits it up, we wouldn't blame the doctor for diagnosing a bleeding ulcer. But what followed the diagnosis in the Rosenhan study was startling. Until being released an average of 19 days later, these eight "patients" showed no other symptoms. Yet after analyzing their (quite normal) life histories, clinicians were able to "discover" the causes of their disorders, such as having mixed emotions about a parent. Even routine note-taking behavior was misinterpreted as a symptom.

Labels matter. When people in another experiment watched videotaped interviews, those told that they were watching job applicants perceived the people as normal (Langer & Abelson, 1974; Langer & Imber,

STRUGGLES AND RECOVERY During his campaign, Boston Mayor Martin Walsh spoke openly about his past struggles with alcohol. In the process, he moved beyond potentially biasing labels, and won a close election.

Paramount Pictures/Photofest

BETTER PORTRAYALS Old stereotypes are slowly being replaced in media portrayals of psychological disorders. Recent films offer fairly realistic depictions. *Iron Man 3* (2013) portrayed a main character, shown here, with posttraumatic stress disorder. *Black Swan* (2010) dramatized a lead character suffering a delusional disorder. *A Single Man* (2009) depicted depression.

1980). Others, who were told they were watching cancer or psychiatric patients, perceived them as "different from most people." One therapist described the person being interviewed as "frightened of his own aggressive impulses," a "passive, dependent type," and so forth. As Rosenhan discovered, a label can have "a life and an influence of its own."

The power of labels is just as real outside the laboratory. Getting a job or finding a place to rent can be a challenge for people recently released from a mental hospital. Label someone as "mentally ill" and people may fear them as potentially violent. That reaction may fade as people better understand that many psychological disorders involve diseases of the brain, not failures of character (Solomon, 1996). Public figures have helped foster this understanding by speaking openly about their own struggles with disorders such as depression and substance abuse.

Despite their risks, diagnostic labels have benefits. They help mental health professionals to communicate about their cases and to study the causes and treatments of disorders. Clients are often relieved to learn that their suffering has a name and that they are not alone in experiencing their symptoms.

In the rest of this chapter, we will discuss some of the major disorders classified in the DSM-5. In Chapter 14, we will consider their *treatment.*

LaunchPad To test your ability to form diagnoses, visit LaunchPad's *PsychSim 6: Classifying Disorders.*

Anxiety Disorders, OCD, and PTSD

Anxiety is part of life. Have you ever felt anxious when speaking in front of a class, peering down from a high ledge, or waiting to play in a big game? We all feel anxious at times. We may occasionally feel enough anxiety to avoid making eye contact or talking with someone—"shyness," we call it. Fortunately for most of us, our uneasiness is not intense and persistent. Some of us, however, are especially prone to notice and remember information perceived as threatening (Mitte, 2008). When our brain's danger-detection system becomes overly active, we are at greater risk for an *anxiety disorder,* or for two other disorders that involve anxiety: *obsessive-compulsive disorder (OCD)* and *posttraumatic stress disorder.*[2]

Anxiety Disorders

LOQ 13-5 How do generalized anxiety disorder, panic disorder, and phobias differ? How do anxiety disorders differ from the ordinary worries and fears we all experience?

The **anxiety disorders** are marked by distressing, persistent anxiety or by maladaptive behaviors that reduce anxiety.

---

2. OCD and PTSD were formerly classified as anxiety disorders, but the DSM-5 now classifies them separately.

For example, people with *social anxiety disorder* become extremely anxious in social settings where others might judge them, such as parties, class presentations, or even eating in a public place. To stave off anxious thoughts and feelings (including physical symptoms such as sweating and trembling), they may avoid going out at all. Even though this behavior reduces their anxiety, it is maladaptive—it does not help them cope with their world.

In this section we focus on three other anxiety disorders:

- *Generalized anxiety disorder,* in which a person is continually tense and uneasy for no apparent reason.
- *Panic disorder,* in which a person experiences *panic attacks*—sudden episodes of intense dread—and often lives in fear of when the next attack might strike.
- *Phobias,* in which a person feels irrationally and intensely afraid of a specific object, activity, or situation.

Generalized Anxiety Disorder

For two years, Tom, a 27-year-old electrician, was bothered by dizziness, sweating palms, and an irregular heartbeat. He felt on edge and sometimes found himself shaking. Tom was fairly successful at hiding his symptoms from his family and co-workers, but sometimes he had to leave work. He allowed himself few other social contacts. Neither his family doctor nor a neurologist was able to find any physical problem.

Tom's unfocused, out-of-control, agitated feelings suggest **generalized anxiety disorder.** The symptoms of this disorder are commonplace; their persistence for six months or more is not. People with this condition (two-thirds are women) worry continually. They are often jittery, on edge, and sleep deprived (McLean & Anderson, 2009). Their gaze becomes fixated on potential threats (Pergamin-Hight et al., 2015). Concentration is difficult as attention switches from worry to worry. Their tension may leak out through furrowed brows, twitching eyelids, trembling, sweating, or fidgeting.

The person may not be able to identify the tension's cause, and therefore cannot relieve or avoid it. To use Sigmund Freud's term, the anxiety is *free-floating* (not linked to a specific stressor or threat). Generalized anxiety disorder and depression often go hand in hand, but even without depression, this disorder tends to be disabling (Hunt et al., 2004; Moffitt et al., 2007). Moreover, it may lead to physical problems, such as high blood pressure.

Panic Disorder

At some point in our life, many of us will experience a terrifying panic attack—a minutes-long feeling of intense fear that something horrible is about to happen. Irregular heartbeat, chest pains, shortness of breath, choking, trembling, or dizziness may accompany the fear. One woman recalled suddenly feeling

> hot and as though I couldn't breathe. My heart was racing and I started to sweat and tremble and I was sure I was going to faint. Then my fingers started to feel numb and tingly and things seemed unreal. It was so bad I wondered if I was dying and asked my husband to take me to the emergency room. By the time we got there (about 10 minutes) the worst of the attack was over and I just felt washed out (Greist et al., 1986).

> **anxiety disorders** psychological disorders characterized by distressing, persistent anxiety or maladaptive behaviors that reduce anxiety.
>
> **generalized anxiety disorder** an anxiety disorder in which a person is continually tense, fearful, and in a state of *autonomic nervous system* arousal.
>
> **panic disorder** an anxiety disorder marked by unpredictable minutes-long episodes of intense dread in which a person may experience terror and accompanying chest pain, choking, or other frightening sensations; often followed by worry over a possible next attack.

For the 1 person in 75 with **panic disorder,** panic attacks are recurrent. These anxiety tornados strike suddenly, do their damage, and disappear, but they are not forgotten. After experiencing even a few panic attacks, people may come to fear the fear itself. Those having (or observing) a panic attack often misread the symptoms as an impending heart attack or other serious physical ailment. Smokers have at least a doubled risk of a panic attack and greater symptoms when they do have an attack (Knuts et al., 2010; Zvolensky & Bernstein, 2005). Because nicotine is a stimulant, lighting up doesn't lighten up.

PANIC ON THE COURSE Golfer Charlie Beljan experienced what he later learned were panic attacks during an important tournament. His thumping heartbeat and shortness of breath led him to think he was having a heart attack. But hospital tests revealed that his symptoms were not related to a physical illness. He recovered, went on to win $846,000, and has become an inspiration to others.

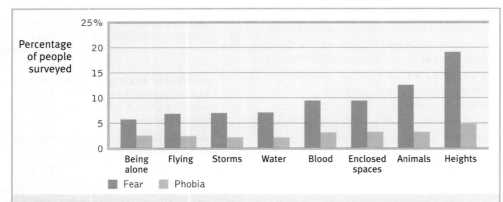

FIGURE 13.1 Some common and uncommon specific fears Researchers surveyed Dutch people to identify the most common events or objects they feared. A strong fear becomes a phobia if it provokes a compelling but irrational desire to avoid the dreaded object or situation. (Data from Depla et al., 2008.)

The constant fear of another attack can lead people with panic disorder to avoid situations where panic might strike. Their avoidance itself may lead to a separate and additional diagnosis of *agoraphobia*, the fear of again experiencing the dreaded tornado of anxiety. Fear of being unable to escape or get help during an attack may cause people with agoraphobia to avoid being outside the home, in a crowd, or at a coffee shop. Not all people with panic disorder develop agoraphobia.

Phobias

We all live with some fears. People with **phobias** are consumed by a persistent, irrational fear and avoidance of some object or situation. *Specific phobias* may focus on particular animals, insects, heights, blood, or enclosed spaces (**FIGURE 13.1**). Many people avoid the triggers (such as high places) that arouse their fear. Marilyn, an otherwise healthy and happy 28-year-old, so feared thunderstorms that she felt anxious as soon as a weather forecaster mentioned possible storms later in the week. If her husband was away and a storm was forecast, she often stayed with a close relative. During a storm, she hid from windows and buried her head to avoid seeing the lightning.

Retrieve + Remember

- Unfocused tension, apprehension, and arousal are symptoms of _____ _____ disorder.

  ANSWER: generalized anxiety

- Those who experience unpredictable periods of terror and intense dread, accompanied by frightening physical sensations, may be diagnosed with a _____ disorder.

  ANSWER: panic

- If a person is focusing anxiety on specific feared objects, activities, or situations, that person may have a _____.

  ANSWER: phobia

Obsessive-Compulsive Disorder (OCD)

LOQ 13-6 What is OCD?

As with the anxiety disorders, we can see aspects of our own behavior in **obsessive-compulsive disorder (OCD)**. *Obsessive thoughts* (recall Marc's focus on cleaning his room) are unwanted and so repetitive it may seem they will never go away. *Compulsive behaviors* are responses to those thoughts (cleaning and cleaning and cleaning).

On a small scale, obsessive thoughts and compulsive behaviors are part of everyday life. Have you ever felt a bit anxious about how your place will appear to others and found yourself checking and cleaning one last time before your guests arrived? Or, perhaps worried about completing an assignment, you caught yourself lining up books or devices "just so" before you began studying? Our lives are full of little rehearsals and fussy behaviors. They cross the fine line between normality and disorder when they persistently *interfere* with everyday life and cause us distress. Checking to see if you locked your door is normal; checking 10 times is not. Washing your hands is normal; washing so often that your skin becomes raw is not. Although people know their anxiety-fueled obsessive thoughts are irrational, these thoughts can become so haunting, and the compulsive rituals so senselessly time-consuming, that effective functioning becomes impossible.

LaunchPad For a 7-minute video illustrating struggles associated with compulsive rituals, visit LaunchPad's *Video: Obsessive-Compulsive Disorder: A Young Mother's Struggle.*

Posttraumatic Stress Disorder (PTSD)

LOQ 13-7 What is PTSD?

While serving his country in war, one soldier, Jesse, saw the killing "of children and women. It was just horrible for anyone to experience." Back home, he suffered "real bad flashbacks" (Welch, 2005).

Jesse is not alone. In one study of 103,788 veterans returning from Iraq and Afghanistan, 25 percent were diagnosed with a psychological disorder (Seal et al., 2007). Some had *traumatic brain injuries (TBI)*, but the most frequent diagnosis was **posttraumatic stress disorder (PTSD)**. Survivors of accidents, disasters, and violent and sexual assaults (including an estimated two-thirds of

BRINGING THE WAR HOME Nearly a quarter-million Iraq and Afghanistan war veterans have been diagnosed with PTSD or traumatic brain injury (TBI). Many vets participate in an intensive recovery program using deep breathing, massage, and group and individual discussion techniques to treat their PTSD or TBI.

prostitutes) have also experienced PTSD symptoms (Brewin et al., 1999; Farley et al., 1998; Taylor et al., 1998b). Typical symptoms include recurring haunting memories and nightmares, a numb feeling of social withdrawal, jumpy anxiety, and trouble sleeping (Germain, 2013; Hoge et al., 2004, 2007; Hoge & Castro, 2006; Kessler, 2000).

About half of us will experience at least one traumatic event in our lifetime. And most of us will display *survivor resiliency*—a tendency to recover after severe stress (Bonanno, 2004, 2005; Bonanno et al., 2006). Some will even experience *posttraumatic growth* (more on this in Chapter 14). But some 5 to 10 percent of us will develop PTSD (Bonanno et al., 2011). Why do some people develop PTSD after a traumatic event, but others don't? One factor seems to be the amount of emotional distress that occurs during the trauma: The higher the distress, the greater the risk for posttraumatic symptoms (Ozer et al., 2003). Some examples:

- Among American military personnel in Afghanistan, 7.6 percent of combatants developed PTSD, compared with 1.4 percent of noncombatants (McNally, 2012).

- Among survivors of the 9/11 terrorist attacks on New York's World Trade Center, the rates of subsequent PTSD diagnoses for those who had been inside were double the rates of those who had been outside (Bonanno et al., 2006).

What else can influence PTSD development after a trauma? Some people may have a more sensitive emotion-processing limbic system that floods their bodies with stress hormones (Kosslyn, 2005; Ozer & Weiss, 2004). Another factor is gender. After a traumatic event, women are twice as likely as men to develop PTSD symptoms (Olff et al., 2007; Ozer & Weiss, 2004).

Some psychologists believe PTSD has been overdiagnosed (Dobbs, 2009; McNally, 2003). Too often, say critics, PTSD gets stretched to include normal stress-related bad memories and dreams. In such cases, some well-intentioned procedures—such as "debriefing" people by asking them to revisit the experience and vent their emotions—may worsen stress reactions (Bonanno et al., 2010; Wakefield & Spitzer, 2002). Other research shows that reliving traumas (such as 9/11 or the Boston Marathon bombing) through media coverage sustains the stress response (Holman et al., 2014). Nevertheless, people diagnosed with PTSD can benefit from other therapies, some of which are discussed in Chapter 14.

Retrieve + Remember

- Those who express anxiety through unwanted repetitive thoughts or actions may have a(n) _____-_____ disorder.

  ANSWER: obsessive-compulsive

- Those with symptoms of recurring memories and nightmares, social withdrawal, jumpy anxiety, numbness of feeling, and/or insomnia for weeks after a traumatic event may be diagnosed with _____ _____ disorder.

  ANSWER: posttraumatic stress

Understanding Anxiety Disorders, OCD, and PTSD

LOQ 13-8 How do conditioning, cognition, and biology contribute to the feelings and thoughts that mark anxiety disorders, OCD, and PTSD?

Anxiety is both a feeling and a thought—a doubt-laden appraisal of one's safety or social skill. How do these anxious feelings and thoughts arise? Sigmund Freud's psychoanalytic theory (Chapter 12) proposed that, beginning in childhood, people *repress* certain impulses, ideas, and feelings. Freud believed that this submerged mental energy sometimes leaks out in odd symptoms, such as anxious hand washing. Few of today's psychologists interpret anxiety this way. Most believe that three modern perspectives—conditioning, cognition, and biology—are more helpful.

Conditioning

Conditioning happens when we learn to associate two or more things that occur together. Through classical conditioning, our fear responses can become linked with formerly neutral objects and events. You may recall from Chapter 6 that an infant—"Little Albert"—learned to fear furry objects that researchers paired with loud noises. In other experiments, researchers have created anxious animals by giving rats unpredictable electric shocks (Schwartz, 1984). The rats,

phobia an anxiety disorder marked by a persistent, irrational fear and avoidance of a specific object, activity, or situation.

obsessive-compulsive disorder (OCD) a disorder characterized by unwanted repetitive thoughts (obsessions), actions (compulsions), or both.

posttraumatic stress disorder (PTSD) a disorder characterized by haunting memories, nightmares, social withdrawal, jumpy anxiety, numbness of feeling, and/or insomnia lingering for four weeks or more after a traumatic experience.

© Lynn Johnson/National Geographic Society/Corbis

like assault victims who report feeling anxious when returning to the scene of the crime, had learned to be uneasy in their lab environment. The lab had become a cue for fear.

Such research helps explain how anxious or traumatized people come to associate their anxiety with certain cues (Bar-Haim et al., 2007; Duits et al., 2015). In one survey, 58 percent of those with social anxiety disorder said their symptoms began after a traumatic event (Ost & Hugdahl, 1981). Anxiety or an anxiety-related disorder is more likely to develop when bad events happen unpredictably and uncontrollably (Field, 2006; Mineka & Oehlberg, 2008). Even a single painful and frightening event may trigger a full-blown phobia, thanks to two processes: classical conditioning's *stimulus generalization* and operant conditioning's *reinforcement*.

Stimulus generalization occurs when a person experiences a fearful event and later develops a fear of similar events. My [DM's] car was once struck by a driver who missed a stop sign. For months afterward, I felt a twinge of unease when any car approached from a side street. Likewise, I [ND] was watching a terrifying movie about spiders, *Arachnophobia*, when a severe thunderstorm struck and the theater lost power. For months, I experienced anxiety at the sight of spiders or cobwebs. Those fears eventually disappeared, but sometimes fears linger and grow. Marilyn's thunderstorm phobia may have similarly generalized after a terrifying or painful experience during a thunderstorm.

Reinforcement helps maintain learned fears and anxieties. Anything that enables us to avoid or escape a feared situation reduces our anxiety. This feeling of relief can reinforce maladaptive behaviors. Fearing a panic attack, a person may decide not to leave the house. Reinforced by feeling calmer, the person is likely to repeat that behavior in the future (Antony et al., 1992). Compulsive behaviors operate similarly. If washing your hands relieves your feelings of anxiety, you may wash your hands again when those feelings return.

Cognition

Learning is more than just conditioning. *Cognition*—our thoughts, memories, interpretations, and expectations—plays a role in many kinds of learning, including what we learn to fear. In one form of cognitive learning, we learn by observing others (Chapter 6). Consider wild monkeys' fear of snakes. Why do nearly all monkeys raised in the wild fear snakes, yet lab-raised monkeys do not? Surely, most wild monkeys do not actually suffer snake bites. Do they learn their fear through observation? To find out, one researcher experimented (Mineka, 1985, 2002). Her study focused on six monkeys raised in the wild (all strongly fearful of snakes) and their lab-raised offspring (none of which feared snakes). During the study, the young monkeys repeatedly observed their parents or peers refusing to reach for food in the presence of a snake. Can you predict what happened? The young monkeys also developed a strong fear of snakes. When they were retested three months later, their learned fear persisted. We humans learn many of our own fears by observing others (Helsen et al., 2011; Olsson et al., 2007).

Our interpretations and expectations also shape our reactions. Whether we panic in response to a creaky sound in an old house depends on whether we interpret the sound as the wind or as a possible knife-wielding intruder. People with anxiety-related disorders tend to be *hypervigilant*. They *attend* more to threatening stimuli. They more often *interpret* unclear stimuli as threatening. (A pounding heart signals a heart attack. A lone spider near the bed indicates an infestation. An everyday disagree-

Hemera Technologies/PhotoObjects.net/360/Getty Images

ment with a partner or boss spells doom for the relationship.) And they more often *remember* threatening events (Van Bockstaele et al., 2014). Anxiety is especially common when people cannot switch off such intrusive thoughts and perceive a loss of control and a sense of helplessness (Franklin & Foa, 2011).

Biology

Learning can't explain all aspects of anxiety disorders, OCD, and PTSD. Why do some of us develop lasting phobias or PTSD after suffering traumas, but others do not? Why do we all learn some fears more readily than others? The answers lie in part in our biology.

GENES Genes matter. Among monkeys, fearfulness runs in families. A monkey reacts more strongly to stress if its close biological relatives have sensitive, high-strung temperaments (Suomi, 1986).

So, too, with people. Some of us have genes that make us like orchids—fragile, yet capable of beauty under favorable circumstances. Others of us are like dandelions—hardy and able to thrive in varied circumstances (Ellis & Boyce, 2008; Pluess & Belsky, 2013). Thus, some of us are genetically predisposed to anxiety, OCD, and PTSD. If one identical twin has an anxiety disorder, the other is likewise at risk (Hettema et al., 2001; Kendler et al., 2002a,b; Van Houtem et al., 2013). Even when raised separately, identical twins may develop similar phobias (Carey, 1990; Eckert et al., 1981). One pair of separated identical twins independently became so afraid of water that, even at age 35, they would wade into the ocean backwards and only up to their knees. Researchers have found genes associated with OCD (Taylor, 2013) and others associated with typical anxiety disorder symptoms (Hovatta et al., 2005).

But as we have seen in so many areas, experience affects whether a gene will be expressed. Experiences such as child abuse can leave tracks in the brain, increasing the chances that a genetic vulnerability to a disorder such as PTSD will be expressed (Mehta et al., 2013; Zannas et al., 2015).

FEARLESS The biological perspective helps us understand why most of us have more fear of heights than does Felix Baumgartner, shown here skydiving from 24 miles above the Earth in 2012.

THE BRAIN Anxiety-related disorders all involve biological events. Traumatic experiences alter our brain, paving new fear pathways, which are easy inroads for more fear experiences (Armony et al., 1998).

Generalized anxiety disorder, panic attacks, phobias, OCD, and PTSD express themselves biologically as overarousal of brain areas involved in impulse control and habitual behaviors. These disorders reflect a brain danger-detection system gone hyperactive—producing anxiety when no danger exists. In OCD, for example, when the brain detects that something is wrong, it seems to generate a mental hiccup of repeating thoughts or actions (Gehring et al., 2000). Brain scans show elevated activity in specific brain areas during behaviors such as compulsive hand washing, checking, ordering, or hoarding (Insel, 2010; Mataix-Cols et al., 2004, 2005).

NATURAL SELECTION No matter how fearful or fearless we are, we humans seem biologically prepared to fear the threats our ancestors faced—spiders and snakes, enclosed spaces and heights, storms and darkness. (In the distant past, those who did not fear these threats were less likely to survive and leave descendants.) Our Stone Age fears are easy to condition and hard to extinguish (Davey, 1995; Öhman, 1986). Even in Britain, which has only one poisonous snake species, people often fear snakes. And we have these fears at very young ages. Nine-month-old infants attend more to sounds signaling ancient threats (hisses, thunder) than they do to sounds representing modern dangers (a bomb exploding, breaking glass) (Erlich et al., 2013). Even some of our modern fears may have their roots in our evolutionary past. Fear of flying includes two ancient fears—of confinement and heights.

Compare our easily conditioned fears to what we *do not* easily learn to fear. World War II air raids, for example, produced remarkably few lasting phobias. As the air strikes continued, the British, Japanese, and German populations did not become more and more panicked. Rather, they grew more indifferent to planes outside their immediate neighborhood (Mineka & Zinbarg, 1996). Evolution has not prepared us to fear bombs dropping from the sky.

Our phobias focus on dangers our ancestors faced. Our compulsive acts typically exaggerate behaviors that helped them survive. Grooming had survival value. Gone wild, it becomes compulsive hair pulling. So too with washing up, which becomes ritual hand washing. And checking territorial boundaries becomes checking and rechecking already locked doors (Rapoport, 1989). Although natural selection shaped our behaviors, when taken to an extreme, these behaviors can interfere with daily life.

psychoactive drug a chemical substance that alters perceptions and mood.

substance use disorder disorder characterized by continued substance craving and use despite significant life disruption and/or physical risk.

Retrieve + Remember

- Researchers believe that conditioning and cognition are aspects of learning that contribute to anxiety-related disorders. What *biological* factors contribute to these disorders?

ANSWER: Biological factors include inherited temperament differences and other gene variations; experience-altered brain pathways; and outdated, inherited responses that had survival value for our distant ancestors.

Substance Use Disorders and Addictive Behaviors

LOQ 13-9 What are substance use disorders, and what roles do tolerance, withdrawal, and addiction play in these disorders?

Do you rely on caffeine pick-me-ups, such as coffee or energy drinks, to keep you going? Caffeine is usually harmless, though it still qualifies as a **psychoactive drug,** a chemical substance that changes perceptions and mood. Most of us manage to use some of these substances—even alcohol and painkillers—in moderation, without disrupting our lives. But sometimes, drug use crosses the line between moderation and **substance use disorder.** This happens when we continue to crave and use a substance that is significantly disrupting our life or putting us at risk physically (**TABLE 13.3**). Substance use disorders can endanger relationships, job and school performance, caretaking abilities, and our own and others' safety.

The three major categories of psychoactive drugs are *depressants, stimulants,*

TABLE 13.3 When Is Drug Use a Disorder?

According to the American Psychiatric Association, a person may be diagnosed with a *substance use disorder* when drug use continues despite significant life disruption. Resulting brain changes may persist after quitting use of the substance (thus leading to strong cravings when exposed to people and situations that trigger memories of drug use). The severity of substance use disorder varies from *mild* (two to three of the indicators listed below) to *moderate* (four to five indicators) to *severe* (six or more indicators). (Source: American Psychiatric Association, 2013.)

Diminished Control
1. Uses more substance, or for longer, than intended.
2. Tries unsuccessfully to regulate use of substance.
3. Spends much time acquiring, using, or recovering from effects of substance.
4. Craves the substance.

Diminished Social Functioning
5. Use disrupts commitments at work, school, or home.
6. Continues use despite social problems.
7. Causes reduced social, recreational, and work activities.

Hazardous Use
8. Continues use despite hazards.
9. Continues use despite worsening physical or psychological problems.

Drug Action
10. Experiences tolerance (needing more substance for the desired effect).
11. Experiences withdrawal when attempting to end use.

Vasca/Shutterstock

and *hallucinogens*. All do their work at the brain's synapses. They stimulate, inhibit, or mimic the activity of the brain's own chemical messengers, the neurotransmitters. But our reaction to psychoactive drugs depends on more than their *biological* effects. *Psychological* influences, including a user's expectations, and *cultural* traditions also play a role (Scott-Sheldon et al., 2012; Ward, 1994). If one culture assumes that a particular drug produces good feelings (or aggression or sexual arousal), and another does not, each culture may find its expectations fulfilled. Later, in the discussions of particular drugs, we'll take a closer look at the interaction of biopsychosocial forces. But first, let's see how our bodies react to the ongoing use of psychoactive drugs.

Tolerance and Addictive Behaviors

Why might a person who rarely drinks alcohol get buzzed on one can of beer, while a long-term drinker shows few effects until the second six-pack? The answer is **tolerance.** With continued use of alcohol and some other drugs (but not marijuana), the user's brain chemistry adapts to offset the drug's effect. To experience the same effect, the user requires larger and larger doses (**FIGURE 13.2**).

Ever-increasing doses of most psychoactive drugs may lead a person to become addicted: The person comes to crave the drug and struggles when attempting to **withdraw** from it, continuing to use the substance despite harmful consequences. Heavy coffee drinkers who skip their usual caffeine intake know the feeling when a headache or grogginess strikes. For people who become addicted to heroin, prescription painkillers, or other depressants, withdrawal may mean much more than a headache. Worldwide, 90 million people are living with such problems related to alcohol and other drugs (WHO, 2008).

Sometimes even *behaviors* become compulsive and dysfunctional, much like abusive drug-taking. Estimates of problematic video game playing in Asia, Europe, and North America have ranged from 3 percent to 12 percent (Anderson & Warburton, 2012; Ferguson et al., 2011). One such "behavior addiction" listed in the DSM-5 is gambling disorder, and the DSM-5 proposes Internet gaming disorder "for further study" (American Psychiatric Association, 2013).

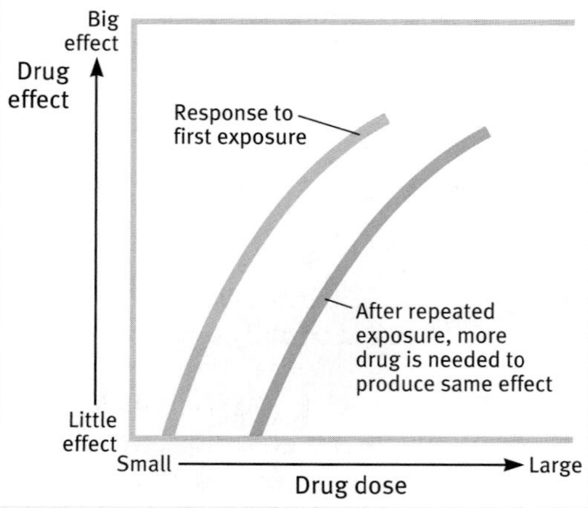

FIGURE 13.2 Drug tolerance

Retrieve + Remember

- What is the process that leads to drug tolerance?

ANSWER: With repeated exposure to a psychoactive drug, the user's brain chemistry adapts and the drug's effect lessens. Thus, it takes bigger doses to get the desired effect.

Depressants

LOQ 13-10 What are depressants, and what are their effects?

Depressants are drugs such as alcohol, barbiturates (tranquilizers), and opiates that calm (depress) neural activity and slow body functions.

ALCOHOL True or false? Alcohol is a depressant in large amounts but is a stimulant in small amounts. *False.* In any amount, alcohol is a depressant—it reduces neural activity and slows body functions.

Slowed neural functions. Low doses of alcohol may, indeed, enliven a drinker, but they do so by acting as a *disinhibitor*. Alcohol slows activity in a part of the brain that controls judgment and inhibitions. As a result, the urges we would feel if sober are the ones we will more likely act upon when intoxicated. Alcohol is an equal-opportunity drug. It increases helpful tendencies, as when tipsy restaurant patrons leave big tips, or social drinkers bond as a group (Hirsh et al., 2011; Lynn, 1988; Sayette et al., 2012). And it increases harmful tendencies, as when sexually aroused men become more aggressive. When drinking, both men and women are more disposed to casual sex (Garcia et al., 2012).

Even the *belief* that we have consumed alcohol can influence our judgment. In one classic experiment (supposedly a study on "alcohol and sexual stimulation"), researchers gave college male volunteers either an alcoholic or a nonalcoholic drink (Abrams & Wilson, 1983). (Both drinks had a strong taste that masked any alcohol.) After watching an erotic movie clip, the men who *thought* they had consumed alcohol were more likely to report having strong sexual fantasies and feeling guilt free—whether they had actually consumed it or not. When people *believe* that alcohol affects social behavior in certain ways, and *believe* that they have been drinking alcohol, they will behave accordingly (Scott-Sheldon et al., 2012). In 14 "intervention studies," college drinkers who were educated about that point came away with lower positive expectations of alcohol, and they drank less in the following month (Scott-Sheldon et al., 2014).

Alcohol does more than lessen our normal inhibitions, however. It produces a sort of short-sightedness by focusing our attention on arousing situations (perhaps a sexually attractive person or some personal slight). This combination of lowered inhibitions and altered perceptions can reduce self-awareness and distract attention from future consequences (Giancola et al., 2010; Hull & Bond, 1986; Steele & Josephs, 1990).

The point to remember: Alcohol's effect lies partly in that powerful sex organ, the mind. Expectations influence behavior.

DRINKING DISASTER DEMO Firefighters reenacted the trauma of an alcohol-related car accident, providing a memorable demonstration for these high school students. Alcohol consumption leads to feelings of invincibility, which become especially dangerous behind the wheel of a car.

Memory disruption. Sometimes, people drink to forget their troubles—a broken relationship, a lost game, a failed exam. And forget they do. Why? Because alcohol disrupts long-term memory processing. It does so in part by suppressing REM sleep, which helps fix the day's experiences into permanent memories. Thus, people recovering from a night of heavy drinking may have blackouts—unable to recall who they met the night before, or what they said or did.

Heavy drinking can have long-term effects on the brain. In rats, at a development period corresponding to human adolescence, binge drinking contributes to the death of nerve cells and reduces the birth rates of new nerve cells. It also impairs the growth of synaptic connections (Crews et al., 2006, 2007).

Slowed body functions. Alcohol slows sympathetic nervous system activity. In low doses, it relaxes the drinker. In larger doses, it causes reactions to slow, speech to slur, and skilled performance to decline.

Paired with lack of sleep, alcohol is a potent sedative. Add these physical effects to lowered inhibitions, and the result can be deadly. Worldwide, several hundred thousand lives are lost each year in alcohol-related accidents and violent crime. When sober, most drinkers believe that driving under the influence of alcohol is wrong, and they insist they would not do so. That belief disappears as blood-alcohol level rises and judgments become fuzzy. Most will drive home from a bar, even if given a Breathalyzer test and told they are intoxicated (Denton & Krebs, 1990; MacDonald et al., 1995).

Alcohol can be life threatening when heavy drinking follows an earlier period of moderate drinking, which suppresses the vomiting response. People may poison themselves with an overdose their body would normally throw up.

Alcohol use disorder. Alcoholism is the popular name for **alcohol use disorder.** Its symptoms are tolerance, withdrawal, and a drive to continue using alcohol despite significant problems associated with that use. Girls and young women are especially vulnerable because they have less of a stomach enzyme that digests alcohol (Wuethrich, 2001). They can become addicted to alcohol more quickly than boys and young men. They also suffer lung, brain, and liver damage at lower consumption levels (CASA, 2003) (**FIGURE 13.3**).

tolerance a dwindling effect with regular use of the same dose of a drug, requiring the user to take larger and larger doses before experiencing the drug's effect.

withdrawal the discomfort and distress that follow ending the use of an addictive drug or behavior.

depressants drugs (such as alcohol, barbiturates, and opiates) that reduce (depress) neural activity and slow body functions.

alcohol use disorder (popularly known as *alcoholism*) alcohol use marked by tolerance, withdrawal, and a drive to continue problematic use.

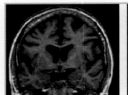
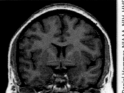

Scan of woman with alcohol use disorder

Scan of woman without alcohol use disorder

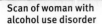

Daniel Hommer, NIAAA, NIH, HHS

FIGURE 13.3 **Disordered drinking shrinks the brain** MRI scans show brain shrinkage in women with alcohol use disorder (left) compared with women in a control group (right).

BARBITURATES Like alcohol, the **barbiturate** drugs, or *tranquilizers,* depress nervous system activity. Barbiturates such as Nembutal, Seconal, and Amytal are sometimes prescribed to induce sleep or reduce anxiety. In larger doses, they can impair memory and judgment. If combined with alcohol, the total depressive effect on body functions can lead to death. This sometimes happens when people take a sleeping pill after an evening of heavy drinking.

OPIATES The **opiates**—opium and its offshoots—also depress nervous system activity. Opiates include heroin and also medically prescribed pain-relief narcotics, such as codeine, morphine, and *methadone* (a synthetic opiate sometimes prescribed as a heroin substitute). As pleasure replaces pain and anxiety, the user's pupils constrict, breathing slows, and *lethargy* (a feeling of extreme relaxation and a lack of energy) sets in. Those who become addicted to this short-term pleasure may pay a long-term price: a gnawing craving for another fix, a need for progressively larger doses (as tolerance develops), and the extreme discomfort of withdrawal. When repeatedly flooded with an artificial opiate, the brain eventually stops producing *endorphins,* its own feel-good opiates. If the artificial opiate is then withdrawn, the brain will lack the normal level of these natural painkillers. Those who cannot or choose not to endure this state may pay an ultimate price—death by overdose.

Retrieve + Remember

- Can someone become "addicted" to shopping?

ANSWER: Unless it becomes compulsive or dysfunctional, simply having a strong interest in shopping is not the same as having a physical addiction to a drug. It does not involve obsessive craving in spite of known negative consequences.

- Alcohol, barbiturates, and opiates are all in a class of drugs called _____.

ANSWER: depressants

Stimulants

LOQ 13-11 What are stimulants, and what are their effects?

A **stimulant** excites neural activity and speeds up body functions. Pupils dilate. Heart and breathing rates increase. Blood-sugar levels rise, causing a drop in appetite. Energy and self-confidence also rise.

Stimulants include caffeine, nicotine, and the more powerful cocaine, amphetamines, methamphetamine, and Ecstasy. People use stimulants to feel alert, lose weight, or boost mood or athletic performance. Unfortunately, stimulants can be addictive, as you may know if you are one of the many who use caffeine daily in your coffee, tea, soda, or energy drinks. Cut off from your usual dose, you may crash into fatigue, headaches, irritability, and depression (Silverman et al., 1992). A mild dose of caffeine typically lasts three or four hours, which—if taken in the evening—may be enough to impair sleep.

NICOTINE One of the most addictive stimulants is **nicotine,** found in cigarettes, e-cigarettes, and other tobacco products. Are tobacco products at least as addictive as heroin and cocaine? *Yes* (see **TABLE 13.4**). Attempts to quit even within the first weeks of smoking often fail (DiFranza, 2008). And, as with other addictions, smokers develop *tolerance.* Those who attempt to quit will experience nicotine-withdrawal symptoms—

craving, insomnia, anxiety, irritability, and distractibility. When trying to focus on a task, their mind wanders at three times the normal rate (Sayette et al., 2010). And to make all this go away, all it takes is a single puff on a cigarette—a portable nicotine dispenser.

Within 7 seconds (twice as fast as intravenous heroin), a rush of nicotine will signal the central nervous system to release a flood of neurotransmitters (**FIGURE 13.4**). Epinephrine and norepinephrine will diminish appetite and boost alertness and mental efficiency. Dopamine and opioids will calm anxiety and reduce sensitivity to pain (Ditre et al., 2011; Gavin, 2004). No wonder some ex-smokers, under stress, return to smoking. Some 1 million Americans did so after the 9/11 terrorist attacks (Pesko, 2014).

These rewards keep people smoking, even among the 3 in 4 smokers who wish they could stop (Newport, 2013b). Each year, fewer than 1 in 7 who want to quit will be able to resist. Smokers die, on average, at least a decade before nonsmokers, but even those who know they are committing slow-motion suicide may be unable to stop (Saad, 2002). By 2030, the number of tobacco-related deaths worldwide is expected to reach 8 million people *each year.* That means that 1 *billion* twenty-first century people may be killed by tobacco (WHO, 2012). Eliminating smoking would increase life expectancy more than any other preventive measure.

The good news is that repeated attempts to quit smoking seem to pay off. Half of all Americans who have ever smoked have quit, some with the aid

TABLE 13.4 The Odds of Getting Hooked After Trying Various Drugs	
Marijuana	9%
Alcohol	15
Cocaine	17
Heroin	23
Tobacco	32

Source: National Academy of Science, Institute of Medicine (Brody, 2003).

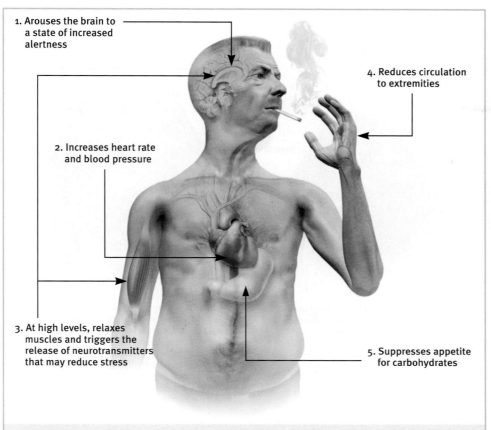

1. Arouses the brain to a state of increased alertness

4. Reduces circulation to extremities

2. Increases heart rate and blood pressure

3. At high levels, relaxes muscles and triggers the release of neurotransmitters that may reduce stress

5. Suppresses appetite for carbohydrates

FIGURE 13.4 Where there's smoke . . . : The physiological effects of nicotine
Nicotine reaches the brain within 7 seconds, twice as fast as intravenous heroin. Within minutes, the amount in the blood soars.

COCAINE Cocaine is a powerful and addictive stimulant derived from the coca plant. The recipe for Coca-Cola originally included an extract of that plant, creating a cocaine tonic for tired elderly people. Between 1896 and 1905, Coke was indeed "the real thing." But no longer. Cocaine is now snorted, injected, or smoked as the street drug *crack cocaine*. It enters the bloodstream quickly, producing a rush of *euphoria*—feelings of great happiness and well-being. Those feelings continue until the brain's supply of the neurotransmitters dopamine, serotonin, and norepinephrine drops off **(FIGURE 13.5)**. Then, within the hour, a crash of agitated depression follows. Many regular cocaine users chasing this high become addicted.

Cocaine use may heighten reactions, such as aggression (Licata et al., 1993). It may also lead to emotional disturbances, suspiciousness, convulsions, cardiac arrest, or respiratory failure. The drug's psychological effects depend in part on the dosage and form consumed, but the situation and the user's expectations and personality also play a role. Given a placebo, cocaine users who *thought* they were taking cocaine often had a cocaine-like experience (Van Dyke & Byck, 1982).

Pictorial Press Ltd/Alamy

NIC-A-TEEN Virtually nobody starts smoking past the vulnerable teen years. Eager to hook customers whose addiction will give them business for years to come, cigarette companies target teens. Portrayals of smoking by popular actors, such as Scarlet Johansson in *Hail, Caesar!*, tempt teens to imitate.

of a nicotine replacement drug and a support group. Success is equally likely whether smokers quit abruptly or gradually (Fiore et al., 2008; Lichtenstein et al., 2010; Lindson et al., 2010). The acute craving and withdrawal symptoms do go away gradually over six months (Ward et al., 1997). After a year's abstinence, only 10 percent return to smoking in the next year (Hughes et al., 2008).

Retrieve + Remember

• What withdrawal symptoms should your friend expect when she finally decides to quit smoking?

ANSWER: Nicotine-withdrawal symptoms include strong cravings, insomnia, anxiety, irritability, distractibility, and difficulty concentrating. However, if your friend sticks with it, her symptoms will gradually go away over the next six months.

barbiturates drugs that depress central nervous system activity, reducing anxiety but impairing memory and judgment.

opiates opium and its derivatives, such as morphine and heroin; depress neural activity, temporarily lessening pain and anxiety.

stimulants drugs (such as caffeine, nicotine, and the more powerful cocaine, amphetamines, methamphetamine, and Ecstasy) that excite neural activity and speed up body functions.

nicotine a stimulating and highly addictive psychoactive drug in tobacco.

cocaine a powerful and addictive stimulant derived from the coca plant; temporarily increases alertness and produces feelings of euphoria.

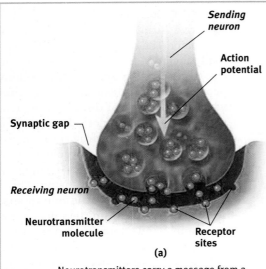

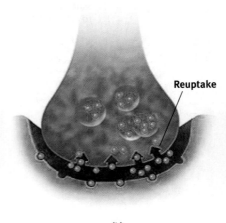

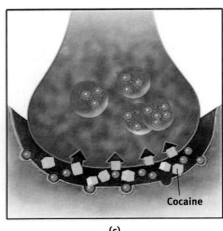

(a)
Neurotransmitters carry a message from a sending neuron across a synapse to receptor sites on a receiving neuron.

(b)
The sending neuron normally reabsorbs excess neurotransmitter molecules, a process called *reuptake*.

(c)
By binding to the sites that normally reabsorb neurotransmitter molecules, cocaine blocks reuptake of dopamine, norepinephrine, and serotonin (Ray & Ksir, 1990). The extra neurotransmitter molecules therefore remain in the synapse, intensifying their normal mood-altering effects and producing a euphoric rush. When the cocaine level drops, the absence of these neurotransmitters produces a crash.

FIGURE 13.5 Cocaine euphoria and crash

METHAMPHETAMINE Amphetamines stimulate neural activity. As body functions speed up, the user's energy rises and mood soars. Amphetamines are the parent drug for the highly addictive **methamphetamine,** which is chemically similar but has greater effects (NIDA, 2002, 2005). Methamphetamine triggers the release of the neurotransmitter dopamine, which stimulates brain cells that enhance energy and mood. Eight or so hours of heightened energy and mood then follow. Aftereffects may include irritability, insomnia, high blood pressure, seizures, social isolation, depression, and occasional violent outbursts (Homer et al., 2008). Over time, methamphetamine may reduce the brain's normal output of dopamine.

ECSTASY Ecstasy is the street name for **MDMA** (methylenedioxymethamphetamine, also known in its powdered form as "Molly"). This powerful drug is both a stimulant and a mild hallucinogen. (*Hallucinogens* distort perceptions and

DRAMATIC DRUG-INDUCED DECLINE This woman's methamphetamine addiction led to obvious physical changes just 18 months after she started.

lead to false sensory images. More on that later.) Ecstasy is an amphetamine derivative that triggers the brain's release of dopamine. But its major effect is releasing stored serotonin and blocking its reuptake, thus prolonging serotonin's feel-good flood (Braun, 2001). Users feel the effect about a half-hour after taking an Ecstasy pill. For three or four hours, they experience high energy and emotional elevation. In a social setting,

they will feel intimately connected to the people around them. ("I love everyone!")

During the late 1990s, Ecstasy's popularity soared as a "club drug" taken at nightclubs and all-night dance parties (Landry, 2002). There are, however, reasons not to be ecstatic about Ecstasy. One is its ability to cause dehydration. With prolonged dancing, this effect can lead to severe overheating, increased blood pressure, and death. Long-term, repeated use can also damage serotonin-producing neurons. Serotonin does more than just make us feel happy. It helps regulate our body rhythms (including sleep), our disease-fighting immune system, and our memory and other cognitive functions (Laws & Kokkalis, 2007; Pacifici et al., 2001; Schilt et al., 2007; Wagner et al., 2012b). Ecstasy interferes with all these functions. The decreased serotonin output can be permanent and can lead to a permanently depressed mood (Croft et al., 2001; McCann et al., 2001; Roiser et al., 2005). Ecstasy delights for the night but darkens our tomorrows.

Hallucinogens

LOQ 13-12 What are hallucinogens, and what are their effects?

Hallucinogens distort perceptions and call up sensory images (such as sounds or sights) without any input from the senses. This helps explain why these drugs are also called *psychedelics,* meaning "mind-manifesting." Some are synthetic. The best known synthetic hallucinogens are MDMA (Ecstasy), discussed earlier, and LSD. Others, such as the mild hallucinogen marijuana, are natural substances.

Whether provoked to hallucinate by drugs, loss of oxygen, or extreme sensory deprivation, the brain hallucinates in basically the same way (Siegel, 1982). The experience typically begins with simple geometric forms, such as a criss-cross, a cobweb, or a spiral. The next phase consists of more meaningful images. Some images may be seen in front of a tunnel; others may be replays of past emotional experiences. As the hallucination peaks, people frequently feel separated from their body. Dreamlike scenes feel so real that people may become panic-stricken or harm themselves.

These sensations are strikingly similar to the **near-death experience.** This altered state of consciousness is reported by about 10 to 15 percent of those revived from cardiac arrest (Agrillo, 2011; Greyson, 2010; Parnia et al., 2014). Many describe visions of tunnels (**FIGURE 13.6**), bright lights or beings of light, a replay of old memories, and out-of-body sensations (Siegel, 1980). Oxygen deprivation and other insults to the brain can produce what one philosopher-neuroscientist calls "neural funny business" (Churchland, 2013, p. 70). During epileptic seizures and migraines, for example, people sometimes experience hallucinations of geometric patterns (Billock & Tsou, 2012). Solitary sailors and polar explorers have reported profound mystical experiences while enduring monotony, isolation, and cold (Suedfeld & Mocellin, 1987).

FIGURE 13.6 Near-death vision or hallucination? People under the influence of hallucinogenic drugs often see "a bright light in the center of the field of vision. . . . The location of this point of light create[s] a tunnel-like perspective" (Siegel, 1977). This is very similar to others' near-death experiences.

LSD In 1943, Albert Hofmann reported perceiving "an uninterrupted stream of fantastic pictures, extraordinary shapes with an intense, kaleidoscopic play of colors" (Siegel, 1984). Hofmann, a chemist, had created and accidentally ingested **LSD** (lysergic acid diethylamide). LSD, like Ecstasy, interferes with the serotonin neurotransmitter system. An LSD "trip" can take users to unexpected places. Emotions may vary from euphoria to detachment to panic, depending in part on the person's mood and expectations.

MARIJUANA For 5000 years, hemp has been cultivated for its fiber. The leaves and flowers of this plant, which are sold as *marijuana,* contain **THC** (delta-9-tetrahydrocannabinol). Whether smoked (getting to the brain in a mere 7 seconds) or eaten (traveling at a slower, less predictable pace), THC produces a mix of effects. Synthetic marijuana ("K-2," also called "Spice") mimics THC but can have harmful side effects—such as agitation, seizures, hallucinations, and suicidal or aggressive thoughts and actions. Lawmakers have passed legislation, such as the U.S. Synthetic Drug Abuse Prevention Act of 2012, to make K-2 illegal.

The straight dope on marijuana: It is usually classified as a mild hallucinogen, because it increases sensitivity to colors, sounds, tastes, and smells. But in other ways, marijuana is like alcohol. It relaxes, disinhibits, and may produce a euphoric high. And, like alcohol, it impairs motor coordination, perceptual skills, and reaction time, so it interferes with safe operation of an automobile or other machine. "THC causes animals to misjudge events," reported Ronald Siegel (1990, p. 163). "Pigeons wait too long to respond to buzzers or lights that tell them food is available for brief periods; and rats turn the wrong way in mazes."

Marijuana and alcohol also differ. The body eliminates alcohol within hours. THC and its by-products linger in the body for more than a week, which means that regular users may experience a less abrupt withdrawal. They may also achieve a high with smaller-than-usual amounts. This is the opposite of typical tolerance, in which repeat users need to take larger doses to feel the same effect.

amphetamines drugs that stimulate neural activity, causing speeded-up body functions and associated energy and mood changes.

methamphetamine a powerfully addictive drug that stimulates the central nervous system with speeded-up body functions and associated energy and mood changes; over time, appears to reduce baseline dopamine levels.

Ecstasy (MDMA) a synthetic stimulant and mild hallucinogen. Produces euphoria and social intimacy, but with short-term health risks and longer-term harm to serotonin-producing neurons and to mood and cognition.

hallucinogens psychedelic ("mind-manifesting") drugs, such as LSD, that distort perceptions and trigger sensory images in the absence of sensory input.

near-death experience an altered state of consciousness reported after a close brush with death (such as cardiac arrest); often similar to drug-induced hallucinations.

LSD a powerful hallucinogenic drug; also known as acid *(lysergic acid diethylamide).*

THC the major active ingredient in marijuana; triggers a variety of effects, including mild hallucinations.

TABLE 13.5 A Guide to Selected Psychoactive Drugs

Drug	Type	Pleasurable Effects	Negative Aftereffects
Alcohol	Depressant	Initial high followed by relaxation and disinhibition	Depression, memory loss, organ damage, impaired reactions
Heroin	Depressant	Rush of euphoria, relief from pain	Depressed physiology, agonizing withdrawal
Caffeine	Stimulant	Increased alertness and wakefulness	Anxiety, restlessness, and insomnia in high doses; uncomfortable withdrawal
Nicotine	Stimulant	Arousal and relaxation, sense of well-being	Heart disease, cancer
Cocaine	Stimulant	Rush of euphoria, confidence, energy	Cardiovascular stress, suspiciousness, depressive crash
Methamphetamine	Stimulant	Euphoria, alertness, energy	Irritability, insomnia, hypertension, seizures
Ecstasy (MDMA)	Stimulant; mild hallucinogen	Emotional elevation, disinhibition	Dehydration, overheating, depressed mood, impaired cognitive and immune functioning
LSD	Hallucinogen	Visual "trip"	Risk of panic
Marijuana (THC)	Mild hallucinogen	Enhanced sensation, relief of pain, distortion of time, relaxation	Impaired learning and memory, increased risk of psychological disorders, lung damage from smoke

A marijuana user's experience can vary with the situation. If the person feels anxious or depressed, marijuana may intensify these feelings. The more often the person uses marijuana, the greater the risk of anxiety, depression, or addiction (Bambico et al., 2010; Hurd et al., 2013; Murray et al., 2007).

Does marijuana harm the brain and impair cognition? Some evidence indicates that it disrupts memory formation (Bossong et al., 2012). Such effects on thinking outlast the period of smoking (Messinis et al., 2006). Heavy adult use for over 20 years has been associated with shrinkage of brain areas that process memories and emotions (Filbey et al., 2014; Yücel et al., 2008). And one long-term study tracking 1000 people from birth found a link between persistent marijuana use before age 18 and lower intelligence test scores in adulthood (Meier et al., 2012b). Other researchers are unconvinced that smoking marijuana harms the brain (Rogeberg, 2013; Weiland et al., 2015).

In some cases, *medical marijuana* use has been legalized as treatment for the pain and nausea associated with diseases such as AIDS and cancer (Munsey, 2010; Watson et al., 2000). In such treatments, the Institute of Medicine recommends delivering the THC with medical inhalers. Marijuana smoke, like cigarette smoke, is toxic and can cause cancer, lung damage, and pregnancy complications (BLF, 2012).

* * *

TABLE 13.5 summarizes the psychoactive drugs discussed in this section. They share some features. All trigger negative aftereffects that offset their immediate positive effects and grow stronger with repetition. This helps explain both tolerance and withdrawal. As the negative aftereffects grow stronger, larger and larger doses are typically needed to produce the desired high (*tolerance*). These increasingly larger doses produce even worse aftereffects in the drug's absence (*withdrawal*). The worsening aftereffects, in turn, create a need to switch off the withdrawal symptoms by taking yet more of the drug.

Retrieve + Remember

"How strange would appear to be this thing that men call pleasure! And how curiously it is related to what is thought to be its opposite, pain! . . . Wherever the one is found, the other follows up behind."

Plato, *Phaedo,* fourth century B.C.E.

- How does this pleasure-pain description apply to the repeated use of psychoactive drugs?

ANSWER: Psychoactive drugs create pleasure by altering brain chemistry. With repeated use of the drug, the brain develops tolerance and needs more of the drug to achieve the desired effect. (Marijuana is an exception). Discontinuing use of the substance then produces painful or psychologically unpleasant withdrawal symptoms.

LaunchPad To review the basic psychoactive drugs and their actions, and to play the role of experimenter as you administer drugs and observe their effects, visit LaunchPad's *PsychSim 6: Your Mind on Drugs.*

Understanding Substance Use Disorders

LOQ 13-13 What biological, psychological, and social-cultural factors help explain why some people abuse mind-altering drugs?

Substance use by North American youth increased during the 1970s. Then, with increased drug education and a shift toward more realism and less glamorous media portrayals of the effects of drugs, substance use declined sharply, except for a small, brief rebound in the mid-1980s. After the early 1990s, the cultural antidrug voice softened, and drugs for a time were again glamorized in music and films. Even so, drug use among high school students has been holding fairly steady (**FIGURE 13.7**).

For many adolescents, occasional drug use represents thrill seeking. Yet why do some adolescents, but not others, become regular drug users? In search of answers, researchers have tried to sort out biological, psychological, and social-cultural influences.

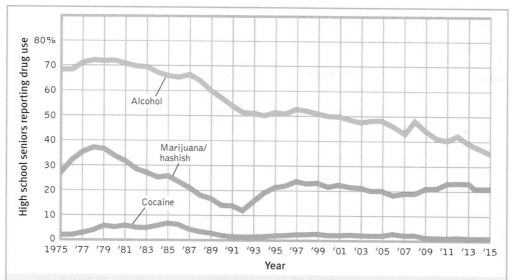

FIGURE 13.7 Trends in drug use The percentage of U.S. high school seniors who said they had used alcohol, marijuana, or cocaine during the past 30 days largely declined from the late 1970s to 1992, when it partially rebounded for a few years. (Data from Johnston et al., 2015.)

Biological Influences

Are some of us biologically vulnerable to particular drugs? Evidence indicates we are (Crabbe, 2002):

- For identical twins, if one twin is diagnosed with alcohol use disorder, the other also has an increased risk for alcohol problems. In marijuana use, too, identical twins more closely resemble each other (Kendler et al., 2002c). This increased risk is not found among fraternal twins.

- Researchers have identified genes associated with alcohol use disorder, and they are seeking genes that contribute to tobacco addiction (Stacey et al., 2012). These culprit genes seem to produce deficiencies in the brain's natural dopamine reward system.

- A large study of 18,115 adopted people also found evidence of both a genetic influence and an environmental influence. Those with drug-abusing *biological parents* were at doubled risk of drug abuse. But those with a drug-abusing *adoptive sibling* also had a doubled risk of

drug abuse (Kendler et al., 2012). So, what might those environmental influences be?

Psychological and Social-Cultural Influences

Throughout this text, you have seen a recurring theme: *Biological, psychological, and social-cultural influences interact to influence behavior.* So, too, with problematic drug use. We have considered some biological influences on substance use and abuse. One psychological factor that has appeared in studies of youth and young adults is the feeling that life is meaningless and directionless (Newcomb & Harlow, 1986). This feeling is common among school dropouts who try to make their way in life without job skills, without privilege, and with little hope.

Sometimes, a psychological influence is obvious. Many heavy users of alcohol, marijuana, and cocaine have experienced significant stress or failure and are depressed. Girls with a history of depression, eating disorders, or sexual or physical abuse are at risk for substance addiction. So are youth

undergoing school or neighborhood transitions (CASA, 2003; Logan et al., 2002). By temporarily dulling the pain of self-awareness, psychoactive drugs may offer a way to avoid coping with depression, anger, anxiety, or insomnia. The relief may be temporary, but as Chapter 6 explains, behavior is often controlled more by its immediate consequences than by its later ones.

Rates of substance use also vary across cultural and ethnic groups. Among actively religious people, alcohol and other substance addiction rates have been low, with extremely low rates among Orthodox Jews, Mormons, Mennonites, and the Amish (Salas-Wright et al., 2012; Vaughn et al., 2011; Yeung et al., 2009). African-American teens' rates of drinking, smoking, and cocaine use are sharply lower than among other U.S. teens (Johnston et al., 2007).

Substance use can also have social roots. Adolescents, self-conscious and often thinking the world is watching them, are especially vulnerable. Smoking, for example, usually begins in the early teen years. Teens may first light up to imitate glamorous celebrities, to project a mature image, to handle stress, or to get the social reward of

SNAPSHOTS

acceptance by other smokers (Cin et al., 2007; DeWall & Pond, 2011; Tickle et al., 2006).

Whether in cities or in rural areas, peers influence attitudes about substance use. They throw the parties and provide (or don't provide) the drugs. If an adolescent's friends abuse drugs, the odds are that he or she will, too. If the friends do not, the opportunity may not even arise.

Peer influence is more than what friends do and say. Adolescents' expectations—what they *believe* their friends are doing and favoring—matter too. One study surveyed sixth-graders in 22 U.S. states. How many believed their friends had smoked marijuana? About 14 percent. How many of those friends said they had smoked it? Only 4 percent (Wren, 1999). College students are not immune to such misperceptions, either. Drinking dominates social occasions partly because students overestimate their fellow students' enthusiasm for alcohol and underestimate their view of its risks (Moreira et al., 2009; Prentice & Miller, 1993; Self, 1994). As always with correlations, the traffic between friends' drug use and our own may be two-way. Our friends influence us, but we also select as friends those who share our likes and dislikes.

Teens rarely abuse drugs if they understand the physical and psychological costs, do well in school, feel good about themselves, and are in a peer group that disapproves of early drinking and using drugs (Bachman et al., 2007; Hingson et al., 2006). These findings suggest three tactics for preventing and treating substance use and addiction among young people:

- Educate them about the long-term costs of a drug's temporary pleasures.
- Boost their self-esteem and help them discover their purpose in life.
- Attempt to modify peer associations or to "inoculate" youth against peer pressures by training them in refusal skills.

Retrieve + Remember

- Studies have found that people who begin drinking in their early teens are much more likely to develop alcohol use disorder than are those who begin at age 21 or after. What possible explanations might there be for this correlation?

ANSWER: Possible explanations include (a) biological factors (a person could have a biological predisposition to both early use and later abuse, or alcohol use could modify a person's neural pathways); (b) psychological factors (early use could establish taste preferences for alcohol); and (c) social-cultural factors (early use could influence enduring habits, attitudes, activities, or peer relationships that could foster alcohol use disorder).

Major Depressive Disorder and Bipolar Disorder

LOQ 13-14 How do major depressive disorder and bipolar disorder differ?

Most of us will have some direct or indirect experience with depression. In the past year, have you at some time "felt so depressed that it was difficult to function"? If so, you were not alone. In one national survey, 31 percent of American college students answered *Yes* (ACHA, 2009).

The college years are an exciting time, but they can also be stressful. Perhaps you wanted to attend college right out of high school but couldn't afford it, and now you are struggling to find time for school amid family and work responsibilities. Perhaps social stresses—such as missing a partner after a breakup or being excluded from a popular group—have left you feeling isolated or down about your future, or about life in general. You may lack the energy to get things done or even to force yourself out of bed. You may be unable to concentrate, eat, or sleep normally.

Occasionally, you may even wonder if you would be better off dead.

Some people's depression has a *seasonal pattern*. It regularly returns each fall or winter and departs each spring. For many others, winter darkness simply means more blue moods. When asked "Have you cried today?," Americans have said *Yes* more often in the winter.

Depression makes sense from an evolutionary perspective. To feel bad in reaction to very sad events is to be in touch with reality. At such times, depression is like a car's low-fuel light—a warning signal that we should stop and take appropriate measures. Biologically speaking, life's purpose is survival and reproduction, not happiness. Just as coughing, vomiting, and various forms of pain protect our body from dangerous toxins, so depression protects us. It slows us down and gives us time to think hard and consider our options (Wrosch & Miller, 2009). It defuses aggression, cuts back on risk taking, and focuses our mind (Allen & Badcock, 2003; Andrews & Thomson, 2009a). As one social psychologist warned, "If someone offered you a pill that would make you permanently happy, you would be well advised to run fast and run far. Emotion is a compass that tells us what to do, and a compass that is perpetually stuck on NORTH is worthless" (Gilbert, 2006).

There is sense to suffering. After reassessing our life, we may redirect our energy in more promising ways. Even mild sadness helps people process and recall faces more accurately (Hills et al., 2011). They also tend to pay more attention to details and make better decisions (Forgas, 2009).

Sometimes, however, depression becomes seriously maladaptive. Abnormal depression can take many forms. Let's look more closely at two of them—*major depressive disorder*, a prolonged state of hopeless depression, and *bipolar disorder*, alternating states of depression and overexcited hyperactivity.

Brad Wenner/Moment Select/Getty Images

TABLE 13.6 Diagnosing Major Depressive Disorder

The DSM-5 classifies major depressive disorder as the presence of at least five of the following symptoms over a two-week period of time (minimally including depressed mood or reduced interest) (American Psychiatric Association, 2013).

- Depressed mood most of the time
- Dramatically reduced interest or enjoyment in most activities most of the time
- Significant challenges regulating appetite and weight
- Significant challenges regulating sleep
- Physical agitation or lethargy
- Feeling listless or with much less energy
- Feeling worthless, or feeling unwarranted guilt
- Problems in thinking, concentrating, or making decisions
- Thinking repetitively of death and suicide

Major Depressive Disorder

Joy, contentment, sadness, and despair are different points on a continuum, points at which any of us may be found at any given moment. The difference between a blue mood after bad news and **major depressive disorder** is like the difference between gasping for breath after a hard run and having chronic asthma. Major depressive disorder occurs when at least five signs of depression last two or more weeks (**TABLE 13.6**). To sense what major depressive disorder feels like, imagine combining the anguish of grief with the exhaustion you feel after pulling an all-nighter.

Although phobias are more common, depression is the number-one reason people seek mental health services. In the United States, 7.6 percent of people interviewed were experiencing moderate or severe depression (CDC, 2014a). Worldwide, depression trails only low back pain as the leading cause of disability (Global Burden of Disease Study, 2015).

Adults diagnosed with *persistent depressive disorder* (formerly called *dysthymia*) have experienced a mildly depressed mood for at least two years (American Psychiatric Association, 2013). They also display at least two of depression's symptoms.

Bipolar Disorder

Our genes dispose some of us, more than others, to respond emotionally to good and bad events (Whisman et al., 2014). In **bipolar disorder,** people bounce from one emotional extreme to the other (week to week, rather than day to day or moment to moment). When a depressive episode ends, a euphoric, overly talkative, wildly energetic, and extremely optimistic state called **mania** follows. But before long, the mood either returns to normal or plunges again into depression.

If depression is living in slow motion, mania is fast forward. During mania, people feel little need for sleep, are easily irritated, and show fewer sexual inhibitions. Feeling extreme optimism and self-esteem, they find advice annoying. Yet they need protection from their poor judgment, which may lead to reckless spending or unsafe sex. Thinking fast feels good, but it also increases risk taking (Chandler & Pronin, 2012; Pronin, 2013).

In milder forms, mania's energy and flood of ideas can fuel creativity. Classical composer George Frideric Handel (1685–1759), who many believe suffered a mild form of bipolar disorder, composed his nearly four-hour-long *Messiah* during three weeks of intense, creative energy (Keynes, 1980). Bipolar disorder strikes more often among people who rely on emotional expression and vivid imagery, such as poets and artists, and less often among those who rely on precision and logic, such as architects, designers, and journalists (Jamison, 1993, 1995; Kaufman & Baer, 2002; Ludwig, 1995).

Bipolar disorder is much less common than major depressive disorder, but is often more dysfunctional. It afflicts as many men as women. The diagnosis has

Actor Russell Brand

Writer Virginia Woolf

Humorist Samuel Clemens (Mark Twain)

CREATIVITY AND BIPOLAR DISORDER There have been many creative artists, composers, writers, and musical performers with bipolar disorder.

major depressive disorder a disorder in which a person experiences, in the absence of drugs or another medical condition, two or more weeks with five or more symptoms, at least one of which must be either (1) depressed mood or (2) loss of interest or pleasure.

bipolar disorder a disorder in which a person alternates between the hopelessness and weariness of depression and the overexcited state of mania. (Formerly called *manic-depressive disorder.*)

mania a hyperactive, wildly optimistic state in which dangerously poor judgment is common.

BIPOLAR DISORDER Artist Abigail Southworth illustrated her experience of bipolar disorder.

risen among adolescents, whose mood swings, sometimes prolonged, range from rage to giddiness. In the decade between 1994 and 2003, bipolar diagnoses in under-20 people showed an astonishing 40-fold increase—from an estimated 20,000 to 800,000 (Carey, 2007; Flora & Bobby, 2008; Moreno et al., 2007). The DSM-5 classifications will likely reduce the number of child and adolescent bipolar diagnoses. Some of those who are persistently irritable and who have frequent and recurring behavior outbursts will now instead be diagnosed with *disruptive mood dysregulation disorder* (Miller, 2010).

Understanding Major Depressive Disorder and Bipolar Disorder

LOQ 13-15 How can the biological and social-cognitive perspectives help us understand major depressive disorder and bipolar disorder?

From thousands of studies of the causes, treatment, and prevention of major depressive disorder and bipolar disorder, researchers have pulled out some common threads. Here, we focus primarily on major depressive disorder. Any theory of depression must explain a number of findings (Lewinsohn et al., 1985, 1998, 2003).

- *Behaviors and thoughts change with depression.* People trapped in a depressed mood are inactive and

feel alone, empty, and without a meaningful future (Bullock & Murray, 2014; Smith & Rhodes, 2014). They are sensitive to negative happenings (Peckham et al., 2010). They recall negative information. And they expect negative outcomes (my team will lose, my grades will fall, my love will fail). When the depression lifts, these behaviors and thoughts disappear. Nearly half the time, people with depression also have symptoms of another disorder, such as anxiety or substance abuse.

- *Depression is widespread.* Worldwide, 300 million people have major depressive or bipolar disorder (Global Burden of Disease, 2015).

- *Women's risk of major depressive disorder is nearly double men's.* In 2009, when Gallup pollsters asked more than a quarter-million Americans if they had ever been diagnosed with depression, 13 percent of men and 22 percent of women said *Yes* (Pelham, 2009). When Gallup asked Americans if they experienced sadness "during a lot of the day yesterday," 17 percent of men and 28 percent of women answered *Yes* (Mendes & McGeeney, 2012). This depression gender gap has been found worldwide (**FIGURE 13.8**). The trend begins in adolescence; preadolescent girls are not more depression-prone than boys are (Hyde et al., 2008).

The depression gender gap fits a bigger pattern. Women are generally more vulnerable to disorders involving internal states, such as depression, anxiety, and inhibited sexual desire. Women experience more situations that may increase their risk for depression, such as receiving less pay for equal work, juggling multiple roles, and caring for children and elderly family members (Freeman & Freeman, 2013). Men's disorders tend to be more external—alcohol use disorder, antisocial conduct, lack of impulse control. When women get sad, they often get sadder than men do. When men get mad, they often get madder than women do.

- *Most major depressive episodes end on their own.* Although therapy often speeds recovery, most people recover from depression and return to normal even without professional help. The black cloud of depression comes and, a few weeks or months later, it often goes. For about half of these people, it eventually returns (Burcusa & Iacono, 2007; Curry et al., 2011; Hardeveld et al., 2010). For about 20 percent, the condition will be chronic (Klein, 2010). An enduring recovery is more likely if the first episode strikes later in life, there were few previous episodes, the person experiences minimal stress, and there is ample social support (Fergusson & Woodward, 2002; Kendler et al., 2001; Richards, 2011).

- *Stressful events sometimes precede depression.* As anxiety is a response to the threat of future loss, depression is often a response to past and current loss. A significant loss or trauma—a loved one's death, a lost job, a marriage break-up, or a physical assault—increase one's risk of depression (Kendler et al., 2008; Monroe & Reid, 2009; Orth et al., 2009). So does moving to a new culture, especially for young people who have not yet formed an identity (Zhang et al., 2013). One long-term study tracked rates of depression in 2000 people

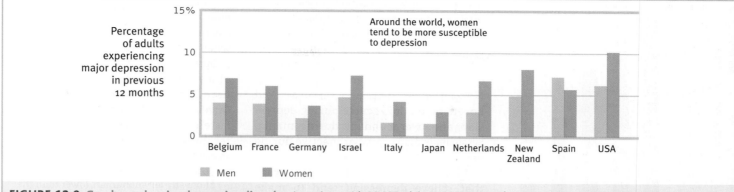

FIGURE 13.8 Gender and major depressive disorder Interviews with 89,037 adults in 18 countries (10 of which are shown here) confirm what many smaller studies have found. Women's risk of major depressive disorder is nearly double that of men's. (Data from Bromet et al., 2011.)

(Kendler, 1998). Among those who had experienced no stressful life event in the preceding month, the risk of depression was less than 1 percent. Among those who had experienced three such events in that month, the risk was 24 percent. Surveys before and after Hurricane Sandy in 2012 revealed a 25 percent increase in clinical depression rates in the most affected areas (Witters & Ander, 2013).

LIFE AFTER DEPRESSION J. K. Rowling, author of the Harry Potter books, reported suffering acute depression—a "dark time," with suicidal thoughts—between ages 25 and 28. It was a "terrible place," she said, but it formed a foundation that allowed her "to come back stronger" (McLaughlin, 2010).

But life's daily minor stressors can also take a toll. One study showed that overreacting to minor stressful events (such as a broken appliance) was a good predictor of depression a decade later (Charles et al., 2013).

• *With each new generation, depression is striking earlier in life (now often in the late teens) and affecting more people.* This has been true in Canada, England, France, Germany, Italy, Lebanon, New Zealand, Puerto Rico, Taiwan, and the United States (Collishaw et al., 2007; Cross-National Collaborative Group, 1992; Kessler et al., 2010; Twenge et al., 2008). In North America, today's young adults are three times more likely than their grandparents to report having recently—or ever—suffered depression. This is true even though their grandparents have been at risk for many more years.

The increased risk among young adults appears partly real, but it may also reflect increased reporting due to cultural differences. Today's young people are more willing to talk openly about their depression. Psychological processes may also contribute. Studies of aging and memory show that we tend to forget many negative experiences over time. Older generations may report fewer instances of depression in part because they overlook depressed feelings they had in earlier years.

Armed with facts, today's researchers propose biological and cognitive explanations of depression, often combined in a biopsychosocial perspective.

LaunchPad For a 9-minute video demonstrating one young man's struggle with depression, visit LaunchPad's *Video: Depression.*

Biological Influences

Depression is a whole-body disorder. It involves genetic predispositions and biochemical imbalances, as well as negative thoughts and a dark mood.

GENES AND DEPRESSION Major depressive disorder and bipolar disorder run in families. The risk of being diagnosed with one of these disorders increases if your parent or sibling has the disorder (Sullivan et al., 2000). If one identical twin is diagnosed with major depressive disorder, the chances are about 1 in 2 that at some time the other twin will be, too. If one identical twin has bipolar disorder, the chances of a similar diagnosis for the co-twin are even higher—7 in 10—even for those twins raised apart (DiLalla et al., 1996). Among fraternal twins, the corresponding odds are just under 2 in 10 (Tsuang & Faraone, 1990). Summarizing the major twin studies (see **FIGURE 13.9**), one research team estimated the heritability of major depressive disorder—the extent to which individual depression differences are attributable to genes—at 37 percent (Bienvenu et al., 2011).

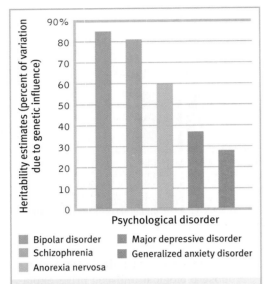

FIGURE 13.9 The heritability of various psychological disorders Using data from multiple studies of identical and fraternal twins, researchers estimated the heritability of bipolar disorder, schizophrenia, anorexia nervosa, major depressive disorder, and generalized anxiety disorder (Bienvenu et al., 2011).

To tease out the genes that put people at risk for depression, some researchers have turned to *linkage analysis*. After finding families in which the disorder appears across several generations, geneticists examine DNA from affected and unaffected family members, looking for differences. Linkage analysis points us to a chromosome neighborhood, note researchers; "a house-to-house search is then needed to find the culprit gene" (Plomin & McGuffin, 2003). But depression is a complex condition. Many genes work together, producing a mosaic of small effects that interact with other factors to put some people at greater risk. If the culprit gene variations can be identified, they may open the door to more effective drug therapy.

THE DEPRESSED BRAIN Scanning devices let us eavesdrop on the brain's activity. During depression, brain activity slows. During mania, it increases (**FIGURE 13.10**). Depression can cause the brain's reward centers to become less active (Miller et al., 2015; Stringaris et al., 2015).

During positive emotions, reward centers become more active (Davidson et al., 2002; Heller et al., 2009; Robinson et al., 2012).

At least two neurotransmitter systems are at work during these periods of brain inactivity and hyperactivity. *Norepinephrine* increases arousal and boosts mood. It is scarce during depression and overabundant during mania. *Serotonin* is also scarce or inactive during depression (Carver et al., 2008).

In Chapter 14, we will see how drugs that relieve depression tend to make more norepinephrine or serotonin available to the depressed brain. Repetitive physical exercise, such as jogging, which increases serotonin, can have a similar effect (Ilardi, 2009; Jacobs, 1994). To run away from a bad mood, you can sometimes use your own two feet.

Psychological and Social Influences

Biological influences contribute to depression, but as we have so often seen, nature and nurture interact. Our life experiences—diet, drugs, stress, and other environmental influences—can place molecular tags on our chromosomes. These *epigenetic* changes do not alter our DNA, but they can trigger our genes to turn on or off. Animal studies suggest that long-lasting epigenetic influences may play a role in depression (Nestler, 2011).

Thinking matters, too. The *social-cognitive perspective* explores how people's assumptions and expectations influence what they perceive. Many depressed people see life through dark glasses of low self-esteem (Orth et al., 2016). They have intensely negative views of themselves, their situation, and their future. Listen to Norman, a college professor, recalling his depression (Endler, 1982, pp. 45–49):

> I [despaired] of ever being human again. I honestly felt subhuman, lower than the lowest vermin. Furthermore, I . . . could not understand why anyone would want to associate with me, let alone love me . . . . I was positive that I was a fraud and a phony and that I didn't deserve my Ph.D. . . . I didn't deserve the research grants I had been awarded; I couldn't understand how I had written books and journal articles. . . . I must have conned a lot of people.

Expecting the worst, depressed people magnify bad experiences and minimize good ones (Wenze et al., 2012). Their *self-defeating beliefs* and *negative explanatory style* feed their depression.

NEGATIVE THOUGHTS AND NEGATIVE MOODS INTERACT Self-defeating beliefs may arise from *learned helplessness*. As we saw in Chapter 10, both dogs and humans act depressed, passive, and withdrawn after experiencing uncontrollable painful events. Learned helplessness is more common in women, who may respond more strongly to

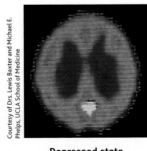 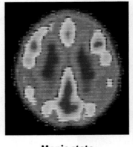 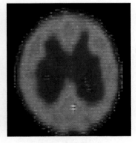

Depressed state (May 17)	**Manic state** (May 18)	**Depressed state** (May 27)

FIGURE 13.10 The ups and downs of bipolar disorder These top-facing PET scans show that brain energy consumption rises and falls with the patient's emotional switches. Red areas are where the brain rapidly consumes glucose.

stress (Hankin & Abramson, 2001; Mazure et al., 2002; Nolen-Hoeksema, 2001, 2003). Do you agree or disagree with the statement, "I feel frequently overwhelmed by all I have to do"? In a survey of students entering American colleges, 38 percent of the women agreed (Pryor et al., 2006). Only 17 percent of the men agreed. (Did your answer fit that pattern?)

Why are women nearly twice as vulnerable to depression (Kessler, 2001)? This higher risk may relate to women's tendency to *ruminate*—to overthink, fret, or brood (Nolen-Hoeksema, 2003). Rumination can be adaptive. Thanks to the continuous firing of an attention-sustaining area of the brain, it can help us focus intently on a problem (Altamirano et al., 2010; Andrews & Thomson, 2009a,b). But relentless, self-focused rumination is not adaptive. It diverts us from thinking about other life tasks, leaves us mired in negative emotions, and disrupts daily activities (Kircanski et al., 2015; Kuppens et al., 2010; Kuster et al., 2012).

Even so, why do life's unavoidable failures lead only some people to become depressed? The answer lies partly in

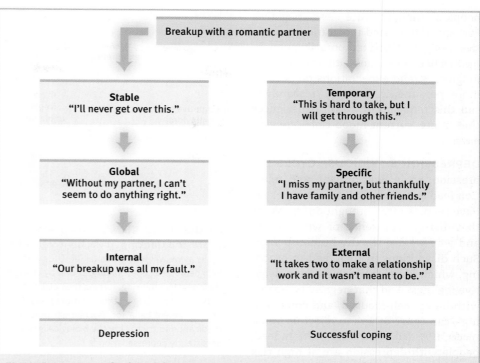

FIGURE 13.11 Outlook and depression After a negative experience, a depression-prone person may respond with a negative explanatory style.

I NEVER KNOW WHAT TO SAY TO PEOPLE.

NO ONE WANTS TO BE AROUND ME.

WILL I EVER GET A JOB?!

DO I SMELL BAD? I'M SO UGLY.

RUMINATION RUNS WILD It's normal to think about our flaws. Sometimes, we do more than that and *ruminate:* We dwell constantly on negative thoughts, particularly negative thoughts about ourselves. Rumination makes it difficult to believe in ourselves and solve problems. In some cases, people seek therapy to reduce their rumination.

their *explanatory style*—who or what they blame for their failures (or credit for their successes). Think how you might feel if you failed a test. If you can blame someone else ("What an unfair test!"), you are more likely to feel angry. If you blame yourself, you probably will feel stupid and depressed.

Depressed people tend to blame themselves. As **FIGURE 13.11** illustrates, they explain bad events in terms that are *stable* ("I'll never get over this"), *global* ("I can't do anything right"), and *internal* ("It's all my fault"). Their explanations are pessimistic, overgeneralized, self-focused, and self-blaming (Huang, 2015; Mor & Winquist, 2002; Wood et al., 1990a,b). The result may be a depressing sense of hopelessness (Abramson et al., 1989; Panzarella et al., 2006). As Martin Seligman has noted, "A recipe for severe depression is preexisting pessimism encountering failure" (1991, p. 78).

Critics point out a chicken-and-egg problem nesting in the social-cognitive

explanation of depression. Which comes first? The pessimistic explanatory style or the depressed mood? The negative explanations *coincide* with a depressed mood, and they are *indicators* of depression (Barnett & Gotlib, 1988). But do they *cause* depression, any more than a speedometer's reading 70 mph *causes* a car's speed? Before or after being depressed,

"*You should never engage in unsupervised introspection.*"

Breakup with a romantic partner

Stable
"I'll never get over this."

Temporary
"This is hard to take, but I will get through this."

Global
"Without my partner, I can't seem to do anything right."

Specific
"I miss my partner, but thankfully I have family and other friends."

Internal
"Our breakup was all my fault."

External
"It takes two to make a relationship work and it wasn't meant to be."

Depression

Successful coping

people's thoughts are less negative. Perhaps a depressed mood *triggers* negative thoughts. If you temporarily put people in a bad or sad mood, their memories, judgments, and expectations do become more pessimistic. Memory researchers call this tendency to recall experiences that fit our current mood *state-dependent memory*.

DEPRESSION'S VICIOUS CYCLE Depression, social withdrawal, and rejection feed one another. Depression, as we have seen, is often brought on by events that disrupt our sense of who we are and why we are worthy human beings. Such disruptions in turn lead to brooding, which is rich soil for growing negative feelings. And that negativity—being withdrawn, self-focused, and complaining—can cause others to reject us (Furr & Funder, 1998; Gotlib & Hammen, 1992). Indeed, people with depression are at high risk for divorce, job loss, and other stressful life events. Weary of the person's fatigue, hopeless attitude, and negative comments, a spouse may threaten to leave, or a boss may question the person's competence. New losses and stress then plunge the already depressed person into even deeper misery. Misery may love another's company, but company does not love another's misery.

We can now assemble pieces of the depression cycle (**FIGURE 13.12**): (1) Stressful experiences interpreted through (2) a brooding, negative explanatory style create (3) a hopeless, depressed state that (4) hampers the way the person thinks and acts. These thoughts and actions in turn fuel (1) further stressful experiences such as rejection. Depression is a snake that bites its own tail.

It is a cycle we can all recognize. When we *feel* down, we *think* negatively and *remember* bad experiences. Britain's Prime Minister Winston Churchill called depression a "black dog" that periodically hounded him. President Abraham Lincoln was so withdrawn and brooding as a young man that his friends feared he might take his own life (Kline, 1974). As their lives remind us, people can and

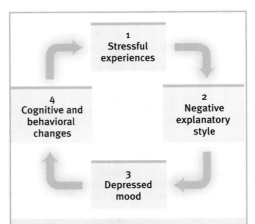

FIGURE 13.12 The vicious cycle of depressed thinking Therapists recognize this cycle, as we will see in Chapter 14. They work to help depressed people break out of it by changing their negative thinking, turning their attention outward, and engaging them in more pleasant and competent behavior. Psychiatrists prescribe medication to try to alter the biological roots of persistently depressed moods.

do struggle through depression. Most regain their capacity to love, to work, to hope, and even to succeed at the highest levels.

Suicide and Self-Injury

LOQ 13-16 What factors increase the risk of suicide, and why do some people injure themselves?

Each year over 800,000 despairing people worldwide will elect a permanent solution to what might have been a temporary problem (WHO, 2014b). The risk of suicide is at least five times greater for those who have been depressed than for the general population (Bostwick & Pankratz, 2000). People seldom elect suicide while in the depths of depression, when energy and will are lacking. The risk increases when they begin to rebound and become capable of following through (Chu et al., 2016).

Suicide is not necessarily an act of hostility or revenge. People—especially older adults—may choose death as an alternative to current or future suffering, a way to switch off unendurable pain

and relieve a perceived burden on family members. "People desire death when two fundamental needs are frustrated to the point of extinction," noted one psychologist: "The need to belong with or connect to others, and the need to feel effective with or to influence others" (Joiner, 2006, p. 47). Suicidal urges typically arise when people feel disconnected from others and a burden to them, or when they feel defeated and trapped by a situation they believe they cannot escape (Joiner, 2010; Taylor et al., 2011). Thus, suicide rates increase with unemployment during economic recessions (DeFina & Hannon, 2015; Reeves et al., 2014). Suicidal thoughts may also increase when people are driven to achieve a goal—to become thin or straight or rich—that proves impossible to reach (Chatard & Selimbegović, 2011).

Looking back, families and friends may recall signs that they believe should have forewarned them—verbal hints, giving possessions away, self-inflicted injuries, or withdrawal and preoccupation with death. But few who talk or think of suicide (a number that includes one-third of all adolescents and college students) actually attempt it. Of those Americans who do attempt it, only about 1 in 25 will die (AAS, 2009). Although most attempts fail, the risk of death by suicide is seven times greater among those who have attempted suicide than those who have not (Al-Sayegh et al., 2015). Each year, about 30,000 people will kill themselves—about two-thirds using guns. (Drug overdoses account for about 80 percent of suicide attempts, but only 14 percent of suicide fatalities.) States with high gun ownership are states with high suicide rates, even after controlling for poverty and urbanization (Miller et al., 2002, 2016; Tavernise, 2013). Thus, although U.S. gun owners often keep a gun to feel safer, the increased risk of suicide and homicide indicates that a gun in the home *increases* the odds of a family member dying (Vyse, 2016).

How can we be helpful to someone who is talking suicide—who says, for example, "I wish I could just end it all" or "I hate my life; I can't go on"? If people write such things online, you can anonymously contact the safety teams at various social media websites (including Facebook, Twitter, Instagram, YouTube, and Tumblr). If a friend or family member talks suicide, you can (1) *listen* and *empathize;* (2) *connect* the person with the Suicide Prevention Lifeline (1-800-273-TALK) or campus health services; and (3) *protect* someone who appears at immediate risk by seeking help from a doctor, the nearest hospital emergency room, or 911. Better to share a secret than to attend a funeral.

Nonsuicidal Self-Injury

Suicide is not the only way to send a message or deal with distress. Some people may engage in *nonsuicidal self-injury (NSSI),* which is more common in adolescence and among females (CDC, 2009). Such behavior, though painful, is not fatal. Those who engage in NSSI cut or burn their skin, hit themselves, pull their hair out, insert objects under their nails or skin, and tattoo themselves (Fikke et al., 2011).

Why do people hurt themselves? They tend to experience bullying and harassment (van Geel et al., 2015). They are generally less able to tolerate and regulate emotional distress (Hamza et al., 2015). They are often extremely self-critical, with poor communication and problem-solving skills (Nock, 2010). Through NSSI, they may

- gain relief from intense negative thoughts through the distraction of pain.
- attract attention and possibly get help.
- relieve guilt by punishing themselves.
- get others to change their negative behavior (bullying, criticism).
- fit in with a peer group.

Does NSSI lead to suicide? Usually not. Those who engage in NSSI are typically suicide gesturers, not suicide attempters (Nock & Kessler, 2006). Suicide gesturers engage in NSSI as a desperate

but non-life-threatening form of communication or when they are feeling overwhelmed. But NSSI is considered a risk factor for suicidal thoughts and future suicide attempts (Hawton et al., 2015; Willoughby et al., 2015). If people do not find help, their nonsuicidal behavior may escalate to suicidal thoughts and, finally, to suicide attempts.

Retrieve + Remember

- What does it mean to say that "depression is a whole-body disorder"?

ANSWER: Many factors contribute to depression, including the biological influences of genetics and brain function. Social-cognitive factors also matter, including the interaction of explanatory style, mood, our responses to stressful experiences, and changes in our patterns of thinking and behaving. Depression involves the whole body and may disrupt sleep, energy, and concentration.

Schizophrenia

During their most severe periods, people with **schizophrenia** live in a private inner world, preoccupied with the strange ideas and images that haunt them. The word itself means "split" *(schizo)* "mind" *(phrenia).* But in this disorder, the mind is not split into multiple personalities. Rather, the mind has suffered a split from reality that shows itself in disturbed perceptions, disorganized thinking and speech, and diminished, inappropriate emotions and actions. Schizophrenia is the chief example of a **psychotic disorder,** a group of disorders marked by irrationality, distorted perceptions, and lost contact with reality.

As you can imagine, these traits profoundly disrupt relationships and make it difficult to hold a job. When people with schizophrenia live in a supportive environment and receive medication, more than 40 percent will enjoy periods of normal life lasting a year or more (Jobe & Harrow, 2010). But only 1 in 7 will have a full and enduring recovery (Jääskeläinen et al., 2013).

Symptoms of Schizophrenia

LOQ 13-17 What patterns of perceiving, thinking, and feeling characterize schizophrenia?

People with schizophrenia display symptoms that are *positive (inappropriate* behaviors are *present)* or *negative (appropriate* behaviors are *absent).* Those with *positive* symptoms may have hallucinations or talk in disorganized and deluded ways. They may laugh or cry or lash out in rage at inappropriate times. Those with *negative* symptoms may have toneless voices, expressionless faces, or mute and rigid bodies.

Disturbed Perceptions and Beliefs

People with schizophrenia sometimes have *hallucinations*—they see, feel, taste, or smell things that exist only in their minds. Most often, the hallucinations are sounds, usually voices making insulting remarks or giving orders. The voices may tell the person that she is bad or that she must burn herself with a cigarette lighter. Imagine your own reaction if a dream broke into your waking consciousness, making it hard to separate your experience from your imagination. Stuart Emmons described his experience:

> When someone asks me to explain schizophrenia I tell them, you know how sometimes in your dreams you are in them yourself and some of them feel like real nightmares? My schizophrenia was like I was walking through a dream. But everything around me was real. At times, today's world seems so boring and I wonder if I would like to step back into the schizophrenic dream, but then I remember all the scary and horrifying experiences (Emmons et al., 1997).

schizophrenia a disorder characterized by delusions, hallucinations, disorganized speech, and/or diminished, inappropriate emotional expression.

psychotic disorders a group of disorders marked by irrational ideas, distorted perceptions, and a loss of contact with reality.

When the unreal seems real, the resulting perceptions are at best bizarre, at worst terrifying.

Hallucinations are false *perceptions.* People with schizophrenia also have disorganized, fragmented thinking often distorted by **delusions,** which are false *beliefs.* If they have *paranoid* tendencies, they may believe they are being threatened or pursued.

Disorganized Speech

Imagine trying to communicate with Maxine, a young woman whose thoughts spill out in no logical order. Her biographer (Sheehan, 1982, p. 25) observed her saying aloud to no one in particular, "This morning, when I was at Hillside [Hospital], I was making a movie. I was surrounded by movie stars. . . . I'm Mary Poppins. Is this room painted blue to get me upset? My grandmother died four weeks after my eighteenth birthday."

Jumbled ideas may make no sense even within sentences, forming what is known as *word salad.* One young man begged for "a little more allegro in the treatment," and suggested that

ART BY SOMEONE DIAGNOSED WITH SCHIZOPHRENIA Commenting on the kind of artwork shown here (from Craig Geiser's 2010 art exhibit in Michigan), poet and art critic John Ashbery wrote: "The lure of the work is strong, but so is the terror of the unanswerable riddles it proposes."

"liberationary movement with a view to the widening of the horizon" will "ergo extort some wit in lectures."

One cause of disorganized thinking may be a breakdown in *selective attention.* Normally, we have a remarkable ability to give our undivided attention to one set of sensory stimuli while filtering out others. People with schizophrenia are easily distracted by tiny unrelated stimuli, such as the grooves on a brick or tones in a voice. But dozens of other cognitive differences are also associated with this disorder (Reichenberg & Harvey, 2007).

Diminished and Inappropriate Emotions and Actions

The expressed emotions of schizophrenia are often utterly inappropriate, split off from reality (Kring & Caponigro, 2010). Maxine laughed after recalling her grandmother's death. On other occasions, she cried when others laughed, or became angry for no apparent reason. Others with schizophrenia lapse into an emotionless *flat affect,* a zombielike state of no apparent feeling. For example, monetary perks fail to provide the normal brain reward center activation (Radua et al., 2015). Most also have an *impaired theory of mind*—they have difficulty reading other people's facial expressions and state of mind (Green & Horan, 2010; Kohler et al., 2010). These emotional traits occur early in the illness and have a genetic basis (Bora & Pantelis, 2013).

Inappropriate motor behavior takes many forms. Some people with schizophrenia perform senseless, compulsive acts, such as continually rocking or rubbing an arm. Others may remain motionless for hours and then become agitated.

Onset and Development of Schizophrenia

LOQ 13-18 How do *acute schizophrenia* and *chronic schizophrenia* differ?

This year, nearly 1 in 100 people (about 60 percent of them men) will join an estimated 24 million others worldwide who have schizophrenia (Global Burden

of Disease, 2015). This disorder knows no national boundaries, and it typically strikes as young people are maturing into adulthood. Men tend to be struck earlier, more severely, and slightly more often (Aleman et al., 2003; Eranti et al., 2013; Picchioni & Murray, 2007).

For some, schizophrenia appears suddenly. Recovery is much more likely when a previously well-adjusted person develops the disorder, called **acute schizophrenia,** seemingly as a rapid reaction to particular life stresses. People with acute schizophrenia often have positive symptoms that respond to drug therapy (Fenton & McGlashan, 1991, 1994; Fowles, 1992).

When schizophrenia is a slow-developing process, called **chronic schizophrenia,** recovery is doubtful (Harrison et al., 2001). This was the case with Maxine, whose schizophrenia developed gradually, emerging from a long history of social inadequacy and poor school performance (MacCabe et al., 2008). Social withdrawal, a negative symptom, is often found among those with chronic schizophrenia (Kirkpatrick et al., 2006). Men, whose schizophrenia develops on average four years earlier than women's, more often exhibit negative symptoms and chronic schizophrenia (Räsänen et al., 2000).

Understanding Schizophrenia

Schizophrenia is one of the most heavily researched psychological disorders. Most studies now link it with abnormal brain tissue and genetic predispositions. Schizophrenia is a disease of the brain made visible in symptoms of the mind.

Brain Abnormalities

LOQ 13-19 What brain abnormalities are associated with schizophrenia?

What sorts of brain abnormalities might explain schizophrenia? Biochemical imbalances? Abnormal brain activity? Problems with brain structures or functions? Researchers are taking a close look at all of these.

Scientists have long known that strange behavior can have strange chemical causes. Have you ever heard the phrase "mad as a hatter"? The saying dates back to the behavior of British hatmakers whose brains were slowly poisoned as they used their mouths to moisten the brims of mercury-laden felt hats (Smith, 1983). Could the hallucinations and other symptoms of schizophrenia have a similar biochemical key?

One possible answer emerged when researchers examined schizophrenia patients' brains after death. They found an excess number of *dopamine* receptors (Seeman et al., 1993; Wong et al., 1986). What could this mean? Perhaps a high level of dopamine could intensify brain signals, creating positive symptoms such as hallucinations and paranoia (Grace, 2010). Sure enough, other evidence confirmed this idea. Drugs that block dopamine receptors often lessen the positive symptoms of schizophrenia. Drugs that increase dopamine levels, such as amphetamines and cocaine, sometimes intensify them (Basu & Basu, 2015; Farnia et al., 2014). But there's more to schizophrenia than abnormal brain chemistry.

Brain scans show that abnormal brain activity and brain structures accompany schizophrenia. Some people with schizophrenia have abnormally low activity in the brain's frontal lobes, which help us reason, plan, and solve problems (Morey et al., 2005; Pettegrew et al., 1993; Resnick, 1992). Others have an unusual corpus callosum, the band of nerve fibers through which the right and left hemispheres communicate (Arnedo et al., 2015).

One study took PET scans of brain activity while people were hallucinating (Silbersweig et al., 1995). When patients heard a voice or saw something, their brain became vigorously active in several core regions. One was the thalamus, the structure that filters incoming sensory signals and transmits them to the brain's cortex. Another PET scan study of people with paranoia found increased activity in the amygdala, a fear-processing center (Epstein et al., 1998).

In schizophrenia, areas of the brain become enlarged and fill with fluid; cerebral tissue also shrinks (Goldman et al., 2009; van Haren et al., 2016; Wright et al., 2000). These brain differences may be inherited. If one identical twin's brain shows the abnormalities, the odds are at least 1 in 2 that the other twin's brain will also have them (van Haren et al., 2012). Some studies have even found brain abnormalities in people who *later* developed this disorder (Karlsgodt et al., 2010). The greater the shrinkage, the more severe the thought disorder (Collinson et al., 2003; Nelson et al., 1998; Shenton, 1992).

The bottom line: Schizophrenia involves not one isolated brain abnormality but problems with several brain regions and their interconnections (Andreasen, 1997, 2001).

Prenatal Environment and Risk

LOQ 13-20 What prenatal events are associated with increased risk of developing schizophrenia?

What causes brain abnormalities in people with schizophrenia? Some researchers blame mishaps during prenatal development or delivery (Fatemi & Folsom, 2009; Walker et al., 2010). Risk factors include low birth weight, mother's diabetes, father's older age, or lack of oxygen during delivery (King et al., 2010). Famine may also increase risks. People conceived during the peak of World War II's Dutch famine developed schizophrenia at twice the normal rate. Those conceived during the famine of 1959 to 1961 in eastern China also displayed this doubled rate (St. Clair et al., 2005; Susser et al., 1996).

Let's consider another possible culprit. Might a midpregnancy viral infection impair fetal brain development (Brown & Patterson, 2011)? To test this fetal-virus idea, scientists have asked these questions:

- *Are people at increased risk of schizophrenia if, during the middle of their fetal development, their country experienced a flu epidemic?* The repeated answer is *Yes* (Mednick et al., 1994; Murray et al., 1992; Wright et al., 1995).

- *Are people who are born in densely populated areas, where viral diseases spread more readily, at greater risk for schizophrenia?* The answer, confirmed in a study of 1.75 million Danes, is *Yes* (Jablensky, 1999; Mortensen, 1999).

- *Are people born during the winter and spring months—after the fall-winter flu season—also at increased risk?* The answer is again *Yes*, and the risk increases from 5 to 8 percent (Fox, 2010; Schwartz, 2011; Torrey et al., 1997; Torrey & Miller, 2002).

- *In the Southern Hemisphere, where the seasons are the reverse of the Northern Hemisphere, are the months of above-average pre-schizophrenia births similarly reversed?* Again, the answer is *Yes*. In Australia, people born between August and October are at greater risk. But people born in the Northern Hemisphere who *later* move to Australia still have a greater risk if they were born between January and March (McGrath et al., 1995; McGrath & Welham, 1999).

- *Are mothers who report being sick with influenza during pregnancy more likely to bear children who develop schizophrenia?* In one study of nearly 8000 women, the answer was *Yes*. The schizophrenia risk increased from the customary

delusion a false belief, often of persecution or grandeur, that may accompany psychotic disorders.

acute schizophrenia (also called *reactive schizophrenia*) a form of schizophrenia that can begin at any age, frequently occurs in response to an emotionally traumatic event, and has extended recovery periods.

chronic schizophrenia (also called *process schizophrenia*) a form of schizophrenia in which symptoms usually appear by late adolescence or early adulthood. As people age, psychotic episodes last longer and recovery periods shorten.

1 percent to about 2 percent. But that increase applied only to mothers who were infected during their second trimester (Brown et al., 2000).

- *Does blood drawn from pregnant women whose offspring develop schizophrenia suggest a viral infection?* In several studies—including one that collected blood samples from some 20,000 pregnant women—the answer has again been *Yes* (Brown et al., 2004; Buka et al., 2001; Canetta et al., 2014).

These converging lines of evidence suggest that fetal-virus infections contribute to the development of schizophrenia. This finding strengthens the U.S. government recommendation that "pregnant women need a flu shot" (CDC, 2014b).

Genetics and Risk

LOQ 13-21 How do genes influence schizophrenia?

Fetal-virus infections may increase the odds that a child will develop schizophrenia. But many women get the flu during their second trimester of pregnancy, and only 2 percent of their children develop schizophrenia. Why does prenatal exposure to the flu virus put some children at risk but not others? Might some people be more vulnerable because they have an inherited predisposition to this disorder? Evidence indicates the answer is *Yes*. For most people, the odds of being diagnosed with schizophrenia are nearly 1 in 100. For those who have a sibling or parent with schizophrenia, the odds increase to about 1 in 10. And if the affected sibling is an identical twin, the odds are close to 1 in 2 (**FIGURE 13.13**). Those odds are unchanged even when the twins are raised apart (Plomin et al., 1997). (Only about a dozen such cases are on record.)

LaunchPad See LaunchPad's *Video: Twin Studies* for a helpful tutorial animation about this type of research design.

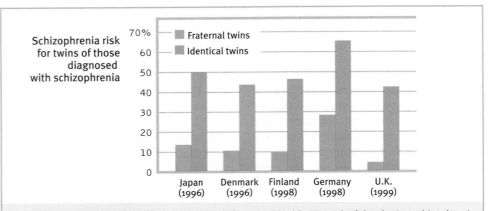

Schizophrenia risk for twins of those diagnosed with schizophrenia

FIGURE 13.13 Risk of developing schizophrenia The lifetime risk of developing schizophrenia varies for family members of a person with this disorder. Across countries, barely more than 1 in 10 fraternal twins, but some 5 in 10 identical twins, share a schizophrenia diagnosis. (Data from Gottesman, 2001.)

But wait! Identical twins also share a prenatal environment. So, is it possible that shared germs as well as shared genes produce identical twin similarities? There is some evidence that supports this idea.

About two-thirds of identical twins also share a placenta and the blood it supplies. Other identical twins have two separate placentas. Sharing a placenta raises the odds of later sharing a schizophrenia diagnosis. If identical twins had separate placentas, the chances are 1 in 10. If they shared a placenta, the co-twin's chances of having the disorder are 6 in 10 (Davis et al., 1995; Davis & Phelps, 1995). A likely explanation: Identical twins who share a placenta are more likely to share the same prenatal viruses (**FIGURE 13.14**).

How, then, can we untangle the genetic influences from the environmental influences on this disorder? Adoption studies offer some clues. Children adopted by someone who develops schizophrenia do not "catch" the disorder. Rather, adopted children have a higher risk if one of their *biological* parents has schizophrenia (Gottesman, 1991). Genes matter.

The search is on for specific genes that, in some combination, might lead to schizophrenia-inducing brain abnormalities. (It is not our genes but our brains that directly control our

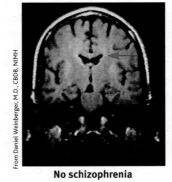
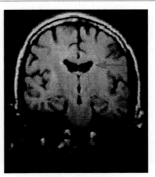

No schizophrenia   **Schizophrenia**

FIGURE 13.14 Schizophrenia in identical twins When twins differ, only the one afflicted with schizophrenia typically has enlarged, fluid-filled cranial cavities (right) (Suddath et al., 1990). The difference between the twins implies some nongenetic factor, such as a virus, is also at work.

behavior.) In the biggest-ever study of the genetics of psychiatric disorder, scientists from 35 countries pooled data from the genomes of 37,000 people with schizophrenia and 113,000 people without (Schizophrenia Working Group, 2014). They found 103 genome locations linked with this disorder. Some genes influence the activity of dopamine and other brain neurotransmitters. Others affect the production of *myelin,* a fatty substance that coats the axons of nerve cells and lets impulses travel at high speed through neural networks.

Although genes matter, the genetic formula is not as straightforward as the inheritance of eye color. Schizophrenia is a group of disorders, influenced by many genes, each with very small effects (Arnedo et al., 2015; International Schizophrenia Consortium, 2009).

As we have seen again and again, nature and nurture interact. Recall again that *epigenetic* (literally "in addition to genetic") factors influence whether genes will be expressed. Like hot water activating a tea bag, environmental factors such as viral infections, nutritional deprivation, and maternal stress can "turn on" the genes that put some of us at higher risk for this disorder. Identical twins' differing histories in the womb and beyond explain why only one may develop a disorder (Dempster et al., 2013; Walker et al., 2010). Our heredity and our life experiences work together. Neither hand claps alone.

LaunchPad Consider how researchers have studied these issues with LaunchPad's *IMMERSIVE LEARNING: How Would You Know If Schizophrenia Is Inherited?*

* * *

Most of us can relate more easily to the ups and downs of anxiety, phobias, and depression than to the strange thoughts, perceptions, and behaviors of schizophrenia. Sometimes our thoughts do jump around, but we rarely talk nonsensically. Occasionally, we feel unjustly suspicious of someone, but we do not believe the world is plotting against us.

Often our perceptions err, but rarely do we see or hear things that are not there. We feel regret after laughing at someone's misfortune, but we rarely giggle in response to our own bad news. At times we just want to be alone, but we do not live in social isolation. However, millions of people around the world do talk strangely, suffer delusions, hear nonexistent voices, see things that are not there, laugh or cry at inappropriate times, or withdraw into private imaginary worlds. The quest to solve the cruel puzzle of schizophrenia therefore continues, more vigorously than ever.

Retrieve + Remember

- A person with schizophrenia who has _____ (positive/negative) symptoms may have an expressionless face and toneless voice.

ANSWER: negative

- What factors contribute to the onset and development of schizophrenia?

ANSWER: Biological factors include abnormalities in brain structure and function and genetic differences. Environmental factors such as nutritional deprivation, exposure to virus, and maternal stress contribute by activating the genes that increase risk.

LaunchPad For an 8-minute description of how clinicians define and treat schizophrenia, visit LaunchPad's *Video— Schizophrenia: New Definitions, New Therapies.*

Other Disorders

Eating Disorders

LOQ 13-22 What are the three main eating disorders, and how do biological, psychological, and social-cultural influences make people more vulnerable to them?

Our bodies are naturally disposed to maintain a steady weight, storing energy reserves in case food becomes unavailable. But psychological influences can overwhelm biological wisdom.

Nowhere is this more painfully clear than in eating disorders.

- In **anorexia nervosa,** people—usually female adolescents, but some women, men, and boys as well— starve themselves. Anorexia often begins as an attempt to lose weight, but the dieting doesn't end. Even when far below normal weight, the self-starved person feels fat, fears being fat, and focuses obsessively on losing weight, sometimes exercising excessively. At some point in their lifetime, 0.6 percent of Americans meet the criteria for anorexia nervosa (Hudson et al., 2007).

SIBLING RIVALRY TO THE EXTREME Twins Maria and Katy Campbell have anorexia nervosa. As children they competed to see who could be thinner. Now, says Maria, her anorexia nervosa is "like a ball and chain around my ankle that I can't throw off" (Foster, 2011).

anorexia nervosa an eating disorder in which a person (usually an adolescent female) maintains a starvation diet despite being significantly underweight; sometimes accompanied by excessive exercise.

- In **bulimia nervosa,** food binges alternate with purges (vomiting and laxative use), sometimes followed by fasting and excessive exercise. Unlike anorexia, bulimia is marked by weight shifts within or above normal ranges, making this disorder easier to hide. Binge-purge eaters are preoccupied with food (especially sweet and high-fat foods) and obsessed with their weight and appearance. They experience bouts of guilt, depression, and anxiety, especially during and following binges (Hinz & Williamson, 1987; Johnson et al., 2002). About 1 percent of Americans, mostly women in their late teens or early twenties (but also some men), have had bulimia.

- Those with **binge-eating disorder** engage in significant bouts of overeating, followed by remorse. But they do not purge, fast, or exercise excessively, and so may be overweight. At some point during their lifetime, 2.8 percent of Americans have had binge-eating disorder (Hudson et al., 2007).

Understanding Eating Disorders

So, how can we explain eating disorders? Heredity matters. Identical twins share these disorders somewhat more often than fraternal twins do (Culbert et al., 2009; Klump et al., 2009; Root et al., 2010). Scientists are searching for culprit genes. Data from 15 studies indicate that having a gene that reduces available serotonin adds 30 percent to a person's risk of anorexia or bulimia (Calati et al., 2011).

But environment also matters. People with anorexia come from families that tend to be competitive, high-achieving, and protective (Berg et al., 2014; Pate et al., 1992; Yates, 1989, 1990). And people with eating disorders often have low self-esteem, set impossible standards, fret about falling short of expectations, and worry about how others perceive them (Brauhardt et al., 2014; Pieters et al., 2007; Yiend et al., 2014).

Our environment includes our culture and our history. Ideal shapes vary across culture and time. In areas with high rates of poverty—where plump means prosperous and thin can signal poverty or illness—bigger is better (Knickmeyer, 2001; Swami et al., 2010).

Bigger does not seem better in Western cultures, where the rise in eating disorders over the last 50 years has coincided with a dramatic increase in women having a poor body image (Feingold & Mazzella, 1998). Those most vulnerable to eating disorders are also those (usually women or gay men) who most idealize thinness and have the greatest body dissatisfaction (Feldman & Meyer, 2010; Kane, 2010; Stice et al., 2010). Part of the pressure stems from images of unnaturally thin models and celebrities (Tovee et al., 1997). One former model recalled walking into a meeting with her agent, starving and with her organs failing as a result of anorexia (Caroll, 2013). Her agent's greeting: "Whatever you are doing, keep doing it."

Should it surprise us, then, that women who view such images often feel ashamed, depressed, and dissatisfied with their own bodies (Myers & Crowther, 2009; Tiggeman & Miller, 2010)? In one study, researchers tested media influences by giving some adolescent girls (but not others) a 15-month subscription to a teen fashion magazine (Stice et al., 2001). Vulnerable magazine readers (girls who felt dissatisfied, idealized thinness, and lacked social support) showed increased body dissatisfaction and eating disorder tendencies.

"Thanks, but we don't eat."

Some critics point out that there's much more to body dissatisfaction and anorexia than media effects (Ferguson et al., 2011). Peer influences, such as teasing, also matter. Nevertheless, the sickness of today's eating disorders stems in part from today's weight-obsessed culture—a culture that says "Fat is bad" in countless ways.

If cultural learning contributes to eating behavior, could prevention programs increase acceptance of one's body? Prevention studies answer Yes. They seem especially effective if the programs are interactive and focused on girls over age 15 (Beintner et al., 2012; Melioli et al., 2016; Vocks et al., 2010).

Dissociative Disorders

LOQ 13-23 What are dissociative disorders, and why are they controversial?

Among the most bewildering disorders are the rare **dissociative disorders.** The person's conscious awareness is said to become separated—*dissociated*—from painful memories, thoughts, and feelings. In this state, people may suddenly lose their memory or change their identity, often in response to an overwhelmingly stressful situation.

Dissociation itself is not so rare. Any one of us may have a fleeting sense of being unreal, of being separated from our body, of watching ourselves as if in a movie. But a massive dissociation of self from ordinary consciousness occurs in **dissociative identity disorder** (DID—formerly called *multiple personality disorder*).

At different times, two or more distinct identities seem to control the person's behavior, each with its own voice and mannerisms. Thus, the person may be prim and proper one moment, loud and flirtatious the next. Typically, the original personality denies any awareness of the other(s).

Skeptics question the genuineness of DID. First, they find it suspicious that *DID has such a short history.* Between 1930 and 1960, the number of North American DID diagnoses was 2 per decade. By the 1980s, when the DSM contained the first formal code for this disorder, the number had exploded to more than 20,000 (McHugh, 1995b). The average number of displayed personalities also mushroomed—from 3 to 12 per patient (Goff & Simms, 1993).

Second, note skeptics, *DID rates vary by culture.* It is much less common outside North America, although in other cultures some people are said to be "possessed" by an alien spirit (Aldridge-Morris, 1989; Kluft, 1991). In Britain, DID—which some consider "a wacky American fad" (Cohen, 1995)—is rare. In India and Japan, it is essentially nonexistent (or at least unreported). Such findings, say skeptics, point to a cultural explanation. They propose that this is a disorder exhibited by suggestible, fantasy-prone people, and that it is created by therapists in a particular social context (Giesbrecht et al., 2008, 2010; Lynn et al., 2014; Merskey, 1992).

Third, some skeptics have asked, could DID be *an extension of our normal capacity for personality shifts?* Perhaps dissociative identities are simply a more extreme version of the varied "selves" we normally present, as when we display a goofy, loud self while hanging out with friends, and a subdued, respectful self around grandparents. If so, say the critics, clinicians who discover multiple personalities may merely have triggered role playing by fantasy-prone people. After all, clients do not enter therapy saying, "Allow me to introduce myselves." Rather, charge the critics, some therapists go fishing for

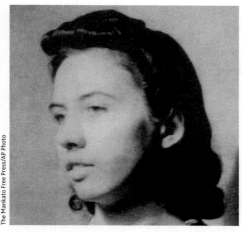

WIDESPREAD DISSOCIATION Shirley Mason was a psychiatric patient diagnosed with dissociative identity disorder (DID). Her life formed the basis of the bestselling book, *Sybil* (Schreiber, 1973), and of two movies. Some argue that the book and movies' popularity fueled the dramatic rise in diagnoses of DID. Skeptics wonder whether Mason actually had DID (Nathan, 2011).

multiple personalities: *"Have you ever felt like another part of you does things you can't control? Does this part of you have a name? Can I talk to the angry part of you?"* Once clients permit a therapist to talk, by name, "to the part of you that says those angry things," they begin acting out the fantasy. Like actors who lose themselves in their roles, vulnerable people may "become" the parts they are acting out. The result may be the experience of another self.

Other researchers and clinicians believe DID is a real disorder. They cite findings of distinct brain and body states associated with differing personalities

"Would it be possible to speak with the personality that pays the bills?"

(Putnam, 1991). People with DID exhibit increased activity in brain areas linked with the control and inhibition of traumatic memories (Elzinga et al., 2007). Brain scans show shrinkage in other areas that aid memory and threat detection (Vermetten et al., 2006).

Understanding Dissociative Identity Disorder

If DID is a real disorder, how can we best understand it? Both the psychodynamic and the learning perspectives have interpreted DID symptoms as ways of coping with anxiety. Some psychodynamic theorists see them as defenses against the anxiety caused by unacceptable impulses. In this view, a second personality could allow the discharge of forbidden impulses. Learning theorists see dissociative disorders as behaviors reinforced by anxiety reduction.

Some clinicians include dissociative disorders under the umbrella of post-traumatic stress disorder. In this view, DID is a natural, protective response to traumatic experiences during childhood (Dalenberg et al., 2012). Many people with DID recall suffering physical, sexual, or emotional abuse as children (Gleaves, 1996; Lilienfeld et al., 1999). In one study of 12 murderers diagnosed with DID, 11 had suffered severe abuse, even torture,

bulimia nervosa an eating disorder in which a person alternates binge eating (usually of high-calorie foods) with purging (by vomiting or laxative use) or fasting.

binge-eating disorder significant binge-eating episodes, followed by distress, disgust, or guilt, but without the purging or fasting that marks bulimia nervosa.

dissociative disorders controversial, rare disorders in which conscious awareness becomes separated (dissociated) from previous memories, thoughts, and feelings.

dissociative identity disorder (DID) a rare dissociative disorder in which a person exhibits two or more distinct and alternating personalities. (Formerly called *multiple personality disorder.*)

in childhood (Lewis et al., 1997). One had been set afire by his parents. Another had been used in child pornography and was scarred from being made to sit on a stove burner. Some critics wonder, however, whether vivid imagination or therapist suggestion contributes to such recollections (Kihlstrom, 2005).

So the debate continues. On one side are those who believe multiple personalities are the desperate efforts of people trying to detach from a horrific existence. On the other are the skeptics who think DID is constructed out of the therapist-client interaction and acted out by fantasy-prone, emotionally vulnerable people.

Retrieve + Remember

- The psychodynamic and learning perspectives agree that dissociative identity disorder symptoms are ways of dealing with anxiety. How do their explanations differ?

ANSWER: The psychodynamic explanation of DID symptoms is that they are defenses against anxiety generated by unacceptable urges. The learning perspective attempts to explain these symptoms as behaviors that have been reinforced by relieving anxiety.

Personality Disorders

LOQ 13-24 What characteristics are typical of personality disorders in general, and what biological and psychological factors are associated with antisocial personality disorder?

There is little debate about the reality of **personality disorders**. These inflexible and enduring behavior patterns interfere with a person's ability to function socially. Some people with these disorders are anxious and withdrawn, and they avoid social contact. Some behave in eccentric or odd ways, or interact without engaging emotionally. Others seem overly dramatic or impulsive, focusing attention on themselves.

The most troubling and heavily researched personality disorder is **antisocial personality disorder.** People with this disorder are typically males whose lack of conscience becomes plain before age 15, as they begin to lie, steal, fight, or display unrestrained sexual behavior (Cale & Lilienfeld, 2002). They behave impulsively and then feel and fear little (Fowles & Dindo, 2009). Not all children with these traits become antisocial adults. Those who do (about half of them) will generally act in violent or otherwise criminal ways, be unable to keep a job, and, if they have a spouse or children, behave irresponsibly toward them (Farrington, 1991). People with antisocial personality (sometimes called *sociopaths* or *psychopaths*) may show lower emotional intelligence—the ability to understand, manage, and perceive emotions (Ermer et al., 2012).

Antisocial does not necessarily mean criminal (Skeem & Cooke, 2010). When lack of conscience combines with keen intelligence, the result may

NO REMORSE Dennis Rader, known as the "BTK killer" in Kansas, was convicted in 2005 of killing 10 people over a 30-year span. Rader exhibited the extreme lack of conscience that marks antisocial personality disorder.

EPA/Jeff Tuttle/Landov

be a charming and clever con artist—or a fearless and ruthless soldier, CEO, or politician (Dutton, 2012).

But do all criminals have antisocial personality disorder? Definitely not. Most criminals show responsible concern for their friends and family members.

Understanding Antisocial Personality Disorder

Antisocial personality disorder is woven of both biological and psychological strands. No single gene codes for a complex behavior such as crime. There is, however, a genetic tendency toward a fearless and uninhibited life. Twin and adoption studies reveal that biological relatives of people with antisocial and unemotional tendencies are at increased risk for antisocial behavior (Frisell et al., 2012; Tuvblad et al., 2011).

Genetic influences and negative environmental factors (such as childhood abuse, family instability, or poverty) can work together to help wire the brain (Dodge, 2009). The genetic vulnerability of those with antisocial and unemotional tendencies appears as low arousal. Awaiting events that most people would find unnerving, such as electric shocks or loud noises, they show little bodily arousal (Hare, 1975; van Goozen et al., 2007). Long-term studies show that their stress hormone levels were lower than average as teenagers, before committing any crime (**FIGURE 13.15**). And those who were slow to develop conditioned fears at age 3 were also more likely to commit a crime later in life (Gao et al., 2010).

Other brain activity differences appear in studies of antisocial criminals. Shown photographs that would produce an emotional response in most people (such as a man holding a knife to a woman's throat), antisocial criminals' heart rate and perspiration responses are lower than normal, and brain areas that typically respond to emotional stimuli are less active (Harenski et al., 2010; Kiehl & Buckholtz, 2010). Other studies have found that people

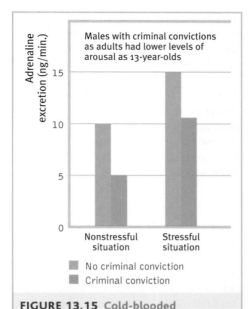

FIGURE 13.15 Cold-blooded arousability and risk of crime Levels of the stress hormone adrenaline were measured in two groups of 13-year-old Swedish boys. In both stressful and nonstressful situations, those who would later be convicted of a crime as 18- to 26-year-olds showed relatively low arousal. (Data from Magnusson, 1990.)

with antisocial criminal tendencies have a smaller-than-normal amygdala, an emotion-controlling part of the brain (Pardini et al., 2014). They also display a hyper-reactive dopamine reward system that predisposes their impulsive drive to do something rewarding, despite the consequences (Buckholtz et al., 2010).

One study compared PET scans of 41 murderers' brains with those from people of similar age and sex. The murderers' frontal lobe, an area that helps control impulses, displayed reduced activity (Raine, 1999, 2005). This reduction was especially apparent in those who murdered impulsively. In a follow-up study, researchers found that violent repeat offenders had 11 percent less frontal lobe tissue than normal (Raine et al., 2000). This helps explain another finding: People with antisocial personality disorder fall far below normal in aspects of thinking such as planning,

organization, and inhibition, which are all frontal lobe functions (Morgan & Lilienfeld, 2000). Such data remind us: Everything psychological is also biological.

Retrieve + Remember

- How do biological and psychological factors contribute to antisocial personality disorder?

ANSWER: Twin and adoption studies show that biological relatives of people with this disorder are at increased risk for antisocial behavior. Researchers have also observed differences in the brain activity and structure of antisocial criminals. Negative environmental factors, such as poverty or childhood abuse, may channel genetic traits such as fearlessness in more dangerous directions—toward aggression and away from social responsibility.

Does "Disorder" Equal "Danger"?

LOQ 13-25 Are people with psychological disorders likely to commit violent acts?

Movies and television sometimes portray people with psychological disorders as homicidal. Mass killings in 2012 by apparently disturbed people in a Colorado theater and a Connecticut elementary school reinforced public perceptions that people with psychological disorders are dangerous (Barry et al., 2013; Jorm et al., 2012). "People with mental illness are getting guns and committing these mass shootings," said Speaker of the U.S. House Paul Ryan (Editorial Board, *New York Times*, 2015). In one survey, 84 percent of Americans agreed that "increased government spending on mental health screening and treatment" would be a "somewhat" or "very" effective "approach to preventing mass shootings at schools" (Newport, 2012).

Do disorders actually increase risk of violence? And can clinicians predict who is likely to do harm? In real life, the vast

personality disorder an inflexible and enduring behavior pattern that impairs social functioning.

antisocial personality disorder a personality disorder in which a person (usually a man) exhibits a lack of conscience for wrongdoing, even toward friends and family members; may be aggressive and ruthless or a clever con artist.

majority of violent crimes are committed by those with no diagnosed disorder (Fazel & Grann, 2006; Skeem et al., 2016). Moreover, mental disorders seldom lead to violence, and clinical prediction of violence is unreliable. Said simply, most violent criminals are not mentally ill, and most mentally ill people are not violent.

The few people with disorders who do commit violent acts tend to be either those who experience threatening delusions and hallucinated voices that command them to act, or those who abuse substances (Douglas et al., 2009; Elbogen & Johnson, 2009; Fazel et al., 2009, 2010). People with disorders also are more likely to be *victims* than perpetrators of violence (Marley & Bulia, 2001). Indeed, reported the U.S. Surgeon General's Office (1999, p. 7), "There is very little risk of violence or harm to a stranger from casual contact

HOW TO PREVENT MASS SHOOTINGS? Following the Newtown, Connecticut, slaughter of 20 young children and 6 adults, people wondered: Could those at risk for violence be identified in advance by mental health workers and reported to police? Would laws that require such reporting discourage disturbed gun owners from seeking mental health treatment?

with an individual who has a mental disorder." People with mental illness commit proportionately little gun violence. Thus, focusing gun restrictions only on mentally ill people is unlikely to significantly reduce gun violence (Friedman, 2012).

Better predictors of violence are use of alcohol or drugs, previous violence, and gun availability. The mass-killing shooters have one more thing in common: They tend to be young males. "We could avoid two-thirds of all crime simply by putting all able-bodied young men in a cryogenic sleep from the age of 12 through 28," said one psychologist (Lykken, 1995).

The findings described in this chapter make clear the need for research and treatment to help the growing number of people, especially teenagers and young adults, who suffer the pain of a psychological disorder. Although mindful of their pain, we can also be encouraged by the many successful people who have pursued brilliant careers while enduring psychological difficulties. Eighteen of them were U.S. presidents, according to one psychiatric analysis of their biographies (Davidson et al., 2006). The bewilderment, fear, and sorrow caused by psychological disorders are real. But, as Chapter 14 shows, hope, too, is real.

CHAPTER REVIEW

Psychological Disorders

Test yourself by taking a moment to answer each of these Learning Objective Questions (repeated here from within the chapter). Then turn to Appendix D, Complete Chapter Reviews, to check your answers. Research suggests that trying to answer these questions on your own will improve your long-term memory of the concepts (McDaniel et al., 2009).

What Is a Psychological Disorder?

13-1: How should we draw the line between normal behavior and psychological disorder?

13-2: Why is there controversy over attention-deficit/hyperactivity disorder?

13-3: How do the medical model and the biopsychosocial approach influence our understanding of psychological disorders?

13-4: How and why do clinicians classify psychological disorders, and why do some psychologists criticize the use of diagnostic labels?

Anxiety Disorders, OCD, and PTSD

13-5: How do generalized anxiety disorder, panic disorder, and phobias differ? How do anxiety disorders differ from the ordinary worries and fears we all experience?

13-6: What is OCD?

13-7: What is PTSD?

13-8: How do conditioning, cognition, and biology contribute to the feelings and thoughts that mark anxiety disorders, OCD, and PTSD?

Substance Use Disorders and Addictive Behaviors

13-9: What are substance use disorders, and what roles do tolerance, withdrawal, and addiction play in these disorders?

13-10: What are depressants, and what are their effects?

13-11: What are stimulants, and what are their effects?

13-12: What are hallucinogens, and what are their effects?

13-13: What biological, psychological, and social-cultural factors help explain why some people abuse mind-altering drugs?

Major Depressive Disorder and Bipolar Disorder

13-14: How do major depressive disorder and bipolar disorder differ?

13-15: How can the biological and social-cognitive perspectives help us understand major depressive disorder and bipolar disorder?

13-16: What factors increase the risk of suicide, and why do some people injure themselves?

Schizophrenia

13-17: What patterns of perceiving, thinking, and feeling characterize schizophrenia?

13-18: How do *acute schizophrenia* and *chronic schizophrenia* differ?

13-19: What brain abnormalities are associated with schizophrenia?

13-20: What prenatal events are associated with increased risk of developing schizophrenia?

13-21: How do genes influence schizophrenia?

Other Disorders

13-22: What are the three main eating disorders, and how do biological, psychological, and social-cultural influences make people more vulnerable to them?

13-23: What are dissociative disorders, and why are they controversial?

13-24: What characteristics are typical of personality disorders in general, and what biological and psychological factors are associated with antisocial personality disorder?

Does "Disorder" Equal "Danger"?

13-25: Are people with psychological disorders likely to commit violent acts?

TERMS AND CONCEPTS TO REMEMBER

Test yourself on these terms by trying to write down the definition in your own words before flipping back to the referenced page to check your answer.

psychological disorder, p. 376

attention-deficit/hyperactivity disorder (ADHD), p. 376

medical model, p. 379

epigenetics, p. 379

DSM-5, p. 379

anxiety disorders, p. 381

generalized anxiety disorder, p. 381

panic disorder, p. 381

phobia, p. 383

obsessive-compulsive disorder (OCD), p. 383

posttraumatic stress disorder (PTSD), p. 383

psychoactive drug, p. 385

substance use disorder, p. 385

tolerance, p. 387

withdrawal, p. 387

depressants, p. 387

alcohol use disorder, p. 387

barbiturates, p. 389

opiates, p. 389

stimulants, p. 389

nicotine, p. 389

cocaine, p. 389

amphetamines, p. 391

methamphetamine, p. 391

Ecstasy (MDMA), p. 391

hallucinogens, p. 391

near-death experience, p. 391

LSD, p. 391

THC, p. 391

major depressive disorder, p. 395

bipolar disorder, p. 395

mania, p. 395

schizophrenia, p. 401

psychotic disorders, p. 401

delusions, p. 403

acute schizophrenia, p. 403

chronic schizophrenia, p. 403

anorexia nervosa, p. 405

bulimia nervosa, p. 407

binge-eating disorder, p. 407

dissociative disorder, p. 407

dissociative identity disorder (DID), p. 407

personality disorder, p. 409

antisocial personality disorder, p. 409

CHAPTER TEST

Test yourself repeatedly throughout your studies. This will not only help you figure out what you know and don't know; the testing itself will help you learn and remember the information more effectively thanks to the testing effect.

1. Anna is embarrassed that it takes her several minutes to parallel-park her car. She usually gets out of the car once or twice to inspect her distance both from the curb and from the nearby cars. Should she worry about having a psychological disorder?

2. Two major disorders that are found worldwide are schizophrenia and _____.

3. A therapist says that psychological disorders are sicknesses and people with these disorders should be treated as patients in a hospital. This therapist believes in the _____ model.

4. Many psychologists reject the disorders-as-illness view and instead maintain that other factors may also be involved—for example, the person's bad habits and poor social skills. This view represents the _____ approach.

   a. medical

   b. epigenetics

   c. biopsychosocial

   d. diagnostic labels

5. Most psychologists and psychiatrists use _____ to classify psychological disorders.

   a. DSM descriptions and codes

   b. in-depth client histories

   c. input from clients' family and friends

   d. the theories of Pinel, Rosenhan, and others

6. A feeling of intense dread that can be accompanied by chest pains, choking sensations, or other frightening sensations is called

   a. an obsession.

   b. a compulsion.

   c. a panic attack.

   d. a specific phobia.

7. Anxiety that takes the form of an irrational fear and avoidance of a specific object, activity, or situation is called a _____.

8. Marina became consumed with the need to clean the entire house and refused to participate in any other activities. Her family consulted a therapist, who diagnosed her as having _____ - _____ disorder.

9. The learning perspective proposes that phobias are
   a. the result of individual genetic makeup.
   b. a way of repressing unacceptable impulses.
   c. conditioned fears.
   d. a symptom of having been abused as a child.

10. After continued use of a psychoactive drug, the drug user needs to take larger doses to get the desired effect. This is referred to as _____.

11. The depressants include alcohol, barbiturates,
    a. and opiates.
    b. cocaine, and morphine.
    c. caffeine, nicotine, and marijuana.
    d. and amphetamines.

12. Why might alcohol make a person more helpful *or* more aggressive?

13. Long-term use of Ecstasy can
    a. depress sympathetic nervous system activity.
    b. deplete the brain's supply of epinephrine.
    c. deplete the brain's supply of dopamine.
    d. damage serotonin-producing neurons.

14. Near-death experiences are strikingly similar to the experiences evoked by _____.

15. Use of marijuana
    a. impairs motor coordination, perception, reaction time, and memory.
    b. inhibits people's emotions.
    c. leads to dehydration and overheating.
    d. stimulates brain cell development.

16. An important psychological contributor to drug use is
    a. inflated self-esteem.
    b. the feeling that life is meaningless and directionless.
    c. a genetic predisposition.
    d. overprotective parents.

17. The "gender gap" in depression refers to the finding that _____ (men's/women's) risk of depression is nearly double that of _____ (men's/women's).

18. Rates of bipolar disorder have risen dramatically in the twenty-first century, especially among
    a. middle-aged women.
    b. middle-aged men.
    c. people 20 and over.
    d. people 19 and under.

19. Treatment for depression often includes drugs that increase supplies of the neurotransmitters _____ and _____.

20. Psychologists who emphasize the importance of negative perceptions, beliefs, and thoughts in depression are working within the _____-_____ perspective.

21. A person with positive symptoms of schizophrenia is most likely to experience
    a. tremors.
    b. delusions.
    c. withdrawal.
    d. flat emotion.

22. People with schizophrenia may hear voices urging self-destruction, an example of a(n) _____.

23. Victor exclaimed, "The weather has been so schizophrenic lately: It's hot one day and freezing the next!" Is this an accurate comparison? Why or why not?

24. Chances for recovery from schizophrenia are best when
    a. onset is sudden, in response to stress.
    b. deterioration occurs gradually, during childhood.
    c. no environmental causes can be identified.
    d. there is a detectable brain abnormality.

25. Which of the following statements is true of bulimia nervosa?
    a. People with bulimia continue to want to lose weight even when they are underweight.
    b. Bulimia is marked by weight fluctuations within or above normal ranges.
    c. Bulimia patients often come from families that are competitive, high-achieving, and protective.
    d. If one twin is diagnosed with bulimia, the chances of the other twin's sharing the disorder are greater if they are fraternal rather than identical twins.

26. Dissociative identity disorder is controversial because
    a. dissociation is quite rare.
    b. it was reported frequently in the 1920s but rarely today.
    c. it is almost never reported outside North America.
    d. its symptoms are nearly identical to those of obsessive-compulsive disorder.

27. A personality disorder, such as antisocial personality, is characterized by
    a. depression.
    b. hallucinations.
    c. enduring and inflexible behavior patterns that impair social functioning.
    d. an elevated level of autonomic nervous system arousal.

28. PET scans of murderers' brains have revealed
    a. higher-than-normal activation in the frontal lobes.
    b. lower-than-normal activation in the frontal lobes.
    c. more frontal lobe tissue than normal.
    d. no differences in brain structures or activity.

Find answers to these questions in Appendix E, in the back of the book.

IN YOUR EVERYDAY LIFE

Answering these questions will help you make these concepts more personally meaningful, and therefore more memorable.

1. Can you recall a fear that you have learned? What role, if any, was played by fear conditioning or by observational learning?

2. Psychoactive drugs such as alcohol, heroin, and methamphetamine all bring pleasure followed by discomfort or depression when the substance wears off. Knowing this, what strategies do you think might keep young teens from abusing substances?

3. Has student life ever made you feel anxious or depressed? What advice would you have for new students?

4. Can you think of a time when feeling depressed actually helped you in some way? Did you re-evaluate your situation or make new plans for the future?

5. Now that you know more about schizophrenia, do you think the media accurately portray the behavior of people with this disorder? Why or why not?

6. As his fans already know, comedian and TV personality Howie Mandel suffers from obsessive-compulsive disorder and a severe germ phobia. How do you think being labeled has helped or hurt Mandel?

7. Dissociative identity disorder is rare, but feeling like a "different person" at times is common. Can you recall ever feeling like a "different person" because of the situation you were in? What was that like?

Use ✖ LearningCurve to create your personalized study plan, which will direct you to the resources that will help you most in ✖ LaunchPad.

SURVEY THE CHAPTER

Therapy

Kay Redfield Jamison is both an award-winning clinical psychologist and a world expert on the emotional extremes of bipolar disorder. She knows her subject firsthand:

> For as long as I can remember, I was frighteningly, although wonderfully, beholden to moods . . . as a child, as a young girl . . . as an adolescent. . . . Caught up in the cycles of manic-depressive illness [bipolar disorder] by the time I began my professional life, I became, both by necessity and intellectual [choice], a student of moods (1995, pp. 4–5).

Jamison's life was blessed with times of intense sensitivity and passionate energy. But like her father's, it was at other times an emotional roller coaster. Reckless spending, racing conversation, and sleeplessness alternated with swings into "the blackest caves of the mind."

Then, "in the midst of utter confusion," she made a life-changing decision. Risking professional embarrassment, she made an appointment with a therapist, a psychiatrist she would visit weekly for years to come.

> He kept me alive a thousand times over. He saw me through madness, despair, wonderful and terrible love affairs, disillusionments and triumphs, recurrences of illness, an almost fatal suicide attempt, the death of a man I greatly loved, and the enormous pleasures and [frustrations] of my professional life. . . . He was very tough, as well as very kind. . . . Even though he understood more than anyone how much I felt I was losing . . . by taking medication, he never [lost] sight of the overall perspective of how costly, damaging, and life threatening my illness was. . . . Although I went to him to be treated for an illness, he taught me . . . the total beholdenness of brain to mind and mind to brain (pp. 87–89).

"Psychotherapy heals," Jamison concluded. "It makes some sense of the confusion, reins in the terrifying thoughts and feelings, returns some control and hope and possibility from it all."

This chapter explores some of the healing options available to therapists and the people who seek their help.

Treating Psychological Disorders

LOQ **L**earning**O**bjective**Q**uestion

14-1 How do psychotherapy and the biomedical therapies differ?

The long history of efforts to treat psychological disorders has included a strange mix of methods, harsh and gentle. Would-be healers have cut holes in people's heads and restrained, bled, or "beat the devil" out of them. But they also have given warm baths and massages and placed people in sunny and peaceful settings. They have given them drugs. And they have talked with them about childhood experiences, current feelings, and maladaptive thoughts and behaviors.

The transition to gentler methods began when reformers such as Philippe Pinel (1745–1826), Dorothea Dix (1802–1887), and others pushed for more humane treatments and for constructing mental hospitals. Since the 1950s, drug therapies and community-based treatment programs have replaced most of those hospitals.

DOROTHEA DIX "I . . . call your attention to the state of the Insane Persons confined within this Commonwealth, in cages."

THE HISTORY OF TREATMENT Visitors to eighteenth-century mental hospitals paid to gawk at patients, as though they were viewing zoo animals. William Hogarth's (1697–1764) painting captured one of these visits to London's St. Mary of Bethlehem hospital (commonly called Bedlam).

Modern Western therapies fall into two main categories.

- In **psychotherapy,** a trained therapist uses psychological techniques to assist someone seeking to overcome difficulties or achieve personal growth. The therapist may explore a client's early relationships, encourage the client to adopt new ways of thinking, or coach the client in replacing old behaviors with new ones.

- **Biomedical therapy** offers medications or other biological treatments. For example, a person with severe depression may receive antidepressants, electroconvulsive shock therapy (ECT), or deep brain stimulation.

The care provider's training and expertise, as well as the disorder itself, influence the choice of treatment. Psychotherapy and medication are often combined. Kay Redfield Jamison received psychotherapy in her meetings with her psychiatrist, and she took medications to control her wild mood swings.

Let's look first at the psychotherapy options for those treated with "talk therapies."

The Psychological Therapies

Among the dozens of psychotherapies, we will focus on the most influential. Each is built on one or more of psychology's major theories: psychodynamic, humanistic, behavioral, and cognitive. Most of these techniques can be used one-on-one or in groups. Psychotherapists often combine multiple methods. Indeed, many psychotherapists describe their approach as **eclectic,** using a blend of therapies.

Psychoanalysis and Psychodynamic Therapy

LOQ **14-2** What are the goals and techniques of psychoanalysis, and how have they been adapted in psychodynamic therapy?

The first major psychological therapy was Sigmund Freud's **psychoanalysis.** Although few clinicians today practice therapy as Freud did, his work deserves discussion. It helped form the foundation for treating psychological disorders, and it continues to influence modern therapists working from the *psychodynamic* perspective.

The Goals of Psychoanalysis

Freud believed that in therapy, people could achieve healthier, less anxious living by releasing the energy they had previously devoted to id-ego-superego conflicts (Chapter 12). Freud assumed that we do not fully know ourselves. He believed that there are threatening things we *repress*—things we do not want to know, so we disown or deny them.

Freud's therapy aimed to bring patients' repressed feelings into conscious awareness. By helping them reclaim their unconscious thoughts and feelings, the therapist *(analyst)* would also help them gain *insight* into the origins of their disorders. This insight could in turn inspire them to take responsibility for their own growth.

The Techniques of Psychoanalysis

Psychoanalytic theory emphasizes the power of childhood experiences to mold us. Thus, its main method is historical reconstruction. It aims to unearth the past in the hope of loosening its bonds on the present. After trying and discarding hypnosis as a possible excavating tool, Freud turned to *free association*.

Imagine yourself as a patient using free association. You begin by relaxing, perhaps by lying on a couch. The psychoanalyst, who sits out of your line of vision, asks you to say aloud whatever comes to mind. At one moment, you're relating a childhood memory. At another, you're describing a dream or recent experience.

It sounds easy, but soon you notice how often you edit your thoughts as you speak. You pause for a second before describing an embarrassing thought. You skip things that seem trivial, off point, or shameful. Sometimes your mind goes blank, unable to remember important details. You may joke or change the subject to something less threatening.

To an analyst, these mental blips are blocks that indicate **resistance.** They hint that anxiety lurks and you are defending against sensitive material. The analyst will note your resistance and then provide insight into its meaning. If offered at the right moment, this **interpretation**—of, say, your not wanting to talk about your mother or call, text, or message her—may reveal the underlying wishes, feelings, and conflicts you are avoiding. The analyst may also offer an explanation of how this resistance fits with other pieces of your psychological puzzle, including those based on an analysis of your dream content.

Multiply that one session by dozens and your relationship patterns will surface in your interactions with your analyst. You may find you have strong positive or negative feelings for your analyst. The analyst may suggest you are **transferring** feelings, such as dependency or mingled love and anger, that you experienced in earlier relationships with family members or other important people. By exposing such feelings, you may gain insight into your current relationships.

Relatively few U.S. therapists now offer traditional psychoanalysis. Much of its underlying theory is not supported by scientific research (Chapter 12). Analysts' interpretations do not follow the scientific method—they cannot be proven or disproven. And psychoanalysis takes considerable time and money, often years of several expensive sessions each week. Some of these problems have been addressed in the modern *psychodynamic perspective* that has evolved from psychoanalysis.

"I'm more interested in hearing about the eggs you're hiding from yourself."

Retrieve + Remember

- In psychoanalysis, when patients experience strong feelings for their analyst, this is called _____. Patients are said to demonstrate anxiety when they put up mental blocks around sensitive memories, showing _____. The analyst will attempt to provide insight into the underlying anxiety by offering a(n) _____ of the mental blocks.

ANSWERS: transference; resistance; interpretation

Psychodynamic Therapy

Although influenced by Freud's ideas, **psychodynamic therapists** don't talk much about id, ego, and superego. Instead, they try to help people understand their current symptoms by focusing on themes across important relationships, including childhood experiences and the therapist-client relationship. "We can have loving feelings and hateful feelings toward the same person," noted one psychodynamic therapist, and "we can desire something and also fear it" (Shedler, 2009). Client-therapist meetings take place once or twice a week (rather than several times weekly) and often for only a few weeks or months. Rather than lying on a couch, out of the therapist's line of vision, clients meet with their therapist face to face.

In these meetings, clients explore and gain perspective on defended-against thoughts and feelings. One therapist illustrated this with the case of a young man who previously had told women that he loved them, when he knew that he didn't (Shapiro, 1999, p. 8). But now with

psychotherapy treatment involving psychological techniques; consists of interactions between a trained therapist and someone seeking to overcome psychological difficulties or achieve personal growth.

biomedical therapy prescribed medications or procedures that act directly on the person's physiology.

eclectic approach an approach to psychotherapy that, depending on the client's problems, uses techniques from various forms of therapy.

psychoanalysis Sigmund Freud's therapeutic technique. Freud believed that the patient's free associations, resistances, dreams, and transferences—and the analyst's interpretations of them—released previously repressed feelings, allowing the patient to gain self-insight.

resistance in psychoanalysis, the blocking from consciousness of anxiety-laden material.

interpretation in psychoanalysis, the analyst's noting supposed dream meanings, resistances, and other significant behaviors and events in order to promote insight.

transference in psychoanalysis, the patient's transfer to the analyst of emotions linked with other relationships (such as love or hatred for a parent).

psychodynamic therapy therapeutic approach derived from the psychoanalytic tradition; views individuals as responding to unconscious forces and childhood experiences, and seeks to enhance self-insight.

FACE-TO-FACE THERAPY In this type of therapy session, the couch has disappeared. But the influence of psychoanalytic theory may not have, especially if the therapist seeks information about the patient's childhood and helps the patient reclaim unconscious feelings.

his wife, who wished he would say that he loved her, he found he *couldn't* do that—"I don't know why, but I can't."

Therapist: *Do you mean, then, that if you could, you would like to?*

Patient: *Well, I don't know. . . . Maybe I can't say it because I'm not sure it's true. Maybe I don't love her.*

Further interactions revealed that the client could not express real love because it would feel "mushy" and "soft" and therefore unmanly. The therapist noted that this young man was "in conflict with himself, and . . . cut off from the nature of that conflict." With such patients, who are estranged from themselves, therapists using psychodynamic techniques "are in a position to introduce them to themselves. We can restore their awareness of their own wishes and feelings, and their awareness, as well, of their reactions against those wishes and feelings" (Shapiro, 1999, p. 8).

Exploring past relationship troubles may help clients understand the origin of their current difficulties. Another therapist (Shedler, 2010a) recalled a client's complaints of difficulty getting along with his colleagues and wife, who saw him as overly critical. The client, "Jeffrey," then "began responding to me as if I were an unpredictable, angry adversary." Seizing the opportunity to help Jeffrey recognize the relationship pattern, the therapist helped him explore the pattern's roots in the attacks and humiliation he had experienced from his father. Jeffrey was then able to work through and let go of this defensive style of responding to people. Without embracing all aspects of Freud's theory, psychodynamic therapists aim to help people gain insight into their childhood experiences and unconscious dynamics.

Humanistic Therapies

LOQ 14-3 What are the basic themes of humanistic therapy, and what are the goals and techniques of Rogers' person-centered approach?

The *humanistic* perspective (Chapter 12) emphasizes people's innate potential for self-fulfillment. Not surprisingly, humanistic therapies attempt to reduce the inner conflicts that interfere with natural development and growth. To achieve this goal, humanistic therapists try to give clients new insights. Indeed, because they share this goal, humanistic and psychodynamic therapies are often referred to as **insight therapies**. But humanistic therapies differ from psychodynamic therapies in many other ways:

- *Humanistic therapists aim to boost people's self-fulfillment by helping them grow in self-awareness and self-acceptance.*

- *Promoting growth, not curing illness, is the therapy focus.* Thus, those in therapy become "clients" or just "persons" rather than "patients" (a change many other therapists have adopted).

- *The path to growth is taking immediate responsibility for one's feelings and actions, rather than uncovering hidden causes.*

- *Conscious thoughts are more important than the unconscious.*

- *The present and future are more important than the past.* Therapy thus focuses on exploring feelings as they occur, rather than on gaining insights into the childhood origins of those feelings.

All these themes are present in a widely used humanistic technique developed by Carl Rogers (1902–1987). **Person-centered therapy** focuses on the person's conscious self-perceptions. It is *nondirective*—the therapist listens, without judging or interpreting, and refrains from directing the client toward certain insights.

Rogers (1961, 1980) believed that most people already possess the resources for growth. He encouraged therapists to foster growth by exhibiting *genuineness*, *acceptance*, and *empathy*. By being *genuine*, therapists hope to encourage clients to likewise express their true feelings. By being *accepting*, therapists may help clients feel freer and more open to change. By showing *empathy*—by sensing and reflecting their clients' feelings—therapists can help clients experience a deeper self-understanding and self-acceptance (Hill & Nakayama, 2000). As Rogers (1980, p. 10) explained,

> Hearing has consequences. When I truly hear a person and the meanings that are important to him at that moment, hearing not simply his words, but him, and when I let him know that I have heard his own private personal meanings, many things happen. There is first of all a grateful look. He feels released. He wants to tell me more about his world. He surges forth in a new sense of freedom. He becomes more open to the process of change.
>
> I have often noticed that the more deeply I hear the meanings of the person, the more there is that happens. Almost always, when a person realizes he has been deeply heard, his eyes moisten. I think in some real sense he is weeping for joy. It is as though he were saying, "Thank God, somebody heard me. Someone knows what it's like to be me."

To Rogers, "hearing" was **active listening.** The therapist echoes, restates, and clarifies what the client expresses (verbally or nonverbally). The therapist also acknowledges those expressed feelings. Active listening is now an accepted part of counseling practices in many

ACTIVE LISTENING Carl Rogers (right) empathized with a client during this group therapy session.

Michael Rougier/The LIFE Picture Collection/Getty Images

schools, colleges, and clinics. Counselors listen attentively. They interrupt only to restate and confirm feelings, to accept what was said, or to check their understanding of something. In the following brief excerpt, note how Rogers tried to provide a psychological mirror that would help the client see himself more clearly.

Rogers: *Feeling that now, hm? That you're just no good to yourself, no good to anybody. Never will be any good to anybody. Just that you're completely worthless, huh?—Those really are lousy feelings. Just feel that you're no good at all, hm?*

Client: Yeah. (Muttering in low, discouraged voice) *That's what this guy I went to town with just the other day told me.*

Rogers: *This guy that you went to town with really told you that you were no good? Is that what you're saying? Did I get that right?*

Client: *M-hm.*

Rogers: *I guess the meaning of that if I get it right is that here's somebody that meant something to you and what does he think of you? Why, he's told you that he thinks you're no good at all. And that just really knocks the props out from under you.* (Client weeps quietly.) *It just brings the tears.* (Silence of 20 seconds)

Client: (Rather defiantly) *I don't care though.*

Rogers: *You tell yourself you don't care at all, but somehow I guess some part of you cares because some part of you weeps over it.* (Meador & Rogers, 1984, p. 167)

Can a therapist be a perfect mirror, critics have asked, without selecting and interpreting what is reflected? Rogers granted that no one can be *totally* nondirective. Nevertheless, he said, the therapist's most important contribution is to accept and understand the client. Given a nonjudgmental, grace-filled environment that provides **unconditional positive regard,** people may accept even their worst traits and feel valued and whole.

How can we improve communication in our own relationships by listening more actively? Three Rogerian hints may help:

1. *Summarize.* Check your understanding by repeating the other person's statements in your own words.

2. *Invite clarification.* "What might be an example of that?" may encourage the person to say more.

3. *Reflect feelings.* "It sounds frustrating" might mirror what you're sensing from the person's body language and emotional intensity.

Behavior Therapies

LOQ 14-4 How does the basic assumption of behavior therapy differ from the assumptions of psychodynamic and humanistic therapies? What techniques are used in exposure therapies and aversive conditioning?

The insight therapies assume that self-awareness and psychological well-being go hand in hand.

- Psychodynamic therapies assume people's problems will lessen as they gain insight into their unresolved and unconscious tensions.

- Humanistic therapies assume people's problems will lessen as they get in touch with their feelings.

Behavior therapies, however, take a different approach. Rather than searching beneath the surface for inner causes, they assume that problem behaviors *are* the problems. (You can become aware of why you are highly anxious during exams and still be anxious.) By harnessing the power of learning principles, behavior therapists offer clients useful tools for getting rid of unwanted

insight therapies therapies that aim to improve psychological functioning by increasing a person's awareness of underlying motives and defenses.

person-centered therapy a humanistic therapy, developed by Rogers, in which the therapist uses techniques such as active listening within a genuine, accepting, empathic environment to promote clients' growth. (Also called *client-centered therapy.*)

active listening empathic listening in which the listener echoes, restates, and clarifies. A feature of Rogers' person-centered therapy.

unconditional positive regard a caring, accepting, nonjudgmental attitude, which Rogers believed would help clients develop self-awareness and self-acceptance.

behavior therapy a therapeutic approach that applies learning principles to the elimination of unwanted behaviors.

behaviors. They view phobias, for example, as learned behaviors. So why not use conditioning techniques to replace them with new behaviors?

Classical Conditioning Techniques

One cluster of behavior therapies draws on principles developed in Ivan Pavlov's conditioning experiments (Chapter 6). As Pavlov and others showed, we learn various behaviors and emotions through *classical conditioning*. If we're attacked by a dog, we may thereafter have a conditioned fear response when other dogs approach. (Our fear generalizes, and all dogs become conditioned stimuli.)

Could other unwanted responses also be explained by conditioning? If so, might reconditioning be a solution? Learning theorist O. H. Mowrer thought so. He developed a successful conditioning therapy for chronic bed-wetters, using a liquid-sensitive pad connected to an alarm. If the sleeping child wets the bed pad, moisture triggers the alarm, waking the child. After a number of trials, the child associates bladder relaxation with waking. In three out of four cases, the treatment has stopped the bed-wetting, and the success has boosted the child's self-image (Christophersen & Edwards, 1992; Houts et al., 1994).

Let's broaden the discussion. What triggers your worst fear responses? Public speaking? Flying? Tight spaces? Circus clowns? Whatever the trigger, do you think you could unlearn your fear responses? With new conditioning, many people have. An example: The fear of riding in an elevator is often a learned response to the stimulus of being con-

fined in a tight space. Therapists have successfully **counterconditioned** people with a fear of confined spaces. They pair the trigger stimulus (the enclosed space of the elevator) with a new response (relaxation) that cannot coexist with fear.

To replace unwanted responses with new responses, therapists may use *exposure therapies* and *aversive conditioning*.

EXPOSURE THERAPIES Picture the animal you fear the most. Maybe it's a snake, a spider, or even a cat or a dog. For 3-year-old Peter, it was a rabbit. To rid Peter of his fear of rabbits and other furry objects, psychologist Mary Cover Jones had a plan: Associate the fear-evoking rabbit with the pleasurable, relaxed response associated with eating.

As Peter began his midafternoon snack, she introduced a caged rabbit on the other side of the huge room. Peter, eagerly munching on his crackers and slurping his milk, hardly noticed the furry animal. Day by day, Jones moved the rabbit closer and closer. Within two months, Peter was holding the rabbit in his lap, even stroking it while he ate. His fear of rabbits and other furry objects had disappeared. It had been *countered,* or replaced, by a relaxed state that could not coexist with fear (Fisher, 1984; Jones, 1924).

Unfortunately for many who might have been helped by Jones' procedures, her story of Peter and the rabbit did not enter psychology's lore when it was reported in 1924. More than 30 years later, psychiatrist Joseph Wolpe (1958; Wolpe & Plaud, 1997) refined Jones' counterconditioning technique into the **exposure therapies** used today. These therapies, in a variety of ways, try to

change people's reactions by repeatedly exposing them to stimuli that trigger unwanted responses. We all experience this process in everyday life. Someone who has moved to a new apartment may be annoyed by loud traffic sounds nearby—but only for a while. With repeated exposure, the person adapts. So, too, with people who have fear reactions to specific events. Exposed repeatedly to the situation that once terrified them, they can learn to react less anxiously (Barrera et al., 2013; Foa et al., 2013).

One form of exposure therapy widely used to treat phobias is **systematic desensitization.** You cannot be anxious and relaxed at the same time. Therefore, if you can repeatedly relax when facing anxiety-provoking stimuli, you can gradually eliminate your anxiety. The trick is to proceed gradually. Imagine you fear public speaking. A behavior therapist first asks you to list all situations that trigger your public speaking anxiety. Your list ranges from situations that cause you to feel mildly anxious (perhaps speaking up in a small group of friends) to those that provoke feelings of panic (having to address a large audience).

The therapist then trains you in *progressive relaxation*. You learn to release tension in one muscle group after another, until you feel comfortable and relaxed. The therapist then asks you to imagine, with your eyes closed, a mildly anxiety-arousing situation—perhaps a mental image of having coffee with a group of friends and trying to decide whether to speak up. You are told to signal, by raising your finger, if you feel any anxiety while imagining this scene. Seeing the signal, the therapist instructs you to switch off the mental image and go back to deep relaxation. This imagined scene is repeatedly paired with relaxation until you feel no trace of anxiety.

The therapist then moves to the next item on your list, again using relaxation techniques to desensitize you to each imagined situation. After several sessions, you move to actual situations and practice what you had only *imagined* before. You begin with relatively

Kim Reinick/Shutterstock
Creativ Studio Heinemann/Getty Images

VIRTUAL REALITY EXPOSURE THERAPY Within the confines of a room, virtual reality technology exposes people to vivid simulations of feared stimuli, such as walking across a rickety bridge high off the ground.

easy tasks and gradually move to more anxiety-filled ones. Conquering your anxiety in an actual situation, not just in your imagination, raises your self-confidence (Foa & Kozak, 1986; Williams, 1987). Eventually, you may even become a confident public speaker.

If an anxiety-arousing situation is too expensive, difficult, or embarrassing to re-create, the therapist may recommend **virtual reality exposure therapy.** You would don a head-mounted display unit that projects a three-dimensional virtual world in front of your eyes. The lifelike scenes (which shift as your head turns) would be tailored to your particular fear. Experimentally treated fears include flying, public speaking, particular animals, and heights (Parsons & Rizzo, 2008). If you fear flying, you could peer out a virtual window of a simulated plane. You would feel the engine's vibrations and hear it roar as the plane taxis down the runway and takes off. In controlled studies, people treated with virtual reality exposure therapy have experienced significant relief from real-life fear (Turner & Casey, 2014).

AVERSIVE CONDITIONING Exposure therapies help you learn what you *should* do. They enable a more relaxed, positive response to an upsetting *harmless* stimulus.

Aversive conditioning helps you to learn what you *should not* do. It creates a negative (aversive) response to a *harmful* stimulus.

The aversive conditioning procedure is simple. It associates the unwanted behavior with *unpleasant* feelings. Is nail biting the problem? The therapist might suggest painting the fingernails with a yucky-tasting nail polish (Baskind, 1997). Is alcohol use disorder the problem? The therapist may offer the client appealing drinks laced with a drug that produces severe nausea. If that therapy links alcohol with violent nausea, the person's reaction to alcohol may change from positive to negative (**FIGURE 14.1**).

counterconditioning behavior therapy procedures that use classical conditioning to evoke new responses to stimuli that are triggering unwanted behaviors; includes *exposure therapies* and *aversive conditioning*.

exposure therapies behavioral techniques, such as *systematic desensitization* and *virtual reality exposure therapy,* that treat anxieties by exposing people (in imagination or actual situations) to the things they fear and avoid.

systematic desensitization a type of exposure therapy that associates a pleasant, relaxed state with gradually increasing, anxiety-triggering stimuli. Commonly used to treat phobias.

virtual reality exposure therapy a counterconditioning technique that treats anxiety through creative electronic simulations in which people can safely face their greatest fears, such as flying, spiders, or public speaking.

aversive conditioning a type of counterconditioning that associates an unpleasant state (such as nausea) with an unwanted behavior (such as drinking alcohol).

Does aversive conditioning work? In the short run it may. In one classic study, 685 patients with alcohol use disorder completed an aversion therapy program

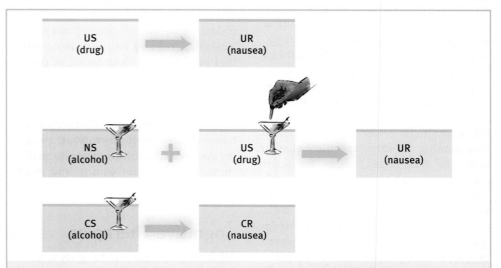

FIGURE 14.1 Aversion therapy for alcohol use disorder After repeatedly drinking an alcoholic beverage mixed with a drug that produces severe nausea, some people with a history of alcohol use disorder develop at least a temporary conditioned aversion to alcohol. (Remember: US is unconditioned stimulus, UR is unconditioned response, NS is neutral stimulus, CS is conditioned stimulus, and CR is conditioned response.)

(Wiens & Menustik, 1983). Over the next year, they returned for several booster treatments that paired alcohol with sickness. At the end of that year, 63 percent were not drinking alcohol. But after three years, only 33 percent were alcohol free.

Aversive conditioning has a built-in problem: Our thoughts can override conditioning processes (Chapter 6). People know that the alcohol-nausea link exists only in certain situations. This knowledge limits the treatment's effectiveness. Thus, therapists often combine aversive conditioning with other treatments.

Operant Conditioning Techniques

LOQ 14-5 What is the basic idea of operant conditioning therapies?

If you swim, you know fear. Through trial, error, and instruction, you learned how to put your head underwater without suffocating, how to pull your body through the water, and perhaps even how to dive safely. Operant conditioning shaped your swimming. You were reinforced for safe, effective behaviors. And you were naturally punished, as when you swallowed water, for improper swimming behaviors.

Remember a basic operant conditioning concept: Consequences drive our voluntary behaviors (Chapter 6). Knowing this, therapists can practice *behavior modification*. They reinforce behaviors they consider desirable. And they do not reinforce, or they sometimes punish, undesirable behavior. Using operant conditioning to solve specific behavior problems has raised hopes for some seemingly hopeless cases. Children with intellectual disabilities have been taught to care for themselves. Socially withdrawn children with autism spectrum disorder (ASD) have learned to interact. People with schizophrenia have learned how to behave more rationally. In each case, therapists used positive reinforcers to *shape* behavior. In a step-by-step manner, they rewarded behaviors that came closer and closer to the desired behaviors.

In extreme cases, treatment must be intensive. One study worked with 19 withdrawn, uncommunicative three-year-olds with ASD. For two years, 40 hours each week, the children's parents attempted to shape their behavior (Lovaas, 1987). They positively reinforced desired behaviors and ignored or punished aggressive and self-abusive behaviors. The combination worked wonders for some children. By first grade, 9 of the 19 were functioning successfully in school and exhibiting normal intelligence. In a control group (not receiving this treatment), only one child showed similar improvement. Later studies focused on positive reinforcement—the effective part of this *early intensive behavioral intervention* (Reichow, 2012).

Not everyone finds the same things rewarding. Hence, the rewards used to modify behavior vary. Some people may respond well to attention or praise. Others require concrete rewards, such as food. Even then, certain foods won't work as reinforcements for everyone. One of us [ND] finds chocolate neither tasty nor rewarding. Pizza is both, so a nice slice would better shape his behaviors. (What might best shape your behaviors?)

To modify behavior, therapists may create a **token economy.** People receive a token or plastic coin when they display a desired behavior—getting out of bed, washing, dressing, eating, talking meaningfully, cleaning their room, or playing cooperatively. Later, they can exchange a number of these tokens for candy, TV time, a day trip, better living quarters, or some other reward. Token economies have worked well in various settings (homes, classrooms, hospitals, institutions for delinquent youth), and among people with various disabilities (Matson & Boisjoli, 2009).

Cognitive Therapies

LOQ 14-6 What are the goals and techniques of the cognitive therapies and of cognitive-behavioral therapy?

People with specific fears and problem behaviors may respond to behavior ther-

apy. But how would you modify the wide assortment of behaviors that accompany depressive disorders? And how would you treat generalized anxiety disorder, where unfocused anxiety doesn't lend itself to a neat list of anxiety-triggering situations? The same *cognitive revolution* that influenced other areas of psychology during the last half-century has influenced therapy as well.

The **cognitive therapies** assume that our thinking colors our feelings (**FIGURE 14.2**). Between an event and our response lies the mind. Self-blaming and overgeneralized explanations of bad events feed depression (Chapter 13). If depressed, we may interpret a suggestion as criticism, disagreement as dislike, praise as flattery, friendliness as pity. Dwelling on such thoughts can sustain our bad mood. Cognitive therapies aim to help people break out of depression's vicious cycle by adopting new ways of perceiving and interpreting events (Kazdin, 2015).

"Life does not consist mainly, or even largely, of facts and happenings; it consists mainly of the storm of thoughts that are forever blowing through one's mind."

Mark Twain (1835–1910)

Retrieve + Remember

- What are the *insight therapies,* and how do they differ from behavior therapies?

  ANSWER: The *insight therapies*—psychodynamic and humanistic therapies—seek to relieve problems by providing an understanding of their origins. Behavior therapies assume the problem behavior is the problem and treat it directly, paying less attention to its origins.

- Some unwanted behaviors are learned. What hope does this fact provide?

  ANSWER: If a behavior can be learned, it can be *unlearned* and replaced by other, more adaptive responses.

- Exposure therapies and aversive conditioning are applications of _____ conditioning. Token economies are an application of _____ conditioning.

  ANSWERS: classical; operant

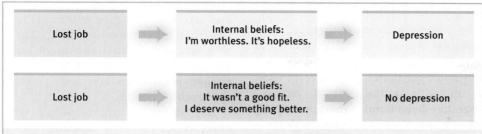

FIGURE 14.2 A cognitive perspective on psychological disorders The person's emotional reactions are produced not directly by the event, but by the person's thoughts in response to the event.

COGNITIVE THERAPY FOR EATING DISORDERS AIDED BY JOURNALING Cognitive therapists guide people toward new ways of explaining their good and bad experiences. By recording positive events and how she has enabled them, this woman may become more mindful of her self-control and more optimistic.

Beck's Therapy for Depression

Depressed people don't see the world through rose-colored glasses. They perceive the world as full of loss, rejection, and abandonment. In daily life, they may be overly attentive to potential threats, and this ongoing focus gives rise to anxiety (MacLeod & Clarke, 2015). In therapy, they often recall and rehearse their own failings and worst impulses (Kelly, 2000).

Cognitive therapist Aaron Beck developed cognitive therapy to show depressed clients the irrational nature of their thinking, and to reverse their negative views of themselves, their situations, and their futures. With this technique, gentle questioning seeks to reveal irrational thinking and then to persuade people to remove the dark glasses through which they view life (Beck et al., 1979, pp. 145–146):

Client: *I agree with the descriptions of me but I guess I don't agree that the way I think makes me depressed.*

Beck: *How do you understand it?*

Client: *I get depressed when things go wrong. Like when I fail a test.*

Beck: *How can failing a test make you depressed?*

Client: *Well, if I fail I'll never get into law school.*

Beck: *So failing the test means a lot to you. But if failing a test could drive people into clinical depression, wouldn't you expect everyone who failed the test to have a depression? . . . Did everyone who failed get depressed enough to require treatment?*

Client: *No, but it depends on how important the test was to the person.*

Beck: *Right, and who decides the importance?*

Client: *I do.*

Beck: *And so, what we have to examine is your way of viewing the test (or the way that you think about the test) and how it affects your chances of getting into law school. Do you agree?*

Client: *Right.*

Beck: *Do you agree that the way you interpret the results of the test will affect you? You might feel depressed, you might have trouble sleeping, not feel like eating, and you might even wonder if you should drop out of the course.*

Client: *I have been thinking that I wasn't going to make it. Yes, I agree.*

Beck: *Now what did failing mean?*

Client: (tearful) *That I couldn't get into law school.*

Beck: *And what does that mean to you?*

Client: *That I'm just not smart enough.*

Beck: *Anything else?*

Client: *That I can never be happy.*

Beck: *And how do these thoughts make you feel?*

Client: *Very unhappy.*

Beck: *So it is the meaning of failing a test that makes you very unhappy. In fact, believing that you can never be happy is a powerful factor in producing unhappiness. So, you get yourself into a trap—by definition, failure to get into law school equals "I can never be happy."*

We often think in words. Therefore, getting people to change what they say to themselves is an effective way to change their thinking. Have you ever studied hard for an exam but felt extremely anxious before taking it? Many well-prepared students make matters worse with self-defeating thoughts: "This exam is going to be impossible. Everyone else seems so relaxed and confident. I wish I were better prepared. I'm so nervous I'll forget everything." Psychologists call this relentless, overgeneralized, self-blaming behavior *catastrophizing.*

To change such negative self-talk, therapists teach people to alter their thinking in stressful situations

token economy an operant conditioning procedure in which people earn a token for exhibiting a desired behavior and can later exchange the tokens for privileges or treats.

cognitive therapy a therapeutic approach that teaches people new, more adaptive ways of thinking; based on the assumption that thoughts intervene between events and our emotional reactions.

PEANUTS

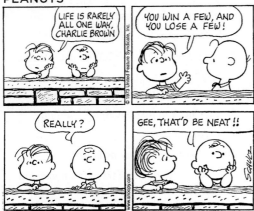

Drawing by Charles Schultz; © 1956. Reprinted by permission of United Features Syndicate

(Meichenbaum, 1977, 1985). Sometimes it may be enough simply to say more positive things to yourself. "Relax. The exam may be hard, but it will be hard for everyone else, too. I studied harder than most people. Besides, I don't need a perfect score to get a good grade." After learning to "talk back" to negative thoughts, depression-prone children, teens, and college students have shown a greatly reduced rate of future depression (Reivich et al., 2013; Seligman et al., 2009). To a large extent, it is the thought that counts. (For a sampling of commonly used cognitive therapy techniques, see **TABLE 14.1**.)

Cognitive-Behavioral Therapy

"The trouble with most therapy," said therapist Albert Ellis (1913–2007), "is that it helps you to feel better. But you don't get better. You have to back it up with action, action, action." **Cognitive-behavioral therapy (CBT)** takes a combined approach to depression and other disorders. This widely practiced *integrative* therapy aims to alter not only the way clients *think* but also the way they *act*. Like other cognitive therapies, CBT seeks to make people aware of their irrational negative thinking and to replace it with new ways of thinking. And like other behavior therapies, it trains people to practice a more positive approach in everyday settings.

Anxiety, depressive disorders, and bipolar disorder share a common problem: emotion regulation (Aldao & Nolen-Hoeksema, 2010). In cognitive-behavioral therapy, people learn to make more realistic appraisals and, as homework, to practice behaviors that are incompatible with their problem (Kazantzis & Dattilio, 2010; Kazantzis et al., 2010; Moses & Barlow, 2006). A person might keep a log of daily situations associated with negative and positive emotions and attempt to engage more in activities that lead to feeling good. Those who fear social situations might learn to shut down negative thoughts that trigger social anxiety and practice approaching people.

CBT effectively treats people with obsessive-compulsive disorder (Öst et al., 2015). In one classic study, people with obsessive-compulsive disorder learned to prevent their compulsive behaviors by relabeling their obsessive thoughts (Schwartz et al., 1996). Feeling the urge to wash their hands again, they would tell themselves, "I'm having a compulsive urge." They would explain to themselves that the hand-washing urge was a result of their brain's abnormal activity, which they had previously viewed in PET scans. Then, instead of giving in, they would spend 15 minutes in some enjoyable alternative behavior—practicing an instrument, taking a walk, gardening. This helped "unstick" the brain by shifting attention and engaging other brain areas. For two or three months, the weekly therapy sessions continued, with relabeling and refocusing practice at home. By the study's end, most participants' symptoms had diminished, and their PET scans revealed normalized brain activity. Many other studies confirm CBT's effectiveness for treating anxiety, depression, and eating disorders (Cristea et al., 2015; Milrod et al., 2015; Turner et al., 2016).

A newer CBT variation, *dialectical behavior therapy (DBT)*, helps change harmful and even suicidal behavior patterns (Linehan et al., 2015; Valentine et al., 2015). *Dialectical* means "opposing," and this therapy attempts to make peace between two opposing forces—acceptance and change. DBT combines cognitive tactics (for tolerating distress and regulating emotions) with social skills training and mindfulness meditation (see Chapter 10). Group training sessions offer additional opportunities to practice new skills in a social context, with further practice as homework.

TABLE 14.1	Selected Cognitive Therapy Techniques	
Aim of Technique	**Technique**	**Therapists' Directives**
Reveal beliefs	Question your interpretations	Explore your beliefs, revealing faulty assumptions such as "I must be liked by everyone."
	Rank thoughts and emotions	Gain perspective by ranking your thoughts and emotions from mildly to extremely upsetting.
Test beliefs	Examine consequences	Explore difficult situations, assessing possible consequences and challenging faulty reasoning.
	Decatastrophize thinking	Work through the actual worst-case consequences of the situation you face (it is often not as bad as imagined). Then determine how to cope with the real situation you face.
Change beliefs	Take appropriate responsibility	Challenge total self-blame and negative thinking, noting aspects for which you may be truly responsible, as well as aspects that aren't your responsibility.
	Resist extremes	Develop new ways of thinking and feeling to replace maladaptive habits. For example, change from thinking "I am a total failure" to "I got a failing grade on that paper, and I can make these changes to succeed next time."

Group and Family Therapies

LOQ 14-7 What are the aims and benefits of group and family therapies?

So far, we have focused mainly on therapies in which one therapist treats one client. Most therapies (though not traditional psychoanalysis) can also occur in small groups.

Group therapy does not provide the same degree of therapist involvement with each client. However, it offers other benefits:

- *It saves therapists' time and clients' money,* and often is no less effective than individual therapy (Fuhriman & Burlingame, 1994; Jónsson et al., 2011).

- *It offers a social laboratory for exploring social behaviors and developing social skills.* Therapists frequently suggest group therapy when clients' problems stem from their interactions with others, as when families have conflicts or an individual's behavior distresses others. The therapist guides people's interactions as they confront issues and try out new behaviors.

John Moore/Getty Images

FAMILY THERAPY This type of therapy often acts as a preventive mental health strategy and may include marriage therapy, as shown here at a retreat for military families. The therapist helps family members understand how their ways of relating to one another create problems. The treatment's emphasis is not on changing the individuals, but on changing their relationships and interactions.

- *It enables clients to see that others share their problems.* It can be a relief to find that others, despite their calm appearance, share your struggles, your troubling feelings, and your potentially harmful thoughts.

- *It provides feedback as clients try out new ways of behaving.* Hearing that you look confident, even though you feel anxious and self-conscious, can be very reassuring.

One special type of group interaction, **family therapy,** assumes that no person is an island. We live and grow in relation to others, especially our family, yet we also work to find an identity outside of our family. These two opposing tendencies can create stress for the individual and the family. This helps explain why therapists tend to view families as systems, in which each person's actions trigger reactions from others. To change negative interactions, the therapist often attempts to guide family members toward positive relationships and improved communication.

LaunchPad   To review the aims and techniques of different psychotherapies, and assess your ability to recognize excerpts from each, visit LaunchPad's *PsychSim 6: Mystery Therapist.*

Evaluating Psychotherapies

Many Americans have great confidence in psychotherapy's effectiveness. "Seek counseling" or "Ask your mate to find a therapist," advice columnists often advise. Before 1950, psychiatrists were the primary providers of mental health care. Today, many others have joined their ranks. Clinical and

cognitive-behavioral therapy (CBT) a popular integrative therapy that combines cognitive therapy (changing self-defeating thinking) with behavior therapy (changing behavior).

group therapy therapy conducted with groups rather than individuals, providing benefits from group interaction.

family therapy therapy that treats the family as a system. Views an individual's unwanted behaviors as influenced by, or directed at, other family members.

counseling psychologists offer psychotherapy, and so do clinical social workers; pastoral, marital, abuse, and school counselors; and psychiatric nurses.

Psychotherapy takes an enormous amount of time, money, and effort. A critical thinker might wonder: Is the faith that millions of people worldwide place in psychotherapy justified? The question, though simply put, is not simply answered.

Is Psychotherapy Effective?

LOQ 14-8 Does psychotherapy work? How do we know?

Imagine that a loved one, knowing that you're studying psychology, has asked for your help. She's been feeling depressed, and she's thinking about making an appointment with a therapist. She wonders: Does psychotherapy really work? You've promised to gather some answers. Where will you start? Who decides whether psychotherapy is effective? Clients? Therapists? Friends and family members?

Clients' Perceptions

If clients' glowing comments were the only measuring stick, your job would be easy. Most clients believe that psychotherapy is effective. Consider 2900

SO HOW LONG HAVE YOU WANTED TO BE A THERAPIST?

THAT'S WHAT I WOULD LIKE TO ASK YOU.

ED WAS IN THERAPY FOR BELIEVING HE WAS A THERAPIST.

Consumer Reports readers who rated their experiences with mental health professionals (1995; Kotkin et al., 1996; Seligman, 1995). How many were at least "fairly well satisfied"? Almost 90 percent (as was Kay Redfield Jamison, as we saw at this chapter's beginning). Among those who recalled feeling *fair* or *very poor* when beginning therapy, 9 in 10 now were feeling *very good, good,* or at least *so-so.* We have their word for it—and who should know better?

But clients' self-reports don't persuade everyone. Critics point out some reasons for skepticism.

- *People often enter therapy in crisis.* Life ebbs and flows. When the crisis passes, people may assume their improvement was a therapy result.

- *Clients believe treatment will be effective.* The *placebo effect* is the healing power of positive expectations.

- *Clients generally speak kindly of their therapists.* Even if their problems remain, clients "work hard to find something positive to say. The therapist had been very understanding, the client had gained a new perspective, he learned to communicate better, his mind was eased, anything at all so as not to have to say treatment was a failure" (Zilbergeld, 1983, p. 117).

- *Clients want to believe the therapy was worth the effort.* If you invested dozens of hours and lots of money in something, wouldn't you be motivated to find something positive about it? Psychologists call this *effort justification.*

Clinicians' Perceptions

If clinicians' perceptions were proof of therapy's effectiveness, we would have even more reason to celebrate. Case studies of successful treatment abound. Furthermore, therapists are like the rest of us. They treasure compliments from clients saying good-bye or later expressing their gratitude. The problem is that clients justify entering psychotherapy

TRAUMA These women were mourning the tragic loss of lives and homes in the 2010 earthquake in China. Those who suffer through such trauma may benefit from counseling, though many people recover on their own or with the help of supportive relationships with family and friends. "Life itself still remains a very effective therapist," noted psychodynamic therapist Karen Horney (*Our Inner Conflicts,* 1945).

by emphasizing their unhappiness. They justify leaving by emphasizing their well-being. And they stay in touch only if satisfied. This means that therapists are most aware of the failures of *other* therapists—those whose clients, having experienced only temporary relief, are now seeking a new therapist for their recurring problems. Thus, the same person, suffering from the same recurring anxiety, depression, or marital difficulty, may be a "success" story in several therapists' files.

Therapists are like the rest of us in another way. We all sometimes suffer from two obstacles to critical thinking (Lilienfeld et al., 2014). The first, *confirmation bias,* is the tendency to unconsciously seek evidence that confirms our beliefs and to ignore evidence that contradicts them. The second is the tendency to see *illusory correlations*—to perceive associations that don't really exist.

Outcome Research

If clients' and therapists' most sincere ratings of their experiences can't inform us about psychotherapy's effectiveness, how can we know what to expect? What types of people and problems are helped, and by what type of psychotherapy?

In search of answers, psychologists have turned to controlled research. This is a well-traveled path. In the 1800s, skeptical medical doctors began to realize that many patients got better on their own and that most of the fashionable treatments (bleeding, purging) were doing no good. Sorting fact from superstition required following patients and recording outcomes with and without a particular treatment. Typhoid fever patients, for example, often improved after being bled, convincing most doctors that the treatment worked. Then came the shock. A control group was given mere bed rest, and after five weeks of fever, 70 percent improved. The study showed that bleeding was worthless (Thomas, 1992).

In the twentieth century, psychology faced a similar challenge. British psychologist Hans Eysenck (1952) launched a spirited debate when he summarized 24 studies of psychotherapy outcomes. He found that two-thirds of those receiving psychotherapy for disorders not involving hallucinations or delusions improved markedly. To this day, no one disputes that optimistic estimate.

Why, then, are we still debating psychotherapy's effectiveness? Because Eysenck also found that *untreated* people, such as those on waiting lists for the same treatment, had similar rates of improvement. With or without psychotherapy, roughly two-thirds improved noticeably. Time was a great healer.

Eysenck's findings sparked an uproar. Some critics pointed out errors in his analyses. Others noted that he based his ideas on only 24 studies. Now, more than a half-century later, there are hundreds of such studies. The best of these studies are *randomized clinical trials*, in which researchers randomly assign people on a waiting list to therapy or to no therapy. Later, they evaluate everyone and compare the outcomes, with assessments by others who don't know whether therapy was given.

Therapists welcomed the result when the first statistical digest combined the results of 475 of these investigations (Smith et al., 1980). The outcome for the average therapy client was better than that for 80 percent of the untreated people (FIGURE 14.3).

Dozens of such summaries have echoed the results of the earlier outcome studies: *Those not undergoing therapy often improve, but those undergoing therapy are more likely to improve, and to improve more quickly and with less risk of relapse.* Moreover, between the treatment sessions for depression and anxiety, many people have sudden reductions in their symptoms. These "sudden gains" offer hope for long-term improvement (Aderka et al., 2012).

So psychotherapy is a good investment of time and money. Like prenatal care, psychotherapy reduces long-term health care costs. One digest of 91 studies showed that after seeking psychotherapy, clients' search for other medical treatment dropped by 16 percent (Chiles et al., 1999).

It's good to know that psychotherapy, in general at least, is somewhat effective. But distressed people—and those paying for their therapy—really want a different question answered. How effective are *particular* treatments for *specific* problems? So what can we tell these people?

Which Psychotherapies Work Best?

LOQ 14-9 Are some psychotherapies more effective than others for specific disorders?

The early statistical summaries and surveys did not find that any one type of psychotherapy was generally better than others (Smith & Glass, 1977; Smith et al., 1980). Later studies have similarly found little connection between clients' outcomes and their clinicians' experience, training, supervision, and licensing (Bickman, 1999; Luborsky et al., 2002; Wampold, 2007). A *Consumer Reports* survey confirmed this result. Were clients treated by a psychiatrist, psychologist, or social worker? Were they seen in a group or individual context? Did the therapist have extensive or relatively limited training and experience? It didn't matter. Clients seemed equally satisfied (Seligman, 1995).

So, was the dodo bird in *Alice in Wonderland* right: "Everyone has won

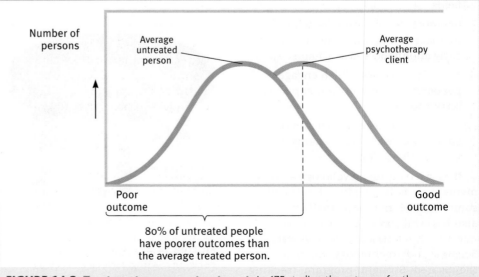

FIGURE 14.3 Treatment versus no treatment In 475 studies, the outcome for the average therapy client was better than that for 80 percent of the untreated people. (Data from Smith et al., 1980.)

and all must have prizes"? Not quite. One general finding emerges from the studies. The more specific the problem, the greater the hope (Singer, 1981; Westen & Morrison, 2001). Moreover, some forms of psychotherapy get prizes for *particular* problems. Behavioral conditioning therapies work well for specific behavior problems, such as bed-wetting, phobias, compulsions, marital problems, and sexual dysfunctions (Baker et al., 2008; Hunsley & Di Giulio, 2002; Shadish & Baldwin, 2005). Psychodynamic therapy has helped treat depression and anxiety (Driessen et al., 2010; Leichsenring & Rabung, 2008; Shedler, 2010b). Nondirective (person-centered) counseling often helps people with mild to moderate depression (Cuijpers et al., 2013). And many studies confirm cognitive and cognitive-behavioral therapies' effectiveness (some say superiority) in helping people cope with anxiety, post-traumatic stress disorder, and depression (Baker et al., 2008; De Los Reyes & Kazdin, 2009; Stewart & Chambless, 2009; Tolin, 2010).

But no prizes would go to certain other psychotherapies (Arkowitz & Lilienfeld, 2006). We would all be wise to avoid approaches that have little or no scientific support, such as

- *energy therapies,* which seek to manipulate people's invisible energy fields.

- *recovered-memory therapies,* which aim to unearth "repressed memories" of early childhood abuse (Chapter 7).

- *rebirthing therapies,* which engage people in reenacting their supposed birth trauma.

- *conversion therapies,* which aim to enable homosexuals to change their sexual orientation.

It is as true for psychological treatments as it is for medical treatments—some can be not only ineffective but also harmful (Barlow, 2010; Castonguay et al., 2010; Dimidjian & Hollon, 2010). The National Science and Technology Council cites the Scared Straight program (seeking to deter children and youth from crime by having them visit with adult inmates) as an example of a well-intentioned

program that has proven unsuccessful or even damaging.

This list of discredited therapies raises another question. *Who should decide which psychotherapies get prizes and which do not?* What role should science play in clinical practice, and how much should science guide health care providers and insurers in setting payment policies for psychotherapy?

This question lies at the heart of a controversy—some call it psychology's civil war. On one side are research psychologists who use scientific methods to extend the list of well-defined therapies with proven results in aiding people with various disorders. They worry that many clinicians "give more weight to their personal experience than to science" (Baker et al., 2008).

On the other side are the nonscientist therapists who view their practices as more art than science. They view psychotherapy as something that cannot be described in a manual or tested in an experiment. People are too complex and psychotherapy is too intuitive for a one-size-fits-all approach, many therapists say.

Between these two camps stand the science-oriented clinicians calling for **evidence-based practice (FIGURE 14.4),**

FIGURE 14.4 Evidence-based clinical decision making Ideal clinical decision making can be visualized as a three-legged stool, upheld by research evidence, clinical expertise, and knowledge of the patient.

(Labels in figure: Clinical decision making; Patient's values, characteristics, preferences, circumstances; Clinical expertise; Best available research evidence)

which has been endorsed by the American Psychological Association and others (2006; Lilienfeld et al., 2013). Therapists using this approach make informed decisions based on research evidence, clinical expertise, and their knowledge of the patient. Increasingly, insurer and government support for mental health services requires evidence-based practice.

Retrieve + Remember

- Therapy is most likely to be helpful for those with problems that (are/are not) well defined.

  ANSWER: are

- What is evidence-based practice?

  ANSWER: Using this approach, therapists make decisions about treatment based on research evidence, clinical expertise, and knowledge of the patient.

How Do Psychotherapies Help People?

LOQ 14-10 What three elements are shared by all forms of psychotherapy?

Why do therapists' training and experience have so little influence on clients' outcomes? The answer seems to be that all psychotherapies offer three basic benefits (Frank, 1982; Goldfried & Padawer, 1982; Strupp, 1986; Wampold, 2001, 2007). They all offer *hope for demoralized people; a new perspective on oneself and the world;* and *an empathic, trusting, caring relationship.*

HOPE FOR DEMORALIZED PEOPLE Many people seek therapy because they feel anxious, depressed, self-disapproving, and unable to turn things around. What any psychotherapy offers is hope—an expectation that, with commitment from the therapy seeker, things can and will get better. By harnessing the person's own healing powers, this belief, apart from any therapy technique, can improve morale, create feelings of inner strength, and reduce symptoms (Corrigan, 2014; Frank, 1982; Prioleau et al., 1983).

A NEW PERSPECTIVE Every psychotherapy also offers people an explanation of their symptoms. Psychotherapy is a new experience that can help people change their behavior and their view of themselves. Armed with a believable fresh perspective, people may approach life with new energy to make needed changes.

AN EMPATHIC, TRUSTING, CARING RELATIONSHIP No matter what technique they use, effective psychotherapists are empathic. They seek to understand people's experiences. They communicate care and concern. And they earn trust through respectful listening, reassurance, and guidance. These qualities were clear in recorded therapy sessions from 36 recognized master therapists (Goldfried et al., 1998). Some took a cognitive-behavioral approach. Others used psychodynamic principles. Regardless, at key moments during the most significant parts of their sessions, they were strikingly similar. They helped clients evaluate themselves, connect different aspects of their life, and gain insight into their interactions with others. At these points, an emotional bond—called a **therapeutic alliance**—forms between psychotherapist and client. This bond is a key aspect of effective psychotherapy (Klein et al., 2003; Wampold, 2001). In one U.S. National Institute of Mental Health depression-treatment study, the most effective therapists were those who formed the closest therapeutic bonds with their clients by showing empathy and care (Blatt et al., 1996).

These three basic benefits—hope, a fresh perspective, and an empathic, caring relationship—help us understand why *paraprofessionals* (briefly trained caregivers) can assist so many troubled people so effectively (Christensen & Jacobson, 1994). They are an important part of what self-help and support groups offer their members. And they also are part of what traditional healers have offered (Jackson, 1992). Healers everywhere—special people to whom others disclose their suffering,

whether psychiatrists, witch doctors, or shamans—have listened in order to understand. And they have empathized, reassured, advised, consoled, interpreted, and explained (Torrey, 1986). These three elements of effective psychotherapy may also explain another finding. People who feel supported by close relationships—who enjoy the fellowship and friendship of caring people—have been less likely to need or seek therapy (Frank, 1982; O'Connor & Brown, 1984).

* * *

To recap, people who seek psychotherapy usually improve. So do many of those who do not undergo psychotherapy, and that is a tribute to our human resourcefulness and our capacity to care for one another. Nevertheless, though the therapist's orientation and experience appear not to matter much, people who receive some psychotherapy usually improve more than those who do not. People with clear-cut, specific problems tend to improve the most.

Retrieve + Remember

- Those who undergo psychotherapy are _____ (more/less) likely to show improvement than those who do not undergo psychotherapy.

ANSWER: more

How Do Culture and Values Influence Psychotherapy?

LOQ 14-11 How do culture and values influence the client-therapist relationship?

All psychotherapies offer hope. Nearly all psychotherapists try to enhance their clients' sensitivity, openness, personal responsibility, and sense of purpose (Jensen & Bergin, 1988). But in matters of culture and values, psychotherapists differ from one another and may differ from their clients (Delaney et al., 2007; Kelly, 1990).

These differences can create a mismatch when a therapist from one culture interacts with a client from another. In North America, Europe, and Australia, for example, many psychotherapists reflect the majority culture's *individualism*, which often gives priority to personal desires and identity. Clients with a *collectivist* perspective, as found in many Asian cultures, may assume people will be more mindful of social and family responsibilities, harmony, and group goals. These clients may have trouble relating to therapies that require them to think only of their individual well-being (Markus & Kitayama, 1991).

Cultural differences help explain some groups' reluctance to use mental health services. People living in "cultures of honor" prize being strong and tough. They may feel that seeking mental health care is an admission of weakness (Brown et al., 2014b). And some minority groups tend to be both reluctant to seek therapy and quick to leave it (Broman, 1996; Chen et al., 2009; Sue, 2006). In one experiment, Asian-American clients matched with counselors who shared their cultural values (rather than mismatched with those who did not) perceived more counselor empathy and felt more alliance with the counselor (Kim et al., 2005).

Client-psychotherapist mismatches may also stem from religious values. Highly religious people may prefer and benefit from therapists who share their values and beliefs (Masters, 2010; Smith et al., 2007; Wade et al., 2006). They may have trouble establishing an emotional bond with a therapist who views the world differently.

evidence-based practice clinical decision making that integrates the best available research with clinical expertise and patient characteristics and preferences.

therapeutic alliance a bond of trust and mutual understanding between a therapist and client, who work together constructively to overcome the client's problem.

A CARING RELATIONSHIP Effective counselors, such as this chaplain working aboard a ship, form a bond of trust with the people they are serving.

Steve Szydlowski/KRT/Newscom

TABLE 14.2   Therapists and Their Training

Type	Description
Clinical psychologists	Most are psychologists with a Ph.D. (includes research training) or Psy.D. (focuses on therapy), supplemented by a supervised internship and, often, postdoctoral training. About half work in agencies and institutions, half in private practice.
Psychiatrists	Psychiatrists are physicians who specialize in the treatment of psychological disorders. Not all psychiatrists have had extensive training in psychotherapy, but as M.D.s or D.O.s they can prescribe medications. Thus, they tend to see those with the most serious problems. Many have their own private practice.
Clinical or psychiatric social workers	A two-year master of social work graduate program plus postgraduate supervision prepares some social workers to offer psychotherapy, mostly to people with everyday personal and family problems. About half have earned the National Association of Social Workers' designation of clinical social worker.
Counselors	Marriage and family counselors specialize in problems arising from family relations. Clergy provide counseling to countless people. Abuse counselors work with substance abusers and with spouse and child abusers and their victims. Mental health and other counselors may be required to have a two-year master's degree.

Finding a Mental Health Professional

LOQ 14-12 What should a person look for when selecting a psychotherapist?

Life for everyone is marked by a mix of calm and stress, blessings and losses, good moods and bad. So when should we seek a mental health professional's help? APA offers these common trouble signals:

- Feelings of hopelessness
- Deep and lasting depression
- Self-destructive behavior, such as substance abuse
- Disruptive fears
- Sudden mood shifts
- Thoughts of suicide
- Compulsive rituals, such as hand washing
- Sexual difficulties
- Hearing voices or seeing things that others don't experience

In looking for a psychotherapist, you may want to have a preliminary meeting with two or three. College health centers are generally good starting points, and they offer some free services. In your meeting, you can describe your problem and learn each therapist's treatment approach. You can ask questions about the therapist's values, credentials (**TABLE 14.2**), and fees. And you can assess your own feelings about each therapist. The emotional bond between therapist and client is perhaps the most important factor in effective therapy.

The American Psychological Association recognizes the importance of a strong therapeutic alliance and it welcomes diverse therapists who can relate well to diverse clients. It accredits programs that provide training in cultural sensitivity (for example, to differing values, communication styles, and language) and that recruit underrepresented cultural groups.

The Biomedical Therapies

Psychotherapy is one way to treat psychological disorders. The other is *biomedical therapy*. Biomedical treatments can change the brain's chemistry with drugs; affect the brain's circuitry with electrical stimulation, magnetic impulses, or psychosurgery; or influence the brain's responses with lifestyle changes.

Are you surprised to see *lifestyle* changes in this list? We find it convenient to talk of separate psychological and biological influences, but everything psychological is also biological. When psychotherapy relieves behaviors associated with obsessive-compulsive disorder or schizophrenia, PET scans reveal a calmer brain (Habel et al., 2010; Schwartz et al., 1996). How about our day-to-day lifestyle—the food we eat, the activities and environments we engage, the social fabric we maintain? Can these choices also be therapeutic? (See Thinking Critically About: Therapeutic Lifestyle Change.)

The influence is two-way. Every thought and feeling depends on the functioning brain. Every creative idea, every moment of joy or anger, every period of depression emerges from the electrochemical activity of the living brain.

Thinking Critically About:
Therapeutic Lifestyle Change

LOQ 14-13 Why is therapeutic lifestyle change considered an effective biomedical therapy, and how does it work?

LIFESTYLE
(exercise, nutrition, relationships, recreation, relaxation, and religious or spiritual engagement) → **influences our BRAIN AND BODY** → **affects our MENTAL HEALTH** [1]

We were designed for physical activity and social engagement.

Our ancestors hunted, gathered, and built in groups.

Modern researchers have found that outdoor activity in a natural environment reduces stress and promotes health. [2]

APPLICATION TO THERAPY

Training seminars promote therapeutic lifestyle change. [3] Small groups of people with depression undergo a 12-week training program with the following goals:

Aerobic exercise, 30 minutes a day, at least three times weekly (increases fitness and vitality, stimulates endorphins)

Regular aerobic exercise rivals the healing power of antidepressant drugs. [4]

Light exposure, 15 to 30 minutes each morning with a light box (amplifies arousal, influences hormones)

Reducing rumination, by identifying and redirecting negative thoughts (enhances positive thinking)

Adequate sleep, with a goal of 7 to 8 hours a night (increases energy and alertness, boosts immunity)

A complete night's sleep improves mood and energy. [5]

zzzzzzzzzzzzzzzzzzzzzzzzz

Social connection, with less alone time and at least two meaningful social engagements weekly (helps satisfy the human need to belong)

Nutritional supplements, including a daily fish oil supplement with omega-3 fatty acids (aids in healthy brain functioning)

Initial small study (74 participants)[6]

 77% of those who completed the program experienced relief from depressive symptoms.

 Only 19% of those assigned to a treatment-as-usual control group showed similar results.

Future research will try to identify which parts of the treatment produce the therapeutic effect.

The biomedical therapies assume that mind and body are a unit: Affect one and you will affect the other.

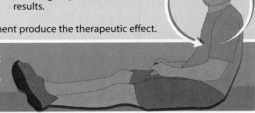

1. Sánchez-Villegas et al., 2015; Walsh, 2011. 2. MacKerron & Mourato, 2013; NEEF, 2015; Phillips, 2011. 3. Ilardi, 2009. 4. Babyak et al., 2000; Salmon, 2001; Schuch et al., 2016. 5. Gregory et al., 2009; Walker & van der Helm, 2009. 6. Ilardi, 2009, 2016.

Drug Therapies

LOQ 14-14 What are the drug therapies? How do double-blind studies help researchers evaluate a drug's effectiveness?

By far, the most widely used biomedical treatments today are the drug therapies. Most drugs for anxiety and depression are prescribed by primary care providers, followed by psychiatrists and, in some states, psychologists. Since the 1950s, drug researchers have written a new chapter in the treatment of people with severe disorders. Thanks to drug therapies and support from community mental health programs, today's resident population of U.S. state and county mental hospitals has dropped to a small fraction of what it was a half-century ago. In one decade alone (1996 to 2005), the number of Americans prescribed antidepressant drugs doubled, from 13 million to 27 million (Olfson & Marcus, 2009).

Almost any new treatment, including drug therapy, is greeted by an initial wave of enthusiasm as many people apparently improve. But that enthusiasm often diminishes on closer examination. To judge the effectiveness of a new treatment, we also need to know:

• Do untreated people also improve? If so, how many, and how quickly?

• Was recovery due to the drug or to the *placebo effect?* When patients and/or mental health workers expect positive results, they may see what they expect, not what really happens. Even mere exposure to

"If this doesn't help you don't worry, it's a placebo."

advertising about a drug's supposed effectiveness can increase its effect (Kamenica et al., 2013).

To control for these influences when testing a new drug, researchers give half the patients the drug, and the other half a similar-appearing placebo. Because neither the staff nor the patients know who gets which, this is called a *double-blind technique.* The good news: In double-blind studies, several types of drugs effectively treat psychological disorders.

* * *

The four most common drug treatments for psychological disorders are *antipsychotic drugs, antianxiety drugs, antidepressant drugs,* and *mood-stabilizing medications.* Let's consider each of these in more detail.

Antipsychotic Drugs

Accidents sometimes launch revolutions. In this instance, an accidental discovery launched a treatment revolution for people with *psychoses.* The discovery was that some drugs used for other medical purposes calmed the hallucinations or delusions that are part of these patients' split from reality. First-generation **antipsychotic drugs,** such as chlorpromazine (sold as Thorazine), reduce patients' overreactions to irrelevant stimuli. Thus, they provide the most help to schizophrenia patients experiencing symptoms such as auditory hallucinations and paranoia (Lehman et al., 1998; Lenzenweger et al., 1989). (Antipsychotic drugs are not equally

effective in changing the schizophrenia symptoms of apathy and withdrawal.)

How do antipsychotic drugs work? They mimic certain neurotransmitters. Some block the activity of dopamine by occupying its receptor sites. This finding reinforces the idea that an overactive dopamine system contributes to schizophrenia. Further support for this idea comes from a side effect of another drug. L-dopa is a drug sometimes given to people with Parkinson's disease to boost their production of dopamine, which is too low. L-dopa raises dopamine levels, but can you guess its occasional side effect? If you guessed hallucinations, you're right.

Do antipsychotic drugs also have side effects? *Yes,* and some are powerful. They may produce sluggishness, tremors, and twitches similar to those of Parkinson's disease (Kaplan & Saddock, 1989). Long-term use of antipsychotics can also produce *tardive dyskinesia,* with involuntary movements of the facial muscles (such as grimacing), tongue, and limbs. Although not more effective in controlling schizophrenia symptoms, many of the newer-generation antipsychotics (such as risperidone and olanzapine) work best for those with severe symptoms and have fewer side effects (Furukawa et al., 2015). These drugs may, however, increase the risk of obesity and diabetes (Buchanan et al., 2010; Tiihonen et al., 2009).

Despite their drawbacks, antipsychotics, combined with life-skills programs and family support, have given new hope to many people with schizophrenia (Guo et al., 2010). Hundreds of thousands of patients have left the wards of mental hospitals and returned to work and to near-normal lives (Leucht et al., 2003). Elyn Saks, a University of Southern California law professor, knows what it means to live with schizophrenia. Thanks to her treatment, which combines an antipsychotic drug and psychotherapy, "Now I'm mostly well. I'm mostly thinking clearly. I do have episodes, but it's not like I'm struggling all of the time to stay on the right side of the line" (Sachs, 2007).

Antianxiety Drugs

Like alcohol, **antianxiety drugs,** such as Xanax or Ativan, depress central nervous system activity (and so should not be used in combination with alcohol). These drugs are often successfully used in combination with psychological therapy to treat anxiety disorders, obsessive-compulsive disorder, and posttraumatic stress disorder. They calm anxiety as the person learns to cope with frightening situations and fear-triggering stimuli.

Some critics fear that antianxiety drugs may reduce symptoms without resolving underlying problems, especially when used as an ongoing treatment. "Popping a Xanax" at the first sign of tension can provide immediate relief, which may reinforce a person's tendency to take drugs when anxious. Anxiety drugs can also be addictive. Regular users who stop taking these drugs may experience increased anxiety, insomnia, and other withdrawal symptoms.

Antidepressant Drugs

The **antidepressant drugs** were named for their ability to lift people up from a state of depression. These drugs are now also used to treat anxiety disorders, obsessive-compulsive disorder, and posttraumatic stress disorder (Wetherell et al., 2013). Many of these drugs work by increasing the availability of norepinephrine or serotonin. These neurotransmitters elevate arousal and mood and are scarce when a person experiences feelings of depression or anxiety.

The most commonly prescribed drugs in this group, including Prozac and its cousins Zoloft and Paxil, lift spirits by prolonging the time serotonin molecules remain in the brain's synapses. They do this by partially blocking the normal reuptake process (see Figure 2.4 in Chapter 2). These drugs are called *selective serotonin reuptake inhibitors (SSRIs)* because they slow (inhibit) the synaptic vacuuming up (reuptake) of serotonin.

Some professionals prefer the SSRIs over other antidepressants (Jakubovski

et al., 2015; Kramer, 2011). SSRIs begin to influence neurotransmission within hours. But their full psychological effect may take four weeks, possibly because these drugs promote the birth of new brain cells (Becker & Wojtowicz, 2007; Jacobs, 2004). Researchers are also exploring the possibility of quicker-acting antidepressants (Grimm & Scheidegger, 2013; McGirr et al., 2015; Naughton et al., 2014).

Drugs are not the only way to lift our mood. Aerobic exercise can calm people who feel anxious, energize those who feel depressed, and offer other positive side effects. Cognitive therapy, which helps people reverse their habits of thinking negatively, can boost the drug-aided relief from depression and reduce posttreatment relapses (Hollon et al., 2002; Keller et al., 2000; Vittengl et al., 2007). The best approach seems to be attacking depression (and anxiety) from both above and below (Cuijpers et al., 2010; Hollon et al., 2014; Kennard et al., 2014; Walkup et al., 2008). Cognitive-behavioral therapy works from the top down to change thought processes. Antidepressant drugs work from the bottom up to affect the emotion-forming limbic system.

People with depression often improve after a month on antidepressant drugs. But after allowing for natural recovery and the placebo effect, how big is the drug effect? Not big, report some researchers (Kirsch, 2010; Kirsch et al., 2002, 2014; Kirsch & Sapirstein, 1998). In double-blind clinical trials, placebos produced improvement comparable with about 75 percent of the active drug's effect. In a follow-up review that included unpublished clinical trials, the antidepressant effect was again modest (Kirsch et al., 2008). The placebo effect was less for those with severe depression, which made the added benefit of the drug somewhat greater for them (Fournier et al., 2010; Kirsch et al., 2008; Olfson & Marcus, 2009). "Given these results, there seems little reason to prescribe antidepressant medication to any but the most severely depressed patients, unless alternative treatments have failed," concluded one researcher (BBC, 2008).

antipsychotic drugs drugs used to treat schizophrenia and other forms of severe thought disorders.

antianxiety drugs drugs used to control anxiety and agitation.

antidepressant drugs drugs used to treat depression, anxiety disorders, obsessive-compulsive disorder, and posttraumatic stress disorder. (Several widely used antidepressant drugs are *selective serotonin reuptake inhibitors—SSRIs.*)

LaunchPad   To better understand how clinical researchers have evaluated drug therapies, complete LaunchPad's *IMMERSIVE LEARNING: How Would You Know How Well Antidepressants Work?*

Mood-Stabilizing Medications

In addition to antipsychotic, antianxiety, and antidepressant drugs, psychiatrists have *mood-stabilizing drugs* in their arsenal. One of them, Depakote, was originally used to treat epilepsy. It was also found effective in controlling the manic episodes associated with bipolar disorder. Another, the simple salt *lithium,* effectively levels the emotional highs and lows of this disorder. Australian physician John Cade discovered this in the 1940s when he administered lithium to a patient with severe mania and the patient became perfectly well in less than a week (Snyder, 1986). Although we do not understand why, lithium works. About 7 in 10 people with bipolar disorder benefit from a long-term daily dose of this cheap salt (Solomon et al., 1995). Their risk of suicide is

"First of all I think you should know that last quarter's sales figures are interfering with my mood-stabilizing drugs."

© John Greim/Age fotostock

but one-sixth that of people with bipolar disorder who are not taking lithium (Oquendo et al., 2011). Kay Redfield Jamison (1995, pp. 88–89) described the effect:

> Lithium prevents my seductive but disastrous highs, diminishes my depressions, clears out the wool and webbing from my disordered thinking, slows me down, gentles me out, keeps me from ruining my career and relationships, keeps me out of a hospital, alive, and makes psychotherapy possible.

Retrieve + Remember

- How do researchers evaluate the effectiveness of particular drug therapies?

ANSWER: Researchers assign people to treatment and no-treatment conditions to see if those who receive the drug therapy improve more than those who don't. *Double-blind* controlled studies are most effective. If neither the therapist nor the client knows which participants have received the drug treatment, then any difference between the treated and untreated groups will reflect the drug treatment's actual effect.

- The drugs given most often to treat depression are called _____. Schizophrenia is often treated with _____ drugs.

ANSWERS: antidepressants; antipsychotic

Brain Stimulation

LOQ 14-15 How are brain stimulation and psychosurgery used in treating specific disorders?

Electroconvulsive Therapy

Another biomedical treatment, **electroconvulsive therapy (ECT)**, manipulates the brain by shocking it. When ECT was first introduced in 1938, the wide-awake patient was strapped to a table and jolted with roughly 100 volts of electricity to the brain. The procedure, which produced racking convulsions and brief unconsciousness, gained a barbaric image. Although that image lingers, today's ECT is much kinder and gentler. The patient receives a general anesthetic and a muscle relaxant to prevent convulsions. A psychiatrist then delivers to the patient's brain 30 to 60 seconds of electric current,

in briefer pulses (**FIGURE 14.5**). Within 30 minutes, the patient awakens and remembers nothing of the treatment or of the preceding hours.

Would you agree to ECT for yourself or a loved one? The decision might be difficult, but the treatment works. Surprising as it may seem, study after study confirms that ECT can effectively treat severe depression in patients who have not responded to drug therapy (Bailine et al., 2010; Fink, 2009; Lima et al., 2013; Medda et al., 2015). After three such sessions each week for two to four weeks, 70 percent or more of those receiving ECT improve markedly. They show some memory loss for the treatment period but no apparent brain damage (Bergsholm et al., 1989; Coffey, 1993). Modern ECT causes less memory disruption than earlier versions did (HMHL, 2007). ECT also reduces suicidal

thoughts and is credited with saving many from suicide (Kellner et al., 2005). The *Journal of the American Medical Association*'s conclusion: "The results of ECT in treating severe depression are among the most positive treatment effects in all of medicine" (Glass, 2001).

How does ECT relieve severe depression? After more than 75 years, no one knows for sure. One patient compared ECT to the smallpox vaccine, which was saving lives before we knew how it worked. Perhaps the brief electric current calms neural centers where overactivity produces depression. Some research indicates that ECT works by weakening connections in a "hyperconnected" neural hub in the left frontal lobe (Perrin et al., 2012).

No matter how impressive the results, the idea of electrically shock-

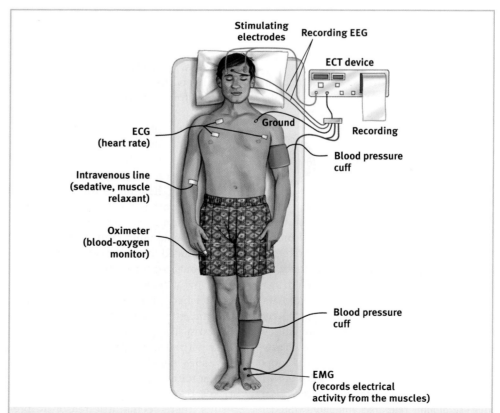

FIGURE 14.5 Electroconvulsive therapy Although controversial, ECT is often an effective treatment for depression that does not respond to drug therapy. ("Electroconvulsive" is no longer accurate, because patients are now given a drug that prevents bodily convulsions.)

ing a person's brain still strikes many as barbaric, especially given our ignorance about why ECT works. Moreover, the mood boost may not last long. About 4 in 10 ECT-treated patients have relapsed into depression within six months, with or without follow-up drug therapy (Kellner et al., 2006; Tew et al., 2007).

Nevertheless, in the minds of many psychiatrists and patients, ECT is a lesser evil than severe depression's misery, anguish, and risk of suicide. As one psychologist reported after ECT relieved his deep depression, "A miracle had happened in two weeks" (Endler, 1982).

Alternative Neurostimulation Therapies

Two other neural stimulation techniques—magnetic stimulation and deep brain stimulation—also treat the depressed brain.

MAGNETIC STIMULATION Depressed moods sometimes improve when repeated pulses surge through a magnetic coil held close to a person's skull (**FIGURE 14.6**). The painless procedure—called **repetitive transcranial magnetic stimulation (rTMS)**—is performed on wide-awake patients over several weeks. Unlike ECT, the rTMS procedure produces no memory loss or other serious side effects, aside from possible headaches.

Initial studies have found a small antidepressant benefit of rTMS (Lepping et al., 2014). How it works is unclear. One possible explanation is that the stimulation energizes the brain's left frontal lobe, which is relatively inactive during depression (Helmuth, 2001). Repeated stimulation may cause nerve cells to form new

A DEPRESSION SWITCH? By comparing the brains of patients with and without depression, researcher Helen Mayberg identified a brain area (highlighted in red) that appears active in people who are depressed or sad, and whose activity may be calmed by deep brain stimulation.

functioning circuits through the process of long-term potentiation. (For more on long-term potentiation, see Chapter 7.) Not all researchers agree that rTMS reduces depressive symptoms (De Raedt et al., 2015). More research will shed light on how rTMS works and whether it's reliable.

DEEP BRAIN STIMULATION Other patients whose depression has resisted both drugs and ECT have benefited from an experimental treatment pinpointing a brain depression center. *Deep brain stimulation* manipulates the depressed brain by means of a pacemaker that activates implanted electrodes in brain areas that feed negative emotions and thoughts (Lozano et al., 2008; Mayberg et al., 2005). The stimulation inhibits activity

electroconvulsive therapy (ECT) a biomedical therapy for severely depressed patients in which a brief electric current is sent through the brain of an anesthetized patient.

repetitive transcranial magnetic stimulation (rTMS) the application of repeated pulses of magnetic energy to the brain; used to stimulate or suppress brain activity.

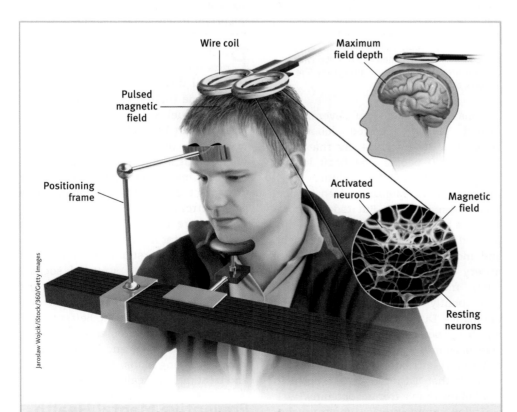

FIGURE 14.6 Magnets for the mind Repetitive transcranial magnetic stimulation (rTMS) sends a painless magnetic field through the skull to the surface of the brain. Pulses can be used to alter activity in various brain areas.

in those brain areas. With deep brain stimulation, some patients have found their depression lifting. Others have become more responsive to drugs or psychotherapy.

Deep brain stimulation may also show promise in other treatment areas. Researchers are exploring whether this technique can relieve obsessive-compulsive disorder and drug and alcohol addictions (Corse et al., 2013; Kisely et al., 2014; Luigjes et al., 2012).

Retrieve + Remember

- Severe depression that has not responded to other therapy may be treated with _____ _____, which can cause memory loss for the immediate past. More moderate neural stimulation techniques designed to help alleviate depression include _____ _____ stimulation and _____ magnetic stimulation.

ANSWERS: electroconvulsive therapy (ECT); repetitive transcranial; deep brain

Psychosurgery

Psychosurgery is surgery that removes or destroys brain tissue in an attempt to change thoughts and behaviors. Because its effects are irreversible, it is the least-used biomedical therapy.

In the 1930s, Portuguese physician Egas Moniz developed what would become the best-known psychosurgical operation: the **lobotomy.** He (and, later, other neurosurgeons) used it to calm uncontrollably emotional and violent patients. This crude but easy and inexpensive procedure took only about 10 minutes:

- *Step* 1. Shock the patient into a coma.
- *Step* 2. Hammer an instrument shaped like an icepick through the top of each eye socket. Drive it into the brain.
- *Step* 3. Wiggle the instrument to cut nerves connecting the frontal lobes with the emotion-controlling centers of the inner brain.

New York Times Co./Getty Images

FAILED LOBOTOMY This 1940 photo shows Rosemary Kennedy (center) at age 22, with brother (and future U.S. president) John and sister Jean. A year later her father, on medical advice, approved a lobotomy that was promised to control her reportedly violent mood swings. The procedure left her confined to a hospital with an infantile mentality for the next 63 years. She died in 2005, at age 86.

Tens of thousands of severely disturbed people received lobotomies between 1936 and 1954. By that time, some 35,000 people had been lobotomized in the United States alone.

For his work, Moniz received a Nobel Prize (Valenstein, 1986). But today, lobotomies are history. Their intention was simply to disconnect emotion from thought, and indeed, they did usually decrease misery or tension. But their effect was often more drastic, leaving people permanently listless, immature, and uncreative. During the 1950s, when calming drugs became available, psychosurgery became scorned—as in the saying sometimes attributed to comedian W. C. Fields that "I'd rather have a bottle in front of me than a frontal lobotomy."

Today, more precise micropsychosurgery is sometimes used in extreme cases. For example, if a patient has uncontrollable seizures, surgeons can destroy the specific nerve clusters that cause or transmit the convulsions. MRI-guided precision surgery is also occasionally done to cut the circuits involved in severe obsessive-compulsive disorder (Carey, 2009, 2011; Sachdev & Sachdev, 1997). Because these procedures cannot be reversed, neurosurgeons perform them only as a last resort.

* * *

TABLE 14.3 summarizes the therapies discussed in this chapter.

Preventing Psychological Disorders and Building Resilience

LOQ 14-16 What may help prevent psychological disorders, and why is it important to develop resilience?

Psychotherapies and biomedical therapies tend to locate the cause of psychological disorders within the person. We assume that people who act cruelly must be cruel and that people who act "crazy" must be "sick." We label people to separate them from "normal" folks. We try to treat "abnormal" people by giving them insight into their problems, by changing their thinking, by helping them gain control with drugs.

But there is another viewpoint. We could interpret many psychological disorders as understandable responses to a disturbing and stressful society. According to this view, it is not just the person who needs treatment, but also the person's social context. Better to prevent mental health problems by reforming a sick situation, and by developing people's coping skills, than to wait for and treat mental health problems.

Preventive Mental Health

A story about the rescue of a drowning person from a rushing river illustrates prevention. Having successfully given

TABLE 14.3 Comparing Therapeutic Approaches

Therapy	Presumed Problem	Therapy Aim	Therapy Technique
Psychodynamic	Unconscious conflicts from childhood experiences	Reduce anxiety through self-insight.	Interpret patients' memories and feelings.
Person-centered	Barriers to self-understanding and self-acceptance	Enable growth via unconditional positive regard, genuineness, acceptance, and empathy.	Listen actively and reflect clients' feelings.
Behavior	Dysfunctional behaviors	Learn adaptive behaviors; extinguish problem behaviors	Use classical conditioning (via exposure or aversion therapy) or operant conditioning (as in token economies).
Cognitive	Negative, self-defeating thinking	Promote healthier thinking and self-talk.	Train people to dispute negative thoughts and attributions.
Cognitive-behavioral	Self-harmful thoughts and behaviors	Promote healthier thinking and adaptive behaviors.	Train people to counter self-harmful thoughts and to act out their new ways of thinking.
Group and family	Stressful relationships	Heal relationships.	Develop an understanding of family and other social systems, explore roles, and improve communication.
Therapeutic lifestyle change	Stress and unhealthy lifestyle	Restore healthy biological state.	Alter lifestyle through adequate exercise, sleep, and other changes.
Drug therapies	Neurotransmitter malfunction	Control symptoms of psychological disorders.	Alter brain chemistry through drugs.
Brain stimulation	Severe, treatment-resistant depression	Alleviate depression that is unresponsive to drug therapy.	Stimulate brain through electroconvulsive shock, magnetic impulses, or deep brain stimulation.
Psychosurgery	Brain malfunction	Relieve severe disorders.	Remove or destroy brain tissue.

first aid to the first victim, the rescuer spots another struggling person and pulls her out, too. After a half-dozen repetitions, the rescuer suddenly turns and starts running away while the river sweeps yet another person into view. "Aren't you going to rescue that fellow?" asks a bystander. "Heck no," the rescuer replies. "I'm going upstream to find out what's pushing all these people in."

Preventive mental health care is upstream work. It aims to prevent psychological casualties by identifying and wiping out the conditions that cause them. Poverty, meaningless work, constant criticism, unemployment, racism, and sexism can undermine people's sense of competence, personal control, and self-esteem (Albee, 1986, 2006). Such stresses increase the risk of depression, alcohol use disorder, and suicide.

To prevent psychological casualties, said psychologist George Albee, caring people should support programs that control or eliminate these stressful situations. We eliminated smallpox not by treating the afflicted but by vaccinating the healthy. We conquered yellow fever by controlling mosquitoes. Better to drain the swamps than just swat the mosquitoes.

Preventing psychological problems means empowering those who have learned an attitude of helplessness and changing environments that breed loneliness. It means renewing fragile family ties. It means boosting parents' and teachers' skills at nurturing children's competence and belief in their abilities. In short, "everything aimed at improving the human condition, at making life more fulfilling and meaningful, may be considered part of primary prevention of mental or emotional disturbance" (Kessler & Albee, 1975, p. 557). Prevention can sometimes provide a double payoff. People with a strong sense of life's meaning are more engaging socially (Stillman et al.,

2011). If we can strengthen people's sense of meaning in life, we may also lessen their loneliness as they grow into more engaging companions.

Among the upstream prevention workers are *community psychologists*. Mindful of how people interact with their environment, they focus on creating environments that support psychological health. Through their research and social action, community psychologists aim to empower people and to enhance their competence, health, and well-being.

psychosurgery surgery that removes or destroys brain tissue in an effort to change behavior.

lobotomy a psychosurgical procedure once used to calm uncontrollably emotional or violent patients. The procedure cut the nerves connecting the frontal lobes to the emotion-controlling centers of the inner brain.

Building Resilience

We have seen that lifestyle change can *lessen* psychological disorders. Might such change also *prevent* some disorders by building individuals' **resilience**—the ability to cope with stress and recover from adversity?

Faced with unforeseen trauma, most adults exhibit resilience. This was true of New Yorkers in the aftermath of the September 11 terror attacks, especially among those who enjoyed supportive close relationships and who had not recently experienced other stressful events (Bonanno et al., 2007). More than 9 in 10 New Yorkers, although stunned and grief-stricken by 9/11, did *not* have a dysfunctional stress reaction. Among those who did have such reactions, the stress symptoms had mostly gone away by the following January (Person et al., 2006). Even most combat-stressed veterans, most political rebels who have survived torture, and most people with spinal cord injuries do not later exhibit posttraumatic stress disorder (Bonanno et al., 2012; Mineka & Zinbarg, 1996).

Struggling with challenging crises can even lead to **posttraumatic growth.** Many cancer survivors have reported a greater appreciation for life, more meaningful relationships, increased personal strength, changed priorities, and a richer spiritual life (Tedeschi & Calhoun, 2004). Out of even our worst experiences, some good can come, especially when we can imagine new possibilities (Roepke, 2015; Roepke & Seligman, 2015). Through preventive efforts, such as community building and personal growth, fewer of us will fall into the rushing river of psychological disorders.

Retrieve + Remember

- What is the difference between preventive mental health and psychological or biomedical therapy?

ANSWER: Psychological and biomedical therapies attempt to relieve people's suffering from psychological disorders. Preventive mental health attempts to prevent suffering by identifying and eliminating the conditions that cause disorders.

* * *

That brings us to the end of this book. Your introduction to psychological science is complete. Navigating through the waters of psychological science has taught us—and you, too?—about our moods and memories, about the inner nooks and crannies of our unconscious, about how our biology and culture in turn shape us. Our hope, as your guides on this tour, is that you have shared some of our fascination, grown in your understanding and compassion, and sharpened your critical thinking. We also hope you enjoyed the ride. We did. With every good wish in your future endeavors,

David Myers

David Myers
DavidMyers.org

Nathan DeWall

Nathan DeWall
NathanDeWall.com

resilience the personal strength that helps most people cope with stress and recover from adversity and even trauma.

posttraumatic growth positive psychological changes as a result of struggling with extremely challenging circumstances and life crises.

CHAPTER REVIEW

Therapy

Test yourself by taking a moment to answer each of these Learning Objective Questions (repeated here from within the chapter). Then turn to Appendix D, Complete Chapter Reviews, to check your answers. Research suggests that trying to answer these questions on your own will improve your long-term memory of the concepts (McDaniel et al., 2009).

Treating Psychological Disorders

14-1: How do psychotherapy and the biomedical therapies differ?

The Psychological Therapies

14-2: What are the goals and techniques of psychoanalysis, and how have they been adapted in psychodynamic therapy?

14-3: What are the basic themes of humanistic therapy, and what are the goals and techniques of Rogers' person-centered approach?

14-4: How does the basic assumption of behavior therapy differ from the assumptions of psychodynamic and humanistic therapies? What techniques are used in exposure therapies and aversive conditioning?

14-5: What is the basic idea of operant conditioning therapies?

14-6: What are the goals and techniques of the cognitive therapies and of cognitive-behavioral therapy?

14-7: What are the aims and benefits of group and family therapies?

Evaluating Psychotherapies

14-8: Does psychotherapy work? How do we know?

14-9: Are some psychotherapies more effective than others for specific disorders?

14-10: What three elements are shared by all forms of psychotherapy?

14-11: How do culture and values influence the client-therapist relationship?

14-12: What should a person look for when selecting a psychotherapist?

The Biomedical Therapies

14-13 Why is therapeutic lifestyle change considered an effective biomedical therapy, and how does it work?

14-14: What are the drug therapies? How do double-blind studies help researchers evaluate a drug's effectiveness?

14-15: How are brain stimulation and psychosurgery used in treating specific disorders?

Preventing Psychological Disorders and Building Resilience

14-16: What may help prevent psychological disorders, and why is it important to develop resilience?

TERMS AND CONCEPTS TO REMEMBER

Test yourself on these terms by trying to write down the definition in your own words before flipping back to the referenced page to check your answer.

psychotherapy, p. 417
biomedical therapy, p. 417
eclectic approach, p. 417
psychoanalysis, p. 417
resistance, p. 417
interpretation, p. 417
transference, p. 417
psychodynamic therapy, p. 417
insight therapies, p. 419
person-centered therapy, p. 419

active listening, p. 419
unconditional positive regard, p. 419
behavior therapy, p. 419
counterconditioning, p. 421
exposure therapies, p. 421
systematic desensitization, p. 421
virtual reality exposure therapy, p. 421

aversive conditioning, p. 421
token economy, p. 423
cognitive therapy, p. 423
cognitive-behavioral therapy (CBT), p. 425
group therapy, p. 425
family therapy, p. 425
evidence-based practice, p. 429
therapeutic alliance, p. 429
antipsychotic drugs, p. 433

antianxiety drugs, p. 433
antidepressant drugs, p. 433
electroconvulsive therapy (ECT), p. 435
repetitive transcranial magnetic stimulation (rTMS), p. 435
psychosurgery, p. 437
lobotomy, p. 437
resilience, p. 438
posttraumatic growth, p. 438

CHAPTER TEST

Test yourself repeatedly throughout your studies. This will not only help you figure out what you know and don't know; the testing itself will help you learn and remember the information more effectively thanks to the *testing effect*.

1. A therapist who helps patients search for the unconscious roots of their problem and offers interpretations of their behaviors, feelings, and dreams, is drawing from
   a. psychoanalysis.
   b. humanistic therapies.
   c. person-centered therapy.
   d. behavior therapy.

2. _____ therapies are designed to help individuals discover the thoughts and feelings that guide their motivation and behavior.

3. Compared with psychoanalysis, humanistic therapies are more likely to emphasize
   a. hidden or repressed feelings.
   b. childhood experiences.
   c. psychological disorders.
   d. self-fulfillment and growth.

4. A therapist who restates and clarifies the client's statements is practicing _____ _____.

5. The goal of behavior therapy is to
   a. identify and treat the underlying causes of the problem.
   b. improve learning and insight.
   c. eliminate the unwanted behavior.
   d. improve communication and social sensitivity.

6. Behavior therapies often use _____ techniques such as systematic desensitization and aversive conditioning to encourage clients to produce new responses to old stimuli.

7. The technique of _____ _____ teaches people to relax in the presence of progressively more anxiety-provoking stimuli.

8. After a near-fatal car accident, Rico developed such an intense fear of driving on the freeway that he takes lengthy alternative routes to work each day. Which psychological therapy might best help Rico overcome his phobia, and why?

9. At a treatment center, people who display a desired behavior receive coins that they can later exchange for other rewards. This is an example of a(n) _____ _____.

10. Cognitive therapy has been especially effective in treating
    a. nail biting.
    b. phobias.
    c. alcohol use disorder.
    d. depression.

11. _____-_____ therapy helps people to change their self-defeating ways of thinking and to act out those changes in their daily behavior.

12. In family therapy, the therapist assumes that
    a. only one family member needs to change.
    b. each person's actions trigger reactions from other family members.
    c. dysfunctional family behaviors are based largely on genetic factors.
    d. therapy is most effective when clients are treated apart from the family unit.

13. The most enthusiastic or optimistic view of the effectiveness of psychotherapy comes from
    a. outcome research.
    b. randomized clinical trials.
    c. reports of clinicians and clients.
    d. a government study of treatment for depression.

14. Studies show that _____ therapy is the most effective treatment for most psychological disorders.
    a. behavior
    b. humanistic
    c. psychodynamic
    d. no one type of

15. What are the three components of evidence-based practice?

16. How does the placebo effect bias patients' attitudes about the effectiveness of drug therapies?

17. Some antipsychotic drugs, used to calm people with schizophrenia, can have unpleasant side effects, including
    a. hyperactivity.
    b. convulsions and momentary memory loss.
    c. sluggishness, tremors, and twitches.
    d. paranoia.

18. Drugs such as Xanax and Ativan, which depress central nervous system activity, can become addictive when used as ongoing treatment. These drugs are referred to as _____ drugs.

19. A simple salt that often brings relief to patients suffering the highs and lows of bipolar disorder is _____.

20. When drug therapies have not been effective, electroconvulsive therapy (ECT) may be used as treatment, largely for people with

 a. severe obsessive-compulsive disorder.

 b. severe depression.

 c. schizophrenia.

 d. anxiety disorders.

21. An approach that seeks to identify and alleviate conditions that put people at high risk for developing psychological disorders is called

 a. deep brain stimulation.

 b. the mood-stabilizing perspective.

 c. natural recovery.

 d. preventive mental health.

Find answers to these questions in Appendix E, in the back of the book.

IN YOUR EVERYDAY LIFE

Answering these questions will help you make these concepts more personally meaningful, and therefore more memorable.

1. What do you think about psychodynamic and humanistic "talk therapy"? Have you ever found yourself using similar ideas when talking with upset friends or family members?

2. Critics say that behavior modification techniques, such as those used in token economies, are not humane. Do you agree or disagree? Why?

3. Have you ever had trouble reaching a goal at school or work because of your own irrational thoughts? How could you challenge these thoughts?

4. How might you use the general helping principles discussed in this chapter during a conversation with a friend who is having family problems?

5. Which lifestyle changes could you make to improve your resilience and enhance your mental health?

6. What were your impressions of biomedical therapies before reading this chapter? Are any of your views different now? Why or why not?

Use **LearningCurve** to create your personalized study plan, which will direct you to the resources that will help you most in **LaunchPad**.

Statistical Reasoning in Everyday Life

Statistics are important tools in psychological research. But accurate statistical understanding benefits everyone. To be an educated person today is to be able to apply simple statistical principles to everyday reasoning. We needn't memorize complicated formulas to think more clearly and critically about data.

Off-the-top-of-the-head estimates often misread reality and can mislead the public. Someone throws out a big, round number. Others echo it, and before long the big, round number becomes public misinformation. Here are a few examples:

- *Ten percent of people are gay or lesbian.* Or is it 2 to 4 percent, as suggested by various national surveys (Chapter 4)?
- *We ordinarily use only 10 percent of our brain.* Or is it closer to 100 percent (Chapter 2)?
- *The human brain has 100 billion nerve cells.* Or is it more like 86 billion, as suggested by one analysis (Chapter 2)?

The point to remember: Doubt big, round, undocumented numbers.

When setting goals, we love big, round numbers. We're far more likely to want to lose 20 pounds than 19 or 21 pounds. And by modifying their behavior, batters are nearly four times more likely to finish the season with a .300 average than with a .299 average (Pope & Simonsohn, 2011).

Statistical illiteracy also feeds needless health scares (Gigerenzer, 2010; Gigerenzer et al., 2008, 2009). In the 1990s, the British press reported a study showing that women taking a particular contraceptive pill had a 100 percent increased risk of blood clots that could produce strokes. This caused thousands of women to stop taking the pill, leading to a wave of unwanted pregnancies and an estimated 13,000 additional abortions (which also are associated with increased blood clot risk). And what did

"*Figures can be misleading—so I've written a song which I think expresses the real story of the firm's performance this quarter.*"

Patrick Hardin

the study actually find? A 100 percent increased risk, indeed—but only from 1 in 7000 to 2 in 7000. Such false alarms underscore the need to teach statistical reasoning and to present statistical information more transparently.

Describing Data

LOQ **L**earning**O**bjective**Q**uestion

A-1 How do we describe data using three measures of central tendency, and what is the relative usefulness of the two measures of variation?

Once researchers have gathered their data, they may organize the data using *descriptive statistics*. One way to do this is to convert the data into a simple *bar graph*, as in **FIGURE A.1**, which displays a distribution of different brands of trucks still on the road after a decade. When reading statistical graphs such as this one, take care. It's easy to design a graph to make a difference look big (Figure A.1a) or small (Figure A.1b). The secret lies in how you label the vertical scale (the *y-axis*).

The point to remember: Think smart. When viewing graphs, read the scale labels and note their range.

Measures of Central Tendency

The next step is to summarize the data using some *measure of central tendency*, a single score that represents a whole set of scores. The simplest measure is

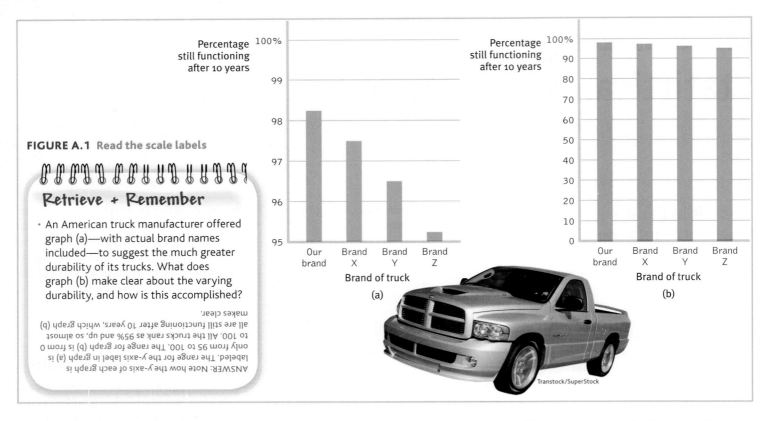

FIGURE A.1 Read the scale labels

Transtock/SuperStock

Retrieve + Remember

- An American truck manufacturer offered graph (a)—with actual brand names included—to suggest the much greater durability of its trucks. What does graph (b) make clear about the varying durability, and how is this accomplished?

ANSWER: Note how the y-axis of each graph is labeled. The range for the y-axis label in graph (a) is only from 95 to 100. The range for graph (b) is from 0 to 100. All the trucks rank as 95% and up, so almost all are still functioning after 10 years, which graph (b) makes clear.

the **mode,** the most frequently occurring score or scores. The most familiar is the **mean,** or arithmetic average—the total sum of all the scores divided by the number of scores. The midpoint—the 50th percentile—is the **median.** On a divided highway, the median is the middle. So, too, with data: If you arrange all the scores in order from the highest to the lowest, half will be above the median and half will be below it.

> The average person has one ovary and one testicle.

Measures of central tendency neatly summarize data. But consider what happens to the mean when a distribution is lopsided, when it's *skewed* by a few way-out scores. With income data, for example, the mode, median, and mean often tell very different stories (**FIGURE A.2**). This happens because the mean is biased by a few extreme scores. When Microsoft co-founder Bill Gates sits down in a small café, its average (mean) customer instantly becomes a billionaire. But the median customer's wealth remains un-

changed. Understanding this, you can see why, according to the 2010 U.S. Census, nearly 65 percent of U.S. households have "below average" income. The bottom half of earners receive much less than half the national income cake. So, most Americans make less than the mean. Mean and median tell different true stories.

The point to remember: Always note which measure of central tendency is reported. If it is a mean, consider whether a few atypical scores could be distorting it.

Measures of Variation

Knowing the value of an appropriate measure of central tendency can tell us a great deal. But the single number omits other information. It helps to know something about the amount of *variation* in the data—how similar or diverse the scores are. Averages derived from scores with low variability are more reliable than averages based on scores with high variability. Consider a basketball player who scored between 13 and 17 points in each of the season's first 10 games. Knowing this, we would be more confident that she would score near 15 points in her next game than

if her scores had varied from 5 to 25 points.

The **range** of scores—the gap between the lowest and highest—provides only a crude estimate of variation. In an otherwise similar group, a couple of extreme scores, such as the $950,000 and $1,420,000 incomes in Figure A.2, will create a deceptively large range.

The more useful standard for measuring how much scores deviate from one another is the **standard deviation.** It better gauges whether scores are packed together or dispersed, because it uses information from each score. The computation[1] assembles information about how much individual scores differ from the mean, which can be very telling. Let's say test scores from Class A and Class B both have the same mean (75 percent), but very different standard deviations (5.0 for Class A and 15.0 for Class B). Have you ever had test experiences like that—where two-thirds of your classmates in one course score in the 70 to 80 percent range, with scores in another

---

[1] The actual standard deviation formula:

$$\sqrt{\dfrac{Sum\ of\ (deviations)^2}{Number\ of\ scores}}$$

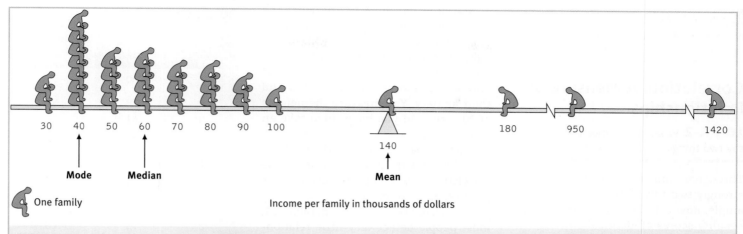

FIGURE A.2 A skewed distribution This graphic representation of the distribution of a village's incomes illustrates the three measures of central tendency—mode, median, and mean. Note how just a few high incomes make the mean—the point that balances the incomes above and below—deceptively high.

course more spread out (two-thirds between 60 and 90)? The standard deviation tells us more about how each class is really faring than does the mean score alone. As another example, consider varsity and intramural sports. A school's varsity volleyball players' ability levels will have a relatively small standard deviation compared with the more diverse ability levels found in those playing on intramural volleyball teams.

You can grasp the meaning of the standard deviation if you consider how scores naturally tend to be distributed. Large numbers of data—heights, weights, intelligence scores, grades (though not

incomes)—often form a symmetrical, bell-shaped distribution. Most cases fall near the mean, and fewer cases fall near either extreme. This bell-shaped distribution is so typical that we call the curve it forms the **normal curve**.

As **FIGURE A.3** shows, a useful property of the normal curve is that roughly 68 percent of the cases fall within one standard deviation on either side of the mean. About 95 percent of cases fall within two standard deviations. Thus, as Chapter 8 notes, about 68 percent of people taking an intelligence test will score within ±15 points of 100. About 95 percent will score within ±30 points.

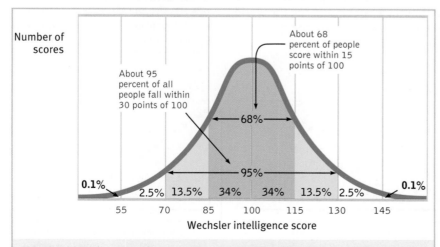

FIGURE A.3 The normal curve Scores on aptitude tests tend to form a normal, or bell-shaped, curve. For example, the most commonly used intelligence test, the Wechsler Adult Intelligence Scale, calls the average score 100.

mode the most frequently occurring score(s) in a distribution.

mean the arithmetic average of a distribution, obtained by adding the scores and then dividing by the number of scores.

median the middle score in a distribution; half the scores are above it and half are below it.

range the difference between the highest and lowest scores in a distribution.

standard deviation a computed measure of how much scores vary around the mean score.

normal curve (normal distribution) a symmetrical, bell-shaped curve that describes the distribution of many types of data; most scores fall near the mean (about 68 percent fall within one standard deviation of it) and fewer and fewer near the extremes.

LaunchPad   For an interactive tutorial on these statistical concepts, visit LaunchPad's *PsychSim 6: Descriptive Statistics*.

Correlation: A Measure of Relationships

LOQ A-2 What does it mean when we say two things are correlated?

Throughout this book, we often ask how strongly two things are related: For example, how closely related are the personality scores of identical twins? How well do intelligence test scores predict career achievement? How closely is stress related to disease?

As we saw in Chapter 1, describing behavior is a first step toward predicting it. When naturalistic observation and surveys reveal that one trait or behavior accompanies another, we say the two *correlate*. A **correlation coefficient** is a statistical measure of relationship. In such cases, **scatterplots** can be very revealing.

Each dot in a scatterplot represents the values of two variables. The three scatterplots in **FIGURE A.4** illustrate the range of possible correlations—from a perfect positive to a perfect negative. (Perfect correlations rarely occur in the real world.) A correlation is positive if two sets of scores, such as height and weight, tend to rise or fall together.

Saying that a correlation is "negative" says nothing about its strength. A correlation is negative if two sets of scores relate inversely, one set going up as the other goes down.

Statistics can help us see what the naked eye sometimes misses. To demonstrate this for yourself, try an imaginary project. You wonder if tall men are more or less easygoing, so you collect two sets of scores: men's heights and their anxiety. You measure the heights of 20 men, and you have them take an anxiety test.

With all the relevant data right in front of you (**TABLE A.1**), can you tell whether the correlation between height and anxiety is positive, negative, or close to zero?

Comparing the columns in Table A.1, most people detect very little relationship between height and anxiety. In fact, the correlation in this imaginary example is positive (+0.63), as we can see if we display the data as a scatterplot (**FIGURE A.5**).

If we fail to see a relationship when data are presented as systematically as in Table A.1, how much less likely are we to notice them in everyday life? To see what is right in front of us, we sometimes need statistical illumination. We can easily see evidence of gender discrimination when given statistically summarized information about job level, seniority, performance, gender, and salary. But we often see no discrimination when the same information dribbles in, case by case (Twiss et al., 1989).

The point to remember: Correlation coefficients tell us nothing about cause and effect, but they can help us see the world more clearly by revealing the extent to which two things relate.

TABLE A.1 Height and Anxiety Scores of 20 Men		
Person	Height in Inches	Anxiety Score
1	80	75
2	63	66
3	61	60
4	79	90
5	74	60
6	69	42
7	62	42
8	75	60
9	77	81
10	60	39
11	64	48
12	76	69
13	71	72
14	66	57
15	73	63
16	70	75
17	63	30
18	71	57
19	68	84
20	70	39

LaunchPad   For an animated tutorial on correlations, see LaunchPad's *Concept Practice: Positive and Negative Correlations*. See also LaunchPad's *Video: Correlational Studies* for another helpful tutorial animation.

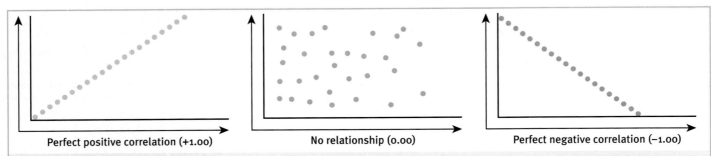

Perfect positive correlation (+1.00)   No relationship (0.00)   Perfect negative correlation (−1.00)

FIGURE A.4 Scatterplots, showing patterns of correlation Correlations can range from +1.00 (scores on one measure increase in direct proportion to scores on another), to 0.00 (no relationship), to −1.00 (scores on one measure decrease precisely as scores rise on the other).

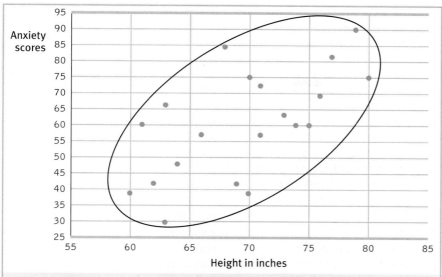

FIGURE A.5 Scatterplot for height and anxiety This display of data from 20 imagined people (each represented by a data point) reveals an upward slope, indicating a positive correlation. The considerable scatter of the data indicates the correlation is much lower than +1.00.

Regression Toward the Mean

LOQ A-3 What is regression toward the mean?

Correlations not only make visible the relationships we might otherwise miss, they also restrain our "seeing" nonexistent relationships. When we believe there is a relationship between two things, we are likely to notice and recall instances that confirm our belief. If we believe that dreams are forecasts of actual events, we may notice and recall confirming instances more than disconfirming instances. The result is an *illusory correlation*.

Illusory correlations feed an illusion of control—that chance events are subject to our personal control. Gamblers, remembering their lucky rolls, may come to believe they can influence the roll of the dice by again throwing gently for low numbers and hard for high numbers. The illusion that uncontrollable events correlate with our actions is also fed by a statistical phenomenon called **regression toward the mean**. Average results are more typical than extreme results. Thus, after an unusual event, things tend to return toward their average level; extraordinary happenings tend to be followed by more ordinary ones.

"Once you become sensitized to it, you see regression everywhere."
Psychologist Daniel Kahneman (1985)

The point may seem obvious, yet we regularly miss it: We sometimes attribute what may be a normal regression (the expected return to normal) to something we have done. Consider two examples:

- Students who score much lower or higher on an exam than they usually do are likely, when retested, to return to their average.

- Unusual ESP subjects who defy chance when first tested nearly always lose their "psychic powers" when retested (a phenomenon parapsychologists have called the *decline effect*).

Failure to recognize regression is the source of many superstitions and of some ineffective practices as well. When day-to-day behavior has a large element of chance fluctuation, we may notice that others' behavior improves (regresses toward average) after we criticize them for very bad performance, and that it worsens (regresses toward average) after we warmly praise them for an exceptionally fine performance. Ironically, then, regression toward the average can mislead us into feeling rewarded for having criticized others and into feeling punished for having praised them (Tversky & Kahneman, 1974).

The point to remember: When a fluctuating behavior returns to normal, there is no need to invent fancy explanations for why it does so. Regression toward the mean is probably at work.

Significant Differences

LOQ A-4 How do we know whether an observed difference can be generalized to other populations?

Data are "noisy." The average score in one group could conceivably differ from the average score in another group

correlation coefficient a statistical index of the relationship between two things (from −1.00 to +1.00).

scatterplot a graphed cluster of dots, each of which represents the values of two variables. The slope of the points suggests the direction of the relationship between the two variables. The amount of scatter suggests the strength of the correlation (little scatter indicates high correlation).

regression toward the mean the tendency for extreme or unusual scores or events to fall back (regress) toward the average.

not because of any real difference but merely because of chance fluctuations in the people sampled. How confidently, then, can we *infer* that an observed difference is not just a fluke—a chance result from the research sample? For guidance, we can ask whether the observed difference between the two groups is reliable and significant. These *inferential statistics* help us determine if results describe a larger population.

When Is an Observed Difference Reliable?

In deciding when it is safe to generalize from a sample, we should keep three principles in mind:

1. **Representative samples are better than biased (unrepresentative) samples.** The best basis for generalizing is from a representative sample of cases, not from the exceptional and memorable cases one finds at the extremes. Research never randomly samples the whole human population. Thus, it pays to keep in mind what population a study has sampled. (To see how an unrepresentative sample can lead you astray, see Thinking Critically About: Cross-Sectional and Longitudinal Studies.)

2. **Less-variable observations are more reliable than those that are more variable.** As we noted earlier in the example of the basketball player whose game-to-game points were consistent, an average is more reliable when it comes from scores with low variability.

3. **More cases are better than fewer cases.** An eager prospective student visits two university campuses, each for a day. At the first, the student randomly attends two classes and discovers both instructors to be witty and engaging. At the next campus, the two sampled instructors seem dull and uninspiring. Returning home, the student (dis-

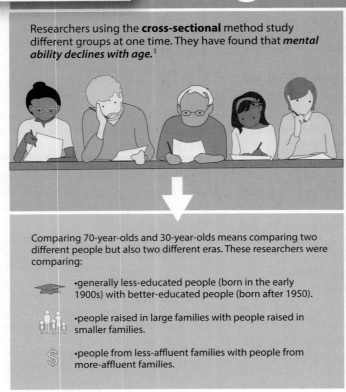
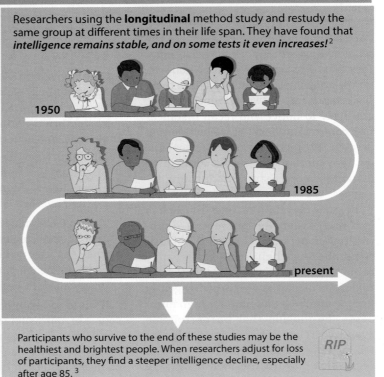

Thinking Critically About:

Cross-Sectional and Longitudinal Studies

LOQ A-5 What are cross-sectional studies and longitudinal studies, and why is it important to know which method was used?

Researchers using the **cross-sectional** method study different groups at one time. They have found that *mental ability declines with age.*[1]

Comparing 70-year-olds and 30-year-olds means comparing two different people but also two different eras. These researchers were comparing:

- •generally less-educated people (born in the early 1900s) with better-educated people (born after 1950).
- •people raised in large families with people raised in smaller families.
- •people from less-affluent families with people from more-affluent families.

Researchers using the **longitudinal** method study and restudy the same group at different times in their life span. They have found that *intelligence remains stable, and on some tests it even increases!*[2]

1950

1985

present

Participants who survive to the end of these studies may be the healthiest and brightest people. When researchers adjust for loss of participants, they find a steeper intelligence decline, especially after age 85.[3]

RIP

1. Wechsler, 1972.   2. Salthouse, 2004, 2010; Schaie & Geiwitz, 1982.   3. Brayne et al., 1999.

counting the small sample size of only two teachers at each institution) tells friends about the "great teachers" at the first school, and the "bores" at the second. Again, we know it but we ignore it: *Averages based on many cases are more reliable (less variable) than averages based on only a few cases.*

The point to remember: Smart thinkers are not overly impressed by a few anecdotes. Generalizations based on a few unrepresentative cases are unreliable.

When Is an Observed Difference "Significant"?

Perhaps you've compared men's and women's scores on a laboratory test of aggression, and you've found a gender difference. But individuals differ. How likely is it that the difference you observed was just a fluke? Statistical testing can estimate the probability of the result occurring by chance.

Here is the underlying logic: When averages from two samples are each reliable measures of their respective populations (as when each is based on many observations that have small variability), then their *difference* is probably reliable as well. (Example: The less the variability in women's and in men's aggression scores, the more confidence we would have that any observed gender difference is reliable.) And when the difference between the sample averages is *large,* we have even more confidence that the difference

between them reflects a real difference in their populations.

In short, when sample averages are reliable, and when the difference between them is relatively large, we say the difference has **statistical significance.** This means that the observed difference is probably not due to chance variation between the samples.

In judging statistical significance, psychologists are conservative. They are like juries who must presume innocence until guilt is proven. For most psychologists, proof beyond a reasonable doubt means not making much of a finding unless the odds of its occurring by chance, if no real effect exists, are less than 5 percent.

When reading about research, you should remember that, given large enough samples, a difference between them may be "statistically significant" yet have little practical significance. For example, comparisons of intelligence test scores among hundreds of thousands of first-born and later-born individuals indicate a highly significant tendency for first-born individuals to have higher average scores than their later-born siblings (Rohrer et al., 2015; Zajonc & Markus, 1975). But because the scores differ by only one to three points, the difference has little practical importance.

The point to remember: Statistical significance indicates the *likelihood* that a result will happen by chance. But this does not say anything about the *importance* of the result.

Retrieve + Remember

- Can you solve this puzzle?

The registrar's office at the University of Michigan has found that usually about 100 students in Arts and Sciences have perfect marks at the end of their first term at the university. However, only about 10 to 15 students graduate with perfect marks. What do you think is the most likely explanation for the fact that there are more perfect marks after one term than at graduation (Jepson et al., 1983)?

ANSWER: Averages based on fewer courses are more variable, which guarantees a greater number of extremely low and high marks at the end of the first term.

- _____ statistics summarize data, while _____ statistics determine if data can be generalized to other populations.

ANSWERS: Descriptive; inferential

LaunchPad For a 9.5-minute video summary of psychology's scientific research strategies, visit LaunchPad's *Video: Research Methods.*

cross-sectional study research in which people of different ages are compared with one another.

longitudinal study research in which the same people are restudied and retested over a long period of time.

statistical significance a statistical statement of how likely it is that an obtained result occurred by chance.

PEANUTS

APPENDIX A REVIEW

Statistical Reasoning in Everyday Life

Test yourself by taking a moment to answer each of these Learning Objective Questions (repeated here from within the appendix). Then turn to Appendix D, Complete Chapter Reviews, to check your answers. Research suggests that trying to answer these questions on your own will improve your long-term memory of the concepts (McDaniel et al., 2009).

Describing Data

A-1: How do we describe data using three measures of central tendency, and what is the relative usefulness of the two measures of variation?

A-2: What does it mean when we say two things are correlated?

A-3: What is regression toward the mean?

Significant Differences

A-4: How do we know whether an observed difference can be generalized to other populations?

A-5: What are cross-sectional studies and longitudinal studies, and why is it important to know which method was used?

TERMS AND CONCEPTS TO REMEMBER

Test yourself on these terms by trying to write down the definition in your own words before flipping back to the referenced page to check your answer.

mode, p. A-3	range, p. A-3	correlation coefficient, p. A-5	cross-sectional study, p. A-7
mean, p. A-3	standard deviation, p. A-3	scatterplot, p. A-5	longitudinal study, p. A-7
median, p. A-3	normal curve, p. A-3	regression toward the mean, p. A-5	statistical significance, p. A-7

APPENDIX A TEST

Test yourself repeatedly throughout your studies. This will not only help you figure out what you know and don't know; the testing itself will help you learn and remember the information more effectively thanks to the *testing effect*.

1. Which of the three measures of central tendency is most easily distorted by a few very large or very small scores?

   a. The mode

   b. The mean

   c. The median

   d. They are all equally vulnerable to distortion from atypical scores.

2. The standard deviation is the most useful measure of variation in a set of data because it tells us

   a. the difference between the highest and lowest scores in the set.

   b. the extent to which the sample being used deviates from the bigger population it represents.

   c. how much individual scores differ from the mode.

   d. how much individual scores differ from the mean.

3. Another name for a bell-shaped distribution, in which most scores fall near the middle and fewer scores fall at each extreme, is a _____ _____.

4. In a _____ correlation, the scores rise and fall together; in a(n) _____ correlation, one score falls as the other rises.

   a. positive; negative   c. negative; inverse

   b. positive; illusory   d. strong; weak

5. If a study revealed that tall people were less intelligent than short people, this would suggest that the correlation between height and intelligence is _____ (positive/negative).

6. A _____ provides a visual representation of the direction and the strength of a relationship between two variables.

7. What is regression toward the mean, and how can it influence our interpretation of events?

8. In _____-_____ studies, a characteristic is assessed across different age groups at the same time.

9. When sample averages are _____ and the difference between them is _____, we can say the difference has statistical significance.

a. reliable; large

c. due to chance; large

b. reliable; small

d. due to chance; small

Find answers to these questions in Appendix E.

Use 📖 LearningCurve to create your personalized study plan, which will direct you to the resources that will help you most in 📖 LaunchPad.

Psychology at Work

———

For most people, to live is to work. Work is life's biggest single waking activity, helping to satisfy several levels of our needs. Work supports us, giving us food, water, and shelter. Work connects us, meeting our social needs. Work defines us, satisfying our self-esteem needs. Work helps us understand people we've met for the first time. Wondering who they are, we may ask, "So, what do you do?"

The answer, however, may give us only a fleeting snapshot of that person at a particular time and place. On the day we retire from the workforce, few of us will look back and say we have followed a predictable career path. We will have changed jobs, some of us often. The trigger for those changes may have been shifting needs in the economy. Or it may have been a desire for better pay, happier on-the-job relationships, or more fulfilling work.

THE JOBS PEOPLE DO: Columnist Gene Weingarten (2002) noted that sometimes a humor writer knows "when to just get out of the way." Here are some sample job titles from the U.S. Department of Labor *Dictionary of Occupational Titles*: animal impersonator, human projectile, banana ripening-room supervisor, impregnator, impregnator helper, dope sprayer, finger waver, rug scratcher, egg smeller, bottom buffer, cookie breaker, brain picker, hand pouncer, bosom presser, mother repairer.

Work and Life Satisfaction

Discovering Your Interests and Strengths

LOQ **L**earning**O**bjective**Q**uestion

B-1 What is *flow?*

Across various occupations, attitudes toward work tend to fall into one of three categories (Wrzesniewski & Dutton, 2001; Wrzesniewski et al.). Some people view their work as a *job*, an unfulfilling but necessary way to make money. Others view their work as a *career*. Their present position may not be ideal, but it is at least a rung on a ladder leading to increasingly better options. The third group views their work as a *calling*. For them, work is a fulfilling and socially useful activity. Of all these groups, those who see their work as a calling report the highest satisfaction with their work and their lives (Dik & Duffy, 2012).

This finding would not surprise Mihaly Csikszentmihalyi (1990, 1999). He observed that quality of life increases when people are purposefully engaged. Between the anxiety of being overwhelmed and stressed, and the apathy of being underwhelmed and bored, lies **flow**. In this intense, focused state, our skills are totally engaged, and we may lose our awareness of self and time. Can you recall being in a zoned-out flow state while texting or playing an online game? If so, then perhaps you can sympathize with the two Northwest Airlines pilots who in 2009 were so focused on their laptops that they missed Earth-to-pilot messages from their control tower. The pilots flew 150 miles past their Minneapolis destination—and lost their jobs.

Csikszentmihalyi [Chick-SENT-me-hi] came up with the flow concept while studying artists who spent hour after

flow a completely involved, focused state, with lowered awareness of self and time; results from full engagement of our skills.

LIFE DISRUPTED Playing and socializing online are ever-present sources of distraction. It takes energy to resist checking our phones, and time to refocus mental concentration after each disruption. Such frequent interruptions disrupt flow, so it's a good idea to instead schedule regular breaks for checking our handheld devices.

hour wrapped up in a project. After painting or sculpting for hours as if nothing else mattered, they finished and appeared to forget about the project. The artists seemed driven less by external rewards—money, praise, promotion—than by the internal rewards for creating the work. They do what they love, and love what they do.

Fascinated, Csikszentmihalyi broadened his observations. He studied dancers, chess players, surgeons, writers, parents, mountain climbers, sailors, and farmers. His research included Australians, North Americans, Koreans, Japanese, and Italians. Participants ranged from the teen years to the golden years. A clear principle emerged: It's exhilarating to flow with an activity that fully engages our skills (Fong et al., 2015). Flow experiences boost our sense of self-esteem, competence, and well-being. Idleness may sound like bliss, but purposeful work enriches our lives. Busy people are happier (Hsee et al., 2010; Robinson & Martin, 2008). One research team interrupted people on about a quarter-million occasions (using a smart-phone app), and found people's minds wandering 47 percent of the time. They were, on average, happier when not mind-wandering (Killingsworth & Gilbert, 2010).

Finding Your Own Flow

Want to identify your own path to flow? You can start by pinpointing your strengths and the types of work that may prove satisfying and successful. Marcus Buckingham and Donald Clifton (2001) have suggested asking yourself four questions.

1. What activities give me pleasure? Bringing order out of chaos? Playing host? Helping others? Challenging sloppy thinking?

2. What activities leave me wondering, "When can I do this again?" rather than, "When will this be over?"

3. What sorts of challenges do I relish? And which do I dread?

4. What sorts of tasks do I learn easily? And which do I struggle with?

You may find your skills engaged and time flying when teaching or selling or writing or cleaning or consoling or creating or repairing. If an activity feels good, if it comes easily, if you look forward to it, then look deeper. You'll see your strengths at work (Buckingham, 2007). For a free (requires registration) assessment of your own strengths, take the "Brief Strengths Test" at AuthenticHappiness.sas.upenn.edu.

The U.S. Department of Labor also offers a career interest questionnaire through its Occupational Information Network (O*NET). At MyNextMove.org/explore/ip you will need about 10 minutes to respond to 60 items, indicating how much you would like or dislike activities ranging from building kitchen cabinets to playing a musical instrument. You will then receive feedback on how strongly your responses reflect six interest types (Holland, 1996):

- *Realistic* (hands-on doers)
- *Investigative* (thinkers)
- *Artistic* (creators)
- *Social* (helpers, teachers)
- *Enterprising* (persuaders, deciders)
- *Conventional* (organizers)

Finally, depending on how much training you are willing to complete, you will

be shown occupations that fit your interest pattern (selected from a national database of 900+ occupations). A more comprehensive (and fee-based) online service, called VIP, assesses people's values, interests, and personalities; suggests occupations; and connects people to job listings at Jobzology.com.

Top performers are "rarely well rounded" (Buckingham & Clifton, 2001, p. 26). Satisfied and successful people devote far less time to correcting their weaknesses than to sharpening their existing skills. Given how stable our traits and temperaments are, this is probably wise. There may be limits to the benefits of assertiveness training if you are shy, or of public speaking courses if you tend to be nervous and soft-spoken. Drawing classes may not help much if you express your artistic side in stick figures. Identifying your talents can help you recognize the activities you learn quickly and find absorbing. Knowing your strengths, you can develop them further.

Retrieve + Remember

- What is the value of finding flow in our work?

ANSWER: We become more likely to view our work as fulfilling and socially useful.

Industrial-Organizational Psychology

LOQ B-2 What are the key fields and subfields related to industrial-organizational psychology?

In developed nations, work has changed, from farming to manufacturing to *knowledge work*. More and more work is *outsourced* to temporary workers who often work off-site, communicating with

THE MODERN WORKFORCE The editorial team that supports the creation of this book and its teaching package works both in-house and from far-flung places. In column 1: Nancy Fleming in Massachusetts, Kathryn Brownson in Michigan, and Katie Pachnos in New York. In column 2: Danielle Slevens in Massachusetts, Lorie Hailey in Kentucky, Trish Morgan in Alberta, and Carlise Stembridge in Minnesota. In column 3: Rachel Losh in New York, Betty Probert in Florida, and Christine Brune in Alaska.

the main office and with one another. (This book and its teaching package are developed and produced by a team of people in a dozen cities, from Alaska to Florida.)

As work changes, have our attitudes toward our work also changed? Has our satisfaction with work increased or decreased? What has happened to the *psychological contract*—that two-way feeling of duty between workers and employers? These are among the questions that fascinate those interested in **industrial-organizational (I/O) psychology**, a profession that applies psychology's principles to the workplace (**TABLE B.1**).

Human factors psychology, now a distinct field allied with I/O psychology, explores how machines and environments can best be designed to fit human abilities. **Personnel psychology** applies psychology's methods and principles to selecting, placing, training, and evaluat-ing workers. **Organizational psychology** is the primary focus of this appendix. This I/O subfield considers an organization's goals, work environments, and management styles, and their influence on worker motivation, satisfaction, and productivity.

Motivating Achievement

LOQ B-3 Why is it important to motivate achievement?

Organizational psychologists help motivate employees and keep them engaged. But what motivates any of us to pursue high standards or difficult goals?

Grit

Think of someone you know who seems driven to be the best—to excel at any task where performance can be judged. Now think of someone who is less driven. For psychologist Henry Murray (1938), the difference between these two people is a reflection of their **achievement motivation**.

TABLE B.1   I/O Psychologists on the Job

As scientists, consultants, and management professionals, industrial-organizational (I/O) psychologists are found working in varied areas:

Human Factors (Engineering) Psychology	Personnel Psychology: Maximizing Human Potential
• Designing optimum work environments • Optimizing person-machine interactions • Developing systems technologies	**Developing training programs to increase job seekers' success** **Selecting and placing employees** • Developing and testing assessment tools for selecting, placing, and promoting workers • Analyzing job content • Optimizing worker placement
Organizational Psychology: Building Better Organizations	
Developing organizations • Analyzing organizational structures • Increasing worker satisfaction and productivity • Fostering organizational change **Enhancing quality of work life** • Expanding individual productivity • Identifying elements of satisfaction • Redesigning jobs • Balancing work and nonwork life in an era of social media, smart phones, and other technologies	**Training and developing employees** • Identifying needs • Designing training programs • Evaluating training programs **Appraising performance** • Developing guidelines • Measuring individual performance • Measuring organizational performance

Source: Information from the Society of Industrial and Organizational Psychology. For more information about I/O psychology and related job opportunities, visit SIOP.org.

industrial-organizational (I/O) psychology the application of psychological concepts and methods to human behavior in workplaces.

human factors psychology a field of psychology allied with I/O psychology that explores how people and machines interact and how machines and physical environments can be made safe and easy to use.

personnel psychology an I/O psychology subfield that helps with job seeking, and with employee recruitment, selection, placement, training, appraisal, and development.

organizational psychology an I/O psychology subfield that examines organizational influences on worker satisfaction and productivity and facilitates organizational change.

achievement motivation a desire for significant accomplishment; for mastery of skills or ideas; for control; and for attaining a high standard.

If you score high in achievement motivation, you have a desire for significant accomplishment, for mastering skills or ideas, for control, and for meeting a high standard.

Achievement motivation matters. Just how much it matters can be seen in a study that followed the lives of 1528 California children. All had scored in the top 1 percent on an intelligence test. Forty years later, researchers compared those who were most and least successful professionally. The most successful were the most highly motivated—they were ambitious, energetic, and persistent. As children, these individuals had enjoyed more active hobbies. As adults, they participated in more groups and preferred *playing* sports over watching sports (Goleman, 1980). Gifted children are able learners. Accomplished adults are determined *doers*. Most of us are energetic doers when starting and finishing a project. It's easiest—have you noticed?—to get "stuck in the middle," which is when high achievers keep going (Bonezzi et al., 2011).

Motivation differences also appear in other studies, including those of high school and college students. Self-discipline, not intelligence score, has been the best predictor of school performance, attendance, and graduation honors. Intense, sustained effort predicts success for teachers, too, especially when combined with a positive enthusiasm. Students of these motivated educators make good academic progress (Duckworth et al., 2009).

"Discipline outdoes talent," conclude researchers Angela Duckworth and Martin Seligman (2005, 2006). It also refines talent. By their early twenties, top violinists have fiddled away 10,000 hours of their life practicing. This is double the practice time of other violin students aiming to be teachers (Ericsson & Pool, 2016).

"*Genius is 1% inspiration and 99% perspiration.*"
Thomas Edison (1847–1931)

Similarly, a study of outstanding scholars, athletes, and artists found that all were highly motivated and self-disciplined. They dedicated hours every day to the pursuit of their goals (Bloom, 1985). These achievers became superstars through daily discipline, not just natural talent. Great achievement, it seems, mixes a teaspoon of inspiration with a gallon of perspiration.

Duckworth (2016) has a name for this passionate dedication to an ambitious, long-term goal: **grit**. Intelligence scores and many other physical and psychological traits can be displayed as a *bell-shaped curve*. Most scores cluster around an average, and fewer scores fall at the two far ends of the bell shape. Achievement scores don't follow this pattern. That is

why organizational psychologists seek ways to engage and motivate ordinary people to be superstars in their own jobs. And that is why training students in *hardiness*—resilience under stress—leads to better grades (Maddi et al., 2009).

Satisfaction and Engagement

I/O psychologists know that everyone wins when workers are satisfied with their jobs. For employees, satisfaction with work, and with one's work-life balance, feeds overall satisfaction with life (Bowling et al., 2010). Moreover, lower job stress feeds improved health (Chapter 10).

How do employers benefit from worker satisfaction? Positive moods

Carol Myers

CALUM'S ROAD: WHAT GRIT CAN ACCOMPLISH Having spent his life on the Scottish island of Raasay, farming a small patch of land, tending its lighthouse, and fishing, Malcolm ("Calum") MacLeod (1911–1988) felt anguished. His local government had repeatedly refused to build a road that would enable vehicles to reach his north end of the island. With the once-flourishing population there having dwindled to two—MacLeod and his wife—he responded with heroic determination. One spring morning in 1964, MacLeod, then in his fifties, gathered an ax, a chopper, a shovel, and a wheelbarrow. By hand, he began to transform the existing footpath into a 1.75 mile road (Miers, 2009).

"With a road," a former neighbor explained, "he hoped new generations of people would return to the north end of Raasay," restoring its culture (Hutchinson, 2006). Day after day he worked through rough hillsides, along hazardous cliff faces, and over peat bogs. Finally, 10 years later, he completed his supreme achievement. The road, which the government has since surfaced, remains a visible example of what vision plus determined grit can accomplish. It bids us each to ponder: What "roads"—what achievements—might we, with sustained effort, build in the years before us?

AN ENGAGED EMPLOYEE Mohamed Mamow, left, was joined by his employer in saying the Pledge of Allegiance as he became a U.S. citizen. Mamow and his wife met in a Somali refugee camp and became parents of five children, whom he has supported by working as a machine operator. Mindful of his responsibility—"I don't like to lose my job. I have a responsibility for my children and my family"—he would arrive for work a half hour early and tend to every detail on his shift. "He is an extremely hard-working employee," noted his employer, and "a reminder to all of us that we are really blessed" (Roelofs, 2010).

Darren Breen/The Grand Rapids Press/Landov

TABLE B.2	Three Types of Employees
Engaged: working with passion and feeling a profound connection to their company or organization.
Not engaged: putting in the time but investing little passion or energy in their work.
Actively disengaged: unhappy workers undermining what their colleagues accomplish.

Source: Information from Gallup via Crabtree, 2005.

can translate into greater creativity, persistence, and helpfulness (Ford et al., 2011; Jeffrey et al., 2014; Shockley et al., 2012). The correlation between individual job satisfaction and performance is modest but real (Judge et al., 2001; Ng et al., 2009; Parker et al., 2003). One analysis tracked 4500 employees at 42 British manufacturing companies. The most productive workers tended to be those in satisfying work environments (Patterson et al., 2004). In the United States, the *Fortune* "100 Best Companies to Work For" have also produced much higher-than-average returns for their investors (Dickler, 2007).

The biggest-ever study of worker satisfaction and job performance was an analysis of Gallup data from more than 198,000 employees (Harter et al., 2002). These people were employed in nearly 8000 business units of 36 large companies, including some 1100 bank branches, 1200 stores, and 4200 teams or departments. The study focused on links between various measures of organizational success and employee engagement—the extent

of workers' involvement, enthusiasm, and identification with their organizations (**TABLE B.2**). The researchers found that engaged workers (compared with not-engaged workers who are just putting in time) know what's expected of them, have what they need to do their work, feel fulfilled in their work, have regular opportunities to do what they do best, perceive that they are part of something significant, and have opportunities to learn and develop. They also found that business units with engaged employees have more loyal customers, less turnover, higher productivity, and greater profits.

But what causal arrows explain this correlation between business success and employee morale and engagement? Does success boost morale, or does high morale boost success? In a follow-up longitudinal study of 142,000 workers, researchers found that, over time, employee attitudes predicted *future* business success (more than the other way around) (Harter et al., 2010). Many other studies confirm that happy workers tend to be good workers (Ford et al., 2011; Seibert et al., 2011; Shockley et al., 2012). One analysis compared companies with top-quartile versus below-average employee engagement levels.

Over a three-year period, earnings grew 2.6 times faster for the companies with highly engaged workers (Ott, 2007).

Leadership

LOQ B-4 How can leaders be most effective?

The best leaders want their organization to be successful. They also want the people who work for them and with them to be satisfied, engaged, and productive. To achieve these ends, effective leaders harness people's strengths, set goals, and choose an appropriate leadership style.

Harnessing Strengths

Engaged employees don't just happen. Effective leaders engage their employees' interests and loyalty. They figure out people's natural talents, adjust roles to suit their talents, and develop those talents into great strengths (**FIGURE B.1**).

grit in psychology, passion and perseverance in the pursuit of long-term goals.

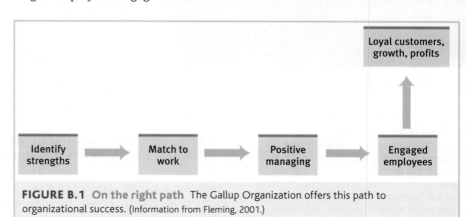

FIGURE B.1 On the right path The Gallup Organization offers this path to organizational success. (Information from Fleming, 2001.)

Trying to create talents that are not there can be a waste of time. Leaders who excel spend more time developing and drawing out strengths that already exist. Effective managers share certain traits (Tucker, 2002). They

- start by helping people identify and measure their strengths.
- match tasks to strengths and then give people freedom to do what they do best.
- care how people feel about their work.
- reinforce positive behaviors through recognition and reward.

Good managers also try not to promote people into roles ill-suited to their strengths. In Gallup surveys, 77 percent of engaged workers strongly agreed that "my supervisor focuses on my strengths or positive characteristics." Only 23 percent of not-engaged workers agreed with that statement (Krueger & Killham, 2005).

THE POWER OF POSITIVE COACHING Football coach Pete Carroll, who led the University of Southern California to two national championships and the Seattle Seahawks to a Super Bowl championship, has combined positive enthusiasm and fun workouts with "a commitment to a nurturing environment that allows people to be themselves while still being accountable to the team" (Trotter, 2014). "It shows you can win with positivity," noted Seahawks star defensive player Richard Sherman. "It's literally all positive reinforcement," said teammate Jimmy Graham (Belson, 2015).

Does all this sound familiar? Bringing out the best in people within an organization builds upon a basic principle of operant conditioning (Chapter 6). To teach a behavior, catch a person doing something right and reinforce it. It sounds simple, but too many managers act like the parents who focus on the one low grade on a child's almost-perfect report card. As a report by the Gallup Organization (2004) observed, "65 percent of Americans received no praise or recognition in their workplace last year."

The bottom line: In the workplace, great managers support employees' well-being. By caring about their employees and engaging and affirming their strengths, they support happier, more creative, more productive workers with less absenteeism and turnover (Amabile & Kramer, 2011; De Neve et al., 2013). People tolerate bad companies more than bad managers (Busteed, 2012). Moreover, the same principles affect college students' satisfaction, retention, and future success (Larkin et al., 2013; Ray & Kafka, 2014). Students who feel supported by caring friends and mentors, and engaged in their campus life, tend to persist and ultimately succeed during and after college.

Setting Specific, Challenging Goals

In study after study, people merely asked to do their best do not do so. Good managers know that a better way to motivate higher achievement is to set specific, challenging goals. For example, you might state your own goal in this course as "Finish studying Appendix B by Friday." Specific goals focus our attention and stimulate us to work hard, persist, and try creative strategies. Such goals are especially effective when workers or team

members participate in setting them. Achieving goals that are challenging yet within our reach boosts our self-evaluation (White et al., 1995).

Stated goals are most effective when combined with progress reports (Harkin et al., 2016). Action plans that break large goals into smaller steps (subgoals) and specify when, where, and how to achieve those steps will increase the chances of completing a project on time (Burgess et al., 2004; Fishbach et al., 2006; Koestner et al., 2002).

Through a task's ups and downs, people best sustain their mood and motivation when they focus on immediate goals (such as daily study) rather than distant goals (such as a course grade). Better to have one's nose to the grindstone than one's eye on the ultimate prize (Houser-Marko & Sheldon, 2008). Thus, before beginning each new edition of this book, our author-editor team *manages by objectives*—we agree on target dates for the completion and editing of each chapter draft. If we focus on achieving each of these short-term goals, the prize—an on-time book—takes care of itself. So, to motivate high productivity, effective leaders work with people to define explicit goals, subgoals, and implementation plans, and then provide feedback on progress.

Choosing an Appropriate Leadership Style

What qualities produce a great leader? Leadership styles vary, depending both on the qualities of the leader and the demands of the situation. In some situations (think of a commander leading troops into battle), a *directive* style may be needed (Fiedler, 1981). In other situations, the strategies that work on the battlefield may smother creativity. If developing a comedy show, for example, a leader might get better results using a *democratic* style that welcomes team member creativity.

Leaders differ in the personal qualities they bring to the job. Some excel at **task leadership**—by setting standards, organizing work, and focusing attention on goals. To keep the group centered on its mission, task leaders typically use a directive style. This style can work well if the leader is smart enough to give good orders (Fiedler, 1987).

Other managers excel at **social leadership.** They explain decisions, help group members solve their conflicts, and build teams that work well together (Evans & Dion, 1991; Pfaff et al., 2013). Social leaders, many of whom are women, often have a democratic style. They share authority and welcome team members' opinions. Social leadership and team-building increases morale and productivity (Shuffler et al., 2011, 2013). We usually feel more satisfied and motivated, and perform better, when we can participate in decision making (Cawley et al., 1998; Pereira & Osburn, 2007). Moreover, when members are sensitive to one another and participate equally, groups solve problems with greater "collective intelligence" (Woolley et al., 2010).

Effective leaders are not overly assertive, which can damage social relationships within the group. And they are not unassertive, which can limit their ability to lead (Ames & Flynn, 2007). Effective leaders of laboratory groups, work teams, corporations, and society tend to be self-confident. They have *charisma* (Goethals & Allison, 2014; House & Singh, 1987; Shamir et al., 1993). People with charisma

- have a *vision* of some goal.
- can *communicate* that vision clearly and simply.
- have enough optimism and faith to *inspire* their group to follow them.

Consider a study of morale at 50 Dutch firms (de Hoogh et al., 2004). Firms with the highest morale ratings had chief executives who inspired their colleagues "to transcend their own self-interests for the sake of the collective." This ability to motivate others to commit themselves to a group's mission is *transformational leadership*. Transformational leaders are often natural extraverts. They set their standards high, and they inspire others to share their vision. They pay attention to other people (Bono & Judge, 2004). The frequent result is a workforce that is more engaged, trusting, and effective (Turner et al., 2002).

Women more than men tend to be transformational leaders. This may help explain why companies with women in top management positions have tended to enjoy superior financial results (Eagly, 2007, 2013). That tendency held even after researchers controlled for variables such as company size.

Effective managers often exhibit a high degree of *both* task and social leadership. This finding applies in many locations, including coal mines, banks, and government offices in India, Taiwan, and Iran (Smith & Tayeb, 1989). As achievement-minded people, effective managers certainly care about how well people do their work. Yet they are sensitive to their workers' needs. That sensitivity is often repaid by worker loyalty. Workers in family-friendly organizations that offer flexible hours report feeling greater job satisfaction and loyalty to their employers (Butts et al., 2013; Roehling et al., 2001).

Employee participation in decision making is common in Sweden, Japan, the United States, and elsewhere (Cawley et al., 1998; Sundstrom et al., 1990). Workers given a chance to voice their opinion and be part of the decision-making process have responded more positively

Courtesy of New Lanark Trust

DOING WELL WHILE DOING GOOD—"THE GREAT EXPERIMENT" At the end of the 1700s, the New Lanark, Scotland, cotton mill had more than 1000 workers. Many were children drawn from Glasgow's poorhouses. They worked 13-hour days and lived in grim conditions.

On a visit to Glasgow, Welsh-born Robert Owen—an idealistic young cotton-mill manager—chanced to meet and marry the mill owner's daughter. Owen and some partners purchased the mill and on the first day of the 1800s began what he said was "the most important experiment for the happiness of the human race that had yet been instituted at any time in any part of the world" (Owen, 1814). The abuse of child and adult labor was, he observed, producing unhappy and inefficient workers. Owen showed transformational leadership skills when he undertook numerous innovations: a nursery for preschool children, education for older children (with encouragement rather than corporal punishment), Sundays off, health care, paid sick days, unemployment pay for days when the mill could not operate, and a company store selling goods at reduced prices.

He also designed a goals- and worker-assessment program that included detailed records of daily productivity and costs but with "no beating, no abusive language."

The financial success fueled a reform movement for better working and living conditions. By 1816, with decades of profitability still ahead, Owen believed he had demonstrated "that society may be formed so as to exist without crime, without poverty, with health greatly improved, with little if any misery, and with intelligence and happiness increased a hundredfold." Although that vision has not been fulfilled, Owen's great experiment laid the groundwork for employment practices that have today become accepted in much of the world.

---

task leadership goal-oriented leadership that sets standards, organizes work, and focuses attention on goals.

social leadership group-oriented leadership that builds teamwork, resolves conflict, and offers support.

to the final decision (van den Bos & Spruijt, 2002). They also feel more empowered and are more creative (Hennessey & Amabile, 2010; Seibert et al., 2011).

The ultimate in employee participation is the employee-owned company. One such company in my [DM's] town is the Fleetwood Group, a thriving 165-employee manufacturer of educational furniture and wireless electronic clickers. Every employee owns part of the company, and as a group they own 100 percent.

As a company that endorses faith-inspired "servant-leadership" and "respect and care for each team member-owner," Fleetwood is free to place people above profits. Thus, when orders lagged during a recession, the employee-owners decided that job security meant more than profits. So the company paid otherwise idle workers to

do community service, such as answering phones at nonprofit agencies and building Habitat for Humanity houses. Employee ownership attracts and retains talented people, which for Fleetwood has meant company success.

Retrieve + Remember

- What characteristics are important for *transformational leaders?*

ANSWER: Transformational leaders are able to inspire others to share a vision and commit themselves to a group's mission. They tend to be naturally extraverted and to set high standards.

APPENDIX B REVIEW

Psychology at Work

Test yourself by taking a moment to answer each of these Learning Objective Questions (repeated here from within the appendix). Then turn to Appendix D, Complete Chapter Reviews, to check your answers. Research suggests that trying to answer these questions on your own will improve your long-term memory of the concepts (McDaniel et al., 2009).

Work and Life Satisfaction

B-1: What is *flow?*

Industrial-Organizational Psychology

B-2: What are the key fields and subfields related to industrial-organizational psychology?

Motivating Achievement

B-3: Why is it important to motivate achievement?

Leadership

B-4: How can leaders be most effective?

TERMS AND CONCEPTS TO REMEMBER

Test yourself on these terms by trying to write down the definition in your own words before flipping back to the referenced page to check your answer.

flow, p. B-1

industrial-organizational (I/O) psychology, p. B-3

human factors psychology, p. B-3

personnel psychology, p. B-3

organizational psychology, p. B-3

achievement motivation, p. B-3

grit, p. B-5

task leadership, p. B-7

social leadership, p. B-7

APPENDIX B TEST

Test yourself repeatedly throughout your studies. This will not only help you figure out what you know and don't know; the testing itself will help you learn and remember the information more effectively thanks to the *testing effect*.

1. People who view their work as a calling often experience _____, a focused state of consciousness, with lowered awareness of themselves and of time.

   a. stress

   b. apathy

   c. flow

   d. facilitation

2. What are the key fields and subfields related to industrial-organizational psychology?

3. _____ psychologists study job seeking, and the recruitment, selection, placement, training, appraisal, and development of employees; _____ _____ psychologists focus on how people and machines interact, and on optimizing devices and work environments.

4. What type of goals will best help you stay focused and motivated to do your finest work in this class?

5. Research indicates that women are often social leaders. They are also more likely than men to have a _____ leadership style.

6. Effective managers often exhibit

   a. only task leadership.

   b. only social leadership.

   c. both task and social leadership, depending on the situation and the person.

   d. task leadership for building teams and social leadership for setting standards.

Find answers to these questions in Appendix E.

Use ⚞ **LearningCurve** to create your personalized study plan, which will direct you to the resources that will help you most in ⚞ **LaunchPad**.

Subfields of Psychology

Jennifer Zwolinski, *University of San Diego*

What can you do with a degree in psychology? Lots!

As a psychology major, you will graduate with a scientific mind-set and an awareness of basic principles of human behavior (biological mechanisms, development, cognition, psychological disorders, social interaction). This background will prepare you for success in many areas, including business, the helping professions, health services, marketing, law, sales, and teaching. You may even go on to graduate school for specialized training to become a psychology professional. This appendix describes psychology's specialized subfields.[1] I also provide updated information about CAREERS IN PSYCHOLOGY at: MacmillanLearning.com/LaunchPad/PEL4e, where you can learn more about the many interesting options available to those with bachelor's, master's, and doctoral degrees in psychology.

If you are like most psychology students, you may be unaware of the wide variety of specialties and work settings available in psychology (Terre & Stoddart, 2000). To date, the American Psychological Association (APA) has formed 56 divisions (**TABLE C.1**). The following paragraphs (arranged alphabetically) describe some careers in the main specialty areas of psychology, most of which require a graduate degree in psychology.

CLINICAL PSYCHOLOGISTS promote psychological health in individuals, groups, and organizations. Some clinical psychologists specialize in specific psychological disorders. Others treat a range of disorders, from adjustment difficulties to severe psychopathology. Clinical psychologists might engage in research, teaching, assessment, and consultation. Some hold workshops and lectures on psychological issues for other professionals or for the public. Clinical psychologists work in a variety of settings, including private practice, industry, mental health service organizations, schools, universities, legal systems, medical systems, counseling centers, government agencies, and military services.

To become a clinical psychologist, you will need to earn a doctorate from a clinical psychology program. The APA sets the standards for clinical psychology graduate programs, offering accreditation (official recognition) to those who meet their standards. In all U.S. states, clinical psychologists working in independent practice must obtain a license to offer services such as therapy and testing.

COGNITIVE PSYCHOLOGISTS study thought processes and focus on such topics as perception, language, attention, problem solving, memory, judgment and decision making, forgetting, and intelligence. Research interests include designing computer-based models of thought processes and identifying biological correlates of cognition. As a cognitive psychologist, you might work as a professor, industrial consultant, or human factors specialist in an educational or business setting.

COMMUNITY PSYCHOLOGISTS move beyond focusing on specific individuals or families and deal with broad problems of mental health in community settings. These psychologists believe that human behavior is powerfully influenced by the interaction between people and their physical, social, political, and economic environments. They seek to promote psychological health by enhancing environmental

COGNITIVE CONSULTING Cognitive psychologists may advise businesses on how to operate more effectively by understanding the human factors involved.

COMMUNITY CARE This community psychologist (left) helped residents work through the emotional challenges that followed the devastating 2010 earthquake in Haiti.

---

[1]Although this text covers the world of psychology, this appendix draws primarily from available U.S. data. Its descriptions of psychology's subfields are, however, also applicable in many other countries.

TABLE C.1   APA Divisions by Number and Name

1. Society for General Psychology	29. Society for the Advancement of Psychotherapy
2. Society for the Teaching of Psychology	30. Society of Psychological Hypnosis
3. Experimental Psychology	31. State, Provincial, and Territorial Psychological Association Affairs
4. *There is no active Division 4.*	32. Society for Humanistic Psychology
5. Evaluation, Measurement, and Statistics Division for Quantitative and Qualitative Methods	33. Intellectual and Developmental Disabilities
6. Behavioral Neuroscience and Comparative Psychology	34. Society for Environmental, Population, and Conservation Psychology
7. Developmental Psychology	35. Society for the Psychology of Women
8. Society for Personality and Social Psychology	36. Society for the Psychology of Religion and Spirituality
9. Society for the Psychological Study of Social Issues (SPSSI)	37. Society for Child and Family Policy and Practice
10. Society for the Psychology of Aesthetics, Creativity, and the Arts	38. Health Psychology
11. *There is no active Division 11.*	39. Psychoanalysis
12. Society of Clinical Psychology	40. Society for Clinical Neuropsychology
13. Society of Consulting Psychology	41. American Psychology-Law Society
14. Society for Industrial and Organizational Psychology	42. Psychologists in Independent Practice
15. Educational Psychology	43. Society for Family Psychology
16. School Psychology	44. Society for the Psychological Study of Lesbian, Gay, Bisexual, and Transgender Issues
17. Society of Counseling Psychology	45. Society for the Psychological Study of Culture, Ethnicity, and Race
18. Psychologists in Public Service	46. Society for Media Psychology and Technology
19. Military Psychology	47. Exercise and Sport Psychology
20. Adult Development and Aging	48. Society for the Study of Peace, Conflict, and Violence: Peace Psychology Division
21. Applied Experimental and Engineering Psychology	49. Society of Group Psychology and Group Psychotherapy
22. Rehabilitation Psychology	50. Society of Addiction Psychology
23. Society for Consumer Psychology	51. Society for the Psychological Study of Men and Masculinity
24. Theoretical and Philosophical Psychology	52. International Psychology
25. Behavior Analysis	53. Society of Clinical Child and Adolescent Psychology
26. Society for the History of Psychology	54. Society of Pediatric Psychology
27. Society for Community Research and Action: Division of Community Psychology	55. American Society for the Advancement of Pharmacotherapy
28. Psychopharmacology and Substance Abuse	56. Trauma Psychology

Source: American Psychological Association

settings, focusing on preventive measures and crisis intervention, with special attention to the problems of underserved groups and ethnic minorities. Given the shared emphasis on prevention, some community psychologists collaborate with professionals in other areas, such as public health. As a community psychologist, your work settings could include federal, state, and local departments of mental health, corrections, and welfare. You might conduct research or help evaluate research in health service settings, serve as an independent consultant for a private or government agency, or teach and consult as a college or university faculty member.

COUNSELING PSYCHOLOGISTS help people adjust to life transitions or make lifestyle changes. Although similar to clinical psychologists, counseling psychologists typically help people with adjustment problems rather than severe psychopathology. Like clinical psychologists, counseling psychologists conduct therapy and provide assessments to individuals and groups. As a counseling psychologist, you would emphasize your clients' strengths, helping them to use their own skills, interests, and abilities to cope during transitions. You might find yourself working in an academic setting as a faculty member or administrator or in a university counseling center, community mental health center, business, or private practice. As with clinical psychology, if you plan to work in independent practice you will need to obtain a state license to provide counseling services to the public.

DEVELOPMENTAL PSYCHOLOGISTS conduct research in age-related behavioral changes and apply their scientific knowledge to educational, child-care, policy, and related settings. As a developmental psychologist, you would investigate change across a broad range of topics, including the biological, psychological, cognitive, and social aspects of development. Developmental psychology informs a number of applied fields, including educational psychology, school psychology, child psychopathology, and gerontology. The field also informs public policy in areas such as education and child-care reform, maternal and child health, and attachment and adoption. You would probably specialize in a specific stage of the life span, such as infancy, childhood, adolescence, or middle or late adulthood. Your work setting could be an educational institution, day-care center, youth group program, or senior center.

EDUCATIONAL PSYCHOLOGISTS are interested in the psychological processes involved in learning. They study the relationship between learning and the physical and social environments, and they develop strategies for enhancing the learning process. As an educational psychologist, working in a university psychology department or school of education, you might conduct basic research on topics related to learning or develop innovative methods of teaching to en-

hance the learning process. You might design effective tests, including measures of aptitude and achievement. You might be employed by a school or government agency or charged with designing and implementing effective employee-training programs in a business setting.

EXPERIMENTAL PSYCHOLOGISTS are a diverse group of scientists who investigate a variety of basic behavioral processes in humans and other animals. Prominent areas of experimental research include comparative methods of science, motivation, learning, thought, attention, memory, perception, and language. Most experimental psychologists identify with a particular subfield, such as cognitive psychology, depending on their interests and training. It is important to note that experimental research methods are not limited to the field of experimental psychology; many other subfields rely on experimental methodology to conduct studies. As an experimental psychologist, you would most likely work in an academic setting, teaching courses and supervising students' research in addition to conducting your own

research. Or you might be employed by a research institution, zoo, business, or government agency.

FORENSIC PSYCHOLOGISTS apply psychological principles to legal issues. They conduct research on the interface of law and psychology, help to create public policies related to mental health, help law-enforcement agencies in criminal investigations, or consult on jury selection and deliberation processes. They also provide assessment to assist the legal community. Although most forensic psychologists are clinical psychologists, they might have expertise in other areas of psychology, such as social or cognitive psychology. Some also hold law degrees. As a forensic psychologist, you might work in a university psychology department, law school, research organization, community mental health agency, law-enforcement agency, court, or correctional setting.

HEALTH PSYCHOLOGISTS are researchers and practitioners concerned with psychology's contribution to promoting health and preventing disease. As

CRIMINAL INVESTIGATION Forensic psychologists may be called on to assist police officers investigating a crime scene, as here after a shooting in Florida. Most forensic work, however, occurs in the lab and for the judicial system.

© ZUMA Press, Inc. / Alamy

applied psychologists or clinicians, they may help individuals lead healthier lives by designing, conducting, and evaluating programs to stop smoking, lose weight, improve sleep, manage pain, prevent the spread of sexually transmitted infections, or treat psychosocial problems associated with chronic and terminal illnesses. As researchers and clinicians, they identify conditions and practices associated with health and illness to help create effective interventions. In public service, health psychologists study and work to improve government policies and health care systems. As a health psychologist, you could be employed in a hospital, medical school, rehabilitation center, public health agency, college or university, or, if you are also a clinical psychologist, in private practice.

INDUSTRIAL-ORGANIZATIONAL (I/O) PSYCHOLOGISTS study the relationship between people and their working environments. They may develop new ways to increase productivity, improve personnel selection, or promote job satisfaction in an organizational setting. Their interests include organizational structure and change, consumer behavior, and personnel selection and training. As an I/O psychologist, you might conduct workplace training or provide organizational analysis and development. You may find yourself working in business, industry, the government, or a college or university. Or you may be self-employed as a consultant or work for a management consulting firm.

NEUROPSYCHOLOGISTS investigate the relationship between neurological processes (structure and function of the brain and nervous system) and behavior. As a neuropsychologist you might assess, diagnose, or treat central nervous system disorders, such as Alzheimer's disease or stroke. You might also evaluate individuals for evidence of head injuries; specific learning disorders; and neurodevelopmental disorders, such

as autism spectrum disorder and attention-deficit/hyperactivity disorder (ADHD). If you are a *clinical neuropsychologist,* you might work in a hospital's neurology, neurosurgery, or psychiatric unit. Neuropsychologists also work in academic settings, where they conduct research and teach.

PSYCHOMETRIC AND QUANTITATIVE PSYCHOLOGISTS study the methods and techniques used to acquire psychological knowledge. A psychometrician may update existing neurocognitive or personality tests or devise new tests for use in clinical and school settings or in business and industry. These psychologists also administer, score, and interpret such tests. Quantitative psychologists collaborate with researchers to design, analyze, and interpret the results of research programs. As a psychometric or quantitative psychologist, you would need to be well trained in research methods, statistics, and computer technology. You would most likely be employed by a university or college, testing company, private research firm, or government agency.

REHABILITATION PSYCHOLO-GISTS are researchers and practitioners who work with people who have lost optimal functioning after an accident, illness, or other event. As a rehabilitation psychologist, you would probably work in a medical rehabilitation institution or hospital. You might also work in a medical school, university, state or federal vocational rehabilitation agency, or in private practice serving people with physical disabilities.

SCHOOL PSYCHOLOGISTS are involved in the assessment of and intervention for children in educational settings. They diagnose and treat cognitive, social, and emotional problems that may negatively influence children's learning or overall functioning at school. As a school psychologist, you would collaborate with teachers, parents, and administrators, making

ASSESSING AND SUPPORTING CHILDREN School psychologists may find themselves working with children individually or in groups. They receive interdisciplinary training in mental health assessment and behavior analysis, research methods and design, and special needs education. They work primarily in schools, but also in a range of other settings, including pediatric hospitals, mental health centers, and correctional facilities.

recommendations to improve student learning. You would work in an academic setting, a federal or state government agency, a child guidance center, or a behavioral research laboratory.

SOCIAL PSYCHOLOGISTS are interested in our interactions with others. Social psychologists study how our beliefs, feelings, and behaviors are affected by and influence other people. They study topics such as attitudes, aggression, prejudice, interpersonal attraction, group behavior, and leadership. As a social psychologist, you would probably be a college or university faculty member. You might also work in organizational consultation, market research, or other applied psychology fields. Some social psychologists work for hospitals, federal agencies, or businesses performing applied research.

SPORT PSYCHOLOGISTS study the psychological factors that influence, and are influenced by, participation in

Phil Walter/Getty Images

CRICKET CURES Sport psychologists often work directly with athletes to help them improve their performance. Here a sport psychologist consults with Brendon McCullum, a record-breaking athlete who plays international cricket for New Zealand.

sports and other physical activities. Their professional activities include coach education and athlete preparation, as well as research and teaching. Sport psychologists who also have a clinical or counseling degree can apply those skills to working with individuals with psychological problems, such as anxiety or substance use disorder, that might interfere with optimal performance. As a sport psychologist, if you were not working in an academic or research setting, you would most likely work as part of a team or an organization or in a private capacity.

* * *

So, the next time someone asks you what you will do with your psychology degree, tell them you have a lot of options. You might use your acquired skills and understanding to get a job and succeed in any number of fields, or you might pursue graduate school and then career opportunities in associated professions. In any case, what you have learned about behavior and mental processes will surely enrich your life (Hammer, 2003).

Complete Chapter Reviews

CHAPTER 1
Psychology's Roots, Big Ideas, and Critical Thinking Tools

Psychology's Roots

1-1 **What are the three key elements of the scientific attitude, and how do they support scientific inquiry?**

- These three basic attitudes helped make modern science possible:
  - Curiosity triggers new ideas. When put to the test, can an idea's predictions be confirmed?
  - Skepticism encourages attention to the facts. Skeptical testing can reveal which claim best matches the facts.
  - Humility helps us discard predictions that can't be verified by research. Researchers must be willing to be surprised and follow new ideas.

1-2 **How has psychology's focus changed over time?**

- Wilhelm Wundt established the first psychological laboratory in Germany in 1879, and studied the basic elements of mental experience.

- Early researchers defined psychology as "the science of mental life." This definition was revised under the influence of the *behaviorists* in the 1920s to the "scientific study of observable behavior."

- Behaviorism was one of psychology's two major forces well into the 1960s. However, the second major force of Freudian psychology, along with the influences of *humanistic psychology* and *cognitive psychology*, revived interest in the study of mental processes.

- *Psychology* is now defined as "the science of behavior and mental processes."

1-3 **What are psychology's current perspectives, and what are some of its subfields?**

- Psychology's current perspectives include neuroscience, evolutionary, behavior genetics, psychodynamic, behavioral, cognitive, and social-cultural.

- Psychology's subfields include biological, developmental, cognitive, personality, social, counseling, health, clinical, industrial-organizational, and community.

- Psychologists may conduct basic research to increase the field's knowledge base or applied research to solve practical problems.

Four Big Ideas in Psychology

1-4 **What four big ideas run throughout this book?**

- *Critical thinking* is smart thinking. It challenges our beliefs and triggers new ways of thinking. The scientific attitude prepares us to examine assumptions, consider the source, uncover hidden values, weigh evidence, and test conclusions.

- Behavior is a *biopsychosocial* event. The biological, psychological, and social-cultural levels of analysis each offer valuable insight into behavior and mental processes.

- We operate with a two-track mind (*dual processing*). Our brains process a surprising amount without our awareness, which affects our thinking, memory, perception, language, and attitudes.

- Psychology explores human strengths (*positive psychology*) as well as challenges (clinical psychology).

Why Do Psychology?

1-5 **How does our everyday thinking sometimes lead us to the wrong conclusion?**

- *Hindsight bias* (the I-knew-it-all-along phenomenon) is believing, after learning the outcome, that we would have foreseen it.

- Overconfidence is the human tendency to be more confident than correct.
- We perceive order in random events due to our natural eagerness to make sense of our world.
- These tendencies lead us to overestimate our intuition and common sense, and then come to the wrong conclusion.

How Do Psychologists Ask and Answer Questions?

1-6 How do theories advance psychological science?

- Psychological *theories* are explanations using principles that organize observations and predict behaviors or events.
- Theories generate *hypotheses*— predictions that can be tested using descriptive, correlational, or experimental methods.
- Research results may validate the theory, or lead to its rejection or revision.
- The precise language used in *operational definitions* allows *replication* by others. If others achieve similar results, confidence in the conclusion will be greater.

1-7 How do psychologists use case studies, naturalistic observations, and surveys to observe and describe behavior, and why is random sampling important?

- *Case studies* study one person or group in depth, in the hope of revealing things true of us all.
- *Naturalistic observation* studies examine behavior in naturally occurring situations without trying to change or control the situation.
- *Surveys* study many people in less depth, using *random sampling* to fairly represent the *population* being studied.

1-8 What are positive and negative correlations, and how can they lead to prediction but not cause-effect explanation?

- In a positive correlation, both items increase or decrease together.
- In a negative correlation, one item increases as the other decreases.
- *Correlations* tell us how well one event predicts another (using a measure called a correlation coefficient), but not whether one event caused the other, or whether some third factor influenced both events.

1-9 How do experiments clarify or reveal cause-effect relationships?

- *Experiments* create a controlled, simplified version of reality to discover cause-effect relationships.
- Psychologists manipulate one or more factors (*independent variables*) while controlling others. The researchers can then measure changes in other factors (*dependent variables*). Experiments minimize *confounding variables* (preexisting differences between groups) through *random assignment*.
- Experiments allow researchers to compare *experimental group* results with *control group* results. Experiments may use a *double-blind procedure* to control for the *placebo effect*.
- Psychological scientists must design studies and choose research methods that will best provide meaningful results. (The Immersive Learning "How Would You Know?" activities in LaunchPad allow you to play the role of the researcher, making choices about the best ways to test interesting questions.)

1-10 How can simplified laboratory experiments help us understand general principles of behavior?

- Studying specific examples in controlled environments can reveal important general principles. These general principles, not the specific findings, help may explain many everyday behaviors.

Psychology's Research Ethics

1-11 Why do psychologists study animals, and what ethical guidelines safeguard human and animal research participants? How do personal values influence psychologists' research and applications?

- Research on animals advances our understanding of other species and sometimes benefits them directly. Animal experimentation also advances our understanding of ourselves and may help solve human problems.
- Professional ethical standards and other legal guidelines, enforced by ethics committees, protect participants. The APA ethics code outlines standards for safeguarding human participants' well-being, including obtaining their *informed consent* and *debriefing* them later.
- Psychologists' values influence their choice of research topics, their theories and observations, their labels for behavior, and their professional advice. Psychology's principles could be used for good or evil, but have been used mainly to enlighten and to achieve positive ends.

Use Psychology to Become a Stronger Person—and a Better Student

1-12 How can psychological principles help you learn, remember, and thrive?

- The *testing effect* shows that learning and memory are enhanced by actively retrieving, rather than simply rereading, previously studied material. The SQ3R study method—

survey, question, read, retrieve, and review—applies principles derived from memory research and can help you learn and remember material.

- Four additional study tips are (1) distribute your study time; (2) learn to think critically; (3) process class information actively; and (4) overlearn.

- Psychological research has shown that people who live happy, thriving lives (1) manage their time to get a full night's sleep; (2) make space for exercise; (3) have a growth mind-set; and (4) prioritize relationships.

CHAPTER 2

The Biology of Mind and Consciousness

The Brain: A Work in Progress

2-1 How do biology and experience interact?

- Everything psychological is simultaneously biological. The links between biology and behavior are a key part of the biopsychosocial approach.

- *Brain plasticity* allows us to adapt to new environments; our brain is a work in progress.

- *Biological psychologists* study the links between biological (genetic, neural, hormonal) and psychological processes. In *cognitive neuroscience,* people from many fields join forces to study the brain activity linked with cognition.

Neural Communication

2-2 What are the parts of a neuron, and what is an *action potential*?

- *Neurons* (nerve cells) are the basic building blocks of the nervous system.

- A neuron has *dendrites* (extensions of the cell body) that receive messages and an *axon* that sends messages to other neurons or to muscles and glands. Some axons are encased in a myelin sheath, which enables faster communication. *Glial cells* provide myelin, and they support, nourish, and protect neurons; they may also play a role in learning, thinking, and memory.

- An *action potential* is a nerve impulse—a brief electrical charge that travels down an axon.

2-3 How do neurons communicate?

- Neurons transmit information in a chemistry-to-electricity process, sending action potentials down their axons. They receive incoming excitatory or inhibitory signals through their dendrites and cell body.

- Neurons fire in an *all-or-none response* when combined incoming signals are strong enough to pass a minimum *threshold.* A brief *refractory period* follows.

- The response triggers a release of chemical messengers *(neurotransmitters)* across the tiny gap *(synapse)* separating a sending neuron from a receiving cell.

2-4 How do neurotransmitters affect our mood and behavior?

- Specific neurotransmitters, such as serotonin and dopamine, travel designated pathways in the brain. Neurotransmitters affect particular behaviors and emotions, such as hunger, movement, and arousal.

- *Endorphins* are natural opiates released in response to pain and intense exercise.

- Drugs and other chemicals affect brain chemistry at synapses.

The Nervous System

2-5 What are the two major divisions of the nervous system, and what are their basic functions?

- The *nervous system's* two major divisions are the *central nervous system (CNS)*—the brain and spinal cord—and the *peripheral nervous system (PNS)*—the sensory and motor neurons connecting the CNS to the rest of the body.

- *Interneurons* communicate within the brain and spinal cord and between *motor neurons* and *sensory neurons.*

- In the PNS, the *somatic nervous system* controls voluntary movements of the skeletal system. The *autonomic nervous system (ANS)* controls the involuntary muscles and the glands. The subdivisions of the ANS are the *sympathetic nervous system* (which arouses) and the *parasympathetic nervous system* (which calms).

The Endocrine System

2-6 How does the endocrine system transmit information and interact with the nervous system?

- The *endocrine system* is the body's slower information system. Its glands secrete *hormones* into the bloodstream, which influence brain and behavior.

- In times of stress or danger, the autonomic nervous system (ANS) activates the *adrenal glands'* fight-or-flight response.

- The *pituitary* (the endocrine system's master gland) triggers other glands, including sex glands, to release hormones, which then affect the brain and behavior. This complex feedback system reveals the interplay between the nervous and endocrine systems.

The Brain

2-7 What are some techniques for studying the brain?

- To study the brain, researchers consider the effects of brain damage.
- They also use *MRI* scans to reveal brain structures.
- Researchers use *EEG* recordings and *PET* and *fMRI* (functional MRI) scans to reveal brain activity.

2-8 What structures make up the brainstem, and what are the functions of the brainstem, thalamus, reticular formation, and cerebellum?

- The *brainstem,* the oldest part of the brain, controls automatic survival functions.
- The *medulla* controls heartbeat and breathing. Just above the medulla, the pons helps coordinate movements and control sleep.
- The *thalamus,* sitting at the top of the brainstem, acts as the brain's sensory control center.
- The *reticular formation* controls arousal.
- The *cerebellum,* attached to the rear of the brainstem, helps process sensory input, coordinate muscle movement, and enable nonverbal learning and memory.

2-9 What are the structures and functions of the limbic system?

- The *limbic system* is linked to emotions, drives, and memory, and its neural centers include the amygdala, hypothalamus, and hippocampus:
  - The *amygdala* is involved in aggressive and fearful responses.
  - The *hypothalamus* monitors various bodily maintenance activities, is linked to emotion and reward, and triggers the pituitary to influence other glands of the endocrine system.

- The *hippocampus* helps process explicit (conscious) memories.

2-10 What are the four lobes of the cerebral cortex, and where are they located?

- The *cerebral cortex* has two hemispheres, and each hemisphere has four lobes:
  - The *frontal lobes* (just behind the forehead) are involved in speaking, muscle movements, planning, and judging.
  - The *parietal lobes* (top-rear of the head) receive sensory input for touch and body position.
  - The *occipital lobes* (back of the head) receive input from the visual fields.
  - The *temporal lobes* (above the ears) receive input from the ears.

2-11 What are the functions of the motor cortex, somatosensory cortex, and association areas?

- The *motor cortex* (at the rear of the frontal lobes) controls voluntary muscle movement.
- The *somatosensory cortex* (at the front of the parietal lobes) registers and processes body touch and movement sensations.
- The cerebral cortex is mostly *association areas,* which are involved primarily in higher-level functions, such as learning, remembering, thinking, and speaking. Higher-level functions require the coordination of many brain areas.

2-12 Do we really use only 10 percent of our brain?

- Association areas, vast in humans, interpret, integrate, and act on sensory information and link it with stored memories. More intelligent animals have larger association areas.
- Evidence from brain damage shows that the neurons in association

areas are busy with higher mental functions, so a bullet would not land in an "unused" area.

2-13 How does the brain modify itself after some kinds of damage?

- The brain's plasticity allows it to modify itself after some types of damage, especially early in life.
- The brain often attempts self-repair by reorganizing existing tissue. *Neurogenesis,* less common, is the formation of new neurons.

2-14 What is a split brain, and what does it reveal about the functions of our two brain hemispheres?

- The *corpus callosum* (a large band of nerve fibers) normally connects the two brain hemispheres. If surgically severed (for example, to treat severe epilepsy), a *split brain* results.
- Split-brain research shows that in most people, the hemispheres are specialized, though they work together in a normal brain. The left hemisphere usually specializes in verbal processing. The right hemisphere usually specializes in visual perception and the recognition of emotion.

Brain States and Consciousness

2-15 What do we mean by *consciousness,* and how does selective attention direct our perceptions?

- *Consciousness* is our awareness of ourselves and our environment. We process information at an explicit, conscious level (*sequential processing* of whatever requires focused attention) and at an implicit, unconscious level (*parallel processing* of routine business).
- We *selectively attend* to, and process, a very limited portion of incoming information, blocking out much and

- often shifting the spotlight of our attention from one thing to another.
- Focused intently on one task, we often display *inattentional blindness* to other events and *change blindness* (a form of inattentional blindness) to changes around us.

2-16 What is the *circadian rhythm,* and what are the stages of our nightly sleep cycle?

- The *circadian rhythm* is our internal biological clock; it regulates our daily cycles of alertness and sleepiness.
- Nightly *sleep* cycles every 90 minutes through recurring stages:
  - NREM-1 sleep is the brief, near-waking sleep with irregular brain waves we enter (after leaving the *alpha waves* of being awake and relaxed); *hallucinations* (sensations such as falling or floating) may occur.
  - NREM-2 sleep, in which we spend about half of our sleep time, includes characteristic bursts of rhythmic brain waves; lengthens as the night goes on.
  - NREM-3 sleep is deep sleep in which large, slow *delta waves* are emitted; this stage shortens as the night goes on.
  - REM *(rapid eye movement) sleep* is described as a paradoxical sleep stage because of internal arousal but external calm (near paralysis). It includes most dreaming and lengthens as the night goes on.

2-17 How do our sleep patterns differ? What five theories describe our need to sleep?

- Age, genetic, and social-cultural factors affect sleep patterns.
- Psychologists suggest five possible reasons why sleep evolved:
  - Sleep may have played a protective role in human evolution by keeping people safe during potentially dangerous periods.

- Sleep also helps restore and repair damaged neurons.
- Sleep helps strengthen neural connections for learning and for building enduring memories.
- Sleep promotes creative problem solving the next day.
- During deep sleep, the pituitary gland secretes a growth hormone necessary for muscle development.

2-18 How does sleep loss affect us, and what are the major sleep disorders?

- Sleep loss causes fatigue and irritability, and impairs concentration, productivity, and memory consolidation. It can also lead to depression, obesity, joint pain, a suppressed immune system, and slowed performance (with greater vulnerability to accidents).
- The major sleep disorders are *insomnia* (recurring wakefulness); *narcolepsy* (sudden, uncontrollable sleepiness, sometimes lapsing directly into REM sleep); *sleep apnea* (the repeated stopping of breathing while asleep); and sleepwalking, sleeptalking, and night terrors.

2-19 What do we dream about, and what are five explanations of *why* we dream?

- Our *dreams* often include ordinary events and everyday experiences, but with a vivid, emotional, and often bizarre flavor. Most dreams are bad dreams—of personal failures, dangers, or misfortunes.
- There are five major views of the function of dreams:
  - Freud's wish fulfillment: Dreams provide a psychic "safety valve," with *manifest content* (story line) acting as a censored version of *latent content* (underlying meaning that gratifies our unconscious wishes).

- Information processing: Dreams help us sort out the day's events and consolidate them in memory.
- Physiological function: Regular brain stimulation may help us develop and preserve neural pathways in the brain.
- Neural activation: The brain attempts to make sense of neural static by weaving it into a story line.
- Cognitive development: Dreams reflect dreamers' cognitive development—their knowledge and understanding.
- Most sleep theorists agree that REM sleep and its associated dreams serve an important function, as shown by the *REM rebound* that occurs following REM deprivation in humans and other species.

CHAPTER 3
Developing Through the Life Span

Developmental Psychology's Major Issues

3-1 What are the three major issues studied by developmental psychologists?

- *Developmental psychologists* study physical, cognitive, and social change throughout the life span with a focus on three major issues:
  - Nature and nurture—how our genetic inheritance (our nature) interacts with our experiences (our nurture) to influence our development.
  - Continuity and stages—what parts of development are gradual and continuous and what parts change abruptly in separate stages.

- Stability and change—which traits persist through life and which change as we age.

Prenatal Development and the Newborn

3-2 How does conception occur, and what are *chromosomes, DNA, genes,* and the human *genome?* How do genes and the environment interact?

- At conception, one sperm cell fuses with one egg cell.
- *Genes* are the basic units of *heredity* that make up *chromosomes,* the threadlike coils of *DNA.* The human *genome* is the shared genetic profile that distinguishes humans from other species.
- The *interaction* between heredity and *environment* influences development. *Epigenetics* is the study of environmental influences on gene expression (making genes active or inactive) that occur without a DNA change.

3-3 How does life develop before birth, and how do *teratogens* put prenatal development at risk?

- From conception to 2 weeks, the *zygote* is in a period of rapid cell development.
- By 6 weeks, the *embryo's* body organs begin to form and function.
- By 9 weeks, the *fetus* is recognizably human.
- *Teratogens* are potentially harmful agents that can pass through the placenta and interfere with normal development, as happens with *fetal alcohol syndrome.*

3-4 What are some of the newborn's abilities and traits?

- Newborns' sensory systems and *reflexes* aid their survival and social interactions with adults.

- Newborns smell and hear well, see what they need to see, and begin using their sensory equipment to learn.
- Inborn *temperament*—emotional reactivity and intensity—heavily influences our developing personality.

3-5 How do twin and adoption studies help us understand the effects of nature and nurture?

- *Identical (monozygotic) twins* develop from a single fertilized egg that splits into two; *fraternal (dizygotic) twins* develop from separate fertilized eggs.
- Studies of separated identical twins allow researchers to maintain the same genes while testing the effects of different home environments. Studies of adoptive families let researchers maintain the same home environment while studying the effects of genetic differences.

Infancy and Childhood

3-6 During infancy and childhood, how do the brain and motor skills develop?

- Most brain cells form before birth. With *maturation* and experience, their interconnections multiply rapidly and become more complex. A pruning process strengthens heavily used links and weakens unused ones, and we seem to have a *critical period* for some skills, such as language.
- Complex motor skills—sitting, standing, walking—develop in a predictable sequence. Timing may vary with individual maturation and with culture.
- We have few conscious memories of events occurring before age 4, a blank space in our conscious memory that psychologists call infantile amnesia.

3-7 From the perspectives of Piaget, Vygotsky, and today's researchers, how does a child's mind develop?

- In his theory of *cognitive* development, Jean Piaget proposed

that children actively construct and modify an understanding of the world through the processes of *assimilation* and *accommodation.* They form *schemas* that help them organize their experiences.

- Piaget believed children construct an understanding of the world by interacting with it while moving through four cognitive stages:
  - *Sensorimotor stage*—first two years; *object permanence* develops.
  - *Preoperational stage*—about age 2 to 6 or 7; preschoolers are *egocentric* but begin to develop a *theory of mind.* Children with *autism spectrum disorder (ASD)* have trouble understanding others' states of mind.
  - *Concrete operational stage*—about 7 to 11 years; mastery of *conservation* and simple math.
  - *Formal operational stage*—about age 12 and up; reasoning expands to abstract thinking.
- Current research supports the sequence Piaget proposed, but finds young children more capable and their development more continuous.
- Lev Vygotsky's studies of child development focused on the ways a child's mind grows by interacting with the social environment. Parents and other caregivers provide temporary scaffolds from which children can step to higher levels of thinking.

3-8 How do the bonds of attachment form between caregivers and infants?

- Infants develop *stranger anxiety* soon after object permanence.
- Infants form *attachments* with caregivers who satisfy nutritional needs but, more importantly, who are comfortable, familiar, and responsive.

3-9 Why do secure and insecure attachments matter, and how does an infant's ability to develop basic trust affect later relationships?

- Attachment styles differ (secure or insecure) due to the child's individual temperament and the responsiveness of the child's caregivers.
- Securely attached children develop *basic trust* and tend to have healthier adult relationships.
- Neglect or abuse can disrupt the attachment process and put children at risk for physical, psychological, and social problems.

3-10 What are the four main parenting styles?

- Parenting styles—authoritarian, permissive, negligent, and authoritative—reflect how responsive and how demanding parents are.
- Child-raising practices reflect both individual and cultural values.

3-11 What outcomes are associated with each parenting style?

- Children with the highest self-esteem, self-reliance, self-regulation, and social competence tend to have authoritative parents. Less positive outcomes are associated with authoritarian, permissive, and negligent parents.
- However, correlation does not equal causation (it's possible that children with positive characteristics are more likely to bring out positive parenting methods).

Adolescence

3-12 How is adolescence defined, and what major physical changes occur during adolescence?

- *Adolescence,* the transition period from childhood to adulthood, begins with *puberty,* a time of sexual maturation.
- The brain's frontal lobes mature during adolescence and the early twenties, enabling improved judgment, impulse control, and long-term planning.

3-13 How did Piaget, Kohlberg, and later researchers describe cognitive and moral development during adolescence?

- In Jean Piaget's view, formal operations (abstract reasoning) develop in adolescence, and this development is the basis for moral judgment. Research indicates that these abilities begin to emerge earlier than Piaget believed.
- Lawrence Kohlberg proposed a stage theory of moral thinking: preconventional morality (self-interest), conventional morality (gaining others' approval or doing one's duty), and postconventional morality (basic rights and self-defined ethical principles). Kohlberg's critics note that the postconventional level is culturally limited, representing morality only from the perspective of an individualist society.
- Other researchers believe that morality lies in moral intuition and moral action as well as thinking.

3-14 What are the social tasks and challenges of adolescence?

- Erik Erikson proposed eight stages of psychosocial development across the life span. He believed we need to achieve the following challenges: trust, autonomy, initiative, competency, identity (in adolescence), *intimacy* (in young adulthood), generativity, and integrity.
- Each life stage has its own psychosocial task, with the chief task of adolescence being solidifying one's sense of self, one's *identity.* This often means trying out a number of different roles. *Social identity* is the part of the self-concept that comes from a person's group memberships.

3-15 How do parents and peers influence adolescents?

- During adolescence, parental influence diminishes and peer influence increases, in part because of the selection effect—the tendency to choose similar others as friends.
- Nature and nurture—genes and experiences—interact to guide our development.
- Parents influence our manners, attitudes, values, faith, and politics. Language and other behaviors are shaped by peer groups, as children adjust to fit in.

3-16 What is emerging adulthood?

- *Emerging adulthood* is the period from age 18 to the mid-twenties, when many young people in Western cultures are no longer adolescents but have not yet achieved full independence as adults.

Adulthood

3-17 How do our bodies and sensory abilities change from early to late adulthood?

- Muscular strength, reaction time, sensory abilities, and cardiac output begin to decline in the late twenties and continue to decline through middle adulthood (to age 65) and late adulthood (after 65).
- Around age 50, *menopause* ends women's period of fertility. Men experience a more gradual decline in sperm count, testosterone level, and speed of erection and ejaculation.

- In late adulthood, the immune system also weakens, but good health habits help to enable better health in later life.

3-18 How does memory change with age?

- Recall begins to decline, especially for meaningless information. Recognition memory remains strong.
- Researchers use *cross-sectional* and *longitudinal studies* to identify mental abilities that do and do not change as people age.

3-19 What are adulthood's two primary commitments, and how do chance events and the social clock influence us?

- Adulthood's two major commitments are love (Erikson's intimacy—forming close relationships) and work (productive activity, or what Erikson called generativity).
- Chance encounters affect many of our important decisions, such as our choice of romantic partners.
- The *social clock* is a culture's expected timing for social events such as marriage, parenthood, and retirement.

3-20 What factors affect our well-being in later life?

- Most older people retain a sense of well-being, partly due to the tendency to focus more on positive emotions and memories.
- People over 65 report as much happiness and satisfaction with life as younger people do.

3-21 How do people vary in their responses to a loved one's death?

- Normal grief reactions vary widely. People do not grieve in predictable stages.
- Death of a loved one is much harder to accept when it comes before its expected time.

- Life can be affirmed even at death, especially for those who experience what Erikson called a sense of integrity—a feeling that one's life has been meaningful.

CHAPTER 4
Sex, Gender, and Sexuality

Gender Development

4-1 How does the meaning of *gender* differ from the meaning of *sex?*

- *Gender* refers to the socially influenced characteristics by which people define men and women. *Sex* refers to the biologically influenced characteristics by which people define male and female. Our understanding of gender arises from the interplay between our biology and our experiences.

4-2 What are some ways in which males and females tend to be alike and to differ?

- Males and females are more alike than different, thanks to our similar genetic makeup—we see, hear, learn, and remember similarly.
- Male-female differences include body fat, muscle, height, age of onset of puberty, life expectancy, and onset of certain disorders.
- Men admit to more *aggression* than women do, and they are more likely to be physically aggressive. Women are slightly more likely than men to commit *relational aggression*.
- In most societies, men have more social power, and their leadership style tends to be directive, whereas women's is more democratic. Women often focus more on social connectedness than do men, and they "tend and befriend."

4-3 What factors contribute to gender bias in the workplace?

- Gender bias in the workplace is seen in such differences as perception, compensation, and child-care responsibility.
- Social norms, leadership styles, interaction styles, and everyday behaviors also contribute.

4-4 How do sex hormones influence prenatal and adolescent development, and what is an *intersex* condition?

- Both sex chromosomes and sex hormones influence development.
- The twenty-third pair of chromosomes determines sex, with the mother contributing an X chromosome and the father contributing either an X *chromosome* (for a girl baby) or a Y *chromosome* (for a boy baby). A Y chromosome triggers additional *testosterone* release and the formation of male sex organs.
- During *puberty*, both *primary* and *secondary sex characteristics* develop. Sex-related genes and physiology influence behavioral and cognitive gender differences between males and females.
- *Intersex* individuals are born possessing biological sexual characteristics of both sexes.

4-5 How do gender roles and gender identity differ?

- *Gender roles* describe how others expect us to act and vary depending on cultural expectations, which change over time and place.
- *Social learning theory* proposes that we learn our *gender identity*—our sense of being male, female, or some combination of the two—as we learn other things: through reinforcement, punishment, and observation. But critics argue that cognition also plays

a role because modeling and rewards cannot explain variation in *gender typing*.

- Some children organize themselves into "boy worlds" and "girl worlds"; others prefer androgyny.

- *Transgender* people's gender identity or expression differs from that associated with their birth sex. Their sexual orientation may be heterosexual, homosexual, bisexual, or asexual.

Human Sexuality

4-6 How do hormones influence human sexual motivation?

- The female *estrogen* and male testosterone hormones influence human sexual behavior less directly than they influence sexual behavior in other species.

- These hormones direct sexual development in the prenatal period; trigger development of sexual characteristics in adolescence; and help activate sexual behavior from puberty to late adulthood.

- Women's sexuality is more responsive to testosterone level than to estrogen level. Short-term shifts in testosterone level are normal in men, partly in response to stimulation.

4-7 What is the human *sexual response cycle,* and how can sexual dysfunctions interfere with this cycle?

- William Masters and Virginia Johnson described four stages in the human *sexual response cycle:* excitement, plateau, orgasm (which involves similar feelings and brain activity in males and females), and resolution. Males then enter a *refractory period* in which renewed arousal and orgasm are impossible.

- *Sexual dysfunctions* are problems that consistently impair sexual arousal or functioning. They can often be successfully treated by behaviorally oriented therapy or drug therapy.

4-8 How can sexually transmitted infections be prevented?

- Safe-sex practices help prevent sexually transmitted infections (STIs). Condoms are especially effective in preventing transmission of HIV, the virus that causes AIDS.

- A vaccination administered before sexual contact can prevent most human papilloma virus (HPV) infections.

4-9 How do external and imagined stimuli contribute to sexual arousal?

- Erotic material and other external stimuli can trigger sexual arousal in both men and women.

- Viewing sexually coercive material can lead to increased acceptance of violence toward women. Viewing sexually explicit materials can cause people to perceive their partners as comparatively less appealing and to devalue their relationships.

- Imagined stimuli (fantasies) help trigger sexual arousal.

4-10 What factors influence teenagers' sexual behaviors and use of contraceptives?

- Rates of teen intercourse vary from culture to culture and era to era.

- Factors contributing to teen pregnancy include minimal communication about birth control with parents, partners, and peers; impulsive sexual behavior, with passion overwhelming self-control; alcohol use; and mass media influences and *social scripts*.

- High intelligence, religious engagement, father presence, and participation in service learning programs have been predictors of teen sexual restraint.

Sexual Orientation

4-11 What has research taught us about sexual orientation?

- *Sexual orientation* is an enduring sexual attraction toward members of one's own sex (homosexual orientation), the other sex (heterosexual orientation), or both sexes (bisexual orientation).

- About 3 or 4 percent of men and 2 percent of women are homosexual. Sexual orientation is enduring.

- Sexual orientation is not an indicator of mental health. There is no evidence that environmental factors influence sexual orientation.

- Evidence for biological influences on homosexuality comes from same-sex attraction in many animal species; gay-straight trait and brain differences; genetic influences; and prenatal influences.

An Evolutionary Explanation of Human Sexuality

4-12 How might an evolutionary psychologist explain male-female differences in sexuality and mating preferences?

- *Evolutionary psychologists* attempt to understand how *natural selection* (how nature selects traits and appetites that contribute to survival and reproduction) has shaped behaviors found in all people.

- They reason that men's attraction to multiple healthy, fertile-appearing partners increases their chances of spreading their genes widely. In contrast, women tend to be choosier than men because of their need to incubate and nurse babies. Women increase their own and their children's chances of survival by searching for mates with the potential for long-term investment in their joint offspring.

4-13 What are the key criticisms of evolutionary explanations of human sexuality, and how do evolutionary psychologists respond?

- Critics argue that evolutionary psychologists (1) start with an effect and work backward to an explanation, (2) do not recognize social and cultural influences, and (3) relieve people from taking responsibility for their sexual behavior.

- Evolutionary psychologists respond that understanding our predispositions can help us overcome them. They recognize the importance of social and cultural influences, but they also cite the value of testable predictions based on evolutionary principles.

Social Influences on Human Sexuality

4-14 What roles do social factors play in our sexuality?

- Scientific research on human sexuality does not aim to define the personal meaning of sex in our own lives, which is influenced by many social factors. Sex is a socially significant act. Intimacy expresses our social nature, and sex at its human best is life uniting and love renewing.

Reflections on the Nature and Nurture of Sex, Gender, and Sexuality

4-15 How do nature, nurture, and our own choices influence gender roles and sexuality?

- Our ancestral history helped form us as a species. Our genes form us,

but our culture and experiences also shape us. Nature and nurture interact in the development of our gender-related traits and our mating behaviors. We are both the creatures and creators of our worlds, with our own hopes, goals, and expectations directing our future.

CHAPTER 5
Sensation and Perception

Basic Concepts of Sensation and Perception

5-1 What are *sensation* and *perception*? What do we mean by *bottom-up processing* and *top-down processing*?

- *Sensation* is the process by which our sensory receptors and nervous system receive information and transmit it to the brain. *Perception* is the process by which our brain organizes and interprets that information.

- *Bottom-up processing* is analysis that begins with the sensory receptors and works up to the brain. *Top-down processing* is information processing guided by higher-level mental processing, such as when we construct perceptions by filtering information through our experience and expectations.

5-2 What three steps are basic to all our sensory systems?

- Our senses (1) receive sensory stimulation (often using specialized receptor cells); (2) transform that stimulation into neural impulses; and (3) deliver the neural information to the brain. *Transduction* is the process

of converting one form of energy into another.

5-3 How do absolute thresholds and difference thresholds differ?

- Our *absolute threshold* is the minimum stimulation needed for us to be consciously aware of any stimulus 50 percent of the time. (Stimuli below that threshold are subliminal.)

- A *difference threshold* (also called the just noticeable difference, or jnd) is the minimum change needed to detect a difference between two stimuli 50 percent of the time.

- *Weber's law* states that two stimuli must differ by a constant minimum percentage (rather than a constant minimum amount).

5-4 How are we affected by subliminal stimuli?

- We do sense some stimuli *subliminally*—less than 50 percent of the time—and can be affected by these sensations. But although we can be *primed*, subliminal stimuli have no powerful, enduring influence on behavior.

5-5 What is the function of sensory adaptation?

- We grow less sensitive to constant sensory input.

- This diminished sensitivity to constant or routine odors, sounds, and touches (*sensory adaptation*) focuses our attention on informative changes in our environment.

5-6 How do our expectations, contexts, motivations, and emotions influence our perceptions?

- Perception is influenced by our *perceptual set*—our mental predisposition to perceive one thing and not another.

- Our physical, emotional, and cultural context, as well as our motivation, can create expectations about what we will perceive, thus affecting those perceptions.

Vision: Sensory and Perceptual Processing

5-7 What are the characteristics of the energy we see as visible light? What structures in the eye help focus that energy?

- The visible light we experience is just a thin slice of the broad spectrum of electromagnetic energy.
- The *hue* (blue, green, and so forth) we perceive in a light depends on its *wavelength,* and its brightness depends on its *intensity.*
- Light entering the eye through the pupil is focused by the lens on the retina—the inner surface of the eye.

5-8 How do the rods and cones process information, and what path does information take from the eye to the brain?

- The retina's light-sensitive *rods* and color-sensitive *cones* convert the light energy into neural impulses.
- After processing by bipolar and ganglion cells in the eyes' retina, neural impulses travel through the *optic nerve* to the thalamus and on to the visual cortex.

5-9 How do we perceive color in the world around us?

- According to the *Young-Helmholtz trichromatic (three-color) theory,* the retina contains three types of color receptors. Contemporary research has found three types of cones, each most sensitive to the wavelengths of one of the three primary colors of light (red, green, or blue).
- According to the *opponent-process theory,* there are three additional color processes (red-versus-green, blue-versus-yellow, black-versus-white). Contemporary research has confirmed that, on the way to the brain, neurons in the retina and the thalamus code the color-related information from the cones into pairs of opponent colors.
- These two theories, and the research supporting them, show that color processing occurs in two stages.

5-10 What are *feature detectors,* and what do they do?

- In the visual cortex, nerve cells called *feature detectors* respond to specific features of the visual stimulus, such as shape, angle, or movement.

5-11 How does the brain use parallel processing to construct visual perceptions?

- Through *parallel processing,* the brain handles many aspects of vision (color, movement, form, and depth) simultaneously. Other neural teams integrate the results, comparing them with stored information and enabling perceptions.

5-12 What was the main message of Gestalt psychology, and how do figure-ground and grouping principles help us perceive forms?

- Gestalt psychologists showed that the brain organizes bits of sensory information into *gestalts,* or meaningful forms. In pointing out that the whole may exceed the sum of its parts, they noted that we filter sensory information and construct our perceptions.
- To recognize an object, we must first perceive it as distinct (see it as a *figure*) from its surroundings (the *ground*).
- We bring order and form to sensory input by organizing it into meaningful groups, following such rules as proximity, continuity, and closure.

5-13 How do we use binocular and monocular cues to see in three dimensions, and how do we perceive motion?

- Humans and many other species perceive depth at, or very soon after, birth. We transform two-dimensional retinal images into three-dimensional *depth perceptions* that allow us to see objects in three dimensions and to judge distance.
- *Binocular cues,* such as *retinal disparity,* are depth cues that rely on information from both eyes.
- *Monocular cues* (such as relative size, interposition, relative height, relative motion, linear perspective, and light and shadow) let us judge depth using information transmitted by only one eye.
- As objects move, we assume that shrinking objects are moving away and enlarging objects are approaching. The brain computes motion imperfectly, with young children especially at risk of incorrectly perceiving approaching hazards such as vehicles.

5-14 How do perceptual constancies help us construct meaningful perceptions?

- *Perceptual constancy* is our ability to recognize an object regardless of the changing image it casts upon our retinas due to its changing angle, distance, or illumination.
- *Color constancy* is our ability to perceive consistent color in an object, even though the lighting and wavelengths shift.
- Shape constancy is our ability to perceive familiar objects (such as an opening door) as unchanging in shape. Size constancy is our ability to perceive objects as unchanging in size despite their changing retinal images. Knowing an object's size gives us clues to its distance; knowing its distance gives clues

about its size, but we sometimes misread monocular distance cues and reach the wrong conclusions, as in the Moon illusion.

5-15 **What does research on restored vision, sensory restriction, and perceptual adaptation reveal about the effects of experience on perception?**

- Experience guides our perceptual interpretations. Some perceptual abilities (such as color and figure-ground perception) are inborn. But people blind from birth who gain sight after surgery lack the experience to visually recognize shapes, forms, and complete faces.

- Sensory restriction research indicates that there is a critical period for some aspects of sensory and perceptual development. Without early stimulation, the brain's neural organization does not develop normally.

- Given eyeglasses that shift the world slightly to the left or right, turn it upside down, or reverse it, people can, through *perceptual adaptation,* learn to move about with ease.

The Nonvisual Senses

5-16 **What are the characteristics of the air pressure waves that we hear as sound?**

- Sound waves vary in amplitude (perceived as loudness) and in *frequency* (perceived as *pitch*—a tone's highness or lowness).

- Sound energy is measured in decibels.

5-17 **How does the ear transform sound energy into neural messages?**

- Through a mechanical chain of events, sound waves travel from the outer ear through the auditory canal, causing tiny vibrations in the eardrum. The bones of the middle ear transmit the vibrations to the fluid-filled *cochlea* in the inner ear,

causing waves of movement in hair cells lining the basilar membrane. This movement triggers nerve cells to send signals along the auditory nerve to the thalamus and then to the brain's auditory cortex.

- Small differences in the loudness and timing of the sounds received by each ear allow us to locate sounds.

- *Sensorineural hearing loss* (or nerve deafness) results from damage to the cochlea's hair cells or their associated nerves. *Conduction hearing loss* results from damage to the mechanical system that transmits sound waves to the cochlea. *Cochlear implants* can restore hearing for some people.

5-18 **What are the four basic touch sensations, and how do we sense touch?**

- Our sense of touch is actually several senses—pressure, warmth, cold, and pain—that combine to produce other sensations, such as "hot."

5-19 **What biological, psychological, and social-cultural influences affect our experience of pain? How do placebos, distraction, and hypnosis help control pain?**

- Pain reflects bottom-up sensations (such as input from nociceptors, the sensory receptors that detect hurtful temperatures, pressure, or chemicals) and top-down processes (such as experience, attention, and culture).

- Pain treatments often combine physical and psychological elements, including distractions. Combining a placebo with distraction, and amplifying the effect with *hypnosis* (which increases our response to suggestions), can help relieve pain. *Posthypnotic suggestion* is used by some clinicians to help control undesired symptoms and behavior.

5-20 **In what ways are our senses of taste and smell similar, and how do they differ?**

- Both taste and smell are chemical senses.

- Taste involves five basic sensations—sweet, sour, salty, bitter, and umami. Taste receptors in the taste buds carry messages to matching partner cells in the brain.

- There are no basic sensations for smell. Some 20 million olfactory receptor cells for smell, located at the top of each nasal cavity, send messages to the brain. These cells work together, combining their messages into patterns that vary, depending on the different odors they detect.

5-21 **How do we sense our body's position and movement?**

- Through *kinesthesia,* we sense the position and movement of individual body parts.

- We monitor our head's (and therefore our body's) position and movement, and maintain our balance, with our *vestibular sense.*

Sensory Interaction

5-22 **How does sensory interaction influence our perceptions, and what is *embodied cognition?***

- *Sensory interaction* is the influence of one sense on another. This occurs, for example, when the smell of a favorite food enhances its taste.

- *Embodied cognition* is the influence of bodily sensations, gestures, and other states on cognitive preferences and judgments.

ESP—Perception Without Sensation?

5-23 **What are the claims of ESP, and what have most research psychologists concluded after putting these claims to the test?**

- The three most testable forms of *extrasensory perception (ESP)* are telepathy (mind-to-mind communication), clairvoyance (perceiving remote events), and precognition (perceiving future events).

- Researchers have not been able to replicate (reproduce) ESP effects under controlled conditions.

CHAPTER 6
Learning

How Do We Learn?

6-1 How do we define *learning*, and what are some basic forms of learning?

- *Learning* is the process of acquiring new and relatively enduring information or behaviors through experience.
- Automatically responding to stimuli we do not control is called *respondent behavior*.
- In *associative learning*, we learn that certain events occur together. These associations produce *operant behaviors*.
- Through *cognitive learning*, we acquire mental information, such as by observation or language, that guides our behavior.

Classical Conditioning

6-2 What is *classical conditioning*, and how does it demonstrate associative learning?

- *Classical conditioning* is a type of learning in which we learn to link two or more stimuli and anticipate events. The process involves stimuli and responses:
  - A UR (*unconditioned response*) is an event that occurs naturally (such as salivation), in response to some stimulus.
  - A US (*unconditioned stimulus*) is something that naturally and automatically (without learning)

triggers the unlearned response (as food in the mouth triggers salivation).
  - A CS (*conditioned stimulus*) is originally an NS (*neutral stimulus*, such as a tone) that, through learning, becomes associated with some unlearned response (salivating).
  - A CR (*conditioned response*) is the learned response (salivating) to the originally neutral but now conditioned stimulus.

6-3 What parts do acquisition, extinction, spontaneous recovery, generalization, and discrimination play in classical conditioning?

- In classical conditioning, the first stage is *acquisition*, or the association of the NS with the US so that the NS begins triggering the CR. Acquisition occurs most readily when the NS is presented just before (ideally, about a half-second before) a US, preparing the organism for the upcoming event. This finding supports the view that classical conditioning is biologically adaptive.
- *Extinction* is diminished responding, which occurs if the CS appears repeatedly by itself (without the US).
- *Spontaneous recovery* is the appearance of a formerly extinguished conditioned response, following a rest period.
- Responses may be triggered by stimuli similar to the CS (*generalization*) but not by dissimilar stimuli (*discrimination*).

6-4 Why is Pavlov's work important, and how is it being applied?

- Ivan Pavlov taught us how to study a psychological process objectively, and that classical conditioning is a basic form of learning that applies to all species.
- Classical conditioning is applied to further human health and well-

being in many areas, including behavioral therapy for some types of psychological disorders.

Operant Conditioning

6-5 What is *operant conditioning*, and how is operant behavior reinforced and shaped?

- *Operant conditioning* is a type of learning in which behavior is strengthened if followed by a *reinforcer* or diminished if followed by a *punisher*.
- Expanding on Edward Thorndike's *law of effect*, B. F. Skinner and others *shaped* the behavior of rats and pigeons placed in *operant chambers* by rewarding successive approximations of a desired behavior.

6-6 How do positive and negative reinforcement differ, and what are the basic types of reinforcers?

- *Positive reinforcers* add a desirable stimulus to increase the frequency of a behavior. *Negative reinforcers* remove or reduce a negative stimulus to increase the frequency of a behavior.
- *Primary reinforcers* (such as receiving food when hungry) are naturally satisfying—no learning is required. *Conditioned* (or *secondary*) *reinforcers* (such as cash) are satisfying because we have learned to associate them with primary reinforcers.
- Reinforcers may be immediate or delayed.

6-7 How do continuous and partial reinforcement schedules affect behavior?

- A *reinforcement schedule* is a pattern that defines how often a desired response will be reinforced.
- In *continuous reinforcement* (reinforcing desired responses every time they occur), learning is rapid, but so is extinction if reinforcement stops.
- In *partial (intermittent) reinforcement* (reinforcing responses only sometimes),

learning is slower, but the behavior is much more resistant to extinction.

- *Fixed-ratio schedules* reinforce behaviors after a set number of responses.
- *Variable-ratio schedules* reinforce behaviors after an unpredictable number of responses.
- *Fixed-interval schedules* reinforce behaviors after set time periods.
- *Variable-interval schedules* reinforce behaviors after unpredictable time periods.

6-8 How does punishment differ from negative reinforcement, and how does punishment affect behavior?

- *Punishment* administers an undesirable consequence (such as spanking) or withdrawing something desirable (such as taking away a favorite toy).
- Negative reinforcement aims to increase frequency of a behavior (such as putting on your seat belt) by taking away something undesirable (the annoying beeping).
- The aim of punishment is to decrease the frequency of a behavior (such as a child's disobedience). Punishment can have unintended drawbacks: it can (1) suppress rather than change unwanted behaviors; (2) encourage discrimination (so that the undesirable behavior appears when the punisher is absent); (3) create fear; and (4) increase aggression.

6-9 Why were Skinner's ideas controversial, and how might his operant conditioning principles be applied at school, at work, in parenting, and for self-improvement?

- Critics say that Skinner's approach dehumanized people by neglecting their personal freedom and seeking to control their actions. Skinner replied that external forces shape us anyway, so we should direct those forces with reinforcement, which is more humane than punishment.
- Teachers can control students' behaviors with shaping techniques, and use interactive media to provide immediate feedback. (For example, the LearningCurve system available with this text provides such feedback and allows students to direct the pace of their own learning.)
- Managers can boost productivity and morale by rewarding well-defined and achievable behaviors.
- Parents can reward desirable behaviors but not undesirable ones.
- We can shape our own behaviors by stating realistic goals, planning how to work toward these goals, monitoring the frequency of our desired behaviors, reinforcing these behaviors, and gradually reducing rewards as our desired behaviors become habitual.

6-10 How does classical conditioning differ from operant conditioning?

- Both types of conditioning are forms of associative learning and involve acquisition, extinction, spontaneous recovery, generalization, and discrimination.
- In classical conditioning, we associate events we do not control and respond automatically (respondent behaviors). In operant conditioning, we link our behaviors (operant behaviors) with their consequences.

Biology, Cognition, and Learning

6-11 What limits does biology place on conditioning?

- We come prepared to learn tendencies, such as taste aversions, that aid our survival. Learning is adaptive.
- Despite operant training, animals may revert to biologically predisposed patterns. Learning some associations is easier than learning others due to these *biological constraints*.

6-12 How do cognitive processes affect classical and operant conditioning?

- More than the *behaviorists* supposed, expectations influence conditioning. In classical conditioning, animals may learn when to expect a US and may be aware of the link between stimuli and responses.
- In operant conditioning, *cognitive mapping* and *latent learning* research illustrate learning that occurs without immediate consequences. This demonstrates the importance of cognitive processes in learning.
- Other research shows that excessive rewards (driving *extrinsic motivation*) can destroy *intrinsic motivation* for an activity.

Learning by Observation

6-13 How does observational learning differ from associative learning? How may observational learning be enabled by mirror neurons?

- *Observational learning,* as shown in Bandura's Bobo doll experiment, involves learning by watching and imitating, rather than learning associations between different events. We learn to anticipate a behavior's consequences because we experience vicarious reinforcement or vicarious punishment.
- Our brain's frontal lobes have a demonstrated ability to mirror the activity of another's brain. (Some psychologists believe *mirror neurons* enable this process.) The same areas fire when we perform certain actions (such as responding to pain or moving our mouth to form words) as when we observe someone else performing those actions.

6-14 What is the impact of prosocial modeling and of antisocial modeling?

- Children tend to imitate what a model does and says, whether the behavior *modeled* is *prosocial* (positive, helpful) or antisocial.

- If a model's actions and words are inconsistent, children may imitate the hypocrisy they observe.

6-15 What is the violence-viewing effect?

- Media violence can contribute to aggression. This violence-viewing effect may be prompted by imitation and desensitization.
- Correlation does not equal causation, but study participants have reacted more cruelly when they have viewed violence (instead of entertaining nonviolence).

CHAPTER 7
Memory

Studying Memory

7-1 What is *memory*, and how do information-processing models help us study memory?

- *Memory* is the persistence of learning over time, through the encoding, storage, and retrieval of information.
- Psychologists use memory models to think about how our brain forms and retrieves memories. Information-processing models involve three processes: *encoding, storage,* and *retrieval.*

7-2 What is the three-stage information-processing model, and how has later research updated this model?

- The three processing stages in the Atkinson and Shiffrin classic three-stage model of memory are *sensory memory, short-term memory,* and *long-term memory.*
- More recent research has updated this model to include two additional concepts: (1) *working memory,* to stress the active processing occurring

in the second memory stage, and (2) *automatic processing,* to address the processing of information outside of conscious awareness.

Building Memories: Encoding

7-3 How do implicit and explicit memories differ?

- *Implicit* (nondeclarative) *memories* are our unconscious memories of skills and classically conditioned associations. They happen without our awareness, through *automatic processing.*
- *Explicit* (declarative) *memories* are our conscious memories of general knowledge, facts, and experiences. They form through *effortful processing.*

7-4 What information do we process automatically?

- In addition to skills and classically conditioned associations, we automatically process incidental information about space, time, and frequency. Our two-track mind works efficiently with the *parallel processing* of different subtasks.

7-5 How does sensory memory work?

- Sensory memory feeds some information into working memory for active processing there.
- An iconic memory is a very brief (a few tenths of a second) picture-image memory of a scene; an echoic memory is a three- or four-second sensory memory of a sound.

7-6 What is our short-term memory capacity?

- Short-term memory capacity is about seven items, give or take two, but this information disappears from memory quickly without rehearsal.

- Our working-memory capacity for active processing varies, depending on age and other factors.

7-7 What are some effortful processing strategies that can help us remember new information?

- Effective effortful processing strategies include *chunking* and *mnemonics.*
- Such strategies help us remember new information because we then focus our attention and make a conscious effort to remember.

7-8 Why is cramming ineffective, and what is the *testing effect?* Why is it important to make new information meaningful?

- Massed practice, or cramming, results in poorer long-term recall than encoding that is spread over time. Psychologists call this result of distributed practice the *spacing effect.* The *testing effect* is the finding that consciously retrieving, rather than simply rereading, information enhances memory.
- If new information is not meaningful, it will be difficult to process. We can avoid some encoding errors by thinking about what we have learned and translating it into personally meaningful terms.

Memory Storage

7-9 What is the capacity of long-term memory? Are our long-term memories processed and stored in specific locations?

- We have an unlimited capacity for storing information permanently in long-term memory.
- Memories are not stored intact in the brain in single specific spots. Many parts of the brain interact as we encode, store, and retrieve memories.

7-10 What roles do the hippocampus and frontal lobes play in memory processing?

- The frontal lobes and *hippocampus* are parts of the brain network dedicated to explicit memory formation.
- Many brain regions send information to the frontal lobes for processing. The hippocampus registers and temporarily holds elements of explicit memories (which are either *semantic* or *episodic*) before moving them for storage elsewhere (*memory consolidation*).

7-11 What roles do the cerebellum and basal ganglia play in memory processing?

- The cerebellum and basal ganglia are parts of the brain network dedicated to implicit memory formation. The cerebellum is important for storing classically conditioned memories.
- The basal ganglia are involved in motor movement and help form procedural memories for skills.

7-12 How do emotions affect our memory processing?

- Emotional arousal causes an outpouring of stress hormones, which lead to activity in the brain's memory-forming areas. Significantly stressful events can trigger very clear *flashbulb memories*.

7-13 How do changes at the synapse level affect our memory processing?

- *Long-term potentiation* (LTP) appears to be the neural process for learning and memory. It involves an increase in a synapse's firing potential as neurons become more efficient and more connections between neurons develop.

Retrieval: Getting Information Out

7-14 How do psychologists assess memory with recall, recognition, and relearning?

- Psychologists assess memory by studying evidence of it in the recall, recognition, and relearning of information:
  - *Recall* is memory demonstrated by retrieving information we learned earlier (as on a fill-in-the-blank test).
  - *Recognition* is memory demonstrated by identifying items previously learned (as on a multiple-choice test).
  - *Relearning* is memory demonstrated by more quickly mastering material that has been previously learned.

7-15 How do external events, internal moods, and order of appearance affect memory retrieval?

- *Retrieval cues*, such as context and mood, are information bits linked with the original encoded memory. These cues activate associations that help us retrieve memories; this process may occur without our awareness, as it does in *priming*.
- Returning to the same physical context or emotional state (*mood congruency*) in which we formed a memory can help us retrieve it.
- The *serial position effect* accounts for our tendency to recall best the last items (which may still be in working memory) and the first items (which we've spent more time rehearsing) in a list.

Forgetting

7-16 Why do we forget?

- Normal forgetting can happen because we have never encoded information (encoding failure); because the physical trace has decayed (storage decay); or because we cannot retrieve what we have encoded and stored (retrieval failure).
- Retrieval problems may result from *proactive* (forward-acting) *interference*, when prior learning interferes with recall of new information, or from *retroactive* (backward-acting) *interference*, when new learning disrupts recall of old information.
- Freud believed that motivated forgetting occurs, but researchers have found little evidence of *repression*.

Memory Construction Errors

7-17 How do misinformation, imagination, and source amnesia influence our memory construction? How do we decide whether a memory is real or false?

- Memories can be continually revised when retrieved, a process memory researchers call *reconsolidation*.
- *Misinformation* (exposure to misleading information) and imagination effects corrupt our stored memories of what actually happened.
- *Source amnesia* leads to faulty memories of how, when, or where we learned something, and may help explain *déjà vu*.
- False memories feel like real memories and can be persistent but are usually limited to the gist (the general idea) of the event.

7-18 Why have reports of repressed and recovered memories been so hotly debated?

- Incest and abuse happen more than was once supposed. But unless the victim was a child too young to remember, such traumas are usually remembered vividly, not repressed.

- Psychologists agree that (1) sexual abuse happens; (2) injustice happens; (3) forgetting happens; (4) recovered memories are common; (5) memories of events that happened before age 4 are unreliable; (6) memories "recovered" under hypnosis are especially unreliable; and (7) memories, whether real or false, can be emotionally upsetting.

7-19 How reliable are young children's eyewitness descriptions?

- Children's eyewitness descriptions are subject to the same memory influences that distort adult reports. If questioned soon after an event in neutral words they understand, children can accurately recall events and people involved in them.

Improving Memory

7-20 How can you use memory research findings to do better in this course and in others?

- Memory research findings suggest the following strategies for improving memory: Study repeatedly, make the material meaningful, activate retrieval cues, use mnemonic devices, minimize proactive and retroactive interference, sleep more, and test yourself to be sure you can retrieve, as well as recognize, material.

CHAPTER 8
Thinking, Language, and Intelligence

Thinking

8-1 What is cognition, and what are the functions of concepts?

- *Cognition* refers to all the mental activities associated with thinking, knowing, remembering, and communicating.
- We use *concepts*, mental groupings of similar objects, events, ideas, or people, to simplify and order the world around us. We form most concepts around *prototypes*, or best examples of a category.

8-2 What cognitive strategies help us solve problems, and what tendencies work against us?

- An *algorithm* is a methodical, logical rule or procedure (such as a step-by-step description for evacuating a building during a fire) that guarantees a solution to a problem.
- A *heuristic* is a simpler strategy (such as running for an exit if you smell smoke) that is usually speedier than an algorithm but is also more error-prone.
- *Insight* is not a strategy-based solution, but rather a sudden flash of inspiration (Aha!) that solves a problem.
- Tendencies that work against us in problem solving include *confirmation bias*, which leads us to verify rather than challenge our hypotheses, and *fixation*, which may prevent us from taking the fresh perspective that would lead to a solution.

8-3 What is intuition, and how can the availability heuristic influence our decisions and judgments?

- *Intuition* involves fast, automatic, unreasoned feelings and thoughts, as contrasted with explicit, conscious reasoning.
- Heuristics enable snap judgments. Using the *availability heuristic*, we judge the likelihood of things based on how readily they come to mind.

8-4 What factors exaggerate our fear of unlikely events?

- The availability heuristic often leads us to fear the wrong things. We also fear what our ancestral history has prepared us to fear, what we cannot control, and what is immediate. We fear too little the ongoing threats that claim lives one by one, such as traffic accidents and diseases.

8-5 How are our decisions and judgments affected by overconfidence, belief perseverance, and framing?

- *Overconfidence* can lead us to overestimate the accuracy of our beliefs.
- When a belief we have formed has been discredited, *belief perseverance* may cause us to cling to that belief. A remedy for belief perseverance is to consider how we might have explained an opposite result.
- *Framing* is the way a question or statement is worded. Subtle wording differences can dramatically alter our responses.

8-6 How do smart thinkers use intuition?

- As people gain expertise, they become skilled at making quick, shrewd judgments. Smart thinkers welcome their intuitions (which are usually adaptive), but when making complex decisions they gather as much information as possible and then take time to let their two-track mind process all available information.

8-7 What is creativity, and what fosters it?

- *Creativity*, the ability to produce new and valuable ideas, requires a certain level of aptitude (ability to learn), but it is more than school smarts. Aptitude tests require *convergent thinking*, but creativity requires *divergent thinking*.
- Robert Sternberg has proposed that creativity has five components: expertise; imaginative thinking skills; a venturesome personality; intrinsic motivation; and a creative

environment that sparks, supports, and refines creative ideas.

8-8 What do we know about thinking in other species?

- Evidence from studies of various species shows that many other animals use concepts, numbers, and tools, and that they transmit learning from one generation to the next (cultural transmission). And, like humans, some other species also show insight, self-awareness, altruism, cooperation, and grief.

Language

8-9 What are the milestones in language development, and when is the critical period for learning language?

- *Language* is our spoken, written, or signed words and the ways we combine them to communicate meaning. Receptive language (the ability to understand what is said to or about you) develops before productive language (the ability to produce words).
- Language development's timing varies, but all children follow the same sequence:
  - By about 4 months of age, infants *babble,* making a wide range of sounds found in languages all over the world.
  - By about 10 months, babbling contains only the sounds of the household language.
  - By about 12 months, children begin to speak in *one-word* sentences.
  - *Two-word (telegraphic)* phrases happen around 24 months, followed by full sentences soon after.
- Childhood is a critical period for learning language. A delay in exposure until age 2 or 3 produces a rush of language. But there is no similar rush of learning in children not exposed to either a spoken or a signed language

until age 7; such deprived children will never master any language.

- Noam Chomsky has proposed that all human languages share a universal grammar—the basic building blocks of language—and that humans are born with a predisposition (a built-in readiness) to learn language. The particular language we learn is the result of our experience.

8-10 What brain areas are involved in language processing and speech?

- Two important language- and speech-processing areas are *Broca's area,* a region of the frontal lobe that controls language expression, and *Wernicke's area,* a region in the left temporal lobe that controls language reception.
- Language processing is spread across other brain areas as well, with different neural networks handling specific linguistic subtasks.

8-11 How can thinking in images be useful?

- Thinking in images can provide useful mental practice if we focus on the steps needed to reach our goal (rather than fantasize about having achieved the goal).

8-12 What do we know about other species' capacity for language?

- A number of chimpanzees and bonobos have (1) learned to communicate with humans by signing or by pushing buttons wired to a computer, (2) developed vocabularies of nearly 400 words, (3) communicated by stringing these words together, (4) taught their skills to younger animals, and (5) demonstrated some understanding of syntax. But only humans possess language—verbal or signed expressions of complex grammar.

Intelligence

8-13 How do psychologists define *intelligence,* and what are the arguments for general intelligence *(g)*?

- *Intelligence* is the ability to learn from experience, solve problems, and use knowledge to adapt to new situations.
- Charles Spearman proposed that we have one *general intelligence (g)* underlying all other specific mental abilities. He helped develop factor analysis, a statistical procedure that searches for clusters of related items.

8-14 How do Gardner's and Sternberg's theories of multiple intelligences differ, and what criticisms have they faced?

- *Savant syndrome* and abilities lost after brain injuries seem to support Howard Gardner's view that we have multiple intelligences. He proposed eight independent intelligences: linguistic, logical-mathematical, musical, spatial, bodily-kinesthetic, intrapersonal, interpersonal, and naturalist. (He later proposed a ninth possible intelligence—existential intelligence.)
- Robert Sternberg's triarchic theory proposes three intelligence areas that predict real-world skills: analytical (academic problem solving), creative (trailblazing smarts), and practical (street smarts).
- Critics note research that has confirmed a general intelligence factor, which widely predicts performance. But highly successful people also tend to be conscientious, well connected, and doggedly energetic, with both ability *and* motivation counting.

8-15 What four abilities make up emotional intelligence?

- *Emotional intelligence,* which is an aspect of social intelligence, includes the abilities to perceive, understand, manage, and use emotions. Emotionally intelligent people achieve greater personal and professional success.

8-16 What is an intelligence test, and how do achievement and aptitude tests differ?

- *Intelligence tests* assess a person's mental aptitudes and compare them with those of others, using numerical scores.

- *Aptitude tests* measure the ability to learn; *achievement tests* measure what we have already learned.

8-17 When and why were intelligence tests created, and how do today's tests differ from early intelligence tests?

- Alfred Binet started the modern intelligence-testing movement in France in the early 1900s, when he developed questions to help predict children's future progress in the Paris school system. Binet hoped his test would improve children's education but feared it might be used to label them.

- During the early twentieth century, Lewis Terman of Stanford University revised Binet's work for use in the United States (which resulted in the *Stanford-Binet* intelligence test). Terman's belief in an intelligence that was fixed at birth and differed among ethnic groups realized Binet's fears that intelligence tests would be used to limit children's opportunities.

- William Stern contributed the concept of the *IQ (intelligence quotient).*

- The most widely used intelligence tests today are the *Wechsler Adult Intelligence Scale (WAIS)* and Wechsler's tests for children. These tests differ from their predecessors in the way they offer an overall intelligence score as well as scores for verbal comprehension, perceptual organization, working memory, and processing speed.

8-18 What is a normal curve, and what does it mean to say that a test has been standardized and is reliable and valid?

- The distribution of test scores often forms a *normal* (bell-shaped) *curve* around the central average score, with fewer and fewer scores at the extremes.

- *Standardization* establishes a basis for meaningful score comparisons by giving a test to a representative sample of future test-takers.

- *Reliability* is the extent to which a test yields consistent results (on two halves of the test, on alternative forms of the test, or on retesting).

- *Validity* is the extent to which a test measures or predicts what it is supposed to. A test should have both *content validity* and *predictive validity*. (Aptitude tests have predictive validity if they can predict future achievements.)

8-19 What are the traits of people who score at the low and high extremes on intelligence tests?

- An intelligence test score of or below 70 is one diagnostic factor in the diagnosis of *intellectual disability;* limited conceptual, social, and practical skills are other factors. Some people with this diagnosis may be able to live independently. One condition included in this category is *Down syndrome,* a developmental disorder caused by an extra copy of chromosome 21.

- People at the high-intelligence extreme tend to be healthy and well-adjusted, as well as unusually successful academically.

8-20 What does it mean when we say that a trait is heritable? What do twin and adoption studies tell us about the nature and nurture of intelligence?

- *Heritability* is the portion of variation among people in a group that can be attributed to genes. Many genes contribute to intelligence; there is no known "genius" gene.

- Studies of twins, family members, and adoptive parents and siblings indicate a significant hereditary contribution to intelligence scores. But these studies also provide evidence of environmental influences.

8-21 How can environmental influences affect cognitive development?

- Heredity and environment interact: Our genes shape the environments that influence us.

- Studies of children raised in extremely impoverished environments with minimal social interaction indicate that life experiences can significantly influence intelligence test performance. No evidence supports the idea that normal, healthy children can be molded into geniuses by growing up in an exceptionally enriched environment.

8-22 How stable are intelligence test scores over the life span, and how do psychologists study this question?

- *Cross-sectional studies* and *longitudinal studies* have shown that intelligence endures. The stability of intelligence test scores increases with age, with scores very stable and predictive by early adolescence.

8-23 What are crystallized and fluid intelligence, and how does aging affect them?

- *Crystallized intelligence,* our accumulated knowledge and verbal skills, tends to increase.

- *Fluid intelligence,* our ability to reason speedily and abstractly, declines in older adults.

8-24 How and why do the genders differ in mental ability scores?

- Males and females tend to have the same average intelligence test scores, but they differ in some specific abilities.

- Girls are better spellers, more verbally fluent, better at locating objects, better at detecting emotions, and more sensitive to touch, taste, and color.

- Boys outperform girls at spatial ability and related mathematics, though in math computation and overall math performance, boys and girls hardly differ. Boys also outnumber girls at the low and high extremes of mental abilities.

- Evolutionary and cultural explanations have been proposed for these gender differences.

8-25 How and why do racial and ethnic groups differ in mental ability scores?

- Racial and ethnic groups differ in their average intelligence test scores. The evidence suggests that environmental differences are responsible for these group differences.

8-26 Are intelligence tests biased and discriminatory? How does stereotype threat affect test-takers' performance?

- Aptitude tests aim to predict how well a test-taker will perform in a given situation. So they are necessarily "biased" in the sense that they are sensitive to performance differences caused by cultural experience.

- But a test should not predict less accurately for one group than for another. In this sense, most experts consider the major aptitude tests unbiased.

- *Stereotype threat,* a self-confirming concern that we will be judged based on a negative stereotype, affects performance on all kinds of tests.

CHAPTER 9
Motivation and Emotion

Motivational Concepts

9-1 What is *motivation,* and what are three key perspectives that help us understand motivated behaviors?

- *Motivation* is a need or desire that energizes and directs behavior.

- *Drive-reduction theory:* We feel motivated when pushed by a *physiological* need to reduce a drive (such as thirst), or when pulled by an *incentive* in our environment (an ice-cold drink). Drive-reduction's goal is *homeostasis,* maintaining a steady internal state.

- Arousal theory: We also feel motivated to behave in ways that maintain arousal (for example, curiosity-driven behaviors). The *Yerkes-Dodson law* describes the relationship between arousal and performance.

- Maslow's *hierarchy of needs:* Our levels of motivation form a pyramid of human needs, from basic needs such as hunger and thirst up to higher-level needs such as self-actualization and self-transcendence.

Hunger

9-2 What physiological factors cause us to feel hungry?

- Hunger's pangs correspond to the stomach's contractions, but hunger also has other causes. Neural areas in the brain, some within the hypothalamus, monitor blood chemistry (including level of *glucose*) and incoming information about the body's state.

- Appetite hormones include ghrelin (secreted by an empty stomach); insulin (controls blood glucose); leptin (secreted by fat cells); orexin (secreted by the hypothalamus); and PYY (secreted by the digestive tract).

- *Basal metabolic rate* is the body's resting rate of energy output. The body may have a *set point* (a biologically fixed tendency to maintain an optimum weight) or a looser settling point (which is also influenced by the environment).

9-3 How do cultural and situational factors affect our taste preferences and eating habits?

- Hunger also reflects our memory of when we last ate and our expectation of when we should eat again.

- Humans as a species prefer certain tastes (such as sweet and salty), but our individual preferences are also influenced by learning, culture, and situation. Some taste preferences, such as the avoidance of new foods, or of foods that have made us ill, have survival value.

9-4 What factors predispose some people to become and remain obese?

- Genes and environment interact to produce obesity.

- Twin and adoption studies indicate that body weight is genetically influenced. Environmental influences include too little sleep and exercise, an abundance of high-calorie food, and social influence.

- Those wishing to lose weight are advised to make a lifelong change in habits: Begin only if you feel motivated and self-disciplined; exercise and get enough sleep; minimize exposure to tempting food cues; limit variety and eat healthy foods; reduce portion sizes; space meals throughout the day; beware of the binge; plan eating to help monitor yourself during social events; forgive the occasional lapse; and connect to a support group.

The Need to Belong

9-5 What evidence points to our human need to belong?

- Social bonds are adaptive and help us to be healthier and happier. Feeling loved activates brain regions associated with rewards and satisfaction.
- *Ostracism* is the deliberate exclusion of individuals or groups. Social isolation can put us at risk mentally and physically.

9-6 How does social networking influence us?

- We connect with others through social networking, strengthening our relationships with those we already know. When networking, people tend toward increased self-disclosure. People with high *narcissism* are especially active on social networking sites.
- Working out strategies for self-control and disciplined usage can help people maintain a healthy balance between their real-world and online time.

Emotion: Arousal, Behavior, and Cognition

9-7 What are the three parts of an emotion, and what theories help us to understand our emotions?

- *Emotions* are psychological responses of the whole organism involving bodily arousal, expressive behaviors, and conscious experience.
- *James-Lange theory:* Emotional feelings follow our body's response to the emotion-arousing stimuli. (We observe our heart pounding and feel fear.)
- *Cannon-Bard theory:* Our body responds to emotion at the same

time that we experience that emotion. (Neither causes the other.)

- *Schachter-Singer two-factor theory:* Emotions have two ingredients, physical arousal and a cognitive label, and the cognitive labels we put on our states of arousal are an essential ingredient of emotion.
- Richard Lazarus agreed that many important emotions arise from our interpretations or inferences. But Robert Zajonc and Joseph LeDoux have contended that some simple emotional responses occur instantly, not only outside our conscious awareness, but before any cognitive processing occurs. This interplay between emotion and cognition illustrates our two-track mind.

Embodied Emotion

9-8 What are some basic emotions?

- Carroll Izard's basic emotions are joy, interest-excitement, surprise, sadness, anger, disgust, contempt, fear, shame, and guilt.

9-9 What is the link between emotional arousal and the autonomic nervous system?

- The arousal component of emotion is regulated by the autonomic nervous system's sympathetic (arousing) and parasympathetic (calming) divisions.
- In a crisis, the fight-or-flight response automatically mobilizes your body for action.

9-10 How do our body states relate to specific emotions?

- The large-scale body changes that accompany sexual arousal, fear, and anger are very similar (increased perspiration, breathing, and heart rate), though they feel different. Emotions may be similarly arousing, but some subtle physiological responses (such as facial muscle movements) distinguish them.

- Emotions use different circuits in the brain. For example, greater activity in the left frontal lobe signals positive rather than negative moods.

9-11 How effective are polygraphs in using body states to detect lies?

- *Polygraphs* (lie detectors) attempt to measure physical evidence of emotions; they are not accurate enough to justify widespread use in business and law enforcement.
- The use of guilty knowledge questions and new forms of technology may produce better indications of lying.

Expressed and Experienced Emotion

9-12 How do we communicate nonverbally? How do women and men differ in these abilities?

- We are good at detecting emotions from body movements, facial expressions, and voice tones. Even seconds-long video clips of behavior can reveal feelings.
- Women tend to read emotional cues more easily and to be more empathic. Their faces also express more emotion.

9-13 How are nonverbal expressions of emotion understood within and across cultures?

- The meaning of gestures varies by culture.
- Facial expressions, such as those of happiness and sadness, are roughly similar all over the world.

9-14 How do facial expressions influence our feelings?

- Research on the *facial feedback effect* shows that our facial expressions can trigger emotional feelings and signal our body to respond accordingly. We also mimic others' expressions, which helps us empathize.

CHAPTER 10
Stress, Health, and Human Flourishing

Stress: Some Basic Concepts

10-1 How does our appraisal of an event affect our stress reaction, and what are the three main types of stressors?

- *Stress* is the process by which we appraise and respond to stressors—events that challenge or threaten us. If we appraise an event as challenging, we will be aroused and focused in preparation for success. If we appraise an event as a threat, we will experience a stress reaction, and our health may suffer.
- The three main types of stressors are catastrophes, significant life changes, and daily hassles.

10-2 How does the body respond to stress?

- Walter Cannon viewed our body's response to stress as a *fight-or-flight* system.
- Hans Selye proposed a general three-phase (alarm, resistance, exhaustion) *general adaptation syndrome (GAS)*.
- People may react to stress by withdrawing, turning to alcohol, or becoming emotionally insensitive (more common in men) or by showing a *tend-and-befriend response* (more common in women), such as when helping others after natural disasters.

Stress Effects and Health

10-3 How does stress influence our immune system?

- Stress takes energy away from the immune system, inhibiting the activities of its B and T lymphocytes, macrophages, and natural killer (NK) cells. This leaves us more vulnerable to illness and disease. *Psychoneuroimmunology* is the study of these mind-body interactions.
- Although stress does not cause diseases such as AIDS and cancer, it may make us more vulnerable to them and influence their progression.

10-4 How does stress increase coronary heart disease risk?

- Stress is directly connected to *coronary heart disease,* the United States' leading cause of death.
- Heart disease has been linked with the competitive, hard-driving, impatient, and (especially) anger-prone *Type A* personality. Type A people secrete more stress hormones. Chronic stress contributes to persistent inflammation, which is associated with heart and other health problems, including depression.
- *Type B* personalities are more relaxed and easygoing and less likely to experience heart disease.
- The fight-or-flight stress reaction may divert blood from the liver to the muscles, leaving excess cholesterol circulating in the bloodstream. Stress can also trigger altered heart rhythms.

10-5 So, does stress *cause* illness?

- Stress may not directly cause illness, but it does make us more vulnerable, by influencing our behaviors and our physiology.

Coping With Stress

10-6 What are two basic ways that people cope with stress?

- We use direct, *problem-focused coping* strategies when we feel a sense of control over a situation, and these are usually most effective.
- When lacking that sense of control, we may need to use *emotion-focused coping* strategies to protect our long-term well-being. These strategies can be harmful if misused.

10-7 How does our sense of control influence stress and health?

- Feelings of loss of *personal control* can trigger physical symptoms, such as increased stress hormones and rising blood pressure. A series of uncontrollable events can lead to *learned helplessness*.
- Those with an *internal locus of control* achieve more in school and work, act more independently, enjoy better health, and feel less depressed than do those with an *external locus of control*.
- Those who develop and maintain *self-control* earn higher income, get better grades, and are healthier.

10-8 How do optimists and pessimists differ, and why does our outlook on life matter?

- *Optimists* (those expecting positive outcomes) tend to be in better health than *pessimists* (those expecting negative outcomes).
- Studies of people with an optimistic outlook show that their immune system is stronger, their blood pressure does not increase as sharply in response to stress, their recovery from heart bypass surgery is faster, and their life expectancy is longer. Yet excessive optimism can blind us to real risks; realistic anxiety over possible future failures can help motivate us to do better.

10-9 How do social support and finding meaning in life influence health?

- Social support promotes health by calming us, by reducing blood pressure and stress hormones, and by fostering stronger immune function. We can significantly reduce our stress and increase our health by building and maintaining relationships with family and friends, and by finding meaning even in difficult times.

Managing Stress Effects

10-10 How well does aerobic exercise help us manage stress and improve well-being?

- *Aerobic exercise* is sustained activity that increases heart and lung fitness, which leads to greater well-being.
- Exercise increases arousal and triggers serotonin activity. It also reduces depression and anxiety.

10-11 In what ways might relaxation and meditation influence stress and health?

- Relaxation and meditation have been shown to reduce stress by relaxing muscles, lowering blood pressure, improving immune functioning, and lessening anxiety and depression. *Mindfulness meditation* is a reflective practice of attending to current experiences in a nonjudgmental and accepting manner. Massage therapy also relaxes muscles and reduces depression.
- Counseling Type A heart attack survivors to slow down and relax has helped lower rates of recurring attacks.

10-12 Does religious involvement relate to health?

- Religious involvement predicts better health and longevity. This may be explained by the healthier lifestyles of religiously active people, the social support that comes along with practicing a faith in community, and the positive emotions often found among people who regularly attend religious services.

Happiness

10-13 What are the causes and consequences of happiness?

- A good mood brightens people's perceptions of the world. Happy people tend to be healthy, energized, and satisfied with life. They also are more willing to help others (the *feel-good, do-good phenomenon*).
- Even significant good or bad events don't usually change our *subjective well-being* for long. Happiness is relative to our own experiences (the *adaptation-level phenomenon*) and to others' success (the *relative deprivation* principle).
- Tips for increasing happiness levels: take charge of your schedule, act happy, seek meaningful work and leisure, buy shared experiences rather than things, exercise, sleep enough, foster friendships, focus beyond the self, and nurture gratitude and spirituality.

CHAPTER 11
Social Psychology

What Is Social Psychology's Focus?

11-1 What are three main focuses of social psychology?

- *Social psychology* focuses on how we think about, influence, and relate to one another. Social psychologists study the social influences that explain why the same person will act differently in different situations.

Social Thinking

11-2 How does the fundamental attribution error describe how we tend to explain others' behavior compared with our own?

- We may commit the *fundamental attribution error* (especially if we come from an individualist Western culture) when explaining others' behavior, by underestimating the influence of the situation and overestimating the effects of personality.
- When we explain our own behavior, however, we more often recognize the influence of the situation.

11-3 What is an attitude, and how do attitudes and actions affect each other?

- *Attitudes* are feelings, often based on our beliefs, that predispose us to respond in certain ways. Attitudes that are stable, specific, and easily recalled can affect our actions when other influences are minimal.
- Persuasion can take two forms: *peripheral route persuasion* and *central route persuasion*.
- Actions also modify our attitudes. This can be seen in the *foot-in-the-door phenomenon* (complying with a large request after having agreed to a small request) and *role* playing (acting a social part by following guidelines for expected behavior).
- When our attitudes don't fit with our actions, *cognitive dissonance theory* suggests that we will reduce tension by changing our attitudes to match our actions.

Social Influence

11-4 What do experiments on conformity and obedience reveal about the power of social influence?

- Solomon Asch and others have found that we are most likely to *conform* to a group standard when (a) we feel incompetent or insecure, (b) our group has at least three people, (c) everyone else agrees, (d) we admire the group's status, (e) we have not already committed to another response, (f) we know we are being observed, and (g) our culture encourages respect for social standards.
- We may conform to gain approval (*normative social influence*) or because we are willing to accept others' opinions as new information (*informational social influence*).

- In Stanley Milgram's famous experiments, people usually obeyed the experimenter's orders even when they thought they were harming another person. Obedience was highest when (a) the experimenter was nearby and (b) was a legitimate authority figure supported by an important institution, (c) the victim was not nearby, and (d) there were no role models for defiance.

11-5 What do the social influence studies teach us about ourselves? How much power do we have as individuals?

- Strong social influences can make people conform to falsehoods or give in to cruelty.
- Even a small minority sometimes sways a group, especially when the minority expresses its views consistently.
- Social control (the power of the situation) and personal control (the power of the individual) interact.

11-6 How does the presence of others influence our actions, via social facilitation, social loafing, or deindividuation?

- In *social facilitation*, the presence of others arouses us, improving performance on easy tasks. Observers can hinder performance on difficult tasks.
- *Social loafing* is the tendency when participating in a group project to feel less responsible, when we may free ride on others' efforts.
- When the presence of others both arouses us and makes us feel less responsible, we may experience *deindividuation*—loss of self-awareness and self-restraint.

11-7 How can group interaction enable group polarization?

- In *group polarization*, group discussions with like-minded others cause us to feel more strongly about our shared beliefs and attitudes.

11-8 What role does the Internet play in group polarization?

- Internet communication magnifies the effect of connecting like-minded people, for better and for worse. People find support, but also often isolation from those with different opinions. Separation plus conversation may thus lead to group polarization.

11-9 How can group interaction enable groupthink?

- *Groupthink* is driven by a desire for harmony within a group, causing its members to overlook important alternatives.

Social Relations

11-10 What are the three parts of prejudice, and how has prejudice changed over time?

- *Prejudice* is an unfair, usually negative, attitude toward a group and its members. Prejudice's three components are (a) beliefs (often *stereotypes*), (b) emotions (negative feelings), and (c) predispositions to action (*discrimination*).
- Open prejudice has decreased, but subtle prejudice and automatic prejudice—occurring without our awareness—continue.
- Prejudice involves both explicit and implicit negative attitudes toward people of a particular ethnic group, gender, sexual orientation, or viewpoint.

11-11 What factors contribute to the social roots of prejudice, and how does scapegoating illustrate the emotional roots of prejudice?

- Social inequalities and social divisions feed prejudice. Favored social groups often justify their higher status with the *just-world phenomenon*.
- We tend to favor our own group (*ingroup bias*) as we divide ourselves into us (the *ingroup*) and them (the *outgroup*).
- We may use prejudice to protect our emotional well-being, such as when focusing anger by blaming events on a *scapegoat*.

11-12 What are the cognitive roots of prejudice?

- The cognitive roots of prejudice grow from our natural ways of processing information: forming categories, remembering vivid cases, and believing that the world is just (and our group's way of doing things is the right way).

11-13 What biological factors predispose us to be aggressive?

- *Aggression* is a complex behavior resulting from the interaction of biology and experience.
- Biology influences our threshold for aggressive behaviors at three levels: genetic (inherited traits), biochemical (such as alcohol or excess testosterone in the bloodstream), and neural (activity in key brain areas).

11-14 What psychological and social-cultural factors may trigger aggressive behavior?

- Frustration (*frustration-aggression principle*), aversive events, getting rewarded for aggression, seeing an aggressive role model, and poor self-control can all contribute to aggression.
- Viewing sexual violence contributes to greater aggression toward women.
- Media portrayals of violence provide *social scripts* that children learn to follow.

11-15 Why do we befriend or fall in love with some people but not others?

- Proximity (geographical nearness) increases liking, in part because of the *mere exposure effect*—exposure to novel stimuli increases liking of those stimuli.
- Physical attractiveness increases social opportunities and improves the way we are perceived.
- Similarity of attitudes and interests greatly increases liking, especially as relationships develop. We also like those who like us.

11-16 How does romantic love typically change as time passes?

- Intimate love relationships start with *passionate love*—an intensely aroused state.
- Over time, the strong affection of *companionate love* may develop, especially if enhanced by an *equitable* relationship and by intimate *self-disclosure*.

11-17 What is altruism? When are we most—and least—likely to help?

- *Altruism* is unselfish regard for the well-being of others.
- We are most likely to help when we (a) notice an incident, (b) interpret it as an emergency, and (c) assume responsibility for helping. Other factors, including our mood and our similarity to the victim, also affect our willingness to help.
- We are least likely to help if other bystanders are present (the *bystander effect*).

11-18 How do social norms explain helping behavior?

- Helping results from socialization, in which we are taught guidelines for expected behaviors in social situations, such as the *reciprocity norm* and the *social-responsibility norm*.

11-19 What social processes fuel conflict? How can we transform feelings of prejudice and conflict into behaviors that promote peace?

- *Conflicts*, perceived incompatibilities of actions, goals, or ideas between individuals and cultures, are often fed by distorted *mirror-image perceptions*—each party views itself as ethical and peaceful and the other as untrustworthy and evil-intentioned. Perceptions can be *self-fulfilling prophecies*.
- Peace can result when individuals or groups cooperate to achieve *superordinate* (shared) *goals*.

CHAPTER 12 Personality

What Is Personality?

12-1 What is *personality*, and what theories inform our understanding of personality?

- *Personality* is an individual's characteristic pattern of thinking, feeling, and acting.
- Psychoanalytic (and later psychodynamic) theory and humanistic theory have become part of our cultural legacy. They also laid the foundation for later theories, such as trait and social-cognitive theories of personality.

Psychodynamic Theories

12-2 How did Sigmund Freud's treatment of psychological disorders lead to his view of the unconscious mind?

- *Psychodynamic theories* view personality from the perspective that behavior is a lively (dynamic) interaction between the conscious and unconscious mind. The theories trace their origin to Sigmund Freud's theory of *psychoanalysis*.
- In treating patients whose disorders had no clear physical explanation, Freud concluded that these problems reflected unacceptable thoughts and feelings, hidden away in the *unconscious* mind. To explore this hidden part of a patient's mind, Freud used *free association* and dream analysis.

12-3 What was Freud's view of personality?

- Freud believed that personality is a result of conflict among the mind's three systems: the *id* (pleasure-seeking impulses), *ego* (reality-oriented executive), and *superego* (internalized set of ideals, or conscience).

12-4 What developmental stages did Freud propose?

- He believed children pass through five *psychosexual stages* (oral, anal, phallic, latency, and genital). Unresolved conflicts at any stage can leave a person's pleasure-seeking impulses *fixated* (stalled) at that stage.

12-5 How did Freud think people defended themselves against anxiety?

- For Freud, anxiety was the product of tensions between the demands of id and superego.
- The ego copes by using unconscious *defense mechanisms,* such as *repression,* which he viewed as the basic mechanism underlying and enabling all the others.

12-6 Which of Freud's ideas did his followers accept or reject?

- Freud's early followers, the neo-Freudians, accepted many of his ideas. They differed in placing more emphasis on the conscious mind and in stressing social motives more than sex or aggression. Neo-Freudian Carl Jung proposed the *collective unconscious*.

- Contemporary psychodynamic theorists and therapists reject Freud's emphasis on sexual motivation. They stress, with support from modern research findings, the view that much of our mental life is unconscious, and they believe that our childhood experiences influence our adult personality and attachment patterns.

12-7 What are projective tests, how are they used, and how are they criticized?

- *Projective tests* attempt to assess personality by showing people an ambiguous image designed to trigger projection of the test-taker's unconscious thoughts and feelings.
- The *Thematic Apperception Test (TAT)* and the *Rorschach inkblot test* are two such tests. The Rorschach has low reliability and validity, but some clinicians value it as a source of suggestive leads, an icebreaker, or a revealing interview technique.

12-8 How do today's psychologists view Freud's psychoanalysis?

- Freud rightly drew our attention to the vast unconscious, to the struggle to cope with anxiety and sexuality, to the conflict between biological impulses and social restraints.
- But his concept of repression, and his view of the unconscious as a collection of repressed and unacceptable thoughts, wishes, feelings, and memories, cannot survive scientific scrutiny.
- Freud offered after-the-fact explanations, which are hard to test scientifically.
- Research does not support many of Freud's specific ideas, such as development being fixed in childhood. (We now know it is lifelong.)

12-9 How has modern research developed our understanding of the unconscious?

- Research confirms that we do not have full access to all that goes on in our mind, but the current view of the unconscious is that it is a separate and parallel track of information processing that occurs outside our awareness. Research also supports reaction formation and projection (the false consensus effect).
- This processing includes schemas that control our perceptions; implicit memories of learned skills; instantly activated emotions; and the self-concept and stereotypes that automatically influence how we process information about ourselves and others.

Humanistic Theories

12-10 How did humanistic psychologists view personality, and what was their goal in studying personality?

- Humanistic theories sought to turn psychology's attention toward human growth potential.
- Abraham Maslow thought that human motivations form a *hierarchy of needs*. If basic needs are fulfilled, people will strive toward *self-actualization* and *self-transcendence*.
- Carl Rogers believed that people are basically good, and that showing *unconditional positive regard* and being genuine, accepting, and empathic can help others develop a more realistic and positive *self-concept*.

12-11 How did humanistic psychologists assess a person's sense of self?

- Some rejected any standardized assessments and relied on interviews and conversations.
- Rogers sometimes used questionnaires in which people described their ideal and actual selves, which he later used to judge progress during therapy.

12-12 How have humanistic theories influenced psychology? What criticisms have they faced?

- Humanistic psychology helped renew interest in the concept of self, and also laid the groundwork for today's scientific subfield of positive psychology.
- Critics have said that humanistic psychology's concepts were vague and subjective, its values self-centered, and its assumptions naively optimistic.

Trait Theories

12-13 How do psychologists use traits to describe personality?

- *Trait* theorists see personality as a stable and enduring pattern of behavior. They have been more interested in describing our differences than in explaining them.
- They identify *factors*—clusters of behavior tendencies that occur together.

12-14 What are some common misunderstandings about introversion?

- Western cultures prize extraversion, but introverts have different, equally important skills. Introversion does not equal shyness, and extraverts don't always outperform introverts as leaders or in sales success. Introverts often experience great achievement; many introverts prosper.

12-15 What are personality inventories?

- *Personality inventories* (such as the *MMPI*) are questionnaires on which people respond to items designed to gauge a wide range of feelings and behaviors.
- Unlike projective tests, these tests are objectively scored. But people can fake their answers to create a good impression; objectivity does not guarantee validity.

12-16 Which traits seem to provide the most useful information about personality variation?

- The Big Five personality factors—conscientiousness, agreeableness, neuroticism, openness, and extraversion (CANOE)—currently offer the clearest picture of personality.
- These factors are stable and appear to be found in all cultures.

12-17 Does research support the consistency of personality traits over time and across situations?

- A person's average traits persist over time and are predictable over many different situations. But traits cannot predict behavior in any one particular situation.

Social-Cognitive Theories

12-18 How do social-cognitive theorists view personality development, and how do they explore behavior?

- *Reciprocal determinism* describes the interaction and mutual influence of behavior, internal personal factors, and environmental factors.
- Albert Bandura first proposed the *social-cognitive perspective,* which views personality as the product of the interaction between a person's traits (including thinking) and the situation—the social world around us.
- Social-cognitive researchers apply principles of learning, cognition, and social behavior to personality.
- A person's average traits are predictable over many different situations, but not in any one particular situation.

12-19 What criticisms have social-cognitive theorists faced?

- Critics note that social-cognitive theorists focus so much on the situation that they fail to appreciate a person's inner traits, underemphasizing the importance of unconscious motives, emotions, and personality characteristics.

Exploring the Self

12-20 Why has psychology generated so much research on the self? How important is self-esteem to our well-being?

- The *self* is the center of personality, organizing our thoughts, feelings, and actions.
- Considering possible selves helps motivate us toward positive development, but focusing too intensely on ourselves can lead to the *spotlight effect.*
- High *self-esteem* is beneficial, but unrealistically high self-esteem, which can be *narcissistic,* is dangerous (linked to aggressive behavior) and fragile. Rather than unrealistically promoting children's feelings of self-worth, it is better to reward their achievements, which leads to feelings of competence.

12-21 What evidence reveals self-serving bias, and how do defensive and secure self-esteem differ?

- *Self-serving bias* is our tendency to perceive ourselves favorably, as when viewing ourselves as better than average or when accepting credit for our successes but not blame for our failures.
- Defensive self-esteem is fragile, focuses on sustaining itself, and views failure or criticism as a threat.
- Secure self-esteem is sturdy, enabling us to feel accepted for who we are.

12-22 How do individualist and collectivist cultures differ in their values and goals?

- Although individuals vary, different cultures tend to emphasize either individualism or collectivism.
- Cultures based on self-reliant *individualism* tend to value personal independence and achievement.
- Cultures based on socially connected *collectivism* tend to value group goals, social identity, and commitments.

CHAPTER 13
Psychological Disorders

What Is a Psychological Disorder?

13-1 How should we draw the line between normal behavior and psychological disorder?

- According to psychologists and psychiatrists, *psychological disorders* are marked by a clinically significant disturbance in an individual's cognition, emotion regulation, or behavior. Such dysfunctional or maladaptive thoughts, emotions, or behaviors interfere with daily life, and thus are disordered.

13-2 Why is there controversy over attention-deficit/hyperactivity disorder?

- A child (or, less commonly, an adult) who displays extreme inattention and/or hyperactivity and impulsivity may be diagnosed with *attention-deficit/hyperactivity disorder (ADHD)* and treated with medication and other therapy.
- The controversy centers on whether the growing number of ADHD cases reflects overdiagnosis or increased awareness of the disorder, and on the long-term effects of stimulant-drug treatment.

13-3 How do the medical model and the biopsychosocial approach influence our understanding of psychological disorders?

- The *medical model* assumes that psychological disorders are mental illnesses with physical causes that can be diagnosed, treated, and, in most cases, cured through therapy, sometimes in a hospital.
- The biopsychosocial approach assumes that disordered behavior comes from the interaction of biological characteristics (genes and physiology), psychological dynamics, and social-cultural circumstances.
- *Epigenetics* also informs our understanding of disorders.

13-4 How and why do clinicians classify psychological disorders, and why do some psychologists criticize the use of diagnostic labels?

- The American Psychiatric Association's *DSM-5 (Diagnostic and Statistical Manual of Mental Disorders, Fifth Edition)* lists and describes psychological disorders. Diagnostic labels provide a common language and shared concepts for communication and research.
- Some critics believe the DSM editions have become too detailed and extensive. Labels can create preconceptions that cause us to view a person differently, and then look for evidence to confirm that view.

Anxiety Disorders, OCD, and PTSD

13-5 How do generalized anxiety disorder, panic disorder, and phobias differ? How do anxiety disorders differ from the ordinary worries and fears we all experience?

- It's common to feel uneasy; when those feelings are intense and persistent they may be classified as disordered.

- *Anxiety disorders* are psychological disorders characterized by distressing, persistent anxiety or maladaptive behaviors that reduce anxiety.
  - People with *generalized anxiety disorder* feel persistently and uncontrollably tense and apprehensive for no apparent reason.
  - In the more extreme *panic disorder,* anxiety escalates into episodes of intense dread.
  - Those with a *phobia* show an irrational fear and avoidance of a specific object, activity, or situation.
- Two other disorders, obsessive-compulsive disorder and posttraumatic stress disorder, involve anxiety (but are classified separately from the anxiety disorders).

13-6 What is OCD?

- Persistent and repetitive thoughts (obsessions), actions (compulsions), or both mark *obsessive-compulsive disorder (OCD)*.

13-7 What is PTSD?

- Symptoms of *posttraumatic stress disorder (PTSD)* include four or more weeks of haunting memories, nightmares, social withdrawal, jumpy anxiety, numbness of feeling, and/or sleep problems following a traumatic event.

13-8 How do conditioning, cognition, and biology contribute to the feelings and thoughts that mark anxiety disorders, OCD, and PTSD?

- The learning perspective views anxiety disorders as a product of fear conditioning, stimulus generalization, fearful-behavior reinforcement, and observational learning of others' fears and cognitions (interpretations, irrational beliefs, and hypervigilance).

- The biological perspective considers genetic predispositions and the role that fears of life-threatening animals, objects, or situations played in natural selection and evolution.

Substance Use Disorders and Addictive Behaviors

13-9 What are substance use disorders, and what roles do tolerance, withdrawal, and addiction play in these disorders?

- Those with a *substance use disorder* experience continued substance craving and use despite significant life disruption and/or physical risk.
- *Psychoactive drugs* are any chemical substances that alter perceptions and moods. They may produce *tolerance*—requiring larger doses to achieve the desired effect—and *withdrawal*—significant discomfort, due to strong addictive cravings, accompanying attempts to quit.

13-10 What are depressants, and what are their effects?

- *Depressants* (alcohol, *barbiturates, opiates*) dampen neural activity and slow body functions.
- Alcohol disinhibits, increasing the likelihood that we will act on our impulses, whether helpful or harmful. User expectations strongly influence alcohol's behavioral effects.
- Alcohol slows neural processing, disrupts memory, and shrinks the brain in those with *alcohol use disorder* (marked by tolerance, withdrawal if use is suspended, and a drive to continue problematic use).

13-11 What are stimulants, and what are their effects?

- *Stimulants* (caffeine, *nicotine, cocaine, amphetamines, methamphetamine, Ecstasy*) excite neural activity, speed up body functions, and lead to heightened energy and mood. All are highly addictive.

- Nicotine's effects make the use of tobacco products a difficult habit to kick, yet repeated attempts to quit seem to pay off.

- Cocaine gives users a fast high, followed shortly by a crash. Its risks include cardiovascular stress and suspiciousness.

- Methamphetamine use may permanently reduce dopamine levels.

- Ecstasy (MDMA), which is also a mild hallucinogen, may damage serotonin-producing neurons and impair physical and cognitive functions.

13-12 What are hallucinogens, and what are their effects?

- *Hallucinogens* (LSD, marijuana) distort perceptions and evoke hallucinations (sensory images in the absence of sensory input), some of which resemble the altered consciousness of *near-death experiences*.

- Marijuana's main ingredient, *THC*, may trigger feelings of disinhibition, euphoria, relaxation, relief from pain, and intense sensitivity to colors, sounds, tastes, and smells. It may also increase feelings of depression or anxiety, impair motor coordination and reaction time, disrupt memory formation, and damage lung tissue (when inhaled).

13-13 What biological, psychological, and social-cultural factors help explain why some people abuse mind-altering drugs?

- Some people are biologically more vulnerable to drugs.

- Psychological factors (such as stress, depression, and hopelessness) and social-cultural influences (peer pressure, cultural values) combine to lead many people to experiment with—and sometimes become addicted to—drugs. Cultural and ethnic groups have differing rates of drug use.

Major Depressive Disorder and Bipolar Disorder

13-14 How do major depressive disorder and bipolar disorder differ?

- A person with *major depressive disorder* experiences two or more weeks with five or more symptoms, at least one of which must be either (1) depressed mood or (2) loss of interest or pleasure.

- A person with the less common condition of *bipolar disorder* experiences not only depression but also *mania* (hyperactive and wildly optimistic, impulsive feelings and behavior).

13-15 How can the biological and social-cognitive perspectives help us understand major depressive disorder and bipolar disorder?

- The biological perspective on major depressive disorder and bipolar disorder focuses on genetic predispositions and on abnormalities in brain function, including those found in neurotransmitter systems.

- The social-cognitive perspective views depression as an ongoing cycle of stressful experiences (interpreted through negative beliefs, attributions, and memories) leading to negative moods and actions and fueling new stressful experiences.

13-16 What factors increase the risk of suicide, and why do some people injure themselves?

- People with depression are more at risk for suicide than others are, but health status and economic and social frustration are also contributing factors.

- Forewarnings of suicide may include verbal hints, giving away possessions, self-inflicted injuries, or withdrawal and preoccupation with death. People who talk about suicide should be taken seriously.

- Nonsuicidal self-injury (NSSI) does not usually lead to suicide but may escalate to suicidal thoughts and acts if untreated. People with NSSI generally do not tolerate stress well and tend to be self-critical, with poor communication and problem-solving skills.

Schizophrenia

13-17 What patterns of perceiving, thinking, and feeling characterize schizophrenia?

- *Schizophrenia* typically strikes during late adolescence and seems to occur in all cultures. It is a disorder characterized by delusions, hallucinations, disorganized speech, and/or diminished, inappropriate emotional expression.

- *Delusions* are false beliefs; hallucinations are sensory experiences without sensory stimulation.

- Schizophrenia symptoms may be positive (the presence of inappropriate behaviors) or negative (the absence of appropriate behaviors).

13-18 How do *acute schizophrenia* and *chronic schizophrenia* differ?

- In *chronic* (or process) *schizophrenia*, the disorder develops gradually and recovery is doubtful. In *acute* (or reactive) *schizophrenia*, the onset is sudden, in reaction to stress, and the prospects for recovery are brighter.

13-19 What brain abnormalities are associated with schizophrenia?

- People with schizophrenia have more receptors for dopamine, which may intensify the positive symptoms such as hallucinations and paranoia.

- Brain scans have revealed abnormal activity in the frontal lobes, thalamus, and amygdala. Brain abnormalities associated with schizophrenia include enlarged, fluid-filled cerebral cavities and loss of cerebral cortex. Schizophrenia involves not one isolated brain abnormality but problems with several brain regions and their interconnections.

13-20 What prenatal events are associated with increased risk of developing schizophrenia?

- Low weight or oxygen deprivation at birth, mother's diabetes, father's older age, and famine conditions during the mother's pregnancy are possible contributing factors. Converging lines of evidence suggest that fetal-virus infections contribute to the development of schizophrenia.

13-21 How do genes influence schizophrenia?

- Twin and adoption studies indicate that the predisposition to schizophrenia is inherited. Multiple genes probably interact to produce schizophrenia.

- No environmental causes invariably produce schizophrenia, but environmental events (such as prenatal viruses or maternal stress) may "turn on" genes for this disorder in those who are predisposed to it.

Other Disorders

13-22 What are the three main eating disorders, and how do biological, psychological, and social-cultural influences make people more vulnerable to them?

- In those with eating disorders, psychological factors can overwhelm the body's tendency to maintain a normal weight.

- Despite being significantly underweight, people with *anorexia*

nervosa (usually adolescent females) continue to diet and sometimes exercise excessively because they view themselves as fat.

- Those with *bulimia nervosa* (usually women in their late teens and early twenties) secretly binge and then compensate with purging, fasting, or excessive exercise.

- Those with *binge-eating disorder* binge but do not follow with purging, fasting, and exercise.

- Cultural pressures, low self-esteem, and negative emotions interact with stressful life experiences and genetics to produce eating disorders.

13-23 What are dissociative disorders, and why are they controversial?

- *Dissociative disorders* are controversial, rare conditions in which conscious awareness seems to become separated (to dissociate) from previous memories, thoughts, and feelings.

- Skeptics note that *dissociative identity disorder* (formerly known as multiple personality disorder) increased dramatically in the late twentieth century, that it is rarely found outside North America, and that it may reflect role playing by people who are vulnerable to therapists' suggestions. Others view this disorder as a protective response to traumatic experience.

13-24 What characteristics are typical of personality disorders in general, and what biological and psychological factors are associated with antisocial personality disorder?

- *Personality disorders* are inflexible and enduring behavior patterns that impair social functioning.

- *Antisocial personality disorder* is characterized by a lack of conscience and, sometimes, by aggressive

and fearless behavior. Genetic predispositions may interact with the environment to produce the altered brain activity associated with this disorder.

Does "Disorder" Equal "Danger"?

13-25 Are people with psychological disorders likely to commit violent acts?

- Mental disorders seldom lead to violence, but when they do, they raise moral and ethical questions about whether society should hold people with disorders responsible for their violent actions. Most people with disorders are nonviolent and are more likely to be victims than attackers.

CHAPTER 14

Therapy

Treating Psychological Disorders

14-1 How do psychotherapy and the biomedical therapies differ?

- *Psychotherapy* is treatment involving psychological techniques. It consists of interactions between a trained therapist and a person seeking to overcome difficulties or achieve personal growth. The major psychotherapies derive from psychology's psychodynamic, humanistic, behavioral, and cognitive perspectives.

- *Biomedical therapy* treats psychological disorders with medications and other biological treatments.

- Therapists who take an *eclectic approach* combine different techniques tailored to the client's problems.

The Psychological Therapies

14-2 What are the goals and techniques of psychoanalysis, and how have they been adapted in psychodynamic therapy?

- Sigmund Freud's *psychoanalysis* aimed to give people self-insight and relief from their disorders by bringing anxiety-laden feelings and thoughts into conscious awareness.

- Techniques included free association, dream analysis, and *interpretation* of instances of *resistance* and *transference.*

- Like psychoanalysis, *psychodynamic therapy* focuses on childhood experiences, therapist interactions, unconscious feelings, and unresolved conflicts. Yet it is briefer, less expensive, and focuses primarily on current symptom relief. Exploring past relationship troubles may help clients understand the origin of their current difficulties.

14-3 What are the basic themes of humanistic therapy, and what are the goals and techniques of Rogers' person-centered approach?

- Both psychoanalytic and humanistic therapies are *insight therapies*—they attempt to improve functioning by increasing clients' awareness of motives and defenses.

- Humanistic therapy's goals have included helping clients grow in self-awareness and self-acceptance; promoting personal growth rather than curing illness; helping clients take responsibility for their own growth; focusing on conscious thoughts rather than unconscious motivations; and seeing the present and future as more important than the past.

- Carl Rogers' *person-centered therapy* proposed that therapists' most important contribution is to function as a psychological mirror through active listening and to provide a growth-fostering environment of *unconditional positive regard* characterized by genuineness, acceptance, and empathy.

14-4 How does the basic assumption of behavior therapy differ from the assumptions of psychodynamic and humanistic therapies? What techniques are used in exposure therapies and aversive conditioning?

- The psychodynamic and humanistic therapies seek to provide insight to help clients address problems. The *behavior therapies* instead assume that problem behaviors *are* the problem. The goal of behavior therapists is to apply learning principles to modify problem behaviors.

- Classical conditioning techniques, including *exposure therapies* (such as *systematic desensitization* or *virtual reality exposure therapy*) and *aversive conditioning*, attempt to change behaviors through *counterconditioning*—evoking new responses to old stimuli that trigger unwanted behaviors.

14-5 What is the basic idea of operant conditioning therapies?

- A basic operant conditioning concept is that consequences drive our voluntary behaviors. Therapy based on operant conditioning principles therefore uses behavior modification techniques to change unwanted behaviors by positively reinforcing desired behaviors and ignoring or punishing undesirable behaviors.

- Therapists may use a *token economy,* in which desired behavior earns privileges.

14-6 What are the goals and techniques of the cognitive therapies and of cognitive-behavioral therapy?

- *Cognitive therapies,* such as Aaron Beck's therapy for depression, assume that our thinking influences our feelings, and that the therapist's role is to change clients' self-defeating thinking by training them to think in healthier ways.

- The widely researched and practiced *cognitive-behavioral therapy (CBT)* combines cognitive therapy and behavior therapy by helping clients regularly act out their new ways of thinking and behaving in their everyday life. A newer CBT variation, dialectical behavior therapy (DBT), combines cognitive tactics for tolerating distress and regulating emotions with social skills training and mindfulness meditation.

14-7 What are the aims and benefits of group and family therapies?

- *Group therapy* can help more people with less cost than individual therapy. Clients may benefit from learning that others have similar problems and from getting feedback on new ways of behaving.

- *Family therapy* treats a family as an interactive system and attempts to help family members discover the roles they play and how to learn to communicate more openly and directly.

Evaluating Psychotherapies

14-8 Does psychotherapy work? How do we know?

- Clients' and therapists' positive testimonials cannot prove that psychotherapy is actually effective. Clients justify their investment, tend to speak kindly of their therapists, and often enter therapy in crisis. Sometimes they are healed by time alone. Therapists tend to track only their "success" stories.

- Outcome research has found that people who remain untreated often improve, but those who receive psychotherapy are more likely to improve, to improve more quickly, and to improve with less chance of a relapse.

14-9 Are some psychotherapies more effective than others for specific disorders?

- No one psychotherapy is superior to all others. Therapy is most effective for those with clear-cut, specific problems.
- Behavior therapies work best with specific behavior problems, such as bed-wetting, phobias, compulsions, marital problems, and sexual dysfunctions.
- Psychodynamic therapy has been effective for depression and anxiety, nondirective (person-centered) counseling often helps with mild to moderate depression, and cognitive-behavioral therapies have been effective in helping people cope with anxiety, depression, and posttraumatic stress disorder.
- *Evidence-based practice* integrates the best available research with clinicians' expertise and patients' characteristics, preferences, and circumstances.

14-10 What three elements are shared by all forms of psychotherapy?

- All effective psychotherapies offer (1) new hope; (2) a fresh perspective; and (3) an empathic, trusting, caring relationship.
- An emotional bond of trust and understanding between therapist and client (the *therapeutic alliance*) is an important element in effective therapy.

14-11 How do culture and values influence the client-therapist relationship?

- Therapists differ from one another and from their clients. These differences may create problems if therapists and clients differ in their cultural or religious perspectives.

14-12 What should a person look for when selecting a psychotherapist?

- College health centers are generally good starting points for counseling options, and they offer some free services.
- A person seeking therapy may want to ask about the therapist's treatment approach, values, credentials, and fees. An important consideration is whether the therapy seeker feels comfortable and able to establish a bond with the therapist.

The Biomedical Therapies

14-13 Why is therapeutic lifestyle change considered an effective biomedical therapy, and how does it work?

- Our lifestyle influences our brain and body, which affects our mental health.
- Depressed people who undergo a program of aerobic exercise, adequate sleep, light exposure, social engagement, negative-thought reduction, and better nutrition have gained some relief. The biomedical therapies assume that mind and body are a unit: Affect one and you will affect the other.

14-14 What are the drug therapies? How do double-blind studies help researchers evaluate a drug's effectiveness?

- Drug therapy is the most widely used biomedical therapy by far.
- *Antipsychotic drugs* are used in treating schizophrenia and other forms of severe thought disorders; some block dopamine activity. Side effects may include tardive dyskinesia (with involuntary movements of facial muscles, tongue, and limbs) or increased risk of obesity and diabetes.
- *Antianxiety drugs,* which depress central nervous system activity, are used to treat anxiety disorders, obsessive-compulsive disorder, and posttraumatic stress disorder, often in combination with psychotherapy. These drugs can reinforce a person's tendency to take drugs and can also cause physical problems.
- *Antidepressant drugs,* which often increase the availability of various neurotransmitters, are used to treat depression, but also anxiety disorders, obsessive-compulsive disorder, and posttraumatic stress disorder, with modest effectiveness. Given their widening use, some professionals prefer the term SSRIs (selective serotonin reuptake inhibitors) for drugs such as Prozac.
- Mood-stabilizing drugs, such as lithium and Depakote, are often prescribed for those with bipolar disorder.
- Studies may use a double-blind procedure to avoid the placebo effect and researchers' and patients' potential bias.

14-15 How are brain stimulation and psychosurgery used in treating specific disorders?

- In *electroconvulsive therapy (ECT)*, a brief electric current is sent through the brain of an anesthetized patient. ECT is an effective treatment for severely depressed people who have not responded to other therapy.
- Newer alternative treatments for depression include *repetitive transcranial magnetic stimulation (rTMS)* and deep brain stimulation.

Psychosurgery (including very precise micropsychosurgery) removes or destroys brain tissue in hopes of modifying behavior. These irreversible psychosurgical procedures are used only as a last resort. *Lobotomies* are no longer performed.

Preventing Psychological Disorders and Building Resilience

14-16 What may help prevent psychological disorders, and why is it important to develop resilience?

- Preventive mental health programs are based on the idea that many psychological disorders could be prevented by changing stressful social contexts and teaching people to cope better with stress. This may help them become more *resilient*, enabling recovery from adversity.
- Community psychologists work to prevent psychological disorders by turning destructive environments into more nurturing places that foster competence, health, and well-being.

APPENDIX A
Statistical Reasoning in Everyday Life

Describing Data

A-1 How do we describe data using three measures of central tendency, and what is the relative usefulness of the two measures of variation?

- Researchers may use descriptive statistics to meaningfully organize the data they've gathered.
- A measure of central tendency is a single score that represents a whole set of scores. Three such measures are the *mode* (the most frequently occurring score), the *mean* (the arithmetic average), and the *median* (the middle score in a group of data).
- Measures of variation tell us how diverse the data are. Two measures of variation are the *range* (which describes the gap between the highest and lowest scores) and the *standard deviation* (which states how much scores vary around the mean, or average, score). The standard deviation uses information from each score, so it is especially useful for showing whether scores are packed together or dispersed.
- Scores often form a *normal* (or bell-shaped) *curve*.

A-2 What does it mean when we say two things are correlated?

- When we say two things are correlated, we are saying that they accompany each other in their movements. The strength of their relationship is expressed as a *correlation coefficient*, which ranges from +1.00 (a perfect positive correlation) through 0 (no correlation) to –1.00 (a perfect negative correlation).
- Their relationship may be displayed in a *scatterplot*, in which each dot represents a value for the two variables.
- Correlations predict but cannot explain.

A-3 What is regression toward the mean?

- *Regression toward the mean* is the tendency for extreme or unusual scores to fall back toward their average.

Significant Differences

A-4 How do we know whether an observed difference can be generalized to other populations?

- Researchers use inferential statistics to help determine the reliability and significance of a study finding.
- To feel confident about generalizing an observed difference to other populations, we would want to know that the sample studied was representative of the larger population being studied; that the observations, on average, had low variability; that the sample consisted of more than a few cases; and that the observed difference was *statistically significant*.

A-5 What are cross-sectional studies and longitudinal studies, and why is it important to know which method was used?

- In a *cross-sectional study*, people of different ages are compared. In a *longitudinal study*, a group of people is studied periodically over a long period of time.
- To draw meaningful conclusions about a study's results, we need to know whether the study used a representative sample to draw its conclusions. Studies of intelligence and aging, for example, have drawn different conclusions depending on whether a cross-sectional or longitudinal study was used.

APPENDIX B
Psychology at Work

Work and Life Satisfaction

B-1 What is *flow*?

- *Flow* is a completely involved, focused state of consciousness with diminished awareness of self and time. It results from fully engaging one's skills.
- Work may be just a job, a somewhat fulfilling career, or a calling, which produces the highest levels of satisfaction.

Industrial-Organizational Psychology

B-2 What are the key fields and subfields related to industrial-organizational psychology?

- *Industrial-organizational (I/O) psychology's* key fields and subfields are human factors, personnel, and organizational psychology:
  - *Human factors psychologists,* now in a distinct field allied with I/O psychology, explore how people and machines interact for optimal safety and effectiveness.
  - *Personnel psychologists* use psychology's principles to select, place, train, and evaluate workers.
  - *Organizational psychologists* consider an organization's goals, environments, and management styles in an effort to improve worker motivation, satisfaction, and productivity.

Motivating Achievement

B-3 Why is it important to motivate achievement?

- *Achievement motivation* is a desire for significant accomplishment; for mastery of skills or ideas; for control; and for attaining a high standard. High achievement motivation leads to greater success, especially when combined with determined, persistent grit.
- The most satisfied and engaged employees tend to be the most productive and successful. Managers motivate most effectively when they make clear what is expected, provide needed materials, allow employees to do what they do best, affirm employees, and ensure opportunities to learn and develop.

Leadership

B-4 How can leaders be most effective?

- Leaders can harness strengths, by matching tasks to talents and reinforcing positive behaviors. They can set specific, challenging goals that stretch employees, but not beyond what they can do.
- Leaders can also choose an appropriate leadership style for the situation, such as *task leadership* when a more directive style is needed, or *social leadership* when a more democratic style fits best. The most effective leaders often combine task and social leadership styles.

Answers to *Chapter Test* Questions

CHAPTER 1

Psychology's Roots, Big Ideas, and Critical Thinking Tools

1. Wilhelm Wundt
2. a
3. d
4. psychiatrist
5. c
6. Critical thinking teaches us to look for evidence instead of relying on our intuition, which is often wrong. In evaluating a claim in the media, look for any signs of scientific evidence, preferably from several studies. Ask the following questions: Are claims based on scientific findings? Have several studies replicated the findings and confirmed them? Are any experts cited? If so, research their background. Are they affiliated with a credible university, college, or institution? Have they conducted or written about scientific research?
7. b
8. The environment (nurture) has an influence on us, but that influence is limited by our biology (nature). Nature and nurture interact. People predisposed to be very tall (nature), for example, are unlikely to become Olympic gymnasts, no matter how hard they work (nurture).
9. Dual processing

10. positive psychology
11. Hindsight bias
12. d
13. hypotheses
14. c
15. random (representative)
16. negative
17. a
18. (a) Alcohol use is associated with violence. (One interpretation: Drinking causes, or triggers, aggressive behavior.) Perhaps anger triggers drinking, or perhaps the same genes or child-raising practices are making both drinking and aggression more likely. (Here researchers have learned that drinking does indeed trigger aggressive behavior.) (b) Educated people live longer, on average, than less-educated people. (One interpretation: Education lengthens life and improves health.) Perhaps richer people can afford more education and better health care. (Research supports this conclusion.) (c) Teens engaged in team sports are less likely to use drugs, smoke, have sex, carry weapons, and eat junk food than are teens who do not engage in team sports. (One interpretation: Team sports encourage healthy living.) Perhaps some third factor explains this correlation—teens who use drugs, smoke, have sex, carry weapons, and eat junk food may be "loners" who do not enjoy playing on any team. (d) Adolescents who frequently see smoking in movies are more likely to smoke. (One interpretation: Movie stars' behav-

ior influences teens.) Perhaps adolescents who smoke and attend movies frequently have less parental supervision and more access to spending money than other adolescents.

19. experiments
20. placebo
21. c
22. independent variable
23. b
24. d

CHAPTER 2

The Biology of Mind and Consciousness

1. axon
2. c
3. a
4. neurotransmitters
5. b
6. b
7. autonomic
8. central
9. a
10. adrenal glands
11. b
12. d
13. c
14. cerebellum
15. b
16. amygdala
17. b

18. hypothalamus
19. d
20. The visual cortex is a neural network of sensory neurons connected via interneurons to other neural networks, including auditory networks. This allows you to integrate visual and auditory information to respond when a friend you recognize greets you at a party.
21. c
22. association areas
23. frontal
24. c
25. ON; HER
26. a
27. b
28. inattentional blindness
29. selective
30. circadian rhythm
31. b
32. NREM-3
33. It increases in duration.
34. c
35. With narcolepsy, the person periodically falls directly into sleep, sometimes REM sleep, with no warning; with sleep apnea, the person repeatedly awakens during the night.
36. d
37. The information-processing explanation of dreaming proposes that brain activity during REM sleep enables us to sift through the daily events and activities we have been thinking about.
38. REM rebound

CHAPTER 3

Developing Through the Life Span

1. continuity/stages
2. b
3. chromosomes
4. gene
5. b
6. c
7. teratogens
8. a
9. c
10. Identical
11. b
12. Epigenetic
13. frontal
14. b
15. We have little conscious memory of events occurring before age 4, in part because major brain areas have not yet matured.
16. Infants in Piaget's *sensorimotor stage* tend to be focused only on their own perceptions of the world and may, for example, be unaware that objects continue to exist when unseen. A child in the *preoperational stage* is still egocentric and incapable of appreciating simple logic, such as the reversibility of operations. A preteen in the *concrete operational stage* is beginning to think logically about concrete events but not about abstract concepts.
17. a
18. stranger anxiety
19. Before these studies, many psychologists believed that infants became attached simply to those who nourished them.
20. temperament
21. b
22. formal operations
23. b
24. emerging adulthood
25. a
26. Cross-sectional studies compare people of different ages. Longitudinal studies restudy and retest the same people over a long period of time.
27. generativity
28. c

CHAPTER 4

Sex, Gender, and Sexuality

1. sex; gender
2. c
3. Y
4. d
5. 11; 12
6. intersex
7. b
8. gender identity
9. b
10. b
11. does; doesn't
12. c
13. c

CHAPTER 5

Sensation and Perception

1. b
2. perception
3. d
4. just noticeable difference
5. b
6. d
7. a
8. wavelength
9. a
10. c
11. c
12. d
13. Your brain constructs this perception of color in two stages. In the first stage, the lemon reflects light energy into your eyes, where it is transformed into neural messages. Three sets of cones, each sensitive to a different light frequency (red, blue, and green) process color. In

this case, the light energy stimulates both red-sensitive and green-sensitive cones. In the second stage, opponent-process cells sensitive to paired opposites of color (red/green, yellow/blue, and black/white) evaluate the incoming neural messages as they pass through your optic nerve to the thalamus and visual cortex. When the yellow-sensitive opponent-process cells are stimulated, you identify the lemon as yellow.

14. feature detectors
15. parallel processing
16. d
17. a
18. b
19. c
20. monocular
21. b
22. b
23. perceptual adaptation
24. cochlea
25. The outer ear collects sound waves, which are translated into mechanical waves by the *middle ear* and turned into fluid waves in the *inner ear*. The auditory nerve then translates the energy into electrical waves and sends them to the brain, which perceives and interprets the sound.
26. nociceptors
27. We have specialized receptors for detecting sweet, salty, sour, bitter, and umami tastes. Being able to detect pleasurable tastes enabled our ancestors to seek out energy- and protein-rich foods. Detecting aversive tastes deterred them from eating toxic substances, increasing their chances of survival.
28. Kinesthesia; vestibular sense
29. Your vestibular sense regulates balance and body positioning through kinesthetic receptors triggered by fluid in your inner ear. Wobbly legs and a spinning world are signs that these receptors are still responding to the ride's turbulence. As your vestibular sense adjusts to solid ground, your balance will be restored.
30. d
31. d

CHAPTER 6

Learning

1. information; behaviors
2. c
3. conditioned
4. discrimination
5. b
6. A sexual image is a US that triggers a UR of interest or arousal. Before the advertisement pairs a product with a sexual image, the product is an NS. Over time the product can become a CS that triggers the CR of interest or arousal.
7. Skinner's
8. shaping
9. b
10. Your instructor could reinforce your attentive behavior by taking away something you dislike. For example, your instructor could offer to shorten the length of an assigned paper or replace lecture time with an in-class activity. In both cases, the instructor would remove something aversive in order to negatively reinforce your focused attention.
11. partial
12. a
13. variable-interval
14. c
15. d
16. b
17. mental map
18. latent learning
19. observational learning

20. vicarious; vicarious
21. a
22. mirror
23. c

CHAPTER 7

Memory

1. encoding; storage; retrieval
2. a
3. iconic; echoic
4. seven
5. mnemonics
6. a
7. implicit
8. c
9. recall
10. retrieval cues
11. Memories are stored within a web of many associations, one of which is mood. When you recall happy moments from your past, you deliberately activate these positive links. You may then experience mood-congruent memory and recall other happy moments, which could improve your mood and brighten your interpretation of current events.
12. a
13. d
14. d
15. retroactive
16. repression
17. b
18. Eliza's immature hippocampus and lack of verbal skills would have prevented her from encoding an explicit memory of the wedding reception at the age of two. It's more likely that Eliza learned information (from hearing the story repeatedly) that she eventually constructed into a memory that feels very real.
19. source amnesia

20. déjà vu
21. b
22. b

CHAPTER 8

Thinking, Language, and Intelligence

1. concept
2. algorithm
3. Oscar will need to guard against *confirmation bias* (searching for support for his own views and ignoring contradictory evidence) as he seeks out opposing viewpoints. Even if Oscar encounters new information that disproves his beliefs, *belief perseverance* may lead him to cling to these views anyway. It will take more compelling evidence to change his beliefs than it took to create them.
4. c
5. availability
6. framing
7. b
8. c
9. telegraphic speech
10. universal grammar
11. a
12. general intelligence (*g*)
13. c
14. academic; practical; creative
15. d
16. d
17. c
18. reliability
19. a
20. c
21. c
22. Writers' work relies more on crystallized intelligence, or accumulated knowledge, which increases with age. For top performance, scientists doing research may need more fluid intelligence (speedy and abstract

reasoning), which tends to decrease with age.
23. c
24. The heritability (difference due to genes) of body weight will be greater in country X, where environmental differences in available nutrition are minimal.
25. Stereotype threat

CHAPTER 9

Motivation and Emotion

1. a
2. incentive
3. Arousal
4. b
5. a
6. Maslow's hierarchy of needs best supports this statement because it addresses the primacy of some motives over others. Once our basic physiological needs are met, safety concerns are addressed next, followed by belongingness and love needs (such as the desire to kiss).
7. homeostasis
8. c
9. glucose; low
10. basal metabolic
11. d
12. Sanjay's plan is problematic. After he gains weight, the extra fat will require less energy to maintain than it did to gain in the first place. Sanjay may have a hard time getting rid of it later, when his metabolism slows down in an effort to retain his body weight.
13. c
14. Monitor the time spent online, as well as your feelings about that time. Hide distracting online friends. Turn off or put away distracting devices. Consider a social media fast, and get outside and away from technology regularly.

15. James-Lange
16. b
17. c
18. A polygraph measures physiological changes, such as heart rate and perspiration, that are associated with emotions. Its use as a lie detector is controversial because the measure cannot distinguish between emotions with similar physiology (such as anxiety and guilt).
19. facial feedback
20. Aiden's droopy posture could negatively affect his mood thanks to the behavior feedback effect, which tends to make us feel the way we act.

CHAPTER 10

Stress, Health, and Human Flourishing

1. resistance; exhaustion
2. tend; befriend
3. b
4. d
5. lymphocytes
6. c
7. Type A individuals frequently experience negative emotions (such as anger and impatience), during which the sympathetic nervous system diverts blood away from the liver. This leaves fat and cholesterol circulating in the bloodstream for deposit near the heart and other organs, increasing the risk of heart disease and other health problems. Thus, Type A individuals actually harm themselves by directing anger at others.
8. negative
9. emotion
10. b
11. internal
12. d
13. aerobic

14. c
15. d
16. b
17. relative deprivation

CHAPTER 11

Social Psychology

1. a
2. foot-in-the-door
3. Cognitive dissonance theory best supports this suggestion. If Jamal acts confident, his behavior will contradict his negative self-thoughts, creating cognitive dissonance. To relieve the tension, Jamal may realign his attitudes with his actions by viewing himself as more outgoing and confident.
4. c
5. a
6. The presence of a large audience generates arousal and strengthens Dr. Huang's most likely response: enhanced performance on a task he has mastered (teaching music history) and impaired performance on a task he finds difficult (statistics).
7. deindividuation
8. group polarization
9. stereotypes
10. b
11. more
12. d
13. frustration-aggression principle
14. c
15. c
16. mere exposure
17. companionate; passionate
18. d
19. c
20. mirror-image
21. superordinate

CHAPTER 12

Personality

1. repression
2. c
3. superego
4. b
5. anxiety
6. Projective
7. d
8. a
9. a
10. d
11. Freud might argue that the criminal may have lacked the proper guidance as a child for developing a strong superego, allowing the id free rein. Rogers might assert that the criminal was raised in an environment lacking genuineness, acceptance (unconditional positive regard), and empathy, which inhibited psychological growth and led to a negative self-concept.
12. unconditional positive regard
13. Trait
14. c
15. b
16. b
17. a
18. social-cognitive
19. b
20. Yes, if that self-love is of the *secure* type. Secure self-esteem promotes a focus beyond the self and a higher quality of life. Excessive self-love may promote artificially high or defensive self-esteem, which may lead to unhappiness if negative external feedback triggers anger or aggression.
21. spotlight effect
22. b

CHAPTER 13

Psychological Disorders

1. No. Anna's behavior is unusual, causes her distress, and may make her a few minutes late on occasion, but it does not appear to significantly disrupt her ability to function. Like most of us, Anna demonstrates some unusual behaviors. Since they are not disabling or dysfunctional, they do not suggest a psychological disorder.
2. depression
3. medical
4. c
5. a
6. c
7. phobia
8. obsessive-compulsive
9. c
10. tolerance
11. a
12. Alcohol is a disinhibitor—it makes us more likely to do what we would have done when sober, whether that is being helpful or being aggressive.
13. d
14. LSD
15. a
16. b
17. women's; men's
18. d
19. norepinephrine; serotonin
20. social-cognitive
21. b
22. hallucination
23. No. Schizophrenia involves the altered perceptions, emotions, and behaviors of a mind split from reality. It does not involve the rapid changes in mood or identity suggested by this comparison.
24. a

25. b
26. c
27. c
28. b

CHAPTER 14

Therapy

1. a
2. Insight
3. d
4. active listening
5. c
6. counterconditioning
7. systematic desensitization
8. Behavior therapies are often the best choice for treating phobias. Viewing Rico's fear of the freeway as a learned response, a behavior therapist might help Rico learn to replace his anxious response to freeway driving with a relaxation response.
9. token economy
10. d
11. Cognitive-behavioral
12. b
13. c
14. d
15. research evidence, clinical expertise, and knowledge of the patient
16. The placebo effect is the healing power of belief in a treatment. When patients expect a treatment to be effective, they may believe it was.
17. c
18. antianxiety
19. lithium
20. b
21. d

APPENDIX A

Statistical Reasoning in Everyday Life

1. b
2. d
3. normal curve
4. a
5. negative
6. scatterplot
7. Regression toward the mean is a statistical phenomenon describing the tendency of extreme scores or outcomes to return to normal after an unusual event. Without knowing this, we may inaccurately decide the return to normal was a result of our own behavior.
8. cross-sectional
9. a

APPENDIX B

Psychology at Work

1. c
2. human factors; personnel; organizational
3. Personnel; human factors
4. Focusing on specific, short-term goals, such as maintaining a regular study schedule, will be more helpful than focusing on more distant general goals, such as earning a good grade in this class.
5. transformational
6. c

Glossary

absolute threshold the minimum stimulus energy needed to detect a particular stimulus 50 percent of the time. (p. 135)

accommodation adapting our current understandings (schemas) to incorporate new information. (p. 79)

achievement motivation a desire for significant accomplishment; for mastery of skills or ideas; for control; and for attaining a high standard. (p. B-3)

achievement test a test designed to assess what a person has learned. (p. 241)

acquisition in classical conditioning, the initial stage, when we link a neutral stimulus and an unconditioned stimulus so that the neutral stimulus begins triggering the conditioned response. (In operant conditioning, the strengthening of a reinforced response.) (p. 173)

action potential a nerve impulse; a brief electrical charge that travels down an axon. (p. 31)

active listening empathic listening in which the listener echoes, restates, and clarifies. A feature of Rogers' person-centered therapy. (p. 419)

acute schizophrenia (also called *reactive schizophrenia*) a form of schizophrenia that can begin at any age, frequently occurs in response to an emotionally traumatic event, and has extended recovery periods. (p. 403)

adaptation-level phenomenon our tendency to form judgments (of sounds, of lights, of income) relative to a neutral level defined by our past experiences. (p. 307)

adolescence the transition period from childhood to adulthood, extending from puberty to independence. (p. 89)

adrenal [ah-DREEN-el] glands a pair of endocrine glands that sit just above the kidneys and secrete hormones (epinephrine and norepinephrine) that help arouse the body in times of stress. (p. 35)

aerobic exercise sustained activity that increases heart and lung fitness; may also reduce depression and anxiety. (p. 299)

aggression any act intended to harm someone physically or emotionally. (pp. 109, 331)

AIDS (acquired immune deficiency syndrome) a life-threatening, sexually transmitted infection caused by the *human immunodeficiency virus* (HIV). AIDS depletes the immune system, leaving the person vulnerable to infections. (p. 117)

alcohol use disorder (popularly known as *alcoholism*) alcohol use marked by tolerance, withdrawal, and a drive to continue problematic use. (p. 387)

algorithm a methodical, logical rule or procedure that guarantees you will solve a particular problem. Contrasts with the usually speedier—but also more error-prone—use of *heuristics*. (p. 223)

all-or-none response a neuron's reaction of either firing (with a full-strength response) or not firing. (p. 33)

alpha waves relatively slow brain waves of a relaxed, awake state. (p. 55)

altruism unselfish concern for the welfare of others. (p. 339)

amnesia literally "without memory"—a loss of memory, often due to brain trauma, injury, or disease. (p. 209)

amphetamines drugs that stimulate neural activity, causing speeded-up body functions and associated energy and mood changes. (p. 391)

amygdala [uh-MIG-duh-la] two lima-bean-sized neural clusters in the limbic system; linked to emotion. (p. 41)

androgyny displaying both traditional masculine and feminine psychological characteristics. (p. 115)

anorexia nervosa an eating disorder in which a person (usually an adolescent female) maintains a starvation diet despite being significantly underweight; sometimes accompanied by excessive exercise. (p. 405)

antianxiety drugs drugs used to control anxiety and agitation. (p. 433)

antidepressant drugs drugs used to treat depression, anxiety disorders, obsessive-compulsive disorder, and posttraumatic stress disorder. (Several widely used antidepressant drugs are *selective serotonin reuptake inhibitors*—SSRIs.) (p. 433)

antipsychotic drugs drugs used to treat schizophrenia and other forms of severe thought disorders. (p. 433)

antisocial personality disorder a personality disorder in which a person (usually a man) exhibits a lack of conscience for wrongdoing, even toward friends and family members; may be aggressive and ruthless or a clever con artist. (p. 407)

anxiety disorders psychological disorders characterized by distressing, persistent anxiety or maladaptive behaviors that reduce anxiety. (p. 381)

aptitude test a test designed to predict a person's future performance; *aptitude* is the capacity to learn. (p. 241)

asexual having no sexual attraction to others. (p. 117)

assimilation interpreting our new experiences in terms of our existing schemas. (p. 79)

association areas cerebral cortex areas involved primarily in higher mental functions, such as learning, remembering, thinking, and speaking. (p. 47)

associative learning learning that certain events occur together. The events may be two stimuli (as in classical conditioning) or a response and its consequences (as in operant conditioning). (p. 171)

attachment an emotional tie with another person; shown in young children by their seeking closeness to their caregiver and showing distress on separation. (p. 83)

attention-deficit/hyperactivity disorder (ADHD) a psychological disorder marked by extreme inattention and/or hyperactivity and impulsivity. (p. 377)

attitude feelings, often based on our beliefs, that predispose us to respond in a particular way to objects, people, and events. (p. 315)

audition the sense or act of hearing. (p. 153)

autism spectrum disorder (ASD) a disorder that appears in childhood and is marked by significant deficiencies in communication and social interaction, and by rigidly fixated interests and repetitive behaviors. (p. 81)

automatic processing unconscious encoding of everyday information, such as space, time, and frequency, and of well-learned information, such as word meanings. (p. 197)

autonomic [aw-tuh-NAHM-ik] nervous system (ANS) peripheral nervous system division that controls the glands and the muscles of the internal organs (such as the heart). Its *sympathetic* subdivision arouses; its *parasympathetic* subdivision calms. (p. 35)

availability heuristic judging the likelihood of an event based on its availability in memory; if an event comes readily to mind (perhaps because it was vivid), we assume it must be common. (p. 224)

aversive conditioning a type of counterconditioning that associates an unpleasant state (such as nausea) with an unwanted behavior (such as drinking alcohol). (p. 421)

axon the neuron extension that sends messages to other neurons or to muscles and glands. (p. 31)

babbling stage beginning at about 4 months, the stage of speech development in which an infant spontaneously utters various sounds, many at first unrelated to the household language. (p. 233)

barbiturates drugs that depress central nervous system activity, reducing anxiety but impairing memory and judgment. (p. 389)

basal metabolic rate the body's resting rate of energy output. (p. 263)

basic trust according to Erik Erikson, a sense that the world is predictable and trustworthy; said to be formed during infancy by appropriate experiences with responsive caregivers. (p. 85)

behaviorism the view that psychology (1) should be an objective science that (2) studies behavior without reference to mental processes. Most psychologists today agree with (1) but not with (2). (pp. 3, 185)

behavior therapy a therapeutic approach that applies learning principles to the elimination of unwanted behaviors. (p. 419)

belief perseverance clinging to beliefs even after evidence has proven them wrong. (p. 227)

binge-eating disorder significant binge-eating episodes, followed by distress, disgust, or guilt, but without the purging or fasting that marks bulimia nervosa. (p. 407)

binocular cue a depth cue, such as retinal disparity, that depends on the use of two eyes. (p. 148)

biological constraints evolved biological tendencies that predispose animals' behavior and learning. Thus, certain behaviors are more easily learned than others. (p. 185)

biological psychology the scientific study of the links between biological and psychological processes. (p. 31)

biomedical therapy prescribed medications or procedures that act directly on the person's physiology. (p. 417)

biopsychosocial approach an approach that integrates different but complementary views from biological, psychological, and social-cultural viewpoints. (p. 9)

bipolar disorder a disorder in which a person alternates between the hopelessness and weariness of depression and the overexcited state of mania. (Formerly called *manic-depressive disorder*.) (p. 395)

blind spot the point at which the optic nerve leaves the eye; this part of the retina is "blind" because it has no receptor cells. (p. 143)

bottom-up processing analysis that begins with the sensory receptors and works up to the brain's integration of sensory information. (p. 135)

brainstem the oldest part and central core of the brain, beginning where the spinal cord swells as it enters the skull; responsible for automatic survival functions. (p. 39)

Broca's area controls language expression; an area of the frontal lobe, usually in the left hemisphere, that directs the muscle movements involved in speech. (p. 235)

bulimia nervosa an eating disorder in which a person alternates binge eating (usually of high-calorie foods) with purging (by vomiting or laxative use) or fasting. (p. 407)

bystander effect the tendency for any given bystander to be less likely to give aid if other bystanders are present. (p. 341)

Cannon-Bard theory the theory that an emotion-arousing stimulus simultaneously triggers (1) physiological responses and (2) the subjective experience of emotion. (p. 271)

case study a descriptive technique in which one individual or group is studied in depth in the hope of revealing universal principles. (p. 15)

central nervous system (CNS) the brain and spinal cord. (p. 35)

central route persuasion occurs when interested people focus on the arguments and respond with favorable thoughts. (p. 315)

cerebellum [sehr-uh-BELL-um] the "little brain" at the rear of the brainstem; functions include processing sensory input, coordinating movement output and balance, and enabling nonverbal learning and memory. (p. 41)

cerebral [seh-REE-bruhl] **cortex** a thin layer of interconnected neurons covering the cerebral hemispheres; the body's ultimate control and information-processing center. (p. 43)

change blindness failing to notice changes in the environment; a form of inattentional blindness. (p. 53)

chromosomes threadlike structures made of DNA molecules that contain the genes. (p. 71)

chronic schizophrenia (also called *process schizophrenia*) a form of schizophrenia in which symptoms usually appear by late adolescence or early adulthood. As people age, psychotic episodes last longer and recovery periods shorten. (p. 403)

chunking organizing items into familiar, manageable units; often occurs automatically. (p. 199)

circadian [ser-KAY-dee-an] **rhythm** our internal biological clock; regular bodily rhythms (for example, of temperature and wakefulness) that occur on a 24-hour cycle. (p. 55)

classical conditioning a type of learning in which we learn to link two or more stimuli and anticipate events. (p. 171)

cocaine a powerful and addictive stimulant derived from the coca plant; temporarily increases alertness and produces feelings of euphoria. (p. 389)

cochlea [KOHK-lee-uh] a coiled, bony, fluid-filled tube in the inner ear; sound waves traveling through the cochlear fluid trigger nerve impulses. (p. 153)

cochlear implant a device for converting sounds into electrical signals and stimulating the auditory nerve through electrodes threaded into the cochlea. (p. 155)

cognition all the mental activities associated with thinking, knowing, remembering, and communicating. (pp. 79, 223)

cognitive-behavioral therapy (CBT) a popular integrative therapy that combines cognitive therapy (changing self-defeating thinking) with behavior therapy (changing behavior). (p. 425)

cognitive dissonance theory the theory that we act to reduce the discomfort (dissonance) we feel when two of our thoughts (cognitions) clash. For example, when we become aware that our attitudes and our actions don't match, we may change our attitudes so that we feel more comfortable. (p. 317)

cognitive learning the acquisition of mental information, whether by observing events, by watching others, or through language. (p. 171)

cognitive map a mental image of the layout of one's environment. (p. 187)

cognitive neuroscience the interdisciplinary study of the brain activity linked with cognition (including perception, thinking, memory, and language). (pp. 4, 31)

cognitive psychology the study of mental processes, such as occur when we perceive, learn, remember, think, communicate, and solve problems. (p. 5)

cognitive therapy a therapeutic approach that teaches people new, more adaptive ways of thinking; based on the assumption that thoughts intervene between events and our emotional reactions. (p. 423)

collective unconscious Carl Jung's concept of a shared, inherited group of memories from our species' history. (p. 355)

collectivism giving priority to the goals of our group (often our extended family or work group) and defining our identity accordingly. (p. 371)

color constancy perceiving familiar objects as having consistent color, even if changing illumination alters the wavelengths reflected by the object. (p. 151)

companionate love the deep affectionate attachment we feel for those with whom our lives are intertwined. (p. 339)

concept a mental grouping of similar objects, events, ideas, or people. (p. 223)

concrete operational stage in Piaget's theory, the stage of cognitive development (from about 7 to 11 years of age) during which children gain the mental operations that enable them to think logically about concrete events. (p. 81)

conditioned reinforcer (also known as *secondary reinforcer*) an event that gains its reinforcing power through its link with a primary reinforcer. (p. 179)

conditioned response (CR) in classical conditioning, a learned response to a previously neutral (but now conditioned) stimulus (CS). (p. 173)

conditioned stimulus (CS) in classical conditioning, an originally irrelevant stimulus that, after association with an unconditioned stimulus (US), comes to trigger a conditioned response (CR). (p. 173)

conduction hearing loss a less common form of hearing loss, caused by damage to the mechanical system that conducts sound waves to the cochlea. (p. 155)

cones retinal receptors that are concentrated near the center of the retina; in daylight or well-lit conditions, cones detect fine detail and give rise to color sensations. (p. 143)

confirmation bias a tendency to search for information that supports your preconceptions and to ignore or distort evidence that contradicts them. (p. 223)

conflict a perceived incompatibility of actions, goals, or ideas. (p. 341)

conformity adjusting our behavior or thinking to coincide with a group standard. (p. 319)

confounding variable a factor other than the factor being studied that might influence a study's results. (p. 19)

consciousness our awareness of ourselves and our environment. (p. 51)

conservation the principle (which Piaget believed to be a part of concrete operational reasoning) that properties such as mass, volume, and number remain the same despite changes in shapes. (p. 79)

content validity the extent to which a test samples the behavior that is of interest. (p. 243)

continuous reinforcement reinforcing a desired response every time it occurs. (p. 179)

control group in an experiment, the group *not* exposed to the treatment; the control group serves as a comparison with the experimental group for judging the effect of the treatment. (p. 19)

convergent thinking narrowing the available solutions to determine the single best solution to a problem. (p. 229)

coping reducing stress using emotional, cognitive, or behavioral methods. (p. 293)

coronary heart disease the clogging of the vessels that nourish the heart muscle; the leading cause of death in the United States and many other countries. (p. 291)

corpus callosum [KOR-pus kah-LOW-sum] a large band of neural fibers connecting the two brain hemispheres and carrying messages between them. (p. 47)

correlation a measure of the extent to which two events vary together, and thus of how well either one predicts the other. The *correlation coefficient* is the mathematical expression of the relationship, ranging from –1.00 to +1.00, with 0 indicating no relationship. (p. 17)

correlation coefficient a statistical index of the relationship between two things (from –1.00 to +1.00). (p. A-5)

counterconditioning behavior therapy procedures that use classical conditioning to evoke new responses to stimuli that are triggering unwanted behaviors; includes *exposure therapies* and *aversive conditioning.* (p. 421)

creativity the ability to produce new and valuable ideas. (p. 229)

critical period a period early in life when exposure to certain stimuli or experiences is needed for proper development. (p. 77)

critical thinking thinking that does not blindly accept arguments and conclusions. Rather, it examines assumptions, uncovers hidden values, weighs evidence, and assesses conclusions. (p. 9)

cross-sectional study research in which people of different ages are compared with one another. (pp. 99, 247, A-7)

crystallized intelligence your accumulated knowledge and verbal skills; tends to increase with age. (p. 249)

culture the enduring behaviors, ideas, attitudes, values, and traditions shared by a group of people and handed down from one generation to the next. (p. 9)

debriefing after an experiment ends, explaining to participants the study's purpose and any deceptions researchers used. (p. 23)

defense mechanisms in psychoanalytic theory, the ego's protective methods of reducing anxiety by unconsciously distorting reality. (p. 353)

deindividuation the loss of self-awareness and self-restraint occurring in group situations that foster arousal and anonymity. (p. 325)

déjà vu that eerie sense that "I've experienced this before." Cues from the current situation may unconsciously trigger retrieval of an earlier experience. (p. 213)

delta waves large, slow brain waves associated with deep sleep. (p. 55)

delusion a false belief, often of persecution or grandeur, that may accompany psychotic disorders. (p. 403)

dendrites neuron extensions that receive messages and conduct them toward the cell body. (p. 31)

dependent variable in an experiment, the factor that is measured; the variable that may change when the independent variable is manipulated. (p. 19)

depressants drugs (such as alcohol, barbiturates, and opiates) that reduce (depress) neural activity and slow body functions. (p. 387)

depth perception the ability to see objects in three dimensions, although the images that strike the retina are two-dimensional; allows us to judge distance. (p. 148)

developmental psychology a branch of psychology that studies physical, cognitive, and social change throughout the life span. (p. 69)

difference threshold the minimum difference between two stimuli required for detection 50 percent of the time. We experience the difference threshold as a *just noticeable difference* (or *jnd*). (p. 135)

discrimination (1) in classical conditioning, the learned ability to distinguish between a conditioned stimulus and other irrelevant stimuli. (In operant conditioning, the ability to distinguish responses that are reinforced from those that are not.) (2) in social psychology, unjustifiable negative behavior toward a group and its members. (pp. 175, 327)

dissociative disorders controversial, rare disorders in which conscious awareness becomes separated (dissociated) from previous memories, thoughts, and feelings. (p. 407)

dissociative identity disorder (DID) a rare dissociative disorder in which a person exhibits two or more distinct and alternating personalities. (Formerly called *multiple personality disorder.*) (p. 407)

divergent thinking expanding the number of possible solutions to a problem; creative thinking that branches out in different directions. (p. 229)

DNA (deoxyribonucleic acid) a molecule containing the genetic information that makes up the chromosomes. (p. 71)

double-blind procedure in an experiment, a procedure in which both the participants and the research staff are ignorant (blind) about who has received the treatment or a placebo. (p. 19)

Down syndrome a condition of mild to severe intellectual disability and associated physical disorders caused by an extra copy of chromosome 21. (p. 245)

dream a sequence of images, emotions, and thoughts passing through a sleeping person's mind. (p. 61)

drive-reduction theory the idea that a physiological need creates an aroused state (a drive) that motivates us to satisfy the need. (p. 259)

DSM-5 the American Psychiatric Association's *Diagnostic and Statistical Manual of Mental Disorders,* Fifth Edition; a widely used system for classifying psychological disorders. (p. 379)

dual processing the principle that our mind processes information at the same time on separate conscious and unconscious tracks. (p. 11)

eclectic approach an approach to psychotherapy that, depending on the client's problems, uses techniques from various forms of therapy. (p. 417)

Ecstasy (MDMA) a synthetic stimulant and mild hallucinogen. Produces euphoria and social intimacy, but with short-term health risks and longer-term harm to serotonin-producing neurons and to mood and cognition. (p. 391)

EEG (electroencephalograph) a device that uses electrodes placed on the scalp to record waves of electrical activity sweeping across the brain's surface. (The record of those brain waves is an *electroencephalogram.*) (p. 39)

effortful processing encoding that requires attention and conscious effort. (p. 197)

egocentrism in Piaget's theory, the preoperational child's difficulty taking another's point of view. (p. 81)

ego the largely conscious, "executive" part of personality that, according to Freud, balances the demands of the id, superego, and reality. The ego operates on the *reality principle,* satisfying the id's desires in ways that will realistically bring pleasure rather than pain. (p. 353)

electroconvulsive therapy (ECT) a biomedical therapy for severely depressed patients in which a brief electric current is sent through the brain of an anesthetized patient. (p. 435)

embodied cognition the influence of bodily sensations, gestures, and other states on cognitive preferences and judgments. (p. 161)

embryo the developing human organism from about 2 weeks after fertilization through the second month. (p. 73)

emerging adulthood a period from about age 18 to the mid-twenties, when many in Western cultures are no longer adolescents but have not yet achieved full independence as adults. (p. 95)

emotion a response of the whole organism, involving (1) bodily arousal, (2) expressive behaviors, and (3) conscious experience. (p. 271)

emotion-focused coping attempting to reduce stress by avoiding or ignoring a stressor and attending to emotional needs related to our stress reaction. (p. 293)

emotional intelligence the ability to perceive, understand, manage, and use emotions. (p. 241)

encoding the process of getting information into the memory system. (p. 197)

endocrine [EN-duh-krin] **system** the body's "slow" chemical communication system; a set of glands that secrete hormones into the bloodstream. (p. 35)

endorphins [en-DOR-fins] "morphine within"—natural, opiate-like neurotransmitters linked to pain control and to pleasure. (p. 35)

environment every external influence, from prenatal nutrition to social support in later life. (p. 71)

epigenetics the study of environmental influences on gene expression that occur without a DNA change. (pp. 73, 377)

episodic memory explicit memory of personally experienced events; one of our two conscious memory systems (the other is *semantic memory*). (p. 201)

equity a condition in which people receive from a relationship in proportion to what they give to it. (p. 339)

erectile disorder inability to develop or maintain an erection due to insufficient bloodflow to the penis. (p. 117)

estrogens sex hormones, such as estradiol, that contribute to female sex characteristics and are secreted in greater amounts by females than by males. Estrogen levels peak during ovulation. In nonhuman mammals this promotes sexual receptivity. (p. 117)

evidence-based practice   clinical decision making that integrates the best available research with clinical expertise and patient characteristics and preferences. (p. 429)

evolutionary psychology   the study of how our behavior and mind have changed in adaptive ways over time due to natural selection. (p. 125)

experiment   a method in which researchers vary one or more factors (independent variables) to observe the effect on some behavior or mental process (the dependent variable). By random assignment of participants, researchers aim to control other factors. (p. 19)

experimental group   in an experiment, the group exposed to the treatment, that is, to one version of the independent variable. (p. 19)

explicit memory   retention of facts and personal events you can consciously retrieve. (Also called *declarative memory*.) (p. 197)

exposure therapies   behavioral techniques, such as *systematic desensitization* and *virtual reality exposure therapy*, that treat anxieties by exposing people (in imagination or actual situations) to the things they fear and avoid. (p. 421)

external locus of control   the perception that chance or outside forces beyond our personal control determine our fate. (p. 295)

extinction   in classical conditioning, the weakening of a conditioned response when an unconditioned stimulus does not follow a conditioned stimulus. (In operant conditioning, the weakening of a response when it is no longer reinforced.) (p. 175)

extrasensory perception (ESP)   the controversial claim that perception can occur apart from sensory input; includes telepathy, clairvoyance, and precognition. (p. 163)

extrinsic motivation   a desire to perform a behavior to gain a reward or avoid punishment. (p. 187)

facial feedback effect   the tendency of facial muscle states to trigger corresponding feelings such as fear, anger, or happiness. (p. 281)

factor   a cluster of behavior tendencies that occur together. (p. 361)

family therapy   therapy that treats the family as a system. Views an individual's unwanted behaviors as influenced by, or directed at, other family members. (p. 425)

feature detectors   nerve cells in the brain that respond to specific features of a stimulus, such as shape, angles, or movement. (p. 145)

feel-good, do-good phenomenon   our tendency to be helpful when already in a good mood. (p. 303)

female orgasmic disorder   distress due to infrequently or never experiencing orgasm. (p. 117)

fetal alcohol syndrome (FAS)   physical and mental abnormalities in children caused by a pregnant woman's heavy drinking. In severe cases, signs include a small, out-of-proportion head and abnormal facial features. (p. 73)

fetus   the developing human organism from 9 weeks after conception to birth. (p. 73)

fight-or-flight response   an emergency response, including activity of the sympathetic nervous system, that mobilizes energy and activity for attacking or escaping a threat. (p. 287)

figure-ground   the organization of the visual field into objects (the *figures*) that stand out from their surroundings (the *ground*). (p. 147)

fixation   (1) in thinking, the inability to see a problem from a new perspective; an obstacle to problem solving. (2) in personality theory, according to Freud, a lingering focus of pleasure-seeking energies at an earlier psychosexual stage, in which conflicts were unresolved. (pp. 223, 353)

fixed-interval schedule   in operant conditioning, a reinforcement schedule that reinforces a response only after a specified time has elapsed. (p. 181)

fixed-ratio schedule   in operant conditioning, a reinforcement schedule that reinforces a response only after a specified number of responses. (p. 179)

flashbulb memory   a clear memory of an emotionally significant moment or event. (p. 203)

flow   a completely involved, focused state, with lowered awareness of self and time; results from full engagement of our skills. (p. B-1)

fluid intelligence   your ability to reason speedily and abstractly; tends to decrease with age, especially during late adulthood. (p. 249)

fMRI (functional MRI)   a technique for revealing bloodflow and, therefore, brain activity by comparing successive MRI scans. fMRI scans show brain function. (p. 39)

foot-in-the-door phenomenon   the tendency for people who have first agreed to a small request to comply later with a larger request. (p. 317)

formal operational stage   in Piaget's theory, the stage of cognitive development (normally beginning about age 12) during which people begin to think logically about abstract concepts. (p. 81)

framing   the way an issue is posed; framing can significantly affect decisions and judgments. (p. 227)

fraternal (dizygotic) twins   twins who develop from separate fertilized eggs. They are genetically no closer than nontwin brothers and sisters, but they share a prenatal environment. (p. 75)

free association   in psychoanalysis, a method of exploring the unconscious in which the person relaxes and says whatever comes to mind, no matter how unimportant or embarrassing. (p. 351)

frequency   the number of complete wavelengths that pass a point in a given time (for example, per second). (p. 153)

frontal lobes   the portion of the cerebral cortex lying just behind the forehead; involved in speaking and muscle movements and in making plans and judgments. (p. 43)

frustration-aggression principle   the principle that frustration—the blocking of an attempt to achieve some goal—creates anger, which can generate aggression. (p. 333)

fundamental attribution error   the tendency, when analyzing others' behavior, to overestimate the influence of personal traits and underestimate the effects of the situation. (p. 315)

gender   in psychology, the socially influenced characteristics by which people define *men* and *women*. (p. 109)

gender identity   our sense of being male, female, or some combination of the two. (p. 115)

gender role   a set of expected behaviors, attitudes, and traits for males or for females. (p. 115)

gender typing   the acquisition of a traditional masculine or feminine role. (p. 115)

general adaptation syndrome (GAS)   Selye's concept of the body's adaptive response to stress in three stages—alarm, resistance, exhaustion. (p. 287)

general intelligence (*g*)   a general intelligence factor that, according to Spearman and others, underlies specific mental abilities and is therefore measured by every task on an intelligence test. (p. 238)

generalization   in classical conditioning, the tendency, after conditioning, to respond similarly to stimuli that resemble the conditioned stimulus. (In operant conditioning, *generalization* occurs when our responses to similar stimuli are also reinforced.) (p. 175)

generalized anxiety disorder   an anxiety disorder in which a person is continually tense, fearful, and in a state of *autonomic nervous system* arousal. (p. 381)

genes   the biochemical units of heredity that make up the chromosomes; segments of DNA. (p. 71)

genome   the complete instructions for making an organism, consisting of all the genetic material in that organism's chromosomes. (p. 71)

gestalt   an organized whole. Gestalt psychologists emphasized our tendency to integrate pieces of information into meaningful wholes. (p. 147)

glial cells (glia)   cells in the nervous system that support, nourish, and protect neurons; they also play a role in learning, thinking, and memory. (p. 31)

glucose   the form of sugar that circulates in the blood and provides the major source of energy for body tissues. When its level is low, we feel hunger. (p. 261)

grammar   in a specific language, a system of rules that enables us to communicate with and understand others. (p. 233)

grit   in psychology, passion and perseverance in the pursuit of long-term goals. (p. B-5)

group polarization   strengthening of a group's preexisting attitudes through discussions within the group. (p. 325)

group therapy   therapy conducted with groups rather than individuals, providing benefits from group interaction. (p. 425)

grouping   the perceptual tendency to organize stimuli into meaningful groups. (p. 147)

groupthink   the mode of thinking that occurs when the desire for harmony in a decision-making group overrides a realistic appraisal of alternatives. (p. 325)

hallucination   a false sensory experience, such as hearing something in the absence of an external auditory stimulus. (p. 45)

hallucinogens   psychedelic ("mind-manifesting") drugs, such as LSD, that distort perceptions and trigger sensory images in the absence of sensory input. (p. 391)

heredity the genetic transfer of characteristics from parents to offspring. (p. 71)

heritability the portion of variation among people in a group that we can attribute to genes. The heritability of a trait may vary, depending on the population and the environment. (p. 245)

heuristic a simple thinking strategy that often allows you to make judgments and solve problems efficiently; usually speedier but also more error-prone than *algorithms*. (p. 223)

hierarchy of needs Maslow's pyramid of human needs; at the base are physiological needs. These basic needs must be satisfied before higher-level safety needs, and then psychological needs, become active. (pp. 259, 357)

hindsight bias the tendency to believe, after learning an outcome, that we could have predicted it. (Also known as the *I-knew-it-all-along phenomenon*.) (p. 11)

hippocampus a neural center located in the limbic system; helps process for storage explicit (conscious) memories of facts and events. (pp. 43, 201)

homeostasis a tendency to maintain a balanced or constant internal state; the regulation of any aspect of body chemistry, such as blood glucose, around a particular level. (p. 259)

hormones chemical messengers that are manufactured by the endocrine glands, travel through the bloodstream, and affect other tissues. (p. 35)

hue the dimension of color that is determined by the wavelength of light; what we know as the color names *blue, green,* and so forth. (p. 141)

human factors psychology a field of psychology allied with I/O psychology that explores how people and machines interact and how machines and physical environments can be made safe and easy to use. (p. B-3)

humanistic psychology historically important perspective that emphasized human growth potential. (p. 3)

hypnosis a social interaction in which one person (the hypnotist) suggests to another person (the subject) that certain perceptions, feelings, thoughts, or behaviors will spontaneously occur. (p. 157)

hypothalamus [hi-po-THAL-uh-muss] a neural structure lying below (*hypo*) the thalamus; directs several maintenance activities (eating, drinking, body temperature), helps govern the endocrine system via the pituitary gland, and is linked to emotion and reward. (p. 43)

hypothesis a testable prediction, often implied by a theory. (p. 13)

id a reservoir of unconscious psychic energy that, according to Freud, strives to satisfy basic sexual and aggressive drives. The id operates on the *pleasure principle*, demanding immediate gratification. (p. 351)

identical (monozygotic) twins twins who develop from a single fertilized egg that splits in two, creating two genetically identical siblings. (p. 75)

identification the process by which, according to Freud, children incorporate their parents' values into their developing superegos. (p. 353)

identity our sense of self; according to Erikson, the adolescent's task is to solidify a sense of self by testing and blending various roles. (p. 93)

implicit memory retention of learned skills, or classically conditioned associations, without conscious awareness. (Also called *nondeclarative memory*.) (p. 197)

inattentional blindness failing to see visible objects when our attention is directed elsewhere. (p. 53)

incentive a positive or negative environmental stimulus that motivates behavior. (p. 259)

independent variable in an experiment, the factor that is manipulated; the variable whose effect is being studied. (p. 19)

individualism giving priority to our own goals over group goals and defining our identity in terms of personal traits rather than group membership. (p. 371)

industrial-organizational (I/O) psychology the application of psychological concepts and methods to human behavior in workplaces. (p. B-3)

informational social influence influence resulting from a person's willingness to accept others' opinions about reality. (p. 319)

informed consent giving people enough information about a study to enable them to decide whether they wish to participate. (p. 23)

ingroup "us"—people with whom we share a common identity. (p. 329)

ingroup bias the tendency to favor our own group. (p. 329)

inner ear the innermost part of the ear, containing the cochlea, semicircular canals, and vestibular sacs. (p. 153)

insight a sudden realization of the solution to a problem; contrasts with strategy-based solutions. (p. 223)

insight therapies therapies that aim to improve psychological functioning by increasing a person's awareness of underlying motives and defenses. (p. 419)

insomnia recurring problems in falling or staying asleep. (p. 61)

intellectual disability a condition of limited mental ability, indicated by an intelligence test score of 70 or below and difficulty adapting to the demands of life. (Formerly referred to as *mental retardation*.) (p. 245)

intelligence the ability to learn from experience, solve problems, and use knowledge to adapt to new situations. (p. 238)

intelligence quotient (IQ) defined originally as the ratio of mental age (*ma*) to chronological age (*ca*) multiplied by 100 (thus, IQ = *ma* ÷ *ca* × 100). On contemporary intelligence tests, the average performance for a given age is assigned a score of 100. (p. 243)

intelligence test a method for assessing an individual's mental aptitudes and comparing them with those of others, using numerical scores. (p. 241)

intensity the amount of energy in a light wave or sound wave, which influences what we perceive as brightness or loudness. Intensity is determined by the wave's amplitude (height). (p. 141)

interaction the interplay that occurs when the effect of one factor (such as environment) depends on another factor (such as heredity). (p. 71)

internal locus of control the perception that we control our own fate. (p. 295)

interneuron neurons within the brain and spinal cord; communicate internally and process information between sensory inputs and motor outputs. (p. 35)

interpretation in psychoanalysis, the analyst's noting supposed dream meanings, resistances, and other significant behaviors and events in order to promote insight. (p. 417)

intersex a condition present at birth; possessing biological sexual characteristics of both sexes. (p. 113)

intimacy in Erikson's theory, the ability to form close, loving relationships; a primary developmental task in early adulthood. (p. 93)

intrinsic motivation a desire to perform a behavior well for its own sake. (p. 187)

intuition an effortless, immediate, automatic feeling or thought, as contrasted with explicit, conscious reasoning. (p. 223)

James-Lange theory the theory that our experience of emotion is our awareness of our physiological responses to an emotion-arousing stimulus. (p. 271)

just-world phenomenon the tendency to believe that the world is just and people therefore get what they deserve and deserve what they get. (p. 329)

kinesthesia [kin-ehs-THEE-zhuh] the system for sensing the position and movement of individual body parts. (p. 161)

language our spoken, written, or signed words, and the ways we combine them to communicate meaning. (p. 231)

latent content according to Freud, the underlying meaning of a dream. (p. 61)

latent learning learning that is not apparent until there is an incentive to demonstrate it. (p. 187)

law of effect Thorndike's principle that behaviors followed by favorable consequences become more likely, and that behaviors followed by unfavorable consequences become less likely. (p. 177)

learned helplessness the hopelessness and passive resignation an animal or person learns when unable to avoid repeated aversive events. (p. 293)

learning the process of acquiring, through experience, new and relatively enduring information or behaviors. (p. 171)

limbic system neural system (including the *amygdala, hypothalamus,* and *hippocampus*) located below the cerebral hemispheres; associated with emotions and drives. (p. 41)

lobotomy a psychosurgical procedure once used to calm uncontrollably emotional or violent patients. The procedure cut the nerves connecting the frontal lobes to the emotion-controlling centers of the inner brain. (p. 437)

longitudinal study research in which the same people are restudied and retested over a long period of time. (pp. 99, 247, A-7)

long-term memory the relatively permanent and limitless storehouse of the memory system. Includes knowledge, skills, and experiences. (p. 197)

long-term potentiation (LTP) an increase in a cell's firing potential. Believed to be a neural basis for learning and memory. (p. 203)

LSD a powerful hallucinogenic drug; also known as acid (*lysergic acid diethylamide*). (p. 391)

major depressive disorder a disorder in which a person experiences, in the absence of drugs or another medical condition, two or more weeks with five or more symptoms, at least one of which must be either (1) depressed mood or (2) loss of interest or pleasure. (p. 395)

mania a hyperactive, wildly optimistic state in which dangerously poor judgment is common. (p. 395)

manifest content according to Freud, the remembered story line of a dream. (p. 61)

maturation biological growth processes leading to orderly changes in behavior, mostly independent of experience. (p. 75)

mean the arithmetic average of a distribution, obtained by adding the scores and then dividing by the number of scores. (p. A-3)

median the middle score in a distribution; half the scores are above it and half are below it. (p. A-3)

medical model the concept that diseases, in this case psychological disorders, have physical causes that can be *diagnosed, treated,* and, in most cases, *cured,* often through treatment in a *hospital.* (p. 377)

medulla [muh-DUL-uh] the base of the brainstem; controls heartbeat and breathing. (p. 39)

memory the persistence of learning over time through the encoding, storage, and retrieval of information. (p. 197)

memory consolidation the neural storage of a long-term memory. (p. 203)

memory trace lasting physical change in the brain as a memory forms. (p. 209)

menarche [meh-NAR-key] first menstrual period. (p. 113)

menopause the end of menstruation. In everyday use, it can also mean the biological transition a woman experiences from before until after the end of menstruation. (p. 97)

mental age a measure of intelligence test performance devised by Binet; the level of performance typically associated with children of a certain chronological age. Thus, a child who does as well as an average 8-year-old is said to have a mental age of 8. (p. 241)

mere exposure effect the phenomenon that repeated exposure to novel stimuli increases liking of them. (p. 335)

methamphetamine a powerfully addictive drug that stimulates the central nervous system with speeded-up body functions and associated energy and mood changes; over time, appears to reduce baseline dopamine levels. (p. 391)

middle ear the chamber between the eardrum and cochlea containing three tiny bones (hammer, anvil, and stirrup) that concentrate the vibrations of the eardrum on the cochlea's oval window. (p. 153)

mindfulness meditation a reflective practice in which people attend to current experiences in a nonjudgmental and accepting manner. (p. 301)

Minnesota Multiphasic Personality Inventory (MMPI) the most widely researched and clinically used of all personality tests. Originally developed to identify emotional disorders (still considered its most appropriate use), this test is now used for many other screening purposes. (p. 361)

mirror-image perceptions mutual views often held by conflicting people, as when each side sees itself as ethical and peaceful and views the other side as evil and aggressive. (p. 343)

mirror neuron a neuron that fires when we perform certain actions and when we observe others performing those actions; a neural basis for imitation and observational learning. (p. 189)

misinformation effect when a memory has been corrupted by misleading information. (p. 213)

mnemonics [nih-MON-iks] memory aids, especially techniques that use vivid imagery and organizational devices. (p. 199)

mode the most frequently occurring score(s) in a distribution. (p. A-3)

modeling the process of observing and imitating a specific behavior. (p. 187)

monocular cue a depth cue, such as interposition or linear perspective, available to either eye alone. (p. 148)

mood-congruent memory the tendency to recall experiences that are consistent with your current good or bad mood. (p. 207)

motivation a need or desire that energizes and directs behavior. (p. 259)

motor cortex the cerebral cortex area at the rear of the frontal lobes; controls voluntary movements. (p. 45)

motor neuron neuron that carries outgoing information from the brain and spinal cord to the muscles and glands. (p. 35)

MRI (magnetic resonance imaging) a technique that uses magnetic fields and radio waves to produce computer-generated images of soft tissue. MRI scans show brain anatomy. (p. 39)

narcissism excessive self-love and self-absorption. (pp. 269, 369)

narcolepsy a sleep disorder in which a person has uncontrollable sleep attacks, sometimes lapsing directly into REM sleep. (p. 61)

natural selection the principle that, among the range of inherited trait variations, the ones most likely to be passed on to succeeding generations are those that increase the organism's chances of surviving and reproducing in its environment. (p. 125)

naturalistic observation a descriptive technique of observing and recording behavior in naturally occurring situations without trying to change or control the situation. (p. 15)

nature–nurture issue the age-old controversy over the relative influence of genes and experience in the development of psychological traits and behaviors. Today's psychological science sees traits and behaviors arising from the interaction of nature and nurture. (p. 9)

near-death experience an altered state of consciousness reported after a close brush with death (such as cardiac arrest); often similar to drug-induced hallucinations. (p. 391)

negative reinforcement increases behaviors by stopping or reducing negative stimuli, such as shock. A negative reinforcer is anything that, when *removed* after a response, strengthens the response. (*Note:* Negative reinforcement is *not* punishment.) (p. 179)

nerves bundled axons that form neural cables connecting the central nervous system with muscles, glands, and sense organs. (p. 35)

nervous system the body's speedy, electrochemical communication network, consisting of all the nerve cells of the central and peripheral nervous systems. (p. 35)

neurogenesis the formation of new neurons. (p. 47)

neuron a nerve cell; the basic building block of the nervous system. (p. 31)

neurotransmitters neuron-produced chemicals that cross the synaptic gap to carry messages to other neurons or to muscles and glands. (p. 33)

neutral stimulus (NS) in classical conditioning, a stimulus that evokes no response before conditioning. (p. 171)

nicotine a stimulating and highly addictive psychoactive drug in tobacco. (p. 389)

normal curve (*normal distribution*) a symmetrical, bell-shaped curve that describes the distribution of many types of data. Most scores fall near the average, or *mean* (about 68 percent fall within one *standard deviation* of it), and fewer and fewer scores lie near the extremes. (pp. 243, A-3)

normative social influence influence resulting from a person's desire to gain approval or avoid disapproval. (p. 319)

object permanence the awareness that things continue to exist even when not perceived. (p. 79)

observational learning learning by observing others. (p. 187)

obsessive-compulsive disorder (OCD) a disorder characterized by unwanted repetitive thoughts (obsessions), actions (compulsions), or both. (p. 383)

occipital [ahk-SIP-uh-tuhl] **lobes** the portion of the cerebral cortex lying at the back of the head; includes areas that receive information from the visual fields. (p. 45)

Oedipus [ED-uh-puss] **complex** according to Freud, a boy's sexual desires toward his mother and feelings of jealousy and hatred for the rival father. (p. 353)

one-word stage the stage in speech development, from about age 1 to 2, during which a child speaks mostly in single words. (p. 233)

operant behavior behavior that operates on the environment, producing consequences. (p. 171)

operant chamber in operant conditioning research, a chamber (also known as a *Skinner box*) containing a bar or key that an animal can manipulate to obtain a food or water reinforcer; attached devices record the animal's rate of bar pressing or key pecking. (p. 177)

operant conditioning a type of learning in which a behavior becomes more probable if followed by a reinforcer or is diminished if followed by a punisher. (p. 177)

operational definition a carefully worded statement of the exact procedures (operations) used in a research study. For example, *human intelligence* may be operationally defined as what an intelligence test measures. (p. 13)

opiates opium and its derivatives, such as morphine and heroin; depress neural activity, temporarily lessening pain and anxiety. (pp. 33, 389)

opponent-process theory the theory that opposing retinal processes (red-green, yellow-blue, white-black) enable color vision. For example, some cells are "turned on" by green and "turned off" by red; others are turned on by red and off by green. (p. 145)

optic nerve the nerve that carries neural impulses from the eye to the brain. (p. 143)

optimism the anticipation of positive outcomes. Optimists are people who expect the best and expect their efforts to lead to good things. (p. 295)

organizational psychology an I/O psychology subfield that examines organizational influences on worker satisfaction and productivity and facilitates organizational change. (p. B-3)

ostracism deliberate social exclusion of individuals or groups. (p. 268)

other-race effect the tendency to recall faces of one's own race more accurately than faces of other races. (p. 331)

outgroup "them"—those perceived as different or apart from our group. (p. 329)

overconfidence the tendency to be more confident than correct—to overestimate the accuracy of our beliefs and judgments. (p. 227)

panic disorder an anxiety disorder marked by unpredictable minutes-long episodes of intense dread in which a person may experience terror and accompanying chest pain, choking, or other frightening sensations; often followed by worry over a possible next attack. (p. 381)

parallel processing processing many aspects of a problem or scene at the same time; the brain's natural mode of information processing for many functions. (pp. 51, 147, 199)

parasympathetic nervous system autonomic nervous system subdivision that calms the body, conserving its energy. (p. 35)

parietal [puh-RYE-uh-tuhl] lobes the portion of the cerebral cortex lying at the top of the head and toward the rear; receives sensory input for touch and body position. (p. 45)

partial (intermittent) reinforcement reinforcing a response only part of the time; results in slower acquisition but much greater resistance to extinction than does continuous reinforcement. (p. 179)

passionate love an aroused state of intense positive absorption in another, usually present at the beginning of romantic love. (p. 339)

perception the process by which our brain organizes and interprets sensory information, transforming it into meaningful objects and events. (p. 135)

perceptual adaptation the ability to adjust to changed sensory input, including an artificially displaced or even inverted visual field. (p. 153)

perceptual constancy perceiving objects as unchanging (having consistent color, brightness, shape, and size) even as illumination and retinal images change. (p. 151)

perceptual set a mental predisposition to perceive one thing and not another. (p. 139)

peripheral nervous system (PNS) the sensory and motor neurons connecting the central nervous system to the rest of the body. (p. 35)

peripheral route persuasion occurs when people are influenced by unimportant cues, such as a speaker's attractiveness. (p. 315)

person-centered therapy a humanistic therapy, developed by Rogers, in which the therapist uses techniques such as active listening within a genuine, accepting, empathic environment to promote clients' growth. (Also called *client-centered therapy*.) (p. 419)

personal control our sense of controlling our environment rather than feeling helpless. (p. 293)

personality an individual's characteristic pattern of thinking, feeling, and acting. (p. 351)

personality disorder an inflexible and enduring behavior pattern that impairs social functioning. (p. 407)

personality inventory a questionnaire (often with *true-false* or *agree-disagree* items) on which people respond to items designed to gauge a wide range of feelings and behaviors; used to assess selected personality traits. (p. 363)

personnel psychology an I/O psychology subfield that helps with job seeking, and with employee recruitment, selection, placement, training, appraisal, and development. (p. B-3)

pessimism the anticipation of negative outcomes. Pessimists are people who expect the worst and doubt that their goals will be achieved. (p. 295)

PET (positron emission tomography) scan a view of brain activity showing where a radioactive form of glucose goes while the brain performs a given task. (p. 39)

phobia an anxiety disorder marked by a persistent, irrational fear and avoidance of a specific object, activity, or situation. (p. 383)

physiological need a basic bodily requirement. (p. 259)

pitch a tone's experienced highness or lowness; depends on frequency. (p. 153)

pituitary gland the most influential endocrine gland. Under the influence of the hypothalamus, the pituitary regulates growth and controls other endocrine glands. (p. 35)

placebo [pluh-SEE-bo; Latin for "I shall please"] an inactive substance or condition that is sometimes given to those in a control group in place of the treatment given to the experimental group. (p. 19)

placebo effect results caused by expectations alone. (p. 19)

plasticity the brain's ability to change, especially during childhood, by reorganizing after damage or by building new pathways based on experience. (p. 31)

polygraph a machine, commonly used in attempts to detect lies, that measures some bodily responses (such as changes in perspiration, heart rate, and breathing) accompanying emotion. (p. 277)

population all those in a group being studied, from which samples may be drawn. (*Note:* Except for national studies, this does *not* refer to a country's whole population.) (p. 17)

positive psychology the scientific study of human functioning, with the goals of discovering and promoting strengths and virtues that help individuals and communities to thrive. (p. 11)

positive reinforcement increases behaviors by presenting positive stimuli, such as food. A positive reinforcer is anything that, when *presented* after a response, strengthens the response. (p. 179)

posthypnotic suggestion a suggestion, made during a hypnosis session, to be carried out after the subject is no longer hypnotized; used by some clinicians to help control undesired symptoms and behaviors. (p. 159)

posttraumatic growth positive psychological changes as a result of struggling with extremely challenging circumstances and life crises. (p. 438)

posttraumatic stress disorder (PTSD) a disorder characterized by haunting memories, nightmares, social withdrawal, jumpy anxiety, numbness of feeling, and/or insomnia lingering for four weeks or more after a traumatic experience. (p. 383)

predictive validity the success with which a test predicts the behavior it is designed to predict. (p. 243)

prejudice an unfair and usually negative attitude toward a group and its members. Prejudice generally involves stereotyped beliefs, negative feelings, and a predisposition to discriminatory action. (p. 327)

preoperational stage in Piaget's theory, the stage (from about 2 to 6 or 7 years of age) in which a child learns to use language but cannot yet perform the mental operations of concrete logic. (p. 79)

primary reinforcer an event that is innately reinforcing, often by satisfying a biological need. (p. 179)

primary sex characteristics the body structures (ovaries, testes, and external genitalia) that make sexual reproduction possible. (p. 113)

priming activating, often unconsciously, associations in our mind, thus setting us up to perceive, remember, or respond to objects or events in certain ways. (pp. 137, 207)

proactive interference the forward-acting disruptive effect of older learning on the recall of *new* information. (p. 211)

problem-focused coping attempting to reduce stress directly—by changing the stressor or the way we interact with that stressor. (p. 293)

projective test a personality test, such as the Rorschach, that provides an ambiguous image designed to trigger projection of the test-taker's unconscious thoughts or feelings. (p. 355)

prosocial behavior positive, constructive, helpful behavior. The opposite of antisocial behavior. (p. 189)

prototype a mental image or best example of a category. Matching new items to a prototype provides a quick and easy method for sorting items into categories (as when you compare a feathered creature to a prototypical bird, such as a robin). (p. 223)

psychoactive drug a chemical substance that alters perceptions and mood. (p. 385)

psychoanalysis (1) Freud's theory of personality that attributes thoughts and actions to unconscious motives and conflicts. (2) Freud's therapeutic technique used in treating psychological disorders. Freud believed the patient's free associations, resistances, dreams, and transferences—and the analyst's interpretations of them—released previously repressed feelings, allowing the patient to gain self-insight. (pp. 351, 417)

psychodynamic theories view personality with a focus on the unconscious and the importance of childhood experiences. (p. 351)

psychodynamic therapy therapeutic approach derived from the psychoanalytic tradition; views individuals as responding to unconscious forces and childhood experiences, and seeks to enhance self-insight. (p. 419)

psychological disorder a syndrome marked by a clinically significant disturbance in a person's cognition, emotion regulation, or behavior. (p. 377)

psychology the science of behavior and mental processes. (p. 5)

psychoneuroimmunology the study of how psychological, neural, and endocrine processes combine to affect our immune system and health. (p. 289)

psychosexual stages the childhood stages of development (oral, anal, phallic, latency, genital) during which, according to Freud, the id's pleasure-seeking energies focus on distinct erogenous zones. (p. 353)

psychosurgery surgery that removes or destroys brain tissue in an effort to change behavior. (p. 437)

psychotherapy treatment involving psychological techniques; consists of interactions between a trained therapist and someone seeking to overcome psychological difficulties or achieve personal growth. (p. 417)

psychotic disorders a group of disorders marked by irrational ideas, distorted perceptions, and a loss of contact with reality. (p. 401)

puberty the period of sexual maturation, during which a person becomes capable of reproducing. (pp. 89, 111)

punishment an event that decreases the behavior it follows. (p. 181)

random assignment assigning participants to experimental and control groups by chance, thus minimizing any preexisting differences between the groups. (p. 19)

random sample a sample that fairly represents a population because each member has an equal chance of inclusion. (p. 17)

range the difference between the highest and lowest scores in a distribution. (p. A-3)

recall memory demonstrated by retrieving information learned earlier, as on a fill-in-the-blank test. (p. 205)

reciprocal determinism the interacting influences of behavior, internal personal factors, and environment. (p. 365)

reciprocity norm an expectation that people will help, not hurt, those who have helped them. (p. 341)

recognition memory demonstrated by identifying items previously learned, as on a multiple-choice test. (p. 205)

reconsolidation a process in which previously stored memories, when retrieved, are potentially altered before being stored again. (p. 211)

reflex a simple, automatic response to a sensory stimulus. (pp. 35, 73)

refractory period (1) in neural processing, a brief resting pause that occurs after a neuron has fired; subsequent action potentials cannot occur until the axon returns to its resting state. (2) in human sexuality, a resting pause that occurs after orgasm, during which a man cannot achieve another orgasm. (pp. 33, 117)

regression toward the mean the tendency for extreme or unusual scores or events to fall back (regress) toward the average. (p. A-5)

reinforcement in operant conditioning, any event that *strengthens* the behavior it follows. (p. 177)

reinforcement schedule a pattern that defines how often a desired response will be reinforced. (p. 179)

relational aggression an act of aggression (physical or verbal) intended to harm a person's relationship or social standing. (p. 109)

relative deprivation the perception that we are worse off relative to those with whom we compare ourselves. (p. 307)

relearning memory demonstrated by time saved when learning material a second time. (p. 205)

reliability the extent to which a test yields consistent results, as assessed by the consistency of scores on two halves of the test, on alternative forms of the test, or on retesting. (p. 243)

REM rebound the tendency for REM sleep to increase following REM sleep deprivation. (p. 62)

REM sleep rapid eye movement sleep; a recurring sleep stage during which vivid dreams commonly occur. Also known as *paradoxical sleep,* because the muscles are relaxed (except for minor twitches) but other body systems are active. (p. 55)

repetitive transcranial magnetic stimulation (rTMS) the application of repeated pulses of magnetic energy to the brain; used to stimulate or suppress brain activity. (p. 435)

replication repeating the essence of a research study, usually with different participants in different situations, to see whether the basic finding can be reproduced. (p. 13)

repression in psychoanalytic theory, the basic defense mechanism that banishes from consciousness the thoughts, feelings, and memories that arouse anxiety. (pp. 211, 353)

resilience the personal strength that helps most people cope with stress and recover from adversity and even trauma. (pp. 303, 438)

resistance in psychoanalysis, the blocking from consciousness of anxiety-laden material. (p. 417)

respondent behavior behavior that occurs as an automatic response to some stimulus. (p. 171)

reticular formation nerve network running through the brainstem and into the thalamus; plays an important role in controlling arousal. (p. 41)

retina the light-sensitive inner surface of the eye; contains the receptor rods and cones plus layers of neurons that begin the processing of visual information. (p. 141)

retinal disparity a binocular cue for perceiving depth. By comparing images from the two eyes, the brain computes distance—the greater the disparity (difference) between the two images, the closer the object. (p. 148)

retrieval the process of getting information out of memory storage. (p. 197)

retrieval cue any stimulus (event, feeling, place, and so on) linked to a specific memory. (p. 207)

retroactive interference the backward-acting disruptive effect of newer learning on the recall of old information. (p. 211)

reuptake a neurotransmitter's reabsorption by the sending neuron. (p. 33)

rods retinal receptors that detect black, white, and gray, and are sensitive to movement; necessary for peripheral and twilight vision, when cones don't respond. (p. 143)

role a set of expectations about a social position, defining how those in the position ought to behave. (pp. 115, 317)

Rorschach inkblot test the most widely used projective test; a set of 10 inkblots, designed by Hermann Rorschach; seeks to identify people's inner feelings by analyzing their interpretations of the blots. (p. 355)

savant syndrome a condition in which a person otherwise limited in mental ability has an exceptional specific skill, such as in computation or drawing. (p. 238)

scapegoat theory the theory that prejudice offers an outlet for anger by providing someone to blame. (p. 329)

scatterplot a graphed cluster of dots, each of which represents the values of two variables. The slope of the points suggests the direction of the relationship between the two variables. The amount of scatter suggests the strength of the correlation (little scatter indicates high correlation). (p. A-5)

schema a concept or framework that organizes and interprets information. (p. 79)

schizophrenia a disorder characterized by delusions, hallucinations, disorganized speech, and/or diminished, inappropriate emotional expression. (p. 401)

secondary sex characteristics nonreproductive sexual traits, such as female breasts and hips, male voice quality, and body hair. (p. 113)

selective attention focusing conscious awareness on a particular stimulus. (p. 51)

self your image and understanding of who you are; in modern psychology, the idea that this is the center of personality, organizing your thoughts, feelings, and actions. (p. 367)

self-actualization according to Maslow, the psychological need that arises after basic physical and psychological needs are met and self-esteem is achieved; the motivation to fulfill our potential. (p. 357)

self-concept all our thoughts and feelings about ourselves, in answer to the question, "Who am I?" (p. 359)

self-control the ability to control impulses and delay short-term gratification for greater long-term rewards. (p. 295)

self-disclosure revealing intimate aspects of ourselves to others. (p. 339)

self-efficacy our sense of competence and effectiveness. (p. 365)

self-esteem our feelings of high or low self-worth. (p. 367)

self-fulfilling prophecy a belief that leads to its own fulfillment. (p. 343)

self-serving bias our readiness to perceive ourselves favorably. (p. 369)

self-transcendence according to Maslow, the striving for identity, meaning, and purpose beyond the self. (p. 357)

semantic memory explicit memory of facts and general knowledge; one of our two conscious memory systems (the other is *episodic memory*). (p. 201)

sensation the process by which our sensory receptors and nervous system receive and represent stimulus energies from our environment. (p. 135)

sensorimotor stage in Piaget's theory, the stage (from birth to nearly 2 years of age) during which infants know the world mostly in terms of their sensory impressions and motor activities. (p. 79)

sensorineural hearing loss hearing loss caused by damage to the cochlea's receptor cells or to the auditory nerves; the most common form of hearing loss, also called *nerve deafness*. (p. 153)

sensory adaptation reduced sensitivity in response to constant stimulation. (p. 137)

sensory interaction the principle that one sense may influence another, as when the smell of food influences its taste. (p. 161)

sensory memory the immediate, very brief recording of sensory information in the memory system. (p. 197)

sensory neuron neuron that carries incoming information from the body's tissues and sensory receptors to the brain and spinal cord. (p. 35)

sequential processing the processing of one aspect of a problem at a time; used when we focus attention on new or complex tasks. (p. 51)

serial position effect our tendency to recall best the last and first items in a list. (p. 207)

set point the point at which your "weight thermostat" may be set. When your body falls below this weight, increased hunger and a lowered metabolic rate may combine to restore lost weight. (p. 263)

sex in psychology, the biologically influenced characteristics by which people define *male* and *female*. (p. 109)

sexual dysfunction a problem that consistently impairs sexual arousal or functioning. (p. 117)

sexual orientation an enduring sexual attraction toward members of one's own sex (homosexual orientation), the other sex (heterosexual orientation), or both sexes (bisexual orientation). (p. 121)

sexual response cycle the four stages of sexual responding described by Masters and Johnson—excitement, plateau, orgasm, and resolution. (p. 117)

shaping an operant conditioning procedure in which reinforcers guide actions closer and closer toward a desired behavior. (p. 177)

short-term memory activated memory that holds a few items briefly (such as the seven digits of a phone number while calling) before the information is stored or forgotten. (p. 197)

sleep a periodic, natural loss of consciousness—as distinct from unconsciousness resulting from a coma, general anesthesia, or hibernation. (Adapted from Dement, 1999.) (p. 55)

sleep apnea a sleep disorder in which a sleeping person repeatedly stops breathing until blood oxygen is so low the person awakens just long enough to draw a breath. (p. 61)

social clock the culturally preferred timing of social events such as marriage, parenthood, and retirement. (p. 99)

social-cognitive perspective views behavior as influenced by the interaction between persons (and their thinking) and their social context. (p. 365)

social facilitation improved performance on simple or well-learned tasks in the presence of others. (p. 324)

social identity the "we" aspect of our self-concept; the part of our answer to "Who am I?" that comes from our group memberships. (p. 93)

social leadership group-oriented leadership that builds teamwork, resolves conflict, and offers support. (p. B-7)

social learning theory the theory that we learn social behavior by observing and imitating and by being rewarded or punished. (p. 115)

social loafing the tendency for people in a group to exert less effort when pooling their efforts toward attaining a common goal than when individually accountable. (p. 325)

social psychology the scientific study of how we think about, influence, and relate to one another. (p. 315)

social-responsibility norm an expectation that people will help those dependent upon them. (p. 341)

social script a culturally modeled guide for how to act in various situations. (pp. 121, 333)

somatic nervous system peripheral nervous system division that controls the body's skeletal muscles. Also called the *skeletal nervous system*. (p. 35)

somatosensory cortex the cerebral cortex area at the front of the parietal lobes; registers and processes body touch and movement sensations. (p. 45)

source amnesia faulty memory for how, when, or where information was learned or imagined. (p. 213)

spacing effect the tendency for distributed study or practice to yield better long-term retention than is achieved through massed study or practice. (p. 201)

spermarche [sper-MAR-key] first ejaculation. (p. 113)

split brain a condition in which the brain's two hemispheres have been isolated by surgery that cut the fibers (mainly those of the corpus callosum) connecting them. (p. 47)

spontaneous recovery the reappearance, after a pause, of an extinguished conditioned response. (p. 175)

spotlight effect overestimating others' noticing and evaluating our appearance, performance, and blunders (as if we presume a spotlight shines on us). (p. 367)

SQ3R a study method incorporating five steps: Survey, Question, Read, Retrieve, Review. (p. 25)

standard deviation a computed measure of how much scores vary around the mean score. (p. A-3)

standardization defining uniform testing procedures and meaningful scores by comparison with the performance of a pretested group. (p. 243)

Stanford-Binet the widely used American revision (by Terman at Stanford University) of Binet's original intelligence test. (p. 241)

statistical significance a statistical statement of how likely it is that an obtained result occurred by chance. (p. A-7)

stereotype a generalized (sometimes accurate but often overgeneralized) belief about a group of people. (p. 327)

stereotype threat a self-confirming concern that you will be judged based on a negative stereotype. (p. 251)

stimulants drugs (such as caffeine, nicotine, and the more powerful cocaine, amphetamines, methamphetamine, and Ecstasy) that excite neural activity and speed up body functions. (p. 389)

stimulus any event or situation that evokes a response. (p. 171)

storage the process of retaining encoded information over time. (p. 197)

stranger anxiety the fear of strangers that infants commonly display, beginning by about 8 months of age. (p. 83)

stress the process by which we perceive and respond to certain events, called *stressors*, that we appraise as threatening or challenging. (p. 287)

subjective well-being self-perceived happiness or satisfaction with life. Used along with measures of objective well-being (for example, physical and economic indicators) to judge our quality of life. (p. 303)

subliminal below a person's absolute threshold for conscious awareness. (p. 135)

substance use disorder disorder characterized by continued substance craving and use despite significant life disruption and/or physical risk. (p. 385)

superego the part of personality that, according to Freud, represents internalized ideals and provides standards for judgment (the conscience) and for future goals. (p. 353)

superordinate goals shared goals that override differences among people and require their cooperation. (p. 343)

suprachiasmatic nucleus (SCN) a pair of cell clusters in the hypothalamus that controls circadian rhythm. In response to light, the SCN adjusts melatonin production, thus modifying our feelings of sleepiness. (p. 57)

survey a descriptive technique for obtaining the self-reported attitudes or behaviors of a group, usually by questioning a representative, *random sample* of that group. (p. 15)

sympathetic nervous system autonomic nervous system subdivision that arouses the body, mobilizing its energy. (p. 35)

synapse [SIN-aps] the junction between the axon tip of a sending neuron and the dendrite or cell body of a receiving neuron. The tiny gap at this junction is called the *synaptic gap* or *synaptic cleft*. (p. 31)

systematic desensitization a type of exposure therapy that associates a pleasant, relaxed state with gradually increasing, anxiety-triggering stimuli. Commonly used to treat phobias. (p. 421)

task leadership goal-oriented leadership that sets standards, organizes work, and focuses attention on goals. (p. B-7)

telegraphic speech early speech stage in which a child speaks in compressed sentences, like a telegram—"want milk" or "Daddy go store"—using mostly nouns and verbs. (p. 233)

temperament a person's characteristic emotional reactivity and intensity. (p. 75)

temporal lobes the portion of the cerebral cortex lying roughly above the ears; includes areas that receive information from the ears. (p. 45)

tend-and-befriend response under stress, people (especially women) often provide support to others (*tend*) and bond with and seek support from others (*befriend*). (p. 289)

teratogen [tuh-RAT-uh-jen] an agent, such as a chemical or virus, that can reach the embryo or fetus during prenatal development and cause harm. (p. 73)

testing effect enhanced memory after retrieving, rather than simply rereading, information. Also sometimes called the *retrieval practice effect* or *test-enhanced learning*. (pp. 25, 201)

testosterone the most important male sex hormone. Both males and females have it, but the additional testosterone in males stimulates the growth of the male sex organs during the fetal period and the development of the male sex characteristics during puberty. (p. 111)

thalamus [THAL-uh-muss] the brain's sensory control center, located on top of the brainstem; directs sensory messages to the cortex and transmits replies to the cerebellum and medulla. (p. 41)

THC the major active ingredient in marijuana; triggers a variety of effects, including mild hallucinations. (p. 391)

Thematic Apperception Test (TAT) a projective test in which people express their inner feelings and interests through the stories they make up about ambiguous scenes. (p. 355)

theory an explanation using principles that organize observations and predict behaviors or events. (p. 13)

theory of mind people's ideas about their own and others' mental states—about their feelings, perceptions, and thoughts, and the behaviors these might predict. (p. 81)

therapeutic alliance a bond of trust and mutual understanding between a therapist and client, who work together constructively to overcome the client's problem. (p. 429)

threshold the level of stimulation required to trigger a neural impulse. (p. 33)

token economy an operant conditioning procedure in which people earn a token for exhibiting a desired behavior and can later exchange the tokens for privileges or treats. (p. 423)

tolerance a dwindling effect with regular use of the same dose of a drug, requiring the user to take larger and larger doses before experiencing the drug's effect. (p. 387)

top-down processing information processing guided by higher-level mental processes, as when we construct perceptions drawing on our experience and expectations. (p. 135)

trait a characteristic pattern of behavior or a tendency to feel and act in a certain way, as assessed by self-report inventories and peer reports. (p. 359)

transduction changing one form of energy into another. In sensation, the transforming of stimulus energies, such as sights, sounds, and smells, into neural impulses our brain can interpret. (p. 135)

transference in psychoanalysis, the patient's transfer to the analyst of emotions linked with other relationships (such as love or hatred for a parent). (p. 417)

transgender an umbrella term describing people whose gender identity or expression differs from that associated with their birth sex. (p. 115)

two-factor theory Schachter and Singer's theory that to experience emotion we must (1) be physically aroused and (2) cognitively label the arousal. (p. 271)

two-word stage beginning about age 2, the stage in speech development during which a child speaks mostly in two-word sentences. (p. 233)

Type A Friedman and Rosenman's term for competitive, hard-driving, impatient, verbally aggressive, and anger-prone people. (p. 291)

Type B Friedman and Rosenman's term for easygoing, relaxed people. (p. 291)

unconditional positive regard a caring, accepting, nonjudgmental attitude, which Rogers believed would help people develop self-awareness and self-acceptance. (pp. 359, 419)

unconditioned response (UR) in classical conditioning, an unlearned, naturally occurring response (such as salivation) to an unconditioned stimulus (US) (such as food in the mouth). (p. 173)

unconditioned stimulus (US) in classical conditioning, a stimulus that unconditionally—naturally and automatically—triggers a response (UR). (p. 173)

unconscious according to Freud, a reservoir of mostly unacceptable thoughts, wishes, feelings, and memories. According to contemporary psychologists, information processing of which we are unaware. (p. 351)

validity the extent to which a test measures or predicts what it is supposed to. (See also *content validity* and *predictive validity*.) (p. 243)

variable-interval schedule in operant conditioning, a reinforcement schedule that reinforces a response at unpredictable time intervals. (p. 181)

variable-ratio schedule in operant conditioning, a reinforcement schedule that reinforces a response after an unpredictable number of responses. (p. 179)

vestibular sense the sense of body movement and position, including the sense of balance. (p. 161)

virtual reality exposure therapy a counterconditioning technique that treats anxiety through creative electronic simulations in which people can safely face their greatest fears, such as airplane flying, spiders, or public speaking. (p. 421)

visual cliff a laboratory device for testing depth perception in infants and young animals. (p. 148)

wavelength the distance from the peak of one light wave or sound wave to the peak of the next. (p. 141)

Weber's law the principle that, to be perceived as different, two stimuli must differ by a constant minimum percentage (rather than a constant amount). (p. 137)

Wechsler Adult Intelligence Scale (WAIS) the WAIS and its companion versions for children are the most widely used intelligence tests; contains verbal and performance (nonverbal) subtests. (p. 243)

Wernicke's area controls language reception; a brain area involved in language comprehension and expression; usually in the left temporal lobe. (p. 235)

withdrawal the discomfort and distress that follow ending the use of an addictive drug or behavior. (p. 387)

working memory a newer understanding of short-term memory that adds conscious, active processing of incoming auditory and visual-spatial information, and of information retrieved from long-term memory. (p. 197)

X chromosome the sex chromosome found in both men and women. Females typically have two X chromosomes; males typically have one. An X chromosome from each parent produces a female child. (p. 111)

Y chromosome the sex chromosome typically found only in males. When paired with an X chromosome from the mother, it produces a male child. (p. 111)

Yerkes-Dodson law the principle that performance increases with arousal only up to a point, beyond which performance decreases. (p. 259)

Young-Helmholtz trichromatic (three-color) theory the theory that the retina contains three different types of color receptors—one most sensitive to red, one to green, one to blue. When stimulated in combination, these receptors can produce the perception of any color. (p. 145)

zygote the fertilized egg; it enters a 2-week period of rapid cell division and develops into an embryo. (p. 73)

absolute threshold/umbral absoluto Energía de estimulación mínima necesaria para detectar una estimulación dada el 50 por ciento del tiempo. (pág. 135)

accommodation/acomodo Adaptación de nuestros entendimientos (esquemas) actuales de manera que incorporen información nueva. (pág. 79)

achievement motivation/motivación de logro Deseo de lograr algo importante, para el dominio maestral de destrezas o ideas; para el control; deseo de alcanzar una norma alta. (pág. B-3)

achievement test/prueba de rendimiento Prueba diseñada para evaluar lo que una persona ha aprendido. (pág. 241)

acquisition/adquisición Según el condicionamiento clásico, etapa inicial en la que relacionamos un estímulo neutral con uno incondicionado, de tal modo que el estímulo neutral comience a desencadenar la respuesta condicionada. (Según el condicionamiento operante, intensificación de una respuesta reforzada.) (pág. 173)

action potential/potencial de acción Impulso nervioso. Carga eléctrica de corta duración que viaja a través del axón. (pág. 31)

active listening/escucha activa Escucha empática en la que el oyente hace eco, reitera y aclara. Característica de la terapia de Rogers centrada en la persona. (pág. 419)

acute schizophrenia/esquizofrenia aguda (también se le dice *esquizofrenia reactiva*). Tipo de esquizofrenia que puede comenzar a cualquier edad; se produce con frecuencia en respuesta a un evento emocionalmente traumático y requiere períodos largos de recuperación. (pág. 403)

adaptation-level phenomenon/fenómeno del nivel de adaptación Nuestra tendencia de formar juicios (de sonidos, de luces, de ingresos) con relación a un nivel neutro definido por nuestras vivencias anteriores. (pág. 307)

adolescence/adolescencia Período de transición de la niñez a la madurez, extendiéndose de la pubertad a la independencia. (pág. 89)

adrenal glands/glándulas suprarrenales Par de glándulas endocrinas ubicadas sobre los riñones que segregan hormonas (epinefrina y norepinefrina) que contribuyen a la estimulación del cuerpo en presencia de situaciones de tensión. (pág. 35)

aerobic exercise/ejercicios aeróbicos Actividad sostenida que mejora la salud cardíaca y pulmonar; posiblemente reduce también la depresión y la ansiedad. (pág. 299)

aggression/agresión Toda conducta que tiene por fin hacerle daño a alguien, sea física o emocionalmente. (págs. 109, 331)

AIDS (acquired immune deficiency syndrome)/sida (síndrome de inmunodeficiencia adquirida) Infección que se transmite sexualmente y que atenta contra la vida misma, causada por el *virus de inmunodeficiencia humana* (VIH). El sida debilita el sistema inmunitario, lo que aumenta la vulnerabilidad de la persona a infecciones. (pág. 117)

alcohol use disorder/trastorno de uso del alcohol (conocido comúnmente como *alcoholismo*) Consumo de alcohol caracterizado por tolerancia, síntomas de abstinencia cuando se interrumpe el consumo, y deseo de seguir consumiéndolo de manera problemática. (pág. 387)

algorithm/algoritmo Regla o procedimiento metódico y lógico que garantiza la resolución de un problema dado. Contrasta con el empleo de la *heurística*, un método generalmente más rápido pero también más propenso a registrar errores. (pág. 223)

all-or-none response/respuesta de todo o nada Reacción que produce una neurona al activarse (con una respuesta de máxima intensidad) o al no activarse. (pág. 33)

alpha waves/ritmo alfa Ritmo con ondas cerebrales relativamente lentas que corresponden a un estado relajado y de vigilia. (pág. 55)

altruism/altruismo Consideración desinteresada por el bienestar de los demás. (pág. 339)

amnesia/amnesia Literalmente significa "sin memoria". Pérdida de la memoria, a menudo a raíz de un trauma, una lesión o una enfermedad. (pág. 209)

amphetamines/anfetaminas Medicamentos que estimulan la actividad neuronal, acelerando las funciones corporales y cambiando el humor y los niveles de energía. (pág. 391)

amygdala/amígdala Dos conjuntos de fibras nerviosas del tamaño de una haba que se hallan en el sistema límbico e intervienen en las emociones. (pág. 41)

androgyny/androginia Que presenta características psicológicas tradicionales tanto masculinas como femeninas. (pág. 115)

anorexia nervosa/anorexia nerviosa Trastorno alimentario en el cual una persona (generalmente una mujer adolescente) se somete a una dieta de hambre a pesar de padecer de delgadez extrema; a veces acompañada de ejercicios excesivos. (pág. 405)

antianxiety drugs/medicamentos ansiolíticos Medicamentos recetados para aliviar los síntomas de la ansiedad y la agitación. (pág. 433)

antidepressant drugs/medicamentos antidepresivos Medicamentos que se usan para tratar la depresión, los trastornos de ansiedad, obsesivo-compulsivo o de estrés postraumático. (Varios de los medicamentos más usados son *inhibidores selectivos de la recaptación de serotonina: ISRS*). (pág. 433)

antipsychotic drugs/medicamentos antipsicóticos Medicamentos recetados para tratar la esquizofrenia y otros tipos de trastornos graves del pensamiento. (pág. 433)

antisocial personality disorder/trastorno de personalidad antisocial Trastorno de la personalidad que se manifiesta cuando la persona (generalmente un hombre) no exhibe sentimiento de culpa por actuar con maldad, incluso hacia los amigos y miembros de la familia; puede ser agresivo y cruel o puede ser un timador listo. (pág. 407)

anxiety disorders/trastornos de ansiedad Trastornos psicológicos que se caracterizan por la preocupación y tensión crónicas o por comportamientos desadaptados que reducen la ansiedad. (pág. 381)

aptitude test/prueba de aptitud Prueba diseñada para predecir el desempeño de una persona en el futuro; *aptitud* es la capacidad de aprender. (pág. 241)

asexual/asexual Ausencia de atracción sexual hacia otros. (pág. 117)

assimilation/asimilación Interpretación de nuestras experiencias nuevas en términos de nuestros esquemas existentes. (pág. 79)

association areas/áreas de asociación Áreas de la corteza cerebral principalmente relacionadas con las funciones mentales superiores como aprender, recordar, pensar y hablar. (pág. 47)

associative learning/aprendizaje asociativo Aprender que ciertos eventos ocurren simultáneamente. Los eventos pueden ser dos estímulos (como en el condicionamiento clásico) o una respuesta y sus consecuencias (como en el condicionamiento operante). (pág. 171)

attachment/apego Vínculo emocional con otra persona; se observa en niños pequeños que buscan cercanía física con la persona que los cuida. Se observan señales de angustia cuando ocurre una separación. (pág. 83)

attention-deficit/hyperactivity disorder (ADHD)/trastorno por déficit de atención con hiperactividad (TDAH) Trastorno psicológico caracterizado por una falta de atención extrema y/o hiperactividad e impulsividad. (pág. 377)

attitude/actitud Sentimientos, a menudo basados en nuestras creencias, que nos predisponen para responder de una manera particular a los objetos, las personas y los eventos. (pág. 315)

audition/audición Sentido o acto de oír. (pág. 153)

autism spectrum disorder (ASD)/autismo Trastorno que se manifiesta en la niñez y que está marcado por deficiencias en las comunicaciones y en la interacción social, y por conductas repetitivas e intereses rigurosamente fijados. (pág. 81)

automatic processing/procesamiento automático Codificación inconsciente de información cotidiana, por ejemplo, de espacio, de tiempo y de frecuencia, y de información bien asimilada, tal como el significado de las palabras. (pág. 197)

autonomic nervous system (ANS)/sistema nervioso autónomo (SNA) División del sistema nervioso periférico que controla las glándulas y los músculos de los órganos internos (tales como el corazón). La subdivisión *simpática* estimula y la subdivisión *parasimpática* relaja. (pág. 35)

availability heuristic/heurística de disponibilidad Acto de estimar la probabilidad de un evento basándose en su disponibilidad en la memoria. Si un evento viene prontamente a la mente (quizás debido a su intensidad), presumimos que es un evento común. (pág. 224)

aversive conditioning/condicionamiento aversivo Tipo de contracondicionamiento que asocia un estado desagradable (por ejemplo, náuseas) con una conducta no deseada (tal como beber alcohol). (pág. 421)

axon/axones Prolongaciones de las neuronas que transmiten mensajes a otras neuronas o a músculos y glándulas. (pág. 31)

babbling stage/fase balbuciente Fase del desarrollo del lenguaje que se da aproximadamente a los 4 meses de edad, y en la que el bebé espontáneamente emite diversos sonidos que al principio no se relacionan con el lenguaje que se usa en casa. (pág. 233)

barbiturates/barbitúricos Medicamentos que deprimen la actividad del sistema nervioso central, reduciendo la ansiedad pero afectando la memoria y el discernimiento. (pág. 389)

basal metabolic rate/tasa de metabolismo basal Cantidad de energía producida por el organismo en reposo absoluto. (pág. 263)

basic trust/confianza básica Según Erik Erikson, una percepción de que el mundo es predecible y fiable; se dice que se forma durante la primera infancia a través de experiencias apropiadas con cuidadores que responden con sensibilidad. (pág. 85)

behaviorism/conductismo Posición de que la psicología (1) debe ser una ciencia objetiva que (2) estudia el comportamiento sin referencia a los procesos mentales. Hoy, la mayoría de los psicólogos que realizan concuerdan con (1) pero no con (2). (págs. 3, 185)

behavior therapy/terapia del comportamiento Enfoque terapéutico que aplica los principios de aprendizaje para lograr la eliminación de comportamientos no deseados. (pág. 419)

belief perseverance/perseverancia en las creencias Empeño en insistir en las creencias incluso después de presentarse pruebas que las desacreditan. (pág. 227)

binge-eating disorder/trastorno alimentario compulsivo Ingestión excesiva de alimentos, seguida de angustia, disgusto o culpa, pero sin las purgas, el ayuno o los ejercicios físicos excesivos que caracterizan a la bulimia nerviosa. (pág. 407)

binocular cue/clave binocular Señal de profundidad, por ejemplo, la disparidad retiniana, para la que se requiere el uso de ambos ojos. (pág. 148)

biological constraints/límites biológicos Tendencias biológicas evolucionadas que predisponen la conducta y el aprendizaje por parte de los animales. Por lo tanto, ciertas conductas son más fáciles de aprender que otras. (pág. 185)

biological psychology/psicología biológica Estudio científico de la relación entre los procesos biológicos y los psicológicos. (pág. 31)

biomedical therapy/terapia biomédica Procedimientos o medicamentos recetados que actúan directamente sobre la fisiología de la persona. (pág. 417)

biopsychosocial approach/enfoque biopsicosocial Enfoque que integra diversos conceptos complementarios en los que se combinan perspectivas biológicas, psicológicas y socioculturales. (pág. 9)

bipolar disorder/trastorno bipolar Trastorno en el que la persona alterna entre la desesperanza y el abatimiento de la depresión y el estado eufórico de la manía. (Anteriormente llamado *trastorno maníaco-depresivo*.) (pág. 395)

blind spot/punto ciego Punto en el cual el nervio óptico sale del ojo; esta parte de la retina es "ciega" porque carece de células receptoras. (pág. 143)

bottom-up processing/procesamiento de abajo hacia arriba Análisis que comienza con los receptores sensoriales y marcha hacia el cerebro y su integración de la información sensorial. (pág. 135)

brainstem/tronco encefálico Parte más antigua y foco central del cerebro, empezando donde la médula espinal se inflama al entrar en el cráneo; el tronco encefálico es responsable por las funciones automáticas de supervivencia. (pág. 39)

Broca's area/área de Broca Parte del lóbulo frontal del cerebro, generalmente en el hemisferio izquierdo, que dirige los movimientos musculares relacionados con el habla y que controla la expresión del lenguaje. (pág. 235)

bulimia nervosa/bulimia nerviosa Trastorno alimentario que se caracteriza por episodios de ingestión excesiva de alimentos (generalmente de alto contenido calórico) seguidos de purgas (vómito o uso de laxantes) o ayuno. (pág. 407)

bystander effect/efecto espectador Tendencia que tienen las personas a no brindar ayuda si hay otras personas presentes. (pág. 341)

Cannon-Bard theory/teoría de Cannon-Bard Teoría de que un estímulo que despierta emociones puede provocar simultáneamente (1) respuestas fisiológicas y (2) la experiencia subjetiva de la emoción. (pág. 271)

case study/caso de estudio Técnica de observación en la cual se estudia a individuo o grupo a profundidad con la esperanza de revelar principios universales. (pág. 15)

central nervous system (CNS)/sistema nervioso central (SNC) El cerebro y la médula espinal. (pág. 35)

central route persuasion/ruta de persuasión central Se produce cuando las personas interesadas se centran en los argumentos y responden con pensamientos favorables. (pág. 315)

cerebellum/cerebelo Es el "cerebro pequeño" y está unido a la parte posterior del tronco encefálico. Sus funciones incluyen el procesamiento de la información sensorial, la coordinación de los movimientos y el equilibrio y la habilitación del lenguaje no verbal y la memoria. (pág. 41)

cerebral cortex/corteza cerebral Capa delgada de neuronas conectadas entre sí, que forman los hemisferios cerebrales; es el principal centro de control y procesamiento de información del organismo. (pág. 43)

change blindness/ceguera al cambio No darse cuenta de cambios en el entorno. Una forma de ceguera por falta de atención. (pág. 53)

chromosomes/cromosomas Estructuras semejantes a hilos conformadas de moléculas de ADN que contienen los genes. (pág. 71)

chronic schizophrenia/esquizofrenia crónica (también se le dice *esquizofrenia procesal*) Tipo de esquizofrenia en la que los síntomas aparecen generalmente en la adolescencia tardía o adultez temprana. A medida que las personas envejecen, los episodios psicóticos duran más y se acortan los períodos de recuperación. (pág. 403)

chunking/agrupamiento Organizar artículos en unidades conocidas y manejables; a menudo ocurre automáticamente. (pág. 199)

circadian rhythm/ritmo circadiano Reloj biológico; ritmos periódicos del organismo (por ejemplo, el de temperatura y estado de vigilia) que ocurren en ciclos de 24 horas. (pág. 55)

classical conditioning/condicionamiento clásico Tipo de aprendizaje en el cual aprendemos a relacionar dos o más estímulos y a anticipar sucesos. (pág. 171)

cocaine/cocaína Estimulante potente y adictivo derivado de la planta de coca; aumenta temporalmente el estado de alerta y produce sensaciones de euforia. (pág. 389)

cochlea/cóclea Estructura tubular en forma de espiral, ósea y rellena de líquido que se halla en el oído interno; las ondas sonoras que pasan por el líquido coclear desencadenan impulsos nerviosos. (pág. 153)

cochlear implant/implante coclear Dispositivo que convierte sonidos en señales eléctricas que estimulan el nervio auditivo mediante electrodos enhebrados en la cóclea. (pág. 155)

cognition/cognición Todas las actividades mentales asociadas con pensar, saber, recordar y comunicar. (págs. 79, 223)

cognitive-behavioral therapy (CBT)/terapia cognitivo-conductual (TCC) Terapia integrada muy difundida que combina la terapia cognitiva (que cambia los pensamientos contraproducentes) con la terapia conductual (que cambia la conducta). (pág. 425)

cognitive dissonance theory/teoría de disonancia cognitiva Teoría según la cual llevamos a cabo una acción con el propósito de reducir la incomodidad (disonancia) que sentimos cuando tenemos dos pensamientos (cogniciones) contradictorios. Por ejemplo, cuando tenemos consciencia de que nuestras actitudes y nuestras acciones entran en conflicto, cambiamos nuestra actitud para sentirnos más cómodos. (pág. 317)

cognitive learning/aprendizaje cognitivo Adquisición de información mental, ya sea a partir de la observación de acontecimientos, la observación de otras personas o a través del lenguaje. (pág. 171)

cognitive map/mapa cognitivo Imagen mental del trazado de nuestro entorno. (pág. 187)

cognitive neuroscience/neurociencia cognitiva Estudio interdisciplinario de las conexiones entre la actividad cerebral relacionada con la cognición (que incluye la percepción, el pensamiento, la memoria y el lenguaje). (págs. 4, 31)

cognitive psychology/psicología cognitiva Estudio de los procesos mentales, tales como los que ocurren cuando percibimos, aprendemos, recordamos, pensamos, nos comunicamos y resolvemos problemas. (pág. 5)

cognitive therapy/terapia cognitiva Enfoque terapéutico en que se les enseña a los pacientes nuevas formas de pensar de un modo más adaptativo. Se basa en el supuesto de que los pensamientos intervienen entre los eventos y nuestras reacciones emocionales. (pág. 423)

collective unconscious/inconsciente colectivo Concepto propuesto por Carl Jung en relación a un grupo común de recuerdos heredados de la historia de nuestra especie. (pág. 355)

collectivism/colectivismo Modo de dar prioridad a las metas del grupo (a menudo de la familia extendida o el grupo de trabajo) y de definir la identidad personal según lo que dicta el grupo. (pág. 371)

color constancy/constancia de color Percibir que objetos conocidos tienen un color constante, incluso si cambios en la iluminación modifican las longitudes de onda que el objeto refleja. (pág. 151)

companionate love/amor compañero Apego afectuoso profundo que sentimos por aquellos con quienes nuestras vidas se entrelazan. (pág. 339)

concept/concepto Agrupamiento mental de objetos, eventos, ideas y personas que tienen un parecido. (pág. 223)

concrete operational stage/etapa del pensamiento lógico-concreto En la teoría de Piaget, la fase del desarrollo cognitivo (desde aproximadamente los 7 años hasta los 11 años de edad) durante la cual los niños adquieren las operaciones mentales que les permiten pensar lógicamente sobre eventos concretos. (pág. 81)

conditioned reinforcer/reforzador condicionado (También denominado *reforzador secundario*) Evento que adquiere su poder de reforzamiento mediante su vínculo con el reforzador primario. (pág. 179)

conditioned response (CR)/respuesta condicionada (RC) En el condicionamiento clásico, la respuesta aprendida a un estímulo previamente neutral (pero ahora condicionado). (pág. 173)

conditioned stimulus (CS)/estímulo condicionado (EC) En el condicionamiento clásico, un estímulo originalmente intrascendente que, después de verse asociado con un estímulo incondicionado (EI) produce una respuesta condicionada. (pág. 173)

conduction hearing loss/pérdida de la audición por conducción Tipo menos común de sordera atribuible a daños en el sistema mecánico que conduce ondas sonoras a la cóclea. (pág. 155)

cones/conos Receptores que se concentran cerca del centro de la retina; con la luz del día o en lugares bien iluminados, los conos detectan detalles finos y producen las sensaciones del color. (pág. 143)

confirmation bias/sesgo confirmatorio Tendencia a buscar información que confirme nuestras ideas preconcebidas y de hacer caso omiso o de distorsionar las pruebas que las contradigan. (pág. 223)

conflict/conflicto Incompatibilidad percibida de acciones, metas o ideas. (pág. 341)

conformity/conformidad Tendencia a ajustar el comportamiento o la forma de pensar hasta hacerlos coincidir con las normas que tiene un grupo. (pág. 319)

confounding variable/variable de confusión Factor distinto del factor que se está estudiando que podría producir un efecto sobre los resultados de un estudio. (pág. 19)

consciousness/consciencia Percepción de nosotros mismos y de nuestro entorno. (pág. 51)

conservation/conservación Principio (que para Piaget forma parte del razonamiento operacional concreto) de que ciertas propiedades (ej., masa, volumen y número) no varían pese a modificaciones en la forma de los objetos. (pág. 79)

content validity/validez del contenido Grado en que las muestras prueban el comportamiento que es de interés. (pág. 243)

continuous reinforcement/reforzamiento continuo Reforzar la respuesta deseada cada vez que ocurre. (pág. 179)

control group/grupo control En un experimento, el grupo de participantes que *no* se expone al tratamiento; el grupo de control sirve de comparación para evaluar el efecto del tratamiento en el grupo sometido al tratamiento. (pág. 19)

convergent thinking/razonamiento convergente Reducción de las soluciones disponibles con el fin de determinar cuál es la mejor solución a un problema. (pág. 229)

coping/mecanismos de manejo Aminoramiento de las tensiones con métodos emocionales, cognitivos o conductuales. (pág. 293)

coronary heart disease/enfermedad coronaria Obstrucción de los vasos que nutren el músculo cardíaco; causa principal de muerte en Estados Unidos y muchos otros países. (pág. 291)

corpus callosum/cuerpo calloso Banda grande de fibras neuronales que conecta los dos hemisferios del cerebro y transmite mensajes entre ellos. (pág. 47)

correlation/correlación Medida del grado en que dos factores varían juntos y por ende, si es que uno de ellos puede predecir, el otro. El *coeficiente de correlación* es la expresión matemática de relación, la cual abarca desde –1.00 hasta +1.00, con el 0 señalando que no hay relación. (pág. 17)

correlation coefficient/coeficiente de correlación Índice estadístico de la relación entre dos cosas (del -1.00 al +1.00). (pág. A-5)

counterconditioning/contracondicionamiento Técnicas de terapia conductual que se valen del condicionamiento clásico para provocar respuestas alternativas a estímulos que producen comportamientos no deseados; incluye las *terapias de exposición* y el *condicionamiento aversivo*. (pág. 421)

creativity/creatividad Capacidad para generar ideas novedosas y valiosas. (pág. 229)

critical period/período crítico Etapa al inicio de la vida, en la cual son necesarios ciertos estímulos o experiencias para que se produzca el desarrollo apropiado del organismo. (pág. 77)

critical thinking/pensamiento crítico Forma de pensar en la que no se aceptan razones ni conclusiones ciegamente; por el contrario, se examinan las suposiciones, se distinguen los valores ocultos, se sopesa la evidencia y se evalúan las conclusiones. (pág. 9)

cross-sectional study/estudio de corte transversal Estudio en el que personas de diferentes edades se comparan unas con otras. (págs. 99, 247)

crystallized intelligence/estudio de corte transversal Estudio en el que personas de diferentes edades se comparan unas con otras. (pág. A-7)

culture/inteligencia cristalizada Todos los conocimientos y capacidades verbales que hemos acumulado; tiende a aumentar con la edad. (pág. 249)

culture/cultura Ideas, actitudes, valores y tradiciones duraderos que comparte un grupo de personas y que se transmiten de generación en generación. (pág. 9)

debriefing/rendición de informes Después de concluir un experimento, explicación que se les da a los participantes objetivo del estudio y toda decepción que los investigadores pudieron haber utilizado. (pág. 23)

defense mechanisms/mecanismos de defensa En la teoría psicoanalítica, los métodos de protección del ego para reducir la ansiedad distorsionando la realidad de manera inconsciente. (pág. 353)

deindividuation/desindividualización Pérdida de la identidad personal y del autocontrol en situaciones de grupo que fomentan la excitación y el anonimato. (pág. 325)

déjà vu/déjà vu Sensación extraña de haber vivido antes una experiencia específica. Señales de la presente situación pueden de manera subconsciente activar la evocación de una vivencia previa. (pág. 213)

delta waves/ondas delta Ondas cerebrales grandes y lentas que se asocian con el sueño profundo. (pág. 55)

delusion/delirios Creencias falsas, a menudo de persecución o de grandeza que pueden acompañar a trastornos psicóticos. (pág. 403)

dendrites/dendritas Prolongaciones de las neuronas que reciben mensajes y envían impulsos hacia el cuerpo neuronal. (pág. 31)

dependent variable/variable dependiente En un experimento, el factor que se mide. Es la variable que puede cambiar cuando se manipula la variable independiente. (pág. 19)

depressants/depresivos Agentes químicos (tales como el alcohol, los barbitúricos y los opiáceos) que reducen (deprimen) la actividad neuronal y enlentecen las funciones del organismo. (pág. 387)

depth perception/percepción de la profundidad Capacidad de ver objetos en tres dimensiones aunque las imágenes percibidas por la retina sean bidimensionales. Nos permite juzgar la distancia. (pág. 148)

developmental psychology/psicología evolutiva   Especialización de la psicología que estudia los cambios físicos, cognitivos y sociales que se ocasionan a lo largo de la vida. (pág. 69)

difference threshold/umbral de diferencia   La diferencia mínima entre dos estímulos que una persona puede detectar el 50 por ciento de las veces. El umbral diferencial se experimenta como una *diferencia apenas perceptible*. (pág. 135)

discrimination/discriminación   (1) Según el condicionamiento clásico, capacidad aprendida de distinguir entre un estímulo condicionado y otros estímulos sin trascendencia. (En el condicionamiento operante, la capacidad de distinguir las respuestas que son reforzadas de las que no lo son.) (2) En la psicología social, el comportamiento negativo injustificado contra un grupo y sus miembros. (págs. 175, 327)

dissociative disorders/trastorno disociativo   Trastornos poco comunes y polémicos en el que el conocimiento consciente se separa (se disocia) de los recuerdos, pensamientos y sentimientos anteriores. (pág. 407)

dissociative identity disorder (DID)/trastorno disociativo de identidad (TDI)   Trastorno disociativo poco común, en el cual una persona exhibe dos o más personalidades claramente definidas que se alternan entre sí. (También se denomina *trastorno de personalidad múltiple*). (pág. 407)

divergent thinking/razonamiento divergente   Expansión del número de soluciones a un problema. Pensamiento creativo que se ramifica en múltiples direcciones. (pág. 229)

DNA (deoxyribonucleic acid)/ADN (ácido desoxirribonucleico)   Molécula que contiene la información genética de la que se constituyen los cromosomas. (pág. 71)

double-blind procedure/procedimiento doble ciego   En un experimento, procedimiento en el cual tanto los participantes como el personal de investigación ignoran (van a ciegas) quién ha recibido el tratamiento y quién el placebo. (pág. 19)

Down syndrome/Síndrome de Down   Trastorno de discapacidad intelectual leve o grave que se presenta junto a otras discapacidades físicas que ocurren a causa de una copia adicional del cromosoma 21. (pág. 245)

dream/sueño   Secuencia de imágenes, emociones y pensamientos que fluyen en la mente de una persona dormida. (pág. 61)

drive-reduction theory/teoría de la reducción del impulso   Concepto de que una necesidad fisiológica crea un estado de excitación (un impulso) que motiva al organismo a satisfacer tal necesidad. (pág. 259)

DSM-5/DSM-5   Manual estadístico y de diagnóstico de trastornos mentales, de la Asociación Norteamericana de Psiquiatría, quinta edición. Sistema ampliamente utilizado para clasificar los trastornos psicológicos. (pág. 379)

dual processing/procesamiento dual   Principio que sostiene que la información se procesa simultáneamente en vías separadas conscientes e inconscientes. (pág. 11)

eclectic approach/enfoque ecléctico   Enfoque de la psicoterapia que, según los problemas del cliente, emplea técnicas tomadas de diversas formas de terapia. (pág. 417)

Ecstasy (MDMA)/éxtasis (MDMA)   Estimulante sintético y alucinógeno ligero. Produce euforia e intimidad social, pero conlleva riesgos de salud a corto plazo. Además, a largo plazo, perjudica las neuronas que producen la serotonina, y afecta el ánimo y el proceso de cognición. (pág. 391)

EEG (electroencephalograph)/(EEG) electroencefalograma   Aparato que emplea electrodos colocados sobre el cuero cabelludo, que produce un registro de las ondas de actividad eléctrica que circulan por la superficie del cerebro. (El trazado de dichas ondas cerebrales es un *electroencefalograma*). (pág. 39)

effortful processing/procesamiento con esfuerzo   Codificación que precisa atención y esfuerzo consciente. (pág. 197)

egocentrism/egocentrismo   Según la teoría de Piaget, la dificultad de los niños en la etapa preoperacional de aceptar el punto de vista ajeno. (pág. 81)

ego/ego   Parte consciente y ejecutiva de la personalidad que, según Freud, media entre las exigencias del id, el superego y la realidad. El ego opera según el *principio de realidad,* satisfaciendo los deseos del id en formas que de manera realista le brindarán placer en lugar de dolor. (pág. 353)

electroconvulsive therapy (ECT)/terapia electroconvulsiva (TEC)   Terapia biomédica para pacientes gravemente deprimidos en la que se envía una corriente eléctrica de corta duración a través del cerebro de un paciente anestesiado. (pág. 435)

embodied cognition/cognición incorporada   La influencia de sensaciones del organismo, y otros estados de preferencias y juicios cognitivos. (pág. 161)

embryo/embrión   Etapa de desarrollo del organismo humano a partir de las dos semanas después de fertilización hasta el segundo mes. (pág. 73)

emerging adulthood/madurez emergente   Etapa que se extiende desde los 18 hasta alrededor de los 25 años, durante la cual muchas personas en los países occidentales ya no son adolescentes pero aún no han alcanzado la independencia plena de un adulto. (pág. 95)

emotion/emoción   Reacción que involucra a todo el organismo e incluye (1) excitación fisiológica, (2) comportamientos expresivos y (3) experiencia consciente. (pág. 271)

emotion-focused coping/superación con enfoque en las emociones   Medidas para sobrellevar las tensiones enfocándose en aliviar o hacer caso omiso de una situación estresante y atender las necesidades emocionales relacionadas con nuestra reacción al estrés. (pág. 293)

emotional intelligence/inteligencia emocional   Capacidad de percibir, entender, administrar y hacer uso de las emociones. (pág. 241)

encoding/codificación   El proceso de ingresar información al sistema de memoria. (pág. 197)

endocrine [EN-duh-krin] system/sistema endocrino   Sistema "lento" de comunicación química del cuerpo; conjunto de glándulas que secretan hormonas al torrente sanguíneo. (pág. 35)

endorphins [en-DOR-fins]/endorfinas   "Morfina adentro"; neurotransmisores naturales similares a los opiáceos que están asociados con el control del dolor y con el placer. (pág. 35)

environment/entorno   Toda influencia externa, desde la alimentación prenatal hasta el apoyo social que se recibe más adelante en la vida. (pág. 71)

epigenetics/epigenética   Estudio de la influencia ambiental sobre la expresión de los genes que ocurre sin un cambio de ADN. (págs. 73, 377)

episodic memory/memora episódica   Memoria explícita de eventos experimentados personalmente. Uno de los dos sistemas de memoria consciente (el otro es la *memoria semántica*). (pág. 201)

equity/equidad   Condición en la cual la persona recibe de manera proporcional lo que aporte a una relación. (pág. 339)

erectile disorder/trastorno eréctil   Incapacidad de desarrollar o mantener una erección debido a un flujo insuficiente de sangre al pene. (pág. 117)

estrogens /estrógenos   Hormonas sexuales, como el estradiol, secretadas en mayor cantidad en la mujer que en el hombre. Los niveles de estrógeno alcanzan su nivel máximo durante la ovulación. En los animales mamíferos esto facilita la receptividad sexual. (pág. 117)

evidence-based practice/práctica basada en la evidencia   Toma de decisiones clínicas que integra lo mejor de las investigaciones disponibles con la pericia clínica y las características y preferencias del paciente. (pág. 429)

evolutionary psychology/psicología evolutiva   Estudio de la evolución del comportamiento y la mente, que emplea los principios de la selección natural para una adaptación efectiva. (pág. 125)

experiment/experimento   Método de investigación en el cual el investigador manipula uno o más factores (variables independientes) para observar su efecto en un comportamiento o proceso mental (variable dependiente). Al ser los participantes asignados de manera aleatoria, los investigadores procuran controlar otros factores. (pág. 19)

experimental group/grupo experimental   Sujetos de un experimento que están expuestos al tratamiento, o sea, a una versión de la variable independiente. (pág. 19)

explicit memory/memoria explícita   Retención de hechos y vivencias personales que tenemos la capacidad de recuperar conscientemente. También se le dice *memoria declarativa*). (pág. 197)

exposure therapies/terapias de exposición   Técnicas conductuales, como la *desensibilización sistemática* y *la terapia de exposición a una realidad virtual* para tratar la ansiedad exponiendo a la persona (en situaciones imaginarias o reales) a las cosas que teme y evita. (pág. 421)

external locus of control/centro de control externo   Impresión de que nuestro destino está determinado por el azar o por fuerzas que están más allá de nuestro control. (pág. 295)

extinction/extinción   Según el condicionamiento clásico, disminución de una respuesta condicionada cuando un estímulo incondicionado no sigue a un estímulo condicionado. (En el condicionamiento operante, disminución de una respuesta cuando deja de ser reforzada). (pág. 175)

extrasensory perception (ESP)/percepción extrasensorial (PES)   La afirmación polémica de que la percepción puede ocurrir aislada de la recepción sensorial; incluye la telepatía, la clarividencia y las premoniciones. (pág. 163)

extrinsic motivation/motivación extrínseca   Deseo de realizar un comportamiento para obtener una recompensa o evitar el castigo. (pág. 187)

facial feedback effect/efecto de reacción facial   Tendencia de los músculos faciales a provocar sentimientos correspondientes como el miedo, el enojo o la felicidad. (pág. 281)

factor/factor   Conjunto de tendencias del comportamiento que ocurren al mismo tiempo. (pág. 361)

family therapy/terapia de familia   Tipo de terapia que trata a la familia como un sistema. Esta terapia considera que los comportamientos no deseados de una persona son influenciados por otros miembros de la familia o están dirigidos hacia ellos (pág. 425)

feature detectors/detectores específicos   Células nerviosas del cerebro que responden a características específicas de un estímulo, como las formas, los ángulos y el movimiento. (pág. 145)

feel-good, do-good phenomenon/fenómeno de sentirse bien y hacer el bien   Tendencia a ayudar a los demás cuando estamos de buen humor. (pág. 303)

female orgasmic disorder/trastorno orgásmico   Sentimiento de angustia debido a nunca haber experimentado un orgasmo o haberlo hecho de manera infrecuente. (pág. 117)

fetal alcohol syndrome (FAS)/síndrome de alcoholismo fetal (SAF)   Anomalías físicas y cognitivas en los niños causadas por la intensa ingestión de alcohol de la madre durante el embarazo. En casos agudos, los síntomas incluyen la cabeza demasiado pequeña y desproporciones faciales observables. (pág. 73)

fetus/feto   Organismo humano en vías de desarrollo a partir de las 9 semanas de concepción hasta el nacimiento. (pág. 73)

fight-or-flight response/respuesta de luchar o huir   Reacción en una emergencia que incluye actividad del sistema nervioso simpático y genera energía y actividad dirigidas a atacar o escapar ante una amenaza. (pág. 287)

figure-ground/figura-trasfondo   Organización del campo visual en objetos (las *figuras*) que se distinguen de sus entornos (los *trasfondos*). (pág. 147)

fixation/obsesión   (1) Incapacidad de ver un problema desde una perspectiva nueva; un impedimento para resolver problemas. (2) Según Freud, un foco persistente de energías en busca del placer en una etapa psicosexual anterior en la que los conflictos todavía no estaban resueltos. (págs. 223, 353)

fixed-interval schedule/cronograma de intervalo fijo   Según el condicionamiento operante, cronograma de reforzamiento que refuerza la respuesta solo después de haber transcurrido un tiempo específico. (pág. 181)

fixed-ratio schedule/cronograma de proporción fija   Según el condicionamiento operante, cronograma de reforzamiento que refuerza la respuesta solo después de darse un número específico de respuestas. (pág. 179)

flashbulb memory/memoria de flash   Memoria clara de un momento o evento emocionalmente significativo. (pág. 203)

flow/fluidez   Estado de participación y concentración totales, con disminución de la conciencia de uno mismo y del tiempo, que ocurre cuando aprovechamos nuestras destrezas al máximo. (pág. B-1)

fluid intelligence/inteligencia fluida   Capacidad que tenemos de razonar de manera rápida y abstracta; tiende a disminuir con la edad, especialmente en la vejez. (pág. 249)

fMRI (functional MRI)/(RMF) resonancia magnética funcional   Técnica para observar la circulación de la sangre y, por lo tanto, la actividad cerebral. Consiste en comparar imágenes de resonancia magnética sucesivas. Las imágenes de resonancia magnética funcional muestran el funcionamiento del cerebro. (pág. 39)

foot-in-the-door phenomenon/fenómeno de pie en la puerta   Tendencia de la gente que ha accedido a algo pequeño en primer lugar, a después satisfacer una exigencia de mayor envergadura. (pág. 317)

formal operational stage/período operacional formal   En la teoría de Piaget, el período en el desarrollo cognitivo (normalmente empieza a los 12 años) durante el que la persona empieza a pensar lógicamente sobre conceptos abstractos. (pág. 81)

framing/encuadre   Forma en que se presenta un asunto; el encuadre puede influenciar considerablemente las decisiones y las opiniones. (pág. 227)

fraternal (dizygotic) twins/gemelos fraternos (dizigóticos)   Se desarrollan de dos óvulos fecundados. Genéticamente no están más cercanos que los hermanos y hermanas, pero comparten un entorno prenatal. (pág. 75)

free association/asociación libre   En psicoanálisis, método de explorar el inconsciente en el que la persona se relaja y dice lo primero que le viene a la mente, no importa cuán poco importante o incómodo. (pág. 351)

frequency/frecuencia   Número de ondas completas que pasan un punto en un tiempo dado (por ejemplo, por segundo). (pág. 153)

frontal lobes/lóbulos frontales   Porción de la corteza cerebral que se halla inmediatamente detrás de la frente; se relaciona con el habla y los movimientos musculares y con la planificación y la formación de opiniones. (pág. 43)

frustration-aggression principle/principio de frustración-agresión   Principio de que la frustración —el bloqueo de un intento para lograr alguna meta— crea ira, la cual puede generar agresión. (pág. 333)

fundamental attribution error/error de atribución fundamental   Tendencia de los observadores, cuando analizan el comportamiento ajeno, a sobrestimar el impacto de las características personales y subestimar el impacto de la situación. (pág. 315)

gender/género   En psicología, las características biológicas y sociales por las cuales la sociedad define *varón* y *mujer*. (pág. 109)

gender identity/identidad de género   Nuestra sensación personal de ser varón o mujer, o combinación de ambos. (pág. 115)

gender role/papel del género   Conjunto de expectativas, actitudes y rasgos de cómo las mujeres y los hombres deben ser o comportarse. (pág. 115)

gender typing/tipificación por género   La adquisición de un papel masculino o femenino tradicional. (pág. 115)

general adaptation syndrome (GAS)/síndrome de adaptación general   Término usado por Selye para referirse a la respuesta adaptativa del cuerpo al estrés que se da en tres etapas: alarma, resistencia y agotamiento. (pág. 287)

general intelligence (g)/factor g de inteligencia general   Factor de inteligencia general que según Spearman y otros subyace habilidades mentales específicas y es, por tanto, cuantificado por cada función en una prueba de inteligencia. (pág. 238)

generalization/generalización   Según el condicionamiento clásico, tendencia posterior al condicionamiento, de responder de manera similar a los estímulos que se parecen al estímulo condicionado. (En el condicionamiento operante, se produce una *generalización* cuando se refuerzan también las respuestas a estímulos similares.) (pág. 175)

generalized anxiety disorder/trastorno de ansiedad generalizado   Trastorno de ansiedad en el cual la persona está constantemente tensa, asustada y con el *sistema nervioso autónomo* activado. (pág. 381)

genes/genes   Unidades bioquímicas de la herencia que forman los cromosomas. Segmentos de ADN. (pág. 71)

genome/genoma   Instrucciones completas para crear un organismo; consiste en todo el material genético en los cromosomas de ese organismo. (pág. 71)

gestalt/Gestalt   Un todo organizado. Los psicólogos de la Gestalt enfatizan nuestra tendencia a integrar segmentos de información en todos significativos. (pág. 147)

glial cells (glia)/células gliales   Células del sistema nervioso que apoyan, alimentan y protegen a las neuronas; también desempeñan un papel en el aprendizaje, el razonamiento y la memoria. (pág. 31)

glucose/glucosa   Forma de azúcar que circula en la sangre y es la mayor fuente de energía para los tejidos del cuerpo. Cuando su nivel está bajo, sentimos hambre. (pág. 261)

grammar/gramática   En un lenguaje específico, sistema de reglas que nos permite comunicarnos y entendernos con otros. (pág. 233)

grit/tenacidad   En psicología, se refiere a la pasión y la perseverancia en la búsqueda de objetivos a largo plazo. (pág. B-5)

group polarization/efecto de polarización de grupo   Solidificación y fortalecimiento de las posiciones imperantes en un grupo mediante diálogos en el grupo. (pág. 325)

group therapy/terapia de grupo Tratamiento que se realiza con grupos en lugar de con personas individuales, que genera beneficios de la interacción del grupo. (pág. 425)

grouping/agrupamiento Tendencia de percepción que clasifica los estímulos en grupos que tienen sentido. (pág. 147)

groupthink/pensamiento colectivo Modo de pensar que ocurre cuando el deseo de armonía en un grupo que toma de decisiones colectivas anula la evaluación objetiva de las alternativas. (pág. 325)

hallucination/alucinaciones Vivencia sensorial falsa, por ejemplo, cuando una persona oye algo sin haber ningún estímulo auditivo externo. (pág. 45)

hallucinogens/alucinógenos Fármacos psicodélicos ("que se manifiestan en la mente"), como el LSD, que distorsionan las percepciones y desencadenan imágenes sensoriales sin que intervengan estímulos sensoriales. (pág. 391)

heredity/herencia Transferencia genética de características, de los padres a los hijos. (pág. 71)

heritability/heredabilidad La porción de variación entre individuos que le podemos atribuir a los genes. La heredabilidad de un rasgo varía de acuerdo con la población y el medio ambiente. (pág. 245)

heuristic/heurística Estrategias de pensamiento sencilla que a menudo nos permite formar juicios y resolver problemas de manera eficiente. Por lo general es más expedita que utilizar *algoritmos*, pero también pueden conducir a más errores. (pág. 223)

hierarchy of needs/jerarquía de necesidades Pirámide de Maslow de las necesidades humanas. En la base de la pirámide están las necesidades fisiológicas, que deben satisfacerse antes que las necesidades de seguridad personal que son de más alto nivel. Las necesidades psicológicas se activan por último, después de satisfacer las anteriores. (págs. 259, 357)

hindsight bias/distorsión retrospectiva Tendencia a creer después de saber un resultado, que uno lo habría previsto. (También conocido como el fenómeno de *ya yo lo sabía*). (pág. 11)

hippocampus/hipocampo Centro neuronal ubicado en el sistema límbico; ayuda a procesar recuerdos explícitos (conscientes) de hechos y eventos para almacenarlos de manera accesible. (págs. 43, 201)

homeostasis/homeostasis Tendencia a mantener un estado interno constante o equilibrado; la regulación de todos los aspectos de la química del organismo, tal como los niveles de glucosa, alrededor de un nivel dado. (pág. 259)

hormones/hormonas Mensajeros químicos producidos por las glándulas endocrinas, que circulan por la sangre y tienen efecto en los tejidos del cuerpo. (pág. 35)

hue/tono Dimensión del color determinada por la longitud de la onda de luz; lo que conocemos como los nombres de los colores: *azul*, *verde*, etc. (pág. 141)

human factors psychology/psicología de factores humanos División de la psicología relacionada con la psicología I/O que explora la interacción entre las personas y las máquinas, y las maneras de hacer que las máquinas y los entornos físicos sean más seguros y fáciles de utilizar. (pág. B-3)

humanistic psychology/psicología humanista Perspectiva de importancia histórica que enfatiza el potencial de crecimiento de las personas. (pág. 3)

hypnosis/hipnosis Interacción social en la cual una persona (el hipnotizador) le sugiere a otra persona (el sujeto) que ciertas percepciones, sentimientos, pensamientos o comportamientos se producirán espontáneamente. (pág. 157)

hypothalamus/hipotálamo Estructura neuronal localizada debajo (*hipo*) del tálamo; regula actividades como comer, beber, y la temperatura del cuerpo; dirige varias actividades de mantenimiento (comer, beber, temperatura corporal); ayuda a dirigir el sistema endocrino a través de la glándula pituitaria, y está conectado a las emociones y las recompensas. (pág. 43)

hypothesis/hipótesis Predicción comprobable, a menudo implicada por una teoría. (pág. 13)

id/id Depósito de energía psíquica inconsciente que, según Freud, aspira a satisfacer los impulsos sexuales y agresivos esenciales. El id funciona según el *principio de placer*, exigiendo satisfacción inmediata. (pág. 351)

identical (monozygotic) twins/gemelos idénticos (monozigóticos) Se desarrollan de un solo óvulo fertilizado que se subdivide en dos para así crear dos organismos genéticamente idénticos. (pág. 75)

identification/identificación Proceso en el que, según Freud, los niños incorporan los valores de sus padres en sus superegos en vías de desarrollo. (pág. 353)

identity/identidad Sentido de autorreconocimiento; según Erikson, la tarea del adolescente consiste en solidificar el sentido de sí mismo probando e integrando una variedad de papeles. (pág. 93)

implicit memory/memoria implícita Retención de destrezas aprendidas o asociaciones condicionadas clásicas, sin tener conciencia del aprendizaje. (También se le dice *memoria no declarativa*). (pág. 197)

inattentional blindness/ceguera por falta de atención No ver los objetos visibles cuando nuestra atención se dirige a otra parte. (pág. 53)

incentive/incentivo Estímulo positivo o negativo del entorno que motiva el comportamiento. (pág. 259)

independent variable/variable independiente Factor que se manipula en un experimento; la variable cuyo efecto es el objeto de estudio. (pág. 19)

individualism/individualismo Darle atención prioritaria a las metas personales antes que a las metas del grupo, y definir la identidad mediante las cualidades personales y no con la pertenencia al grupo. (pág. 371)

industrial-organizational (I/O) psychology/psicología industrial y organizacional (I/O) Aplicación de conceptos y métodos psicológicos al comportamiento humano en el entorno laboral. (pág. B-3)

informational social influence/influencia social informativa Influencia resultante de la disposición de una persona a aceptar las opiniones de otros acerca de la realidad. (pág. 319)

informed consent/autorización informada Darles a las personas información suficiente sobre un estudio para permitirles decidir si desean o no participar. (pág. 23)

ingroup/endogrupo "Nosotros". Personas con quienes uno comparte una identidad común. (pág. 329)

ingroup bias/estereotipo de grupo propio Tendencia a favorecer al grupo al que se pertenece.

inner ear/oído interno Parte más interna del oído; contiene la cóclea, los canales semicirculares y los sacos vestibulares. (pág. 153)

insight/agudeza Entendimiento repentino de cómo se resuelve un problema; contrasta con las soluciones basadas en estrategias. (pág. 223)

insight therapies/tratamientos con agudeza Terapias que aspiran a mejorar el funcionamiento psicológico mediante el aumento en la conciencia de la persona de los motivos y las defensas subyacentes. (pág. 419)

insomnia/insomnio Dificultades recurrentes para dormirse y conciliar el sueño. (pág. 61)

intellectual disability/discapacidad intelectual Estado de capacidad mental limitada, que se expresa a través de una puntuación de prueba de inteligencia de 70 o menos y de la dificultad para adaptarse a las exigencias de la vida. (Anteriormente conocida como *retardo mental*). (pág. 245)

intelligence/inteligencia Capacidad de aprender de las experiencias, de resolver problemas y de utilizar el conocimiento para adaptarse a situaciones nuevas. (pág. 238)

intelligence quotient (IQ)/coeficiente intelectual (CI) Cifra definida originalmente como la edad mental (*em*) dividida entre la edad cronológica (*ec*) y el resultado multiplicado por 100 (por lo tanto, CI = *em* ÷ *ec* × 100). En las pruebas actuales de inteligencia, al desempeño promedio para una edad dada se le asigna una puntuación de 100. (pág. 243)

intelligence test/prueba de inteligencia Método para evaluar las aptitudes mentales de la persona y compararlas con las de otras personas utilizando puntuaciones numéricas. (pág. 241)

intensity/intensidad Cantidad de energía en una onda de luz o en una onda sonora que percibimos como brillo o volumen. La intensidad la determina la amplitud (altura) de la onda. (pág. 141)

interaction/interacción Interacción que se produce cuando el efecto de un factor (por ejemplo, el entorno) depende de otro factor (por ejemplo, la herencia). (pág. 71)

internal locus of control/foco de control interno Impresión de que controlamos nuestro propio destino. (pág. 295)

interneuron/interneurona Neuronas ubicadas dentro del cerebro y la médula espinal. Se comunican internamente y procesan la información entre los estímulos sensoriales y las respuestas motoras. (pág. 35)

interpretation/interpretación En psicoanálisis, las observaciones del analista con relación al significado de los sueños, las resistencias, y otras conductas y eventos significativos, a fin de promover la sagacidad. (pág. 417)

intersex/intersexo Condición al momento del nacimiento en la que el recién nacido presenta características sexuales biológicas de ambos sexos. (pág. 113)

intimacy/intimidad Según la teoría de Erikson, capacidad de formar relaciones cercanas y afectivas; función primordial del desarrollo en la adolescencia y al comienzo de la vida adulta. (pág. 93)

intrinsic motivation/motivación intrínseca Deseo de realizar una conducta de manera adecuada simplemente por la mera satisfacción de hacerlo bien. (pág. 187)

intuition/intuición Sentimiento o pensamiento automático e inmediato, que no precisa esfuerzo alguno, que se contrasta con el razonamiento explícito y consciente. (pág. 223)

James-Lange theory/teoría de James-Lange Teoría que expone que nuestra experiencia emocional es la conciencia que tenemos de nuestras respuestas fisiológicas a los estímulos que despiertan emociones. (pág. 271)

just-world phenomenon/hipótesis del "mundo justo" Tendencia a creer que el mundo es justo y que por tanto, las personas obtienen lo que se merecen y se merecen lo que obtienen. (pág. 329)

kinesthesia/cinestesia Sistema que siente la posición y el movimiento de las partes individuales de cuerpo. (pág. 161)

language/lenguaje Palabras habladas, escritas o en señas y las maneras que se combinan para comunicar significado. (pág. 231)

latent content/contenido latente Según Freud, significado subyacente de un sueño. (pág. 61)

latent learning/aprendizaje latente Aprendizaje que no es aparente sino hasta que hay un incentivo para demostrarlo. (pág. 187)

law of effect/ley de efecto Principio propuesto por Thorndike en el que se propone que las conductas seguidas por consecuencias favorables se tornan más comunes, mientras que las conductas seguidas por consecuencias desfavorables se repiten con menos frecuencia. (pág. 177)

learned helplessness/indefensión aprendida Desesperación y resignación pasiva que un animal o persona desarrollan cuando son incapaces de evitar repetidos eventos de aversión. (pág. 293)

learning/aprendizaje Proceso de adquirir, mediante la experiencia información o conductas nuevas y relativamente permanentes. (pág. 171)

limbic system/sistema límbico Sistema de neuronas (incluye la *amígdala, el hipotálamo y el hipocampo*), ubicado debajo de los hemisferios cerebrales; se lo asocia con las emociones y los impulsos. (pág. 41)

lobotomy/lobotomía Procedimiento psicoquirúrgico que otrora se usó para calmar a pacientes emocionalmente incontrolables o violentos. En el procedimiento se cortaban los nervios entre los lóbulos frontales y los centros en el interior del cerebro que controlan las emociones. (pág. 437)

long-term memory/memoria a largo plazo El almacenaje relativamente permanente e ilimitado del sistema de la memoria. Incluye los conocimientos, las habilidades y las experiencias. (pág. 197)

long-term potentiation (LTP)/potenciación a largo plazo (PLP) Aumento en la eficacia de una célula para transmitir impulsos sinápticos. Se considera la base neuronal del aprendizaje y la memoria. (pág. 203)

longitudinal study/estudio longitudinal Investigación en la que las mismas personas se estudian una y otra vez durante un lapso prolongado. (págs. 99, 247)

longitudinal study/estudio longitudinal Investigación en la que las mismas personas se estudian una y otra vez durante un lapso de tiempo prolongado. (pág. A-7)

LSD/ácido lisérgico Poderoso fármaco alucinógeno; también se conoce como ácido (*dietilamida de ácido lisérgico*). (pág. 391)

major depressive disorder/trastorno depresivo mayor Trastorno en el cual una persona —sin padecer alguna afección médica y sin usar drogas— pasa dos o más semanas con cinco o más síntomas, de los cuales al menos uno tiene que ser ya sea (1) un estado de ánimo deprimido o (2) la pérdida de interés o placer. (pág. 395)

mania/manía Estado de ánimo marcado por un estado de hiperactividad y optimismo desenfrenado, caracterizado por la falta de juicio. (pág. 395)

manifest content/contenido manifiesto Según Freud, trama del sueño que se recuerda al despertarse. (pág. 61)

maturation/maduración Procesos de crecimiento biológico que casi siempre conducen a cambios ordenados en el comportamiento y son independientes de la experiencia. (pág. 75)

mean/promedio Promedio aritmético de una distribución que se obtiene sumando las puntuaciones y luego dividiendo el total entre el número de puntuaciones. (pág. A-3)

median/media Puntuación central de una distribución; la mitad de las puntuaciones se encuentran por encima y la mitad se encuentran por dejado de la media.

medical model/modelo médico Concepto que afirma que las enfermedades, en este caso los trastornos psicológicos, tienen causas físicas que se pueden *diagnosticar, tratar* y, en la mayoría de los casos, *curar,* generalmente por medio de tratamientos que se llevan a cabo en un *hospital.* (pág. 377)

medulla/médula Base del tronco encefálico; controla la frecuencia cardíaca y la respiración. (pág. 39)

memory/memoria Aprender de manera persistente a través del tiempo usando la codificación, el almacenaje y la recuperación de la información. (pág. 197)

memory consolidation/consolidación de la memoria Almacenaje neural de la memoria a largo plazo. (pág. 203)

memory trace/rastro de memoria Cambios físicos duraderos que ocurren en el cerebro al formarse un recuerdo. (pág. 209)

menarche/menarquia Primer período menstrual. (pág. 113)

menopause/menopausia Cesación de la menstruación. En el uso cotidiano, el término se refiere a la transición biológica que experimenta la mujer desde antes hasta después de acabar de menstruar. (pág. 97)

mental age/edad mental Medida de desempeño en la prueba de inteligencia diseñada por Binet. La edad cronológica del niño que corresponde característicamente a un nivel dado de desempeño. Por ende, se dice que un niño que se desempeña como una persona normal de 8 años, tiene una edad mental de 8 años. (pág. 241)

mere exposure effect/efecto de la mera exposición Fenómeno que sostiene que la exposición repetida a estímulos novedosos aumenta la atracción a tales estímulos. (pág. 335)

methamphetamine/metanfetamina Fármaco poderosamente adictivo que estimula el sistema nervioso central con funciones corporales aceleradas y los cambios correspondientes de la energía y el estado de ánimo. Con el tiempo, parece reducir los niveles de referencia de dopamina. (pág. 391)

middle ear/oído medio Cámara ubicada entre el tímpano y la cóclea; contiene tres huesos pequeños (el martillo, el yunque y el estribo) que concentran las vibraciones del tímpano y de la ventana oval de la cóclea. (pág. 153)

mindfulness meditation/meditación a conciencia plena Práctica reflexiva en la que las personas atienden a las vivencias vigentes de una manera tolerante y no condenatoria. (pág. 301)

Minnesota Multiphasic Personality Inventory (MMPI)/ Inventario de Personalidad Polifacética de Minnesota (IPPM) La más ampliamente investigada y utilizada de todas las pruebas de personalidad. Se creó originalmente para identificar trastornos emocionales (y todavía se la utiliza con tal fin). Esta prueba se utiliza en la actualidad para muchas actividades de preselección. (pág. 361)

mirror-image perceptions/percepciones idénticas Opiniones mutuas que generalmente sostienen las personas que discrepan o experimentan conflictos entre sí, como cuando cada parte se ve a sí misma como ética y pacifica, y a la otra parte la ve como malvada y agresiva. (pág. 343)

mirror neuron/neurona espejo Neurona que se activa cuando llevamos a cabo ciertas acciones y cuando observamos a otros realizando tales acciones; la base neuronal para el aprendizaje por imitación y por observación. (pág. 189)

misinformation effect/efecto de información errónea Recuerdo que se deforma al recibir información engañosa. (pág. 213)

mnemonics/nemotécnica Ayudas para la memoria, sobre todo técnicas que utilizan imágenes brillantes y dispositivos organizacionales. (pág. 199)

mode/modo Puntuación o puntuaciones que ocurren con mayor frecuencia en una distribución. (pág. A-3)

modeling/modelar Proceso de observar e imitar un comportamiento en particular. (pág. 187)

monocular cue/indicación monocular Señal de profundidad como la interposición y la perspectiva lineal, que puede ser extraída de las imágenes de cada uno de los ojos. (pág. 148)

mood-congruent memory/memoria congruente con el estado de ánimo Tendencia a recordar experiencias que concuerdan con el buen o mal estado de ánimo que estamos viviendo. (pág. 207)

motivation/motivación Necesidad o deseo que promueve y dirige el comportamiento. (pág. 259)

motor cortex/corteza motora Parte de la corteza cerebral en la parte posterior de los lóbulos frontales. Controla los movimientos voluntarios. (pág. 45)

motor neuron/neurona motriz Neurona que lleva la información desde cerebro y la médula espinal hacia los músculos y las glándulas.

MRI (magnetic resonance imaging)/resonancia magnética nuclear (RMN) Técnica que emplea campos magnéticos y ondas de radio para producir imágenes computarizadas de tejidos blandos. Las imágenes de RMN nos permiten visualizar la anatomía del cerebro. (pág. 39)

narcissism/narcisismo Amor propio y ensimismamiento excesivos. (págs. 269, 369)

narcolepsy/narcolepsia Trastorno caracterizado por ataques incontrolables de sueño, en el que a veces el individuo entra directamente en el sueño MOR. (pág. 61)

natural selection/selección natural Principio según el cual, de entre la variedad de rasgos heredados, aquellos que contribuyen al aumento de la reproducción y la supervivencia tienen mayor probabilidad de pasar a las generaciones futuras. (pág. 125)

naturalistic observation/observación naturalista Técnica de observar y registrar la conducta en situaciones reales sin tratar de manipular ni controlar la situación. (pág. 15)

nature–nurture issue/debate de naturaleza–crianza Controversia de antaño acerca del aporte relativo que ejercen los genes y las vivencias en el desarrollo de los rasgos y comportamientos psicológicos. En la ciencia psicológica actual se opina que los rasgos y comportamientos tienen origen en la interrelación entre la naturaleza y la crianza. (pág. 9)

near-death experience/experiencia al borde de la muerte Estado de alteración de la consciencia experimentado por personas que tienen un encuentro cercano con la muerte (por ejemplo, cuando se sufre un paro cardíaco). A menudo es similar a las alucinaciones inducidas por los estupefacientes. (pág. 391)

negative reinforcement/reforzamiento negativo Aumento en la expresión de comportamientos mediante la interrupción o reducción de los estímulos negativos tales como un correntazo. Un reforzamiento negativo es cualquier cosa que, *cuando se elimina* después de una reacción, refuerza la reacción. (*Nota*: el reforzamiento negativo *no significa* castigo). (pág. 179)

nerves/nervios Haces de axones neuronales que forman "cables" de nervios y conectan el sistema nervioso central con los músculos, las glándulas y los órganos sensoriales. (pág. 35)

nervous system/sistema nervioso Veloz red electroquímica de comunicación del cuerpo que consta de todas las células nerviosas de los sistemas nerviosos central y periférico. (pág. 35)

neurogenesis/neurogénesis Formación de neuronas nuevas. (pág. 47)

neuron/neurona Célula nerviosa; el componente básico del sistema nervioso. (pág. 31)

neurotransmitters/neurotransmisores Agentes químicos producidos por las neuronas que atraviesan la brecha sináptica y transmiten mensajes a otras neuronas o a los músculos y las glándulas. (pág. 33)

neutral stimulus (NS)/estímulos neutrales (EN) Según el condicionamiento clásico, un estímulo que no produce respuesta antes del condicionamiento. (pág. 171)

nicotine/nicotina Fármaco estimulante, altamente adictivo y psicoactivo que se halla en el tabaco. (pág. 389)

normal curve/curva normal Curva en forma de campana que describe la distribución de muchos atributos físicos y psicológicos. La mayoría de las puntuaciones yacen cerca de la media y otras, cada vez menos, yacen cerca de los extremos. (pág. 243)

normative social influence/influencia social normativa Influencia resultante del deseo de una persona de obtener la aprobación o evitar la desaprobación de los demás. (pág. 319)

object permanence/permanencia de los objetos Reconocimiento de que las cosas siguen existiendo aunque no las veamos. (pág. 79)

observational learning/aprendizaje observacional Aprender observando a los demás. (pág. 187)

obsessive-compulsive disorder (OCD)/trastorno obsesivo-compulsivo (TOC) Trastorno que se caracteriza por pensamientos (obsesiones) y/o acciones (compulsiones) repetitivos y no deseados. (pág. 383)

occipital lobes/lóbulos occipitales Porción de la corteza cerebral ubicada en la parte posterior de la cabeza; incluye las áreas que reciben información de los campos visuales. (pág. 45)

Oedipus complex/complejo de Edipo Según Freud, los deseos sexuales de un niño hacia su madre y sentimientos de celos y odio para con el padre rival. (pág. 353)

one-word stage/etapa holofrástica Etapa en el desarrollo del habla, entre el primero y segundo años, en la que el niño se expresa principalmente con palabras aisladas. (pág. 233)

operant behavior/comportamiento operante Comportamiento que opera en el entorno, produciendo consecuencias. (pág. 171)

operant chamber/cámara operante Caja que contiene una barra o tecla que un animal puede manipular para obtener un reforzamiento de comida o agua. Está dotada de un aparato de grabación que registra la frecuencia con la que el animal dentro de la caja presiona la barra u oprime la tecla. Se emplea en investigaciones de condicionamiento operante. (También se conoce como *caja de Skinner*). (pág. 177)

operant conditioning/condicionamiento operante Aprendizaje en el que el comportamiento se torna más probable si está seguido por un reforzamiento o se atenúa si está seguido por un castigo. (pág. 177)

operational definition/definición operacional Declaración redactada con gran cuidado en la que se detallan los procedimientos (operaciones) exactos que se usan en un estudio de investigación. Por ejemplo, *la inteligencia* humana puede ser operacionalmente definida como lo que se mide en una prueba de inteligencia. (pág. 13)

opiates/opiáceos El opio y sus derivados, tales como la morfina y la heroína. Deprimen la actividad neuronal y alivian temporalmente el dolor y la ansiedad. (págs. 33, 389)

opponent-process theory/teoría de proceso de oponentes Teoría que manifiesta que los procesos opuestos de la retina (rojo-verde, amarillo- azul, blanco-negro) posibilitan la visualización de los colores. Por ejemplo, el verde "enciende" algunas células y "apaga" otras; y el rojo "enciende" otras células y el verde las "apaga". (pág. 145)

optic nerve/nervio óptico Nervio que transporta los impulsos neuronales del ojo al cerebro. (pág. 143)

optimism/optimismo Anticipación de resultados positivos. Son optimistas las personas que esperan lo mejor y creen que sus esfuerzos llevan a obtener buenos resultados. (pág. 295)

organizational psychology/psicología organizacional Subdivisión de la psicología I/O que examina las influencias organizacionales en la satisfacción y productividad de los trabajadores y facilita cambios organizacionales. (pág. B-3)

ostracism/ostracismo Exclusión social deliberada de individuos o grupos. (pág. 268)

other-race effect/efecto de otras razas Tendencia a recordar caras de la raza de uno mismo con mayor precisión que las caras de otras razas. (pág. 331)

outgroup/grupo ajeno "Ellos", o sea, las personas a las que percibimos como distintas o separadas, que no forman parte de nuestro grupo. (pág. 329)

overconfidence/exceso de confianza Tendencia a ser más confiado que acertado, o sea, a sobreestimar las creencias y las opiniones propias. (pág. 227)

panic disorder/trastorno de pánico Trastorno de ansiedad marcado por el inicio repentino y recurrente de episodios de aprehensión intensa o terror que pueden durar varios minutos. Pueden incluir dolor de pecho, sofocamiento, y otras sensaciones atemorizantes, a menudo seguidas por preocupaciones de un posible ataque posterior. (pág. 381)

parallel processing/procesamiento en paralelo Procesamiento simultáneo de muchos aspectos de un problema o escena; modo natural del cerebro de procesar la información de varias funciones. (págs. 51, 147, 199)

parasympathetic nervous system/sistema nervioso autónomico parasimpático Subdivisión del sistema nervioso autónomico que calma el cuerpo y conserva su energía. (pág. 35)

parietal lobes/lóbulos parietales Área de la corteza cerebral en la parte superior y hacia la parte posterior de la cabeza; recibe aportes sensoriales del tacto y la posición del cuerpo. (pág. 45)

partial (intermittent) reinforcement/reforzamiento parcial (intermitente) Reforzamiento de una respuesta tan solo una parte del tiempo; tiene como resultado la adquisición más lenta de una respuesta pero mucho más resistente a la extinción que el reforzamiento continuo. (pág. 179)

passionate love/amor apasionado Estado excitado de intensa y positiva absorción en otro ser. Por lo general se observa al comienzo de una relación de amor romántica. (pág. 339)

perception/percepción Proceso mediante el cual el cerebro organiza e interpreta la información sensorial transformándola en objetos y sucesos que tienen sentido. (pág. 135)

perceptual adaptation/adaptación perceptiva Capacidad de acomodarnos a un estímulo sensorial cambiado, como por ejemplo un campo visual artificialmente desplazado o incluso invertido. (pág. 153)

perceptual constancy/constancia perceptiva Tendencia a percibir objetos como si fueran constantes e inalterables (como si mantuvieran el color, el brillo, la forma y el tamaño), a pesar de los cambios que se produzcan en la iluminación y en las imágenes que llegan a la retina. (pág. 151)

perceptual set/predisposición perceptiva Predisposición mental para percibir una cosa y no otra. (pág. 139)

peripheral nervous system (PNS)/sistema nervioso periférico (SNP) Neuronas sensoriales y motrices que conectan el sistema nervioso central con el resto del organismo. (pág. 35)

peripheral route persuasion/ruta de persuasión periférica Se produce cuando las personas se ven influenciadas por señales triviales, como el atractivo del orador. (pág. 315)

person-centered therapy/terapia centrada en la persona Tipo de terapia humanista creada por Rogers, en la cual el terapeuta se vale de técnicas tales como escuchar activamente dentro de un entorno genuino, con aceptación y empatía, para facilitar el crecimiento personal del cliente. (También se denomina *terapia centrada en el cliente*). (pág. 419)

personal control/control personal Nuestro sentido de controlar el entorno en lugar de sentirnos impotentes. (pág. 293)

personality/personalidad Forma característica de pensar, sentir y actuar de una persona. (pág. 351)

personality disorder/trastornos de la personalidad Patrón de comportamientos inflexibles y duraderos que se interponen ante el desempeño social. (pág. 407)

personality inventory/inventario de personalidad Cuestionario (a menudo de preguntas de *falso verdadero* o de *desacuerdo acuerdo*) en el que las personas responden a consultas diseñadas para medir una amplia gama de sentimientos y conductas. Se usa para evaluar ciertas características escogidas de la personalidad. (pág. 363)

personnel psychology/psicología de personal Subdivisión de la psicología I/O que ayuda con la búsqueda de empleo y con el reclutamiento, selección, colocación, capacitación, evaluación y desarrollo de los empleados. (pág. B-3)

pessimism/pesimismo Anticipación de resultados negativos. Son pesimistas las personas que esperan lo peor y dudan de que puedan alcanzar sus metas. (pág. 295)

PET (positron emission tomography) scan/TEP (tomografía por emisión de positrones) Muestra visual de la actividad cerebral que detecta hacia dónde se dirige un tipo de glucosa radiactiva en el momento en que el cerebro realiza una función dada. (pág. 39)

phobia/fobia Trastorno de ansiedad marcado por un temor persistente e irracional y la evasión de un objeto, actividad o situación específicos. (pág. 383)

physiological need/necesidad fisiológica Exigencia básica del cuerpo. (pág. 259)

pitch/tono Propiedad de los sonidos que los caracteriza como agudos o graves, en función de su frecuencia. (pág. 153)

pituitary gland/glándula pituitaria La glándula más influyente del sistema endocrino. Bajo la influencia del hipotálamo, la glándula pituitaria regula el crecimiento y controla las demás glándulas endocrinas. (pág. 35)

placebo/placebo Substancia o condición inactiva que a veces se suministra a los miembros de un grupo de control en lugar del tratamiento que se le da al grupo experimental. En latín significa "complaceré". (pág. 19)

placebo effect/efecto placebo Resultados producidos por las expectativas únicamente. (pág. 19)

plasticity/plasticidad Capacidad del cerebro de modificarse, sobre todo durante la niñez, reordenándose después de un daño cerebral o formando nuevas trayectorias basadas en la experiencia. (pág. 31)

polygraph/polígrafo Máquina, utilizada comúnmente con la intención de detectar mentiras, que mide ciertas reacciones corporales (como los cambios en la transpiración, el ritmo cardíaco y la respiración) que acompañan a las emociones. (pág. 277)

population/población Todos aquellos que constituyen el grupo que se está estudiando, a partir del cual se pueden tomar muestras. (*Nota:* Salvo en estudios de alcance nacional, *no* se refiere a la totalidad de la población de un país). (pág. 17)

positive psychology/psicología positiva Estudio científico del funcionamiento humano, que tiene las metas de descubrir y promover las fortalezas y las virtudes que ayudan a los individuos y a las comunidades a prosperar. (pág. 11)

positive reinforcement/reforzamiento positivo Aumento en la expresión de comportamientos mediante la presentación de estímulos positivos, por ejemplo, un alimento. Un reforzamiento positivo es cualquier cosa que, *presentada* después de una respuesta, refuerza la respuesta. (pág. 179)

posthypnotic suggestion/sugerencia poshipnótica Sugerencia que se hace durante una sesión de hipnotismo, que el sujeto debe realizar cuando ya no está hipnotizado; la utilizando algunos practicantes para ayudar a controlar síntomas y conductas no deseadas. (pág. 159)

posttraumatic growth/crecimiento postraumático Cambios psicológicos positivos como resultado de la lucha contra circunstancias extremadamente difíciles y crisis de la vida. (pág. 438)

posttraumatic stress disorder (PTSD)/trastorno por estrés postraumático (TEPT) Trastorno de ansiedad caracterizado por recuerdos obsesionantes, pesadillas, aislamiento social, ansiedad asustadiza, y/o insomnio que perdura por cuatro semanas o más después de una experiencia traumática. (pág. 383)

predictive validity/validez predictiva Nivel de éxito con el que una prueba predice el comportamiento para el que ha sido diseñada para predecir. (pág. 243)

prejudice/prejuicio Actitud injusta y normalmente negativa hacia un grupo y sus integrantes. El prejuicio generalmente implica creencias estereotipadas, sentimientos negativos y una predisposición a acción discriminatoria. (pág. 327)

preoperational stage/etapa preoperacional En la teoría de Piaget, la etapa (desde alrededor de los 2 hasta los 6 o 7 años de edad) durante la que el niño aprende a utilizar el lenguaje; pero todavía no comprende las operaciones mentales de la lógica concreta. (pág. 79)

primary reinforcer/reforzador primario Suceso que es inherentemente reforzador y a menudo satisface una necesidad biológica. (pág. 179)

primary sex characteristics/características primarias del sexo Estructuras del organismo (ovarios, testículos y aparatos genitales externos) que posibilitan la reproducción sexual. (pág. 113)

priming/preparación Activación de asociaciones en nuestra mente, a menudo de manera inconsciente, que nos dispone a percibir o recordar objetos o sucesos de una manera determinada. (págs. 137, 207)

proactive interference/interferencia proactiva Efecto interruptor del aprendizaje anterior sobre la manera de recordar información *nueva*. (pág. 211)

problem-focused coping/superación con enfoque en los problemas Intento de sobrellevar el estrés de manera directa cambiando ya sea lo que produce la tensión o la forma en que nos relacionamos con dicho tensionador. (pág. 293)

projective test/prueba de proyección Tipo de prueba de la personalidad, como la prueba de Rorschach, en la cual se le da a una persona una imagen ambigua diseñada para provocar una proyección de pensamientos o sentimientos inconscientes. (pág. 355)

prosocial behavior/comportamiento prosocial Comportamiento positivo, constructivo, útil. Lo contrario del comportamiento antisocial. (pág. 189)

prototype/prototipo Imagen mental o mejor ejemplo de una categoría. Al cotejar artículos nuevos con un prototipo se trabaja con un método rápido y sencillo para clasificar artículos en categorías (tal como cuando se comparan animales de plumas con un ave prototípico, como un petirrojo). (pág. 223)

psychoactive drug/fármaco psicoactivo Sustancia química que altera las percepciones y el estado de ánimo. (pág. 385)

psychoanalysis/psicoanálisis (1) Teoría de Freud sobre la personalidad que atribuye los pensamientos y las acciones a motivos y conflictos inconscientes. (2) El método terapéutico de Freud usado para el tratamiento de trastornos psicológicos. Freud creía que las asociaciones libres, las resistencias, los sueños y las transferencias del paciente (así como la interpretación de ellas por parte del analista) liberaban sentimientos antes reprimidos, permitiendo que el paciente adquiriera agudeza introspectiva. (págs. 351, 417)

psychodynamic theories/teorías psicodinámicas Visión de la personalidad con una concentración en el subconsciente y en la importancia de las vivencias en la niñez. (pág. 351)

psychodynamic therapy/terapia psicodinámica Enfoque terapéutico que se deriva de la tradición psicoanalítica; se observa a los individuos como si respondieran a fuerzas inconscientes y experiencias de la niñez, y se busca agudizar la introspección. (pág. 419)

psychological disorder/trastorno psicológico Síndrome caracterizado por la alteración clínicamente significativa de los pensamientos, los sentimientos y los comportamientos de una persona. (pág. 377)

psychology/psicología Estudio científico de cómo los procesos psicológicos, neuronales y endocrinos se combinan para afectar nuestro sistema inmunitario y la salud en general. (pág. 5)

psychoneuroimmunology/psiconeuroinmunología Estudio de cómo los procesos psicológicos, neuronales y endocrinos se combinan en nuestro organismo para influenciar el sistema inmunitario y la salud en general. (pág. 289)

psychosexual stages/etapas psicosexuales Etapas del desarrollo infantil (oral, anal, fálica, latente, genital), durante las cuales, según Freud, las energías del id que buscan el placer se enfocan en zonas erógenas específicas. (pág. 353)

psychosurgery/psicocirugía Cirugía que extrae o destruye tejido cerebral para cambiar el comportamiento. (pág. 437)

psychotherapy/psicoterapia Tratamiento que incluye técnicas psicológicas; consiste en interacciones entre un terapeuta cualificado y una persona que desea superar dificultades psicológicas o lograr un crecimiento personal. (pág. 417)

psychotic disorders/trastornos psicóticos Grupo de trastornos caracterizados por ideas irracionales, percepciones distorsionadas y pérdida de contacto con la realidad. (pág. 401)

puberty/pubertad Período de maduración sexual durante el cual la persona adquiere la capacidad de reproducirse. (págs. 89, 111)

punishment/castigo Evento que disminuye el comportamiento que le precede. (pág. 181)

random assignment/asignación aleatoria Asignación de participantes a los grupos experimental y de control. Se realiza al azar para minimizar las diferencias preexistentes que pudiese haber entre los asignados. (pág. 19)

random sample/muestra aleatoria Muestra que representa justamente la población, gracias a que cada elemento de la población tiene igual oportunidad de ser seleccionado. (pág. 17)

range/alcance Diferencia entre las puntuaciones más alta y más baja en una distribución. (pág. A-3)

recall/recordación Memoria que se demuestra recuperando información aprendida anteriormente, tal como en las pruebas que consisten en rellenar espacios en blanco. (pág. 205)

reciprocal determinism/determinismo recíproco Influencias de la interacción entre la conducta, los factores personales internos y el entorno. (pág. 365)

reciprocity norm/norma de reciprocidad Expectativa de que las personas ayudarán, y no harán daño, a aquellos que las han ayudado. (pág. 341)

recognition/reconocimiento Memoria que se demuestra identificando cosas que se aprendieron anteriormente, tal como en las pruebas de opciones múltiples. (pág. 205)

reconsolidation/reconsolidación Proceso en el que los recuerdos almacenados, al ser recuperados, son potencialmente alterados antes de ser almacenados nuevamente. (pág. 211)

reflex/reflejo Respuesta simple y automática a un estímulo sensorial. (págs. 35, 73)

refractory period/período refractario (1) En el procesamiento neuronal, una breve fase de descanso que se produce después de que una neurona ha disparado. No se pueden producir potenciales de acción subsiguientes hasta que el axón vuelva a su estado de reposo. (2) En la sexualidad humana, fase de descanso que se produce después del orgasmo, en la que el varón es incapaz de tener otro orgasmo. (págs. 33, 117)

regression toward the mean/regresión hacia la media Tendencia hacia las puntuaciones o eventos extremos o poco comunes para así retornar (regresar) hacia el promedio. (pág. A-5)

reinforcement/reforzamiento Según el condicionamiento operante, todo suceso que *fortalezca* el comportamiento al que sigue. (pág. 177)

reinforcement schedule/plan de reforzamiento Patrón que define la frecuencia con que se reforzará una respuesta deseada. (pág. 179)

relational aggression/regresión relacional Acto de agresión (sea física o verbal) que tiene por intención hacerle daño a las relaciones de la persona o a su estatus social. (pág. 109)

relative deprivation/privación relativa Impresión de que estamos en peor situación que aquellos con quienes nos comparamos. (pág. 307)

relearning/reaprendizaje Memoria que se demuestra por el tiempo que se ahorra cuando se aprende algo por segunda vez. (pág. 205)

reliability/fiabilidad Grado hasta el que una prueba produce resultados coherentes, comprobados por la uniformidad de las puntuaciones en las dos mitades de la prueba, en formas distintas de la prueba, o al retomar la prueba. (pág. 243)

REM rebound/rebote de MOR Tendencia al aumento del sueño MOR como consecuencia de la privación del sueño MOR. (pág. 62)

REM sleep/sueño MOR (movimiento ocular rápido) Etapa recurrente del sueño durante la cual generalmente ocurren sueños gráficos. También se conoce como *sueño paradójico,* porque los músculos están relajados (salvo unos espasmos mínimos) pero los demás sistemas del cuerpo están activos. (pág. 55)

repetitive transcranial magnetic stimulation (rTMS)/estimulación magnética transcraneal repetitiva (EMTR) Aplicación repetitiva de pulsos de energía magnética al cerebro. Se utiliza para estimular o suprimir la actividad cerebral. (pág. 435)

replication/replicación Repetir la esencia de un estudio de investigación, por lo general con participantes diferentes y en situaciones diferentes, para ver si las conclusiones básicas se pueden reproducir. (pág. 13)

repression/represión En la teoría del psicoanálisis, el mecanismo básico de defensa por medio del cual el sujeto elimina de su consciente aquellos pensamientos, emociones o recuerdos que le producen ansiedad. (págs. 211, 353)

resilience/resiliencia Fuerza personal que ayuda a la mayoría de las personas a asumir con flexibilidad situaciones de estrés y recuperarse de la adversidad e incluso de un trauma. (págs. 303, 438)

resistance/resistencia En el psicoanálisis, bloquear del consciente aquello que está cargado de ansiedad. (pág. 417)

respondent behavior/comportamiento de respuesta Comportamiento que ocurre como respuesta automática a un estímulo. (pág. 171)

reticular formation/formación reticular Red de nervios que atraviesa el tronco encefálico e ingresa en el tálamo y que desempeña un papel importante en el control de la excitación. (pág. 41)

retina/retina Superficie en la parte interior del ojo que es sensible a la luz y que contiene los receptores de luz llamados bastoncillos y conos, además de capas de neuronas que inician el procesamiento de la información visual. (pág. 141)

retinal disparity/disparidad retiniana Clave binocular para la percepción de la profundidad. Mediante la comparación de las imágenes que provienen de ambos ojos, el cerebro calcula la distancia. Cuanto mayor sea la disparidad (diferencia) entre dos imágenes, más cerca estará el objeto. (pág. 148)

retrieval/recuperación Proceso de extraer la información que está almacenada en la memoria. (pág. 197)

retrieval cue/clave de recuperación Todo estímulo (suceso, sentimiento, lugar, etc.) relacionado con un recuerdo específico. (pág. 207)

retroactive interference/interferencia retroactiva Efecto interruptor de algo nuevo que se ha aprendido en la capacidad de recordar información *vieja*. (pág. 211)

reuptake/recaptación Reabsorción de un neurotransmisor por la neurona emisora. (pág. 33)

rods/bastoncillos Receptores de la retina que detectan el negro, el blanco y el gris, y que son sensibles al movimiento; necesarios para la visión periférica y en la penumbra cuando los conos no responden. (pág. 143)

role/rol Conjunto de expectativas (normas) acerca de una posición social, que definen la forma en que deben comportarse las personas que ocupan esa posición. (págs. 115, 317)

Rorschach inkblot test/prueba de Rorschach Prueba proyectiva de amplio uso. Conjunto de 10 manchas de tinta, diseñado por Hermann Rorschach; busca identificar los sentimientos internos de las personas mediante el análisis de sus interpretaciones de las manchas. (pág. 355)

savant syndrome/síndrome de savant Condición según la cual una persona de capacidad mental limitada, cuenta con una destreza excepcional en un campo como la computación o el dibujo. (pág. 238)

scapegoat theory/teoría del chivo expiatorio Teoría que expone que el prejuicio ofrece un escape para la cólera porque nos brinda a alguien a quien culpar. (pág. 329)

scatterplot/gráfico de aspersión Conjunto de datos graficados, cada uno de los cuales representa los valores de dos variables. La pendiente de los puntos sugiere el sentido de la relación entre los dos variables. El nivel de aspersión sugiere la fuerza de la correlación (un bajo nivel de aspersión indica alta correlación). (pág. A-5)

schema/esquema Concepto o marco referencial que organiza e interpreta la información. (pág. 79)

schizophrenia/esquizofrenia Trastorno caracterizado por delirios, alucinaciones, habla desorganizada y/o expresión emocional disminuida o inapropiada. (pág. 401)

secondary sex characteristics/características secundarias del sexo Rasgos sexuales no relacionados con la reproducción, tales como los senos y las caderas de las mujeres, la calidad de la voz del varón, y el pelo corporal. (pág. 113)

selective attention/atención selectiva Capacidad de enfocar la consciencia en un estímulo en particular. (pág. 51)

self/yo Imagen que tenemos de nosotros mismos y entendimiento de quiénes somos. Según la psicología moderna, el concepto de que este es el centro de la personalidad, que organiza los pensamientos, los sentimientos y las acciones. (pág. 367)

self-actualization/autorrealización Según Maslow, necesidad psicológica que surge después de satisfacer las necesidades físicas y psicológicas y de lograr la autoestima; motivación para realizar nuestro potencial pleno. (pág. 357)

self-concept/concepto de uno mismo Todo lo que pensamos y sentimos acerca de nosotros mismos cuando respondemos a la pregunta: "¿Quién soy?". (pág. 359)

self-control/autocontrol Capacidad de controlar los impulsos y demorar la gratificación a corto plazo con el fin de obtener mayores recompensas a largo plazo. (pág. 295)

self-disclosure/revelación personal Revelación a los demás de cosas íntimas de nuestro ser. (pág. 339)

self-efficacy/autoeficacia Nuestros sentimientos de competencia y eficacia. (pág. 365)

self-esteem/autoestima Sentimientos altos o bajos con que nos valoramos a nosotros mismos. (pág. 367)

self-fulfilling prophecy/profecía autorrealizada Creencia que conduce a su propia realización. (pág. 343)

self-serving bias/parcialidad interesada Disposición para percibirnos a nosotros mismos de manera favorable. (pág. 369)

self-transcendence/autotrascendencia Según Maslow, esfuerzo por alcanzar una identidad, un sentido y un propósito que vaya más allá de uno mismo. (pág. 357)

semantic memory/memora semántica Memoria explícita de hechos y conocimientos generales. Uno de los dos sistemas de memoria conscientes (el otro es la *memoria episódica*). (pág. 201)

sensation/sensación Proceso mediante el cual los receptores sensoriales y el sistema nervioso reciben las energías de los estímulos provenientes de nuestro entorno. (pág. 135)

sensorimotor stage/etapa sensoriomotriz En la teoría de Piaget, la etapa (de los 0 a los 2 años de edad) durante la cual los bebés conocen el mundo principalmente en términos de sus impresiones sensoriales y actividades motoras. (pág. 79)

sensorineural hearing loss/pérdida de la audición sensorineuronal Sordera causada por daños a la células receptoras de la cóclea o a los nervios de la audición; la forma más común de sordera. También se le dice *sordera nerviosa*. (pág. 153)

sensory adaptation/adaptación sensorial Disminución en la sensibilidad como respuesta a la estimulación constante. (pág. 137)

sensory interaction/interacción sensorial Principio que un sentido puede influir en otro, como cuando el olor de la comida influye en su sabor. (pág. 161)

sensory memory/memoria sensorial Registro breve e inmediato de la información sensorial en el sistema de la memoria. (pág. 197)

sensory neuron/neurona sensorial Neurona que conduce la información que le llega desde los tejidos del cuerpo y los receptores sensoriales al cerebro y la médula espinal. (pág. 35)

sequential processing/procesamiento secuencial Procesamiento de un aspecto de un problema a la vez; se utiliza cuando centramos la atención en tareas nuevas o complejas. (pág. 51)

serial position effect/efecto de posición serial Tendencia a recordar con mayor facilidad los elementos del comienzo y el final de una lista. (pág. 207)

set point/punto fijo Punto de supuesto equilibrio en el "termostato del peso" de una persona. Cuando el cuerpo alcanza un peso por debajo de este punto, se produce un aumento en el hambre y una disminución en el índice metabólico, los cuales pueden actuar para restablecer el peso perdido. (pág. 263)

sex/sexo En psicología, las características biológicas por las cuales la sociedad define al *hombre* y la *mujer*. (pág. 109)

sexual dysfunction/disfunción sexual Problema que complica de manera constante la excitación y el funcionamiento sexuales. (pág. 117)

sexual orientation/orientación sexual Atracción sexual duradera hacia miembros de nuestro mismo sexo (orientación homosexual), del sexo opuesto (orientación heterosexual) o de ambos sexos (orientación bisexual). (pág. 121)

sexual response cycle/ciclo de respuesta sexual Las cuatro etapas de respuesta sexual descritas por Masters y Johnson: excitación, meseta, orgasmo y resolución. (pág. 117)

shaping/modelamiento Procedimiento del condicionamiento operante en el cual los reforzadores conducen una acción con aproximaciones sucesivas hasta lograr el comportamiento deseado. (pág. 177)

short-term memory/memoria a corto plazo Memoria activada que retiene algunos elementos por un corto tiempo, tales como los siete dígitos de un número telefónico mientras se marca, antes de que la información se almacene o se olvide. (pág. 197)

sleep/sueño Pérdida del conocimiento que es periódica y natural. Es distinta de la inconsciencia que puede resultar del estado de coma, de la anestesia general o de la hibernación. (Adaptado de Dement, 1999). (pág. 55)

sleep apnea/apnea del sueño Trastorno del sueño en el que se interrumpe repetidamente la respiración hasta tal punto de que el nivel de oxígeno en sangre llega a ser tan bajo que la persona tiene que despertarse para respirar. (pág. 61)

social clock/reloj social Manera que la sociedad prefiere para marcar el tiempo adecuado de los eventos sociales, tales como el matrimonio, la paternidad y la jubilación. (pág. 99)

social-cognitive perspective/perspectiva sociocognoscitiva Ver la conducta como influida por la interacción entre las personas (y sus pensamientos) y su contexto social. (pág. 365)

social facilitation/facilitación social Mejoramiento del desempeño en funciones sencillas o bien aprendidas en la presencia de otros. (pág. 324)

social identity/identidad social Aspecto "nosotros" del concepto de nosotros mismos; parte de nuestra respuesta a "¿Quién soy?" que proviene de nuestra pertenencia a grupos. (pág. 93)

social leadership/liderazgo social Liderazgo orientado hacia el grupo que fortalece el trabajo en equipo, que media en conflictos y que ofrece apoyo. (pág. B-7)

social learning theory/teoría de aprendizaje social Teoría que señala que aprendemos la conducta social observando e imitando, y al ser recompensados o castigados. (pág. 115)

social loafing/holgazanería social Tendencia de las personas en un grupo de realizar menos esfuerzo cuando juntan sus esfuerzos para lograr una meta común que cuando son responsables individualmente. (pág. 325)

social psychology/psicología social Estudio científico de cómo pensamos, influimos y nos relacionamos con los demás. (pág. 315)

social-responsibility norm/norma de responsabilidad social Expectativa de que las personas ayudarán a aquellos que dependen de ellas. (pág. 341)

social script/guión social Guía modelada culturalmente acerca de cómo actuar en diversas situaciones. (págs. 121, 333)

somatic nervous system/sistema nervioso somático División del sistema nervioso periférico que controla los músculos esqueléticos del cuerpo. También llamado *sistema nervioso esquelético*. (pág. 35)

somatosensory cortex/corteza somatosensorial Área de la corteza cerebral en la parte delantera de los lóbulos parietales. Registra y procesa el tacto y las sensaciones de movimiento. (pág. 45)

source amnesia/amnesia de la fuente Recuerdo errado de cómo, cuándo o dónde se aprendió o se imaginó la información. (pág. 213)

spacing effect/efecto del aprendizaje espaciado Tendencia a que el estudio o la práctica distribuidos logren mejor retención a largo plazo que la que se logra a través del estudio o la práctica en volumen masivo. (pág. 201)

spermarche/espermarca Primera eyaculación. (pág. 113)

split brain/cerebro dividido Condición en la que los dos hemisferios cerebrales se privan de la comunicación mediante el corte quirúrgico de las fibras que los conectan (principalmente las del cuerpo calloso). (pág. 47)

spontaneous recovery/recuperación espontánea Reaparición, después de una pausa, de una respuesta condicionada extinguida. (pág. 175)

spotlight effect/efecto reflector Sobreestimación de lo que los demás advierten y evalúan de nuestro aspecto, desempeño y desatinos (como si nos estuviera apuntando un reflector). (pág. 367)

SQ3R/inspeccionar, preguntar, leer, recitar, repasar Método de estudio en el que se siguen cinco pasos: Inspeccionar, Preguntar, Leer, Recitar, Repasar. (pág. 25)

standard deviation/desviación estándar Medición computada de cuánto varía cierta puntuación con respecto a la puntuación media. (pág. A-3)

standardization/estandarización Definir procedimientos de medición uniformes y puntuaciones significativos mediante la comparación del desempeño de un grupo examinado con anterioridad. (pág. 243)

Stanford-Binet/Stanford-Binet Revisión norteamericana (por Terman en la Universidad de Stanford) de la prueba original de inteligencia de Binet. Esta prueba se usa extensamente. (pág. 241)

statistical significance/significado estadístico Declaración estadística de la probabilidad de que un resultado obtenido haya sido producto del azar. (pág. A-7)

stereotype/estereotipo Creencia (a veces acertada, pero frecuentemente demasiado generalizada) sobre las características de un grupo. (pág. 327)

stereotype threat/amenaza de estereotipos Preocupación autoconfirmada de que nos evaluarán con base en un estereotipo negativo. (pág. 251)

stimulants/estimulantes Fármacos (tales como la cafeína, la nicotina y las más poderosas cocaína, anfetamina, metanfetamina y éxtasis) que excitan la actividad neuronal y aceleran las funciones corporales. (pág. 389)

stimulus/estímulo Todo suceso o situación que provoca una respuesta. (pág. 171)

storage/almacenamiento Retención a través del tiempo de información codificada. (pág. 197)

stranger anxiety/miedo a los extraños Miedo a los extraños que los bebé manifiestan normalmente a partir de alrededor de los 8 meses de edad. (pág. 83)

stress/estrés Proceso mediante el cual percibimos y respondemos a ciertos eventos llamados *estresores*, los cuales evaluamos como amenazantes o desafiantes. (pág. 287)

subjective well-being/bienestar subjetivo Felicidad o satisfacción con la vida de uno mismo. Se emplea junto con medidas de bienestar objetivas (por ejemplo, con indicadores físicos y económicos) para evaluar nuestra calidad de vida. (pág. 303)

subliminal/subliminal Aquello que ocurre por debajo de nuestro umbral absoluto de la consciencia. (pág. 135)

substance use disorder/trastornos causados por el uso de estupefacientes Trastorno caracterizado por la continuación de las ansias y el uso de estupefacientes pese a que han interrumpido el estilo de vida de manera significativa y/o representan un riesgo físico. (pág. 385)

superego/supergo En el psicoanálisis freudiano, componente de la personalidad que representa ideales internalizados y proporciona parámetros de juicio (la consciencia) y para fijarse metas futuras. (pág. 353)

superordinate goals/metas comunes Metas compartidas que hacen caso omiso de las diferencias entre las personas y que requieren su cooperación. (pág. 343)

suprachiasmatic nucleus (SCN)/núcleo supraquiasmático (NSQ) Par de grupos de células en el hipotálamo que controlan el ritmo circadiano. En respuesta a la luz, el núcleo supraquiasmático ajusta la producción de melatonina, modificando de esta manera los niveles de somnolencia. (pág. 57)

survey/encuesta Técnica descriptiva para obtener actitudes o conductas del grupo autoinformadas por las personas; generalmente mediante preguntas que se le plantean a una *muestra aleatoria y representativa* de dicho grupo. (pág. 15)

sympathetic nervous system/sistema nervioso simpático Subdivisión del sistema nervioso autonómico que en despierta al cuerpo y moviliza su energía. (pág. 35)

synapse/sinapsis Intersección entre el extremo del axón de una neurona que envía un mensaje y la dendrita o cuerpo celular de la neurona receptora. El pequeño espacio entre estos puntos de contacto se denomina *brecha sináptica* o *hendidura sináptica*. (pág. 31)

systematic desensitization/desensibilización sistemática Tipo de terapia de exposición en la cual se asocia un estado tranquilo y agradable con estímulos que van aumentando paulatinamente y que provocan ansiedad. De uso común para tratar fobias. (pág. 421)

task leadership/liderazgo específico Liderazgo orientado a metas específicas que establece las normas, organiza el trabajo y centra la atención en metas. (pág. B-7)

telegraphic speech/habla telegráfica Etapa inicial del habla de un niño, que tiene forma de telegrama y está formada mayormente por sustantivos y verbos; por ejemplo, "quiero leche" o "papá va trabajo". (pág. 233)

temperament/temperamento Reactividad e intensidad emocionales características de una persona. (pág. 75)

temporal lobes/lóbulos temporales Porción de la corteza cerebral que yace más o menos encima de las orejas; incluye las áreas que reciben información de los oídos. (pág. 45)

tend-and-befriend response/respuesta de cuidarse y amigarse En situaciones de estrés, las personas (sobre todo las mujeres) a menudo se dan apoyo (*cuidar*), a la vez que forman vínculos y buscan apoyo de otros (*amigarse*). (pág. 289)

teratogen/teratógeno Agente, podría ser químico o viral, que pueden afectar al embrión o al feto durante el desarrollo prenatal, produciéndole daño. (pág. 73)

testing effect/efecto de prueba Recuerdo aumentado luego de recuperar la información, en lugar de simplemente volver a leerla. También conocido como *efecto de práctica de recuperación* o *aprendizaje intensificado por pruebas*. (pág. 25)

testosterone/testosterona La hormona sexual masculina más importante. La tienen tanto los varones como las mujeres pero la cantidad adicional en los varones estimula el crecimiento de los órganos sexuales masculinos durante el período fetal y el desarrollo de las características sexuales masculinas secundarias en la pubertad. (pág. 111)

thalamus/tálamo Centro sensorial de control del cerebro ubicado encima del tronco encefálico; dirige mensajes sensoriales a la corteza cerebral y transmite respuestas al cerebelo y la médula. (pág. 41)

THC/THC Principal sustancia activa que se encuentra en la marihuana, produce distintos efectos, inclusive alucinaciones leves. (pág. 391)

Thematic Apperception Test (TAT)/Prueba de apercepción temática (PAT) Prueba proyectiva en la que el individuo expresa sus sentimientos e intereses internos mediante historias que inventa en torno a escenas ambiguas. (pág. 355)

theory/teoría Explicación que emplea principios que organizan observaciones y predicen comportamientos o sucesos. (pág. 13)

theory of mind/teoría de la mente Conceptos que tienen las personas acerca de sus propios procesos mentales y de los de los demás; es decir, de sus sentimientos, percepciones y pensamientos y de los comportamientos que estos podrían predecir. (pág. 81)

therapeutic alliance/alianza terapéutica Vínculo de confianza y comprensión mutua que se establece entre el terapeuta y el cliente, que trabajan juntos de manera constructiva para superar el problema del cliente. (pág. 429)

threshold/umbral   Nivel de estimulación requerido para activar un impulso neuronal. (pág. 33)

token economy/economía de fichas   Procedimiento del condicionamiento operante en el que las personas ganan una ficha cuando exhiben un comportamiento deseado y luego pueden intercambiar las fichas ganadas por privilegios o para darse algún gusto. (pág. 423)

tolerance/tolerancia   Disminución del efecto con el uso regular de la misma dosis de un fármaco, lo que requiere que el usuario tome dosis cada vez mayores para poder experimentar el efecto del fármaco. (pág. 387)

top-down processing/procesamiento de arriba hacia abajo   Procesamiento de la información orientado por procesos mentales de alto nivel, como cuando construimos percepciones basándonos en nuestras vivencias y expectativas. (pág. 135)

trait/rasgo   Patrón de comportamiento característico o disposición a sentirse y actuar de cierta forma, según se evalúa en los inventarios de autoinformes e informes de pares. (pág. 359)

transduction/transducción   Transformación de un tipo de energía en otro. En las sensaciones, transformación de las energías de los estímulos, tales como las imágenes, los sonidos y los olores, en impulsos neuronales que el cerebro tiene la capacidad de interpretar. (pág. 135)

transference/transferencia   En el psicoanálisis, la transferencia de emociones ligadas a otras relaciones, del paciente al analista (tales como el amor o el odio hacia el padre o la madre). (pág. 417)

transgender/transexual   Término genérico que describe a personas cuya identidad o expresión de género difiere de la que se asocia con su sexo al nacer. (pág. 115)

two-factor theory/teoría de los dos factores   Teoría de Schachter y Singer que propone que para experimentar emociones debemos (1) recibir estimulación física y (2) identificar el estímulo a nivel cognitivo. (pág. 271)

two-word stage/etapa de dos palabras   A partir de los 2 años de edad, etapa del desarrollo del lenguaje durante la cual el niño emite mayormente frases de dos palabras. (pág. 233)

Type A/Tipo A   Término de Friedman y Rosenman para referirse a las personas competitivas, compulsivas, impacientes, verbalmente agresivas y con tendencia a enojarse. (pág. 291)

Type B/Tipo B   Término de Friedman y Rosenman para referirse a las personas tolerantes, relajadas y tranquilas. (pág. 291)

unconditional positive regard/consideración positiva incondicional   Actitud de cuidado, aceptación y parcialidad. Según Rogers, así los clientes desarrollarían consciencia y aceptación de sí mismos. (págs. 359, 419)

unconditioned response (UR)/respuesta incondicionada (RI)   En el condicionamiento clásico, la respuesta no aprendida e innata que es producida por un estímulo incondicionado (EI) (como la salivación cuando la comida está en la boca). (pág. 173)

unconditioned stimulus (US)/estímulo incondicionado (EI)   En el condicionamiento clásico, estímulo que provoca una respuesta incondicionalmente (RI) y de manera natural y automática. (pág. 173)

unconscious/inconsciente   Según Freud, un depósito de pensamientos, deseos, sentimientos y recuerdos, en su mayoría inaceptables. Según los psicólogos contemporáneos, el procesamiento de información del cual no tenemos consciencia. (pág. 351)

validity/validez   Grado en que una prueba mide o predice lo que se supone debe medir o predecir. (Ver también *validez del contenido* y *validez predictiva*.) (pág. 243)

variable-interval schedule/calendario de intervalo variable   Según el condicionamiento operante, calendario de reforzamientos que refuerza una respuesta en intervalos de tiempo impredecibles. (pág. 181)

variable-ratio schedule/plan de proporción variable   En el condicionamiento operante, plan de reforzamientos que refuerza una respuesta después de un número impredecible de respuestas. (pág. 179)

vestibular sense/sentido vestibular   Sentido de movimiento y posición del cuerpo, inclusive el sentido de equilibrio. (pág. 161)

virtual reality exposure therapy/terapia de exposición a una realidad virtual   Técnica del contracondicionamiento que trata la ansiedad mediante estimulaciones electrónicas creativas en la que las personas puede hacerles frente a mayores temores, tales como volar en avión, ver una araña o hablar en público. (pág. 421)

visual cliff/precipicio visual   Dispositivo del laboratorio con el que se examina la percepción de profundidad en los bebés y en animales de corta edad. (pág. 148)

wavelength/longitud de onda   Distancia entre la cresta de una onda de luz o de sonido y la cresta de la siguiente onda. (pág. 141)

Weber's law/ley de Weber   Principio que sostiene que para que dos estímulos se perciban como distintos, estos deben diferir por un porcentaje mínimo constante (en vez de por una cantidad constante). (pág. 137)

Wechsler Adult Intelligence Scale (WAIS)/escala de la Inteligencia de Wechsler para adultos (EIWA)   La prueba EIWA y su versión adaptada para niños son las prueba de inteligencia más ampliamente utilizadas. Incluyen subpruebas verbales y de desempeño (no verbales). (pág. 243)

Wernicke's area/área de Wernicke   Parte del cerebro generalmente ubicada en el lóbulo temporal izquierdo, que participa en la comprensión y la expresión del lenguaje, y que controla la recepción del mismo. (pág. 235)

withdrawal/síndrome de abstinencia   La incomodidad y angustia que sigue cuando se deja de utilizar un estupefaciente adictivo o se suspende una conducta. (pág. 387)

working memory/memoria operativa   Entendimiento más reciente de la memoria a corto plazo que añade el procesamiento consciente y activo de información auditiva y visual-espacial, y de información recuperada de la memoria a largo plazo. (pág. 197)

X chromosome/cromosoma X   Cromosoma del sexo que se encuentra en el varón y la mujer. Las mujeres por lo general tienen dos cromosomas X; los hombres por lo general tienen un cromosoma X y un cromosoma Y. Con un cromosoma X del padre y otro de la madre, se produce una mujer. (pág. 111)

Y chromosome/cromosoma Y   Cromosoma del sexo que solamente se halla en los hombres. Cuando se aparea con un cromosoma X de la madre, se produce un varón. (pág. 111)

Yerkes-Dodson law/Ley de Yerkes-Dodson   Principio que establece que el rendimiento aumenta con la excitación solamente hasta un punto; más allá de este punto el rendimiento disminuye. (pág. 259)

Young-Helmholtz trichromatic (three-color) theory/teoría tricromática de Young-Helmholtz   Teoría de que la retina contiene tres tipos distintos de receptores de color: uno más sensible al rojo, otro al verde y otro al azul. Al estimularse en combinación, estos receptores son capaces de producir la percepción de cualquier color. (pág. 145)

zygote/cigoto   Huevo fertilizado. Atraviesa por un período de dos semanas de división celular rápida y se convierte en un embrión. (pág. 73)

References

AAA. (2010). *Asleep at the wheel: the prevalence and impact of drowsy driving.* AAA Foundation for Traffic Safety (aaafoundation.org/pdf/2010DrowsyDrivingReport.pdf).

AAA. (2015). *Teen driver safety: Environmental factors and driver behaviors in teen driver crashes.* AAA Foundation for Traffic Safety (aaafoundation.org/sites/default/files/2015TeenCrashCausationFS.pdf).

AAMC. (2014). Medical students, selected years, 1965–2013. Association of American Medical Colleges (aamc.org/download/411782/data/2014_table1.pdf).

AAS. (2009, April 25). *USA suicide: 2006 final data.* Prepared for the American Association of Suicidology by J. L. McIntosh (suicidology.org).

Abrams, D. B., & Wilson, G. T. (1983). Alcohol, sexual arousal, and self-control. *Journal of Personality and Social Psychology, 45,* 188–198.

Abrams, L. (2008). Tip-of-the-tongue states yield language insights. *American Scientist, 96,* 234–239.

Abrams, M. (2002, June). Sight unseen—Restoring a blind man's vision is now a real possibility through stem-cell surgery. But even perfect eyes cannot see unless the brain has been taught to use them. *Discover, 23,* 54–60.

Abramson, L. Y., Metalsky, G. I., & Alloy, L. B. (1989). Hopelessness depression: A theory-based subtype. *Psychological Review, 96,* 358–372.

Abramson, L. Y., Seligman, M. E. P., & Teasdale, J. D. (1978). Learned helplessness in humans: Critique and reformulation. *Journal of Abnormal Psychology, 87,* 49–74.

Academy of Science of South Africa. (2015). *Diversity in human sexuality: Implications for policy in Africa* (p. 36). Academy of Science of South Africa (assaf.org.za).

Acevedo, B. P., & Aron, A. (2009). Does a long-term relationship kill romantic love? *Review of General Psychology, 13,* 59–65.

Acevedo, B. P., Aron, A., Fisher, H. E., & Brown, L. L. (2012). Neural correlates of long-term intense romantic love. *Social Cognitive and Affective Neuroscience, 7,* 145–159.

ACHA. (2009). *American College Health Association-National College Health Assessment II: Reference group executive summary. Fall 2008.* Baltimore: American College Health Association.

Ackerman, D. (2004). *An alchemy of mind: The marvel and mystery of the brain.* New York: Scribner.

Adachi, T., Fujino, H., Nakae, A., Mashimo, T., & Sasaki, J. (2014). A meta-analysis of hypnosis for chronic pain problems: A comparison between hypnosis, standard care, and other psychological interventions. *International Journal of Clinical and Experimental Hypnosis, 62,* 1–28.

Adams, H. E., Wright, L. W., Jr., & Lohr, B. A. (1996). Is homophobia associated with homosexual arousal? *Journal of Abnormal Psychology, 105,* 440–446.

Adelmann, P. K., Antonucci, T. C., Crohan, S. F., & Coleman, L. M. (1989). Empty nest, cohort, and employment in the well-being of midlife women. *Sex Roles, 20,* 173–189.

Adelstein, J. S., Shehzad, Z., Mennes, M., DeYoung, C. G., Zuo, X.-N., Kelly, C., . . . Milham, M. P. (2011). Personality is reflected in the brain's intrinsic functional architecture. *PLoS ONE, 6,* e27633.

Aderka, I. M., Nickerson, A., Bøe, H. J., & Hofmann, S. G. (2012). Sudden gains during psychological treatments of anxiety and depression: A meta-analysis. *Journal of Consulting and Clinical Psychology, 80,* 93–101.

Adler, J. M., Lodi-Smith, J., Philippe, F. L., & Houle, I. (2016). The incremental validity of narrative identity in predicting well-being: A review of the field and recommendations for the future. *Personality and Social Psychology Review, 20*(2), 142–175.

Adolph, K. E., Kretch, K. S., & LoBue, V. (2014). Fear of heights in infants? *Current Directions in Psychological Science, 23,* 60–66.

Affleck, G., Tennen, H., Urrows, S., & Higgins, P. (1994). Person and contextual features of daily stress reactivity: Individual differences in relations of undesirable daily events with mood disturbance and chronic pain intensity. *Journal of Personality and Social Psychology, 66,* 329–340.

Agerström, J., Björklund, F., Carlsson, R., & Rooth, D.-O. (2012). Warm and competent Hassan = cold and incompetent Eric: A harsh equation of real-life hiring discrimination. *Basic and Applied Social Psychology, 34,* 359–366.

Agrillo, C. (2011). Near-death experience: Out-of-body and out-of-brain? *Review of General Psychology, 15,* 1–10.

Agudelo, L. Z., Femenía, T., Orhan, F., Porsmyr-Palmertz, M., Goiny, M., Martinez-Redondo, V., . . . Ruas, J. L. (2014). Skeletal muscle PGC-1 1 modulates kynurenine metabolism and mediates resilience to stress-induced depression. *Cell, 159,* 33–45.

Aiello, J. R., Thompson, D. D., & Brodzinsky, D. M. (1983). How funny is crowding anyway? Effects of room size, group size, and the introduction of humor. *Basic and Applied Social Psychology, 4,* 193–207.

Aimone, J. B., Jessberger, S., & Gage, F. H. (2010, last modified February 5). Adult neurogenesis. Scholarpedia (scholarpedia.org).

Ainsworth, M. D. S. (1973). The development of infant-mother attachment. In B. Caldwell & H. Ricciuti (Eds.), *Review of child development research* (Vol. 3). Chicago: University of Chicago Press.

Ainsworth, M. D. S. (1979). Infant-mother attachment. *American Psychologist, 34,* 932–937.

Ainsworth, M. D. S. (1989). Attachments beyond infancy. *American Psychologist, 44,* 709–716.

Aknin, L. B., Barrington-Leigh, C. P., Dunn, E. W., Helliwell, J. F., Burns, J., Biswas-Diener, R., & Norton, M. I. (2013). Prosocial spending and well-being: Cross-cultural evidence for a psychological universal. *Journal of Personality and Social Psychology, 104,* 635–652.

Aknin, L. B., Broesch, T., Kiley Hamlin, J., & Van de Vondervoort, J. W. (2015). Pro-social behavior leads to happiness in a small-scale rural society. *Journal of Experimental Psychology: General, 144,* 788–795.

Alanko, K., Santtila, P., Harlaar, N., Witting, K., Varjonen, M., Jern, P., . . . Sandnabba, N. K. (2010). Common genetic effects of gender atypical behavior in childhood and sexual orientation in adulthood: A study of Finnish twins. *Archives of Sexual Behavior, 39,* 81–92.

Albee, G. W. (1986). Toward a just society: Lessons from observations on the primary prevention of psychopathology. *American Psychologist, 41,* 891–898.

Albee, G. W. (2006). Historical overview of primary prevention of psychopathology: Address to the 3rd world conference on the promotion of mental health and prevention of mental and behavioral disorders. September 15–17, 2004, Auckland, New Zealand. *The Journal of Primary Prevention, 27,* 449–456.

Albert, D., Chein, J., & Steinberg, L. (2013). Peer influences on adolescent decision making. *Current Directions in Psychological Science, 22,* 80–86.

Alcock, J. E. (2011, March/April). Back from the future: Parapsychology and the Bem affair. *Skeptical Inquirer,* pp. 31–39.

Aldao, A., & Nolen-Hoeksema, S. (2010). Emotion-regulation strategies across psychopathology: A meta-analytic review. *Clinical Psychology Review, 30,* 217–237.

Aldridge-Morris, R. (1989). *Multiple personality: An exercise in deception.* Hillsdale, NJ: Erlbaum.

Aleman, A., Kahn, R. S., & Selten, J.-P. (2003). Sex differences in the risk of schizophrenia: Evidence from meta-analysis. *Archives of General Psychiatry, 60,* 565–571.

Alexander, L., & Tredoux, C. (2010). The spaces between us: A spatial analysis of informal segregation. *Journal of Social Issues, 66,* 367–386.

Allen, J. R., & Setlow, V. P. (1991). Heterosexual transmission of HIV: A view of the future. *Journal of the American Medical Association, 266,* 1695–1696.

Allen, K. (2003). Are pets a healthy pleasure? The influence of pets on blood pressure. *Current Directions in Psychological Science, 12,* 236–239.

Allen, M., D'Alessio, D., & Emmers-Sommer, T. M. (2000). Reactions of criminal sexual offenders to pornography: A meta-analytic summary. In M. Roloff (Ed.), *Communication yearbook 22* (pp. 139–169). Thousand Oaks, CA: Sage.

Allen, M., Emmers, T. M., Gebhardt, L., & Giery, M. (1995). Pornography and rape myth acceptance. *Journal of Communication, 45,* 5–26.

Allen, M. S., & Jones, M. V. (2014). The "home advantage" in athletic competitions. *Current Directions in Psychological Science, 23,* 48–53.

Allen, M. W., Gupta, R., & Monnier, A. (2008). The interactive effect of cultural symbols and human values on taste evaluation. *Journal of Consumer Research, 35,* 294–308.

Allen, N. B., & Badcock, P. B. T. (2003). The social risk hypothesis of depressed mood: Evolutionary, psychosocial, and neurobiological perspectives. *Psychological Bulletin, 129,* 887–913.

Allen, T., & Sherman, J. (2011). Ego threat and intergroup bias: A test of motivated-activation versus self-regulatory accounts. *Psychological Science, 22,* 331–333.

Allport, G. W. (1954). *The nature of prejudice.* New York: Addison-Wesley.

Ally, B. A., Hussey, E. P., & Donahue, M. J. (2013). A case of hyperthymesia: Rethinking the role of the amygdala in autobiographical memory. *Neurocase, 19,* 166–181.

Al-Sayegh, H., Lowry, J., Polur, R. N., Hines, R. B., Liu, F., & Zhang, J. (2015). Suicide history and mortality: A follow-up of a national cohort in the United States. *Archives of Suicide Research, 19,* 35–47.

Altamirano, L. J., Miyake, A., & Whitmer, A. J. (2010). When mental inflexibility facilitates executive control: Beneficial side effects of ruminative tendencies on goal maintenance. *Psychological Science, 21,* 1377–1382.

Alwin, D. F. (1990). Historical changes in parental orientations to children. In N. Mandell (Ed.), *Sociological studies of child development* (Vol. 3). Greenwich, CT: JAI Press.

Amabile, T. M. (1983). *The social psychology of creativity.* New York: Springer-Verlag.

Amabile, T. M., & Hennessey, B. A. (1992). The motivation for creativity in children. In A. K. Boggiano & T. S. Pittman (Eds.), *Achievement and motivation: A social-developmental perspective.* New York: Cambridge University Press.

Amabile, T. M., & Kramer, S. J. (2011). *The progress principle: Using small wins to ignite joy, engagement, and creativity at work.* Cambridge, MA: Harvard Business Review Press.

Ambady, N. (2010). The perils of pondering: Intuition and thin slice judgments. *Psychological Inquiry, 21,* 271–278.

Ambrose, C. T. (2010). The widening gyrus. *American Scientist, 98,* 270–274.

Amedi, A., Merabet, L. B., Bermpohl, F., & Pascual-Leone, A. (2005). The occipital cortex in the blind: Lessons about plasticity and vision. *Current Directions in Psychological Science, 14,* 306–311.

Amen, D. G., Stubblefield, M., Carmichael, B., & Thisted, R. (1996). BrainSPECT findings and aggressiveness. *Annals of Clinical Psychiatry, 8,* 129–137.

American Enterprise. (1992, January/February). Women, men, marriages and ministers. *The American Enterprise,* p. 106.

American Psychiatric Association. (2013). *Diagnostic and statistical manual of mental disorders* (5th ed.). Arlington, VA: American Psychiatric Publishing.

American Psychological Association [APA Presidential Task Force on Evidence-Based Practice]. (2006). Evidence-based practice in psychology. *American Psychologist, 61,* 271–285.

Ames, D. R., & Flynn, F. J. (2007). What breaks a leader: The curvilinear relation between assertiveness and leadership. *Journal of Personality and Social Psychology, 92,* 307–324.

Ammori, B. (2013, January 4). Viewpoint: Benefits of bariatric surgery. *GP* (gponline.com).

Andersen, R. A., Hwang, E. J., & Mulliken, G. H. (2010). Cognitive neural prosthetics. *Annual Review of Psychology, 61,* 169–190.

Andersen, S. M. (1998). *Service learning: A national strategy for youth development.* A position paper issued by the Task Force on Education Policy. Washington, DC: Institute for Communitarian Policy Studies, George Washington University.

Anderson, B. L. (2002). Biobehavioral outcomes following psychological interventions for cancer patients. *Journal of Consulting and Clinical Psychology, 70,* 590–610.

Anderson, C. A. (2004). An update on the effects of playing violent video games. *Journal of Adolescence, 27,* 113–122.

Anderson, C. A. (2013, June). Guns, games, and mass shootings in the U.S. *Bulletin of the International Society for Research on Aggression,* pp. 14–19.

Anderson, C. A., Anderson, K. B., Dorr, N., DeNeve, K. M., & Flanagan, M. (2000). Temperature and aggression. In M. P. Zanna (Ed.), *Advances in experimental social psychology* (pp. 63–133). San Diego: Academic Press.

Anderson, C. A., Brion, S., Moore, D. A., & Kennedy, J. A. (2012). A status enhancement account of overconfidence. *Journal of Personality and Social Psychology, 103,* 718–735.

Anderson, C. A., Bushman, B. J., & Groom, R. W. (1997). Hot years and serious and deadly assault: Empirical tests of the heat hypothesis. *Journal of Personality and Social Psychology, 73,* 1213–1223.

Anderson, C. A., & Delisi, M. (2011). Implications of global climate change for violence in developed and developing countries. In J. Forgas, A. Kruglanski., & K. Williams (Eds.), *The psychology of social conflict and aggression* (pp. 249–265). New York: Psychology Press.

Anderson, C. A., & Dill, K. E. (2000). Video games and aggressive thoughts, feelings, and behavior in the laboratory and in life. *Journal of Personality and Social Psychology, 78,* 772–790.

Anderson, C. A., Lindsay, J. J., & Bushman, B. J. (1999). Research in the psychological laboratory: Truth or triviality? *Current Directions in Psychological Science, 8,* 3–9.

Anderson, C. A., Shibuya, A., Ihori, N., Swing, E. L., Bushman, B. J., Sakamoto, A., . . . Saleem, M. (2010a). Violent video game effects on aggression, empathy, and prosocial behavior in Eastern and Western countries: A meta-analytic review. *Psychological Bulletin, 136,* 151–173.

Anderson, C. A., & Warburton, W. A. (2012). The impact of violent video games: An overview. In W. Warburton & D. Braunstein (Eds.), *Growing up fast and furious: Reviewing the impacts of violent and sexualized media on children* (pp. 56–84). Annandale, New South Wales, Australia: Federation Press.

Anderson, J. R., Gillies, A., & Lock, L. (2010b). Pan thanatology. *Current Biology, 20,* R349–R351.

Anderson, R. C., Pichert, J. W., Goetz, E. T., Schallert, D. L., Stevens, K. V., & Trollip, S. R. (1976). Instantiation of general terms. *Journal of Verbal Learning and Verbal Behavior, 15,* 667–679.

Anderson, S. E., Dallal, G. E., & Must, A. (2003). Relative weight and race influence average age at menarche: Results from two nationally representative surveys of U.S. girls studied 25 years apart. *Pediatrics, 111,* 844–850.

Anderson, S. R. (2004). *Doctor Dolittle's delusion: Animals and the uniqueness of human language.* New Haven: Yale University Press.

Andreasen, N. C. (1997). Linking mind and brain in the study of mental illnesses: A project for a scientific psychopathology. *Science, 275,* 1586–1593.

Andreasen, N. C. (2001). *Brave new brain: Conquering mental illness in the era of the genome.* New York: Oxford University Press.

Andrews, P. W., & Thomson, J. A., Jr. (2009a). The bright side of being blue: Depression as an adaptation for analyzing complex problems. *Psychological Review, 116,* 620–654.

Andrews, P. W., & Thomson, J. A., Jr. (2009b, January/February). Depression's evolutionary roots. *Scientific American Mind,* pp. 57–61.

Anglemyer, A., Horvath, T., & Rutherford, G. (2014). The accessibility of firearms and risk for suicide and homicide victimization among household members. *Annals of Internal Medicine, 160,* 101–112.

Annan, K. A. (2001, December 10). We can love what we are, without hating who—and what—we are not. Lecture delivered on receipt of the 2001 Nobel Peace Prize, Oslo, Norway.

Antonaccio, O., Botchkovar, E. V., & Tittle, C. R. (2011). Attracted to crime: Exploration of criminal motivation among respondents in three European cities. *Criminal Justice and Behavior, 38,* 1200–1221.

Antony, M. M., Brown, T. A., & Barlow, D. H. (1992). Current perspectives on panic and panic disorder. *Current Directions in Psychological Science, 1,* 79–82.

Antrobus, J. (1991). Dreaming: Cognitive processes during cortical activation and high afferent thresholds. *Psychological Review, 98,* 96–121.

Anzures, G., Quinn, P. C., Pascalis, O., Slater, A. M., Tanaka, J. W., & Lee, K. (2013). Developmental origins of the other-race effect. *Current Directions in Psychological Science, 22,* 173–178.

AP. (2007, October 25). AP/Ipsos poll: One-third in AP poll believe in ghosts and UFOs, half accept ESP. Associated Press (ap-ipsosresults.com/).

AP. (2009, May 9). AP-mtvU AP 2009 Economy, College Stress and Mental Health Poll. Associated Press (ap.org).

APA. (2002). *Ethical principles of psychologists and code of conduct.* Washington, DC: American Psychological Association.

APA. (2007). Report of the APA Task Force on the Sexualization of Girls. Washington, DC: American Psychological Association.

APA. (2009). Stress in America 2009. American Psychological Association (apa.org).

APA. (2010, accessed April 28). Answers to your questions about transgender individuals and gender identity. (apa.org/pi/women/programs/girls/report.aspx).

APA Task Force on Violent Media. (2015). *Technical report on the review of the violent video game literature.* American Psychological Association (apa.org/pi/families/review-video-games.pdf).

Archer, J. (2000). Sex differences in aggression between heterosexual partners: A meta-analytic review. *Psychological Bulletin, 126,* 651–680.

Archer, J. (2004). Sex differences in aggression in real-world settings: A meta-analytic review. *Review of General Psychology, 8,* 291–322.

Archer, J. (2007). A cross-cultural perspective on physical aggression between partners. *Issues in Forensic Psychology, No. 6,* 125–131.

Archer, J. (2009). Does sexual selection explain human sex differences in aggression? *Behavioral and Brain Sciences, 32,* 249–311.

Arent, S. M., Landers, D. M., & Etnier, J. L. (2000). The effects of exercise on mood in older adults: A meta-analytic review. *Journal of Aging and Physical Activity, 8,* 407–430.

Ariely, D. (2010). *Predictably irrational, revised and expanded edition: The hidden forces that shape our decisions.* New York: Harper Perennial.

Ariely, D., & Loewenstein, G. (2006). The heat of the moment: The effect of sexual arousal on sexual decision making. *Journal of Behavioral Decision Making, 19,* 87–98.

Aries, E. (1987). Gender and communication. In P. Shaver & C. Henrick (Eds.), *Review of Personality and Social Psychology, 7,* 149–176.

Arkowitz, H., & Lilienfeld, S. O. (2006, April/May). Psychotherapy on trial. *Scientific American Mind,* pp. 42–49.

Armony, J. L., Quirk, G. J., & LeDoux, J. E. (1998). Differential effects of amygdala lesions on early and late plastic components of auditory cortex spike trains during fear conditioning. *Journal of Neuroscience, 18,* 2592–2601.

Armstrong, E. A., England, P., & Fogarty, A. C. K. (2012). Accounting for women's orgasm and sexual enjoyment in college hookups and relationships. *American Sociological Review, 77,* 435–462.

Arnedo, J., Mamah, D., Baranger, D. A., Harms, M. P., Barch, D. M., Svrakic, D. M., . . . Zwir, I. (2015). Decomposition of brain diffusion imaging data uncovers latent schizophrenias with distinct patterns of white matter anisotropy. *NeuroImage, 120,* 43–54.

Arneson, J. J., Sackett, P. R., & Beatty, A. S. (2011). Ability-performance relationships in education and employment settings: Critical tests of the more-is-better and the good-enough hypotheses. *Psychological Science, 22,* 1336–1342.

Arnett, J. J. (2006). Emerging adulthood: Understanding the new way of coming of age. In J. J. Arnett & J. L.

Tanner (Eds.), *Emerging adults in America: Coming of age in the 21st century.* Washington, DC: American Psychological Association.

Arnett, J. J. (2007). Socialization in emerging adulthood: From the family to the wider world, from socialization to self-socialization. In J. E. Grusec & P. D. Hastings (Eds.), *Handbook of socialization: Theory and research.* New York: Guilford Press.

Aron, A., Melinat, E., Aron, E. N., Vallone, R. D., & Bator, R. J. (1997). The experimental generation of interpersonal closeness: A procedure and some preliminary findings. *Personality and Social Psychology Bulletin, 23,* 363–377.

Aron, A., Norman, C. C., Aron, E. N., McKenna, C., & Heyman, R. E. (2000). Couples' shared participation in novel and arousing activities and experienced relationship quality. *Journal of Personality and Social Psychology, 78,* 273–284.

Aronson, E. (2001, April 13). Newsworthy violence. E-mail to SPSP discussion list, drawing from *Nobody Left to Hate.* New York: Freeman, 2000.

Artiga, A. I., Viana, J. B., Maldonado, C. R., Chandler-Laney, P. C., Oswald, K. D., & Boggiano, M. M. (2007). Body composition and endocrine status of long-term stress-induced binge-eating rats. *Physiology and Behavior, 91,* 424–431.

Asch, S. E. (1955). Opinions and social pressure. *Scientific American, 193,* 31–35.

Asendorpf, J. B., Penke, L., & Back, M. D. (2011). From dating to mating and relating: Predictors of initial and long-term outcomes of speed-dating in a community sample. *European Journal of Personality, 25,* 16–30.

Aserinsky, E. (1988, January 17). Personal communication.

Askay, S. W., & Patterson, D. R. (2007). Hypnotic analgesia. *Expert Review of Neurotherapeutics, 7,* 1675–1683.

Aspinwall, L. G., & Tedeschi, R. G. (2010). The value of positive psychology for health psychology: Progress and pitfalls in examining the relation of positive phenomena to health. *Annals of Behavioral Medicine, 39,* 4–15.

Aspy, C. B., Vesely, S. K., Oman, R. F., Rodine, S., Marshall, L., & McLeroy, K. (2007). Parental communication and youth sexual behaviour. *Journal of Adolescence, 30,* 449–466.

Assanand, S., Pinel, J. P. J., & Lehman, D. R. (1998). Personal theories of hunger and eating. *Journal of Applied Social Psychology, 28,* 998–1015.

Atkinson, R. C., & Shiffrin, R. M. (1968). Human memory: A control system and its control processes. In K. Spence (Ed.), *The psychology of learning and motivation* (Vol. 2). New York: Academic Press.

Austin, E. J., Deary, I. J., Whiteman, M. C., Fowkes, F. G. R., Pedersen, N. L., Rabbitt, P., . . . McInnes, L. (2002). Relationships between ability and personality: Does intelligence contribute positively to personal and social adjustment? *Personality and Individual Differences, 32,* 1391–1411.

Auyeung, B., Baron-Cohen, S., Ashwin, E., Knickmeyer, R., Taylor, K., Hackett, G., & Hines, M. (2009). Fetal testosterone predicts sexually differentiated childhood behavior in girls and in boys. *Psychological Science, 20,* 144–148.

Averill, J. R. (1993). William James's other theory of emotion. In M. E. Donnelly (Ed.), *Reinterpreting the legacy of William James.* Washington, DC: American Psychological Association.

Aviezer, H., Hassin, R. R., Ryan, J., Grady, C., Susskind, J., Anderson, A., . . . Bentin, S. (2008). Angry, disgusted, or afraid? Studies on the malleability of emotion perception. *Psychological Science, 19,* 724–732.

Ax, A. F. (1953). The physiological differentiation of fear and anger in humans. *Psychosomatic Medicine, 15,* 433–442.

Ayan, S. (2009, April/May). Laughing matters. *Scientific American Mind,* pp. 24–31.

Azar, B. (1998, June). Why can't this man feel whether or not he's standing up? *APA Monitor* (apa.org/monitor /jun98/touch.html).

Azevedo, F. A., Carvalho, L. R., Grinberg, L. T., Farfel, J. M., Ferretti, R. E., Leite, R. E., . . . Herculano-Houzel, S. (2009). Equal numbers of neuronal and nonneuronal cells make the human brain an isometrically scaled-up primate brain. *Journal of Comparative Neurology, 513,* 532–541.

Baas, M., De Dreu, C. K. W., & Nijstad, B. A. (2008). A meta-analysis of 25 years of mood-creativity research: Hedonic tone, activation, or regulatory focus? *Psychological Bulletin, 134,* 779–806.

Babyak, M., Blumenthal, J. A., Herman, S., Khatri, P., Doraiswamy, M., Moore, K., . . . Krishnan, K. R. (2000). Exercise treatment for major depression: Maintenance of therapeutic benefit at ten months. *Psychosomatic Medicine, 62,* 633–638.

Bachman, J., O'Malley, P. M., Schulenberg, J. E., Johnston, L. D., Freedman-Doan, P., & Messersmith, E. E. (2007). *The education-drug use connection: How successes and failures in school relate to adolescent smoking, drinking, drug use, and delinquency.* Mahwah, NJ: Erlbaum.

Back, M. D., Stopfer, J. M., Vazire, S., Gaddis, S., Schmukle, S. C., Egloff, B., & Gosling, S. D. (2010). Facebook profiles reflect actual personality not self-idealization. *Psychological Science, 21,* 372–274.

Backman, L., & MacDonald, S. W. S. (2006). Death and cognition: Synthesis and outlook. *European Psychologist, 11,* 224 –235.

Baddeley, A. D. (1982). *Your memory: A user's guide.* New York: Macmillan.

Baddeley, A. D., Thomson, N., & Buchanan, M. (1975). Word length and the structure of short-term memory. *Journal of Verbal Learning and Verbal Behavior, 14,* 575–589.

Baddeley, J. L., & Singer, J. A. (2009). A social interactional model of bereavement narrative disclosure. *Review of General Psychology, 13,* 202–218.

Badgett, M. V. L., & Mallory, C. (2014, December). *Relationship recognition patterns of same-sex couples by gender.* The Williams Institute, U.C.L.A. (williamsinstitute.law. ucla.edu/wp-content/uploads/Badgett-Mallory-Gender-Dec-2014.pdf).

Bagemihl, B. (1999). *Biological exuberance: Animal homosexuality and natural diversity.* New York: St. Martins.

Bahrick, H. P. (1984). Semantic memory content in permastore: 50 years of memory for Spanish learned in school. *Journal of Experimental Psychology: General, 111,* 1–29.

Bahrick, H. P., Bahrick, P. O., & Wittlinger, R. P. (1975). Fifty years of memory for names and faces: A cross-sectional approach. *Journal of Experimental Psychology: General, 104,* 54–75.

Bailey, J. M., Dunne, M. P., & Martin, N. G. (2000). Genetic and environmental influences on sexual orientation and its correlates in an Australian twin sample. *Journal of Personality and Social Psychology, 78,* 524–536.

Bailey, J. M., Gaulin, S., Agyei, Y., & Gladue, B. A. (1994). Effects of gender and sexual orientation on evolutionarily relevant aspects of human mating psychology. *Journal of Personality and Social Psychology, 66,* 1081–1093.

Bailey, R. E., & Gillaspy, J. A., Jr. (2005). Operant psychology goes to the fair: Marian and Keller Breland in the popular press, 1947–1966. *The Behavior Analyst, 28,* 143–159.

Bailine, S., Fink, M., Knapp, R. Petrides, G., Husain, M. M., Rasmussen, K., . . . Kellner, C. H. (2010). Electroconvulsive therapy is equally effective in unipolar and bipolar depression. *Acta Psychiatrica Scandinavica, 121,* 431–436.

Baillargeon, R. (1995). A model of physical reasoning in infancy. In C. Rovee-Collier & L. P. Lipsitt (Eds.), *Advances in infancy research* (Vol. 9). Stamford, CT: Ablex.

Baillargeon, R. (2008). Innate ideas revisited: For a principle of persistence in infants' physical reasoning. *Perspectives in Psychological Science, 3,* 2–13.

Baker, M. & Maner, J. (2009). Male risk-taking as a context-sensitive signaling device. *Journal of Experimental Social Psychology, 45,* 1136–1139.

Baker, T. B., McFall, R. M., & Shoham, V. (2008). Current status and future prospects of clinical psychology: Toward a scientifically principled approach to mental and behavioral health care. *Psychological Science in the Public Interest, 9,* 67–103.

Baker, T. B., Piper, M. E., McCarthy, D. E., Majeskie, M. R., & Fiore, M. C. (2004). Addiction motivation reformulated: An affective processing model of negative reinforcement. *Psychological Review, 111,* 33–51.

Bakermans-Kranenburg, M. J., van IJzendoorn, M. H., & Juffer, F. (2003). Less is more: Meta-analyses of sensitivity and attachment interventions in early childhood. *Psychological Bulletin, 129,* 195–215.

Bakshy, E., Messing, S., & Adamic, L. A. (2015). Exposure to ideologically diverse news and opinion on Facebook. *Science, 348,* 1130–1132.

Balcetis, E., & Dunning, D. (2010). Wishful seeing: More desired objects are seen as closer. *Psychological Science, 21,* 147–152.

Ballini, A., Cantore, S., Fatone, L., Montenegro, V., De Vito, D., Pettini, F., . . . Foti, C. (2012). Transmission of nonviral sexually transmitted infections and oral sex. *Journal of Sexual Medicine, 9,* 372–384.

Balsam, K. F., Beauchaine, T. P., Rothblum, E. S., & Solomon, S. E. (2008). Three-year follow-up of same-sex couples who had civil unions in Vermont, same-sex couples not in civil unions, and heterosexual married couples. *Developmental Psychology, 44,* 102–116.

Balter, M. (2010). Animal communication helps reveal roots of language. *Science, 328,* 969–970.

Bambico, F. R., Nguyen N.-T., Katz, N., & Gobbi, G. (2010). Chronic exposure to cannabinoids during adolescence but not during adulthood impairs emotional behavior and monoaminergic neurotransmission. *Neurobiology of Disease, 37,* 641–655.

Bancroft, J., Loftus, J., & Long, J. S. (2003). Distress about sex: A national survey of women in heterosexual relationships. *Archives of Sexual Behavior, 32,* 193–208.

Bandura, A. (1977). Self-efficacy: Toward a unifying theory of behavior. *Psychological Review, 84,* 191–215.

Bandura, A. (1982). The psychology of chance encounters and life paths. *American Psychologist, 37,* 747–755.

Bandura, A. (1986). *Social foundations of thought and action: A social-cognitive theory.* Englewood Cliffs, NJ: Prentice-Hall.

Bandura, A. (2005). The evolution of social cognitive theory. In K. G. Smith & M. A. Hitt (Eds.), *Great minds in management: The process of theory development.* Oxford: Oxford University Press.

Bandura, A. (2006). Toward a psychology of human agency. *Perspectives on Psychological Science, 1,* 164–180.

Bandura, A. (2008). An agentic perspective on positive psychology. In S. J. Lopez (Ed.), *Positive psychology: Exploring the best in people: Vol. 1. Discovering human strengths* (pp. 167–196). Westport, CT: Praeger.

Bandura, A., Ross, D., & Ross, S. A. (1961). Transmission of aggression through imitation of aggressive models. *Journal of Abnormal and Social Psychology, 63,* 575–582.

Bar-Haim, Y., Lamy, D., Pergamin, L., Bakermans-Kranenburg, M. J., & van IJzendoorn, M. H. (2007). Threat-related attentional bias in anxious and nonanxious individuals: A meta-analytic study. *Psychological Bulletin, 133*, 1–24.

Barash, D. P. (2012). *Homo mysterius: Evolutionary puzzles of human nature.* New York: Oxford University Press.

Barbaresi, W. J., Katusic, S. K., Colligan, R. C., Weaver, A. L., & Jacobsen, S. J. (2007). Modifiers of long-term school outcomes for children with attention-deficit/hyperactivity disorder: Does treatment with stimulant medication make a difference? Results from a population-based study. *Journal of Developmental and Behavioral Pediatrics, 28*, 274–287.

Barberá, P., Jost, J. T., Nagler, J., Tucker, J. A., & Bonneau, R. (2015). Tweeting from left to right: Is online political communication more than an echo chamber? *Psychological Science, 26*, 1531–1542.

Bargh, J. A., & Chartrand, T. L. (1999). The unbearable automaticity of being. *American Psychologist, 54*, 462–479.

Barinaga, M. B. (1997). How exercise works its magic. *Science, 276*, 1325.

Barkley, R. A., Cook, E. H., Jr., Diamond, A., Zametkin, A., Thapar, A., Teeter, A., . . . Pelham, W., Jr. (2002). International consensus statement on ADHD: January 2002. *Clinical Child and Family Psychology Review, 5*, 89–111.

Barlow, D. H. (2010). Negative effects from psychological treatments: A perspective. *American Psychologist, 65*, 13–20.

Barlow, F. K., Paolini, S., Pedersen, A., Hornsey, M. J., Radke, H. R. M., Harwood, J., . . . Sibley, C. G. (2012). The contact caveat: Negative contact predicts increased prejudice more than positive contact predicts reduced prejudice. *Personality and Social Psychology Bulletin, 38*, 1629–1643.

Barnett, P. A., & Gotlib, I. H. (1988). Psychosocial functioning and depression: Distinguishing among antecedents, concomitants, and consequences. *Psychological Bulletin, 104*, 97–126.

Barnier, A. J., & McConkey, K. M. (2004). Defining and identifying the highly hypnotizable person. In M. Heap, R. J. Brown, & D. A. Oakley (Eds.), *The highly hypnotizable person: Theoretical, experimental and clinical issues* (pp. 30–60). London: Brunner-Routledge.

Baron, C. E., Smith, T. W., Uchino, B. N., Baucom, B. R., & Birmingham, W. C. (2016). Getting along and getting ahead: Affiliation and dominance predict ambulatory blood pressure. *Health Psychology, 35*, 253–261.

Baron-Cohen, S. (2008). Autism, hypersystemizing, and truth. *Quarterly Journal of Experimental Psychology, 61*, 64–75.

Baron-Cohen, S. (2009). Autism: The empathizing-systemizing (E-S) theory. *The Year in Cognitive Neuroscience, 1156*, 68–80.

Baron-Cohen, S., Bowen, D. C., Rosemary, J. H., Allison, C., Auyeung, B., Lombardo, M. V., & Lai, M.-C. (2015). The "reading the mind in the eyes" test: Complete absence of typical difference in ~400 men and women with autism. *PLoS One, 10*, e0136521.

Barrera, T. L., Mott, J. M., Hofstein, R. F., & Teng, E. J. (2013). A meta-analytic review of exposure in group cognitive behavioral therapy for posttraumatic stress disorder. *Clinical Psychology Review, 33*, 24–32.

Barrett, D. (2011, November/December). Answers in your dreams. *Scientific American Mind*, 26–33.

Barrett, L. F. (2006). Are emotions natural kinds? *Perspectives on Psychological Science, 1*, 28–58.

Barretto, R. P., Gillis-Smith, S., Chandrashekar, J., Yarmolinsky, D. A., Schnitzer, M. J., Ryba, N. J., & Zuker, C. S. (2015). The neural representation of taste quality at the periphery. *Nature, 517*, 373–376.

Barrick, M. R., Mount, M. K., & Judge, T. A. (2001). Personality and performance at the beginning of the new millennium: What do we know and where do we go next? *International Journal of Selection and Assessment, 9*, 9–30.

Barry, C. L., McGinty, E. E., Vernick, J. S., & Webster, D. W. (2013). After Newtown—Public opinion on gun policy and mental illness. *New England Journal of Medicine, 368*, 1077–1081.

Bashore, T. R., Ridderinkhof, K. R., & van der Molen, M. W. (1997). The decline of cognitive processing speed in old age. *Current Directions in Psychological Science, 6*, 163–169.

Baskind, D. E. (1997, December 14). Personal communication, from Delta College.

Basu, S., & Basu, D. (2015). The relationship between psychoactive drugs, the brain and psychosis. *International Archives of Addiction Research and Medicine, 1*(003).

Bates, T. C. (2015). The glass is half full and half empty: A population-representative twin study testing if optimism and pessimism are distinct systems. *Journal of Positive Psychology, 10*, 533–542.

Bathje, G. J., & Pryor, J. B. (2011). The relationships of public and self-stigma to seeking mental health services. *Journal of Mental Health Counseling, 33*, 161–177.

Bauer, M., Cassar, A., Chytilová, J., & Henrich, J. (2014). War's enduring effects on the development of egalitarian motivations and in-group biases. *Psychological Science, 25*, 47–57.

Baum, A., & Posluszny, D. M. (1999). Health psychology: Mapping biobehavioral contributions to health and illness. *Annual Review of Psychology, 50*, 137–163.

Baumeister, H., & Härter, M. (2007). Prevalence of mental disorders based on general population surveys. *Social Psychiatry and Psychiatric Epidemiology, 42*, 537–546.

Baumeister, R. F. (2000). Gender differences in erotic plasticity: The female sex drive as socially flexible and responsive. *Psychological Bulletin, 126*, 347–374.

Baumeister, R. F. (2001, April). Violent pride: Do people turn violent because of self-hate, or self-love? *Scientific American*, pp. 96–101.

Baumeister, R. F. (2006, August/September). Violent pride. *Scientific American Mind*, pp. 54–59.

Baumeister, R. F. (2010). *Is there anything good about men? How cultures flourish by exploiting men.* New York: Oxford.

Baumeister, R. F. (2015, April). Conquer yourself, conquer the world. *Scientific American*, pp. 61–65.

Baumeister, R. F., & Bratslavsky, E. (1999). Passion, intimacy, and time: Passionate love as a function of change in intimacy. *Personality and Social Psychology Review, 3*, 49–67.

Baumeister, R. F., Bratslavsky, E., Muraven, M., & Tice, D. M. (1998a). Ego depletion: Is the active self a limited resource? *Journal of Personality and Social Psychology, 74*, 1252–1265.

Baumeister, R. F., Campbell, J. D., Krueger, J. I., & Vohs, K. D. (2003). Does high self-esteem cause better performance, interpersonal success, happiness, or healthier lifestyles? *Psychological Science in the Public Interest, 4*, 1–44.

Baumeister, R. F., Catanese, K. R., & Vohs, K. D. (2001). Is there a gender difference in strength of sex drive? Theoretical views, conceptual distinctions, and a review of relevant evidence. *Personality and Social Psychology Review, 5*, 242–273.

Baumeister, R. F., Dale, K., & Sommer, K. L. (1998b). Freudian defense mechanisms and empirical findings in modern personality and social psychology: Reaction formation, projection, displacement, undoing, isolation, sublimation, and denial. *Journal of Personality, 66*, 1081–1125.

Baumeister, R. F., & Leary, M. R. (1995). The need to belong: Desire for interpersonal attachments as a fundamental human motivation. *Psychological Bulletin, 117*, 497–529.

Baumeister, R. F., & Tice, D. M. (1986). How adolescence became the struggle for self: A historical transformation of psychological development. In J. Suls & A. G. Greenwald (Eds.), *Psychological perspectives on the self* (Vol. 3). Hillsdale, NJ: Erlbaum.

Baumeister, R. F., & Tierney, J. (2012). *Willpower: Rediscovering the greatest human strength.* New York: Penguin.

Baumgardner, A. H., Kaufman, C. M., & Levy, P. E. (1989). Regulating affect interpersonally: When low esteem leads to greater enhancement. *Journal of Personality and Social Psychology, 56*, 907–921.

Baumrind, D. (1966). Effects of authoritative parental control on child behavior. *Child Development*, 887–907.

Baumrind, D. (1967). Child care practices anteceding three patterns of preschool behavior. *Genetic Psychology Monographs, 75*, 43–88.

Baumrind, D. (1996). The discipline controversy revisited. *Family Relations, 45*, 405–414.

Baumrind, D. (2013). Authoritative parenting revisited: History and current status. In R. E. Larzelere, A. S. E. Morris, & A. W. Harrist, (Eds.), *Authoritative parenting: Synthesizing nurturance and discipline for optimal child development* (pp. 11–34). Washington, DC: American Psychological Association.

Baumrind, D., Larzelere, R. E., & Cowan, P. A. (2002). Ordinary physical punishment: Is it harmful? Comment on Gershoff (2002). *Psychological Bulletin, 128*, 602–611.

Bavelier, D., Newport, E. L., & Supalla, T. (2003). Children need natural languages, signed or spoken. *Cerebrum, 5*(1), 19–32.

BBC. (2008, February 26). Anti-depressants "of little use." *BBC News* (news.bbc.co.uk).

Beaman, A. L., & Klentz, B. (1983). The supposed physical attractiveness bias against supporters of the women's movement: A meta-analysis. *Personality and Social Psychology Bulletin, 9*, 544–550.

Beardsley, L. M. (1994). Medical diagnosis and treatment across cultures. In W. J. Lonner & R. Malpass (Eds.), *Psychology and culture* (pp. 279–284). Boston: Allyn & Bacon.

Beauchamp, G. K. (1987). The human preference for excess salt. *American Scientist, 75*, 27–33.

Beauvois, J.-L., Courbet, D., & Oberlé, D. (2012). The prescriptive power of the television host: A transposition of Milgram's obedience paradigm to the context of TV game show. *European Review of Applied Psychology/ Revue Européenne de Psychologie Appliquée, 62*, 111–119.

Beck, A. T., Rush, A. J., Shaw, B. F., & Emery, G. (1979). *Cognitive therapy of depression.* New York: Guilford Press.

Becker, D. V., Kenrick, D. T., Neuberg, S. L., Blackwell, K. C., & Smith, D. M. (2007). The confounded nature of angry men and happy women. *Journal of Personality and Social Psychology, 92*, 179–190.

Becker, M., Cortina, K. S., Tsai, Y., & Eccles, J. S. (2014). Sexual orientation, psychological well-being, and mental health: A longitudinal analysis from adolescence to young adulthood. *Psychology of Sexual Orientation and Gender Diversity, 1*, 132–145.

Becker, S., & Wojtowicz, J. M. (2007). A model of hippocampal neurogenesis in memory and mood disorders. *Trends in Cognitive Sciences, 11*, 70–76.

Becklen, R., & Cervone, D. (1983). Selective looking and the noticing of unexpected events. *Memory and Cognition, 11*, 601–608.

Beckman, M. (2004). Crime, culpability, and the adolescent brain. *Science, 305*, 596–599.

Beeman, M. J., & Chiarello, C. (1998). Complementary right- and left-hemisphere language comprehension. *Current Directions in Psychological Science, 7*, 2–8.

Beer, J. S., & Hughes, B. L. (2010). Neural systems of social comparison and the "above-average" effect. *NeuroImage, 49*, 2671–2679.

Bègue, L., Subra, B., Arvers, P., Muller, D., Bricout, V., & Zorman, M. (2009). A message in a bottle: Extrapharmacological effects of alcohol on aggression. *Journal of Experimental Social Psychology, 45*, 137–142.

Beilock, S. (2010). *Choke: What the secrets of the brain reveal about getting it right when you have to.* New York: Free Press.

Beintner, I., Jacobi, C., & Taylor, C. B. (2012). Effects of an Internet-based prevention programme for eating disorders in the USA and Germany: A meta-analytic review. *European Eating Disorders Review, 20*, 1–8.

Bell, A. P., Weinberg, M. S., & Hammersmith, S. K. (1981). *Sexual preference: Its development in men and women.* Bloomington: Indiana University Press.

Belluck, P. (2013, February 5). People with mental illness more likely to be smokers, study finds. *The New York Times* (nytimes.com).

Belot, M., & Francesconi, M. (2006, November). Can anyone be "the one"? Evidence on mate selection from speed dating. London: Centre for Economic Policy Research (cepr.org).

Belson, K. (2015, September 6). No foul mouths on this field: Football with a New Age twist. *The New York Times* (nytimes.com).

Bem, D., Tressoldi, P. E., Rabeyron, T., & Duggan, M. (2014, April 11). Feeling the future: A meta-analysis of 90 experiments on the anomalous anticipation of random future events. Retrieved from http://papers.ssrn.com/sol3/papers.cfm?abstract_id=2423692

Bem, D. J. (1984). Quoted in *The Skeptical Inquirer, 8*, 194.

Bem, D. J. (2011). Feeling the future: Experimental evidence for anomalous retroactive influences on cognition and affect. *Journal of Personality and Social Psychology, 100*, 407–425.

Bem, S. L. (1987). Masculinity and femininity exist only in the mind of the perceiver. In J. M. Reinisch, L. A. Rosenblum, & S. A. Sanders (Eds.), *Masculinity/femininity: Basic perspectives.* New York: Oxford University Press.

Bem, S. L. (1993). *The lenses of gender.* New Haven, CT: Yale University Press.

Benartzi, S., & Thaler, R. H. (2013). Behavioral economics and the retirement savings crisis. *Science, 339*, 1152–1153.

Benedict, C., Brooks, S. J., O'Daly, O. G., Almen, M. S., Morell, A., Åberg, K., . . . Schiöth, H. B. (2012). Acute sleep deprivation enhances the brain's response to hedonic food stimuli: An fMRI study. *Journal of Clinical Endocrinology and Metabolism, 97*, 2011–2759.

Bennett, W. I. (1995). Beyond overeating. *New England Journal of Medicine, 332*, 673–674.

Ben-Shakhar, G., & Elaad, E. (2003). The validity of psychophysiological detection of information with the guilty knowledge test: A meta-analytic review. *Journal of Applied Psychology, 88*, 131–151.

Benson, P. L., Sharma, A. R., & Roehlkepartain, E. C. (1994). *Growing up adopted: A portrait of adolescents and their families.* Minneapolis: Search Institute.

Berg, J. M., Wall, M., Larson, N., Eisenberg, M. E., Loth, K. A., & Neumark-Sztainer, D. (2014). The unique and additive associations of family functioning and parenting practices with disordered eating behaviors in diverse adolescents. *Journal of Behavioral Medicine, 37*, 205–217.

Berger, B. G., & Motl, R. W. (2000). Exercise and mood: A selective review and synthesis of research employing the profile of mood states. *Journal of Applied Sports Psychology, 12*, 69–92.

Bergsholm, P., Larsen, J. L., Rosendahl, K., & Holsten, F. (1989). Electroconvulsive therapy and cerebral computed tomography. *Acta Psychiatrica Scandinavia, 80*, 566–572.

Berk, L. S., Felten, D. L., Tan, S. A., Bittman, B. B., & Westengard, J. (2001). Modulation of neuroimmune parameters during the eustress of humor-associated mirthful laughter. *Alternative Therapies, 7*, 62–76.

Berkovich-Ohana, A., Glickson, J., & Goldstein, A. (2014). Studying the default mode and its mindfulness-induced changes using EEF functional connectivity. *Social Cognitive and Affective Neuroscience, 9*, 1616–1624.

Berkowitz, L. (1983). Aversively stimulated aggression: Some parallels and differences in research with animals and humans. *American Psychologist, 38*, 1135–1144.

Berkowitz, L. (1989). Frustration-aggression hypothesis: Examination and reformulation. *Psychological Bulletin, 106*, 59–73.

Berman, M., Gladue, B., & Taylor, S. (1993). The effects of hormones, Type A behavior pattern, and provocation on aggression in men. *Motivation and Emotion, 17*, 125–138.

Berman, M. G., Jonides, J., & Kaplan, S. (2008). The cognitive benefits of interacting with nature. *Psychological Science, 19*, 1207–1212.

Bernieri, F., Davis, J., Rosenthal, R., & Knee, C. (1994). Interactional synchrony and rapport: Measuring synchrony in displays devoid of sound and facial affect. *Personality and Social Psychology Bulletin, 20*, 303–311.

Bernstein, D. M., & Loftus, E. F. (2009). The consequences of false memories for food preferences and choices. *Perspectives on Psychological Science, 4*, 135–139.

Bernstein, M. J., & Claypool, H. M. (2012). Social exclusion and pain sensitivity: Why exclusion sometimes hurts and sometimes numbs. *Personality and Social Psychology Bulletin, 38*, 185–196.

Berry, C. M., & Zhao, P. (2015). Addressing criticisms of existing predictive bias research: Cognitive ability test scores still overpredict African Americans' job performance. *Journal of Applied Psychology, 100*, 162–179.

Berscheid, E. (1981). An overview of the psychological effects of physical attractiveness and some comments upon the psychological effects of knowledge of the effects of physical attractiveness. In G. W. Lucker, K. Ribbens, & J. A. McNamara (Eds.), *Psychological aspects of facial form (Craniofacial growth series)* (pp. 1–23). Ann Arbor: Center for Human Growth and Development, University of Michigan.

Berscheid, E. (2010). Love in the fourth dimension. *Annual Review of Psychology, 61*, 1–25.

Berscheid, E., Gangestad, S. W., & Kulakowski, D. (1984). Emotion in close relationships: Implications for relationship counseling. In S. D. Brown & R. W. Lent (Eds.), *Handbook of counseling psychology* (pp. 435–476). New York: Wiley.

Berti, A., Cottini, G., Gandola, M., Pia, L., Smania, N., Stracciari, A., . . . Paulesu, E. (2005). Shared cortical anatomy for motor awareness and motor control. *Science, 309*, 488–491.

Bertrand, M., & Mullainathan, S. (2003). Are Emily and Greg more employable than Lakisha and Jamal? A field experiment on labor market discrimination. Massachusetts Institute of Technology, Department of Economics, Working Paper 03–22.

Bhatt, R. S., Wasserman, E. A., Reynolds, W. F., Jr., & Knauss, K. S. (1988). Conceptual behavior in pigeons: Categorization of both familiar and novel examples from four classes of natural and artificial stimuli. *Journal of Experimental Psychology: Animal Behavior Processes, 14*, 219–234.

Bick, J., Zhu, T., Stamoulis, C., Fox, N. A., Zeanah, C., & Nelson, C. A. (2015). Effect of early institutionalization and foster care on long-term white matter development: A randomized clinical trial. *JAMA Pediatrics, 169*, 211–219.

Bickman, L. (1999). Practice makes perfect and other myths about mental health services. *American Psychologist, 54*, 965–978.

Biederman, I., & Vessel, E. A. (2006). Perceptual pleasure and the brain. *American Scientist, 94*, 247–253.

Bienvenu, O. J., Davydow, D. S., & Kendler, K. S. (2011). Psychiatric "diseases" versus behavioral disorders and degree of genetic influence. *Psychological Medicine, 41*, 33–40.

Bilefsky, D. (2009, March 11). Europeans debate castration of sex offenders. *The New York Times* (nytimes.com).

Billock, V. A., & Tsou, B. H. (2012). Elementary visual hallucinations and their relationships to neural pattern-forming mechanisms. *Psychological Bulletin, 138*, 744–774.

Bird, C. D., & Emery, N. J. (2009). Rooks use stones to raise the water level to reach a floating worm. *Current Biology, 19*, 1410–1414.

Birnbaum, G. E., & Reis, H. T. (2012). When does responsiveness pique sexual interest? Attachment and sexual desire in initial acquaintanceships. *Personality and Social Psychology Bulletin, 38*(7), 946–958.

Birnbaum, G. E., Reis, H. T., Mikulincer, M., Gillath, O., & Orpaz, A. (2006). When sex is more than just sex: Attachment orientations, sexual experience, and relationship quality. *Journal of Personality and Social Psychology, 91*, 929–943.

Birnbaum, S. G., Yuan, P. X., Wang, M., Vijayraghavan, S., Bloom, A. K., Davis, D. J., . . . Arnsten, A. F. T. (2004). Protein kinase C overactivity impairs prefrontal cortical regulation of working memory. *Science, 306*, 882–884.

Biro, D., Humle, T., Koops, K., Sousa, C., Hayashi, M., & Matsuzawa, T. (2010a). Chimpanzee mothers at Bossou, Guinea carry the mummified remains of their dead infants. *Current Biology, 20*, R351–R352.

Biro, F. M., Galvez, M. D., Greenspan, L. C., Succop, P. A., Vangeepuram, N., Pinney, S. M., . . . Wolff, M. S. (2010b). Pubertal assessment method and baseline characteristics in a mixed longitudinal study of girls. *Pediatrics, 126*, e583–e590.

Biro, F. M., Greenspan, L. C., & Galvez, M. P. (2012). Puberty in girls of the 21st century. *Journal of Pediatric and Adolescent Gynecology, 25*, 289–294.

Bishop, G. D. (1991). Understanding the understanding of illness: Lay disease representations. In J. A. Skelton & R. T. Croyle (Eds.), *Mental representation in health and illness* (pp. 32–59). New York: Springer-Verlag.

Bjork, E. L., & Bjork, R. (2011). Making things hard on yourself, but in a good way: Creating desirable difficulties to enhance learning. In M. A. Gernsbacher, M. A. Pew, L. M. Hough, & J. R. Pomerantz (Eds.), *Psychology and the real world.* New York: Worth Publishers.

Bjorklund, D. F., & Green, B. L. (1992). The adaptive nature of cognitive immaturity. *American Psychologist, 47*, 46–54.

Blake, A., Nazarian, M., & Castel, A. (2015). The Apple of the mind's eye: Everyday attention, metamemory, and reconstructive memory for the Apple logo. *Quarterly Journal of Experimental Psychology, 68*, 858–865.

Blake, W. (2013, March). Voices from solitary: A sentence worse than death. Solitary Watch (solitarywatch.com).

Blakemore, S.-J. (2008). Development of the social brain during adolescence. *Quarterly Journal of Experimental Psychology, 61*, 40–49.

Blakeslee, S. (2006, January 10). Cells that read minds. *The New York Times* (nytimes.com).

Blanchard, R. (2004). Quantitative and theoretical analyses of the relation between older brothers and homosexuality in men. *Journal of Theoretical Biology, 230,* 173–187.

Blanchard, R. (2008a). Review and theory of handedness, birth order, and homosexuality in men. *Laterality, 13,* 51–70.

Blanchard, R. (2008b). Sex ratio of older siblings in heterosexual and homosexual, right-handed and non-right-handed men. *Archives of Sexual Behavior, 37,* 977–981.

Blanchard, R. (2014, July). Detecting and correcting for family size differences in the study of sexual orientation and fraternal birth order. *Archives of Sexual Behavior, 43,* 845–852.

Blanchard-Fields, F. (2007). Everyday problem solving and emotion: An adult developmental perspective. *Current Directions in Psychological Science, 16,* 26–31.

Blanke, O. (2012). Multisensory brain mechanisms of bodily self-consciousness. *Nature Reviews Neuroscience, 13,* 556–571.

Blanken, L. M. E., Mous, S. E., Ghassabian, A., Muetzel, R. L., Schoemaker, N. K., El Marroun, H., . . . White, T. (2015). Cortical morphology in 6- to 10-year old children with autistic traits: A population-based neuroimaging study. *The American Journal of Psychiatry, 172,* 479–486.

Blascovich, J. & Mendes, W. B. (2010). Social psychophysiology and embodiment. In S. T. Fiske, D. T. Gilbert, & G. Lindzey (Eds.), *The handbook of social psychology* (5th ed., pp. 194–227). New York: John Wiley & Sons.

Blass, T. (1999). The Milgram paradigm after 35 years: Some things we now know about obedience to authority. *Journal of Applied Social Psychology, 29,* 955–978.

Blatt, S. J., Sanislow, C. A., III, Zuroff, D. C., & Pilkonis, P. (1996). Characteristics of effective therapists: Further analyses of data from the National Institute of Mental Health Treatment of Depression Collaborative Research Program. *Journal of Consulting and Clinical Psychology, 64,* 1276–1284.

Bleidorn, W., Arslan, R. C., Denissen, J. J. A., Rentfrow, P. J., Gebauer, J. E., Potter, J., & Gosling, S. D. (2016). Age and gender differences in self-esteem—A cross-cultural window. *Journal of Personality and Social Psychology.* Advance online publication. http://dx.doi.org/10.1037/pspp0000078

BLF. (2012). *The impact of cannabis on your lungs.* London: British Lung Foundation.

Blinkhorn, V., Lyons, M., & Almond, L. (2015). The ultimate femme fatale: Narcissism predicts serious and aggressive sexually coercive behavior in females. *Personality and Individual Differences, 87,* 219–223.

Bloom, B. C. (Ed.). (1985). *Developing talent in young people.* New York: Ballantine.

Bloom, F. E. (1993, January/February). What's new in neurotransmitters. *Brain-Work,* pp. 7–9.

Bloom, P. (2000). *How children learn the meanings of words.* Cambridge, MA: MIT Press.

Bockting, W. O. (2014). Transgender identity development. In W. O. Bockting (Ed.), *APA handbook of sexuality and psychology* (Vol. 1, pp. 739–758). Washington, DC: American Psychological Association.

Bodenmann, G., Meuwly, N., Germann, J., Nussbeck, F. W., Heinrichs, M. & Bradbury, T. N. (2015). Effects of stress on the social support provided by men and women in intimate relationships. *Psychological Science, 26,* 1584–1594.

Boecker, H., Sprenger, T., Spilker, M. E., Henriksen, G., Koppenhoefer, M., Wagner, K. J., . . . Tolle, T. R. (2008). The runner's high: Opioidergic mechanisms in the human brain. *Cerebral Cortex, 18,* 2523–2531.

Boehm, J. K., & Kubzansky, L. D. (2012). The heart's content: The association between positive psychological

well-being and cardiovascular health. *Psychological Bulletin, 138,* 655–691.

Boehm, J. K., Trudel-Fitzgerald, C., Kivimaki, M., & Kubzansky, L. D. (2015). The prospective association between positive psychological well-being and diabetes. *Health Psychology, 34,* 1013–1021.

Boesch-Achermann, H., & Boesch, C. (1993). Tool use in wild chimpanzees: New light from dark forests. *Current Directions in Psychological Science, 2,* 18–21.

Bogaert, A. F. (2003). Number of older brothers and sexual orientation: New texts and the attraction/behavior distinction in two national probability samples. *Journal of Personality and Social Psychology, 84,* 644–652.

Bogaert, A. F. (2004). Asexuality: Prevalence and associated factors in a national probability sample. *Journal of Sex Research, 41,* 279–287.

Bogaert, A. F. (2006a). Biological versus nonbiological older brothers and men's sexual orientation. *PNAS, 103,* 10771–10774.

Bogaert, A. F. (2006b). Toward a conceptual understanding of asexuality. *Review of General Psychology, 10,* 241–250.

Bogaert, A. F. (2010). Physical development and sexual orientation in men and women: An analysis of NATSAL-2000. *Archives of Sexual Behavior, 39,* 110–116.

Bogaert, A. F. (2012). *Understanding asexuality.* Lanham, MD: Rowman & Littlefield.

Bogaert, A. F. (2015). Asexuality: What it is and why it matters. *Journal of Sex Research, 52,* 362–379.

Boggiano, A. K., Harackiewicz, J. M., Bessette, M. M., & Main, D. S. (1985). Increasing children's interest through performance-contingent reward. *Social Cognition, 3,* 400–411.

Bolger, N., DeLongis, A., Kessler, R. C., & Schilling, E. A. (1989). Effects of daily stress on negative mood. *Journal of Personality and Social Psychology, 57,* 808–818.

Bolmont, M., Cacioppo, J. T., & Cacioppo, S. (2014). Love is in the gaze: An eye-tracking study of love and sexual desire. *Psychological Science, 25,* 1748–1756.

Boly, M., Garrido, M. I., Gosseries, O., Bruno, M.-A., Boveroux, P., Schnakers, C., . . . Friston, K. (2011). Preserved feed-forward but impaired top-down processes in the vegetative state. *Science, 332,* 858–862.

Bonanno, G. A. (2004). Loss, trauma, and human resilience: Have we underestimated the human capacity to thrive after extremely aversive events? *American Psychologist, 59,* 20–38.

Bonanno, G. A. (2005). Adult resilience to potential trauma. *Current Directions in Psychological Science, 14,* 135–137.

Bonanno, G. A. (2009). *The other side of sadness: What the new science of bereavement tells us about life after loss.* New York: Basic Books.

Bonanno, G. A., Brewin, C. R., Kaniasty, K., & La Greca, A. M. (2010). Weighing the costs of disaster: Consequences, risks, and resilience in individuals, families, and communities. *Psychological Science in the Public Interest, 11,* 1–49.

Bonanno, G. A., Galea, S., Bucciarelli, A., & Vlahov, D. (2006). Psychological resilience after disaster. *Psychological Science, 17,* 181–186.

Bonanno, G. A., Galea, S., Bucciarelli, A., & Vlahov, D. (2007). What predicts psychological resilience after disaster? The role of demographics, resources, and life stress. *Journal of Consulting and Clinical Psychology, 75*(5), 671–682.

Bonanno, G. A., & Kaltman, S. (1999). Toward an integrative perspective on bereavement. *Psychological Bulletin, 125,* 760–777.

Bonanno, G. A., Kennedy, P., Galatzer-Levy, I. R., Lude, P., & Elfström, M. L. (2012). Trajectories of resilience, depression, and anxiety following spinal cord injury. *Rehabilitation Psychology, 57,* 236–247.

Bonanno, G. A., Westphal, M., & Mancini, A. D. (2011). Resilience to loss and potential trauma. *Annual Review of Clinical Psychology, 11,* 511–535.

Bond, C. F., Jr., & DePaulo, B. M. (2006). Accuracy of deception judgments. *Personality and Social Psychology Review, 10,* 214–234.

Bond, C. F., Jr., & DePaulo, B. M. (2008). Individual differences in detecting deception: Accuracy and bias. *Psychological Bulletin, 134,* 477–492.

Bond, M. H., Lun, V. M.-C., Chan, J., Chan, W. W.-Y., & Wong, D. (2012). Enacting modesty in Chinese culture: The joint contribution of personal characteristics and contextual features. *Asian Journal of Social Psychology, 15,* 14–25.

Bond, R., & Smith, P. B. (1996). Culture and conformity: A meta-analysis of studies using Asch's (1952b, 1956) line judgment task. *Psychological Bulletin, 119,* 111–137.

Bonetti, L., Campbell, M. A., & Gilmore, L. (2010). The relationship of loneliness and social anxiety with children's and adolescents' online communication. *Cyberpsychology, Behavior, and Social Networking, 13,* 279–285.

Bonezzi, A., Brendl, C. M., & DeAngelis, M. (2011). Stuck in the middle: The psychophysics of goal pursuit. *Psychological Science, 22,* 607–612.

Bono, J. E., & Judge, T. A. (2004). Personality and transformational and transactional leadership: A meta-analysis. *Journal of Applied Psychology, 89,* 901–910.

Bora, E., & Pantelis, C. (2013). Theory of mind impairments in first-episode psychosis, individuals at ultra-high risk for psychosis and in first-degree relatives of schizophrenia: Systematic review and meta-analysis. *Schizophrenia Research, 144,* 31–36.

Bornstein, M. H., Cote, L. R., Maital, S., Painter, K., Park, S.-Y., Pascual, L., . . . Vyt, A. (2004). Cross-linguistic analysis of vocabulary in young children: Spanish, Dutch, French, Hebrew, Italian, Korean, and American English. *Child Development, 75,* 1115–1139.

Bornstein, M. H., Tal, J., Rahn, C., Galperin, C. Z., Pêcheux, M.-G., Lamour, M., . . . Tamis-LeMonda, C. S. (1992a). Functional analysis of the contents of maternal speech to infants of 5 and 13 months in four cultures: Argentina, France, Japan, and the United States. *Developmental Psychology, 28,* 593–603.

Bornstein, M. H., Tamis-LeMonda, C. S., Tal, J., Ludemann, P., Toda, S., Rahn, C. W., . . . Vardi, D. (1992b). Maternal responsiveness to infants in three societies: The United States, France, and Japan. *Child Development, 63,* 808–821.

Bornstein, R. F. (1989). Exposure and affect: Overview and meta-analysis of research, 1968–1987. *Psychological Bulletin, 106,* 265–289.

Bornstein, R. F. (1999). Source amnesia, misattribution, and the power of unconscious perceptions and memories. *Psychoanalytic Psychology, 16,* 155–178.

Bornstein, R. F., Galley, D. J., Leone, D. R., & Kale, A. R. (1991). The temporal stability of ratings of parents: Test-retest reliability and influence of parental contact. *Journal of Social Behavior and Personality, 6,* 641–649.

Boroditsky, L. (2009, June 12). How does our language shape the way we think? *The Edge* (edge.org).

Boron, J. B., Willis, S. L., & Schaie, K. W. (2007). Cognitive training gain as a predictor of mental status. *Journal of Gerontology: Series B: Psychological Sciences and Social Sciences, 62B*(1), 45–52.

Bossong, M. G., Jansma, J. M., van Hell, H. H., Jagerm, G., Oudman, E., Saliasi, E., . . . Ramsey, N. F. (2012). Effects of delta-9-tetrahydrocannabinol in human working memory function. *Biological Psychiatry, 71,* 693–699.

Bostwick, J. M., & Pankratz, V. S. (2000). Affective disorders and suicide risk: A re-examination. *American Journal of Psychiatry, 157,* 1925–1932.

Bosworth, R. G., & Dobkins, K. R. (1999). Left-hemisphere dominance for motion processing in deaf signers. *Psychological Science, 10,* 256–262.

Bothwell, R. K., Brigham, J. C., & Malpass, R. S. (1989). Cross-racial identification. *Personality and Social Psychology Bulletin, 15,* 19–25.

Bouchard, T. J., Jr. (2004). Genetic influence on human psychological traits. *Current Directions in Psychological Science, 13,* 148–151.

Bouchard, T. J., Jr. (2014). Genes, evolution and intelligence. *Behavior Genetics, 44,* 549–577.

Boucher, J., Mayes, A., & Bigham, S. (2012). Memory in autistic spectrum disorder. *Psychological Bulletin, 138,* 458–496.

Bowden, E. M., & Beeman, M. J. (1998). Getting the right idea: Semantic activation in the right hemisphere may help solve insight problems. *Psychological Science, 9,* 435–440.

Bowen, S., Witkiewitz, K., Dillworth, T. M., Chawla, N., Simpson, T. L., Ostafin, B. D., . . . Marlatt, G. A. (2006). Mindfulness meditation and substance use in an incarcerated population. *Psychology of Addictive Behaviors, 20,* 343–347.

Bower, B. (2009, February 14). The dating go round. *Science News,* pp. 22–25.

Bower, G. H. (1986). Prime time in cognitive psychology. In P. Eelen & O. Fontaine (Eds.), *Behavior therapy: Beyond the conditioning paradigm* (pp. 22–47). Leuven, Belgium: Leuven University Press.

Bower, G. H., & Morrow, D. G. (1990). Mental models in narrative comprehension. *Science, 247,* 44–48.

Bower, J. M., & Parsons, L. M. (2003, August). Rethinking the "lesser brain." *Scientific American,* pp. 50–57.

Bowers, J. S., Mattys, S. L., & Gage, S. H. (2009). Preserved implicit knowledge of a forgotten childhood language. *Psychological Science, 20,* 1064–1069.

Bowler, M. C., & Woehr, D. J. (2006). A meta-analytic evaluation of the impact of dimension and exercise factors on assessment center ratings. *Journal of Applied Psychology, 91,* 1114–1124.

Bowling, N. A., Eschleman, K. J., & Wang, Q. (2010). A meta-analytic examination of the relationship between job satisfaction and subjective well-being. *Journal of Occupational and Organizational Psychology, 83,* 915–934.

Boxer, P., Huesmann, L. R., Bushman, B. J., O'Brien, M., & Moceri, D. (2009). The role of violent media preference in cumulative developmental risk for violence and general aggression. *Journal of Youth and Adolescence, 38,* 417–428.

Boyatzis, C. J. (2012). Spiritual development during childhood and adolescence. In L. J. Miller (Ed.), *The Oxford handbook of psychology and spirituality* (pp. 151–164). New York: Oxford University Press.

Boyatzis, C. J., Matillo, G. M., & Nebitt, K. M. (1995). Effects of the "Mighty Morphin Power Rangers" on children's aggression with peers. *Child Study Journal, 25,* 45–55.

Boyce, C. J., & Wood, A. M. (2011). Personality prior to disability determines adaptation: Agreeable individuals recover lost life satisfaction faster and more completely. *Psychological Science, 22,* 1397–1402.

Boyce, C. J., Wood, A. M., Daly, M., & Sedikides, C. (2015). Personality change following unemployment. *Journal of Applied Psychology, 100,* 991–1011.

Braden, J. P. (1994). *Deafness, deprivation, and IQ.* New York: Plenum.

Bradley, D. R., Dumais, S. T., & Petry, H. M. (1976). Reply to Cavonius. *Nature, 261,* 78.

Bradley, R. B., Binder, E. B., Epstein, M. P., Tang, Y., Nair, H. P., Liu, W., . . . Ressler, K. J. (2008). Influence of child abuse on adult depression: Moderation by the corticotropin-releasing hormone receptor gene. *Archives of General Psychiatry, 65,* 190–200.

Brainerd, C. J. (1996). Piaget: A centennial celebration. *Psychological Science, 7,* 191–195.

Brang, D., Edwards, L., Ramachandran, V. S., & Coulson, S. (2008). Is the sky 2? Contextual priming in grapheme-color synaesthesia. *Psychological Science, 19,* 421–428.

Brannan, D., Biswas-Diener, R., Mohr, C., Mortazavi, S., & Stein, N. (2013). Friends and family: A cross-cultural investigation of social support and subjective well-being among college students. *Journal of Positive Psychology, 8,* 65–75.

Brannon, L. A., & Brock, T. C. (1993). Comment on report of HIV infection in rural Florida: Failure of instructions to correct for gross underestimation of phantom sex partners in perception of AIDS risk. *New England Journal of Medicine, 328,* 1351–1352.

Bransford, J. D., & Johnson, M. K. (1972). Contextual prerequisites for understanding: Some investigations of comprehension and recall. *Journal of Verbal Learning and Verbal Behavior, 11,* 717–726.

Brasel, S. A., & Gips, J. (2011). Media multitasking behavior: Concurrent television and computer usage. *Cyberpsychology, Behavior, and Social Networking, 14,* 527–534.

Brauhardt, A., Rudolph, A., & Hilbert, A. (2014). Implicit cognitive processes in binge-eating disorder and obesity. *Journal of Behavioral Therapy and Experimental Psychiatry, 45,* 285–290.

Braun, S. (1996). New experiments underscore warnings on maternal drinking. *Science, 273,* 738–739.

Braun, S. (2001, Spring). Seeking insight by prescription. *Cerebrum,* pp. 10–21.

Braunstein, G. D., Sundwall, D. A., Katz, M., Shifren, J. L., Buster, J. E., Simon, J. A., . . . Watts, N. B. (2005). Safety and efficacy of a testosterone patch for the treatment of hypoactive sexual desire disorder in surgically menopausal women: A randomized, placebo-controlled trial. *Archives of Internal Medicine, 165,* 1582–1589.

Bray, D. W., & Byham, W. C. (1991, Winter). Assessment centers and their derivatives. *Journal of Continuing Higher Education,* pp. 8–11.

Bray, D. W., & Byham, W. C., interviewed by Mayes, B. T. (1997). Insights into the history and future of assessment centers: An interview with Dr. Douglas W. Bray and Dr. William Byham. *Journal of Social Behavior and Personality, 12,* 3–12.

Brayne, C., Spiegelhalter, D. J., Dufouil, C., Chi, L.-Y., Dening, T. R., Paykel, E. S., . . . Huppert, F. A. (1999). Estimating the true extent of cognitive decline in the old old. *Journal of the American Geriatrics Society, 47,* 1283–1288.

Breedlove, S. M. (1997). Sex on the brain. *Nature, 389,* 801.

Brehm, S., & Brehm, J. W. (1981). *Psychological reactance: A theory of freedom and control.* New York: Academic Press.

Breslin, C. W., & Safer, M. A. (2011). Effects of event valence on long-term memory for two baseball championship games. *Psychological Science, 22,* 1408–1412.

Brewer, J. A., Malik, S., Babuscio, T. A., Nich, C., Johnson, H. E., Deleone, C. M., . . . Rounsaville, B. J. (2011). Mindfulness training for smoking cessation: Results from a randomized controlled trial. *Drug and Alcohol Dependence, 119,* 72–80.

Brewer, W. F. (1977). Memory for the pragmatic implications of sentences. *Memory & Cognition, 5,* 673–678.

Brewin, C. R., Andrews, B., Rose, S., & Kirk, M. (1999). Acute stress disorder and posttraumatic stress disorder in victims of violent crime. *American Journal of Psychiatry, 156,* 360–366.

Briley, D. A., & Tucker-Drob, E. (2014). Genetic and environmental continuity in personality development: A meta-analysis. *Psychological Bulletin, 140,* 1303–1331.

Briscoe, D. (1997, February 16). Women lawmakers still not in charge. *Grand Rapids Press,* p. A23.

Brislin, R. W. (1988). Increasing awareness of class, ethnicity, culture, and race by expanding on students' own experiences. In I. Cohen (Ed.), *The G. Stanley Hall lecture series.* Washington, DC: American Psychological Association.

Broadbent, E., Kahokehr, A., Booth, R. J., Thomas, J., Windsor, J. A., Buchanan, C. M., . . . Hill, A. G. (2012). A brief relaxation intervention reduces stress and improves surgical wound healing response: A randomized trial. *Brain, Behavior, and Immunity, 26,* 212–217.

Brody, J. E. (2003, September 30). Addiction: A brain ailment, not a moral lapse. *The New York Times* (nytimes.com).

Brody, S., & Tillmann, H. C. (2006). The post-orgasmic prolactin increase following intercourse is greater than following masturbation and suggests greater satiety. *Biological Psychology, 71,* 312–315.

Broman, C. L. (1996). Coping with personal problems. In H. W. Neighbors & J. S. Jackson (Eds.), *Mental health in Black America* (pp. 117–129). Thousand Oaks, CA: Sage.

Bromet, E., Andrade, L. H., Hwang, I., Sampson, N. A., Alonso, J., de Girolamo, G., . . . Kessler, R. C. (2011). Cross-national epidemiology of DSM-IV major depressive episode. *BMC Medicine, 9,* 90. http://www.biomedcentral.com/1741-7015/9/90

Brooks, R. (2012). "Asia's missing women" as a problem in applied evolutionary psychology? *Evolutionary Psychology, 12,* 910–925.

Brose, A., de Roover, K., Ceulemans, E., & Kuppens, P. (2015). Older adults' affective experiences across 100 days are less variable and less complex than younger adults'. *Psychology and Aging, 30,* 194–208.

Brown, A. S., & Patterson, P. H. (2011). Maternal infection and schizophrenia: Implications for prevention. *Schizophrenia Bulletin, 37,* 284–290.

Brown, A. S., Begg, M. D., Gravenstein, S., Schaefer, C. A., Wyatt, R. J., Bresnahan, M., . . . Susser, E. S. (2004). Serologic evidence of prenatal influenza in the etiology of schizophrenia. *Archives of General Psychiatry, 61,* 774–780.

Brown, A. S., Schaefer, C. A., Wyatt, R. J., Goetz, R., Begg, M. D., Gorman, J. M., & Susser, E. S. (2000). Maternal exposure to respiratory infections and adult schizophrenia spectrum disorders: A prospective birth cohort study. *Schizophrenia Bulletin, 26,* 287–295.

Brown, E. L., & Deffenbacher, K. (1979). *Perception and the senses.* New York: Oxford University Press.

Brown, J. A. (1958). Some tests of the decay theory of immediate memory. *Quarterly Journal of Experimental Psychology, 10,* 12–21.

Brown, K. W., Goodman, R. J., & Inzlicht, M. (2013). Dispositional mindfulness and the attenuation of neural responses to emotional stimuli. *Social Cognitive and Affective Neuroscience, 8,* 93–99.

Brown, P. C., Roediger, H. L., III, & McDaniel, M. A. (2014a). *Make it stick: The science of successful learning.* Cambridge, MA: Harvard University Press.

Brown, R. P., Imura, M., & Mayeux, L. (2014b). Honor and the stigma of mental healthcare. *Personality and Social Psychology Bulletin, 40*, 1119–1131.

Brown, S. L., Brown, R. M., House, J. S., & Smith, D. M. (2008). Coping with spousal loss: Potential buffering effects of self-reported helping behavior. *Personality and Social Psychology Bulletin, 34*, 849–861.

Browning, C. (1992). *Ordinary men: Reserve police battalion 101 and the final solution in Poland.* New York: HarperCollins.

Browning, R. (1868). "The ring and the book. IV—Tertium quid." New York: Thomas Y. Crowell.

Bruce-Keller, A. J., Keller, J. N., & Morrison, C. D. (2009). Obesity and vulnerability of the CNS. *Biochemica et Biophysica Acta, 1792*, 395–400.

Bruck, M., & Ceci, S. J. (1999). The suggestibility of children's memory. *Annual Review of Psychology, 50*, 419–439.

Bruck, M., & Ceci, S. J. (2004). Forensic developmental psychology: Unveiling four common misconceptions. *Current Directions in Psychological Science, 15*, 229–232.

Bruer, J. T. (1999). *The myth of the first three years: A new understanding of early brain development and lifelong learning.* New York: Free Press.

Brummelman, E., Thomaes, S., Nelemans, S. A., Orobio de Castro, B., Overbeek, G., & Bushman, B. J. (2015). Origins of narcissism in children. *PNAS, 112*, 3659–3662.

Brunner, M., Gogol, K. M., Sonnleitner, P., Keller, U., Krauss, S., & Preckel, F. (2013). Gender differences in the mean level, variability, and profile shape of student achievement: Results from 41 countries. *Intelligence, 41*, 378–395.

Buchanan, R. W., Kreyenbuhl, J., Kelly, D. L., Noel, J. M., Boggs, D. L., Fischer, B. A., . . . Schizophrenic Patient Outcomes Research Team (PORT). (2010). The 2009 schizophrenia PORT psychopharmacological treatment recommendations and summary statements. *Schizophrenia Bulletin, 36*, 71–93.

Buchanan, T. W. (2007). Retrieval of emotional memories. *Psychological Bulletin, 133*, 761–779.

Buck, L. B., & Axel, R. (1991). A novel multigene family may encode odorant receptors: A molecular basis for odor recognition. *Cell, 65*, 175–187.

Buckholtz, J. W., Treadway, M. T., Cowan, R. L., Woodward, N. D., Benning, S. D., Li, R., . . . Zald, D. H. (2010). Mesolimbic dopamine reward system hypersensitivity in individuals with psychopathic traits. *Nature Neuroscience, 13*, 419–421.

Buckingham, M. (2007). *Go put your strengths to work: 6 powerful steps to achieve outstanding performance.* New York: Free Press.

Buckingham, M., & Clifton, D. O. (2001). *Now, discover your strengths.* New York: Free Press.

Buckley, C. (2007, January 3). Man is rescued by stranger on subway tracks. *The New York Times* (nytimes.com).

Buckley, K. E., & Leary, M. R. (2001). *Perceived acceptance as a predictor of social, emotional, and academic outcomes.* Paper presented at the Society of Personality and Social Psychology annual convention.

Buehler, R., Griffin, D., & Ross, M. (1994). Exploring the "planning fallacy": Why people underestimate their task completion times. *Journal of Personality and Social Psychology, 67*, 366–381.

Buehler, R., Griffin, D., & Ross, M. (2002). Inside the planning fallacy: The causes and consequences of optimistic time predictions. In T. Gilovich, D. Griffin, & D. Kahneman (Eds.), *Heuristics and biases: The psychology of intuitive judgment* (pp. 250–270). Cambridge: Cambridge University Press.

Buffardi, L. E., & Campbell, W. K. (2008). Narcissism and social networking web sites. *Personality and Social Psychology Bulletin, 34*, 1303–1314.

Buhle, J. T., Stevens, B. L., Friedman, J. J., & Wager, T. D. (2012). Distraction and placebo: Two separate routes to pain control. *Psychological Science, 23*, 246–253.

Buka, S. L., Tsuang, M. T., Torrey, E. F., Klebanoff, M. A., Wagner, R. L., & Yolken, R. H. (2001). Maternal infections and subsequent psychosis among offspring. *Archives of General Psychiatry, 58*, 1032–1037.

Bullock, B., & Murray, G. (2014). Reduced amplitude of the 24 hour activity rhythm: A biomarker of vulnerability to bipolar disorder? *Clinical Psychological Science, 2*, 86–96.

Burcusa, S. L., & Iacono, W. G. (2007). Risk for recurrence in depression. *Clinical Psychology Review, 27*, 959–985.

Burger, J. M. (2009). Replicating Milgram: Would people still obey today? *American Psychologist, 64*, 1–11.

Burgess, M., Enzle, M. E., & Schmaltz, R. (2004). Defeating the potentially deleterious effects of externally imposed deadlines: Practitioners' rules-of-thumb. *Personality and Social Psychology Bulletin, 30*, 868–877.

Buri, J. R., Louiselle, P. A., Misukanis, T. M., & Mueller, R. A. (1988). Effects of parental authoritarianism and authoritativeness on self-esteem. *Personality and Social Psychology Bulletin, 14*, 271–282.

Burish, T. G., & Carey, M. P. (1986). Conditioned aversive responses in cancer chemotherapy patients: Theoretical and developmental analysis. *Journal of Counseling and Clinical Psychology, 54*, 593–600.

Burke, D. M., & Shafto, M. A. (2004). Aging and language production. *Current Directions in Psychological Science, 13*, 21–24.

Burke, M., Adamic, L. A., & Marciniak, K. (2013, July). *Families on Facebook.* Paper presented at the Seventh International AAAI Conference on Weblogs and Social Media, Cambridge, MA. Retrieved from http://www.aaai.org/ocs/index.php/ICWSM/ICWSM13/paper/view/5992

Burns, B. C. (2004). The effects of speed on skilled chess performance. *Psychological Science, 15*, 442–447.

Busby, D. M., Carroll, J. S., & Willoughby, B. J. (2010). Compatibility or restraint? The effects of sexual timing on marriage relationships. *Journal of Family Psychology, 24*, 766–774.

Bushdid, C., Magnasco, M. O., Vosshall, L. B., & Keller, A. (2014). Humans can discriminate more than 1 trillion olfactory stimuli. *Science, 343*, 1370–1372.

Bushman, B. J., & Anderson, C. A. (2009). Comfortably numb: Desensitizing effects of violent media on helping others. *Psychological Science, 20*, 273–277.

Bushman, B. J., Bonacci, A. M., van Dijk, M., & Baumeister, R. F. (2003). Narcissism, sexual refusal, and aggression: Testing a narcissistic reactance model of sexual coercion. *Journal of Personality and Social Psychology, 84*, 1027–1040.

Bushman, B. J., & Huesmann, L. R. (2010). Aggression. In S. T. Fiske, D. T. Gilbert, & G. Lindzey (Eds.), *Handbook of social psychology* (5th ed., Ch. 23, pp. 833–863). New York: John Wiley & Sons.

Bushman, B. J., Moeller, S. J., & Crocker, J. (2011). Sweets, sex, or self-esteem? Comparing the value of self-esteem boosts with other pleasant rewards. *Journal of Personality, 79*, 993–1012.

Bushman, B. J., Ridge, R. D., Das, E., Key, C. W., & Busath, G. L. (2007). When God sanctions killing: Effects of scriptural violence on aggression. *Psychological Science, 18*, 204–207.

Buss, A. H. (1989). Personality as traits. *American Psychologist, 44*, 1378–1388.

Buss, D. M. (1994). The strategies of human mating: People worldwide are attracted to the same qualities in the opposite sex. *American Scientist, 82*, 238–249.

Buss, D. M. (1995). Evolutionary psychology: A new paradigm for psychological science. *Psychological Inquiry, 6*, 1–30.

Buss, D. M. (2008). Female sexual psychology. World Question Center 2008 (edge.org).

Busteed, B. (2012, August 27). College grads need to interview the job. *Huffington Post* (huffingtonpost.com).

Buster, J. E., Kingsberg, S. A., Aguirre, O., Brown, C., Breaux, J. G., Buch, A., . . . Casson, P. (2005). Testosterone patch for low sexual desire in surgically menopausal women: A randomized trial. *Obstetrics and Gynecology, 105*, 944–952.

Butler, A., Oruc, I., Fox, C. J., & Barton, J. J. S. (2008). Factors contributing to the adaptation aftereffects of facial expression. *Brain Research, 1191*, 116–126.

Butler, R. A. (1954, February). Curiosity in monkeys. *Scientific American*, pp. 70–75.

Butts, M. M., Casper, W. J., & Yang, T. S. (2013). How important are work–family support policies? A meta-analytic investigation of their effects on employee outcomes. *Journal of Applied Psychology, 98*, 1–25.

Buxton, O. M., Cain, S. W., O'Connor, S. P., Porter, J. H., Duffy, J. F., Wang, W., . . . Shea, S. A. (2012). Adverse metabolic consequences in humans of prolonged sleep restriction combined with circadian disruption. *Science Translational Medicine, 4*, 129–143.

Byrne, D. (1982). Predicting human sexual behavior. In A. G. Kraut (Ed.), *The G. Stanley Hall lecture series* (Vol. 2). Washington, DC: American Psychological Association.

Byrne, R. W. (1991, May/June). Brute intellect. *The Sciences*, pp. 42–47.

Byrne, R. W., Bates, L. A., & Moss, C. J. (2009). Elephant cognition in primate perspective. *Comparative Cognition & Behavior Reviews, 4*, 1–15.

Byron, K., & Khazanchi, S. (2011). A meta-analytic investigation of the relationship of state and trait anxiety to performance on figural and verbal creative tasks. *Personality and Social Psychology Bulletin, 37*, 269–283.

Cacioppo, J. T., Cacioppo, S., Gonzaga, G. C., Ogburn, E. L., & VanderWeele, T. J. (2013). Marital satisfaction and break-ups differ across on-line and off-line meeting venues. *PNAS, 110*, 10135–10140.

Cacioppo, J. T., & Hawkley, L. C. (2009). Perceived social isolation and cognition. *Trends in Cognitive Sciences, 13*, 447–454.

Cacioppo, J. T., & Patrick, C. (2008). *Loneliness.* New York: W. W. Norton.

Caddick, A., & Porter, L. E. (2012). Exploring a model of professionalism in multiple perpetrator violent crime in the UK. *Criminological & Criminal Justice: An International Journal, 12*, 61–82.

Cain, S. (2012). *Quiet: The power of introverts in a world that can't stop talking.* New York: Crown.

Calati, R., De Ronchi, D., Bellini, M., & Serretti, A. (2011). The 5-HTTLPR polymorphism and eating disorders: A meta-analysis. *International Journal of Eating Disorders, 44*, 191–199.

Caldwell, J. A. (2012). Crew schedules, sleep deprivation, and aviation performance. *Current Directions in Psychological Science, 21*, 85–89.

Cale, E. M., & Lilienfeld, S. O. (2002). Sex differences in psychopathy and antisocial personality disorder: A review and integration. *Clinical Psychology Review, 22*, 1179–1207.

Callaghan, T., Rochat, P., Lillard, A., Claux, M. L., Odden, H., Itakura, S., . . . Singh, S. (2005). Synchrony in the onset of mental-state reasoning. *Psychological Science, 16*, 378–384.

Calvin, C. M., Deary, I. J., Webbink, D., Smith, P., Fernandes, C., Lee, S. H., . . . Visscher, P. M. (2012). Multivariate genetic analyses of cognition and academic achievement from two population samples of 174,000 and 166,000 school children. *Behavior Genetics, 42*, 699–710.

Calvo-Merino, B., Glaser, D. E., Grèzes, J., Passingham, R. E., & Haggard, P. (2004). Action observation and acquired motor skills: An fMRI study with expert dancers. *Cerebral Cortex, 15*, 1243–1249.

Cameron, L., & Rutland, A. (2006). Extended contact through story reading in school: Reducing children's prejudice toward the disabled. *Journal of Social Issues, 62*, 469–488.

Campbell, D. T. (1975). On the conflicts between biological and social evolution and between psychology and moral tradition. *American Psychologist, 30*, 1103–1126.

Campbell, D. T., & Specht, J. C. (1985). Altruism: Biology, culture, and religion. *Journal of Social and Clinical Psychology, 3*(1), 33–42.

Campbell, L., & Marshall, T. (2011). Anxious attachment and relationship processes: An interactionist perspective. *Journal of Personality, 79*, 1219–1249.

Campbell, S. (1986). *The Loch Ness Monster: The evidence.* Willingborough, Northamptonshire, U.K.: Aquarian Press.

Campbell, W. K., Foster, C. A., & Finkel, E. J. (2002). Does self-love lead to love for others? A story of narcissistic game-playing. *Journal of Personality and Social Psychology, 83*, 340–354.

Camperio-Ciani, A., Corna, F., & Capiluppi, C. (2004). Evidence for maternally inherited factors favouring male homosexuality and promoting female fecundity. *Proceedings of the Royal Society of London B, 271*, 2217–2221.

Camperio-Ciani, A., Lemmola, F., & Blecher, S. R. (2009). Genetic factors increase fecundity in female maternal relatives of bisexual men as in homosexuals. *Journal of Sexual Medicine, 6*, 449–455.

Camperio-Ciani, A., & Pellizzari, E. (2012). Fecundity of paternal and maternal non-parental female relatives of homosexual and heterosexual men. *PLoS One, 7*, e51088.

Campitelli, G., & Gobet, F. (2011). Deliberate practice: Necessary but not sufficient. *Current Directions in Psychological Science, 20*, 280–285.

Campos, J. J., Bertenthal, B. I., & Kermoian, R. (1992). Early experience and emotional development: The emergence of wariness of heights. *Psychological Science, 3*, 61–64.

Canetta, S., Sourander, A., Surcel, H., Hinkka-Yli-Salomäki, S., Leiviskä, J., Kellendonk, C., . . . Brown, A. S. (2014). Elevated maternal C-reactive protein and increased risk of schizophrenia in a national birth cohort. *American Journal of Psychiatry, 171*, 960–968.

Canli, T., Desmond, J. E., Zhao, Z., & Gabrieli, J. D. E. (2002). Sex differences in the neural basis of emotional memories. *PNAS, 99*, 10789–10794.

Cannon, W. B. (1929). *Bodily changes in pain, hunger, fear, and rage.* New York: Branford.

Cannon, W. B., & Washburn, A. L. (1912). An explanation of hunger. *American Journal of Physiology, 29*, 441–454.

Cantor, N., & Kihlstrom, J. F. (1987). *Personality and social intelligence.* Englewood Cliffs, NJ: Prentice-Hall.

Caplan, N., Choy, M. H., & Whitmore, J. K. (1992, February). Indochinese refugee families and academic achievement. *Scientific American*, pp. 36–42.

Caprariello, P. A., & Reis, H. T. (2013). To do, to have, or to share? Valuing experiences over material possessions depends on the involvement of others. *Journal of Personality and Social Psychology, 104*, 199–215.

Carey, B. (2007, September 4). Bipolar illness soars as a diagnosis for the young. *The New York Times* (nytimes.com).

Carey, B. (2009, November 27). Surgery for mental ills offers both hope and risk. *The New York Times* (nytimes.com).

Carey, B. (2011, February 14). Wariness on surgery of the mind. *The New York Times* (nytimes.com).

Carey, G. (1990). Genes, fears, phobias, and phobic disorders. *Journal of Counseling and Development, 68*, 628–632.

Carlson, M. (1995, August 29). Quoted by S. Blakeslee, In brain's early growth, timetable may be crucial. *The New York Times*, pp. C1, C3.

Carlson, M., Charlin, V., & Miller, N. (1988). Positive mood and helping behavior: A test of six hypotheses. *Journal of Personality and Social Psychology, 55*, 211–229.

Carnahan, T., & McFarland, S. (2007). Revisiting the Stanford Prison Experiment: Could participant self-selection have led to the cruelty? *Personality and Social Psychology Bulletin, 33*, 603–614.

Carney, D. R., Cuddy, A. J. C., & Yap, A. J. (2015). Review and summary of research on the embodied effects of expansive (vs. contractive) nonverbal displays. *Psychological Science, 26*, 657–663.

Carpusor, A., & Loges, W. E. (2006). Rental discrimination and ethnicity in names. *Journal of Applied Social Psychology, 36*, 934–952.

Carroll, H. (2013, October). Teen fashion model Georgina got so thin her organs were failing. But fashion designers still queued up to book her. Now she's telling her story to shame the whole industry. *The Daily Mail* (dailymail.co.uk).

Carroll, J. M., & Russell, J. A. (1996). Do facial expressions signal specific emotions? Judging emotion from the face in context. *Journal of Personality and Social Psychology, 70*, 205–218.

Carstensen, L. L. (2011). *A long bright future: Happiness, health and financial security in an age of increased longevity.* New York: PublicAffairs.

Carstensen, L. L., & Mikels, J. A. (2005). At the intersection of emotion and cognition: Aging and the positivity effect. *Current Directions in Psychological Science, 14*, 117–121.

Carstensen, L. L., Turan, B., Scheibe, S., Ram, N., Ersner-Hershfield, H., Samanez-Larkin, G. R., . . . Nesselroade, J. R. (2011). Emotional experience improves with age: Evidence based on over 10 years of experience sampling. *Psychology and Aging, 26*, 21–33.

Carter, T. J., & Gilovich, T. (2010). The relative relativity of material and experiential purchases. *Journal of Personality and Social Psychology, 98*, 146–159.

Carver, C. S., Johnson, S. L., & Joormann, J. (2008). Serotonergic function, two-mode models of self-regulation, and vulnerability to depression: What depression has in common with impulsive aggression. *Psychological Bulletin, 134*, 912–943.

Carver, C. S., Scheier, M. F., & Segerstrom, S. C. (2010). Optimism. *Clinical Psychology Review, 30*, 879–889.

CASA. (2003). *The formative years: Pathways to substance abuse among girls and young women ages 8–22.* New York: National Center on Addiction and Substance Abuse, Columbia University.

Casey, B. J., & Caudle, K. (2013). The teenage brain: Self-control. *Current Directions in Psychological Science, 22*, 82–87.

Casey, B. J., Getz, S., & Galvan, A. (2008). The adolescent brain. *Developmental Review, 28*, 62–77.

Cash, T., & Janda, L. H. (1984, December). The eye of the beholder. *Psychology Today*, pp. 46–52.

Caspi, A., McClay, J., Moffitt, T., Mill, J., Martin, J., Craig, I. W., . . . Poulton, R. (2002). Role of genotype in the cycle of violence in maltreated children. *Science, 297*, 851–854.

Cassidy, J., & Shaver, P. R. (1999). *Handbook of attachment.* New York: Guilford.

Castillo, R. J. (1997). *Culture and mental illness: A client-centered approach.* Pacific Grove, CA: Brooks/Cole.

Castonguay, L. G., Boswell, J. F., Constantino, M. J., Goldfried, M. R., & Hill, C. E. (2010). Training implications of harmful effects of psychological treatments. *American Psychologist, 65*, 34–49.

Cattell, R. B. (1963). Theory of fluid and crystallized intelligence: A critical experiment. *Journal of Educational Psychology, 54*, 1–22.

Cavalli-Sforza, L., Menozzi, P., & Piazza, A. (1994). *The history and geography of human genes.* Princeton, NJ: Princeton University Press.

Cavigelli, S. A., & McClintock, M. K. (2003). Fear of novelty in infant rats predicts adult corticosterone dynamics and an early death. *PNAS, 100*, 16131–16136.

Cawley, B. D., Keeping, L. M., & Levy, P. E. (1998). Participation in the performance appraisal process and employee reactions: A meta-analytic review of field investigations. *Journal of Applied Psychology, 83*, 615–633.

CDC. (2009). *Self-harm, all injury causes, nonfatal injuries and rates per 100,000.* Centers for Disease Control and Prevention. Retrieved from http://webappa.cdc.gov/cgi-bin/broker.exe

CDC. (2013). Diagnoses of HIV infection in the United States and dependent areas, 2013. *HIV Surveillance Report, Volume 25.* Washington, DC: Centers for Disease Control and Prevention.

CDC. (2014a, December). Depression in the U.S. household population, 2009–2012 (NCHS Data Brief No. 172). Centers for Disease Control and Prevention (cdc.gov /nchs/data/databriefs/db172.htm).

CDC. (2014b). *Pregnant women need a flu shot.* Centers for Disease Control and Prevention (cdc.gov/flu/pdf /freeresources/pregnant/flushot_pregnant_factsheet.pdf).

CDC. (2016a). Heart disease facts. Centers for Disease Control and Prevention (cdc.gov/heartdisease/facts.htm).

CDC. (2016b, accessed January 21). Reproductive health: Teen pregnancy. Centers for Disease Control and Prevention (cdc.gov/teenpregnancy).

CDC. (2016c, accessed January 21). STDs in adolescents and young adults. Centers for Disease Control and Prevention (cdc.gov/std/stats14/adol.htm).

CEA. (2014). Nine facts about American families and work. Office of the President of the United States: Council of Economic Advisers.

Ceci, S. J. (1993). Cognitive and social factors in children's testimony. Master lecture, American Psychological Association convention.

Ceci, S. J., & Bruck, M. (1993). Child witnesses: Translating research into policy. *Social Policy Report* (Society for Research in Child Development), 7(3), 1–30.

Ceci, S. J., & Bruck, M. (1995). *Jeopardy in the courtroom: A scientific analysis of children's testimony.* Washington, DC: American Psychological Association.

Ceci, S. J., Ginther, D. K., Kahn, S., & Williams, W. M. (2014). Women in academic science: A changing landscape. *Psychological Science in the Public Interest, 15*, 75–141.

Ceci, S. J., Huffman, M. L. C., Smith, E., & Loftus, E. F. (1994). Repeatedly thinking about a non-event: Source misattributions among preschoolers. *Consciousness and Cognition, 3*, 388–407.

Census Bureau. (2014). Industry and occupation. Table 1: Full-time, year-round workers and median earnings in the past 12 months by sex and detailed occupation. Washington, DC: Bureau of the Census.

Centerwall, B. S. (1989). Exposure to television as a risk factor for violence. *American Journal of Epidemiology*, 129, 643–652.

Cepeda, N. J., Pashler, H., Vul, E., Wixted, J. T., & Rohrer, D. (2006). Distributed practice in verbal recall tasks: A review and quantitative synthesis. *Psychological Bulletin*, 132, 354–380.

Cepeda, N. J., Vul, E., Rohrer, D., Wixted, J. T., & Pashler, H. (2008). Spacing effects in learning: A temporal ridgeline of optimal retention. *Psychological Science*, 19, 1095–1102.

Cerella, J. (1985). Information processing rates in the elderly. *Psychological Bulletin*, 98, 67–83.

CFI. (2003, July). *International developments*. Report. Amherst, NY: Center for Inquiry International.

Chabris, C. F., & Simons, D. (2010). *The invisible gorilla: And other ways our intuitions deceive us*. New York: Crown.

Chambers, E. S., Bridge, M. W., & Jones, D. A. (2009). Carbohydrate sensing in the human mouth: Effects on exercise performance and brain activity. *Journal of Physiology*, 587, 1779–1794.

Chamove, A. S. (1980). Nongenetic induction of acquired levels of aggression. *Journal of Abnormal Psychology*, 89, 469–488.

Champagne, F. A. (2010). Early adversity and developmental outcomes: Interaction between genetics, epigenetics, and social experiences across the life span. *Perspectives on Psychological Science*, 5, 564–574.

Chance News. (1997, 25 November). More on the frequency of letters in texts. Dartmouth College (Chance@Dartmouth.edu).

Chandler, J. J., & Pronin, E. (2012). Fast thought speed induces risk taking. *Psychological Science*, 23, 370–374.

Chandra, A., Mosher, W. D., & Copen, C. (2011, March). *Sexual behavior, sexual attraction, and sexual identity in the United States: Data from the 2006–2008 National Survey of Family Growth*. National Health Statistics Reports, Number 36 (Centers for Disease Control and Prevention).

Chang, A.-M., Aeschbach, D., Duggy, J. F., & Czeisler, C. A. (2015). Evening use of light-emitting eReaders negatively affects sleep, circadian timing, and next-morning alertness. *PNAS*, 112, 1232–1237.

Chang, E. C. (2001). Cultural influences on optimism and pessimism: Differences in Western and Eastern construals of the self. In E. C. Chang (Ed.), *Optimism and pessimism* (pp. 257–280). Washington, DC: APA Books.

Chang, Y. T., Chen, Y. C., Hayter, M., & Lin, M. L. (2009). Menstrual and menarche experience among pubescent female students in Taiwan: Implications for health education and promotion service. *Journal of Clinical Nursing*, 18, 2040–2048.

Chaplin, T. M. (2015). Gender and emotion expression: A developmental contextual perspective. *Emotion Review*, 7, 14–21.

Chaplin, T. M., & Aldao, A. (2013). Gender differences in emotion expression in children: A meta-analytic review. *Psychological Bulletin*, 139, 735–765.

Chaplin, W. F., Phillips, J. B., Brown, J. D., Clanton, N. R., & Stein, J. L. (2000). Handshaking, gender, personality, and first impressions. *Journal of Personality and Social Psychology*, 79, 110–117.

Charles, S. T., Piazza, J. R., Mogle, J., Sliwinski, M. J., & Almeida, D. M. (2013). The wear and tear of daily stressors on mental health. *Psychological Science*, 24, 733–741.

Charness, N., & Boot, W. R. (2009). Aging and information technology use. *Current Directions in Psychological Science*, 18, 253–258.

Charpak, G., & Broch, H. (2004). *Debunked! ESP, telekinesis, and other pseudoscience*. Baltimore, MD: Johns Hopkins University Press.

Chartrand, T. L., & Bargh, J. A. (1999). The chameleon effect: The perception-behavior link and social interaction. *Journal of Personality and Social Psychology*, 76, 893–910.

Chartrand, T. L., & van Baaren, R. (2009). Human mimicry. In M. P. Zanna (Ed.), *Advances in experimental social psychology* (pp. 219–274). San Diego, CA: Elsevier Academic Press.

Chassy, P., & Gobet, F. (2011). A hypothesis about the biological basis of expert intuition. *Review of General Psychology*, 15, 198–212.

Chatard, A., & Selimbegović, L. (2011). When self-destructive thoughts flash through the mind: Failure to meet standards affects the accessibility of suicide-related thoughts. *Journal of Personality and Social Psychology*, 100, 587–605.

Cheek, J. M., & Melchior, L. A. (1990). Shyness, self-esteem, and self-consciousness. In H. Leitenberg (Ed.), *Handbook of social and evaluation anxiety* (pp. 47–82). New York: Plenum Press.

Chein, J., Albert, D., O'Brien, L., Uckert, K., & Steinberg, L. (2011). Peers increase adolescent risk taking by enhancing activity in the brain's reward circuitry. *Developmental Science*, 14, F1–F10.

Chein, J. M., & Schneider, W. (2012). The brain's learning and control architecture. *Current Directions in Psychological Science*, 21, 78–84.

Chen, A. W., Kazanjian, A., & Wong, H. (2009). Why do Chinese Canadians not consult mental health services: Health status, language or culture? *Transcultural Psychiatry*, 46, 623–640.

Chen, S.-Y., & Fu, Y.-C. (2008). Internet use and academic achievement: Gender differences in early adolescence. *Adolescence*, 44, 797–812.

Chennu, S., Pinoia, P., Kamau, E., Allanson, J., Williams, G. B., Monti, M. M., . . . Bekinschtein, T. A. (2014). Spectral signatures of reorganised brain network in disorders of consciousness. *PLoS Computational Biology*, 10:e1003887.

Chess, S., & Thomas, A. (1987). *Know your child: An authoritative guide for today's parents*. New York: Basic Books.

Cheung, B. Y., Chudek, M., & Heine, S. J. (2011). Evidence for a sensitive period for acculturation: Younger immigrants report acculturating at a faster rate. *Psychological Science*, 22, 147–152.

Chick, C. F. (2015). Reward processing in the adolescent brain: Individual differences and relation to risk taking. *Journal of Neuroscience*, 35, 13539–13541.

Chida, Y., & Hamer, M. (2008). Chronic psychosocial factors and acute physiological responses to laboratory-induced stress in healthy populations: A quantitative review of 30 years of investigations. *Psychological Bulletin*, 134, 829–885.

Chida, Y., & Steptoe, A. (2009). The association of anger and hostility with future coronary heart disease: A meta-analytic review of prospective evidence. *Journal of the American College of Cardiology*, 17, 936–946.

Chida, Y., Steptoe, A., & Powell, L. H. (2009). Religiosity/spirituality and mortality. *Psychotherapy and Psychosomatics*, 78, 81–90.

Chida, Y., & Vedhara, K. (2009). Adverse psychosocial factors predict poorer prognosis in HIV disease: A meta-analytic review of prospective investigations. *Brain, Behavior, and Immunity*, 23, 434–445.

Child Trends. (2013). Attitudes toward spanking. Child Trends Data Bank (childtrends.org/?indicators=attitudes-towardspanking).

Chiles, J. A., Lambert, M. J., & Hatch, A. L. (1999). The impact of psychological interventions on medical cost offset: A meta-analytic review. *Clinical Psychology: Science and Practice*, 6, 204–220.

Chisholm, K. (1998). A three-year follow-up of attachment and indiscriminate friendliness in children adopted from Romanian orphanages. *Child Development*, 69, 1092–1106.

Chivers, M. L. (2005). A brief review and discussion of sex differences in the specificity of sexual arousal. *Sexual and Relationship Therapy*, 20, 377–390.

Chivers, M. L., Seto, M. C., Lalumière, M. L., Laan, E., & Grimbos, T. (2010). Agreement of self-reported and genital measures of sexual arousal in men and women: A meta-analysis. *Archives of Sexual Behavior*, 39, 5–56.

Choi, C. Q. (2008, March). Do you need only half your brain? *Scientific American*, p. 104.

Chomsky, N. (1972). *Language and mind*. New York: Harcourt Brace.

Chopik, W. J., Edelstein, R. S., & Fraley, R. C. (2013). From the cradle to the grave: Age differences in attachment from early adulthood to old age. *Journal of Personality*, 81, 171–183.

Chopik, W. J., Kim, E. S., & Smith, J. (2015). Changes in optimism are associated with changes in health over time among older adults. *Social Psychological and Personality Science*, 6(7), 814–822.

Christakis, D. A., Garrison, M. M., Herrenkohl, T., Haggerty, K., Rivara, K. P., Zhou, C., & Liekweg, K. (2013). Modifying media content for preschool children: A randomized control trial. *Pediatrics*, 131, 431–438.

Christakis, N. A., & Fowler, J. H. (2007). The spread of obesity in a large social network over 32 years. *New England Journal of Medicine*, 357, 370–379.

Christakis, N. A., & Fowler, J. H. (2009). *Connected: The surprising power of social networks and how they shape our lives*. New York: Little, Brown.

Christensen, A., & Jacobson, N. S. (1994). Who (or what) can do psychotherapy: The status and challenge of nonprofessional therapies. *Psychological Science*, 5, 8–14.

Christophersen, E. R., & Edwards, K. J. (1992). Treatment of elimination disorders: State of the art 1991. *Applied & Preventive Psychology*, 1, 15–22.

Chu, C., Podlogar, M. C., Hagan, C. R., Buchman-Schmitt, J. M., Silva, C., Chiurliza, B., . . . Joiner, T. E. (2016). The interactive effects of the capability for suicide and major depressive episodes on suicidal behavior in a military sample. *Cognitive Therapy and Research*, 40, 22–30.

Chu, P. S., Saucier, D. A., & Hafner, E. (2010). Meta-analysis of the relationships between social support and well-being in children and adolescents. *Journal of Social and Clinical Psychology*, 29, 624–645.

Chua, H. F., Boland, J. E., & Nisbett, R. E. (2005). Cultural variation in eye movements during scene perception. *PNAS*, 102, 12629–12633.

Chugani, H. T., & Phelps, M. E. (1986). Maturational changes in cerebral function in infants determined by 18FDG positron emission tomography. *Science*, 231, 840–843.

Chung, J. M., Robins, R. W., Trzesniewski, K. H., Noftle, E. E., Roberts, B. W., & Widaman, K. F. (2014). Continuity and change in self-esteem during emerging adulthood. *Journal of Personality and Social Psychology*, 106, 469–483.

Church, T. S., Thomas, D. M., Tudor-Locke, C., Katzmarzyk, P. T., Earnest, C. P., Rodarte, R. Q., . . . Bouchard, C. (2011). Trends over 5 decades in U.S. occupation-related physical activity and their associations with obesity. *PLoS ONE*, 6(5), e19657.

Churchland, P. S. (2013). *Touching a nerve: The self as brain.* New York: Norton.

CIA. (2010). The World Fact Book: Literacy. Washington, DC: Central Intelligence Agency (cia.gov/library/publications/the-world-factbook/fields/2103.html).

Cialdini, R. B. (1993). *Influence: Science and practice* (3rd ed.). New York: HarperCollins.

Cialdini, R. B., & Richardson, K. D. (1980). Two indirect tactics of image management: Basking and blasting. *Journal of Personality and Social Psychology, 39,* 406–415.

Ciarrochi, J., Forgas, J. P., & Mayer, J. D. (2006). *Emotional intelligence in everyday life* (2nd ed.). New York: Psychology Press.

Cin, S. D., Gibson, B., Zanna, M. P., Shumate, R., & Fong, G. T. (2007). Smoking in movies, implicit associations of smoking with the self, and intentions to smoke. *Psychological Science, 18,* 559–563.

Cincotta, A. L., Gehrman, P., Gooneratne, N. S., & Baime, M. J. (2011). The effects of a mindfulness-based stress reduction programme on presleep cognitive arousal and insomnia symptoms: A pilot study. *Stress and Health, 27,* e299–e305.

Clack, B., Dixon, J., & Tredoux, C. (2005). Eating together apart: Patterns of segregation in a multi-ethnic cafeteria. *Journal of Community and Applied Social Psychology, 15,* 1–16.

Clancy, S. A. (2005). *Abducted: How people come to believe they were kidnapped by aliens.* Cambridge, MA: Harvard University Press.

Clark, A., Seidler, A., & Miller, M. (2001). Inverse association between sense of humor and coronary heart disease. *International Journal of Cardiology, 80,* 87–88.

Clark, C. J., Luguri, J. B., Ditto, P. H., Knobe, J., Shariff, A. F., & Baumeister, R. F. (2014). Free to punish: A motivated account of free will belief. *Journal of Personality and Social Psychology, 106,* 501–513.

Clark, K. B., & Clark, M. P. (1947). Racial identification and preference in Negro children. In T. M. Newcomb & E. L. Hartley (Eds.), *Readings in social psychology.* New York: Holt.

Clark, R. D., III, & Hatfield, E. (1989). Gender differences in receptivity to sexual offers. *Journal of Psychology & Human Sexuality, 2,* 39–55.

Cleary, A. M. (2008). Recognition memory, familiarity, and déjà vu experiences. *Current Directions in Psychological Science, 17,* 353–357.

Coan, J. A., Schaefer, H. S., & Davidson, R. J. (2006). Lending a hand: Social regulation of the neural response to threat. *Psychological Science, 17,* 1032–1039.

Coffey, C. E. (Ed.) (1993). *Clinical science of electroconvulsive therapy.* Washington, DC: American Psychiatric Press.

Cohen, D. (1995, June 17). Now we are one, or two, or three. *New Scientist,* pp. 14–15.

Cohen, P. (2010, June 11). Long road to adulthood is growing even longer. *The New York Times* (nytimes.com).

Cohen, S. (2004). Social relationships and health. *American Psychologist, 59,* 676–684.

Cohen, S., Alper, C. M., Doyle, W. J., Treanor, J. J., & Turner, R. B. (2006). Positive emotional style predicts resistance to illness after experimental exposure to rhinovirus or influenza A virus. *Psychosomatic Medicine, 68,* 809–815.

Cohen, S., Doyle, W. J., Alper, C. M., Janicki-Deverts, D., & Turner, R. B. (2009). Sleep habits and susceptibility to the common cold. *Archives of Internal Medicine, 169,* 62–67.

Cohen, S., Doyle, W. J., Skoner, D. P., Rabin, B. S., & Gwaltney, J. M., Jr. (1997). Social ties and susceptibility to the common cold. *Journal of the American Medical Association, 277,* 1940–1944.

Cohen, S., Doyle, W. J., Turner, R., Alper, C. M., & Skoner, D. P. (2003). Sociability and susceptibility to the common cold. *Psychological Science, 14,* 389–395.

Cohen, S., Janicki-Deverts, D., Turner, R. B., & Doyle, W. J. (2015). Does hugging provide stress-buffering social support? A study of susceptibility to upper respiratory infection and illness. *Psychological Science, 26,* 135–147.

Cohen, S., Kaplan, J. R., Cunnick, J. E., Manuck, S. B., & Rabin, B. S. (1992). Chronic social stress, affiliation, and cellular immune response in nonhuman primates. *Psychological Science, 3,* 301–304.

Cohen, S., & Pressman, S. D. (2006). Positive affect and health. *Current Directions in Psychological Science, 15,* 122–125.

Cohen, S., Tyrrell, D. A. J., & Smith, A. P. (1991). Psychological stress and susceptibility to the common cold. *New England Journal of Medicine, 325,* 606–612.

Colapinto, J. (2000). *As nature made him: The boy who was raised as a girl.* New York: HarperCollins.

Colarelli, S. M., Spranger, J. L., & Hechanova, M. R. (2006). Women, power, and sex composition in small groups: An evolutionary perspective. *Journal of Organizational Behavior, 27,* 163–184.

Collier, K. L., Bos, H. M. W., & Sandfort, T. G. M. (2012). Intergroup contact, attitudes toward homosexuality, and the role of acceptance of gender nonconformity in young adolescents. *Journal of Adolescence, 35,* 899–907.

Collinger, J. L., Wodlinger, B., Downey, J. E., Wang, W., Tyler-Kabara, E. C., Weber, D. J., . . . Schwartz, A. B. (2013). High-performance neuroprosthetic control by an individual with tetraplegia. *The Lancet, 381,* 557–564.

Collins, F. (2007, February 1). In the cathedral or the laboratory, it's the same God, National Prayer Breakfast told. On Faith (faithstreet.com/onfaith/2007/02/01/whether-cathedral-or-laborator/1867).

Collins, F. S., & Tabak, L. A. (2014). Policy: NIH plans to enhance reproducibility. *Nature, 505,* 612–613.

Collins, G. (2009, March 9). The rant list. *The New York Times* (nytimes.com).

Collins, R. L., Elliott, M. N., Berry, S. H., Danouse, D. E., Kunkel, D., Hunter, S. B., & Miu, A. (2004). Watching sex on television predicts adolescent initiation of sexual behavior. *Pediatrics, 114,* 280–289.

Collinson, S. L., MacKay, C. E., James, A. C., Quested, D. J., Phillips, T., Roberts, N., & Crow, T. J. (2003). Brain volume, asymmetry and intellectual impairment in relation to sex in early-onset schizophrenia. *British Journal of Psychiatry, 183,* 114–120.

Collishaw, S., Pickles, A., Natarajan, L., & Maughan, B. (2007, June). *20-year trends in depression and anxiety in England.* Paper presented at the Thirteenth Scientific Meeting on the Brain and the Developing Child, London.

Colvert, E., Beata, T., McEwen, F., Stewart, C., Curran, S. R., Woodhouse, E., . . . Bolton, P. (2015). Heritability of autism spectrum disorder in a UK population-based twin sample. *JAMA Psychiatry, 72,* 415–423.

Confer, J. C., Easton, J. A., Fleischman, D. S., Goetz, C. D., Lewis, D. M. G., Perilloux, C., & Buss, D. M. (2010). Evolutionary psychology: Controversies, questions, prospects, and limitations. *American Psychologist, 65,* 110–126.

Conley, C. S., & Rudolph, K. D. (2009). The emerging sex difference in adolescent depression: Interacting contributions of puberty and peer stress. *Development and Psychopathology, 21,* 593–620.

Conley, K. M. & Lehman, B. J. (2012). Test anxiety and cardiovascular responses to daily academic stressors. *Stress and Health, 28,* 41–50.

Conley, T. D. (2011). Perceived proposer personality characteristics and gender differences in acceptance of casual sex offers. *Journal of Personality and Social Psychology, 100,* 300–329.

Connor, C. E. (2010). A new viewpoint on faces. *Science, 330,* 764–765.

Conroy-Beam, D., Buss, D. M., Pham, M. N., & Shackelford, T. K. (2015). How sexually dimorphic are human mate preferences? *Personality and Social Psychology Bulletin, 41,* 1082–1093.

Consumer Reports. (1995, November). Does therapy help? pp. 734–739.

Conway, A. R. A., Skitka, L. J., Hemmerich, J. A., & Kershaw, T. C. (2009). Flashbulb memory for 11 September 2001. *Applied Cognitive Psychology, 23,* 605–623.

Conway, M. A., Wang, Q., Hanyu, K., & Haque, S. (2005). A cross-cultural investigation of autobiographical memory: On the universality and cultural variation of the reminiscence bump. *Journal of Cross-Cultural Psychology, 36,* 739–749.

Cooke, L. J., Wardle, J., & Gibson, E. L. (2003). Relationship between parental report of food neophobia and everyday food consumption in 2–6-year-old children. *Appetite, 41,* 205–206.

Cooper, M. (2010, October 18). From Obama, the tax cut nobody heard of. *The New York Times* (nytimes.com).

Cooper, W. H., & Withey, M. J. (2009). The strong situation hypothesis. *Personality and Social Psychology Review, 13,* 62–72.

Coopersmith, S. (1967). *The antecedents of self-esteem.* San Francisco: Freeman.

Copeland, W., Shanahan, L., Miller, S., Costello, E. J., Angold, A., & Maughan, B. (2010). Outcomes of early pubertal timing in young women: A prospective population-based study. *American Journal of Psychiatry, 167,* 1218–1225.

Corcoran, D. W. J. (1964). The relation between introversion and salivation. *The American Journal of Psychology, 77,* 298–300.

Coren, S. (1996). *Sleep thieves: An eye-opening exploration into the science and mysteries of sleep.* New York: Free Press.

Corey, D. P., Garcia-Añoveros, J., Holt, J. R., Kwan, K. Y., Lin, S. Y., Vollrath, M. A., & Zhang, D. S. (2004). TRPA1 is a candidate for the mechano-sensitive transduction channel of vertebrate hair cells. *Nature, 432,* 723–730.

Corina, D. P. (1998). The processing of sign language: Evidence from aphasia. In B. Stemmer & H. A. Whittaker (Eds.), *Handbook of neurolinguistics.* San Diego: Academic Press.

Corina, D. P., Vaid, J., & Bellugi, U. (1992). The linguistic basis of left hemisphere specialization. *Science, 255,* 1258–1260.

Corkin, S. (2013). *Permanent present tense: The unforgettable life of the amnesic patient.* New York: Basic Books.

Corkin, S., quoted by R. Adelson. (2005, September). Lessons from H. M. *Monitor on Psychology,* p. 59.

Cornier, M.-A. (2011). Is your brain to blame for weight regain? *Physiology & Behavior, 104,* 608–612.

Correll, J., Park, B., Judd, C. M., Wittenbrink, B., Sadler, M. S., & Keesee, T. (2007). Across the thin blue line: Police officers and racial bias in the decision to shoot. *Journal of Personality and Social Psychology, 92,* 1006–1023.

Correll, J., Wittenbrink, B., Crawford, M. T., & Sadler, M. S. (2015). Stereotypic vision: How stereotypes disambiguate visual stimuli. *Journal of Personality and Social Psychology, 108,* 219–233.

Corrigan, P. W. (2014). Can there be false hope in recovery? *British Journal of Psychiatry, 205*, 423–424.

Corse, A. K., Chou, T., Arulpragasm, A. R., Kaur, N., Deckersbach, T., & Cusin, C. (2013). Deep brain stimulation for obsessive-compulsive disorder. *Psychiatric Annals, 43*, 351–357.

Costa, P. T., Jr., & McCrae, R. R. (2011). The five-factor model, five-factor theory, and interpersonal psychology. In L. M. Horowitz & S. Strack (Eds.), *Handbook of interpersonal psychology: Theory, research, assessment, and therapeutic interventions* (pp. 91–104). Hoboken, NJ: John Wiley & Sons.

Costa, P. T., Jr., Terracciano, A., & McCrae, R. R. (2001). Gender differences in personality traits across cultures: Robust and surprising findings. *Journal of Personality and Social Psychology, 81*, 322–331.

Costello, E. J., Compton, S. N., Keeler, G., & Angold, A. (2003). Relationships between poverty and psychopathology: A natural experiment. *Journal of the American Medical Association, 290*, 2023–2029.

Coulter, K. C., & Malouff, J. M. (2013). Effects of an intervention designed to enhance romantic relationship excitement: A randomized-control trial. *Couple and Family Psychology: Research and Practice, 2*, 34–44.

Courtney, J. G., Longnecker, M. P., Theorell, T., & de Verdier, M. G. (1993). Stressful life events and the risk of colorectal cancer. *Epidemiology, 4*, 407–414.

Cowan, N. (2010). The magical mystery four: How is working memory capacity limited, and why? *Current Directions in Psychological Science, 19*, 51–57.

Cowart, B. J. (1981). Development of taste perception in humans: Sensitivity and preference throughout the life span. *Psychological Bulletin, 90*, 43–73.

Cox, J. J., Reimann, F. Nicholas, A. K., Thornton, G., Roberts, E., & Springell, K., & Woods, C. G. (2006). An SCN9A channelopathy causes congenital inability to experience pain. *Nature, 444*, 894–898.

Coyne, J. C. (1976a). Toward an interactional description of depression. *Psychiatry, 39*, 28–40.

Coyne, J. C. (1976b). Depression and the response of others. *Journal of Abnormal Psychology, 85*, 186–193.

Crabbe, J. C. (2002). Genetic contributions to addiction. *Annual Review of Psychology, 53*, 435–462.

Crabtree, S. (2005, January 13). Engagement keeps the doctor away. *Gallup Management Journal* (gmj.gallup.com).

Crabtree, S. (2011, December 12). *U.S. seniors maintain happiness highs with less social time.* Gallup Poll (gallup.com).

Credé, M., & Kuncel, N. R. (2008). Study habits, skills, and attitudes: The third pillar supporting collegiate academic performance. *Perspectives on Psychological Science, 3*, 425–453.

Creswell, J. D., Bursley, J. K., & Satpute, A. B. (2013). Neural reactivation links unconscious thought to decision making performance. *Social Cognitive and Affective Neuroscience, 8*, 863–869.

Creswell, J. D., Way, B. M., Eisenberger, N. I., & Lieberman, M. D. (2007). Neural correlates of dispositional mindfulness during affect labeling. *Psychosomatic Medicine, 69*, 560–565.

Crews, F. T., He, J., & Hodge, C. (2007). Adolescent cortical development: A critical period of vulnerability for addiction. *Pharmacology, Biochemistry and Behavior, 86*, 189–199.

Crews, F. T., Mdzinarishvili, A., Kim, D., He, J., & Nixon, K. (2006). Neurogenesis in adolescent brain is potently inhibited by ethanol. *Neuroscience, 137*, 437–445.

Cristea, I. A., Huibers, M. J., David, D., Hollon, S. D., Andersson, G., & Cuijpers, P. (2015). The effects of cognitive behavior therapy for adult depression on dysfunctional thinking: A meta-analysis. *Clinical Psychology Review, 42*, 62–71.

Crocker, J., & Park, L. E. (2004). The costly pursuit of self-esteem. *Psychological Bulletin, 130*, 392–414.

Crocker, J., Thompson, L. L., McGraw, K. M., & Ingerman, C. (1987). Downward comparison, prejudice, and evaluation of others: Effects of self-esteem and threat. *Journal of Personality and Social Psychology, 52*, 907–916.

Crockett, M. J., Kurth-Nelson, Z., Siegel, J. Z., Dayan, P., & Dolan, R. J. (2014). Harm to others outweighs harm to self in moral decision making. *PNAS, 111*, 17320–17325.

Croft, R. J., Klugman, A., Baldeweg, T., & Gruzelier, J. H. (2001). Electrophysiological evidence of serotonergic impairment in long-term MDMA ("Ecstasy") users. *American Journal of Psychiatry, 158*, 1687–1692.

Crook, T. H., & West, R. L. (1990). Name recall performance across the adult life-span. *British Journal of Psychology, 81*, 335–340.

Crosier, B. S., Webster, G. D., & Dillon, H. M. (2012). Wired to connect: Evolutionary psychology and social networks. *Review of General Psychology, 16*, 230–239.

Cross, S., & Markus, H. (1991). Possible selves across the life span. *Human Development, 34*, 230–255.

Cross-National Collaborative Group. (1992). The changing rate of major depression. *Journal of the American Medical Association, 268*, 3098–3105.

Crowell, J. A., & Waters, E. (1994). Bowlby's theory grown up: The role of attachment in adult love relationships. *Psychological Inquiry, 5*, 1–22.

Csikszentmihalyi, M. (1990). *Flow: The psychology of optimal experience.* New York: Harper & Row.

Csikszentmihalyi, M. (1999). If we are so rich, why aren't we happy? *American Psychologist, 54*, 821–827.

Csikszentmihalyi, M., & Hunter, J. (2003). Happiness in everyday life: The uses of experience sampling. *Journal of Happiness Studies, 4*, 185–199.

Cuijpers, P., Sijbrandij, M., Koole, S. L., Andersson, G., Beekman, A. T., & Reynolds, C. F. (2013). The efficacy of psychotherapy and pharmacotherapy in treating depressive and anxiety disorders: A meta-analysis of direct comparisons. *World Psychiatry, 12*(2), 137–148.

Cuijpers, P., van Straten, A., Schuurmans, J., van Oppen, P., Hollon, S. D., & Andersson, G. (2010). Psychotherapy for chronic major depression and dysthymia: A meta-analysis. *Clinical Psychology Review, 30*, 51–62.

Culbert, K. M., Burt, S. A., McGue, M., Iacono, W. G., & Klump, K. L. (2009). Puberty and the genetic diathesis of disordered eating attitudes and behaviors. *Journal of Abnormal Psychology, 118*, 788–796.

Currie, T. E., & Little, A. C. (2009). The relative importance of the face and body in judgments of human physical attractiveness. *Evolution and Human Behavior, 30*, 409–416.

Curry, J., Silva, S., Rohde, P., Ginsburg, G., Kratochvil, C., Simons, A., . . . March, J. (2011). Recovery and recurrence following treatment for adolescent major depression. *Archives of General Psychiatry, 68*, 263–269.

Curtis, R. C., & Miller, K. (1986). Believing another likes or dislikes you: Behaviors making the beliefs come true. *Journal of Personality and Social Psychology, 51*, 284–290.

Custers, R., & Aarts, H. (2010). The unconscious will: How the pursuit of goals operates outside of conscious awareness. *Science, 329*, 47–50.

Cyders, M. A., & Smith, G. T. (2008). Emotion-based dispositions to rash action: Positive and negative urgency. *Psychological Bulletin, 134*, 807–828.

Dabbs, J. M., Jr., Bernieri, F. J., Strong, R. K., Campo, R., & Milun, R. (2001). Going on stage: Testosterone in greetings and meetings. *Journal of Research in Personality, 35*, 27–40.

Dabbs, J. M., Jr., & Morris, R. (1990). Testosterone, social class, and antisocial behavior in a sample of 4,462 men. *Psychological Science, 1*, 209–211.

Dalenberg, C. J., Brand, B. L., Gleaves, D. H., Dorahy, M. J., Loewenstein, R. J., Cardeña, E., . . . Spiegel, D. (2012). Evaluation of the evidence for the trauma and fantasy models of dissociation. *Psychological Bulletin, 138*, 550–588.

Daley, J. (2011, July/August). What you don't know can kill you. *Discover* (discovermagazine.com).

Daly, M., Delaney, L., Egan, R. F., & Baumeister, R. F. (2015). Childhood self-control and unemployment throughout the life span: Evidence from two British cohort studies. *Psychological Science, 26*, 709–723.

Damasio, A. R. (2003). *Looking for Spinoza: Joy, sorrow, and the feeling brain.* New York: Harcourt.

Dambacher, F., Sack, A. T., Lobbestael, J., Arntz, A., Brugman, S., & Schuhmann, T. (2015). Out of control: Evidence for anterior insula involvement in motor impulsivity and reactive aggression. *Social Cognitive and Affective Neuroscience, 10*, 508–516.

Danelli, L., Cossu, G., Berlingeri, M., Bottini, G., Sberna, M., & Paulesu, E. (2013). Is a lone right hemisphere enough? Neurolinguistic architecture in a case with a very early left hemispherectomy. *Neurocase, 19*, 209–231.

Danner, D. D., Snowdon, D. A., & Friesen, W. V. (2001). Positive emotions in early life and longevity: Findings from the Nun Study. *Journal of Personality and Social Psychology, 80*, 804–813.

Danso, H., & Esses, V. (2001). Black experimenters and the intellectual test performance of white participants: The tables are turned. *Journal of Experimental Social Psychology, 37*, 158–165.

Darley, J. M., & Alter, A. (2013). Behavioral issues of punishment, retribution, and deterrence. In E. Shafir (Ed.), *The behavioral foundations of public policy* (pp. 181–194). Princeton, NJ: Princeton University Press.

Darley, J. M., & Latané, B. (1968a). Bystander intervention in emergencies: Diffusion of responsibility. *Journal of Personality and Social Psychology, 8*, 377–383.

Darley, J. M., & Latané, B. (1968b, December). When will people help in a crisis? *Psychology Today*, pp. 54–57, 70–71.

Darwin, C. (1872). *The expression of the emotions in man and animals.* London: John Murray, Albemarle Street.

Daum, I., & Schugens, M. M. (1996). On the cerebellum and classical conditioning. *Psychological Science, 5*, 58–61.

Davey, G., & Rato, R. (2012). Subjective well-being in China: A review. *Journal of Happiness Studies, 13*, 333–346.

Davey, G. C. L. (1995). Preparedness and phobias: Specific evolved associations or a generalized expectancy bias? *Behavioral and Brain Sciences, 18*, 289–297.

Davidson, J. R. T., Connor, K. M., & Swartz, M. (2006). Mental illness in U.S. presidents between 1776 and 1974: A review of biographical sources. *Journal of Nervous and Mental Disease, 194*, 47–51.

Davidson, R. J., & Begley, S. (2012). *The emotional life of your brain: How its unique patterns affect the way you think, feel, and live—and how you can change them.* New York: Hudson Street Press.

Davidson, R. J., Kabat-Zinn, J., Schumacher, J., Rosenkranz, M., Muller, D., Santorelli, S. F., . . . Sheridan, J. F. (2003). Alterations in brain and immune function produced by mindfulness meditation. *Psychosomatic Medicine, 65*, 564–570.

Davidson, R. J., Pizzagalli, D., Nitschke, J. B., & Putnam, K. (2002). Depression: Perspectives from affective neuroscience. *Annual Review of Psychology, 53*, 545–574.

Davidson, R. J., Putnam, K. M., & Larson, C. L. (2000). Dysfunction in the neural circuitry of emotion regulation—a possible prelude to violence. *Science, 289*, 591–594.

Davidson, T. L., & Riley, A. L. (2015). Taste, sickness, and learning. *American Scientist, 103*, 204–211.

Davies, P. (2007). *Cosmic jackpot: Why our universe is just right for life.* Boston: Houghton Mifflin.

Davis, B. E., Moon, R. Y., Sachs, H. C., & Ottolini, M. C. (1998). Effects of sleep position on infant motor development. *Pediatrics, 102*, 1135–1140.

Davis, D. E., Choe, E., Meyers, J., Wade, N., Varias, K., Gifford, A., . . . Worthington, E. L. (2016). Thankful for the little things: A meta-analysis of gratitude interventions. *Journal of Counseling Psychology, 63*, 20–31.

Davis, J. O., & Phelps, J. A. (1995). Twins with schizophrenia: Genes or germs? *Schizophrenia Bulletin, 21*, 13–18.

Davis, J. O., Phelps, J. A., & Bracha, H. S. (1995). Prenatal development of monozygotic twins and concordance for schizophrenia. *Schizophrenia Bulletin, 21*, 357–366.

Davis, J. P., Lander, K., & Jansari, A. (2013). I never forget a face. *The Psychologist, 26*, 726–729.

Davis, K., Christodoulou, J., Seider, S., & Gardner, H. (2011). The theory of multiple intelligences. In R. J. Sternberg & S. B. Kaufman (Eds.), *Cambridge handbook of intelligence* (pp. 485–503). Cambridge, UK; New York: Cambridge University Press.

Davison, S. L., & Davis, S. R. (2011). Androgenic hormones and aging—The link with female function. *Hormones and Behavior, 59*, 745–753.

Dawes, R. M. (1994). *House of cards: Psychology and psychotherapy built on myth.* New York: Free Press.

Dawkins, L., Shahzad, F.-Z., Ahmed, S. S., & Edmonds, C. J. (2011). Expectation of having consumed caffeine can improve performance and moods. *Appetite, 57*, 597–600.

de Boysson-Bardies, B., Halle, P., Sagart, L., & Durand, C. (1989). A cross-linguistic investigation of vowel formants in babbling. *Journal of Child Language, 16*, 1–17.

de Courten-Myers, G. M. (2005, February 4). Personal correspondence (estimating total brain neurons, extrapolating from her carefully estimated 20 to 23 billion cortical neurons).

de Dios, M. A., Herman, D. S., Britton, W. B., Hagerty, C. E., Anderson, B. J., & Stein, M. D. (2012). Motivational and mindfulness intervention for young adult female marijuana users. *Journal of Substance Abuse Treatment, 42*, 56–64.

De Dreu, C. K. W., Greer, L. L., Handgraaf, M. J. J., Shalvi, S., Van Kleef, G. A., Baas, M., . . . Feith, S. W. W. (2010). The neuropeptide oxytocin regulated parochial altruism in intergroup conflict among humans. *Science, 328*, 1409–1411.

De Dreu, C. K. W., Nijstad, B. A., Baas, M., Wolsink, I., & Roskes, M. (2012). Working memory benefits creative insight, musical improvisation, and original ideation through maintained task-focused attention. *Personality and Social Psychology Bulletin, 38*, 656–669.

de Gee, J., Knapen, T., & Donner, T. H. (2014). Decision-related pupil dilation reflects upcoming choice and individual bias. *PNAS, 111*, E618–E625.

de Hoogh, A. H. B., den Hartog, D. N., Koopman, P. L., Thierry, H., van den Berg, P. T., van der Weide, J. G., & Wilderom, C. P. M. (2004). Charismatic leadership, environmental dynamism, and performance. *European Journal of Work and Organisational Psychology, 13*, 447–471.

De Koninck, J. (2000). Waking experiences and dreaming. In M. Kryger, T. Roth, & W. Dement (Eds.), *Principles and practice of sleep medicine* (3rd ed.). Philadelphia: Saunders.

de Lange, M., Debets, L., Ruitenberg, K., & Holland, R. (2012). Making less of a mess: Scent exposure as a tool for behavioral change. *Social Influence, 7*, 90–97.

De Los Reyes, A., & Kazdin, A. E. (2009). Identifying evidence-based interventions for children and adolescents using the range of possible changes model: A meta-analytic illustration. *Behavior Modification, 33*, 583–617.

De Neve, J.-E., Diener, E., Tay, L., & Xuereb, C. (2013). The objective benefits of subjective well-being. In J. F. Helliwell, R. Layard, & J. Sachs (Eds.), *World happiness report 2013* (Vol. 2., pp. 54–79). New York: UN Sustainable Network Development Solutions Network.

De Raedt, R., Vanderhasselt, M. A., & Baeken, C. (2015). Neurostimulation as an intervention for treatment resistant depression: From research on mechanisms towards targeted neurocognitive strategies. *Clinical Psychology Review, 41*, 61–69.

de Vries, J., Byrne, M., & Kehoe, E. (2015). Cognitive dissonance induction in everyday life: An fMRI study. *Social Neuroscience, 10*, 268–281.

de Waal, F. (2011). Back cover quote for D. Blum, *Love at Goon Park: Harry Harlow and the science of affection.* New York: Basic Books.

de Wit, L., Luppino, F., van Straten, A., Penninx, B., Zitman, F., & Cuijpers, P. (2010). Depression and obesity: A meta-analysis of community-based studies. *Psychiatry Research, 178*, 230–235.

De Wolff, M. S., & van IJzendoorn, M. H. (1997). Sensitivity and attachment: A meta-analysis on parental antecedents of infant attachment. *Child Development, 68*, 571–591

Deary, I. J. (2008). Why do intelligent people live longer? *Nature, 456*, 175–176.

Deary, I. J., Batty, G. D., & Gale, C. R. (2008). Bright children become enlightened adults. *Psychological Science, 19*, 1–6.

Deary, I. J., Pattie, A., & Starr, J. M. (2013). The stability of intelligence from age 11 to age 90 years: The Lothian birth cohort of 1921. *Psychological Science, 24*, 2361–2368.

Deary, I. J., Thorpe, G., Wilson, V., Starr, J. M., & Whalley, L. J. (2003). Population sex differences in IQ at age 11: The Scottish mental survey 1932. *Intelligence, 31*, 533–541.

Deary, I. J., Whalley, L. J., & Starr, J. M. (2009). *A lifetime of intelligence: Follow-up studies of the Scottish Mental Surveys of 1932 and 1947.* Washington, DC: American Psychological Association.

Deary, I. J., Whiteman, M. C., Starr, J. M., Whalley, L. J., & Fox, H. C. (2004). The impact of childhood intelligence on later life: Following up the Scottish mental surveys of 1932 and 1947. *Journal of Personality and Social Psychology, 86*, 130–147.

Dechesne, M., Pyszczynski, T., Arndt, J., Ransom, S., Sheldon, K. M., van Knippenberg, A., & Janssen, J. (2003). Literal and symbolic immortality: The effect of evidence of literal immortality on self-esteem striving in response to mortality salience. *Journal of Personality and Social Psychology, 84*, 722–737.

Deci, E. L., & Ryan, R. M. (Eds.) (2002). *Handbook of self-determination research.* Rochester, NY: University of Rochester Press.

Deci, E. L., & Ryan, R. M. (2009). Self-determination theory: A consideration of human motivational universals. In P. J. Corr & G. Matthews (Eds.), *The Cambridge handbook of personality psychology* (pp. 441–456). New York: Cambridge University Press.

DeFina, L. F., Willis, B. L., Radford, N. B., Gao, A., Leonard, D., Haskell, W. L., . . . Berry, J. D. (2013). The association between midlife cardiorespiratory fitness levels and later-life dementia. *Annals of Internal Medicine, 158*, 162–168.

DeFina, R., & Hannon, L. (2015). The changing relationship between unemployment and suicide. *Suicide and Life-Threatening Behavior, 45*, 217–229.

Dehne, K. L., & Riedner, G. (2005). *Sexually transmitted infections among adolescents: The need for adequate health services.* Geneva: World Health Organization.

DeLamater, J. D. (2012). Sexual expression in later life: A review and synthesis. *Journal of Sex Research, 49*, 125–141.

DeLamater, J. D., & Sill, M. (2005). Sexual desire in later life. *Journal of Sex Research, 42*, 138–149.

Delaney, H. D., Miller, W. R., & Bisonó, A. M. (2007). Religiosity and spirituality among psychologists: A survey of clinician members of the American Psychological Association. *Professional Psychology: Research and Practice, 38*, 538–546.

Delaunay-El Allam, M., Soussignan, R., Patris, B., Marlier, L., & Schaal, B. (2010). Long-lasting memory for an odor acquired at the mother's breast. *Developmental Science, 13*, 849–863.

DeLoache, J. S., & Brown, A. L. (1987, October-December). Differences in the memory-based searching of delayed and normally developing young children. *Intelligence, 11*(4), 277–289.

DeLoache, J. S., Chiong, C., Sherman, K., Islam, N., Vanderborght, M., Troseth, G. L., . . . O'Doherty, K. (2010). Do babies learn from baby media? *Psychological Science, 21*, 1570–1574.

DeLongis, A., Coyne, J. C., Dakof, G., Folkman, S., & Lazarus, R. S. (1982). Relationship of daily hassles, uplifts, and major life events to health status. *Health Psychology, 1*, 119–136.

DeLongis, A., Folkman, S., & Lazarus, R. S. (1988). The impact of daily stress on health and mood: Psychological and social resources as mediators. *Journal of Personality and Social Psychology, 54*, 486–495.

DelPriore, D. J., & Hill, S. E. (2013). The effects of paternal disengagement on women's sexual decision making: An experimental approach. *Journal of Personality and Social Psychology, 105*, 234–246.

Dement, W. C. (1978). *Some must watch while some must sleep.* New York: Norton.

Dement, W. C. (1999). *The promise of sleep.* New York: Delacorte Press.

Dement, W. C., & Wolpert, E. A. (1958). The relation of eye movements, body mobility, and external stimuli to dream content. *Journal of Experimental Psychology, 55*, 543–553.

Demicheli, V., Rivetti, A., Debalini, M. G., & Di Pietrantonj, C. (2012, February 15). Vaccines for measles, mumps and rubella in children. *Cochrane Database of Systematic Reviews,* Issue 2, CD004407.

Demir, E., & Dickson, B. J. (2005). Fruitless splicing specifies male courtship behavior in *Drosophila. Cell, 121*, 785–794.

Dempster, E., Viana, J., Pidsley, R., & Mill, J. (2013). Epigenetic studies of schizophrenia: Progress, predicaments, and promises for the future. *Schizophrenia Bulletin, 39,* 11–16.

DeNeve, K. M., & Cooper, H. (1998). The happy personality: A meta-analysis of 137 personality traits and subjective well-being. *Psychological Bulletin, 124,* 197–229.

Denollet, J. (2005). DS14: Standard assessment of negative affectivity, social inhibition, and Type D personality. *Psychosomatic Medicine, 67,* 89–97.

Denollet, J., Sys, S. U., Stroobant, N., Rombouts, H. Gillebert, T. C., & Brutsaert, D. L. (1996). Personality as independent predictor of long-term mortality in patients with coronary heart disease. *The Lancet, 347,* 417–421.

Denson, T. F. (2011). A social neuroscience perspective on the neurobiological bases of aggression. In P. R. Shaver, & M. Mikulincer (Eds.), *Human aggression and violence: Causes, manifestations, and consequences* (pp. 105–120). Washington, DC: American Psychological Association.

Denton, K., & Krebs, D. (1990). From the scene to the crime: The effect of alcohol and social context on moral judgment. *Journal of Personality and Social Psychology, 59,* 242–248.

Depla, M. F. I. A., ten Have, M. L., van Balkom, A. J. L. M., & de Graaf, R. (2008). Specific fears and phobias in the general population: Results from the Netherlands Mental Health Survey and Incidence Study (NEMESIS). *Social Psychiatry and Psychiatric Epidemiology, 43,* 200–208.

Dermer, M., Cohen, S. J., Jacobsen, E., & Anderson, E. A. (1979). Evaluative judgments of aspects of life as a function of vicarious exposure to hedonic extremes. *Journal of Personality and Social Psychology, 37,* 247–260.

Desikan, R. S., Cabral, H. J., Hess, C. P., Dillon, W. P., Glastonbury, C. M., Weiner, M. W., . . . Alzheimer's Disease Neuroimaging Initiative. (2009). Automated MRI measures identify individuals with mild cognitive impairment and Alzheimer's disease. *Brain, 132,* 2048–2057.

DeSteno, D., Petty, R. E., Wegener, D. T., & Rucker, D. D. (2000). Beyond valence in the perception of likelihood: The role of emotion specificity. *Journal of Personality and Social Psychology, 78,* 397–416.

Dettman, S. J., Pinder, D., Briggs, R. J. S., Dowell, R. C., & Leigh, J. R. (2007). Communication development in children who receive the cochlear implant younger than 12 months: Risk versus benefits. *Ear and Hearing, 28*(2), Supplement 11S–18S.

Deutsch, J. A. (1972, July). Brain reward: ESP and ecstasy. *Psychology Today,* 46–48.

DeValois, R. L., & DeValois, K. K. (1975). Neural coding of color. In E. C. Carterette & M. P. Friedman (Eds.), *Handbook of perception: Vol. V. Seeing.* New York: Academic Press.

Dew, M. A., Hoch, C. C., Buysse, D. J., Monk, T. H., Begley, A. E., Houck, P. R., . . . Reynolds, C. F., III. (2003). Healthy older adults' sleep predicts all-cause mortality at 4 to 19 years of follow-up. *Psychosomatic Medicine, 65,* 63–73.

DeWall, C. N., Baumeister, R. F., Stillman, T. F., & Gaillot, M. T. (2007). Violence restrained: Effects of self-regulation and its depletion on aggression. *Journal of Experimental Social Psychology, 43,* 62–76.

DeWall, C. N., Lambert, N. M., Slotter, E. B., Pond, R. S., Jr., Deckman, T., Finkel, E. J., . . . Fincham, F. D. (2011). So far away from one's partner, yet so close to romantic alternatives: Avoidant attachment, interest in alternatives, and infidelity. *Journal of Personality and Social Psychology, 101,* 1302–1316.

DeWall, C. N., MacDonald, G., Webster, G. D., Masten, C. L., Baumeister, R. F., Powell, C., . . . Eisenberger, N. I. (2010). Acetaminophen reduces social pain: Behavioral and neural evidence. *Psychological Science, 21,* 931–937.

DeWall, C. N., & Pond, R. S., Jr. (2011). Loneliness and smoking: The costs of the desire to reconnect. *Self and Identity, 10,* 375–385.

Dewar, M., Alber, J., Butler, C., Cowan, N., & Sala, S. D. (2012). Brief wakeful resting boosts new memories over the long term. *Psychological Science, 23,* 955–960.

DeYoung, C. G., Hirsch, J. B., Shane, M. S., Papademetris, X., Rajeevan, N., & Gray, J. R. (2010). Testing predictions from personality neuroscience: Brain structure and the Big Five. *Psychological Science, 21,* 820–828.

Di Tella, R., Haisken-De New, J., & MacCulloch, R. (2010). Happiness adaptation to income and to status in an individual panel. *Journal of Economic Behavior & Organization, 76,* 834–852.

Diaconis, P., & Mosteller, F. (1989). Methods for studying coincidences. *Journal of the American Statistical Association, 84,* 853–861.

Diamond, L. (2008). *Sexual fluidity: Understanding women's love and desire.* Cambridge, MA: Harvard University Press.

Dickens, W. T., & Flynn, J. R. (2006). Black Americans reduce the racial IQ gap: Evidence from standardization samples. *Psychological Science, 17,* 913–920.

Dickler, J. (2007, January 18). Best employers, great returns. *CNN Money* (CNNMoney.com).

Dickson, B. J. (2005, June 3). Quoted in E. Rosenthal, For fruit flies, gene shift tilts sex orientation. *The New York Times* (nytimes.com).

Dickson, N., van Roode, T., Cameron, C., & Paul, C. (2013). Stability and change in same-sex attraction, experience, and identity by sex and age in a New Zealand birth cohort. *Archives of Sexual Behavior, 42,* 753–763.

Diekelmann, S., & Born, J. (2010). The memory function of sleep. *Nature Neuroscience, 11,* 114–126.

Diener, E., Nickerson, C., Lucas, R. E., & Sandvik, E. (2002). Dispositional affect and job outcomes. *Social Indicators Research, 59,* 229–259.

Diener, E., & Oishi, S. (2000). Money and happiness: Income and subjective well-being across nations. In E. Diener & E. M. Suh (Eds.), *Subjective well-being across cultures* (pp. 185–218). Cambridge, MA: MIT Press.

Diener, E., Oishi, S., & Lucas, R. E. (2003). Personality, culture, and subjective well-being: Emotional and cognitive evaluations of life. *Annual Review of Psychology, 54,* 403–425.

Diener, E., Oishi, S., & Lucas, R. E. (2015). National accounts of subjective well-being. *American Psychologist, 70,* 234–242.

Diener, E., Oishi, S., & Park, J. Y. (2014). An incomplete list of eminent psychologists of the modern era. *Archives of Scientific Psychology, 21,* 20–31.

Diener, E., Tay, L., & Myers, D. G. (2011). The religion paradox: If religion makes people happy, why are so many dropping out? *Journal of Personality and Social Psychology, 101,* 1278–1290.

Diener, E., Wolsic, B., & Fujita, F. (1995). Physical attractiveness and subjective well-being. *Journal of Personality and Social Psychology, 69,* 120–129.

DiFranza, J. R. (2008, May). Hooked from the first cigarette. *Scientific American,* pp. 82–87.

Dijksterhuis, A., & Strick, M. (2016). A case for thinking without consciousness. *Perspectives on Psychological Science, 11,* 117–132.

Dik, B. J., & Duffy, R. D. (2012). *Make your job a calling: How the psychology of vocation can change your life at work.* Conshohocken, PA: Templeton Press.

DiLalla, D. L., Carey, G., Gottesman, I. I., & Bouchard, T. J., Jr. (1996). Heritability of MMPI personality indicators of psychopathology in twins reared apart. *Journal of Abnormal Psychology, 105,* 491–499.

Dimberg, U., Thunberg, M., & Elmehed, K. (2000). Unconscious facial reactions to emotional facial expressions. *Psychological Science, 11,* 86–89.

Dimidjian, S., & Hollon, S. D. (2010). How would we know if psychotherapy were harmful? *American Psychologist, 65,* 21–33.

Dingfelder, S. F. (2010, November). A second chance for the Mexican wolf. *Monitor on Psychology,* pp. 20–21.

Dion, K. K., & Dion, K. L. (1993). Individualistic and collectivistic perspectives on gender and the cultural context of love and intimacy. *Journal of Social Issues, 49,* 53–69.

DiSalvo, D. (2010, January/February). Are social networks messing with your head? *Scientific American Mind,* pp. 48–55.

Ditre, J. W., Brandon, T. H., Zale, E. L., & Meagher, M. M. (2011). Pain, nicotine, and smoking: Research findings and mechanistic considerations. *Psychological Bulletin, 137,* 1065–1093.

Dixon, J., Durrheim, K., & Tredoux, C. (2007). Intergroup contact and attitudes toward the principle and practice of racial equality. *Psychological Science, 18,* 867–872.

Dobbs, D. (2009, April). The post-traumatic stress trap. *Scientific American,* pp. 64–69.

Dodge, K. A. (2009). Mechanisms of gene–environment interaction effects in the development of conduct disorder. *Perspectives on Psychological Science, 4,* 408–414.

Dohrenwend, B. P., Pearlin, L., Clayton, P., Hamburg, B., Dohrenwend, B. S., Riley, M., & Rose, R. (1982). Report on stress and life events. In G. R. Elliott & C. Eisdorfer (Eds.), *Stress and human health: Analysis and implications of research* (pp. 55–80). New York: Springer.

DOL. (2015, accessed March 4). *Women in labor force.* U.S. Department of Labor (dol.gov/wb/stats/facts_over_time .htm).

Dolezal, H. (1982). *Living in a world transformed.* New York: Academic Press.

Domhoff, G. W. (1996). *Finding meaning in dreams: A quantitative approach.* New York: Plenum.

Domhoff, G. W. (2003). *The scientific study of dreams: Neural networks, cognitive development, and content analysis.* Washington, DC: American Psychological Association.

Domhoff, G. W. (2007). Realistic simulations and bizarreness in dream content: Past findings and suggestions for future research. In D. Barrett & P. McNamara (Eds.), *The new science of dreaming: Content, recall, and personality characteristics.* Westport, CT: Praeger.

Domhoff, G. W. (2010). *The case for a cognitive theory of dreams.* Unpublished manuscript: University of California at Santa Cruz (dreamresearch.net/Library /domhoff_2010.html).

Domhoff, G. W. (2011). The neural substrate for dreaming: Is it a subsystem of the default network? *Consciousness and Cognition, 20*(4), 1163–1174.

Domjan, M. (1992). Adult learning and mate choice: Possibilities and experimental evidence. *American Zoologist, 32,* 48–61.

Domjan, M. (1994). Formulation of a behavior system for sexual conditioning. *Psychonomic Bulletin & Review, 1,* 421–428.

Domjan, M. (2005). Pavlovian conditioning: A functional perspective. *Annual Review of Psychology, 56,* 179–206.

Donlea, J. M., Ramanan, N., & Shaw, P. J. (2009). Use-dependent plasticity in clock neurons regulates sleep need in Drosophila. *Science, 324,* 105–108.

Donnellan, M. B., Trzesniewski, K. H., Robins, R. W., Moffitt, T. E., & Caspi, A. (2005). Low self-esteem is related to aggression, antisocial behavior, and delinquency. *Psychological Science, 16,* 328–335.

Donnerstein, E. (1998). Why do we have those new ratings on television? Invited address to the National Institute on the Teaching of Psychology.

Donnerstein, E. (2011). The media and aggression: From TV to the Internet. In J. Forgas, A. Kruglanski, & K. Williams (Eds.), *The psychology of social conflict and aggression* (pp. 267–284). New York: Psychology Press.

Donohue, J., & Gebhard, P. (1995). The Kinsey Institute/Indiana University report on sexuality and spinal cord injury. *Sexuality and Disability, 1,* 7–85.

Donvan, J., & Zucker, C. (2010, October). Autism's first child. *The Atlantic* (theatlantic.com/magazine/archive/2010/10/autismsfirst-child/308227/).

Douglas, K. S., Guy, L. S., & Hart, S. D. (2009). Psychosis as a risk factor for violence to others: A meta-analysis. *Psychological Bulletin, 135,* 679–706.

Douthat, R. (2010, November 28). The partisan mind. *The New York Times* (nytimes.com).

Dovidio, J. F., & Gaertner, S. L. (1999). Reducing prejudice: Combating intergroup biases. *Current Directions in Psychological Science, 8,* 101–105.

Downs, E., & Smith, S. L. (2010). Keeping abreast of hypersexuality: A video game character content analysis. *Sex Roles, 62,* 721–733.

Doyle, R. (2005, March). Gay and lesbian census. *Scientific American,* p. 28.

Draganski, B., Gaser, C., Busch, V., Schuierer, G., Bogdahn, U., & May, A. (2004). Neuroplasticity: changes in grey matter induced by training. *Nature, 427*(6972), 311–312.

Draguns, J. G. (1990a). Normal and abnormal behavior in cross-cultural perspective: Specifying the nature of their relationship. *Nebraska Symposium on Motivation 1989, 37,* 235–277.

Draguns, J. G. (1990b). Applications of cross-cultural psychology in the field of mental health. In R. W. Brislin (Ed.), *Applied cross-cultural psychology* (pp. 302–324). Newbury Park, CA: Sage.

Draguns, J. G. (1997). Abnormal behavior patterns across cultures: Implications for counseling and psychotherapy. *International Journal of Intercultural Relations, 21,* 213–248.

Drew, T., Võ, M. L.-H., & Wolfe, J. M. (2013). The invisible gorilla strikes again: Sustained inattentional blindness in expert observers. *Psychological Science, 24,* 1848–1853.

Driessen, E., Cuijpers, P., de Maat, S. C. M., Abbas, A. A., de Jonghe, F., & Dekker, J. J. M. (2010). The efficacy of short-term psychodynamic psychotherapy for depression: A meta-analysis. *Clinical Psychology Review, 30,* 25–36.

Drydakis, N. (2009). Sexual orientation discrimination in the labour market. *Labour Economics, 16,* 364–372.

Duckworth, A. (2016). *Grit: The power of passion and perseverance.* New York: Scribner.

Duckworth, A. L., Quinn, P. D., Lynam, D. R., Loeber, R., & Stouthamer- Loeber, M. (2011). Role of test motivation in intelligence testing. *PNAS, 108,* 7716–7720.

Duckworth, A. L., Quinn, P. D., & Seligman, M. E. P. (2009). Positive predictors of teacher effectiveness. *Journal of Positive Psychology, 4,* 540–547.

Duckworth, A. L., & Seligman, M. E. P. (2005). Discipline outdoes talent: Self-discipline predicts academic performance in adolescents. *Psychological Science, 12,* 939–944.

Duckworth, A. L., & Seligman, M. E. P. (2006). Self-discipline gives girls the edge: Gender in self-discipline, grades, and achievement tests. *Journal of Educational Psychology, 98,* 198–208.

Duckworth, A. L., Tsukayama, E., & Kirby, T. A. (2013). Is it really self-control? Examining the predictive power of the delay of gratification task. *Personality and Social Psychology Bulletin, 39,* 843–855.

Duclos, S. E., Laird, J. D., Sexter, M., Stern, L., & Van Lighten, O. (1989). Emotion-specific effects of facial expressions and postures on emotional experience. *Journal of Personality and Social Psychology, 57,* 100–108.

Duggan, J. P., & Booth, D. A. (1986). Obesity, overeating, and rapid gastric emptying in rats with ventromedial hypothalamic lesions. *Science, 231,* 609–611.

Duits, P., Cath, D. C., Lissek, S., Hox, J. J., Hamm, A. O., Engelhard, I. M., . . . Baas, J. M. P. (2015). Updated meta-analysis of classical fear conditioning in the anxiety disorders. *Depression and Anxiety, 32,* 239–253.

DuMont, K. A., Widom, C. S., & Czaja, S. J. (2007). Predictors of resilience in abused and neglected children grown-up: The role of individual and neighborhood characteristics. *Child Abuse & Neglect, 31,* 255–274.

Dunbar, R. I. M., Baron, R., Frangou, A., Pearce, E., van Leeuwin, E. J. C., Stow, J., . . . van Vugt, M. (2011). Social laughter is correlated with an elevated pain threshold. *Proceedings of the Royal Society: Series B, 279,* 1161–1167.

Duncan, B. L. (1976). Differential social perception and attribution of intergroup violence: Testing the lower limits of stereotyping of blacks. *Journal of Personality and Social Psychology, 34,* 590–598.

Dunham, Y., Chen, E. E., & Banaji, M. R. (2013). Two signatures of implicit intergroup attitudes: Developmental invariance and early enculturation. *Psychological Science, 24,* 860–868.

Dunn, A. L., Trivedi, M. H., Kampert, J. B., Clark, C. G., & Chambliss, H. O. (2005). Exercise treatment for depression: Efficacy and dose response. *American Journal of Preventive Medicine, 28,* 1–8.

Dunn, E., & Norton, M. (2013). *Happy money: The science of smarter spending.* New York: Simon & Schuster.

Dunn, E. W., Aknin, L. B., & Norton, M. I. (2008). Spending money on others promotes happiness. *Science, 319,* 1687–1688.

Dunn, E. W., Aknin, L. B., & Norton, M. I. (2014). Pro-social spending and happiness: Using money to benefit others pays off. *Current Directions in Psychological Science, 13,* 347–355.

Dunn, M., & Searle, R. (2010). Effect of manipulated prestige-car ownership on both sex attractiveness ratings. *British Journal of Psychology, 101,* 69–80.

Dunson, D. B., Colombo, B., & Baird, D. D. (2002). Changes with age in the level and duration of fertility in the menstrual cycle. *Human Reproduction, 17,* 1399–1403.

Dutton, D. G., & Aron, A. P. (1974). Some evidence for heightened sexual attraction under conditions of high anxiety. *Journal of Personality and Social Psychology, 30,* 510–517.

Dutton, D. G., & Aron, A. P. (1989). Romantic attraction and generalized liking for others who are sources of conflict-based arousal. *Canadian Journal of Behavioural Sciences, 21,* 246–257.

Dutton, K. (2012). *The wisdom of psychopaths: What saints, spies, and serial killers can teach us about success.* New York: Scientific American/Farrar, Straus and Giroux.

Dweck, C. S. (2012a). Implicit theories. In P. A. M. Van Lange, A. Kruglanski, & E. T. Higgins (Eds.), *Handbook of theories of social psychology* (Vol. 2, pp. 43–61). Thousand Oaks, CA: Sage.

Dweck, C. S. (2012b). Mindsets and human nature: Promoting change in the Middle East, the schoolyard, the racial divide, and willpower. *American Psychologist, 67,* 614–622.

Dweck, C. S. (2015a, January 1). The secret to raising smart kids. *Scientific American* (scientificamerican.com).

Dweck, C. S. (2015b, September 23). Carol Dweck revists the "growth mindset." *Education Week* (edweek.org)

Dweck, C. S. (2016, January/February). The remarkable reach of growth mindsets. *Scientific American Mind,* pp. 35–41.

Eagan, K., Stolzenberg, E. B., Bates, A. K., Aragon, M. C. Suchard, M. R., & Rios-Aguilar, C. R. (2016). *The American freshman: National norms 2015.* Los Angeles, Higher Education Research Institute, UCLA.

Eagan, K., Stolzenberg, E. B., Ramirez, J. J., Aragon, M. C., Suchard, M. R., & Hurtado, S. (2014). *The American freshman: National norms fall 2014.* Los Angeles: UCLA Higher Education Research Institute.

Eagly, A. H. (2007). Female leadership advantage and disadvantage: Resolving the contradictions. *Psychology of Women Quarterly, 31,* 1–12.

Eagly, A. H. (2009). The his and hers of prosocial behavior: An examination of the social psychology of gender. *American Psychologist, 64,* 644–658.

Eagly, A. H. (2013, March 20). Hybrid style works, and women are best at it. *The New York Times* (nytimes.com).

Eagly, A. H., Ashmore, R. D., Makhijani, M. G., & Kennedy, L. C. (1991). What is beautiful is good, but . . .: A meta-analytic review of research on the physical attractiveness stereotype. *Psychological Bulletin, 110,* 109–128.

Eagly, A. H., & Carli, L. (2007). *Through the labyrinth: The truth about how women become leaders.* Cambridge, MA: Harvard University Press.

Eagly, A. H., & Wood, W. (1999). The origins of sex differences in human behavior: Evolved dispositions versus social roles. *American Psychologist, 54,* 408–423.

Eagly, A. H., & Wood, W. (2013). The nature-nurture debates: 25 years of challenges in understanding the psychology of gender. *Perspectives on Psychological Science, 8,* 340–357.

Easterlin, R. A., Morgan, R., Switek, M., & Wang, F. (2012). China's life satisfaction, 1990–2010. *PNAS, 109,* 9670–9671.

Eastwick, P. W., Luchies, L. B., Finkel, E. J., & Hunt, L. L. (2014a). The many voices of Darwin's descendants: Reply to Schmitt (2014). *Psychological Bulletin, 140,* 673–681.

Eastwick, P. W., Luchies, L. B., Finkel, E. J., & Hunt, L. L. (2014b). The predictive validity of ideal partner preferences: A review and meta-analysis. *Psychological Bulletin, 140,* 623–665.

Eckensberger, L. H. (1994). Moral development and its measurement across cultures. In W. J. Lonner & R. Malpass (Eds.), *Psychology and culture.* Boston: Allyn & Bacon.

Eckert, E. D., Heston, L. L., & Bouchard, T. J., Jr. (1981). MZ twins reared apart: Preliminary findings of psychiatric disturbances and traits. In L. Gedda, P. Paris, & W. D. Nance (Eds.), *Twin research: Vol. 3. Pt. B. Intelligence, personality, and development* (pp. 178–188). New York: Alan Liss.

Economist. (2001, December 20). An anthropology of happiness. *The Economist* (economist.com/world/asia).

Edelman, S., & Kidman, A. D. (1997). Mind and cancer: Is there a relationship? A review of the evidence. *Australian Psychologist, 32,* 1–7.

Editorial Board of *The New York Times.* (2015, December 15). Don't blame mental illness for gun violence. *The New York Times* (nytimes.com).

Edwards, R. R., Campbell, C., Jamison, R. N., & Wiech, K. (2009). The neurobiological underpinnings of coping with pain. *Current Directions in Psychological Science*, 18, 237–241.

Egeland, M., Zunszain, P. A., & Pariante, C. M. (2015). Molecular mechanisms in the regulation of adult neurogenesis during stress. *Nature Reviews Neuroscience*, 16, 189–200.

Eichstaedt, J. C., Schwartz, H. A., Kern, M. L., Park, G., Labarthe, D. R., Merchant, R. M., . . . Seligman, M. E. P. (2015). Psychological language on Twitter predicts county-level heart disease mortality. *Psychological Science*, 26, 159–169.

Eippert, F., Finsterbush, J., Bingel, U., & Bùchel, C. (2009). Direct evidence for spinal cord involvement in placebo analgesia. *Science*, 326, 404.

Eisenberg, D., Hunt, J., Speer, N., & Zivin, K. (2011). Mental health service utilization among college students in the United States. *Journal of Nervous and Mental Disease*, 199, 301–308.

Eisenberg, N., & Lennon, R. (1983). Sex differences in empathy and related capacities. *Psychological Bulletin*, 94, 100–131.

Eisenberger, N. I., Master, S. L., Inagaki, T. K., Taylor, S. E., Shirinyan, D., Lieberman, M. D., & Naliboff, B. D. (2011). Attachment figures activate a safety signal-related neural region and reduce pain experience. PNAS, 108, 11721–11726.

Eisenberger, R., & Rhoades, L. (2001). Incremental effects of reward on creativity. *Journal of Personality and Social Psychology*, 81, 728–741.

Eisenbruch, A. B., Simmons, Z. L., & Roney, J. R. (2015). Lady in red: Hormonal predictors of women's clothing choices. *Psychological Science*, 26, 1332–1338.

Ekman, P. (1994). Strong evidence for universals in facial expressions: A reply to Russell's mistaken critique. *Psychological Bulletin*, 115, 268–287.

Ekman, P., & Friesen, W. V. (1971). Constants across cultures in the face and emotion. *Journal of Personality and Social Psychology*, 17, 124–129.

Ekman, P., & Friesen, W. V. (1975). *Unmasking the face.* Englewood Cliffs, NJ: Prentice-Hall.

Ekman, P., Friesen, W. V., O'Sullivan, M., Chan, A., Diacoyanni-Tarlatzis, I., Heider, K., . . . Tzavaras, A. (1987). Universals and cultural differences in the judgments of facial expressions of emotion. *Journal of Personality and Social Psychology*, 53, 712–717.

Elbogen, E. B., & Johnson, S. C. (2009). The intricate link between violence and mental disorder: Results from the National Epidemiologic Survey on Alcohol and Related Conditions. *Archives of General Psychiatry*, 66, 152–161.

Elfenbein, H. A., & Ambady, N. (2002). On the universality and cultural specificity of emotion recognition: A meta-analysis. *Psychological Bulletin*, 128, 203–235.

Elfenbein, H. A., & Ambady, N. (2003a). When familiarity breeds accuracy: Cultural exposure and facial emotion recognition. *Journal of Personality and Social Psychology*, 85, 276–290.

Elfenbein, H. A., & Ambady, N. (2003b). Universals and cultural differences in recognizing emotions. *Current Directions in Psychological Science*, 12, 159–164.

Elkind, D. (1970). The origins of religion in the child. *Review of Religious Research*, 12, 35–42.

Elkind, D. (1978). *The child's reality: Three developmental themes.* Hillsdale, NJ: Erlbaum.

Ellenbogen, J. M., Hu, P. T., Payne, J. D., Titone, D., & Walker, M. P. (2007). Human relational memory requires time and sleep. PNAS, 104, 7723–7728.

Ellin, A. (2009, February 12). The recession. Isn't it romantic? *The New York Times* (nytimes.com).

Elliot, A. J., & Niesta, D. (2008). Romantic red: Red enhances men's attraction to women. *Journal of Personality and Social Psychology*, 95, 1150–1164.

Elliot, A. J., Tracy, J. L., Pazda, A. D., & Beall, A. T. (2013). Red enhances women's attractiveness to men: First evidence suggesting universality. *Journal of Experimental Social Psychology*, 49, 165–168.

Ellis, B. J., Bates, J. E., Dodge, K. A., Fergusson, D. M., John, H. L., Pettit, G. S., & Woodward, L. (2003). Does father absence place daughters at special risk for early sexual activity and teenage pregnancy? *Child Development*, 74, 801–821.

Ellis, B. J., & Boyce, W. T. (2008). Biological sensitivity to context. *Current Directions in Psychological Science*, 17, 183–187.

Ellis, L., & Ames, M. A. (1987). Neurohormonal functioning and sexual orientation: A theory of homosexuality-heterosexuality. *Psychological Bulletin*, 101, 233–258.

Else-Quest, N. M., Hyde, J. S., & Linn, M. C. (2010). Cross-national patterns of gender differences in mathematics: A meta-analysis. *Psychological Bulletin*, 136, 103–127.

Elzinga, B. M., Ardon, A. M., Heijnis, M. K., De Ruiter, M. B., Van Dyck, R., & Veltman, D. J. (2007). Neural correlates of enhanced working-memory performance in dissociative disorder: A functional MRI study. *Psychological Medicine*, 37, 235–245.

Emerging Trends. (1997, September). Teens turn more to parents than friends on whether to attend church. Princeton, NJ: Princeton Religion Research Center.

Emery, G., Jr. (2004). *Psychic predictions 2004.* Committee for the Scientific Investigation of Claims of the Paranormal (csicop.org).

Emery, G., Jr. (2006, January 17). Psychic predictions 2005. *Skeptical Inquirer* (csicop.org).

Emmons, S., Geisler, C., Kaplan, K. J., & Harrow, M. (1997). *Living with schizophrenia.* Muncie, IN: Taylor and Francis (Accelerated Development).

Endler, N. S. (1982). *Holiday of darkness: A psychologist's personal journey out of his depression.* New York: Wiley.

Engemann, K. M., & Owyang, M. T. (2005, April). So much for that merit raise: The link between wages and appearance. *Regional Economist* (stlouisfed.org).

Engen, T. (1987). Remembering odors and their names. *American Scientist*, 75, 497–503.

English, T., & Chen, S. (2011) Self-concept consistency and culture: The differential impact of two forms of consistency. *Personality and Social Psychology Bulletin*, 37, 838–849.

Entringer, S., Buss, C., Andersen, J., Chicz-DeMet, A., & Wadhwa, P. D. (2011). Ecological momentary assessment of maternal cortisol profiles over a multipleday period predicts the length of human gestation. *Psychosomatic Medicine*, 73, 469–474.

Epel, E. S. (2009). Telomeres in a life-span perspective: A new "psychobiomarker"? *Current Directions in Psychological Science*, 18, 6–9.

Epley, N., Keysar, B., Van Boven, L., & Gilovich, T. (2004). Perspective taking as egocentric anchoring and adjustment. *Journal of Personality and Social Psychology*, 87, 327–339.

Epley, N., Savitsky, K., & Gilovich, T. (2002). Empathy neglect: Reconciling the spotlight effect and the correspondence bias. *Journal of Personality and Social Psychology*, 83, 300–312.

Epstein, J., Stern, E., & Silbersweig, D. (1998). Mesolimbic activity associated with psychosis in schizophrenia: Symptom-specific PET studies. *Annals of the New York Academy of Sciences*, 877, 562–574.

Epstein, S. (1983a). Aggregation and beyond: Some basic issues on the prediction of behavior. *Journal of Personality*, 51, 360–392.

Epstein, S. (1983b). The stability of behavior across time and situations. In R. Zucker, J. Aronoff, & A. I. Rabin (Eds.), *Personality and the prediction of behavior.* San Diego: Academic Press.

Eranti, S. V., MacCabe, J. H., Bundy, H., & Murray, R. M. (2013). Gender difference in age at onset of schizophrenia: A meta-analysis. *Psychological Medicine*, 43, 155–167.

Erdelyi, M. H. (1985). *Psychoanalysis: Freud's cognitive psychology.* New York: Freeman.

Erdelyi, M. H. (1988). Repression, reconstruction, and defense: History and integration of the psychoanalytic and experimental frameworks. In J. Singer (Ed.), *Repression: Defense mechanism and cognitive style* (pp. 1–31). Chicago: University of Chicago Press.

Erdelyi, M. H. (2006). The unified theory of repression. *Behavioral and Brain Sciences*, 29, 499–551.

Erickson, K. I. (2009). Aerobic fitness is associated with hippocampal volume in elderly humans. *Hippocampus*, 19, 1030–1039.

Erickson, K. I., Raji, C. A., Lopez, O. L., Becker, J. T., Rosano, C., Newman, A. B., . . . Kuller, L. H. (2010). Physical activity predicts gray matter volume in late adulthood: The Cardiovascular Health Study. *Neurology*, 75, 1415–1422.

Erickson, M. F., & Aird, E. G. (2005). *The motherhood study: Fresh insights on mothers' attitudes and concerns.* New York: The Motherhood Project, Institute for American Values.

Ericsson, K. A., & Pool, R. (2016). *PEAK: Secrets from the new science of expertise.* Boston: Houghton Mifflin.

Ericsson, K. A., Roring, R. W., & Nandagopal, K. (2007). Giftedness and evidence for reproducibly superior performance: An account based on the expert performance framework. *High Ability Studies*, 18, 3–56.

Erikson, E. H. (1963). *Childhood and society.* New York: Norton.

Erlich, N., Lipp, O. V., & Slaughter, V. (2013). Of hissing snakes and angry voices: Human infants are differentially responsive to evolutionary fear-relevant sounds. *Developmental Science*, 16, 894–904.

Ermer, E., Cope, L. M., Nyalakanti, P. K., Calhoun, V. D., & Kiehl, K. A. (2012). Aberrant paralimbic gray matter in criminal psychopathy. *Journal of Abnormal Psychology*, 121, 649–658.

Ertmer, D. J., Young, N. M., & Nathani, S. (2007). Profiles of focal development in young cochlear implant recipients. *Journal of Speech, Language, and Hearing Research*, 50, 393–407.

Escasa, M. J., Casey, J. F., & Gray, P. B. (2011). Salivary testosterone levels in men at a U.S. sex club. *Archives of Sexual Behavior*, 40, 921–926.

Escobar-Chaves, S. L., Tortolero, S. R., Markham, C. M., Low, B. J., Eitel, P., & Thickstun, P. (2005). Impact of the media on adolescent sexual attitudes and behaviors. *Pediatrics*, 116, 303–326.

Esposito, G., Yoshida, S., Ohnishi, R., Tsuneoka, Y., Rostagno, M., Yokota, S., . . . Kuroda, K. O. (2013). Infant calming responses during maternal carrying in humans and mice. *Current Biology*, 23, 739–745.

Esser, J. K., & Lindoerfer, J. S. (1989). Groupthink and the space shuttle *Challenger* accident: Toward a quantitative case analysis. *Journal of Behavioral Decision Making*, 2, 167–177.

Esterling, B. A., L'Abate, L., Murray, E. J., & Pennebaker, J. W. (1999). Empirical foundations for writing in prevention and psychotherapy: Mental and physical health outcomes. *Clinical Psychology Review*, 19, 79–96.

Esterson, A. (2001). The mythologizing of psychoanalytic history: Deception and self-deception in Freud's accounts of the seduction theory episode. *History of Psychiatry, 12,* 329–352.

Eurich, T. L., Krause, D. E., Cigularov, K., & Thornton, G. C., III. (2009). Assessment centers: Current practices in the United States. *Journal of Business Psychology, 24,* 387–407.

Evans, C. R., & Dion, K. L. (1991). Group cohesion and performance: A meta-analysis. *Small Group Research, 22,* 175–186.

Evans, N., & Levinson, S. C. (2009). The myth of language universals: Language diversity and its importance for cognitive science. *Behavioral and Brain Sciences, 32,* 429–492.

Everett, J. A. C., Caviola, L., Kahane, G., Savulescu, J., & Faber, N. S. (2015). Doing good by doing nothing? The role of social norms in explaining default effects in altruistic contexts. *European Journal of Social Psychology, 45,* 230–241.

Evers, A., Muñiz, J., Bartram, D., Boben, D., Egeland, J., Fernández-Hermida, J. R., . . . Urbánek, T. (2012). Testing practices in the 21st century: Developments and European psychologists' opinions. *European Psychologist, 17,* 300–319.

Exelmans, L., Custers, K., & Van den Bulck, J. (2015). Violent video games and delinquent behavior in adolescents: A risk factor perspective. *Aggressive Behavior, 41,* 267–279.

Exline, J. J., Baumeister, R. F., Bushman, B. J., Campbell, W. K., & Finkel, E. J. (2004). Too proud to let go: Narcissistic entitlement as a barrier to forgiveness. *Journal of Personality and Social Psychology, 87,* 894–912.

Eysenck, H. J. (1952). The effects of psychotherapy: An evaluation. *Journal of Consulting Psychology, 16,* 319–324.

Eysenck, H. J. (1990, April 30). An improvement on personality inventory. *Current Contents: Social and Behavioral Sciences, 22*(18), 20.

Eysenck, H. J. (1992). Four ways five factors are not basic. *Personality and Individual Differences, 13,* 667–673.

Eysenck, H. J., & Grossarth-Maticek, R. (1991). Creative novation behavior therapy as a prophylactic treatment for cancer and coronary heart disease: Part II—Effects of treatment. *Behaviour Research and Therapy, 29,* 17–31.

Eysenck, H. J., Wakefield, J. A., Jr., & Friedman, A. F. (1983). Diagnosis and clinical assessment: The DSM-III. *Annual Review of Psychology, 34,* 167–193.

Eysenck, S. B. G., & Eysenck, H. J. (1963). The validity of questionnaire and rating assessments of extraversion and neuroticism, and their factorial stability. *British Journal of Psychology, 54,* 51–62.

Fabiano, G. A., Pelham, W. E., Jr., Coles, E. K., Gnagy, E. M., Chronis-Tuscano, A., & O'Connor, B. C. (2008). A meta-analysis of behavioral treatments for attention-deficit/hyperactivity disorder. *Clinical Psychology Review, 29,* 129–140.

Fagan, J. F., & Holland, C. R. (2007). Equal opportunity and racial differences in IQ. *Intelligence, 30,* 361–387.

Fairfield, H. (2012, February 4). Girls lead in science exam, but NOT in the United States. *The New York Times* (nytimes.com).

Falk, R., Falk, R., & Ayton, P. (2009). Subjective patterns of randomness and choice: Some consequences of collective responses. *Journal of Experimental Psychology: Human Perception and Performance, 35,* 203–224.

Fanti, K. A., Vanman, E., Henrich, C. C., & Avraamides, M. N. (2009). Desensitization to media violence over a short period of time. *Aggressive Behavior, 35,* 179–187.

Farah, M. J., Rabinowitz, C., Quinn, G. E., & Liu, G. T. (2000). Early commitment of neural substrates for face recognition. *Cognitive Neuropsychology, 17,* 117–124.

Farb, N. A. S., Anderson, A. K., Mayberg, H., Bean, J., McKeon, D., & Segal, Z. V. (2010). Minding one's emotions: Mindfulness training alters the neural expression of sadness. *Emotion, 10,* 25–33.

Farina, A. (1982). The stigma of mental disorders. In A. G. Miller (Ed.), *In the eye of the beholder* (pp. 305–363). New York: Praeger.

Farley, M., Baral, I., Kiremire, M., & Sezgin, U. (1998). Prostitution in five countries: Violence and post-traumatic stress disorder. *Feminism and Psychology, 8,* 405–426.

Farnia, V., Shakeri, J., Tatari, F., Juibari, T. A., Yazdchi, K., Bajoghli, H., . . . Aghaei, A. (2014). Randomized controlled trial of aripiprazole versus risperidone for the treatment of amphetamine-induced psychosis. *The American Journal of Drug and Alcohol Abuse, 40*(1), 10–15.

Farrington, D. P. (1991). Antisocial personality from childhood to adulthood. *The Psychologist: Bulletin of the British Psychological Society, 4,* 389–394.

Farruggia, S. P., Chen, C., Greenberger, E., Dmitrieva, J., & Macek, P. (2004). Adolescent self-esteem in cross-cultural perspective: Testing measurement equivalence and a mediation model. *Journal of Cross-Cultural Psychology, 35,* 719–733.

Fatemi, S. H., & Folsom, T. D. (2009). The neurodevelopmental hypothesis of schizophrenia, revisited. *Schizophrenia Bulletin, 35,* 528–548.

Fazel, S., & Grann, M. (2006). The population impact of severe mental illness on violent crime. *American Journal of Psychiatry, 163,* 1397–1403.

Fazel, S., Langstrom, N., Hjern, A., Grann, M., & Lichtenstein, P. (2009). Schizophrenia, substance abuse, and violent crime. *JAMA, 301,* 2016–2023.

Fazel, S., Lichtenstein, P., Grann, M., Goodwin, G. M., & Långström, N. (2010). Bipolar disorder and violent crime: New evidence from population-based longitudinal studies and systematic review. *Archives of General Psychiatry, 67,* 931–938.

Federal Trade Commission. (2016). Lumosity to pay $2 million to settle FTC deceptive advertising charges for its "brain training" program. [Press release]. Retrieved from ftc.gov/news-events/press-releases/2016/01/lumosity-pay-2-million-settle-ftc-deceptive-advertising-charges

Feingold, A. (1992). Good-looking people are not what we think. *Psychological Bulletin, 111,* 304–341.

Feingold, A., & Mazzella, R. (1998). Gender differences in body image are increasing. *Psychological Science, 9,* 190–195.

Feinstein, J. S., Buzza, C., Hurlemann, R., Follmer, R. L., Dahdaleh, N. S., Coryell, W. H., . . . Wemmie, J. A. (2013). Fear and panic in humans with bilateral amygdala damage. *Nature Neuroscience, 16,* 270–272.

Feinstein, J. S., Duff, M. C., & Tranel, D. (2010, April 27). Sustained experiences of emotion after loss of memory in patients with amnesia. *PNAS, 107,* 7674–7679.

Feldman, G., Baumeister, R. F., & Wong, K. F. E. (2014a). Free will is about choosing: The link between choice and the belief in free will. *Personality and Social Psychology Bulletin, 55,* 239–245.

Feldman, M. B., & Meyer, I. H. (2010). Comorbidity and age of onset of eating disorders in gay men, lesbians, and bisexuals. *Psychiatry Research, 180,* 126–131.

Feldman, R., Rosenthal, Z., & Eidelman, A. I. (2014b). Maternal-preterm skin-to-skin contact enhances child physiologic organization and cognitive control across the first 10 years of life. *Biological Psychiatry, 75,* 56–64.

Fenigstein, A. (2015). Milgram's shock experiments and the Nazi perpetrators: A contrarian perspective on the role of obedience pressures during the Holocaust. *Theory and Psychology, 25,* 581–598.

Fenn, K. M., & Hambrick, D. Z. (2012). Individual differences in working memory capacity predict sleep-dependent memory consolidation. *Journal of Experimental Psychology: General, 141*(3), 404–410.

Fenton, W. S., & McGlashan, T. H. (1991). Natural history of schizophrenia subtypes: II. Positive and negative symptoms and long-term course. *Archives of General Psychiatry, 48,* 978–986.

Fenton, W. S., & McGlashan, T. H. (1994). Antecedents, symptom progression, and long-term outcome of the deficit syndrome in schizophrenia. *American Journal of Psychiatry, 151,* 351–356.

Ferguson, C. J. (2009, June 14). Not every child is secretly a genius. *The Chronicle Review* (chronicle.com /article/Not-Every-Child-Is-Secretly/48001).

Ferguson, C. J. (2013). Spanking, corporal punishment and negative long-term outcomes: A meta-analytic review of longitudinal studies. *Clinical Psychology Review, 33,* 196–208.

Ferguson, C. J. (2014). Is video game violence bad? *The Psychologist, 27,* 324–327.

Ferguson, C. J. (2015). Do angry birds make for angry children? A meta-analysis of video game influences on children's and adolescents' aggression, mental health, prosocial behavior, and academic performance. *Perspectives on Psychological Science, 10,* 646–666.

Ferguson, C. J., Winegard, B., & Winegard, B. M. (2011). Who is the fairest one of all? How evolution guides peer and media influences on female body dissatisfaction. *Review of General Psychology, 15,* 11–28.

Ferguson, M. J., & Zayas, V. (2009). Automatic evaluation. *Current Directions in Psychological Science, 18,* 362–366.

Fergusson, D. M., & Woodward, L. G. (2002). Mental health, educational, and social role outcomes of adolescents with depression. *Archives of General Psychiatry, 59,* 225–231.

Fernández-Dols, J.-M., & Ruiz-Belda, M.-A. (1995). Are smiles a sign of happiness? Gold medal winners at the Olympic Games. *Journal of Personality and Social Psychology, 69,* 1113–1119.

Fernie, G., Peeters, M., Gullo, M. J., Christianson, P., Cole, J. C., Sumnall, H., & Field, M. (2013). Multiple behavioral impulsivity tasks predict prospective alcohol involvement in adolescents. *Addiction, 108,* 1916–1923.

Fernyhough, C. (2008). Getting Vygotskian about theory of mind: Mediation, dialogue, and the development of social understanding. *Developmental Review, 28,* 225–262.

Ferriman, K., Lubinski, D., & Benbow, C. P. (2009). Work preferences, life values, and personal views of top math/science graduate students and the profoundly gifted: Developmental changes and gender differences during emerging adulthood and parenthood. *Journal of Personality and Social Psychology, 97,* 517–522.

Ferris, C. F. (1996, March). The rage of innocents. *The Sciences,* pp. 22–26.

Ficks, C. A., & Waldman, I. D. (2014). Candidate genes for aggression and antisocial behavior: A meta-analysis of association studies of the 5HTTLPR and MAOA-uVNTR. *Behavior Genetics, 44,* 427–444.

Fiedler, F. E. (1981). Leadership effectiveness. *American Behavioral Scientist, 24,* 619–632.

Fiedler, F. E. (1987, September). When to lead, when to stand back. *Psychology Today,* pp. 26–27.

Field, A. P. (2006). Is conditioning a useful framework for understanding the development and treatment of phobias? *Clinical Psychology Review, 26,* 857–875.

Field, T. (2010). Touch for socioemotional and physical well-being: A review. *Developmental Review, 30,* 367–383.

Field, T., Hernandez-Reif, M., Feijo, L., & Freedman, J. (2006). Prenatal, perinatal and neonatal stimulation: A survey of neonatal nurseries. *Infant Behavior & Development, 29,* 24–31.

Fielder, R. L., Walsh, J. L., Carey, K. B., & Carey, M. P. (2013). Predictors of sexual hookups: A theory-based, prospective study of first-year college women. *Archives of Sexual Behavior, 42,* 1425–1441.

Fields, R. D. (2011, May/June). The hidden brain. *Scientific American,* pp. 53–59.

Fikke, L. T., Melinder, A., & Landrø, N. I. (2011). Executive functions are impaired in adolescents engaging in non-suicidal self-injury. *Psychological Medicine, 41,* 601–610.

Filbey, F. M., Aslan, S., Calhoun, V. D., Spence, J. S., Damaraju, E., Caprihan, A., & Segall, J. (2014). Long-term effects of marijuana use on the brain. *PNAS, 111,* 16913–16918.

Fincham, F. D., & Bradbury, T. N. (1993). Marital satisfaction, depression, and attributions: A longitudinal analysis. *Journal of Personality and Social Psychology, 64,* 442–452.

Finchilescu, G., & Tredoux, C. (Eds.) (2010). Intergroup relations in post apartheid South Africa: Change, and obstacles to change. *Journal of Social Issues, 66,* 223–236.

Finer, L. B., & Philbin, J. M. (2014). Trends in ages at key reproductive transitions in the United States, 1951–2010. *Women's Health Issues, 24,* e271–e279. Retrieved from http://dx.doi.org/10.1016/j.whi.2014.02.002

Fingelkurts, A. A., & Fingelkurts, A. A. (2009). Is our brain hardwired to produce God, or is our brain hardwired to perceive God? A systematic review on the role of the brain in mediating religious experience. *Cognitive Processes, 10,* 293–326.

Fingerman, K. L., & Charles, S. T. (2010). It takes two to tango: Why older people have the best relationships. *Current Directions in Psychological Science, 19,* 172–176.

Fink, M. (2009). *Electroconvulsive therapy: A guide for professionals and their patients.* New York: Oxford University Press.

Finkel, E. J., Cheung, E. O., Emery, L. F., Carswell, K. L., & Larson, G. M. (2015a). The suffocation model: Why marriage in America is becoming an all-or-nothing institution. *Current Directions in Psychological Science, 24,* 238–244.

Finkel, E. J., DeWall, C. N., Slotter, E. B., McNulty, J. K., Pond, R. S., Jr., & Atkins, D. C. (2012a). Using I3 theory to clarify when dispositional aggressiveness predicts intimate partner violence perpetration. *Journal of Personality and Social Psychology, 102,* 533–549.

Finkel, E. J., & Eastwick, P. W. (2008). Speed-dating. *Current Directions in Psychological Science, 17,* 193–197.

Finkel, E. J., & Eastwick, P. W. (2009). Arbitrary social norms influence sex differences in romantic selectivity. *Psychological Science, 20,* 1290–1295.

Finkel, E. J., Eastwick, P. W., Karney, B. R., Reis, H. T., & Sprecher, S. (2012b, September/October). Dating in a digital world. *Scientific American Mind,* pp. 26–33.

Finkel, E. J., Eastwick, P. W., Karney, B. R., Reis, H. T., & Sprecher, S. (2012c). Online dating: A critical analysis from the perspective of psychological science. *Psychological Science in the Public Interest, 13,* 3–66.

Finkel, E. J., Norton, M. I., Reis, H. T., Ariely, D., Caprariello, P. A., Eastwick, P. W., . . . Maniaci, M. R. (2015b). When does familiarity promote versus undermine interpersonal attraction? A proposed integrative model from erstwhile adversaries. *Perspectives on Psychological Science, 10,* 3–19.

Fiore, M. C., Jaén, C. R., Baker, T. B., Bailey, W. C., Benowitz, N. L., Curry, S. J., . . . Wewers, M. E. (2008). *Treating tobacco use and dependence: 2008 update. Clinical practice guideline.* Rockville, MD: U.S. Department of Health and Human Services, Public Health Service.

Fischer, A., & LaFrance, M. (2015). What drives the smile and the tear: Why women are more emotionally expressive than men. *Emotion Review, 7,* 22–29.

Fischer, P., & Greitemeyer, T. (2006). Music and aggression: The impact of sexual-aggressive song lyrics on aggression-related thoughts, emotions, and behavior toward the same and the opposite sex. *Personality and Social Psychology Bulletin, 32,* 1165–1176.

Fischer, P., Greitemeyer, T., Kastenmüller, A., Vogrincic, C., & Sauer, A. (2011). The effects of risk-glorifying media exposure on risk-positive cognitions, emotions, and behaviors: A meta-analytic review. *Psychological Bulletin, 137,* 367–390.

Fischer, R., & Boer, D. (2011). What is more important for national well-being: money or autonomy? A meta-analysis of well-being, burnout, and anxiety across 63 societies. *Journal of Personality and Social Psychology, 101,* 164–184.

Fischhoff, B., Slovic, P., & Lichtenstein, S. (1977). Knowing with certainty: The appropriateness of extreme confidence. *Journal of Experimental Psychology: Human Perception and Performance, 3,* 552–564.

Fishbach, A., Dhar, R., & Zhang, Y. (2006). Subgoals as substitutes or complements: The role of goal accessibility. *Journal of Personality and Social Psychology, 91,* 232–242.

Fisher, E. L., & Borgida, E. (2012). Intergroup disparities and implicit bias: A commentary. *Journal of Social Issues, 68,* 385–398.

Fisher, H. E. (1993, March/April). After all, maybe it's biology. *Psychology Today,* pp. 40–45.

Fisher, H. T. (1984). Little Albert and Little Peter. *Bulletin of the British Psychological Society, 37,* 269.

Flack, W. F. (2006). Peripheral feedback effects of facial expressions, bodily postures, and vocal expressions on emotional feelings. *Cognition and Emotion, 20,* 177–195.

Flaherty, D. K. (2011). The vaccine-autism connection: a public health crisis caused by unethical medical practices and fraudulent science. *Annals of Pharmacotherapy, 45,* 1302–1304.

Flegal, K. M., Carroll, M. D., Kit, B. K., Ogden, C. L. (2012). Prevalence of obesity and trends in the distribution of body mass index among US adults, 1999–2010. *JAMA, 307,* 491–497.

Fleming, I., Baum, A., & Weiss, L. (1987). Social density and perceived control as mediator of crowding stress in high-density residential neighborhoods. *Journal of Personality and Social Psychology, 52,* 899–906.

Fleming, J. H. (2001, Winter/Spring). Introduction to the special issue on linkage analysis. *Gallup Research Journal,* pp. i–vi.

Fleming, J. H., & Scott, B. A. (1991). The costs of confession: The Persian Gulf War POW tapes in historical and theoretical perspective. *Contemporary Social Psychology, 15,* 127–138.

Fletcher, G. J. O., Fitness, J., & Blampied, N. M. (1990). The link between attributions and happiness in close relationships: The roles of depression and explanatory style. *Journal of Social and Clinical Psychology, 9,* 243–255.

Flora, S. R. (2004). *The power of reinforcement.* Albany, NJ: SUNY Press.

Flora, S. R., & Bobby, S. E. (2008, September/October). The bipolar bamboozle. *Skeptical Inquirer,* pp. 41–45.

Flueckiger, L., Lieb, R., Meyer, A., Witthauer, C., & Mata, J. (2016). The importance of physical activity and sleep for affect on stressful days: Two intensive longitudinal studies. *Emotion, 16*(4), 488–497.

Flynn, J. R. (2003). Movies about intelligence: The limitations of *g. Current Directions in Psychological Science, 12,* 95–99.

Flynn, J. R. (2007). *What is intelligence?* New York: Cambridge University Press.

Flynn, J. R. (2012). *Are we getting smarter? Rising IQ in the twenty-first century.* Cambridge: Cambridge University Press.

Foa, E. B., Gillihan, S. J., & Bryant, R. A. (2013). Challenges and successes in dissemination of evidence-based treatments for posttraumatic stress: Lessons learned from prolonged exposure therapy for PTSD. *Psychological Science in the Public Interest, 14,* 65–111.

Foa, E. B., & Kozak, M. J. (1986). Emotional processing of fear: Exposure to corrective information. *Psychological Bulletin, 99,* 20–35.

Foer, J. (2011a). *Moonwalking with Einstein: The art and science of remembering everything.* New York: Penguin.

Foer, J. (2011b, February 20). Secrets of a mind-gamer. *The New York Times* (nytimes.com).

Fong, C. J., Zaleski, D. J., & Leach, J. K. (2015). The challenge–skill balance and antecedents of flow: A meta-analytic investigation. *Journal of Positive Psychology, 10,* 425–446.

Fong, K., & Mar, R. A. (2015). What does my avatar say about me? Inferring personality from avatars. *Personality and Social Psychology Bulletin, 41,* 237–249.

Ford, E. S. (2002). Does exercise reduce inflammation? Physical activity and B-reactive protein among U.S. adults. *Epidemiology, 13,* 561–569.

Ford, M. T., Cerasoli, C. P., Higgins, J. A., & Deccesare, A. L. (2011). Relationships between psychological, physical, and behavioural health and work performance: A review and meta-analysis. *Work & Stress, 25,* 185–204.

Foree, D. D., & LoLordo, V. M. (1973). Attention in the pigeon: Differential effects of food-getting versus shock-avoidance procedures. *Journal of Comparative and Physiological Psychology, 85,* 551–558.

Forgas, J. P. (2008). Affect and cognition. *Perspectives on Psychological Science, 3,* 94–101.

Forgas, J. P. (2009, November/December). Think negative! *Australian Science,* pp. 14–17.

Forgas, J. P., Bower, G. H., & Krantz, S. E. (1984). The influence of mood on perceptions of social interactions. *Journal of Experimental Social Psychology, 20,* 497–513.

Forsyth, D. R., Lawrence, N. K., Burnette, J. L., & Baumeister, R. F. (2007). Attempting to improve academic performance of struggling college students by bolstering their self-esteem: An intervention that backfired. *Journal of Social and Clinical Psychology, 26,* 447–459.

Foss, D. J., & Hakes, D. T. (1978). *Psycholinguistics: An introduction to the psychology of language.* Englewood Cliffs, NJ: Prentice-Hall.

Foster, J. (2011, June 16). Our deadly anorexic pact. *The Daily Mail* (dailymail.co.uk).

Foubert, J. D., Brosi, M. W., & Bannon, R. S. (2011). Pornography viewing among fraternity men: Effects on bystander intervention, rape myth acceptance, and behavioral intent to commit sexual assault. *Sexual Addiction & Compulsivity, 18,* 212–231.

Foulkes, D. (1999). *Children's dreaming and the development of consciousness.* Cambridge, MA: Harvard University Press.

Fournier, J. C., DeRubeis, R. J., Hollon, S. D., Dimidjian, S., Amsterdam, J. D., Shelton, R. C., & Fawcett, J. (2010). Antidepressant drug effects and depression severity: A patient-level meta-analysis. *Journal of the American Medical Association, 303,* 47–53.

Fouts, R. S. (1992). Transmission of a human gestural language in a chimpanzee mother-infant relationship. *Friends of Washoe, 12/13,* pp. 2–8.

Fouts, R. S. (1997). *Next of kin: What chimpanzees have taught me about who we are.* New York: Morrow.

Fowles, D. C. (1992). Schizophrenia: Diathesis-stress revisited. *Annual Review of Psychology, 43,* 303–336.

Fowles, D. C., & Dindo, L. (2009). Temperament and psychopathy: A dual-pathway model. *Current Directions in Psychological Science, 18,* 179–183.

Fox, B. H. (1998). Psychosocial factors in cancer incidence and prognosis. In J. C. Holland (Ed.) *Psycho-oncology* (pp. 110–124). New York: Oxford University Press.

Fox, C. R., & Tannenbaum, D. (2015, September 26). The curious politics of the "nudge." *The New York Times* (nytimes.com)

Fox, D. (2010, June). The insanity virus. *Discover,* pp. 58–64.

Fox, E., Lester, V., Russo, R., Bowles, R. J., Pichler, A., & Dutton, K. (2000). Facial expression of emotion: Are angry faces detected more efficiently? *Cognition and Emotion, 14,* 61–92.

Fox, M. L., Dwyer, D. J., & Ganster, D. C. (1993). Effects of stressful job demands and control on physiological and attitudinal outcomes in a hospital setting. *Academy of Management Journal, 36,* 289–318.

Fraley, R. C., Roisman, G. I., Booth-LaForce, C., Owen, M. T., & Holland, A. S. (2013). Interpersonal and genetic origins of adult attachment styles: A longitudinal study from infancy to early adulthood. *Journal of Personality and Social Psychology, 104,* 817–838.

Fraley, R. C., Vicary, A. M., Brumbaugh, C. C., & Roisman, G. I. (2011). Patterns of stability in adult attachment: An empirical test of two models of continuity and change. *Journal of Personality and Social Psychology, 101,* 974–992.

Frances, A. J. (2013). *Saving normal: An insider's revolt against out-of-control psychiatric diagnosis, DSM-5, big pharma, and the medicalization of ordinary life.* New York: HarperCollins.

Frances, A. J. (2014, September/October). No child left undiagnosed. *Psychology Today,* pp. 49–50.

Frank, J. D. (1982). Therapeutic components shared by all psychotherapies. In J. H. Harvey & M. M. Parks (Eds.), *The Master Lecture Series: Vol. 1. Psychotherapy research and behavior change* (pp. 9–37). Washington, DC: American Psychological Association.

Frankenburg, W., Dodds, J., Archer, P., Shapiro, H., & Bresnick, B. (1992). The Denver II: A major revision and restandardization of the Denver Developmental Screening Test. *Pediatrics, 89,* 91–97.

Frankl, V. E. (1962). *Man's search for meaning: An introduction to logotherapy.* Boston: Beacon Press.

Franklin, M., & Foa, E. B. (2011). Treatment of obsessive-compulsive disorder. *Annual Review of Clinical Psychology, 7,* 229–243.

Frasure-Smith, N., & Lesperance, F. (2005). Depression and coronary heart disease: Complex synergism of mind, body, and environment. *Current Directions in Psychological Science, 14,* 39–43.

Frattaroli, J. (2006). Experimental disclosure and its moderators: A meta-analysis. *Psychological Bulletin, 132,* 823–865.

Fredrickson, B. L. (2013). Updated thinking on positivity ratios. *American Psychologist, 68,* 814–822.

Freedman, D. H. (2011, February). How to fix the obesity crisis. *Scientific American,* pp. 40–47.

Freedman, D. J., Riesenhuber, M., Poggio, T., & Miller, E. K. (2001). Categorical representation of visual stimuli in the primate prefrontal cortex. *Science, 291,* 312–316.

Freedman, J. L., & Perlick, D. (1979). Crowding, contagion, and laughter. *Journal of Experimental Social Psychology, 15,* 295–303.

Freedman, R., Lewis, D. A., Michels, R., Pine, D. S., Schultz, S. K., Tamminga, C. A., . . . Yager, J. (2013). The initial field trials of DSM-5: New blooms and old thorns. *American Journal of Psychiatry, 170,* 1–5.

Freeman, D., & Freeman, J. (2013). *The stressed sex: Uncovering the truth about men, women, and mental health.* Oxford, England: Oxford University Press.

Freeman, E. C., & Twenge, J. M. (2010, January). *Using MySpace increases the endorsement of narcissistic personality traits.* Poster presented at the annual conference of the Society for Personality and Social Psychology, Las Vegas, NV.

Freeman, W. J. (1991, February). The physiology of perception. *Scientific American,* pp. 78–85.

Frenda, S. J., Patihis, L., Loftus, E. F., Lewis, H. C., & Fenn, K. M. (2014). Sleep deprivation and false memories. *Clinical Psychological Science, 25,* 1674–1681.

Freud, S. (1935: reprinted 1960). *A general introduction to psychoanalysis.* New York: Washington Square Press.

Freyd, J. J., DePrince, A. P., & Gleaves, D. H. (2007). The state of betrayal trauma theory: Reply to McNally—Conceptual issues and future directions. *Memory, 15,* 295–311.

Freyd, J. J., Putnam, F. W., Lyon, T. D., Becker-Blease, K. A., Cheit, R. E., Siegel, N. B., & Pezdek, K. (2005). The science of child sexual abuse. *Science, 308,* 501.

Friedel, J. E., DeHart, W. B., Madden, G. J., & Odum, A. L. (2014). Impulsivity and cigarette smoking: Discounting of monetary and consumable outcomes in current and non-smokers. *Psychopharmacology, 231,* 4517–4526.

Friedman, H. S., & Martin, L. R. (2012). *The longevity project.* New York: Penguin (Plume).

Friedman, M., & Ulmer, D. (1984). *Treating Type A behavior—and your heart.* New York: Knopf.

Friedman, R., & James, J. W. (2008). The myth of the stages of dying, death and grief. *Skeptic, 14(2),* 37–41.

Friedman, R. A. (2012, December 17). In gun debate, a misguided focus on mental illness. *The New York Times* (nytimes.com).

Friedrich, M., Wilhelm, I., Born, J., & Friederici, A. D. (2015). Generalization of word meanings during infant sleep. *Nature Communications, 6,* Article 6004. doi:10.1038/ncomms7004

Friend, T. (2004). *Animal talk: Breaking the codes of animal language.* New York: Free Press.

Frisch, M., & Zdravkovic, S. (2010). Body size at birth and same-sex marriage in young adulthood. *Archives of Sexual Behavior, 39,* 117–123.

Frisell, T., Pawitan, Y., Långström, N., & Lichtenstein, P. (2012). Heritability, assortative mating and gender differences in violent crime: Results from a total population sample using twin, adoption, and sibling models. *Behavior Genetics, 42,* 3–18.

Frith, U., & Frith, C. (2001). The biological basis of social interaction. *Current Directions in Psychological Science, 10,* 151–155.

Fritz, T., Jentschke, S., Gosselin, N., Sammler, D., Peretz, I., Turner, R., . . . Koelsch, S. (2009). Universal recognition of three basic emotions in music. *Current Biology, 19,* 573–576.

Fromkin, V., & Rodman, R. (1983). *An introduction to language* (3rd ed.). New York: Holt, Rinehart & Winston.

Frühauf, S., Gerger, H., Schmidt, H. M., Munder, T., & Barth, J. (2013). Efficacy of psychological interventions for sexual dysfunction: A systematic review and meta-analysis. *Archives of Sexual Behavior, 42,* 915–933.

Fry, A. F., & Hale, S. (1996). Processing speed, working memory, and fluid intelligence: Evidence for a developmental cascade. *Psychological Science, 7,* 237–241.

Fry, D. P. (2012). Life without war. *Science, 336,* 879–884.

Fuhriman, A., & Burlingame, G. M. (1994). Group psychotherapy: Research and practice. In A. Fuhriman & G. M. Burlingame (Eds.), *Handbook of group psychotherapy* (pp. 3–40). New York: Wiley.

Fuhrmann, D., Knoll, L. J., & Blakemore, S. J. (2015). Adolescence as a sensitive period of brain development. *Trends in Cognitive Sciences, 19(10),* 558–566.

Fuller, M. J., & Downs, A. C. (1990). *Spermarche is a salient biological marker in men's development.* Poster presented at the American Psychological Society convention.

Fuller, T. D., Edwards, J. N., Sermsri, S., & Vorakitphokatorn, S. (1993). Housing, stress, and physical well-being: Evidence from Thailand. *Social Science & Medicine, 36,* 1417–1428.

Fulmer, C. A., Gelfand, M. J., Kruglanski, A. W., Kim-Prieto, C., Diener, E., Pierro, A., & Higgins, E. T. (2010). On "feeling right" in cultural contexts: How person–culture match affects self-esteem and subjective well-being. *Psychological Science, 21,* 1563–1569.

Funder, D. C., & Block, J. (1989). The role of ego-control, ego-resiliency, and IQ in delay of gratification in adolescence. *Journal of Personality and Social Psychology, 57,* 1041–1050.

Furnham, A. (1982). Explanations for unemployment in Britain. *European Journal of Social Psychology, 12,* 335–352.

Furnham, A., & Baguma, P. (1994). Cross-cultural differences in the evaluation of male and female body shapes. *International Journal of Eating Disorders, 15,* 81–89.

Furnham, A., & Wu, J. (2008). Gender differences in estimates of one's own and parental intelligence in China. *Individual Differences Research, 6,* 1–12.

Furr, R. M., & Funder, D. C. (1998). A multimodal analysis of personal negativity. *Journal of Personality and Social Psychology, 74,* 1580–1591.

Furukawa, T. A., Levine, S. Z., Tanaka, S., Goldberg, Y., Samara, M., Davis, J. M., . . . Leucht, S. (2015). Initial severity of schizophrenia and efficacy of antipsychotics: Participant-level meta-analysis of 6 placebo-controlled studies. *JAMA Psychiatry, 72,* 14–21.

Gable, S. L., Gosnell, C. L., Maisel, N. C., & Strachman, A. (2012). Safely testing the alarm: Close others' responses to personal positive events. *Journal of Personality and Social Psychology, 103,* 963–981.

Gaddy, M. A., & Ingram, R. E. (2014). A meta-analytic review of mood-congruent implicit memory in depressed mood. *Clinical Psychology Review, 34,* 402–416.

Gaertner, L., Iuzzini, J., & O'Mara, E. M. (2008). When rejection by one fosters aggression against many: Multiple-victim aggression as a consequence of social rejection and perceived groupness. *Journal of Experimental Social Psychology, 44,* 958–970.

Gaillard, R., Dehaene, S., Adam, C., Clémenceau, S., Hasboun, D., Baulac, M., . . . Naccache, L. (2009). Converging intracranial markers of conscious access. *PLoS Biology, 7(e):* e1000061.

Gaissmaier, W., & Gigerenzer, G. (2012). 9/11, Act II: A fine-grained analysis of regional variations in traffic fatalities in the aftermath of the terrorist attacks. *Psychological Science, 23,* 1449–1454.

Galak, J., Leboeuf, R. A., Nelson, L. D., & Simmons, J. P. (2012). Correcting the past: Failures to replicate psi. *Journal of Personality and Social Psychology, 103,* 933–948.

Galambos, N. L. (1992). Parent-adolescent relations. *Current Directions in Psychological Science, 1,* 146–149.

Galanter, E. (1962). Contemporary psychophysics. In R. Brown, E. Galanter, E. H. Hess, & G. Mandler (Eds.), *New directions in psychology.* New York: Holt Rinehart & Winston.

Gale, C. R., Batty, G. D., & Deary, I. J. (2008). Locus of control at age 10 years and health outcomes and behaviors at age 30 years: The 1970 British Cohort Study. *Psychosomatic Medicine, 70,* 397–403.

Galinsky, A. M., & Sonenstein, F. L. (2013). Relationship commitment, perceived equity, and sexual enjoyment among young adults in the United States. *Archives of Sexual Behavior, 42,* 93–104.

Galla, B. M., & Duckworth, A. L. (2015). More than resisting temptation: Beneficial habits mediate the relationship between self-control and positive life outcomes. *Journal of Personality and Social Psychology, 109,* 508–525.

Gallace, A. (2012). Living with touch. *The Psychologist, 25,* 896–899.

Gallace, A., & Spence, C. (2011). To what extent do Gestalt grouping principles influence tactile perception? *Psychological Bulletin, 137,* 538–561.

Gallese, V., Gernsbacher, M. A., Heyes, C., Hickok, G., & Iacoboni, M. (2011). Mirror neuron forum. *Perspectives on Psychological Science, 6,* 369–407.

Gallup, G. G., Jr., & Frederick, D. A. (2010). The science of sex appeal: An evolutionary perspective. *Review of General Psychology, 14,* 240–250.

Gallup, G. H. (1972). *The Gallup poll: Public opinion 1935–1971 (Vol. 3).* New York: Random House.

Gallup Organization. (2004, August 16). Personal communication [T. Rath: bucketbook@gallup.com].

Gandhi, A. V., Mosser, E. A., Oikonomou, G., & Prober, D. A. (2015). Melatonin is required for the circadian regulation of sleep. *Neuron, 85,* 1193–1199.

Gangestad, S. W., & Simpson, J. A. (2000). The evolution of human mating: Tradeoffs and strategic pluralism. *Behavioral and Brain Sciences, 23,* 573–587.

Gangestad, S. W., Thornhill, R., & Garver-Apgar, C. E. (2010). Men's facial masculinity predicts changes in their female partners' sexual interests across the ovulatory cycle, whereas men's intelligence does not. *Evolution and Human Behavior, 31,* 412–424.

Gangwisch, J. E., Babiss, L. A., Malaspina, D., Turner, J. B., Zammit, G. K., & Posner, K. (2010). Earlier parental set bedtimes as a protective factor against depression and suicidal ideation. *Sleep, 33,* 97–106.

Gao, Y., Raine, A., Venables, P. H., Dawson, M. E., & Mednick, S. A. (2010). Association of poor childhood fear conditioning and adult crime. *American Journal of Psychiatry, 167,* 56–60.

Garcia, J., & Gustavson, A. R. (1997, January). Carl R. Gustavson (1946–1996): Pioneering wildlife psychologist. *APS Observer,* pp. 34–35.

Garcia, J., & Koelling, R. A. (1966). Relation of cue to consequence in avoidance learning. *Psychonomic Science, 4,* 123–124.

Garcia, J. R., Massey, S. G., Merriwether, A. M., & Seibold-Simpson, S. M. (2013). *Orgasm experience among emerging adult men and women: Relationship context and attitudes toward uncommitted sex.* Poster presentation at the Association for Psychological Science convention, Washington, DC.

Garcia, J. R., Reiber, C., Massey, S. G., & Merriwether, A. M. (2012). Sexual hookup culture: A review. *Review of General Psychology, 16,* 161–176.

Garcia, J. R., Reiber, C., Massey, S. G., & Merriwether, A. M. (2013, February). Sexual hook-up culture. *Monitor on Psychology,* pp. 60–66.

Garcia-Falgueras, A., & Swaab, D. F. (2010). Sexual hormones and the brain: An essential alliance for sexual identity and sexual orientation. *Endocrine Development, 17,* 22–35.

Gardner, H. (1983). *Frames of mind: The theory of multiple intelligences.* New York: Basic Books.

Gardner, H. (1998, March 19). An intelligent way to progress. *The Independent* (London), p. E4.

Gardner, H. (2006). *The development and education of the mind: The selected works of Howard Gardner.* New York: Routledge/Taylor & Francis.

Gardner, H. (2011). *The theory of multiple intelligences: As psychology, as education, as social science.* Address on the receipt of an honorary degree from José Cela University in Madrid and the Prince of Asturias Prize for Social Science.

Gardner, J., & Oswald, A. J. (2007). Money and mental well-being: A longitudinal study of medium–sized lottery wins. *Journal of Health Economics, 6,* 49–60.

Gardner, R. A., & Gardner, B. I. (1969). Teaching sign language to a chimpanzee. *Science, 165,* 664–672.

Garfield, C. (1986). *Peak performers: The new heroes of American business.* New York: Morrow.

Garon, N., Bryson, S. E., & Smith, I. M. (2008). Executive function in preschoolers: A review using an integrative framework. *Psychological Bulletin, 134,* 31–60.

Gartrell, N., & Bos, H. (2010). U.S. national longitudinal lesbian family study: Psychological adjustment of 17-year-old adolescents. *Pediatrics, 126,* 28–36.

Gatchel, R. J., Peng, Y. B., Peters, M. L., Fuchs, P. N., & Turk, D. C. (2007). The biopsychosocial approach to chronic pain: Scientific advances and future directions. *Psychological Bulletin, 133,* 581–624.

Gates, G. J., & Newport, F. (2012, October 18). *Special report: 3.4% of U.S. adults identify as LGBT.* (gallup.com).

Gavin, K. (2004, November 9). *U-M team reports evidence that smoking affects human brain's natural "feel good" chemical system* [Press release]. Retrieved from https://www.sciencedaily.com/releases/2004/10/041027141507.htm

Gawronski, B., & Quinn, K. (2013). Guilty by mere similarity: Assimilative effects of facial resemblance on automatic evaluation. *Journal of Experimental Social Psychology, 49,* 120–125.

Gazzaniga, M. S. (1967, August). The split brain in man. *Scientific American,* pp. 24–29.

Gazzaniga, M. S. (1983). Right hemisphere language following brain bisection: A 20-year perspective. *American Psychologist, 38,* 525–537.

Gazzaniga, M. S. (1988). Organization of the human brain. *Science, 245,* 947–952.

Gazzaniga, M. S. (2016). *Tales from both sides of the brain: A life in neuroscience.* New York: Ecco.

Gazzola, V., Spezio, M. L., Etzel, J. A., Catelli, F., Adolphs, R., & Keysers, C. (2012). Primary somatosensory cortex discriminates affective significance in social touch. *PNAS, 109,* E1657–E1666.

Ge, X., & Natsuaki, M. N. (2009). In search of explanations for early pubertal timing effects on developmental psychopathology. *Current Directions in Psychological Science, 18,* 327–441.

Geary, D. C. (1995). Sexual selection and sex differences in spatial cognition. *Learning and Individual Differences, 7,* 289–301.

Geary, D. C. (1996). Sexual selection and sex differences in mathematical abilities. *Behavioral and Brain Sciences, 19,* 229–247.

Geary, D. C. (2010). *Male, female: The evolution of human sex differences* (2nd ed.). Washington, DC: American Psychological Association.

Geary, D. C., Salthouse, T. A., Chen, G.-P., & Fan, L. (1996). Are East Asian versus American differences in arithmetical ability a recent phenomenon? *Developmental Psychology, 32,* 254–262.

Gehring, W. J., Wimke, J., & Nisenson, L. G. (2000). Action monitoring dysfunction in obsessive-compulsive disorder. *Psychological Science, 11*(1), 1–6.

Geier, A. B., Rozin, P., & Doros, G. (2006). Unit bias: A new heuristic that helps explain the effects of portion size on food intake. *Psychological Science, 17,* 521–525.

Gellis, L. A., Arigo, D., & Elliott, J. C. (2013). Cognitive refocusing treatment for insomnia: A randomized controlled trial in university students. *Behavior Therapy, 44,* 100–110.

Gentile, D. A. (2009). Pathological video-game use among youth ages 8 to 18: A national study. *Psychological Science, 20,* 594–602.

Gentile, D. A., & Bushman, B. J. (2012). Reassessing media violence effects using a risk and resilience approach to understanding aggression. *Psychology of Popular Media Culture, 1,* 138–151.

Gentile, D. A., Coyne, S., & Walsh, D. A. (2011). Media violence, physical aggression and relational aggression in school age children: A short-term longitudinal study. *Aggressive Behavior, 37,* 193–206.

George, L. K., Larson, D. B., Koenig, H. G., & McCullough, M. E. (2000). Spirituality and health: What we know, what we need to know. *Journal of Social and Clinical Psychology, 19,* 102–116.

Geraerts, E., Bernstein, D. M., Merckelbach, H., Linders, C., Raymaekers, L., & Loftus, E. F. (2008). Lasting false beliefs and their behavioral consequences. *Psychological Science, 19,* 749–753.

Geraerts, E., Schooler, J. W., Merckelback, H., Jelicic, M., Hauer, B. J. A., & Ambadar, Z. (2007). The reality of recovered memories: Corroborating continuous and discontinuous memories of childhood sexual abuse. *Psychological Science, 18,* 564–568.

Gerber, J., & Wheeler, L. (2009). On being rejected: A meta-analysis of experimental research on rejection. *Perspectives on Psychological Science, 4,* 468–488.

Gerhart, K. A., Koziol-McLain, J., Lowenstein, S. R., & Whiteneck, G. G. (1994). Quality of life following spinal cord injury: Knowledge and attitudes of emergency care providers. *Annals of Emergency Medicine, 23,* 807–812.

Germain, A. (2013). Sleep disturbances as the hallmark of PTSD: Where are we now? *Archives of Journal of Psychiatry, 170,* 372–382.

Gerrard, M., & Luus, C. A. E. (1995). Judgments of vulnerability to pregnancy: The role of risk factors and individual differences. *Personality and Social Psychology Bulletin, 21,* 160–171.

Gershoff, E. T. (2002). Parental corporal punishment and associated child behaviors and experiences: A meta-analytic and theoretical review. *Psychological Bulletin, 128,* 539–579.

Gershoff, E. T., Grogan-Kaylor, A., Lansford, J. E., Chang, L., Zelli, A., Deater-Deckard, K., & Dodge, K. A. (2010). Parent discipline practices in an international sample: Associations with child behaviors and moderation by perceived normativeness. *Child Development, 81,* 487–502.

Giancola, P. R., Josephs, R. A., Parrott, D. J., & Duke, A. A. (2010). Alcohol myopia revisited: Clarifying aggression and other acts of disinhibition through a distorted lens. *Perspectives on Psychological Science, 5,* 265–278.

Gibbons, F. X. (1986). Social comparison and depression: Company's effect on misery. *Journal of Personality and Social Psychology, 51*, 140–148.

Gibson, E. J., & Walk, R. D. (1960, April). The "visual cliff." *Scientific American*, pp. 64–71.

Giesbrecht, T., Lynn, S. J., Lilienfeld, S. O., & Merckelbach, H. (2008). Cognitive processes in dissociation: An analysis of core theoretical assumptions. *Psychological Bulletin, 134*, 617–647.

Giesbrecht, T., Lynn, S. J., Lilienfeld, S. O., & Merckelbach, H. (2010). Cognitive processes, trauma, and dissociation—Misconceptions and misrepresentations: Reply to Bremmer (2010). *Psychological bulletin, 136*, 7–11.

Gigantesco, A., Stazi, M. A., Alessandri, G., Medda, E., Tarolla, E., & Fagnani, C. (2011). Psychological well-being (PWB): A natural life outlook? An Italian twin study of heritability on PWB in young adults. *Psychological Medicine, 41*, 2637–2649.

Gigerenzer, G. (2004). Dread risk, September 11, and fatal traffic accidents. *Psychological Science, 15*, 286–287.

Gigerenzer, G. (2006). Out of the frying pan into the fire: Behavioral reactions to terrorist attacks. *Risk Analysis, 26*, 347–351.

Gigerenzer, G. (2010). *Rationality for mortals: How people cope with uncertainty*. New York: Oxford University Press.

Gigerenzer, G., Gaissmaier, W., Kurz-Milcke, E., Schwartz, L. M., & Woloshin, S. (2008). Helping doctors and patients make sense of health statistics. *Psychological Science in the Public Interest, 8*, 53–96.

Gigerenzer, G., Gaissmaier, W., Kurz-Milcke, E., Schwartz, L. M., & Woloshin, S. (2009, April/May). Knowing your chances. *Scientific American Mind*, pp. 41–51.

Gilbert, D. T. (2006). *Stumbling on happiness*. New York: Knopf.

Gilbert, D. T., King, G., Pettigrew, S., & Wilson, T. D. (2016). Comment on "Estimating the reproducibility of psychological science." *Science, 351*, 1037-b.

Gildersleeve, K., Haselton, M., & Fales, M. R. (2014). Do women's mate preferences change across the menstrual cycle? A meta-analytic review. *Psychological Bulletin, 140*, 1205–1259.

Gilestro, G. F., Tononi, G., & Cirelli, C. (2009). Widespread changes in synaptic markers as a function of sleep and wakefulness in Drosophila. *Science, 324*, 109–112.

Gill, A. J., Oberlander, J., & Austin, E. (2006). Rating e-mail personality at zero acquaintance. *Personality and Individual Differences, 40*, 497–507.

Gillen-O'Neel, C., Huynh, V. W., & Fuligni, A. J. (2013). To study or to sleep? The academic costs of extra studying at the expense of sleep. *Child Development, 84*, 133–142.

Gillison, M. L., Broutian, T., Pickard, R. K. L., Tong, Z.-Y., Xiao, W., Kahle, L., . . . Chaturvedi, A. K. (2012). Prevalence of oral HPV infection in the United States, 2009–2010. *JAMA, 307*, 693–703.

Gilovich, T. D. (1996). *The spotlight effect: Exaggerated impressions of the self as a social stimulus*. Unpublished manuscript, Cornell University.

Gilovich, T. D., & Medvec, V. H. (1995). The experience of regret: What, when, and why. *Psychological Review, 102*, 379–395.

Gilovich, T. D., & Savitsky, K. (1999). The spotlight effect and the illusion of transparency: Egocentric assessments of how we are seen by others. *Current Directions in Psychological Science, 8*, 165–168.

Giltay, E. J., Geleijnse, J. M., Zitman, F. G., Buijsse, B., & Kromhout, D. (2007). Lifestyle and dietary correlates of dispositional optimism in men: The Zutphen Elderly Study. *Journal of Psychosomatic Research, 63*, 483–490.

Giltay, E. J., Geleijnse, J. M., Zitman, F. G., Hoekstra, T., & Schouten, E. G. (2004). Dispositional optimism and all-cause and cardiovascular mortality in a prospective cohort of elderly Dutch men and women. *Archives of General Psychiatry, 61*, 1126–1135.

Gingerich, O. (1999, February 6). Is there a role for natural theology today? *The Real Issue* (origins.org/real/n9501/natural.html).

Gino, G., Wilmuth, C. A., & Brooks, A. W. (2015). Compared to men, women view professional advancement as equally attainable, but less desirable. *PNAS, 112*, 12354–12359.

Glasman, L. R., & Albarracin, D. (2006). Forming attitudes that predict future behavior: A meta-analysis of the attitude-behavior relation. *Psychological Bulletin, 132*, 778–822.

Glass, R. M. (2001). Electroconvulsive therapy: Time to bring it out of the shadows. *Journal of the American Medical Association, 285*, 1346–1348.

Gleaves, D. H. (1996). The sociocognitive model of dissociative identity disorder: A reexamination of the evidence. *Psychological Bulletin, 120*, 42–59.

Global Burden of Disease Study 2013 Collaborators. (2015). Global, regional, and national incidence, prevalence, and years lived with disability for 301 acute and chronic diseases and injuries in 188 countries, 1990–2013: A systematic analysis for the Global Burden of Disease Study 2013. *The Lancet, 386*, 743–800.

Gluszek, A., & Dovidio, J. F. (2010). The way they speak: A social psychological perspective on the stigma of nonnative accents in communication. *Personality and Social Psychology Review, 14*, 214–237.

Godden, D. R., & Baddeley, A. D. (1975). Context-dependent memory in two natural environments: On land and underwater. *British Journal of Psychology, 66*, 325–331.

Goethals, G. R., & Allison, S. T. (2014). Kings and charisma, Lincoln and leadership: An evolutionary perspective. In G. R. Goethals, S. T. Allison, R. M. Kramer, & D. M. Messick (Eds.), *Conceptions of leadership: Enduring ideas and emerging insights* (pp. 111–124). New York: Palgrave Macmillan.

Goff, D. C., & Simms, C. A. (1993). Has multiple personality disorder remained consistent over time? *Journal of Nervous and Mental Disease, 181*, 595–600.

Gold, M., & Yanof, D. S. (1985). Mothers, daughters, and girlfriends. *Journal of Personality and Social Psychology, 49*, 654–659.

Goldberg, J. (2007, accessed May 31). *Quivering bundles that let us hear*. Howard Hughes Medical Institute (hhmi.org/senses/c120.html).

Goldberg, L. R. (1992). The development of markers for the Big-Five factor structure. *Psychological Assessment, 4*, 26–42.

Golder, S. A., & Macy, M. W. (2011). Diurnal and seasonal mood vary with work, sleep, and day-length across diverse cultures. *Science, 333*, 1878–1881.

Goldfried, M. R., & Padawer, W. (1982). Current status and future directions in psychotherapy. In M. R. Goldfried (Ed.), *Converging themes in psychotherapy: Trends in psychodynamic, humanistic, and behavioral practice* (pp. 3–49). New York: Springer.

Goldfried, M. R., Raue, P. J., & Castonguay, L. G. (1998). The therapeutic focus in significant sessions of master therapists: A comparison of cognitive-behavioral and psychodynamic-interpersonal interventions. *Journal of Consulting and Clinical Psychology, 66*, 803–810.

Goldinger, S. D., & Papesh, M. H. (2012). Pupil dilation reflects the creation and retrieval of memories. *Current Directions in Psychological Science, 21*, 90–95.

Goldman, A. L., Pezawas, L., Mattay, V. S., Fischl, B., Verchinski, B. A., Chen, Q., . . . Meyer-Lindenberg, A. (2009). Widespread reductions of cortical thickness in schizophrenia and spectrum disorders and evidence of heritability. *Archives of General Psychiatry, 66*, 467–477.

Goldstein, I. (2000, August). Male sexual circuitry. *Scientific American*, pp. 70–75.

Goldstein, I., Lue, T. F., Padma-Nathan, H., Rosen, R. C., Steers, W. D., & Wicker, P. A. (1998). Oral sildenafil in the treatment of erectile dysfunction. *New England Journal of Medicine, 338*, 1397–1404.

Goleman, D. (1980, February). 1,528 little geniuses and how they grew. *Psychology Today*, pp. 28–53.

Goleman, D. (1995). *Emotional intelligence*. New York: Bantam.

Goleman, D. (2006). *Social intelligence*. New York: Bantam Books.

Golkar, A., Selbing, I., Flygare, O., Öhman, A., & Olsson, A. (2013). Other people as means to a safe end: Vicarious extinction blocks the return of learned fear. *Psychological Science, 24*, 2182–2190.

Gollwitzer, P. M., & Oettingen, G. (2012). Goal pursuit. In P. M. Gollwitzer & G. Oettingen (Eds.), *The Oxford handbook of human motivation* (pp. 208–231). New York: Oxford University Press.

Gómez-Robles, A., Hopkins, W. D., Schapiro, S. J., & Sherwood, C. C. (2015). Relaxed genetic control of cortical organization in human brains compared with chimpanzees. *PNAS, 112*, 14799–14804.

Goodale, M. A., & Milner, D. A. (2004). *Sight unseen: An exploration of conscious and unconscious vision*. Oxford: Oxford University Press.

Goodale, M. A., & Milner, D. A. (2006). One brain—two visual systems. *The Psychologist, 19*, 660–663.

Goode, E. (1999, April 13). If things taste bad, 'phantoms' may be at work. *The New York Times* (nytimes.com).

Goode, E. (2012, June 19). Senators start a review of solitary confinement. *The New York Times* (nytimes.com).

Goodhart, D. E. (1986). The effects of positive and negative thinking on performance in an achievement situation. *Journal of Personality and Social Psychology, 51*, 117–124.

Goodman, G. S., Ghetti, S. Quas, J. A., Edelstein, R. S., Alexander, K. W., Redlick, A. D., . . . Jones, D. P. H. (2003). A prospective study of memory for child sexual abuse: New findings relevant to the repressed-memory controversy. *Psychological Science, 14*, 113–118.

Goodman, G. S., & Quas, J. A. (2008). Repeated interviews and children's memory. *Current Directions in Psychological Science, 17*, 386–389.

Goodwin, P. Y., Mosher, W. D., & Chandra, A. (2010). Marriage and cohabitation in the United States: A statistical portrait based on Cycle 6 (2002) of the National Survey of Family Growth. National Center for Health Statistics. *Vital Health Statistics, 23*(28).

Gopnik, A., Griffiths, T. L., & Lucas, C. G. (2015). When younger learners can be better (or at least more open-minded) than older ones. *Current Directions in Psychological Science, 24*, 87–92.

Goranson, R. E. (1978). *The hindsight effect in problem solving*. Unpublished manuscript, cited by G. Wood (1984), Research methodology: A decision-making perspective. In A. M. Rogers & C. J. Scheirer (Eds.), *The G. Stanley Hall lecture series* (Vol. 4). Washington, DC.

Gorchoff, S. M., John, O. P., & Helson, R. (2008). Contextualizing change in marital satisfaction during middle age. *Psychological Science, 19*, 1194–1200.

Gordon, A. M., & Chen, S. (2010). When you accept me for me: The relational benefits of intrinsic affirmations from one's relationship partner. *Personality and Social Psychology Bulletin, 36*, 1439–1453.

Gordon, A. M., & Chen, S. (2014). The role of sleep in interpersonal conflict: Do sleepless nights mean worse fights? *Social Psychological and Personality Science, 5,* 168–175.

Gore, J., & Sadler-Smith, E. (2011). Unpacking intuition: A process and outcome framework. *Review of General Psychology, 15,* 304–316.

Gore-Felton, C., Koopman, C., Thoresen, C., Arnow, B., Bridges, E., & Spiegel, D. (2000). Psychologists' beliefs and clinical characteristics: Judging the veracity of childhood sexual abuse memories. *Professional Psychology: Research and Practice, 31,* 372–377.

Gorlick, A. (2010, January 13). Stanford scientists link brain development to chances of recovering vision after blindness. *Stanford Report* (news.stanford.edu).

Gorman, J. (2014, January 6). The brain, in exquisite detail. *The New York Times* (nytimes.com).

Gorrese, A., & Ruggieri, R. (2012). Peer attachment: A meta-analytic review of gender and age differences and associations with parent attachment. *Journal of Youth and Adolescence, 41,* 650–672.

Gosling, S. D. (2008). *Snoop: What your stuff says about you.* New York: Basic Books.

Gosling, S. D., Kwan, V. S. Y., & John, O. P. (2003). A dog's got personality: A cross-species comparative approach to personality judgments in dogs and humans. *Journal of Personality and Social Psychology, 85,* 1161–1169.

Gotlib, I. H., & Hammen, C. L. (1992). *Psychological aspects of depression: Toward a cognitive-interpersonal integration.* New York: Wiley.

Gottesman, I. I. (1991). *Schizophrenia genesis: The origins of madness.* New York: Freeman.

Gottesman, I. I. (2001). Psychopathology through a life span-genetic prism. *American Psychologist, 56,* 867–881.

Gottfredson, L. S. (2002a). Where and why *g* matters: Not a mystery. *Human Performance, 15,* 25–46.

Gottfredson, L. S. (2002b). *g:* Highly general and highly practical. In R. J. Sternberg & E. L. Grigorenko (Eds.), *The general factor of intelligence: How general is it?* (pp. 331–380). Mahwah, NJ: Erlbaum.

Gottfredson, L. S. (2003a). Dissecting practical intelligence theory: Its claims and evidence. *Intelligence, 31,* 343–397.

Gottfredson, L. S. (2003b). On Sternberg's "Reply to Gottfredson." *Intelligence, 31,* 415–424.

Gould, E. (2007). How widespread is adult neurogenesis in mammals? *Nature Neuroscience, 8,* 481–488.

Gould, S. J. (1981). *The mismeasure of man.* New York: Norton.

Goyal, M., Singh, S., Sibinga, E. S., Gould, N. F., Rowland-Seymour, A., Sharma, R., . . . Haythornthwaite, J. A. (2014). Meditation programs for psychological stress and well-being: A systematic review and meta-analysis. *JAMA Internal Medicine, 174,* 357–368.

Grace, A. A. (2010). Ventral hippocampus, interneurons, and schizophrenia: A new understanding of the pathophysiology of schizophrenia and its implications for treatment and prevention. *Current Directions in Psychological Science, 19,* 232–237.

Grady, C. L., McIntosh, A. R., Horwitz, B., Maisog, J. M., Ungeleider, L. G., Mentis, M. J., . . . Haxby, J. V. (1995). Age-related reductions in human recognition memory due to impaired encoding. *Science, 269,* 218–221.

Grande, G., Romppel, M., & Barth, J. (2012). Association between type D personality and prognosis in patients with cardiovascular diseases: A systematic review and meta-analysis. *Annals of Behavioral Medicine, 43,* 299–310.

Granic, I., Lobel, A., & Engels, R. C. M. E. (2014). The benefits of playing video games. *American Psychologist, 69,* 66–78.

Grant, A. M., Gino, F., & Hoffmann, D. A. (2011). Reversing the extraverted leadership advantage: The role of employee proactivity. *Academy of Management Journal, 54,* 528–550.

Gray-Little, B., & Burks, N. (1983). Power and satisfaction in marriage: A review and critique. *Psychological Bulletin, 93,* 513–538.

Graybiel, A. M., & Smith, K. S. (2014, June). Good habits, bad habits. *Scientific American,* pp. 39–43.

Green, J. D., Sedikides, C., & Gregg, A. P. (2008). Forgotten but not gone: The recall and recognition of self-threatening memories. *Journal of Experimental Social Psychology, 44,* 547–561.

Green, J. T., & Woodruff-Pak, D. S. (2000). Eyeblink classical conditioning: Hippocampal formation is for neutral stimulus associations as cerebellum is for association-response. *Psychological Bulletin, 126,* 138–158.

Green, M. F., & Horan, W. P. (2010). Social cognition in schizophrenia. *Current Directions in Psychological Science, 19,* 243–248.

Greenberg, J. (2008). Understanding the vital human quest for self-esteem. *Perspectives on Psychological Science, 3,* 48–55.

Greene, J. (2010). Remarks to an Edge conference: The new science of morality. Retrieved from edge.org

Greene, J., Sommerville, R. B., Nystrom, L. E., Darley, J. M., & Cohen, J. D. (2001). An fMRI investigation of emotional engagement in moral judgment. *Science, 293,* 2105.

Greenwald, A. G. (1992). *Subliminal semantic activation and subliminal snake oil.* Paper presented to the American Psychological Association Convention, Washington, DC.

Greenwald, A. G., Banaji, M. R., & Nosek, B. A. (2015). Statistically small effects of the implicit association test can have societally large effects. *Journal of Personality and Social Psychology, 108,* 553–561.

Greenwald, A. G., McGhee, D. E., & Schwartz, J. L. K. (1998). Measuring individual differences in implicit cognition: The implicit association test. *Journal of Personality and Social Psychology, 74,* 1464–1480.

Greenwald, A. G., Oakes, M. A., & Hoffman, H. (2003). Targets of discrimination: Effects of race on responses to weapons holders. *Journal of Experimental Social Psychology, 39,* 399.

Greenwald, A. G., & Pettigrew, T. F. (2014). With malice toward none and charity for some: Ingroup favoritism enables discrimination. *American Psychologist, 69,* 645–655.

Greenwald, A. G., Spangenberg, E. R., Pratkanis, A. R., & Eskenazi, J. (1991). Double-blind tests of subliminal self-help audiotapes. *Psychological Science, 2,* 119–122.

Greer, S. G., Goldstein, A. N., & Walker, M. P. (2013). The impact of sleep deprivation on food desire in the human brain. *Nature Communications, 4,* Article 2259. doi:10.1038/ncomms3259

Greers, A. E. (2004). Speech, language, and reading skills after early cochlear implantation. *Archives of Otolaryngology—Head & Neck Surgery, 130,* 634–638.

Gregory, A. M., Rijksdijk, F. V., Lau, J. Y., Dahl, R. E., & Eley, T. C. (2009). The direction of longitudinal associations between sleep problems and depression symptoms: A study of twins aged 8 and 10 years. *Sleep, 32,* 189–199.

Gregory, R. L. (1978). *Eye and brain: The psychology of seeing* (3rd ed.). New York: McGraw-Hill.

Gregory, R. L., & Gombrich, E. H. (Eds.). (1973). *Illusion in nature and art.* New York: Charles Scribner's Sons.

Greif, E. B., & Ulman, K. J. (1982). The psychological impact of menarche on early adolescent females: A review of the literature. *Child Development, 53,* 1413–1430.

Greist, J. H., Jefferson, J. W., & Marks, I. M. (1986). *Anxiety and its treatment: Help is available.* Washington, DC: American Psychiatric Press.

Greitemeyer, T., & Osswald, S. (2010). Effects of prosocial video games on prosocial behavior. *Journal of Personality and Social Psychology, 98,* 211–221.

Greitemeyer, T., & Osswald, S. (2011). Playing prosocial video games increases the accessibility of prosocial thoughts. *Journal of Social Psychology, 151,* 121–128.

Greyson, B. (2010). Implications of near-death experiences for a postmaterialist psychology. *Review of Religion and Spirituality, 2,* 37–45.

Grèzes, J., & Decety, J. (2001). Functional anatomy of execution, mental simulation, observation, and verb generation of actions: A meta-analysis. *Human Brain Mapping, 12,* 1–19.

Griggs, R. (2014). Coverage of the Stanford Prison Experiment in introductory psychology textbooks. *Teaching of Psychology, 41,* 195–203.

Grillon, C., Quispe-Escudero, D., Mathur, A., & Ernst, M. (2015). Mental fatigue impairs emotion regulation. *Emotion, 15,* 383–389.

Grilo, C. M., & Pogue-Geile, M. F. (1991). The nature of environmental influences on weight and obesity: A behavior genetic analysis. *Psychological Bulletin, 110,* 520–537.

Grimm, S., & Scheidegger, M. (2013, May/June). A trip out of depression. *Scientific American Mind,* pp. 67–71.

Griskevicius, V., Tybur, J. M., Gangestad, S. W., Perea, E. F., Shapiro, J. R., & Kenrick, D. T. (2009). Aggress to impress: Hostility as an evolved context-dependent strategy. *Journal of Personality and Social Psychology, 96,* 980–994.

Grobstein, C. (1979, June). External human fertilization. *Scientific American,* pp. 57–67.

Grodin, E. N., & White, T. L. (2015). The neuroanatomical delineation of agentic and affiliative extraversion. *Cognitive, Affective, and Behavioral Neuroscience, 15,* 321–334.

Groothuis, T. G. G., & Carere, C. (2005). Avian personalities: Characterization and epigenesis. *Neuroscience and Biobehavioral Reviews, 29,* 137–150.

Gross, A. E., & Crofton, C. (1977). What is good is beautiful. *Sociometry, 40,* 85–90.

Grossberg, S. (1995). The attentive brain. *American Scientist, 83,* 438–449.

Grossmann, I., Na, J., Varnum, M. E. W., Park, D. C., Kitayama, S., & Nisbett, R. E. (2010). Reasoning about social conflicts improves into old age. *PNAS, 107,* 7246–7250.

Gruder, C. L. (1977). Choice of comparison persons in evaluating oneself. In J. M. Suls & R. L. Miller (Eds.), *Social comparison processes* (pp. 21–41). New York: Hemisphere.

Guéguen, N. (2011). Effects of solicitor sex and attractiveness on receptivity to sexual offers: A field study. *Archives of Sexual Behavior, 40,* 915–919.

Guerin, B. (1986). Mere presence effects in humans: A review. *Journal of Personality and Social Psychology, 22,* 38–77.

Guiso, L., Monte, F., Sapienza, P., & Zingales, L. (2008). Culture, gender, and math. *Science, 320,* 1164–1165.

Gunderson, E. A., Gripshover, S. J., Romero, C., Dweck, C. S., Goldin-Meadow, S., & Levine, S. C. (2013). Parent praise to 1- to 3-year-olds predicts children's motivational frameworks 5 years later. *Child Development, 84,* 1526–1541.

Gunstad, J., Strain, G., Devlin, M. J., Wing, R., Cohen, R. A., Paul, R. H., . . . Mitchell, J. E. (2011). Improved memory function 12 weeks after bariatric surgery. *Surgery for Obesity and Related Diseases, 7*, 465–472.

Guo, M., Gan, Y., & Tong, J. (2013). The role of meaning-focused coping in significant loss. *Anxiety, Stress, & Coping, 26*, 87–102.

Guo, X., Zhai, J., Liu, Z., Fang, M., Wang, B., Wang, C., . . . Zhao, J. (2010). Effect of antipsychotic medication alone vs combined with psychosocial intervention on outcomes of early-stage schizophrenia. *Archives of General Psychiatry, 67*, 895–904.

Gustavson, C. R., Garcia, J., Hankins, W. G., & Rusiniak, K. W. (1974). Coyote predation control by aversive conditioning. *Science, 184*, 581–583.

Gustavson, C. R., Kelly, D. J., & Sweeney, M. (1976). Prey lithium aversions I: Coyotes and wolves. *Behavioral Biology, 17*, 61–72.

Gutchess, A. (2014). Plasticity in the aging brain: New directions in cognitive neuroscience. *Science, 346*, 579–582.

Guttmacher Institute. (1994). *Sex and America's teenagers.* New York: Alan Guttmacher Institute.

Guttmacher Institute. (2012). *Facts on American teens' sexual and reproductive health.* Retrieved from guttmacher.org/pubs/FB-ATSRH.html

H., Sally. (1979, August). *Videotape recording number T–3, Fortunoff Video Archive of Holocaust Testimonies.* New Haven, CT: Yale University Library.

Haapakoski, R., Mathieu, J., Ebmeier, K. P., Alenius, H., & Kivimäki, M. (2015). Cumulative meta-analysis of interleukins 6 and 1β, tumour necrosis factor α and C-reactive protein in patients with major depressive disorder. *Brain, Behavior, and Immunity, 49*, 206–215.

Habel, U., Koch, K., Kellerman, T., Reske, M., Frommann, N., Wolwer, W., . . . Schneider, F. (2010). Training of affect recognition in schizophrenia: Neurobiological correlates. *Social Neuroscience, 5*, 92–104.

Hadjistavropoulos, T., Craig, K. D., Duck, S., Cano, A., Goubert, L., Jackson, P. L., . . . Fitzgerald, T. D. (2011). A biopsychosocial formulation of pain communication. *Psychological Bulletin, 137*, 910–939.

Hagger, M. S., & Chatzisarantis, N. L. D. (2013). The sweet taste of success: The presence of glucose in the oral cavity moderates the depletion of self-control resources. *Personality and Social Psychology Bulletin, 39*, 28–42.

Hagger, M. S., Wood, C., Stiff, C., & Chatzisarantis, N. L. D. (2010). Ego depletion and the strength model of self-control: A meta-analysis. *Psychological Bulletin, 136*, 495–525.

Haidt, J. (2002). The moral emotions. In R. J. Davidson, K. Scherer, & H. H. Goldsmith (Eds.), *Handbook of affective sciences* (pp. 852–870). New York: Oxford University Press.

Haidt, J. (2006). *The happiness hypothesis: Finding modern truth in ancient wisdom.* New York: Basic Books.

Haidt, J. (2010). Moral psychology must not be based on faith and hope: Commentary on Narvaez. *Perspectives on Psychological Science, 5*, 182–184.

Hajhosseini, B., Stewart, B., Tan, J. C., Busque, S., & Melcher, M. L. (2013). Evaluating deceased donor registries: Identifying predictive factors of donor designation. *American Surgeon, 79*, 235–241.

Hakuta, K., Bialystok, E., & Wiley, E. (2003). Critical evidence: A test of the critical-period hypothesis for second-language acquisition. *Psychological Science, 14*, 31–38.

Halberstadt, J. B., Niedenthal, P. M., & Kushner, J. (1995). Resolution of lexical ambiguity by emotional state. *Psychological Science, 6*, 278–281.

Halberstadt, J., Sherman, S. J., & Sherman, J. W. (2011). Why Barack Obama is black. *Psychological Science, 22*, 29–33.

Haldeman, D. C. (1994). The practice and ethics of sexual orientation conversion therapy. *Journal of Consulting and Clinical Psychology, 62*, 221–227.

Haldeman, D. C. (2002). Gay rights, patient rights: The implications of sexual orientation conversion therapy. *Professional Psychology: Research and Practice, 33*, 260–264.

Hall, A. (2016, May 9). "They keep me young!": German grandmother who had IVF quads at 65 poses with her children on their first birthday and insists she is a fit mother. *Daily Mail* (dailymail.co.uk).

Hall, C. S., Dornhoff, W., Blick, K. A., & Weesner, K. E. (1982). The dreams of college men and women in 1950 and 1980: A comparison of dream contents and sex differences. *Sleep, 5*, 188–194.

Hall, C. S., & Lindzey, G. (1978). *Theories of personality* (2nd ed.). New York: Wiley.

Hall, D. T., & Chandler, D. E. (2005). Psychological success: When the career is a calling. *Journal of Organizational Behavior, 26*, 155–176.

Hall, G. (1997). Context aversion, Pavlovian conditioning, and the psychological side effects of chemotherapy. *European Psychologist, 2*, 118–124.

Hall, J. A. (1984). *Nonverbal sex differences: Communication accuracy and expressive style.* Baltimore: Johns Hopkins University Press.

Hall, J. A. (1987). On explaining gender differences: The case of nonverbal communication. In P. Shaver & C. Hendrick (Eds.), *Review of personality and social psychology* (Vol. 7, pp. 177–200). Thousand Oaks, CA: Sage Publications.

Hall, S. S. (2004, May). The good egg. *Discover*, pp. 30–39.

Haller, R., Rummel, C., Henneberg, S., Pollmer, U., & Köster, E. P. (1999). The influence of early experience with vanillin on food preference later in life. *Chemical Senses, 24*, 465–467.

Halpern, D. F., Benbow, C. P., Geary, D. C., Gur, R. C., Hyde, J. S., & Gernsbacher, M. A. (2007). The science of sex differences in science and mathematics. *Psychological Science in the Public Interest, 8*, 1–51.

Hammack, P. L., (2005). The life course development of human sexual orientation: An integrative paradigm. *Human Development, 48*, 267–290.

Hammer, E. (2003). How lucky you are to be a psychology major. *Eye on Psi Chi*, 4–5.

Hammersmith, S. K. (1982, August). *Sexual preference: An empirical study from the Alfred C. Kinsey Institute for Sex Research.* Paper presented at the meeting of the American Psychological Association, Washington, DC.

Hammond, D. C. (2008). Hypnosis as sole anesthesia for major surgeries: Historical and contemporary perspectives. *American Journal of Clinical Hypnosis, 51*, 101–121.

Hampshire, A., Highfield, R. R., Parkin, B. L., & Owen, A. M. (2012). Fractionating human intelligence. *Neuron, 76*, 1225–1237.

Hampson, R. (2000, April 10). In the end, people just need more room. *USA Today*, p. 19A.

Hamza, C. A., Willoughby, T., & Heffer, T. (2015). Impulsivity and nonsuicidal self-injury: A review and meta-analysis. *Clinical Psychology Review, 38*, 13–24.

Hänggi, J., Koeneke, S., Bezzola, L., Jäncke, L. (2010). Structural neuroplasticity in the sensorimotor network of professional female ballet dancers. *Human Brain Mapping, 31*, 1196–1206.

Hankin, B. L., & Abramson, L. Y. (2001). Development of gender differences in depression: An elaborated cognitive vulnerability–transactional stress theory. *Psychological Bulletin, 127*, 773–796.

Hansen, C. H., & Hansen, R. D. (1988). Finding the face-in-the-crowd: An anger superiority effect. *Journal of Personality and Social Psychology, 54*, 917–924.

Harbaugh, W. T., Mayr, U., & Burghart, D. R. (2007). Neural responses to taxation and voluntary giving reveal motives for charitable donations. *Science, 316*, 1622–1625.

Harden, K. P., & Mendle, J. (2011). Why don't smart teens have sex? A behavioral genetic approach. *Child Development, 82*, 1327–1344.

Hardeveld, H. S., De Graaf, R., Nolen, W. A., & Beckman, A. T. F. (2010). Prevalence and predictors of recurrence of major depressive disorder in the adult population. *Acta Psychiatrica Scandinavia, 122*, 184–191.

Hardt, O., Einarsson, E. O., & Nader, K. (2010). A bridge over troubled water: Reconsolidation as a link between cognitive and neuroscientific memory research traditions. *Annual Review of Psychology, 61*, 141–167.

Hare, R. D. (1975). Psychophysiological studies of psychopathy. In D. C. Fowles (Ed.), *Clinical applications of psychophysiology* (pp. 77–105). New York: Columbia University Press.

Harenski, C. L., Harenski, K. A., Shane, M. W., & Kiehl, K. A. (2010). Aberrant neural processing of moral violations in criminal psychopaths. *Journal of Abnormal Psychology, 119*, 863–874.

Harkin, B., Webb, T. L., Chang, B. P. I., Prestwich, A., Conner, M., Kellar, I., . . . Sheeran, P. (2016). Does monitoring goal progress promote goal attainment? A meta-analysis of the experimental evidence. *Psychological Bulletin, 142*, 198–229.

Harkins, S. G., & Szymanski, K. (1989). Social loafing and group evaluation. *Journal of Personality and Social Psychology, 56*, 934–941.

Harlow, H. F., Harlow, M. K., & Suomi, S. J. (1971). From thought to therapy: Lessons from a primate laboratory. *American Scientist, 59*, 538–549.

Harmon-Jones, E., Abramson, L. Y., Sigelman, J., Bohlig, A., Hogan, M. E., & Harmon-Jones, C. (2002). Proneness to hypomania/mania symptoms or depression symptoms and asymmetrical frontal cortical responses to an anger-evoking event. *Journal of Personality and Social Psychology, 82*, 610–618.

Harms, P. D., Roberts, B. W., & Winter, D. (2006). Becoming the Harvard man: Person-environment fit, personality development, and academic success. *Personality and Social Psychology Bulletin, 32*, 851–865.

Harper, C., & McLanahan, S. (2004). Father absence and youth incarceration. *Journal of Research on Adolescence, 14*, 369–397.

Harris, B. (1979). Whatever happened to Little Albert? *American Psychologist, 34*, 151–160.

Harris Interactive. (2010). 2009 eHarmony® marriage metrics study: Methodological notes. eHarmony (http://www.eharmony.com/press-release/31/).

Harris, J. R. (1998). *The nurture assumption.* New York: Free Press.

Harris, J. R. (2002). Beyond the nurture assumption: Testing hypotheses about the child's environment. In J. G. Borkowski, S. L. Ramey, & M. Bristol-Power (Eds.), *Parenting and the child's world: Influences on academic, intellectual, and social-emotional development* (pp. 3–20). Mahwah, NJ: Erlbaum.

Harris, R. J. (1994). The impact of sexually explicit media. In J. Brant & D. Zillmann (Eds.), *Media effects: Advances in theory and research* (pp. 247–272). Hillsdale, NJ: Erlbaum.

Harrison, G., Hopper, K. I. M., Craig, T., Laska, E., Siegel, C., Wanderling, J., . . . Holmberg, S. K. (2001). Recovery from psychotic illness: A 15-and 25-year international follow-up study. *The British Journal of Psychiatry, 178*(6), 506–517.

Harrison, L. A., Hurlemann, R., & Adolphs, R. (2015). An enhanced default approach bias following amygdala lesions in humans. *Psychological Science, 26*, 1543–1555.

Harriston, K. A. (1993, December 24). 1 shakes, 1 snoozes: Both win $45 million. *The Washington Post* release (in *Tacoma News Tribune*, pp. A1, A2).

Harter, J. K., Schmidt, F. L., Asplund, J. W., Killham, E. A., & Agrawal, S. (2010). Causal impact of employee work perceptions on the bottom line of organizations. *Perspectives on Psychological Science, 5,* 378–389.

Harter, J. K., Schmidt, F. L., & Hayes, T. L. (2002). Business-unit-level relationship between employee satisfaction, employee engagement, and business outcomes: A meta-analysis. *Journal of Applied Psychology, 87,* 268–279.

Hartwig, M., & Bond, C. F., Jr. (2011). Why do lie-catchers fail? A lens model meta-analysis of human lie judgments. *Psychological Bulletin, 137,* 643–659.

Hasan, Y., Bègue, L., Scharkow, M., & Bushman, B. J. (2013). The more you play, the more aggressive you become: A long-term experimental study of cumulative violent video game effects on hostile expectations and aggressive behavior. *Journal of Experimental Social Psychology, 49,* 224–227.

Haselton, M. G., & Gildersleeve, K. (2011). Can men detect ovulation? *Current Directions in Psychological Science, 20,* 87–92.

Haslam, S. A., & Reicher, S. (2007). Beyond the banality of evil: Three dynamics of an interactionist social psychology of tyranny. *Personality and Social Psychology Bulletin, 33,* 615–622.

Haslam, S. A., & Reicher, S. D. (2012). Contesting the "nature" of conformity: What Milgram and Zimbardo's studies really show. *PLOS Biology, 10*(11), e1001426. doi:10.1371/journal.pbio.1001426

Hassan, B., & Rahman, Q. (2007). Selective sexual orientation-related differences in object location memory. *Behavioral Neuroscience, 121,* 625–633.

Hassin, R. R. (2013). Yes it can: On the functional abilities of the human unconscious. *Perspectives on Psychological Science, 8,* 195–207.

Hatfield, E. (1988). Passionate and companionate love. In R. J. Sternberg & M. L. Barnes (Eds.), *The psychology of love* (pp. 191–217). New Haven, CT: Yale University Press.

Hatfield, E., Mo, Y., & Rapson, R. L. (2015). Love, sex, and marriage across cultures. *Oxford Handbooks Online* (oxfordhandbooks.com).

Hatfield, E., & Sprecher, S. (1986). *Mirror, mirror . . . The importance of looks in everyday life.* Albany: State University of New York Press.

Havas, D. A., Glenberg, A. M., Gutowski, K. A., Lucarelli, M. J., & Davidson, R. J. (2010). Cosmetic use of botulinum toxin-A affects processing of emotional language. *Psychological Science, 21,* 895–900.

Haworth, C. M. A., Wright, M. J., Martin, N. W., Martin, N. G., Boomsma, D. I., Bartels, M., . . . Plomin, R. (2009). A twin study of the genetics of high cognitive ability selected from 11,000 twin pairs in six studies from four countries. *Behavior Genetics, 39,* 359–370.

Hawton, K., Bergen, H., Cooper, J., Turnbull, P., Waters, K., Ness, J., & Kapur, N. (2015). Suicide following self-harm: Findings from the Multicentre Study of self-harm in England, 2000–2012. *Journal of Affective Disorders, 175,* 147–151.

Haxby, J. V. (2001, July 7). Quoted by B. Bower, Faces of perception. *Science News,* pp. 10–12. See also J. V. Haxby, M. I. Gobbini, M. L. Furey, A. Ishai, J. L. Schouten & P. Pietrini, Distributed and overlapping representations of faces and objects in ventral temporal cortex. *Science, 293,* 2425–2430.

Headey, B., Muffels, R., & Wagner, G. G. (2010). Long-running German panel survey shows that personal and economic choices, not just genes, matter for happiness. *PNAS, 107,* 17922–17926.

Heckert, J. (2012, November 15). The hazards of growing up painlessly. *The New York Times* (nytimes.com).

Heider, F. (1958). *The psychology of interpersonal relations.* New York: Wiley.

Heiman, J. R. (1975, April). The physiology of erotica: Women's sexual arousal. *Psychology Today,* pp. 90–94.

Heine, S. J., & Buchtel, E. E. (2009). Personality: The universal and the culturally specific. *Annual Review of Psychology, 60,* 369–394.

Heine, S. J., & Hamamura, T. (2007). In search of East Asian self-enhancement. *Personality and Social Psychology Review, 11,* 4–27.

Heine, S. J., Proulx, T., & Vohs, K. D. (2006). Meaning maintenance model: On the coherence of human motivations. *Personality and Social Psychology Review, 10,* 88–110.

Hejmadi, A., Davidson, R. J., & Rozin, P. (2000). Exploring Hindu Indian emotion expressions: Evidence for accurate recognition by Americans and Indians. *Psychological Science, 11,* 183–187.

Helfand, D. (2011, January 7). An assault on rationality. *The New York Times* (nytimes.com).

Heller, A. S., Johnstone, T., Schackman, A. J., Light, S. N., Peterson, M. J., Kolden, G. G., . . . Davidson, R. J. (2009). Reduced capacity to sustain positive emotion in major depression reflects diminished maintenance of fronto-striatal brain activation. *PNAS, 106,* 22445–22450.

Heller, W. (1990, May/June). Of one mind: Second thoughts about the brain's dual nature. *The Sciences,* pp. 38–44.

Helliwell, J., Layard, R., & Sachs, J. (Eds.) (2013). *World happiness report.* New York: Earth Institute, Columbia University.

Helliwell, J. F., & Wang, S. (2015). How was the weekend? How the social context underlies weekend effects in happiness and other emotions for US workers. *PLoS One, 10,* e0145123.

Helmreich, W. B. (1992). *Against all odds: Holocaust survivors and the successful lives they made in America.* New York: Simon & Schuster.

Helmreich, W. B. (1994). Personal correspondence. Department of Sociology, City University of New York.

Helms, J. E., Jernigan, M., & Mascher, J. (2005). The meaning of race in psychology and how to change it: A methodological perspective. *American Psychologist, 60,* 27–36.

Helmuth, L. (2001). Boosting brain activity from the outside in. *Science, 292,* 1284–1286.

Helsen, K., Goubert, L., Peters, M. L., & Vlaeyen, J. W. S. (2011). Observational learning and pain-related fear: An experimental study with colored cold pressor tasks. *Journal of Pain, 12,* 1230–1239.

Hembree, R. (1988). Correlates, causes, effects, and treatment of test anxiety. *Review of Educational Research, 58,* 47–77.

Henderlong, J., & Lepper, M. R. (2002). The effects of praise on children's intrinsic motivation: A review and synthesis. *Psychological Bulletin, 128,* 774–795.

Henig, R. M. (2010, August 18). What is it about 20-somethings? *The New York Times* (nytimes.com).

Henkel, L. A., Franklin, N., & Johnson, M. K. (2000, March). Cross-modal source monitoring confusions between perceived and imagined events. *Journal of Experimental Psychology: Learning, Memory, & Cognition, 26,* 321–335.

Hennenlotter, A., Dresel, C., Castrop, F., Ceballos Baumann, A., Wohlschlager, A., & Haslinger, B. (2008). The link between facial feedback and neural activity within central circuitries of emotion: New insights from botulinum toxin-induced denervation of frown muscles. *Cerebral Cortex, 19,* 537–542.

Hennessey, B. A., & Amabile, T. M. (2010). Creativity. *Annual Review of Psychology, 61,* 569–598.

Henrich, J., Heine, S. J., & Norenzayan, A. (2010). The weirdest people in the world? *Behavioral and Brain Sciences, 33,* 61–135.

Herbenick, D., Reece, M., Schick, V., & Sanders, S. A. (2014). Erect penile length and circumference dimensions of 1,661 sexually active men in the United States. *Journal of Sexual Medicine, 11,* 93–101.

Herbenick, D., Reece, M., Schick, V., Sanders, S. A., Dodge, B., & Fortenberry, J. D. (2010). Sexual behavior in the United States: Results from a national probability sample of men and women ages 14–94. *Journal of Sexual Medicine, 7*(suppl. 5), 255–265.

Herculano-Houzel, S. (2012). The remarkable, yet not extraordinary, human brain as a scaled-up primate brain and its associated cost. *PNAS, 109*(Suppl. 1), 10661–10668.

Herholz, S. C., & Zatorre, R. J. (2012). Musical training as a framework for brain plasticity: Behavior, function, and structure. *Neuron, 76,* 486–502.

Herman, C. P., & Polivy, J. (1980). Restrained eating. In A. J. Stunkard (Ed.), *Obesity* (pp. 208–225). Philadelphia: Saunders.

Herman, C. P., Roth, D. A., & Polivy, J. (2003). Effects of the presence of others on food intake: A normative interpretation. *Psychological Bulletin, 129,* 873–886.

Herman-Giddens, M. E., Steffes, J., Harris, D., Slora, E., Hussey, M., Dowshen, S. A., . . . Reiter, E. O. (2012). Secondary sexual characteristics in boys: Data from the pediatric research in office settings network. *Pediatrics, 130,* 1058–1068.

Herman-Giddens, M. E., Wang, L., & Koch, G. (2001). Secondary sexual characteristics in boys: Estimates from the National Health and Nutrition Examination Survey III, 1988–1994. *Archives of Pediatrics and Adolescent Medicine, 155,* 1022–1028.

Hernandez, A. E., & Li, P. (2007). Age of acquisition: Its neural and computational mechanisms. *Psychological Bulletin, 133,* 638–650.

Hernandez, R., Kershaw, K. N., Siddique, J., Boehm, J. K., Kubzansky, L. D., Diez-Roux, A., . . . Lloyd-Jones, D. M. (2015). Optimism and cardiovascular health: Multi-Ethnic Study of Atherosclerosis (MESA). *Health Behavior and Policy Review, 2,* 62–73.

Herrmann, E., Call, J., Hernández-Lloreda, M. V., Hare, B., & Tomasello, M. (2007). Humans have evolved specialized skills of social cognition: The cultural intelligence hypothesis. *Science, 317,* 1360–1365.

Herrnstein, R. J., & Loveland, D. H. (1964). Complex visual concept in the pigeon. *Science, 146,* 549–551.

Hertenstein, M. J., Hansel, C., Butts, S., Hile, S. (2009). Smile intensity in photographs predicts divorce later in life. *Motivation and Emotion, 33,* 99–105.

Hertenstein, M. J., Keltner, D., App, B., Bulleit, B., & Jaskolka, A. (2006). Touch communicates distinct emotions. *Emotion, 6,* 528–533.

Herz, R. (2007). *The scent of desire: Discovering our enigmatic sense of smell.* New York: Morrow/HarperCollins.

Herz, R. (2012, January 28). You eat that? *The Wall Street Journal* (online.wsj.com).

Herz, R. S. (2001, October). Ah, sweet skunk! Why we like or dislike what we smell. *Cerebrum,* pp. 31–47.

Hess, E. H. (1956, July). Space perception in the chick. *Scientific American,* pp. 71–80.

Hess, U., & Thibault, P. (2009). Darwin and emotion expression. *American Psychologist, 64,* 120–128.

Hetherington, M. M., Anderson, A. S., Norton, G. N. M., & Newson, L. (2006). Situational effects on meal intake: A comparison of eating alone and eating with others. *Physiology and Behavior, 88,* 498–505.

Hettema, J. M., Neale, M. C., & Kendler, K. S. (2001). A review and meta-analysis of the genetic epidemiology of anxiety disorders. *American Journal of Psychiatry, 158,* 1568–1578.

Hickok, G. (2014). *The myth of mirror neurons: The real neuroscience of communication and cognition.* New York: Norton.

Hickok, G., Bellugi, U., & Klima, E. S. (2001, June). Sign language in the brain. *Scientific American,* pp. 58–65.

Hilgard, E. R. (1986). *Divided consciousness: Multiple controls in human thought and action.* New York: Wiley.

Hilgard, E. R. (1992). Dissociation and theories of hypnosis. In E. Fromm & M. R. Nash (Eds.), *Contemporary hypnosis research.* New York: Guilford.

Hill, C. E., & Nakayama, E. Y. (2000). Client-centered therapy: Where has it been and where is it going? A comment on Hathaway. *Journal of Clinical Psychology, 56,* 961–875.

Hills, P. J., Werno, M. A., & Lewis, M. B. (2011). Sad people are more accurate at face recognition than happy people. *Consciousness and Cognition, 20,* 1502–1517.

Hines, M. (2004). *Brain gender.* New York: Oxford University Press.

Hingson, R. W., Heeren, T., & Winter M. R. (2006). Age at drinking onset and alcohol dependence. *Archives of Pediatrics & Adolescent Medicine, 160,* 739–746.

Hintzman, D. L. (1978). *The psychology of learning and memory.* San Francisco: Freeman.

Hinz, L. D., & Williamson, D. A. (1987). Bulimia and depression: A review of the affective variant hypothesis. *Psychological Bulletin, 102,* 150–158.

Hirsh, J. B., Galinsky, A. D., & Zhong, C.-B. (2011). Drunk, powerful, and in the dark: How general processes of disinhibition produce both prosocial and antisocial behavior. *Perspectives on Psychological Science, 6,* 415–427.

Hirst, W., Phelps, E. A., Buckner, R. L., Budson, A. E., Cuc, A., Gabrieli, J. D., . . . Vaidya, C. J. (2009). Long-term memory for the terrorist attack of September 11: Flashbulb memories, event memories, and the factors that influence their retention. *Journal of Experimental Psychology: General, 138,* 161–176.

HMHL. (2007, February). Electroconvulsive therapy. *Harvard Mental Health Letter,* Harvard Medical School, pp. 1–4.

Hobson, J. A. (2003). *Dreaming: An introduction to the science of sleep.* New York: Oxford.

Hobson, J. A. (2004). *13 dreams Freud never had: The new mind science.* New York: Pi Press.

Hobson, J. A. (2009). REM sleep and dreaming: Towards a theory of protoconsciousness. *Nature Reviews, 10,* 803–814.

Hochberg, L. R., Bacher, D., Jarosiewicz, B., Masse, N. Y., Simeral, J. D., Vogel, J., . . . Donoghue, J. P. (2012). Reach and grasp by people with tetraplegia using a neutrally controlled robotic arm. *Nature, 485,* 375–375.

Hochmair, I. (2013, September). Cochlear implants: The size of the task concerning children born deaf. MED-EL (medel.com).

Hoebel, B. G., & Teitelbaum, P. (1966). Effects of force-feeding and starvation on food intake and body weight in a rat with ventromedial hypothalamic lesions. *Journal of Comparative and Physiological Psychology, 61,* 189–193.

Hoffman, B. M., Babyak, M. A., Craighead, W. E., Sherwood, A., Doraiswamy, P. M., Coons, M. J., & Blumenthal, J. A. (2011). Exercise and pharmacotherapy in patients with major depression: One-year follow-up of the SMILE study. *Psychosomatic Medicine, 73,* 127–133.

Hoffman, D. D. (1998). *Visual intelligence: How we create what we see.* New York: Norton.

Hoffman, H. (2012). Considering the role of conditioning in sexual orientation. *Archives of Sexual Behavior, 41,* 63–71.

Hoffman, H. G. (2004, August). Virtual-reality therapy. *Scientific American,* pp. 58–65.

Hofmann, S. G., Sawyer, A. T., Witt, A. A., & Oh, D. (2010). The effect of mindfulness-based therapy on anxiety and depression: A meta-analytic review. *Journal of Consulting and Clinical Psychology, 78,* 169–183.

Hogan, C. L., Catalino, L. I., Mata, J., & Fredrickson, B. L. (2015). Beyond emotional benefits: Physical activity and sedentary behavior affect psychosocial resources through emotions. *Psychology & Health, 30,* 354–369.

Hoge, C. W., & Castro, C. A. (2006). Post-traumatic stress disorder in UK and US forces deployed to Iraq. *The Lancet, 368,* 837.

Hoge, C. W., Castro, C. A., Messer, S. C., McGurk, D., Cotting, D. I., & Koffman, R. L. (2004). Combat duty in Iraq and Afghanistan, mental health problems, and barriers to care. New *England Journal of Medicine, 351,* 13–22.

Hoge, C. W., Terhakopian, A., Castro, C. A., Messer, S. C., & Engel, C. C. (2007). Association of posttraumatic stress disorder with somatic symptoms, health care visits, and absenteeism among Iraq War veterans. *American Journal of Psychiatry, 164,* 150–153.

Hogg, M. A. (2006). Social identity theory. In P. J. Burke (Ed.), *Contemporary social psychological theories* (pp. 111–136). Stanford, CA: Stanford University Press.

Hohmann, G. W. (1966). Some effects of spinal cord lesions on experienced emotional feelings. *Psychophysiology, 3,* 143–156.

Holahan, C. K., & Sears, R. R. (1995). *The gifted group in later maturity.* Stanford, CA: Stanford University Press.

Holden, C. (2008). Poles apart. *Science, 321,* 193–195.

Holland, D., Chang, L., Ernst, T. M., Curran, M., Buchthal, S. D., Alicata, D., . . . Dale, A. M. (2014). Structural growth trajectories and rates of change in the first 3 months of infant brain development. *JAMA Neurology, 71,* 1266–1274.

Holland, J. L. (1996). Exploring careers with a typology: What we have learned and some new directions. *American Psychologist, 51,* 397–406.

Holle, H., Warne, K., Seth, A. K., Critchley, H. D., & Ward, J. (2012). Neural basis of contagious itch and why some people are more prone to it. *PNAS, 109,* 19816–19821.

Hollis, K. L. (1997). Contemporary research on Pavlovian conditioning: A "new" functional analysis. *American Psychologist, 52,* 956–965.

Hollon, S. D., DeRubeis, R. J., Fawcett, J., Amsterdam, J. D., Shelton, R. C., Zajecka, J., . . . Gallop, R. (2014). Effect of cognitive therapy with antidepressant medications vs. antidepressants alone on the rate of recovery in major depressive disorder. *JAMA Psychiatry, 71,* 1157–1164.

Hollon, S. D., Thase, M. E., & Markowitz, J. C. (2002). Treatment and prevention of depression. *Psychological Science in the Public Interest, 3,* 39–77.

Holman, E. A., Garfin, D. R., & Silver, R. C. (2014). Media's role in broadcasting acute stress following the Boston marathon bombings. *PNAS, 111,* 93–98.

Holstege, G., Georgiadis, J. R., Paans, A. M. J., Meiners, L. C., van der Graaf, F. H. C. E., & Reinders, A. A. T. S. (2003a). Brain activation during male ejaculation. *Journal of Neuroscience, 23,* 9185–9193.

Holstege, G., Reinders, A. A. T., Paans, A. M. J., Meiners, L. C., Pruim, J., & Georgiadis, J. R. (2003b). *Brain activation during female sexual orgasm.* Program No. 727.7. Washington, DC: Society for Neuroscience.

Homer, B. D., Solomon, T. M., Moeller, R. W., Mascia, A., DeRaleau, L., & Halkitis, P. N. (2008). Methamphetamine abuse and impairment of social functioning: A review of the underlying neurophysiological causes and behavioral implications. *Psychological Bulletin, 134,* 301–310.

Hooper, J., & Teresi, D. (1986). *The three-pound universe.* New York: Macmillan.

Hopkins, E. D., & Cantalupo, C. (2008). Theoretical speculations on the evolutionary origins of hemispheric specialization. *Current Directions in Psychological Science, 17,* 233–237.

Hor, H., & Tafti, M. (2009). How much sleep do we need? *Science, 325,* 825–826.

Horn, J. L. (1982). The aging of human abilities. In J. Wolman (Ed.), *Handbook of developmental psychology.* Englewood Cliffs, NJ: Prentice-Hall.

Horne, J. (2011). The end of sleep: "Sleep debt" versus biological adaptation of human sleep to waking needs. *Biological Psychology, 87,* 1–14.

Horowitz, S. S. (2012). The science and art of listening. *The New York Times* (nytimes.com).

Horwood, L. J., & Fergusson, D. M. (1998). Breast-feeding and later cognitive and academic outcomes. *Pediatrics, 101*(1), E9.

Hou, W.-H., Chiang, P.-T., Hsu, T.-Y., Chiu, S.-Y., & Yen, Y.-C. (2010). Treatment effects of massage therapy in depressed people: A meta-analysis. *Journal of Clinical Psychiatry, 71,* 894–901.

House, R. J., & Singh, J. V. (1987). Organizational behavior: Some new directions for I/O psychology. *Annual Review of Psychology, 38,* 669–718.

Houser-Marko, L., & Sheldon, K. M. (2008). Eyes on the prize or nose to the grindstone? The effects of level of goal evaluation on mood and motivation. *Personality and Social Psychology Bulletin, 34,* 1556–1569.

Houts, A. C., Berman, J. S., & Abramson, H. (1994). Effectiveness of psychological and pharmacological treatments for nocturnal enuresis. *Journal of Consulting and Clinical Psychology, 62,* 737–745.

Hovatta, I., Tennant, R. S., Helton, R., Marr, R. A., Singer, O., Redwine, J. M., . . . Barlow, C. (2005). Glyoxalase 1 and glutathione reductase 1 regulate anxiety in mice. *Nature, 438,* 662–666.

Hsee, C. K., Yang, A. X., & Wang, L. (2010). Idleness aversion and the need for justifiable busyness. *Psychological Science, 21,* 926–930.

Hsiang, S. M., Burke, M., & Miguel, E. (2013). Quantifying the influence of climate on human conflict. *Science, 341,* 1212.

Huang, C. (2010). Mean-level change in self-esteem from childhood through adulthood: Meta-analysis of longitudinal studies. *Review of General Psychology, 14,* 251–260.

Huang, C. (2015). Relation between attributional style and subsequent depressive symptoms: A systematic review and meta-analysis of longitudinal studies. *Cognitive Therapy and Research, 39*(6), 721–735.

Huang, J., Chaloupka, F. J., & Fong, G. T. (2013). Cigarette graphic warning labels and smoking prevalence in Canada: A critical examination and reformulation of the FDA regulatory impact analysis. *Tobacco Control,* published online.

Huang, M.-E., Wu, Z.-Q., & Tang, G.-Q. (2010). How does personality relate to mental health in service industry setting? The mediating effects of emotional labor strategies. *Acta Psychologica Sinica, 42,* 1175–1189.

Hubbard, E. M., Arman, A. C., Ramachandran, V. S., & Boynton, G. M. (2005). Individual differences among grapheme-color synesthetes: Brain-behavior correlations. *Neuron, 45,* 975–985.

Hubel, D. H. (1979, September). The brain. *Scientific American,* pp. 45–53.

Hubel, D. H., & Wiesel, T. N. (1979, September). Brain mechanisms of vision. *Scientific American,* pp. 150–162.

Huber, E., Webster, J. M., Brewer, A. A., MacLeod, D. I. A., Wandell, B. A., Boynton, G. M., . . . Fine, I. (2015). A lack of experience-dependent plasticity after more than a decade of recovered sight. *Psychological Science, 26,* 393–401.

Hucker, S. J., & Bain, J. (1990). Androgenic hormones and sexual assault. In W. Marshall, R. Law, & H. Barbaree (Eds.), *The handbook on sexual assault.* New York: Plenum.

Hudson, J. I., Hiripi, E., Pope, H. G., & Kessler, R. C. (2007). The prevalence and correlates of eating disorders in the National Comorbidity Survey Replication. *Biological Psychiatry, 61,* 348–358.

Hudson, N. W., & Roberts, B. W. (2014). Goals to change personality traits: Concurrent links between personality traits, daily behavior, and goals to change oneself. *Journal of Research in Personality, 53,* 68–83.

Huey, E. D., Krueger, F., & Grafman, J. (2006). Representations in the human prefrontal cortex. *Current Directions in Psychological Science, 15,* 167–171.

Hughes, J. R., Peters, E. N., & Naud, S. (2008). Relapse to smoking after 1 year of abstinence: A meta-analysis. *Addictive Behaviors, 33,* 1516–1520.

Hughes, M. L., Geraci, L., & De Forrest, R. L. (2013). Aging 5 years in 5 minutes: The effect of taking a memory test on older adults' subjective age. *Psychological Science, 24,* 2481–2488.

Hull, J. G., & Bond, C. F., Jr. (1986). Social and behavioral consequences of alcohol consumption and expectancy: A meta-analysis. *Psychological Bulletin, 99,* 347–360.

Hull, J. M. (1990). *Touching the rock: An experience of blindness.* New York: Vintage Books.

Hull, S. J., Hennessy, M., Bleakley, A., Fishbein, M., & Jordan, A. (2011). Identifying the causal pathways from religiosity to delayed adolescent sexual behavior. *Journal of Sex Research, 48,* 543–553.

Human Connectome Project. (2013). The Human Connectome Project (humanconnectome.org/).

Hummer, R. A., Rogers, R. G., Nam, C. B., & Ellison, C. G. (1999). Religious involvement and U.S. adult mortality. *Demography, 36,* 273–285.

Humphrey, S. E., Nahrgang, J. D., & Morgeson, F. P. (2007). Integrating motivational, social, and contextual work design features: A meta-analytic summary and theoretical extension of the work design literature. *Journal of Applied Psychology, 92,* 1332–1356.

Hunsley, J., & Bailey, J. M. (1999). The clinical utility of the Rorschach: Unfulfilled promises and an uncertain future. *Psychological Assessment, 11,* 266–277.

Hunsley, J., & Di Giulio, G. (2002). Dodo bird, phoenix, or urban legend? The question of psychotherapy equivalence. *Scientific Review of Mental Health Practice, 1,* 11–22.

Hunt, C., Slade, T., & Andrews, G. (2004). Generalized anxiety disorder and major depressive disorder comorbidity in the National Survey of Mental Health and Well-Being. *Depression and Anxiety, 20,* 23–31.

Hunt, J. M. (1982). Toward equalizing the developmental opportunities of infants and preschool children. *Journal of Social Issues, 38*(4), 163–191.

Hunt, L. L., Eastwick, P. W., & Finkel, E. J. (2015). Leveling the playing field: Longer acquaintance predicts reduced assortative mating on attractiveness. *Psychological Science, 26,* 1046–1053.

Hunt, M. (1990). *The compassionate beast: What science is discovering about the humane side of humankind.* New York: William Morrow.

Hunt, M. (1993). *The story of psychology.* New York: Doubleday.

Hunter, S., & Sundel, M. (Eds.). (1989). *Midlife myths: Issues, findings, and practice implications.* Newbury Park, CA: Sage.

Hurd, Y. L., Michaelides, M., Miller, M. L., & Jutras-Aswad, D. (2013). Trajectory of adolescent cannabis use on addiction vulnerability. *Neuropharmacology, 76,* 416–424.

Hutchinson, R. (2006). *Calum's road.* Edinburgh, Scotland: Burlinn Limited.

Hvistendahl, M. (2011). China's population growing slowly, changing fast. *Science, 332,* 650–651.

Hyde, J. S. (2005). The gender similarities hypothesis. *American Psychologist, 60,* 581–592.

Hyde, J. S. (2014). Gender similarities and differences. *Annual Review of Psychology, 65,* 373–398.

Hyde, J. S., & Mertz, J. E. (2009). Gender, culture, and mathematics performance. *PNAS, 106,* 8801–8807.

Hyde, J. S., Mezulis, A. H., & Abramson, L. Y. (2008). The ABCs of depression: Integrating affective, biological, and cognitive models to explain the emergence of the gender difference in depression. *Psychological Review, 115,* 291–313.

Iacoboni, M. (2009). Imitation, empathy, and mirror neurons. *Annual Review of Psychology, 60,* 653–670.

Ibos, G., & Freedman, D. J. (2014). Dynamic integration of task-relevant visual features in posterior parietal cortex. *Neuron, 83,* 1468–1480.

Ickes, W., Snyder, M., & Garcia, S. (1997). Personality influences on the choice of situations. In R. Hogan, J. Johnson, & S. Briggs (Eds.). *Handbook of personality psychology* (pp. 165–195). San Diego, CA: Academic Press.

Idson, L. C., & Mischel, W. (2001). The personality of familiar and significant people: The lay perceiver as a social-cognitive theorist. *Journal of Personality and Social Psychology, 80,* 585–596.

IJzerman, H., & Semin, G. R. (2009). The thermometer of social proximity: Mapping social proximity on temperature. *Psychological Science, 20,* 1214–1220.

Ikonomidou, C. C., Bittigau, P., Ishimaru, M. J., Wozniak, D. F., Koch, C., Genz, K., . . . Olney, J. W. (2000). Ethanol-induced apoptotic neurodegeneration and fetal alcohol syndrome. *Science, 287,* 1056–1060.

Ilardi, S. (2016, accessed May 2). Therapeutic lifestyle change (TLC). University of Kansas (tlc.ku.edu).

Ilardi, S. S. (2009). *The depression cure: The six-step program to beat depression without drugs.* Cambridge, MA: De Capo Lifelong Books.

Inbar, Y., Cone, J., & Gilovich, T. (2010). People's intuitions about intuitive insight and intuitive choice. *Journal of Personality and Social Psychology, 99,* 232–247.

Ingalhalikar, M., Smith, A., Parker, D., Satterthwaite, T. D., Elliott, M. A., Ruparel, K., . . . Verma, R. (2013). Sex differences in the structural connectome of the human brain. *PNAS, 111,* 823–828.

Ingham, A. G., Levinger, G., Graves, J., & Peckham, V. (1974). The Ringelmann effect: Studies of group size and group performance. *Journal of Experimental Social Psychology, 10,* 371–384.

Inglehart, R. (1990). *Culture shift in advanced industrial society.* Princeton, NJ: Princeton University Press.

Inglehart, R., Foa, R., Peterson, C., & Welzel, C. (2008). Development, freedom, and rising happiness: A global perspective (1981–2007). *Perspectives on Psychological Science, 3,* 264–285.

Innocence Project. (2015). Eyewitness misidentification. Retrieved from http://www.innocenceproject.org/understand/Eyewitness-Misidentification.php

Insel, T. R. (2010, April). Faulty circuits. *Scientific American,* pp. 44–51.

International Schizophrenia Consortium. (2009). Common polygenic variation contributes to risk of schizophrenia and bipolar disorder. *Nature, 460,* 748–752.

Inzlicht, M., & Ben-Zeev, T. (2000). A threatening intellectual environment: Why females are susceptible to experiencing problem-solving deficits in the presence of males. *Psychological Science, 11,* 365–371.

Inzlicht, M., & Kang, S. K. (2010). Stereotype threat spillover: How coping with threats to social identity affects aggression, eating, decision making, and attention. *Journal of Personality and Social Psychology, 99,* 467–481.

Ipsos. (2010, April 8). One in five (20%) global citizens believe that alien beings have come down to earth and walk amongst us in our communities disguised as humans. Ipsos (ipsos-na.com).

IPU. (2015, January 1). Women in national parliaments: Situation as of 1 January 2015. International Parliamentary Union (ipu.org/wmn-e/world.htm).

Ireland, M. E., & Pennebaker, J. W. (2010). Language style matching in writing: Synchrony in essays, correspondence, and poetry. *Journal of Personality and Social Psychology, 99,* 549–571.

Ironson, G., Solomon, G. F., Balbin, E. G., O'Cleirigh, C., George, A., Kumar, M., . . . Woods, T. E. (2002). The Ironson-Woods spiritual/religiousness index is associated with long survival, health behaviors, less distress, and low cortisol in people with HIV/AIDS. *Annals of Behavioral Medicine, 24,* 34–48.

Isaacowitz, D. M. (2012). Mood regulation in real time: Age differences in the role of looking. *Current Directions in Psychological Science, 21,* 237–242.

Islam, S. S., & Johnson, C. (2003). Correlates of smoking behavior among Muslim Arab-American adolescents. *Ethnicity & Health, 8,* 319–337.

Iso, H., Simoda, S., & Matsuyama, T. (2007). Environmental change during postnatal development alters behaviour. *Behavioural Brain Research, 179,* 90–98.

ITU. (2016, accessed April 20). ICT facts and figures. International Telecommunications Union (itu.int/en/ITU-D/Statistics/Documents/facts/ICTFactsFigures2015.pdf).

Ives-Deliperi, V. L., Solms, M., & Meintjes, E. M. (2011). The neural substrates of mindfulness: An fMRI investigation. *Social Neuroscience, 6,* 231–242.

Iyengar, S. S., & Lepper, M. R. (2000). When choice is demotivating: Can one desire too much of a good thing? *Journal of Personality and Social Psychology, 79,* 995–1006.

Izard, C. E. (1977). *Human emotions.* New York: Plenum Press.

Izard, C. E. (1994). Innate and universal facial expressions: Evidence from developmental and cross-cultural research. *Psychological Bulletin, 114,* 288–299.

Jääskeläinen, E., Juola, P., Hirvonen, N., McGrath, J. J., Saha, S., Isohanni, M., . . . Miettunen, J. (2013). A systematic review and meta-analysis of recovery in schizophrenia. *Schizophrenia Bulletin, 39,* 1296–1306.

Jablensky, A. (1999). Schizophrenia: Epidemiology. *Current Opinion in Psychiatry, 12,* 19–28.

Jack, R. E., Garrod, O. G. B., Yu, H., Caldara, R., & Schyns, P. G. (2012). Facial expressions of emotion are not culturally universal. *PNAS, 109*, 7241–7244.

Jäckle, S., & Wenzelburger, G. (2015). Religion, religiosity, and the attitudes toward homosexuality—A multilevel analysis of 79 countries. *Journal of Homosexuality, 62*, 207–241.

Jackson, G. (2009). Sexual response in cardiovascular disease. *Journal of Sex Research, 46*, 233–236.

Jackson, J. M., & Williams, K. D. (1988). *Social loafing: A review and theoretical analysis.* Unpublished manuscript, Fordham University.

Jackson, S. W. (1992). The listening healer in the history of psychological healing. *American Journal Psychiatry, 149*, 1623–1632.

Jacobs, B. L. (1994). Serotonin, motor activity, and depression-related disorders. *American Scientist, 82*, 456–463.

Jacobs, B. L. (2004). Depression: The brain finally gets into the act. *Current Directions in Psychological Science, 13*, 103–106.

Jacques, C., & Rossion, B. (2006). The speed of individual face categorization. *Psychological Science, 17*, 485–492.

Jaffe, E. (2004, October). Peace in the Middle East may be impossible: Lee D. Ross on naive realism and conflict resolution. *APS Observer*, pp. 9–11.

Jakubovski, E., Varigonda, A. L., Freemantle, N., Taylor, M. J., & Bloch, M. H. (2015). Systematic review and meta-analysis: Dose-response relationship of selective serotonin reuptake inhibitors in major depressive disorder. *American Journal of Psychiatry, 173*(2), 174–183.

James, W. (1890). *The principles of psychology* (Vol. 2). New York: Holt.

Jamieson, J. P. (2010). The home field advantage in athletics: A meta-analysis. *Journal of Applied Social Psychology, 40*, 1819–1848.

Jamison, K. R. (1993). *Touched with fire: Manic-depressive illness and the artistic temperament.* New York: Free Press.

Jamison, K. R. (1995). *An unquiet mind.* New York: Knopf.

Janis, I. L. (1982). *Groupthink: Psychological studies of policy decisions and fiascoes.* Boston: Houghton Mifflin.

Janis, I. L. (1986). Problems of international crisis management in the nuclear age. *Journal of Social Issues, 42*(2), 201–220.

Jaremka, L. M., Gabriel, S., & Carvallo, M. (2011). What makes us feel the best also makes us feel the worst: The emotional impact of independent and interdependent experiences. *Self and Identity, 10*, 44–63.

Jaschik, S. (2013, January 14). Spoiled children. Inside Higher Education (insidehighered.com).

Jayakar, R., King, T. Z., Morris, R., & Na, S. (2015). Hippocampal volume and auditory attention on a verbal memory task with adult survivors of pediatric brain tumor. *Neuropsychology, 29*, 303–319.

Jedrychowski, W., Perera, F., Jankowski, J., Butscher, M., Mroz, E., Flak, E., . . . Sowa, A. (2012). Effect of exclusive breastfeeding on the development of children's cognitive function in the Krakow prospective birth cohort study. *European Journal of Pediatrics, 171*, 151–158.

Jeffrey, K., Mahoney, S., Michaelson, J., & Abdallah, S. (2014). *Well-being at work: A review of the literature.* Retrieved from http://www.neweconomics.org/publications/entry/well-being-at-work

Jenkins, J. G., & Dallenbach, K. M. (1924). Obliviscence during sleep and waking. *American Journal of Psychology, 35*, 605–612.

Jenkins, J. M., & Astington, J. W. (1996). Cognitive factors and family structure associated with theory of mind development in young children. *Developmental Psychology, 32*, 70–78.

Jensen, J. P., & Bergin, A. E. (1988). Mental health values of professional therapists: A national interdisciplinary survey. *Professional Psychology: Research and Practice, 19*, 290–297.

Jepson, C., Krantz, D. H., & Nisbett, R. E. (1983). Inductive reasoning: Competence or skill? *The Behavioral and Brain Sciences, 3*, 494–501.

Jessberger, S., Aimone, J. B., & Gage, F. H. (2008). Neurogenesis. In *Learning and memory: A comprehensive reference.* Oxford: Elsevier.

Ji, D., & Wilson, M. A. (2007). Coordinated memory replay in the visual cortex and hippocampus during sleep. *Nature Neuroscience, 10*, 100–107.

Jobe, T. H., & Harrow, M. (2010). Schizophrenia course, long-term outcome, recovery, and prognosis. *Current Directions in Psychological Science, 19*, 220–225.

Joel, D., Berman, Z, Tavor, I., Wexler, N., Gaber, O., Stein, Y., . . . Assaf, Y. (2015, December) Sex beyond the genitalia: The human brain mosaic. *PNAS, 112*(50), 15468–15473.

John, O. P., & Srivastava, S. (1999). The Big Five trait taxonomy: History, measurement, and theoretical perspectives. In L. A. Pervin & O. P. John (Eds.), *Handbook of personality: Theory and research* (Vol. 2, pp. 102–138). New York: Guilford.

Johnson, D. L., Wiebe, J. S., Gold, S. M., Andreasen, N. C., Hichwa, R. D., Watkins, G. L., & Ponto, L. L. B. (1999). Cerebral blood flow and personality: A positron emission tomography study. *American Journal of Psychiatry, 156*, 252–257.

Johnson, E., & Novak, W. (1992). *My life.* New York: Fawcett Books.

Johnson, E. J., & Goldstein, D. (2003). Do defaults save lives? *Science, 302*, 1338–1339.

Johnson, J. A. (2007, June 26). Not so situational. Commentary on the SPSP listserv (spsp-discuss@stolaf.edu).

Johnson, J. G., Cohen, P., Kotler, L., Kasen, S., & Brook, J. S. (2002). Psychiatric disorders associated with risk for the development of eating disorders during adolescence and early adulthood. *Journal of Consulting and Clinical Psychology, 70*, 1119–1128.

Johnson, J. S., & Newport, E. L. (1991). Critical period effects on universal properties of language: The status of subjacency in the acquisition of a second language. *Cognition, 39*, 215–258.

Johnson, M. (2014). *Morality for humans: Ethical understanding from the perspective of cognitive science.* Chicago: University of Chicago Press.

Johnson, M. D., & Chen, J. (2015). Blame it on the alcohol: The influence of alcohol consumption during adolescence, the transition to adulthood, and young adulthood on one-time sexual hookups. *Journal of Sex Research, 52*, 570–579.

Johnson, M. H., & Morton, J. (1991). *Biology and cognitive development: The case of face recognition.* Oxford, England: Blackwell.

Johnson, M. P. (2008). *A typology of domestic violence: Intimate terrorism, violent resistance, and situational couple violence.* Boston: Northeastern University Press.

Johnson, W. (2010). Understanding the genetics of intelligence: Can height help? Can corn oil? *Current Directions in Psychological Science, 19*, 177–182.

Johnson, W., Carothers, A., & Deary, I. J. (2008). Sex differences in variability in general intelligence: A new look at the old question. *Perspectives on Psychological Science, 3*, 518–531.

Johnson, W., Turkheimer, E., Gottesman, I. I., & Bouchard, T. J., Jr. (2009). Beyond heritability: Twin studies in behavioral research. *Current Directions in Psychological Science, 18*, 217–220.

Johnston, L. D., O'Malley, P. M., Bachman, J. G., & Schulenberg, J. E. (2007, May). *Monitoring the Future national results on adolescent drug use: Overview of key findings, 2006.* Bethesda, MD: National Institute on Drug Abuse.

Johnston, L. D., O'Malley, P. M., Miech, R. A., Bachman, J. G., & Schulenberg, J. E. (2015, February). *Monitoring the Future national results on drug use: 1975–2014: 2014 overview, key findings on adolescent drug use.* Ann Arbor: Institute for Social Research, University of Michigan.

Joiner, T. E., Jr. (2006). *Why people die by suicide.* Cambridge, MA: Harvard University Press.

Joiner, T. E., Jr. (2010). *Myths about suicide.* Cambridge, MA: Harvard University Press.

Jonason, P. K., Garcia, J. R., Webster, G. D., Li, N. P., & Fisher, H. E. (2015). Relationship dealbreakers: Traits people avoid in potential mates. *Personality and Social Psychology Bulletin, 41*, 1697–1711.

Jones, A. C., & Gosling, S. D. (2005). Temperament and personality in dogs (*Canis familiaris*): A review and evaluation of past research. *Applied Animal Behaviour Science, 95*, 1–53.

Jones, B., Reedy, E. J., & Weinberg, B. A. (2014, January). *Age and scientific genius.* NBER Working Paper Series (nber.org/papers/w19866).

Jones, E. (1957). *The life and work of Sigmund Freud: Vol. 3. The last phase (1919–1939)* (Pt. 1, chap. 4). New York: Basic Books.

Jones, J. M. (2013, December 19). *In U.S., 40% get less than recommended amount of sleep.* Gallup Poll (gallup .com).

Jones, J. T., Pelham, B. W., Carvallo, M., & Mirenberg, M. C. (2004). How do I love thee? Let me count the Js: Implicit egotism and interpersonal attraction. *Journal of Personality and Social Psychology, 87*, 665–683.

Jones, M. C. (1924). A laboratory study of fear: The case of Peter. *Journal of Genetic Psychology, 31*, 308–315.

Jones, S. S. (2007). Imitation in infancy: The development of mimicry. *Psychological Science, 18*, 593–599.

Jónsson, H., Hougaard, E., Bennedsen, B. E. (2011). Randomized comparative study of group versus individual cognitive behavioural therapy for obsessive compulsive disorder. *Acta Psychiatrica Scandinavica, 123*, 387–397.

Jorm, A. F., Reavley, N. J., & Ross, A. M. (2012). Belief in the dangerousness of people with mental disorders: A review. *Australian and New Zealand Journal of Psychiatry, 46*, 1029–1045.

Jose, A., O'Leary, D., & Moyer, A. (2010). Does premarital cohabitation predict subsequent marital stability and marital quality? A meta-analysis. *Journal of Marriage and Family, 72*, 105–116.

Jost, J. T., Kay, A. C., & Thorisdottir, H. (Eds.) (2009). *Social and psychological bases of ideology and system justification.* New York: Oxford University Press.

Judge, T. A., Thoresen, C. J., Bono, J. E., & Patton, G. K. (2001). The job satisfaction/job performance relationship: A qualitative and quantitative review. *Psychological Bulletin, 127*, 376–407.

Jung-Beeman, M., Bowden, E. M., Haberman, J., Frymiare, J. L., Arambel-Liu, S., Greenblatt, R., . . . Kounios, J. (2004). Neural activity when people solve verbal problems with insight. *PloS Biology 2*(4), e111.

Just, M. A., Keller, T. A., & Cynkar, J. (2008). A decrease in brain activation associated with driving when listening to someone speak. *Brain Research, 1205*, 70–80.

Kabat-Zinn, J. (2001). Mindfulness-based interventions in context: Past, present, and future. *Clinical Psychology: Science and Practice, 10,* 144–156.

Kagan, J. (1976). Emergent themes in human development. *American Scientist, 64,* 186–196.

Kagan, J. (1984). *The nature of the child.* New York: Basic Books.

Kagan, J. (1995). On attachment. *Harvard Review of Psychiatry, 3,* 104–106.

Kagan, J. (1998). *Three seductive ideas.* Cambridge, MA: Harvard University Press.

Kagan, J. (2010). *The temperamental thread: How genes, culture, time, and luck make us who we are.* Washington, DC: Dana Press.

Kagan, J., Lapidus, D. R., & Moore, M. (1978, December) Infant antecedents of cognitive functioning: A longitudinal study. *Child Development, 49*(4), 1005–1023.

Kagan, J., & Snidman, N. (2004). *The long shadow of temperament.* Cambridge, MA: Belknap Press.

Kahneman, D. (1985, June). Quoted by K. McKean, Decisions, decisions. *Discover,* pp. 22–31.

Kahneman, D. (1999). Assessments of objective happiness: A bottom-up approach. In D. Kahneman, E. Diener, & N. Schwartz (Eds.), *Understanding well-being: Scientific perspectives on enjoyment and suffering.* New York: Russell Sage Foundation.

Kahneman, D. (2005, January 13). What were they thinking? Q&A with Daniel Kahneman. *Gallup Management Journal* (gmj.gallup.com).

Kahneman, D. (2011). *Thinking, fast and slow.* New York: Farrar, Straus, and Giroux.

Kahneman, D., Fredrickson, B. L., Schreiber, C. A., & Redelmeier, D. A. (1993). When more pain is preferred to less: Adding a better end. *Psychological Science, 4,* 401–405.

Kahneman, D., Krueger, A. B., Schkade, D. A., Schwarz, N., & Stone, A. A. (2004). A survey method for characterizing daily life experience: The day reconstruction method. *Science, 306,* 1776–1780.

Kahneman, D., & Tversky, A. (1972). Subjective probability: A judgment of representativeness. *Cognitive Psychology 3,* 430–454.

Kail, R. (1991). Developmental change in speed of processing during childhood and adolescence. *Psychological Bulletin, 109,* 490–501.

Kail, R., & Hall, L. K. (2001). Distinguishing short-term memory from working memory. *Memory & Cognition, 29,* 1–9.

Kaiser Family Foundation. (2010, January). *Generation M2: Media in the lives of 8- to 18-year-olds* (by V. J. Rideout, U. G. Foeher, & D. F. Roberts). Menlo Park, CA: Henry J. Kaiser Family Foundation.

Kakinami, L., Barnett, T. A., Séguin, L., & Paradis, G. (2015). Parenting style and obesity risk in children. *Preventive Medicine, 75,* 18–22.

Kamarck, T., & Jennings, J. R. (1991). Biobehavioral factors in sudden cardiac death. *Psychological Bulletin, 109,* 42–75.

Kamel, N. S., & Gammack, J. K. (2006). Insomnia in the elderly: Cause, approach, and treatment. *American Journal of Medicine, 119,* 463–469.

Kamenica, E., Naclerio, R., & Malani, A. (2013). Advertisements impact the physiological efficacy of a branded drug. *PNAS, 110,* 12931–12935.

Kamil, A. C., & Cheng, K. (2001). Way-finding and landmarks: The multiple-bearings hypothesis. *Journal of Experimental Biology, 204,* 103–113.

Kaminski, J., Cali, J., & Fischer, J. (2004). Word learning in a domestic dog: Evidence for "fast mapping." *Science, 304,* 1682–1683.

Kandel, E. (2008, October/November). Quoted in S. Avan, Speaking of memory. *Scientific American Mind,* pp. 16–17.

Kandel, E. R. (2012, March 5). Interview by Claudia Dreifus: A quest to understand how memory works. *The New York Times* (nytimes.com).

Kandel, E. R., & Schwartz, J. H. (1982). Molecular biology of learning: Modulation of transmitter release. *Science, 218,* 433–443.

Kane, G. D. (2010). Revisiting gay men's body image issues: Exposing the fault lines. *Review of General Psychology, 14,* 311–317.

Kaplan, H. I., & Saddock, B. J. (Eds.). (1989). *Comprehensive textbook of psychiatry, V.* Baltimore, MD: Williams & Wilkins.

Kaprio, J., Koskenvuo, M., & Rita, H. (1987). Mortality after bereavement: A prospective study of 95,647 widowed persons. *American Journal of Public Health, 77,* 283–287.

Karacan, I., Goodenough, D. R., Shapiro, A., & Starker, S. (1966). Erection cycle during sleep in relation to dream anxiety. *Archives of General Psychiatry, 15,* 183–189.

Karasik, L. B., Adolph, K. E., Tamis-LeMonda, C. S., & Bornstein, M. H. (2010). WEIRD walking: Cross-cultural research on motor development. *Behavioral and Brain Sciences, 33,* 95–96.

Karau, S. J., & Williams, K. D. (1993). Social loafing: A meta-analytic review and theoretical integration. *Journal of Personality and Social Psychology, 65,* 681–706.

Kark, J. D., Shemi, G., Friedlander, Y., Martin, O., Manor, O., & Blondheim, S. H. (1996). Does religious observance promote health? Mortality in secular vs. religious kibbutzim in Israel. *American Journal of Public Health, 86,* 341–346.

Karlén, J., Ludvigsson, J., Hedmark, M., Faresjö, Å., Theodorsson, E., & Faresjö, T. (2015). Early psychosocial exposures, hair cortisol levels, and disease risk. *Pediatrics, 135,* e1450–e1457. doi:10.1542/peds.2014-2561

Karlsgodt, K. H., Sun, D., & Cannon, T. D. (2010). Structural and functional brain abnormalities in schizophrenia. *Current Directions in Psychological Science, 19,* 226–231.

Karpicke, J. D. (2012). Retrieval-based learning: Active retrieval promotes meaningful learning. *Current Directions in Psychological Science, 21,* 157–163.

Karpicke, J. D., & Roediger, H. L., III. (2008). The critical importance of retrieval for learning. *Science, 319,* 966–968.

Karremans, J. C., Frankenhis, W. E., & Arons, S. (2010). Blind men prefer a low waist-to-hip ratio. *Evolution and Human Behavior, 31,* 182–186.

Kasen, S., Chen, H., Sneed, J., Crawford, T., & Cohen, P. (2006). Social role and birth cohort influences on gender-linked personality traits in women: A 20-year longitudinal analysis. *Journal of Personality and Social Psychology, 91,* 944–958.

Kashdan, T. B. (2009). *Curious? Discover the missing ingredient to a fulfilling life.* New York: William Morrow.

Katz-Wise, S. L., & Hyde, J. S. (2012). Victimization experiences of lesbian, gay, and bisexual individuals: A meta-analysis. *Journal of Sex Research, 49,* 142–167.

Katz-Wise, S. L., Priess, H. A., & Hyde, J. S. (2010). Gender-role attitudes and behavior across the transition to parenthood. *Developmental Psychology, 46,* 18–28.

Kaufman, G., & Libby, L. K. (2012). Changing beliefs and behavior through experience-taking. *Journal of Personality and Social Psychology, 103,* 1–19.

Kaufman, J. C., & Baer, J. (2002). I bask in dreams of suicide: Mental illness, poetry, and women. *Review of General Psychology, 6,* 271–286.

Kaufman, L., & Kaufman, J. H. (2000). Explaining the moon illusion. *PNAS, 97,* 500–505.

Kawamichi, H., Yoshihara, K., Sugawara, S. K., Matsunaga, M., Makita, K., Hamano, Y. H., . . . Sadato, N. (2015). Helping behavior induced by empathic concern attenuates anterior cingulate activation in response to others' distress. *Social Neuroscience, 11*(2), 109–122. doi:10.1080/17470919.2015.1049709

Kay, A. C., Baucher, D., Peach, J. M., Laurin, K., Friesen, J., Zanna, M. P., & Spencer, S. J. (2009). Inequality, discrimination, and the power of the status quo: Direct evidence for a motivation to see the way things are as the way they should be. *Journal of Personality and Social Psychology, 97,* 421–434.

Kayser, C. (2007, April/May). Listening with your eyes. *Scientific American Mind,* pp. 24–29.

Kazantzis, N., & Dattilio, F. M. (2010). Definitions of homework, types of homework and ratings of the importance of homework among psychologists with cognitive behavior therapy and psychoanalytic theoretical orientations. *Journal of Clinical Psychology, 66,* 758–773.

Kazantzis, N., Whittington, C., & Dattilio, F. M. (2010). Meta-analysis of homework effects in cognitive and behavioral therapy: A replication and extension. *Clinical Psychology: Science and Practice, 17,* 144 –156.

Kazdin, A. E. (2015). Editor's introduction to the special series: Targeted training of cognitive processes for behavioral and emotional disorders. *Clinical Psychological Science, 3,* 38.

Kearney, M. S., & Levine, P. B. (2014). *Media influences on social outcomes: The impact of MTV's 16 and Pregnant on teen childbearing.* The National Bureau of Economic Research: NBER Working Paper No. 19795.

Keesey, R. E., & Corbett, S. W. (1983). Metabolic defense of the body weight set-point. In A. J. Stunkard & E. Stellar (Eds.), *Eating and its disorders* (pp. 87–96). New York: Raven Press.

Keith, S. W., Redden, D. T., Katzmarzyk, P. T., Boggiano, M. M., Hanlon, E. C., Benca, R. M., . . . Allison, D. B. (2006). Putative contributors to the secular increase in obesity: Exploring the roads less traveled. *International Journal of Obesity, 30,* 1585–1594.

Kell, H. J., Lubinski, D., & Benbow, C. P. (2013). Who rises to the top? Early indicators. *Psychological Science, 24,* 648–659.

Keller, M. B., McCullough, J. P., Klein, D. N., Arnow, B., Dunner, D. L., Gelenberg, M. D., . . . Zajecka J. (2000), A comparison of nefazodone, the cognitive behavioral-analysis system of psychotherapy, and their combination for the treatment of chronic depression. *New England Journal of Medicine, 342,* 1462–1470.

Kellerman, J., Lewis, J., & Laird, J. D. (1989). Looking and loving: The effects of mutual gaze on feelings of romantic love. *Journal of Research in Personality, 23,* 145–161.

Kelley, J., & De Graaf, N. D. (1997). National context, parental socialization, and religious belief: Results from 15 nations. *American Sociological Review, 62,* 639–659.

Kelling, S. T., & Halpern, B. P. (1983). Taste flashes: Reaction times, intensity, and quality. *Science, 219,* 412–414.

Kellner, C. H., Fink, M., Knapp, R., Petrides, G. Husain, M., Rummans, T., . . . Malur, C. (2005). Relief of expressed suicidal intent by ECT: A consortium for research in ECT study. *American Journal of Psychiatry, 162,* 977–982.

Kellner, C. H., Knapp, R. G., Petrides, G., Rummans, T. A., Husain, M. M., Rasmussen, K., . . . Fin, M. (2006). Continuation electroconvulsive therapy vs. pharmacotherapy for relapse prevention in major depression: A multisite study from the Consortium for Research in Electroconvulsive Therapy (CORE). *Archives of General Psychiatry, 63,* 1337–1344.

Kelly, A. E. (2000). Helping construct desirable identities: A self-presentational view of psychotherapy. *Psychological Bulletin, 126,* 475–494.

Kelly, D. J., Quinn, P. C., Slater, A. M., Lee, K., Ge, L., & Pascalis, O. (2007). The other-race effect develops during infancy: Evidence of perceptual narrowing. *Psychological Science, 18,* 1084–1089.

Kelly, T. A. (1990). The role of values in psychotherapy: A critical review of process and outcome effects. *Clinical Psychology Review, 10,* 171–186.

Kendall-Tackett, K. A. (Ed.) (2004). *Health consequences of abuse in the family: A clinical guide for evidence-based practice.* Washington, DC: American Psychological Association.

Kendall-Tackett, K. A., Williams, L. M., & Finkelhor, D. (1993). Impact of sexual abuse on children: A review and synthesis of recent empirical studies. *Psychological Bulletin, 113,* 164–180.

Kendler, K. S. (1998, January). Major depression and the environment: A psychiatric genetic perspective. *Pharmacopsychiatry, 31*(1), 5–9.

Kendler, K. S. (2011). A statement from Kenneth S. Kendler, M.D., on the proposal to eliminate the grief exclusion criterion from major depression. American Psychiatric Association DSM-5 Development (www.dsm5.org).

Kendler, K. S., Jacobson, K. C., Myers, J., & Prescott, C. A. (2002a). Sex differences in genetic and environmental risk factors for irrational fears and phobias. *Psychological Medicine, 32,* 209–217.

Kendler, K. S., Maes, H. H., Lönn, S. L., Morris, N. A., Lichtenstein, P., Sundquist, J., & Sundquist, K. (2015). A Swedish national twin study of criminal behavior and its violent, white-collar and property subtypes. *Psychological Medicine, 45,* 2253–2262.

Kendler, K. S., Myers, J., & Prescott, C. A. (2002b). The etiology of phobias: An evaluation of the stress-diathesis model. *Archives of General Psychiatry, 59,* 242–248.

Kendler, K. S., Myers, J., & Zisook, S. (2008). Does bereavement-related major depression differ from major depression associated with other stressful life events? *American Journal of Psychiatry, 165,* 1449–1455.

Kendler, K. S., Neale, M. C., Thornton, L. M., Aggen, S. H., Gilman, S. E., & Kessler, R. C. (2002c). Cannabis use in the last year in a U.S. national sample of twin and sibling pairs. *Psychological Medicine, 32,* 551–554.

Kendler, K. S., Sundquist, K., Ohlsson, H., Palmer, K., Maes, H., Winkleby, M. A., & Sundquist, J. (2012). Genetic and familial environmental influences on the risk for drug abuse: A Swedish adoption study. *Archives of General Psychiatry, 69,* 690–697.

Kendler, K. S., Thornton, L. M., & Gardner, C. O. (2001). Genetic risk, number of previous depressive episodes, and stressful life events in predicting onset of major depression. *American Journal of Psychiatry, 158,* 582–586.

Kendler, K. S., Turkheimer, E., Ohlsson, H., Sundquist, J., & Sundquist, K. (2015). Family environment and the malleability of cognitive ability: A Swedish national home-reared and adopted-away cosibling control study. *PNAS, 112,* 4612–4617.

Kendrick, K. M., & Feng, J. (2011). Neural encoding principles in face perception revealed using nonprimate models. In G. Rhodes, A. Calder, M. Johnson, & J. V. Haxby (Eds.), *The Oxford handbook of face perception* (pp. 675–690). Oxford, England: Oxford University Press.

Kennard, B. D., Emslie, G. J., Mayes, T. L., Nakonezny, P. A., Jones, J. M., Foxwell, A. A., & King, J. (2014). Sequential treatment of fluoxetine and relapse-prevention CBT to improve outcomes in pediatric depression. *American Journal of Psychiatry, 171,* 1083–1090.

Kennedy, S., & Over, R. (1990). Psychophysiological assessment of male sexual arousal following spinal cord injury. *Archives of Sexual Behavior, 19,* 15–27.

Kenrick, D. T., & Gutierres, S. E. (1980). Contrast effects and judgments of physical attractiveness: When beauty becomes a social problem. *Journal of Personality and Social Psychology, 38,* 131–140.

Kenrick, D. T., Gutierres, S. E., & Goldberg, L. L. (1989). Influence of popular erotica on judgments of strangers and mates. *Journal of Experimental Social Psychology, 25,* 159–167.

Kenrick, D. T., Nieuweboer, S., & Bunnk, A. P. (2009). Universal mechanisms and cultural diversity: Replacing the blank slate with a coloring book. In M. Schaller, S. Heine, A. Norenzayan, T. Yamagishi, & T. Kameda (Eds.), *Evolution, culture, and the human mind* (pp. 257–271). Mahwah, NJ: Erlbaum.

Kensinger, E. A. (2007). Negative emotion enhances memory accuracy: Behavioral and neuroimaging evidence. *Current Directions in Psychological Science, 16,* 213–218.

Keough, K. A., Zimbardo, P. G., & Boyd, J. N. (1999). Who's smoking, drinking, and using drugs? Time perspective as a predictor of substance use. *Basic and Applied Social Psychology, 2,* 149–164.

Kernis, M. H. (2003). Toward a conceptualization of optimal self-esteem. *Psychological Inquiry, 14,* 1–26.

Kerr, N. L., & Bruun, S. E. (1983). Dispensability of member effort and group motivation losses: Free-rider effects. *Journal of Personality and Social Psychology, 44,* 78–94.

Kessler, M., & Albee, G. (1975). Primary prevention. *Annual Review of Psychology, 26,* 557–591.

Kessler, R. C. (2000). Posttraumatic stress disorder: The burden to the individual and to society. *Journal of Clinical Psychiatry, 61*(suppl. 5), 4–12.

Kessler, R. C. (2001). Epidemiology of women and depression. *Journal of Affective Disorders, 74,* 5–1.

Kessler, R. C., Brinbaum, H. G., Shahly, V., Bromet, E., Hwang, I., McLaughlin, K. A., . . . Stein, D. J. (2010). Age differences in the prevalence and co-morbidity of DSM-IV major depressive episodes: Results from the WHO World Mental Health Survey Initiative. *Depression and Anxiety, 27,* 351–364.

Kessler, R. C., Foster, C., Joseph, J., Ostrow, D., Wortman, C., Phair, J., & Chmiel, J. (1991). Stressful life events and symptom onset in HIV infection. *American Journal of Psychiatry, 148,* 733–738.

Keyes, K. M., Maslowsky, J., Hamilton, A., & Schulenberg, J. (2015). The great sleep recession: Changes in sleep duration among U.S. adolescents, 1991–2012. *Pediatrics, 135,* 460–468.

Keynes, M. (1980, December 20/27). Handel's illnesses. *The Lancet,* pp. 1354–1355.

Keys, A., Brozek, J., Henschel, A., Mickelsen, O., & Taylor, H. L. (1950). *The biology of human starvation.* Minneapolis: University of Minnesota Press.

Khera, M., Bhattacharya, R. K., Blick, G., Kushner, H., Nguyen, D., & Miner, M. M. (2011). Improved sexual function with testosterone replacement therapy in hypogonadal men: Real-world data from the Testim Registry in the United States (TriUS). *Journal of Sexual Medicine, 8,* 3204–3213.

Kiecolt-Glaser, J. K. (2009). Psychoneuroimmunology: Psychology's gateway to the biomedical future. *Perspectives on Psychological Science, 4,* 367–369.

Kiecolt-Glaser, J. K., Page, G. G., Marucha, P. T., MacCallum, R. C., & Glaser, R. (1998). Psychological influences on surgical recovery: Perspectives from psychoneuroimmunology. *American Psychologist, 53,* 1209–1218.

Kiehl, K. A., & Buckholtz, J. W. (2010, September/October). Inside the mind of a psychopath. *Scientific American Mind,* pp. 22–29.

Kihlstrom, J. F. (1990). Awareness, the psychological unconscious, and the self. Address to the American Psychological Association convention.

Kihlstrom, J. F. (2005). Dissociative disorders. *Annual Review of Clinical Psychology, 1,* 227–253.

Kihlstrom, J. F. (2006). Repression: A unified theory of a will-o'-the-wisp. *Behavioral and Brain Sciences, 29,* 523.

Kille, D. R., Forest, A. L., & Wood, J. V. (2013). Tall, dark, and stable: Embodiment motivates mate selection preferences. *Psychological Science, 24,* 112–114.

Killingsworth, M. A., & Gilbert, D. T. (2010). A wandering mind is an unhappy mind. *Science, 330,* 932.

Kilpatrick, L. A., Suyenobu, B. Y., Smith, S. R., Bueller, J. A., Goodman, T., Creswell, J. D., . . . Naliboff, B. D. (2011). Impact of mindfulness-based stress reduction training on intrinsic brain activity. *Neuroimage, 56,* 290–298.

Kilpeläinen, T. O., Qi, L., Brage, S., Sharp, S. J., Sonestedt, E., Demerath, E., . . . Loos, R. J. F. (2012). Physical activity attenuates the influence of FTO variants on obesity risk: A meta-analysis of 218,166 adults and 19,268 children. *PLoS Medicine.* http://www.plosmedicine.org/article/info%3Adoi%2F10.1371%2Fjournal.pmed.1001116

Kim, B. S. K., Ng, G. F., & Ahn, A. J. (2005). Effects of client expectation for counseling success, client-counselor worldview match, and client adherence to Asian and European American cultural values on counseling process with Asian Americans. *Journal of Counseling Psychology, 52,* 67–76.

Kim, D. A., Hwong, A. R., Stafford, D., Hughes, D. A., O'Malley, A. J., Fowler, J. H., & Christakis, N. A. (2015). Social network targeting to maximize population behaviour change: A cluster randomized controlled trial. *The Lancet, 386,* 145–153.

Kim, G., & Tong, A. (2010, February 23). Airline passengers have grown, seats haven't. *Sacramento Bee* (reprinted by *Grand Rapids Press,* pp. B1, B3).

Kim, J. L., & Ward, L. M. (2012). Striving for pleasure without fear: Short-term effects of reading a women's magazine on women's sexual attitudes. *Psychology of Women Quarterly, 36,* 326–336.

Kim, S. H., Vincent, L. C., & Goncalo, J. A. (2013). Outside advantage: Can social rejection fuel creative thought? *Journal of Experimental Psychology: General, 142,* 605–611.

Kimata, H. (2001). Effect of humor on allergen-induced wheal reactions. *Journal of the American Medical Association, 285,* 737.

Kim-Yeary, K. H., Ounpraseuth, S., Moore, P., Bursac, Z., & Greene, P. (2012). Religion, social capital, and health. *Review of Religious Research, 54,* 331–347.

King, S., St.-Hilaire, A., & Heidkamp, D. (2010). Prenatal factors in schizophrenia. *Current Directions in Psychological Science, 19,* 209–213.

Kinnier, R. T., & Metha, A. T. (1989). Regrets and priorities at three stages of life. *Counseling and Values, 33,* 182–193.

Kinsella, E. L., Ritchie, T. D., & Igou, E. R. (2015). Zeroing in on heroes: A prototype analysis of hero features. *Journal of Personality and Social Psychology, 108,* 114–127.

Kinzler, K. D., Shutts, K., Dejesus, J., & Spelke, E. S. (2009). Accent trumps race in guiding children's social preferences. *Social Cognition, 27,* 623–634.

Kirby, D. (2002). Effective approaches to reducing adolescent unprotected sex, pregnancy, and childbearing. *Journal of Sex Research, 39,* 51–57.

Kircanski, K., Thompson, R. J., Sorenson, J. E., Sherdell, L., & Gotlib, I. H. (2015). Rumination and worry in daily life: Examining the naturalistic validity of theoretical constructs. *Clinical Psychological Science, 3*(6), 926–939.

Kirkpatrick, B., Fenton, W. S., Carpenter, W. T., Jr., & Marder, S. R. (2006). The NIMHMATRICS consensus statement on negative symptoms. *Schizophrenia Bulletin, 32,* 214–219.

Kirsch, I. (2010). *The emperor's new drugs: Exploding the antidepressant myth.* New York: Basic Books.

Kirsch, I., Deacon, B. J., Huedo-Medina, T. B., Scoboria, A., Moore, T. J., & Johnson, B. T. (2008) Initial severity and antidepressant benefits: A meta-analysis of data submitted to the Food and Drug Administration. *Public Library of Science Medicine, 5,* e45.

Kirsch, I., Kong, J., Sadler, P., Spaeth, R., Cook, A., Kaptchuk, T. J., & Gollub, R. (2014). Expectancy and conditioning in placebo analgesia: Separate or connected processes? *Psychology of Consciousness: Theory, Research, and Practice, 1,* 51–59.

Kirsch, I., Moore, T. J., Scoboria, A., & Nicholls, S. S. (2002, July 15). New study finds little difference between effects of antidepressants and placebo. *Prevention and Treatment* (journals.apa.org/prevention).

Kirsch, I., & Sapirstein, G. (1998). Listening to Prozac but hearing placebo: A meta-analysis of antidepressant medication. *Prevention and Treatment, 1,* posted June 26 at (journals.apa.org/prevention/volume1).

Kisely, S., Hall, K., Siskind, D., Frater, J., Olson, S., & Crompton, D. (2014). Deep brain stimulation for obsessive-compulsive disorder: A systematic review and meta-analysis. *Psychological Medicine, 44,* 3533–3542.

Kish, D. (2015, March). How I use sonar to navigate the world. Retrieved from ted.com/talks/daniel_kish_how_i_use_sonar_to_navigate_the_world?language=en.

Kitahara, C. M., Flint, A. J., de Gonzalez, A. B., Bernstein, L., Brotzman, M., MacInnis, R. J., . . . Hartge, P. (2014, July 8). Association between class III obesity (BMI of 40–59 kg/m²) and mortality: A pooled analysis of 20 prospective studies. *PLOS Medicine.* doi:10.1371/journal.pmed.1001673

Kitayama, S., Chua, H. F., Tompson, S., & Han, S. (2013). Neural mechanisms of dissonance: An fMRI investigation of choice justification. *NeuroImage, 69,* 206–212.

Kitayama, S., Conway, L. G., III, Pietromonaci, P. R., Park, H., & Plaut, V. C. (2010). Ethos of independence across regions in the United States: The production–adoption model of cultural change. *American Psychologist, 65,* 559–574.

Klayman, J., & Ha, Y.-W. (1987). Confirmation, disconfirmation, and information in hypothesis testing. *Psychological Review, 94,* 211–228.

Klein, D. N. (2010). Chronic depression: Diagnosis and classification. *Current Directions in Psychological Science, 19,* 96–100.

Klein, D. N., Schwartz, J. E., Santiago, N. J., Vivian, D., Vocisano, C., Castonguay, L. G., . . . Keller, M. B. (2003). Therapeutic alliance in depression treatment: Controlling for prior change and patient characteristics. *Journal of Consulting and Clinical Psychology, 71,* 997–1006.

Kleinke, C. L. (1986). Gaze and eye contact: A research review. *Psychological Bulletin, 1000,* 78–100.

Kleinmuntz, B., & Szucko, J. J. (1984). A field study of the fallibility of polygraph lie detection. *Nature, 308,* 449–450.

Kleitman, N. (1960, November). Patterns of dreaming. *Scientific American,* pp. 82–88.

Klemm, W. R. (1990). Historical and introductory perspectives on brainstem-mediated behaviors. In W. R. Klemm & R. P. Vertes (Eds.), *Brainstem mechanisms of behavior.* New York: Wiley.

Klimstra, T. A., Hale, W. W., III, Raaijmakers, Q. A. W., Branje, S. J. T., & Meeus, W. H. J. (2009). Maturation of personality in adolescence. *Journal of Personality and Social Psychology, 96,* 898–912.

Kline, D., & Schieber, F. (1985). Vision and aging. In J. E. Birren & K. W. Schaie (Eds.), *Handbook of the psychology of aging.* New York: Van Nostrand Reinhold.

Kline, N. S. (1974). *From sad to glad.* New York: Ballantine Books.

Klinke, R., Kral, A., Heid, S., Tillein, J., & Hartmann, R. (1999). Recruitment of the auditory cortex in congenitally deaf cats by long-term cochlear electrostimulation. *Science, 285,* 1729–1733.

Kluft, R. P. (1991). Multiple personality disorder. In A. Tasman & S. M. Goldfinger (Eds.), *Review of Psychiatry* (Vol. 10, pp. 161–188). Washington, DC: American Psychiatric Press.

Klump, K. L., Suisman, J. L., Burt, S. A., McGue, M., & Iacono, W. G. (2009). Genetic and environmental influences on disordered eating: An adoption study. *Journal of Abnormal Psychology, 118,* 797–805.

Klüver, H., & Bucy, P. C. (1939). Preliminary analysis of functions of the temporal lobes in monkeys. *Archives of Neurology and Psychiatry, 42,* 979–1000.

Knapp, S., & VandeCreek, L. (2000, August). Recovered memories of childhood abuse: Is there an underlying professional consensus? *Professional Psychology: Research and Practice, 31,* 365–371.

Knickmeyer, E. (2001, August 7). In Africa, big is definitely better. *Seattle Times,* p. A7.

Knight, R. T. (2007). Neural networks debunk phrenology. *Science, 316,* 1578–1579.

Knight, W. (2004, August 2). Animated face helps deaf with phone chat. *New Scientist* (NewScientist.com).

Knuts, I. J. E., Cosci, F., Esquivel, G., Goossens, L., van Duinen, M., Bareman, M., . . . Schruers, K. R. J. (2010). Cigarette smoking and 35% CO2 induced panic in panic disorder patients. *Journal of Affective Disorders, 124,* 215–218.

Koenen, K. C., Moffitt, T. E., Roberts, A. L., Martin, L. T., Kubzansky, L., Harrington, H., . . . Caspi, A. (2009). Childhood IQ and adult mental disorders: A test of the cognitive reserve hypothesis. *American Journal of Psychiatry, 166,* 50–57.

Koenig, H. G., King, D. E., & Carson, V. B. (2012). *Handbook of religion and health* (2nd ed.). New York: Oxford University Press.

Koenig, H. G., & Larson, D. B. (1998). Use of hospital services, religious attendance, and religious affiliation. *Southern Medical Journal, 91,* 925–932.

Koenig, L. B., McGue, M., Krueger, R. F., & Bouchard, T. J., Jr. (2005). Genetic and environmental influences on religiousness: Findings for retrospective and current religiousness ratings. *Journal of Personality, 73,* 471–488.

Koenig, L. B., & Vaillant, G. E. (2009). A prospective study of church attendance and health over the lifespan. *Health Psychology, 28,* 117–124.

Koenigs, M., Young, L., Adolphs, R., Tranel, D., Cushman, F., Hauser, M., & Damasio, A. (2007). Damage to the prefrontal cortex increases utilitarian moral judgements. *Nature, 446,* 908–911.

Koestner, R., Lekes, N., Powers, T. A., & Chicoine, E. (2002). Attaining personal goals: Self-concordance plus implementation intentions equals success. *Journal of Personality and Social Psychology, 83,* 231–244.

Kohlberg, L. (1981). *The philosophy of moral development: Essays on moral development* (Vol. I). San Francisco: Harper & Row.

Kohlberg, L. (1984). *The psychology of moral development: Essays on moral development* (Vol. II). San Francisco: Harper & Row.

Kohler, C. G., Walker, J. B., Martin, E. A., Healey, K. M., & Moberg, P. J. (2010). Facial emotion perception in schizophrenia: A meta-analytic review. *Schizophrenia Bulletin, 36,* 1009–1019.

Kohler, I. (1962, May). Experiments with goggles. *Scientific American,* pp. 62–72.

Köhler, W. (1925; reprinted 1957). *The mentality of apes.* London: Pelican.

Kolata, G. (1987). Metabolic catch-22 of exercise regimens. *Science, 236,* 146–147.

Kolb, B. (1989). Brain development, plasticity, and behavior. *American Psychologist, 44,* 1203–1212.

Kolb, B., & Whishaw, I. Q. (1998). Brain plasticity and behavior. *Annual Review of Psychology, 49,* 43–64.

Kolker, K. (2002, December 8). Video violence disturbs some: Others scoff at influence. *Grand Rapids Press,* pp. A1, A12.

Koltko-Rivera, M. E. (2006). Rediscovering the later version of Maslow's hierarchy of needs: Self-transcendence and opportunities for theory, research, and unification. *Review of General Psychology, 10,* 302–317.

Komisaruk, B. R., & Whipple, B. (2011). Non-genital orgasms. *Sexual and Relationship Therapy, 26,* 356–372.

Konkle, T., Brady, T. F., Alvarez, G. A., & Oliva, A. (2010). Conceptual distinctiveness supports detailed visual long-term memory for real-world objects. *Journal of Experimental Psychology: General, 139,* 558–578.

Koopmans, J. R., Slutske, W. S., van Baal, G. C. M., & Boomsma, D. I. (1999). The influence of religion on alcohol use initiation: Evidence for a genotype x environment interaction. *Behavior Genetics, 29,* 445–453.

Kosslyn, S. M. (2005). Reflective thinking and mental imagery: A perspective on the development of posttraumatic stress disorder. *Development and Psychopathology, 17,* 851–863.

Kosslyn, S. M. (2008). The world in the brain. In 2008: What have you changed your mind about? Why? *The Edge* (edge.org).

Kosslyn, S. M., & Koenig, O. (1992). *Wet mind: The new cognitive neuroscience.* New York: Free Press.

Kotchick, B. A., Shaffer, A., & Forehand, R. (2001). Adolescent sexual risk behavior: A multi-system perspective. *Clinical Psychology Review, 21,* 493–519.

Kotkin, M., Daviet, C., & Gurin, J. (1996). The Consumer Reports mental health survey. *American Psychologist, 51,* 1080–1082.

Kounios, J., & Beeman, M. (2009). The Aha! moment: The cognitive neuroscience of insight. *Current Directions in Psychological Science, 18,* 210–215.

Kraft, T., & Pressman, S. (2012). Grin and bear it: The influence of the manipulated facial expression on the stress response. *Psychological Science, 23,* 1372–1378.

Kramer, A. (2010). Personal correspondence.

Kramer, A. D. I. (2012). The spread of emotion via Facebook. In *Proceedings of the SIGCHI Conference on Human Factors in Computing Systems* (pp. 767–770). New York: Association for Computing Machinery.

Kramer, P. D. (2011, July 9). In defense of antidepressants. *The New York Times* (nytimes.com).

Kranz, F., & Ishai, A. (2006). Face perception is modulated by sexual preference. *Current Biology, 16,* 63–68.

Kranz, G. S., Hahn, A., Kaufmann, U., Küblböck, M., Hummer, A., Ganger, S., . . . Lanzenberger, R. (2014). White matter microstructure in transsexuals and controls investigated by diffusion tensor imaging. *The Journal of Neuroscience, 34*, 15466–15475.

Kring, A. M., & Caponigro, J. M. (2010). Emotion in schizophrenia: Where feeling meets thinking. *Current Directions in Psychological Science, 19*, 255–259.

Kring, A. M., & Gordon, A. H. (1998). Sex differences in emotion: Expression, experience, and physiology. *Journal of Personality and Social Psychology, 74*, 686–703.

Kringelbach, M. L., & Berridge, K. C. (2012, August). The joyful mind. *Scientific American*, pp. 40–45.

Kristeller, J. L., Baer, R. A., & Quillian-Wolever, R. (2006). Mindfulness-based approaches to eating disorders. In R. A. Baer (Ed.), *Mindfulness-based treatment approaches: A clinician's guide to evidence base and applications* (pp. 75–91). San Diego, CA: Academic Press.

Kroes, M. C. W., Tendolkar, I., van Wingen, G. A., van Waarde, J. A., Strange, B. A., & Fernández, G. (2014). An electroconvulsive therapy procedure impairs reconsolidation of episodic memories in humans. *Nature Neuroscience, 17*, 204–206.

Krosnick, J. A., & Alwin, D. F. (1989). Aging and susceptibility to attitude change. *Journal of Personality and Social Psychology, 57*, 416–425.

Krosnick, J. A., Betz, A. L., Jussim, L. J., & Lynn, A. R. (1992). Subliminal conditioning of attitudes. *Personality and Social Psychology Bulletin, 18*, 152–162.

Kross, E., Bruehlman-Senecal, E., Park, J., Burson, A., Dougherty, A., Shablack, H., . . . Ayduk, O. (2014). Self-talk as a regulatory mechanism: How you do it matters. *Journal of Personality and Social Psychology, 106*, 304–324.

Krueger, A. B., & Malecková, J. (2009). Attitudes and action: Public opinion and the occurrence of international terrorism. *Science, 325*, 1534–1536.

Krueger, J., & Killham, E. (2005, December 8). At work, feeling good matters. *Gallup Management Journal* (gmj.gallup.com).

Krueger, J., & Killham, E. (2006, March 9). Why Dilbert is right: Uncomfortable work environments make for disgruntled employees—just like the cartoon says. *Gallup Management Journal* (gmj.gallup.com).

Kruger, J., Epley, N., Parker, J., & Ng, Z.-W. (2005). Egocentrism over e-mail: Can we communicate as well as we think? *Journal of Personality and Social Psychology, 89*, 925–936.

Krumhansl, C. L. (2010). Plink: "Thin slices" of music. *Music Perception, 27*, 337–354.

Kubzansky, L. D., Sparrow, D., Vokanas, P., & Kawachi, I. (2001). Is the glass half empty or half full? A prospective study of optimism and coronary heart disease in the normative aging study. *Psychosomatic Medicine, 63*, 910–916.

Kuhl, P. K., & Meltzoff, A. N. (1982). The bimodal perception of speech in infancy. *Science, 218*, 1138–1141.

Kuhnle, C., Hofer, M., & Kilian, B. (2012). Self-control as predictor of school grades, life balance, and flow in adolescents. *British Journal of Educational Psychology, 82*, 533–548.

Kumar, A. & Gilovich, T. (2013). *Talking about what you did and what you have: The differential story utility of experiential and material purchases.* http://www.acrwebsite.org/volumes/1014578/volumes/v41/NA-41

Kumsta, R., Kreppner, J., Kennedy, M., Knights, N., Rutter, M., & Sonuga-Barke, E. (2015). Psychological consequences of early global deprivation: An overview of findings from the English & Romanian adoptees study. *European Psychologist, 20*, 138–151.

Kupfer, D. J. (2012, June 1). Dr Kupfer defends DSM-5. *Medscape Psychiatry* (medscape.com/viewarticle/764735).

Kuppens, P., Allen, N. B., & Sheeber, L. B. (2010). Emotional inertia and psychological maladjustment. *Psychological Science, 21*, 984–991.

Kurdziel, L., Duclos, K., & Spencer, R. M. C. (2013). Sleep spindles in midday naps enhance learning in preschool children. *PNAS, 110*, 17267–17272.

Kuster, F., Orth, U., & Meier, L. L. (2012). Rumination mediates the prospective effect of low self-esteem on depression: A five-wave longitudinal study. *Personality and Social Psychology Bulletin, 38*, 747–759.

Kutas, M. (1990). Event-related brain potential (ERP) studies of cognition during sleep: Is it more than a dream? In R. R. Bootzin, J. F. Kihlstrom, & D. Schacter (Eds.), *Sleep and cognition* (pp. 43–57). Washington, DC: American Psychological Association.

Kuttler, A. F., La Greca, A. M., & Prinstein, M. J. (1999). Friendship qualities and social-emotional functioning of adolescents with close, cross-sex friendships. *Journal of Research on Adolescence, 9*, 339–366.

Kvavilashvili, L., Mirani, J., Schlagman, S., Foley, K., & Kornbrot, D. E. (2009). Consistency of flashbulb memories of September 11 over long delays: Implications for consolidation and wrong time slice hypotheses. *Journal of Memory and Language, 61*, 556–572.

Kwon, P. (2013). Resilience in lesbian, gay, and bisexual individuals. *Personality and Social Psychology Review, 17*, 371–383.

Lacayo, R. (1995, June 12). Violent reaction. *Time*, pp. 25–39.

Lacey, M. (2010, December 11). He found bag of cash, but did the unexpected. *The New York Times* (nytimes.com).

Lafer-Sousa, R., Hermann, K. L., & Conway, B. R. (2015). Striking individual differences in color perception uncovered by "the dress" photograph. *Current Biology, 25*, R545–R546.

Lai, M.-C., Lombardo, M. V., Auyeung, B., Chakrabarti, B., & Baron-Cohen, S. (2015). Sex/gender differences and autism: Setting the scene for future research. *Journal of the American Academy of Child & Adolescent Psychiatry, 54*, 11–24.

Laird, J. D. (1974). Self-attribution of emotion: The effects of expressive behavior on the quality of emotional experience. *Journal of Personality and Social Psychology, 29*, 475–486.

Laird, J. D. (1984). The real role of facial response in the experience of emotion: A reply to Tourangeau and Ellsworth, and others. *Journal of Personality and Social Psychology, 47*, 909–917.

Laird, J. D., Cuniff, M., Sheehan, K., Shulman, D., & Strum, G. (1989). Emotion specific effects of facial expressions on memory for life events. *Journal of Social Behavior and Personality, 4*, 87–98.

Lakin, J. L., Chartrand, T. L., & Arkin, R. M. (2008). I am too just like you: Nonconscious mimicry as an automatic behavioral response to social exclusion. *Psychological Science, 19*, 816–822.

Lally, P., Van Jaarsveld, C. H. M., Potts, H. W. W., & Wardle, J. (2010). How are habits formed: Modelling habit formation in the real world. *European Journal of Social Psychology, 40*, 998–1009.

Lam, C. B., & McBride-Chang, C. A. (2007). Resilience in young adulthood: The moderating influences of gender-related personality traits and coping flexibility. *Sex Roles, 56*, 159–172.

Lambert, N. M., DeWall, C. N., Bushman, B. J., Tillman, T. F., Fincham, F. D., Pond, R. S., Jr., & Gwinn, A. M. (2011). *Lashing out in lust: Effect of pornography on nonsexual, physical aggression against relationship partners.* Paper presentation at the Society for Personality and Social Psychology convention.

Lambert, N. M., Negash, S., Stillman, T. F., Olmstead, S. B., & Fincham, F. D. (2012). A love that doesn't last: Pornography consumption and weakened commitment to a romantic partner. *Journal of Social and Clinical Psychology, 31*, 410–438.

Lambird, K. H., & Mann, T. (2006). When do ego threats lead to self-regulation failure? Negative consequences of defensive high self-esteem. *Personality and Social Psychology Bulletin, 32*, 1177–1187.

Landau, M. J., Oyserman, D., Keefer, L. A., & Smith, G. C. (2014). The college journey and academic engagement: How metaphor use enhances identity-based motivation. *Journal of Personality and Social Psychology, 106*, 679–698.

Landauer, T. (2001, September). Quoted in R. Herbert, You must remember this. *APS Observer*, p. 11.

Landauer, T. K., & Whiting, J. W. M. (1979). Correlates and consequences of stress in infancy. In R. Munroe, B. Munroe, & B. Whiting (Eds.), *Handbook of Cross-Cultural Human Development*. New York: Garland.

Landberg, J., & Norström, T. (2011). Alcohol and homicide in Russia and the United States: A comparative analysis. *Journal of Studies on Alcohol and Drugs, 72*, 723–730.

Landry, M. J. (2002). MDMA: A review of epidemiologic data. *Journal of Psychoactive Drugs, 34*, 163–169.

Langer, E. J. (1983). *The psychology of control*. Beverly Hills, CA: Sage.

Langer, E. J., & Abelson, R. P. (1974). A patient by any other name . . .: Clinician group differences in labeling bias. *Journal of Consulting and Clinical Psychology, 42*, 4–9.

Langer, E. J., & Imber, L. (1980). The role of mindlessness in the perception of deviance. *Journal of Personality and Social Psychology, 39*, 360–367.

Langlois, J. H., Kalakanis, L., Rubenstein, A. J., Larson, A., Hallam, M., & Smoot, M. (2000). Maxims or myths of beauty? A meta-analytic and theoretical review. *Psychological Bulletin, 126*, 390–423.

Langmeyer, A., Guglhör-Rudan, A., & Tarnai, C. (2012). What do music preferences reveal about personality? A cross-cultural replication using self-ratings and ratings of music samples. *Journal of Individual Differences, 33*, 119–130.

Lángström, N. H., Rahman, Q., Carlström, E., & Lichtenstein, P. (2010). Genetic and environmental effects on same-sex sexual behavior: A population study of twins in Sweden. *Archives of Sexual Behavior, 39*, 75–80.

Lankford, A. (2009). Promoting aggression and violence at Abu Ghraib: The U.S. military's transformation of ordinary people into torturers. *Aggression and Violent Behavior, 14*, 388–395.

Larkin, J. E., Brasel, A. M., & Pines, H. A. (2013). Cross-disciplinary applications of I/O psychology concepts: Predicting student retention and employee turnover. *Review of General Psychology, 17*, 82–92.

Larkin, K., Resko, J. A., Stormshak, F., Stellflug, J. N., & Roselli, C. E. (2002). *Neuroanatomical correlates of sex and sexual partner preference in sheep.* Paper presented at Society for Neuroscience convention.

Larrick, R. P., Timmerman, T. A., Carton, A. M., & Abrevaya, J. (2011). Temper, temperature, and temptation: Heat-related retaliation in baseball. *Psychological Science, 22*, 423–428.

Larson, R. W., & Verma, S. (1999). How children and adolescents spend time across the world: Work, play, and developmental opportunities. *Psychological Bulletin, 125*, 701–736.

Larzelere, R. E. (2000). Child outcomes of non-abusive and customary physical punishment by parents: An updated literature review. *Clinical Child and Family Psychology Review, 3*, 199–221.

Larzelere, R. E., & Kuhn, B. R. (2005). Comparing child outcomes of physical punishment and alternative disciplinary tactics: A meta-analysis. *Clinical Child and Family Psychology Review, 8,* 1–37.

Larzelere, R. E., Kuhn, B. R., & Johnson, B. (2004). The intervention selection bias: An underrecognized confound in intervention research. *Psychological Bulletin, 130,* 289–303.

Lassiter, G. D., & Irvine, A. A. (1986). Video-taped confessions: The impact of camera point of view on judgments of coercion. *Journal of Personality and Social Psychology, 16,* 268–276.

Lassiter, G. D., Lindberg, M. J., Gonzáles-Vallego, C., Bellezza, F. S., & Phillips, N. D. (2009). The deliberation-without-attention effect: Evidence for an artifactual interpretation. *Psychological Science, 20,* 671–675.

Latané, B. (1981). The psychology of social impact. *American Psychologist, 36,* 343–356.

Latané, B., & Dabbs, J. M., Jr. (1975). Sex, group size and helping in three cities. *Sociometry, 38,* 180–194.

Laumann, E. O., Gagnon, J. H., Michael, R. T., & Michaels, S. (1994). *The social organization of sexuality: Sexual practices in the United States.* Chicago: University of Chicago Press.

Laws, K. R., & Kokkalis, J. (2007). Ecstasy (MDMA) and memory function: A meta-analytic update. *Human Psychopharmacology: Clinical and Experimental, 22,* 381–388.

Lazarus, R. S. (1990). Theory-based stress measurement. *Psychological Inquiry, 1,* 3–13.

Lazarus, R. S. (1991). Progress on a cognitive-motivational-relational theory of emotion. *American Psychologist, 46,* 352–367.

Lazarus, R. S. (1998). *Fifty years of the research and theory of R. S. Lazarus: An analysis of historical and perennial issues.* Mahwah, NJ: Erlbaum.

Lea, S. E. G. (2000). Towards an ethical use of animals. *The Psychologist, 13,* 556–557.

Leaper, C., & Ayres, M. M. (2007). A meta-analytic review of gender variations in adults' language use: Talkativeness, affiliative speech, and assertive speech. *Personality and Social Psychology Review, 11,* 328–363.

Leary, M. R. (1999). The social and psychological importance of self-esteem. In R. M. Kowalski & M. R. Leary (Eds.), *The social psychology of emotional and behavioral problems: Interfaces of social and clinical psychology* (pp. 197–221). Washington, DC: American Psychological Association.

Leary, M. R. (2012). Sociometer theory. In L. Van Lange, A. W. Kruglanski, & E. T. Higgins (Eds.), *Handbook of theories of social psychology* (Vol. 2, pp. 141–159). Los Angeles: Sage Publications.

LeDoux, J. (2015). *Anxious: Using the brain to understand and treat fear and anxiety.* New York: Viking.

LeDoux, J. E. (1996). *The emotional brain: The mysterious underpinnings of emotional life.* New York: Simon & Schuster.

LeDoux, J. E. (2002). *The synaptic self.* London: Macmillan.

LeDoux, J. E. (2009, July/August). Quoted by K. McGowan, Out of the past. *Discover,* pp. 28–37.

LeDoux, J. E., & Armony, J. (1999). Can neurobiology tell us anything about human feelings? In D. Kahneman, E. Diener, & N. Schwartz (Eds.), *Well-being: The foundations of hedonic psychology* (pp. 489–499). New York: Sage.

Lee, C. S., Therriault, D. J., & Linderholm, T. (2012). On the cognitive benefits of cultural experience: Exploring the relationship between studying abroad and creative thinking. *Applied Cognitive Psychology, 26,* 768–778.

Lee, L., Frederick, S., & Ariely, D. (2006). Try it, you'll like it: The influence of expectation, consumption, and revelation on preferences for beer. *Psychological Science, 17,* 1054–1058.

Lee, S. W. S., & Schwarz, N. (2012). Bidirectionality, mediation, and moderation of metaphorical effects: The embodiment of social suspicions and fishy smells. *Journal of Personality and Social Psychology, 103,* 737–749.

Lefcourt, H. M. (1982). *Locus of control: Current trends in theory and research.* Hillsdale, NJ: Erlbaum.

Lehman, A. F., Steinwachs, D. M., Dixon, L. B., Goldman, H. H., Osher, F., Postrado, L., . . . Zito, J. (1998). Translating research into practice: The schizophrenic patient outcomes research team (PORT) treatment recommendations. *Schizophrenia Bulletin, 24,* 1–10.

Lehman, D. R., Wortman, C. B., & Williams, A. F. (1987). Long-term effects of losing a spouse or child in a motor vehicle crash. *Journal of Personality and Social Psychology, 52,* 218–231.

Leichsenring, F., & Rabung, S. (2008). Effectiveness of long-term psychodynamic psychotherapy: A meta-analysis. *JAMA, 300,* 1551–1565.

Leitenberg, H., & Henning, K. (1995). Sexual fantasy. *Psychological Bulletin, 117,* 469–496.

Lemmer, G., & Wagner, U. (2015). Can we really reduce ethnic prejudice outside the lab? A meta-analysis of direct and indirect contact interventions. *European Journal of Social Psychology, 45,* 152–168.

Lemonick, M. D. (2002, June 3). Lean and hungrier. *Time,* p. 54.

Lench, H. C., Flores, S. A., & Bench, S. W. (2011). Discrete emotions predict changes in cognition, judgment, experience, behavior, and physiology: A meta-analysis of experimental emotion elicitations. *Psychological Bulletin, 137,* 834–855.

Lenhart, A. (2012, March 19). Teens, smartphones & texting. Pew Internet & American Life Project (pewinternet.org).

Lenhart, A. (2015, April 9). Teens, social media & technology overview 2015. Pew Internet & Research Center (pewinternet.org).

Lenhart, A., & Duggan, M. (2014, February 11). Couples, the Internet, and social media. Pew Research Center (pewinternet.org).

Lenneberg, E. H. (1967). *Biological foundations of language.* New York: Wiley.

Lennox, B. R., Bert, S., Park, G., Jones, P. B., & Morris, P. G. (1999). Spatial and temporal mapping of neural activity associated with auditory hallucinations. *Lancet, 353,* 644.

Lenton, A. P., & Francesconi, M. (2010). How humans cognitively manage an abundance of mate options. *Psychological Science, 21,* 528–533.

Lenton, A. P., & Francesconi, M. (2012). Too much of a good thing? Variety is confusing in mate choice. *Biology Letters, 7,* 528–531.

Lenzenweger, M. F., Dworkin, R. H., & Wethington, E. (1989). Models of positive and negative symptoms in schizophrenia: An empirical evaluation of latent structures. *Journal of Abnormal Psychology, 98,* 62–70.

Leonhard, C., & Randler, C. (2009). In sync with the family: Children and partners influence the sleep-wake circadian rhythm and social habits of women. *Chronobiology International, 26,* 510–525.

LePort, A. K. R., Mattfeld, A. T., Dickinson-Anson, H., Fallon, J. H., Stark, C. E. L., Kruggel, F., . . . McGaugh, J. L. (2012). Behavioral and neuroanatomical investigation of highly superior autobiographical memory (HSAM). *Neurobiology of Learning and Memory, 98,* 78–92.

Lepping, P., Schönfeldt-Lecuona, C., Sambhi, R. S., Lanka, S. V. N., Lane, S., Whittington, R., . . . Poole, R. (2014). A systematic review of the clinical relevance of repetitive transcranial magnetic stimulation. *Acta Psychiatrica Scandinavica, 130,* 326–341.

Lereya, S. T., Copeland, W. E., Costello, E. J., & Wolke, D. (2015). Adult mental health consequences of peer bullying and maltreatment in childhood: Two cohorts in two countries. *Lancet Psychiatry, 2,* 524–531.

Leslie, M. (2011). Are telomere tests ready for prime time? *Science, 322,* 414–415.

Leucht, S., Barnes, T. R. E., Kissling, W., Engel, R. R., Correll, C., & Kane, J. M. (2003). Relapse prevention in schizophrenia with new-generation antipsychotics: A systematic review and exploratory meta-analysis of randomized, controlled trials. *American Journal of Psychiatry, 160,* 1209–1222.

Leuner, B., Glasper, E. R., & Gould, E. (2010). Sexual experience promotes adult neurogenesis in the hippocampus despite an initial elevation in stress hormones. *PLoS One, 5,* e11597.

LeVay, S. (1991). A difference in hypothalamic structure between heterosexual and homosexual men. *Science, 253,* 1034–1037.

LeVay, S. (1994, March). Quoted in D. Nimmons, Sex and the brain. *Discover,* p. 64–71.

LeVay, S. (2011). *Gay, straight, and the reason why: The science of sexual orientation.* New York: Oxford University Press.

Levenson, R. M., Krupinski, E. A., Navarro, V. M., & Wasserman, E. A. (2015, November 18). Pigeons (*Columba livia*) as trainable observers of pathology and radiology breast cancer images. *PLoS ONE, 10:*e0141357.

Levenson, R. W. (1992). Autonomic nervous system differences among emotions. *Psychological Science, 3,* 23–27.

Levine, J. A., Lanningham-Foster, L. M., McCrady, S. K., Krizan, A. C., Olson, L. R., Kane, P. H., . . . Clark, M. M. (2005). Interindividual variation in posture allocation: Possible role in human obesity. *Science, 307,* 584–586.

Levine, R., Sato, S., Hashimoto, T., & Verma, J. (1995). Love and marriage in eleven cultures. *Journal of Cross-Cultural Psychology, 26,* 554–571.

Lewandowski, G. W., Jr., Aron, A., & Gee, J. (2007). Personality goes a long way: The malleability of opposite-sex physical attractiveness. *Personality Relationships, 14,* 571–585.

Lewinsohn, P. M., Hoberman, H., Teri, L., & Hautziner, M. (1985). An integrative theory of depression. In S. Reiss & R. Bootzin (Eds.), *Theoretical issues in behavior therapy* (pp. 331–359). Orlando, FL: Academic Press.

Lewinsohn, P. M., Petit, J., Joiner, T. E., Jr., & Seeley, J. R. (2003). The symptomatic expression of major depressive disorder in adolescents and young adults. *Journal of Abnormal Psychology, 112,* 244–252.

Lewinsohn, P. M., Rohde, P., & Seeley, J. R. (1998). Major depressive disorder in older adolescents: Prevalence, risk factors, and clinical implications. *Clinical Psychology Review, 18,* 765–794.

Lewinsohn, P. M., & Rosenbaum, M. (1987). Recall of parental behavior by acute depressives, remitted depressives, and nondepressives. *Journal of Personality and Social Psychology, 52,* 611–619.

Lewis, D. O., Yeager, C. A., Swica, Y., Pincus, J. H., & Lewis, M. (1997). Objective documentation of child abuse and dissociation in 12 murderers with dissociative identity disorder. *American Journal of Psychiatry, 154,* 1703–1710.

Lewis, M. (1992). Commentary. *Human Development, 35,* 44–51.

Lewontin, R. (1976). Race and intelligence. In N. J. Block & G. Dworkin (Eds.), *The IQ controversy: Critical readings.* New York: Pantheon.

Li, J., Laursen, T. M., Precht, D. H., Olsen, J., & Mortensen, P. B. (2005). Hospitalization for mental illness among parents after the death of a child. *New England Journal of Medicine, 352*, 1190–1196.

Li, T., & Chan, D. K.-S. (2012). How anxious and avoidant attachment affect romantic relationship quality differently: A meta-analytic review. *European Journal of Social Psychology, 42*, 406–419.

Liang, K. Y., Mintun, M. A., Fagan, A. M., Goate, A.M., Bugg, J. M., Holtzman, D. M., . . . Head, D. (2010). Exercise and Alzheimer's disease biomarkers in cognitively normal older adults. *Annals of Neurology, 68,* 311–318.

Liberman, M. C. (2015, August). Hidden hearing loss. *Scientific American,* pp. 49–53.

Licata, A., Taylor, S., Berman, M., & Cranston, J. (1993). Effects of cocaine on human aggression. *Pharmacology Biochemistry and Behavior, 45,* 549–552.

Lichtenstein, E., Zhu, S.-H., & Tedeschi, G. J. (2010). Smoking cessation quitlines: An underrecognized intervention success story. *American Psychologist, 65,* 252–261.

Liddle, J. R., Shackelford, T. K., & Weekes-Shackelford, V. W. (2012). Why can't we all just get along?: Evolutionary perspectives on violence, homicide, and war. *Review of General Psychology, 16,* 24–36.

Lieberman, M. D., & Eisenberger, N. I. (2015). The dorsal anterior cingulate is selective for pain: Results from large-scale fMRI reverse inference. *PNAS, 12,* 15250–15255.

Lieberman, M. D., Eisenberger, N. L., Crockett, M. J., Tom, S. M., Pfeifer, J. H., & Way, B. M. (2007). Putting feelings into words: Affect labeling disrupts amygdala activity in response to affective stimuli. *Psychological Science, 18,* 421–428.

Lilienfeld, S. O. (2009, Winter). Tips for spotting psychological pseudoscience: A student-friendly guide. *Eye on Psi Chi,* pp. 23–26.

Lilienfeld, S. O., Lynn, S. J., Kirsch, I., Chaves, J. F., Sarbin, T. R., Ganaway, G. K., & Powell, R. A. (1999). Dissociative identity disorder and the socio-cognitive model: Recalling the lessons of the past. *Psychological Bulletin, 125,* 507–523.

Lilienfeld, S. O., Ritschel, L. A., Lynn, S. J., Cautin, R. L., & Latzman, R. D. (2013). Why many clinical psychologists are resistant to evidence-based practice: Root causes and constructive remedies. *Clinical Psychology Review, 33,* 883–900.

Lilienfeld, S. O., Ritschel, L. A., Lynn, S. J., Cautin, R. L., & Latzman, R. D. (2014). Why ineffective psychotherapies appear to work: A taxonomy of causes of spurious therapeutic effectiveness. *Perspectives on Psychological Science, 9,* 355–387.

Lim, D., & DeSteno, D. (2016). Suffering and compassion: The links among adverse life experiences, empathy, compassion, and prosocial behavior. *Emotion, 16*(2), 175–182.

Lim, J., & Dinges, D. F. (2010). A meta-analysis of the impact of short-term sleep deprivation on cognitive variables. *Psychological Bulletin, 136,* 375–389.

Lima, N., Nascimento, V., Peixoto, J. A. C., Moreira, M. M., Neto, M. L. R., Almeida, J. C., . . . Reis, A. O. A. (2013). Electroconvulsive therapy use in adolescents: A systematic review. *Annals of General Psychiatry, 12,* 17. http://www.annals-generalpsychiatry.com/content/12/1/17

Lin, Z., & Murray, S. O. (2015). More power to the unconscious: Conscious, but not unconscious, exogenous attention requires location variation. *Psychological Science, 26,* 221–230.

Lindau, S. T., Schumm, L. P., Laumann, E. O., Levinson, W., O'Muircheartaigh, C. A., & Waite, L. J. (2007). A study of sexuality and health among older adults in the United States. *New England Journal of Medicine, 357,* 762–774.

Lindberg, S. M., Hyde, J. S., Linn, M. C., & Petersen, J. L. (2010). New trends in gender and mathematics performance: A meta-analysis. *Psychological Bulletin, 136,* 1125–1135.

Lindner, I., Echterhoff, G., Davidson, P. S. R., & Brand, M. (2010). Observation inflation: Your actions become mine. *Psychological Science, 21,* 1291–1299.

Lindson, N., Aveyard, P., & Hughes, J. R. (2010). Reduction versus abrupt cessation in smokers who want to quit (review). *Cochrane Collaboration* (Cochrane Library, Issue 3; thecochranelibrary.com).

Linehan, M. M., Korslund, K. E., Harned, M. S., Gallop, R. J., Lungu, A., Neacsiu, A. D., . . . Murray-Gregory, A. M. (2015). Dialectical behavior therapy for high suicide risk in individuals with borderline personality disorder: A randomized clinical trial and component analysis. *JAMA Psychiatry, 72,* 475–482.

Lippa, R. A. (2007). The relation between sex drive and sexual attraction to men and women: A cross-national study of heterosexual, bisexual, and homosexual men and women. *Archives of Sexual Behavior, 36,* 209–222.

Lippa, R. A. (2009). Sex differences in sex drive, sociosexuality, and height across 53 nations: Testing evolutionary and social structural theories. *Archives of Sexual Behavior, 38,* 631–651.

Lipps, H. M. (1999). *A new psychology of women: Gender, culture, and ethnicity.* Mountain View, CA: Mayfield Publishing.

Lipsitt, L. P. (2003). Crib death: A biobehavioral phenomenon? *Current Directions in Psychological Science, 12,* 164–170.

Liu, Y., Balaraman, Y., Wang, G., Nephew, K. P., & Zhou, F. C. (2009). Alcohol exposure alters DNA methylation profiles in mouse embryos at early neurulation. *Epigenetics, 4,* 500–511.

Livingstone, M., & Hubel, D. (1988). Segregation of form, color, movement, and depth: Anatomy, physiology, and perception. *Science, 240,* 740–749.

Locke, A. E., Kahali, B., Berndt, S. I., Justice, A. E., Pers, T. H., Day, F. R., . . . Speliotes, E. K. (2015). Genetic studies of body mass index yield new insights for obesity biology. *Nature, 518,* 195–206.

Loewenstein, G., & Furstenberg, F. (1991). Is teenage sexual behavior rational? *Journal of Applied Social Psychology, 21,* 957–986.

Loftus, E. F. (1995, March/April). Remembering dangerously. *Skeptical Inquirer,* pp. 20–29.

Loftus, E. F. (2012, July). Manufacturing memories. Invited address to the International Congress of Psychology, Cape Town.

Loftus, E. F., & Ketcham, K. (1994). *The myth of repressed memory: False memories and allegations of sexual abuse.* New York: St. Martin's Press.

Loftus, E. F., Levidow, B., & Duensing, S. (1992). Who remembers best? Individual differences in memory for events that occurred in a science museum. *Applied Cognitive Psychology, 6,* 93–107.

Loftus, E. F., & Loftus, G. R. (1980). On the permanence of stored information in the human brain. *American Psychologist, 35,* 409–420.

Loftus, E. F., & Palmer, J. C. (October, 1974). Reconstruction of automobile destruction: An example of the interaction between language and memory. *Journal of Verbal Learning & Verbal Behavior, 13*(5), 585–589.

Logan, T. K., Walker, R., Cole, J., & Leukefeld, C. (2002). Victimization and substance abuse among women: Contributing factors, interventions, and implications. *Review of General Psychology, 6,* 325–397.

Logue, A. W. (1998a). Laboratory research on self-control: Applications to administration. *Review of General Psychology, 2,* 221–238.

Logue, A. W. (1998b). Self-control. In W. T. O'Donohue (Ed.), *Learning and behavior therapy* (pp. 252–273). Boston, MA: Allyn & Bacon.

London, P. (1970). The rescuers: Motivational hypotheses about Christians who saved Jews from the Nazis. In J. Macaulay & L. Berkowitz (Eds.), *Altruism and helping behavior* (pp. 241–250). New York: Academic Press.

Lonergan, M. H., Olivera-Figueroa, L., Pitman, R. K., & Brunet, A. (2013). Propranolol's effects on the consolidation and reconsolidation of long-term emotional memory in healthy participants: A meta-analysis. *Journal of Psychiatry & Neuroscience, 38,* 222–231.

Lopes, P. N., Brackett, M. A., Nezlek, J. B., Schutz, A., Sellin, II, & Salovey, P. (2004). Emotional intelligence and social interaction. *Personality and Social Psychology Bulletin, 30,* 1018–1034.

Loprinzi, P. D., Loenneke, J. P., & Blackburn, E. H. (2015). Movement-based behaviors and leukocyte telomere length among US adults. *Medical Science and Sports Exercise, 47,* 2347–2352.

Lord, C. G., Lepper, M. R., & Preston, E. (1984). Considering the opposite: A corrective strategy for social judgment. *Journal of Personality and Social Psychology, 47,* 1231–1247.

Lord, C. G., Ross, L., & Lepper, M. (1979). Biased assimilation and attitude polarization: The effects of prior theories on subsequently considered evidence. *Journal of Personality and Social Psychology, 37,* 2098–2109.

Louie, K., & Wilson, M. A. (2001). Temporally structured replay of awake hippocampal ensemble activity during rapid eye movement sleep. *Neuron, 29,* 145–156.

Lourenco, O., & Machado, A. (1996). In defense of Piaget's theory: A reply to 10 common criticisms. *Psychological Review, 103,* 143–164.

Lovaas, O. I. (1987). Behavioral treatment and normal educational and intellectual functioning in young autistic children. *Journal of Consulting and Clinical Psychology, 55,* 3–9.

Low, P. (2012). *The Cambridge Declaration on Consciousness.* Publicly proclaimed in Cambridge, UK, on July 7, 2012, at the Francis Crick Memorial Conference on Consciousness in Human and non-Human Animals (fcmconference.org/img/CambridgeDeclarationOnConsciousness.pdf).

Lowry, P. E. (1997). The assessment center process: New directions. *Journal of Social Behavior and Personality, 12,* 53–62.

Lozano, A., Mayberg, H., Giacobbe, P., Hami, C., Craddock, R., & Kennedy, S. (2008). Subcallosal cingulate gyrus deep brain stimulation for treatment-resistant depression. *Biological Psychiatry, 64,* 461–467.

Lubinski, D. (2009a). Cognitive epidemiology: With emphasis on untangling cognitive ability and socioeconomic status. *Intelligence, 37,* 625–633.

Lubinski, D. (2009b). Exceptional cognitive ability: The phenotype. *Behavioral Genetics, 39,* 350–358.

Lubinski, D., Benbow, C. P., & Kell, H. J. (2014). Life paths and accomplishments of mathematically precocious males and females four decades later. *Psychological Science, 25,* 2217–2232.

Luborsky, L., Rosenthal, R., Diguer, L., Andrusyna, T. P., Berman, J. S., Levitt, J. T., . . . Krause, E. D. (2002). The dodo bird verdict is alive and well—mostly. *Clinical Psychology: Science and Practice, 9,* 2–34.

Lucas, A., Morley, R., Cole, T. J., Lister, G., & Leeson-Payne, C. (1992). Breast milk and subsequent intelligence quotient in children born preterm. *Lancet, 339,* 261–264.

Lucas, R. E., Clark, A. E., Georgellis, Y., & Diener, E. (2004). Unemployment alters the set point for life satisfaction. *Psychological Science, 15*, 8–13.

Lucas, R. E., & Donnellan, M. B. (2007). How stable is happiness? Using the STARTS model to estimate the stability of life satisfaction. *Journal of Research in Personality, 41*, 1091–1098.

Lucas, R. E., & Donnellan, M. B. (2011). Personality development across the life span: Longitudinal analyses with a national sample from Germany. *Journal of Personality and Social Psychology, 101*, 847–861.

Ludwig, A. M. (1995). *The price of greatness: Resolving the creativity and madness controversy.* New York: Guilford Press.

Ludwig, D. S., & Friedman, M. I. (2014). Increasing adiposity: Consequence or cause of overeating? *JAMA, 311*, 2167–2168.

Luigjes, J., van den Brink, W., Feenstra, M., van den Munckhof, P., Schuurman, P. R., Schippers, R., . . . Denys, D. (2012). Deep brain stimulation in addiction: A review of potential brain targets. *Molecular Psychiatry, 17*, 572–583.

Lumeng, J. C., Forrest, P., Appugliese, D. P., Kaciroti, N., Corwyn, R. F., & Bradley, R. H. (2010). Weight status as a predictor of being bullied in third through sixth grades. *Pediatrics, 125*, e1301–1307.

Lund, T. J., & Dearing, E. (2012). Is growing up affluent risky for adolescents or is the problem growing up in an affluent neighborhood? *Journal of Research on Adolescence, 23*, 274–282.

Luppino, F. S., de Wit, L. M., Bouvy, P. F., Stijnen, T., Cuijpers, P., Penninx, W. J. H., & Zitman, F. G. (2010). Overweight, obesity, and depression. *Archives of General Psychiatry, 67*, 220–229.

Luria, A. M. (1968). In L. Solotaroff (Trans.), *The mind of a mnemonist.* New York: Basic Books.

Lutfey, K. E., Link, C. L., Rosen, R. C., Wiegel, M., & McKinlay, J. B. (2009). Prevalence and correlates of sexual activity and function in women: Results from the Boston Area Community Health (BACH) survey. *Archives of Sexual Behavior, 38*, 514–527.

Lutgendorf, S. K., & Andersen, B. L. (2015). Biobehavioral approaches to cancer progression and survival. *American Psychologist, 70*, 186–197.

Lutgendorf, S. K., Lamkin, D. M., Jennings, N. B., Arevalo, J. M. G., Penedo, F., DeGeest, K., . . . Sood, A. K. (2008). Biobehavioral influences on matrix metalloproteinase expression in ovarian carcinoma. *Clinical Cancer Research, 14*, 6839–6846.

Lutgendorf, S. K., Russell, D., Ullrich, P., Harris, T. B., & Wallace, R. (2004). Religious participation, interleukin-6, and mortality in older adults. *Health Psychology, 23*, 465–475.

Luthar, S. S., Barkin, S. H., & Crossman, E. J. (2013). "I can, therefore I must": Fragility in the upper-middle classes. *Development and Psychopathology, 25*, 1529–1549.

Luyckx, K., Tildesley, E. A., Soenens, B., Andrews, J. A., Hampson, S. E., Peterson, M., & Duriez, B. (2011). Parenting and trajectories of children's maladaptive behaviors: A 12-year prospective community study. *Journal of Clinical Child and Adolescent Psychology, 40*, 468–478.

Lykken, D. T. (1991, August). *Science, lies, and controversy: An epitaph for the polygraph.* Invited address at the 99th Annual Convention of the American Psychological Association, San Francisco, CA.

Lykken, D. T. (1995). *The antisocial personalities.* New York: Erlbaum.

Lykken, D. T. (1999). *Happiness: The nature and nurture of joy and contentment.* New York: Golden Books.

Lykken, D. T., & Tellegen, A. (1996). Happiness is a stochastic phenomenon. *Psychological Science, 7*, 186–189.

Lynch, G. (2002). Memory enhancement: The search for mechanism-based drugs. *Nature Neuroscience, 5* (suppl.), 1035–1038.

Lynch, G., & Staubli, U. (1991). Possible contributions of long-term potentiation to the encoding and organization of memory. *Brain Research Reviews, 16*, 204–206.

Lynn, M. (1988). The effects of alcohol consumption on restaurant tipping. *Personality and Social Psychology Bulletin, 14*, 87–91.

Lynn, S. J., Laurence, J., & Kirsch, I. (2015). Hypnosis, suggestion, and suggestibility: An integrative model. *American Journal of Clinical Hypnosis, 57*, 314–329.

Lynn, S. J., Lilienfeld, S. O., Merckelbach, H., Giesbrecht, T., McNally, R. J., Loftus, E. F., . . . Malaktaris, A. (2014). The trauma model of dissociation: Inconvenient truths and stubborn fictions. Comment on Dalenberg et al. (2012). *Psychological Bulletin, 140*, 896–910.

Lynn, S. J., Rhue, J. W., & Weekes, J. R. (1990). Hypnotic involuntariness: A social cognitive analysis. *Psychological Review, 97*, 169–184.

Lynne, S. D., Graber, J. A., Nichols, T. R., Brooks-Gunn, J., & Botvin, G. J. (2007). Links between pubertal timing, peer influences, and externalizing behaviors among urban students followed through middle school. *Journal of Adolescent Health, 40*, 181.e7–181.e13.

Lyons, B. D., Hoffman, B. J., Michel, J. W., & Williams, K. J. (2011). On the predictive efficiency of past performance and physical ability: The case of the National Football League. *Human Performance, 24*, 158–172.

Lyons, H. A., Manning, W. D., Longmore, M. A., & Giordano, P. C. (2015). Gender and casual sexual activity from adolescence to emerging adulthood: Social and life course correlates. *Journal of Sex Research, 52*, 543–557.

Lyons, L. (2005, January 4). *Teens stay true to parents' political perspectives.* Gallup Poll News Service (gallup.com).

Lyubomirsky, S. (2001). Why are some people happier than others? The role of cognitive and motivational processes in well-being. *American Psychologist, 56*, 239–249.

Lyubomirsky, S. (2008). *The how of happiness.* New York: Penguin.

Maas, J. B., & Robbins, R. S. (2010). *Sleep for success: Everything you must know about sleep but are too tired to ask.* Bloomington, IN: Author House.

Maass, A., D'Ettole, C., & Cadinu, M. (2008). Checkmate? The role of gender stereotypes in the ultimate intellectual sport. *European Journal of Social Psychology, 38*, 231–245.

Macapagal, K. R., Janssen, E., Fridberg, D. J., Finn, P. R., & Heiman, J. R. (2011). The effects of impulsivity, sexual arousability, and abstract intellectual ability on men's and women's go/no-go task performance. *Archives of Sexual Behavior, 40*, 995–1006.

MacCabe, J. H., Lambe, M. P., Cnattingius, S., Torrång, A., Björk, C., Sham, P. C., . . . Hultman, C. M. (2008). Scholastic achievement at age 16 and risk of schizophrenia and other psychoses: A national cohort study. *Psychological Medicine, 38*, 1133–1140.

Maccoby, E. E. (1990). Gender and relationships: A developmental account. *American Psychologist, 45*, 513–520.

Maccoby, E. E. (1998). *The paradox of gender.* Cambridge, MA: Harvard University Press.

Maccoby, E. E. (2002). Gender and group process: A developmental perspective. *Current Directions in Psychological Science, 11*, 54–58.

MacDonald, G., & Leary, M. R. (2005). Why does social exclusion hurt? The relationship between social and physical pain. *Psychological Bulletin, 131*, 202–223.

MacDonald, T. K., & Hynie, M. (2008). Ambivalence and unprotected sex: Failure to predict sexual activity and decreased condom use. *Journal of Applied Social Psychology, 38*, 1092–1107.

MacDonald, T. K., Zanna, M. P., & Fong, G. T. (1995). Decision making in altered states: Effects of alcohol on attitudes toward drinking and driving. *Journal of Personality and Social Psychology, 68*, 973–985.

MacFarlane, A. (1978, February). What a baby knows. *Human Nature,* pp. 74–81.

Mackenzie, J. L., Aggen, S. H., Kirkpatrick, R. M., Kendler, K. S., & Amstadter, A. B. (2015). A longitudinal twin study of insomnia symptoms in adults. *Sleep, 38*, 1423–1430.

MacKenzie, M. J., Nicklas, E., Waldfogel, J., & Brooks-Gunn, J. (2013). Spanking and child development across the first decade of life. *Pediatrics, 132*, e1118–e1125. doi:10.1542/peds.2013-1227

MacKerron, G., & Mourato, S. (2013). Happiness is greater in natural environments. *Global Environmental Change, 23*, 992–1000.

MacLeod, C., & Clarke, P. J. F. (2015). The attentional bias modification approach to anxiety intervention. *Clinical Psychological Science, 3*, 58–78.

Macmillan, M., & Lena, M. L. (2010). Rehabilitating Phineas Gage. *Neuropsychological Rehabilitation, 17*, 1–18.

Macnamara, B. N., Hambrick, D. Z., & Oswald, F. L. (2014). Deliberate practice and performance in music, games, sports, education, and professions: A meta-analysis. *Psychological Science, 25*, 1608–1618.

MacNeilage, P. F., Rogers, L. J., & Vallortigara, G. (2009, July). Origins of the left and right brain. *Scientific American,* pp. 60–67.

Maddi, S. R., Harvey, R. H., Khoshaba, D. M., Fazel, M., & Resurreccion, N. (2009). Hardiness training facilitates performance in college. *Journal of Positive Psychology, 4*, 566–577.

Maeda, Y., & Yoon, S. Y. (2013). A meta-analysis on gender differences in mental rotation ability measured by the Purdue spatial visualization tests: Visualization of rotations (PSVT:R). *Educational Psychology Review, 25*, 69–94.

Maes, H. H. M., Neale, M. C., & Eaves, L. J. (1997). Genetic and environmental factors in relative body weight and human adiposity. *Behavior Genetics, 27*, 325–351.

Magnusson, D. (1990). Personality research—Challenges for the future. *European Journal of Personality, 4*, 1–17.

Maguire, E. A., Gadian, D. G., Johnsrude, I. S., Good, C. D., Ashburner, J., Frackowiak, R. S. J., & Frith, C. D. (2000). Navigation-related structural change in the hippocampi of taxi drivers. *PNAS, 97*, 4398–4403.

Maguire, E. A., Valentine, E. R., Wilding, J. M., & Kapur, N. (2003). Routes to remembering: The brains behind superior memory. *Nature Neuroscience, 6*, 90–95.

Maguire, E. A., Woollett, & Spiers, H. J. (2006). London taxi drivers and bus drivers: A structural MRI and neuropsychological analysis. *Hippocampus, 16*, 1091–1101.

Maher, S., Ekstrom, T., & Chen, Y. (2014). Greater perceptual sensitivity to happy facial expression. *Perception, 43*, 1353–1364.

Maier, S. F., Watkins, L. R., & Fleshner, M. (1994). Psychoneuroimmunology: The interface between behavior, brain, and immunity. *American Psychologist, 49*, 1004–1017.

Major, B., Carrington, P. I., & Carnevale, P. J. D. (1984). Physical attractiveness and self-esteem: Attribution for praise from an other-sex evaluator. *Personality and Social Psychology Bulletin, 10*, 43–50.

Major, B., Schmidlin, A. M., & Williams, L. (1990). Gender patterns in social touch: The impact of setting and age. *Journal of Personality and Social Psychology, 58*, 634–643.

Makin, S. (2015a, November/December). What really causes autism. *Scientific American*, pp. 57–63.

Makin, S. (2015b, July/August). Can you train your brain? *Scientific American Mind*, pp. 64–69.

Malamuth, N. M., & Check, J. V. P. (1981). The effects of media exposure on acceptance of violence against women: A field experiment. *Journal of Research in Personality, 15*, 436–446.

Malmquist, C. P. (1986). Children who witness parental murder: Posttraumatic aspects. *Journal of the American Academy of Child Psychiatry, 25*, 320–325.

Maner, J. K., Kenrick, D. T., Neuberg, S. L., Becker, D. V., Robertson, T., Hofer, B., . . . Schaller, M. (2005). Functional projection: How fundamental social motives can bias interpersonal perception. *Journal of Personality and Social Psychology, 88*, 63–78.

Mann, T., Tomiyama, A. J., & Ward, A. (2015). Promoting public health in the context of the "obesity epidemic": False starts and promising new directions. *Perspectives on Psychological Science, 10*, 706–710.

Manning, W., & Cohen, J. A. (2012). Premarital cohabitation and marital dissolution: An examination of recent marriages. *Journal of Marriage and Family, 74*, 377–387.

Manson, J. E. (2002). Walking compared with vigorous exercise for the prevention of cardiovascular events in women. *New England Journal of Medicine, 347*, 716–725.

Maquet, P. (2001). The role of sleep in learning and memory. *Science, 294*, 1048–1052.

Mar, R. A., & Oatley, K. (2008). The function of fiction is the abstraction and simulation of social experience. *Perspectives on Psychological Science, 3*, 173–192.

Margolis, M. L. (2000). Brahms' lullaby revisited: Did the composer have obstructive sleep apnea? *Chest, 118*, 210–213.

Marinak, B. A., & Gambrell, L. B. (2008). Intrinsic motivation and rewards: What sustains young children's engagement with text? *Literacy Research and Instruction, 47*, 9–26.

Marjonen, H., Sierra, A., Nyman, A., Rogojin, V., Gröhn, O., Linden, A.-M., . . . Kaminen-Ahola, N. (2015). Early maternal alcohol consumption alters hippocampal DNA methylation, gene expression and volume in a mouse model. *PLOS ONE, 10*(5), e0124931. doi:10.1371/journal.pone.0124931

Markus, H. R., & Kitayama, S. (1991). Culture and the self: Implications for cognition, emotion, and motivation. *Psychological Review, 98*, 224–253.

Markus, H. R., & Nurius, P. (1986). Possible selves. *American Psychologist, 41*, 954–969.

Marley, J., & Bulia, S. (2001). Crimes against people with mental illness: Types, perpetrators and influencing factors. *Social Work, 46*, 115–124.

Marshall, M. J. (2002). *Why spanking doesn't work.* Springville, UT: Bonneville Minds.

Marshall, P. J., & Meltzoff, A. N. (2014). Neural mirroring mechanisms and imitation in human infants. *Philosophical Transactions of the Royal Society: Series B, 369*(1644). doi:10.1098/rstb.2013.0620

Marshall, R. D., Bryant, R. A., Amsel, L., Suh, E. J., Cook, J. M., & Neria, Y. (2007). The psychology of ongoing threat: Relative risk appraisal, the September 11 attacks, and terrorism-related fears. *American Psychologist, 62*, 304–316.

Marteau, T. M. (1989). Framing of information: Its influences upon decisions of doctors and patients. *British Journal of Social Psychology, 28*, 89–94.

Marteau, T. M., Hollands, G. J., & Fletcher, P. C. (2012). Changing human behavior to prevent disease: The importance of targeting automatic processes. *Science, 337*, 1492–1495.

Martin, C. K., Anton, S. D., Walden, H., Arnett, C., Greenway, F. L., & Williamson, D. A. (2007). Slower eating rate reduces the food intake of men, but not women: Implications for behavioural weight control. *Behaviour Research and Therapy, 45*, 2349–2359.

Martin, C. L., & Ruble, D. (2004). Children's search for gender cues. *Current Directions in Psychological Science, 13*, 67–70.

Martin, C. L., Ruble, D. N., & Szkrybalo, J. (2002). Cognitive theories of early gender development. *Psychological Bulletin, 128*, 903–933.

Martín, R., Bajo-Grañeras, R., Moratalla, R., Perea, G., & Araque, A. (2015). Circuit-specific signaling in astrocyte-neuron networks in basal ganglia pathways. *Science, 349*, 730–734.

Martins, Y., Preti, G., Crabtree, C. R., & Wysocki, C. J. (2005). Preference for human body odors is influenced by gender and sexual orientation. *Psychological Science, 16*, 694–701.

Maslow, A. H. (1970). *Motivation and personality* (2nd ed.). New York: Harper & Row.

Maslow, A. H. (1971). *The farther reaches of human nature.* New York: Viking Press.

Mason, C., & Kandel, E. R. (1991). Central visual pathways. In E. R. Kandel, J. H. Schwartz, & T. M. Jessell (Eds.), *Principles of neural science* (3rd ed.). New York: Elsevier.

Mason, R. A., & Just, M. A. (2004). How the brain processes causal inferences in text. *Psychological Science, 15*, 1–7.

Massimini, M., Ferrarelli, F., Huber, R., Esser, S. K., Singh, H., & Tononi, G. (2005). Breakdown of cortical effective connectivity during sleep. *Science, 309*, 2228–2232.

Master, S. L., Eisenberger, N. I., Taylor, S. E., Naliboff, B. D., Shirinyan, D., & Lieberman, M. D. (2009). A picture's worth: Partner photographs reduce experimentally induced pain. *Psychological Science, 20*, 1316–1318.

Masters, K. S. (2010). The role of religion in therapy: Time for psychologists to have a little faith? *Cognitive and Behavioral Practice, 17*, 393–400.

Masters, W. H., & Johnson, V. E. (1966). *Human sexual response.* Boston: Little, Brown.

Mastroianni, G. R. (2015). Obedience in perspective: Psychology and the Holocaust. *Theory and Psychology, 25*, 657–669.

Mastroianni, G. R., & Reed, G. (2006). Apples, barrels, and Abu Ghraib. *Sociological Focus, 39*, 239–250.

Masuda, T., & Kitayama, S. (2004). Perceiver-induced constraint and attitude attribution in Japan and the US: A case for the cultural dependence of the correspondence bias. *Journal of Experimental Social Psychology, 40*, 409–416.

Mataix-Cols, D., Rosario-Campos, M. C., & Leckman, J. F. (2005). A multi-dimensional model of obsessive-compulsive disorder. *American Journal of Psychiatry, 162*, 228–238.

Mataix-Cols, D., Wooderson, S., Lawrence, N., Brammer, M. J., Speckens, A., & Phillips, M. L. (2004). Distinct neural correlates of washing, checking, and hoarding symptom dimensions in obsessive-compulsive disorder. *Archives of General Psychiatry, 61*, 564–576.

Mather, M., & Sutherland, M. (2012, February). The selective effects of emotional arousal on memory. *APA Science Brief* (apa.org).

Matson, J. L., & Boisjoli, J. A. (2009). The token economy for children with intellectual disability and/or autism: A review. *Research on Developmental Disabilities, 30*, 240–248.

Matsumoto, D., & Ekman, P. (1989). American-Japanese cultural differences in intensity ratings of facial expressions of emotion. *Motivation and Emotion, 13*, 143–157.

Matsumoto, D., Frank, M. G., & Hwang, H. C. (2015). The role of intergroup emotions on political violence. *Current Directions in Psychological Science, 24*, 369–373.

Matsumoto, D., & Willingham, B. (2006). The thrill of victory and the agony of defeat: Spontaneous expressions of medal winners of the 2004 Athens Olympic Games. *Journal of Personality and Social Psychology, 91*, 568–581.

Matsumoto, D., & Willingham, B. (2009). Spontaneous facial expressions of emotion of congenitally and noncongenitally blind individuals. *Journal of Personality and Social Psychology, 96*, 1–10.

Matthews, R. N., Domjan, M., Ramsey, M., & Crews, D. (2007). Learning effects on sperm competition and reproductive fitness. *Psychological Science, 18*, 758–762.

Maurer, D., & Maurer, C. (1988). *The world of the newborn.* New York: Basic Books.

Mauss, I. B., Shallcross, A. J., Troy, A. S., John, O. P., Ferrer, E., Wilhelm, F. H., & Gross, J. J. (2011). Don't hide your happiness! Positive emotion dissociation, social connectedness, and psychological functioning. *Journal of Personality and Social Psychology, 100*, 738–748.

Mautz, B., Wong, B., Peters, R., & Jennions, M. (2013). Penis size interacts with body shape and height to influence male attractiveness. *PNAS, 110*, 6925–6693.

Maxwell, S. E., Lau, M. Y., & Howard, G. S. (2015). Is psychology suffering from a replication crisis? What does "failure to replicate" really mean? *American Psychologist, 70*, 487–498.

May, C., & Hasher, L. (1998). Synchrony effects in inhibitory control over thought and action. *Journal of Experimental Psychology: Human Perception and Performance, 24*, 363–380.

May, P. A., Baete, J., Russo, A. J., Elliott, J., Blankenship, J., Kalberg, W. O., . . . Hoyme, H. E. (2014). Prevalence and characteristics of fetal alcohol spectrum disorders. *Pediatrics, 134*, 855–866.

May, R. (1982). The problem of evil: An open letter to Carl Rogers. *Journal of Humanistic Psychology, 22*, 10–21.

Mayberg, H. S., Lozano, A. M., Voon, V., McNeely, H. E., Seminowicz, D., Hamani, C., . . . Kennedy, S. H. (2005). Deep brain stimulation for treatment-resistant depression. *Neuron, 45*, 651–660.

Mayer, J. D., Salovey, P., & Caruso, D. R. (2002). *The Mayer-Salovey-Caruso emotional intelligence test (MSCEIT).* Toronto: Multi-Health Systems, Inc.

Mayer, J. D., Salovey, P., & Caruso, D. R. (2012). The validity of the MSCEIT: Additional analyses and evidence. *Emotion Review, 4*, 403–408.

Mayer, J. D., Salovey, P., Caruso, D. R., & Cherkasskiy, L. (2011). Emotional intelligence. In R. J. Sternberg & S. B. Kaufman (Eds.), *The Cambridge handbook of intelligence* (pp. 528–249). New York: Cambridge University Press.

Mazure, C., Keita, G., & Blehar, M. (2002). *Summit on women and depression: Proceedings and recommendations.* Washington, DC: American Psychological Association (apa.org/pi/women/programs/depression/summit-2002.pdf).

Mazzoni, G., Scoboria, A., & Harvey, L. (2010). Nonbelieved memories. *Psychological Science, 21*, 1334–1340.

McAdams, D. P., & Guo, J. (2015). Narrating the generative life. *Psychological Science, 26,* 475–483.

McAndrew, F. T. (2009). The interacting roles of testosterone and challenges to status in human male aggression. *Aggression and Violent Behavior, 14,* 330–335.

McBurney, D. H. (1996). *How to think like a psychologist: Critical thinking in psychology.* Upper Saddle River, NJ: Prentice-Hall.

McBurney, D. H., & Collings, V. B. (1984). *Introduction to sensation and perception* (2nd ed.). Englewood Cliffs, NJ: Prentice-Hall.

McBurney, D. H., & Gent, J. F. (1979). On the nature of taste qualities. *Psychological Bulletin, 86,* 151–167.

McCabe, K. O., & Fleeson, W. (2016). Are traits useful? Explaining trait manifestations as tools in the pursuit of goals. *Journal of Personality and Social Psychology, 110,* 287–301.

McCain, N. L., Gray, D. P., Elswick, R. K., Jr., Robins, J. W., Tuck, I., Walter, J. M., . . . Ketchum, J. M. (2008). A randomized clinical trial of alternative stress management interventions in persons with HIV infection. *Journal of Consulting and Clinical Psychology, 76,* 431–441.

McCann, I. L., & Holmes, D. S. (1984). Influence of aerobic exercise on depression. *Journal of Personality and Social Psychology, 46,* 1142–1147.

McCann, U. D., Eligulashvili, V., & Ricaurte, G. A. (2001). (+/–)3,4 Methylenedioxymethamphetamine ("Ecstasy")-induced serotonin neurotoxicity: Clinical studies. *Neuropsychobiology, 42,* 11–16.

McCarthy, P. (1986, July). Scent: The tie that binds? *Psychology Today,* pp. 6, 10.

McCauley, C. R. (2002). Psychological issues in understanding terrorism and the response to terrorism. In C. E. Stout (Ed.), *The psychology of terrorism* (Vol. 3, pp. 3–29). Westport, CT: Praeger/Greenwood.

McCauley, C. R., & Segal, M. E. (1987). Social psychology of terrorist groups. In C. Hendrick (Ed.), *Group processes and intergroup relations: Review of personality and social psychology* (Vol. 9, pp. 231–256). Beverly Hills, CA: Sage.

McClendon, B. T., & Prentice-Dunn, S. (2001). Reducing skin cancer risk: An intervention based on protection motivation theory. *Journal of Health Psychology, 6,* 321–328.

McClintock, M. K., & Herdt, G. (1996, December). Rethinking puberty: The development of sexual attraction. *Current Directions in Psychological Science, 5,* 178–183.

McClung, M., & Collins, D. (2007). "Because I know it will!": Placebo effects of an ergogenic aid on athletic performance. *Journal of Sport & Exercise Psychology, 29,* 382–394.

McClure, E. B. (2000). A meta-analytic review of sex differences in facial expression processing and their development in infants, children, and adolescents. *Psychological Bulletin, 126,* 424–453.

McClure, M. J., & Lydon, J. E. (2014). Anxiety doesn't become you: How attachment compromises relational opportunities. *Journal of Personality and Social Psychology, 106,* 89–111.

McConnell, A. R., Brown, C. M., Shoda, T. M., Stayton, L. E., & Martin, C. E. (2011). Friends with benefits: On the positive consequences of pet ownership. *Journal of Personality and Social Psychology, 101,* 1239–1252.

McConnell, R. A. (1991). National Academy of Sciences opinion on parapsychology. *Journal of the American Society for Psychical Research, 85,* 333–365.

McCool, G. (1999, October 26). Mirror-gazing Venezuelans top of vanity stakes. *The Toronto Star.* Retrieved from web.lexis-nexis.com

McCrae, R. R., & Costa, P. T., Jr. (1986). Clinical assessment can benefit from recent advances in personality psychology. *American Psychologist, 41,* 1001–1003.

McCrae, R. R., & Costa, P. T., Jr. (2008). The Five-Factor Theory of personality. In O. P. John, R. W. Robins, & L. A. Pervin (Eds.), *Handbook of personality: Theory and research* (3rd ed., pp. 159–181). New York: Guilford.

McCrae, R. R., Costa, P. T., Jr., Ostendorf, F., Angleitner, A., Hrebicková, M., Avia, M. D., . . . Smith, P. B. (2000). Nature over nurture: Temperament, personality, and life span development. *Journal of Personality and Social Psychology, 78,* 173–186.

McCrae, R. R., Terracciano, A., & 78 Members of the Personality Profiles of Cultures Project. (2005). Universal features of personality traits from the observer's perspective: Data from 50 cultures. *Journal of Personality and Social Psychology, 88,* 547–561.

McCrae, R. R., Terracciano, A., & Khoury, B. (2007). Dolce far niente: The positive psychology of personality stability and invariance. In A. D. Ong & M. H. Van Dulmen (Eds.), *Oxford handbook of methods in positive psychology* (pp. 176–188). New York: Oxford University Press.

McCullough, M. E., Hoyt, W. T., Larson, D. B., Koenig, H. G., & Thoresen, C. (2000). Religious involvement and mortality: A meta-analytic review. *Health Psychology, 19,* 211–222.

McCullough, M. E., & Laurenceau, J.-P. (2005). Religiousness and the trajectory of self-rated health across adulthood. *Personality and Social Psychology Bulletin, 31,* 560–573.

McDaniel, M. A., Howard, D. C., & Einstein, G. O. (2009). The read-recite-review study strategy: Effective and portable. *Psychological Science, 20,* 516–522.

McEvoy, S. P., Stevenson, M. R., McCartt, A. T., Woodward, M., Haworth, C., Palamara, P., & Cercarelli, R. (2005). Role of mobile phones in motor vehicle crashes resulting in hospital attendance: A case-crossover study. *British Medical Journal, 331,* 428. http://dx.doi.org/10.1136/bmj.38537.397512.55

McEvoy, S. P., Stevenson, M. R., & Woodward, M. (2007). The contribution of passengers versus mobile phone use to motor vehicle crashes resulting in hospital attendance by the driver. *Accident Analysis and Prevention, 39,* 1170–1176.

McGaugh, J. L. (1994). Quoted by B. Bower, Stress hormones hike emotional memories. *Science News, 146,* 262.

McGaugh, J. L. (2003). *Memory and emotion: The making of lasting memories.* New York: Columbia University Press.

McGaugh, J. L. (2015). Consolidating memories. *Annual Review of Psychology, 66,* 1–24.

McGaugh, J. L., & LePort, A. (2014, February). Remembrance of all things past. *Scientific American,* pp. 41–45.

McGhee, P. E. (1976, June). Children's appreciation of humor: A test of the cognitive congruency principle. *Child Development, 47*(2), 420–426.

McGirr, A., Berlim, M. T., Bond, D. J., Fleck, M. P., Yatham, L. N., & Lam, R. W. (2015). A systematic review and meta-analysis of randomized, double-blind, placebo-controlled trials of ketamine in the rapid treatment of major depressive episodes. *Psychological Medicine, 45,* 693–704.

McGrath, J. J., & Welham, J. L. (1999). Season of birth and schizophrenia: A systematic review and meta-analysis of data from the Southern hemisphere. *Schizophrenia Research, 35,* 237–242.

McGrath, J. J., Welham, J., & Pemberton, M. (1995). Month of birth, hemisphere of birth and schizophrenia. *British Journal of Psychiatry, 167,* 783–785.

McGue, M., & Bouchard, T. J., Jr. (1998). Genetic and environmental influences on human behavioral differences. *Annual Review of Neuroscience, 21,* 1–24.

McGue, M., Bouchard, T. J., Jr., Iacono, W. G., & Lykken, D. T. (1993). Behavioral genetics of cognitive ability: A life-span perspective. In R. Plomin & G. E. McClearn (Eds.), *Nature, nurture and psychology* (pp. 59–76). Washington, DC: American Psychological Association.

McGurk, H., & MacDonald, J. (1976). Hearing lips and seeing voices. *Nature, 264,* 746–748.

McHugh, P. R. (1995b). Witches, multiple personalities, and other psychiatric artifacts. *Nature Medicine, 1*(2), 110–114.

McLaughlin, M. (2010, October 2). J. K. Rowling: Depression, the "terrible place that allowed me to come back stronger." *The Scotsman* (scotsman.com).

McLean, C. P., & Anderson, E. R. (2009). Brave men and timid women? A review of the gender differences in fear and anxiety. *Clinical Psychology Review, 29,* 496–505.

McMurray, B. (2007). Defusing the childhood vocabulary explosion. *Science, 317,* 631.

McNally, R. J. (2003). *Remembering trauma.* Cambridge, MA: Harvard University Press.

McNally, R. J. (2007). Betrayal trauma theory: A critical appraisal. *Memory, 15,* 280–292.

McNally, R. J. (2012). Are we winning the war against posttraumatic stress disorder? *Science, 336,* 872–874.

McNally, R. J., & Geraerts, E. (2009). A new solution to the recovered memory debate. *Perspectives on Psychological Science, 4,* 126–134.

McNeil, B. J., Pauker, S. G., & Tversky, A. (1988). On the framing of medical decisions. In D. E. Bell, H. Raiffa, & A. Tversky (Eds.), *Decision making: Descriptive, normative, and prescriptive interactions* (pp. 562–568). New York: Cambridge University Press.

McNulty, J. K., Olson, M. A., Meltzer, A. L., & Shaffer, M. J. (2013). Though they may be unaware, newlyweds implicitly know whether their marriage will be satisfying. *Science, 342,* 1119–1120.

McWhorter, J. (2012, April 23). Talking with your fingers. *The New York Times* (nytimes.com).

Meador, B. D., & Rogers, C. R. (1984). Person-centered therapy. In R. J. Corsini (Ed.), *Current psychotherapies* (3rd ed.). Itasca, IL: Peacock.

Medda, P., Toni, C., Mariani, M. G., De Simone, L., Mauri, M., & Perugi, G. (2015). Electroconvulsive therapy in 197 patients with a severe, drug-resistant bipolar mixed state: Treatment outcome and predictors of response. *The Journal of Clinical Psychiatry, 76*(9), 1168–1173.

Mednick, S. A., Huttunen, M. O., & Machon, R. A. (1994). Prenatal influenza infections and adult schizophrenia. *Schizophrenia Bulletin, 20,* 263–267.

Medvec, V. H., Madey, S. F., & Gilovich, T. (1995). When less is more: Counterfactual thinking and satisfaction among Olympic medalists. *Journal of Personality and Social Psychology, 69,* 603–610.

Mehl, M. R., Vazire, S., Holleran, S. E., & Clark, C. S. (2010). Eavesdropping on happiness: Well-being is related to having less small talk and more substantive conversations. *Psychological Science, 21,* 539–541.

Mehta, D., Klengel, T., Conneely, K. N., Smith, A. K., Altmann, A., Pace, T. W., . . . Binder, E. B. (2013). Childhood maltreatment is associated with distinct genomic and epigenetic profiles in posttraumatic stress disorder. *PNAS, 110,* 8302–8307.

Mehta, M. R. (2007). Cortico-hippocampal interaction during up-down states and memory consolidation. *Nature Neuroscience, 10,* 13–15.

Meichenbaum, D. (1977). *Cognitive-behavior modification: An integrative approach.* New York: Plenum Press.

Meichenbaum, D. (1985). *Stress inoculation training*. New York: Pergamon.

Meier, B. P., Moeller, S. K., Riemer-Peltz, M., & Robinson, M. D. (2012a). Sweet taste preferences and experiences predict prosocial inferences, personalities, and behaviors. *Journal of Personality and Social Psychology, 102*, 163–174.

Meier, M. H., Caspi, A., Ambler, A., Harrington, H., Houts, R., Keefe, R. S., . . . Moffitt, T. E. (2012b). Persistent cannabis users show neuropsychological decline from childhood to midlife. PNAS, 109, E2657–2664.

Melby-Lervåg, M., & Hulme, C. (2013). Is working memory training effective? A meta-analytic review. *Developmental Psychology, 49*, 270–291.

Melioli, T., Bauer, S., Franko, D. L., Moessner, M., Ozer, F., Chabrol, H., & Rodgers, R. F. (2016). Reducing eating disorder symptoms and risk factors using the internet: A meta-analytic review. *International Journal of Eating Disorders, 49*(1), 19–31.

Meltzoff, A. N., Kuhl, P. K., Movellan, J., & Sejnowski, T. J. (2009). Foundations for a new science of learning. Science, 325, 284–288.

Meltzoff, A. N., & Moore, M. K. (1997). Explaining facial imitation: A theoretical model. *Early Development and Parenting, 6*, 179–192.

Melzack, R. (1992, April). Phantom limbs. *Scientific American*, pp. 120–126.

Melzack, R. (2005). Evolution of the neuromatrix theory of pain. *Pain Practice, 5*, 85–94.

Mendes, E., & McGeeney, K. (2012, July 9). *Women's health trails men's most in former Soviet Union*. Gallup (gallup.com).

Mendle, J., Turkheimer, E., & Emery, R. E. (2007). Detrimental psychological outcomes associated with early pubertal timing in adolescent girls. *Developmental Review, 27*, 151–171.

Mendolia, M., & Kleck, R. E. (1993). Effects of talking about a stressful event on arousal: Does what we talk about make a difference? *Journal of Personality and Social Psychology, 64*, 283–292.

Merari, A. (2002). Explaining suicidal terrorism: Theories versus empirical evidence. Invited address to the American Psychological Association.

Merskey, H. (1992). The manufacture of personalities: The production of multiple personality disorder. *British Journal of Psychiatry, 160*, 327–340.

Merzenich, M. (2007). Quoted at Posit Science Brain Fitness Program (positscience.com).

Messias, E., Eaton, W. W., & Grooms, A. N. (2011). Economic grand rounds: Income inequality and depression prevalence across the United States: An ecological study. *Psychiatric Services, 62*, 710–712.

Messinis, L., Kyprianidou, A., Malefaki, S., & Papathanasopoulos, P. (2006). Neuropsychological deficits in long-term frequent cannabis users. *Neurology, 66*, 737–739.

Meston, C. M., & Buss, D. M. (2007). Why humans have sex. *Archives of Sexual Behavior, 36*, 477–507.

Metzler, D. (2011, Spring). Vocabulary growth in adult cross-fostered chimpanzees. *Friends of Washoe, 32*(3), 11–13.

Meyer, A., Proudfit, G. H., Bufferd, S. J., Kujawa, A. J., Laptook, R. S., Torpey, D. C., & Klein, D. N. (2015). Self-reported and observed punitive parenting prospectively predicts increased error-related brain activity in six-year-old children. *Journal of Abnormal Child Psychology, 43*, 821–829.

Meyer-Bahlburg, H. F. L. (1995). Psychoneuroendocrinology and sexual pleasure: The aspect of sexual orientation. In P. R. Abramson & S. D. Pinkerton (Eds.), *Sexual nature/sexual culture* (pp. 135–153). Chicago: University of Chicago Press.

Michael, R. B., Garry, M., & Kirsch, I. (2012). Suggestion, cognition, and behavior. *Current Directions in Psychological Science, 21*, 151–156.

Middlebrooks, J. C., & Green, D. M. (1991). Sound localization by human listeners. *Annual Review of Psychology, 42*, 135–159.

Miers, R. (2009, Spring). Calum's road. *Scottish Life*, pp. 36–39, 75.

Mikulincer, M., & Shaver, P. R. (2001). Attachment theory and intergroup bias: Evidence that priming the secure base schema attenuates negative reactions to out-groups. *Journal of Personality and Social Psychology, 81*, 97–115.

Milan, R. J., Jr., & Kilmann, P. R. (1987). Interpersonal factors in premarital contraception. *Journal of Sex Research, 23*, 289–321.

Miles, D. R., & Carey, G. (1997). Genetic and environmental architecture of human aggression. *Journal of Personality and Social Psychology, 72*, 207–217.

Milgram, S. (1963). Behavioral study of obedience. *Journal of Abnormal & Social Psychology, 67*(4), 371–378.

Milgram, S. (1974). *Obedience to authority*. New York: Harper & Row.

Miller, C. H., Hamilton, J. P., Sacchet, M. D., & Gotlib, I. H. (2015). Meta-analysis of functional neuroimaging of major depressive disorder in youth. *JAMA Psychiatry, 72*(10), 1045–1053.

Miller, G. (2004). Axel, Buck share award for deciphering how the nose knows. Science, 306, 207.

Miller, G. (2010). Anything but child's play. Science, 327, 1192–1193.

Miller, G. (2012a). Drone wars: Are remotely piloted aircraft changing the nature of war? *Science, 336*, 842–843.

Miller, G. A. (1956). The magical number seven, plus or minus two: Some limits on our capacity for processing information. *Psychological Review, 63*, 81–97.

Miller, H. C., Pattison, K. F., DeWall, C. N., Rayburn-Reeves, R., & Zentall, T. R. (2010). Self-control without a "self"? Common self-control processes in humans and dogs. *Psychological Science, 21*, 534–538.

Miller, J. G., & Bersoff, D. M. (1995). Development in the context of everyday family relationships: Culture, interpersonal morality and adaptation. In M. Killen & D. Hart (Eds.), *Morality in everyday life: A developmental perspective*. New York: Cambridge University Press.

Miller, L. K. (1999). The savant syndrome: Intellectual impairment and exceptional skill. *Psychological Bulletin, 125*, 31–46.

Miller, M., Azrael, D., & Hemenway, D. (2002). Household firearm ownership levels and suicide across U.S. regions and states, 1988–1997. *Epidemiology, 13*, 517–524.

Miller, M., Swanson, S. A., & Azrael, D. (2016). Are we missing something pertinent? A bias analysis of unmeasured confounding in the firearm-suicide literature. *Epidemiologic Reviews, 38*, 62–69.

Miller, P. (2012b, January). A thing or two about twins. *National Geographic*, pp. 38–65.

Milrod, B., Chambless, D. L., Gallop, R., Busch, F. N., Schwalberg, M., McCarthy, K. S., . . . Barber, J. P. (2015, June 9). Psychotherapies for panic disorder: A tale of two sites. *Journal of Clinical Psychiatry*.

Milyavskaya, M., Gingras, I., Mageau, G. A., Koestner, R., Gagnon, H., Fang, J., & Bolché, J. (2009). Balance across contexts: Importance of balanced need satisfaction across various life domains. *Personality and Social Psychology Bulletin, 35*, 1031–1045.

Mineka, S. (1985). The frightful complexity of the origins of fears. In F. R. Brush & J. B. Overmier (Eds.), *Affect, conditioning and cognition: Essays on the determinants of behavior* (pp. 55–73). Hillsdale, NJ: Erlbaum.

Mineka, S. (2002). Animal models of clinical psychology. In N. Smelser & P. Baltes (Eds.), *International encyclopedia of the social and behavioral sciences* (pp. 2020–2025). Oxford, England: Elsevier Science.

Mineka, S., & Oehlberg, K. (2008). The relevance of recent developments in classical conditioning to understanding the etiology and maintenance of anxiety disorders. *Acta Psychologica, 127*, 567–580.

Mineka, S., & Zinbarg, R. (1996). Conditioning and ethological models of anxiety disorders: Stress-in-dynamic-context anxiety models. In D. Hope (Ed.), *Perspectives on anxiety, panic, and fear* (Nebraska Symposium on Motivation, pp. 135–210). Lincoln: University of Nebraska Press.

Minsky, M. (1986). *The society of mind*. New York: Simon & Schuster.

Mischel, W. (1968). *Personality and assessment*. New York: Wiley.

Mischel, W. (1981). Current issues and challenges in personality. In L. T. Benjamin, Jr. (Ed.), *The G. Stanley Hall lecture series* (Vol. 1, pp. 85–99). Washington, DC: American Psychological Association.

Mischel, W. (1984). Convergences and challenges in the search for consistency. *American Psychologist, 39*, 351–364.

Mischel, W. (2004). Toward an integrative science of the person. *Annual Review of Psychology, 55*, 1–22.

Mischel, W. (2014). *The marshmallow test: Mastering self-control*. Boston: Little, Brown.

Mischel, W., & Shoda, Y. (1995). A cognitive-affective system theory of personality: Reconceptualizing situations, dispositions, dynamics, and invariance in personality structure. *Psychological Review, 102*, 246–268.

Mischel, W., Shoda, Y., & Peake, P. K. (1988). The nature of adolescent competencies predicted by preschool delay of gratification. *Journal of Personality and Social Psychology, 54*, 687–696.

Mischel, W., Shoda, Y., & Rodriguez, M. L. (1989). Delay of gratification in children. Science, 244, 933–938.

Mishkin, M. (1982). A memory system in the monkey. *Philosophical Transactions of the Royal Society of London: Biological Sciences, 298*, 83–95.

Mishkin, M., Suzuki, W. A., Gadian, D. G., & Vargha-Khadem, F. (1997). Hierarchical organization of cognitive memory. *Philosophical Transactions of the Royal Society of London: Biological Sciences, 352*, 1461–1467.

Mita, T. H., Dermer, M., & Knight, J. (1977). Reversed facial images and the mere-exposure hypothesis. *Journal of Personality and Social Psychology, 35*, 597–601.

Mitani, J. C., Watts, D. P., & Amsler, S. J. (2010). Lethal intergroup aggression leads to territorial expansion in wild chimpanzees. *Current Biology, 20*, R507–R509.

Mitte, K. (2008). Memory bias for threatening information in anxiety and anxiety disorders: A meta-analytic review. *Psychological Bulletin, 134*, 886–911.

Mobbs, D., Yu, R., Meyer, M., Passamonti, L., Seymour, B., Calder, A. J., . . . Dalgeish, T. (2009). A key role for similarity in vicarious reward. Science, 324, 900.

Moffitt, T. E., Arsenault, L., Belsky, D., Dickson, N., Hancox, R. J., Harrington, H., . . . Caspi, A. (2011). A gradient of childhood self-control predicts health, wealth, and public safety. PNAS, 108, 2693–2698.

Moffitt, T. E., Caspi, A., Harrington, H., & Milne, B. J. (2002). Males on the life-course-persistent and adolescence-limited antisocial pathways: Follow-up at age 26 years. *Development and Psychopathology, 14*, 179–207.

Moffitt, T. E., Harrington, H., Caspi, A., Kim-Cohen, J., Goldberg, D., Gregory, A. M., & Poulton, R. (2007). Depression and generalized anxiety disorder: Cumulative and sequential comorbidity in a birth cohort followed prospectively to age 32 years. *Archives of General Psychiatry, 64,* 651–660.

Moghaddam, F. M. (2005). The staircase to terrorism: A psychological exploration. *American Psychologist, 60,* 161–169.

Molenberghs, P., Ogilivie, C., Louis, W. R., Decety, J., Bagnall, J., & Bain, P. G. (2015). The neural correlates of justified and unjustified killing: An fMRI study. *Social Cognitive and Affective Neuroscience, 10,* 1397–1404.

Möller-Levet, C. S., Archer, S. N., Bucca, G., Laing, E. E., Slak, A., Kabijo, R., . . . Dijk, D.-J. (2013). Effects of insufficient sleep on circadian rhythmicity and expression amplitude of the human blood transcriptome. *PNAS, 110,* E1132–E1141.

Mondloch, C. J., Lewis, T. L., Budreau, D. R., Maurer, D., Dannemiller, J. L., Stephens, B. R., & Kleiner-Gathercoal, K. A. (1999). Face perception during early infancy. *Psychological Science, 10,* 419–422.

Money, J. (1987). Sin, sickness, or status? Homosexual gender identity and psychoneuroendocrinology. *American Psychologist, 42,* 384–399.

Money, J., Berlin, F. S., Falck, A., & Stein, M. (1983). *Antiandrogenic and counseling treatment of sex offenders.* Baltimore, MD: Department of Psychiatry and Behavioral Sciences, The Johns Hopkins University School of Medicine.

Monroe, S. M., & Reid, M. W. (2009). Life stress and major depression. *Current Directions in Psychological Science, 18,* 68–72.

Montag, C., Weber, B., Trautner, P., Newport, B., Markett, S., Walter, N. T., . . . Reuter, M. (2012). Does excessive play of violent first-person-shooter-videogames dampen brain activity in response to emotional stimuli? *Biological Psychology, 89,* 107–111.

Montoya, E. R., Terburg, D., Box, P. A., & van Honk, J. (2012). Testosterone, cortisol, and serotonin as key regulators of social aggression: A review and theoretical perspective. *Motivation and Emotion, 36,* 65–73.

Montoya, R. M., & Horton, R. S. (2013). A meta-analytic investigation of the processes underlying the similarity-attraction effect. *Journal of Social and Personal Relationships, 30,* 64–94.

Montoya, R. M., & Horton, R. S. (2014). A two-dimensional model for the study of interpersonal attraction. *Personality and Social Psychology Review, 18,* 59–86.

Mook, D. G. (1983). In defense of external invalidity. *American Psychologist, 38,* 379–387.

Moore, D. W. (2004, December 17). *Sweet dreams go with a good night's sleep.* Gallup News Service (gallup.com).

Moore, D. W. (2005, June 16). *Three in four Americans believe in paranormal.* Gallup Poll (gallup.com).

Moore, S. C., Patel, A. V., Matthews, C. E., Berrington de Gonzalez, A., Park, Y., Katki, H. A., . . . Lee, I.-M. (2012). Leisure time physical activity of moderate to vigorous intensity and mortality: A large pooled cohort analysis. *PLOS Medicine, 9*(11), e1001335. doi:10.1371/journal.pmed.1001335

Mor, N., & Winquist, J. (2002). Self-focused attention and negative affect: A meta-analysis. *Psychological Bulletin, 128,* 638–662.

More, H. L., Hutchinson, J. R., Collins, D. F., Weber, D. J., Aung, S. K. H., & Donelan, J. M. (2010). Scaling of sensorimotor control in terrestrial mammals. *Proceedings of the Royal Society B, 277,* 3563–3568.

Moreira, M. T., Smith, L. A., & Foxcroft, D. (2009). Social norms interventions to reduce alcohol misuse in university or college students. *Cochrane Database of Systematic Reviews,* Issue 3, Art. No. C06748.

Moreland, R. L., & Beach, S. R. (1992). Exposure effects in the classroom: The development of affinity among students. *Journal of Experimental Social Psychology, 28,* 255–276.

Moreland, R. L., & Zajonc, R. B. (1982). Exposure effects in person perception: Familiarity, similarity, and attraction. *Journal of Experimental Social Psychology, 18,* 395–415.

Morelli, G. A., Rogoff, B., Oppenheim, D., & Goldsmith, D. (1992). Cultural variation in infants' sleeping arrangements: Questions of independence. *Developmental Psychology, 26,* 604–613.

Moreno, C., Laje, G., Blanco, C., Jiang, H., Schmidt, A. B., & Olfson, M. (2007). National trends in the outpatient diagnosis and treatment of bipolar disorder in youth. *Archives of General Psychiatry, 64,* 1032–1039.

Morey, R. A., Inan, S., Mitchell, T. V., Perkins, D. O., Lieberman, J. A., & Belger, A. (2005). Imaging frontostriatal function in ultra-high-risk, early, and chronic schizophrenia during executive processing. *Archives of General Psychiatry, 62,* 254–262.

Morgan, A. B., & Lilienfeld, S. O. (2000). A meta-analytic review of the relation between antisocial behavior and neuropsychological measures of executive function. *Clinical Psychology Review, 20,* 113–136.

Mori, K., & Mori, H. (2009). Another test of the passive facial feedback hypothesis: When your face smiles, you feel happy. *Perceptual and Motor Skills, 109,* 1–3.

Morris, M. (2015, September 18). Damaging labels do transgender people a disservice. *Edmonton Journal* (edmontonjournal.com).

Morrison, A. R. (2003, July). The brain on night shift. *Cerebrum,* pp. 23–36.

Morrison, M., Tay, L., & Diener, E. (2014). *Subjective well-being across the lifespan worldwide.* Paper presented at the Society for Personality and Social Psychology convention, Austin, Texas.

Mortensen, P. B. (1999). Effects of family history and place and season of birth on the risk of schizophrenia. *New England Journal of Medicine, 340,* 603–608.

Moruzzi, G., & Magoun, H. W. (1949). Brain stem reticular formation and activation of the EEG. *Electroencephalography and Clinical Neurophysiology, 1,* 455–473.

Moscovici, S. (1985). Social influence and conformity. In G. Lindzey & E. Aronson (Eds.), *The handbook of social psychology* (3rd ed., pp. 347–412). Hillsdale, NJ: Erlbaum.

Moses, E. B., & Barlow, D. H. (2006). A new unified treatment approach for emotional disorders based on emotion science. *Current Directions in Psychological Science, 15,* 146–150.

Mosher, C. E., & Danoff-Burg, S. (2008). Agentic and communal personality traits: Relations to disordered eating behavior, body shape concern, and depressive symptoms. *Eating Behaviors, 9,* 497–500.

Mosing, M. A., Zietsch, B. P., Shekar, S. N., Wright, M. J., & Martin, N. G. (2009). Genetic and environmental influences on optimism and its relationship to mental and self-rated health: A study of aging twins. *Behavior Genetics, 39,* 597–604.

Moskowitz, T. J., & Wertheim, L. J. (2011). *Scorecasting: The hidden influences behind how sports are played and games are won.* New York: Crown Archetype.

Motivala, S. J., & Irwin, M. R. (2007). Sleep and immunity: Cytokine pathways linking sleep and health outcomes. *Current Directions in Psychological Science, 16,* 21–25.

Moulin, S., Waldfogel, J., & Washbrook, E. (2014). Baby bonds: Parenting, attachment, and a secure base for children. *Sutton Trust, 1–42.*

Moyer, K. E. (1983). The physiology of motivation: Aggression as a model. In C. J. Scheier & A. M. Rogers (Eds.), *The G. Stanley Hall lecture series* (Vol. 3, pp. 123–139). Washington, DC: American Psychological Association.

Mroczek, D. K., & Kolarz, D. M. (1998). The effect of age on positive and negative affect: A developmental perspective on happiness. *Journal of Personality and Social Psychology, 75,* 1333–1349.

Mroczek, D. K., & Spiro, A., III. (2003). Modeling intra-individual change in personality traits: Findings from the Normative Aging Study. *Journals of Gerontology: Series B. Psychological Sciences and Social Sciences, 58,* P153–P165.

Mueller, P. A., & Oppenheimer, D. M. (2014). The pen is mightier than the keyboard: Advantages of longhand over laptop note-taking. *Psychological Science, 25,* 1159–1168.

Muller, J. E., Mittleman, M. A., Maclure, M., Sherwood, J. B., & Tofler, G. H. (1996). Triggering myocardial infarction by sexual activity. *Journal of the American Medical Association, 275,* 1405–1409.

Mullin, C. R., & Linz, D. (1995). Desensitization and resensitization to violence against women: Effects of exposure to sexually violent films on judgments of domestic violence victims. *Journal of Psychiatric Research, 26,* 225–235.

Munsey, C. (2010, June). Medicine or menace? Psychologists' research can inform the growing debate over legalizing marijuana. *Monitor on Psychology,* pp. 50–55.

Murayama, K., Pekrun, R., Lichtenfeld, S., & vom Hofe, R. (2013). Predicting long-term growth in students' mathematics achievement: The unique contributions of motivation and cognitive strategies. *Child Development, 84,* 1475–1490.

Murray, H. A. (1938). *Explorations in personality.* New York: Oxford University Press.

Murray, H. A., & Wheeler, D. R. (1937). A note on the possible clairvoyance of dreams. *Journal of Psychology, 3,* 309–313.

Murray, R., Jones, P., O'Callaghan, E., Takei, N., & Sham, P. (1992). Genes, viruses, and neurodevelopmental schizophrenia. *Journal of Psychiatric Research, 26,* 225–235.

Murray, R. M., Morrison, P. D., Henquet, C., & Di Forti, M. (2007). Cannabis, the mind and society: The hash realities. *Nature Reviews: Neuroscience, 8,* 885–895.

Musick, M. A., Herzog, A. R., & House, J. S. (1999). Volunteering and mortality among older adults: Findings from a national sample. *Journals of Gerontology, 54B,* 173–180.

Mustanski, B. S., & Bailey, J. M. (2003). A therapist's guide to the genetics of human sexual orientation. *Sexual and Relationship Therapy, 18,* 1468–1479.

Muusses, L. D., Kerkhof, P., & Finkenauer, C. (2015). Internet pornography and relationship quality: A longitudinal study of within and between partner effects of adjustment, sexual satisfaction and sexually explicit internet material among newly-weds. *Computers in Human Behavior, 45,* 77–84.

Myers, D. G. (1993). *The pursuit of happiness.* New York: Harper.

Myers, D. G. (2000). *The American paradox: Spiritual hunger in an age of plenty.* New Haven, CT: Yale University Press.

Myers, D. G. (2010). *Social psychology* (10th ed.). New York: McGraw-Hill.

Myers, D. G., & Bishop, G. D. (1970). Discussion effects on racial attitudes. *Science, 169,* 778–779.

Myers, D. G., & Diener, E. (1995). Who is happy? *Psychological Science, 6,* 10–19.

Myers, D. G., & Diener, E. (1996, May). The pursuit of happiness. *Scientific American* (scientificamerican.com).

Myers, D. G., & Scanzoni, L. D. (2005). *What God has joined together*. San Francisco: HarperSanFrancisco.

Myers, T. A., & Crowther, J. H. (2009). Social comparison as a predictor of body dissatisfaction: A meta-analytic review. *Journal of Abnormal Psychology, 118*, 683–698.

Nagamatsu, L. S., Chan, A., Davis, J. C., Beattie, B. L., Graf, P., Voss, M. W., . . . Liu-Ambrose, T. (2013). Physical activity improves verbal and spatial memory in older adults with probable mild cognitive impairment: A 6-month randomized controlled trial. *Journal of Aging Research, 2013*, Article 861893. doi:10.1155/2013/861893

Nagourney, A. (2002, September 25). For remarks on Iraq, Gore gets praise and scorn. *The New York Times* (nytimes.com).

Nanni, V., Uher, R., & Danese, A. (2012). Childhood maltreatment predicts unfavorable course of illness and treatment outcome in depression: A meta-analysis. *American Journal of Psychiatry, 169*, 141–151.

Napolitan, D. A., & Goethals, G. R. (1979). The attribution of friendliness. *Journal of Experimental Social Psychology, 15*, 105–113.

Narvaez, D. (2010). Moral complexity: The fatal attraction of truthiness and the importance of mature moral functioning. *Perspectives on Psychological Science, 5*, 163–181.

Nathan, D. (2011). *Sybil exposed: The extraordinary story behind the famous multiple personality case*. New York: Simon & Schuster.

National Academy of Sciences. (2001). *Exploring the biological contributions to human health: Does sex matter?* Washington, DC: Institute of Medicine, National Academy Press.

National Academy of Sciences. (2002). *The polygraph and lie detection*. Washington, DC: National Academies Press.

National Center for Health Statistics. (1990). *Health, United States, 1989*. Washington, DC: U.S. Department of Health and Human Services.

National Institute of Mental Health. (2013, October 1). *The numbers count: Mental disorders in America*. Retrieved from http://www.lb7.uscourts.gov/documents/12-cv-1072url2.pdf

National Safety Council. (2015). Transportation mode comparison in *Injury Facts*. (nsc.org)

National Sleep Foundation. (2013). 2013 International Bedroom Poll: Summary of findings. Retrieved from sleepfoundation.org/sites/default/files/RPT495a.pdf

Naughton, M., Clarke, G., O'Leary, O. F, Cryan, J. F., & Dinan, T. G. (2014). A review of ketamine in affective disorders: Current evidence of clinical efficacy, limitations of use and pre-clinical evidence on proposed mechanisms of action. *Journal of Affective Disorders, 156*, 24–35.

Naumann, L. P., Vazire, S., Rentfrow, P. J., & Gosling, S. D. (2009). Personality judgments based on physical appearance. *Personality and Social Psychology Bulletin, 35*, 1661–1671.

Nausheen, B., Carr, N. J., Peveler, R. C., Moss-Morris, R., Verrill, C., Robbins, E., . . . Gidron, Y. (2010). Relationship between loneliness and proangiogenic cytokines in newly diagnosed tumors of colon and rectum. *Psychosomatic Medicine, 72*, 912–916.

Neal, D. T., Wood, W., & Drolet, A. (2013). How do people adhere to goals when willpower is low? The profits (and pitfalls) of strong habits. *Journal of Personality and Social Psychology, 104*, 959–975.

Nedeltcheva, A. V., Kilkus, J. M., Imperial, J., Schoeller, D. A., & Penev, P. D. (2010). Insufficient sleep undermines dietary efforts to reduce adiposity. *Annals of Internal Medicine, 153*, 435–441.

NEEF. (2015). Fact sheet: Children's health and nature. National Environmental Education Foundation (neefusa.org/resource/children%E2%80%99s-health-and-nature-fact-sheet).

Neel, R., Kenrick, D. T., White, A. E., & Neuberg, S. L. (2016). Individual differences in fundamental social motives. *Journal of Personality and Social Psychology*. Advance online publication. http://dx.doi.org/10.1037/pspp0000068

Neese, R. M. (1991, November/December). What good is feeling bad? The evolutionary benefits of psychic pain. *The Sciences*, pp. 30–37.

Neimeyer, R. A., & Currier, J. M. (2009). Grief therapy: Evidence of efficacy and emerging directions. *Current Directions in Psychological Science, 18*, 352–356.

Neisser, U. (1979). The control of information pickup in selective looking. In A. D. Pick (Ed.), *Perception and its development: A tribute to Eleanor J. Gibson* (pp. 209–219). Hillsdale, NJ: Erlbaum.

Neisser, U., Boodoo, G., Bouchard, T. J., Jr., Boykin, A. W., Brody, N., Ceci, S. J., . . . Urbina, S. (1996). Intelligence: Knowns and unknowns. *American Psychologist, 51*, 77–101.

Neitz, J., Carroll, J., & Neitz, M. (2001). Color vision: Almost reason enough for having eyes. *Optics & Photonics News, 12*, 26–33.

Nelson, C. A., III, Fox, N. A., & Zeanah, C. H., Jr. (2013a, April). Anguish of the abandoned child. *Scientific American*, pp. 62–67.

Nelson, C. A., III, Fox, N. A., & Zeanah, C. H., Jr. (2014). *Romania's abandoned children*. Cambridge, MA: Harvard University Press.

Nelson, C. A., III, Furtado, E. Z., Fox, N. A., & Zeanah, C. H., Jr. (2009). The deprived human brain. *American Scientist, 97*, 222–229.

Nelson, M. D., Saykin, A. J., Flashman, L. A., & Riordan, H. J. (1998). Hippocampal volume reduction in schizophrenia as assessed by magnetic resonance imaging. *Archives of General Psychiatry, 55*, 433–440.

Nelson, S. K., Kushlev, K., English, T., Dunn, E. W., & Lyubomirsky, S. (2013b). In defense of parenthood: Children are associated with more joy than misery. *Psychological Science, 24*, 3–10.

Nes, R. B. (2010). Happiness in behaviour genetics: Findings and implications. *Journal of Happiness Studies, 11*, 369–381.

Nesca, M., & Koulack, D. (1994). Recognition memory, sleep and circadian rhythms. *Canadian Journal of Experimental Psychology, 48*, 359–379.

Nestler, E. J. (2011, December). Hidden switches in the mind. *Scientific American*, pp. 77–83.

Nestoriuc, Y., Rief, W., & Martin, A. (2008). Meta-analysis of biofeedback for tension-type headache: Efficacy, specificity, and treatment moderators. *Journal of Consulting and Clinical Psychology, 76*, 379–396.

Neubauer, D. N. (1999). Sleep problems in the elderly. *American Family Physician, 59*, 2551–2558.

Neumann, R., & Strack, F. (2000). "Mood contagion": The automatic transfer of mood between persons. *Journal of Personality and Social Psychology, 79*, 211–223.

Newcomb, M. D., & Harlow, L. L. (1986). Life events and substance use among adolescents: Mediating effects of perceived loss of control and meaninglessness in life. *Journal of Personality and Social Psychology, 51*, 564–577.

Newell, B. R. (2015). "Wait! Just let me not think about that for a minute": What role do implicit processes play in higher-level cognition? *Current Directions in Psychological Science, 24*, 65–70.

Newport, E. L. (1990). Maturational constraints on language learning. *Cognitive Science, 14*, 11–28.

Newport, F. (2001, February). Americans see women as emotional and affectionate, men as more aggressive. *The Gallup Poll Monthly*, pp. 34–38.

Newport, F. (2012, December 19). To stop shootings, Americans focus on police, mental health. Gallup (gallup.com).

Newport, F. (2013a, July 25). *In U.S. 87% approve of Black-White marriage, vs. 4% in 1958*. Gallup Poll (gallup.com).

Newport, F. (2013b, July 31). *Most U.S. smokers want to quit, have tried multiple times: Former smokers say best way to quit is just to stop "cold turkey."* Gallup (gallup.com).

Newport, F. (2015, July 9). *Most U.S. smartphone owners check phone at least hourly*. Gallup Poll (gallup.com).

Newport, F., Argrawal, S., & Witters, D. (2010, December 23). *Very religious Americans lead healthier lives*. Gallup (gallup.com).

Newport, F., & Pelham, B. (2009, December 14). *Don't worry, be 80: Worry and stress decline with age*. Gallup (gallup.com).

Newport, F., & Wilke, J. (2013, August 2). *Most in U.S. want marriage, but its importance has dropped*. Gallup Poll (gallup.com).

Newton, I. (1704). *Opticks: Or, a treatise of the reflexions, refractions, inflexions and colours of light*. London: Royal Society.

Ng, T. W. H., Sorensen, K. L., & Eby, L. T. (2006). Locus of control at work: A meta-analysis. *Journal of Organizational Behavior, 27*, 1057–1087.

Ng, T. W. H., Sorensen, K. L., & Yim, F. H. K. (2009). Does the job satisfaction–job performance relationship vary across cultures? *Journal of Cross-Cultural Psychology, 40*, 761–796.

Nguyen, H.-H. D., & Ryan, A. M. (2008). Does stereotype threat affect test performance of minorities and women? A meta-analysis of experimental evidence. *Journal of Applied Psychology, 93*, 1314–1334.

Nickell, J. (Ed.). (1994). *Psychic sleuths: ESP and sensational cases*. Buffalo, NY: Prometheus Books.

Nickell, J. (2005, July/August). The case of the psychic detectives. *Skeptical Inquirer* (skeptically.org/skepticism/id10.html).

Nickerson, R. S. (2002). The production and perception of randomness. *Psychological Review, 109*, 330–357.

Nickerson, R. S. (2005). Bertrand's chord, Buffon's needles, and the concept of randomness. *Thinking & Reasoning, 11*, 67–96.

Nicolas, S., & Levine, Z. (2012). Beyond intelligence testing: Remembering Alfred Binet after a century. *European Psychologist, 17*, 320–325.

NIDA. (2002). Methamphetamine abuse and addiction. *Research Report Series*. National Institute on Drug Abuse, NIH Publication Number 02–4210.

NIDA. (2005, May). Methamphetamine. *NIDA Info Facts*. National Institute on Drug Abuse.

Nieuwenstein, M. R., Wierenga, T., Morey, R. D., Wicherts, J. M., Blom, T. N., Wagenmakers, E., & van Rijn, H. (2015). On making the right choice: A meta-analysis and large-scale replication attempt of the unconscious thought advantage. *Judgment and Decision Making, 10*, 1–17.

NIH. (2001, July 20). *Workshop summary: Scientific evidence on condom effectiveness for sexually transmitted disease (STD) prevention*. Bethesda: National Institute of Allergy and Infectious Diseases, National Institutes of Health.

NIH. (2010). Teacher's guide: Information about sleep. National Institutes of Health (science.education.nih.gov/).

Nikolas, M. A., & Burt, A. (2010). Genetic and environmental influences on ADHD symptom dimensions of inattention and hyperactivity: A meta-analysis. *Journal of Abnormal Psychology, 119*, 1–17.

Niles, A. N., Craske, M. G., Lieberman, M. D., & Hur, C. (2015). Affect labeling enhances exposure effectiveness for public speaking anxiety. *Behavior Research and Therapy, 68,* 27–36.

Nisbett, R. E. (2003). *The geography of thought: How Asians and Westerners think differently . . . and why.* New York: Free Press.

Nisbett, R. E. (2009). *Intelligence and how to get it: Why schools and culture count.* New York: Norton.

Nisbett, R. E., Aronson, J., Blair, C., Dickens, W., Flynn, J., Halpern, D. F., & Turkheimer, E. (2012). Intelligence: New findings and theoretical developments. *American Psychologist, 67,* 130–159.

Nizzi, M. C., Demertzi, A., Gosseries, O., Bruno, M. A., Jouen, F., & Laureys, S. (2012). From armchair to wheelchair: How patients with a locked-in syndrome integrate bodily changes in experienced identity. *Consciousness and Cognition, 21,* 431–437.

Nock, M. K. (2010). Self-injury. *Annual Review of Clinical Psychology, 6,* 339–363.

Nock, M. K., & Kessler, R. C. (2006). Prevalence of and risk factors for suicide attempts versus suicide gestures: Analysis of the National Comorbidity Survey. *Journal of Abnormal Psychology, 115,* 616–623.

Nolen-Hoeksema, S. (2001). Gender differences in depression. *Current Directions in Psychological Science, 10,* 173–176.

Nolen-Hoeksema, S. (2003). *Women who think too much: How to break free of overthinking and reclaim your life.* New York: Holt.

Nolen-Hoeksema, S., & Larson, J. (1999). *Coping with loss.* Mahwah, NJ: Erlbaum.

Nørby, S. (2015). Why forget? On the adaptive value of memory loss. *Perspectives on Psychological Science, 10,* 551–578.

NORC. (2007). National Opinion Research Center (University of Chicago) General Social Survey data, 1972 through 2004 (accessed via sda.berkeley.edu).

Norem, J. K. (2001). *The positive power of negative thinking: Using defensive pessimism to harness anxiety and perform at your peak.* New York: Basic Books.

Norris, A. L., Marcus, D. K., & Green, B. A. (2015). Homosexuality as a discrete class. *Psychological Science, 26,* 1843–1853.

Nowak, A., Gelfand, M. J., Borkowski, W., Cohen, D., & Hernandez, I. (2016). The evolutionary basis of honor cultures. *Psychological Science, 27,* 12–24.

NPR. (2009, July 11). Afraid to fly? Try living on a plane. National Public Radio (npr.org).

NSC. (2010, January 12). NSC estimates 1.6 million crashes caused by cell phone use and texting. National Safety Council (nsc.org).

Nurmikko, A. V., Donoghue, J. P., Hochberg, L. R., Patterson, W. R., Song, Y.-K., Bull, C. W., . . . Aceros, J. (2010). Listening to brain microcircuits for interfacing with external world—Progress in wireless implantable microelectronic neuroengineering devices. *Proceedings of the IEEE, 98,* 375–388.

Nussinovitch, U., & Shoenfeld, Y. (2012). The role of gender and organ specific autoimmunity. *Autoimmunity Reviews, 11,* A377–A385.

Nuttin, J. M., Jr. (1987). Affective consequences of mere ownership: The name letter effect in twelve European languages. *European Journal of Social Psychology, 17,* 381–402.

O'Boyle, E. H., Jr., Humphrey, R. H., Pollack, J. M., Hawyer, T. H., & Story, P. A. (2011). The relation between emotional intelligence and job performance: A meta-analysis. *Journal of Organizational Behavior, 32,* 788–818.

O'Brien, L., Albert, D., Chein, J., & Steinberg, L. (2011). Adolescents prefer more immediate rewards when in the presence of their peers. *Journal of Research on Adolescence, 21,* 747–753.

O'Connor, P., & Brown, G. W. (1984). Supportive relationships: Fact or fancy? *Journal of Social and Personal Relationships, 1,* 159–175.

O'Donnell, L., Stueve, A., O'Donnell, C., Duran, R., San Doval, A., Wilson, R. F., . . . Pleck, J. H. (2002). Long-term reduction in sexual initiation and sexual activity among urban middle schoolers in the reach for health service learning program. *Journal of Adolescent Health, 31,* 93–100.

O'Donovan, A., Neylan, T. C., Metzler, T., & Cohen, B. E. (2012). Lifetime exposure to traumatic psychological stress is associated with elevated inflammation in the Heart and Soul Study. *Brain, Behavior, and Immunity, 26,* 642–649.

O'Hara, R. E., Gibbons, F. X., Gerrard, M., Li, Z., & Sargent, J. D. (2012). Greater exposure to sexual content in popular movies predicts earlier sexual debut and increased sexual risk taking. *Psychological Science, 23,* 984–993.

O'Sullivan, M., Frank, M. G., Hurley, C. M., & Tiwana, J. (2009). Police lie detection accuracy: The effect of lie scenario. *Law and Human Behavior, 33,* 530–538.

Oakley, D. A., & Halligan, P. W. (2013). Hypnotic suggestion: Opportunities for cognitive neuroscience. *Nature Reviews Neuroscience, 14,* 565–576.

Oaten, M., & Cheng, K. (2006a). Improved self-control: The benefits of a regular program of academic study. *Basic and Applied Social Psychology, 28,* 1–16.

Oaten, M., & Cheng, K. (2006b). Longitudinal gains in self-regulation from regular physical exercise. *British Journal of Health Psychology, 11,* 717–733.

Oelschläger, M., Pfannmöller, J., Langer, I., & Lotze, M. (2014). Usage of the middle finger shapes reorganization of the primary somatosensory cortex in patients with index finger amputation. *Restorative Neurology and Neuroscience, 32,* 507–515.

Offer, D., Ostrov, E., Howard, K. I., & Atkinson, R. (1988). *The teenage world: Adolescents' self-image in ten countries.* New York: Plenum.

Ogden, J. (2012, January 16). HM, the man with no memory. *Psychology Today* (psychologytoday.com).

Öhman, A. (1986). Face the beast and fear the face: Animal and social fears as prototypes for evolutionary analyses of emotion. *Psychophysiology, 23,* 123–145.

Öhman, A., Lundqvist, D., & Esteves, F. (2001). The face in the crowd revisited: A threat advantage with schematic stimuli. *Journal of Personality and Social Psychology, 80,* 381–396.

Oishi, S., Diener, E. F., Lucas, R. E., & Suh, E. M. (1999). Cross-cultural variations in predictors of life satisfaction: Perspectives from needs and values. *Personality and Social Psychology Bulletin, 25,* 980–990.

Oishi, S., Kesebir, S., & Diener, E. (2011). Income inequality and happiness. *Psychological Science, 22,* 1095–1100.

Oishi, S., Schiller, J., & Blair, E. G. (2013). Felt understanding and misunderstanding affect the perception of pain, slant, and distance. *Social Psychological and Personality Science, 4,* 259–266.

Oishi, S., & Schimmack, U. (2010). Culture and well-being: A new inquiry into the psychological wealth of nations. *Perspectives in Psychological Science, 5,* 463–471.

Okimoto, T. G., & Brescoll, V. L. (2010). The price of power: Power seeking and backlash against female politicians. *Personality and Social Psychology Bulletin, 36,* 923–936.

Olds, J. (1975). Mapping the mind onto the brain. In F. G. Worden, J. P. Swazey, & G. Adelman (Eds.), *The neurosciences: Paths of discovery.* Cambridge, MA: MIT Press.

Olds, J., & Milner, P. (1954). Positive reinforcement produced by electrical stimulation of the septal area and other regions of rat brain. *Journal of Comparative and Physiological Psychology, 47,* 419–427.

Olff, M., Langeland, W., Draijer, N., & Gersons, B. P. R. (2007). Gender differences in posttraumatic stress disorder. *Psychological Bulletin, 135,* 183–204.

Olfson, M., & Marcus, S. C. (2009). National patterns in antidepressant medication treatment. *Archives of General Psychiatry, 66,* 848–856.

Oliner, S. P., & Oliner, P. M. (1988). *The altruistic personality: Rescuers of Jews in Nazi Europe.* New York: Free Press.

Olivé, I., Templemann, C., Berthoz, A., & Heinze, H.-J. (2015). Increased functional connectivity between superior colliculus and brain regions implicated in bodily self-consciousness during the rubber band illusion. *Human Brain Mapping, 36,* 717–730.

Olson, K. R., Key, A. C., & Eaton, N. R. (2015). Gender cognition in transgender children. *Psychological Science, 26,* 467–474.

Olson, R. L., Hanowski, R. J., Hickman, J. S., & Bocanegra, J. (2009, September). Driver distraction in commercial vehicle operations. Washington, DC: U.S. Department of Transportation, Federal Motor Carrier Safety Administration.

Olsson, A., Nearing, K. I., & Phelps, E. A. (2007). Learning fears by observing others: The neural systems of social fear transmission. *Social Cognitive and Affective Neuroscience, 2,* 3–11.

Olweus, D., Mattsson, A., Schalling, D., & Low, H. (1988). Circulating testosterone levels and aggression in adolescent males: A causal analysis. *Psychosomatic Medicine, 50,* 261–272.

Oman, D., Kurata, J. H., Strawbridge, W. J., & Cohen, R. D. (2002). Religious attendance and cause of death over 31 years. *International Journal of Psychiatry in Medicine, 32,* 69–89.

Open Science Collaboration. (2015). Estimating the reproducibility of psychological science. *Science, 349,* 943.

Oquendo, M. A., Galfalvy, H. C., Currier, D., Grunebaum, M. F., Sher, L., Sullivan, G. M., . . . Mann, J. J. (2011). Treatment of suicide attempters with bipolar disorder: A randomized clinical trial comparing lithium and valproate in the prevention of suicidal behavior. *American Journal of Psychiatry, 168,* 1050–1056.

Orth, U., Maes, J., & Schmitt, M. (2015). Self-esteem development across the life span: A longitudinal study with a large sample from Germany. *Developmental Psychology, 51,* 248–259.

Orth, U., & Robins, R. W. (2014). The development of self-esteem. *Current Directions in Psychological Science, 23,* 381–387.

Orth, U., Robins, R. W., Meier, L. L., & Conger, R. D. (2016). Refining the vulnerability model of low self-esteem and depression: Disentangling the effects of genuine self-esteem and narcissism. *Journal of Personality and Social Psychology, 110,* 133–149.

Orth, U., Robins, R. W., Trzesniewski, K. H., Maes, J., & Schmitt, M. (2009). Low self-esteem is a risk factor for depressive symptoms from young adulthood to old age. *Journal of Abnormal Psychology, 118,* 472–478.

Osborne, L. (1999, October 27). A linguistic big bang. *The New York Times Magazine* (nytimes.com).

Oskarsson, A. T., Van Voven, L., McClelland, G. H., & Hastie, R. (2009). What's next? Judging sequences of binary events. *Psychological Bulletin, 135,* 262–285.

Ossher, L., Flegal, K. E., & Lustig, C. (2012). Everyday memory errors in older adults. *Aging, Neuropsychology, and Cognition, 20,* 220–242.

Öst, L. G., Havnen, A., Hansen, B., & Kvale, G. (2015). Cognitive behavioral treatments of obsessive–compulsive disorder. A systematic review and meta-analysis of studies published 1993–2014. *Clinical Psychology Review, 40,* 156–169.

Öst, L. G., & Hugdahl, K. (1981). Acquisition of phobias and anxiety response patterns in clinical patients. *Behaviour Research and Therapy, 16,* 439–447.

Ostfeld, A. M., Kasl, S. V., D'Atri, D. A., & Fitzgerald, E. F. (1987). *Stress, crowding, and blood pressure in prison.* Hillsdale, NJ: Erlbaum.

Osvath, M., & Karvonen, E. (2012). Spontaneous innovation for future deception in a male chimpanzee. *PLoS ONE, 7*(5), e36782.

Oswald, F. L., Mitchell, G., Blanton, H., Jaccard, J., & Tetlock, P. E. (2015). Using the IAT to predict ethnic and racial discrimination: Small effect sizes of unknown societal significance. *Journal of Personality and Social Psychology, 108,* 562–571.

Ott, B. (2007, June 14). Investors, take note: Engagement boosts earnings. *Gallup Management Journal* (gallup.com).

Ott, C. H., Lueger, R. J., Kelber, S. T., & Prigerson, H. G. (2007). Spousal bereavement in older adults: Common, resilient, and chronic grief with defining characteristics. *Journal of Nervous and Mental Disease, 195,* 332–341.

Owen, A. M. (2014). Disorders of consciousness: Diagnostic accuracy of brain imaging in the vegetative state. *Nature Reviews Neurology, 10,* 370–371.

Owen, A. M., Coleman, M. R., Boly, M., Davis, M. H., Laureys, S., & Pickard, J. D. (2006). Detecting awareness in the vegetative state. *Science, 313,* 1402.

Owen, R. (1814). First essay in *New view of society, Or the formation of character.* Quoted in *The story of New Lanark Mills,* Lanark, Scotland: New Lanark Conservation Trust, 1993.

Owens, J. A., Belon, K., & Moss, P. (2010). Impact of delaying school start time on adolescent sleep, mood, and behavior. *Archives of Pediatric Adolescent Medicine, 164,* 608–614.

Oxfam. (2005, March 26). *Three months on: New figures show tsunami may have killed up to four times as many women as men.* Oxfam Press Release (oxfam.org.uk).

Ozer, E. J., Best, S. R., Lipsey, T. L., & Weiss, D. S. (2003). Predictors of posttraumatic stress disorder and symptoms in adults: A meta-analysis. *Psychological Bulletin, 1*(9), 52–73.

Ozer, E. J., & Weiss, D. S. (2004). Who develops posttraumatic stress disorder? *Current Directions in Psychological Science, 13,* 169–172.

Pacifici, R., Zuccaro, P., Farre, M., Pichini, S., Di Carlo, S., Roset, P. N., . . . de la Torre, R. (2001). Effects of repeated doses of MDMA ("Ecstasy") on cell-mediated immune response in humans. *Life Sciences, 69,* 2931–2941.

Padgett, V. R. (1989). *Predicting organizational violence: An application of 11 powerful principles of obedience.* Paper presented at the American Psychological Association convention.

Pagani, L. S., Fitzpatrick, C., Barnett, T. A., & Dubow, E. (2010). Prospective associations between early childhood television exposure and academic, psychosocial, and physical well-being by middle childhood. *Archives of Pediatric and Adolescent Medicine, 164,* 425–431.

Paller, K. A., & Suzuki, S. (2014). The source of consciousness. *Trends in Cognitive Sciences, 18,* 387–389.

Pallier, C., Colomé, A., & Sebastián-Gallés, N. (2001). The influence of native-language phonology on lexical access: Exemplar-based versus abstract lexical entries. *Psychological Science, 12,* 445–448.

Palmer, D. C. (1989). A behavioral interpretation of memory. In L. J. Hayes (Ed.), *Dialogues on verbal behavior: The first international institute on verbal relations* (pp. 261–279). Reno, NV: Context Press.

Pandey, J., Sinha, Y., Prakash, A., & Tripathi, R. C. (1982). Right-left political ideologies and attribution of the causes of poverty. *European Journal of Social Psychology, 12,* 327–331.

Panksepp, J. (2007). Neurologizing the psychology of affects: How appraisal-based constructivism and basic emotion theory can coexist. *Perspectives on Psychological Science, 2,* 281–295.

Panzarella, C., Alloy, L. B., & Whitehouse, W. G. (2006). Expanded hopelessness theory of depression: On the mechanisms by which social support protects against depression. *Cognitive Theory and Research, 30,* 307–333.

Pardini, D. A., Raine, A., Erickson, K., & Loeber, R. (2014). Lower amygdala volume in men is associated with childhood aggression, early psychopathic traits, and future violence. *Biological Psychiatry, 75,* 73–80.

Park, D. C., & McDonough, I. M. (2013). The dynamic aging mind: Revelations from functional neuroimaging research. *Perspectives on Psychological Science, 8,* 62–67.

Park, G., Schwartz, H. A., Eichstaedt, J. C., Kern, M. L., Kosinski, M., Stillwell, D. J., . . . Seligman, M. E. P. (2015). Automatic personality assessment through social media language. *Journal of Personality and Social Psychology, 108,* 934–952.

Parker, C. P., Baltes, B. B., Young, S. A., Huff, J. W., Altmann, R. A., LaCost, H. A., & Roberts, J. E. (2003). Relationships between psychological climate perceptions and work outcomes: A meta-analytic review. *Journal of Organizational Behavior, 24,* 389–416.

Parker, E. S., Cahill, L., & McGaugh, J. L. (2006). A case of unusual autobiographical remembering. *Neurocase, 12,* 35–49.

Parker, K., & Wang, W. (2013). Modern parenthood. *Pew Research Center, Social & Demographic Trends.* (Accessed August 10, 2015, pewsocialtrends.org/2013/03/14/modern-parenthood-roles-of-moms-and-dads-converge-as-they-balance-work-and-family).

Parkes, A., Wight, D., Hunt, K., Henderson, M., & Sargent, J. (2013). Are sexual media exposure, parental restrictions on media use and co-viewing TV and DVDs with parents and friends associated with teenagers' early sexual behavior? *Journal of Adolescence, 36,* 1121–1133.

Parnia, S., Fenwick, P., Spearpoint K., & Devos, G. (2014). Awareness during resuscitation (AWARE). *Circulation, 128,* A236.

Parsons, T. D., & Rizzo, A. A. (2008). Affective outcomes of virtual reality exposure therapy for anxiety and specific phobias: A meta-analysis. *Journal of Behavior Therapy and Experimental Psychiatry, 39,* 250–261.

Parthasarathy, S., Vasquez, M. M., Halonen, M., Bootzin, R., Quan, S. F., Martinez, F. D., & Guerra, S. (2015). Persistent insomnia is associated with mortality risk. *American Journal of Medicine, 128,* 268–275.

Pascoe, E. A., & Richman, L. S. (2009). Perceived discrimination and health: A meta-analytic review. *Psychological Bulletin, 135,* 531–554.

Pate, J. E., Pumariega, A. J., Hester, C., & Garner, D. M. (1992). Cross-cultural patterns in eating disorders: A review. *Journal of the American Academy of Child and Adolescent Psychiatry, 31,* 802–809.

Patihis, L., Ho, L. Y., Tingen, I. W., Lilienfeld, S. O., & Loftus, E. F. (2014a). Are the "memory wars" over? A scientist–practitioner gap in beliefs about repressed memory. *Psychological Science, 25,* 519–530.

Patihis, L., Lilienfeld, S. O., Ho, L. Y., & Loftus, E. F. (2014b). Unconscious repressed memory is scientifically questionable. *Psychological Science, 25,* 1967–1968.

Patterson, F. (1978, October). Conversations with a gorilla. *National Geographic,* pp. 438–465.

Patterson, G. R., Chamberlain, P., & Reid, J. B. (1982). A comparative evaluation of parent training procedures. *Behavior Therapy, 13,* 638–650.

Patterson, M., Warr, P., & West, M. (2004). Organizational climate and company productivity: The role of employee affect and employee level. *Journal of Occupational and Organizational Psychology, 77,* 193–216.

Pauker, K., Weisbuch, M., Ambady, N., Sommers, S. R., Adams, R. B., Jr., & Ivcevic, Z. (2009). Not so Black and White: Memory for ambiguous group members. *Journal of Personality and Social Psychology, 96,* 795–810.

Paunesku, D., Walton, G. M., Romero, C., Smith, E. N., Yeager, D. S., & Dweck, C. S. (2015). Mindset interventions are a scalable treatment for academic underachievement. *Psychological Science, 26,* 784–793.

Paus, T., Zijdenbos, A., Worsley, K., Collins, D. L., Blumenthal, J., Giedd, J. N., Rapaport, J. L., & Evans, A. C. (1999). Structural maturation of neural pathways in children and adolescents: In vivo study. *Science, 283,* 1908–1911.

Pavlov, I. (1927). *Conditioned reflexes: An investigation of the physiological activity of the cerebral cortex.* Oxford: Oxford University Press.

Payne, B. K. (2006). Weapon bias: Split-second decisions and unintended stereotyping. *Current Directions in Psychological Science, 15,* 287–291.

Payne, B. K., & Corrigan, E. (2007). Emotional constraints on intentional forgetting. *Journal of Experimental Social Psychology, 43,* 780–786.

Payne, J. W., Samper, A., Bettman, J. R., & Luce, M. F. (2008). Boundary conditions on unconscious thought in complex decision making. *Psychological Science, 19,* 1118–1123.

Pazda, A. D., & Elliot, A. J. (2012). The color of attraction: How red influences physical appeal. In M. Paludi (Ed.), *The psychology of love.* Santa Barbara, CA: Praeger.

Pazda, A. D., Prokop, P., & Elliot, A. J. (2014). Red and romantic rivalry: Viewing another woman in red increases perceptions of sexual receptivity, derogation, and intentions to mate-guard. *Personality and Social Psychology Bulletin, 40,* 1260–1269.

Peck, E. (2015, April 29). Harvard Business School launches new effort to attract women. *Huffington Post* (huffingtonpost.com).

Peckham, A. D., McHugh, R. K., & Otto, M. W. (2010). A meta-analysis of the magnitude of biased attention in depression. *Depression and Anxiety, 27,* 1135–1142.

Pelham, B. W. (1993). On the highly positive thoughts of the highly depressed. In R. F. Baumeister (Ed.), *Self-esteem: The puzzle of low self-regard.* New York: Plenum.

Pelham, B. W. (2009, October 22). About one in six Americans report history of depression. Gallup (gallup.com).

Pelham, B., & Crabtree, S. (2008, October 8). *Worldwide, highly religious more likely to help others.* Gallup (gallup.com).

Pennebaker, J. W. (1990). *Opening up: The healing power of confiding in others.* New York: William Morrow.

Pennebaker, J. W. (2011). *The secret life of pronouns: What our words say about us.* New York: Bloomsbury Press.

Pennebaker, J. W., Barger, S. D., & Tiebout, J. (1989). Disclosure of traumas and health among Holocaust survivors. *Psychosomatic Medicine, 51,* 577–589.

Pennebaker, J. W., Gosling, S. D., & Ferrell, J. D. (2013). Daily online testing in large classes: Boosting college performance while reducing achievement gaps. *PLOS ONE, 8*(11), e79774.

Pennebaker, J. W., & O'Heeron, R. C. (1984). Confiding in others and illness rate among spouses of suicide and accidental death victims. *Journal of Abnormal Psychology, 93,* 473–476.

Peplau, L. A., & Fingerhut, A. W. (2007). The close relationships of lesbians and gay men. *Annual Review of Psychology, 58,* 405–424.

Pepperberg, I. M. (2009). *Alex & me: How a scientist and a parrot discovered a hidden world of animal intelligence—and formed a deep bond in the process.* New York: Harper.

Pepperberg, I. M. (2012). Further evidence for addition and numerical competence by a grey parrot (*Psittacus erithacus*). *Animal Cognition, 15,* 711–717.

Pepperberg, I. M. (2013). Abstract concepts: Data from a grey parrot. *Behavioural Processes, 93,* 82–90.

Perani, D., & Abutalebi, J. (2005). The neural basis of first and second language processing. *Current Opinion in Neurobiology, 15,* 202–206.

Pereg, D., Gow, R., Mosseri, M., Lishner, M., Rieder, M., Van Uum, S., & Koren, G. (2011). Hair cortisol and the risk for acute myocardial infarction in adult men. *Stress, 14,* 73–81.

Pereira, A. C., Huddleston, D. E., Brickman, A. M., Sosunov, A. A., Hen, R., McKhann, G. M., . . . Small, S. A. (2007). An in vivo correlate of exercise-induced neurogenesis in the adult dentate gyrus. *PNAS, 104,* 5638–5643.

Pereira, G. M., & Osburn, H. G. (2007). Effects of participation in decision making on performance and employee attitudes: A quality circles meta-analysis. *Journal of Business Psychology, 22,* 145–153.

Pergamin-Hight, L., Naim, R., Bakermans-Kranenburg, M. J., van IJzendoorn, M. H., & Bar-Haim, Y. (2015). Content specificity of attention bias to threat in anxiety disorders: A meta-analysis. *Clinical Psychology Review, 35,* 10–18.

Perilloux, H. K., Webster, G. D., & Gaulin, S. J. (2010). Signals of genetic quality and maternal investment capacity: The dynamic effects of fluctuating asymmetry and waist-to-hip ratio on men's ratings of women's attractiveness. *Social Psychological and Personality Science, 1,* 34–42.

Perkins, A. M., Inchley-Mort, S. L., Pickering, A. D., Corr, P. J., & Burgess, A. P. (2012). A facial expression for anxiety. *Journal of Personality and Social Psychology, 102,* 910–924.

Perkins, A., & Fitzgerald, J. A. (1997). Sexual orientation in domestic rams: Some biological and social correlates. In L. Ellis & L. Ebertz (Eds.), *Sexual orientation: Toward biological understanding* (pp. 107–128). Westport, CT: Praeger Publishers.

Perrachione, T. K., Del Tufo, S. N., & Gabrieli, J. D. E. (2011). Human voice recognition depends on language ability. *Science, 333,* 595.

Perrin, J. S., Merz, S., Bennett, D. M., Currie, J., Steele, D. J., Reid, I. C., & Schwarzbauer, C. (2012). Electroconvulsive therapy reduced frontal cortical connectivity in severe depressive disorder. *PNAS, 109,* 5464–5468.

Perry, J. R. B., Day, F., Elks, C. E., Sulem, P., Thompson, D. J., Ferreira, T., & 260 others. (2014). Parent-of-specific allelic associations among 106 genomic loci for age at menarche. *Nature, 514,* 92–97.

Person, C., Tracy, M., & Galea, S. (2006). Risk factors for depression after a disaster. *Journal of Nervous and Mental Disease, 194,* 659–666.

Pert, C. B., & Snyder, S. H. (1973). Opiate receptor: Demonstration in nervous tissue. *Science, 179,* 1011–1014.

Perugini, E. M., Kirsch, I., Allen, S. T., Coldwell, E., Meredith, J., Montgomery, G. H., & Sheehan, J. (1998). Surreptitious observation of responses to hypnotically suggested hallucinations: A test of the compliance hypothesis. *International Journal of Clinical and Experimental Hypnosis, 46,* 191–203.

Peschel, E. R., & Peschel, R. E. (1987). Medical insights into the castrati in opera. *American Scientist, 75,* 578–583.

Pesko, M. F. (2014). Stress and smoking: Associations with terrorism and causal impact. *Contemporary Economic Policy, 32,* 351–371.

Peters, M., Rhodes, G., & Simmons, L. W. (2007). Contributions of the face and body to overall attractiveness. *Animal Behaviour, 73,* 937–942.

Peters, T. J., & Waterman, R. H., Jr. (1982). *In search of excellence: Lessons from America's best-run companies.* New York: Harper & Row.

Petersen, J. L., & Hyde, J. S. (2010). A meta-analytic review of research on gender differences in sexuality, 1993–2007. *Psychological Bulletin, 136,* 21–38.

Petersen, J. L., & Hyde, J. S. (2011). Gender differences in sexual attitudes and behaviors: A review of meta-analytic results and large datasets. *Journal of Sex Research, 48,* 149–165.

Peterson, C., Peterson, J., & Skevington, S. (1986). Heated argument and adolescent development. *Journal of Social and Personal Relationships, 3,* 229–240.

Peterson, L. R., & Peterson, M. J. (1959). Short-term retention of individual verbal items. *Journal of Experimental Psychology, 58,* 193–198.

Petitto, L. A., & Marentette, P. F. (1991). Babbling in the manual mode: Evidence for the ontogeny of language. *Science, 251,* 1493–1496.

Pettegrew, J. W., Keshavan, M. S., & Minshew, N. J. (1993). ³¹P nuclear magnetic resonance spectroscopy: Neurodevelopment and schizophrenia. *Schizophrenia Bulletin, 19,* 35–53.

Petticrew, C., Bell, R., & Hunter, D. (2002). Influence of psychological coping on survival and recurrence in people with cancer: Systematic review. *British Medical Journal, 325,* 1066.

Petticrew, M., Fraser, J. M., & Regan, M. F. (1999). Adverse life events and risk of breast cancer: A meta-analysis. *British Journal of Health Psychology, 4,* 1–17.

Pettigrew, T. F., Christ, O., Wagner, U., & Stellmacher, J. (2007). Direct and indirect intergroup contact effects on prejudice: A normative interpretation. *International Journal of Intercultural Relations, 31,* 411–425.

Pettigrew, T. F., & Tropp, L. R. (2011). *When groups meet: The dynamics of intergroup contact.* New York: Psychology Press.

Pew. (2006). *Remembering 9/11.* Pew Research Center (pewresearch.org).

Pew. (2007, July 18). *Modern marriage: "I like hugs. I like kisses. But what I really love is help with the dishes."* Pew Research Center (pewresearch.org).

Pew. (2010, July 1). *Gender equality universally embraced, but inequalities acknowledged.* Pew Research Center Publications (pewresearch.org).

Pew. (2011, December 15). *17% and 61%—Texting, talking on the phone and driving.* Pew Research Center (pewresearch.org).

Pew. (2012, June 4). *Section 8: Values about immigration and race.* Pew Research Center (people-press.org/2012/06/04/section-8-values-about-immigration-and-race/).

Pew. (2013). *The global divide on homosexuality: Greater acceptance in more secular and affluent countries.* [Data file]. Pew Research Center (pewglobal.org/files/2013/06/Pew-Global-Attitudes-Homosexuality-Report-FINAL-JUNE-4-2013.pdf).

Pew. (2015a). *Broadband technology fact sheet.* Pew Research Center (pewinternet.org/fact-sheets/broadband-technology-fact-sheet/).

Pew. (2015b, November 4). *Raising kids and running a household: How working parents share the load.* Pew Research Center (pewsocialtrends.org).

Pfaff, L. A., Boatwright, K. J., Potthoff, A. L., Finan, C., Ulrey, L. A., & Huber, D. M. (2013). Perceptions of women and men leaders following 360-degree feedback evaluations. *Performance Improvement Quarterly, 26,* 35–56.

Pfundmair, M., DeWall, C. N., Fries, V., Geiger, B., Krämer, T., Krug, S., . . . Aydin, N. (2015). Sugar or spice: Using I3 metatheory to understand how and why glucose reduces rejection-related aggression. *Aggressive behavior, 41*(6), 537–543.

Phillips, A. L. (2011). A walk in the woods. *American Scientist, 69,* 301–302.

Piaget, J. (1930). *The child's conception of physical causality* (M. Gabain, Trans.). London: Routledge & Kegan Paul.

Piaget, J. (1932). *The moral judgment of the child.* New York: Harcourt, Brace & World.

Piazza, J. R., Charles, S. T., Silwinski, M. J., Mogle, J., & Almeida, D. M. (2013). Affective reactivity to daily stressors and long-term risk of reporting a chronic health condition. *Annals of Behavioral Medicine, 45,* 110–120.

Picardi, A., Fagnani, C., Nisticò, L., & Stazi, M. A. (2011). A twin study of attachment style in young adults. *Journal of Personality, 79,* 965–992.

Picchioni, M. M., & Murray, R. M. (2007). Schizophrenia. *British Medical Journal, 335,* 91–95.

Piekarski, D. J., Routman, D. M., Schoomer, E. E., Driscoll, J. R., Park, J. H., Butler, M. P., & Zucker, I. (2009). Infrequent low dose testosterone treatment maintains male sexual behavior in Syrian hamsters. *Hormones and Behavior, 55,* 182–189.

Pieters, G. L. M., de Bruijn, E. R. A., Maas, Y., Hultjin, W., Vandereycken, W., Peuskens, J., & Sabbe, B. G. (2007). Action monitoring and perfectionism in anorexia nervosa. *Brain and Cognition, 63,* 42–50.

Pietschnig, J., & Voracek, M. (2015). One century of global IQ gains: A formal meta-analysis of the Flynn effect (1909–2013). *Perspectives on Psychological Science, 10,* 282–306.

Piliavin, J. A. (2003). Doing well by doing good: Benefits for the benefactor. In C. L. M. Keyes & J. Haidt (Eds.), *Flourishing: Positive psychology and the life well-lived.* Washington, DC: American Psychological Association.

Pillemer, D. B. (1998). *Momentous events, vivid memories.* Cambridge, MA: Harvard University Press.

Pilley, J. W., & Reid, A. K. (2011). Border collie comprehends object names as verbal referents. *Behavioural Processes, 86,* 184–195.

Pinker, S. (1995). The language instinct. *The General Psychologist, 31,* 63–65.

Pinker, S. (1998). Words and rules. *Lingua, 106,* 219–242.

Pinker, S. (2008). *The sexual paradox: Men, women, and the real gender gap.* New York: Scribner.

Pinker, S. (2010a). 2010: How is the Internet changing the way you think? Not at all. *Edge* (edge.org).

Pinker, S. (2010b, June 10). Mind over mass media. *The New York Times,* A31.

Pinker, S. (2011, September 27). A history of violence. *Edge* (edge.org).

Pinquart, M. (2015). Associations of parenting styles and dimensions with academic achievement in children and adolescents: A meta-analysis. *Educational Psychology Review*, 1–19. doi:10.1007/s10648-015-9338-y

Pipe, M.-E., Lamb, M. E., Orbach, Y., & Esplin, P. W. (2004). Recent research on children's testimony about experienced and witnessed events. *Developmental Review*, 24, 440–468.

Pipher, M. (2002). *The middle of everywhere: The world's refugees come to our town.* New York: Harcourt Brace.

Place, S. S., Todd, P. M., Penke, L., & Asendorph, J. B. (2009). The ability to judge the romantic interest of others. *Psychological Science*, 20, 22–26.

Plant, E. A., & Peruche, B. M. (2005). The consequences of race for police officers' responses to criminal suspects. *Psychological Science*, 16, 180–183.

Plassmann, H., O'Doherty, J., Shiv, B., & Rangel, A. (2008). Marketing actions can modulate neural representations of experienced pleasantness. *PNAS*, 105, 1050–1054.

Platek, S. M., & Singh, D. (2010) Optimal waist-to-hip ratios in women activate neural reward centers in men. *PLoS ONE* 5(2): e9042. doi:10.1371/journal.pone.0009042.

Plöderl, M., Wagenmakers, E., Tremblay, P., Ramsay, R., Kralovec, K., Fartacek, C., & Fartacek, R. (2013). Suicide risk and sexual orientation: A critical review. *Archives of Sexual Behavior*, 42, 715–727.

Plomin, R. (2011). Why are children in the same family so different? Nonshared environment three decades later. *International Journal of Epidemiology*, 40, 582–592.

Plomin, R., & Daniels, D. (1987). Why are children in the same family so different from one another? *Behavioral and Brain Sciences*, 10, 1–60.

Plomin, R., & DeFries, J. C. (1998, May). The genetics of cognitive abilities and disabilities. *Scientific American*, pp. 62–69.

Plomin, R., DeFries, J. C., Knopik, V. S., & Neiderhiser, J. M. (2016). Top 10 replicated findings from behavioral genetics. *Perspectives on Psychological Science*, 11, 3–23.

Plomin, R., DeFries, J. C., McClearn, G. E., & Rutter, M. (1997). *Behavioral genetics.* New York: Freeman.

Plomin, R., McClearn, G. E., Pedersen, N. L., Nesselroade, J. R., & Bergeman, C. S. (1988). Genetic influence on childhood family environment perceived retrospectively from the last half of the life span. *Developmental Psychology*, 24, 37–45.

Plomin, R., & McGuffin, P. (2003). Psychopathology in the postgenomic era. *Annual Review of Psychology*, 54, 205–228.

Plous, S., & Herzog, H. A. (2000). Poll shows researchers favor lab animal protection. *Science*, 290, 711.

Pluess, M., & Belsky, J. (2013). Vantage sensitivity: Individual differences in response to positive experiences. *Psychological Bulletin*, 139, 901–916.

Poelmans, G., Pauls, D. L., Buitelaar, J. K., & Franke, B. (2011). Integrated genomewide association study findings: Identification of a neurodevelopmental network for attention deficit hyperactivity disorder. *American Journal of Psychiatry*, 168, 365–377.

Polderman, T. J. C., Benyamin, B., de Leeuw, C., Sullivan, P. F., van Bochoven, A., Visscher, P. M., & Posthuma, D. (2015). Meta-analysis of the heritability of human traits based on fifty years of twin studies. *Nature Genetics*, 47, 702–709.

Poldrack, R. A., Halchenko, Y. O., & Hanson, S. J. (2009). Decoding the large-scale structure of brain function by classifying mental states across individuals. *Psychological Science*, 20, 1364–1372.

Polivy, J., Herman, C. P., & Coelho, J. S. (2008). Caloric restriction in the presence of attractive food cues: External cues, eating, and weight. *Physiology and Behavior*, 94, 729–733.

Pollak, S., Cicchetti, D., & Klorman, R. (1998). Stress, memory, and emotion: Developmental considerations from the study of child maltreatment. *Developmental Psychopathology*, 10, 811–828.

Polusny, M. A., & Follette, V. M. (1995). Long-term correlates of child sexual abuse: Theory and review of the empirical literature. *Applied & Preventive Psychology*, 4, 143–166.

Poon, L. W. (1987). Myths and truisms: Beyond extant analyses of speed of behavior and age. Address to the Eastern Psychological Association convention.

Pope, D., & Simonsohn, U. (2011). Round numbers as goals: Evidence from baseball, SAT takers, and the lab. *Psychological Science*, 22, 71–79.

Popenoe, D. (1993, October). *The evolution of marriage and the problem of stepfamilies: A biosocial perspective.* Paper presented at the First Annual Symposium on Stepfamilies, State College, PA.

Poropat, A. E. (2014). Other-rated personality and academic performance: Evidence and implications. *Learning and Individual Differences*, 34, 24–32.

Porter, S., & Peace, K. A. (2007). The scars of memory: A prospective, longitudinal investigation of the consistency of traumatic and positive emotional memories in adulthood. *Psychological Science*, 18, 435–441.

Porter, S., & ten Brinke, L. (2008). Reading between the lies: Identifying concealed and falsified emotions in universal facial expressions. *Psychological Science*, 19, 508–514.

Posner, M. I., & Carr, T. H. (1992). Lexical access and the brain: Anatomical constraints on cognitive models of word recognition. *American Journal of Psychology*, 105, 1–26.

Poundstone, W. (2014). *How to predict the unpredictable. The art of outsmarting almost everyone.* London: OneWorld Publications.

Powell, K. E., Thompson, P. D., Caspersen, C. J., & Kendrick, J. S. (1987). Physical activity and the incidence of coronary heart disease. *Annual Review of Public Health*, 8, 253–287.

Powell, L. H., Schahabi, L., & Thoresen, C. E. (2003). Religion and spirituality: Linkages to physical health. *American Psychologist*, 58, 36–52.

Powell, R., Digdon, N. A., Harris, B., & Smithson, C. (2014). Correcting the record on Watson, Rayner and Little Albert: Albert Barger as "Psychology's Lost Boy." *American Psychologist*, 69, 600–611.

Powell, R. A., & Boer, D. P. (1994). Did Freud mislead patients to confabulate memories of abuse? *Psychological Reports*, 74, 1283–1298.

Prentice, D. A., & Miller, D. T. (1993). Pluralistic ignorance and alcohol use on campus: Some consequences of misperceiving the social norm. *Journal of Personality and Social Psychology*, 64, 243–256.

Prince Charles. (2000). BBC Reith Lecture.

Prioleau, L., Murdock, M., & Brody, N. (1983). An analysis of psychotherapy versus placebo studies. *The Behavioral and Brain Sciences*, 6, 275–310.

Pronin, E. (2007). Perception and misperception of bias in human judgment. *Trends in Cognitive Sciences*, 11, 37–43.

Pronin, E. (2013). When the mind races: Effects of thought speed on feeling and action. *Current Directions in Psychological Science*, 22, 283–288.

Pronin, E., Berger, J., & Molouki, S. (2007). Alone in a crowd of sheep: Asymmetric perceptions of conformity and their roots in an introspection illusion. *Journal of Personality and Social Psychology*, 92, 585–595.

Pronin, E., & Ross, L. (2006). Temporal differences in trait self-ascription: When the self is seen as another. *Journal of Personality and Social Psychology*, 90, 197–209.

Prot, S., Gentile, D., Anderson, C. A., Suzuli, K., Swing, E., Lim, K. M., . . . Lam, B. C. P. (2014). Long-term relations among prosocial-media use, empathy, and prosocial behavior. *Psychological Science*, 25, 358–368.

Protzko, J., Aronson, J., & Blair, C. (2013). How to make a young child smarter: Evidence from the database of raising intelligence. *Perspectives on Psychological Science*, 8, 25–40.

Provine, R. R. (2011). Emotional tears and NGF: A biographical appreciation and research beginning. *Archives Italiennes de Biologie*, 149, 271–276.

Provine, R. R. (2012). *Curious behavior: Yawning, laughing, hiccupping, and beyond.* Cambridge, MA: Harvard University Press.

Provine, R. R., Krosnowski, K. A., & Brocato, N. W. (2009). Tearing: Breakthrough in human emotional signaling. *Evolutionary Psychology*, 7, 52–56.

Pryor, J. H., Hurtado, S., DeAngelo, L., Blake, L. P., & Tran, S. (2011). *The American freshman: national norms fall 2010.* Los Angeles: Higher Education Research Institute, UCLA.

Pryor, J. H., Hurtado, S., Saenz, V. B., Korn, J. S., Santos, J. L., & Korn, W. S. (2006). *The American freshman: National norms for fall 2006.* Los Angeles: Higher Education Research Institute, UCLA.

Pryor, J. H., Hurtado, S., Saenz, V. B., Lindholm, J. A., Korn, W. S., & Mahoney, K. M. (2005). *The American freshman: National norms for fall 2005.* Los Angeles: Higher Education Research Institute, UCLA.

Pryor, J. H., Hurtado, S., Sharkness, J., & Korn, W. S. (2007). *The American freshman: National norms for fall 2007.* Los Angeles: UCLA Higher Education Research Institute.

Psychologist. (2003). Who's the greatest? *The Psychologist*, 16, 170–175.

Putnam, F. W. (1991). Recent research on multiple personality disorder. *Psychiatric Clinics of North America*, 14, 489–502.

Pyszczynski, T. A., Motyl, M., Vail, K. E., III, Hirschberger, G., Arndt, J., & Kesebir, P. (2012). Drawing attention to global climate change decreases support for war. *Peace and Conflict: Journal of Peace Psychology*, 18, 354–368.

Pyszczynski, T. A., Rothschild, Z., & Abdollahi, A. (2008). Terrorism, violence, and hope for peace: A terror management perspective. *Current Directions in Psychological Science* 17, 318–322.

Pyszczynski, T. A., Solomon, S., & Greenberg, J. (2002). *In the wake of 9/11: The psychology of terror.* Washington, DC: American Psychological Association.

Qin, H.-F., & Piao, T.-J. (2011). Dispositional optimism and life satisfaction of Chinese and Japanese college students: Examining the mediating effects of affects and coping efficacy. *Chinese Journal of Clinical Psychology*, 19, 259–261.

Qirko, H. N. (2004) "Fictive kin" and suicide terrorism. *Science*, 304, 49–50.

Quinn, P. C., Bhatt, R. S., Brush, D., Grimes, A., & Sharpnack, H. (2002). Development of form similarity as a Gestalt grouping principle in infancy. *Psychological Science*, 13, 320–328.

Quoidbach, J., Gilbert, D. T., & Wilson, T. D. (2013). The end of history illusion. *Science*, 339, 96–98.

Raby, K. L., Cicchetti, D., Carlson, E. A., Cutuli, J. J., Englund, M. M., & Egeland, B. (2012). Genetic and care-giving-based contributions to infant attachment: Unique associations with distress reactivity and attachment security. *Psychological Science, 23,* 1016–1023.

Raby, K. L., Roisman, G. I., Fraley, R. C., & Simpson, J. A. (2014). The enduring predictive significance of early maternal sensitivity: Social and academic competence through age 32 years. *Child Development, 86,* 695–708.

Racsmány, M., Conway, M. A., & Demeter, G. (2010). Consolidation of episodic memories during sleep: Long-term effects of retrieval practice. *Psychological Science, 21,* 80–85.

Radford, B. (2010, March 5). Missing persons and abductions reveal psychics' failures. *DiscoveryNews* (news .discovery.com).

Radua, J., Schmidt, A., Borgwardt, S., Heinz, A., Schlagenhauf, F., McGuire, P., & Fusar-Poli, P. (2015). Ventral striatal activation during reward processing in psychosis: A neurofunctional meta-analysis. *JAMA Psychiatry, 72*(12), 1243–1251.

Rahman, Q. (2015, July 24). "Gay genes": Science is on the right track, we're born this way. Let's deal with it. *The Guardian* (theguardian.com).

Rahman, Q., & Koerting, J. (2008). Sexual orientation-related differences in allocentric spatial memory tasks. *Hippocampus, 18,* 55–63.

Rahman, Q., & Wilson, G. D. (2003). Born gay? The psychobiology of human sexual orientation. *Personality and Individual Differences, 34,* 1337–1382.

Rahman, Q., Wilson, G. D., & Abrahams, S. (2004). Biosocial factors, sexual orientation and neurocognitive functioning. *Psychoneuroendocrinology, 29,* 867–881.

Raila, H., Scholl, B. J., & Gruber, J. (2015). Seeing the world through rose-colored glasses: People who are happy and satisfied with life preferentially attend to positive stimuli. *Emotion, 15,* 449–462.

Raine, A. (1999). Murderous minds: Can we see the mark of Cain? *Cerebrum: The Dana Forum on Brain Science 1*(1), 15–29.

Raine, A. (2005). The interaction of biological and social measures in the explanation of antisocial and violent behavior. In D. M. Stoff & E. J. Susman (Eds.) *Developmental psychobiology of aggression* (pp. 13–42). New York: Cambridge University Press.

Raine, A. (2013). *The anatomy of violence: The biological roots of crime.* New York: Pantheon.

Raine, A., Lencz, T., Bihrle, S., LaCasse, L., & Colletti, P. (2000). Reduced prefrontal gray matter volume and reduced autonomic activity in antisocial personality disorder. *Archives of General Psychiatry, 57,* 119–127.

Rainie, L., Purcell, K., Goulet, L. S., & Hampton, K. H. (2011, June 16). *Social networking sites and our lives.* Pew Research Center (pewresearch.org).

Rainville, P., Duncan, G. H., Price, D. D., Carrier, B., & Bushnell, M. C. (1997). Pain affect encoded in human anterior cingulate but not somatosensory cortex. *Science, 277,* 968–971.

Rajendran, G., & Mitchell, P. (2007). Cognitive theories of autism. *Developmental Review, 27,* 224–260.

Ramachandran, V. S., & Blakeslee, S. (1998). *Phantoms in the brain: Probing the mysteries of the human mind.* New York: Morrow.

Ramos, M. R., Cassidy, C., Reicher, S., & Haslam, S. A. (2012). A longitudinal investigation of the rejection-identification hypothesis. *British Journal of Social Psychology, 51,* 642–660.

Randall, D. K. (2012, September 22). Rethinking sleep. *The New York Times* (nytimes.com).

Randi, J. (1999, February 4). 2000 club mailing list e-mail letter.

Randler, C., & Bausback, V. (2010). Morningness-eveningness in women around the transition through menopause and its relationship with climacteric complaints. *Biological Rhythm Research, 41,* 415–431.

Rapoport, J. L. (1989, March). The biology of obsessions and compulsions. *Scientific American,* pp. 83–89.

Räsänen, S., Pakaslahti, A., Syvalahti, E., Jones, P. B., & Isohanni, M. (2000). Sex differences in schizophrenia: A review. *Nordic Journal of Psychiatry, 54,* 37–45.

Rasmussen, H. N., Scheier, M. F., & Greenhouse, J. B. (2009). Optimism and physical health: A meta-analytic review. *Annals of Behavioral Medicine, 37,* 239–256.

Rasmussen, K. (2016). Entitled vengeance: A meta-analysis relating narcissism to provoked aggression. *Aggressive Behavior. 42*(4), 362–379. doi:10.1002 /ab.21632

Rattan, A., Savani, K., Naidu, N. V. R., & Dweck, C. S. (2012). Can everyone become highly intelligent? Cultural differences in and societal consequences of beliefs about the universal potential for intelligence. *Journal of Personality and Social Psychology, 103,* 787–803.

Ray, J., & Kafka, S. (2014, May 6). *Life in college matters for life after college.* Gallup Poll (gallup.com).

Raynor, H. A., & Epstein, L. H. (2001). Dietary variety, energy regulation, and obesity. *Psychological Bulletin, 127,* 325–341.

Reason, J. (1987). The Chernobyl errors. *Bulletin of the British Psychological Society, 40,* 201–206.

Reason, J., & Mycielska, K. (1982). *Absent-minded? The psychology of mental lapses and everyday errors.* Englewood Cliffs, NJ: Prentice-Hall.

Rebar, A. L., Stanton, R., Geard, D., Short, C., Duncan, M. J., & Vandelanotte, C. (2015). A meta-meta-analysis of the effect of physical activity on depression and anxiety in non-clinical adult populations. *Health Psychology Review, 9,* 366–378.

Redden, J. P., Mann, T., Vickers, Z., Mykerezi, E., Reicks, M., & Elsbernd, E. (2015). Serving first in isolation increases vegetable intake among elementary schoolchildren. *PLoS ONE, 10*(4), e0121283. doi:10.1371/ journal.pone.0121283

Redick, T. S., Shipstead, Z., Harrison, T. L., Hicks, K. L., Fried, D.E., Hambrick, D. Z., . . . Engle, R. W. (2013). No evidence of intelligence improvement after working memory training: A randomized, placebo-controlled study. *Journal of Experimental Psychology: General, 142,* 359–379.

Reed, P. (2000). Serial position effects in recognition memory for odors. *Journal of Experimental Psychology: Learning, Memory, and Cognition, 26,* 411–422.

Reeves, A., McKee, M., & Stuckler, D. (2014). Economic suicides in the Great Recession in Europe and North America. *British Journal of Psychiatry, 205,* 246–247.

Reichenberg, A., & Harvey, P. D. (2007). Neuropsychological impairments in schizophrenia: Integration of performance-based and brain imaging findings. *Psychological Bulletin, 133,* 833–858.

Reichert, R. A., Robb, M. B., Fender, J. G., & Wartella, E. (2010). Word learning from baby videos. *Archives of Pediatrics & Adolescent Medicine, 164,* 432–437.

Reichow, B. (2012). Overview of meta-analyses on early intensive behavioral intervention for young children with autism spectrum disorders. *Journal of Autism and Developmental Disorders, 42,* 512–520.

Reifman, A., & Cleveland, H. H. (2007). *Shared environment: A quantitative review.* Paper presented to the

Society for Research in Child Development, Boston, MA.

Reifman, A. S., Larrick, R. P., & Fein, S. (1991). Temper and temperature on the diamond: The heat-aggression relationship in Major League Baseball. *Personality and Social Psychology Bulletin, 17,* 580–585.

Reimann, F., Cox, J. J., Belfer, I., Diatchenko, L., Zaykin, D. V., McHale, D. P., & Woods, C. G. (2010). Pain perception is altered by a nucleotide polymorphism in SCN9A. *PNAS, 107,* 5148–5153.

Reiner, W. G., & Gearhart, J. P. (2004). Discordant sexual identity in some genetic males with cloacal exstrophy assigned to female sex at birth. *New England Journal of Medicine, 350,* 333–341.

Reis, H. T., & Aron, A. (2008). Love: What is it, why does it matter, and how does it operate? *Perspectives on Psychological Science, 3,* 80–86.

Reis, S. M. (2001). Toward a theory of creativity in diverse creative women. In M. Bloom & T. Gullotta (Eds.), *Promoting creativity across the life span* (pp. 231–276). Washington, DC: CWLA Press.

Reisenzein, R. (1983). The Schachter theory of emotion: Two decades later. *Psychological Bulletin, 94,* 239–264.

Reiser, M. (1982). *Police psychology.* Los Angeles: LEHI.

Reitz, A. K., Motti-Stefanidi, F., & Asendorpf, J. B. (2016, June). Me, us, and them: Testing sociometer theory in a socially diverse real-life context. *Journal of Personality and Social Psychology. 110*(6), 908–920. http:// dx.doi.org/10.1037/pspp0000078

Reivich, K., Gillham, J. E., Chaplin, T. M., & Seligman, M. E. P. (2013). From helplessness to optimism: The role of resilience in treating and preventing depression in youth. In S. Goldstein & R. B. Brooks (Eds.), *Handbook of resilience in children* (pp. 201–214). New York: Springer Science+Business Media.

Rekker, R., Keijsers, L., Branje, S., & Meeus, W. (2015). Political attitudes in adolescence and emerging adulthood: Developmental changes in mean level, polarization, rank-order stability, and correlates. *Journal of Adolescence, 41,* 136–147.

Remick, A. K., Polivy, J., & Pliner, P. (2009). Internal and external moderators of the effect of variety on food intake. *Psychological Bulletin, 135,* 434–451.

Remington, A., Swettenham, J., Campbell, R., & Coleman, M. (2009). Selective attention and perceptual load in autism spectrum disorder. *Psychological Science, 20,* 1388–1393.

Remley, A. (1988, October). From obedience to independence. *Psychology Today,* pp. 56–59.

Ren, D., Tan, K., Arriaga, X. B., & Chan, K. Q. (2015). Sweet love: The effects of sweet taste experience on romantic perceptions. *Journal of Social and Personal Relationships.* Advance online publication. doi:10.1177/0265407514554512

Renner, M. J., & Renner, C. H. (1993). Expert and novice intuitive judgments about animal behavior. *Bulletin of the Psychonomic Society, 31,* 551–552.

Renner, M. J., & Rosenzweig, M. R. (1987). *Enriched and impoverished environments: Effects on brain and behavior.* New York: Springer-Verlag.

Renninger, K. A., & Granott, N. (2005). The process of scaffolding in learning and development. *New Ideas in Psychology, 23*(3), 111–114.

Rentfrow, P. J., & Gosling, S. D. (2003). The Do Re Mi's of everyday life: The structure and personality correlates of music preferences. *Journal of Personality and Social Psychology, 84,* 1236–1256.

Rentfrow, P. J., & Gosling, S. D. (2006). Message in a ballad: The role of music preferences in interpersonal perception. *Psychological Science, 17,* 236–242.

Rescorla, R. A., & Wagner, A. R. (1972). A theory of Pavlovian conditioning: Variations in the effectiveness of reinforcement and nonreinforcement. In A. H. Black & W. F. Perokasy (Eds.), Classical conditioning II: Current theory (pp. 64–99). New York: Appleton-Century-Crofts.

Resnick, M. D., Bearman, P. S., Blum, R. W., Bauman, K. E., Harris, K. M., Jones, J., . . . Udry, J. R. (1997). Protecting adolescents from harm: Findings from the National Longitudinal Study on Adolescent Health. Journal of the American Medical Association, 278, 823–832.

Resnick, S. M. (1992). Positron emission tomography in psychiatric illness. Current Directions in Psychological Science, 1, 92–98.

Reuters. (2000, July 5). Many teens regret decision to have sex (National Campaign to Prevent Teen Pregnancy survey). The Washington Post (washingtonpost.com).

Reuters. (2015, November 25). Most important problem facing the US today. Reuters Polling (polling. reuters.com/#!poll/SC8/type/smallest/dates/20150901-20151125/collapsed/true/spotlight/1).

Reyna, V. F., Chick, C. F., Corbin, J. C., & Hsia, A. N. (2013). Developmental reversals in risky decision making: Intelligence agents show larger decision biases than college students. Psychological Science, 25, 76–84.

Reyna, V. F., & Farley, F. (2006). Risk and rationality in adolescent decision making: Implications for theory, practice, and public policy. Psychological Science in the Public Interest, 7(1), 1–44.

Rhoades, G. K., Stanley, S. M., & Markman, H. J. (2009). The pre-engagement cohabitation effect: A replication and extension of previous findings. Journal of Family Psychology, 23, 107–111.

Rhodes, M. G., & Anastasi, J. S. (2012). The own-age bias in face recognition: A meta-analytic and theoretical review. Psychological Bulletin, 138, 146–174.

Rhodes, S. R. (1983). Age-related differences in work attitudes and behavior: A review and conceptual analysis. Psychological Bulletin, 93, 328–367.

Rice, E., Gibbs, J., Winetrobe, H. Rhoades, H., Plant, A., Montoya, J., & Kordic, T. (2014). Sexting and sexual behavior among middle school students. Pediatrics, 134, e21–e28.

Rice, M. E., & Grusec, J. E. (1975). Saying and doing: Effects on observer performance. Journal of Personality and Social Psychology, 32, 584–593.

Richards, D. (2011). Prevalence and clinical course of depression: A review. Clinical Psychology Review, 31, 1117–1125.

Richardson, M., Abraham, C., & Bond, R. (2012). Psychological correlates of university students' academic performance: A systematic review and meta-analysis. Psychological Bulletin, 138, 353–387.

Richeson, J. A., & Shelton, J. N. (2007). Negotiating interracial interactions. Current Directions in Psychological Science, 16, 316–320.

Rickard, I. J., Frankenhuis, W. E., & Nettle, D. (2014). Why are childhood family factors associated with timing of maturation? A role for internal prediction. Perspectives on Psychological Science, 9, 3–15.

Rieff, P. (1979). Freud: The mind of a moralist (3rd ed.). Chicago: University of Chicago Press.

Riemer, H., Shavitt, S., Koo, M., & Markus, H. R. (2014). Preferences don't have to be personal: Expanding attitude theorizing with a cross-cultural perspective. Psychological Review, 121, 619–648.

Rietveld, C. A., Medland, S. E., Derringer, J., Yang, J., Esko, T., Martin, N. W., . . . Koellinger, P. D. (2013). GWAS of 126,559 individuals identifies genetic variants associated with educational attainment. Science, 340, 1467–1471.

Riffkin, R. (2014, July 9). Obesity linked to lower social well-being. Gallup-Healthways Well-Being Index (gallup.com).

Riis, J., Loewenstein, G., Baron, J., Jepson, C., Fagerlin, A., & Ubel, P. A. (2005). Ignorance of hedonic adaptation to hemodialysis: A study using ecological momentary assessment. Journal of Experimental Psychology: General, 134, 3–9.

Rindermann, H., & Ceci, S. J. (2009). Educational policy and country outcomes in international cognitive competence studies. Perspectives on Psychological Science, 4, 551–577.

Riordan, M. (2013, March 19). Tobacco warning labels: Evidence of effectiveness. Washington, DC: The Campaign for Tobacco-Free Kids (tobaccofreekids.org).

Ritchie, S. J., Dickie, D. A., Cox, S. R., Hernandez, M. del C. V., Corley, J., Royle, N. A., . . . Deary, I. J. (2015). Brain volumetric changes and cognitive ageing during the eighth decade of life. Human Brain Mapping, 36, 4910–4925.

Ritchie, S. J., Wiseman, R., & French, C. C. (2012). Failing the future: Three unsuccessful attempts to replicate Bem's "retroactive facilitation of recall" effect. PLOS ONE, 7(3), e33r23. doi:10.1371/journal.pone.0033423

Ritter, S. M., Damian, R. I., Simonton, D. K., van Baaren, R. B., Strick, M., Derks, J., & Dijksterhuis, A. (2012). Diversifying experiences enhance cognitive flexibility. Journal of Experimental Social Psychology, 48, 961–964.

Rizzolatti, G., Fadiga, L., Fogassi, L., & Gallese, V. (2002). From mirror neurons to imitation: Facts and speculations. In A. N. Meltzoff & W. Prinz (Eds.), The imitative mind: Development, evolution, and brain bases. Cambridge, UK: Cambridge University Press.

Rizzolatti, G., Fogassi, L., & Gallese, V. (2006, November). Mirrors in the mind. Scientific American, pp. 54–61.

Roberti, J. W., Storch, E. A., & Bravata, E. A. (2004). Sensation seeking, exposure to psychosocial stressors, and body modifications in a college population. Personality and Individual Differences, 37, 1167–1177.

Roberts, B. W., Caspi, A., & Moffitt, T. E. (2001). The kids are alright: Growth and stability in personality development from adolescence to adulthood. Journal of Personality and Social Psychology, 81, 670–683.

Roberts, B. W., Caspi, A., & Moffitt, T. E. (2003). Work experiences and personality development in young adulthood. Journal of Personality and Social Psychology, 84, 582–593.

Roberts, B. W., Walton, K. E., & Viechtbauer, W. (2006). Patterns of mean-level change in personality traits across the life course: A meta-analysis of longitudinal studies. Psychological Bulletin, 132, 1–25.

Roberts, L. (1988). Beyond Noah's ark: What do we need to know? Science, 242, 1247.

Roberts, T.-A. (1991). Determinants of gender differences in responsiveness to others' evaluations. Dissertation Abstracts International, 51(8–B).

Robins, R. W., & Trzesniewski, K. H. (2005). Self-esteem development across the lifespan. Current Directions in Psychological Science, 14(3), 158–162.

Robinson, F. P. (1970). Effective study. New York: Harper & Row.

Robinson, J. P., & Martin, S. (2008). What do happy people do? Social Indicators Research, 89, 565–571.

Robinson, J. P., & Martin, S. (2009). Changes in American daily life: 1965–2005. Social Indicators Research, 93, 47–56.

Robinson, O. J., Cools, R., Carlisi, C. O., & Drevets, W. C. (2012). Ventral striatum response during reward and punishment reversal learning in unmedicated major depressive disorder. American Journal of Psychiatry, 169, 152–159.

Robinson, T. N., Borzekowski, D. L. G., Matheson, D. M., & Kraemer, H. C. (2007). Effects of fast food branding on young children's taste preferences. Archives of Pediatrics and Adolescent Medicine, 161, 792–797.

Robinson, V. M. (1983). Humor and health. In P. E. McGhee & J. H. Goldstein (Eds.), Handbook of humor research: Vol. 2. Applied studies (pp. 109–128). New York: Springer-Verlag.

Robles, T. F. (2015). Marital quality and health: Implications for marriage in the 21st century. Current Directions in Psychological Science, 23, 427–432.

Robles, T. F., Slatcher, R. B., Trombello, J. M., & McGinn, M. M. (2014). Marital quality and health: A meta-analytic review. Psychological Bulletin, 140, 140–187.

Rochat, F. (1993). How did they resist authority? Protecting refugees in Le Chambon during World War II. Paper presented at the American Psychological Association convention.

Rock, I., & Palmer, S. (1990, December). The legacy of Gestalt psychology. Scientific American, pp. 84–90.

Rodin, J. (1986). Aging and health: Effects of the sense of control. Science, 233, 1271–1276.

Rodriguez, T. (2015, June 11). Teenagers who don't get enough sleep at higher risk for mental health problems. Scientific American (scientificamerican.com).

Roediger, H. L., III. (2013). Applying cognitive psychology to education: Translational educational science. Psychological Science in the Public Interest, 14, 1–3.

Roediger, H. L., III, & Finn, B. (2010, March/April). The pluses of getting it wrong. Scientific American Mind, pp. 39–41.

Roediger, H. L., III, & Karpicke, J. D. (2006). Test-enhanced learning: Taking memory tests improves long-term retention. Psychological Science, 17, 249–255.

Roediger, H. L., III, & McDermott, K. B. (1995). Creating false memories: Remembering words not presented in lists. Journal of Experimental Psychology: Learning, Memory, and Cognition, 21, 803–814.

Roediger, H. L., III, Wheeler, M. A., & Rajaram, S. (1993). Remembering, knowing, and reconstructing the past. In D. L. Medin (Ed.), The psychology of learning and motivation: Advances in research and theory (Vol. 30, pp. 97–134). Orlando, FL: Academic Press.

Roehling, P. V., Roehling, M. V., & Moen, P. (2001). The relationship between worklife policies and practices and employee loyalty: A life course perspective. Journal of Family and Economic Issues, 22, 141–170.

Roelofs, T. (2010, September 22). Somali refugee takes oath of U.S. citizenship year after his brother. The Grand Rapids Press. Retrieved from http://www.mlive.com/news/grand-rapids/index.ssf/2010/09/somali_refugee_takes_oath_of_u.html

Roenneberg, T., Kuehnle, T., Pramstaller, P. P., Ricken, J., Havel, M., Guth, A., & Merrow, M. (2004). A marker for the end of adolescence. Current Biology, 14, R1038–R1039.

Roepke, A. M. (2015). Psychosocial interventions and posttraumatic growth: A meta-analysis. Journal of Consulting and Clinical Psychology, 83(1), 129.

Roepke, A. M., & Seligman, M. E. P. (2015). Doors opening: A mechanism for growth after adversity. Journal of Positive Psychology, 10, 107–115.

Roese, N. J., & Summerville, A. (2005). What we regret most . . . and why. Personality and Social Psychology Bulletin, 31, 1273–1285.

Roese, N. J., & Vohs, K. D. (2012). Hindsight bias. Perspectives on Psychological Science, 7, 411–426.

Roesser, R. (1998). What you should know about hearing conservation. Better Hearing Institute (betterhearing.org).

Rogeberg, O. (2013). Correlations between cannabis use and IQ change in the Dunedin cohort are consistent with confounding from socioeconomic status. PNAS, 110, 4251–4254.

Rogers, C. R. (1961). *On becoming a person: A therapist's view of psychotherapy.* Boston: Houghton Mifflin.

Rogers, C. R. (1980). *A way of being.* Boston: Houghton Mifflin.

Rohan, M. J., & Zanna, M. P. (1996). Value transmission in families. In C. Seligman, J. M. Olson, & M. P. Zanna (Eds.), *The psychology of values: The Ontario Symposium* (Vol. 8, pp. 253–276). Mahwah, NJ: Erlbaum.

Rohner, R. P. (1986). *The warmth dimension: Foundations of parental acceptance-rejection theory.* Newbury Park, CA: Sage.

Rohrer, J. M., Egloff, B., & Schmukle, S. C. (2015). Examining the effects of birth order on personality. *PNAS, 112*(6), 14224–14229. doi:10.1073/pnas.1506451112

Roiser, J. P., Cook, L. J., Cooper, J. D., Rubinsztein, D. C., & Sahakian, B. J. (2005). Association of a functional polymorphism in the serotonin transporter gene with abnormal emotional processing in Ecstasy users. *American Journal of Psychiatry, 162,* 609–612.

Romens, S. E., McDonald, J., Svaren, J., & Pollak, S. D. (2015). Associations between early life stress and gene methylation in children. *Child Development, 86,* 303–309.

Ronay, R., & von Hippel, W. (2010). The presence of an attractive woman elevates testosterone and physical risk taking in young men. *Social Psychology and Personality Science, 1,* 57–64.

Root, T. L., Thornton, L. M., Lindroos, A. K., Stunkard, A. J., Lichtenstein, P., Pedersen, N. L., . . . Bulik, C. M. (2010). Shared and unique genetic and environmental influences on binge eating and night eating: A Swedish twin study. *Eating Behaviors, 11,* 92–98.

Roque, L., Verissimo, M., Oliveira, T. F., & Oliveira, R. F. (2012). Attachment security and HPA axis reactivity to positive and challenging emotional situations in child–mother dyads in naturalistic settings. *Developmental Psychobiology, 54,* 401–411.

Rosch, E. (1978). Principles of categorization. In E. Rosch & B. L. Lloyd (Eds.), *Cognition and categorization* (pp. 27–48). Hillsdale, NJ: Erlbaum.

Rose, A. J., & Rudolph, K. D. (2006). A review of sex differences in peer relationship processes: Potential trade-offs for the emotional and behavioral development of girls and boys. *Psychological Bulletin, 132,* 98–131.

Rose, J. S., Chassin, L., Presson, C. C., & Sherman, S. J. (1999). Peer influences on adolescent cigarette smoking: A prospective sibling analysis. *Merrill-Palmer Quarterly, 45,* 62–84.

Rose, R. J., Viken, R. J., Dick, D. M., Bates, J. E., Pulkkinen, L., & Kaprio, J. (2003). It does take a village: Nonfamiliar environments and children's behavior. *Psychological Science, 14,* 273–277.

Roselli, C. E., Larkin, K., Schrunk, J. M., & Stormshak, F. (2004). Sexual partner preference, hypothalamic morphology and aromatase in rams. *Physiology and Behavior, 83,* 233–245.

Roselli, C. E., Resko, J. A., & Stormshak, F. (2002). Hormonal influences on sexual partner preference in rams. *Archives of Sexual Behavior, 31,* 43–49.

Rosenbaum, M. (1986). The repulsion hypothesis: On the nondevelopment of relationships. *Journal of Personality and Social Psychology, 51,* 1156–1166.

Rosenberg, E. L., Zanesco, A. P., King, B. G., Aichele, S. R., Jacobs, R. L., Bridwell, D. A., . . . Saron, C. D. (2015). Intensive meditation training influences emotional responses to suffering. *Emotion, 15,* 775–790.

Rosenberg, N. A., Pritchard, J. K., Weber, J. L., Cann, H. M., Kidd, K. K., Zhivotosky, L. A., & Feldman, M. W. (2002). Genetic structure of human populations. *Science, 298,* 2381–2385.

Rosenblum, L. D. (2013, January). A confederacy of senses. *Scientific American,* pp. 73–78.

Rosenfeld, M. J. (2013, August 26). Personal communication.

Rosenfeld, M. J. (2014). Couple longevity in the era of same-sex marriage in the United States. *Journal of Marriage and Family, 76,* 905–911.

Rosenfeld, M. J., & Thomas, R. J. (2012). Searching for a mate: The rise of the Internet as a social intermediary. *American Sociological Review, 77,* 523–547.

Rosenhan, D. L. (1973). On being sane in insane places. *Science, 179,* 250–258.

Rosenthal, R., Hall, J. A., Archer, D., DiMatteo, M. R., & Rogers, P. L. (1979). The PONS test: Measuring sensitivity to nonverbal cues. In S. Weitz (Ed.), *Nonverbal communication* (2nd ed., pp. 357–370). New York: Oxford University Press.

Rosenzweig, M. R. (1984). Experience, memory, and the brain. *American Psychologist, 39,* 365–376.

Roseth, C. J., Johnson, D. W., & Johnson, R. T. (2008). Promoting early adolescents' achievement and peer relationships: The effects of cooperative, competitive, and individualistic goal structures. *Psychological Bulletin, 134,* 223–246.

Rosin, H. (2010, July, August). The end of men. *The Atlantic* (theatlantic.com).

Rossi, P. J. (1968). Adaptation and negative aftereffect to lateral optical displacement in newly hatched chicks. *Science, 160,* 430–432.

Rotge, J.-Y., Lemogne, C., Hinfray, S., Huguet, P., Grynszpan, O., Tartour, E., . . . Fossati, P. (2015). A meta-analysis of the anterior cingulate contribution to social pain. *Social Cognitive and Affective Neuroscience, 10,* 19–27.

Rothbart, M., Fulero, S., Jensen, C., Howard, J., & Birrell, P. (1978). From individual to group impressions: Availability heuristics in stereotype formation. *Journal of Experimental Social Psychology, 14,* 237–255.

Rothbart, M. K. (2007). Temperament, development, and personality. *Current Directions in Psychological Science, 16,* 207–212.

Rothman, A. J., & Salovey, P. (1997). Shaping perceptions to motivate healthy behavior: The role of message framing. *Psychological Bulletin, 121,* 3–19.

Rottensteiner, M., Leskinen, T., Niskanen, E., Aaltonen, S., Mutikainen, S., Wikgren, J., . . . Kujala, U. M. (2015). Physical activity, fitness, glucose homeostasis, and brain morphology in twins. *Medicine and Science in Sports and Exercise, 47,* 509–518.

Rovee-Collier, C. (1989). The joy of kicking: Memories, motives, and mobiles. In P. R. Solomon, G. R. Goethals, C. M. Kelley, & B. R. Stephens (Eds.), *Memory: Interdisciplinary approaches* (pp. 151–179). New York: Springer-Verlag.

Rovee-Collier, C. (1997). Dissociations in infant memory: Rethinking the development of implicit and explicit memory. *Psychological Review, 104,* 467–498.

Rovee-Collier, C. (1999). The development of infant memory. *Current Directions in Psychological Science, 8,* 80–85.

Rowe, D. C. (1990). As the twig is bent? The myth of child-rearing influences on personality development. *Journal of Counseling and Development, 68,* 606–611.

Rowe, D. C., Vazsonyi, A. T., & Flannery, D. J. (1994). No more than skin deep: Ethnic and racial similarity in developmental process. *Psychological Review, 101*(3), 396.

Rowland, C. A. (2014). The effect of testing versus restudy on retention: A meta-analytic review of the testing effect. *Psychological Bulletin, 140,* 1432–1463.

Rozin, P., Dow, S., Mosovitch, M., & Rajaram, S. (1998). What causes humans to begin and end a meal? A role for memory for what has been eaten, as evidenced by a study of multiple meal eating in amnesic patients. *Psychological Science, 9,* 392–396.

Ruau, D., Liu, L. Y., Clark, J. D., Angst, M. S., & Butte, A. J. (2012). Sex differences in reported pain across 11,000 patients captured in electronic medical records. *Journal of Pain, 13,* 228–234.

Ruback, R. B., Carr, T. S., & Hopper, C. H. (1986). Perceived control in prison: Its relation to reported crowding, stress, and symptoms. *Journal of Applied Social Psychology, 16,* 375–386.

Rubenstein, J. S., Meyer, D. E., & Evans, J. E. (2001). Executive control of cognitive processes in task switching. *Journal of Experimental Psychology: Human Perception and Performance, 27,* 763–797.

Rubenstein, L. M., Freed, R. D., Shapero, B. G., Fauber, R. L., & Alloy, L. B. (2016, June). Cognitive attributions in depression: Bridging the gap between research and clinical practice. *Journal of Psychotherapy Integration, 26,* 103–115. http://dx.doi.org/10.1037/int0000030

Rubin, D. C., Rahhal, T. A., & Poon, L. W. (1998). Things learned in early adulthood are remembered best. *Memory and Cognition, 26,* 3–19.

Rubin, L. B. (1985). *Just friends: The role of friendship in our lives.* New York: Harper & Row.

Rubin, Z. (1970). Measurement of romantic love. *Journal of Personality and Social Psychology, 16,* 265–273.

Rubio-Fernández, P., & Geurts, B. (2013). How to pass the false-belief task before your fourth birthday. *Psychological Science, 24,* 27–33.

Ruchlis, H. (1990). *Clear thinking: A practical introduction.* Buffalo, NY: Prometheus Books.

Rueckert, L., Doan, T., & Branch, B. (2010). *Emotion and relationship effects on gender differences in empathy.* Presented at the annual meeting of the Association for Psychological Science, Boston, MA, May, 2010.

Ruffin, C. L. (1993). Stress and health—little hassles vs. major life events. *Australian Psychologist, 28,* 201–208.

Rule, B. G., & Ferguson, T. J. (1986). The effects of media violence on attitudes, emotions, and cognitions. *Journal of Social Issues, 42*(3), 29–50.

Rule, N. O., Ambady, N., & Hallett, K. C. (2009). Female sexual orientation is perceived accurately, rapidly, and automatically from the face and its features. *Journal of Experimental Social Psychology, 45,* 1245–1251.

Rumbaugh, D. M. (1977). *Language learning by a chimpanzee: The Lana project.* New York: Academic Press.

Rumbaugh, D. M., & Washburn, D. A. (2003). *Intelligence of apes and other rational beings.* New Haven, CT: Yale University Press.

Rushton, J. P. (1975). Generosity in children: Immediate and long-term effects of modeling, preaching, and moral judgment. *Journal of Personality and Social Psychology, 31,* 459–466.

Rutledge, R. B., Skandali, N., Dayan, P., & Dolan, R. J. (2014). A computational and neural model of momentary subjective well-being. *PNAS, 111,* 12252–12257.

Ryan, C., Huebner, D., Diaz, R. M., & Sanchez, J. (2009). Family rejection as a predictor of negative health outcomes in White and Latino lesbian, gay, and bisexual young adults. *Pediatrics, 123,* 346–352.

Ryan, R. M., & Deci, E. L. (2004). Avoiding death or engaging life as accounts of meaning and culture: Comment on Pyszczynski et al. (2004). *Psychological Bulletin, 130,* 473–477.

Rydell, R. J., Rydell, M. T., & Boucher, K. L. (2010). The effect of negative performance stereotypes on learning. *Journal of Personality and Social Psychology, 99,* 883–896.

Saad, L. (2002, November 21). *Most smokers wish they could quit.* Gallup (gallup.com).

Saad, L. (2015, July 13). *Nearly half of smartphone users can't imagine life without it.* Gallup (gallup.com).

Sabbagh, M. A., Xu, F., Carlson, S. M., Moses, L. J., & Lee, K. (2006). The development of executive functioning and theory of mind: A comparison of Chinese and U.S. preschoolers. *Psychological Science, 17,* 74–81.

Sabini, J. (1986). Stanley Milgram (1933–1984). *American Psychologist, 41,* 1378–1379.

Sachdev, P., & Sachdev, J. (1997). Sixty years of psychosurgery: Its present status and its future. *Australian and New Zealand Journal of Psychiatry, 31,* 457–464.

Sachs, A. (2007, August 27). A memoir of schizophrenia. *Time* (time.com).

Sachs, J. (2012). Introduction. In J. Helliwell, R. Layard, & J. Sachs (Eds.), *World happiness report.* New York: The Earth Institute, Columbia University.

Sacks, O. (1985). *The man who mistook his wife for a hat.* New York: Summit Books.

Sadler, M. S., Correll, J., Park, B., & Judd, C. M. (2012a). The world is not Black and White: Racial bias in the decision to shoot in a multiethnic context. *Journal of Social Issues, 68,* 286–313.

Sadler, M. S., Meagor, E. L., & Kaye, M. E. (2012b). Stereotypes of mental disorders differ in competence and warmth. *Social Science and Medicine, 74,* 915–922.

Sagan, C. (1977). *The dragons of Eden: Speculations on the evolution of human intelligence.* New York: Ballantine.

Salas-Wright, C. P., Vaughn, M. G., Hodge, D. R., & Perron, B. E. (2012). Religiosity profiles of American youth in relation to substance use, violence, and delinquency. *Journal of Youth and Adolescence, 41,* 1560–1575.

Salmon, P. (2001). Effects of physical exercise on anxiety, depression, and sensitivity to stress: A unifying theory. *Clinical Psychology Review, 21,* 33–61.

Salovey, P. (1990, January/February). Interview. *American Scientist,* pp. 25–29.

Salthouse, T. A. (2004). What and when of cognitive aging. *Current Directions in Psychological Science, 13,* 140–144.

Salthouse, T. A. (2009). When does age-related cognitive decline begin? *Neurobiology of Aging, 30,* 507–514.

Salthouse, T. A. (2010). Selective review of cognitive aging. *Journal of the International Neuropsychological Society, 16,* 754–760.

Salthouse, T. A. (2013). Within-cohort age-related differences in cognitive functioning. *Psychological Science, 24,* 123–130.

Salthouse, T. A., & Mandell, A. R. (2013). Do age-related increases in tip-of-the tongue experiences signify episodic memory impairments? *Psychological Science, 24,* 2489–2497.

Sampson, E. E. (2000). Reinterpreting individualism and collectivism: Their religious roots and monologic versus dialogic person–other relationship. *American Psychologist, 55,* 1425–1432.

Sánchez-Álvarez, N., Extremera, N., & Fernández-Berrocal, P. (2015). The relation between emotional intelligence and subjective well-being: A meta-analytic investigation. *The Journal of Positive Psychology,* 1–10.

Sánchez-Villegas, A., Henríquez-Sánchez, P., Ruiz-Canela, M., Lahortiga, F., Molero, P., Toledo, E., & Martínez-González, M. A. (2015). A longitudinal analysis of diet quality scores and the risk of incident depression in the SUN Project. *BMC Medicine, 13(1),* 1.

Sanders, A. R., Martin, E. R., Beecham, G. W., Guo, S., Dawood, K. Rieger, G. . . Bailey, J. M. (2015). Genome-wide scan demonstrates significant linkage for male sexual orientation. *Psychological Medicine, 45,* 1379–1388.

Sanders, M. A., Shirk, S. D., Burgin, C. J., & Martin, L. L. (2012). The gargle effect: Rinsing the mouth with glucose enhances self-control. *Psychological Science, 23,* 1470–1472.

Sandfort, T. G. M., de Graaf, R., Bijl, R., & Schnabel, P. (2001). Same-sex sexual behavior and psychiatric disorders. *Archives of General Psychiatry, 58,* 85–91.

Sandkühler, S., & Bhattacharya, J. (2008). Deconstructing insight: EEG correlates of insightful problem solving. *PloS ONE, 3,* e1459.

Sandler, W., Meir, I., Padden, C., & Aronoff, M. (2005). The emergence of grammar: Systematic structure in a new language. *PNAS, 102,* 2261–2265.

Sandstrom, A. (2015, December 2). *Religious groups' policies on transgender members vary widely.* Pew Research Center (pewresearch.org).

Sanz, C., Blicher, A., Dalke, K., Gratton-Fabri, L., McClure-Richards, T., & Fouts, R. (1998, Winter–Spring). Enrichment object use: Five chimpanzees' use of temporary and semi-permanent enrichment objects. *Friends of Washoe, 19(1,2),* 9–14.

Sanz, C., Morgan, D., & Gulick, S. (2004). New insights into chimpanzees, tools, and termites from the Congo Basin. *American Naturalist, 164,* 567–581.

Sapadin, L. A. (1988). Friendship and gender: Perspectives of professional men and women. *Journal of Social and Personal Relationships, 5,* 387–403.

Saphire-Bernstein, S., Way, B. M., Kim, H. S, Sherman, D. K., & Taylor, S. E. (2011). Oxytocin receptor gene (OXTR) is related to psychological resources. *PNAS, 108,* 15118–15122.

Sapolsky, R. (2005). The influence of social hierarchy on primate health. *Science, 308,* 648–652.

Sarro, E. C., Wilson, D. A., & Sullivan, R. M. (2014). Maternal regulation of infant brain state. *Current Biology, 24,* 1664–1669.

Savage-Rumbaugh, E. S., Murphy, J., Sevcik, R. A., Brakke, K. E., Williams, S. L., & Rumbaugh, D. M., with commentary by Bates, E. (1993). Language comprehension in ape and child. *Monographs of the Society for Research in Child Development, 58(233),* 1–254.

Savage-Rumbaugh, E. S., Rumbaugh, D., & Fields, W. M. (2009). Empirical Kanzi: The ape language controversy revisited. *Skeptic, 15,* 25–33.

Savani, K., & Rattan, A. (2012). A choice mind-set increases the acceptance and maintenance of wealth inequality. *Psychological Science, 23,* 796–804.

Savic, I., Berglund, H., & Lindstrom, P. (2005). Brain response to putative pheromones in homosexual men. *PNAS, 102,* 7356–7361.

Savin-Williams, R., Joyner, K., & Rieger, G. (2012). Prevalence and stability of self-reported sexual orientation identity during young adulthood. *Archives of Sexual Behavior, 41,* 103–110.

Savitsky, K., Epley, N., & Gilovich, T. (2001). Do others judge us as harshly as we think? Overestimating the impact of our failures, shortcomings, and mishaps. *Journal of Personality and Social Psychology, 81,* 44–56.

Savitsky, K., & Gilovich, T. (2003). The illusion of transparency and the alleviation of speech anxiety. *Journal of Experimental Social Psychology, 39,* 618–625.

Savoy, C., & Beitel, P. (1996). Mental imagery for basketball. *International Journal of Sport Psychology, 27,* 454–462.

Sawyer, A. C. P., Miller-Lewis, L. R., Searle, A. K., & Sawyer, M. G. (2015). Is greater improvement in early self-regulation associated with fewer behavioral problems later in childhood? *Developmental Psychology, 51,* 1740–1755.

Sayal, K., Heron, J., Golding, J., Alati, R., Smith, G. D., Gray, R., & Emond, A. (2009). Binge pattern of alcohol consumption during pregnancy and childhood mental health outcomes: Longitudinal population-based study. *Pediatrics, 123,* e289.

Sayette, M. A., Creswell, K. G., Kimoff, J. D., Fairbairn, C. E., Cohn, J. F., Heckman, B. W., . . . Moreland, R. L. (2012). Alcohol and group formation: A multimodal investigation of the effects of alcohol on emotion and social bonding. *Psychological Science, 23,* 869–878.

Sayette, M. A., Schooler, J. W., & Reichle, E. D. (2010). Out for a smoke: The impact of cigarette craving on zoning out during reading. *Psychological Science, 21,* 26–30.

Sbarra, D. A., Hasselmo, K., & Bourassa, K. J. (2015). Divorce and health: Beyond individual differences. *Current Directions in Psychological Science, 24,* 109–113.

Sbarra, D. A., Law, R. W., & Portley, R. M. (2011). Divorce and death: A meta-analysis and research agenda for clinical, social, and health psychology. *Perspectives on Psychological Science, 6,* 454–474.

Scarr, S. (1984, May). What's a parent to do? A conversation with E. Hall. *Psychology Today,* pp. 58–63.

Scarr, S. (1989). Protecting general intelligence: Constructs and consequences for interventions. In R. J. Linn (Ed.), *Intelligence: Measurement, theory, and public policy.* Champaign: University of Illinois Press.

Scarr, S. (1993, May/June). Quoted in Nature's thumbprint: So long, superparents. *Psychology Today,* p. 16.

Schab, F. R. (1991). Odor memory: Taking stock. *Psychological Bulletin, 109,* 242–251.

Schachter, S., & Singer, J. E. (1962). Cognitive, social and physiological determinants of emotional state. *Psychological Review, 69,* 379–399.

Schacter, D. L. (1992). Understanding implicit memory: A cognitive neuroscience approach. *American Psychologist, 47,* 559–569.

Schacter, D. L. (1996). *Searching for memory: The brain, the mind, and the past.* New York: Basic Books.

Schafer, S. M., Colloca, L., & Wager, T. D. (2015). Conditioned placebo analgesia persists when subjects know they are receiving a placebo. *Journal of Pain, 16,* 412–420.

Schaie, K. W., & Geiwitz, J. (1982). *Adult development and aging.* Boston: Little, Brown.

Schalock, R. L., Borthwick-Duffy, S., Bradley, V. J., Buntinx, W. H. E., Coulter, D. L., Craig, E. M. (2010). *Intellectual disability: Definition, classification, and systems of supports* (11th edition). Washington, DC: American Association on Intellectual and Developmental Disabilities.

Scheier, M. F., & Carver, C. S. (1992). Effects of optimism on psychological and physical well-being: Theoretical overview and empirical update. *Cognitive Therapy and Research, 16,* 201–228.

Schein, E. H. (1956). The Chinese indoctrination program for prisoners of war: A study of attempted brainwashing. *Psychiatry, 19,* 149–172.

Schick, V., Herbenick, D., Reece, M., Sanders, S. A., Dodge, B., Middlestadt, S. E., & Fortenberry, J. D. (2010). Sexual behaviors, condom use, and sexual health of Americans over 50: Implications for sexual health promotion for older adults. *Journal of Sexual Medicine, 7(suppl 5),* 315–329.

Schiffenbauer, A., & Schiavo, R. S. (1976). Physical distance and attraction: An intensification effect. *Journal of Experimental Social Psychology, 12,* 274–282.

Schilt, T., de Win, M. M. L, Koeter, M., Jager, G., Korf, D. J., van den Brink, W., & Schmand, B. (2007). Cognition in novice ecstasy users with minimal exposure to other drugs. *Archives of General Psychiatry, 64,* 728–736.

Schizophrenia Working Group of the Psychiatric Genomics Consortium. (2014). Biological insights from 108 schizophrenia-associated genetic loci. *Nature*, 511, 421–427.

Schlaffke, L., Golisch, A., Haag, L. M., Lenz, M., Heba, S., Lissek, S., . . . Tegenthoff, M. (2015). The brain's dress code: How the dress allows to decode the neuronal pathway of an optical illusion. *Cortex*, 73, 271–275.

Schlomer, G. L., Del Giudice, M., & Ellis, B. J. (2011). Parent-offspring conflict theory: An evolutionary framework for understanding conflict within human families. *Psychological Review*, 118, 496–521.

Schmader, T. (2010). Stereotype threat deconstructed. *Current Directions in Psychological Science*, 19, 14–18.

Schmidt, F. L., & Hunter, J. E. (1998). The validity and utility of selection methods in personnel psychology: Practical and theoretical implications of 85 years of research findings. *Psychological Bulletin*, 124, 262–274.

Schmitt, D. P. (2007). Sexual strategies across sexual orientations: How personality traits and culture relate to sociosexuality among gays, lesbians, bisexuals, and heterosexuals. *Journal of Psychology and Human Sexuality*, 18, 183–214.

Schmitt, D. P., & Allik, J. (2005). Simultaneous administration of the Rosenberg Self-esteem Scale in 53 nations: Exploring the universal and culture-specific features of global self-esteem. *Journal of Personality and Social Psychology*, 89, 623–642.

Schmitt, D. P., Allik, J., McCrae, R. R., & Benet-Martínez, V. (2007). The geographic distribution of Big Five personality traits: Patterns and profiles of human self-description across 56 nations. *Journal of Cross-Cultural Psychology*, 38, 173–212.

Schmitt, D. P., Jonason, P. K., Byerley, G. J., Flores, S. D., Illbeck, B. E., O'Leary, K. N., & Qudrat, A. (2012). A reexamination of sex differences in sexuality: New studies reveal old truths. *Current Directions in Psychological Science*, 21, 135–139.

Schnall, E., Wassertheil-Smnoller, S., Swencionis, C., Zemon, V., Tinker, L., O'Sullivan, M. J., . . . Goodwin, M. (2010). The relationship between religion and cardiovascular outcomes and all-cause mortality in the Women's Health Initiative Observational Study. *Psychology and Health*, 25, 249–263.

Schneider, S. L. (2001). In search of realistic optimism: Meaning, knowledge, and warm fuzziness. *American Psychologist*, 56, 250–263.

Schneiderman, N. (1999). Behavioral medicine and the management of HIV/AIDS. *International Journal of Behavioral Medicine*, 6, 3–12.

Schneier, B. (2007, May 17). Virginia Tech lesson: Rare risks breed irrational responses. *Wired* (wired.com).

Schoen, R., & Canudas-Romo, V. (2006). Timing effects on divorce: 20th century experience in the United States. *Journal of Marriage and Family*, 68, 749–758.

Schoeneman, T. J. (1994). Individualism. In V. S. Ramachandran (Ed.), *Encyclopedia of human behavior*. San Diego: Academic Press.

Schofield, J. W. (1986). Black-White contact in desegregated schools. In M. Hewstone & R. Brown (Eds.), *Contact and conflict in intergroup encounters* (pp. 79–92). Oxford: Basil Blackwell.

Schonfield, D., & Robertson, B. A. (1966). Memory storage and aging. *Canadian Journal of Psychology*, 20, 228–236.

Schooler, J. W., Gerhard, D., & Loftus, E. F. (1986). Qualities of the unreal. *Journal of Experimental Psychology: Learning, Memory, and Cognition*, 12, 171–181.

Schorr, E. A., Fox, N.A., van Wassenhove, V., & Knudsen, E. I. (2005). Auditory-visual fusion in speech perception in children with cochlear implants. *PNAS*, 102, 18748–18750.

Schreiber, F. R. (1973). *Sybil*. Chicago: Regnery.

Schuch, F. B., Vancampfort, D., Richards, J., Rosenbaum, S., Ward, P. B., & Stubbs, B. (2016). Exercise as a treatment for depression: a meta-analysis adjusting for publication bias. *Journal of Psychiatric Research*, 77, 42–51.

Schultheiss, O., Wiemers, U. & Wolf, O. (2014). Implicit need for achievement predicts attenuated cortisol responses to difficult tasks. *Journal of Research in Personality*, 48, 84–92.

Schuman, H., & Scott, J. (June, 1989). Generations and collective memories. *American Sociological Review*, 54(3), 359–381.

Schumann, K., & Ross, M. (2010). Why women apologize more than men: Gender differences in thresholds for perceiving offensive behavior. *Psychological Science*, 21, 1649–1655.

Schurger, A., Pereira, F., Treisman, A., Cohen, J. D. (2010, January). Reproducibility distinguishes conscious from nonconscious neural representations. *Science*, 327, 97–99.

Schutte, N. S., Malouff, J. M., Thorsteinsson, E. B., Bhullar, N., & Rooke, S. E. (2007). A meta-analytic investigation of the relationship between emotional intelligence and health. *Personality and Individual Differences*, 42, 921–933.

Schwartz, B. (1984). *Psychology of learning and behavior* (2nd ed.). New York: Norton.

Schwartz, B. (2000). Self-determination: The tyranny of freedom. *American Psychologist*, 55, 79–88.

Schwartz, B. (2004). *The paradox of choice: Why more is less*. New York: Ecco/HarperCollins.

Schwartz, H. W., Eichstaedt, J., Kern, M. L., Dziurzynski, L., Ramones, S., Agrawal, M., . . . Ungar, L. (2013). Personality, gender, and age in the language of social media: The open-vocabulary approach. *PLOS ONE*, 8, e73791.

Schwartz, J. M., Stoessel, P. W., Baxter, L. R., Jr., Martin, K. M., & Phelps, M. E. (1996). Systematic changes in cerebral glucose metabolic rate after successful behavior modification treatment of obsessive-compulsive disorder. *Archives of General Psychiatry*, 53, 109–113.

Schwartz, P. J. (2011). Season of birth in schizophrenia: A maternal–fetal chronobiological hypothesis. *Medical Hypotheses*, 76, 785–793.

Schwartz, S. H., & Rubel-Lifschitz, T. (2009). Cross-national variation in the size of sex differences in values: Effects of gender equality. *Journal of Personality and Social Psychology*, 97, 171–185.

Schwartzman-Morris, J., & Putterman, C. (2012). Gender differences in the pathogenesis and outcome of lupus and of lupus nephritis. *Clinical and Developmental Immunology*, 2012, 604892. doi:10.1155/2012/604892.

Schwarz, A. (2012, June 9). Risky rise of the good-grade pill. *The New York Times* (nytimes.com).

Schwarz, A., & Cohen, S. (2013, March 31). A.D.H.D. seen in 11% of U.S. children as diagnoses rise. *The New York Times* (nytimes.com).

Schwarz, N., Strack, F., Kommer, D., & Wagner, D. (1987). Soccer, rooms, and the quality of your life: Mood effects on judgments of satisfaction with life in general and with specific domains. *European Journal of Social Psychology*, 17, 69–79.

Sclafani, A. (1995). How food preferences are learned: Laboratory animal models. *Proceedings of the Nutrition Society*, 54, 419–427.

Scott, D. J., Stohler, C. S., Egnatuk, C. M., Wang, H., Koeppe, R. A., & Zubieta, J.-K. (2007). Individual differences in reward responding explain placebo-induced expectations and effects. *Neuron*, 55, 325–336.

Scott, K. M., Wells, J. E. Angermeyer, M., Brugha, T. S., Bromet, E., Demyttenaere, K., . . . Kessler, R. C. (2010). Gender and the relationship between marital status and first onset of mood, anxiety and substance use disorders. *Psychological Medicine*, 40, 1495–1505.

Scott, W. A., Scott, R., & McCabe, M. (1991). Family relationships and children's personality: A cross-cultural, cross-source comparison. *British Journal of Social Psychology*, 30, 1–20.

Scott-Sheldon, L. A. J., Carey, K. B., Elliott, J. C., Garey, L., & Carey, M. P. (2014). Efficacy of alcohol interventions for first-year college students: A meta-analytic review of randomized controlled trials. *Journal of Consulting and Clinical Psychology*, 82, 177–188.

Scott-Sheldon, L. A. J., Terry, D. L., Carey, K. B., Garey, L., & Carey, M. P. (2012). Efficacy of expectancy challenge interventions to reduce college student drinking: A meta-analytic review. *Psychology of Addictive Behaviors*, 26, 393–405.

Scullin, M. K., & McDaniel, M. A. (2010). Remembering to execute a goal: Sleep on it! *Psychological Science*, 21, 1028–1035.

Sdorow, L. M. (2005). The people behind psychology. In B. Perlman, L. McCann, & W. Buskist (Eds.), *Voices of experience: Memorable talks from the National Institute on the Teaching of Psychology* (pp. 1–16). Washington, DC: American Psychological Society.

Seal, K. H., Bertenthal, D., Miner, C. R., Sen, S., & Marmar, C. (2007). Bringing the war back home: Mental health disorders among 103,788 U.S. veterans returning from Iraq and Afghanistan seen at Department of Veterans Affairs facilities. *Archives of Internal Medicine*, 167, 467–482.

Sechrest, L., Stickle, T. R., & Stewart, M. (1998). The role of assessment in clinical psychology. In A. Bellack, M. Hersen (series eds.), & C. R. Reynolds (vol. ed.), *Comprehensive clinical psychology: Vol. 4. Assessment* (pp. 1–32). New York: Pergamon.

Sedgh, G., Finer, L. B., Bankole, A., Eilers, M. A., & Singh, S. (2015). Adolescent pregnancy, birth, and abortion rates across countries: Levels and recent trends. *Journal of Adolescent Health*, 56, 223–230.

Sedlmeier, P., Eberth, J., Schwarz, M., Zimmermann, D., Haarig, F., Jaeger, S., & Kunze, S. (2012). The psychological effects of meditation: A meta-analysis. *Psychological Bulletin*, 138, 1139–1171.

Seeman, P., Guan, H.-C., & Van Tol, H. H. M. (1993). Dopamine D4 receptors elevated in schizophrenia. *Nature*, 365, 441–445.

Seery, M. D. (2011). Resilience: A silver lining to experiencing adverse life events. *Current Directions in Psychological Science*, 20, 390–394.

Segal, N. L., McGuire, S. A., & Stohs, J. H. (2012). What virtual twins reveal about general intelligence and other behaviors. *Personality and Individual Differences*, 53, 405–410.

Segall, M. H., Dasen, P. R., Berry, J. W., & Poortinga, Y. H. (1990). *Human behavior in global perspective: An introduction to cross-cultural psychology*. New York: Pergamon.

Segerstrom, S. C., Hardy, J. K., Evans, D. R., & Greenberg, R. N. (2012). Vulnerability, distress, and immune response to vaccination in older adults. *Brain, Behavior, and Immunity*, 26, 747–753.

Segerstrom, S. C., Taylor, S. E., Kemeny, M. E., & Fahey, J. L. (1998). Optimism is associated with mood, coping, and immune change in response to stress. *Journal of Personality and Social Psychology*, 74, 1646–1655.

Seibert, S. E., Wang, G., & Courtright, S. H. (2011). Antecedents and consequences of psychological and team empowerment in organizations: A meta-analytic review. *Journal of Applied Psychology, 96,* 981–1003.

Seidel, A., & Prinz, J. (2013). Sound morality: Irritating and icky noises amplify judgments in divergent moral domains. *Cognition, 127,* 1–5.

Self, C. E. (1994). *Moral culture and victimization in residence halls.* Dissertation: Thesis (M.A.). Bowling Green University.

Seligman, M. E. P. (1975). *Helplessness: On depression, development and death.* San Francisco: Freeman.

Seligman, M. E. P. (1991). *Learned optimism.* New York: Knopf.

Seligman, M. E. P. (1994). *What you can change and what you can't.* New York: Knopf.

Seligman, M. E. P. (1995). The effectiveness of psychotherapy: The Consumer Reports study. *American Psychologist, 50,* 965–974.

Seligman, M. E. P. (2002). *Authentic happiness: Using the new positive psychology to realize your potential for lasting fulfillment.* New York: Free Press.

Seligman, M. E. P. (2011). *Flourish: A visionary new understanding of happiness and well-being.* New York: Free Press.

Seligman, M. E. P. (2012, May 8). Quoted in A. C. Brooks, America and the value of "earned success." *The Wall Street Journal* (wsj.com).

Seligman, M. E. P., Ernst, R. M., Gillham, J., Reivich, K., & Linkins, M. (2009). Positive education: Positive psychology and classroom interventions. *Oxford Review of Education, 35,* 293–311.

Seligman, M. E. P., & Maier, S. F. (1967). Failure to escape traumatic shock. *Journal of Experimental Psychology, 74,* 1–9.

Seligman, M. E. P., Steen, T. A., Park, N., & Peterson, C. (2005). Positive psychology progress: Empirical validation of interventions. *American Psychologist, 60,* 410–421.

Seligman, M. E. P., & Yellen, A. (1987). What is a dream? *Behavior Research and Therapy, 25,* 1–24.

Sellers, H. (2010). *You don't look like anyone I know.* New York: Riverhead Books.

Selye, H. (1936). A syndrome produced by diverse noxious agents. *Nature, 138,* 32.

Selye, H. (1976). *The stress of life.* New York: McGraw-Hill.

Senghas, A., & Coppola, M. (2001). Children creating language: How Nicaraguan Sign Language acquired a spatial grammar. *Psychological Science, 12,* 323–328.

Sengupta, S. (2001, October 10). Sept. 11 attack narrows the racial divide. *The New York Times* (nytimes.com).

Senju, A., Southgate, V., White, S., & Frith, U. (2009). Mindblind eyes: An absence of spontaneous theory of mind in Asperger syndrome. *Science, 325,* 883–885.

Service, R. F. (1994). Will a new type of drug make memory-making easier? *Science, 266,* 218–219.

Shadish, W. R., & Baldwin, S. A. (2005). Effects of behavioral marital therapy: A meta-analysis of randomized controlled trials. *Journal of Consulting and Clinical Psychology, 73,* 6–14.

Shafir, E., & LeBoeuf, R. A. (2002). Rationality. *Annual Review of Psychology, 53,* 491–517.

Shaki, S. (2013). What's in a kiss? Spatial experience shapes directional bias during kissing. *Journal of Nonverbal Behavior, 37,* 43–50.

Shalev, I., Moffitt, T. E., Sugden, K., Williams, B., Houts, R. M., Danese, A., . . . Caspi, A. (2013). Exposure to violence during childhood is associated with telomere erosion from 5 to 10 years of age: A longitudinal study. *Molecular Psychiatry, 18,* 576–581.

Shallcross, A. J., Ford, B. Q., Floerke, V. A., & Mauss, I. B. (2013). Getting better with age: The relationship between age, acceptance, and negative affect. *Journal of Personality and Social Psychology, 104,* 734–749.

Shamir, B., House, R. J., & Arthur, M. B. (1993). The motivational effects of charismatic leadership: A self-concept based theory. *Organizational Science, 4,* 577–594.

Shan, W., Shengua, J., Davis, H., Hunter, M., Peng, K., Shao, X., . . . Wang, Y. (2012). Mating strategies in Chinese culture: Female risk-avoiding vs. male risk-taking. *Evolution and Human Behavior, 33,* 182–192.

Shanahan, L., McHale, S. M., Osgood, D. W., & Crouter, A. C. (2007). Conflict frequency with mothers and fathers from middle childhood to late adolescence: Within- and between-families comparisons. *Developmental Psychology, 43,* 539–550.

Shane, S. (2015, June 24). Homegrown extremists tied to deadlier toll than jihadis in U.S. since 9/11. *The New York Times* (nytimes.com).

Shannon, B. J., Raichle, M. E., Snyder, A. Z., Fair, D. A., Mills, K. L., Zhang, D., . . . Kiehl, K. A. (2011). Premotor functional connectivity predicts impulsivity in juvenile offenders. *PNAS, 108,* 11241–11245.

Shapiro, D. (1999). *Psychotherapy of neurotic character.* New York: Basic Books.

Shapiro, K. A., Moo, L. R., & Caramazza, A. (2006). Cortical signatures of noun and verb production. *PNAS, 103,* 1644–1649.

Shargorodsky, J., Curhan, S. G., Curhan, G. C., & Eavey, R. (2010). Changes of prevalence of hearing loss in US adolescents. *Journal of the American Medical Association, 304,* 772–778.

Shariff, A. F., Greene, J. D., Karremans, J. C., Luguri, J. B., Clark, C. J., Schooler, J. W., . . . Vohs, K. D. (2014). Free will and punishment: A mechanistic view of human nature reduces retribution. *Psychological Science, 25,* 1563–1570.

Sharma, A. R., McGue, M. K., & Benson, P. L. (1998). The psychological adjustment of United States adopted adolescents and their nonadopted siblings. *Child Development, 69,* 791–802.

Shaver, P. R., Morgan, H. J., & Wu, S. (1996). Is love a basic emotion? *Personal Relationships, 3,* 81–96.

Shaw, B. A., Liang, J., & Krause, N. (2010). Age and race differences in the trajectories of self-esteem. *Psychology and Aging, 25,* 84–94.

Shaw, J., & Porter, S. (2015). Constructing rich false memories of committing crime. *Psychological Science, 26,* 291–301.

Shedler, J. (2009, March 23). *That was then, this is now: Psychoanalytic psychotherapy for the rest of us.* Unpublished manuscript, Department of Psychiatry, University of Colorado Health Sciences Center.

Shedler, J. (2010a, November/December). Getting to know me. *Scientific American Mind,* pp. 53–57.

Shedler, J. (2010b). The efficacy of psychodynamic psychotherapy. *American Psychologist, 65,* 98–109.

Sheehan, S. (1982). *Is there no place on earth for me?* Boston: Houghton Mifflin.

Sheltzer, J. M., & Smith, J. C. (2014). Elite male faculty in the life sciences employ fewer females. *PNAS, 111,* 10107–10112.

Shenton, M. E. (1992). Abnormalities of the left temporal lobe and thought disorder in schizophrenia: A quantitative magnetic resonance imaging study. *New England Journal of Medicine, 327,* 604–612.

Shepard, R. N. (1990). *Mind sights.* New York: Freeman.

Shepherd, C. (1999, June). News of the weird. *Funny Times,* p. 21.

Shergill, S. S., Bays, P. M., Frith, C. D., & Wolpert, D. M. (2003). Two eyes for an eye: The neuroscience of force escalation. *Science, 301,* 187.

Sherif, M. (1966). *In common predicament: Social psychology of intergroup conflict and cooperation.* Boston: Houghton Mifflin.

Sherman, P. W., & Flaxman, S. M. (2001). Protecting ourselves from food. *American Scientist, 89,* 142–151.

Sherman, R. A., Rauthmann, J. F., Brown, N. A., Serfass, D. S., & Jones, A. B. (2015). The independent effects of personality and situations on real-time expressions of behavior and emotion. *Journal of Personality and Social Psychology, 109,* 872–888.

Sherry, D., & Vaccarino, A. L. (1989). Hippocampus and memory for food caches in black-capped chickadees. *Behavioral Neuroscience, 103,* 308–318.

Shettleworth, S. J. (1973). Food reinforcement and the organization of behavior in golden hamsters. In R. A. Hinde & J. Stevenson-Hinde (Eds.), *Constraints on learning.* London: Academic Press.

Shettleworth, S. J. (1993). Where is the comparison in comparative cognition? Alternative research programs. *Psychological Science, 4,* 179–184.

Shiell, M. M., Champoux, F., & Zatorre, R. (2014). Enhancement of visual motion detection thresholds in early deaf people. *PLOS ONE, 9*(2), e90498. doi:10.1371/journal.pone.0090498

Shifren, J. L., Monz, B. U., Russo, P. A., Segreti, A., Johannes, C. B. (2008). Sexual problems and distress in United States women: Prevalence and correlates. *Obstetrics & Gynecology, 112,* 970–978.

Shilsky, J. D., Hartman, T. J., Kris-Etherton, P. M., Rogers, C. J., Sharkey, N. A., & Nickols-Richardson, S. M. (2012). Partial sleep deprivation and energy balance in adults: An emerging issue for consideration by dietetics practitioners. *Journal of the Academy of Nutrition and Dietetics, 112,* 1785–1797.

Shipstead, Z., Hicks, K. L., & Engle, R. W. (2012a). Cogmed working memory training: Does the evidence support the claims? *Journal of Applied Research in Memory and Cognition, 1,* 185–193.

Shipstead, Z., Redick, T. S., & Engle, R. W. (2012b). Is working memory training effective? *Psychological Bulletin, 138,* 628–654.

Shiromani, P. J., Horvath, T., Redline, S., & Van Cauter E. (Eds.) (2012). *Sleep loss and obesity: Intersecting epidemics.* New York: Springer Science.

Shockley, K. M., Ispas, D., Rossi, M. E., & Levine, E. L. (2012). A meta-analytic investigation of the relationship between state affect, discrete emotions, and job performance. *Human Performance, 25,* 377–411.

Shor, E., Roelfs, D. J., & Yogev, T. (2013). The strength of family ties: A meta-analysis and meta-regression of self-reported social support and mortality. *Social Networks, 35,* 626–638.

Shors, T. J. (2014). The adult brain makes new neurons, and effortful learning keeps them alive. *Current Directions in Psychological Science, 23,* 311–318.

Showers, C. (1992). The motivational and emotional consequences of considering positive or negative possibilities for an upcoming event. *Journal of Personality and Social Psychology, 63,* 474–484.

Shrestha, A., Nohr, E. A., Bech, B. H., Ramlau-Hansen, C. H., & Olsen, J. (2011). Smoking and alcohol during pregnancy and age of menarche in daughters. *Human Reproduction, 26,* 259–265.

Shuffler, M. L., Burke, C. S., Kramer, W. S., & Salas, E. (2013). Leading teams: Past, present, and future perspectives. In M. G. Rumsey (Ed.), *The Oxford handbook of leadership* (pp. 144–166). New York: Oxford University Press.

Shuffler, M. L., DiazGranados, D., & Salas, E. (2011). There's a science for that: Team development interventions in organizations. *Current Directions in Psychological Science, 20,* 365–372.

Shuwairi, S. M., & Johnson, S. P. (2013). Oculomotor exploration of impossible figures in early infancy. *Infancy, 18,* 221–232.

Siegel, J. M. (2012). Suppression of sleep for mating. *Science, 337,* 1610–1611.

Siegel, R. K. (1977, October). Hallucinations. *Scientific American,* pp. 132–140.

Siegel, R. K. (1980). The psychology of life after death. *American Psychologist, 35,* 911–931.

Siegel, R. K. (1982, October). Quoted by J. Hooper, Mind tripping. *Omni,* pp. 72–82, 159–160.

Siegel, R. K. (1984, March 15). Personal communication.

Siegel, R. K. (1990). *Intoxication.* New York: Pocket Books.

Siegel, S. (2005). Drug tolerance, drug addiction, and drug anticipation. *Current Directions in Psychological Science, 14,* 296–300.

Siegler, R. S., & Ellis, S. (1996). Piaget on childhood. *Psychological Science, 7,* 211–215.

Silber, M. H., Ancoli-Israel, S., Bonnet, M. H., Chokroverty, S., Grigg-Damberger, M. M., Hirshkowitz, M., . . . Iber, C. (2008). The visual scoring of sleep in adults. *Journal of Clinical Sleep Medicine, 3,* 121–131.

Silbersweig, D. A., Stern, E., Frith, C., Cahill, C., Holmes, A., Grootoonk, S., . . . Frackowiak, R. S. J. (1995). A functional neuroanatomy of hallucinations in schizophrenia. *Nature, 378,* 176–179.

Silva, A. J., Stevens, C. F., Tonegawa, S., & Wang, Y. (1992). Deficient hippocampal long-term potentiation in alpha-calcium-calmodulin kinase II mutant mice. *Science, 257,* 201–206.

Silva, C. E., & Kirsch, I. (1992). Interpretive sets, expectancy, fantasy proneness, and dissociation as predictors of hypnotic response. *Journal of Personality and Social Psychology, 63,* 847–856.

Silver, M., & Geller, D. (1978). On the irrelevance of evil: The organization and individual action. *Journal of Social Issues, 34,* 125–136.

Silver, N. (2012). *The signal and the noise: Why so many predictions fail—but some don't.* New York: Penguin.

Silver, R. C., Holman, E. A., Anderson, J. P., Poulin, M., McIntosh, D. N., & Gil-Rivas, V. (2013). Mental- and physical-health effects of acute exposure to media images of the September 11, 2001 attacks and Iraq War. *Psychological Science, 24,* 1623–1634.

Silver, R. C., Holman, E. A., McIntosh, D. N., Poulin, M., & Gil-Rivas, V. (2002). Nationwide longitudinal study of psychological responses to September 11. *Journal of the American Medical Association, 288,* 1235–1244.

Silverman, K., Evans, S. M., Strain, E. C., & Griffiths, R. R. (1992). Withdrawal syndrome after the double-blind cessation of caffeine consumption. *New England Journal of Medicine, 327,* 1109–1114.

Simon, H. (2001, February). Quoted by A. M. Hayashi, When to trust your gut. *Harvard Business Review,* pp. 59–65.

Simon, H. A., & Chase, W. G. (1973) Skill in chess. *American Scientist, 61,* 394–403.

Simon, V., Czobor, P., Bálint, S., Mésáros, A., & Bitter, I. (2009). Prevalence and correlates of adult attention-deficit hyperactivity disorder: Meta-analysis. *British Journal of Psychiatry, 194,* 204–211.

Simons, D. J., & Chabris, C. F. (1999). Gorillas in our midst: Sustained inattentional blindness for dynamic events. *Perception, 28,* 1059–1074.

Simons, D. J., & Levin, D. T. (1998). Failure to detect changes to people during a real-world interaction. *Psychonomic Bulletin & Review, 5,* 644–649.

Simonton, D. K. (1988). Age and outstanding achievement: What do we know after a century of research? *Psychological Bulletin, 104,* 251–267.

Simonton, D. K. (1990). Creativity in the later years: Optimistic prospects for achievement. *The Gerontologist, 30,* 626–631.

Simonton, D. K. (1992). The social context of career success and course for 2,026 scientists and inventors. *Personality and Social Psychology Bulletin, 18,* 452–463.

Simonton, D. K. (2012a). Teaching creativity: Current findings, trends, and controversies in the psychology of creativity. *Teaching of Psychology, 39,* 217–222.

Simonton, D. K. (2012b, November–December). The science of genius. *Scientific American Mind,* pp. 35–41.

Sin, N. L., Graham-Engeland, J. E., Ong, A. D., & Almeida, D. M. (2015). Affective reactivity to daily stressors is associated with elevated inflammation. *Health Psychology, 34,* 1154–1165.

Sin, N. L., & Lyubomirsky, S. (2009). Enhancing well-being and alleviating depressive symptoms with positive psychology interventions: A practice-friendly meta-analysis. *Journal of Clinical Psychology: In session, 65,* 467–487.

Sinclair, R. C., Hoffman, C., Mark, M. M., Martin, L. L., & Pickering, T. L. (1994). Construct accessibility and the misattribution of arousal: Schachter and Singer revisited. *Psychological Science, 5,* 15–18.

Singer, J. L. (1981). Clinical intervention: New developments in methods and evaluation. In L. T. Benjamin, Jr. (Ed.), *The G. Stanley Hall lecture series* (Vol. 1, pp. 105–128). Washington, DC: American Psychological Association.

Singer, T., Seymour, B., O'Doherty, J., Kaube, H., Dolan, R. J., & Frith, C. (2004). Empathy for pain involves the affective but not sensory components of pain. *Science, 303,* 1157–1162.

Singh, S. (1997). *Fermat's enigma: The epic quest to solve the world's greatest mathematical problem.* New York: Bantam Books.

Singh, S., & Riber, K. A. (1997, November). Fermat's last stand. *Scientific American,* pp. 68–73.

Sinha, P. (2013, July). Once blind and now they see. *Scientific American,* pp. 49–55.

Sio, U. N., Monahan, P., & Ormerod, T. (2013). Sleep on it, but only if it is difficult: Effects of sleep on problem solving. *Memory and Cognition, 41,* 159–166.

Sipski, M. L., Alexander, C. J., & Rosen, R. C. (1999). Sexual response in women with spinal cord injuries: Implications for our understanding of the able bodied. *Journal of Sexual & Marital Therapy, 25,* 11–22.

Sireteanu, R. (1999). Switching on the infant brain. *Science, 286,* 59, 61.

Skeem, J., Kennealy, P., Monahan, J., Peterson, J., & Appelbaum, P. (2016). Psychosis uncommonly and inconsistently precedes violence among high-risk individuals. *Clinical Psychological Science, 4*(1), 40–49.

Skeem, J. L., & Cooke, D. J. (2010). Is criminal behavior a central component of psychopathy? Conceptual directions for resolving the debate. *Psychological Assessment, 22,* 433–445.

Skinner, B. F. (1953). *Science and human behavior.* New York: Macmillan.

Skinner, B. F. (1956). A case history in scientific method. *American Psychologist, 11,* 221–233.

Skinner, B. F. (1961, November). Teaching machines. *Scientific American,* pp. 91–102.

Skinner, B. F. (1983, September). Origins of a behaviorist. *Psychology Today,* pp. 22–33.

Skinner, B. F. (1989). Teaching machines. *Science, 243,* 1535.

Sklar, L. S., & Anisman, H. (1981). Stress and cancer. *Psychological Bulletin, 89,* 369–406.

Skov, R. B., & Sherman, S. J. (1986). Information-gathering processes: Diagnosticity, hypothesis-confirmatory strategies, and perceived hypothesis confirmation. *Journal of Experimental Social Psychology, 22,* 93–121.

Slaughter, V., Imuta, K., Peterson, C. C., & Henry, J. D. (2015). Meta-analysis of theory of mind and peer popularity in the preschool and early school years. *Child Development, 86,* 1159–1174.

Slutske, W. S., Moffitt, T. E., Poulton, R., & Caspi A. (2012). Undercontrolled temperament at age 3 predicts disordered gambling at age 32: A longitudinal study of a complete birth cohort. *Psychological Science, 23,* 510–516.

Smalarz, L., & Wells, G. L. (2015). Contamination of eyewitness self-reports and the mistaken identification problem. *Current Directions in Psychological Science, 24,* 120–124.

Small, D. A., Loewenstein, G., & Slovic, P. (2007). Sympathy and callousness: The impact of deliberative thought on donations to identifiable and statistical victims. *Organizational Behavior and Human Decision Processes, 102,* 143–153.

Small, M. F. (1997). Making connections. *American Scientist, 85,* 502–504.

Smedley, A., & Smedley, B. D. (2005). Race as biology is fiction, racism as a social problem is real: Anthropological and historical perspectives on the social construction of race. *American Psychologist, 60,* 16–26.

Smelser, N. J., & Mitchell, F. (Eds.). (2002). *Terrorism: Perspectives from the behavioral and social sciences.* Washington, DC: National Academies Press.

Smith, A. (1983). Personal correspondence.

Smith, B. C. (2011, January 16). The senses and the multi-sensory. World Question Center, *Edge* (edge.org).

Smith, D. M., Loewenstein, G., Jankovic, A., & Ubel, P. A. (2009a). Happily hopeless: Adaptation to a permanent, but not to a temporary, disability. *Health Psychology, 28,* 787–791.

Smith, E., & Delargy, M. (2005). Clinical review: Locked-in syndrome. *British Medical Journal, 330,* 406–409.

Smith, J. A., & Rhodes, J. E. (2014). Being depleted and being shaken: An interpretative phenomenological analysis of the experiential features of a first episode of depression. *Psychology and Psychotherapy: Theory, Research and Practice, 88,* 197–209.

Smith, M. B. (1978). Psychology and values. *Journal of Social Issues, 34,* 181–199.

Smith, M. L., & Glass, G. V. (1977). Meta-analysis of psychotherapy outcome studies. *American Psychologist, 32,* 752–760.

Smith, M. L., Glass, G. V., & Miller, R. L. (1980). *The benefits of psychotherapy.* Baltimore: Johns Hopkins Press.

Smith, P. B., & Tayeb, M. (1989). Organizational structure and processes. In M. Bond (Ed.), *The cross-cultural challenge to social psychology* (pp. 116–127). Newbury Park, CA: Sage.

Smith, S. J., Axelton, A. M., & Saucier, D. A. (2009b). The effects of contact on sexual prejudice: A meta-analysis. *Sex Roles, 61,* 178–191.

Smith, T. B., Bartz, J., & Richards, P. S. (2007). Outcomes of religious and spiritual adaptations to psychotherapy: A meta-analytic review. *Psychotherapy Research, 17*, 643–655.

Smith, T. W. (1998, December). *American sexual behavior: Trends, sociodemographic differences, and risk behavior.* National Opinion Research Center GSS Topical Report No. 25.

Smith, T. W. (2006). Personality as risk and resilience in physical health. *Current Directions in Psychological Science, 15*, 227–231.

Smits, I. A. M., Dolan, C. V., Vorst, H. C. M., Wicherts, J. M., & Timmerman, M. E. (2011). Cohort differences in big five personality traits over a period of 25 years. *Journal of Personality and Social Psychology, 100*, 1124–1138.

Snedeker, J., Geren, J., & Shafto, C. L. (2007). Starting over: International adoption as a natural experiment in language development. *Psychological Science, 18*, 79–86.

Snyder, S. H. (1984). Neurosciences: An integrative discipline. *Science, 225*, 1255–1257.

Snyder, S. H. (1986). *Drugs and the brain.* New York: Scientific American Library .

Solomon, D. A., Keitner, G. I., Miller, I. W., Shea, M. T., & Keller, M. B. (1995). Course of illness and maintenance treatments for patients with bipolar disorder. *Journal of Clinical Psychiatry, 56*, 5–13.

Solomon, J. (1996, May 20). Breaking the silence. *Newsweek*, pp. 20–22.

Solomon, M. (1987, December). Standard issue. *Psychology Today*, pp. 30–31.

Solomon, Z., Greene, T., Ein-Dor, T., Zerach, G., Benyamini, Y., & Ohry, A. (2014). The long-term implications of war captivity for mortality and health. *Journal of Behavioral Medicine, 37*, 849–859.

Song, S. (2006, March 27). Mind over medicine. *Time*, p. 47.

Sood, A. K., Armaiz-Pena, G. N., Halder, J., Nick, A. M., Stone, R. L., Hu, W., . . . Lutgendorf, S. K. (2010). Adrenergic modulation of focal adhesion kinase protects human ovarian cancer cells from anoikis. *Journal of Clinical Investigation, 120*, 1515–1523.

Soto, C. J., John, O. P., Gosling, S. D., & Potter, J. (2011). Age differences in personality traits from 10 to 65: Big five domains and facets in a large cross-sectional sample. *Journal of Personality and Social Psychology, 100*, 330–348.

Spanos, N. P., & Coe, W. C. (1992). A social-psychological approach to hypnosis. In E. Fromm & M. R. Nash (Eds.), *Contemporary hypnosis research.* New York: Guilford.

Sparrow, B., Liu, J., & Wegner, D. M. (2011). Google effects on memory: Cognitive consequences of having information at our fingertips. *Science, 333*, 776–778.

Speer, N. K., Reynolds, J. R., Swallow, K. M., & Zacks, J. M. (2009). Reading stories activates neural representations of visual and motor experiences. *Psychological Science, 20*, 989–999.

Spencer, S. J., Steele, C. M., & Quinn, D. M. (1997). *Stereotype threat and women's math performance.* Unpublished manuscript, Hope College.

Spengler, M., Brunner, M., Damian, R. I., Lüdtke, O., Martin, R., & Roberts, B. W. (2015). Student characteristics and behaviors at age 12 predict occupational success 40 years later over and above childhood IQ and parental socioeconomic status. *Developmental Psychology, 51*(9), 1329.

Sperling, G. (1960). The information available in brief visual presentations. *Psychological Monographs, 74* (Whole No. 498).

Sperry, R. W. (1964). Problems outstanding in the evolution of brain function. James Arthur Lecture, American Museum of Natural History, New York. Cited by R.

Ornstein (1977), *The psychology of consciousness* (2nd ed.). New York: Harcourt Brace Jovanovich.

Spiegel, D. (2007). The mind prepared: Hypnosis in surgery. *Journal of the National Cancer Institute, 99*, 1280–1281.

Spielberger, C., & London, P. (1982). Rage boomerangs. *American Health, 1*, 52–56.

Spielmann, S. S., MacDonald, G., Joel, S., & Impett, E. A. (2015). Longing for ex-partners out of fear of being single. *Journal of Personality.* doi:10.1111/jopy.12222

Spring, B., Pingitore, R., Bourgeois, M., Kessler, K. H., & Bruckner, E. (1992). *The effects and non-effects of skipping breakfast: Results of three studies.* Paper presented at the American Psychological Association convention.

Sproesser, G., Schupp, H. T., & Renner, B. (2014). The bright side of stress-induced eating: Eating more when stressed but less when pleased. *Psychological Science, 25*, 58–65.

Squire, L. R., & Wixted, J. T. (2011). The cognitive neuroscience of human memory since H.M. *Annual Review of Neuroscience, 34*, 259–288.

Srivastava, S., John, O. P., Gosling, S. D., & Potter, J. (2003). Development of personality in early and middle adulthood: Set like plaster or persistent change? *Journal of Personality & Social Psychology, 84*, 1041–1053.

Srivastava, S., McGonigal, K. M., Richards, J. M., Butler, E. A., & Gross, J. J. (2006). Optimism in close relationships: How seeing things in a positive light makes them so. *Journal of Personality and Social Psychology, 91*, 143–153.

St. Clair, D., Xu, M., Wang, P., Yu, Y., Fang, Y., Zhang, F., . . . He, L. (2005). Rates of adult schizophrenia following prenatal exposure to the Chinese famine of 1959–1961. *Journal of the American Medical Association, 294*, 557–562.

Stacey, D., Bilbao, A., Maroteaux, M., Jia, T., Easton, A. E., Longueville, S., . . . the IMAGEN Consortium. (2012). RASGRF2 regulates alcohol-induced reinforcement by influencing mesolimbic dopamine neuron activity and dopamine release. *PNAS, 109*, 21128–21133.

Stafford, T., & Dewar, M. (2014). Tracing the trajectory of skill learning with a very large sample of online game players. *Psychological Science, 25*, 511–518.

Stager, C. L., & Werker, J. F. (1997). Infants listen for more phonetic detail in speech perception than in word-learning tasks. *Nature, 388*, 381–382.

Stahl, A. E., & Feigenson, L. (2015). Observing the unexpected enhances infants' learning and exploration. *Science, 348*, 91–94.

Stanley, S. M., Rhoades, G. K., Amato, P. R., Markman, H. J., & Johnson, C. A. (2010). The timing of cohabitation and engagement: Impact on first and second marriages. *Journal of Marriage and Family, 72*, 906–918.

Stanovich, K. E. (1996). *How to think straight about psychology.* New York: HarperCollins.

Stanovich, K. E., & West, R. F. (2008). On the relative independence of thinking biases and cognitive ability. *Journal of Personality and Social Psychology, 94*, 672–695.

State, M. W., & Šestan, N. (2012). The emerging biology of autism spectrum disorders. *Science, 337*, 1301–1304.

Staub, E. (1989). *The roots of evil: The psychological and cultural sources of genocide.* New York: Cambridge University Press.

Steel, P., Schmidt, J., & Schultz, J. (2008). Refining the relationship between personality and subjective well-being. *Psychological Bulletin, 134*, 138–161.

Steele, C. M. (1990, May). A conversation with Claude Steele. *APS Observer*, pp. 11–17.

Steele, C. M., & Josephs, R. A. (1990). Alcohol myopia: Its prized and dangerous effects. *American Psychologist, 45*, 921–933.

Steele, C. M., Spencer, S. J., & Aronson, J. (2002). Contending with group image: The psychology of stereotype and social identity threat. *Advances in Experimental Social Psychology, 34*, 379–440.

Steinberg, L. (1987, September). Bound to bicker. *Psychology Today*, pp. 36–39.

Steinberg, L. (2001). We know some things: Parent–adolescent relationships in retrospect and prospect. *Journal of Research on Adolescence, 11*(1), 1–19.

Steinberg, L. (2010, March). Analyzing adolescence. Interview with Sara Martin. *Monitor on Psychology*, pp. 26–29.

Steinberg, L. (2013). The influence of neuroscience on U.S. Supreme Court decisions involving adolescents' criminal culpability. *Nature Reviews Neuroscience, 14*, 513–518.

Steinberg, L., Cauffman, E., Woolard, J., Graham, S., & Banich, M. (2009). Are adolescents less mature than adults? Minors' access to abortion, the juvenile death penalty, and the alleged APA "flip-flop." *American Psychologist, 64*, 583–594.

Steinberg, L., Lamborn, S. D., Darling, N., Mounts, N. S., & Dornbusch, S. M. (1994). Overtime changes in adjustment and competence among adolescents from authoritative, authoritarian, indulgent, and neglectful families. *Child Development, 65*, 754–770.

Steinberg, L., & Morris, A. S. (2001). Adolescent development. *Annual Review of Psychology, 52*, 83–110.

Steinberg, L., & Scott, E. S. (2003). Less guilty by reason of adolescence: Developmental immaturity, diminished responsibility, and the juvenile death penalty. *American Psychologist, 58*, 1009–1018.

Steinberg, N. (1993, February). Astonishing love stories (from an earlier United Press International report). *Games*, p. 47.

Stellar, J. E., John-Henderson, N., Anderson, C. L., Gordon, A. M., McNeil, G. D., & Keltner, D. (2015). Positive affect and markers of inflammation: Discrete positive emotions predict lower levels of inflammatory cytokines. *Emotion, 15*, 129–133.

Stepanikova, I., Nie, N. H., & He, X. (2010). Time on the Internet at home, loneliness, and life satisfaction: Evidence from panel time-diary data. *Computers in Human Behavior, 26*, 329–338.

Steptoe, A., & Wardle, J. (2011). Positive affect measured using ecological momentary assessment and survival in older men and woman. *PNAS, 108*, 18244–18248.

Sternberg, R. J. (1985). *Beyond IQ: A triarchic theory of human intelligence.* New York: Cambridge University Press.

Sternberg, R. J. (1988). Applying cognitive theory to the testing and teaching of intelligence. *Applied Cognitive Psychology, 2*, 231–255.

Sternberg, R. J. (2003). Our research program validating the triarchic theory of successful intelligence: Reply to Gottfredson. *Intelligence, 31*, 399–413.

Sternberg, R. J. (2006). The Rainbow Project: Enhance the SAT through assessments of analytical, practical, and creative skills. *Intelligence, 34*, 321–350.

Sternberg, R. J. (2011). The theory of successful intelligence. In R. J. Sternberg & S. B. Kaufman (Eds.), *The Cambridge handbook of intelligence.* New York: Cambridge University Press.

Sternberg, R. J., & Grajek, S. (1984). The nature of love. *Journal of Personality and Social Psychology, 47*, 312–329.

Sternberg, R. J., & Kaufman, J. C. (1998). Human abilities. *Annual Review of Psychology, 49*, 479–502.

Sternberg, R. J., & Lubart, T. I. (1991). An investment theory of creativity and its development. *Human Development, 34*, 1–31.

Sternberg, R. J., & Lubart, T. I. (1992). Buy low and sell high: An investment approach to creativity. *Psychological Science, 1*, 1–5.

Stetter, F., & Kupper, S. (2002). Autogenic training: A meta-analysis of clinical outcome studies. *Applied Psychophysiology and Biofeedback, 27*, 45–98.

Stevenson, H. W. (1992, December). Learning from Asian schools. *Scientific American*, pp. 70–76.

Stewart, R. E., & Chambless, D. L. (2009). Cognitive–behavioral therapy for adult anxiety disorders in clinical practice: A meta-analysis of effectiveness studies. *Journal of Consulting and Clinical Psychology, 77*, 595–606.

Stice, E., Ng, J., & Shaw, H. (2010). Risk factors and prodromal eating pathology. *Journal of Child Psychology and Psychiatry, 51*, 518–525.

Stice, E., Spangler, D., & Agras, W. S. (2001). Exposure to media-portrayed thin-ideal images adversely affects vulnerable girls: A longitudinal experiment. *Journal of Social and Clinical Psychology, 20*, 270–288.

Stickgold, R. (2000, March 7). Quoted by S. Blakeslee, For better learning, researchers endorse, "sleep on it" adage. *The New York Times*, p. F2.

Stickgold, R. (2012). Sleep, memory and dreams: Putting it all together. In *Aquém e além do cérebro* [Behind and beyond the brain]. Bial: Fundação Bial Institution of Public Utility.

Stickgold, R., & Ellenbogen, J. M. (2008, August/September). Quiet! Sleeping brain at work. *Scientific American Mind*, pp. 23–29.

Stillman, T. F., Baumeister, R. F., Vohs, K. D., Lambert, N. M., Fincham, F. D., & Brewer, L. E. (2010). Personal philosophy and personnel achievement: Belief in free will predicts better job performance. *Social Psychological and Personality Science, 1*, 43–50.

Stillman, T. F., Lambet, N. M., Fincham, F. D., & Baumeister, R. F. (2011). Meaning as magnetic force: Evidence that meaning in life promotes interpersonal appeal. *Social Psychological and Personality Science, 2*, 13–20.

Stith, S. M., Rosen, K. H., Middleton, K. A., Busch, A. L., Lunderberg, K., & Carlton, R. P. (2000). The intergenerational transmission of spouse abuse: A meta-analysis. *Journal of Marriage and the Family, 62*, 640–654.

Stockton, M. C., & Murnen, S. K. (1992). *Gender and sexual arousal in response to sexual stimuli: A meta-analytic review*. Paper presented at the American Psychological Society convention.

Stone, A. A., & Neale, J. M. (1984). Effects of severe daily events on mood. *Journal of Personality and Social Psychology, 46*, 137–144.

Stone, A. A., Schneider, S., & Harter, J. K. (2012). Day-of-week mood patterns in the United States: On the existence of "Blue Monday," "Thank God it's Friday" and weekend effects. *Journal of Positive Psychology, 7*, 306–314.

Stone, A. A., Schwartz, J. E., Broderick, J. E., & Deaton, A. (2010). A snapshot of the age distribution of psychological well-being in the United States. *PNAS, 107*, 9985–9990.

St-Onge, M. P., McReynolds, A., Trivedi, Z. B., Roberts, A. L., Sy, M., & Hirsch, J. (2012). Sleep restriction leads to increased activation of brain regions sensitive to food stimuli. *American Journal of Clinical Nutrition, 95*, 818–824.

Storbeck, J., Robinson, M. D., & McCourt, M. E. (2006). Semantic processing precedes affect retrieval: The neurological case for cognitive primary in visual processing. *Review of General Psychology, 10*, 41–55.

Storm, B. C., & Jobe, T. A. (2012). Retrieval-induced forgetting predicts failure to recall negative autobiographical memories. *Psychological Science, 23*, 1356–1363.

Storms, M. D. (1973). Videotape and the attribution process: Reversing actors' and observers' points of view. *Journal of Personality and Social Psychology, 27*, 165–175.

Storms, M. D. (1983). *Development of sexual orientation*. Washington, DC: Office of Social and Ethical Responsibility, American Psychological Association.

Storms, M. D., & Thomas, G. C. (1977). Reactions to physical closeness. *Journal of Personality and Social Psychology, 35*, 412–418.

Stowell, J. R., Oldham, T., & Bennett, D. (2010). Using student response systems ("clickers") to combat conformity and shyness. *Teaching of Psychology, 37*, 135–140.

Strain, J. F., Womack, K. B., Didenbani, N., Spence, J. S., Conover, H., Hart, J., Jr., . . . Cullum, C. M. (2015). Imaging correlates of memory and concussion history in retired National Football League athletes. *JAMA Neurology, 72*, 773–780.

Stranahan, A. M., Khalil, D., & Gould, E. (2006). Social isolation delays the positive effects of running on adult neurogenesis. *Nature Neuroscience, 9*, 526–533.

Strange, B. A., & Dolan, R. J. (2004). b-Adrenergic modulation of emotional memory-evoked human amygdala and hippocampal responses. *PNAS, 101*, 11454–11458.

Strange, D., Hayne, H., & Garry, M. (2008). A photo, a suggestion, a false memory. *Applied Cognitive Psychology, 22*, 587–603.

Strasburger, V. C., Jordan, A. B., & Donnerstein, E. (2010). Health effects of media on children and adolescents. *Pediatrics, 125*, 756–767.

Stratton, G. M. (1896). Some preliminary experiments on vision without inversion of the retinal image. *Psychological Review, 3*, 611–617.

Straub, R. O., Seidenberg, M. S., Bever, T. G., & Terrace, H. S. (1979). Serial learning in the pigeon. *Journal of the Experimental Analysis of Behavior, 32*, 137–148.

Straus, M. A., Sugarman, D. B., & Giles-Sims, J. (1997). Spanking by parents and subsequent antisocial behavior of children. *Archives of Pediatric Adolescent Medicine, 151*, 761–767.

Strawbridge, W. J. (1999). *Mortality and religious involvement: A review and critique of the results, the methods, and the measures*. Paper presented at Harvard University conference on religion and health sponsored by the National Institute for Health Research and the John Templeton Foundation.

Strawbridge, W. J., Cohen, R. D., & Shema, S. J. (1997). Frequent attendance at religious services and mortality over 28 years. *American Journal of Public Health, 87*, 957–961.

Strick, M., Dijksterhuis, A., & van Baaren, R. B. (2010). Unconscious thought effects take place off-line, not on-line. *Psychological Science, 21*, 484–488.

Stringaris, A., Vidal-Ribas Belil, P., Artiges, E., Lemaitre, H., Gollier-Briant, F., Wolke, S., . . . Fadai, T. (2015). The brain's response to reward anticipation and depression in adolescence: Dimensionality, specificity, and longitudinal predictions in a community-based sample. *American Journal of Psychiatry, 172*(12), 1215–1223.

Stroebe, M., Finenauer, C., Wijngaards-de Meij, L., Schut, H., van den Bout, J., & Stroebe, W. (2013). Partner-oriented self-regulation among bereaved parents: The costs of holding in grief for the partner's sake. *Psychological Science, 24*, 395–402.

Stroebe, W. (2013). Firearm possession and violent death: A critical review. *Aggression and Violent Behavior, 18*, 709–721.

Stroebe, W., Schut, H., & Stroebe, M. S. (2005). Grief work, disclosure and counseling: Do they help the bereaved? *Clinical Psychology Review, 25*, 395–414.

Stroud, L. R., Panadonatos, G. D., Rodriguez, D., McCallum, M., Salisbury, A. L., Phipps, M. G., . . . Marsit, C. J. (2014). Maternal smoking during pregnancy and infant stress response: Test of a prenatal programming hypothesis. *Psychoneuroendocrinology, 48*, 29–40.

Strully, K. W. (2009). Job loss and health in the U.S. labor market. *Demography, 46*, 221–246.

Strupp, H. H. (1986). Psychotherapy: Research, practice, and public policy (how to avoid dead ends). *American Psychologist, 41*, 120–130.

Štulhofer, A., Šoh, D., Jelaska, N., Baćak, V., & Landripet, I. (2011). Religiosity and sexual risk behavior among Croatian college students, 1998–2008. *Journal of Sex Research, 48*, 360–371.

Stunkard, A. J., Harris, J. R., Pedersen, N. L., & McClearn, G. E. (1990). A separated twin study of the body mass index. *New England Journal of Medicine, 322*, 1483–1487.

Stutzer, A., & Frey, B. S. (2006). Does marriage make people happy, or do happy people get married? *Journal of Socio-Economics, 35*, 326–347.

Su, R., Rounds, J., & Armstrong, P. I. (2009). Men and things, women and people: A meta-analysis of sex differences in interests. *Psychological Bulletin, 135*, 859–884.

Subrahmanyam, K., & Greenfield, P. (2008). Online communication and adolescent relationships. *The Future of Children, 18*, 119–146.

Suddath, R. L., Christison, G. W., Torrey, E. F., Casanova, M. F., & Weinberger, D. R. (1990). Anatomical abnormalities in the brains of monozygotic twins discordant for schizophrenia. *New England Journal of Medicine, 322*, 789–794.

Sue, S. (2006). Research to address racial and ethnic disparities in mental health: Some lessons learned. In S. I. Donaldson, D. E. Berger, & K. Pezdek (Eds.), *Applied psychology: New frontiers and rewarding careers*. (pp. 119–134). Mahwah, NJ: Erlbaum.

Suedfeld, P., & Mocellin, J. S. P. (1987). The "sensed presence" in unusual environments. *Environment and Behavior, 19*, 33–52.

Sulik, M. J., Blair, C., Mills-Koonce, R., Berry, D., Greenberg, M., & Family Life Project Investigators. (2015). Early parenting and the development of externalizing behavior problems: Longitudinal mediation through children's executive function. *Child Development, 86*, 1588–1603.

Sullivan, P. F., Neale, M. C., & Kendler, K. S. (2000). Genetic epidemiology of major depression: Review and meta-analysis. *American Journal of Psychiatry, 157*, 1552–1562.

Suls, J. M., & Tesch, F. (1978). Students' preferences for information about their test performance: A social comparison study. *Journal of Experimental Social Psychology, 8*, 189–197.

Summers, M. (1996, December 9). Mister Clean. *People Weekly*, pp. 139–142.

Sundie, J. M., Kenrick, D. T., Griskevicius, V., Tybur, J. M., Vohs, K. D., & Beal, D. J. (2011). Peacocks, Porsches, and Thorsten Veblen: Conspicuous consumption as a sexual signaling system. *Journal of Personality and Social Psychology, 100*, 664–680.

Sundstrom, E., De Meuse, K. P., & Futrell, D. (1990). Work teams: Applications and effectiveness. *American Psychologist, 45*, 120–133.

Sunstein, C. R. (2007). On the divergent American reactions to terrorism and climate change. *Columbia Law Review, 107*, 503–557.

Suomi, S. J. (1986). Anxiety-like disorders in young nonhuman primates. In R. Gettleman (Ed.), *Anxiety disorders of childhood* (pp. 1–23). New York: Guilford Press.

Suomi, S. J., Collins, M. L., Harlow, H. F., & Ruppenthal, G. C. (1976). Effects of maternal and peer separations on young monkeys. *Journal of Child Psychology and Psychiatry, 17*, 101–112.

Surgeon General. (1986). *The Surgeon General's workshop on pornography and public health*, June 22–24. Report prepared by E. P. Mulvey & J. L. Haugaard and released by Office of the Surgeon General on August 4, 1986.

Surgeon General. (1999). *Mental health: A report of the Surgeon General*. Rockville, MD: U.S. Department of Health and Human Services.

Susser, E., Neugenbauer, R., Hoek, H. W., Brown, A. S., Lin, S., Labovitz, D., & Gorman, J. M. (1996). Schizophrenia after prenatal famine. *Archives of General Psychiatry, 53*(1), 25–31.

Sutherland, A. (2006a). *Bitten and scratched: Life and lessons at the premier school for exotic animal trainers*. New York: Viking.

Sutherland, A. (2006b, June 25). What Shamu taught me about a happy marriage. *The New York Times* (nytimes.com).

Swami, V. (2015). Cultural influences on body size ideals: Unpacking the impact of Westernization and modernization. *European Psychologist, 20*, 44–51.

Swami, V., Frederick, D. A., Aavik, T., Alcalay, L., Allik, J., Anderson, D., . . . Zivcic-Becirevic, I. (2010). The attractive female body weight and female body dissatisfaction in 26 countries across 10 world regions: Results of the international body project I. *Personality and Social Psychology Bulletin, 36*, 309–325.

Swami, V., Henderson, G., Custance, D., & Tovée, M. J. (2011). A cross-cultural investigation of men's judgments of female body weight in Britain and Indonesia. *Journal of Cross-Cultural Psychology, 42*, 140–145.

Swann, W. B., Jr., Chang-Schneider, C., & McClarty, K. L. (2007). Do people's self-views matter? Self-concept and self-esteem in everyday life. *American Psychologist, 62*, 84–94.

Swinburn, B. A., Sacks, G., Hall, K. D., McPherson, K., Finegood, D. T., Moodie, M. L., & Gortmaker, S. L. (2011). The global obesity pandemic: Shaped by global drivers and local environments. *The Lancet, 378*, 804–814.

Symbaluk, D. G., Heth, C. D., Cameron, J., & Pierce, W. D. (1997). Social modeling, monetary incentives, and pain endurance: The role of self-efficacy and pain perception. *Personality and Social Psychology Bulletin, 23*, 258–269.

Tadmor, C. T., Galinsky, A. D., & Maddux, W. W. (2012). Getting the most out of living abroad: Biculturalism and integrative complexity as key drivers of creative and professional success. *Journal of Personality and Social Psychology, 103*, 520–542.

Taheri, S. (2004, 20 December). Does the lack of sleep make you fat? *University of Bristol Research News* (bristol.ac.uk).

Taheri, S., Lin, L., Austin, D., Young, T., & Mignot, E. (2004). Short sleep duration is associated with reduced leptin, elevated ghrelin, and increased body mass index. *PloS Medicine, 1*(3), e62.

Tajfel, H. (Ed.). (1982). *Social identity and intergroup relations*. New York: Cambridge University Press.

Takizawa, R., Maughan, B., & Arseneault, L. (2014). Adult health outcomes of childhood bullying victimization: Evidence from a five-decade longitudinal British birth cohort. *American Journal of Psychiatry, 171*, 777–784.

Talarico, J. M., & Moore, K. M. (2012). Memories of "The Rivalry": Differences in how fans of the winning and losing teams remember the same game. *Applied Cognitive Psychology, 26*, 746–756.

Tamres, L. K., Janicki, D., & Helgeson, V. S. (2002). Sex differences in coping behavior: A meta-analytic review and an examination of relative coping. *Personality and Social Psychology Review, 6*, 2–30.

Tangney, J. P., Baumeister, R. F., & Boone, A. L. (2004). High self-control predicts good adjustment, less pathology, better grades, and interpersonal success. *Journal of Personality, 72*, 271–324.

Tannen, D. (1990). *You just don't understand: Women and men in conversation*. New York: Morrow.

Tannenbaum, P. (2002, February). Quoted by R. Kubey & M. Csikszentmihalyi, Television addiction is no mere metaphor. *Scientific American*, pp. 74–80.

Tanner, J. M. (1978). *Fetus into man: Physical growth from conception to maturity*. Cambridge, MA: Harvard University Press.

Tardif, T., Fletcher, P., Liang, W., Zhang, Z., Kaciroti, N., & Marchman, V. A. (2008). Baby's first 10 words. *Developmental Psychology, 44*, 929–938.

Taubes, G. (2001). The soft science of dietary fat. *Science, 291*, 2536–2545.

Taubes, G. (2002, July 7). What if it's all been a big fat lie? *The New York Times* (nytimes.com).

Tavernier, R., & Willoughby, T. (2014). Bidirectional associations between sleep (quality and duration) and psychosocial functioning across the university years. *Developmental Psychology, 50*, 674–682.

Tavernise, S. (2013, February 13). To reduce suicide rates, new focus turns to guns. *The New York Times* (nytimes.com).

Taylor, C. A., Manganello, J. A., Lee, S. J., & Rice, J. C. (2010a). Mothers' spanking of 3-year-old children and subsequent risk of children's aggressive behavior. *Pediatrics, 125*, 1057–1065.

Taylor, P. J., Gooding, P., Wood, A. M., & Tarrier, N. (2011). The role of defeat and entrapment in depression, anxiety, and suicide. *Psychological Bulletin, 137*, 391–420.

Taylor, S. (2013). Molecular genetics of obsessive-compulsive disorder: A comprehensive meta-analysis of genetic association studies. *Molecular Psychiatry, 18*, 799–805.

Taylor, S., Kuch, K., Koch, W. J., Crockett, D. J., & Passey, G. (1998b). The structure of posttraumatic stress symptoms. *Journal of Abnormal Psychology, 107*, 154–160.

Taylor, S. E. (1983). Adjustment to threatening events: A theory of cognitive adaptation. *American Psychologist, 38*, 1161–1173.

Taylor, S. E. (2002). *The tending instinct: How nurturing is essential to who we are and how we live*. New York: Times Books.

Taylor, S. E. (2006). Tend and befriend: Biobehavioral bases of affiliation under stress. *Current Directions in Psychological Science, 15*, 273–277.

Taylor, S. E., Cousino, L. K., Lewis, B. P., Gruenewald, T. L., Gurung, R. A. R., & Updegraff, J. A. (2000). Biobehavioral responses to stress in females: Tend-and-befriend, not fight-or-flight. *Psychological Review, 107*, 411–430.

Taylor, S. E., Pham, L. B., Rivkin, I. D., & Armor, D. A. (1998a). Harnessing the imagination: Mental simulation, self-regulation, and coping. *American Psychologist, 53*, 429–439.

Taylor, S. E., Saphire-Bernstein, S., & Seeman, T. E. (2010b). Are plasma oxytocin in women and plasma vasopressin in men biomarkers of distressed pair-bond relationships? *Psychological Science, 21*, 3–7.

Tedeschi, R. G., & Calhoun, L. G. (2004). Posttraumatic growth: Conceptual foundations and empirical evidence. *Psychological Inquiry, 15*, 1–18.

Teghtsoonian, R. (1971). On the exponents in Stevens' law and the constant in Ekman's law. *Psychological Review, 78*, 71–80.

Teller. (2009, April 20). Quoted by J. Lehrer, Magic and the brain: Teller reveals the neuroscience of illusion. *Wired* (wired.com).

Telzer, E. H., Flannery, J., Shapiro, M., Humphreys, K. L., Goff, B., Gabard-Durman, L., . . . Tottenham, N. (2013). Early experience shapes amygdala sensitivity to race: An international adoption design. *Journal of Neuroscience, 33*, 13484–13488.

Tenenbaum, H. R., & Leaper, C. (2002). Are parents' gender schemas related to their children's gender-related cognitions? A meta-analysis. *Developmental Psychology, 38*, 615–630.

Terrace, H. S. (1979, November). How Nim Chimpsky changed my mind. *Psychology Today*, pp. 65–76.

Terre, L., & Stoddart, R. (2000). Cutting edge specialties for graduate study in psychology. *Eye on Psi Chi, 23*–26.

Tesser, A., Forehand, R., Brody, G., & Long, N. (1989). Conflict: The role of calm and angry parent-child discussion in adolescent development. *Journal of Social and Clinical Psychology, 8*, 317–330.

Tew, J. D., Mulsant, B. H., Haskett, R. F., Joan, P., Begley, A. E., Sackeim, H. A. (2007). Relapse during continuation pharmacotherapy after acute response to ECT: A comparison of usual care versus protocolized treatment. *Annals of Clinical Psychiatry, 19*, 1–4.

Thaler, L., Arnott, S. R., & Goodale, M. A. (2011). Neural correlates of natural human echolocation in early and late blind echolocation experts. *PLoS One, 6*, e20162.

Thaler, L., Milne, J. L., Arnott, S. R., Kish, D., & Goodale, M. A. (2014). Neural correlates of motion processing through echolocation, source hearing, and vision in blind echolocation experts and sighted echolocation novices. *Journal of Neurophysiology, 111*, 112–127.

Thaler, R. H. (2015, May 8). Unless you are Spock, irrelevant things matter in economic behavior. *The New York Times* (nytimes.com).

Thaler, R. H., & Sunstein, C. R. (2008). *Nudge: Improving decisions about health, wealth, and happiness*. New Haven, CT: Yale University Press.

Thatcher, R. W., Walker, R. A., & Giudice, S. (1987). Human cerebral hemispheres develop at different rates and ages. *Science, 236*, 1110–1113.

Thiel, A., Hadedank, B., Herholz, K., Kessler, J., Winhuisen, L., Haupt, W. F., & Heiss, W.-D. (2006). From the left to the right: How the brain compensates progressive loss of language function. *Brain and Language, 98*, 57–65.

Thomas, A., & Chess, S. (1986). The New York Longitudinal Study: From infancy to early adult life. In R. Plomin & J. Dunn (Eds.), *The study of temperament: Changes, continuities, and challenges*. Hillsdale, NJ: Erlbaum.

Thomas, L. (1992). *The fragile species*. New York: Scribner's.

Thompson, G. (2010). The $1 million dollar challenge. *Skeptic Magazine, 15*, 8–9.

Thompson, J. K., Jarvie, G. J., Lahey, B. B., & Cureton, K. J. (1982). Exercise and obesity: Etiology, physiology, and intervention. *Psychological Bulletin, 91*, 55–79.

Thompson, P. M., Giedd, J. N., Woods, R. P., MacDonald, D., Evans, A. C., & Toga, A. W. (2000). Growth patterns in the developing brain detected by using continuum mechanical tensor maps. *Nature, 404*, 190–193.

Thompson, R., Emmorey, K., & Gollan, T. H. (2005). "Tip of the fingers" experiences by Deaf signers. *Psychological Science, 16*, 856–860.

Thompson-Schill, S. L., Ramscar, M., & Chrysikou, E. G. (2009). Cognition without control: When a little frontal lobe goes a long way. *Current Directions in Psychological Science, 18,* 259–263.

Thorndike, E. L. (1898). Animal intelligence: An experimental study of the associative processes in animals. *Psychological Review Monograph Supplement 2,* 4–160.

Thorne, J., with Larry Rothstein. (1993). *You are not alone: Words of experience and hope for the journey through depression.* New York: HarperPerennial.

Thornton, B., & Moore, S. (1993). Physical attractiveness contrast effect: Implications for self-esteem and evaluations of the social self. *Personality and Social Psychology Bulletin, 19,* 474–480.

Thorpe, W. H. (1974). *Animal nature and human nature.* London: Metheun.

Tickle, J. J., Hull, J. G., Sargent, J. D., Dalton, M. A., & Heatherton, T. F. (2006). A structural equation model of social influences and exposure to media smoking on adolescent smoking. *Basic and Applied Social Psychology, 28,* 117–129.

Tiggemann, M., & Miller, J. (2010). The Internet and adolescent girls' weight satisfaction and drive for thinness. *Sex Roles, 63,* 79–90.

Tiihonen, J., Lönnqvist, J., Wahlbeck, K., Klaukka, T., Niskanen, L., Tanskanen, A., & Haukka, J. (2009). 11-year follow-up of mortality in patients with schizophrenia: A population-based cohort study (FIN11 study). *The Lancet, 374,* 260–267.

Timmerman, T. A. (2007) "It was a thought pitch": Personal, situational, and target influences on hit-by-pitch events across time. *Journal of Applied Psychology, 92,* 876–884.

Tirrell, M. E. (1990). Personal communication.

Tobin, D. D., Menon, M., Menon, M., Spatta, B. C., Hodges, E. V. E., & Perry, D. G. (2010). The intrapsychics of gender: A model of self-socialization. *Psychological Review, 117,* 601–622.

Toews, P. (2004, December 30). *Dirk Willems: A heart undivided.* Mennonite Brethren Historical Commission (nbhistory.org/profiles/dirk.en.html).

Tolin, D. F. (2010). Is cognitive–behavioral therapy more effective than other therapies? A meta-analytic review. *Clinical Psychology Review, 30,* 710–720.

Tolman, E. C., & Honzik, C. H. (1930). Introduction and removal of reward, and maze performance in rats. *University of California Publications in Psychology, 4,* 257–275.

Tomaka, J., Blascovich, J., & Kelsey, R. M. (1992). Effects of self-deception, social desirability, and repressive coping on psychophysiological reactivity to stress. *Personality and Social Psychology Bulletin, 18,* 616–624.

Tononi, G., & Cirelli, C. (2013, August). Perchance to prune. *Scientific American,* pp. 34–39.

Topolinski, S., & Reber, R. (2010). Gaining insight into the "aha" experience. *Current Directions in Psychological Science, 19,* 401–405.

Torrey, E. F. (1986). *Witchdoctors and psychiatrists.* New York: Harper & Row.

Torrey, E. F., & Miller, J. (2002). *The invisible plague: The rise of mental illness from 1750 to the present.* New Brunswick, NJ: Rutgers University Press.

Torrey, E. F., Miller, J., Rawlings, R., & Yolken, R. H. (1997). Seasonality of births in schizophrenia and bipolar disorder: A review of the literature. *Schizophrenia Research, 28,* 1–38.

Totterdell, P., Kellett, S., Briner, R. B., & Teuchmann, K. (1998). Evidence of mood linkage in work groups. *Journal of Personality and Social Psychology, 74,* 1504–1515.

Tovee, M. J., Mason, S. M., Emery, J. L., McCluskey, S. E., & Cohen-Tovee, E. M. (1997). Supermodels: Stick insects or hourglasses? *The Lancet, 350,* 1474–1475.

Tracey, J. L., & Robins, R. W. (2004). Show your pride: Evidence for a discrete emotion expression. *Psychological Science, 15,* 194–197.

Trahan, L. H., Stuebing, K. K., Fletcher, J. M., & Hiscock, M. (2014). The Flynn effect: A meta-analysis. *Psychological Bulletin, 140,* 1332–1360.

Treffert, D. A., & Christensen, D. D. (2005, December). Inside the mind of a savant. *Scientific American,* pp. 108–113.

Treffert, D. A., & Wallace, G. L. (2002). Island of genius—The artistic brilliance and dazzling memory that sometimes accompany autism and other disorders hint at how all brains work. *Scientific American, 286,* 76–86.

Treisman, A. (1987). Properties, parts, and objects. In K. R. Boff, L. Kaufman, & J. P. Thomas (Eds.), *Handbook of perception and human performance* (pp. 35-1–35-70). New York: Wiley.

Triandis, H. C. (1994). *Culture and social behavior.* New York: McGraw-Hill.

Triandis, H. C., Bontempo, R., Villareal, M. J., Asai, M., & Lucca, N. (1988). Individualism and collectivism: Cross-cultural perspectives on self–ingroup relationships. *Journal of Personality and Social Psychology, 54,* 323–338.

Trickett, P. K., & McBride-Chang, C. (1995). The developmental impact of different forms of child abuse and neglect. *Developmental Review, 15,* 311–337.

Trillin, C. (2006, March 27). Alice off the page. *The New Yorker,* p. 44.

Triplett, N. (1898). The dynamogenic factors in pacemaking and competition. *American Journal of Psychology, 9,* 507–533.

Trotter, J. (2014, January 23). The power of positive coaching. *Sports Illustrated* (http://mmqb.si.com/2014/01/23/pete-carroll-seattle-seahawkssuper-bowl-48).

Tsai, J. L., Ang, J. Y. Z., Blevins, E., Goernandt, J., Fung, H. H., Jiang, D., . . . Haddouk, L. (2016). Leaders' smiles reflect cultural differences in ideal affect. *Emotion, 16*(2), 183–195.

Tsai, J. L., Knutson, B., & Fung, H. H. (2006). Cultural variation in affect valuation. *Journal of Personality and Social Psychology, 90,* 288–307.

Tsang, Y. C. (1938). Hunger motivation in gastrectomized rats. *Journal of Comparative Psychology, 26,* 1–17.

Tse, T., Langston, R. F., Kakeyama, M., Bethus, I., Spooner P. A., Wood, E. R., . . . Morris, R. G. M. (2007). Schemas and memory consolidation. *Science, 316,* 76–82.

Tsuang, M. T., & Faraone, S. V. (1990). *The genetics of mood disorders.* Baltimore, MD: Johns Hopkins University Press.

Tsvetkova, M., & Macy, M. W. (2014). The social contagion of generosity. *PLOS ONE, 9*(2), e87275. doi:10.1371/journal.pone.0087275

Tuber, D. S., Miller, D. D., Caris, K. A., Halter, R., Linden, F., & Hennessy, M. B. (1999). Dogs in animal shelters: Problems, suggestions, and needed expertise. *Psychological Science, 10,* 379–386.

Tucker, K. A. (2002, May 20). I believe you can fly. *Gallup Management Journal* (gallup.com).

Tuk, M. A., Zhang, K., & Sweldens, S. (2015). The propagation of self-control: Self-control in one domain simultaneously improves self-control in other domains. *Journal of Experimental Psychology: General, 144,* 639–654.

Turner, H., Marshall, E., Wood, F., Stopa, L., & Waller, G. (2016). CBT for eating disorders: The impact of early changes in eating pathology on later changes in personality pathology, anxiety and depression. *Behaviour Research and Therapy, 77,* 1–6.

Turner, J. C. (2007) Self-categorization theory. In R. Baumeister & K. Vohs (Eds.), *Encyclopedia of social psychology* (pp. 793–795). Thousand Oaks, CA: Sage.

Turner, N., Barling, J., & Zacharatos, A. (2002). Positive psychology at work. In C. R. Snyder & S. J. Lopez (Eds.), *The handbook of positive psychology* (pp. 715–728). New York: Oxford University Press.

Turner, W. A., & Casey, L. M. (2014). Outcomes associated with virtual reality in psychological interventions: Where are we now? *Clinical Psychology Review, 34,* 634–644.

Tuvblad, C., Narusyte, J., Grann, M., Sarnecki, J., & Lichtenstein, P. (2011). The genetic and environmental etiology of antisocial behavior from childhood to emerging adulthood. *Behavior Genetics, 41,* 629–640.

Tversky, A. (1985, June). Quoted in K. McKean, Decisions, decisions. *Discover,* pp. 22–31.

Tversky, A., & Kahneman, D. (1974). Judgment under uncertainty: Heuristics and biases. *Science, 185,* 1124–1131.

Twenge, J. M. (2001). Birth cohort changes in extraversion: A cross-temporal meta-analysis, 1966–1993. *Personality and Individual Differences, 30,* 735–748.

Twenge, J. M., Baumeister, R. F., DeWall, C. N., Ciarocco, N. J., & Bartels, J. M. (2007). Social exclusion decreases prosocial behavior. *Journal of Personality and Social Psychology, 92,* 56–66.

Twenge, J. M., Baumeister, R. F., Tice, D. M., & Stucke, T. S. (2001). If you can't join them, beat them: Effects of social exclusion on aggressive behavior. *Journal of Personality and Social Psychology, 81,* 1058–1069.

Twenge, J. M., & Campbell, W. K. (2008). Increases in positive self-views among high school students: Birth-cohort changes in anticipated performance, self-satisfaction, self-liking, and self-competence. *Psychological Science, 19,* 1082–1086.

Twenge, J. M., Campbell, W. K., & Freeman, E. C. (2012). Generational differences in young adults' life goals, concern for others, and civic orientation, 1966–2009. *Journal of Personality and Social Psychology, 102,* 1045–1062.

Twenge, J. M., Gentile, B., DeWall, C. D., Ma, D., & Lacefield, K. (2008). *A growing disturbance: Increasing psychopathology in young people 1938–2007 in a meta-analysis of the MMPI.* Unpublished manuscript, San Diego State University.

Twenge, J. M., Gentile, B., DeWall, C. N., Ma, D., Lacefield, K., & Schurtz, D. R. (2010). Birth cohort increases in psychopathology among young Americans, 1938–2007: A cross-temporal meta-analysis of the MMPI. *Clinical Psychology Review, 30,* 145–154.

Twenge, J. M., Zhang, L., & Im, C. (2004). It's beyond my control: A cross-temporal meta-analysis of increasing externality in locus of control, 1960–2002. *Personality and Social Psychology Review, 8,* 308–319.

Twiss, C., Tabb, S., Crosby, F. (1989). Affirmative action and aggregate data: The importance of patterns in the perception of discrimination. In F. Blanchard & F. Crosby (Eds.), *Affirmative action: Social psychological perspectives* (pp. 159–167). New York: Springer-Verlag.

Tyler, K. A. (2002). Social and emotional outcomes of childhood sexual abuse: A review of recent research. *Aggression and Violent Behavior, 7,* 567–589.

U.S. Senate Select Committee on Intelligence. (2004, July 9). *Report of the Select Committee on Intelligence on the U.S. intelligence community's prewar intelligence assessments on Iraq.* Washington, DC: U.S. Senate Select Committee on Intelligence.

Uchida, Y., & Kitayama, S. (2009). Happiness and unhappiness in East and West: Themes and variations. *Emotion, 9,* 441–456.

Uchino, B. N., Cacioppo, J. T., & Kiecolt-Glaser, J. K. (1996). The relationship between social support and physiological processes: A review with emphasis on underlying mechanisms and implications for health. *Psychological Bulletin, 119,* 488–531.

Uchino, B. N., Uno, D., & Holt-Lunstad, J. (1999). Social support, physiological processes, and health. *Current Directions in Psychological Science, 8,* 145–148.

Udry, J. R. (2000). Biological limits of gender construction. *American Sociological Review, 65,* 443–457.

Ugander, J., Backstrom, L., Marlow, C., & Kleinberg, J. (2012). Structural diversity in social contagion. *PNAS, 109,* 5962–5966.

UNAIDS. (2013, accessed May 17). *Data and analysis.* Joint United Nations Programme on HIV/AIDS (unaids.org/en/data-analysis).

United Nations. (2011, November 17). *Discriminatory laws and practices and acts of violence against individuals based on their sexual orientation and gender identity.* Report of the United Nations High Commissioner for Human Rights.

United Nations. (2015). *Human development report 2015.* New York: United Nations Development Programme.

Urry, H. L., & Gross, J. J. (2010). Emotion regulation in older age. *Current Directions in Psychological Science, 19,* 352–357.

Urry, H. L., Nitschke, J. B., Dolski, I., Jackson, D. C., Dalton, K. M., Mueller, C. J., . . . Davidson, R. J. (2004). Making a life worth living: Neural correlates of well-being. *Psychological Science, 15,* 367–372.

Vaillant, G. (2013, May). Quoted in S. Stossel, What makes us happy, revisited. *The Atlantic* (theatlantic.com/magazine/archive/2013/05/thanks-mom/309287/).

Vaillant, G. E. (2002). *Aging well: Surprising guideposts to a happier life from the landmark Harvard study of adult development.* Boston: Little, Brown.

Valenstein, E. S. (1986). *Great and desperate cures: The rise and decline of psychosurgery.* New York: Basic Books.

Valentine, S. E., Bankoff, S. M., Poulin, R. M., Reidler, E. B., & Pantalone, D. W. (2015). The use of dialectical behavior therapy skills training as standalone treatment: A systematic review of the treatment outcome literature. *Journal of Clinical Psychology, 71,* 1–20.

Valkenburg, P. M., & Peter, J. (2009). Social consequences of the Internet for adolescents: A decade of research. *Current Directions in Psychological Science, 18,* 1–5.

Vallone, R. P., Griffin, D. W., Lin, S., & Ross, L. (1990). Overconfident prediction of future actions and outcomes by self and others. *Journal of Personality and Social Psychology, 58,* 582–592.

van Anders, S. M. (2012). Testosterone and sexual desire in healthy women and men. *Archives of Sexual Behavior, 41,* 1471–1484.

Van Bockstaele, B., Verschuere, B., Tibboel, H., De Houwer, J., Crombez, G., & Koster, E. H. W. (2014). A review of current evidence for the causal impact of attentional bias on fear and anxiety. *Psychological Bulletin, 140,* 682–721.

van de Bongardt, D., Reitz, E., Sandfort, T., & Deković, M. (2015). A meta-analysis of the relations between three types of peer norms and adolescent sexual behavior. *Personality and Social Psychology Review, 19,* 203–234.

van den Boom, D. C. (1990). Preventive intervention and the quality of mother-infant interaction and infant exploration in irritable infants. In W. Koops, H. J. G. Soppe, J. L. van der Linden, P. C. M. Molenaar, & J. J. F. Schroots (Eds.), *Developmental psychology research in The Netherlands.* The Netherlands: Uitgeverij Eburon. Cited by C. Hazan & P. R. Shaver (1994). Deeper into attachment theory. *Psychological Inquiry, 5,* 68–79.

van den Boom, D. C. (1995). Do first-year intervention effects endure? Follow-up during toddlerhood of a sample of Dutch irritable infants. *Child Development, 66,* 1798–1816.

van den Bos, K., & Spruijt, N. (2002). Appropriateness of decisions as a moderator of the psychology of voice. *European Journal of Social Psychology, 32,* 57–72.

van der Lee, R., & Ellemers, N. (2015). Gender contributes to personal research funding success in The Netherlands. *PNAS, 112*(40), 12349–12353.

Van Dijk, W. W., Van Koningsbruggen, G. M., Ouwerkerk, J. W., & Wesseling, Y. M. (2011). Self-esteem, self-affirmation, and schadenfreude. *Emotion, 11,* 1445–1449.

van Dyke, C., & Byck, R. (1982, March). Cocaine. *Scientific American,* pp. 128–141.

van Engen, M. L., & Willemsen, T. M. (2004). Sex and leadership styles: A meta-analysis of research published in the 1990s. *Psychological Reports, 94,* 3–18.

van Geel, M., Goemans, A., & Vedder, P. (2015). A meta-analysis on the relation between peer victimization and adolescent non-suicidal self-injury. *Psychiatry Research, 230*(2), 364–368.

van Goozen, S. H. M., Fairchild, G., Snoek, H., & Harold, G. T. (2007). The evidence for a neurobiological model of childhood antisocial behavior. *Psychological Bulletin, 133,* 149–182.

van Haren, N. E., Schnack, H. G., Koevoets, M. G., Cahn, W., Pol, H. E. H., & Kahn, R. S. (2016). Trajectories of subcortical volume change in schizophrenia: A 5-year follow-up. *Schizophrenia Research, 173*(3), 140–145.

van Haren, N. M., Rijsdijk, F., Schnack, H. G., Picchioni, M. M., Toulopoulou, T., Weisbrod, M., . . . Kahn, R. S. (2012). The genetic and environmental determinants of the association between brain abnormalities and schizophrenia: The Schizophrenia Twins and Relatives Consortium. *Biological Psychiatry, 71,* 915–921.

van Honk, J., Schutter, D. J., Bos, P. A., Kruijt, A.-W., Lentje, E. G. & Baron-Cohen, S. (2011). Testosterone administration impairs cognitive empathy in women depending on second-to-fourth digit ratio. *PNAS, 108,* 3448–3452.

Van Horn, J., Irimia, A., Torgerson, C., Chambers, M., Kikinis, R., & Toga, A. (2012). Mapping connectivity damage in the case of Phineas Gage. *PLOS ONE, 7*(5), e37454. doi:10.1371/journal.pone.0037454

Van Houtem, C. M. H. H., Lain, M. L., Boomsma, D. I., Ligthart, L., van Wijk, A. J., & De Jongh, A. (2013). A review and meta-analysis of the heritability of specific phobia subtypes and corresponding fears. *Journal of Anxiety Disorders, 27,* 379–388.

van IJzendoorn, M. H., & Juffer, F. (2005). Adoption is a successful natural intervention enhancing adopted children's IQ and school performance. *Current Directions in Psychological Science, 14,* 326–330.

van IJzendoorn, M. H., & Juffer, F. (2006). The Emanual Miller Memorial Lecture 2006: Adoption as intervention. Meta-analytic evidence for massive catch-up and plasticity in physical, socio-emotional, and cognitive development. *Journal of Child Psychology and Psychiatry, 47,* 1228–1245.

van Ijzendoorn, M. H., Juffer, F., & Poelhuis, C. W. K. (2005). Adoption and cognitive development: A meta-analytic comparison of adopted and nonadopted children's IQ and school performance. *Psychological Bulletin, 131,* 301–316.

van IJzendoorn, M. H., & Kroonenberg, P. M. (1988). Cross-cultural patterns of attachment: A meta-analysis of the strange situation. *Child Development, 59,* 147–156.

van IJzendoorn, M. H., Luijk, M. P. C. M., & Juffer, F. (2008). IQ of children growing up in children's homes: A meta-analysis on IQ delays in orphanages. *Merrill-Palmer Quarterly, 54,* 341–366.

Van Ittersum, K., & Wansink, B. (2012). Plate size and color suggestibility: The Delboeuf illusion's bias on serving and eating behavior. *Journal of Consumer Research, 39,* 215–228.

Van Kesteren, P. J. M., Asscheman, H., Megens, J. A. J., & Gooren, J. G. (1997). Mortality and morbidity in transsexual subjects treated with cross-sex hormones. *Clinical Endocrinology, 47,* 337–342.

Van Yperen, N. W., & Buunk, B. P. (1990). A longitudinal study of equity and satisfaction in intimate relationships. *European Journal of Social Psychology, 20,* 287–309.

Van Zeijl, J., Mesman, J., van IJzendoorn, M. H., Bakermans-Kranenburg, M. J., Juffer, F., Stolk, M. N., . . . Alink, L. R. A. (2006). Attachment-based intervention for enhancing sensitive discipline in mothers of 1- to 3-year-old children at risk for externalizing behavior problems: A randomized controlled trial. *Journal of Consulting and Clinical Psychology, 74,* 994–1005.

vanDellen, M. R., Campbell, W. K., Hoyle, R. H., & Bradfield, E. K. (2011). Compensating, resisting, and breaking: A meta-analytic examination of reactions to self-esteem threat. *Personality and Social Psychological Review, 15,* 51–74.

Vandenberg, S. G., & Kuse, A. R. (1978). Mental rotations: A group test of three-dimensional spatial visualization. *Perceptual and Motor Skills, 47,* 599–604.

VanderLaan, D. P., Forrester, D. L., Petterson, L. J., & Vasey, P. L. (2012). Offspring production among the extended relatives of Samoan men and fa'afafine. *PloS One, 7,* e36088.

VanderLaan, D. P., & Vasey, P. L. (2011). Male sexual orientation in Independent Samoa: Evidence for fraternal birth order and maternal fecundity effects. *Archives of Sexual Behavior, 40,* 495–503.

Vanhalst, J., Soenens, B., Luyckx, K., Van Petegem, S., Weeks, M. S., & Asher, S. R. (2015). Why do the lonely stay lonely? Chronically lonely adolescents' attributions and emotions in situations of social inclusion and exclusion. *Journal of Personality and Social Psychology, 109,* 932–948.

Vaughn, E. L., de Dios, M. A., Steinfeldt, J. A., & Kratz, L. M. (2011). Religiosity, alcohol use attitudes, and alcohol use in a national sample of adolescents. *Psychology of Addictive Behaviors, 25,* 547–553.

Vaughn, K. B., & Lanzetta, J. T. (1981). The effect of modification of expressive displays on vicarious emotional arousal. *Journal of Experimental Social Psychology, 17,* 16–30.

Vazsonyi, A., Ksinan, A., Mikuška, J., & Jiskrova, G. (2015). The Big Five and adolescent adjustment: An empirical test across six cultures. *Personality and Individual Differences, 83,* 234–244.

Vecera, S. P., Vogel, E. K., & Woodman, G. F. (2002). Lower region: A new cue for figure-ground assignment. *Journal of Experimental Psychology: General, 13,* 194–205.

Veenhoven, R. (2014). *World database of happiness.* Retrieved from worlddatabaseofhappiness.eur.nl/

Verbeek, M. E. M., Drent, P. J., & Wiepkema, P. R. (1994). Consistent individual differences in early exploratory behaviour of male great tits. *Animal Behaviour, 48,* 1113–1121.

Verduyn, P., Lee, D. S., Park, J., Shablack, H., Orvell, A., Bayer, J., . . . Kross, E. (2015). Passive Facebook usage undermines affective well-being: Experimental and longitudinal evidence. *Journal of Experimental Psychology: General, 144,* 480–488.

Verhaeghen, P., & Salthouse, T. A. (1997). Meta-analyses of age-cognition relations in adulthood: Estimates of linear and nonlinear age effects and structural models. *Psychological Bulletin, 122,* 231–249.

Vermetten, E., Schmahl, C., Lindner, S., Loewenstein, R. J., & Bremner, J. D. (2006). Hippocampal and amygdalar volumes in dissociative identity disorder. *American Journal of Psychiatry, 163*, 630–636.

Vezzali, L., Stathi, S., Giovannini, D., Capozza, D., & Trifiletti, E. (2015). The greatest magic of Harry Potter: Reducing prejudice. *Journal of Applied Social Psychology, 45*, 105–121.

Victora, C. G., Horta, B. L., de Mola, C. L., Quevedo, L., Pinheiro, R. T., Gigante, D. P., . . . Barros, F. C. (2015). Association between breastfeeding and intelligence, educational attainment, and income at 30 years of age: A prospective birth cohort study from Brazil. *Lancet Global Health, 3*, e199–205 (thelancet.com/lancetgh).

Vidoni, E. D., Johnson, D. K., Morris, J. K., Van Sciver, A., Greer, C. S., Billinger, S. A., & Burns, J. M. (2015). Dose-response of aerobic exercise on cognition: A community-based, pilot randomized controlled trial. *PLoS One, 10*, e0131647.

Vigil, J. M. (2009). A socio-relational framework of sex differences in the expression of emotion. *Behavioral and Brain Sciences, 32*, 375–428.

Vigliocco, G., & Hartsuiker, R. J. (2002). The interplay of meaning, sound, and syntax in sentence production. *Psychological Bulletin, 128*, 442–472.

Vining, E. P. G., Freeman, J. M., Pillas, D. J., Uematsu, S., Carson, B. S., Brandt, J., . . . Zukerberg, A. (1997). Why would you remove half a brain? The outcome of 58 children after hemispherectomy—The Johns Hopkins Experience: 1968 to 1996. *Pediatrics, 100*, 163–171.

Vinkhuyzen, A. A. E., van der Sluis, S., Posthuma, D., & Boomsma, D. I. (2009). The heritability of aptitude and exceptional talent across different domains in adolescents and young adults. *Behavior Genetics, 39*, 380–392.

Visich, P. S., & Fletcher, E. (2009). Myocardial infarction. In J. K. Ehrman P. M. Gordon, P. S. Visich, & S. J. Keleyian (Eds.). *Clinical exercise physiology* (2nd ed.). Champaign, IL: Human Kinetics.

Vitello, P. (2012, August 1). George A. Miller, a pioneer in cognitive psychology, is dead at 92. *The New York Times* (nytimes.com).

Vittengl, J. R., Clark, L. A., Dunn, T. W., & Jarrett, R. B. (2007). Reducing relapse and recurrence in unipolar depression: A comparative meta-analysis of cognitive-behavioral therapy's effects. *Journal of Consulting and Clinical Psychology, 75*, 475–488.

Vliegenthart, J., Noppe, G., van Rossum, E. F. C., Koper, J. W., Raat, H., & van den Akker, E. L. T. (2016). Socioeconomic status in children is associated with hair cortisol levels as a biological measure of chronic stress. *Psychoneuroendocrinology, 65*, 9–14.

Vocks, S., Tuschen-Caffier, B., Pietrowsky, R., Rustenbach, S. J., Kersting, A., & Herpertz, S. (2010). Meta-analysis of the effectiveness of psychological and pharmacological treatments for binge eating disorder. *International Journal of Eating Disorders, 43*, 205–217.

Vogel, N., Schilling, Wahl, H.-W., Beekman, A. T. F., & Penninx, B. W. J. H. (2013). Time-to-death-related change in positive and negative affect among older adults approaching the end of life. *Psychology and Aging, 28*, 128–141.

Vohs, K. D., & Baumeister, R. F. (Eds.) (2011). *Handbook of self-regulation*, (2nd ed.). New York: Guilford.

Vohs, K. D., Baumeister, R. F., & Schmeichel, B. J. (2012). Motivation, personal beliefs, and limited resources all contribute to self-control. *Journal of Experimental Social Psychology, 48*, 943–947.

Volkow, N. D., Wang, G. J., Kollins, S. H., Wigal, T. L., Newcorn, J. H., Telang, F., . . . Swanson, J. M. (2009). Evaluating dopamine reward pathway in ADHD: Clinical implications. *Journal of the American Medical Association, 302*, 1084–1091.

von Hippel, W. (2007). Aging, executive functioning, and social control. *Current Directions in Psychological Science, 16*, 240–244.

von Hippel, W. (2015, July 17). Do people become more prejudiced as they grow older? *BBC News Magazine* (bbc.com/news/magazine-33523313).

von Hippel, W., & Trivers, R. (2011). The evolution and psychology of self-deception. *Behavioral and Brain Sciences, 34*, 1–56.

von Senden, M. (1932). *The perception of space and shape in the congenitally blind before and after operation.* Glencoe, IL: Free Press.

von Stumm, S., Hell, B., & Chamorro-Premuzic, T. (2011). The hungry mind: Intellectual curiosity is the third pillar of academic performance. *Perspectives on Psychological Science, 6*, 574–588.

von Stumm, S., & Plomin, R. (2015). Breastfeeding and IQ growth from toddlerhood through adolescence. *PLoS ONE, 10*(9), e0138676.

Vonk, J., Jett, S. E., & Mosteller, K. W. (2012). Concept formation in American black bears, *Ursus americanus. Animal Behaviour, 84*, 953–964.

Vorona, R. D., Szklo-Coxe, M., Wu, A., Dubik, M., Zhao, Y., & Ware, J. C. (2011). Dissimilar teen crash rates in two neighboring Southeastern Virginia cities with different high school start times. *Journal of Clinical Sleep Medicine, 7*, 145–151.

Voyer, D., & Voyer, S. D. (2014). Gender differences in scholastic achievement: A meta-analysis. *Psychological Bulletin, 140*, 1174–1204.

VPC. (2013, February 7). States with higher gun ownership and weak gun laws lead nation in gun death. Violence Policy Center (vpc.org/press/press-release-archive/states-with-higher-gun-ownership-andweak-gun-laws-lead-nation-in-gun-death/).

Vukasović, T., & Bratko, D. (2015). Heritablity of personality: A meta-analysis of behavior genetic studies. *Psychological Bulletin, 141*, 769–785.

Vyse, S. (2016, March/April). Guns: feeling safe ≠ being safe. *Skeptical Inquirer*, pp. 27–30.

Waber, R. L., Shiv, B., Carmon, Z., & Ariely, D. (2008). Commercial features of placebo and therapeutic efficacy. *Journal of the American Medical Association, 299*, 1016–1017.

Wade, K. A., Garry, M., Read, J. D., & Lindsay, D. S. (2002). A picture is worth a thousand lies: Using false photographs to create false childhood memories. *Psychonomic Bulletin & Review, 9*, 597–603.

Wade, N. G., Worthington, E. L., Jr., & Vogel, D. L. (2006). Effectiveness of religiously tailored interventions in Christian therapy. *Psychotherapy Research, 17*, 91–105.

Wagenmakers, E.-J. (2014, June 25). Bem is back: A skeptic's review of a meta-analysis on psi. Open Science Collaboration (centerforopenscience.github.io/osc/2014/06/25/a-skeptics-review).

Wagenmakers, E.-J., Wetzels, R., Borsboom, D., & van der Maas, H. (2011). Why psychologists must change the way they analyze their data: The case of psi. *Journal of Personality and Social Psychology, 100*, 1–12.

Wager, R. D., & Atlas, L. Y. (2013). How is pain influenced by cognition? Neuroimaging weighs in. *Perspectives on Psychological Science, 8*, 91–97.

Wagner, D., Becker, B., Koester, P., Gouzoulis-Mayfrank, E., & Daumann, J. (2012b). A prospective study of learning, memory, and executive function in new MDMA users. *Addiction, 108*, 136–145.

Wagner, D. D., Altman, M., Boswell, R. G., Kelley, W. M., & Heatherton, T. F. (2013). Self-regulatory depletion enhances neural responses to rewards and impairs top-down control. *Psychological Science, 24*, 2262–2271.

Wagner, D. T., Barnes, C. M., Lim, V. K. G., & Ferris, D. L. (2012a). Lost sleep and cyberloafing: Evidence from the laboratory and a daylight saving time quasiexperiment. *Journal of Applied Psychology, 97*, 1068–1076.

Wagstaff, G. (1982). Attitudes to rape: The "just world" strikes again? *Bulletin of the British Psychological Society, 13*, 275–283.

Wakefield, J. C., & Spitzer, R. L. (2002). Lowered estimates—but of what? *Archives of General Psychiatry, 59*, 129–130.

Walfisch, A., Sermer, C., Cressman, A., & Koren, G. (2014). Breast milk and cognitive development—the role of confounders: A systematic review. *BMJ Open, 3*, e003259.

Walker, E., Shapiro, D., Esterberg, M., & Trotman, H. (2010). Neurodevelopment and schizophrenia: Broadening the focus. *Current Directions in Psychological Science, 19*, 204–208.

Walker, M. P., & van der Helm, E. (2009). Overnight therapy? The role of sleep in emotional brain processing. *Psychological Bulletin, 135*, 731–748.

Walker, W. R., Skowronski, J. J., & Thompson, C. P. (2003). Life is pleasant—and memory helps to keep it that way! *Review of General Psychology, 7*, 203–210.

Walkup, J. T., Albano, A. M., Piacentini, J., Bermaher, B., Compton, S. N., Sherrill, J. T., . . . Kendall, P. C. (2008). Cognitive behavioral therapy, sertraline, or a combination in childhood anxiety. *New England Journal of Medicine, 359*, 2753–2766.

Wallach, M. A., & Wallach, L. (1983). *Psychology's sanction for selfishness: The error of egoism in theory and therapy.* New York: Freeman.

Wallach, M. A., & Wallach, L. (1985, February). How psychology sanctions the cult of the self. *Washington Monthly*, pp. 46–56.

Walsh, R. (2011). Lifestyle and mental health. *American Psychologist, 66*, 579–592.

Walster (Hatfield), E., Aronson, V., Abrahams, D., & Rottman, L. (1966). Importance of physical attractiveness in dating behavior. *Journal of Personality and Social Psychology, 4*, 508–516.

Walton, G. M., & Cohen, G. L. (2011). A brief social-belonging intervention improves academic and health outcomes of minority students. *Science, 331*, 1447–1451.

Walton, G. M., & Spencer, S. J. (2009). Latent ability: Grades and test scores systematically underestimate the intellectual ability of negatively stereotyped students. *Psychological Science, 20*, 1132–1139.

Wampold, B. E. (2001). *The great psychotherapy debate: Models, methods, and findings.* Mahwah, NJ: Erlbaum.

Wampold, B. E. (2007). Psychotherapy: The humanistic (and effective) treatment. *American Psychologist, 62*, 857–873.

Wang, F., DesMeules, M., Luo, W., Dai, S., Lagace, C., & Morrison, H. (2011a). Leisure-time physical activity and marital status in relation to depression between men and women: A prospective study. *Health Psychology, 30*, 204–211.

Wang, J., Häusermann, M., Wydler, H., Mohler-Kuo, M., & Weiss, M. G. (2012). Suicidality and sexual orientation among men in Switzerland: Findings from 3 probability surveys. *Journal of Psychiatric Research, 46*, 980–986.

Wang, J., He, L., Liping, J., Tian, J., & Benson, V. (2015a). The "positive effect" is present in older Chinese adults: Evidence from an eye tracking study. *PLOS ONE, 10*(4), e0121372. doi:10.1371/journal.pone.0121372

Wang, J., Leu, J., & Shoda, Y. (2011b). When the seemingly innocuous "stings": Racial microaggressions and their emotional consequences. *Personality and Social Psychology Bulletin, 37*, 1666–1678.

Wang, J. X., Rogers, L. M., Gross, E. Z., Ryals, A. J., Dokucu, M. E., Brandstatt, K. L., . . . Voss, J. L. (2014). Targeted enhancement of cortical-hippocampal brain networks and associative memory. *Science, 345*, 1054–1057.

Wang, X. T., & Dvorak, R. D. (2010). Sweet future: Fluctuating blood glucose levels affect future discounting. *Psychological Science, 21*, 183–188.

Wang, Z., Lukowski, S. L., Hart, S. A., Lyons, I. M., Thompson, L. A., Kovas, Y., . . . Petrill, S. A. (2015b). Is math anxiety always bad for math learning? The role of math motivation. *Psychological Science, 26*, 1863–1876.

Wann, J. P. Poulter, D. R., & Purcell, C. (2011). Reduced sensitivity to visual looming inflates the risk posed by speeding vehicles when children try to cross the road. *Psychological Science, 22*, 429–434.

Wansink, B. (2014). *Slim by design: Mindless eating solutions for everyday life.* New York: Morrow.

Warburton, W. A., Williams, K. D., & Cairns, D. R. (2006). When ostracism leads to aggression: The moderating effects of control deprivation. *Journal of Experimental Social Psychology, 42*, 213–220.

Ward, A., & Mann, T. (2000). Don't mind if I do: Disinhibited eating under cognitive load. *Journal of Personality and Social Psychology, 78*, 753–763.

Ward, B. W., Dahlhamer, J. M., Galinsky, A. M., & Joestl, S. S. (2014, July 15). *Sexual orientation and health among U.S. adults: National Health Interview Survey, 2013.* Centers for Disease Control and Prevention: National Health Statistics Reports, Number 77.

Ward, C. (1994). Culture and altered states of consciousness. In W. J. Lonner & R. Malpass (Eds.), *Psychology and culture* (pp. 59–64). Boston: Allyn & Bacon.

Ward, C. A. (2000). Models and measurements of psychological androgyny: A cross-cultural extension of theory and research. *Sex Roles, 43*, 529–552.

Ward, J. (2003). State of the art synaesthesia. *The Psychologist, 16*, 196–199.

Ward, K. D., Klesges, R. C., & Halpern, M. T. (1997). Predictors of smoking cessation and state-of-the-art smoking interventions. *Journal of Social Issues, 53*, 129–145.

Wardle, J., Cooke, L. J., Gibson, L., Sapochnik, M., Sheiham, A., & Lawson, M. (2003). Increasing children's acceptance of vegetables: A randomized trial of parent-led exposure. *Appetite, 40*, 155–162.

Wason, P. C. (1960). On the failure to eliminate hypotheses in a conceptual task. *Quarterly Journal of Experimental Psychology, 12*, 129–140.

Wasserman, E. A. (1993). Comparative cognition: Toward a general understanding of cognition in behavior. *Psychological Science, 4*, 156–161.

Wasserman, E. A. (1995). The conceptual abilities of pigeons. *American Scientist, 83*, 246–255.

Watson, D. (2000). *Mood and temperament.* New York: Guilford Press.

Watson, J. B. (1913). Psychology as the behaviorist views it. *Psychological Review, 20*, 158–177.

Watson, J. B. (1924). The unverbalized in human behavior. *Psychological Review, 31*, 339–347.

Watson, J. B., & Rayner, R. (1920). Conditioned emotional reactions. *Journal of Experimental Psychology, 3*, 1–14.

Watson, R. I., Jr. (1973). Investigation into deindividuation using a cross-cultural survey technique. *Journal of Personality and Social Psychology, 25*, 342–345.

Watson, S. J., Benson, J. A., Jr., & Joy, J. E. (2000). Marijuana and medicine: Assessing the science base: A summary of the 1999 Institute of Medicine report. *Archives of General Psychiatry, 57*, 547–553.

Watters, E. (2010). *Crazy like us: The globalization of the American psyche.* New York: Free Press.

Way, B. M., Creswell, J. D., Eisenberger, N. I., & Lieberman, M. D. (2010). Dispositional mindfulness and depressive symptomatology: Correlations with limbic and self-referential neural activity during rest. *Emotion, 10*, 12–24.

Wayment, H. A., & Peplau, L. A. (1995). Social support and well-being among lesbian and heterosexual women: A structural modeling approach. *Personality and Social Psychology Bulletin, 21*, 1189–1199.

Weaver, J. B., Masland, J. L., & Zillmann, D. (1984). Effect of erotica on young men's aesthetic perception of their female sexual partners. *Perceptual and Motor Skills, 58*, 929–930.

Webster, G. D., DeWall, C. N., Pond, R. S., Jr., Deckman, T., Jonason, P. K., Le, B. M., . . . Bator, R. J. (2014). The Brief Aggression Questionnaire: Psychometric and behavioral evidence for an efficient measure of trait aggression. *Aggressive Behavior, 40*, 120–139.

Wechsler, D. (1972). "Hold" and "Don't Hold" tests. In S. M. Chown (Ed.), *Human aging.* New York: Penguin.

Wegner, D. M., & Ward, A. F. (2013, December). How Google is changing your brain. *Scientific American*, pp. 58–61.

Wei, W., Lu, H., Zhao, H., Chen, C., Dong, Q., & Zhou, X. (2012). Gender differences in children's arithmetic performance are accounted for by gender differences in language abilities. *Psychological Science, 23*, 320–330.

Weiland, B. J., Thayer, R. E., Depue, B. E., Sabbineni, A., Bryan, A. D., & Hutchison, K. E. (2015). Daily marijuana use is not associated with brain morphometric measures in adolescents or adults. *Journal of Neuroscience, 35*, 1505–1512.

Weingarten, G. (2002, March 10). Below the beltway. *The Washington Post*, p. WO3.

Weinstein, N., Ryan, W. S., DeHaan, C. R., Przybylski, A. K., Legate, N., & Ryan, R. M. (2012). Parental autonomy support and discrepancies between implicit and explicit sexual identities: Dynamics of self-acceptance and defense. *Journal of Personality and Social Psychology, 102*, 815–832.

Weinstein, N. D. (1980). Unrealistic optimism about future life events. *Journal of Personality and Social Psychology, 39*, 806–820.

Weinstein, N. D. (1982). Unrealistic optimism about susceptibility to health problems. *Journal of Behavioral Medicine, 5*, 441–460.

Weinstein, N. D. (1996, October 4). 1996 optimistic bias bibliography. (weinstein_c@aesop.rutgers.edu).

Weir, K. (2013, May). Captive audience. *Monitor on Psychology*, pp. 44–49.

Weisbuch, M., Ivcevic, Z., & Ambady, N. (2009). On being liked on the web and in the "real world": Consistency in first impressions across personal webpages and spontaneous behavior. *Journal of Experimental Social Psychology, 45*, 573–576.

Weiser, E. B. (2015). #Me: Narcissism and its facets as predictors of selfie-posting frequency. *Personality and Individual Differences, 86*, 477–481.

Weiss, A., King, J. E., & Perkins, L. (2006). Personality and subjective well-being in orangutans (*Pongo pygmaeus* and *Pongo abelii*). *Journal of Personality and Social Psychology, 90*, 501–511.

Weiss, A., Staes, N., Pereboom, J. J. M., Stevens, J. M. G., & Eens, M. (2015). Personality in bonobos. *Psychological Science, 26*, 1430–1439.

Welch, W. W. (2005, February 28). Trauma of Iraq war haunting thousands returning home. *USA Today* (usatoday.com).

Weller, S., & Davis-Beaty, K. (2002). The effectiveness of male condoms in prevention of sexually transmitted diseases (protocol). *Cochrane Database of Systematic Reviews*, Issue 4, Art. No. CD004090.

Wells, D. L. (2009). The effects of animals on human health and well-being. *Journal of Social Issues, 65*, 523–543.

Wells, G. L. (1981). Lay analyses of causal forces on behavior. In J. Harvey (Ed.), *Cognition, social behavior and the environment.* Hillsdale, NJ: Erlbaum.

Wenze, S. J., Gunthert, K. C., & German, R. E. (2012). Biases in affective forecasting and recall in individuals with depression and anxiety symptoms. *Personality and Social Psychology Bulletin, 38*, 895–906.

Westen, D. (1996). *Is Freud really dead? Teaching psychodynamic theory to introductory psychology.* Presentation to the Annual Institute on the Teaching of Psychology, St. Petersburg Beach, FL.

Westen, D. (1998). The scientific legacy of Sigmund Freud: Toward a psychodynamically informed psychological science. *Psychological Bulletin, 124*, 333–371.

Westen, D. (2007). *The political brain: The role of emotion in deciding the fate of the nation.* New York: PublicAffairs.

Westen, D., & Morrison, K. (2001). A multidimensional meta-analysis of treatments for depression, panic, and generalized anxiety disorder: An empirical examination of the status of empirically supported therapies. *Journal of Consulting and Clinical Psychology, 69*, 875–899.

Wetherell, J. L., Petkus, A. J., White, K. S., Nguyen, H., Kornblith, S., Andreescu, C., . . . Lenze, E. J. (2013). Antidepressant medication augmented with cognitive-behavioral therapy for generalized anxiety disorder in older adults. *American Journal of Psychiatry, 170*, 782–789.

Whelan, R., Conrod, P. J., Poline, J.-B., Lourdusamy, A., Banaschewski, T., Barker, G. J., . . . the IMAGEN Consortium. (2012). Adolescent impulsivity phenotypes characterized by distinct brain networks. *Nature Neuroscience, 15*, 920–925.

Whisman, M. A., Johnson, D. P., & Rhee, S. H. (2014). A behavior genetic analysis of pleasant events, depressive symptoms, and their covariation. *Clinical Psychological Science, 2*, 535–544.

White, H. R., Brick, J., & Hansell, S. (1993). A longitudinal investigation of alcohol use and aggression in adolescence. *Journal of Studies on Alcohol, Supplement No. 11*, 62–77.

White, L., & Edwards, J. (1990). Emptying the nest and parental well-being: An analysis of national panel data. *American Sociological Review, 55*, 235–242.

White, P. H., Kjelgaard, M. M., & Harkins, S. G. (1995). Testing the contribution of self-evaluation to goal-setting effects. *Journal of Personality and Social Psychology, 69*, 69–79.

Whitehead, B. D., & Popenoe, D. (2001). *The state of our unions 2001: The social health of marriage in America.* Rutgers University: The National Marriage Project.

Whiten, A., & Boesch, C. (2001, January). Cultures of chimpanzees. *Scientific American*, pp. 60–67.

Whiting, B. B., & Edwards, C. P. (1988). *Children of different worlds: The formation of social behavior.* Cambridge, MA: Harvard University Press.

Whitlock, J. R., Heynen, A. L., Shuler, M. G., & Bear, M. F. (2006). Learning induces long-term potentiation in the hippocampus. *Science, 313*, 1093–1097.

Whitmer, R. A., Gustafson, D. R., Barrett-Connor, E. B., Haan, M. N., Gunderson, E. P., & Yaffe, K. (2008). Central obesity and increased risk of dementia more than three decades later. *Neurology, 71*, 1057–1064.

WHO. (2000). *Effectiveness of male latex condoms in protecting against pregnancy and sexually transmitted infections.* World Health Organization (who.int).

WHO. (2003). *The male latex condom: Specification and guidelines for condom procurement.* Department of Reproductive Health and Research, Family and Community Health, World Health Organization.

WHO. (2008). Mental health (nearly 1 million annual suicide deaths). World Health Organization (who.int).

WHO. (2010, September). *Mental health: strengthening our response.* Geneva: World Health Organization (who.int).

WHO. (2012, May). *Tobacco: Fact sheet* No. 339. Geneva: World Health Organization (who.int).

WHO. (2013, November). *Sexually transmitted infections (STIs).* Fact sheet No. 110. World Health Organization (who.int).

WHO. (2014a). *Chain-free initiative.* World Health Organization (emro.who.int).

WHO. (2014b, October). *Mental disorders.* World Health Organization (who.int/mediacentre/factsheets/fs396/en/).

WHO. (2015a, accessed March 4). *Gender inequalities and HIV.* World Health Organization (who.int/gender/hiv_aids/en).

WHO. (2015b, January). *Obesity and overweight: Fact sheet.* Geneva: World Health Organization (who.int/mediacentre/factsheets/fs311/en/).

Wickelgren, I. (2009, September/October). I do not feel your pain. *Scientific American Mind,* pp. 51–57.

Wickelgren, W. A. (1977). *Learning and memory.* Englewood Cliffs, NJ: Prentice-Hall.

Widiger, T. A., Gore, W. L., Crego, C., Rojas, S. L., & Oltmanns, J. R. (2016). Five-factor model and personality disorder. In T. A. Widiger (Ed.), *The Oxford handbook of the five factor model of personality.* New York: Oxford University Press.

Widom, C. S. (1989a). Does violence beget violence? A critical examination of the literature. *Psychological Bulletin, 106,* 3–28.

Widom, C. S. (1989b). The cycle of violence. *Science, 244,* 160–166.

Wiens, A. N., & Menustik, C. E. (1983). Treatment outcome and patient characteristics in an aversion therapy program for alcoholism. *American Psychologist, 38,* 1089–1096.

Wierson, M., & Forehand, R. (1994). Parent behavioral training for child noncompliance: Rationale, concepts, and effectiveness. *Current Directions in Psychological Science, 3,* 146–149.

Wierzbicki, M. (1993). Psychological adjustment of adoptees: A meta-analysis. *Journal of Clinical Child Psychology, 22,* 447–454.

Wiesel, T. N. (1982). Postnatal development of the visual cortex and the influence of environment. *Nature, 299,* 583–591.

Wigdor, A. K., & Garner, W. R. (1982). *Ability testing: Uses, consequences, and controversies.* Washington, DC: National Academy Press.

Wilder, D. A. (1981). Perceiving persons as a group: Categorization and intergroup relations. In D. L. Hamilton (Ed.), *Cognitive processes in stereotyping and intergroup behavior* (pp. 213–257). Hillsdale, NJ: Erlbaum.

Wiley, J., & Jarosz, A. F. (2012). Working memory capacity, attentional focus, and problem solving. *Current Directions in Psychological Science, 21,* 258–262.

Wilkinson, R., & Pickett, K. (2009). *The spirit level: Why greater equality makes societies stronger.* London: Bloomsbury Press.

Willett, L. L., Halvorsen, A. J., McDonald, F. S., Chaudhry, S. I., & Arora, V. M. (2015). Gender differences in salary of internal medicine residency directors: A national survey. *The American Journal of Medicine, 128,* 659–665.

Williams, J. E., & Best, D. L. (1990). *Measuring sex stereotypes: A multination study.* Newbury Park, CA: Sage.

Williams, K. D. (2007). Ostracism. *Annual Review of Psychology, 58,* 425–452.

Williams, K. D. (2009). Ostracism: A temporal need-threat model. *Advances in Experimental Social Psychology, 41,* 275–313.

Williams, K. D., & Sommer, K. L. (1997). Social ostracism by coworkers: Does rejection lead to loafing or compensation? *Personality and Social Psychology Bulletin, 23,* 693–706.

Williams, L. E., & Bargh, J. A. (2008). Experiencing physical warmth promotes interpersonal warmth. *Science, 322,* 606–607.

Williams, N. M., Zaharieva, I., Martin, A., Langley, K., Mantripragada, K., Fossdal, R., . . . Thapar, A. (2010). Rare chromosomal deletions and duplications in attention-deficit hyperactivity disorder: A genome-wide analysis. *The Lancet, 376,* 1401–1408.

Williams, R. (1993). *Anger kills.* New York: Times Books.

Williams, S. L. (1987). *Self-efficacy and mastery-oriented treatment for severe phobias.* Paper presented at the American Psychological Association convention.

Williams, T. (2015, March 17). Missouri executes killer who had brain injury. *The New York Times* (nytimes.com).

Williams, W. W., & Ceci, S. (2015). National hiring experiments reveal 2:1 faculty preference for women on tenure track. *PNAS, 112,* 5360–5365.

Willingham, D. T. (2010, Summer). Have technology and multitasking rewired how students learn? *American Educator, 42,* 23–28.

Willis, J., & Todorov, A. (2006). First impressions: Making up your mind after a 100-ms. exposure to a face. *Psychological Science, 17,* 592–598.

Willis, S. L., Tennstedt, S. L., Marsiske, M., Ball, K., Elias, J., Koepke, K. M., . . . Wright, E. (2006). Long-term effects of cognitive training on everyday functional outcomes in older adults. *JAMA, 296,* 2805–2814.

Willmuth, M. E. (1987). Sexuality after spinal cord injury: A critical review. *Clinical Psychology Review, 7,* 389–412.

Willoughby, B. J., Carroll, J. S., & Busby, D. M. (2014). Differing relationship outcomes when sex happens before, on, or after first dates. *Journal of Sex Research, 51,* 52–61.

Willoughby, T., Heffer, T., & Hamza, C. A. (2015). The link between nonsuicidal self-injury and acquired capability for suicide: A longitudinal study. *Journal of Abnormal Psychology, 124,* 1110–1115.

Wilson, A. E., & Ross, M. (2001). From chump to champ: People's appraisals of their earlier and present selves. *Journal of Personality and Social Psychology, 80,* 572–584.

Wilson, R. S. (1979). Analysis of longitudinal twin data: Basic model and applications to physical growth measures. *Acta Geneticae Medicae et Gemellologiae, 28,* 93–105.

Wilson, R. S., Beck, T. L., Bienias, J. L., & Bennett, D. A. (2007). Terminal cognitive decline: Accelerated loss of cognition in the last years of life. *Psychosomatic Medicine, 69,* 131–137.

Wilson, T. D. (2006). The power of social psychological interventions. *Science, 313,* 1251–1252.

Wilson, T. D., Reinhard, D. A., Westgate, E. C., Gilbert, D. T., Ellerbeck, N., Hahn, C., . . . Shaked, A. (2014). Just think: The challenges of the disengaged mind. *Science, 345,* 75–77.

Windholz, G. (1989, April-June). The discovery of the principles of reinforcement, extinction, generalization, and differentiation of conditional reflexes in Pavlov's laboratories. *Pavlovian Journal of Biological Science, 26,* 64–74.

Windholz, G. (1997). Ivan P. Pavlov: An overview of his life and psychological work. *American Psychologist, 52,* 941–946.

Winter, W. C., Hammond, W. R., Green, N. H., Zhang, Z., & Bilwise, D. L. (2009). Measuring circadian advantage in Major League Baseball: A 10-year retrospective study. *International Journal of Sports Physiology and Performance, 4,* 394–401.

Wirth, J. H., Sacco, D. F., Hugenberg, K., & Williams, K. D. (2010). Eye gaze as relational evaluation: Averted eye gaze leads to feelings of ostracism and relational devaluation. *Personality and Social Psychology Bulletin, 36,* 869–882.

Wiseman, R., & Greening, E. (2002). The Mind Machine: A mass participation experiment into the possible existence of extra-sensory perception. *British Journal of Psychology, 93,* 487–499.

Witek-Janusek, L., Albuquerque, K., Chroniak, K. R., Chroniak, C., Durazo, R., & Mathews, H. L. (2008). Effect of mindfulness based stress reduction on immune function, quality of life and coping in women newly diagnosed with early stage breast cancer. *Brain Behavior and Immunity, 22(6),* 969–981.

Witt, J. K., & Brockmole, J. R. (2012). Action alters object identification: Wielding a gun increases the bias to see guns. *Journal of Experimental Psychology: Human Perception and Performance, 38,* 1159–1167.

Witt, J. K., & Proffitt, D. R. (2005). See the ball, hit the ball: Apparent ball size is correlated with batting average. *Psychological Science, 16,* 937–938.

Witters, D. (2014, October 20). *U.S. adults with children at home have greater joy, stress.* Retrieved from gallup.com /poll/178631/adults-childrenhome-greater-joy-stress.aspx

Witters, D., & Ander, S. (2013, January 4). *Depression increases in areas Superstorm Sandy hit hardest.* Gallup (gallup.com).

Witters, D., & Wood, J. (2015, January 14). *Heart attacks and depression closely linked.* Gallup (gallup.com).

Witvliet, C. V. O., & Vrana, S. R. (1995). Psychophysiological responses as indices of affective dimensions. *Psychophysiology, 32,* 436–443.

Wixted, J. T., & Ebbesen, E. B. (1991). On the form of forgetting. *Psychological Science, 2,* 409–415.

Wölfer, R., & Hewstone, M. (2015, August). Intra- versus intersex aggression. Testing theories of sex differences using aggression networks. *Psychological Science, 26,* 1285–1294.

Wolfinger, N. H. (2015). *Want to avoid divorce? Wait to get married, but not too long.* Institute for Family Studies (family-studies.org/want-to-avoid-divorce-wait-to-get-married-but-not-too-long/).

Wolfson, A. R., & Carskadon, M. A. (1998). Sleep schedules and daytime functioning in adolescents. *Child Development, 69,* 875–887.

Wollmer, M. A., de Boer, C., Kalak, N., Beck, J., Götz, T., Schmidt, T., . . . Kruger, T. H. (2012). Facing depression with botulinum toxin: A randomized controlled trial. *Journal of Psychiatric Research, 46,* 574–581.

Wolpe, J. (1958). *Psychotherapy by reciprocal inhibition.* Stanford, CA: Stanford University Press.

Wolpe, J., & Plaud, J. J. (1997). Pavlov's contributions to behavior therapy: The obvious and the not so obvious. *American Psychologist, 52,* 966–972.

Wong, D. F., Wagner, H. N., Tune, L. E., Dannals, R. F., Pearlson, G. D., Links, J. M., . . . Giedde, A. (1986). Positron emission tomography reveals elevated D2 dopamine receptors in drug-naive schizophrenics. *Science, 234,* 1588–1593.

Wong, M. M., & Csikszentmihalyi, M. (1991). Affiliation motivation and daily experience: Some issues on gender differences. *Journal of Personality and Social Psychology, 60,* 154–164.

Wood, J. M. (2003, May 19). Quoted by R. Mestel, Rorschach tested: Blot out the famous method? Some experts say it has no place in psychiatry. *Los Angeles Times* (latimes.com).

Wood, J. M., Bootzin, R. R., Kihlstrom, J. F., & Schacter, D. L. (1992). Implicit and explicit memory for verbal information presented during sleep. *Psychological Science, 3,* 236–239.

Wood, J. M., Nezworski, M. T., Garb, H. N., & Lilienfeld, S. O. (2006). The controversy over Exner's comprehensive system for the Rorschach: The critics speak. *Independent Practitioner, 26,* 73–82.

Wood, J. V., Saltzberg, J. A., & Goldsamt, L. A. (1990a). Does affect induce self-focused attention? *Journal of Personality and Social Psychology, 58,* 899–908.

Wood, J. V., Saltzberg, J. A., Neale, J. M., Stone, A. A., & Rachmiel, T. B. (1990b). Self-focused attention, coping responses, and distressed mood in everyday life. *Journal of Personality and Social Psychology, 58,* 1027–1036.

Wood, W. (1987). Meta-analytic review of sex differences in group performance. *Psychological Bulletin, 102,* 53–71.

Wood, W., & Eagly, A. H. (2002). A cross-cultural analysis of the behavior of women and men: Implications for the origins of sex differences. *Psychological Bulletin, 128,* 699–727.

Wood, W., & Eagly, A. H. (2007). Social structural origins of sex differences in human mating. In S. W. Gangestad & J. A. Simpson (Eds.), *The evolution of mind: Fundamental questions and controversies.* New York: Guilford Press.

Wood, W., Kressel, L., Joshi, P. D., & Louie, B. (2014a). Meta-analysis of menstrual cycle effects on women's mate preferences. *Emotion Review, 6,* 229–249.

Wood, W., Labrecque, J. S., Lin, P.-Y., & Rünger, D. (2014b). Habits in dual process models. In J. Sherman, B. Gawronski, & Y. Trope (Eds.), *Dual process theories of the social mind* (pp. 371–385). New York: Guilford Press.

Wood, W., Lundgren, S., Ouellette, J. A., Busceme, S., & Blackstone, T. (1994). Minority influence: A meta-analytic review of social influence processes. *Psychological Bulletin, 115,* 323–345.

Woods, N. F., Dery, G. K., & Most, A. (1983). Recollections of menarche, current menstrual attitudes, and premenstrual symptoms. In S. Golub (Ed.), *Menarche: The transition from girl to woman.* Lexington, MA: Lexington Books.

Woolett, K., & Maguire, E. A. (2011). Acquiring "the knowledge" of London's layout drives structural brain changes. *Current Biology, 21,* 2109–2114.

Woolley, A. W., Chabris, C. F., Pentland, A., Hasmi, N., & Malone, T. W. (2010). Evidence for a collective intelligence factor in the performance of human groups. *Science, 330,* 686–688.

World Federation for Mental Health. (2005). *ADHD: The hope behind the hype.* Accessed May 25, 2016, from webcontent.hkcss.org.hk/rh/rpp/HKPaediatricSociety-20050909ADHD_guideline_WFMH1.pdf

Worldwatch. (2013). Meat production continues to rise. Worldwatch Institute (worldwatch.org/node/5443#notes).

Wortham, J. (2010, May 13). Cellphones now used more for data than for calls. *The New York Times* (nytimes.com).

Wortman, C. B., & Silver, R. C. (1989). The myths of coping with loss. *Journal of Consulting and Clinical Psychology, 57,* 349–357.

Wren, C. S. (1999, April 8). Drug survey of children finds middle school a pivotal time. *The New York Times* (nytimes.com).

Wright, I. C., Rabe-Hesketh, S., Woodruff, P. W. R., David, A. S., Murray, R. M., & Bullmore, E. T. (2000). Meta-analysis of regional brain volumes in schizophrenia. *American Journal of Psychiatry, 157,* 16–25.

Wright, P., Takei, N., Rifkin, L., & Murray, R. M. (1995). Maternal influenza, obstetric complications, and schizophrenia. *American Journal of Psychiatry, 152,* 1714–1720.

Wright, P. H. (1989). Gender differences in adults' same- and cross-gender friendships. In R. G. Adams & R. Blieszner (Eds.), *Older adult friendships: Structure and process.* Newbury Park, CA: Sage.

Wrosch, C., & Miller, G. E. (2009). Depressive symptoms can be useful: Self-regulatory and emotional benefits of dysphoric mood in adolescence. *Journal of Personality and Social Psychology, 96,* 1181–1190.

Wrzesniewski, A., & Dutton, J. E. (2001). Crafting a job: Revisioning employees as active crafters of their work. *Academy of Management Review, 26,* 179–201.

Wrzesniewski, A., McCauley, C. R., Rozin, P., & Schwartz, B. (1997). Jobs, careers, and callings: People's relations to their work. *Journal of Research in Personality, 31,* 21–33.

Wrzesniewski, A., Schwartz, B., Cong, X., Kane, M., Omar, A., & Kolditz, T. (2014). Multiple types of motives don't multiply the motivation of West Point cadets. PNAS, 111, 10990–10995.

Wuethrich, B. (2001, March). Getting stupid: Surprising new neurological behavioral research reveals that teenagers who drink too much may permanently damage their brains and seriously compromise their ability to learn. *Discover, 56,* 56–64.

Wulsin, L. R., Vaillant, G. E., & Wells, V. E. (1999). A systematic review of the mortality of depression. *Psychosomatic Medicine, 61,* 6–17.

Wyatt, J. K., & Bootzin, R. R. (1994). Cognitive processing and sleep: Implications for enhancing job performance. *Human Performance, 7,* 119–139.

Wynne, C. D. L. (2004). *Do animals think?* Princeton, NJ: Princeton University Press.

Wynne, C. D. L. (2008). Aping language: A skeptical analysis of the evidence for nonhuman primate language. *Skeptic, 13*(4), 10–13.

Xie, L., Kang, H., Xu, Q., Chen, M. J., Liao, Y., Thiyagarajan, M., . . . Nedergaard, M. (2013). Sleep drives metabolite clearance from the adult brain. *Science, 342,* 373–377.

Xu, J., Murphy, S. L., Kochanek, K. D., & Bastian B. A. (2016, February 16). Deaths: Final data for 2013. *National Vital Statistics Report, 64* (2). Centers for Disease Control and Prevention (cdc.gov).

Xu, Y., & Corkin, S. (2001). H. M. revisits the Tower of Hanoi puzzle. *Neuropsychology, 15,* 69–79.

Yamagata, S., Suzuki, A. Ando, J., Ono, Y., Kilima, N. Yoshimura, K., . . . Jang, K. L. (2006). Is the genetic structure of human personality universal? A cross-cultural twin study from North America, Europe, and Asia. *Journal of Personality and Social Psychology, 90,* 987–998.

Yamaguchi, M., Masuchi, A., Nakanishi, D., Suga, S., Konishi, N., Yu, Y. Y., & Ohtsubo, Y. (2015). Experiential purchases and prosocial spending promote happiness by enhancing social relationships. *The Journal of Positive Psychology, 11,* 1–9.

Yang, G., Lai, G. S. W., Cichon, J., Ma, L., Li, W., & Gan, W. B. (2014). Sleep promotes branch-specific formation of dendritic spines after learning. *Science, 344,* 173–1178.

Yang, S., Markoczy, L., & Qi, M. (2006). Unrealistic optimism in consumer credit card adoption. *Journal of Economic Psychology, 28,* 170–185.

Yang, Y., & Raine, A. (2009). Prefrontal structural and functional brain imaging findings in antisocial, violent, and psychopathic individuals: A meta-analysis. *Psychiatry Research: Neuroimaging, 174,* 81–88.

Yang, Y. C., Boen, C., Gerken, K., Li, T., Schorpp, K., & Harris, K. M. (2016). Social relationships and physiological determinants of longevity across the human life span. PNAS, 113, 578–583.

Yarkoni, T. (2010). Personality in 100,000 words: A large-scale analysis of personality and word use among bloggers. *Journal of Research in Personality, 44,* 363–373.

Yarnell, P. R., & Lynch, S. (1970, April 25). Retrograde memory immediately after concussion. *Lancet, 1,* 863–865.

Yates, A. (1989). Current perspectives on the eating disorders: I. History, psychological and biological aspects. *Journal of the American Academy of Child and Adolescent Psychiatry, 28,* 813–828.

Yates, A. (1990). Current perspectives on the eating disorders: II. Treatment, outcome, and research directions. *Journal of the American Academy of Child and Adolescent Psychiatry, 29,* 1–9.

Ybarra, O. (1999). Misanthropic person memory when the need to self-enhance is absent. *Personality and Social Psychology Bulletin, 25,* 261–269.

Yeager, D. S., Johnson, R., Spitzer, B. J., Trzesniewski, K. H., Powers, J., & Dweck, C. S. (2014). The far-reaching effects of believing people can change: Implicit theories of personality shape stress, health, and achievement during adolescence. *Journal of Personality and Social Psychology, 106,* 867–884.

Yeager, D. S., Miu, A. S., Powers, J., & Dweck, C. S. (2013). Implicit theories of personality and attributions of hostile intent: A meta-analysis, an experiment, and a longitudinal intervention. *Child Development, 84,* 1651–1667.

Yerkes, R. M., & Dodson, J. D. (1908). The relation of strength of stimulus to rapidity of habit-formation. *Journal of Comparative Neurology and Psychology, 18,* 459–482.

Yeung, J. W. K., Chan, Y., & Lee, B. L. K. (2009). Youth religiosity and substance use: A meta-analysis from 1995 to 2007. *Psychological Reports, 105,* 255–266.

Yiend, J., Parnes, C., Shepherd, K., Roche, M.-K., & Cooper, M. J. (2014). Negative self-beliefs in eating disorders: A cognitive-bias-modification study. *Clinical Psychological Science, 2,* 756–766.

Young, C., & Lim, C. (2014). Time as a network good: Evidence from unemployment and the standard workweek. *Sociological Science, 1,* 10–27.

Young, S. G., Hugenberg, K., Bernstein, M. J., & Sacco, D. F. (2012). Perception and motivation in face recognition: A critical review of theories of the cross-race effect. *Personality and Social Psychology Review, 16,* 116–142.

Younger, J., Aron, A., Parke, S., Chatterjee, N., & Mackey, S. (2010). Viewing pictures of a romantic partner reduces experimental pain: Involvement of neural reward systems. *PLoS ONE 5*(10), e13309. doi:10.1371/journal.pone.0013309.

Yücel, M., Solowij, N., Respondek, C., Whittle, S., Fornito, A., Pantelis, C., & Lubman, D. I. (2008). Regional brain abnormalities associated with long-term cannabis use. *Archives of General Psychiatry, 65,* 694–701.

Zagorsky, J. L. (2007). Do you have to be smart to be rich? The impact of IQ on wealth, income and financial distress. *Intelligence, 35,* 489–501.

Zajonc, R. B. (1965). Social facilitation. *Science, 149,* 269–274.

Zajonc, R. B. (1980). Feeling and thinking: Preferences need no inferences. *American Psychologist, 35,* 151–175.

Zajonc, R. B. (1984). On the primacy of affect. *American Psychologist, 39,* 117–123.

Zajonc, R. B. (2001). Mere exposure: A gateway to the subliminal. *Current Directions in Psychological Science, 10,* 224–228.

Zajonc, R. B., & Markus, G. B. (1975). Birth order and intellectual development. *Psychological Review, 82,* 74–88.

Zak, P. J. (2012). *The moral molecule: The source of love and prosperity.* New York: Dutton.

Zannas, A. S., Provençal, N., & Binder, E. B. (2015). Epigenetics of posttraumatic stress disorder: Current evidence, challenges, and future directions. *Biological Psychiatry, 78(5),* 327–335.

Zauberman, G., & Lynch, J. G., Jr. (2005). Resource slack and propensity to discount delayed investments of time versus money. *Journal of Experimental Psychology: General, 134,* 23–37.

Zeidner, M. (1990). Perceptions of ethnic group modal intelligence: Reflections of cultural stereotypes or intelligence test scores? *Journal of Cross-Cultural Psychology, 21,* 214–231.

Zell, E., & Alicke, M. D. (2010). The local dominance effect in self-evaluation: Evidence and explanations. *Personality and Social Psychology Review, 14,* 368–384.

Zell, E., Krizan, Z., & Teeter, S. R. (2015). Evaluating gender similarities and differences using metasynthesis. *American Psychologist, 70,* 10–20.

Zhang, J., Fang, L., Yow-Wu, B. W., & Wieczorek, W. F. (2013). Depression, anxiety, and suicidal ideation among Chinese Americans: A study of immigration-related factors. *Journal of Nervous and Mental Disease, 201,* 17–22.

Zhong, C.-B., Dijksterhuis, A., & Galinsky, A. D. (2008). The merits of unconscious thought in creativity. *Psychological Science, 19,* 912–918.

Zhong, C.-B., & Leonardelli, G. J. (2008). Cold and lonely: Does social exclusion literally feel cold? *Psychological Science, 19,* 838–842.

Zhu, W. X., Lu, L., & Hesketh, T. (2009). China's excess males, sex selective abortion, and one child policy: Analysis of data from 2005 national intercensus survey. *British Medical Journal, 338,* b1211. http://dx.doi.org/10.1136/bmj.b1211

Zilbergeld, B. (1983). *The shrinking of America: Myths of psychological change.* Boston: Little, Brown.

Zillmann, D. (1986). *Effects of prolonged consumption of pornography.* Background paper for The Surgeon General's Workshop on Pornography and Public Health, June 22–24. Report prepared by E. P. Mulvey & J. L. Haugaard and released by Office of the Surgeon General on August 4, 1986.

Zillmann, D. (1989). Effects of prolonged consumption of pornography. In D. Zillmann & J. Bryant (Eds.), *Pornography: Research advances and policy considerations.* Hillsdale, NJ: Erlbaum.

Zillmann, D., & Bryant, J. (1984). Effects of massive exposure to pornography. In N. Malamuth & E. Donnerstein (Eds.), *Pornography and sexual aggression* (pp. 115–138). Orlando, FL: Academic Press.

Zimbardo, P. G. (1970). The human choice: Individuation, reason, and order versus deindividuation, impulse, and chaos. In W. J. Arnold & D. Levine (Eds.), *Nebraska symposium on motivation, 1969* (pp. 237–307). Lincoln, NE: University of Nebraska Press.

Zimbardo, P. G. (1972, April). Pathology of imprisonment. *Society, 9,* pp. 4–8.

Zimbardo, P. G. (2001, September 16). *Fighting terrorism by understanding man's capacity for evil.* Op-ed essay distributed by spsp-discuss@stolaf.edu.

Zimbardo, P. G. (2004, May 25). Journalist interview re: *Abu Ghraib prison abuses: Eleven answers to eleven questions.* Unpublished manuscript, Stanford University, Stanford, CA.

Zimbardo, P. G. (2007, September). Person x situation x system dynamics. *The Observer* (Association for Psychological Science), p. 43.

Zogby, J. (2006, March). *Survey of teens and adults about the use of personal electronic devices and headphones.* Utica, NY: Zogby International.

Zou, Z., & Buck, L. B. (2006, March). Combinatorial effects of odorant mixes in olfactory cortex. *Science, 311,* 1477–1481.

Zubieta, J.-K., Bueller, J. A., Jackson, L. R., Scott, D. J., Xu, Y., Koeppe, R. A., . . . Stohler, C. S. (2005). Placebo effects mediated by endogenous opioid activity on μ-opioid receptors. *Journal of Neuroscience, 25,* 7754–7762.

Zubieta, J.-K., Heitzeg, M. M., Smith, Y. R., Bueller, J. A., Xu, K., Xu, Y., . . . Goldman, D. (2003). COMT val158met genotype affects μ-opioid neurotransmitter responses to a pain stressor. *Science, 299,* 1240–1243.

Zucker, G. S., & Weiner, B. (1993). Conservatism and perceptions of poverty: An attributional analysis. *Journal of Applied Social Psychology, 23,* 925–943.

Zuckerberg, M. (2012, February 1). Letter to potential investors. Quoted by S. Sengupta & C. C. Miller, "Social mission" vision meets Wall Street. *The New York Times* (nytimes.com).

Zuckerman, M. (1979). *Sensation seeking: Beyond the optimal level of arousal.* Hillsdale, NJ: Erlbaum.

Zuckerman, M. (2009). Sensation seeking. In M. R. Leary & R. H. Hoye (Eds.), *Handbook of individual differences in social behavior* (pp. 455–465). New York: Guilford Press.

Zvolensky, M. J., & Bernstein, A. (2005). Cigarette smoking and panic psychopathology. *Current Directions in Psychological Science, 14,* 301–305.

Name Index

Subject Index

How Does Psychology Apply to YOUR Everyday Life?